11th Edition

Organizational Behavior

Managing People and Organizations

©Pal Teravagimov/Shutterstock

RICKY W. GRIFFIN
Texas A&M University

GREGORY MOORHEAD
Emeritus, Arizona State University

CENGAGE Learning®

Andover • Melbourne • Mexico City • Stamford, CT • Toronto • Hong Kong • New Delhi • Seoul • Singapore • Tokyo

Organizational Behavior: Managing People and Organizations, 11e
Ricky W. Griffin and Gregory Moorhead

ISBN-13: 978-81-315-3335-2
ISBN-10: 81-315-3335-2

Cengage Learning India Private Limited
418, F.I.E., Patparganj
Delhi 110092
India

Tel: 91-11-43641111
Fax: 91-11-43641100
Email: asia.infoindia@cengage.com

Cengage Learning is a leading provider of customized learning solutions with office locations around the globe, including Andover, Melbourne, Mexico City, Stamford (CT), Toronto, Hong Kong, New Delhi, Seoul, Singapore, and Tokyo. Locate your local office at: www.cengage.com/global

Cengage Learning Products are represented in Canada by Nelson Education, Ltd.

For product information, visit our website at **www.cengage.co.in**

Printed in India
First Indian Reprint 2017

Disclaimer:
This book contains link to resources which are a part of the US edition. The same may not be available with the Indian edition. The buyer needs to purchase a copy of the US edition to have full access to those resources. In no event the publisher shall be liable for any limitation or performance due to unavailability of these resources.

Brief Contents

Contents

PART 3 Interpersonal Processes in Organizations

PART 4 Organizational Processes and Characteristics

Preface

It has been said that the only constant is change. And change continues to be the watchword for managers everywhere. Now more than ever, managers need a comprehensive and sophisticated understanding of the assets, tools, and resources they can draw upon to compete most effectively. And understanding the people who comprise organizations—operating employees, managers, engineers, support staff, sales representatives, decision makers, professionals, maintenance workers, and administrative employees—is critical for any manager who aspires to understand change and how his or her organization needs to respond to that change.

As we prepared this edition of *Organizational Behavior: Managing People and Organizations*, we once again relied on a fundamental assumption that has helped the book remain a market leader since the publication of its first edition more than two decades ago: we must equip today's students (and tomorrow's managers) with a perspective on managing people that allows them to create, interpret, judge, imagine, and build behaviors and relationships. This perspective requires students to gain a firm grasp of the fundamentals of human behavior in organizations—the basic foundations of behavior—so that they can develop new answers to the new problems they encounter. As new challenges are thrust upon us from around the world by global competition, new technologies, newer and faster information processes, new worldwide uncertainties, and customers who demand the best in quality and service, the next generation of managers will need to go back to basics—the fundamentals—and then combine those basics with valid new experiences in a complex world, and ultimately develop creative new solutions, processes, products, or services to gain competitive advantage.

THE TEXT THAT MEETS THE CHALLENGE

This edition of *Organizational Behavior: Managing People and Organizations* takes on that charge by providing the basics in each area, bolstered by the latest research in the field and infused with examples of what companies are doing in each area. We open each chapter with a textual introduction that weaves in a new opening incident and provides an immediate example of how the chapter topic is relevant in organizations. Chapter outlines and learning objectives are also presented at the beginning of each chapter. We continue to build and reinforce learning techniques at the end of each chapter in order to provide more opportunities to work with the chapter content. In addition to the end-of-chapter case, experiential exercise, and self-assessment exercise, we have added an exercise that will give students the opportunity to build their own managerial skills. *Organizational Behavior: Managing People and Organizations* prepares and energizes managers of the future for the complex and challenging tasks of the new century while it preserves the past contributions of the classics. It is comprehensive in its presentation of practical perspectives, backed up by the research and learning of the experts. We expect each reader to be inspired by the most exciting task of the new century: managing people in organizations.

CONTENT AND ORGANIZATION

The eleventh edition of *Organizational Behavior: Managing People and Organizations* retains the same basic overall organization that has worked so well for over 25 years. But within that framework, we also introduce several exciting and innovative changes that will further enhance the book's usefulness.

Part I discusses the managerial context of organizational behavior. In Chapter 1 we introduce the basic concepts of the field, discuss the importance of the study of organizational behavior, and relate organizational behavior to the broader field of management. Our new Chapter 2 focuses on the changing environment of organizations. The key topics addressed in this chapter are globalization, diversity, technology, ethics and corporate governance, and new employment relationships.

Part II includes six chapters that focus on the fundamental individual processes in organizations: individual behavior, motivation, employee performance, work stress, and decision making. Chapter 3 presents the foundations for understanding individual behavior in organizations by discussing the psychological nature of people, elements of personality, individual attitudes, perceptual processes, and workplace behavior. Coverage of emotional intelligence has also been added to this chapter. Chapter 4 focuses on the two primary categories of motivation theories: need-based approaches and process-based approaches. Chapters 5 and 6, meanwhile, move away from theory per se and describe some of the more important methods and techniques used by organizations to actually implement the theories of motivation, with Chapter 5 discussing work-related methods for motivating employees and Chapter 6 addressing reward-based approaches to motivation. Work stress, another important element of individual behavior in organizations, is covered in Chapter 7. Finally, Chapter 8 is devoted to decision making and problem solving.

In Part III we move from the individual aspects of organizational behavior to the more interpersonal aspects of the field, including communication, groups and teams, leadership and influence processes, power and politics, and conflict and negotiations. Chapters 9 and 10 are a two-chapter sequence on groups and teams in organizations. We believe there is too much important material to just have one chapter on these topics. Therefore, we present the basics of understanding the dynamics of small-group behavior in Chapter 9 and discuss the more applied material on teams in Chapter 10. In this manner, readers get to understand the more basic processes first before tackling the more complex issues in developing teams in organizations. Chapter 11 describes the behavioral aspects of communication in organizations. We present leadership in a two-chapter sequence, examining models and concepts in Chapter 12 and contemporary views in Chapter 13. We believe users will especially enjoy Chapter 13, with its coverage of strategic, ethical, and virtual leadership, as well as gender and cross-cultural impacts on leadership. Closely related to leadership are the concepts of power, politics, and workplace justice. This material is covered in Chapter 14. Part III closes with Chapter 15, devoted to conflict and negotiations in organizations.

In Part IV we address more macro and system-wide aspects of organizational behavior. Chapter 16, the first of a two-chapter sequence on organizational structure and design, presents the classical view of organizations and then describes the basic building blocks of organizations—division of labor, specialization, centralization, formalization, responsibility, and authority. Chapter 17 describes more about the factors and the process through which the structure of an organization is matched to fit the demands of change, new technology, and expanding competition, including global issues. Chapter 18 moves on to the more elusive concept of organizational culture. The final chapter,

Chapter 19, could really be the cornerstone of every chapter, because it presents the classical and contemporary views of organizational change. Due to the demands on organizations today, as stated earlier and by every management writer alive, change is the order of the day, the year, the decade, and the new century.

FEATURES OF THE BOOK

This edition of *Organizational Behavior: Managing People and Organizations* is guided by our continuing devotion to the preparation of the next generation of managers. This is reflected in several key elements of the book that stem, we believe, from this guiding principle: a strong student orientation; contemporary content; a real-world, applied approach; and effective pedagogy.

Student Orientation

We believe that students, instructors, and other readers will agree with our students' reactions to the book as being easy and even enjoyable to read with its direct and active style. We have tried to retain the comprehensive nature of the book while writing in a style that is active and lively and geared to the student reader. We want students to enjoy reading the book while they learn from it. All of the figures include meaningful captions to tie the figure directly to the concepts. The end-of-chapter features retain the popular experiential exercises and the diagnostic questionnaire, or self-assessments, and the real-world cases that show how the chapter material relates to actual practice.

Contemporary Content Coverage

This edition continues our tradition of presenting the most modern management approaches as expressed in the popular press and in academic research. The basic structure of the book remains the same, but you will find new coverage that represents the most recent research in many areas of the book.

Real-World, Applied Approach

The organizations cited in the opening incidents, examples, cases, and boxed features throughout this edition represent a blend of large, well-known and smaller, less well-known organizations so that students will see the applicability of the material in a variety of organizational settings. Each chapter opens and closes with concrete examples of relevant topics from the chapter. Each chapter also contains one or two topical boxes dealing with issues such as change, diversity, and ethics. Each box has a unique, identifying icon that distinguishes it and makes it easier for students to identify.

Effective Pedagogy

Our guiding objective continues to be to put together a package that enhances student learning. The package includes several features of the book, many of which have already been mentioned.

- Each chapter begins with a "Chapter Outline and Objectives" and ends with a "Synopsis."
- "Discussion Questions" at the end of each chapter stimulate interaction among students and provide a guide to complete studying of the chapter concepts.
- An "Experiencing Organizational Behavior" exercise at the end of each chapter helps students make the transition from textbook learning to real-world

applications. The end-of-chapter case, "How Do You See It?" also assists in this transition.

- A "Self-Assessment Exercise" activity at the end of each chapter gives students the opportunity to apply a concept from the chapter to a brief self-assessment or diagnostic activity.
- The "Building Managerial Skills" activity provides an opportunity for students to "get their hands dirty" and really use something discussed in the chapter.
- Figures, tables, photographs, and cartoons offer visual and humorous support for the text content. Explanatory captions to figures, photographs, and cartoons enhance their pedagogical value.
- A running marginal glossary and a complete glossary found on the textbook website provide additional support for identifying and learning key concepts.

A new design reflects this edition's content, style, and pedagogical program. The colors remain bold to reflect the dynamic nature of the behavioral and managerial challenges facing managers today, and the interior photographs in this edition have been specially selected to highlight the dynamic world of organizational behavior.

CHANGES TO THIS EDITION

While our book retains its proven basic framework and approach, we have also made many changes in this edition. Some of these changes are revisions and updates, and others are new features and new content. The major changes are as follows:

Updates and Revisions

All of the cases and boxed inserts are either new to this edition or heavily revised and updated versions from the previous edition. In addition, the newest research is cited throughout the book and examples updated to reflect the very latest events.

New Pedagogy

We have added two significant new pedagogical elements to this edition as well. First, while our book has always presented a balanced view of both service and non-service businesses, in this edition we decided to emphasize the growing service component of the business world in an even clearer manner. Specifically, we have added a "Service" box in each chapter that highlights the chapter content from a direct service orientation. In addition, we have also replaced the traditional chapter-closing case with a series of interesting and current video cases. We believe you will find these to be both valuable and engaging.

New Content

Finally, we have also added a substantial amount of new coverage of emerging topics and concepts. The major ones include:

- Chapter 2: A revised section focusing on how to frame ethical issues
- Chapter 5: A new discussion of extended work schedules as they relate to employee motivation
- Chapter 6: A new discussion of the balanced scorecard approach to performance management
- Chapter 8: A new chapter organization and new coverage of both evidence-based decision making and prospect theory
- Chapter 13: New coverage of the GLOBE leadership project

- Chapter 16: New discussion of Sony Corporation's reorganization by product in 2009 and 2012. Additional comments on how authority and responsibility may differ across cultures.
- Chapter 17: New discussion of the "boss-less" or "boss-free" organization
- Chapter 18: Expanded discussion of innovation with examples
- Chapter 19: Revised discussion (with data) on people working from home and the "office-less" office as workplace changes

SUPPLEMENTS

Instructor Supplements

- **Instructor's Resource CD-ROM (ISBN-10: 1435462831 | ISBN-13: 9781435462830)**
  Find all of the helpful, time-saving teaching resources you need to create a dynamic, interactive management course in this all-in-one Instructor's Resource CD. The Instructor's Resource CD includes the Instructor's Manual (IM) files, ExamView® testing files, Test Bank files in Word®, PowerPoint® slides, and a DVD Guide to help you most effectively use this edition's accompanying video cases. Updated content throughout the IM and PowerPoint slides reflects the latest editions on the text. Almost one third of the Test Bank questions are new. The IM, PowerPoints, and DVD Guide are also available on the instructor website.
- **DVD for Organizational Behavior (ISBN-10: 1435462076 | ISBN-13: 9781435462076)**
  Completely revised from the previous edition, nineteen NEW clips bring organizational behavior to life by challenging students' understanding and reinforcing concepts from the book. The clips are tied to the end of chapter, "How Do You See It?" Cases. The accompanying DVD guide (available on the Instructor's Companion Website) offers detailed descriptions of the segments, including chapter learning goals, chapter concepts spotlighted in segments, a synopsis, case discussion questions and suggested answers. These videos can also be found streaming on the CourseMate site as well as being offered as homework quizzing in CengageNOW.

Student Supplements

- **Management CourseMate with eBook Instant Access Code (ISBN-10: 1133629644 | ISBN-13: 9781133629641)**
  The more you study, the better the results. Make the most of your study time by accessing everything you need to succeed in one place. Read your textbook online, take notes, review flashcards, watch videos, play games, and take practice quizzes—online with CourseMate.
- **CengageNOW with eBook Instant Access Code (ISBN-10: 1133663664 | ISBN-13: 9781133663669)**
  CengageNOW is an easy-to-use online resource that helps you study in LESS TIME to get the grade you want NOW. A Personalized Study diagnostic tool assists you in accessing areas where you need to focus study. Built-in technology tools help you master concepts and prepare for exams and daily class.

- **Cengage Learning Write Experience 2.0 Powered by MyAccess with eBook Instant Access Code (ISBN-10: 1133663656 | ISBN-13: 9781133663652)**
  Cengage Learning's Write Experience is a new technology that is the first in higher education to offer students the opportunity to improve their writing and analytical skills without adding to professors' workload. Offered through an exclusive agreement with Vantage Learning, creator of the software used for GMAT essay grading, Write Experience evaluates students' answers to a select set of assignments for writing for voice, style, format, and originality. For more information about this unique course solution, contact your local sales representative or visit www.cengage .com/writeexperience. Better Writing. Better Outcomes. Write Experience.

ZEBRAS?!?

But why zebras on the cover? Well, for one thing, they present an attractive image. But more seriously, if we look a bit closer we can see that while all zebras look similar to one another, in reality the markings and patterns on each are unique. They are social animals that live and travel in groups. Within each group there is a well defined hierarchy based on power and status, and each group has a leader. And the group itself works with certain other groups (such as impala and wildebeests) to protect itself from other groups (most notably lions). When you have finished reading and studying this book, you will come to understand that, like zebras, each of us as a human being has certain things in common with all other humans, but each of us is also unique. We are social, live and travel in groups, have hierarchies and leaders, and both collaborate and compete with others. So, what can managers learn from zebras? Maybe not much, but they are still wonderful creatures to watch!

We would like to hear from you about your experiences in using the book. We want to know what you like and what you do not like about it. Please write to us via e-mail to tell us about your learning experiences. You may contact us at:

Ricky Griffin
rgriffin@tamu.edu

Greg Moorhead
greg.moorhead@asu.edu

Acknowledgments

Although this book bears our two names, numerous people have contributed to it. Through the years we have had the good fortune to work with many fine professionals who helped us to sharpen our thinking about this complex field and to develop new and more effective ways of discussing it. Their contributions were essential to the development of this edition. Any and all errors of omission, interpretation, and emphasis remain the responsibility of the authors.

Several reviewers made essential contributions to the development of this and previous editions. We would like to express a special thanks to them for taking the time to provide us with their valuable assistance:

LUCY ARENDT,
University of Wisconsin-Green Bay

ABDUL AZIZ,
College of Charleston

STEVE BALL,
Cleary College

BRENDAN BANNISTER,
Northeastern University

GREG BAXTER,
Southeastern Oklahoma State University

JON W. BEARD,
Purdue University

MARY-BETH BERES,
Mercer University Atlanta

RONALD A. BIGONESS,
Stephen F. Austin State University

ALLEN BLUEDORN,
University of Missouri Columbia

KRISTEN BOHLANDER,
Eckerd College

BRYAN BONNER,
University of Utah

WAYNE BOSS,
University of Colorado Boulder

MURRAY BRUNTON,
Central Ohio Technical College

JOHN BUNCH,
Kansas State University

MARK BUTLER,
San Diego State University

KEN BUTTERFIELD,
Washington State University

RICHARD R. CAMP,
Eastern Michigan University

ANTHONY CHELTE,
Western New England College

ANNE COOPER,
St. Petersburg Community College

JOHN L. COTTON,
Marquette University

DAN R. DALTON,
Indiana University Bloomington

CARLA L. DANDO,
Idaho State University

T. K. DAS,
Baruch College

ROGER DEAN,
Washington & Lee University

GEORGE DELODZIA,
University of Rhode Island

RONALD A. DIBATTISTA,
Bryant College

CRAIG DOMECK,
Palm Beach Atlantic University

HARRY DOMICONE,
California Lutheran University

THOMAS W. DOUGHERTY,
University of Missouri–Columbia

CATHY DUBOIS,
Kent State University

EARLINDA ELDER-ALBRITTON,
Detroit College of Business

STEVEN ELIAS,
New Mexico State University

LESLIE ELROD,
University of Cincinnati Blue Ash College

STANLEY W. ELSEA,
Kansas State University

JAN FELDBAUER,
Austin Community College

MAUREEN J. FLEMING,
The University of Montana—Missoula

JOSEPH FOREST,
Georgia State University

PHIL GALLAGHER,
Stevenson University

ELIEZER GEISLER,
Northeastern Illinois University

ROBERT GIACALONE,
University of Richmond

BOB GODDARD,
Appalachian State University

LYNN HARLAND,
University of Nebraska at Omaha

STAN HARRIS,
Lawrence Tech University

NELL HARTLEY,
Robert Morris College

PETER HEINE,
Stetson University

WILLIAM HENDRIX,
Clemson University

JOHN JERMIER,
University of South Florida

AVIS L. JOHNSON,
University of Akron

BRUCE JOHNSON,
Gustavus Adolphus College

GWEN JONES,
Bowling Green State University

KATHLEEN JOHNSON,
Keene State College

ROBERT T. KELLER,
University of Houston

MICHAEL KLAUSNER,
University of Pittsburgh at Bradford

STEPHEN KLEISATH,
University of Wisconsin

BARBARA E. KOVATCH,
Rutgers University

DAVID R. LEE,
University of Dayton

RICHARD LEIFER,
Rensselaer Polytechnic Institute

ROBERT W. LEONARD,
Lebanon Valley College

FENGRU LI,
University of Montana

PETER LORENZI,
University of Central Arkansas

JOSEPH B. LOVELL,
California State University,
San Bernardino

PATRICIA MANNINEN,
North Shore Community College

EDWARD K. MARLOW,
Eastern Illinois University

EDWARD MILES,
Georgia State University

C. W. MILLARD,
University of Puget Sound

ALAN N. MILLER,
University of Nevada, Las Vegas

HERFF L. MOORE,
University of Central Arkansas

ROBERT MOORMAN,
West Virginia University

STEPHAN J. MOTOWIDLO,
Pennsylvania State University

RICHARD T. MOWDAY,
University of Oregon

MARGARET A. NEALE,
Northwestern University

CHRISTOPHER P. NECK,
Virginia Tech

LINDA L. NEIDER,
University of Miami

MARY LIPPITT NICHOLS,
University of Minnesota Minneapolis

RANJNA PATEL,
Bethune-Cookman College

ROBERT J. PAUL,
Kansas State University

JOHN PERRY,
Pennsylvania State University

PAMELA POMMERENKE,
Michigan State University

JAMES C. QUICK,
University of Texas at Arlington

RICHARD RASPEN,
Wilkes University

ELIZABETH RAWLIN,
University of South Carolina

GARY REINKE,
University of Maryland

JOAN B. RIVERA,
West Texas A&M University

BILL ROBINSON,
Indiana University of Pennsylvania

HANNAH ROTHSTEIN,
Baruch College

GOLI SADRI,
California State University–Fullerton

CAROL S. SAUNDERS,
University of Oklahoma

DANIEL SAUERS,
Winona State University

CONSTANCE SAVAGE,
Ashland University

MARY JANE SAXTON,
University of Colorado at Denver

RALPH L. SCHMITT,
Macomb Community College

RANDALL S. SCHULER,
Rutgers University

AMIT SHAH,
Frostburg State University

GARY SHIELDS,
Wayne State University

PAMELA K. SIGAFOOSE,
Palm Beach Atlantic University

RANDALL G. SLEETH,
Virginia Commonwealth University

DAYLE SMITH,
University of San Francisco

DR. ANDREA SMITH-HUNTER,
Siena College

RIEANN SPENCE-GALE,
Northern Virginia Community College (Alexandria)

WILLIAM R. STEVENS,
Missouri Southern State College

DIANNA L. STONE,
University of Texas at San Antonio

NAREATHA STUDDARD,
Arkansas State University

CHRISTY SUCIU,
Boise State University

STEVE TAYLOR,
Boston College

DONALD TOMPKINS,
Slippery Rock University

AHMAD TOOTOONCHI,
Frostburg State University

MATTHEW VALLE,
Troy State University at Dothan

LINN VAN DYNE,
Michigan State University

DAVID D. VAN FLEET,
Arizona State University

BOBBY C. VAUGHT,
Southwest Missouri State University

SEAN VALENTINE,
University of Wyoming

JACK W. WALDRIP,
American Graduate School of International Management

JOHN P. WANOUS,
The Ohio State University

JUDITH Y. WEISINGER,
Northeastern University

JOSEPH W. WEISS,
Bentley College

ALBERT D. WIDMAN,
Berkeley College

The eleventh edition could never have been completed without the support of Texas A&M University, whose leadership team facilitated our work by providing the environment that encourages scholarly activities and contributions to the field. Several assistants and graduate and undergraduate assistants were also involved in the development of the eleventh edition.

We would also like to acknowledge the outstanding team of professionals at Cengage Learning who helped us prepare this book. Julia Chase has been steadfast in her commitment to quality and her charge to us to raise quality throughout the book. Jennifer Ziegler, Viswanath Prasanna, Amber Hosea, Kristina Mose-Libon, Punitha Rajamohan, Susan Buschorn, Mike Schenk, Scott Person, Robin LeFevre, Stacy Shirley, and Tammy Grega were also key players in the creation of this text and support program.

Finally, we would like to acknowledge the role of change in our own lives. One of us has successfully fought cancer, and the other has had a complete lower leg reconstruction. The techniques that led us to where we are today did not exist when we wrote the first edition of this book. Hence, change has touched the two of us in profound ways. We also continue to be mindful of the daily reminders that we get about change in our personal lives. Our children, for example, were born in the early days of our partnership and have now gone on to start families of their own and further enrich our lives with grandchildren. Indeed, without the love and support of our families, our lives would be far less meaningful. It is with all of our love that we dedicate this book to them.

R.W.G.
G.M.

For my daughter Ashley, still her daddy's sweet and shining star
(and sometimes his boss!).

— R.W.G.

For my family: Linda, Alex, Erin, Lindsay, Kevin, and Bennett.

—G.M.

CHAPTER 1

An Overview of Organizational Behavior

Chapter Outline

- What is Organizational Behavior?
- Organizational Behavior and the Management Process
- Organizational Behavior and the Manager's Job
- Contemporary Organizational Behavior
- Contextual Perspectives on Organizational Behavior
- Managing for Effectiveness

Chapter Learning Objectives

After studying this chapter, you should be able to:

1. Define organizational behavior.
2. Identify the functions that comprise the management process and relate them to organizational behavior.
3. Relate organizational behavior to basic managerial roles and skills.
4. Describe contemporary organizational behavior characteristics.
5. Discuss contextual perspectives on organizational behavior.
6. Describe the role of organizational behavior in managing for effectiveness.

No Company for Old-Fashioned Management

"When you think about employees first, the bottom line is better."

—Kevin Stickles, VP for Human Resources, Wegmans Food Markets

If you're looking for the best Parmesan cheese for your chicken parmigiana recipe, you might try Wegmans, especially if you happen to live in the vicinity of Pittsford, New York. Cheese department manager Carol Kent will be happy to recommend the best brand because her job calls for knowing cheese as well as managing some 20 subordinates. Kent is a knowledgeable employee, and knowledgeable employees, boasts Wegmans CEO Danny Wegman, are "something our competitors don't have and our customers couldn't get anywhere else."

Wegmans Food Markets, a family-owned East Coast chain with nearly 80 outlets in 6 states, prides itself on its commitment to customers, and it shows: It ranks at the top of the latest *Consumer Reports* survey of the best national and regional grocery stores. But commitment to customers is only half of the overall Wegmans strategy, which calls for reaching the company's customers through its employees. "How do we differentiate ourselves?" asks Wegman, who then proceeds to answer his own question: "If we can sell products that require knowledge in terms of how you use them, that's our strategy. Anything that requires knowledge and service gives us a reason to be." That's the logic behind one of Carol Kent's recent assignments—one which she understandably regards as a perk: Wegmans sent her to Italy to conduct a personal study of Italian cheese. "We sat with the families [that make the cheeses]," she recalls, "broke bread with them. It helped me understand that we're not just selling a piece of cheese. We're selling a tradition, a quality."

Kent and the employees in her department also enjoy the best benefits package in the industry, including fully paid health insurance. And that includes part-timers, who make up about two-thirds of the company's workforce of more than 42,000. In part, the strategy of extending benefits to this large segment of the labor force is intended to make sure that stores have enough good workers for crucial peak periods, but there's no denying that the costs of employee-friendly policies can mount up. At 15 to 17 percent of sales, for example, Wegmans' labor costs are well above the 12 percent figure for most supermarkets. But according to one

Tracy A. Woodward/Washington Post/Getty Images

Wegmans is known as one of the most effectively managed supermarket chains in the world. Mark Lewis, a Wegmans baker, has a thorough understanding of the bread baking process and is happy to explain it to customers.

company HR executive, holding down labor costs isn't necessarily a strategic priority: "We would have stopped offering free health insurance [to part-timers] a long time ago," she admits, "if we tried to justify the costs."

Besides, employee turnover at Wegmans is just 6 percent—about half the industry average. And this is an industry in which total turnover costs have been known to outstrip total annual profits by 40 percent. Wegmans employees tend to be knowledgeable because about 20 percent of them have been with the company for at least 10 years, and many have logged at least a quarter century. Says one 19-year-old college student who works at an upstate New York Wegmans while pursuing a career as a high school history teacher, "I love this place. If teaching doesn't work out, I would so totally work at Wegmans." Edward McLaughlin, who directs the Food Industry Management Program at Cornell University, understands this sort of attitude: "When you're a 16-year-old kid, the last thing you want to do is wear a geeky shirt and work for a supermarket," but at Wegmans, he explains, "it's a badge of honor. You're not a geeky cashier. You're part of the social fabric."

In 2012, Wegmans placed fourth in *Fortune* magazine's annual list of "100 Best Companies to Work For"—good for 15 consecutive years on the list and 8 straight top-7 finishes. "It says that we're doing something right," says a company spokesperson, "and that there's no better way to take care of our customers than to be a great place for our employees to work." "Our employees," explains VP for Human Resources Kevin Stickles, "are our number-one asset, period. The first question you ask is: 'Is this the best thing for the employee?' " The approach, argues Stickles, anchors a solid business model: "When you think about employees first, the bottom line is better. We want our employees to extend the brand to our customers."

In addition to its healthcare package, Wegmans has been cited for such perks as fitness center discounts, compressed work weeks, telecommuting, and domestic-partner benefits (which extend to same-sex partners). Under the company's Employee Scholarship Program, full-time workers can also receive up to $2,200 a year for four years, and part-timers up to $1,500.

Since its inception in 1984, the program has handed out more than $81 million in scholarships to more than 25,000 employees, including $4.5 million in 2011. Like most Wegman policies, this one combines employee outreach with long-term corporate strategy: "This program has made a real difference in the lives of many young people," says president Colleen Wegman, who adds that it's also "one of the reasons we've been able to attract the best and the brightest to work at Wegmans."

Granted, Wegmans, which has remained in family hands since its founding in 1916, has an advantage in being as generous with its resources as its family of top executives wants to be: It doesn't have to do everything with quarterly profits in mind. Mired in a "public mentality," says Stickles, "the first thing [other companies] think about is the quarter. The first thing is that you cut labor." The Wegman family, adds senior VP Mary Ellen Burris, has no intention of taking the company public: "It takes away your ability to focus on your people and your customers."

Wegmans likes to point out that taking care of its employees is a longstanding priority. Profit sharing and fully funded medical coverage were introduced in 1950 by Robert Wegman, son and nephew of brothers Walter and John, who opened the firm's original flagship store in Rochester, New York, in 1930. Why did Robert Wegman make such generous gestures to his employees way back then? "Because," he says simply, "I was no different from them."

What Do You Think?

1. Why don't more firms adopt the kind of management practices that have contributed to Wegmans' success?
2. Under what circumstances might Wegmans be forced to change its approach to dealing with its employees?

References: Maria Panaritis, "Wegmans Tops List in Consumer Survey," *Philadelphia Inquirer*, April 3, 2012, www.philly.com on April 5, 2012; Jon Springer, "Danny Wegman," *Supermarket News*, July 14, 2009, http://supermarketnews.com on April 15, 2011; David Rohde, "The Anti-Walmart: The Secret Sauce of Wegmans Is People," *The Atlantic*, March 23, 2012, www.theatlantic.com on April 5, 2012; Michael A. Prospero, "Employee Innovator: Wegmans," *Fast Company*, October 2004, www.fastcompany.com on April 5, 2012; "100 Best Companies to Work For," *Fortune*, February 6, 2012, http://money.cnn.com on April 5, 2012; "Wegmans Scholarships" (2012), www.wegmans.com on April 5, 2012; "Wegmans Announces 2011 Employee Scholarship Recipients," press release, June 17, 2011, www.wegmans.com on April 5, 2012.

In many ways a Wegmans store may not look substantially different from a large national chain store. But its dual emphasis on both customer and employee satisfaction had paid big dividends as the firm continues to thrive through good times and bad. Regardless of their size, scope, or location, all organizations have at least one thing in common—they are comprised of people. It is these people who make decisions about the strategic direction of a firm, it is they who acquire the resources the firm uses to create new products, and it is they who sell those products. People manage a firm's corporate headquarters, its warehouses, and its information technology, and it is people who clean up at the end of the day. No matter how effective a manager might be, all organizational successes—and failures—are the result of the behaviors of many people. Indeed, no manager can succeed without the assistance of others.

Thus, any manager—whether responsible for a big business such as Google, Abercrombie & Fitch, General Electric, Apple, Starbucks, or British Airways; for a niche business such as the Boston Celtics basketball team or the Mayo Clinic; or for a local Pizza Hut restaurant or neighborhood dry cleaning establishment—must strive to understand the people who work in the organization. This book is about those people. It is also about the organization itself and the managers who operate it. The study of organizations and the study of the people who work in them together constitute the field of organizational behavior. Our starting point in exploring this field begins with a more detailed discussion of its meaning and its importance to managers.

WHAT IS ORGANIZATIONAL BEHAVIOR?

What exactly is meant by the term "organizational behavior"? And why should it be studied? Answers to these two fundamental questions will both help establish our foundation for discussion and analysis and help you better appreciate the rationale as to how and why understanding the field can be of value to you in the future.

The Meaning of Organizational Behavior

Organizational behavior is the study of human behavior in organizational settings, the interface between human behavior and the organization, and the organization itself.

Organizational behavior (OB) is the study of human behavior in organizational settings, of the interface between human behavior and the organization, and of the organization itself.[1] Although we can focus on any one of these three areas, we must also remember that all three are ultimately necessary for a comprehensive understanding of organizational behavior. For example, we can study individual behavior without explicitly considering the organization. But because the organization influences and is influenced by the individual, we cannot fully understand the individual's behavior without learning something about the organization. Similarly, we can study organizations without focusing explicitly on the people within them. But again, we are looking at only a portion of the puzzle. Eventually we must consider the other pieces, as well as the whole.

Figure 1.1 illustrates this view of organizational behavior. It shows the linkages among human behavior in organizational settings, the individual–organization interface, the organization itself, and the environment surrounding the organization. Each individual brings to an organization a unique set of personal characteristics and a unique personal background and set of experiences from other organizations. Therefore, in considering the people who work in their organizations, managers must look at the unique perspective each individual brings to the work setting. For example, suppose managers at The Home Depot review data showing that employee turnover within the firm is gradually but consistently increasing. Further suppose that they hire a consultant to help them better understand the problem. As a starting point, the consultant might analyze the types of people the company usually hires. The goal would be to learn as much as possible about the nature of the company's workforce as individuals—their expectations, their personal goals, and so forth.

But individuals do not work in isolation. They come in contact with other people and with the organization in a variety of ways. Points of contact include managers, coworkers, the formal policies and procedures of the organization, and various changes implemented by the organization. In addition, over time, individuals change, as a function of personal experiences and maturity as well as through work experiences and

FIGURE 1.1

The Nature of Organizational Behavior

The field of organizational behavior attempts to understand human behavior in organizational settings, the organization itself, and the individual–organization interface. As illustrated here, these areas are highly interrelated. Thus, although it is possible to focus on only one of these areas at a time, a complete understanding of organizational behavior requires knowledge of all three areas.

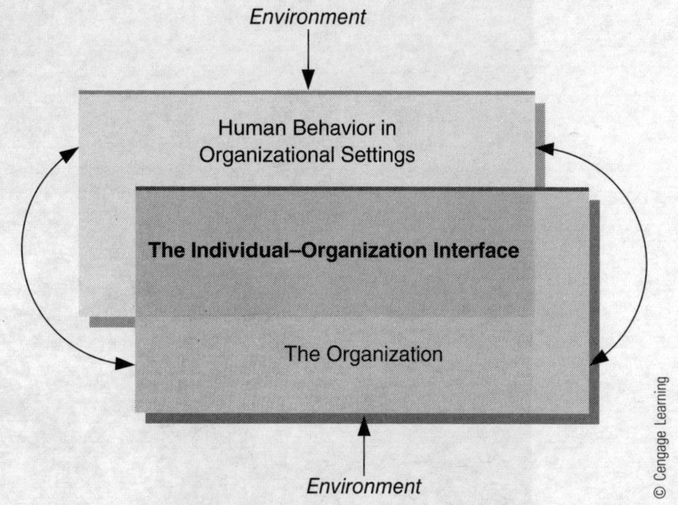

organizational developments. The organization, in turn, is affected by the presence and eventual absence of the individual. Clearly, then, managers must also consider how the individual and the organization interact. Thus, the consultant studying turnover at The Home Depot might next look at the orientation procedures and initial training for newcomers to the organization. The goal of this phase of the study would be to understand some of the dynamics of how incoming individuals are introduced to and interact with the broader organizational context.

An organization, of course, exists before a particular person joins it and continues to exist after he or she leaves. Thus, the organization itself represents a crucial third perspective from which to view organizational behavior. For instance, the consultant studying turnover would also need to study the structure and culture of The Home Depot. An understanding of factors such as a firm's performance evaluation and reward systems, its decision-making and communication patterns, and the structure of the firm itself can provide added insight into why some people choose to leave a company and others elect to stay.

Clearly, then, the field of organizational behavior is both exciting and complex. Myriad variables and concepts accompany the interactions just described, and together these factors greatly complicate the manager's ability to understand, appreciate, and manage others in the organization. They also provide unique and important opportunities to enhance personal and organizational effectiveness.

The Importance of Organizational Behavior

The importance of organizational behavior may now be clear, but we should nonetheless take a few moments to make it even more explicit. Most people are raised and educated in organizations, acquire most of their material possessions from organizations, and die as members of organizations. Many of our activities are regulated by the various organizations that make up our governments. And most adults spend the better part of their lives working in organizations. Because organizations influence our lives so powerfully, we have every reason to be concerned about how and why those organizations function.

In our relationships with organizations, we may adopt any one of several roles or identities. For example, we can be consumers, employees, suppliers, competitors, owners, or investors. Since most readers of this book are either present or future managers, we will adopt a managerial perspective throughout our discussion. The study of

Southwest Airlines is consistently ranked among the most admired businesses in the United States. One key to Southwest's success is its commitment to hiring, training, rewarding, and retaining outstanding employees. Concepts and ideas from the field of organizational behavior reinforce many of the employment practices used at Southwest.

organizational behavior can greatly clarify the factors that affect how managers manage. Hence, the field attempts to describe the complex human context of organizations and to define the opportunities, problems, challenges, and issues associated with that realm.

The value of organizational behavior is that it isolates important aspects of the manager's job and offers specific perspectives on the human side of management: people as organizations, people as resources, and people as people. To further underscore the importance of organizational behavior to managers, we should consider this simple fact: Year in and year out, most of the firms on *Fortune*'s list of the world's most admired companies have impeccable reputations for valuing and respecting the people who work for them.[2] Clearly, then, an understanding of organizational behavior can play a vital role in managerial work. To most effectively use the knowledge provided by this field, managers must thoroughly understand its various concepts, assumptions, and premises. To provide this foundation, we next tie organizational behavior even more explicitly to management and then turn to a more detailed examination of the manager's job itself.

Organizational Behavior and Management

Virtually all organizations have managers with titles such as chief financial officer, marketing manager, director of public relations, vice president for human resources, and plant manager. But probably no organization has a position called "organizational behavior manager." The reason for this is simple: Organizational behavior is not a defined business function or area of responsibility similar to finance or marketing. Rather, understanding of organizational behavior provides a set of insights and tools that all managers can use to carry out their jobs more effectively.

An appreciation and understanding of organizational behavior helps managers better understand why others in the organization behave as they do. For example, most managers in an organization are directly responsible for the work-related behaviors of a certain set of other people—their immediate subordinates. Typical managerial activities in this realm include motivating employees to work harder, ensuring that employees' jobs are properly designed, resolving conflicts, evaluating performance, and helping workers set goals to achieve rewards. The field of organizational behavior abounds with models and research relevant to each of these activities.[3]

Unless they happen to be chief executive officers (CEOs), managers also report to others in the organization (and even the CEO reports to the board of directors). In dealing with these individuals, an understanding of basic issues associated with leadership, power and political behavior, decision making, organization structure and design, and organizational culture can be extremely beneficial. Again, the field of organizational behavior provides numerous valuable insights into these processes.

Managers can also use their knowledge of organizational behavior to better understand their own needs, motives, behaviors, and feelings, which will help them improve decision-making capabilities, control stress, communicate better, and comprehend how career dynamics unfold. The study of organizational behavior provides insights into all of these concepts and processes.

Managers interact with a variety of colleagues, peers, and coworkers inside the organization. An understanding of attitudinal processes, individual differences, group dynamics, intergroup dynamics, organizational culture, and power and political behavior can help managers handle such interactions more effectively. Organizational behavior provides a variety of practical insights into these processes. Virtually all of the insights into behavioral processes already mentioned are also valuable in interactions with people outside the organization—suppliers, customers, competitors, government officials, representatives of citizens' groups, union officials, and potential joint-venture partners. In addition, a special understanding of the environment, technology, and global issues is valuable. Again, organizational behavior offers managers many different insights into how and why things happen as they do.

Finally, these patterns of interactions hold true regardless of the type of organization. Whether a business is large or small, domestic or international, growing or stagnating, its managers perform their work within a social context. And the same can be said of managers in health care, education, and government, as well as those in student organizations such as fraternities, sororities, and professional clubs. We see, then, that it is essentially impossible to understand and practice management without considering the numerous areas of organizational behavior. Further, as more and more organizations hire managers from other countries, the processes of understanding human behavior in organizations will almost certainly grow increasingly complex. We now address the nature of the manager's job in more detail before returning to our primary focus on organizational behavior.

ORGANIZATIONAL BEHAVIOR AND THE MANAGEMENT PROCESS

Managerial work is fraught with complexity and unpredictability and enriched with opportunity and excitement. However, in characterizing managerial work, most educators and other experts find it useful to conceptualize the activities performed by managers as reflecting one or more of four basic functions. These functions are generally referred to as *planning*, *organizing*, *leading*, and *controlling*. While these functions are

FIGURE 1.2

Basic Managerial Functions

Managers engage in the four basic functions of planning, organizing, leading, and controlling. These functions are applied to human, financial, physical, and information resources with the ultimate purpose of efficiently and effectively attaining organizational goals.

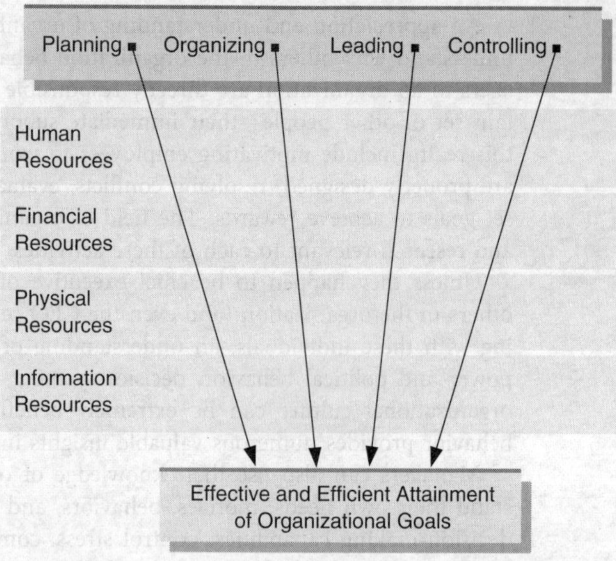

often described in a sequential manner, in reality, of course, most managerial work involves all four functions simultaneously.

Similarly, organizations use many different resources in the pursuit of their goals and objectives. As with management functions, though, these resources can also generally be classified into four groups: *human, financial, physical,* and/or *information* resources. As illustrated in Figure 1.2, managers combine these resources through the four basic functions, with the ultimate purpose of efficiently and effectively attaining the goals of the organization. That is, the figure shows how managers apply the basic functions across resources to advance the organization toward its goals.

Planning is the process of determining an organization's desired future position and the best means of getting there.

Planning, the first managerial function, is the process of determining the organization's desired future position and deciding how best to get there. The planning process at Sears, for example, includes studying and analyzing the environment, deciding on appropriate goals, outlining strategies for achieving those goals, and developing tactics to help execute the strategies. Behavioral processes and characteristics pervade each of these activities. Perception, for instance, plays a major role in environmental scanning, and creativity and motivation influence how managers set goals, strategies, and tactics for their organization. Larger corporations such as Walmart and Starbucks usually rely on their top management teams to handle most planning activities. In smaller firms, the owner usually takes care of planning.

Organizing is the process of designing jobs, grouping jobs into units, and establishing patterns of authority between jobs and units.

The second managerial function is **organizing**—the process of designing jobs, grouping jobs into manageable units, and establishing patterns of authority among jobs and groups of jobs. This process produces the basic structure, or framework, of the organization. For large organizations such as Apple and Toyota, that structure can be extensive and complicated. The structure includes several hierarchical layers and spans myriad activities and areas of responsibility. Smaller firms can often function with a relatively simple and straightforward form of organization. As noted earlier, the processes and characteristics of the organization itself are a major theme of organizational behavior.

Leading is the process of getting the organization's members to work together toward the organization's goals.

Leading, the third major managerial function, is the process of motivating members of the organization to work together toward the organization's goals. An Old Navy store manager, for example, must hire people, train them, and motivate them. Major components of leading include motivating employees, managing group dynamics, and the actual process of leadership itself. These are all closely related to major areas of organizational behavior. All managers, whether they work in a huge multinational corporation spanning dozens of countries or in a small neighborhood business serving a few square city blocks, must understand the importance of leading.

Controlling is the process of monitoring and correcting the actions of the organization and its members to keep them directed toward their goals.

The fourth managerial function, **controlling**, is the process of monitoring and correcting the actions of the organization and its people to keep them headed toward their goals. A manager at Best Buy has to control costs, inventory, and so on. Again, behavioral processes and characteristics are a key part of this function. Performance evaluation, reward systems, and motivation, for example, all apply to control. Control is of vital importance to all businesses, but it may be especially critical to smaller ones. Walmart, for example, can withstand with relative ease a loss of several thousand dollars due to poor control, but an equivalent loss may be devastating to a small firm.

ORGANIZATIONAL BEHAVIOR AND THE MANAGER'S JOB

As they engage in the basic management functions previously described, managers often find themselves playing a variety of different roles. Moreover, to perform their functions most effectively and to be successful in their various roles, managers must also draw upon a set of critical skills. This section first introduces the basic managerial roles and then describes the core skills necessary for success in an organization.

Basic Managerial Roles

In an organization, as in a play or a movie, a role is the part a person plays in a given situation. Managers often play a number of different roles. In general, as summarized in Table 1.1, there are ten basic managerial roles, which cluster into three general categories.[4]

Table 1.1 Important Managerial Roles

CATEGORY	ROLE	EXAMPLE
Interpersonal	Figurehead	Attend employee retirement ceremony
	Leader	Encourage workers to increase productivity
	Liaison	Coordinate activities of two committees
Informational	Monitor	Scan *Business Week* for information about competition
	Disseminator	Send out memos outlining new policies
	Spokesperson	Hold press conference to announce new plant
Decision-Making	Entrepreneur	Develop idea for new product and convince others of its merits
	Disturbance handler	Resolve dispute
	Resource allocator	Allocate budget requests
	Negotiator	Settle new labor contract

interpersonal roles are the figurehead, the leader, and the liaison.

Interpersonal Roles The **interpersonal roles** are primarily social in nature; that is, they are roles in which the manager's main task is to relate to other people in certain ways. The manager sometimes may serve as a *figurehead* for the organization. Taking visitors to dinner and attending ribbon-cutting ceremonies are part of the figurehead role. In the role of *leader*, the manager works to hire, train, and motivate employees. Finally, the *liaison* role consists of relating to others outside the group or organization. For example, a manager at Intel might be responsible for handling all price negotiations with a key supplier of microchips. Obviously, each of these interpersonal roles involves behavioral processes.

informational roles are the monitor, the disseminator, and the spokesperson.

Informational Roles The three **informational roles** involve some aspect of information processing. The *monitor* actively seeks information that might be of value to the organization in general or to specific managers. The manager who transmits this information to others is carrying out the role of *disseminator*. The *spokesperson* speaks for the organization to outsiders. A manager chosen by Dell Computer to appear at a press conference announcing a new product launch or other major deal, such as a recent decision to undertake a joint venture with Microsoft or Amazon, would be serving in this role. Again, behavioral processes are part of each of these roles, because information is almost always exchanged between people.

decision-making roles are the entrepreneur, the disturbance handler, the resource allocator, and the negotiator.

Decision-Making Roles Finally, there are also four **decision-making roles**. The *entrepreneur* voluntarily initiates change—such as innovations or new strategies—within the organization. The *disturbance handler* helps settle disputes between various parties, such as other managers and their subordinates. The *resource allocator* decides who will get what—how resources in the organization will be distributed among various individuals and groups. The *negotiator* represents the organization in reaching agreements with other organizations, such as contracts between management and labor unions. Again, behavioral processes clearly are crucial in each of these decisional roles.

Critical Managerial Skills

Another important element of managerial work is mastery of the skills necessary to carry out basic functions and fill fundamental roles. In general, most successful managers have a strong combination of technical, interpersonal, conceptual, and diagnostic skills.[5]

Technical skills are the skills necessary to accomplish specific tasks within the organization.

Technical Skills **Technical skills** are skills necessary to accomplish specific tasks within the organization. Designing a new computer for Hewlett-Packard, developing a new formula for a frozen-food additive for Conagra, or writing a press release for Halliburton all require technical skills. Hence, these skills are generally associated with the operations employed by the organization in its production processes. For example, David Packard and Bill Hewlett, founders of Hewlett-Packard, started out their careers as engineers. Other examples of managers with strong technical skills include Eric Molson (CEO of Molson Coors Brewing, who began his career as a brewmaster) and Ron Meyer (COO of Universal Studios, who began his career as a filmmaker). The CEOs of the Big Four accounting firms also began their careers as accountants.

The manager uses **interpersonal skills** to communicate with, understand, and motivate individuals and groups.

Interpersonal Skills The manager uses **interpersonal skills** to communicate with, understand, and motivate individuals and groups. As we have noted, managers spend a large portion of their time interacting with others, so it is clearly important that they get along well with other people. For instance, David Novak is CEO of YUM! Brands, the firm that owns KFC, Pizza Hut, and Taco Bell. Novak is able to relate to employees

Christinne Muschi cm/Reuters

Eric Molson began his career as a brewmaster and eventually became CEO of Molson Coors Brewing. His technical understanding of beer making processes contributed to his success many times as he climbed the corporate ladder.

throughout the firm. He is also known to his employees as a caring, compassionate, and an honest person. These qualities inspire others throughout the firm and motivate them to work hard to help Novak reach the firm's goals.

The manager uses **conceptual skills** to think in the abstract.

Conceptual Skills **Conceptual skills** are the manager's ability to think in the abstract. A manager with strong conceptual skills is able to see the "big picture." That is, she or he can see opportunity where others see roadblocks or problems. For example, after Steve Wozniak and Steve Jobs built a small computer of their own design in a garage, Wozniak essentially saw a new toy that could be tinkered with. Jobs, however, saw far more and convinced his partner that they should start a company to make and sell the computers. The result? Apple Computer. In subsequent years Jobs also used his conceptual skills to identify the potential in digital media technologies, leading to the introduction of such products as the iPod, the iPhone, iTunes, and the iPad as well as his overseeing the creation of Pixar Animation Studios. When he died in 2011 Jobs was hailed as one of the most innovative managers of all time.

The manager uses **diagnostic skills** to understand cause-and-effect relationships and to recognize the optimal solutions to problems.

Diagnostic Skills Most successful managers also bring diagnostic skills to the organization. **Diagnostic skills** allow managers to better understand cause-and-effect relationships and to recognize the optimal solutions to problems. For instance, when Ed Whitacre was chairman and CEO of SBC Communications, he recognized that, though his firm was performing well in the consumer market, it lacked strong brand identification in the business environment. He first carefully identified and then implemented an action to remedy the firm's shortcoming—SBC would buy AT&T (for $16 billion), acquiring in the process the very name recognition that his company needed. After the

FIGURE 1.3

Managerial Skills at Different Organizational Levels

Most managers need technical, interpersonal, conceptual, and diagnostic skills, but the importance of these skills varies by level in the organization. As illustrated here, conceptual and diagnostic skills are usually more important for top managers in organizations, whereas technical and interpersonal skills may be more important for first-line managers.

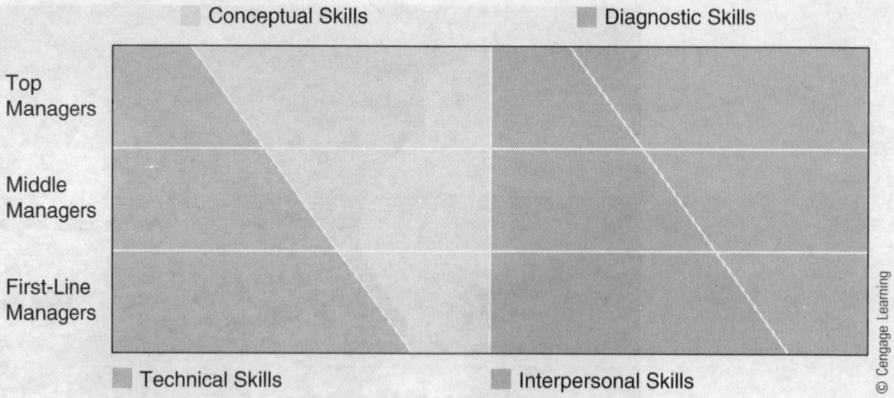

acquisition was completed, the firm changed its corporate name from SBC to AT&T. And it was Whitacre's diagnostic skills that pulled it all together.[6] Indeed, his legacy of strong diagnostic skills led to his being asked to lead the corporate turnaround at General Motors in 2009.

Of course, not every manager has an equal measure of these four basic types of skills. Nor are equal measures critical. As shown in Figure 1.3, for example, the optimal skills mix tends to vary with the manager's level in the organization. First-line managers generally need to depend more on their technical and interpersonal skills and less on their conceptual and diagnostic skills. Top managers tend to exhibit the reverse combination—more emphasis on conceptual and diagnostic skills and less dependence on technical and interpersonal skills. Middle managers require a more even distribution of skills. Similarly, the mix of needed skills can vary depending on economic circumstances. One recent survey suggested that during very tough economic times, the most important skills for a CEO are to be an effective communicator and motivator, be decisive, and be a visionary.[7]

You probably possess all of these skills to a greater or lesser degree, but what about your *disruptive skills*? At first glance, this doesn't sound like a particularly desirable skill set, but it certainly can be. To find out how, read the *Change* box entitled "Do You Have What It Takes to Disrupt Your Work Life?" on page 13.

CONTEMPORARY ORGANIZATIONAL BEHAVIOR

Now, with this additional understanding of managerial work, we can return to our discussion of organizational behavior. We first introduce two fundamental characteristics of contemporary organizational behavior that warrant special discussion; we then identify the particular set of concepts that are generally accepted as defining the field's domain.

Characteristics of the Field

Managers and researchers who use concepts and ideas from organizational behavior must recognize that it has an interdisciplinary focus and a descriptive nature; that is, it draws from a variety of other fields and it attempts to describe behavior (rather than to predict how behavior can be changed in consistent and generalizable ways).

CHANGE Do You Have What It Takes to Disrupt Your Work Life?

Let's say that you're a doctor who's tired of practicing medicine. It happens. One female physician wrote to Philippa Kennealy, a career coach for medical professionals, to say, "I don't want to practice clinical medicine anymore and am currently at home with my children. I am at a loss as to what I can do with my knowledge and skills." Kennealy suggested that her attention to detail and commitment to high performance might make her valuable in the field of electronic medical records (EMR)—creating computerized medical records for such healthcare deliverers as hospitals or physicians' offices. Kennealy also cites the example of a Stanford-trained general surgeon who switched to entrepreneurship to cofound four medical-device startups.

> ***"We often overlook our best skills—our innate talents—simply because we perform them without even thinking."***
>
> —WHITNEY JOHNSON, FOUNDING PARTNER, ROSE PARK ADVISORS

Granted, when it comes to making such career- (and life-) changing decisions, the average physician is at a certain advantage over most of the rest of us. At the very least, your doctor is probably good at listening, "connect-the-dot" problem solving, and remembering extremely complex details. HR experts call these *disruptive skills*—what Whitney Johnson, a founding partner of the investment firm Rose Park Advisors, identifies as "our distinctive innate talents rather than 'me-too' skills.... These are the skills," says Johnson, "that can help you carve out a disruptive niche—consequently upping your value in the marketplace." She adds that your disruptive skill might actually be "a confluence of skills." Take, for example, our career-disaffected physician. Many job candidates can claim to be good listeners; many others may claim above-average problem-solving ability and still others a remarkable capacity for remembering things. A physician, however, can honestly put all three skills on her résumé, and "for the right customer," observes Johnson, "that combination is your disruptive skill."

At this point, you're probably saying to yourself, "Never mind spoiled doctors. I'm just looking for a job to help pay for a college education in which I haven't even decided on a major." True enough, but most us have things that we're pretty good at—abilities that may in fact be potential disruptive skills. One big problem is the fact that a lot of us don't even know *what* they are, much less what workplace *value* they might have. According to Johnson, "we often overlook our best skills—our innate talents—simply because we perform them without even thinking." You could even have a certain "genius" at some activity, but as Alana Cates, president of the consultancy and training firm Accelerated Profit Solutions, puts it, "the frustration in genius is in believing that if it is easy for you, it must be easy for everyone else."

Johnson suggests that you begin thinking about your disruptive skills by asking yourself three questions:

1. *What do you do reflexively well?* These are usually the things that you do well—and often with pleasure—without thinking about them. Business consultant and motivational speaker Marcus Buckingham suggests that you think about what you're doing whenever you feel "invigorated, inquisitive, successful."
2. *What do others identify as being your best skills?* "Too many people," quipped the late publisher Malcolm Forbes, "overvalue what they are not and undervalue what they are." If you want to be an actor but everyone else keeps saying that you'd make a great set designer, you'd probably do well to heed the feedback. Otherwise, warns Johnson, "over the course of your career, it will leave you trading at a discount to what you are worth."
3. *Do you have a confluence of skills?* In other words, is your disruptive skill actually a skill *set*—what Johnson characterizes as "an unusual intersection of ordinary proficiencies"?

References: Philippa Kennealy, "Physicians Considering a Career Change Need to Figure Out Their 'Disruptive' Skills," The Entrepreneurial MD for Women, September 29, 2010, www.mommd.com on April 6, 2012; Philippa Kennealy, "The General Surgeon Who Sculpted a New Physician Career," The Entrepreneurial MD, February 27, 2012, www.entrepreneurialmd.com on April 6, 2012; Whitney Johnson, "How to Identify Your Disruptive Skills," HBR Blog Network, October 4, 2010, http://blogs.hbr.org on April 6, 2012; Whitney Johnson, "To Get Paid What You're Worth, Know Your Disruptive Skills," HBR Blog Network, September 14, 2010, http://blogs.hbr.org on April 6, 2012.

An Interdisciplinary Focus In many ways, organizational behavior synthesizes several other fields of study. Perhaps the greatest contribution is from psychology, especially organizational psychology. Psychologists study human behavior, whereas organizational psychologists deal specifically with the behavior of people in organizational settings. Many of the concepts that interest psychologists, such as individual differences and motivation, are also central to students of organizational behavior. These concepts are covered in Chapters 3–8.

Sociology, too, has had a major impact on the field of organizational behavior. Sociologists study social systems such as families, occupational classes, and organizations. Because a major concern of organizational behavior is the study of organization structures, the field clearly overlaps with areas of sociology that focus on the organization as a social system. Chapters 16–19 reflect the influence of sociology on the field of organizational behavior.

Anthropology is concerned with the interactions between people and their environments, especially their cultural environment. Culture is a major influence on the structure of organizations and on the behavior of people in organizations. Culture is discussed in Chapters 2 and 18.

Political science also interests organizational behaviorists. We usually think of political science as the study of political systems such as governments. But themes of interest to political scientists include how and why people acquire power and such topics as political behavior, decision making, conflict, the behavior of interest groups, and coalition formation. These are also major areas of interest in organizational behavior, as is reflected in Chapters 9–15.

Economists study the production, distribution, and consumption of goods and services. Students of organizational behavior share the economist's interest in areas such as labor market dynamics, productivity, human resource planning and forecasting, and cost-benefit analysis. Chapters 2, 5, and 6 most strongly illustrate these issues.

Engineering has also influenced the field of organizational behavior. Industrial engineering in particular has long been concerned with work measurement, productivity measurement, work flow analysis and design, job design, and labor relations. Obviously these areas are also relevant to organizational behavior and are discussed in Chapters 2, 5, and 10.

Most recently, medicine has come into play in connection with the study of human behavior at work, specifically in the area of stress. Increasingly, research is showing that controlling the causes and consequences of stress in and out of organizational settings is important for the well-being of both the individual and the organization. Chapter 7 is devoted to stress.

Stockbyte/Photos.com

Some people believe that work stress is approaching epidemic proportions. Researchers in the field of organizational behavior are helping to combat this epidemic by studying the causes of stress and how it can be most effectively managed.

A Descriptive Nature A primary goal of studying organizational behavior is to describe relationships between two or more behavioral variables. The theories and concepts of the field, for example, cannot predict with certainty that changing a specific set of workplace variables will improve an individual employee's performance by a certain amount.[8] At best, the field can suggest that certain general concepts or variables tend to be related to one another in particular settings. For instance, research might indicate that in one organization, employee satisfaction and individual perceptions of working conditions are positively related. However, we may not know whether that correlation occurs because better working conditions lead to more satisfaction, because more-satisfied people see their jobs differently than dissatisfied people, or because both satisfaction and perceptions of working conditions are actually related through other intervening variables. Also, the relationship between satisfaction and perceptions of working conditions observed in one setting may be considerably stronger, weaker, or nonexistent in other settings.

Organizational behavior is descriptive for several reasons: the immaturity of the field, the complexities inherent in studying human behavior, and the lack of valid, reliable, and accepted definitions and measures. Whether the field will ever be able to make definitive predictions and prescriptions is still an open question. But even if it never succeeds in these endeavors, the value of studying organizational behavior is firmly established. Because behavioral processes pervade most managerial functions and roles, and because the work of organizations is done primarily by people, the knowledge and understanding gained from the field can significantly help managers in many ways.[9]

Basic Concepts of the Field

The central concepts of organizational behavior can be grouped into three basic categories: (1) individual processes, (2) interpersonal processes, and (3) organizational processes and characteristics. As Figure 1.4 shows, these categories provide the basic framework for this book.

This chapter and the next develop a managerial perspective on organizational behavior and link the core concepts of organizational behavior with actual management for organizational effectiveness. Chapter 2 describes the changing environment of organizations, especially relating to diversity, globalization, and similar trends and issues. Together, the two chapters in Part I provide a fundamental introduction to organizational behavior.

The six chapters of Part II cover individual processes in organizations. Chapter 3 explores key individual differences in such characteristics as personality and attitudes. Chapter 4 provides an introduction to and discussion of basic models useful for understanding employee work motivation. Chapters 5 and 6 are devoted to various methods and strategies that managers can use to enhance employee motivation and performance. Chapter 7 covers the causes and consequences of stress in the workplace. Finally, Chapter 8 explores decision making, problem solving, and creativity.

Part III is devoted to interpersonal processes in organizations. Chapter 9 introduces the foundations of interpersonal behavior through its coverage of group dynamics. Chapter 10 describes how managers are using teams in organizations today, while Chapter 11 explores communications processes in organizations. Chapter 12 discusses leadership models and concepts, while Chapter 13 describes contemporary views of leadership in organizations. Power, politics, and workplace justice are covered in Chapter 14. Chapter 15 covers conflict and negotiation processes in organizations.

Part IV is devoted to organizational processes and characteristics. Chapter 16 sets the stage with its coverage of the foundations of organization structure; Chapter 17 is an in-depth treatment of organization design. Organizational culture is discussed in Chapter 18. Organizational change and development are covered in Chapter 19. Finally, research methods in organizational behavior and the field's historical development are covered in Appendices A and B.

FIGURE 1.4

The Framework for Understanding Organizational Behavior

Organizational behavior is an exciting and complex field of study. The specific concepts and topics that constitute the field can be grouped into three categories: individual, interpersonal, and organizational processes and characteristics. Here these concepts and classifications are used to provide an overall framework for the organization of this book.

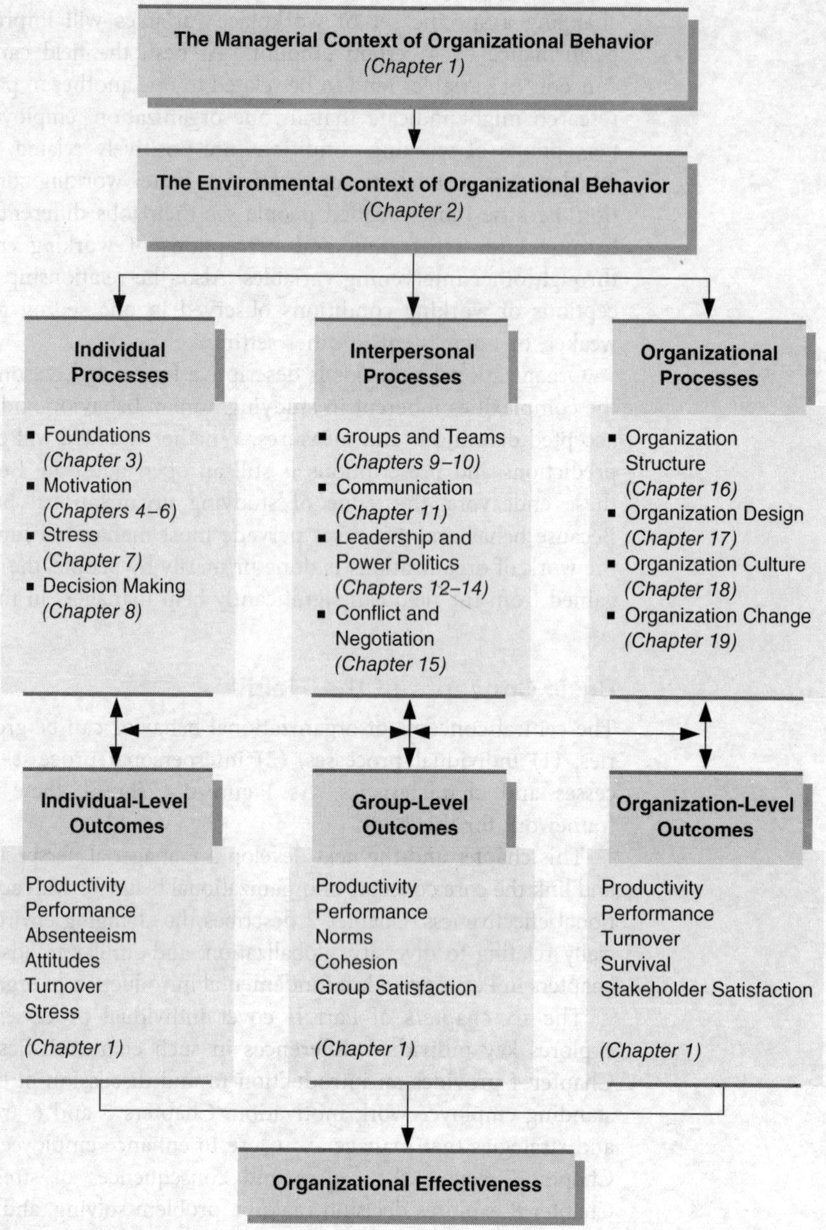

CONTEXTUAL PERSPECTIVES ON ORGANIZATIONAL BEHAVIOR

Several contextual perspectives—most notably the systems and contingency perspectives and the interactional view—also influence our understanding of organizational behavior. Many of the concepts and theories discussed in the chapters that follow reflect these perspectives; they represent basic points of view that influence much of our contemporary thinking about behavior in organizations. In addition, they allow us to see more clearly how managers use behavioral processes as they strive for organizational effectiveness.

FIGURE 1.5

The Systems Approach to Organizations

The systems approach to organizations provides a useful framework for understanding how the elements of an organization interact among themselves and with their environment. Various inputs are transformed into different outputs, with important feedback from the environment. If managers do not understand these interrelations, they may tend to ignore their environment or overlook important interrelationships within their organizations.

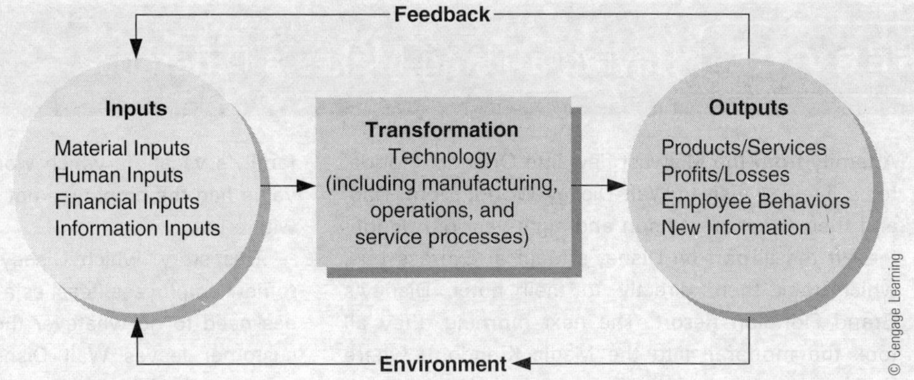

Systems and Situational Perspectives

The systems and situational perspectives share related viewpoints on organizations and how they function. Each is concerned with interrelationships among organizational elements and between organizational and environmental elements.

The Systems Perspective The systems perspective, or the theory of systems, was first developed in the physical sciences, but it has been extended to other areas, such as management.[10] A **system** is an interrelated set of elements that function as a whole. Figure 1.5 shows a general framework for viewing organizations as systems.

A **system** is a set of interrelated elements functioning as a whole.

According to this perspective, an organizational system receives four kinds of inputs from its environment: material, human, financial, and informational (note that this is consistent with our earlier description of management functions). The organization's managers then combine and transform these inputs and return them to the environment in the form of products or services, employee behaviors, profits or losses, and additional information. Then the system receives feedback from the environment regarding these outputs.

As an example, we can apply systems theory to the Shell Oil Company. Material inputs include pipelines, crude oil, and the machinery used to refine petroleum. Human inputs are oil field workers, refinery workers, office staff, and other people employed by the company. Financial inputs take the form of money received from oil and gas sales, stockholder investment, and so forth. Finally, the company receives information inputs from forecasts about future oil supplies, geological surveys on potential drilling sites, sales projections, and similar analyses.

Through complex refining and other processes, these inputs are combined and transformed to create products such as gasoline and motor oil. As outputs, these products are sold to the consuming public. Profits from operations are fed back into the environment through taxes, investments, and dividends; losses, when they occur, hit the environment by reducing stockholders' incomes. In addition to having on-the-job contacts with customers and suppliers, employees live in the community and participate in a variety of activities away from the workplace, and their behavior is influenced in part by their experiences as Shell workers. Finally, information about the company and its operations is also released into the environment. The environment, in turn, responds to these outputs and influences future inputs. For example, consumers may buy more or less gasoline depending on the quality and price of Shell's product, and banks may be more or less willing to lend Shell money based on financial information released about the company.

The systems perspective is valuable to managers for a variety of reasons. First, it underscores the importance of an organization's environment. For instance, failing to

SERVICE Having a Thing Makes a Difference

A family from the Midwest flew into Orlando, Florida, for a five-day visit to Walt Disney World. Mom, Dad, and their five-year-old son and eight-year-old daughter left the airport on Disney's Magical Express bus, which took them directly to their hotel, Disney's Grand Floridian Resort. The next morning, they all took the monorail into the Magic Kingdom, where Dad immediately bought two mouse-ear hats embroidered with the kids' names. Over the next few days, the five-year-old did as many five-year-olds will do, and kept his hat on night and day. It was his treasured possession, and he wore it everywhere he went. On the day before the end of the visit, the family returned to the Magic Kingdom for a second time. After exiting the Pirates of the Caribbean attraction, the little boy discovered he no longer had his beloved hat and began crying. Dad realized he had a problem, and the problem got worse when the little girl, seeing that her brother was getting attention by crying, started to cry herself.

After three fun-filled and magical days, the whole vacation was becoming a disaster because of a lost hat. Dad, hoping the hat might be found, asked the ride attendant to look in the boats to see whether the hat could be found. The ride attendant looked and found nothing. The boy was crying as only a little boy who lost his most prized possession could cry. Mom was unhappy, Dad was frustrated, and Sister was in tears. Seeing this unhappy situation in what is supposed to be the happiest place on earth, the ride attendant went across the aisle, grabbed two Mickey hats, and placed one on the boy's head and the other on Dad's. The crying stopped, and smiles returned.

Later, when the family returned home, dad wrote a letter to the head of Walt Disney World to tell him what a splendid time they'd had. Interestingly, while the letter included only one page about the various attractions in the parks and the amenities of the hotel, there were several pages devoted to describing the way this high-school-aged employee had saved this family's vacation by his prompt action in replacing his son's Mickey hat. The question is, what is a Mickey hat worth? The answer is the entire cost of that family's vacation, which would have lost most of its value had the employee not taken action and saved it with a hat.

This story, which Disney trainers like to recount to new employees, teaches a simple point. All employees need to do whatever they can to ensure that no customer leaves Walt Disney World unhappy. The employee in this case listened, learned, and saved the family's vacation by noticing how distressed the family was and acting on what Disney had taught him.

As a way to introduce the service inserts seen in each chapter, this example illustrates well the challenges that service managers face when customers enter their organizations and interact directly with employees to create an intangible service experience. The challenge of managing an employee who must coproduce such experiences is far different from that of supervising someone whose only task is to add a wheel to a car coming down the assembly line. From an organizational behavior perspective, managers must not only understand the personality characteristics, attitudes, and behaviors of their own employees but also teach those employees how to understand and respond to the personality characteristics, attitudes, and behaviors of the customers they interact with on a daily basis.

There are several key differences between producing a physical "thing" and creating an intangible "experience" that lives in the memory. The most important are the intangible features of experiences. Because there is no inventory to balance supply with demand, customer waits must be managed by employees in ways that make the waiting time acceptable. Moreover, there is no inventory to count, store, keep track of, or reorder when supplies get low. A second feature of intangibility is that the experience invariably requires interaction between a customer and an employee, especially at the customer contact points where the customer looks for and expects excellent service from what often proves to be the lowest-paid, shortest-tenured, and least-trained employee. As a result, the role of supervisors must change. Unlike in a manufacturing organization, where the production worker can be monitored in a set place doing a repetitive task, service employees often go to the customers, interact with them outside the view of their supervisors, and not only perform their tasks but also build relationships and fix any problems that customers may have. The fourth difference is that the customer is almost always involved in some coproduction activity. Thus, the employee not only must know how to effectively perform his or her role in the creation of a service experience but must also supervise and sometimes teach customers how to perform their roles, as well. If customers can't perform their roles successfully, that failure will inevitably be attributed to the company. The fifth difference is that the setting in which the experience occurs is important to both customer and employee. The mood, attitude, and emotions of both the employee and the customer affect the quality of the service experience and that is directly impacted by the environment of the experience itself. Finally, the quality measures, performance measures, and productivity measures are all subjective. This last point brings out the second major difference between experience-creating and product-producing organizations: the value and quality of the experience are subjectively determined by the customer. It doesn't matter what your organization's quality control team assesses, what the service planners plan, or what your employees believe is the best service possible. It is all determined by the customer and only the customer. The impact of these differences on organizational behavior will become the focal point of the inserts throughout the remainder of this book. Not having a thing to produce, hold, and show makes a difference in organizational behavior.

Discussion Question: How is managing people making things different from managing customer experiences?

acquire the appropriate resources and failing to heed feedback from the environment can be disastrous. The systems perspective also helps managers conceptualize the flow and interaction of various elements of the organization itself as they work together to transform inputs into outputs.

The **situational perspective** suggests that in most organizations, situations and outcomes are influenced by other variables.

The Situational Perspective Another useful viewpoint for understanding behavior in organizations comes from the **situational perspective**. In the earlier days of management studies, managers searched for universal answers to organizational questions. They sought prescriptions, the "one best way" that could be used in any organization under any conditions, searching, for example, for forms of leadership behavior that would always lead employees to be more satisfied and to work harder. Eventually, however, researchers realized that the complexities of human behavior and organizational settings make universal conclusions virtually impossible. They discovered that in organizations, most situations and outcomes are contingent; that is, the precise relationship between any two variables is likely to be situational (i.e., dependent on other variables).[11]

Figure 1.6 distinguishes the universal and situational perspectives. The universal model, shown at the top of the figure, presumes a direct cause-and-effect linkage between variables. For example, it suggests that whenever a manager encounters a particular problem or situation (such as motivating employees to work harder), a universal approach exists (such as raising pay or increasing autonomy) that will lead to the desired outcome. The situational perspective, on the other hand, acknowledges that several other variables alter the direct relationship. In other words, the appropriate managerial action or behavior in any given situation depends on elements of that situation.

The field of organizational behavior has gradually shifted from a universal approach in the 1950s and early 1960s to a situational perspective. The situational perspective is especially strong in the areas of motivation (Chapter 4), job design (Chapter 5), leadership (Chapters 12 and 13), and organizational design (Chapter 17), but it is becoming increasingly important throughout the entire field.

FIGURE 1.6

Universal Versus Situational Approach

Managers once believed that they could identify the "one best way" of solving problems or reacting to situations. Here we illustrate a more realistic view, the situational approach. The situational approach suggests that approaches to problems and situations are contingent on elements of the situation.

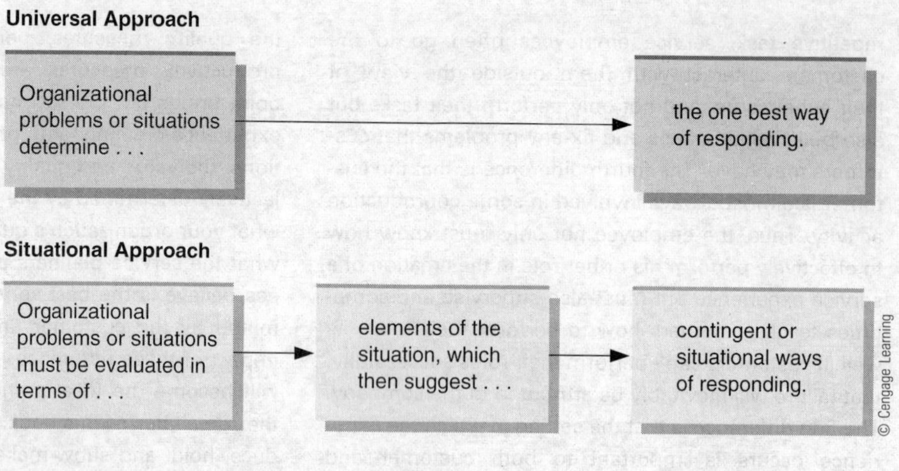

Interactionalism: People and Situations

Interactionalism suggests that individuals and situations interact continuously to determine individuals' behavior.

Interactionalism is another useful perspective to help better understand behavior in organizational settings. First presented in terms of interactional psychology, this view assumes that individual behavior results from a continuous and multidirectional interaction between characteristics of the person and characteristics of the situation. More specifically, **interactionalism** attempts to explain how people select, interpret, and change various situations.[12] Figure 1.7 illustrates this perspective. Note that the individual and the situation are presumed to interact continuously. This interaction is what determines the individual's behavior.

The interactional view implies that simple cause-and-effect descriptions of organizational phenomena are not enough. For example, one set of research studies may suggest that job changes lead to improved employee attitudes. Other studies may propose that attitudes influence how people perceive their jobs in the first place. Both positions probably are incomplete: Employee attitudes may influence job perceptions, but these perceptions may in turn influence future attitudes. Because interactionalism is a fairly recent contribution to the field, it is less prominent in the chapters that follow than the systems and contingency theories. Nonetheless, the interactional view appears to offer many promising ideas for future development.

FIGURE 1.7

The Interactionist Perspective on Behavior in Organizations

When people enter an organization, their own behaviors and actions shape that organization in various ways. Similarly, the organization itself shapes the behaviors and actions of each individual who becomes a part of it. This interactionist perspective can be useful in explaining organizational behavior.

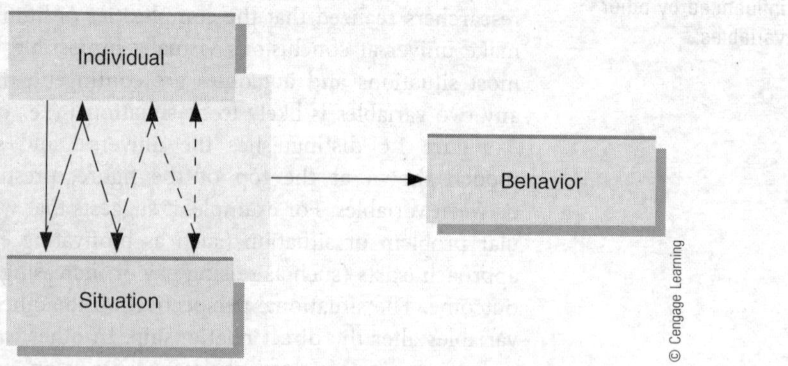

MANAGING FOR EFFECTIVENESS

Earlier in this chapter, we noted that managers work toward various goals. We are now in a position to elaborate on the nature of these goals in detail. In particular, as shown in Figure 1.8, goals—or outcomes—exist at three specific levels in an organization:

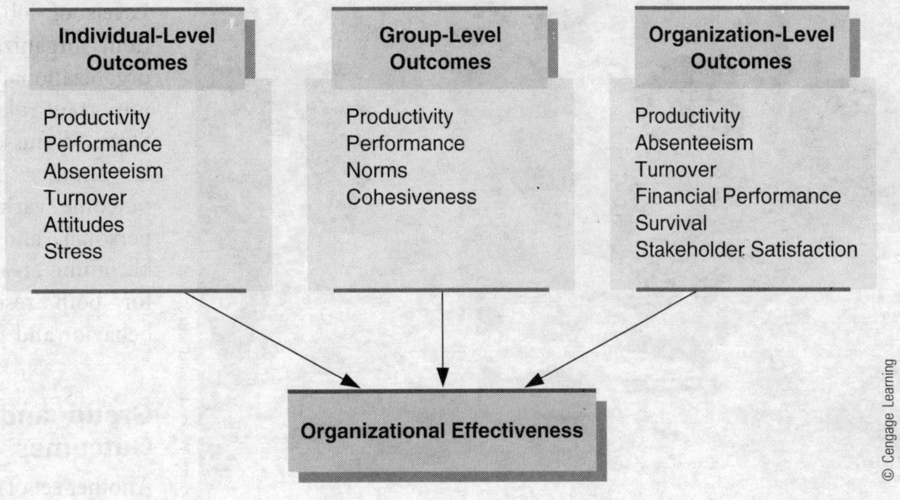

FIGURE 1.8

Managing for Effectiveness

Managers work to optimize a variety of individual-level, group-level, and organization-level outcomes. It is sometimes necessary to make trade-offs among the different types and levels of outcomes, but each is an important determinant of organizational effectiveness.

individual-level outcomes, group-level outcomes, and organizational-level outcomes. Of course, it may sometimes be necessary to make trade-offs among these different kinds of outcomes, but in general each is seen as a critical component of organizational effectiveness. The sections that follow elaborate on these different levels in more detail.

Individual-Level Outcomes

Several different outcomes at the individual level are important to managers. Given the focus of the field of organizational behavior, it should not be surprising that most of these outcomes are directly or indirectly addressed by various theories and models. (We provide a richer and more detailed analysis of individual-level outcomes in Chapter 3.)

Individual Behaviors First, several individual behaviors result from a person's participation in an organization. One important behavior is productivity. A person's productivity is an indicator of his or her efficiency and is measured in terms of the products or services created per unit of input. For example, if Bill makes 100 units of a product in a day and Sara makes only 90 units in a day, then, assuming that the units are of the same quality and that Bill and Sara make the same wages, Bill is more productive than Sara.

Performance, another important individual-level outcome variable, is a somewhat broader concept. It is made up of all work-related behaviors. For example, even though Bill is highly productive, it may also be that he refuses to work overtime, expresses negative opinions about the organization at every opportunity, and will do nothing unless it falls precisely within the boundaries of his job. Sara, on the other hand, may always be willing to work overtime, is a positive representative of the organization, and goes out of her way to make as many contributions to the organization as possible. Based on the full array of behaviors, then, we might conclude that Sara actually is the better performer.

Two other important individual-level behaviors are absenteeism and turnover. Absenteeism is a measure of attendance. Although virtually everyone misses work occasionally, some people miss far more than others. Some look for excuses to miss work and call in sick regularly just for some time off; others miss work only when absolutely necessary. Turnover occurs when a person leaves the organization. If the individual who leaves is a good performer or if the organization has invested heavily in training the person, turnover can be costly.

Individual Attitudes and Stress Another set of individual-level outcomes influenced by managers consists of individual attitudes. (We discuss attitudes more fully in Chapter 3.)

Jacob Wackerhausen/iStockphoto.com

Group- and team-level outcomes are becoming increasingly important to all organizations. Because so much work today is done by groups and teams, managers need to understand how to effectively create a team, how to direct and motivate that team, and then how to assess the team's performance. In this team, one member is presenting a proposal for how to complete a project to his five teammates. The team as a whole will then decide whether to accept the proposal, modify it, or start over looking for a new approach.

Levels of job satisfaction or dissatisfaction, organizational commitment, and organizational involvement all play an important role in organizational behavior. Stress, discussed more fully in Chapter 7, is another important individual-level outcome variable. Given its costs, both personal and organizational, stress is becoming an increasingly important topic for both researchers in organizational behavior and practicing managers.

Group- and Team-Level Outcomes

Another set of outcomes exists at the group and team level. Some of these outcomes parallel the individual-level outcomes just discussed. For example, if an organization makes extensive use of work teams, team productivity and performance are important outcome variables. On the other hand, even if all the people in a group or team have the same or similar attitudes toward their jobs, the attitudes themselves are individual-level phenomena. Individuals, not groups, have attitudes.

But groups or teams can also have unique outcomes that individuals do not share. For example, as we will discuss in Chapter 9, groups develop norms that govern the behavior of individual group members. Groups also develop different levels of cohesiveness. Thus, managers need to assess both common and unique outcomes when considering the individual and group levels.

Organization-Level Outcomes

Finally, a set of outcome variables exists at the organization level. As before, some of these outcomes parallel those at the individual and group levels, but others are unique. For example, we can measure and compare organizational productivity. We can also develop organization-level indicators of absenteeism and turnover. But profitability is generally assessed only at the organizational level.

Organizations are also commonly assessed in terms of financial performance: stock price, return on investment, growth rates, and so on. They are also evaluated in terms of their ability to survive and the extent to which they satisfy important stakeholders such as investors, government regulators, employees, and unions.

Clearly, then, the manager must balance different outcomes across all three levels of analysis. In many cases, these outcomes appear to contradict one another. For example, paying workers high salaries can enhance satisfaction and reduce turnover, but it also may detract from bottom-line performance. Similarly, exerting strong pressure to increase individual performance may boost short-term profitability but increase turnover and job stress. Thus, the manager must look at the full array of outcomes and attempt to balance them in an optimal fashion. The manager's ability to do this is a major determinant of the organization's success.

SYNOPSIS

Organizational behavior is the study of human behavior in organizational settings, the interface between human behavior and the organization, and the organization itself. The study of organizational behavior is important because organizations have a powerful influence on our lives. It also directly relates to management in organizations. Indeed, by its very nature, management requires an understanding of human behavior to help managers better comprehend behaviors at different levels in the organization, at the same level in the organization, in other organizations, and in themselves.

The manager's job can be characterized in terms of four functions. These basic managerial functions are planning, organizing, leading, and controlling. Planning is the process of determining the organization's desired future position and deciding how best to get there. Organizing is the process of designing jobs, grouping jobs into manageable units, and establishing patterns of authority among jobs and groups of jobs. Leading is the process of motivating members of the organization to work together toward the organization's goals. Controlling is the process of monitoring and correcting the actions of the organization and its people to keep them headed toward their goals.

Managerial work involves ten basic roles and requires the use of four skills. The roles consist of three interpersonal roles (figurehead, leader, and liaison), three informational roles (monitor, disseminator, and spokesperson), and four decision-making roles (entrepreneur, disturbance handler, resource allocator, and negotiator). The four basic skills necessary for effective management are technical, interpersonal, conceptual, and diagnostic skills.

Contemporary organizational behavior attempts to describe, rather than prescribe, behavioral forces in organizations. Ties to psychology, sociology, anthropology, political science, economics, engineering, and medicine make organizational behavior an interdisciplinary field. The basic concepts of the field are divided into three categories: individual processes, interpersonal processes, and organizational processes and characteristics. Those categories form the framework for the organization of this book.

Important contextual perspectives on the field of organizational behavior are the systems and situational perspectives and interactionalism. There are also a number of very important individual-, group-, and organizational-level outcomes related to organizational effectiveness.

DISCUSSION QUESTIONS

1. Some people have suggested that understanding human behavior at work is the single most important requirement for managerial success. Do you agree or disagree with this statement? Why?
2. In what ways is organizational behavior comparable to functional areas such as finance, marketing, and production? In what ways is it different from these areas? Is it similar to statistics in any way?
3. Identify some managerial jobs that are highly affected by human behavior and others that are less so. Which would you prefer? Why?
4. The text identifies four basic managerial functions. Based on your own experiences or observations, provide examples of each function.
5. Which managerial skills do you think are among your strengths? Which are among your weaknesses? How might you improve the latter?
6. Suppose you have to hire a new manager. One candidate has outstanding technical skills but poor interpersonal skills. The other has exactly the opposite mix of skills. Which would you hire? Why?
7. Some people believe that individuals working in an organization have basic human rights to satisfaction with their work and to the opportunity to grow and develop. How would you defend this position? How would you argue against it?
8. Many universities offer a course in industrial or organizational psychology. The content of those courses is quite similar to the content of this one. Do you think that behavioral material is best taught in a business or in a psychology program, or is it best to teach it in both?
9. Do you believe the field of organizational behavior has the potential to become prescriptive as opposed to descriptive? Why or why not?

10. Are the notions of systems, situationalism, and interactionalism mutually exclusive? If not, describe ways in which they are related.

11. Get a recent issue of a popular business magazine such as *Business Week* or *Fortune* and scan its major articles. Do any of them reflect concepts from organizational behavior? Describe.

12. Do you read *Dilbert*? Do you think it accurately describes organization life? Are there other comic strips that reflect life and work in contemporary organizations?

HOW DO YOU SEE IT?

In the Company of Hounds

"I definitely went into it wanting a more relaxed culture. Not just for my staff, but for myself as well."

—CAMP BOW WOW FRANCHISEE SUE RYAN

Sue Ryan is a veteran of the managerial ranks at Avnet Technology Solutions and GE, and to judge by her account in our video, she came away from the experience with a somewhat ambivalent attitude. "I had this manager," she recalls (though she doesn't say where), "who was just miserable to work for but taught me an incredible amount.... I probably learned more from her than anybody else, but it was painful."

She left the corporate world to open her own business in 2004, presumably to enjoy—and pass on—the better managerial practices that she'd encountered in her career. "I definitely went into it," says Ryan, "wanting a more relaxed culture. Not just for my staff, but for myself as well." The business she chose was a *franchise*—a form of ownership in which a *franchiser* grants a *franchisee* the right to use its brand name and sell its products. Ryan's franchise is sold by a Denver-based company called Camp Bow Wow, which was started in 2000 by a dog-loving entrepreneur named Heidi Ganahl.

Like most franchises, Camp Bow Wow—a sort of combination day camp/B&B for dogs—requires a certain degree of consistency in the operation of each location, but Ryan appreciated Ganahl's openness to creative input from owners on the front lines. Ryan, for example, bought an already established location in Boulder, Colorado, which came equipped with a staff hired by the previous franchisee. "When I started," she says, "it was just me and a staff that was all at the same level." The existing structure was "very flat" (there were few layers of management), and it unfortunately required Ryan to do all of the day-to-day managing. "It was just me doing absolutely everything," she recalls. "I was consumed with the business."

It wasn't exactly what Ryan had in mind when she decided to find a less stressful way of putting her managerial experience to work on her own behalf. Her solution was to find employees who could develop the managerial skills needed to take some of the burden off of her shoulders. She wanted to create a system "where I could start promoting [employees] and mentoring them into lead positions."

Thus the video introduces us to Candace Stathis, who has turned out to be Ryan's most successful managerial protégée. "The biggest misconception I had about managers," admits Stathis, "is that they sat around in offices and kind of did nothing." Not surprisingly, Stathis has since been disabused of this notion, and she gives a concise account of what she's learned as a manager at Camp Bow Wow, including a few things about leadership and operational effectiveness (she's found, for example, that people "are way harder to train" than dogs).

Sue Ryan's approach to managing her business—including her strategy for developing managers to help her do it—seems to be getting results. In 2011, Camp Bow Wow Boulder won the franchiser's Golden Paw Award for top safety standards and percentage revenue as well as support for the Bow Wow Buddies Foundation, a nonprofit arm of the company dedicated to improving the lives and health of dogs through fostering and rehoming and other programs.

CASE QUESTIONS

1. In what ways does Sue Ryan perform each of the three *basic managerial roles—interpersonal, informational,* and *decision making*? How about Candace Stathis? How must both Ryan and Stathis make use of the four *critical managerial skills—technical, interpersonal, conceptual,* and *diagnostic*? In the case of each manager, which of these skills seems most in evidence in the video? Which of these skills would you consider most important for a manager at a business such as Camp Bow Wow Boulder?

2. What can you say about managerial practices at Camp Bow Wow Boulder by applying each of the three *contextual perspectives* on organizational behaviour—*systems, situational*, and *interactional*? Which perspective seems to be the most useful in describing the way the business's managers go about their jobs?
3. What does Candace Stathis mean when she says that "customer service has to be effective as opposed to efficient"? Under what circumstances does Sue Ryan most often feel the "tension" between the need to be effective and the need to be efficient? How does she try to resolve that tension?
4. As managers with goals, in what ways do Ryan and Stathis recognize the need to balance the three levels of business *outcomes—individual, group and team*, and *organizational*? In what order would each manager probably rank the importance of these outcomes? Whether you think that their rankings would be the same or different, explain why.

ADDITIONAL SOURCES

Camp Bow Wow, "Camp Bow Wow Boulder Dog Daycare and Boarding" (2012), www.campbowwow.com on April 23, 2012; Aimee Heckel, "The Surprising Rules, Etiquette and Offerings at Boulder County's Dog Daycares," Boulder (CO) *DailyCamera.com*, August 31, 2011, www.dailycamera.com on April 23, 2012; "Heidi Ganahl, Founder & CEO, Camp Bow Wow," *SmartGirls Way*, August 4, 2011, http://smartgirlsway.com on April 23, 2012; Susan de Castro McCann, "Camp Bow Wow Comes to the Rescue to Sop Up Oil in the Gulf," *Redstone Review*, May 24, 2010, www.redstonereview.com on April 23, 2012; Megan Allen, "Camp Bow Wow Announces 2011 Second Quarter Golden Paw and Golden Wags + Whiskers Winners," Camp Bow Wow, September 9, 2011, www.bowwowbuddies.com on April 23, 2012.

EXPERIENCING ORGANIZATIONAL BEHAVIOR

Relating OB and Popular Culture

Purpose This exercise will help you appreciate the importance and pervasiveness of organizational behavior concepts and processes in both contemporary organizational settings and popular culture.

Format Your instructor will divide the class into groups of three to five members. Each group will be assigned a specific television program to watch before the next class meeting.

Procedure Arrange to watch the program as a group. Each person should have a pad of paper and a pencil handy. As you watch the show, jot down examples of individual behavior, interpersonal dynamics, organizational characteristics, and other concepts and processes relevant to organizational behavior. After the show, spend a few minutes comparing notes. Compile one list for the entire group. (It is advisable to turn off the television set during this discussion!)

During the next class meeting, have someone in the group summarize the plot of the show and list the concepts it illustrated. The following television shows are especially good for illustrating behavioral concepts in organizational settings:

The Big Bang Theory	*N.C.I.S.*
American Chopper	*Hawaii Five-0*
The Office	*Star Trek*
Grey's Anatomy	*Modern Family*
The Deadliest Catch	*Glee*
Pawn Stars	*Storage Wars*

Follow-Up Questions

1. What does this exercise illustrate about the pervasiveness of organizations in our contemporary society?
2. What recent or classic movies might provide similar kinds of examples?
3. Do you think television programs from countries other than the United States would provide more or fewer examples of shows set in organizations?

Variation: Do the same exercise but use a recent popular movie such as *The Avengers, The Hunger Games*, or something similar instead of a television program.

BUILDING MANAGERIAL SKILLS

Exercise Overview Your conceptual skills reflect your ability to think in the abstract. This exercise will help you extend your conceptual skills by identifying and analyzing situations that call for different kinds of management functions, roles, and skills in different kinds of organizations.

Exercise Background This chapter includes discussions of four management *functions*, ten management *roles*, and seven management *skills*. It also stresses the idea that management activities are necessary in many different kinds of organizations.

Start by identifying five different types of organizations: one large business, one small business, one educational organization, one health care organization, and one government organization. You might choose organizations about which you have some personal knowledge or organizations that you simply recognize by name and industry. Next, put yourself in the position of a top manager in each of your five specific organizations.

Write the names of these five organizations across the top of a sheet of paper. Then list the four functions, ten roles, and seven skills down the left side of the sheet. Now put your imagination to work: Think of a situation, a problem, or an opportunity that fits at the intersection of each row and column on the sheet. The dean of your college, for example, must perform a leadership role and apply interpersonal skills. The manager of an all-night diner must perform an organizing function and play the role of monitor.

Exercise Task

1. Do you notice any patterns of meaningful similarities in functions, roles, or skills across the five columns? Are there, for example, similarities in performing leadership roles or applying communication skills in most or all of the five types of organization? Do you notice any patterns of meaningful differences?
2. Based on your assessment of the patterns of similarities and differences that you identified in task 1, give two or three reasons why managers might find it easy to move from one type of organization to another. Give two or three reasons why managers might find it difficult to move from one type of organization to another.
3. Identify two or three places on your grid where the intersection between a type of organization and a function, role, or skill suggests something at which you might be particularly good. How about something at which, at least right now, you think you wouldn't be very good. Explain your reasoning.

SELF-ASSESSMENT EXERCISE

Assessing Your Own Management Skills

How Do I Rate as a Manager?

The following self-assessment should help you understand your current understanding of the practice of management and your own approach to management. This assessment outlines four important functions of management: planning, organizing, leading, and controlling. You should respond to this in one of three ways:

(a) respond based on your own managerial experience if you have any,

(b) respond about effective (or ineffective) managers you have observed in your work experience, or

(c) respond in terms of how you think an ideal manager should behave.

Instructions: Recall a situation in which you were a member of a group or team that had a specific task or project to complete. This may have been at work, in a class, or in a church, club, or civic organization. Now assess your behavior in each of the functions. For each question, rate yourself according to the following scale:

Rating Scale

5 Definitely true of me

4 Probably true of me

3 Neither true nor not true; undecided

2 Probably not true of me

1 Definitely not true of me

I. Planning

_______1. I prepare an agenda for meetings.

_______2. I try to anticipate what will happen in the future as a result of my current actions and decisions.

_______3. I establish clear goals for myself and others.

_______4. I carefully analyze the pros and cons involved in situations before reaching decisions.

_______5. I am quite willing to try new things, to experiment.

_______6. I have a clear vision for accomplishing the task at hand.

_______7. I put plans in writing so that others can know exactly what they are.

_______8. I try to remain flexible so that I can adapt to changing conditions.

_______9. I try to anticipate barriers to goal accomplishment and how to overcome them.

_______10. I discuss plans and involve others in arriving at those plans.

_______ **Section I Total**

II. Organizing

_______1. I try to follow the plan while working on the task.

_______2. I try to develop any understanding of the different steps or parts needed to accomplish the task at hand.

_______3. I evaluate different ways of working on the task before deciding on which course of action to follow.

_______4. I have a clear sense of the priorities necessary to accomplish the task.

_______5. I arrange for others to be informed about the degree of progress in accomplishing the task.

_______6. I am open to alternative, even novel, ways of working on the task.

_______7. I adapt the sequence of activities involved if circumstances change.

_______8. I have a clear sense of how the steps involved in accomplishing the task should be structured.

_______9. I lead or follow where appropriate to see that progress is made toward accomplishing the task.

_______10. I coordinate with others to assure steady progress on the task.

_______ **Section II Total**

III. Leading

_______1. I set an example for others to follow.

_______2. I am effective at motivating others.

_______3. I try to keep a balance between getting the work done and keeping a spirit of teamwork.

_______4. I try to handle conflict in nonthreatening, constructive ways.

_______5. I help others in the group and provide guidance and training to better perform their roles.

_______6. I am open to suggestions from others.

_______7. I keep everyone informed about the group's activities and progress.

_______8. I show a genuine interest in the work of others.

_______9. I am considerate when providing constructive suggestions to others.

_______10. I understand the needs of others and encourage initiative in their meeting those needs.

_______ **Section III Total**

IV. Controlling

_______1. I regularly assess the quantity and quality of progress on the task at hand.

_______2. I try to assure that the information I have is timely, accurate, complete, and relevant.

_______3. I routinely share information with others to help them accomplish their tasks.

_______4. I compare progress with plans and take corrective action as warranted.

_______5. I manage my time and help others to manage theirs.

_______ 6. I have good sources of information or methods for obtaining information.

_______ 7. I use technology (computers, tablets, smart phones, etc.) to aid in monitoring progress and communicating with others.

_______ 8. I anticipate possible negative reactions and take action to minimize them.

_______ 9. I recognize that "fixing problems before they occur" is better than "fixing problems after they occur."

_______ 10. I try to balance my attention on the many different steps in accomplishing the task at hand.

_______ **Section IV Total**

Source: Adapted from Van Fleet, D. D., Van Fleet, E. W., & Seperich, G. J. 2013. *Principles of Management for Agribusiness.* Clifton Park, NY: Delmar/Cengage Learning; Griffin, R. W. 2011. *Management*. Mason, OH: South-Western Cengage Learning; and Van Fleet, D. D. 1991. *Behavior in Organizations*. Boston: Houghton Mifflin, in collaboration with G. Moorhead and R. W. Griffin. Adapted from David Van Fleet, Ella Van Fleet, and George J. Seperich, *Agribusiness: Principles of Management* (Clifton Park, NY: Delmar/Cengage Learning, 2013); Ricky Griffin, *Management*, 11th ed. (Mason, OH: South-Western Cengage Learning, 2013); and David Van Fleet, *Behavior in Organizations* (Boston: Houghton Mifflin, 1991).

CHAPTER 2

The Changing Environment of Organizations

Chapter Outline

- Globalization and Business
- Diversity and Business
- Technology and Business
- Ethics and Corporate Governance
- New Employment Relationships

Chapter Learning Objectives

After studying this chapter, you should be able to:

1. Discuss the emergence of international management and its impact on organizations.
2. Describe the nature of diversity in organizations and identify and explain key dimensions of diversity.
3. Discuss the changing nature of technology and its impact on business.
4. Describe emerging perspectives on ethics and corporate governance.
5. Discuss the key issues in new employment relationships.

Adventures in Social Entrepreneuring

"We function much as venture capitalists do in the private sector. You could say we're social VCs."

—Neal Keny-Guyer, CEO of Mercy Corps

In the aftermath of the devastating earthquake that struck the island nation of Haiti in January 2010, Oregon-based Mercy Corps arrived with a team of emergency-response experts from around the world. Focusing on immediate humanitarian needs, the team delivered food to overwhelmed hospitals and set up services to provide clean water. Mercy Corps also initiated a work-for-cash program that paid survivors to aid in clearing debris and restoring buildings, thus providing them with a little dignity along with the means to purchase supplies for their families and jump-start the local economy. In addition, the organization set up trauma centers for children, using counseling methods that it had helped to develop in the wake of the 9/11 terrorist attacks in New York City eight years earlier. In the aftermath of the devastating earthquake and tsunami that struck Japan in March 2011, Mercy Corps delivered emergency supplies and set up such programs as Comfort for Kids to help children deal with the emotional effects of a large-scale disaster.

Obviously, Mercy Corps isn't a newcomer to the enterprise of providing humanitarian aid. Founded in 1979 as the Save the Refugees Fund, a task force to help victims of famine and genocide in Cambodia, it expanded in 1982, becoming Mercy Corps International to reflect its broader mission. Since its founding, the nonprofit organization has provided $2.2 billion in humanitarian aid and development assistance to people in 114 countries and annually reaches nearly 19 million people in 36 nations.

Mercy Corps's approach to on-the-ground assistance also involves more than immediate-response and emergency-relief services. According to its mission statement,

> *Mercy Corps has learned that communities recovering from war or social upheaval must be the agents of their own transformation for change to endure. It's only when communities set their own agendas,*

Miguel Samper for Mercy Corps

Mercy Corps provides relief to people victimized by disasters. This volunteer is a part of Mercy Corps' Comfort for Kids program. She is proving support for the victims of the earthquake that devastated Haiti.

raise their own resources, and implement programs themselves that the first successes result in the renewed hope, confidence, and skills to continue their development independently.

Mercy Corps thus works to foster "sustainable community development that integrates agriculture, health, housing and infrastructure, economic development, education, and environment and local management," as well as launching "initiatives that promote citizen participation, accountability, conflict management, and the rule of law." In India, for example, Mercy Corps has taught small-scale tea farmers sustainable ways to grow organic teas and get fair prices for them. On plantations owned by big tea companies, it's helped not only to improve living and economic conditions in worker villages but to form self-governing Community Initiative Groups to manage ongoing community needs in education, infrastructure, and employment. In southern Sudan, which has been torn by Africa's longest civil war, Mercy Corps has built networks of local organizations to provide such essential services as adult literacy, orphan care, and HIV/AIDS counseling; other programs have helped to build roads and community centers and to electrify villages.

In Indonesia, where sanitation is a major area of concern, Mercy Corps has launched a long-term Hygiene Promotion Program. On Hand Washing Day, for instance, community representatives take to the streets with colorful buckets and teach children how to wash their hands with soap and water; similarly equipped hand-washing stations have been set up in neighborhoods throughout the capital of Djakarta. (Dirty hands can cause diarrhea, which kills 2 million children under the age of 5 every year.) Other programs focus on education and equipment for harvesting rainwater and removing solid waste from residential neighborhoods.

In addition to the devastating effects of war, social upheaval, and natural disaster, Mercy Corps is also concerned with the effects of climate change on developing communities. It therefore works to provide "viable economic options as communities adapt to new environmental realities," especially in helping poor communities to cope with "the rising incidence of climate-related disasters such as flooding and drought." According to Mercy Corps, its climate-related programs fall into three main areas:

- *Alternative energy:* promoting energy sources that support sustainable economic activities
- *Sustainable resource management:* supporting a community's ability to provide its own environmental and ecological services
- *Advocacy, outreach, and models that work:* inspiring governments and communities to rely on proven environment- and climate-friendly programs

In 2010, for example, when drought in the African nation of Niger threatened nearly 8 million people with malnutrition and starvation, Mercy Corps not only mobilized efforts to provide food commodities but also helped local farmers deal with chronic debt arising from inefficient methods and prior crop failures. A year later, Mercy Corps responded when Timor-Leste, an island nation northwest of Australia, faced just the opposite in climate-related crises: Because seasonal rains continued throughout the dry season, when farmers plant and harvest the country's food supply, drainage systems failed and crops could not be delivered over impassable roads. In addition to providing immediate relief, Mercy Corps trained local blacksmiths to make portable silos for storing rice and corn, the country's main staples.

What Do You Think?

1. If we say that Mercy Corps responds to "environmental forces," what do we mean by the term *environment*? Why is *environment* in the sense of "*natural* environment" not quite adequate?

2. Would you be interested in working for an SBE instead of a for-profit organization? Why or why not? If you were in a position to do so, would you be willing to invest in an SBE? Why or why not?

References: Mercy Corps, "What We're Doing in Haiti," January 23, 2010, www.mercycorps.org on April 7, 2012; Mercy Corps, "Our History," 2012, www.mercycorps.org on April 7, 2012; Roger Burks, "Change Brewing in the Tea Lands," Mercy Corps, April 9, 2008, www.mercycorps.org on April 7, 2012; Mercy Corps, "Sudan," 2012, www.mercycorps.org on April 7, 2012; Mercy Corps Indonesia, 2012, http://indonesia.mercycorps.org on April 7, 2012; Roger Burks, "Responding to Niger's Latest Hunger Crisis," Mercy Corps, July 23, 2010, www.mercycorps.org on April 7, 2012; USAID, "USAID Helps Drought-Affected Niger with First Award under the Emergency Food Security Program," press release, June 17, 2010, www.usaid.gov on April 7, 2012; Wahyu Nugroho, "Farmers in Timor-Leste Store Up for a Better Future," Mercy Corps, March 22, 2011, www.mercycorps.org on April 7, 2012.

The environment of all organizations is changing at an unprecedented rate. The rise of social entrepreneurship by organizations such as Mercy Corps represents only one perspective on environmental change. Indeed, in some industries, such as consumer electronics, popular entertainment, and information technology, the speed and magnitude of change are truly breathtaking. YouTube, for instance, uploads over 60 hours of new video footage every hour. And it's only been during the last decade or so that smartphone technologies, Facebook, and social networking have become commonplace.

Even industries characterized by what have been staid and predictable environments, such as traditional retail and heavy manufacturing, also face sweeping environmental changes today. Understanding and addressing the environment of a business has traditionally been the purview of top managers. But the effects of today's changing environment permeate the entire organization. Hence, to truly understand the behavior of people in organizational settings, it is also necessary to understand the changing environment of business.[1] This chapter is intended to provide the framework for such understanding. Specifically, as illustrated in Figure 2.1, we introduce and examine five of the central environmental forces for change faced by today's organizations: globalization, diversity, technology, ethics and corporate governance, and new employment relationships. An understanding of these forces will then set the stage for our in-depth discussion of contemporary organizational behavior that begins in Chapter 3.

GLOBALIZATION AND BUSINESS

Globalization is the internationalization of business activities and the shift toward an integrated global economy.

Perhaps the most significant source of change affecting many organizations today is the increasing **globalization** of organizations and management. Of course, in many ways, international management is nothing new. Centuries ago, the Roman army was forced to develop a management system to deal with its widespread empire.[2] Moreover, many notable early explorers such as Christopher Columbus and Magellan were not actually seeking new territory but instead were looking for new trade routes to boost international trade. Likewise, the Olympic Games, the Red Cross, and other organizations have international roots. From a business standpoint, however, the widespread effects of globalization are relatively new, at least in the United States.

FIGURE 2.1

The Changing Environment of Business

The changing environment of business presents both opportunities and challenges for managers today. Five important environmental forces are globalization, diversity, technology, ethics and corporate governance, and new employment relationships.

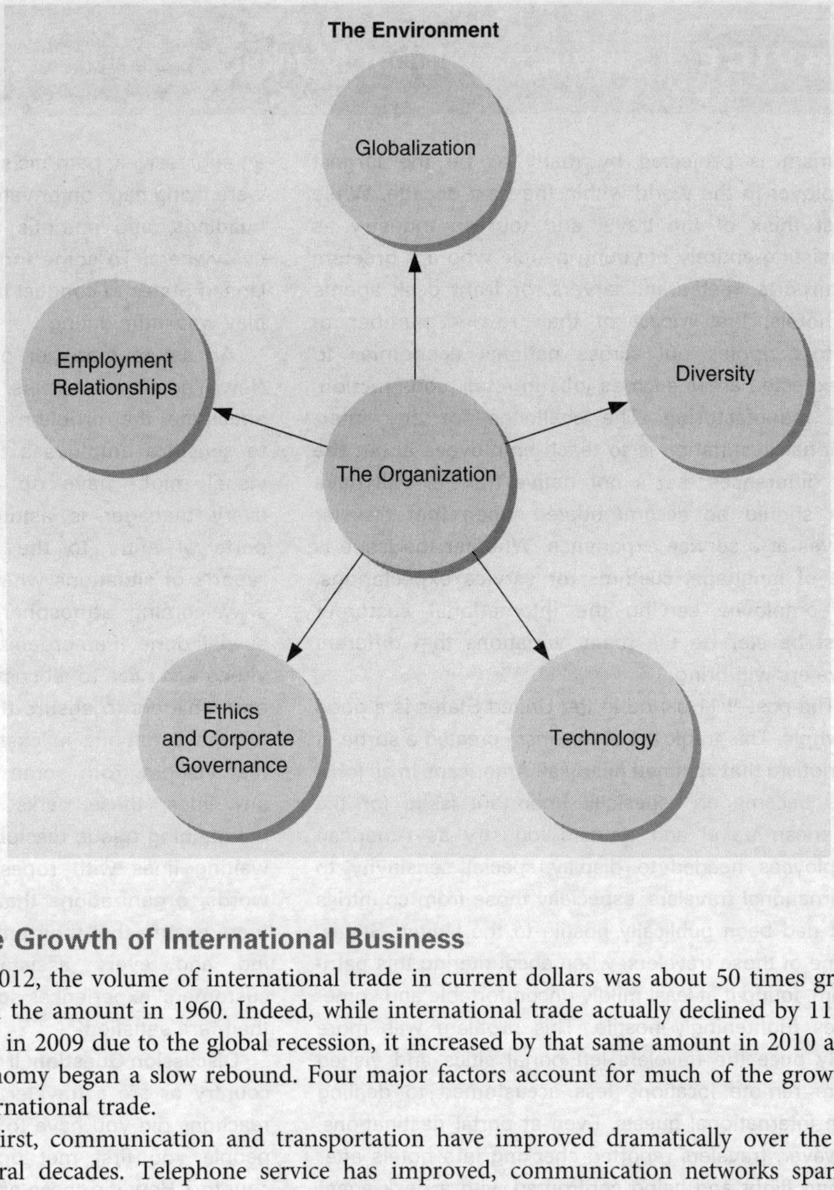

The Growth of International Business

In 2012, the volume of international trade in current dollars was about 50 times greater than the amount in 1960. Indeed, while international trade actually declined by 11 percent in 2009 due to the global recession, it increased by that same amount in 2010 as the economy began a slow rebound. Four major factors account for much of the growth in international trade.

First, communication and transportation have improved dramatically over the past several decades. Telephone service has improved, communication networks span the globe and can interact via satellite, and once-remote areas have become routinely accessible. Telephone service in some developing countries is now almost entirely by cellular phone technology rather than land-based wired telephone service. Fax and electronic mail technologies allow managers to send documents around the world in seconds as opposed to the days it took just a few years ago. And newer applications such as text messaging and Skype have made global communication even easier. In short, it is simply easier to conduct international business today than was the case just a few years ago.

Second, businesses have expanded internationally to increase their markets. Companies in smaller countries, such as Nestlé in Switzerland and Heineken in the Netherlands, recognized long ago that their domestic markets were too small to sustain much growth and therefore moved into the international arena. Many U.S. firms, on the other hand, have only found it advantageous to enter foreign markets in the last half-century. Now, though, most midsize and even many small firms routinely buy and/or sell products and services in other countries.

SERVICE Serving a Global Market

©rangizzz/Shutterstock

Tourism is projected by many to be the largest employer in the world within the next decade. While most think of the travel and tourism industry as consisting entirely of young people who are greeters at airports, restaurant servers, or front desk agents at hotels, the impact of the growing number of visitors ripples out across national economies to unexpected areas such as jobs in retail, construction, and manufacturing. The challenge for any international destination is to teach employees about the key differences that a non-native traveler will have that should be accommodated when that traveler arrives at a service experience. Whether the issue is one of language, customs, or service expectations, the employee serving the international customer must be alert to the many variations that different travelers will bring.

The post–9/11 period in the United States is a good example. This tragic act of terrorism created a surge of patriotism that spanned nearly all Americans in all jobs. This became an especially important issue for the American travel and tourism industry as American employees needed to display special sensitivity to international travelers, especially those from countries that had been publically hostile to the United States. Some of those travelers, when encountering this patriotism, found it at least mildly uncomfortable and sometimes frighteningly hostile. This problem was more likely once the travelers left portal cities and visited more remote locations less accustomed to dealing with international guests. Even at portal destinations, however, travelers reported checking into hotels after a long flight and being confronted with a desk agent wearing an American flag and a lapel button displaying an aggressively patriotic slogan. On the streets, people were flying flags on private residences and commercial buildings, and patriotic auto bumper stickers were everywhere. To some foreign travelers coming to the United States to conduct business or vacation, this display was intimidating.

An astute manager of a business-class hotel in New York, Los Angeles, or Washington, DC, might anticipate the problem and provide extra training to sensitize employees to the impact these strong visual might have on guests. Unfortunately, not every manager is astute, and outside the major ports of entry to the United States there were reports of situations where the hospitality to ensure a welcoming atmosphere for all visitors was not so well done. If an organization is supposed to be providing a service to all customers, then it is incumbent on managers to ensure that employees are prepared for the variations in customers. Theme parks know that visitors from some cultures avoid standing in any lines; these parks assist their employees in maintaining queue discipline by clearly defining their waiting lines with ropes and stanchions. In other words, organizations that serve international customers ensure that their employees are provided training and every assistance in managing those customers' experiences so that they and those around them are satisfied.

Discussion Question: If you have traveled to another country or are a traveler from another county, what reactions did you have to the things you saw and the people you first met upon entry into the foreign country? How did these affect your feelings about and perceptions of the country you entered?

Third, more and more firms are moving into international markets to control costs, especially to reduce labor costs. Plans to cut costs in this way do not always work out as planned, but many firms are successfully using inexpensive labor in Asia and Mexico.[3] In searching for lower labor costs, some companies have discovered well-trained workers and built more efficient plants that are closer to international markets. India, for instance, has emerged as a major force in the high-tech sector. Turkey and Indonesia are also growing in importance. And many foreign automakers have built plants in the United States.

Finally, many organizations have become international in response to competition. If an organization starts gaining strength in international markets, its competitors often must follow suit to avoid falling too far behind in sales and profitability. Exxon Mobil Corporation and Chevron realized they had to increase their international market share to keep pace with foreign competitors such as BP and Royal Dutch Shell.

Cross-Cultural Differences and Similarities

The primary concern of this book is human behavior in organizational settings, so we now turn our attention to differences and similarities in behavior across cultures. While there is relatively little research in this area, interesting findings have begun to emerge.[4]

General Observations At one level, it is possible to make several general observations about similarities and differences across cultures. For one thing, cultural and national boundaries do not necessarily coincide. Some areas of Switzerland are very much like Italy, other parts like France, and still other parts like Germany. Similarly, within the United States there are large cultural differences across, say, Southern California, Texas, and the East Coast.[5]

Given this basic assumption, one major review of the literature on international management reached five basic conclusions.[6] First, behavior in organizational settings does indeed vary across cultures. Thus, employees in companies based in Japan, the United States, and Germany are likely to have different attitudes and patterns of behavior. The behavior patterns are also likely to be widespread and pervasive within an organization.

Culture is the set of shared values, often taken for granted, that help people in a group, organization, or society understand which actions are considered acceptable and which are deemed unacceptable.

Second, culture itself is one major cause of this variation. **Culture** is the set of shared values, often taken for granted, that help people in a group, organization, or society understand which actions are considered acceptable and which are deemed unacceptable (we use this same definition to frame our discussion of organizational culture in Chapter 18). Thus, although the behavioral differences just noted may be caused in part by different standards of living, different geographical conditions, and so forth, culture itself is a major factor apart from other considerations.

People behave differently in different cultural contexts. This business meeting, for example, includes managers from different countries. Each manager's behavior will almost certainly be affected by the diverse behaviors of others at the meeting.

Digital Vision/Photodisc/Jupiter Images

Third, although the causes and consequences of behavior within organizational settings remain quite diverse across cultures, organizations and the ways they are structured appear to be growing increasingly similar. Hence, managerial practices at a general level may be becoming more and more alike, but the people who work within organizations still differ markedly.

Fourth, the same individual behaves differently in different cultural settings. A manager may adopt one set of behaviors when working in one culture but change those behaviors when moved to a different culture. For example, Japanese executives who come to work in the United States may slowly begin to act more like U.S. managers and less like Japanese managers. This, in turn, may be source of concern for them when they are transferred back to Japan.

Finally, cultural diversity can be an important source of synergy in enhancing organizational effectiveness. More and more organizations are coming to

Table 2.1 Work-Related Differences in 10 Countries

COUNTRY	INDIVIDUALISM/ COLLECTIVISM	POWER DISTANCE	UNCERTAINTY AVOIDANCE	MASCULINITY	LONG-TERM ORIENTATION
CANADA	H	M	M	M	L
GERMANY	M	M	M	M	M
ISRAEL	M	L	M	M	(no data)
ITALY	H	M	M	H	(no data)
JAPAN	M	M	H	H	H
MEXICO	H	H	H	M	(no data)
PAKISTAN	L	M	M	M	L
SWEDEN	H	M	L	L	M
UNITED STATES	H	M	M	M	L
VENEZUELA	L	H	M	H	(no data)

Note: H = high; M = moderate; L = low for INDIVIDUALISM/COLLECTIVISM H means High Individualism, L means High Collectivism and M means a balance of individualism and collectivism. These are only 10 of the more than 60 countries that Hofstede and others have studied.

References: Adapted from Geert Hofstede and Michael Harris Bond, "The Confucius Connection: From Cultural Roots to Economic Growth," *Organizational Dynamics,* Spring 1988, pp. 5–21; Geert Hofstede, "Motivation, Leadership, and Organization: Do American Theories Apply Abroad?" *Organizational Dynamics,* Summer 1980, pp. 42–63.

appreciate the virtues of diversity, but they still know surprisingly little about how to manage it. Organizations that adopt a multinational strategy can—with effort—become more than a sum of their parts. Operations in each culture can benefit from operations in other cultures through an enhanced understanding of how the world works.[7]

Specific Cultural Issues Geert Hofstede, a Dutch researcher, studied workers and managers in 60 countries and found that specific attitudes and behaviors differed significantly because of the values and beliefs that characterized those countries.[8] Table 2.1 shows how Hofstede's categories help us summarize differences for several countries.

Individualism exists to the extent that people in a culture define themselves primarily as individuals rather than as part of one or more groups or organizations.

Collectivism is characterized by tight social frameworks in which people tend to base their identities on the group or organization to which they belong.

The two primary dimensions that Hofstede found are the individualism/collectivism continuum and power distance. **Individualism** exists to the extent that people in a culture define themselves primarily as individuals rather than as part of one or more groups or organizations. At work, people from more individualistic cultures tend to be more concerned about themselves as individuals than about their work group, individual tasks are more important than relationships, and hiring and promotion are usually based on skills and rules. **Collectivism**, on the other hand, is characterized by tight social frameworks in which people tend to base their identities on the group or organization to which they belong. At work, this means that employee–employer links are more like family relationships, relationships are more important than individuals or tasks, and hiring and promotion are based on group membership. In the United States, a very individualistic culture, it is important to perform better than others and to stand out from the crowd. In Japan, a more collectivist culture, an individual tries to fit in with the group, strives for harmony, and prefers stability.

Power distance, which can also be called **orientation to authority**, is the extent to which people accept as normal an unequal distribution of power.

Uncertainty avoidance, which can also be called **preference for stability**, is the extent to which people feel threatened by unknown situations and prefer to be in clear and unambiguous situations.

Masculinity, which might be more accurately called **assertiveness** or **materialism**, is the extent to which the dominant values in a society emphasize aggressiveness and the acquisition of money and other possessions as opposed to concern for people, relationships among people, and overall quality of life.

Long-term values include focusing on the future, working on projects that have a distant payoff, persistence, and thrift.

Short-term values are more oriented toward the past and the present and include respect for traditions and social obligations.

Power distance, which can also be called **orientation to authority**, is the extent to which people accept as normal an unequal distribution of power. In countries such as Mexico and Venezuela, for example, people prefer to be in a situation in which authority is clearly understood and lines of authority are never bypassed. On the other hand, in countries such as Israel and Denmark, authority is not as highly respected and employees are quite comfortable circumventing lines of authority to accomplish something. People in the United States tend to be mixed, accepting authority in some situations but not in others.

Hofstede also identified other dimensions of culture. **Uncertainty avoidance**, which can also be called **preference for stability**, is the extent to which people feel threatened by unknown situations and prefer to be in clear and unambiguous situations. People in Japan and Mexico prefer stability to uncertainty, whereas uncertainty is normal and accepted in Sweden, Hong Kong, and the United Kingdom. **Masculinity**, which might be more accurately called **assertiveness** or **materialism**, is the extent to which the dominant values in a society emphasize aggressiveness and the acquisition of money and other possessions as opposed to concern for people, relationships among people, and overall quality of life. People in the United States tend to be moderate on both the uncertainty avoidance and masculinity scales. Japan and Italy score high on the masculinity scale while Sweden scores low.

Hofstede's framework has recently been expanded to include **long-term** versus **short-term orientation**. Long-term values include focusing on the future, working on projects that have a distant payoff, persistence, and thrift. Short-term values are more oriented toward the past and the present and include respect for traditions and social obligations. Japan, Hong Kong, and China are highly long-term oriented. The Netherlands, the United States, and Germany are moderately long-term oriented. Pakistan and West Africa tend to be more short-term oriented.

Hofstede's research presents only one of several ways of categorizing differences across many different countries and cultures. His findings, however, are now widely accepted and have been used by many companies. They have also prompted ongoing research by others. The important issue to remember is that people from diverse cultures value things differently from each other and that people need to take these differences into account as they work.

Managerial Behavior Across Cultures

Some individual variations in people from different cultures shape the behavior of both managers and employees. Other differences are much more likely to influence managerial behavior per se.[9] In general, these differences relate to managerial beliefs about the role of authority and power in the organization. For example, managers in Indonesia, Italy, and Japan tend to believe that the purpose of an organization's structure is to let everyone know who his or her boss is (medium to high power distance). Managers in the United States, Germany, and the Great Britain, in contrast, believe that organizational structure is intended to coordinate group behavior and effort (low power distance). On another dimension, Italian and German managers believe it is acceptable to bypass one's boss to get things done, but among Swedish and British managers, bypassing one's superior is strongly prohibited.

Figure 2.2 illustrates findings on another interesting point. Managers in Japan strongly believe that a manager should be able to answer any question he or she is asked. Thus, they place a premium on expertise and experience. At the other extreme are Swedish managers, who have the least concern about knowing all the answers. They view themselves as problem solvers and facilitators who make no claim to omniscience.

FIGURE 2.2

Differences Across Cultures in Managers' Beliefs about Answering Questions from Subordinates

Subordinates in various cultures have different beliefs regarding managers' ability to provide definite, precise answers to questions. Japan has the strongest expectations; Sweden has the weakest.

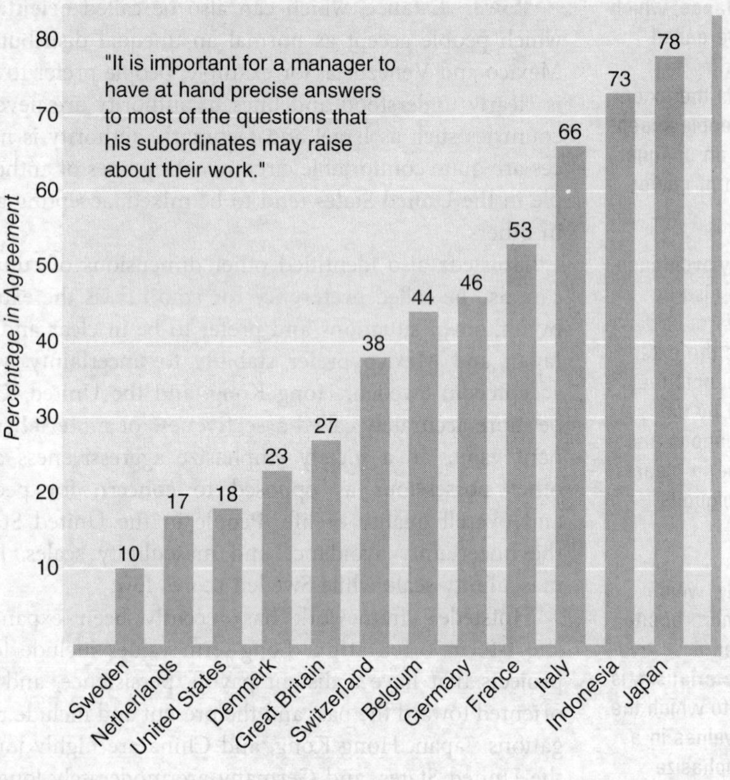

Reference: Reprinted from *International Studies of Management and Organizations,* vol. XIII, no. 1–2, Spring–Summer 1983, by permission of M. E. Sharpe, Inc., Armonk, N.Y. 10504

Some evidence also suggests that managerial behavior is rapidly changing, at least among European managers. In general, these managers are becoming more career oriented, better educated, more willing to work cooperatively with labor, more willing to delegate, and more cosmopolitan. Finally, a recent major global research project has investigated differences in leadership in different countries and produced some interesting results. We explore this research in Chapter 13.

DIVERSITY AND BUSINESS

Workforce diversity refers to the important similarities and differences among the employees of organizations.

A second major environmental shift in recent years has been the increased attention devoted to the concept of diversity. **Workforce diversity** refers to the important similarities and differences among the employees of organizations. 3M defines its goals regarding workforce diversity as "valuing uniqueness, while respecting differences, maximizing individual potentials, and synergizing collective talents and experiences for the growth and success of 3M."[10] In a diverse workforce, managers are compelled to recognize and handle the similarities and differences that exist among the people in the organization.[11]

Employees' conceptions of work, expectations of rewards from the organization, and practices in relating to others are all influenced by diversity. Managers of diverse work groups need to understand how the social environment affects employees' beliefs about work, and they must have the communication skills required to develop confidence and self-esteem in members of diverse work groups.[12]

Stereotypes are generalizations about a person or a group of persons based on certain characteristics or traits.

Unfortunately, many people tend to stereotype others in organizations. A **stereotype** is a generalization about a person or a group of persons based on certain characteristics or traits. Many managers fall into the trap of stereotyping workers as being like themselves and sharing a manager's orientation toward work, rewards, and relating to coworkers. However, if workers do not share those views, values, and beliefs, problems can arise. A second situation involving stereotyping occurs when managers classify workers into some particular group based on traits such as age or gender. It is often easier for managers to group people based on easily identifiable characteristics and to treat these groups as "different." Managers who stereotype workers based on assumptions about the characteristics of their group tend to ignore individual differences and therefore to make rigid judgments about others that do not take into account the specific person and the current situation.

Prejudices are judgments about others that reinforce beliefs about superiority and inferiority.

Stereotypes can lead to the even more dangerous process of prejudice toward others. **Prejudices** are judgments about others that reinforce beliefs about superiority and inferiority. They can lead to an exaggerated assessment of the worth of one group and a diminished assessment of the worth of others. When people prejudge others, they make assumptions about the nature of the others that may or may not be true, and they manage accordingly. In other words, people build job descriptions, reward systems, performance appraisal systems, and management systems and policies that fit their stereotypes.

Management systems built on stereotypes and prejudices do not meet the needs of a diverse workforce. An incentive system may offer rewards that people do not value, job descriptions might not fit the jobs and the people who do them, and performance evaluation systems might measure the wrong things. In addition, those who engage in prejudice and stereotyping fail to recognize employees' distinctive individual talents, a situation that often leads these employees to lose self-esteem and possibly have lower levels of job satisfaction and performance. Stereotypes can also become self-fulfilling prophecies. If we assume someone is incompetent and treat the person as though he or she is incompetent, then over time the employee may begin to share the same belief. This can lead to reduced productivity, lower creativity, and lower morale.

Of course, managers caught in this counterproductive cycle can change. As a first step, they must recognize that diversity exists in organizations. Only then can they begin to manage it appropriately. Managers who do not recognize diversity may face an unhappy, disillusioned, and underutilized workforce.

Dimensions of Diversity

In the United States, race and gender have been considered the primary dimensions of diversity. The earliest civil rights laws, for instance, were aimed at correcting racial segregation. Other more recent laws have dealt with discrimination on the basis of gender, age, and disability. However, diversity entails broader issues than these. In the largest sense, the diversity of the workforce refers to all of the ways that employees are similar and different. The importance of renewed interest in diversity is that it helps organizations reap the benefits of all the similarities and differences among workers.

Primary dimensions of diversity are those factors that are either inborn or exert extraordinary influence on early socialization.

The **primary dimensions of diversity** are those factors that are either inborn or exert extraordinary influence on early socialization. These include age, race and ethnicity, gender, physical and mental abilities, and sexual orientation.[13] These factors make up the essence of who we are as human beings. They define us to others, and because of how others react to them, these factors also define us to ourselves. These characteristics are enduring aspects of our human personality, and they sometimes present extremely complex problems to managers.

Secondary dimensions of diversity include factors that matter to us as individuals and that to some extent define us to others; however, they may be less permanent than primary dimensions and can be adapted or changed.

Secondary dimensions of diversity include factors that matter to us as individuals and that to some extent define us to others; however, they may be less permanent than primary dimensions and can be adapted or changed. These include educational background, geographical location, income, marital status, military experience, parental status, religious beliefs, and work experience. These factors may influence any given individual as much as the primary dimensions. Many veterans of the wars in Afghanistan and Iraq, for example, have been profoundly affected by their experience of serving in the military.

Who Will Be the Workforce of the Future?

Employment statistics can help us understand just how different the workforce of the future will be. Figure 2.3 compares the workforce composition of 1984, 1994, 2004, and projections for 2014. All workforce segments have increased as a percentage of the total workforce except the white male segment, which has declined steadily. This may not seem too dramatic, but it follows decades in which the white males have dominated the workforce, making up well over 50 percent of it. When one considers that the total U.S. workforce is over 150 million people, a small percentage decline is still large in absolute numbers.[14]

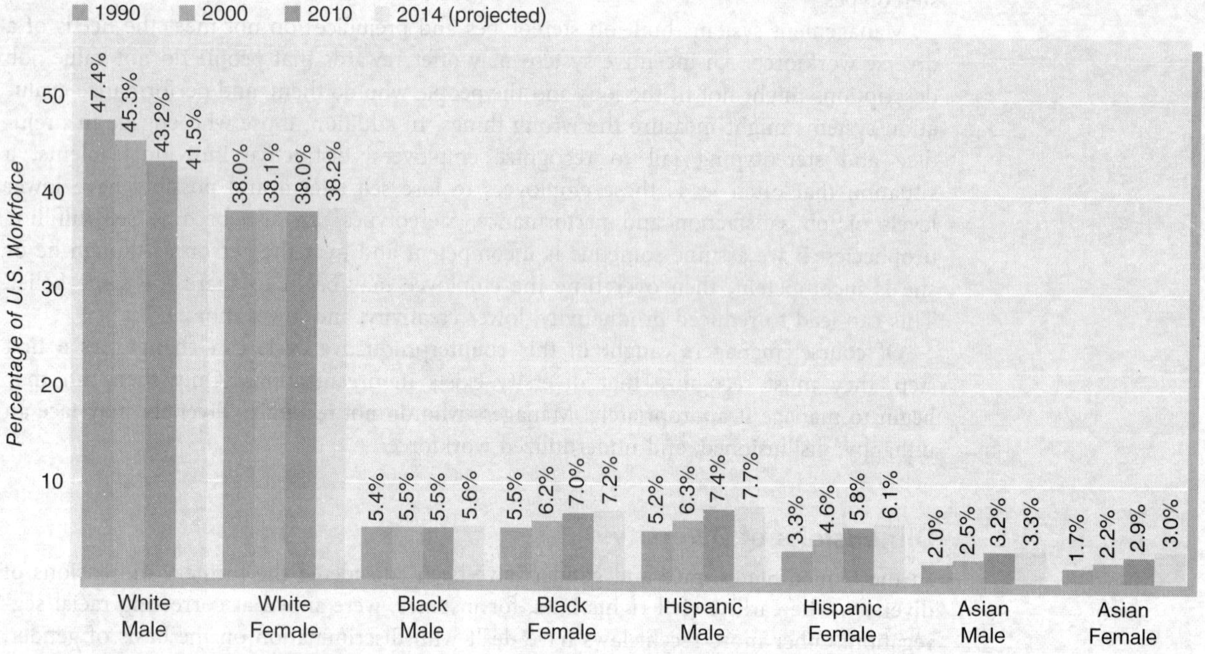

FIGURE 2.3

Workforce Composition 1990–2014

In the period between 1990 and 2014, all workforce segments are expected to increase as a percentage of the total workforce except the white male segment, which is has declined from 47.4% in 1990 to 43.2% in 2010 and is expected to decline further to 41.5 % by 2014.

Note: The percentages for each year exceed 100 because of the number of individuals who report dual or multiple ethnicities.

Source: Bureau of Labor Statistics, Labor Force Projections to 2014: Retiring Boomers, http://www.bls.gov/opub/mlr/2010/11/art3full.pdf

FIGURE 2.4

Projected Workforce Growth by Segment from 2004 to 2014

As this figure illustrates, while the overall workforce is expected to grow by 1% between 2004 and 2014, the smallest growth will occur in the white male and white female categories, while the largest growth will occur in the Asian female category.

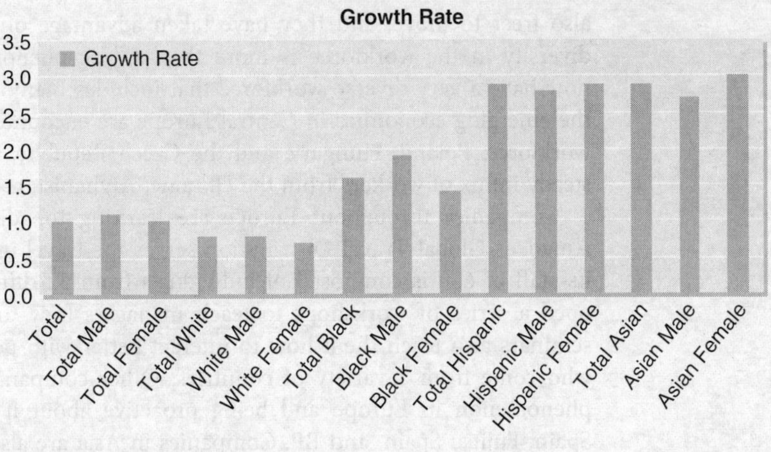

Source: Bureau of Labor Statistics, Labor Force Projections to 2014; http://www.bls.gov/opub/mlr/2005/11/art3full.pdf

We can also examine the nature of the growth in the workforce over the 10-year period from 2004 to 2014 (projected). Figure 2.4 shows the percentage of the growth attributable to each segment. For instance, over this 10-year period the total male portion of the workforce is expected to grow by 1.1 percent. Within this category, though, white males are expected to increase only by .8 percent while black males are projected to increase by 1.9 percent, Hispanic males by 2.8 percent, and Asian males by 2.7 percent. As can be seen, both white males and white females are expected to decline slightly as a percentage of the overall workforce while all other groups are projected to increase.

Examining the age ranges of the workforce gives us another view of the changes. In contrast to its standing in earlier decades, the 16–24 age group is growing more rapidly than the overall population—an increase of 3.4 million (14.8 percent) between 2000 and 2010. The number of workers in the 25–54 age group has increased by 5 million (5.0 percent), and the number of workers in the 55 and older group has increased by 8.5 million (46.6 percent).[15]

Global Workforce Diversity

Similar statistics on workforce diversity are found in other countries. In Canada, for instance, minorities are the fastest-growing segment of the population and the workforce. In addition, women make up two-thirds of the growth in the Canadian workforce, increasing from 35 percent in the 1970s to over 50 percent in 2010. These changes have initiated a workforce revolution in offices and factories throughout Canada. Managers and employees are learning to adapt to changing demographics. One study found that 81 percent of the organizations surveyed by the Conference Board of Canada include diversity management programs for their employees.[16]

Increasing diversity in the workplace is even more dramatic in Europe, where employees have been crossing borders for many years. In fact, in 1991 more than 2 million Europeans were living in one country and working in another. When the European Union further eased border crossings for its citizens in 1992, this number increased significantly. It was expected that opening borders among the European community members primarily would mean relaxing trade restrictions so that goods and services could move more freely among the member countries. In addition, however, workers were also freer to move, and they have taken advantage of the opportunity. It is clear that diversity in the workforce is more than a U.S. phenomenon. Many German factories now have a very diverse workforce that includes many workers from Turkey. Several of the emerging economies in Central Europe are encountering increasing diversity in their workforce. Poland, Hungary, and the Czech Republic, for instance, have experienced a steady influx of workers from the Ukraine, Afghanistan, Sri Lanka, China, and Somalia.[17]

Companies throughout Europe are learning to adjust to the changing workforce. Amadeus Global Travel Distribution serves the travel industry, primarily in Europe, but its staff of 650 is composed of individuals from 32 different countries. Amadeus developed a series of workshops to teach managers how to lead multicultural teams. Such seminars also teach them how to interact better with peers, subordinates, and superiors who come from a variety of countries. Other companies experiencing much the same phenomenon in Europe and being proactive about it include Mars, Hewlett-Packard Spain, Fujitsu Spain, and BP. Companies in Asia are also encountering increasing diversity. In Thailand, where there is a shortage of skilled and unskilled workers because of rapid industrialization and slow population growth, there is a growing demand for foreign workers to fill the gap, which creates problems integrating local and foreign workers.[18] Thus, the issue of workforce diversity is not limited to the United States.

The Value of Diversity

The United States has historically been seen as a "melting pot" of people from many different countries, cultures, and backgrounds. For centuries, it was assumed that people who came from other countries should assimilate into the existing cultural context they were entering. Although equal employment opportunity and accompanying affirmative action legislation have had significant effects on diversifying workplaces, they sometimes focused on bringing into the workplace people from culturally different groups and fully assimilating them into the existing organization. In organizations, however, integration proved difficult to implement. Members of the majority were slow to adapt and usually resistant to the change. Substantive career advancement opportunities rarely materialized for those who were "different."

The issue of workforce diversity has become increasingly important in the last few years as employees, managers, consultants, and the government finally realized that the composition of the workforce affects organizational productivity. Today, instead of a melting pot, the workplace in the United States might be regarded as more of a "tossed salad" made up of a mosaic of different flavors, colors, and textures. Rather than trying to assimilate those who are different into a single organizational culture, the current view holds that organizations need to celebrate the differences and utilize the variety of talents, perspectives, and backgrounds of all employees.[19]

Assimilation is the process through which members of a minority group are socialized into learning the ways of the majority group.

Assimilation **Assimilation** is the process through which members of a minority group become socialized into learning the ways of the majority group. In organizations this entails hiring people from diverse backgrounds and attempting to mold them to fit into the existing organizational culture. One way that companies attempt to make people fit in is by requiring that employees speak only one language. For instance, Carlos Solero was fired after he refused to sign a work agreement that included a policy of English-only at a suburban manufacturing plant near Chicago. Management said the intent of the English-only policy was to improve communication among workers at the plant. In response, Solero and seven other Spanish speakers filed lawsuits against the plant. Attempts to assimilate diverse workers by imposing English-only rules can lead to a variety of organizational problems. Most organizations develop systems such as performance evaluation and incentive programs that reinforce the values of the dominant group.

Ed Quinn/Corbis News/Corbis

Diversity training is a common method used in businesses today to better enable their employees to accept and value differences. These Pilgrim Health Care workers, for instance, are participating in a role-playing exercise as part of a diversity training program. Various individuals wear labels branding themselves as "complainer," "rookie-new hire," "opposed to change," "overweight," and so forth. As they interact with one another, they begin to see how labels affect their interactions with others at work.

(Chapter 18 discusses organizational culture as a means of reinforcing the organizational values and affecting the behavior of workers.) By universally applying the values of the majority group throughout the organization, assimilation tends to perpetuate false stereotypes and prejudices. Workers who are different are expected to meet the standards for dominant group members.[20]

Dominant groups tend to be self-perpetuating. Majority group members may avoid people who are "different" simply because they find communication difficult. Moreover, informal discussions over coffee and lunch and during after-hours socializing tend to be limited to people in the dominant group. As a result, those who are not in the dominant group miss out on the informal communication opportunities in which office politics, company policy, and other issues are often discussed in rich detail. Subsequently, employees not in the dominant group often do not understand the more formal communications and may not be included in necessary actions taken in response. The dominant group likewise remains unaware of opinions from the "outside."

Similarly, since the dominant group makes decisions based on its own values and beliefs, the minority group has little say in decisions regarding compensation, facility location, benefit plans, performance standards, and other work issues that pertain directly to all workers. Workers who differ from the majority very quickly get the idea that to succeed in such a system, one must be like the dominant group in terms of values and beliefs, dress, and most other characteristics. Because success depends on assimilation, differences are driven underground.

Not paying attention to diversity can be very costly to the organization. In addition to blocking minority involvement in communication and decision making, it can result in tensions among workers, lower productivity, increased costs due to increasing absenteeism, increased employee turnover, increased equal employment opportunity and harassment suits, and lower morale among the workers.

Valuing diversity means putting an end to the assumption that everyone who is not a member of the dominant group must assimilate.

Benefits of Valuing Diversity **Valuing diversity** means putting an end to the assumption that everyone who is not a member of the dominant group must assimilate. This is not easily accomplished in most organizations. Truly valuing diversity is not merely giving lip service to an ideal, putting up with a necessary evil, promoting a level of tolerance for those who are different, or tapping into the latest fad. It is providing an opportunity to develop and utilize all of the human resources available to the organization for the benefit of the workers and the organization as a whole.

Valuing diversity is not just the right thing to do for workers; it is the right thing to do for the organization, both financially and economically.[21] One of the most important benefits of diversity is the richness of ideas and perspectives that it makes available to the organization. Rather than relying on one homogeneous dominant group for new ideas and alternative solutions to increasingly complex problems, companies that value diversity have access to more perspectives on a problem. These fresh perspectives may lead to development of new products, opening of new markets, or improving service to existing customers.[22]

Overall, the organization wins when it truly values diversity. Workers who recognize that the organization truly values them are likely to be more creative, motivated, and productive. Valued workers in diverse organizations experience less interpersonal conflict because the employees understand each other. When employees of different cultural groups, backgrounds, and values understand each other, they have a greater sense of teamwork, a stronger identification with the team, and a deeper commitment to the organization and its goals.

TECHNOLOGY AND BUSINESS

Technology refers to the methods used to create products, including both physical goods and intangible services.

Technology refers to the methods used to create products, including both physical goods and intangible services. Technological change has become a major driver for other forms of organization change. Moreover, it also has widespread effects on the behaviors of people inside an organization. Three specific areas of technology worth noting here are: (1) the shift toward a service-based economy, (2) the growing use of technology for competitive advantage, and (3) mushrooming change in information technology.[23]

Manufacturing and Service Technologies

Manufacturing is a form of business that combines and transforms resources into tangible outcomes that are then sold to others.

Manufacturing is a form of business that combines and transforms resources into tangible outcomes that are then sold to others. The Goodyear Tire and Rubber Company is a manufacturer because it combines rubber and chemical compounds and uses blending equipment and molding machines to create tires. Broyhill is a manufacturer because it buys wood and metal components, pads, and fabric and then combines them into furniture. And Apple is a manufacturer because it uses electronic, metal, plastic, and composite components to build smartphones, computers, and other digital products.

Manufacturing was once the dominant technology in the United States. During the 1970s, manufacturing entered a long period of decline, primarily because of foreign competition. U.S. firms had grown lax and sluggish, and new foreign competitors came onto the scene with better equipment and much higher levels of efficiency. For example, steel companies in the Far East were able to produce high-quality steel for much lower prices than large U.S. steel companies like such as Bethlehem Steel and U.S. Steel. Faced with a battle for survival, some companies disappeared, but many others underwent a long and difficult period of change by eliminating waste and transforming themselves into leaner and more efficient and responsive entities. They reduced their workforces dramatically, closed antiquated or unnecessary plants, and modernized their remaining plants. Over the last decade or so, however, their efforts have started to pay dividends as U.S. manufacturing has regained a competitive position in many different industries. While low wages continue to center a great deal of global manufacturing in Asia, some manufacturers are now thriving in the United States.

A **service organization** is one that transforms resources into an intangible output and creates time or place utility for its customers.

During the decline of the manufacturing sector, a tremendous growth in the service sector kept the overall U.S. economy from declining at the same rate. A **service organization** is one that transforms resources into an intangible output and creates time or place utility for its customers. For example, Merrill Lynch makes stock transactions for its customers, Avis leases cars to its customers, and your local hairdresser cuts your hair. In 1947, the service sector was responsible for less than half of the U.S. gross national product (GNP). By 1975, however, this figure reached 65 percent, and by 2006 had surpassed 75 percent. The service sector has been responsible for almost 90 percent of all new jobs created in the United States since 1990. Moreover, employment in service occupations is expected to grow 26.8 percent between 2010 and 2020.[24]

Antony Souter/Alamy Limited

Service businesses like Avis must work to insure that their employees are well-trained in the procedures the firm uses to rent automobiles. But their employees must also demonstrate strong customer service skills. Both skill sets are especially important in settings like this Cape Town rental counter where employees will deal with customers from around the world.

Managers have come to see that many of the tools, techniques, and methods that are used in a factory are also useful to a service firm. For example, managers of automobile plants and hair salons each have to decide how to design their facility, identify the best location for it, determine optimal capacity, make decisions about inventory storage, set procedures for purchasing raw materials, and set standards for productivity and quality. At the same time, though, service-based firms must hire and train employees based on a different skill set than is required by most manufacturers. For instance, consumers seldom come into contact with the Toyota employee who installs the seats in their car, so that person can be hired based on technical skills. But Avis must recruit people who not only know how to do a job but who can also effectively interface with a variety of consumers. These and related service technology issues are explored throughout our book in a our new Services boxed insert.

Technology and Competition

Technology is the basis of competition for some firms, especially those whose goals include being the technology leaders in their industries. A company, for example, might focus its efforts on being the lowest-cost producer or on always having the most technologically advanced products on the market. But because of the rapid pace of new developments, keeping a leadership position based on technology is becoming increasingly challenging. Another challenge is meeting constant demands to decrease cycle time (the time that it takes a firm to accomplish some recurring activity or function from beginning to end).

Businesses have increasingly found that they can be more competitive if they can systematically decrease cycle times. Many companies, therefore, now focus on decreasing cycle times in areas ranging from developing products to making deliveries and collecting credit payments. Twenty years ago, it took a carmaker about five years from the decision to launch a new product until it was available in dealer showrooms. Now most companies can complete the cycle in less than two years. The speedier process allows them to more quickly respond to changing economic conditions, consumer preferences, and new competitor products while recouping more quickly their product-development costs. Some firms compete directly on how quickly they can get things done for consumers. In the early days of personal computers, for instance, getting a made-to-order system took six to eight weeks. Today, firms such as Dell can usually ship exactly what the customer wants in a matter of days.

Information Technology

Most people are very familiar with advances in information technology. Cellular telephones, electronic books, smart phones such as the iPhone and Blackberry, the iPad, and digital cameras, as well as technologically based social networking sites like Facebook, are just a few of the many recent innovations that have changed how people live and work.[25] Breakthroughs in information technology have resulted in leaner organizations, more flexible operations, increased collaboration among employees, more flexible work sites, and improved management processes and systems. On the other hand, they have also resulted in less personal communication, less "down time" for managers and employees, and an increased sense of urgency vis-à-vis decision making and communication—changes that have not necessarily always been beneficial. We discuss information technology and its relationship to organizational behavior in more detail in Chapter 11.

ETHICS AND CORPORATE GOVERNANCE

Ethics are a person's beliefs regarding what is right or wrong in a given situation.

While **ethics** have long been of relevance to businesses, what seems like an epidemic of ethical breaches in recent years has placed ethics in the mainstream of managerial thought today. One special aspect of business ethics, corporate governance, has also taken on increased importance. Ethics also increasingly relate to information technology. Before discussing these issues, however, it is useful to understand how best to frame ethical relationships in organizations.

Framing Ethical Issues

Figure 2.5 illustrates how many ethical situations can be framed. Specifically, most ethical dilemmas faced by managers relate to how the organization treats its employees, how employees treat the organization, and how employees and organizations treat other economic agents.

How an Organization Treats Its Employees One important area of managerial ethics is the treatment of employees by the organization. This area includes policies such as hiring and firing, wages and working conditions, and employee privacy and respect. For example, both ethical and legal guidelines suggest that hiring and firing decisions should be based solely on an individual's ability to perform the job. A manager who discriminates against African Americans in hiring is exhibiting both unethical and illegal behavior. But consider the case of a manager who does not discriminate in general but who hires a family friend when other applicants might be just as—or perhaps more—qualified. Although these hiring decisions may not be illegal, they may be objectionable on ethical grounds.

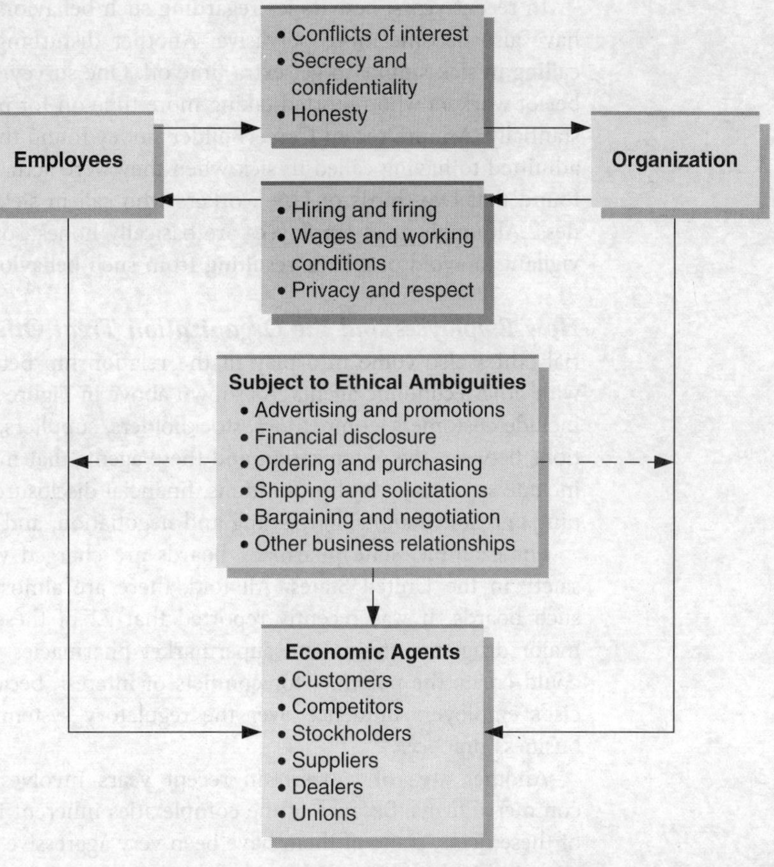

FIGURE 2.5

Managerial Ethics

Managers face a variety of ethical situations. In most cases these situations involve how the organization treats its employees, how employees treat the organization, and how employees and organizations treat other economic agents.

Wages and working conditions, although tightly regulated, are also areas for potential controversy. For example, a manager paying an employee less than he deserves, simply because the manager knows the employee cannot afford to quit or risk losing his job by complaining, might be considered unethical. The same goes for employee benefits, especially if an organization takes action that affects the compensation packages—and welfare—of an entire workforce. Finally, most observers would also agree that an organization is obligated to protect the privacy of its employees. A manager's divulging to employees that one of their coworkers is having financial problems or an affair is generally seen as an unethical breach of privacy. Likewise, the manner in which an organization addresses issues associated with sexual harassment involves employee privacy and related rights.

How Employees Treat the Organization Numerous ethical issues also stem from how employees treat the organization, especially in regard to conflicts of interest, secrecy and confidentiality, and honesty. A conflict of interest occurs when a decision potentially benefits the individual to the possible detriment of the organization. To guard against such practices, most companies have policies that forbid their buyers to accept gifts from suppliers. Divulging company secrets is also clearly unethical. Employees who work for businesses in highly competitive industries—electronics, software, and fashion apparel, for example—might be tempted to sell information about company plans to competitors. A third area of concern is honesty in general. Relatively common problems in this area include such activities as using a business telephone to make personal long-distance calls, stealing supplies, and padding expense accounts.

In recent years, new issues regarding such behaviors as personal Internet use at work have also become more pervasive. Another disturbing trend is that more workers are calling in sick simply to get extra time off. One survey, for instance, found that the number of workers who reported taking more time off for personal needs was increasing substantially. A more recent CareerBuilder survey found that 29 percent of workers surveyed admitted to having called in sick when they were actually well.[26] And yet another survey found that two-thirds of U.S. workers who call in sick do so for reasons other than illness. Although most employees are basically honest, organizations must nevertheless be vigilant to avoid problems resulting from such behaviors.

How Employees and the Organization Treat Other Economic Agents Managerial ethics also come into play in the relationship between the firm and its employees with other economic agents. As shown above in Figure 2.5, the primary agents of interest include customers, competitors, stockholders, suppliers, dealers, and unions. The interactions between the organization and these agents that may be subject to ethical ambiguity include advertising and promotions, financial disclosures, ordering and purchasing, shipping and solicitations, bargaining and negotiation, and other business relationships.

For example, state pharmacy boards are charged with overseeing prescription drug safety in the United States. All told, there are almost 300 pharmacists who serve on such boards. It was recently reported that 72 of these pharmacists were employees of major drugstore chains and supermarket pharmacies. These arrangements, while legal, could create the potential for conflicts of interest, because they might give the pharmacist's employers influence over the regulatory system designed to monitor their own business practices.[27]

Another area of concern in recent years involves financial reporting by some e-commerce firms. Because of the complexities inherent in valuing the assets and revenues of these firms, some of them have been very aggressive in presenting their financial positions in highly positive lights. In at least a few cases, some firms have substantially overstated their earnings projections to entice more investment. After Time-Warner merged with AOL, it discovered that its new online partner had overstated its value through various inappropriate accounting methods. Some of today's accounting scandals in traditional firms have stemmed from similarly questionable practices.[28] For instance, Diamond Foods, maker of Emerald snack nuts and Pop Secret popcorn, recently had to restate its earnings after an audit uncovered several accounting irregularities.[29]

Hilton Hotels recently hired two senior executives away from rival Starwood Hotels. It was later determined that the executives took eight boxes of electronic and paper documents with them; much of the material in the boxes related to plans and details for starting a new luxury-hotel brand. When Hilton announced plans to start such a chain itself, to be called Denizen Hotels, officials at Starwood became suspicious and investigated. When they learned about the theft of confidential materials, which Hilton subsequently returned, Starwood filed a lawsuit against Hilton.[30]

Additional complexities faced by many firms today include the variations in ethical business practices in different countries. In some countries, bribes and side payments are a normal and customary part of doing business. However, U.S. laws forbid these practices, even if a firm's rivals from other countries are paying them. For example, a U.S. power-generating company once lost a $320 million contract in the Middle East because government officials demanded a $3 million bribe. A Japanese firm paid the bribe and won the contract. Another major American company once had a big project in India cancelled because newly elected officials demanded bribes. And Walmart has recently been charged with paying $24 million in bribes to Mexican officials to sidestep local regulations and obtain expedited building permits for new stores.[31] Although such

Andrew Burton/Reuters/Landov Media

Walmart was recently charged with paying $24 million in bribes to Mexican officials to avoid local regulations and expedite permits for new stores. These protestors in New York are speaking out against the giant discounter's efforts to open stores in their city, in park by invoking Walmart's recent scandal in Mexico.

payments are illegal under U.S. law, other situations are more ambiguous. In China, for example, local journalists expect their cab fare to be paid if they are covering a business-sponsored news conference. In Indonesia, the normal time for a foreigner to get a driver's license is over a year, but it can be "expedited" for an extra $100. In Romania, building inspectors routinely expect a "tip" for a favorable review.[32] And the government of Bahrain recently charged Alcoa with involvement in a 15-year conspiracy involving overcharging, fraud, and bribery.[33] Alcoa, for instance, billed Bahraini clients for "overhead," a normal and understood charge in some countries but not in parts of the Middle East. Similarly, gifts provided to some local officials by Alcoa were seen by other officials as bribes.

Ethical Issues in Corporate Governance

Corporate governance refers to the oversight of a public corporation by its board of directors.

A related area of emerging concern relates to ethical issues in **corporate governance**—the oversight of a public corporation by its board of directors. The board of a public corporation is expected to ensure that the business is being properly managed and that the decisions made by its senior management are in the best interests of shareholders and other stakeholders. But in far too many cases the recent ethical scandals alluded to previously have actually started with a breakdown in the corporate governance structure. For instance, in a now-classic ethical scandal involving governance issues, WorldCom's board approved a personal loan to the firm's CEO, Bernard Ebbers, for $366 million even though there was little evidence that he could repay it. Likewise, Tyco's board approved a $20 million bonus for one of its own members for helping with the acquisition of a firm owned by that individual (this bonus was in addition to the purchase price!).

But boards of directors are also increasingly being criticized even when they are not directly implicated in wrongdoing. The biggest complaint here often relates to board independence. Disney, for instance, has faced this problem in the past. Several key members of the firm's board of directors were from companies that do business with Disney, and others were long-time friends of senior Disney executives. While board members need to have some familiarity with both the firm and its industry in order to function effectively, they also need to have sufficient independence to carry out their oversight function.[34]

Ethical Issues in Information Technology

Another set of issues that have emerged in recent times involves information technology. Among the specific questions in this area are individual rights to privacy and the potential abuse of information technology by companies. Indeed, online privacy has become a hot issue as companies sort out the related ethical and management issues. DoubleClick, an online advertising network, is one of the firms at the center of the privacy debate. The company has collected data on the habits of millions of web surfers, recording which sites they visit and which ads they click on. DoubleClick insists that the profiles are anonymous and are used to better match surfers with appropriate ads. However, after the company announced a plan to add names and addresses to its database, it was forced to back down because of public concerns over invasion of online privacy.

DoubleClick isn't the only firm gathering personal data about people's Internet activities. People who register at Yahoo! are asked to list date of birth, among other details. Amazon.com, eBay, and other sites also ask for personal information. And GPS and other tracking technologies allow firms to potentially know where their subscribers are physically located at any point in time. As awareness of these capabilities increases, surveys show that people are troubled by the amount of information being collected, who gets to see it, and other issues associated with privacy.

One way management can address these concerns is by posting a privacy policy on its website. The policy should explain exactly what data the company collects and who gets to see the data. It should also allow people a choice about having their information shared with others and indicate how people can opt out of data collection. Disney, IBM, and other companies support this position by refusing to advertise on websites that have no posted privacy policies.

In addition, companies can offer web surfers the opportunity to review and correct information that has been collected, especially medical and financial data. In the offline world, consumers are legally allowed to inspect credit and medical records. In the online world, this kind of access can be costly and cumbersome, because data are often spread across several computer systems. Despite the technical difficulties, government agencies are already working on Internet privacy guidelines; this means, in turn, that companies will also need internal guidelines, training, and leadership to ensure compliance.

NEW EMPLOYMENT RELATIONSHIPS

A final significant area of environmental change that is particularly relevant for businesses today involves what we call new employment relationships. While we discuss employment relationships from numerous perspectives in Part 2 of this book, two particularly important areas today involve the management of knowledge workers and the outsourcing of jobs to other businesses, especially when those businesses are in other countries. Managing temporary and contingency workers and tiered workforces is also becoming increasingly complex.

The Management of Knowledge Workers

Knowledge workers are those employees who add value in an organization simply because of what they know.

Traditionally, employees added value to organizations because of what they did or because of their experience. However, during today's "information age," many employees add value simply because of what they know.[35] These employees are often referred to as **knowledge workers**. How well these employees are managed is seen as a major factor in determining which firms will be successful in the future.[36] Knowledge workers include computer scientists, physical scientists, engineers, product designers, and video game developers. They tend to work in high-technology firms and are usually experts in some abstract knowledge base. They often believe they have the right to work in an autonomous fashion, and they identify more strongly with their profession than with any organization—even to the extent of defining performance primarily in terms recognized by other members of their profession.[37]

As the importance of information-driven jobs grows, the need for knowledge workers will grow as well. But these employees require extensive and highly specialized training, and not everyone is willing to make the human capital investments necessary to move into these jobs. In fact, even after knowledge workers are on the job, retraining and training updates are critical so that their skills do not become obsolete. It has been suggested, for example, that the "half-life" for a technical education in engineering is about three years. Further, the failure to update the required skills will not only result in the organization's losing competitive advantage but will also increase the likelihood that the knowledge worker will go to another firm that is more committed to updating those skills.[38]

Compensation and related policies for knowledge workers must also be specially tailored. For example, in many high-tech organizations, engineers and scientists have the option of entering a technical career path that parallels a management career path. This allows the knowledge worker to continue to carry out specialized work without taking on large management responsibilities, while at the same time offering that worker compensation that is equivalent to that available to management. But in other high-tech firms, the emphasis is on pay for performance, with profit sharing based on projects or products developed by the knowledge workers. In addition, in most firms employing these workers there has been a tendency to reduce the number of levels of the organization to allow the knowledge workers to react more quickly to the external environment by reducing the need for bureaucratic approvals.[39]

Outsourcing

Outsourcing is the practice of hiring other firms to do work previously performed by the organization itself; when this work is moved overseas, it is often called offshoring.

Outsourcing is the practice of hiring other firms to do work previously performed by the organization itself. It is an increasingly popular strategy because it helps firms focus on their core activities and avoid getting sidetracked by secondary activities. The snack bar at a large commercial bank may be important to employees and some customers, but running it is not the bank's main line of business and expertise. Bankers need to focus on money management and financial services, not food-service operations. That's why most banks outsource snack bar operations to food-service management companies whose main line of business includes cafeterias. The result, ideally, is more attention to banking by bankers, better food service for snack bar customers, and formation of a new supplier–client relationship (food-service company/bank). Firms today often outsource numerous activities, including payroll, employee training, facility maintenance, and research and development.

Up to a point, at least, outsourcing makes good business sense in areas that are highly unrelated to a firm's core business activities. However, it has attracted considerably more attention in recent years because of the growing trend toward outsourcing abroad in order to lower labor costs; this practice is often called *offshoring*. One recent estimate suggests that 3.3 million white-collar jobs currently being performed in the United States will likely be moved abroad by 2015; this same study suggests that 1 out of 10 IT jobs once held by U.S. workers will be handled by non-U.S. workers by that same date.[40]

Many software firms, for example, have found that there is an abundance of talented programmers in India who are willing to work for much lower salaries than their American counterparts. Likewise, many firms that operate large call centers find that they can handle those operations for much lower costs from other parts of the world. As a result, domestic jobs may be lost. And some firms attract additional criticism when they require their domestic workers—soon to be out of jobs—to train their newly hired foreign replacements! Clearly, there are numerous behavioral and motivational issues involved in practices such as these. Several of them are detailed in the *Diversity* box entitled "The BOSS in Indian BPO" on page 53, which discusses problems faced by outsource employees in India.

Temp and Contingency Workers

A **contingent worker** is a person who works for an organization on something other than a permanent or full-time basis.

Another trend that has impacted employment relationships in business involves the use of contingent or temporary workers. Indeed, recent years have seen an explosion in the use of such workers by organizations. A **contingent worker** is a person who works for an organization on something other than a permanent or full-time basis. Categories of contingent workers include independent contractors, on-call workers, temporary employees (usually hired through outside agencies), and contract and leased employees. Another category is part-time workers. The financial services giant Citigroup, for example, makes extensive use of part-time sales agents to pursue new clients. About 10 percent of the U.S. workforce currently uses one of these alternative forms of employment relationships. Experts suggest, however, that this percentage is increasing at a consistent pace.

Managing contingent workers is not always straightforward, however, especially from a behavioral perspective. Expecting too much from such workers, for example, is a mistake that managers should avoid. An organization with a large contingent workforce must make some decisions about the treatment of contingent workers relative to the treatment of permanent, full-time workers. Should contingent workers be invited to the company holiday party? Should they have the same access to such employee benefits as counseling services and childcare? There are no right or wrong answers to such questions. Managers must understand that they need to develop a strategy for integrating contingent workers according to some sound logic and then follow that strategy consistently over time.[41]

Tiered Workforce

A **tiered workforce** exists when one group of an organization's workforce has a contractual arrangement with the organization objectively different from another group performing the same jobs.

A final emerging issue dealing with new employment relationships is what we might call the tiered workforce. A **tiered workforce** exists when one group of an organization's workforce has a contractual arrangement with the organization objectively different from that of another group performing the same jobs. For example, Harley-Davidson recently negotiated a new agreement with its labor union for wages and job security at its large motorcycle factory in York, Pennsylvania. The change was needed to help the plant remain competitive and to prevent Harley from moving York jobs to other factories. Under terms of the new agreement, the lowest-paid production worker currently on staff earns \$24.10 an hour. All new employees hired for that same job in the future, however, will earn \$19.28 an hour. Yet another group of employees, called "casual" workers, work on an "as needed" basis and will earn \$16.75 an hour.[42] Similarly, under a new contract

DIVERSITY The BOSS in Indian BPO

Twenty-one-year-old Anurag Verma has one of those jobs that tend to come up in the conversation when Americans are talking about U.S. unemployment: He works in India's burgeoning *business process outsourcing* (*BPO*) industry. He makes very good money—about $800 a month, which is 12 times the average Indian salary. He uses a Blackberry and doesn't have to ride a crowded bus to work because he owns a car. He was getting ready to put money down on a condo until one day he collapsed at his desk and had to be taken to the hospital. In the weeks leading up to his collapse, he had been suffering from dizzy spells and migraines; he'd lost his appetite and 22 pounds.

> ***"Those who put in 10 hours of work every night are unable to get adequate sleep during daytime no matter how hard they try. This causes a cumulative sleep debt leading to significant sleep deprivation, fatigue, mood swings, [and] lack of concentration."***
>
> —DR. ANUPAM MITTAL, MAX HOSPITAL IN DELHI, INDIA

Anurag had been on the job for eight months, and in the BPO industry, his problem is known as *BOSS—Burn Out Stress Syndrome*. Symptoms include chronic fatigue, insomnia, loss of appetite, and gastrointestinal problems. Back and shoulder pain are common, as are ear and eye ailments. Experts say that BOSS affects about one-third of India's 7 million BPO workers. In the city of Bangalore (known as "the Silicon Valley of India" because it's the country's leading information technology exporter), a study of IT professionals conducted by the National Institute for Mental Health and Neurosciences (NIMHANS) found that 1 in 20 workers regularly considered suicide and classified 36 percent as "probable psychiatric cases."

"You are making nice money," reports 26-year-old Vaibhav Vats, whose weight ballooned to 265 pounds after two years at an outsourced IBM call center, "but the tradeoff," he warns young people just entering the industry out of college, "is also big." Those tradeoffs typically include long night shifts and disrupted eating and sleeping schedules. A common result, according to doctors, is the alteration of biorhythms—the patterns by which our bodies adapt to the patterns of day and night. One study, for example, found that BPO workers tend to develop markedly different sleeping patterns. According to researchers, they were not only sleepier but were "more depressed and suffered from anxiety disorders." Explains Dr. Anupam Mittal of Delhi's Max Hospital: "Those who put in 10 hours of work every night are unable to get adequate sleep during daytime no matter how hard they try. This causes a cumulative sleep debt leading to significant sleep deprivation, fatigue, mood swings, [and] lack of concentration."

There are also physiological repercussions. Women, for instance, suffer from menstrual and hormonal disorders when disrupted sleep patterns create imbalances in melatonin and cortisol, two hormones related to sleep and stress. "Sleep deprivation and exposure to light at night," says Dr. Swati Bhargava, a Mumbai gynecologist, "interrupts melatonin production, thereby stimulating the body to produce more estrogen, which is a known hormonal promoter of breast cancer." Bhargava's diagnosis is supported by research showing that women who work nights have a 60 percent higher risk of breast cancer.

References: Neeta Lal, "India's Outsourcing Blues," *Asia Sentinel*, May 6, 2008, www.asiasentinel.com on April 9, 2012; Pawan Budhwar, "The Good and Bad of Outsourcing to India: Emerging Problems in the Sector and the Way Forward" (Birmingham, UK: Aston University, January 26, 2010), www1.aston.ac.uk on April 9, 2012; Saritha Rai, "India Outsourcing Workers Stressed to the Limit," *ZDNet*, August 26, 2009, www.zdnet.com on April 9, 2012; "India's Outsourcing Industry Facing Mass Level Health Problems," *BPO Tiger*, January 23, 2008, www.bpotiger.com on April 9, 2012.

with the United Auto Workers, new hires at Ford, General Motors, and Chrysler will earn a lower hourly wage and reduced benefits compared to workers already on the payroll when the agreement was signed.[43] General Motors, for example, pays its pre-contract employees a minimum of $28 an hour, but all new employees start at $14 an hour.

These and other arrangements will pose challenges in the future. For instance, newly hired workers may come to feel resentment towards their more senior colleagues who are getting paid more for the same work. Likewise, when the job market improves and workers have more options, firms may face higher turnover among their newer lower-paid employees.

SYNOPSIS

Globalization is playing a major role in the environment of many firms today. The volume of international trade has grown significantly and continues to grow at a very rapid pace. There are four basic reasons for this growth: (1) communication and transportation have advanced dramatically over the past several decades; (2) businesses have expanded internationally to increase their markets; (3) firms are moving into international markets to control costs, especially to reduce labor costs; and (4) many organizations have become international in response to competition. There are numerous cross-cultural differences and similarities that affect behavior within organizations.

A second major environmental shift in recent years has been the increased attention devoted to the concept of diversity. Workforce diversity refers to the important similarities and differences among the employees of organizations. Unfortunately, many people tend to stereotype others in organizations. Stereotypes can lead to the even more dangerous process of prejudice toward others. Managers should be cognizant of both primary and secondary dimensions of diversity, as well as the wide array of benefits to be derived from having a diverse workforce.

Technology refers to the methods used to create products, including both physical goods and intangible services. Technological change has become a major driver for other forms of organization change. Moreover, it also has widespread effects on the behaviors of people inside an organization. Three specific areas of technology relevant to the study of organizational behavior are (1) the shift toward a service-based economy, (2) the growing use of technology for competitive advantage, and (3) mushrooming change in information technology.

While ethics have long been of relevance to businesses, what seems like an epidemic of ethical breaches in recent years has placed ethics in the mainstream of managerial thought today. One special aspect of business ethics, corporate governance, has also taken on increased importance. Ethics also increasingly relate to information technology. A central issue today revolves around the fact that rapid changes in business relationships, organizational structures, and financial systems pose unsurpassed difficulties in keeping accurate track of a company's financial position.

Another significant area of environmental change that is particularly relevant for businesses today involves new employment relationships. Knowledge workers are those who add value to an organization because of what they know. How well these employees are managed is seen as a major factor in determining which firms will be successful in the future. Outsourcing is the practice of hiring other firms to do work previously performed by the organization itself. It is an increasingly popular strategy because it helps firms focus on their core activities and avoid getting sidetracked by secondary activities. However, it grows controversial when the jobs being outsourced are really being exported to foreign countries in ways that reduce domestic job opportunities. Contingent and temporary workers and the creation of a tiered workforce also pose special challenges. These challenges center around the treatment of various groups (such as contingent or lower-tier workers) compared to other groups (such as permanent or higher-tier employees).

DISCUSSION QUESTIONS

1. Identify ways in which the globalization of business affects businesses in your community.
2. What would you imagine to be the major differences among working for a domestic firm inside the United States, working for a foreign company's operations inside the United States, and working for an American firm's operations abroad?
3. Why do organizations need to be interested in managing diversity? Is it a legal or moral obligation, or does it have some other purpose?

4. Summarize in your own words what the statistics tell us about the workforce of the future.
5. All things considered, do you think people from diverse cultures are more alike or more different? Explain the reasons for your answer.
6. What role does changing technology play in your daily activities?
7. How concerned are you regarding technology-related privacy? Are your concerns increasing? Why or why not?
8. Do you think concerns regarding ethics will remain central in managerial thinking, or will these concerns eventually become less important? Why?
9. Do you anticipate becoming a "knowledge worker"? How do you think this will shape your own thinking regarding your employer, compensation, and so forth?
10. What are your personal opinions about the use of international outsourcing?
11. Does multiculturalism contribute to competitive advantage for an organization?

HOW DO YOU SEE IT?

Snow Job

"If we were to produce garments in the U.S., I'd say our prices would be doubled."

—HOLDEN OUTERWEAR FOUNDER MIKEY LEBLANC

In 2000, Mikey LeBlanc was a prominent professional snowboarder* who found most of the clothing available to winter-sports enthusiasts "silly looking." Fellow snowboarder Scott Zergebel agreed. Moreover, said Zergebel, "everything on the market felt like it was machine made and mass produced." Their solution? Start up a company, as LeBlanc put it, for "making garments that looked great [while] hiding a ton of technical features." And while they were at it, adds Zergebel, they wanted to "bring back a sense of Old World tailoring and craftsmanship."

So in 2002, LeBlanc and Zergebel launched Holden Outerwear to make pants and jackets for snowboarders and skiers. At first, they entered the market under a licensing agreement with Earth Products, itself a subsidiary of K2 Sports, the world's biggest maker of snow-sports equipment and apparel. They broke off the agreement in 2007 and set out on their own, officially locating in Portland, Oregon. LeBlanc, who introduces himself in our video as "one of the guys that helps with the marketing around here," is usually referred to as "marketing director." Zergebel (who does not appear in the video) is generally identified as "creative director." As of August 2011, Holden has had an official CEO in the person of former Adidas executive Ben Pruess.

As a startup, Holden was among the approximately 7 percent of new businesses that venture into the manufacturing arena, where high costs often discourage entry into many industries. LeBlanc and Zergebel, however, wanted to *make* something—better cold-weather outerwear—and that meant finding the right resources and the means to transform them into tangible products that people would buy. Because the company makes clothes, LeBlanc reminds us, "fashion definitely figures into Holden" products, and he stresses that the company looks far and wide for inspiration: "A lot of our competitors," he explains, "look inside our industry for inspiration, and it kind of becomes incestuous. We've always looked outside, whether it was to stores, to current trends, to friends wearing stuff, to our travel around the world." In addition, Holden makes garments designed to perform specific functions—in particular, keeping winter-sports enthusiasts warm and dry while allowing them to perform well in their chosen activities. Stitched seams, for instance, are always waterproofed with a plastic adhesive film (from South Korea), and fabrics are finished with a proprietary DWR (durable water repellent) called Ricochet, which outlasts finishes made to industry standards.

LeBlanc adds that Holden's choice of fabrics also reflects the company's "big push in eco-friendlier attributes." Japanese Recyclon, for example, is made of 59 percent recycled nylon, and Holden's Hemp/PET Poly Fabric combines hemp and recycled synthetic fibers derived from plastic bottles otherwise destined for landfills. Lining using S.Cafe yarn, developed and produced in Taiwan, is made by weaving recycled coffee grounds into the fabric (a process which, oddly enough, aids in odor control).

Finally, all Holden garments are manufactured overseas (primarily in China) and shipped to the United States and Canada and, from there, to distribution outlets around the world. "I'm throwing a guess here," says Le Blanc, "but if we were to produce garments in the U.S., I'd say our prices would be doubled. At a minimum. It's really hard to beat the prices coming out of China." Holden products are also sold overseas, primarily in Asia and Europe. "When we started," recalls LeBlanc, "I totally envisioned us being a global company," but while Holden has met with some success in Asia, LeBlanc admits that the company is still taking baby steps in Europe. Most of its sales (about $10 million in 2011) are still in the United States, and its best market segment remains its first: According to *Snowboarder Magazine*, Holden is tied for third among 16 companies that sell snowboarding outerwear.

CASE QUESTIONS

1. Google "Holden Outerwear" and check out some of the company's online advertising (much of which appears in the advertising of distributors and retailers). Typically, what product features are stressed? Which features are designed to make products "look great"? Which features qualify as "technical features"? In general, does Holden seem to live up to LeBlanc's ideal of "making garments that look great [while] hiding a ton of technical features"?
2. As of this writing, Holden has a grand total of 10 employees. We're introduced to a few of them during the video, although only briefly. What does Hillary Lloyd do? What *cultural issues* does she probably face in working with the outside vendor for whom she's responsible? [*Hint:* Go to http://geert-hofstede.com/south-korea.html.]
3. In explaining Holden's choice of *outsourcing* as a strategy, LeBlanc discusses three areas of product and marketing management. What are they, and what advantages does LeBlanc attribute to each? Which of the three has proved to be the biggest challenge, and what has Holden done to solve problems in this area?
4. In May 2012, Holden announced that it was moving its headquarters from Portland to Los Angeles, where operating expenses will be about 15 percent lower. The company also said that it intended to extend its product lines into apparel for hiking, skateboarding, bicycling, and, eventually, surfing. "We are a reflection of the global community that inspires us," explained Ben Pruess. Give some reasons why you think the strategy decisions were made and why you think they were good ones. Do you think that the two decisions are related? If so, in what ways?
5. A recent article entitled "Manufacturing Startups: What You Need to Know" begins this way:**

   With ever-advancing technology, cheap outsourced labor, and globalized logistics providers, it should be easy to start up a manufacturing company, right? Wrong. The challenges have simply become greater.

   In what ways—specifically—does this statement apply to Holden Outerwear? The article goes on to offer two suggestions for would-be manufacturing entrepreneurs: (1) reduce costs and (2) remember that "everything is global." In what ways—specifically—has Holden heeded this advice?

ADDITIONAL SOURCES

Holden Outerwear, "Holden History" (2012), www.holdenouterwear.com on May 3, 2012; Erik Siemers, "Growing Holden Hires First CEO," *Portland* (OR) *Business Journal*, August 12, 2011, www.bizjournals.com on May 3, 2012; Allan Brettman, "Holden Outerwear Exits Portland in Search of New Markets, Lower Expenses," *OregonLive.com*, May 2, 2012, http://blog.oregonlive.com on May 3, 2012; Brettman, "Snowboarding's Holden Outerwear Announces It's Leaving Portland for LA," *OregonLive.com*, May 2, 2012, http://impact.oregonlive.com on May 3, 2012; Scott Zergebel, "My Inspiration Comes from Trying to Live My Life to the Fullest," *SIA's Latest*, March 28, 2012, www.snowsports.com on May 3, 2012; "Industry Profile: Holden Owner Mikey LeBlanc," *Shayboarder.com*, July 1, 2010, www.shayboarder.com on May 3, 2012; David Benedek, "David Benedek Interviews Mikey LeBlanc," *Snowboarder Magazine*, December 17, 2009, www.snowboardermag.com on May 3, 2012.

*According to *TransWorld SNOWboarding* magazine, it was LeBlanc who brought attention to the tech-backcountry aerial movement and spearheaded the resurgence of rail, jib, and street boards.
**Staci Wood, "Manufacturing Startups: What You Need to Know," *Small Business Trends Radio*, December 9, 2008, www.smbtrendwire.com on May 3, 2012.

EXPERIENCING ORGANIZATIONAL BEHAVIOR

Understanding Your Own Stereotypes about Others

Purpose This exercise will help you better understand your own stereotypes and attitudes toward others.

Format You will be asked to evaluate a situation and the assumptions you make in doing so. Then you will compare your results with those of the rest of the class.

Procedure

1. Read the following description of the situation to yourself and decide who it is that is standing at your door and why you believe it to be that person. Make some notes that explain your rationale for eliminating the other possibilities and selecting the one that you did. Then answer the follow-up questions.
2. Working in small groups or with the class as a whole, discuss who might be standing at your door and why you believe it to be that person. Record the responses of your class members.
3. In class discussion, reflect on the stereotypes used to reach a decision and consider the following:
   a. How hard was it to let go of your original belief once you had formed it?
   b. What implications do first impressions of people have concerning how you treat them, what you expect of them, and your assessment of whether the acquaintance is likely to go beyond the initial stage?
   c. What are the implications of your responses to these questions concerning how you, as a manager, might treat a new employee? What will the impact be on that employee?
   d. What are the implications of your answers for yourself in terms of job hunting?

Situation You have just checked into a hospital room for some minor surgery the next day. When you get to your room, you are told that the following people will be coming to speak with you within the next several hours.

1. The surgeon who will do the operation
2. A nurse
3. The secretary for the department of surgery
4. A representative of the company that supplies televisions to the hospital rooms
5. A technician who does laboratory tests
6. A hospital business manager
7. The dietitian

[Note: You have never met any of these people before and do not know what to expect.]

About half an hour after your arrival, a woman who seems to be of Asian ancestry appears at your door dressed in a straight red wool skirt, a pink-and-white-striped polyester blouse with a bow at the neck, and red medium-high-heeled shoes that match the skirt. She is wearing gold earrings, a gold chain necklace, a gold wedding band, and a white hospital laboratory coat. She is carrying a clipboard.

Follow-Up Questions

1. Of the seven people listed, which of them is standing at your door? How did you reach this conclusion?
2. If the woman had not been wearing a white hospital laboratory coat, how might your perceptions of her have differed? Why?
3. If you find out that she is the surgeon who will be operating on you in the morning, and you thought initially that she was someone else, how confident do you now feel in her ability as a surgeon? Why?
4. What implications can you draw from this exercise regarding the management of knowledge workers?

BUILDING MANAGERIAL SKILLS

Exercise Overview Communications skills refer to your ability to convey ideas and information to other people. The task, of course, is easier when the person to whom you're communicating is familiar with the same language as you are; but in an increasingly diverse business environment, you won't always have the luxury of expressing yourself strictly on your own terms. This exercise asks you to communicate information by carefully crafting the terms in which you express yourself.

Exercise Background You're the owner of a store that sells unfinished furniture made of fine woods.

Customers, both individual consumers and retailers, buy your furniture and finish the pieces themselves, usually with oil-based finishes. One of your best customers is the owner of a small furniture store catering to the members of a local ethnic community. She is not a native speaker of English. She has learned that waste rags used in the application of oil-based finishes have been known to explode—a phenomenon known as "spontaneous combustion"—and has become worried, both about the safety of her customers and about her own liability. You need to send her a letter reassuring her that the problem, while real, can be dealt with easily and safely. You also need to tell her what to tell her customers.

Exercise Task Now do the following:

1. Review the following sampling of guidelines for "internationalizing" the English language. It's designed to help you write clear messages to nonnative speakers and to reduce the possibility of creating a misunderstanding between you and a person from a different culture. (You can also follow the same guidelines when communicating to another native speaker of English.)*
   - Use the most common words in the language (there are 3,000 to 4,000 to choose from).
   - Use only the most common meaning of words that have multiple meanings (the word "high" has 20 meanings, the word "expensive" only one).
   - Avoid sports terms ("ballpark figure") and words that require mental pictures ("red tape").
   - Use words only in the most common way (don't make verbs out of nouns, as in "*faxing* a letter").
   - Don't create or use new words; avoid slang.
   - Avoid two-word verbs (use "apply" instead of "put on").
   - Use more short, simple sentences than you normally would.
   - Avoid acronyms ("ASAP"), emoticons (:-o), and shorthand ("4" for "for").
   - Adopt a formal tone and use maximum punctuation for the greatest clarity.
2. Go online to locate a manufacturer of oil-based finishes. Find out what the maker of the product has to say about dealing with the problem of spontaneous combustion.
3. Write a letter to your nonnative-speaking customer. Explain the problem of spontaneous combustion, tell her what the manufacturer recommends, and sum up your own advice.

*List adapted from D.I. Riddle and Z.D. Lanham, "Internationalizing Written Business English: 20 Propositions for Native English Speakers," *Journal of Language for International Business*, vol. 1 (1984–1985), pp. 1–11.

SELF-ASSESSMENT EXERCISE

Cross-Cultural Awareness

The following questions are intended to provide insights into your awareness of other cultures. Please indicate the best answers to the questions listed below. There is no passing or failing answer. Use the following scale, recording it in the space before each question.

1 = definitely no

2 = not likely

3 = not sure

4 = likely

5 = definitely yes

_____ 1. I can effectively conduct business in a language other than my native language.

_____ 2. I can read and write a language other than my native language with great ease.

_____ 3. I understand the proper protocol for conducting a business card exchange in at least two countries other than my own.

_____ 4. I understand the role of the *keiretsu* in Japan or the *chaebol* in Korea.

_____ 5. I understand the differences in manager-subordinate relationships in two countries other than my own.

_____ 6. I understand the differences in negotiation styles in at least two countries other than my own.

_____ 7. I understand the proper protocols for gift giving in at least three countries.

_____ 8. I understand how a country's characteristic preference for individualism versus collectivism can influence business practices.

______ 9. I understand the nature and importance of demographic diversity in at least three countries.

______ 10. I understand my own country's laws regarding giving gifts or favors while on international assignments.

______ 11. I understand how cultural factors influence the sales, marketing, and distribution systems of different countries.

______ 12. I understand how differences in male-female relationships influence business practices in at least three countries.

______ 13. I have studied and understood the history of a country other than my native country.

______ 14. I can identify the countries of the European Union without looking them up.

______ 15. I know which gestures to avoid using overseas because of their obscene meanings.

______ 16. I understand how the communication styles practiced in specific countries can influence business practices.

______ 17. I know in which countries I can use my first name with recent business acquaintances.

______ 18. I understand the culture and business trends in major countries in which my organization conducts business.

______ 19. I regularly receive and review news and information from and about overseas locations.

______ 20. I have access to and utilize a cultural informant before conducting business at an overseas location.

______ = Total Score

When you have finished, add up your score and compare it with those of others in your group. Discuss the areas of strength and weakness of the group members.

[Note: This brief instrument has not been scientifically validated and is to be used for classroom discussion purposes only.]

Reference: Neal R. Goodman, "Cross-Cultural Training for the Global Executive," in Richard W. Brislin and Tomoko Yoshida (eds.), *Improving Intercultural Interactions,* pp. 35–36, copyright © 1994 by Sage Publications, Inc. Reprinted by permission of Sage Publications, Inc.

CHAPTER 3 Foundations of Individual Behavior

Chapter Outline

- People in Organizations
- Personality and Organizations
- Attitudes in Organizations
- Perception in Organizations
- Types of Workplace Behavior

Chapter Learning Objectives

After studying this chapter, you should be able to:

1. **Explain the nature of the individual–organization relationship.**
2. **Define personality and describe personality attributes that affect behavior in organizations.**
3. **Discuss individual attitudes in organizations and how they affect behavior.**
4. **Describe basic perceptual processes and the role of attributions in organizations.**
5. **Explain how workplace behaviors can directly or indirectly influence organizational effectiveness.**

What to Do When the Boss Releases His Inner Toddler

"Most tantrums don't involve things being thrown across the room."

—Organizational consultant Lynn Taylor, on TOTs

Put yourself in the following scenario:

You're one of 10 VPs at a small chain of regional clothing stores, where you're in charge of the women's apparel departments. One of your jobs is to review each month's performance at a meeting of all 10 department heads and the company president. Like your fellow VPs, you prepare a PowerPoint presentation showing the results for the previous month and your projections for the upcoming month, and during your presentation you take the podium and lead the discussion from the front of the room.

On the whole, the meeting is part of a pretty sound overall strategy that allows everyone to know what's going on and what to expect across the board. Typically, the only drawback to an informative and productive session is the president's apparent inability to deal with bad news. He gets irritable and likes to lambaste "underperformers," and as a result, you and your colleagues always enter the meeting with stomachs in knots and leave it with full-blown gastric distress. The president himself thinks he's fostering open and honest discussion, but everyone else in the room knows plain old-fashioned bullying when they see it.

As luck would have it, you now find yourself at the front of the room, looking up at the floor-to-ceiling screen on which are emblazoned, in what looks to you like 500-point font (red, of course), your less than stellar monthly numbers. Sweating profusely, you're attempting to explain some disappointing sales figures when you hear a noise—a sort of thudding and rattling—against the wall behind you. Startled, you spin around toward the room and are surprised to see that everyone seems to be looking for

Iromaya Images/Jupiter Images

Some bosses engage in behaviors that others find intimidating or even abusive in nature. Fortunately, people who understand organizational behavior can often develop insights in such behaviors and develop strategies for countering or at least coping with them.

something on the floor or checking the weather through the windows on one side of the room. Finally you glance toward the wall behind you, where you discover a bent meeting-room chair lying on the floor, and as you look up again, you see that the president is standing, his arms crossed and his face scowling. "The next time you show me numbers like those," he snarls, "I won't miss!"

Believe it or not, this is a true story (although we've changed a few details—very few—in the interest of plausibility and dramatic impact). It's told by John McKee, a consultant to professionals and businesspeople who want to move up the management ladder as quickly—and, presumably, with as little violence—as possible. McKee was actually an eye witness to the episode, and although he admits that it's "the clearest example of a boss behaving badly" that he's ever seen, he hastens to add that he won't be the least bit surprised when someone comes up with an even better one.

Consultant Lynn Taylor, who specializes in the development of work and management teams, calls bosses like the one in our scenario *Terrible Office Tyrants*, or *TOTs*—managers who can't control their power when they're placed under stress. Taylor believes that the characterization is apt in light of research showing that bosses like the one we've described actually "return to their misbehaving 'inner toddler' to handle unwieldy pressures." In other words, they revert to the kind of behavior that produced "self-serving results" when they were children. In the adult workplace, explains Taylor, they "occasionally find that their ability to master the world is limited, as it is with most mortal beings. This revelation, on top of their inability to communicate clearly in the moment, makes them furious and frustrated."

According to Taylor, there are 20 "core, parallel traits [shared by] TOTs and toddlers." The following, which are fairly aggressive, she catalogs under "Bratty Behavior":

- Bragging
- Bullying

- Demanding
- Ignoring
- Impulsiveness
- Lying
- Self-centeredness
- Stubbornness
- Tantrums
- Territorialism
- Whining

"Most tantrums," Taylor assures us, "don't involve things being thrown across the room," and TOT behavior, especially in its less aggressive forms—fickleness, mood swings, neediness—can be "proactively managed" by employees who don't care to be treated as emotional punching bags. She recommends "humor, common sense, rational thinking, and setting limits to bad behavior." And remember, she adds, "You are the parent with the proverbial cookie jar when it comes to managing a TOT."

Taylor's approach to understanding and dealing with bad bosses isn't entirely metaphorical, and she does suggest that beleaguered employees translate her general advice into some concrete coping techniques. When confronted by managerial neediness, for example, a good "pacifier" might be a reply such as: "It'll be the first thing on my to-do list tomorrow." If you're looking for a handy toolbox of effective techniques, you can find dozens on the Internet, most of them posted by psychologists and organizational consultants. The following was complied by Karen Burns, *U.S. News* columnist and specialist on career advice for women:

- *Put everything in writing.* Write and date progress reports. When you get verbal instructions, summarize them in a reply e-mail.
- *Be a star performer.* Beyond just being a good employee, maintain a positive demeanor; it's hard for someone to ambush you when you're doing your job and smiling in the process.
- *Pick your moments.* Rather than simply avoiding your boss, study her patterns. Steer clear when she's a nutcase and schedule interactions for times when she's stabilized.
- *Seek community.* Anchor your sanity in ties to coworkers and other managers. Find a mentor inside the workplace and someone outside to talk (and vent) to.
- *Control what you can.* You can't control your boss's irrational behavior, so control what you can—namely, the way you respond to it. Ignore the cranky tone of voice and respond to the substance of what she says. Also, eat right, exercise, get enough sleep, and spend the rest of your time with sane people.

- *Know your rights.* If you want to take your grievance to the HR department (or further), be sure that you've documented your problem and your efforts to resolve it, and be specific about the remedy you're asking for (transfer, severance package, etc.).
- *Identify the exits.* Come up with a plan, and don't be bullied into taking action before you're ready.

What Do You Think?

1. According to some experts, the sort of behavior recorded here is more prevalent in the business world than in the rest of society. Assuming that this is true, why do you suppose that's the case?
2. Are you something of a perfectionist? Are you easily frustrated? How well suited are you—at this point in your life—to the task of managing other people?

References: John McKee, "Worst Boss Ever," *TechRepublic*, February 8, 2007, www.techrepublic.com on April 10, 2012; Lynn Taylor, "Why Bad Bosses Act Like Toddlers," *Psychology Today*, August 27, 2009, www.psychologytoday.com on April 10, 2012; Lynn Taylor, "10 Ways to Manage Bad Bosses," *CNN Living*, December 15, 2009, http://articles.cnn.com on April 10, 2012; Karen Burns, "How to Survive a Bad Boss," *U.S. News & World Report*, November 4, 2009, http://money.usnews.com on April 10, 2012.

Think about human behavior as a jigsaw puzzle. Puzzles consist of various pieces that fit together in precise ways. And of course, no two puzzles are exactly alike. They have different numbers of pieces, the pieces are of different sizes and shapes, and they fit together in different ways. The same can be said of human behavior and its determinants. Each of us is a whole picture, like a fully assembled jigsaw puzzle, but the puzzle pieces that define us and the way those pieces fit together are unique. Every person in an organization is fundamentally different from everyone else. To be successful, managers must recognize that these differences exist and attempt to understand them.

In this chapter we explore some of the key characteristics that differentiate people from one another in organizations. We first investigate the psychological nature of individuals in organizations. We then look at elements of people's personalities that can influence behavior and consider individual attitudes and their role in organizations. Next, we examine the role of perception in organizations. We close this chapter with an examination of various kinds of workplace behaviors that affect organizational performance.

PEOPLE IN ORGANIZATIONS

As a starting point for understanding the behavior of people in organizations, we first examine the basic nature of the individual–organization relationship. Understanding this relationship helps us appreciate the nature of individual differences. That is, these

FIGURE 3.1

The Psychological Contract

Psychological contracts govern the basic relationship between people and organizations. Individuals contribute such things as effort and loyalty. In turn, organizations offer such inducements as pay and job security.

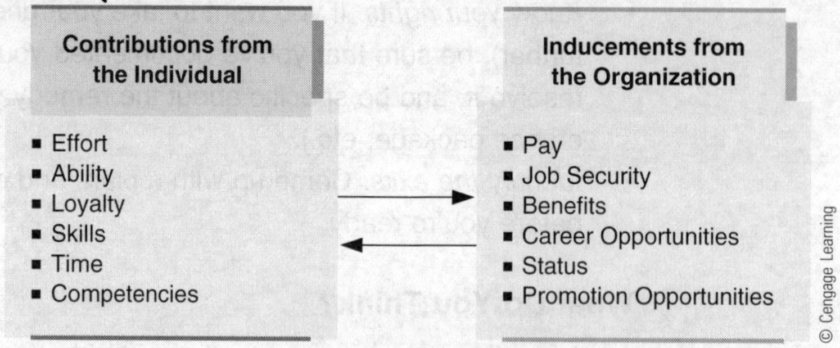

differences play a critical role in determining various important workplace behaviors of special relevance to managers.

Psychological Contracts

Whenever we buy a car or sell a house, both buyer and seller sign a contract that specifies the terms of the agreement—who pays what to whom, when it's paid, and so forth. A psychological contract resembles a standard legal contract in some ways, but it is less formal and less well defined. Specifically, a **psychological contract** is a person's overall set of expectations regarding what he or she will contribute to the organization and what the organization will provide in return.[1] Unlike any other kind of business contract, a psychological contract is not written on paper, nor are all of its terms explicitly negotiated.

A **psychological contract** is a person's set of expectations regarding what he or she will contribute to an organization and what the organization, in return, will provide to the individual.

Figure 3.1 illustrates the essential nature of a psychological contract. The individual makes a variety of **contributions** to the organization—such things as effort, skills, ability, time, and loyalty. Jill Henderson, a branch manager for Merrill Lynch, uses her knowledge of financial markets and investment opportunities to help her clients make profitable investments. Her MBA in finance, coupled with hard work and motivation, have allowed her to become one of the firm's most promising young managers. The firm believed she had these attributes when it hired her, of course, and expected that she would do well.

An individual's **contributions** to an organization include such things as effort, skills, ability, time, and loyalty.

In return for these contributions, the organization provides **inducements** to the individual. Some inducements, such as pay and career opportunities, are tangible rewards. Others, such as job security and status, are more intangible. Jill Henderson started at Merrill Lynch at a very competitive salary and has received an attractive salary increase each of the six years she has been with the firm. She has also been promoted twice and expects another promotion—perhaps to a larger office—in the near future.

Organizations provide **inducements** to individuals in the form of tangible and intangible rewards.

In this instance, both Jill Henderson and Merrill Lynch apparently perceive that the psychological contract is fair and equitable. Both will be satisfied with the relationship and will do what they can to continue it. Henderson is likely to continue to work hard and effectively, and Merrill Lynch is likely to continue to increase her salary and give her promotions. In other situations, however, things might not work out as well. If either party sees an inequity in the contract, that party may initiate a change. The employee might ask for a pay raise or promotion, put forth less effort, or look for a better job elsewhere. The organization can also initiate change by training the worker to improve his skills, by transferring him to another job, or by firing him.

All organizations face the basic challenge of managing psychological contracts. They want value from their employees, and they need to give employees the right inducements. For instance, underpaid employees may perform poorly or leave for better jobs elsewhere. An employee may even occasionally start to steal organizational resources as a way to balance the psychological contract. Overpaying employees who contribute little to the organization, though, incurs unnecessary costs.

Recent trends in downsizing and cutbacks have complicated the process of managing psychological contracts, especially during the recession of 2008–2010. For example, many organizations used to offer at least reasonable assurances of job permanence as a fundamental inducement to employees. Now, however, job permanence is less likely, so alternative inducements may be needed.[2] Among the new forms of inducements that some companies are providing are additional training opportunities and increased flexibility in working schedules.

Increased globalization of business also complicates the management of psychological contracts. For example, the array of inducements that employees deem to be of value varies across cultures. U.S. workers tend to value individual rewards and recognition, but Japanese workers are more likely to value group-based rewards and recognition. Workers in Mexico and Germany highly value leisure time and may thus prefer more time off from work, whereas workers in China may place a lower premium on time off. The Lionel Train Company, maker of toy electric trains, once moved its operations to Mexico to capitalize on cheaper labor. The firm encountered problems, however, when it could not hire enough motivated employees to maintain quality standards and ended up making a costly move back to the United States. That is, the prevailing low wages in Mexico (which prompted the firm to move there to begin with) were not sufficient inducement to motivate the high quality performance the firm expected.

A related problem faced by international businesses is the management of psychological contracts for expatriate managers. In some ways, this process is more like a formal contract than are other employment relationships. Managers selected for a foreign assignment, for instance, are usually given some estimate of the duration of the assignment and receive various adjustments in their compensation package, including cost-of-living adjustments, education subsidies for children, reimbursement of personal travel expenses, and so forth. When the assignment is over, the manager must then be integrated back into the domestic organization. During the time of the assignment, however, the organization itself may have changed in many ways—new managers, new coworkers, new procedures, new business practices, and so forth. Thus, returning managers may very well come back to an organization that is quite different from the one they left and to a job quite different from what they expected.[3]

The Person-Job Fit

Person-job fit is the extent to which the contributions made by the individual match the inducements offered by the organization.

One specific aspect of managing psychological contracts is management of the **person-job fit**. A good person-job fit is one in which the employee's contributions match the inducements the organization offers. In theory, each employee has a specific set of needs to be fulfilled and a set of job-related behaviors and abilities to contribute. If the organization can take perfect advantage of those behaviors and abilities and exactly fulfill the employee's needs, it will have achieved a perfect person-job fit.

Of course, such a precise person-job fit is seldom achieved. For one thing, hiring procedures are imperfect. Managers can estimate employee skill levels when making hiring decisions and can improve them through training, but even simple performance dimensions are hard to measure objectively and validly. For another thing, both people and organizations change. An employee who finds a new job stimulating and exciting to begin with may find the same job boring and monotonous a few years later. An organization that adopts new technology needs new skills from its employees. Finally, each person is unique. Measuring skills and performance is difficult enough. Assessing attitudes and personality is far more complex. Each of these individual differences makes matching individuals with jobs a difficult and complex process.[4]

Individual Differences

Individual differences are personal attributes that vary from one person to another.

As already noted, every individual is unique. **Individual differences** are personal attributes that vary from one person to another. Individual differences may be physical, psychological, and emotional. The individual differences that characterize a specific person make that person unique.[5] As we see in the sections that follow, basic categories of individual differences include personality, attitudes, perception, and creativity. First, however, we need to note the importance of the situation in assessing the individual's behavior.

Are the specific differences that characterize a given person good or bad? Do they contribute to or detract from performance? The answer, of course, is that it depends on the circumstances. One person may be dissatisfied, withdrawn, and negative in one job setting but satisfied, outgoing, and positive in another. Working conditions, coworkers, and leadership are just a few of the factors that affect how a person performs and feels about a job. Thus, whenever a manager attempts to assess or account for individual differences among her employees, she must also be sure to consider the situation in which behavior occurs.

Since managers need to establish effective psychological contracts with their employees and achieve optimal fits between people and jobs, they face a major challenge in attempting to understand both individual differences and contributions in relation to inducements and contexts. A good starting point in developing this understanding is to appreciate the role of personality in organizations.

PERSONALITY AND ORGANIZATIONS

Personality is the relatively stable set of psychological attributes that distinguish one person from another.

Personality is the relatively stable set of psychological attributes that distinguish one person from another. A longstanding debate among psychologists—often expressed as "nature versus nurture"—concerns the extent to which personality attributes are inherited from our parents (the "nature" argument) or shaped by our environment (the "nurture" argument). In reality, both biological and environmental factors play important roles in determining our personalities.[6] Although the details of this debate are beyond the scope of our discussion here, managers should strive to understand basic personality attributes and how they can affect people's behavior in organizational situations, not to mention their perceptions of and attitudes toward the organization.

The "Big Five" Personality Traits

The **"big five" personality traits** are a set of fundamental traits that are especially relevant to organizations.

Agreeableness is the ability to get along with others.

Psychologists have identified literally thousands of personality traits and dimensions that differentiate one person from another. But in recent years, researchers have identified five fundamental personality traits that are especially relevant to organizations.[7] These traits, illustrated in Figure 3.2, are now commonly called the **"big five" personality traits.**

Agreeableness refers to a person's ability to get along with others. Agreeableness causes some people to be gentle, cooperative, forgiving, understanding, and good-natured in their dealings with others. But lack of it results in others' being irritable, short-tempered, uncooperative, and generally antagonistic toward other people. Researchers have not yet fully investigated the effects of agreeableness, but it seems likely that highly agreeable people are better at developing good working relationships with coworkers, subordinates, and higher-level managers, whereas less agreeable people are not likely to have particularly good working relationships. The same pattern might extend to relationships with customers, suppliers, and other key organizational constituents.

Conscientiousness refers to the number of goals on which a person focuses.

Conscientiousness refers to the number of goals on which a person focuses. People who focus on relatively few goals at one time are likely to be organized, systematic, careful, thorough, responsible, and self-disciplined. Others, however, tend to pursue a wider

FIGURE 3.2

The "Big Five" Personality Framework

The "big five" personality framework is currently very popular among researchers and managers. These five dimensions represent fundamental personality traits presumed to be important in determining the behaviors of individuals in organizations. In general, experts agree that personality traits closer to the left end of each dimension are more positive in organizational settings, whereas traits closer to the right are less positive.

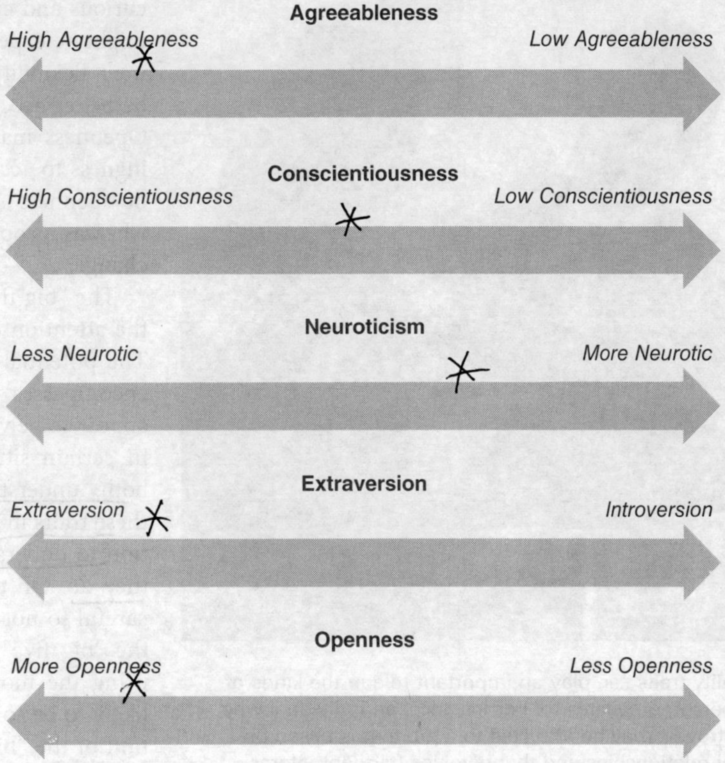

array of goals, and, as a result, tend to be more disorganized, careless, and irresponsible, as well as less thorough and self-disciplined. Research has found that more conscientious people tend to be higher performers than less conscientious people in a variety of different jobs. This pattern seems logical, of course, since conscientious people take their jobs seriously and approach their jobs in a highly responsible fashion.

Neuroticism is characterized by a person's tendency to experience unpleasant emotions such as anger, anxiety, depression, and feelings of vulnerability.

The third of the "big five" personality dimensions is **neuroticism.** People who are relatively more neurotic tend to experience unpleasant emotions such as anger, anxiety, depression, and feelings of vulnerability more often than do people who are relatively less neurotic. People who are less neurotic are relatively poised, calm, resilient, and secure; people who are more neurotic are more excitable, insecure, reactive, and subject to extreme mood swings. People with less neuroticism might be expected to better handle job stress, pressure, and tension. Their stability might also lead them to be seen as being more reliable than their less stable counterparts.

Extraversion is the quality of being comfortable with relationships; the opposite extreme, introversion, is characterized by more social discomfort.

Extraversion reflects a person's comfort level with relationships. Extroverts are sociable, talkative, assertive, and open to establishing new relationships. Introverts are much less sociable, talkative, and assertive, and more reluctant to begin new relationships. Research suggests that extroverts tend to be higher overall job performers than introverts and that they are more likely to be attracted to jobs based on personal relationships, such as sales and marketing positions.

Openness is the capacity to entertain new ideas and to change as a result of new information.

Finally, **openness** reflects a person's rigidity of beliefs and range of interests. People with high levels of openness are willing to listen to new ideas and to change their own ideas, beliefs, and attitudes in response to new information. They also tend to have broad interests and to be curious, imaginative, and creative. On the other hand, people with low levels of openness tend to be less receptive to new ideas and less willing to change their minds. Further, they tend to have fewer and narrower interests and to be less

Tetra Images/PhotoLibrary

Personality traits can play an important role in the kinds of jobs a person gravitates to. For instance, an individual who is an extrovert may be attracted to a job that is based on personal relationships and that involves frequent interactions with other people. This salesperson, for example, seems to be genuinely enjoying his interactions with his customer.

curious and creative. People with more openness might be expected to be better performers due to their flexibility and the likelihood that they will be better accepted by others in the organization. Openness may also encompass a person's willingness to accept change; people with high levels of openness may be more receptive to change, whereas people with little openness may resist change.

The "big five" framework continues to attract the attention of both researchers and managers. The potential value of this framework is that it encompasses an integrated set of traits that appear to be valid predictors of certain behaviors in certain situations. Thus, managers who can both understand the framework and assess these traits in their employees are in a good position to understand how and why they behave as they do. On the other hand, managers must be careful to not overestimate their ability to assess the "big five" traits in others. Even assessment using the most rigorous and valid measures is likely to be somewhat imprecise. Another limitation of the "big five" framework is that it is primarily based on research conducted in the United States. Thus, its generalizability to other cultures presents unanswered questions. Even within the United States, a variety of other factors and traits are also likely to affect behavior in organizations.

The Myers-Briggs Framework

Another interesting approach to understanding personalities in organizations is the Myers-Briggs framework. This framework, based on the classical work of Carl Jung, differentiates people in terms of four general dimensions: sensing, intuiting, judging, and perceiving. Higher and lower positions in each of the dimensions are used to classify people into one of sixteen different personality categories.

The Myers-Briggs Type Indicator (MBTI) is a popular questionnaire that some organizations use to assess personality types. Indeed, it is among the most popular selection instruments used today, with as many as 2 million people taking it each year. Research suggests that the MBTI is a useful method for determining communication styles and interaction preferences. In terms of personality attributes, however, questions exist about both the validity and the stability of the MBTI.

Emotional intelligence, or **EQ**, is the extent to which people are self-aware, can manage their emotions, can motivate themselves, express empathy for others, and possess social skills.

Emotional Intelligence

The concept of emotional intelligence has been identified in recent years and provides some interesting insights into personality. **Emotional intelligence**, or **EQ**, refers to the extent to which people are self-aware, can manage their emotions, can motivate themselves, express empathy for others, and possess social skills.[8] (EQ is used to parallel the traditional term IQ, which of course stands for "intelligence quotient.") These various dimensions can be described as follows:

- *Self-awareness* This is the basis for the other components. It refers to a person's capacity for being aware of how he or she is feeling. In general, more self-awareness allows a person to more effectively guide his or her own life and behaviors.
- *Managing emotions* This refers to a person's capacities to balance anxiety, fear, and anger so that they do not interfere with getting things accomplished.
- *Motivating oneself* This dimension refers to a person's ability to remain optimistic and to continue striving in the face of setbacks, barriers, and failure.
- *Empathy* Empathy refers to a person's ability to understand how others are feeling even without being explicitly told.
- *Social skill* This refers to a person's ability to get along with others and to establish positive relationships.

Preliminary research suggests that people with high EQs may perform better than others, especially in jobs that require a high degree of interpersonal interaction and that involve influencing or directing the work of others. Moreover, EQ appears to be something that isn't biologically based but instead can be developed.[9]

Other Personality Traits at Work

Besides these complex models of personality, several other specific personality traits are also likely to influence behavior in organizations. Among the most important are locus of control, self-efficacy, authoritarianism, Machiavellianism, self-esteem, and risk propensity.

A person's **locus of control** is the extent to which he believes his circumstances are a function of either his own actions or of external factors beyond his control.

Locus of control is the extent to which people believe that their behavior has a real effect on what happens to them.[10] Some people, for example, believe that if they work hard they will succeed. They may also believe that people who fail do so because they lack ability or motivation. People who believe that individuals are in control of their lives are said to have an internal locus of control. Other people think that fate, chance, luck, or other people's behavior determines what happens to them. For example, an employee who fails to get a promotion may attribute that failure to a politically motivated boss or just bad luck, rather than to her or his own lack of skills or poor performance record. People who think that forces beyond their control dictate what happens to them are said to have an external locus of control.

A person's **self-efficacy** is that person's beliefs about his or her capabilities to perform a task.

Self-efficacy is a related but subtly different personality characteristic. A person's self-efficacy is that person's belief about his or her capabilities to perform a task. People with high self-efficacy believe that they can perform well on a specific task, whereas people with low self-efficacy tend to doubt their ability to perform a specific task. Self-assessments of ability contribute to self-efficacy, but so does the individual's personality. Some people simply have more self-confidence than others. This belief in their ability to perform a task effectively results in their being more self-assured and better able to focus their attention on performance.[11]

Authoritarianism is the belief that power and status differences are appropriate within hierarchical social systems such as organizations.

Another important personality characteristic is **authoritarianism**, the extent to which a person believes that power and status differences are appropriate within hierarchical social systems such as organizations.[12] For example, a person who is highly authoritarian may accept directives or orders from someone with more authority purely because the other person is "the boss." On the other hand, a person who is not highly authoritarian, although she or he may still carry out reasonable directives from the boss, is more likely to question things, express disagreement with the boss, and even refuse to carry out orders if they are for some reason objectionable.

Najiah Feanny/Corbis

Many people consider disgraced former CEO Dennis Kozlowski to be a poster child for Machiavellianism. During his tenure as CEO of Tyco Kozlowski apparently thought his position gave him carte blanche to use corporate resources to fund his own extravagant lifestyle including such excesses as a gold shower curtain!

A highly authoritarian manager may be relatively autocratic and demanding, and highly authoritarian subordinates are more likely to accept this behavior from their leader. On the other hand, a less authoritarian manager may allow subordinates a bigger role in making decisions, and less authoritarian subordinates might respond more positively to this behavior.

Machiavellianism is another important personality trait. This concept is named after Niccolo Machiavelli, a sixteenth-century author. In his book *The Prince*, Machiavelli explained how the nobility could more easily gain and use power. The term "Machiavellianism" is now used to describe behavior directed at gaining power and controlling the behavior of others. Research suggests that the degree of Machiavellianism varies from person to person. More Machiavellian individuals tend to be rational and nonemotional, may be willing to lie to attain their personal goals, put little emphasis on loyalty and friendship, and enjoy manipulating others' behavior. Less Machiavellian individuals are more emotional, less willing to lie to succeed, value loyalty and friendship highly, and get little personal pleasure from manipulating others. By all accounts, Dennis Kozlowski, the indicted former CEO of Tyco International, had a high degree of Machiavellianism. He apparently came to believe that his position of power in the company gave him the right to do just about anything he wanted with company resources.[13]

People who possess the personality trait of **Machiavellianism** behave to gain power and control the behavior of others.

A person's **self-esteem** is the extent to which that person believes he or she is a worthwhile and deserving individual.

A person's **risk propensity** is the degree to which he or she is willing to take chances and make risky decisions.

Self-esteem is the extent to which a person believes that he or she is a worthwhile and deserving individual. A person with high self-esteem is more likely to seek higher-status jobs, be more confident in his or her ability to achieve higher levels of performance, and derive greater intrinsic satisfaction from his or her accomplishments. In contrast, a person with less self-esteem may be more content to remain in a lower-level job, be less confident of his or her ability, and focus more on extrinsic rewards (extrinsic rewards are tangible and observable rewards like a paycheck, job promotion, and so forth). Among the major personality dimensions, self-esteem is the one that has been most widely studied in other countries. Although more research is clearly needed, the published evidence suggests that self-esteem as a personality trait does indeed exist in a variety of countries and that its role in organizations is reasonably important across different cultures.

Risk propensity is the degree to which a person is willing to take chances and make risky decisions. A manager with a high risk propensity, for example, might experiment with new ideas and gamble on new products. Such a manager might also lead the organization in new and different directions. This manager might be a catalyst for innovation or, if the risky decisions prove to be bad ones, might jeopardize the continued well-being of the organization. A manager with low risk propensity might lead an organization to stagnation and excessive conservatism, or might help the organization successfully weather turbulent and unpredictable times by maintaining stability and calm. Thus, the potential consequences of a manager's risk propensity depend heavily on the organization's environment.

SERVICE Customer Self-Efficacy

©rangizzz/Shutterstock

Imagine you lead a company that offers customers the opportunity to bungee jump off a 100-foot bridge spanning a raging river. You have employees whose jobs include hooking up customers properly, filling out legal waiver of liability forms, and ensuring that the jumps go off without errors and that customers have some scary fun. Your revenue stream and profits require that this process proceeds with a minimum of delay, as you have learned that making customers wait too long leads to many who lose their courage, run out of time, or get impatient and leave. The challenge for you is to enhance your customers' belief in their ability to make the jump—their self-efficacy—so they will take the plunge with the confidence that they are capable of successfully performing this task.

In reviewing your knowledge of ways to enhance self-efficacy from your organizational behavior course, you realize that the same strategies you learned about for enhancing employee self-efficacy can also be used for customers. You recall that there are four ways to promote self-efficacy. These are, from most to least influential, enactive mastery, vicarious experience, verbal persuasion, and emotional (physiological) arousal. Enactive mastery is learned through repeated experiences in which a person discovers the level of performance of which he or she is capable. The second way to develop self-efficacy is through vicarious experiences or modeling, whether by self-modeling or by observing another person. The third strategy for developing self-efficacy is verbal persuasion. The final strategy for developing self-efficacy is the individual's physiological state.

With this knowledge, you quickly realize that you can use some or all of these in designing how your bungee jump is set up and in training your employees how to enhance your customers' self-efficacy and improve their ability to co-produce the value of the bungee experience. The easiest strategy to implement is to redesign the waiting line in a way that the customers waiting to jump can observe others taking the plunge. This allows you to use vicarious experiences of others to enhance the self-efficacy of the customers in line. Watching others, especially those that look like them or those who are inferior to them in some way (age, size, etc.) is an effective strategy for building self-efficacy: "If that person can do it, so can I."

You might also include a television monitor for waiting customers to observe that broadcasts footage of prior jumpers, carefully edited to include a diverse array of people similar to those typically seeking out this experience. A related physical setting strategy is to find ways to evoke a physiological response that inspires people to take on difficult challenges, such as playing the theme song from *Rocky*.

The second step is to train your employees on things they can do to enhance customer self-efficacy. Employees can be taught to observe and determine guest performance capabilities for co-producing the required tasks, to intervene in ways that enhance self-efficacy, and to provide persuasive encouragement. Disney cast members, for example, are extensively trained to train guests in the use of its FASTPASS system from a machine that is not easy for all guests to use. Cast members are trained to recognize and train those guests who need assistance to build mastery in a way similar to the training that airline desk agents must go through to teach the airline passenger how to co-produce the self-ticketing procedure.

For our bungee example, we can teach employees what to say to encourage waiting customers to jump. Another strategy is to teach your employees how to identify pairing or groupings of customers so that friends or significant others waiting can be encouraged to chant encouragement to the first person in the group. Not only will those chanting encouragement enhance the self-efficacy of the person waiting to jump, but the employee can also point out to the person about to jump that he or she will be serving as a role model for the others to follow.

The point is simple—not only does knowledge of self-efficacy and how it operates help in developing strategies for better managing your employees' perceptions of their ability to successfully perform their tasks, but the same strategies that enhance employee performance in doing their jobs will enhance your customers' ability to do their parts in the co-production of a service experience. In our bungee example, if the customer doesn't jump, that customer leaves disappointed and our revenue stream suffers.

Discussion Question: Reflect on service experiences you have had and discuss the things the organization did to enhance your self-efficacy.

ATTITUDES IN ORGANIZATIONS

Attitudes are a person's complexes of beliefs and feelings about specific ideas, situations, or other people.

People's attitudes also affect their behavior in organizations. **Attitudes** are complexes of beliefs and feelings that people have about specific ideas, situations, or other people. Attitudes are important because they are the mechanism through which most people express their feelings. An employee's statement that he feels underpaid by an organization reflects his feelings about his pay. Similarly, when a manager says that she likes a new advertising campaign, she is expressing her feelings about the organization's marketing efforts.

How Attitudes Are Formed

Attitudes are formed by a variety of forces, including our personal values, our experiences, and our personalities. For example, if we value honesty and integrity, we may form especially favorable attitudes toward a manager whom we believe to be very honest and moral. Similarly, if we have had negative and unpleasant experiences with a particular coworker, we may form an unfavorable attitude toward that person. Any of the "big five" or individual personality traits may also influence our attitudes. Understanding the basic structure of an attitude helps us see how attitudes are formed and can be changed.

Attitude Structure Attitudes are usually viewed as stable dispositions to behave toward objects in a certain way. For any number of reasons, a person might decide that he or she does not like a particular political figure or a certain restaurant (a disposition). We would expect that person to express consistently negative opinions of the candidate or restaurant and to maintain the consistent, predictable intention of not voting for the political candidate or not eating at the restaurant. In this view, attitudes contain three components: cognition, affect, and intention.

A person's **cognitions** constitute the knowledge a person presumes to have about something.

Cognition is the knowledge a person presumes to have about something. You may believe you like a class because the textbook is excellent, the class meets at your favorite time, the instructor is outstanding, and the workload is light. This "knowledge" may be true, partially true, or totally false. For example, you may intend to vote for a particular candidate because you think you know where the candidate stands on several issues. In reality, depending on the candidate's honesty and your understanding of his or her statements, the candidate's thinking on the issues may be exactly the same as yours, partly the same, or totally different. Cognitions are based on perceptions of truth and reality, and, as we note later, perceptions agree with reality to varying degrees.

A person's **affect** is his or her feelings toward something.

A person's affect is his or her feelings toward something. In many ways, affect is similar to emotion—it is something over which we have little or no conscious control.

FIGURE 3.3

Attitude Formation

Attitudes are generally formed around a sequence of cognition, affect, and behavioral intention. That is, we come to know something that we believe to be true (cognition). This knowledge triggers a feeling (affect). Cognition and affect then together influence how we intend to behave in the future.

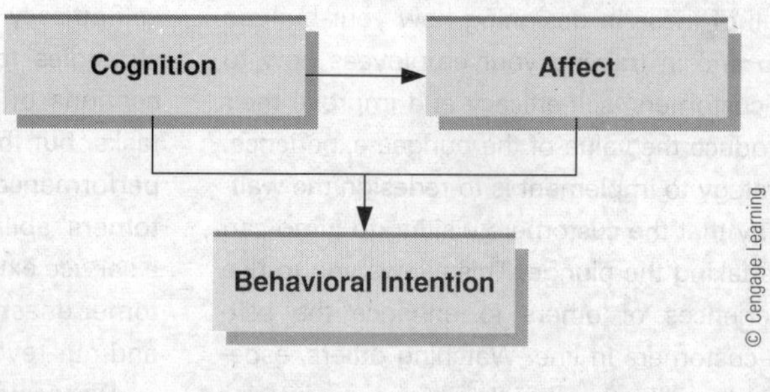

For example, most people react to words such as "love," "hate," "sex," and "war" in a manner that reflects their feelings about what those words convey. Similarly, you may like one of your classes, dislike another, and be indifferent toward a third. If the class you dislike is an elective, you may not be particularly concerned. But if it is the first course in your chosen major, your affective reaction may cause you considerable anxiety.

An **intention** is a component of an attitude that guides a person's behavior.

Intention guides a person's behavior. If you like your instructor, you may intend to take another class from him or her next semester. Intentions are not always translated into actual behavior, however. If the instructor's course next semester is scheduled for 8 a.m., you may decide that another instructor is just as good. Some attitudes, and their corresponding intentions, are much more central and significant to an individual than others. You may intend to do one thing (take a particular class) but later alter your intentions because of a more significant and central attitude (fondness for sleeping late).

Cognitive dissonance is the anxiety a person experiences when simultaneously possessing two sets of knowledge or perceptions that are contradictory or incongruent.

Cognitive Dissonance When two sets of cognitions or perceptions are contradictory or incongruent, a person experiences a level of conflict and anxiety called **cognitive dissonance**. Cognitive dissonance also occurs when people behave in a fashion that is inconsistent with their attitudes. For example, a person may realize that smoking and overeating are dangerous yet continue to do both. Because the attitudes and behaviors are inconsistent with each other, the person probably will experience a certain amount of tension and discomfort and may try to reduce these feelings by changing the attitude, altering the behavior, or perceptually distorting the circumstances. For example, the dissonance associated with overeating might be resolved by continually deciding to go on a diet "next week."

Cognitive dissonance affects people in a variety of ways. We frequently encounter situations in which our attitudes conflict with each other or with our behaviors. Dissonance reduction is the way we deal with these feelings of discomfort and tension. In organizational settings, people contemplating leaving the organization may wonder why they continue to stay and work hard. As a result of this dissonance, they may conclude that the company is not so bad after all, that they have no immediate options elsewhere, or that they will leave "soon."

Attitude Change Attitudes are not as stable as personality attributes. For example, new information may change attitudes. A manager may have a negative attitude about a new colleague because of the colleague's lack of job-related experience. After working with the new person for a while, however, the manager may come to realize that he is actually very talented and subsequently develop a more positive attitude. Likewise, if the object of an attitude changes, a person's attitude toward that object may also change. Suppose, for example, that employees feel underpaid and as a result have negative attitudes toward the company's reward system. A big salary increase may cause these attitudes to become more positive.

Attitudes can also change when the object of the attitude becomes less important or less relevant to the person. For example, suppose an employee has a negative attitude about his company's health insurance. When his spouse gets a new job with an organization that has outstanding insurance benefits, his attitude toward his own insurance may become more moderate simply because he no longer has to worry about it. Finally, as noted earlier, individuals may change their attitudes as a way to reduce cognitive dissonance.

Deeply rooted attitudes that have a long history are, of course, resistant to change. For example, over a period of years a former airline executive named Frank Lorenzo developed a reputation in the industry of being antiunion and of cutting wages and benefits. As a result, employees throughout the industry came to dislike and distrust him. When he took over Eastern Airlines, its employees had such a strong attitude of distrust toward him that they could never agree to cooperate with any of his programs or ideas. Some of them actually cheered months later when Eastern went bankrupt, even though it was costing them their own jobs!

Key Work-Related Attitudes

People in an organization form attitudes about many different things. Employees are likely to have attitudes about their salary, their promotion possibilities, their boss, employee benefits, the food in the company cafeteria, and the color of the company softball team uniforms. Of course, some of these attitudes are more important than others. Especially important attitudes are job satisfaction and organizational commitment.

Job satisfaction is the extent to which a person is gratified or fulfilled by his or her work.

Job Satisfaction **Job satisfaction** reflects the extent to which people find gratification or fulfillment in their work. Extensive research on job satisfaction shows that personal factors such as an individual's needs and aspirations determine this attitude, along with group and organizational factors such as relationships with coworkers and supervisors and working conditions, work policies, and compensation.[14]

A satisfied employee tends to be absent less often, to make positive contributions, and to stay with the organization.[15] In contrast, a dissatisfied employee may be absent more often, may experience stress that disrupts coworkers, and may be continually looking for another job. Contrary to what a lot of managers believe, however, high levels of job satisfaction do not necessarily lead to higher levels of productivity.[16] One survey indicated that, also contrary to popular opinion, Japanese workers are less satisfied with their jobs than their counterparts in the United States.[17]

Organizational commitment is a person's identification with and attachment to an organization.

Organizational Commitment **Organizational commitment**, sometimes called job commitment, reflects an individual's identification with and attachment to the organization. A highly committed person will probably see herself as a true member of the firm (for example, referring to the organization in personal terms such as "we make high-quality products"), overlook minor sources of dissatisfaction, and see herself remaining a member of the organization. In contrast, a less committed person is more likely to see herself as an outsider (for example, referring to the organization in less personal terms such as "they don't pay their employees very well"), to express more dissatisfaction about things, and to not see herself as a long-term member of the organization.[18]

Organizations can do few definitive things to promote satisfaction and commitment, but some specific guidelines are available. For one thing, if the organization treats its employees fairly and provides reasonable rewards and job security, its employees are more likely to be satisfied and committed. Allowing employees to have a say in how things are done can also promote these attitudes. Designing jobs so that they are stimulating can enhance both satisfaction and commitment. Research suggests that Japanese workers may be more committed to their organizations than are U.S. workers.[19] Other research suggests that some of the factors that may lead to commitment, including extrinsic rewards, role clarity, and participative management, are the same across different cultures.[20]

Job satisfaction, of course, is not just an American attitude. Workers in other countries also experience various degrees of satisfaction with their jobs. While one early study suggested that Japanese workers are less satisfied with their jobs than their U.S. counterparts, other research has suggested just the opposite!

~~Hoepft~~
~~2pm wed.~~

Affect and Mood in Organizations

Researchers have recently started to renew their interest in the affective component of attitudes. Recall from our previous discussion that the affective component of an attitude reflects our emotions. Managers once believed that emotion and feelings varied among people from day to day, but research now suggests that although some short-term fluctuation does indeed occur, there are also underlying stable predispositions toward fairly constant and predictable moods and emotional states.[21]

People who possess **positive affectivity** are upbeat and optimistic, have an overall sense of well-being, and see things in a positive light.

Some people, for example, tend to have a higher degree of **positive affectivity**. This means that they are relatively upbeat and optimistic, that they have an overall sense of well-being, and that they usually see things in a positive light. Thus, they always seem to be in a good mood. People with more **negative affectivity** are just the opposite. They are generally downbeat and pessimistic and they usually see things in a negative way. They seem to be in a bad mood most of the time.

People characterized by **negative affectivity** are generally downbeat and pessimistic, see things in a negative way, and seem to be in a bad mood.

Of course, as noted above, short-term variations can occur among even the most extreme types. People with a lot of positive affectivity, for example, may still be in a bad mood if they have just been passed over for a promotion, gotten extremely negative performance feedback, or have been laid off or fired, for instance. Similarly, those with negative affectivity may be in a good mood—at least for a short time—if they have just been promoted, received very positive performance feedback, or had other good things befall them. After the initial impact of these events wears off, however, those with positive affectivity generally return to their normal positive mood, whereas those with negative affectivity gravitate back to their normal bad mood.[22]

PERCEPTION IN ORGANIZATIONS

Perception is the set of processes by which an individual becomes aware of and interprets information about the environment.

Perception—the set of processes by which an individual becomes aware of and interprets information about the environment—is another important element of workplace behavior. If everyone perceived everything the same way, things would be a lot simpler (and a lot less exciting!). Of course, just the opposite is true: People perceive the same things in very different ways.[23] Moreover, people often assume that reality is objective and that we all perceive the same things in the same way.

To test this idea, we could ask students at the University of Texas and the University of Oklahoma to describe the most recent football game between their schools. We probably would hear two conflicting stories. These differences would arise primarily because of perception. The fans "saw" the same game but interpreted it in sharply contrasting ways.

Since perception plays a role in a variety of workplace behaviors, managers should understand basic perceptual processes. As implied in our definition, perception actually consists of several distinct processes. Moreover, in perceiving we receive information in many guises, from spoken words to visual images of movements and forms. Through perceptual processes, the receiver assimilates the varied types of incoming information for the purpose of interpreting it.[24]

Basic Perceptual Processes

Selective perception is the process of screening out information that we are uncomfortable with or that contradicts our beliefs.

Figure 3.4 shows two basic perceptual processes that are particularly relevant to managers—selective perception and stereotyping.

Selective Perception **Selective perception** is the process of screening out information that we are uncomfortable with or that contradicts our beliefs. For example, suppose a manager is exceptionally fond of a particular worker. The manager has a very positive

FIGURE 3.4

Basic Perceptual Processes

Perception determines how we become aware of information from our environment and how we interpret it. Selective perception and stereotyping are particularly important perceptual processes that affect behavior in organizations.

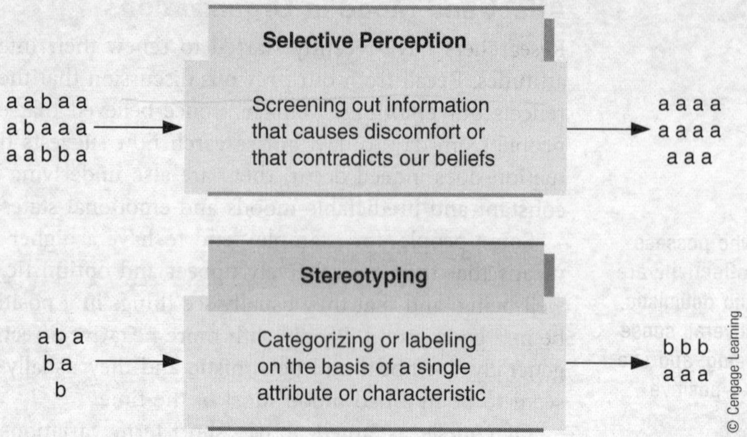

attitude about the worker and thinks he is a top performer. One day the manager notices that the worker seems to be goofing off. Selective perception may cause the manager to quickly forget what he observed. Similarly, suppose a manager has formed a very negative image of a particular worker. She thinks this worker is a poor performer who never does a good job. When she happens to observe an example of high performance from the worker, she may quickly forget it. In one sense, selective perception is beneficial because it allows us to disregard minor bits of information. Of course, the benefit occurs only if our basic perception is accurate. If selective perception causes us to ignore important information, however, it can become quite detrimental.

Stereotyping

Stereotyping is the process of categorizing or labeling people on the basis of a single attribute.

Stereotyping is categorizing or labeling people on the basis of a single attribute. Certain forms of stereotyping can be useful and efficient. Suppose, for example, that a manager believes that communication skills are important for a particular job and that speech communication majors tend to have exceptionally good communication skills. As a result, whenever he interviews candidates for jobs he pays especially close attention to speech communication majors. To the extent that communication skills truly predict job performance and that majoring in speech communication does indeed provide those skills, this form of stereotyping can be beneficial. Common attributes from which people often stereotype are race and sex. Of course, stereotypes along these lines are inaccurate and can be harmful. For example, suppose a human resource manager forms the stereotype that women can only perform certain tasks and that men are best suited for other tasks. To the extent that this affects the manager's hiring practices, he or she is (1) costing the organization valuable talent for both sets of jobs, (2) violating federal law, and (3) behaving unethically.

It's bad enough when other people subject you to stereotyping. To see what can happen when you make matters worse by stereotyping *yourself*, see the *Diversity* box entitled "Do You Have an Excessive Need to Be Yourself?" on page 77.

Perception and Attribution

Attribution theory suggests that we attribute causes to behavior based on our observations of certain characteristics of that behavior.

Attribution theory has extended our understanding of how perception affects behavior in organizations.[25] Attribution theory suggests that we observe behavior and then attribute causes to it. That is, we attempt to explain why people behave as they do. The process of attribution is based on perceptions of reality, and these perceptions may vary widely among individuals.

DIVERSITY Do You Have an Excessive Need to Be Yourself?

As manager of a restaurant supply warehouse, Harry "Hands-On" Hinderson likes to keep a close watch on how his subordinates go about the tasks he assigns them. He corrects minor errors in order to avoid rough edges on the final product, requires workers to check with him on most decisions, and reassigns unpromising projects before they turn into major disasters. The demands on his own time and energy, of course, are quite high, so Harry once decided to try the hands-off approach: He gave a couple of veteran employees projects and deadlines and then backed off. One worker broke down and asked for guidance before the deadline, and the other turned in a report that fell short of both her own standards and Harry's.

I was right in the first place, Harry concluded. *If I don't look over their shoulders, people just don't get the job done.* When he complained about his own workload, a fellow manager said, "You're micromanaging yourself into an early grave." "I'm a micromanager," replied Harry. "That's just the way I am."

Not surprisingly, some employees don't like to work with Harry. "He's one of those crazy micromanagers," they say. In a sense, they're guilty of stereotyping Harry by lumping him in the category of "crazy micromanagers" and reducing him to his micromanagerial traits, but, ironically, they're probably stereotyping him because Harry is guilty of stereotyping *himself*.

Basically, *self-stereotyping* means that people tend to identify themselves according to the characteristics of some "in group" to which they believe they belong. Whenever someone says something like "I'm always late" or "I'm not a good listener" or "I'm terrible at math," he or she is self-stereotyping. Harry has self-stereotyped himself as a micromanager, but one has to wonder: Was he always a micromanager? How (and why) did he become a micromanager? One of the most serious drawbacks of self-stereotyped assessments is the fact that they tend to become self-fulfilling prophecies. Studies show, for example, that when women are reminded that they're "no good at math," they perform worse on math tasks. In turn, they're perceived by others as a poor at math and treated accordingly—say, by teachers and employers.

Before long, says executive coach Marshall Goldsmith, we begin to define ourselves by our beliefs about ourselves, evolving into "a pile of behaviors that we define as 'me.'... If we buy into our behavior definition of 'me'... we can learn to excuse almost any annoying action"—or unacceptable workplace performance—"by saying, 'That's just the way I am!'" Obviously, such an attitude is not a prescription for change and improvement.

> ***"Each of us has a pile of behaviors that we define as 'me.'... If we buy into our behavioral definition of 'me'... we can learn to excuse almost any annoying action by saying, 'That's just the way I am!'"***
>
> —CAREER COACH MARSHALL GOLDSMITH

In Harry's case, his belief that he *is* a micromanager at his core—along with his micromanagerial behavior—could have negative consequences. In particular, micromanagers aren't generally the best managers: According to MindTools, a website dedicated to enhancing career skills,

> *a truly effective manager sets up those around him to succeed. Micromanagers, on the other hand, prevent employees from making... their own decisions.... Good managers empower their employees to do well by giving [them] opportunities to excel; bad managers disempower their employees by hoarding those opportunities. And a disempowered employee is an ineffective one.*

Harry's entrenched practice of self-stereotyping may well contribute to career disappointment down the road. Like his subordinates, his superiors will eventually stereotype him as a micromanager, and if they have any managerial savvy, they'll hold micromanagers responsible for producing ineffective employees. When it comes time to reward managerial performance, Harry will probably get passed over because he'll be perceived as a member of the group known as "micromanagers." And this will probably happen regardless of Harry's *individual* strengths as a manager. That's the way stereotyping works.

References: "Avoiding Micromanagement," MindTools (1996–2012), www.mindtools.com on April 11, 2012; Marshall Goldsmith, "Do You Have an Excessive Need to Be Yourself?" *Harvard Business Review*, July 13, 2009, http://blobgs.hbr.org on April 11, 2012; Sean Silverthorne, "Self-Stereotyping Can Damage Your Career," *CBSNews.com*, July 16, 2009, www.cbsnews.com on April 11, 2012; John Grohol, "Stereotyping That Hurts, Stereotyping That Helps," *PsychCentral.com*, April 10, 2008, http://psychcentral.com on April 11, 2012; Linda Talley, "Are You Personally Stereotyping Yourself?" *Linda Talley dot Com*, February 1, 2012, www.lindatalley.com on April 11, 2012; Dave Franzetta, "Have You Stereotyped Yourself?" *Ubiquitous Wisdom*, December 26, 2011, www.ubiquitouswisdom.com on April 11, 2012.

FIGURE 3.5

The Attribution Process

The attribution process involves observing behavior and then attributing causes to it. Observed behaviors are interpreted in terms of their consensus, their consistency, and their distinctiveness. Based on these interpretations, behavior is attributed to either internal or external causes.

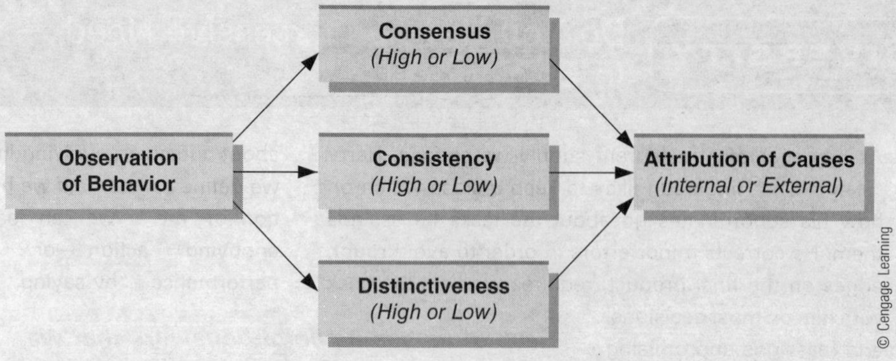

Figure 3.5 illustrates the basic attribution theory framework. To start the process, we observe behavior, either our own or someone else's. We then evaluate that behavior in terms of its degrees of consensus, consistency, and distinctiveness. Consensus is the extent to which other people in the same situation behave in the same way. Consistency is the degree to which the same person behaves in the same way at different times. Distinctiveness is the extent to which the same person behaves in the same way in different situations. We form impressions or attributions as to the causes of behavior based on various combinations of consensus, consistency, and distinctiveness. We may believe the behavior is caused internally (by forces within the person) or externally (by forces in the person's environment).

For example, suppose you observe one of your subordinates being rowdy, disrupting others' work, and generally making a nuisance of himself. If you can understand the causes of this behavior, you may be able to change it. If the employee is the only one engaging in the disruptive behavior (low consensus), if he behaves like this several times each week (high consistency), and if you have seen him behave like this in other settings (low distinctiveness), a logical conclusion would be that internal factors are causing his behavior.

Suppose, however, that you observe a different pattern: Everyone in the person's work group is rowdy (high consensus); and although the particular employee often is rowdy at work (high consistency), you have never seen him behave this way in other settings (high distinctiveness). This pattern indicates that something in the situation is causing the behavior—that is, that the causes of the behavior are external.

TYPES OF WORKPLACE BEHAVIOR

Workplace behavior is a pattern of action by the members of an organization that directly or indirectly influences organizational effectiveness.

Now that we have looked closely at how individual differences can influence behavior in organizations, let's turn our attention to what we mean by workplace behavior. **Workplace behavior** is a pattern of action by the members of an organization that directly or indirectly influences the organization's effectiveness. One way to talk about workplace behavior is to describe its impact on performance and productivity, absenteeism and turnover, and organizational citizenship. Unfortunately, employees can exhibit dysfunctional behaviors as well.

Performance Behaviors

Performance behaviors are all of the total set of work-related behaviors that the organization expects the individual to display.

Performance behaviors are the total set of work-related behaviors that the organization expects the individual to display. You might think of these as the "terms" of the psychological contract. For some jobs, performance behaviors can be narrowly defined and easily measured. For example, an assembly-line worker who sits by a moving conveyor and attaches parts to a product as it passes by has relatively few performance behaviors. He or she is expected to remain at the workstation and correctly attach the parts. Performance can often be assessed quantitatively by counting the percentage of parts correctly attached.

For many other jobs, however, performance behaviors are more diverse and much more difficult to assess. For example, consider the case of a research-and-development scientist at Merck. The scientist works in a lab trying to find new scientific breakthroughs that have commercial potential. The scientist must apply knowledge learned in graduate school and experience gained from previous research. Intuition and creativity are also important. And the desired breakthrough may take months or even years to accomplish. Organizations rely on a number of different methods to evaluate performance. The key, of course, is to match the evaluation mechanism with the job being performed.

Dysfunctional Behaviors

Dysfunctional behaviors are those that detract from organizational performance.

Absenteeism occurs when an individual does not show up for work.

Some work-related behaviors are dysfunctional in nature. That is, **dysfunctional behaviors** are those that detract from, rather than contribute to, organizational performance. Two of the more common ones are absenteeism and turnover. **Absenteeism** occurs when an employee does not show up for work. Some absenteeism has a legitimate cause, such as illness, jury duty, or a death or illness in the family. At other times, the employee may report a feigned legitimate cause that's actually just an excuse to stay home. When an employee is absent, legitimately or not, her or his work does not get done at all or a substitute must be hired to do it. In either case, the quantity or quality of actual output is likely to suffer. Obviously, some absenteeism is expected, but organizations strive to minimize feigned absenteeism and reduce legitimate absences as much as possible.

Bloomberg/Getty Images

Chick-fil-A owners provide a number of attractive benefits compared to other fast-food chains, in part as a way to keep their turnover lower. One Chick-fil-A operator in Texas offers college scholarships to high school students with a good work history with the firm.

Turnover occurs when people quit their jobs.

Turnover occurs when people quit their jobs. An organization usually incurs costs in replacing workers who have quit, and if turnover involves especially productive people, it is even more costly. Turnover seems to result from a number of factors, including aspects of the job, the organization, the individual, the labor market, and family influences. In general, a poor person-job fit is also a likely cause of turnover. People may also be prone to leave an organization if its inflexibility makes it difficult to manage family and other personal matters and may be more likely to stay if an organization provides sufficient flexibility to make it easier to balance work and non-work considerations.[26] One Chick-fil-A operator in Texas has cut the turnover rate in his stores by offering flexible work schedules, college scholarships, and such perks as free bowling trips.[27]

Other forms of dysfunctional behavior may be even more costly for an organization.[28] Theft and sabotage, for example, result in direct financial costs for an organization. Sexual and racial harassment also cost an organization, both indirectly (by lowering morale, producing fear, and driving off valuable employees) and directly (through financial liability if the organization responds inappropriately). Workplace violence is also a growing concern in many organizations. Violence by disgruntled workers or former workers results in dozens of deaths and injuries each year.[29]

Organizational Citizenship

A person's degree of **organizational citizenship** is the extent to which his or her behavior makes a positive overall contribution to the organization.

Managers strive to minimize dysfunctional behaviors while trying to promote organizational citizenship. **Organizational citizenship** refers to the behavior of individuals who make a positive overall contribution to the organization.[30] Consider, for example, an employee who does work that is acceptable in terms of both quantity and quality. However, she refuses to work overtime, won't help newcomers learn the ropes, and is generally unwilling to make any contribution beyond the strict performance of her job. This person may be seen as a good performer, but she is not likely to be seen as a good organizational citizen.

Another employee may exhibit a comparable level of performance. In addition, however, he always works late when the boss asks him to, he takes time to help newcomers learn their way around, and he is perceived as being helpful and committed to the organization's success. He is likely to be seen as a better organizational citizen.

A complex mosaic of individual, social, and organizational variables determines organizational citizenship behaviors. For example, the personality, attitudes, and needs (discussed in Chapter 4) of the individual must be consistent with citizenship behaviors. Similarly, the social context, or work group, in which the individual works must facilitate and promote such behaviors (we discuss group dynamics in Chapter 9). And the organization itself, especially its culture, must be capable of promoting, recognizing, and rewarding these types of behaviors if they are to be maintained. The study of organizational citizenship is still in its infancy, but preliminary research suggests that it may play a powerful role in organizational effectiveness.

SYNOPSIS

Understanding individuals in organizations is important for all managers. A basic framework for facilitating this understanding is the psychological contract—people's expectations regarding what they will contribute to the organization and what they will get in return. Organizations strive to achieve an optimal person-job fit, but this process is complicated by the existence of individual differences.

Personalities are the relatively stable sets of psychological and behavioral attributes that distinguish one person from another. The "big five" personality traits are agreeableness, conscientiousness, neuroticism, extraversion, and openness. Myers-Briggs dimensions and emotional intelligence also offer insights into personalities in organizations. Other important personality traits include locus of control, self-efficacy, authoritarianism, Machiavellianism, self-esteem, and risk propensity.

Attitudes are based on emotion, knowledge, and intended behavior. Cognitive dissonance results from contradictory or incongruent attitudes, behaviors, or both. Job satisfaction or dissatisfaction and organizational commitment are important work-related attitudes. Employees' moods, assessed in terms of positive or negative affectivity, also affect attitudes in organizations.

Perception is the set of processes by which a person becomes aware of and interprets information about the environment. Basic perceptual processes include selective perception and stereotyping. Perception and attribution are also closely related.

Workplace behavior is a pattern of action by the members of an organization that directly or indirectly influences organizational effectiveness. Performance behaviors are the set of work-related behaviors the organization expects the individual to display in order to fulfill the psychological contract. Dysfunctional behaviors include absenteeism and turnover, as well as theft, sabotage, and violence. Organizational citizenship entails behaviors that make a positive overall contribution to the organization.

DISCUSSION QUESTIONS

1. What is a psychological contract? Why is it important? What psychological contracts do you currently have?
2. Sometimes people describe an individual as having "no personality." What is wrong with this statement? What does this statement actually mean?
3. Describe how the "big five" personality attributes might affect a manager's own behavior in dealing with subordinates.
4. What are the components of an individual's attitude?
5. Think of a person you know who seems to have positive affectivity. Think of another who has more negative affectivity. How constant are they in their expressions of mood and attitude?
6. How does perception affect behavior?
7. What stereotypes do you form about people? Are they good or bad?
8. Recall a situation in which you made attributions and describe them using the framework supplied in Figure 3.4.
9. Identify and describe several important workplace behaviors.
10. As a manager, how would you go about trying to make someone a better organizational citizen?

HOW DO YOU SEE IT?

Advances in Technology

"I really didn't expect things to take the course that they've taken here."

—KIM CLAY, IT MANAGER AT MITCHELL GOLD + BOB WILLIAMS

"I think I've grown a lot here," says Kim Clay, who's currently the information technology (IT) manager at furniture maker Mitchell Gold + Bob Williams (MG+BW). "I really didn't expect things to take the course that they've taken here," she adds. "I really didn't expect it to lead into what it's become." As our video makes clear, Clay has certainly followed an unusual career trajectory at the company, which sells home furnishings out of its own MG+BW Signature Stores as well as such national chains as Pottery Barn and Williams-Sonoma and a number of independent retailers. She started out in a department called Consumer Inquiry, in which most of her professional contact with technology involved the telephone over which she fielded queries from *consumers*—that is, from individuals shopping for slip-covered sectionals or down-blend ottomans.

Clay's next position, in Customer Care, also called upon her telephone skills, this time in managing relations with a portfolio of *retail customers*—that is, with stores that carry MG+BW products. This job, she reports, demanded a little more of her skills in dealing with the people on the other end of the line. In working with the company's retail partners, she had more to do than simply satisfy inquisitive shoppers: She was responsible for resolving the often complex issues that arise in handling customer orders and managing other facets of business-to-business relations.

As Clay tells us later in the video, the process of getting products from MG+BW's factory in Taylorsville, North

Carolina, to stores located all over the country—the process of taking, tracking, shipping, and invoicing orders—is largely "technology driven," and her ability to handle that technology was obviously the key to both her subsequent change of direction and job enhancement at the company. "I think she just had this natural ability as it relates to technology and computers," says VP of Human Resources Dan Gauthreaux, and although she had no formal education in computer technology, both superiors and coworkers had noticed Clay's mastery of the informal learning curve entailed by her job. "It just seems that when people had problems with their computers," remarks Clay, "they typically came to me and asked for help."

Fortunately, she works for a company that places a premium on the ability to learn new things and put them to use. As Gauthreaux recalls, Clay's boss in Customer Care first told him about somebody in her department "'that's terrific, bright, and talented, and I think it's our job to kind of foster that development.'" Gauthreaux agreed, and so the company created a Help Desk for Clay to be in charge of. "I'd never really done anything with computers" in an official capacity, "so I was really excited to try it," says Clay, who also admits that "it was a big challenge to move from Customer Care to technology."

Her success at developing and running a new high-tech department came as no surprise to Gauthreaux. "You knew that if Kim was given an assignment or project… she would make it happen," he says, although he emphasizes that the company isn't in the habit of putting valuable employees in sink-or-swim situations. "We're the kind of company," he explains, "that whoever Kim reports to, they're not going to let her step off that ledge and not be successful…. Whether it's from an HR perspective or a coworkers' perspective, there's a real… 'your success is my success' kind of mentality" at MG+BW.

Before long, Clay was assigned to the company's IT department as a specialist, and today, as she informs us at the outset of the video, she's head of the department. Once again, of course, the move was a challenge, but this time, the shift in focus and responsibility wasn't quite so pronounced. Like her job in Customer Care, Clay's IT job requires her to keep up with role of technology in supporting both internal and external company activities. "It's a constantly changing field," explains Clay, "and we have to stay on top of it to keep the business competitive. And we have to know the new technology that's out there and try to incorporate it into our business as quickly as we can."

"It's been real growth for me personally," she adds. "… I really don't think it's an experience that you can get [at] a lot of places, with the opportunities that I've been given here."

CASE QUESTIONS

1. The manager of an IT department is responsible for the resources used by an organization to manage the information that it needs in order to carry out its mission. As for MG+BW, you can check out its mission at **www.mgbwhome.com**. Given this information, try to identify and describe some of the activities that Kim Clay performs in her current job.
2. Here's how Clay describes her former job in Customer Care:

   I dealt directly with our customers at the retail level, answering questions about orders that they [had] placed with us and that sort of thing. I had a large variety of our customers that I was directly responsible for.

   Rank the importance of *positive "big five" personality traits* in the performance of a job like Clay's Customer Care job. Now do the same thing for her job as IT manager. Do you see any interesting differences—positive traits, for example, that are clearly more important in one job than in the other? Can you identify which positive traits probably contribute to Clay's adaptability in performing both jobs successfully?
3. Assess Clay's personality in terms of each of the following traits—*emotional intelligence*, *locus of control*, and *self-efficacy*. Be specific in explaining each of your assessments. Now compare yourself to Clay: Being as honest as you can, assess yourself—at this stage of your life and/or career—in terms of the same traits.
4. Describe the approach of MG+BW managers in dealing with the following *work-related attitudes—job satisfaction*, *organizational commitment*, and *affectivity*.
5. Clay picked up her computer skills while on the job. What about you? How do you learn best? If you want to jumpstart your thinking about this question, go to http://blog.nextdayflyers.com. Search for the post *Learning Styles in the Workplace: Why you should care* (March 5, 2009), where you'll find a brief survey of the three different ways in which, according to many experts, most people learn in the workplace.*

ADDITIONAL SOURCES

Mitchell Gold + Bob Williams, "About Us," "Our Mission," "Our History" (2012), www.mgbwhome.com on June 11, 2012; "Household Durables: Company Overview of Mitchell Gold + Bob Williams," *Bloomberg Businessweek*, June 11, 2012, http://investing.businessweek.com on June 11, 2012; "The Rowe Companies Announces Sale of the Mitchell Gold Co.," *PR Newswire*, April 4, 2003, www.prnewswire.com on June 11, 2012.

*Karen Daniels, "Learning Styles in the Workplace: Why You Should Care," *NextDayFlyers.com Blog*, March 5, 2009, http://blog.nextdayflyers.com on June 11, 2012.

EXPERIENCING ORGANIZATIONAL BEHAVIOR

Matching Jobs and Personalities

Purpose This exercise is designed to give you some insight into the importance of matching personalities both to workplaces and to specific jobs. It should also give you a good idea of how hard it is to perform this task well.

Format The exercise asks you to perform two tasks:

- Match personality traits with specific jobs.
- Develop a series of questions to assess personality traits in job applicants.

Procedure Read each of the following job descriptions:

Page Conducts visitors on tours of radio and television station facilities and explains duties of staff, operation of equipment, and methods of broadcasting. Utilizes general knowledge of various phases of radio and television station operations. Runs errands within studio. May relieve telephone switchboard operator. May perform general clerical duties such as taking messages, filing, and typing.

Young-Adult Librarian Plans and conducts library program to provide special services for young adults. Selects books and audiovisual materials of interest to young adults to be acquired by library. Assists young adults in selecting materials. Plans and organizes young-adult activities, such as film programs, chess clubs, creative writing clubs, and photography contests. Delivers talks on books to stimulate reading. Compiles lists of library materials of interest to young adults. Confers with parents, teachers, and community organizations to assist in developing programs to stimulate reading and develop communication skills.

Mortgage Loan Interviewer Interviews applicants applying for mortgage loans to document income, debt, and credit history. Requests documents for verification, such as income tax returns, bank account numbers, purchase agreements, and property descriptions. Determines whether applicant meets establishment standards for further consideration, following the manual and using a calculator. Informs applicant of closing costs, such as appraisal, credit report, and notary fees. Answers applicant's questions and asks for signature on information authorization forms. Submits application forms for verification of application information. Calls applicant or other persons to resolve discrepancies, such as credit report showing late payment history. Informs applicant of loan denial or acceptance.

Park Ranger Enforces laws, regulations, and policies in state or national park. Registers vehicles and visitors, collects fees, and issues parking and use permits. Provides information pertaining to park use, safety requirements, and points of interest. Directs traffic, investigates accidents, and patrols area to prevent fires, vandalism, and theft. Cautions, evicts, or apprehends violators of laws and regulations. Directs or participates in first-aid and rescue activities. May compile specified park-use statistics, keep records, and prepare reports of area activities. May train and supervise park workers and concession attendants.

Headwaiter/Headwaitress Supervises and coordinates activities of dining room personnel to serve food aboard ship. Assigns duties, work stations, and responsibilities to personnel and directs their performances. Inspects dining tables and work areas for cleanliness. Greets patrons and shows them to dining tables. Requisitions supplies, such as glassware, china, and silverware. Authorizes personnel to work overtime. May suggest entrees, dinner courses, and wines to guests.

Exercise Task Working alone, you need to prepare by doing two things:

1. Select any **three** of these jobs, and for each, determine a personality trait that you think is especially important for a person performing the job (i.e., three jobs and three personality traits).
2. For each of the three jobs that you've analyzed, write up a series of five questions that will help you assess how an applicant for the job scores on the trait that you've selected for it. Make sure that your questions can be answered on a five-point scale (i.e., *strongly agree, agree, neither agree nor disagree, disagree, strongly disagree*).

After you've finished these preparatory steps, do the following:

1. Exchange your lists of questions with one of your classmates. You'll pretend to be a job applicant, and your partner will pretend to be a job interviewer. He or she will choose one of your lists and ask those questions to you,

and you will provide honest and truthful answers.

2. Repeat the process, taking the role of the interviewer while your partner takes the role of the applicant.
3. When you've finished the role-playing part of the exercise, discuss the experience with one another. First, each of you should reveal the trait that you had in mind when you drew up the list of five questions that you were asked in your "interview." Second, you should discuss how well each of your question sets measured the trait that you had in mind when you compiled them. If you have time remaining, you can have the same discussion about one or more of your remaining lists of questions.

BUILDING MANAGERIAL SKILLS

Exercise Overview Interpersonal skills refer to the ability to communicate with, understand, and motivate individuals and groups. Implicit in this definition is the notion that a manager should try to understand important characteristics of others, including their personalities. This exercise will give you insights into both the importance of personality in the workplace and some of the difficulties associated with assessing personality traits.

Exercise Background You will first try to determine which personality traits are most relevant for different jobs. You will then write a series of questions that you think may help assess or measure those traits in prospective employees. First, read each of the following job descriptions:

Sales representative: This position involves calling on existing customers to ensure that they are happy with the firm's products. It also requires the sales representative to work to get customers to increase the quantity of your products they are buying, as well as to attract new customers. A sales representative must be aggressive but not pushy.

Office manager: The office manager oversees the work of a staff of 20 secretaries, receptionists, and clerks. The manager hires them, trains them, evaluates their performance, and sets their pay. The manager also schedules working hours and, when necessary, disciplines or fires workers.

Warehouse worker: Warehouse workers unload trucks and carry shipments to shelves for storage. They also pull customer orders from shelves and take products for packing. The job requires workers to follow orders precisely and has little room for autonomy or interaction with others during work.

Exercise Task Working alone, identify a single personality trait that you think is especially important for a person to be able to effectively perform each of these three jobs. Next, write five questions that, when answered by a job applicant, will help you assess how that applicant scores on that particular trait. These questions should be of the type that can be answered on a five-point scale (for example, *strongly agree, agree, neither agree or disagree, disagree, strongly disagree*).

Exchange questions with a classmate. Pretend you are a job applicant. Provide honest and truthful answers to each question. Discuss the traits each of you identified for each position. How well you think your classmate's questions actually measure those traits?

Conclude by addressing the following questions:

1. How easy is it to measure personality?
2. How important do you believe it is for organizations to consider personality in hiring decisions?
3. Do perception and attitudes affect how people answer personality questions?

SELF-ASSESSMENT EXERCISE

What's Your Learning Style?

"Learning style" refers to the ways you prefer to approach new information. We all learn and process information in our own special style, although we share some learning patterns, preferences, and approaches. Knowing your own style also can help you to realize that other people may approach the same situation in a different way from your own.

Take a few minutes to complete the following questionnaire to assess your preferred learning style. Begin by reading the words in the left-hand column. Of the three responses to the right, circle the one that best characterizes you, answering as honestly as possible with the description that applies to you right now. Count the number of circled items and write your total at the bottom of each column. The questions you prefer provide insight into how you learn.

1. When I try to **concentrate…**	I grow distracted by clutter or movement, and I notice things around me other people don't notice.	I get distracted by sounds, and I attempt to control the amount and type of noise around me.	I become distracted by commotion, and I tend to retreat inside myself.
2. When I **visualize…**	I see vivid, detailed pictures in my thoughts.	I think in voices and sounds.	I see images in my thoughts that involve movement.
3. When I **talk with others…**	I find it difficult to listen for very long.	I enjoy listening, or I get impatient to talk myself.	I gesture and communicate with my hands.
4. When I **contact people…**	I prefer face-to-face meetings.	I prefer speaking by telephone for serious conversations.	I prefer to interact while walking or participating in some activity.
5. When I **see an acquaintance…**	I forget names but remember faces, and I tend to replay where we met for the first time.	I know people's names and I can usually quote what we discussed.	I remember what we did together and I may almost "feel" our time together.
6. When I **relax…**	I watch TV, see a play, visit an exhibit, or go to a movie.	I listen to the radio, play music, read, or talk with a friend.	I play sports, make crafts, or build something with my hands.
7. When I **read…**	I like descriptive examples and I may pause to imagine the scene.	I enjoy the narrative most and I can almost "hear" the characters talk.	I prefer action-oriented stories, but I do not often read for pleasure.
8. When I **spell…**	I envision the word in my mind or imagine what the word looks like when written.	I sound out the word, sometimes aloud, and tend to recall rules about letter order.	I get a feel for the word by writing it out or pretending to type it.
9. When I **do something new…**	I seek out demonstrations, pictures, or diagrams.	I want verbal and written instructions, and to talk it over with someone else.	I jump right in to try it, keep trying, and try different approaches.

10. When I **assemble an object…**	I look at the picture first and then, maybe, read the directions.	I read the directions, or I talk aloud as I work.	I usually ignore the directions and figure it out as I go along.
11. When I **interpret someone's mood…**	I examine facial expressions.	I rely on listening to tone of voice.	I focus on body language.
12. When I **teach other people…**	I show them.	I tell them, write it out, or I ask them a series of questions.	I demonstrate how it is done and then ask them to try.
Total	Visual:_____	Auditory:_____	Tactile/Kinesthetic:_____

The column with the highest total represents your primary processing style. The column with the second-most choices is your secondary style.

Your primary learning style: ___

Your secondary learning style: ___

Source: Adapted from Marcia L. Conner, *Learn More Now: 10 Simple Steps to Learning Better, Smarter, and Faster* (Hoboken, NJ: John Wiley & Sons, March 2004).

CHAPTER 4 Motivation in Organizations

Chapter Outline

- The Nature of Motivation
- Need-Based Perspectives on Motivation
- Process-Based Perspectives on Motivation
- Learning-Based Perspectives on Motivation

Chapter Learning Objectives

After studying this chapter, you should be able to:

1. **Characterize the nature of motivation, including its importance and basic historical perspectives.**
2. **Identify and describe the need-based perspectives on motivation.**
3. **Identify and describe the major process-based perspectives on motivation.**
4. **Describe learning-based perspectives on motivation.**

Are You Happily Productive or Productively Happy?

"If you're not happy doing what you do on a daily basis ... you'll just be getting things done for the sake of getting things done."

—Productivity consultant Sara Caputo M.A.

Sara Caputo is the founder and owner of Radiant Organizing, a training and coaching firm located in Santa Barbara, California. As a productivity consultant, her work includes both one-on-one sessions with clients and speaking engagements on how to get things done in the workplace. One day, she recalls, as she was in the middle of a presentation at a professional conference, "I just felt myself really loving what I do.... This got me thinking," she says. "What comes first—happiness in your work or productivity in your work? Are we *more productive* in our jobs and at work because we enjoy what we do and [because] that in itself is a motivator? Or are we *happier* in our jobs and at work because we're productive?"

At first, Caputo admits, she was willing to accept the likelihood that her question came down to "sort of a chicken/egg dilemma." Upon further reflection, however, she decided that happiness probably comes first. "At one point in your life," she reasons,

> *you had a calling to do what you're doing right now. Then time goes by, and what gets in the way? All the "other stuff." At the end of the day, if you're not happy doing what you do on a daily basis, you'll have a hard time sustaining your productivity because you'll just be getting things done for the sake of getting things done.*

One rather suspects that Caputo's workplace experience has been somewhat happier than average, but her bottom-line perspective on the cause-and-effect relationship between happiness and productivity is pretty much in line with most thinking on the subject. Another productivity consultant, for example, advises that "if you want to get more done at work … you should start by liking what you do…."

Sara Caputo is the owner of Radiant Organizing, a training and development firm in Santa Barbara, California.

[T]he productivity gurus out there," warns Alexander Kjerulf, founder and CHO ("Chief Happiness Officer") of Spoing!, a Danish consulting firm,

> *will tell you that it's all about having the right system. You need to prioritize your tasks. You must keep detailed logs of how you spend your time, [and] to-do lists are of course essential. You must learn to structure your calendar, and much, much more.... [But] no system, no tool or methodology in the world can beat the productivity boost you get from really, really enjoying your work.*

Happiness at work, says Kjerulf, "is the #1 productivity booster," and he cites a number of reasons why: Happy people work better with others, fix problems rather than complain about them, and make better decisions; they're optimistic and "way more motivated," and they have more energy and get sick less often.

Kjerulf admits that there's still a "question of causation"—the chicken-or-egg issue of which came first, happiness or productivity. "The link," he concludes, "goes both ways," but "the link is strongest from happiness to productivity—which means that if you want to be more productive, the very best thing you can do is focus on being happy with what you do."

Not everyone, however, sees the happiness-productivity link from the same perspective. For Paul Larson, a veteran of operations management in a variety of industries, the "legend that happy workers are productive employees has been a part of our organizational thinking for so long that many just take for granted that it has to be true." Larson, founder and president of The Myrddin Group, a Texas-based consultancy specializing in organizational design and development, agrees that "productive workers do seem to be happier." But that, he suggests, is "where the confusion is coming from.... [P]roductivity leads to satisfaction and happiness," he argues, "not the other way around. People who do a good job tend to feel intrinsically good about it." To boost productivity, Larson advises, companies should train and support managers "in their efforts to keep the troops fully engaged. It's that engagement that provides the venues for achievement and recognition."

Charles Kerns, a behavioral psychologist at Pepperdine University's Graziado School of Business and Management, agrees with Larson that engagement is the best goal for a manager who wants "to influence the happiness level of his or her employees." He's not quite so sure, however, that enhancing either personal or organizational productivity hinges on solving the chicken/egg dilemma. "Job satisfaction researchers," he points out, "have had a long-standing debate as to whether employees are happy first and performers second, or performers first and happy second," and he doesn't think that the matter is going to be resolved any time soon. For practical purposes, he suggests, "both happiness and job performance need to be addressed."

This is where *engagement* comes in. On the one hand, according to Kerns, managers should probably resign themselves to the fact that improving engagement is about the best they can hope for. On the other hand, improving an employee's engagement with his or her work is no small achievement. Engagement can be measured by the extent to which an individual has *more happy or positive experiences than negative ones*, and the key to increasing positive experiences, says Kerns, is engaging an employee's strengths: "An employee's level of engagement … and subsequent happiness," he contends, "is likely boosted when he or she has the opportunity to do what he or she does best at work: Utilizing one's strengths is a positive experience." With engagement as a starting point, Kerns thinks that the happiness-productivity equation can be formulated in more practical terms: Happiness, he explains, "comes from work experiences that yield positive emotions [and] positive thoughts," and "people who approach tasks with positivity [are] more productive."

What Do You Think?

1. Judging from your own experience, do you think that there's really a significant relationship between happiness and productivity?
2. Judging again from your own experience, is engagement enough to make you productive, or do you need some kind of more tangible motivation?

References: Sara Caputo, "Which Comes First: Happiness or Productivity?" *Toolbox for HR*, April 15, 2009, http://hr.toolbox.com on April 16, 2012; Alexander Kjerulf, "Top 10 Reasons Why Happiness at Work Is the Ultimate Productivity Booster," *PositiveSharing.com*, March 27, 2007, http://positivesharing.com on April 16, 2012; Paul Larson, "Employee Motivation in the Workplace," *Suite101.com*, May 4, 2009, http://paul-larson.suite101.com on April 16, 2012; Charles Kerns, "Putting Performance and Happiness Together in the Workplace," *Graziado Business Report*, 2008, vol. 11, http://gbr.pepperdine.edu on April 16, 2012.

Given the complex array of individual differences discussed in Chapter 3, it should be obvious that people work for a wide variety of different reasons. Some people want money, some want a challenge, and some want power. What people in an organization want from work and how they think they can achieve it plays an instrumental role in determining their motivation to work. As we see in this chapter, motivation is vital to all organizations. Indeed, the difference between highly effective organizations and less effective ones often lies in the motivations of their members (as evidenced by NetApp at the beginning of this chapter). Thus, managers need to understand the nature of individual motivation, especially as it applies to work situations. In this chapter we first explore various need-based perspectives on motivation. We then turn our attention to the more sophisticated process-based perspectives. We conclude with a discussion of learning-based perspectives on motivation.[1]

THE NATURE OF MOTIVATION

Motivation is the set of forces that leads people to behave in particular ways.

Motivation is the set of forces that causes people to engage in one behavior rather than some alternative behavior.[2] Students who stay up all night to ensure that their term papers are the best they can be, salespeople who work on Saturdays to get ahead, and doctors who make follow-up phone calls to patients to check on their conditions are all motivated people. Of course, students who avoid the term paper by spending the day at the beach, salespeople who go home early to escape a tedious sales call, and doctors who skip follow-up calls to have more time for golf are also motivated, but their goals are different. From the manager's viewpoint, the objective is to motivate people to behave in ways that are in the organization's best interest.[3]

The Importance of Motivation

Managers strive to motivate people in the organization to perform at high levels. This means getting them to work hard, to come to work regularly, and to make positive contributions to the organization's mission. But job performance depends on ability and environment as well as motivation. This relationship can be stated as follows:

$$P = M + A + E$$

where

P = performance, M = motivation,
A = ability, and E = environment.

To reach high levels of performance, an employee must want to do the job well (motivation); must be able to do the job effectively (ability); and must have the materials, resources, equipment, and information required to do the job (environment). A deficiency in any one of these areas hurts performance. A manager should thus strive to ensure that all three conditions are met.[4]

In most settings motivation is the most difficult of these factors to manage. If an employee lacks the ability to perform, she or he can be sent to training programs to learn new job skills. If the person cannot learn those skills, she or he can be transferred to a simpler job and replaced with a more skilled worker. If an employee lacks materials, resources, equipment, and/or information, the manager can take steps to provide them. For example, if a worker cannot complete a project without sales forecast data from marketing, the manager can contact marketing and request that information. But if motivation

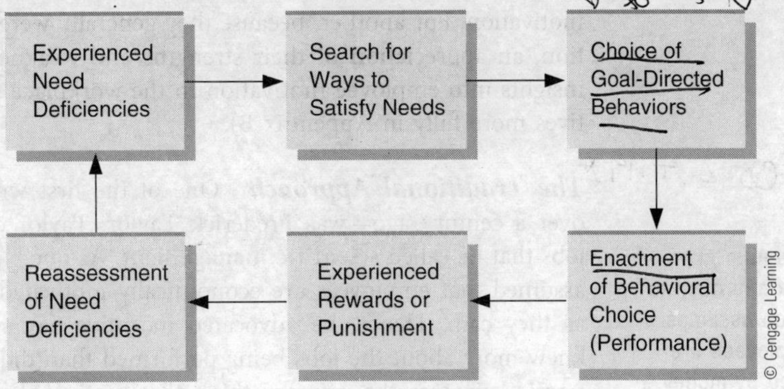

FIGURE 4.1

Motivational Framework

This framework provides a useful way to see how motivational processes occur. When people experience a need deficiency, they seek ways to satisfy it, which results in a choice of goal-directed behaviors. After performing the behavior, the individual experiences rewards or punishments that affect the original need deficiency.

is deficient, the manager faces the more complex situation of determining what will motivate the employee to work harder.[5]

The Motivational Framework

We can start to understand motivation by looking at need deficiencies and goal-directed behaviors. Figure 4.1 shows the basic motivational framework we use to organize our discussion. A need—something an individual requires or wants—is the starting point.[6] Motivated behavior usually begins when a person has one or more important **needs**. Although a need that is already satisfied may also motivate behavior (for example, the need to maintain a standard of living one has already achieved), unmet needs usually result in more intense feelings and behavioral changes. For example, if a person has yet to attain the standard of living she desires, this unmet need may stimulate her to action.

A **need** is anything an individual requires or wants.

A need deficiency usually triggers a search for ways to satisfy it. Consider a person who feels her salary and position are deficient because they do not reflect the importance to the organization of the work she does and because she wants more income. She may feel she has three options: to simply ask for a raise and a promotion, to work harder in the hope of earning a raise and a promotion, or to look for a new job with a higher salary and a more prestigious title.

Next comes a choice of goal-directed behaviors. Although a person might pursue more than one option at a time (such as working harder while also looking for another job), most effort is likely to be directed at one option. In the next phase, the person actually carries out the behavior chosen to satisfy the need. She will probably begin putting in longer hours, working harder, and so forth. She will next experience either rewards or punishment as a result of this choice. She may perceive her situation to be punishing if she ends up earning no additional recognition and not getting a promotion or pay raise. Alternatively, she may actually be rewarded by getting the raise and promotion because of her higher performance.

Finally, the person assesses the extent to which the outcome achieved fully addresses the original need deficiency. Suppose the person wanted a 10 percent raise and a promotion to vice president. If she got both, she should be satisfied. On the other hand, if she got only a 7 percent raise and a promotion to associate vice president, she will have to decide whether to keep trying, to accept what she got, or to choose one of the other options considered earlier. (Sometimes, of course, a need may go unsatisfied altogether, despite the person's best efforts.)

Historical Perspectives on Motivation

Historical views on motivation, although not always accurate, are of interest for several reasons. For one thing, they provide a foundation for contemporary thinking about motivation. For another, because they generally were based on common sense and intuition, an appreciation of their strengths and weaknesses can help managers gain useful insights into employee motivation in the workplace (we discuss these historical perspectives more fully in Appendix B).

The **scientific management approach** to motivation assumes that employees are motivated by money.

The Traditional Approach One of the first writers to address work motivation—over a century ago—was Frederick Taylor. Taylor developed a method for structuring jobs that he called **scientific management**. As one basic premise of this approach, Taylor assumed that employees are economically motivated and work to earn as much money as they can.[7] Hence, he advocated incentive pay systems. He believed that managers knew more about the jobs being performed than did workers, and he assumed that economic gain was the primary thing that motivated everyone. Other assumptions of the traditional approach were that work is inherently unpleasant for most people and that the money they earn is more important to employees than the nature of the job they are performing. Hence, people could be expected to perform any kind of job if they were paid enough. Although the role of money as a motivating factor cannot be dismissed, proponents of the traditional approach took too narrow a view of the role of monetary compensation and also failed to consider other motivational factors.

The **human relations approach** to motivation suggests that favorable employee attitudes result in motivation to work hard.

The Human Relations Approach The human relations approach supplanted scientific management in the 1930s.[8] The **human relations approach** assumed that employees want to feel useful and important, that employees have strong social needs, and that these needs are more important than money in motivating employees. Advocates of the human relations approach advised managers to make workers feel important and to allow them a modicum of self-direction and self-control in carrying out routine activities. The illusion of involvement and importance were expected to satisfy workers' basic social needs and result in higher motivation to perform. For example, a manager might allow a work group to participate in making a decision even though he had already determined what the decision would be. The symbolic gesture of seeming to allow participation was expected to enhance motivation, even though no real participation took place.

The **human resource approach** to motivation assumes that people want to contribute and are able to make genuine contributions.

The Human Resource Approach The **human resource approach** to motivation carries the concepts of needs and motivation one step farther. Whereas the human relationists believed that the illusion of contribution and participation would enhance motivation, the human resource view, which began to emerge in the 1950s, assumes that the contributions themselves are valuable to both individuals and organizations. It assumes that people want to contribute and are able to make genuine contributions. Management's task, then, is to encourage participation and to create a work environment that makes full use of the human resources available. This philosophy guides most contemporary thinking about employee motivation. At Ford, Apple, Texas Instruments, and Hewlett-Packard, for example, work teams are being called upon to solve a variety of problems and to make substantive contributions to the organization.

NEED-BASED PERSPECTIVES ON MOTIVATION

Need-based theories of motivation assume that need deficiencies cause behavior.

Need-based perspectives represent the starting point for most contemporary thought on motivation, although these theories also attracted critics.[9] The basic premise of **need-based theories** and models, consistent with our motivation framework introduced earlier, is that humans are motivated primarily by deficiencies in one or more important needs or need categories. Need theorists have attempted to identify and categorize the needs that are most important to people.[10] (Some observers call these "content theories" because they deal with the content, or substance, of what motivates behavior.) The best-known need theories are the hierarchy of needs and the ERG theory.

The Hierarchy of Needs

The hierarchy of needs, developed by psychologist Abraham Maslow in the 1940s, is the best-known need theory.[11] Influenced by the human relations school, Maslow argued that human beings are "wanting" animals: They have innate desires to satisfy a given set of needs. Furthermore, Maslow believed that these needs are arranged in a hierarchy of importance, with the most basic needs at the foundation of the hierarchy.

Maslow's hierarchy of needs theory assumes that human needs are arranged in a hierarchy of importance.

Figure 4.2 shows **Maslow's hierarchy of needs**. The three sets of needs at the bottom of the hierarchy are called *deficiency needs* because they must be satisfied for the individual to be fundamentally comfortable. The top two sets of needs are termed *growth needs* because they focus on personal growth and development.

The most basic needs in the hierarchy are *physiological needs*. These include the needs for food, sex, and air. Next in the hierarchy are *security needs*: things that offer safety and security, such as adequate housing and clothing and freedom from worry and anxiety. *Belongingness needs*, the third level in the hierarchy, are primarily social. Examples include the need for love and affection and the need to be accepted by peers. The fourth level, *esteem needs*, actually encompasses two slightly different kinds of needs: the need for a positive self-image and self-respect and the need to be respected by others. At the top of the hierarchy are *self-actualization needs*. These involve a person's realizing his or her full potential and becoming all that he or she can be.

Maslow believed that each need level must be satisfied before the level above it can become important. Thus, once physiological needs have been satisfied, their importance diminishes, and security needs emerge as the primary sources of motivation. This escalation up the hierarchy continues until the self-actualization needs become the primary motivators. Suppose, for example, that Jennifer Wallace earns all the money she needs and is very satisfied with her standard of living. Additional income may have little or

FIGURE 4.2

The Hierarchy of Needs

Maslow's hierarchy of needs consists of five basic categories of needs. This figure illustrates both general and organizational examples of each type of need. Of course, each individual has a wide variety of specific needs within each category.

Source: Adapted from Abraham H. Maslow, "A Theory of Human Motivation," *Psychological Review,* 1943, vol., 50, pp. 374–396.

no motivational impact on her behavior. Instead, Jennifer will strive to satisfy other needs, such as a desire for higher self-esteem.

However, if a previously satisfied lower-level set of needs becomes deficient again, the individual returns to that level. For example, suppose that Jennifer unexpectedly loses her job. At first, she may not be too worried because she has savings and confidence that she can find another good job. As her savings dwindle, however, she will become increasingly motivated to seek new income. Initially, she may seek a job that both pays well and satisfies her esteem needs. But as her financial situation grows worse, she may lower her expectations regarding esteem and instead focus almost exclusively on simply finding a job with a reliable paycheck.

In most businesses, physiological needs are probably the easiest to evaluate and to meet. Adequate wages, toilet facilities, ventilation, and comfortable temperatures and working conditions are measures taken to satisfy this most basic level of needs. Security needs in organizations can be satisfied by such things as job continuity (no layoffs), a grievance system (to protect against arbitrary supervisory actions), and an adequate insurance and retirement system (to guard against financial loss from illness and to ensure retirement income).

Most employees' belongingness needs are satisfied by family ties and group relationships both inside and outside the organization. In the workplace, people usually develop friendships that provide a basis for social interaction and can play a major role in satisfying social needs. Managers can help satisfy these needs by fostering interaction and a sense of group identity among employees. At the same time, managers can be sensitive to the probable effects on employees (such as low performance and absenteeism) of family problems or lack of acceptance by coworkers. Esteem needs in the workplace are met at least partially by job titles, choice offices, merit pay increases, awards, and other forms of recognition. Of course, to be sources of long-term motivation, tangible rewards such as these must be distributed equitably and be based on performance.

Self-actualization needs are perhaps the hardest to understand and the most difficult to satisfy. For example, it is difficult to assess how many people completely meet their full potential. In most cases, people who are doing well on Maslow's hierarchy will have satisfied their esteem needs and will be moving toward self-actualization. Working toward self-actualization, rather than actually achieving it, may be the ultimate motivation for most people. In recent years there has been a pronounced trend toward people leaving well-paying but less fulfilling jobs to take lower-paying but more fulfilling jobs such as nursing and teaching. This might indicate that they are actively working toward self-actualization.[12]

Research shows that the need hierarchy does not generalize very well to other countries. For example, in Greece and Japan, security needs may motivate employees more than self-actualization needs. Likewise, belongingness needs are especially important in Sweden, Norway, and Denmark. Research has also found differences in the relative importance of different needs in Mexico, India, Peru, Canada, Thailand, Turkey, and Puerto Rico.[13]

Maslow's needs hierarchy makes a certain amount of intuitive sense. And because it was the first motivation theory to become popular, it is also one of the best known among practicing managers. However, research has revealed a number of deficiencies in the theory. For example, five levels of needs are not always present; the actual hierarchy of needs does not always conform to Maslow's model; and need structures are more unstable and variable than the theory would lead us to believe.[14] And sometimes managers are overly clumsy or superficial in their attempts to use a theory such as this one. Thus, the theory's primary contribution seems to lie in providing a general framework for categorizing needs.

ERG Theory

The **ERG theory** describes existence, relatedness, and growth needs.

The **ERG theory**, developed by Yale psychologist Clayton Alderfer, is another historically important need theory of motivation.[15] In many respects, ERG theory extends and refines Maslow's needs hierarchy concept, although there are also several important differences between the two. The *E*, *R*, and *G* stand for three basic need categories: existence, relatedness, and growth. *Existence needs*—those necessary for basic human survival—roughly correspond to the physiological and security needs of Maslow's hierarchy. *Relatedness needs*—those involving the need to relate to others—are similar to Maslow's belongingness and esteem needs. Finally, *growth needs* are analogous to Maslow's needs for self-esteem and self-actualization.

In contrast to Maslow's approach, ERG theory suggests that more than one kind of need—for example, both relatedness and growth needs—may motivate a person at the same time. A more important difference from Maslow's hierarchy is that ERG theory includes a satisfaction-progression component and a frustration-regression component. The satisfaction-progression concept suggests that after satisfying one category of needs, a person progresses to the next level. On this point, the need hierarchy and ERG theory agree. The need hierarchy, however, assumes that the individual remains at the next level until the needs at that level are satisfied. In contrast, the frustration-regression component of ERG theory suggests that a person who is frustrated by trying to satisfy a higher level of needs eventually will regress to the preceding level.[16]

Suppose, for instance, that Nick Hernandez has satisfied his basic needs at the relatedness level and now is trying to satisfy his growth needs. That is, he has many friends and social relationships and is now trying to learn new skills and advance in his career. For a variety of reasons, such as organizational constraints (i.e., few challenging jobs, a glass ceiling, etc.) and the lack of opportunities to advance, he is unable to satisfy those needs. No matter how hard he tries, he seems stuck in his current position. According to ERG theory, frustration of his growth needs will cause Nick's relatedness needs to once again become dominant as motivators. As a result, he will put renewed interest into making friends and developing social relationships.

The Dual-Structure Theory

The **dual-structure theory** identifies motivation factors, which affect satisfaction, and hygiene factors, which determine dissatisfaction.

Another important need-based theory of motivation is the **dual-structure theory**, which is in many ways similar to the need theories just discussed. This theory was originally called the "two-factor theory," but the more contemporary name used here is more descriptive. This theory has played a major role in managerial thinking about motivation, and though few researchers today accept the theory, it is nevertheless widely known and accepted among practicing managers.

Development of the Theory Frederick Herzberg and his associates developed the dual-structure theory in the late 1950s and early 1960s.[17] Herzberg began by interviewing approximately 200 accountants and engineers in Pittsburgh. He asked them to recall times when they felt especially satisfied and motivated by their jobs and times when they felt particularly dissatisfied and unmotivated. He then asked them to describe what caused the good and bad feelings. The responses to the questions were recorded by the interviewers and later subjected to content analysis. (In a content analysis, the words, phrases, and sentences used by respondents are analyzed and categorized according to their meanings.)

To his surprise, Herzberg found that entirely different sets of factors were associated with the two kinds of feelings about work. For example, a person who indicated "low pay" as a source of dissatisfaction would not necessarily identify "high pay" as a source of satisfaction and motivation. Instead, people associated entirely different

SERVICE The Need for Fun at Work

©rangizzz/Shutterstock

When you enter a retail shop, restaurant, or classroom, you like to be greeted with a happy smile. When you join a group of employees to start another work day, you also like being greeted with happy smiles from your coworkers. It's hard to find anyone that would prefer being around people who are frowning instead of smiling. A smile is a universal signal that the person you are dealing with is glad to see you and glad you are there. Managers of service organizations know how important it is to make their employees smile for their customers. The question is how to get employees to smile to send the desired friendly welcome to each and every customer. Not only is it hard to smile at customers all day, every day for most employees, it is hard to smile when those customers are rude and offensive or when the employee is just having a bad day. On the other hand, service organizations know that the next customer in line doesn't care that the last customer encountered by your employee was so frustrating and offensive to deal with that the employee is in tears. To the next customer, the impact of the last customer on the service experience is irrelevant history. They just want a friendly greeting with a smile.

Although we will deal further with the management of emotional labor in a later chapter, here we focus on creating an employee environment that promotes happiness and a sense of fun in order to get our employees to smile. Some motivational theorists, such as William Glasser, consider fun to be one of the fundamental human needs. Glasser's choice theory explicitly includes fun as part of his approach to explaining an individual's needs hierarchy. Glasser's hierarchy begins with survival needs and proceeds to the needs for love and belongingness. Once reaching this level, Glasser suggests that the satisfaction of these lower-level needs is logically followed by the needs for power and recognition and then by the needs for freedom and autonomy. However, after these needs are met, Glasser proposes a fifth and powerful employee need—the drive to have fun.

Unfortunately, many organizations are unconcerned with this need and their role in helping employees meet it. Benchmark service organizations, however, know how important it is for their employees to have fun at work, not only because it puts a smile on the employees' faces when dealing with coworkers but also because of the contagious influence that employee fun can have on customers. Well-known examples include Southwest Airlines, where founder Herb Kelleher often referred to himself as the "High Priest of Ha Ha" as part of his efforts to encourage employees to have fun at work. And it worked. Southwest is famous for its employee- and customer-centered culture in which employees take their work seriously but don't take themselves too seriously while doing it. Southwest's customers tell tales of cabin attendants hiding in overhead bins to surprise boarding passengers, singing the FAA-prescribed safety instructions to a rap beat, or decorating themselves and check-in counters to celebrate holidays.

Other organizations have taken different approaches to promote fun at work. Hotels celebrate with pizza or ice cream parties when an employee receives a complimentary letter from a customer; restaurants have pre-shift "alley rallies" for servers, both to familiarize them with the menu and to make them smile before serving customers; and hospitals have celebrations with patients for special occasions that make everyone smile. Not only do people who are smiling find it impossible to simultaneously frown and look unhappy to customers and coworkers, but having fun and laughing release endorphins, epinephrine, and adrenaline that actually make people feel better. In the movie *Patch Adams*, Robin Williams famously portrayed a doctor who used laughter and clown dress to help speed his patients' healing process.

Many popular books have been written on how to create a fun work environment. One study that asked human resource managers what makes a fun work environment identified 10 separate items. These were celebrations of personal milestones (e.g., birthdays), celebrations of professional milestones (e.g., award banquets), social events, opportunities to participate in volunteer and civic groups, stress release activities (massage, exercise facilities), humor, games, friendly competitions, opportunities for personal development (book clubs), and entertainment (bands, skits). When the researchers analyzed their data, they found all items loaded on a single factor. In trying to explain how so many different items could cluster together, the researchers concluded that fun at work activities actually reflected a bigger issue: management showing a positive message of its respect and appreciation for its employees with a smile on its face. They offered the following definition: "A fun work environment intentionally encourages, initiates, and supports a variety of enjoyable and pleasurable activities that positively impact the attitude and productivity of individuals and groups," or, more succinctly, "a work environment that makes people smile."

The point is simple. We want people to have fun at work in order to increase the likelihood that these employees will smile at their internal and external customers, because everyone prefers to be served by and work with people who greet them as a friend that they are glad to see.

Discussion Question: What things can managers do to ensure that their employees are smiling when they encounter either internal or external customers? Why is it important for them to smile?

causes, such as recognition or achievement, with satisfaction and motivation. The findings led Herzberg to conclude that the prevailing thinking about satisfaction and motivation was incorrect. As Figure 4.3 shows, at the time, job satisfaction was being viewed as a single construct ranging from satisfaction to dissatisfaction. If this were the case, Herzberg reasoned, one set of factors should therefore influence movement back and forth along the continuum. But because his research had identified differential influences from two different sets of factors, Herzberg argued that two different dimensions must be involved. Thus, he saw motivation as a dual-structured phenomenon.

Figure 4.3 also illustrates the dual-structure concept that there is one dimension ranging from satisfaction to no satisfaction and another ranging from dissatisfaction to no

FIGURE 4.3

The Dual-Structure Theory of Motivation

The traditional view of satisfaction suggested that satisfaction and dissatisfaction were opposite ends of a single dimension. Herzberg's dual-structure theory found evidence of a more complex view. In this theory, motivation factors affect one dimension, ranging from satisfaction to no satisfaction. Other workplace characteristics, called "hygiene factors," are assumed to affect another dimension, ranging from dissatisfaction to no dissatisfaction.

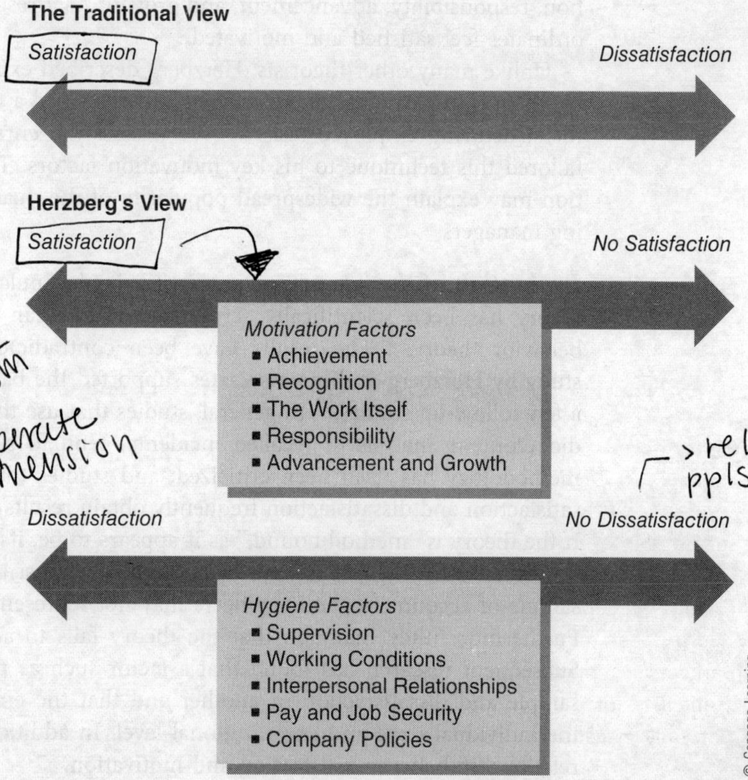

dissatisfaction. The two dimensions must presumably be associated with the two sets of factors identified in the initial interviews. Thus, this theory proposed, employees might be either satisfied or not satisfied and, at the same time, dissatisfied or not dissatisfied.[18]

Motivation factors are intrinsic to the work itself and include factors such as achievement and recognition.

Hygiene factors are extrinsic to the work itself and include factors such as pay and job security.

In addition, Figure 4.3 lists the primary factors identified in Herzberg's interviews. **Motivation factors** such as achievement and recognition were often cited by people as primary causes of satisfaction and motivation. When present in a job, these factors apparently could cause satisfaction and motivation; when they were absent, the result was feelings of no satisfaction rather than dissatisfaction. The other set of factors, **hygiene factors**, came out in response to the questions about dissatisfaction and lack of motivation. The respondents suggested that pay, job security, supervisors, and working conditions, if seen as inadequate, could lead to feelings of dissatisfaction. When these factors were considered acceptable, however, the person still was not necessarily satisfied; rather, he or she was simply not dissatisfied.[19]

To use the dual-structure theory in the workplace, Herzberg recommended a two-stage process. First, the manager should try to eliminate situations that cause dissatisfaction, which Herzberg assumed to be the more basic of the two dimensions. For example, suppose that Susan Kowalski wants to use the dual-structure theory to enhance motivation in the group of seven technicians she supervises. Her first goal would be to achieve a state of no dissatisfaction by addressing hygiene factors. Imagine, for example, that she discovers that their pay is a bit below market rates and that a few of them are worried about job security. Her response would be to secure a pay raise for them and to allay their concerns about job security.

According to the theory, once a state of no dissatisfaction exists, trying to improve motivation further through hygiene factors is a waste of time.[20] At that point, the motivation factors enter the picture. Thus, when Susan is sure that she has adequately dealt with hygiene issues, she should try to increase opportunities for achievement, recognition, responsibility, advancement, and growth. As a result, she would be helping her subordinates feel satisfied and motivated.

Unlike many other theorists, Herzberg described explicitly how managers could apply his theory. In particular, he developed and described a technique called "job enrichment" for structuring employee tasks.[21] (We discuss job enrichment in Chapter 5.) Herzberg tailored this technique to his key motivation factors. This unusual attention to application may explain the widespread popularity of the dual-structure theory among practicing managers.

Evaluation of the Theory Because it gained popularity so quickly, the dual-structure theory has been scientifically scrutinized more than almost any other organizational behavior theory.[22] The results have been contradictory, to say the least. The initial study by Herzberg and his associates supported the basic premises of the theory, as did a few follow-up studies.[23] In general, studies that use the same methodology as Herzberg did (content analysis of recalled incidents) tend to support the theory. However, this methodology has itself been criticized, and studies that use other methods to measure satisfaction and dissatisfaction frequently obtain results quite different from Herzberg's.[24] If the theory is "method bound," as it appears to be, its validity is therefore questionable.

Several other criticisms have been directed against the theory. Critics say the original sample of accountants and engineers may not represent the general working population. Furthermore, they maintain that the theory fails to account for individual differences. Subsequent research has found that a factor such as pay may affect satisfaction in one sample and dissatisfaction in another and that the effect of a given factor depends on the individual's age and organizational level. In addition, the theory does not define the relationship between satisfaction and motivation.

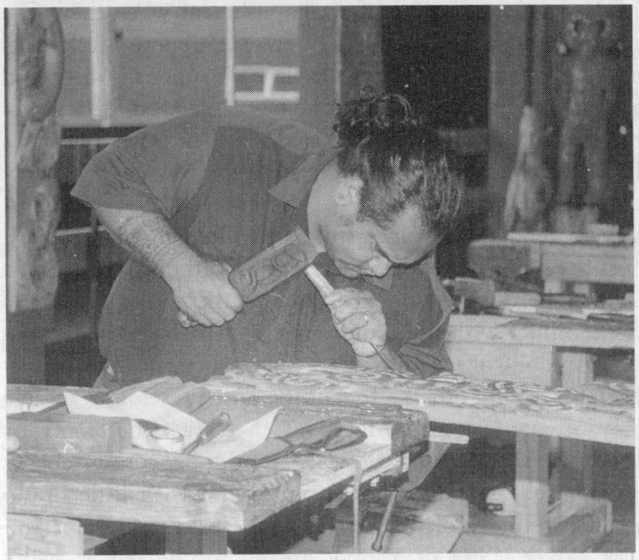

WoodyStock/Alamy

The two-factor theory makes specific predictions about what factors do and do not motivate people at work. One study, however, found that these factors are different in New Zealand. This New Zealander is working on an ancient carving to represent his Maori heritage.

Research has also suggested that the dual-structure framework varies across cultures. Only limited studies have been conducted, but findings suggest that employees in New Zealand and Panama assess the impact of motivation and hygiene factors differently from U.S. workers.[25] It is not surprising, then, that the dual-structure theory is no longer held in high esteem by organizational behavior researchers. Indeed, the field has since adopted far more complex and valid conceptualizations of motivation, most of which we discuss in Chapter 6. But because of its initial popularity and its specific guidance for application, the dual-structure theory merits a special place in the history of motivation research.

Other Important Needs

Each theory discussed so far describes interrelated sets of important individual needs within specific frameworks. Several other key needs have been identified, but these needs are not allied with any single integrated theoretical perspective. The three most frequently mentioned are the needs for achievement, affiliation, and power.

The **need for achievement** is the desire to accomplish a task or goal more effectively than was done in the past.

The Need for Achievement The **need for achievement** is most frequently associated with the work of David McClelland.[26] This need arises from an individual's desire to accomplish a goal or task more effectively than in the past. Individuals who have a high need for achievement tend to set moderately difficult goals and to make moderately risky decisions. Suppose, for example, that Mark Cohen, a regional manager for a national retailer, sets a sales increase goal for his stores of either 1 percent or 50 percent. The first goal is probably too easy, and the second is probably impossible to reach; either would suggest a low need for achievement. But a mid-range goal of, say, 15 percent might present a reasonable challenge but also be within reach. Setting this goal might more accurately reflect a high need for achievement.

High-need achievers also want immediate, specific feedback on their performance. They want to know how well they did something as quickly after finishing it as possible. For this reason, high-need achievers frequently take jobs in sales, where they get almost immediate feedback from customers, and avoid jobs in areas such as research and development, where tangible progress is slower and feedback comes at longer intervals. If Mark only asks his managers for their sales performance on a periodic basis, he might not have a high need for achievement. But if he is constantly calling each store manager in his territory to ask about their sales increases, this activity indicates a high need for achievement on his part.

Preoccupation with work is another characteristic of high-need achievers. They think about it on their way to the workplace, during lunch, and at home. They find it difficult to put their work aside, and they become frustrated when they must stop working on a partly completed project. If Mark seldom thinks about his business in the evening, he may not be a high-need achiever. However, if work is always on his mind, he might indeed be a high-need achiever.

Finally, high-need achievers tend to assume personal responsibility for getting things done. They often volunteer for extra duties and find it difficult to delegate part of a job to someone else. Accordingly, they derive a feeling of accomplishment when they have done more work than their peers without the assistance of others. Suppose Mark visits a store one day and finds that the merchandise is poorly displayed, the floor is dirty, and the sales clerks don't seem motivated to help customers. If he has a low need for achievement, he might point the problems out to the store manager and then leave. But if his need for achievement is high, he may very well stay in the store for a while, personally supervising the changes that need to be made.

Although high-need achievers tend to be successful, they often do not achieve top management posts. The most common explanation is that although high need for achievement helps these people advance quickly through the ranks, the traits associated with the need often conflict with the requirements of high-level management positions. Because of the amount of work they are expected to do, top executives must be able to delegate tasks to others. In addition, they seldom receive immediate feedback, and they often must make decisions that are either more or less risky than those with which a high-need achiever would be comfortable.[27] High-need achievers tend to do well as individual entrepreneurs with little or no group reinforcement Bill Gates, cofounder of Microsoft, Reed Hasting, founder and CEO of Netflix, and Marissa Mayer, CEO of Yahoo! are all recognized as being high-need achievers.

The **need for affiliation** is the need for human companionship.

The Need for Affiliation Individuals also experience the **need for affiliation**—the need for human companionship.[28] Researchers recognize several ways that people with a high need for affiliation differ from those with a lower need. Individuals with a high need tend to want reassurance and approval from others and usually are genuinely concerned about others' feelings. They are likely to act and think as they believe others want them to, especially those with whom they strongly identify and desire friendship. As we might expect, people with a strong need for affiliation most often work in jobs with a lot of interpersonal contact, such as sales and teaching positions.

For example, suppose that Watanka Jackson is seeking a job as a geologist or petroleum field engineer, a job that will take her into remote areas for long periods of time with little interaction with coworkers. Aside from her academic training, one reason for the nature of her job search might be that she has a low need for affiliation. In contrast, a classmate of hers, William Pfeffer, may be seeking a job in the corporate headquarters of a petroleum company. His preferences might be dictated, at least in part, by a desire to be around other people in the workplace; thus, he has a higher need for affiliation. A recent Gallup survey suggests that people who have at least one good friend at work are much more likely to be highly engaged with their work and to indicate higher levels of job satisfaction.[29]

The **need for power** is the desire to control the resources in one's environment.

The Need for Power A third major individual need is the **need for power**—the desire to control one's environment, including financial, material, informational, and human resources.[30] People vary greatly along this dimension. Some individuals spend much time and energy seeking power; others avoid power if at all possible. People with a high need for power can be successful managers if three conditions are met. First, they must seek power for the betterment of the organization rather than for their own interests. Second, they must have a fairly low need for affiliation because fulfilling a personal need for power may well alienate others in the workplace. Third, they need plenty of self-control to curb their desire for power when it threatens to interfere with effective organizational or interpersonal relationships.[31]

PROCESS-BASED PERSPECTIVES ON MOTIVATION

The **process-based perspectives on motivation** focus on how people behave in their efforts to satisfy their needs.

Process-based perspectives are concerned with how motivation occurs. Rather than attempting to identify motivational stimuli, process perspectives focus on why people choose certain behavioral options to satisfy their needs and how they evaluate their satisfaction after they have attained these goals. Three useful process perspectives on motivation are the equity, expectancy, and goal-setting theories.

The Equity Theory of Motivation

Equity theory focuses on people's desire to be treated with what they perceive as equity and to avoid perceived inequity.

Equity is the belief that we are being treated fairly in relation to others; inequity is the belief that we are being treated unfairly in relation to others.

The equity theory of motivation is based on the relatively simple premise that people in organizations want to be treated fairly.[32] The theory defines equity as the belief that we are being treated fairly in relation to others and inequity as the belief that we are being treated unfairly compared with others. Equity theory is just one of several theoretical formulations derived from social comparison processes. Social comparisons involve evaluating our own situation in terms of others' situations. In this chapter, we focus mainly on equity theory because it is the most highly developed of the social comparison approaches and the one that applies most directly to the work motivation of people in organizations.

Forming Equity Perceptions People in organizations form perceptions of the equity of their treatment through a four-step process. First, they evaluate how they are being treated by the firm. Second, they form a perception of how a "comparison-other" is being treated. The comparison-other might be a person in the same work group, someone in another part of the organization, or even a composite of several people scattered throughout the organization.[33] Third, they compare their own circumstances with those of the comparison-other and then use this comparison as the basis for forming an impression of either equity or inequity. Fourth, depending on the strength of this feeling, the person may choose to pursue one or more of the alternatives discussed in the next section.

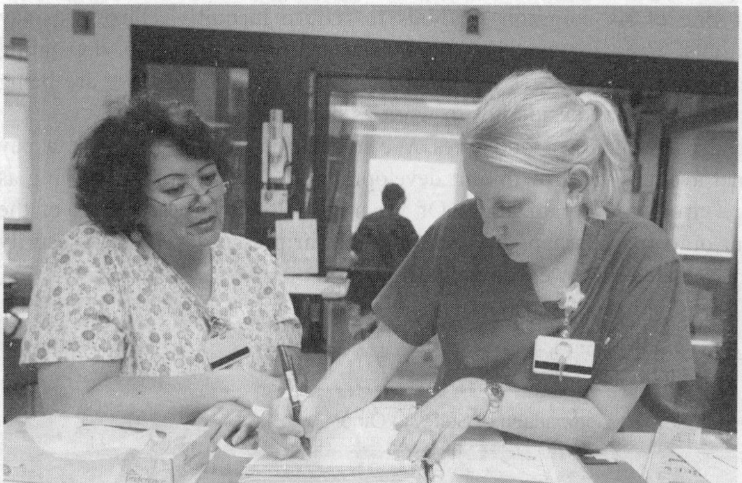

AP Photo/Rich Pedroncelli

The equity theory of motivation suggests that people compare themselves with others in terms of their inputs to their organization relative to their outcomes. But in these days of high-stress jobs and overworked employees, equity perceptions may be about as stable as a house of cards. Take Sherri Stoddard, for example. Stoddard is a registered nurse. Efforts to lower healthcare costs have caused nurses to take on ever-growing patient loads. In addition, they often have mandatory overtime requirements and mountains of paperwork. While their compensation has grown slightly, many nurses like Stoddard are feeling that they are being asked to do too much for what they are paid.

Equity theory describes the equity comparison process in terms of an input-to-outcome ratio. Inputs are an individual's contributions to the organization—such factors as education, experience, effort, and loyalty. Outcomes are what the person receives in return—pay, recognition, social relationships, intrinsic rewards, and similar things. In effect, then, this part of the equity process is essentially a personal assessment of one's psychological contract. A person's assessments of inputs and outcomes for both self and others are based partly on objective data (for example, the person's own salary) and partly on perceptions (such as the comparison-other's level of recognition). The equity comparison thus takes the following form:

$$\frac{\text{Outcome (self)}}{\text{Inputs (self)}} \text{ compared with } \frac{\text{Outcomes (other)}}{\text{Inputs (other)}}$$

If the two sides of this psychological equation are comparable, the person experiences a feeling of equity; if the two sides do not balance, a feeling of inequity results. We should stress, however, that a perception of equity does not require that the perceived outcomes and inputs be equal, but only that their ratios be the same. A person may believe that his comparison-other deserves to make more money because she works harder, thus making her outcomes (higher pay) acceptable because it is proportional to her higher input (harder work). Only if the other person's outcomes seem disproportionate to her inputs does the comparison provoke a perception of inequity.

Responses to Equity and Inequity Figure 4.4 summarizes the results of an equity comparison. If a person feels equitably treated, she is generally motivated to maintain the status quo. For example, she will continue to provide the same level of input to the organization as long as her outcomes do not change and the ratio of inputs and outcomes of the comparison-other do not change. But a person who is experiencing inequity—real or imagined—is motivated to reduce it. Moreover, the greater the inequity, the stronger the level of motivation.

People may use one of six common methods to reduce inequity.[34] First, we may change our own inputs. Thus, we may put more or less effort into the job, depending on which way the inequity lies, as a way to alter our ratio. If we believe we are being underpaid, for example, we may decide not to work as hard.

Second, we may change our own outcomes. We might, for example, demand a pay raise, seek additional avenues for growth and development, or even resort to stealing as a way to "get more" from the organization. Or we might alter our perceptions of the value of our current outcomes, perhaps by deciding that our present level of job security is greater and more valuable than we originally thought.

FIGURE 4.4

Responses to Perceptions of Equity and Inequity

People form equity perceptions by comparing their situation with that of someone else's. If they perceive equity, they are motivated to maintain the current situation. If they perceive inequity, they are motivated to use one or more of the strategies shown here to reduce the inequity.

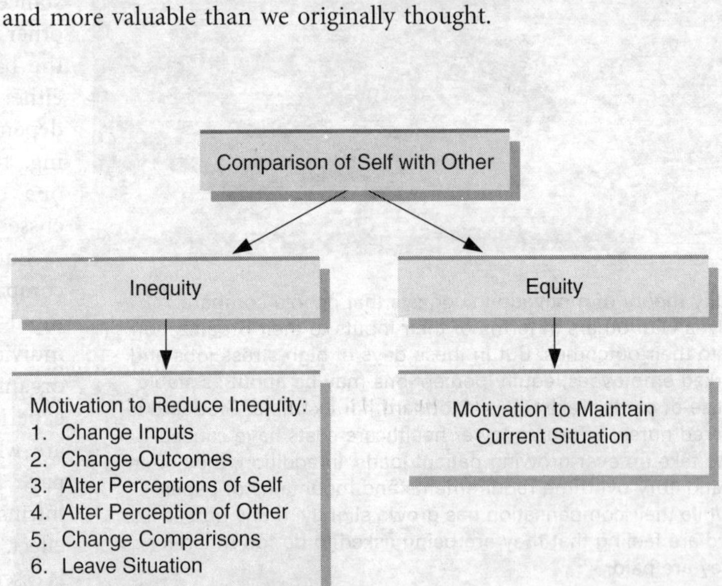

A third, more complex response is to alter our perceptions of ourselves and our behavior. After perceiving an inequity, for example, we may change our original self-assessment and decide that we are really contributing less but receiving more than we originally believed. For example, we might decide that we are not really working as many hours as we had first thought—admitting, perhaps, that some of our time spent in the office is really just socializing and not actually contributing to the organization.

Fourth, we may alter our perception of the comparison-other's inputs or outcomes. After all, much of our assessment of other people is based on perceptions, and perceptions can be changed. For example, if we feel underrewarded, we may decide that our comparison-other is working more hours than we originally believed—say by coming in on weekends and taking work home at night.

Fifth, we may change the object of comparison. We may conclude, for instance, that the current comparison-other is the boss's personal favorite, is unusually lucky, or has special skills and abilities. A different person would thus provide a more valid basis for comparison. Indeed, we might change comparison-others fairly often.

Finally, as a last resort, we may simply leave the situation. That is, we might decide that the only way to feel better about things is to be in a different situation altogether. Transferring to another department or seeking a new job may be the only way to reduce the inequity.

Evaluation and Implications Most research on equity theory has been narrowly focused, dealing with only one ratio—between pay (hourly and piece-rate) and the quality or quantity of worker output given overpayment and underpayment.[35] Findings support the predictions of equity theory quite consistently, especially when the worker feels underpaid. When workers being paid on a piece-rate basis experience inequity, they tend to reduce their inputs by decreasing quality and tend to increase their outcomes by producing more units of work. When a person paid by the hour experiences inequity, the theory predicts an increase in quality and quantity if the person feels overpaid and a decrease in quality and quantity if the person feels underpaid. Research provides stronger support for responses to underpayment than for responses to overpayment; overall, however, most studies appear to uphold the basic premises of the theory. One interesting new twist on equity theory suggests that some people are more sensitive than others to perceptions of inequity. That is, some people pay a good deal of attention to their relative standing within the organization. Others focus more on their own situation without considering the situations of others.[36]

Social comparisons clearly are a powerful factor in the workplace. For managers, the most important implication of equity theory concerns organizational rewards and reward systems. Because "formal" organizational rewards (pay, task assignments, and so forth) are more easily observable than "informal" rewards (intrinsic satisfaction, feelings of accomplishment, and so forth), they are often central to a person's perceptions of equity.

Equity theory offers managers three messages. First, everyone in the organization needs to understand the basis for rewards. If people are to be rewarded more for the quality of work rather than for quantity of work, for instance, that fact needs to be clearly communicated to everyone. Second, people tend to take a multifaceted view of their rewards; they perceive and experience a variety of rewards, some tangible and others intangible. Finally, people base their actions on their perceptions of reality. If two people make exactly the same salary but each thinks the other makes more, each will base his or her experience of equity on the perception, not the reality. Hence, even if a manager believes two employees are being fairly rewarded, the employees themselves may not necessarily agree if their perceptions differ from the manager's.

The Expectancy Theory of Motivation

Expectancy theory suggests that people are motivated by how much they want something and the likelihood they perceive of getting it.

Expectancy theory is a more encompassing model of motivation than equity theory. Over the years since its original formulation, the theory's scope and complexity have continued to grow.

The Basic Expectancy Model Victor Vroom is generally credited with first applying the theory to motivation in the workplace.[37] The theory attempts to determine how individuals choose among alternative behaviors. The basic premise of expectancy theory is that motivation depends on how much we want something and how likely we think we are to get it.

A simple example further illustrates this premise. Suppose a recent college graduate is looking for her first managerial job. While scanning the want ads, she sees that Shell Oil is seeking a new executive vice president to oversee its foreign operations. The starting salary is $1,500,000. The student would love the job, but she does not bother to apply because she recognizes that she has no chance of getting it. Reading on, she sees a position that involves scraping bubble gum from underneath desks in college classrooms. The starting pay is $7.25 an hour, and no experience is necessary. Again, she is unlikely to apply—even though she assumes she could get the job, she does not want it.

Then she comes across an advertisement for a management training position with a large company known for being an excellent place to work. No experience is necessary, the primary requirement is a college degree, and the starting salary is $40,000. She will probably apply for this position because (1) she wants it and (2) she thinks she has a reasonable chance of getting it. (Of course, this simple example understates the true complexity of most choices. Job-seeking students may have strong geographic preferences, have other job opportunities, and also be considering graduate school. Most decisions of this type, in fact, are quite complex.)

Figure 4.5 summarizes the basic expectancy model. The model's general components are effort (the result of motivated behavior), performance, and outcomes. Expectancy theory emphasizes the linkages among these elements, which are described in terms of expectancies and valences.

Effort-to-performance expectancy is a person's perception of the probability that effort will lead to performance.

Effort-to-Performance Expectancy **Effort-to-performance expectancy** is a person's perception of the probability that effort will lead to successful performance. If we believe our effort will lead to higher performance, this expectancy is very strong, perhaps

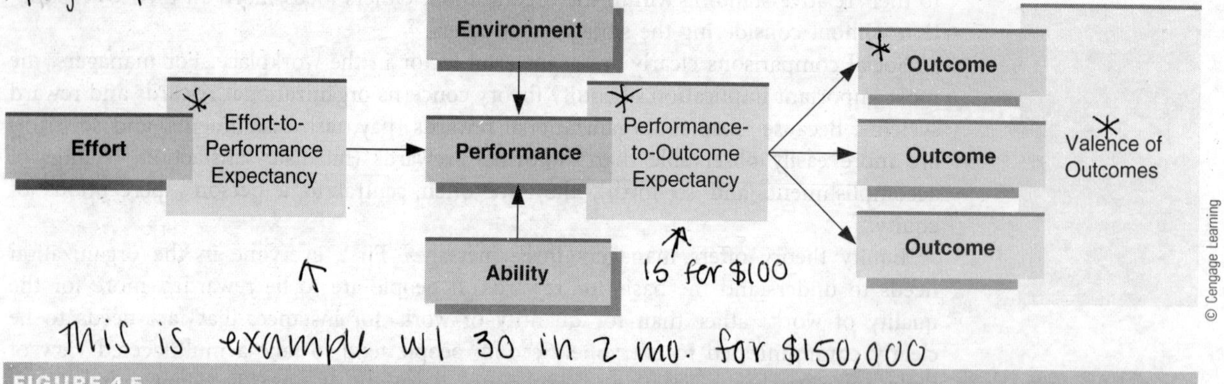

FIGURE 4.5

The Expectancy Theory of Motivation

The expectancy theory is the most complex model of employee motivation in organizations. As shown here, the key components of expectancy theory are effort-to-performance expectancy, performance-to-outcome expectancy, and outcomes, each of which has an associated valence. These components interact with effort, the environment, and the ability to determine an individual's performance.

Performance-to-outcome expectancy is the individual's perception of the probability that performance will lead to certain outcomes.

An **outcome** is anything that results from performing a particular behavior.

Valence is the degree of attractiveness or unattractiveness a particular outcome has for a person.

approaching a probability of 1.0, where 1.0 equals absolute certainty that the outcome will occur. If we believe our performance will be the same no matter how much effort we make, our expectancy is very low—perhaps as low as 0, meaning that there is no probability that the outcome will occur. A person who thinks there is a moderate relationship between effort and subsequent performance—the normal circumstance—has an expectancy somewhere between 1.0 and 0. Mia Hamm, a star soccer player who believes that when she puts forth maximum effort she has a great chance of scoring higher than any opponent, clearly sees a link between her effort and performance.

Performance-to-Outcome Expectancy **Performance-to-outcome expectancy** is a person's perception of the probability that performance will lead to certain other outcomes. If a person thinks a high performer is certain to get a pay raise, this expectancy is close to 1.0. At the other extreme, a person who believes raises are entirely independent of performance has an expectancy close to 0. Finally, if a person thinks performance has some bearing on the prospects for a pay raise, his or her expectancy is somewhere between 1.0 and 0. In a work setting, several performance-to-outcome expectancies are relevant because, as Figure 4.5 shows, several outcomes might logically result from performance. Each outcome, then, has its own expectancy. Denver Broncos quarterback Peyton Manning may believe that if he plays aggressively all the time (performance), he has a great chance of leading his team to the playoffs. Playing aggressively may win him individual honors like the Most Valuable Player award, but he may also experience more physical trauma and throw more interceptions. (All three anticipated results are outcomes.)

Isaiah Downing/Newscom

NFL quarterback Peyton Manning has clear expectancies regarding his capabilities. When an injury led his former team, the Indianapolis Colts, to release him Manning signed a new contract with the Denver Broncos because he believed that he still had the skills necessary to lead a team to the playoffs.

Outcomes and Valences An **outcome** is anything that might potentially result from performance. High-level performance conceivably might produce such outcomes as a pay raise, a promotion, recognition from the boss, fatigue, stress, or less time to rest, among others. The **valence** of an outcome is the relative attractiveness or unattractiveness—the value—of that outcome to the person. Pay raises, promotions, and recognition might all have positive valences, whereas fatigue, stress, and less time to rest might all have negative valences.

The strength of outcome valences varies from person to person. Work-related stress may be a significant negative factor for one person but only a slight annoyance to another. Similarly, a pay increase may have a strong positive valence for someone desperately in need of money, a slight positive valence for someone interested mostly in getting a promotion, or—for someone in an unfavorable tax position—even a negative valence!

The basic expectancy framework suggests that three conditions must be met before motivated behavior occurs. First, the effort-to-performance expectancy must be well above zero. That is, the worker must reasonably expect that exerting effort will produce high levels of performance. Second, the performance-to-outcome expectancies must be well above zero. In other words, the person must believe that performance will realistically result in valued outcomes. Third, the sum of all the valences for the potential outcomes relevant to the person

FIGURE 4.6

The Porter-Lawler Model

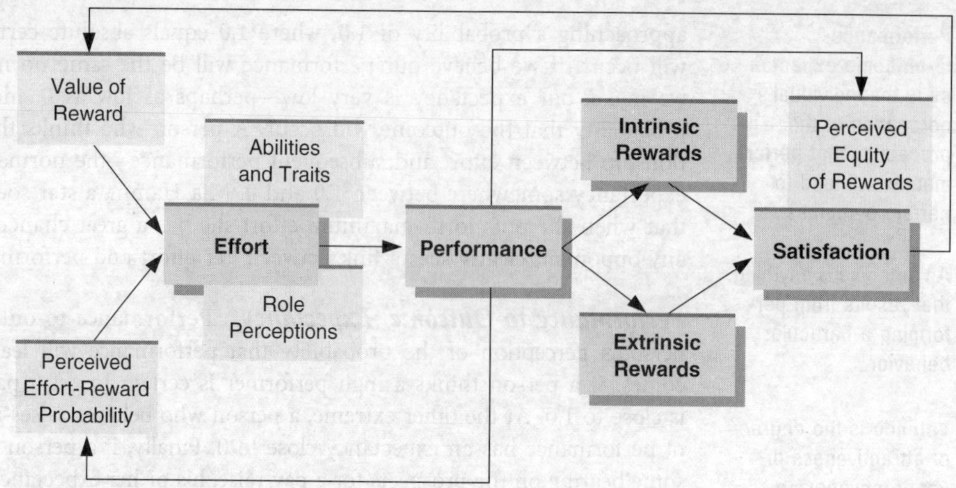

The Porter and Lawler expectancy model provides interesting insights into the relationships between satisfaction and performance. As illustrated here, this model predicts that satisfaction is determined by the perceived equity of intrinsic and extrinsic rewards for performance. That is, rather than satisfaction causing performance, which many people might predict, this model argues that it is actually performance that eventually leads to satisfaction.

Reference: Figure from Lyman W. Porter and Edward E. Lawler, *Managerial Attitudes and Performance.* Copyright © 1968. McGraw-Hill, Inc. Used by permission of Lyman W. Porter.

must be positive. One or more valences may be negative as long as the positives outweigh the negatives. For example, stress and fatigue may have moderately negative valences, but if pay, promotion, and recognition have very high positive valences, the overall valence of the set of outcomes associated with performance will still be positive.

Conceptually, the valences of all relevant outcomes and the corresponding pattern of expectancies are assumed to interact in an almost mathematical fashion to determine a person's level of motivation. Most people do assess likelihoods of and preferences for various consequences of behavior, but they seldom approach them in such a calculating manner.

The Porter-Lawler Model The original presentation of expectancy theory placed it squarely in the mainstream of contemporary motivation theory. Since then, the model has been refined and extended many times. Most modifications have focused on identifying and measuring outcomes and expectancies. An exception is the variation of expectancy theory developed by Porter and Lawler. These researchers used expectancy theory to develop a novel view of the relationship between employee satisfaction and performance.[38] Although the conventional wisdom was that satisfaction leads to performance, Porter and Lawler argued the reverse: If rewards are adequate, high levels of performance may lead to satisfaction.

The Porter-Lawler model appears in Figure 4.6. Some of its features are quite different from the original version of expectancy theory. For example, the extended model includes abilities, traits, and role perceptions. At the beginning of the motivational cycle, effort is a function of the value of the potential reward for the employee (its valence) and the perceived effort-reward probability (an expectancy). Effort then combines with abilities, traits, and role perceptions to determine actual performance.

Performance results in two kinds of rewards. Intrinsic rewards are intangible—a feeling of accomplishment, a sense of achievement, and so forth. Extrinsic rewards are tangible outcomes such as pay and promotion. The individual judges the value of his or her performance to the organization and uses social comparison processes (as in equity theory) to form an impression of the equity of the rewards received. If the rewards are regarded as equitable, the employee feels satisfied. In subsequent cycles, satisfaction with rewards influences the value of the rewards anticipated, and actual performance following effort influences future perceived effort-reward probabilities.

Evaluation and Implications Expectancy theory has been tested by many different researchers in a variety of settings and using a variety of methods.[39] As noted earlier, the complexity of the theory has been both a blessing and a curse.[40] Nowhere is this double-edged quality more apparent than in the research undertaken to evaluate the theory. Several studies have supported various parts of the theory. For example, both kinds of expectancy and valence have been found to be associated with effort and performance in the workplace.[41] Research has also confirmed expectancy theory's claims that people will not engage in motivated behavior unless they (1) value the expected rewards, (2) believe their efforts will lead to performance, and (3) believe their performance will result in the desired rewards.[42]

However, expectancy theory is so complicated that researchers have found it quite difficult to test. In particular, the measures of various parts of the model may lack validity, and the procedures for investigating relationships among the variables have often been less scientific than researchers would like. Moreover, people are seldom as rational and objective in choosing behaviors as expectancy theory implies. Still, the logic of the model, combined with the consistent, albeit modest, research support for it, suggests that the theory has much to offer.

Research has also suggested that expectancy theory is more likely to explain motivation in the United States than in other countries. People from the United States tend to be very goal oriented and tend to think that they can influence their own success. Thus, under the right combinations of expectancies, valences, and outcomes, they will be highly motivated. But different patterns may exist in other countries. For example, many people from Muslim countries think that God determines the outcome of every behavior, so the concept of expectancy is not applicable.[43]

Because expectancy theory is so complex, it is difficult to apply directly in the workplace. A manager would need to figure out what rewards each employee wants and how valuable those rewards are to each person, measure the various expectancies, and finally adjust the relationships to create motivation. Nevertheless, expectancy theory offers several important guidelines for the practicing manager. The following are some of the more fundamental guidelines:

1. Determine the primary outcomes each employee wants.
2. Decide what levels and kinds of performance are needed to meet organizational goals.
3. Make sure the desired levels of performance are possible.
4. Link desired outcomes and desired performance.
5. Analyze the situation for conflicting expectancies.
6. Make sure the rewards are large enough.
7. Make sure the overall system is equitable for everyone.[44]

LEARNING-BASED PERSPECTIVES ON MOTIVATION

Learning is a relatively permanent change in behavior or behavioral potential resulting from direct or indirect experience.

Learning is another key component in employee motivation. In any organization, employees quickly learn which behaviors are rewarded and which are ignored or punished. Thus, learning plays a critical role in maintaining motivated behavior. **Learning** is a relatively permanent change in behavior or behavioral potential that results from direct or indirect experience. For example, we can learn to use a new software application program by practicing and experimenting with its various functions and options.

How Learning Occurs

Classical conditioning is a simple form of learning that links a conditioned response with an unconditioned stimulus.

The Traditional View: Classical Conditioning The most influential historical approach to learning is classical conditioning, developed by Ivan Pavlov in his famous experiments with dogs.[45] **Classical conditioning** is a simple form of learning in which a conditioned response is linked with an unconditioned stimulus. In organizations, however, only simple behaviors and responses can be learned in this manner. For example, suppose an employee receives very bad news one day from his boss. It's possible that the employee could come to associate, say, the color of the boss's suit that day with bad news. Thus, the next time the boss wears that same suit to the office, the employee may experience dread and foreboding.

But this form of learning is obviously simplistic and not directly relevant to motivation. Learning theorists soon recognized that although classical conditioning offered some interesting insights into the learning process, it was inadequate as an explanation of human learning. For one thing, classical conditioning relies on simple cause-and-effect relationships between one stimulus and one response; it cannot deal with the more complex forms of learned behavior that typify human beings. For another, classical conditioning ignores the concept of choice; it assumes that behavior is reflexive, or involuntary. Therefore, this perspective cannot explain situations in which people consciously and rationally choose one course of action from among many. Because of these shortcomings of classical conditioning, theorists eventually moved on to other approaches that seemed more useful in explaining the processes associated with complex learning.

The Contemporary View: Learning as a Cognitive Process Although it is not tied to a single theory or model, contemporary learning theory generally views learning as a cognitive process; that is, it assumes that people are conscious, active participants in how they learn.[46]

First, the cognitive view suggests that people draw on their experiences and use past learning as a basis for their present behavior. These experiences represent knowledge, or cognitions. For example, an employee faced with a choice of job assignments will use previous experiences in deciding which one to accept. Second, people make choices about their behavior. The employee recognizes that she has two alternatives and chooses one. Third, people recognize the consequences of their choices. Thus, when the employee finds the job assignment rewarding and fulfilling, she will recognize that the choice was a good one and will understand why. Finally, people evaluate those consequences and add them to prior learning, which affects future choices. Faced with the same job choices next year, the employee will probably be motivated to choose the same one. As implied earlier, several perspectives on learning take a cognitive view. Perhaps foremost among them is reinforcement theory. Although reinforcement theory per se is not really new, it has only been applied to organizational settings in the last few years.

*we try to avoid negative consequences -> carrot + stick -> theory x

Reinforcement Theory and Learning

Reinforcement theory is based on the idea that behavior is a function of its consequences.

Reinforcement theory (also called "operant conditioning") is generally associated with the work of B. F. Skinner.[47] In its simplest form, **reinforcement theory** suggests that behavior is a function of its consequences.[48] Behavior that results in pleasant consequences is more likely to be repeated (the employee will be motivated to repeat the current behavior), and behavior that results in unpleasant consequences is less likely to be repeated (the employee will be motivated to engage in different behaviors). Reinforcement theory also suggests that in any given situation, people explore a variety of possible behaviors. Future behavioral choices are affected by the consequences of earlier behaviors. Cognitions, as already noted, also play an important role. Therefore, rather than

*types of reinforcement
+/-
extinction
punishment

assuming the mechanical stimulus-response linkage suggested by the traditional classical view of learning, contemporary theorists believe that people consciously explore different behaviors and systematically choose those that result in the most desirable outcomes.

Suppose a new employee at Monsanto in St. Louis wants to learn the best way to get along with his boss. At first, the employee is very friendly and informal, but the boss responds by acting aloof and, at times, annoyed. Because the boss does not react positively, the employee is unlikely to continue this behavior. In fact, the employee next starts acting more formal and professional and finds the boss much more receptive to this posture. The employee will probably continue this new set of behaviors because they have resulted in positive consequences.

The reinforcement process, however, isn't quite as clear cut as we may have suggested. The *Ethics* box entitled "What Does Reinforcement *Mean*?" on this page shows that certain other factors—factors that might skew a manager's judgment—may well be involved in an employee's performance.

ETHICS What Does Reinforcement *Mean*?

You're the general manager of a supermarket, and you've just finished a department-by-department year-end review of your managers' performances. Every department—meats, dairy, seafood, deli, bakery, and so forth—has performed up to or beyond expectations. All except one: Produce fell 12 percent short of upper management's forecast. You decide to reward all your managers with healthy bonuses except for your produce manager. In other words, you plan to use *punishment* in order to motivate your produce manager and *positive reinforcement* to motivate all of your other managers. You congratulate yourself for having reached a fair and logical decision.

> **"It's very difficult for people to detect their own errors. You're too busy making a mistake to detect it at the same time."**
> —PSYCHOLOGIST DANIEL KAHNEMAN

According to Daniel Kahneman, a psychologist who won the Nobel Prize in economics for his work on behavioral and decision-making models, your decision is probably not fair (at least not altogether), and it's certainly not logical—at least not when the reality of the situation is taken into consideration. Here's how Kahneman sees your two-pronged decision-making model:

Manager's department performs well →
You reward manager →
Department continues to perform well

Manager's department performs poorly →
You punish manager → Department performs better

The key to Kahneman's criticism is called *regression to the mean*—the principle that, *from one performance measurement to the next, the change in performance will be toward the overall average level of performance*. Say, for example, that you're a par golfer and that par for your course is 72. If you shoot 68 in one round, your next round will probably be *in the direction* of 72—not necessarily 72 exactly, which is your average, or 76, which would bring you exactly back to a two-round average of 72. Technically, regression to the mean is a *law*, and not a *rule*: You could shoot a second round of 70 or even 67, but *most of the time*, your second-round score won't be as good as your first-round score.

Why does regression to the mean occur? Because usually—and probably—a complex combination of factors determines any outcome. And because this combination is complex, it's not likely that the same combination will repeat itself the next time you measure the outcome. Which brings us back to your produce manager: *It's not likely that his managerial performance was the sole (or even necessarily the primary) factor in his department's poor performance.* Other factors might include variations in competition, economic and market conditions, and decisions made by managers above him—all of which are largely random and which will undoubtedly be different from one performance measurement to the next.

Now that you understand a little about the reality of regression to the mean, compare your decision-making model to a model that reflects reality:

Manager's department performs well →
Department probably does not perform as well

Manager's department performs poorly →
Department probably performs better

Your reinforcement decision will *probably* have little or nothing to do with next year's outcome in any of your store's departments. And you've *probably* been unfair to your produce manager.

Kahneman isn't inclined to be overly critical of your mistaken belief that you've made a logical, fair, and effective decision: "It's very difficult for people to detect their own errors," he admits. "You're too busy making a mistake to detect it at the same time." He does, however, reserve the right to be pessimistic: "The failure to recognize the import of regression," he warns,

> *can have pernicious consequences.... We normally reinforce others when their behavior is good and punish them when their behavior is bad. By regression alone [however], they are most likely to improve after being punished and most likely to deteriorate after being rewarded. Consequently, we are exposed to a lifetime schedule in which we are most often rewarded for punishing others and punished for rewarding [them].*

References: Bryan Burke, "Fighter Pilots and Firing Coaches," *Advanced NFL Stats*, February 19, 2009, www.advancednflstats.com on April 21, 2012; David Hall, "Daniel Kahneman Interview," *New Zealand Listener*, January 21, 2012, www.listener.co.nz on April 21, 2012; Steve Miller, "We're Not Very Good Statisticians," *Information Management*, March 26, 2012, www.information-management.com on April 21, 2012; Galen Strawson, "*Thinking, Fast and Slow* by Daniel Kahneman—Review," *The Guardian*, December 13, 2011, www.guardian.co.uk on April 21, 2012; *Judgment under Uncertainty: Heuristics and Biases*, ed. Daniel Kahneman, Paul Slovic, and Amos Tversky (Cambridge, UK: Cambridge University Press, 1982), http://books.google.com on April 21, 2012.

Reinforcements are the consequences of behavior.

Positive reinforcement is a reward or other desirable consequence that a person receives after exhibiting behavior.

Avoidance, or **negative reinforcement**, is the opportunity to avoid or escape from an unpleasant circumstance after exhibiting behavior.

Extinction decreases the frequency of behavior by eliminating a reward or desirable consequence that follows that behavior.

Types of Reinforcement in Organizations The consequences of behavior are called **reinforcement**. Managers can use various kinds of reinforcement to affect employee behavior. There are four basic forms of reinforcement—positive reinforcement, avoidance, extinction, and punishment.

Positive reinforcement is a reward or other desirable consequence that follows behavior. Providing positive reinforcement after a particular behavior motivates employees to maintain or increase the frequency of that behavior. A compliment from the boss after an employee has completed a difficult job and a salary increase following a worker's period of high performance are examples of positive reinforcement. This type of reinforcement has been used at Corning's ceramics factory in Virginia, where workers receive bonuses for pulling blemished materials from assembly lines before they go into more expensive stages of production. Intuit has started a program of giving relatively small but relatively frequent rewards when workers perform well. So, for example, rather than getting one large bonus at the end of the year, a high performer may get several smaller ones throughout the year.[49]

Avoidance, also known as **negative reinforcement**, is another means of increasing the frequency of desirable behavior. Rather than receiving a reward following a desirable behavior, the person is given the opportunity to avoid an unpleasant consequence. For example, suppose that a boss habitually criticizes employees who dress casually. To avoid criticism, an employee may routinely dress to suit the supervisor's tastes. The employee is thus motivated to engage in desirable behavior (at least from the supervisor's viewpoint) to avoid an unpleasant, or aversive, consequence.

Extinction decreases the frequency of behavior, especially behavior that was previously rewarded. If rewards are withdrawn for behaviors that were previously reinforced, the behaviors will probably become less frequent and eventually die out. For example, a manager with a small staff may encourage frequent visits from subordinates as a way of keeping in touch with what is going on. Positive reinforcement might include cordial conversation, attention to subordinates' concerns, and encouragement to come in again soon. As the staff grows, however, the manager may find that such unstructured conversations make it difficult to get her own job done. She then might begin to brush off casual conversation and reward only to-the-point "business" conversations. Withdrawing the rewards for casual chatting will probably extinguish that behavior. We should also note that if managers, inadvertently or otherwise, stop rewarding valuable behaviors such as good performance, those behaviors also may become extinct.

Punishment is an unpleasant, or aversive, consequence that results from behavior.

Punishment, like extinction, also tends to decrease the frequency of undesirable behaviors. Punishment is an unpleasant, or aversive, consequence of a behavior.[50] Examples of punishment are verbal or written reprimands, pay cuts, loss of privileges, layoffs, and termination. Many experts question the value of punishment and believe that managers use it too often and use it inappropriately. In some situations, however, punishment may be an appropriate tool for altering behavior. Many instances of life's unpleasantness teach us what to do by means of punishment. Falling off a bike, drinking too much, or going out in the rain without an umbrella all lead to punishing consequences (getting bruised, suffering a hangover, and getting wet), and we often learn to change our behavior as a result. Furthermore, certain types of undesirable behavior may have far-reaching negative effects if they go unpunished. For instance, an employee who sexually harasses a coworker, a clerk who steals money from the petty cash account, and an executive who engages in illegal stock transactions all deserve punishment.

Schedules of reinforcement indicate when or how often managers should reinforce certain behaviors.

Schedules of Reinforcement in Organizations Should the manager try to reward every instance of desirable behavior and punish every instance of undesirable behavior? Or is it better to apply reinforcement according to some plan or schedule? As you might expect, it depends on the situation. Table 4.1 summarizes five basic **schedules of reinforcement** that managers can use.

With **continuous reinforcement**, behavior is rewarded every time it occurs.

Continuous reinforcement rewards behavior every time it occurs. Continuous reinforcement is very effective in motivating desirable behaviors, especially in the early stages of learning. When reinforcement is withdrawn, however, extinction sets in very quickly. But continuous reinforcement poses serious difficulties because the manager must

Table 4.1 Schedules of Reinforcement

SCHEDULE OF REINFORCEMENT	NATURE OF REINFORCEMENT
Command Groups	**Task Groups**
Continuous	Behavior is reinforced every time it occurs.
Fixed-Interval	Behavior is reinforced according to some predetermined, constant schedule based on time.
Variable-Interval	Behavior is reinforced after periods of time, but the time span varies from one time to the next.
Fixed-Ratio	Behavior is reinforced according to the number of behaviors exhibited, with the number of behaviors needed to gain reinforcement held constant.
Variable-Ratio	Behavior is reinforced according to the number of behaviors exhibited, but the number of behaviors needed to gain reinforcement varies from one time to the next.

Nuccio DiNuzzo/KRT/Newscom

Fixed-interval reinforcement schedules are among the most widely used but least effective ways of supplying reinforcement. One method managers can use to offset this is to drop by on a variable ratio basis and supply verbal encouragement like this manager is doing. But of course if the schedule for verbal encouragement becomes too predictable then it, too, becomes fixed interval in nature.

monitor every behavior of an employee and provide effective reinforcement. This approach, then, is of little practical value to managers. Offering partial reinforcement according to one of the other four schedules is much more typical.

Fixed-interval reinforcement is reinforcement provided on a predetermined, constant schedule. The Friday-afternoon paycheck is a good example of a fixed-interval reinforcement. Unfortunately, in many situations the fixed-interval schedule does not necessarily maintain high performance levels. If employees know the boss will drop by to check on them every day at 1:00 p.m., they may be motivated to work hard at that time, hoping to gain praise and recognition or to avoid the boss's wrath. At other times of the day, the employees probably will not work as hard because they have learned that reinforcement is unlikely except during the daily visit.

Fixed-interval reinforcement provides reinforcement on a fixed time schedule.

Variable-interval reinforcement varies the amount of time between reinforcements.

Variable-interval reinforcement also uses time as the basis for applying reinforcement, but it varies the interval between reinforcements. This schedule is inappropriate for paying wages, but it can work well for other types of positive reinforcement, such as praise and recognition, and for avoidance. Consider again the group of employees just described. Suppose that instead of coming by at exactly 1:00 p.m. every day, the boss visits at a different time each day: 9:30 a.m. on Monday, 2:00 p.m. on Tuesday, 11:00 a.m. on Wednesday, and so on. The following week, the times change. Because the employees do not know exactly when to expect the boss, they may be motivated to work hard for a longer period—until her visit. Afterward, though, they may drop back to lower levels because they have learned that she will not be back until the next day.

Fixed-ratio reinforcement provides reinforcement after a fixed number of behaviors.

The fixed- and variable-ratio schedules gear reinforcement to the number of desirable or undesirable behaviors rather than to blocks of time. With **fixed-ratio reinforcement**, the number of behaviors needed to obtain reinforcement is constant. Assume, for instance, that a work group enters its cumulative performance totals into the firm's computer network every hour. The manager of the group uses the network to monitor its activities. He might adopt a practice of dropping by to praise the group every time it reaches a performance level of 500 units. Thus, if the group does this three times on Monday, he stops by each time; if it reaches the mark only once on Tuesday, he stops by only once. The fixed-ratio schedule can be fairly effective in maintaining desirable behavior. Employees may acquire a sense of what it takes to be reinforced and may be motivated to maintain their performance.

Variable-ratio reinforcement varies the number of behaviors between reinforcements.

With **variable-ratio reinforcement**, the number of behaviors required for reinforcement varies over time. An employee performing under a variable-ratio schedule is motivated to work hard because each successful behavior increases the probability that the next one will result in reinforcement. With this schedule, the exact number of behaviors needed to obtain reinforcement is not crucial; what is important is that the intervals between reinforcement not be so long that the worker gets discouraged and stops trying. The supervisor in the fixed-ratio example could reinforce his work group after it reaches performance levels of 325, 525, 450, 600, and so on. A variable-ratio schedule can be quite effective, but it is difficult and cumbersome to use when formal organizational rewards, such as pay increases and promotions, are the reinforcers. A fixed-interval system is the best way to administer these rewards.

Social Learning in Organizations

Social learning occurs when people observe the behaviors of others, recognize their consequences, and alter their own behavior as a result.

In recent years, managers have begun to recognize the power of social learning. **Social learning** occurs when people observe the behaviors of others, recognize their consequences, and alter their own behavior as a result. A person can learn to do a new job by observing others or by watching videotapes. Or an employee may learn to avoid being late by seeing the boss chew out fellow workers. Social learning theory, then, suggests that individual behavior is determined by a person's cognitions and social environment. More specifically, people are presumed to learn behaviors and attitudes at least partly in response to what others expect of them.

Several conditions must be met to produce an appropriate environment for social learning. First, the behavior being observed and imitated must be relatively simple. Although we can learn by watching someone else how to push three or four buttons to set specifications on a machine or to turn on a computer, we probably cannot learn a complicated sequence of operations for the machine or how to run a complex software package without also practicing the various steps ourselves. Second, social learning usually involves observed and imitated behavior that is concrete, not intellectual. We can learn by watching others how to respond to the different behaviors of a particular manager or how to assemble a few component parts into a final assembled product. But we probably cannot learn through simple observation how to write computer software, how to write complicated text, how to conceptualize, or how to think abstractly. Finally, for social learning to occur, we must possess the physical ability to imitate the behavior observed. Most of us, even if we watch televised baseball games or tennis matches every weekend, cannot hit a fastball like Miguel Cabrera or execute a backhand like Venus Williams.

Social learning influences motivation in a variety of ways. Many of the behaviors we exhibit in our daily work lives are learned from others. Suppose a new employee joins an existing work group. She already has some basis for knowing how to behave from her education and previous experience. However, the group provides a set of very specific cues she can use to tailor her behavior to fit her new situation. The group may indicate how the organization expects its members to dress, how people are "supposed" to feel about the boss, and so forth. Hence, the employee learns how to behave in the new situation partly in response to what she already knows and partly in response to what others suggest and demonstrate.

As we showed in our opening vignette on NetApp, social learning can be a significant factor in developing a satisfying workplace. In continuing our discussion of NetApp, the "Change" box shows that, under certain adverse conditions, even the most successful motivational techniques have limitations.

Organizational Behavior Modification

Learning theory alone has important implications for managers, but organizational behavior modification has even more practical applications. Organizational behavior modification is an important application of reinforcement theory some managers use to enhance motivation and performance.

Organizational behavior modification, or **OB mod**, is the application of reinforcement theory to people in organizational settings.

Behavior Modification in Organizations **Organizational behavior modification**, or **OB mod**, is the application of reinforcement theory to people in organizational settings.[51] Reinforcement theory says that we can increase the frequency of desirable behaviors by linking those behaviors with positive consequences and decrease undesirable

FIGURE 4.7

Steps in Organizational Behavior Modification

Organizational behavior modification involves using reinforcement theory to motivate employee behavior. By employing the steps shown here, managers can often isolate behaviors they value and then link specific rewards to those behaviors. As a result, employees will be more likely to engage in those behaviors in the future.

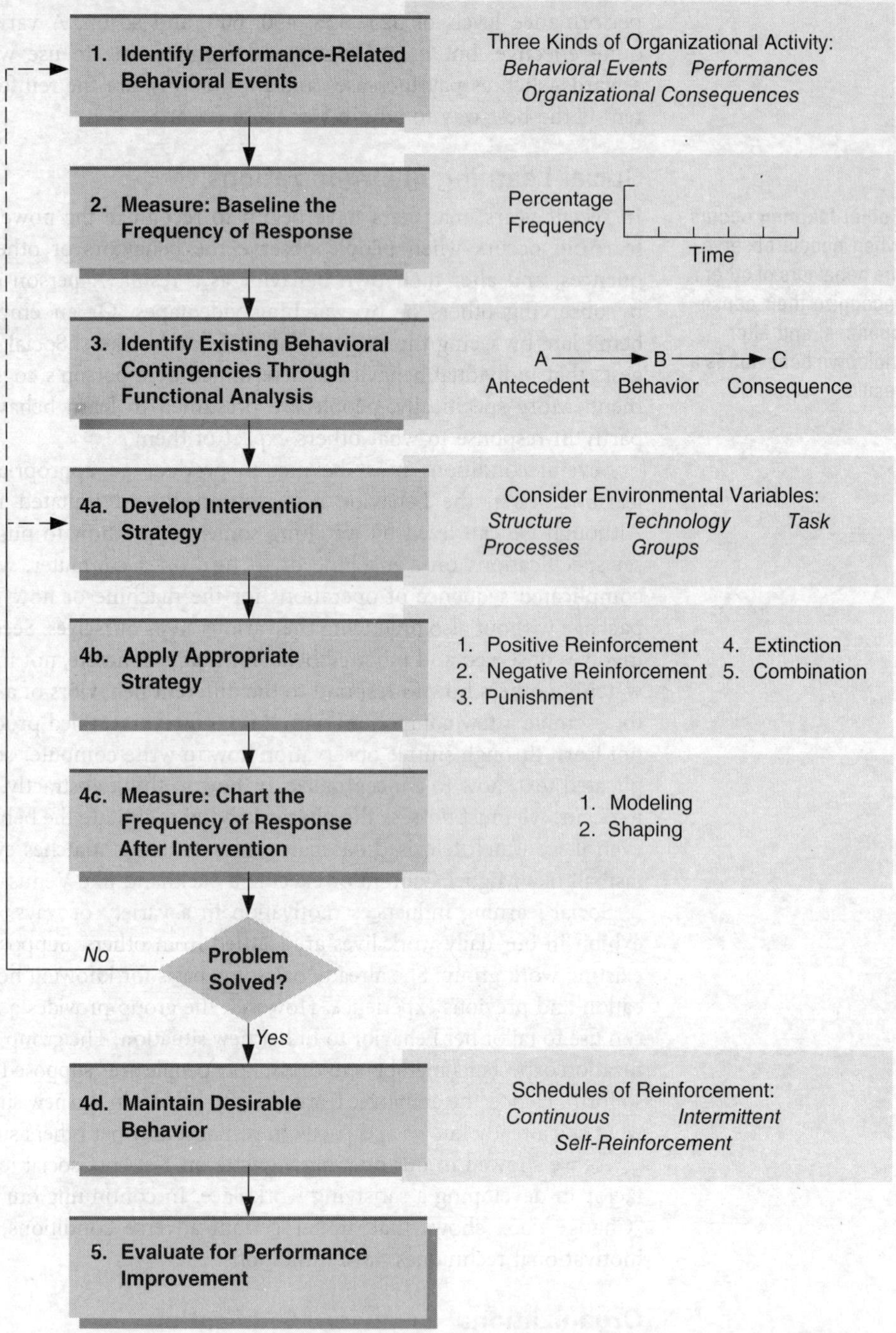

Reference: "Steps in Organizational Behavior Modification" from *Personnel,* July–August 1974. Copyright © 1974 American Management Association. Reprinted by permission.

behaviors by linking them with negative consequences. OB mod characteristically uses positive reinforcement to encourage desirable behaviors in employees. Figure 4.7 illustrates the basic steps in OB mod.

The first step is to identify performance-related behavioral events—that is, desirable and undesirable behaviors. A manager of an electronics store might decide that the most important behavior for salespeople working on commission is to greet customers warmly and show them the exact merchandise they came in to see. Note in Figure 4.7 that three kinds of organizational activity are associated with this behavior: the behavioral event itself, the performance that results, and the organizational consequences that befall the individual.

Next, the manager measures baseline performance—the existing level of performance for each individual. This usually is stated in terms of a percentage frequency across different time intervals. For example, the electronics store manager may observe that a particular salesperson presently is greeting around 40 percent of the customers each day as desired. Performance management techniques, described in Chapter 6, are used for this purpose.

The third step is to identify the existing behavioral contingencies, or consequences, of performance; that is, what happens now to employees who perform at various levels? If an employee works hard, does he or she get a reward or just get tired? The electronics store manager may observe that when customers are greeted warmly and assisted competently, they buy something 40 percent of the time, whereas customers who are not properly greeted and assisted make a purchase only 20 percent of the time.

At this point, the manager develops and applies an appropriate intervention strategy. In other words, some element of the performance-reward linkage—structure, process, technology, groups, or task—is changed to make high-level performance more rewarding. Various kinds of positive reinforcement are used to guide employee behavior in desired directions. The electronics store manager might offer a sales commission plan whereby salespeople earn a percentage of the dollar amount taken in by each sale. The manager might also compliment salespeople who give appropriate greetings and ignore those who do not. This reinforcement helps shape the behavior of salespeople. In addition, an individual salesperson who does not get reinforced may imitate the behavior of more successful salespersons. In general, this step relies on the reward system in the organization, as discussed previously.

After the intervention step, the manager again measures performance to determine whether the desired effect has been achieved. If not, the manager must redesign the intervention strategy or repeat the entire process. For instance, if the salespeople in the electronics store are still not greeting customers properly, the manager may need to look for other forms of positive reinforcement—perhaps a higher commission.

If performance has increased, the manager must try to maintain the desirable behavior through some schedule of positive reinforcement. For example, higher commissions might be granted for every other sale, for sales over a certain dollar amount, and so forth. (As we saw earlier, a reinforcement schedule defines the interval at which reinforcement is given.)

Finally, the manager looks for improvements in individual employees' behavior. Here the emphasis is on offering significant longer-term rewards, such as promotions and salary adjustments, to sustain ongoing efforts to improve performance.

The Effectiveness of OB Mod Because the OB mod approach is relatively simple, it has been used by many types of organizations, with varying levels of success.[52] A program at Emery Air Freight prompted much of the initial enthusiasm for OB mod, and other success stories have caught the attention of practicing managers.[53] B. F. Goodrich increased productivity more than 300 percent and Weyerhaeuser increased productivity by at least 8 percent in three different work groups.[54] These results suggest that OB mod is a valuable method for improving employee motivation in many situations.

OB mod also has certain drawbacks. For one thing, not all applications have worked. A program at Standard Oil of Ohio was discontinued because it failed to meet its objectives; another program at Michigan Bell was only modestly successful. In addition, managers frequently have only limited means for providing meaningful reinforcement for their employees. Furthermore, much of the research testing OB mod has gone on in laboratories and thus is hard to generalize to the real world. And even if OB mod works for a while, the impact of the positive reinforcement may wane once the novelty has worn off, and employees may come to view it as a routine part of the compensation system.[55]

The Ethics of OB Mod Although OB mod has considerable potential for enhancing motivated behavior in organizations, its critics raise ethical issues about its use. The primary ethical argument is that use of OB mod compromises individual freedom of choice. Managers may tend to select reinforcement contingencies that produce advantages for the organization with little or no regard for what is best for the individual employee. Thus, workers may be rewarded for working hard, producing high-quality products, and so forth. Behaviors that promote their own personal growth and development or that reduce their level of personal stress may go unrewarded.

An element of manipulation is also involved in OB mod. Indeed, its very purpose is to shape the behaviors of others. Thus, rather than giving employees an array of behaviors from which to choose, managers may continually funnel employee efforts through an increasingly narrow array of behavioral options so that they eventually have little choice but to select the limited set behaviors approved of by managers.

These ethical issues are, of course, real concerns that should not be ignored. At the same time, many other methods and approaches used by managers have the same goal of shaping behavior. Thus, OB mod is not really unique in its potential for misuse or misrepresentation. The keys are for managers to recognize and not abuse their ability to alter subordinate behavior and for employees to maintain control of their own work environment to the point that they are fully cognizant of the behavioral choices they are making.

SYNOPSIS

Motivation is the set of forces that cause people to behave as they do. Motivation starts with a need. People search for ways to satisfy their needs and then behave accordingly. Their behavior results in rewards or punishment. To varying degrees, an outcome may satisfy the original need. Scientific management asserted that money is the primary human motivator in the workplace. The human relations view suggested that social factors are primary motivators.

According to Abraham Maslow, human needs are arranged in a hierarchy of importance, from physiological to security to belongingness to esteem to, finally, self-actualization. The ERG theory is a refinement of Maslow's original hierarchy that includes a frustration-regression component. In Herzberg's dual-structure theory, satisfaction and dissatisfaction are two distinct dimensions instead of opposite ends of the same dimension. Motivation factors are presumed to affect satisfaction and hygiene factors are presumed to affect dissatisfaction. Herzberg's theory is well known among managers but has several deficiencies. Other important individual needs include the needs for achievement, affiliation, and power.

The equity theory of motivation assumes that people want to be treated fairly. It hypothesizes that people compare their own input-to-outcome ratio in the organization with the ratio of a comparison-other. If they feel their treatment has been inequitable, they take steps to reduce the inequity. Expectancy theory, a somewhat more complicated model, follows from the assumption that people are motivated to work toward a goal if they want it and think that they have a reasonable chance of achieving it. Effort-to-performance expectancy is the belief that effort will lead to performance. Performance-to-outcome expectancy is the belief that performance will lead to certain outcomes. Valence is the desirability to the individual of the various possible outcomes of performance. The Porter-Lawler version of expectancy theory provides useful insights into the relationship between satisfaction and performance. This model suggests that performance may lead to a variety of intrinsic and extrinsic rewards. When perceived as equitable, these rewards lead to satisfaction.

Learning also plays a role in employee motivation. Various kinds of reinforcement provided according to different schedules can increase or decrease motivated behavior. People are affected by social learning processes. Organizational behavior modification is a strategy for using learning and reinforcement principles to enhance employee motivation and performance. This strategy relies heavily on the effective measurement of performance and the provision of rewards to employees after they perform at a high level.

DISCUSSION QUESTIONS

1. Is it possible for someone to be unmotivated, or is all behavior motivated?
2. When has your level of performance been directly affected by your motivation? By your ability? By the environment?
3. Identify examples from your own experience that support, and others that refute, Maslow's hierarchy of needs theory.
4. Do you agree or disagree with the basic assumptions of Herzberg's dual-structure theory? Why?
5. How do you evaluate yourself in terms of your needs for achievement, affiliation, and power?
6. Have you ever experienced inequity in a job or a class? How did it affect you?
7. Which is likely to be a more serious problem—perceptions of being underrewarded or perceptions of being overrewarded?
8. What are some managerial implications of equity theory beyond those discussed in the chapter?
9. Do you think expectancy theory is too complex for direct use in organizational settings? Why or why not?
10. Do the relationships between performance and satisfaction suggested by Porter and Lawler seem valid? Cite examples that both support and refute the model.
11. Think of occasions on which you experienced each of the four types of reinforcement.
12. Identify the five forms of reinforcement that you receive most often (i.e., wages, grades, etc.). On what schedule do you receive each of them?
13. What is your opinion about the ethics of OB mod?

HOW DO YOU SEE IT?

A Socially Conscious Company

"When people are excited about something, they'll do virtually anything."

—BRAM LEVY, GLOBAL DIRECTOR, LIVINGSOCIAL ADVENTURES

When she was a student at Dartmouth, Maia Josebachvili wanted to go skydiving but couldn't afford it. It occurred to her, however, that if she organized a whole group of paying customers for a skydiving excursion, she could go along for free. Thus was born the idea for Urban Escapes, which Josebachvili started in 2008 to offer excursions for New Yorkers looking for a weekend of white-water rafting, mountain climbing, or perhaps just apple picking.

In looking around for a career, says Josebachvili in our video, "I was most drawn to creating my own thing," and as she adds elsewhere, Urban Escapes "started as a passion product. I mean, this is who I am. I spend my weekends mountain biking, rock climbing, and skydiving and then drinking beers at a brewery." The fun factor is what also attracted Josebachvili's eventual co-owner: "I was motivated to join Urban Escapes," says Bram Levy, "purely because it seemed like something fun to do. I was really lucky to have the opportunity to try something new and fun and exciting, and if it didn't work out," he admits, "… I could always come back to the safe world" (which, for Levy, was "the consulting world").

About four months after starting out, 25-year-old Josebachvili had sought out 29-year-old Levy to help her expand the business, and by mid-2010, Urban Escapes had outlets in Boston, Philadelphia, and Washington, D.C. The company soon added offices in San Francisco, Chicago, and Austin, Texas, bringing the workforce to a grand total of nine full-time employees (New York also required a full-time manager) and 50 part-timers to run weekend events. Levy admits that he was surprised by the eagerness of people to buy into the Urban Escapes concept. It wasn't the money: "If someone is working for us solely to get rich," he advises, "I'm guessing they made a poor choice." From the beginning, however, "we had employees across the country working for us for virtually no income and no stability, merely because they enjoyed what we had to offer. And," Levy hastens to point out, "they were having fun."

Since joining Urban Escapes, Levy has come to the conclusion that "when people are excited about something, they'll do virtually anything." Josebachvili agrees that it's a matter of "passion," but she's also convinced that people gravitate toward Urban Escapes because it offers them an opportunity for satisfaction in their work lives: "It sounds so cheesy," she says, "but I think it was really the passion and everyone's belief that this was going to work" that allowed Urban Escapes to take off.

Similarly, Levy's motives for joining the company involved both personal and career goals. Becoming part of Urban Escapes, he explains, "was really a unique opportunity." Josebachvili "was somebody who was really passionate and exciting to work with," but equally important was the promise of satisfying his desire to help run a successful business. Urban Escapes, he tells us, was "an idea that I truly believed in [and] thought could work," and it offered him "a chance to run my own business again without a tremendous amount of financial or personal risk."

In fact, the most important decision that Josebachvili and Levy have made during their company's brief existence was a major business decision. In October 2010, they sold Urban Escapes—as well as themselves and their first six full-time employees—to a company called LivingSocial. Founded in the same year as Urban Escapes, LivingSocial is an online coupon or "daily deal" site that allows members to search its "local activity discovery engine" to find restaurants, activities, and services offering discounts of up to 50 to 70 percent. (Its best-known competitor is market leader Groupon.) In 2010 (its last year as a stand-alone business), Urban Escapes attracted about 12,000 customers and took in $1 million in revenue. LivingSocial, which now has 60 million members worldwide and 4,900 employees, had revenues of $100 million in 2010 and $224 million in 2011.

The "acquisition thing," says Josebachvili, reflects the commitment of both companies to doing things that are both fun and worthwhile. "LivingSocial contacted us, and they said, 'Hey, we love what you do, and we think that if we all do it together, we can all do it better.' And we thought about it for about a day" and agreed. She also foresees a synergy of passion and expansion: "We're passionate," she explains in another interview, "about organizing experiences you could never arrange on your own, and this acquisition is the perfect opportunity for us to expand these completely unique, guided experiences around the globe."

CASE QUESTIONS

1. Clearly, both Josebachvili and Levy are highly *self-motivated* people and managers. Judging from the video, what traits do you see in them that probably contribute to self-motivated behavior, both in and out of the workplace? And what about you? What traits do you share with Josebachvili and/or Levy? In what respects do you differ? In what areas would you make personal improvements?
2. Apply the *human resource approach* to motivation to Josebachvili and Levy's practices as managers. How well—and in what specific ways—does it seem to characterize their approach to managing employees? How might these practices change as a result of the acquisition of Urban Escapes by LivingSocial?
3. Maslow's *hierarchy of needs* theory is also used by some psychologists to describe people's personalities. What can you tell about Josebachvili's personality by applying this theory to her? As a theory of motivation, how well—or poorly—does Maslow's hierarchy of needs theory of motivation apply to Josebachvili? Perform the same exercise by applying *ERG theory* to Josebachvili.
4. In what ways do Levy and, especially, Josebachvili appear to be satisfying *needs for achievement, affiliation,* and *power*? Rank these three needs in order of importance to each of them. In what ways do they appear to recognize these same needs in their employees?
5. In what ways does the *expectancy theory* of motivation explain Josebachvili's life and career choices since she left high school? Be methodical in your response: In order, apply the *basic model* by explaining the roles of *effort-to-performance expectancy, performance-to-outcome expectancy,* and *outcomes and valences.*

ADDITIONAL SOURCES

"How Maia Josebachvili Turned Her Skydiving Hobby into a Business," *Fast Company.com*, October 19, 2010, www.fastcompany.com on June 13, 2012; Dave Blake, "Interview with Maia Josebachvili, CEO of Urban Escapes NYC," *New York City Interview*, May 29, 2009, www.nycinterviews.com on June 13, 2012; Tiffany Black, "30 under 30: Maia Josebachvili and Bram Levy, Owners of Urban Escapes," *Inc.*, July 19, 2010, www.inc.com on June 13, 2012; Donna Fenn, "Living Social and Urban Escapes: A 30 under 30 Marriage," *Inc.*, October 19, 2010, www.inc.com on June 13, 2012; Riley McDermid, "LivingSocial Acquires Urban Escapes to Take Lead in Daily Deal War," *VentureBeat*, October 19, 2010, www.venturebeat .com on June 13, 2012.

EXPERIENCING ORGANIZATIONAL BEHAVIOR

Understanding the Dynamics of Expectancy Theory

Purpose: This exercise will help you recognize both the potential value and the complexity of expectancy theory.

Format: Working alone, you will be asked to identify the various aspects of expectancy theory that are pertinent to your class. You will then share your thoughts and results with some of your classmates.

Procedure: Considering your class as a workplace and your effort in the class as a surrogate for a job, do the following:

1. Identify six or seven things that might happen as a result of good performance in your class (for example, getting a good grade or a recommendation from your instructor). Your list must include at least one undesirable outcome (for example, a loss of free time).
2. Using a value of 10 for "extremely desirable," 10 for "extremely undesirable," and 0 for "complete neutrality," assign a valence to each outcome. In other words, the valence you assign to each outcome should be somewhere between 10 and 10, inclusive.
3. Assume you are a high performer. On that basis, estimate the probability of each potential outcome. Express this probability as a percentage.
4. Multiply each valence by its associated probability and add the results. This total is your overall valence for high performance.
5. Assess the probability that if you exert effort, you will be a high performer. Express that probability as a percentage.
6. Multiply this probability by the overall valence for high performance calculated in step 4. This score reflects your motivational force—that is, your motivation to exert strong effort.

Now form groups of three or four. Compare your scores on motivational force. Discuss why some scores differ widely. Also, note whether any group members had similar force scores but different combinations of factors leading to those scores.

Follow-Up Questions

1. What does this exercise tell you about the strengths and limitations of expectancy theory?
2. Would this exercise be useful for a manager to run with a group of subordinates? Why or why not?

BUILDING MANAGERIAL SKILLS

Exercise Overview Interpersonal skills refer to the ability to communicate with, understand, and motivate individuals and groups, and communication skills refer to the ability to send and receive information effectively. This exercise is designed to demonstrate the essential roles played in employee motivation by an understanding of what motivates people and an ability to communicate that understanding.

Exercise Background One implication of reinforcement theory is that both positive reinforcement (reward) and punishment can be effective in altering employee behavior. The use of punishment, however, may result in resentment on the employee's part, and over the long term, the resentment can diminish the effectiveness of the punishment. By and large, positive reinforcement is more effective over time.

Exercise Task Your instructor will ask for volunteers to perform a demonstration in front of the class. Consider volunteering, but if you don't want to participate, observe the behavior of the volunteers closely. When the demonstration is over, respond to the following questions:

1. Based on what you saw, which is more effective—positive reinforcement or punishment?
2. How did positive reinforcement and punishment affect the "employee" in the demonstration? How did it affect the "boss"?
3. What, in your opinion, are the likely long-term consequences of positive reinforcement and punishment?

Reference

Ricky W. Griffin, *Management*, 10th ed. (Mason, OH: South Western Educational Publishing, 2010).

SELF-ASSESSMENT EXERCISE

Assessing Your Equity Sensitivity

The questions that follow are intended to help you better understand your equity sensitivity. Answer each question on the scales by circling the number that best reflects your personal feelings.

1. I think it is important for everyone to be treated fairly.

5	4	3	2	1
Strongly Agree	Agree	Neither Agree nor Disagree	Disagree	Strongly Disagree

2. I pay a lot of attention to how I am treated in comparison to how others are treated.

5	4	3	2	1
Strongly Agree	Agree	Neither Agree nor Disagree	Disagree	Strongly Disagree

3. I get really angry if I think I'm being treated unfairly.

5	4	3	2	1
Strongly Agree	Agree	Neither Agree nor Disagree	Disagree	Strongly Disagree

4. It makes me uncomfortable if I think someone else is not being treated fairly.

5	4	3	2	1
Strongly Agree	Agree	Neither Agree nor Disagree	Disagree	Strongly Disagree

5. If I thought I was being treated unfairly, I would be very motivated to change things.

5	4	3	2	1
Strongly Agree	Agree	Neither Agree nor Disagree	Disagree	Strongly Disagree

6. It doesn't really bother me if someone else gets a better deal than I do.

1	2	3	4	5
Strongly Agree	Agree	Neither Agree nor Disagree	Disagree	Strongly Disagree

7. It is impossible for everyone to be treated fairly all the time.

1	2	3	4	5
Strongly Agree	Agree	Neither Agree nor Disagree	Disagree	Strongly Disagree

8. When I'm a manager, I'll make sure that all of my employees are treated fairly.

5	4	3	2	1
Strongly Agree	Agree	Neither Agree nor Disagree	Disagree	Strongly Disagree

9. I would quit my job if I thought I was being treated unfairly.

5	4	3	2	1
Strongly Agree	Agree	Neither Agree nor Disagree	Disagree	Strongly Disagree

10. Short-term inequities are okay because things all even out in the long run.

1	2	3	4	5
Strongly Agree	Agree	Neither Agree nor Disagree	Disagree	Strongly Disagree

Instructions: Add up your total points (note that some items have a "reversed" numbering arrangement). If you scored 35 or higher, you are highly sensitive to equity and fairness; 15 or lower, you have very little sensitivity to equity and fairness; between 35 and 15, you have moderate equity sensitivity.

CHAPTER 5 Motivating Employee Performance Through Work

Chapter Outline

- Motivation and Employee Performance
- Work Design in Organizations
- Employee Involvement and Motivation
- Flexible Work Arrangements

Chapter Learning Objectives

After studying this chapter, you should be able to:

1. Relate motivation and employee performance.
2. Discuss work design, including its evolution and alternative approaches.
3. Relate employment involvement in work and motivation.
4. Identify and describe key flexible work arrangements.

Orchestrating Outcomes

"[T]hey feel empowered. They don't have anyone telling them what to do. They walk into the rehearsal hall and it's their opportunity to influence [and] shape music."

—Executive Director Graham Parker on the musicians of the Orpheus Chamber Orchestra

Reviewing a concert by the Orpheus Chamber Orchestra, *New York Times* music critic Vivien Schweitzer wrote that the orchestra played Robert Schumann's Symphony No. 2 "with remarkable coordination"; the "balance among strings, winds, and brass," she added, "was impressively well proportioned."

Was Schweitzer, as we sometimes say, damning with faint praise? Isn't a *symphony*, which means "harmony of sounds," *supposed* to be played with remarkable coordination? Aren't the various sections of the orchestra *supposed* to

Svemir, 2009/Used under license from Shutterstock.com

The Orpheus Chamber Orchestra is unique in that it practices and performs without a conductor. This autonomy, in turn, helps motivate the musicians to perform at the highest level possible.

be well balanced? Had the conductor, whose job is to ensure a consummate performance of the music, achieved little more than coordination and balance? Actually, New York–based Orpheus doesn't play with a conductor, and Schweitzer was remarking on the fact that the orchestra had "bravely—and successfully—attempted" such a complex work without the artistic and managerial leadership of someone who directs rehearsals and stands at a podium waving an authoritative baton.

"For us at Orpheus," explains executive director Graham Parker, "it's the *way* we make the music that's the difference." Orpheus holds to the principle that its product—the music performed for audiences—is of the highest quality when its workers—the musicians—are highly satisfied with their jobs. All professional orchestra musicians, of course, are highly trained and skilled, but make no mistake about it: A lot of them are not very happy workers. J. Richard Hackman, an organizational psychologist at Harvard, surveyed workers in 13 different occupational categories, including orchestra players, to determine relative levels of job motivation and satisfaction. On the one hand, musicians ranked at the top in motivation, "fueled by their own pride and professionalism," according to Hackman. But when it came to general satisfaction with their jobs, orchestra players ranked seventh (just below federal prison guards and slightly above beer sales and delivery teams). On the question of satisfaction with growth opportunities, they ranked ninth (again, below prison guards, though a little higher than O.R. nurses and hockey players).

It's this disconnect between motivation and satisfaction—and between motivation and product quality—that Orpheus was conceived to rectify, and the first principle in what's now known as the "Orpheus Process" is this: "Put power in the hands of the people doing the work." According to Harvey Seifter, a consultant specializing in relationships between business and the arts, the Orpheus Process consists of five elements designed to put this principle into practice:

1. *Choosing Leaders.* For each piece of music that the orchestra decides to perform, members select a leadership team composed of five to seven musicians. This "core team" then leads rehearsals and serves as a conduit for members' input. It's also responsible for seeing that the final performance reflects "a unified vision."
2. *Developing Strategies.* Prior to rehearsals, the core team decides how a piece of music will be played. Its ultimate goal is to ensure "an overall interpretive approach to the music," and it works to meet this goal by trying out various approaches to the music during rehearsals with the full orchestra.
3. *Developing the Product.* Once an interpretive approach has been chosen, rehearsals are geared toward refining it. At this point, players make suggestions and critique the playing of their colleagues. It is, of course,

a highly collaborative stage in the process, and its success depends on mutual respect. "We're all specialists—that's the beginning of the discussion," says violinist Martha Caplin. "When I talk to ... another musician in the group, it's on an equal level. It's absolutely crucial that we have that attitude." When disagreements arise, everyone works toward a consensus, and if a consensus can't be reached, the issue is settled by a vote. Violinist Eriko Sato also emphasizes that the process of collaborative input works best when members focus their contributions on outcomes of the highest possible quality: "Fundamentally," she says, "I don't think everybody's opinion should be addressed at all times. There are certain places and times for certain things to be said. The appropriate moment. Everybody knows what's wrong, everybody can feel what's wrong. But do you have a *solution*? Do you know how to solve a *problem*?"

4. *Perfecting the Product.* Just before each concert, a couple of members take seats in the hall to listen to the performance from the audience's perspective. Then they report to the full ensemble and may suggest some final adjustments.
5. *Delivering the Product.* The final performance is the ultimate result of the Orpheus Process, but it isn't the last step. When the concert is over, members get together to share their impressions of the performance and to make suggestions for even further refinements.

"If you ask any musician in the orchestra why they love playing with Orpheus," says Parker, "it's because they feel empowered. They don't have anyone telling them what to do. They walk into the rehearsal hall and it's their opportunity to influence [and] shape music, to make music with all their experience, all their training coming together." Ask double bass player Don Palma, for instance. Palma took a sabbatical after one year with Orpheus to play with the Los Angeles Philharmonic. "I just hated it," he says. "I didn't like to be told what to do all the time, being treated like I wasn't really worth anything other than to be a good soldier and just sit there and do as I was told. I felt powerless to affect things.... I felt frustrated, and there was nothing I could ... do to help make things better." By contrast, says Palma, "Orpheus keeps me involved. I have some measure of participation in the direction the music is going to take. I think that's why a lot of us have stayed involved so long."

In most orchestras, the conductor makes more or less autocratic decisions about what will be played and how. The input of musicians is neither sought nor welcomed, and unsolicited advice may be sharply rebuffed—and may, in fact, serve as grounds for dismissal. At Orpheus, says Parker, "we have a completely different structure to the way we approach rehearsal": A core team of players selected by the orchestra from each instrument section plans and leads rehearsals for a given piece of music.

To assist in meeting the inevitable challenges posed by its democratic structure, Orpheus recruited Harvard's Hackman to its board of trustees in 2007. Hackman immediately helped the orchestra organize itself around two leadership groups. An *artistic planning group* consists of two staff members and three "artistic directors." The executive director serves as a sort of moderator for group discussions, and the general manager keeps everyone posted on market-related events and initiatives. The three artistic directors, who are members of the orchestra, work with other members to find out what they're interested in working on and to convey their ideas to the planning group. They also serve on a *senior leadership team* with the executive director, the general manager, and the directors of finance, marketing, and operations. This team determines the best ways to do things given the organization's commitment to democratic structure, leadership, and roles—the best way to develop artistic agendas; to choose players, soloists, and composers; and to make the team accountable for its own artistic decisions.

It's important to remember, however, that neither the Orpheus Process nor the Orpheus two-team structure is any guarantee of organizational effectiveness. As in any organizational endeavor, execution is the difference between success and failure, and a study of the Orpheus approach to management has revealed a variety of reasons for the effectiveness of teamwork within the ensemble. Every member, for example, clearly understands the group's purpose and mission; every member's role is clearly stated and agreed upon, and all members perform an equal amount of work in meeting the group's objectives.

What Do You Think?

1. Can you think of any other occupational groups that might share the motivational needs and values of professional musicians? In what ways might the task of motivating musicians differ from that of motivating people in more conventional work settings?
2. Can you identify differences in the actual "work" of playing in the Orpheus Chamber Orchestra versus playing in a traditional orchestra? How might these differences affect the motivation of musicians in each setting?

References: Vivien Schweitzer, "Players with No Conductor and, Increasingly, with No Fear," *New York Times*, May 7, 2007, http://query.nytimes.com on April 18, 2012; Anthony Tommasini, "The Pluses and Minuses of Lacking a Conductor," *New York Times*, October 18, 2008, www.nytimes.com on April 18, 2012; Jennifer Higgs, "Orpheus Chamber Orchestra Embodies Democratic Principles," *Axiom News*, October 28, 2008, www.axiomnews.ca on April 18, 2012; Amanda Gordon, "Self-Governing Orpheus Chamber Orchestra Has Broader Lessons to Offer, Says Banking and Civic Leader John Whitehead," *New York Sun,* April 25, 2009, www.nysun.com on April 18, 2012; Harvey Seifter, "The Conductorless Orchestra," *Leader to Leader Journal*, no. 21 (Summer 2001), www.life-bv.nl on April 18, 2012; J. Richard Hackman, *Leading Teams: Setting the Stage for Great Performances* (Cambridge, MA: Harvard Business School Press, 2002), http://books.google.com on April 18, 2012.

Managers determine what jobs will be performed in their organizations and how those jobs will be performed. But managers must also determine how to motivate people and how to optimize their performance. The long-term key to success in business is to create jobs that optimize the organization's requirements for productivity and efficiency while simultaneously motivating and satisfying the employees who perform those jobs. As people and organizations change, and as we continue to learn more about management, it is important to look back occasionally at those jobs and make whatever changes are necessary to improve them.

This chapter is the first of two that address the strategies managers use to optimize the performance of their employees. We begin with a discussion of work design, starting with a look at historical approaches. Then we discuss an important contemporary perspective on jobs, the job characteristics theory. Next, we review the importance of employee involvement through participation in their work. Finally, we discuss flexible work arrangements that can be used to enhance motivation and performance. To begin, we will introduce a general framework that can guide managers as they attempt to put into practice various theories and models of motivation.

MOTIVATION AND EMPLOYEE PERFORMANCE

Chapter 4 described a variety of perspectives on motivation. But no single theory or model completely explains motivation—each covers only some of the factors that actually result in motivated behavior. Moreover, even if one theory were applicable in a particular situation, a manager might still need to translate that theory into operational terms. Thus, while using the actual theories as tools, managers need to understand various operational procedures, systems, and methods for enhancing motivation and performance.

Figure 5.1 illustrates a basic framework for relating various theories of motivation to potential and actual motivation and to operational methods for translating this potential and actual motivation into performance. The left side of the figure illustrates that motivated behavior can be induced by need-based or process-based circumstances. That is, people may be motivated to satisfy various specific needs or through various processes such as perceptions of inequity, expectancy relationships, and reinforcement contingencies.

These need-, process-, and learning-based concepts result in the situation illustrated in the center of the figure—a certain potential exists for motivated behavior directed at enhanced performance. For example, suppose that an employee wants more social relationships—that is, he wants to satisfy belongingness, relatedness, or affiliation needs. This means that there is potential for the employee to want to perform at a higher level if he thinks that higher performance will satisfy those social needs. Likewise, if an employee's high performance in the past was followed by strong positive reinforcement, there is again a potential for motivation directed at enhanced performance.

But managers may need to take certain steps to translate the potential for motivation directed at enhanced performance into real motivation and real enhanced performance. In some cases, these steps may be tied to the specific need or process that has created the existing potential. For example, providing more opportunities for social interaction contingent on improved performance might capitalize on an employee's social needs. More typically, however, a manager needs to go further to help translate potential into real performance.

The right side of Figure 5.1 names some of the more common methods used to enhance performance. This chapter covers the first three—job design, employee participation and empowerment, and flexible work arrangements. The other three—goal setting, performance management, and organizational rewards—are discussed in Chapter 6.

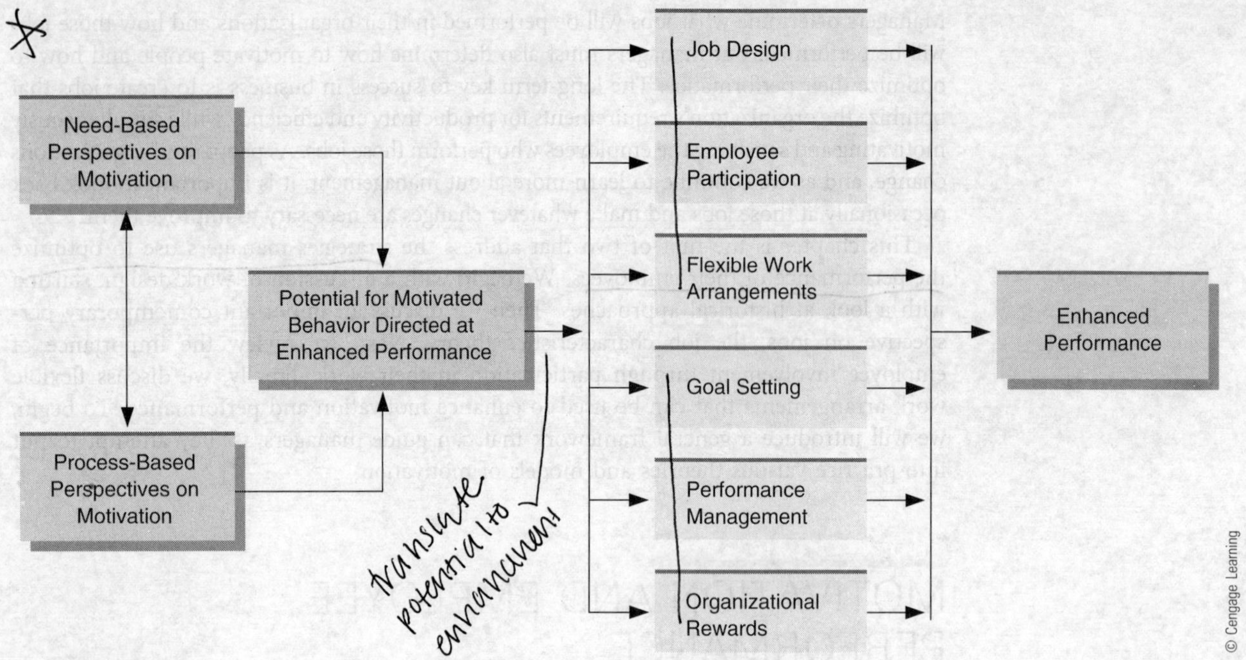

FIGURE 5.1

Enhancing Performance in Organizations

Managers can use a variety of methods to enhance performance in organizations. The need- and process-based perspectives on motivation explain some of the factors involved in increasing the potential for motivated behavior directed at enhanced performance. Managers can then use such means as goal setting, job design, flexible work arrangements, performance management, rewards, and organizational behavior motivation to help translate this potential into actual enhanced performance.

WORK DESIGN IN ORGANIZATIONS

Job design is how organizations define and structure jobs.

Work design is an important method managers can use to enhance employee performance.[1] When work design is addressed at the individual level, it is most commonly referred to as **job design**; it can be defined as how organizations define and structure jobs. As we will see, properly designed jobs can have a positive impact on the motivation, performance, and job satisfaction of those who perform them. On the other hand, poorly designed jobs can impair motivation, performance, and job satisfaction. The first widespread model of how individual work should be designed was job specialization. For example, a worker who applies safety decals to a piece of equipment as that equipment moves down an assembly line is performing a specialized job.

Job Specialization

Job specialization, as advocated by scientific management, can help improve efficiency, but it can also promote monotony and boredom.

Frederick Taylor, the chief proponent of **job specialization**, argued that jobs should be scientifically studied, broken down into small component tasks, and then standardized across all workers doing those jobs.[2] Taylor's view grew from the historical writings about division of labor advocated by Scottish economist Adam Smith. In practice, job specialization generally brought most, if not all, of the advantages its advocates claimed. Specialization paved the way for large-scale assembly lines and was at least

Job specialization is the basis for all assembly line jobs like these. Workers perform precisely configured jobs as work passes by them on a moving belt. In theory this promotes efficiency. However, it also leads to boredom and monotony.

partly responsible for the dramatic gains in output U.S. industry achieved for several decades after the turn of the century.

On the surface, job specialization appears to be a rational and efficient way to structure jobs. The jobs in many factories, for instance, are highly specialized and are often designed to maximize productivity. In practice, however, performing those jobs can cause problems, foremost among them the extreme monotony of highly specialized tasks. Consider the job of assembling toasters. A person who does the entire assembly may find the job complex and challenging, albeit inefficient. If the job is specialized so that the worker simply inserts a heating coil into the toaster as it passes along on an assembly line, the process may be efficient, but it is unlikely to interest or challenge the worker. A worker numbed by boredom and monotony may be less motivated to work hard and more inclined to do poor-quality work or to complain about the job. For these reasons, managers began to search for job design alternatives to specialization.

One of the primary catalysts for this search was a famous study of jobs in the automobile industry. The purpose of this study was to assess how satisfied automobile workers were with various aspects of their jobs.[3] The workers indicated that they were reasonably satisfied with their pay, working conditions, and the quality of their supervision. However, they expressed extreme dissatisfaction with the actual work they did. The plants were very noisy, and the moving assembly line dictated a rigid, grueling pace. Jobs were highly specialized and standardized.

The workers complained about six facets of their jobs: mechanical pacing by an assembly line, repetitiveness, low skill requirements, involvement with only a portion of the total production cycle, limited social interaction with others in the workplace, and lack of control over the tools and techniques used in the job. These sources of dissatisfaction were a consequence of the job design prescriptions of scientific management. Thus, managers began to recognize that although job specialization might lead to efficiency, if carried too far, it would have a number of negative consequences.[4]

Early Alternatives to Job Specialization

In response to the automobile plant study, other reported problems with job specialization, and a general desire to explore ways to create less monotonous jobs, managers began to seek alternative ways to design jobs. Managers initially formulated two alternative approaches: job rotation and job enlargement.

Job rotation is systematically moving workers from one job to another in an attempt to minimize monotony and boredom.

Job Rotation **Job rotation** involves systematically shifting workers from one job to another to sustain their motivation and interest. Under specialization, each task is broken down into small parts. For example, assembling fine writing pens such as those made by Mont Blanc or Cross might involve four discrete steps: testing the ink cartridge, inserting the cartridge into the barrel of the pen, screwing the cap onto the barrel, and inserting the assembled pen into a box. One worker might perform step one, another step two, and so forth.

When job rotation is introduced, the tasks themselves stay the same. However, the workers who perform them are systematically rotated across the various tasks. Jones, for example, starts out with task 1 (testing ink cartridges). On a regular basis—perhaps weekly or monthly—she is systematically rotated to task 2, to task 3, to task 4, and back to task 1. Gonzalez, who starts out on task 2 (inserting cartridges into barrels), rotates ahead of Jones to tasks 3, 4, 1, and back to 2.

Numerous firms have used job rotation, including American Cyanamid, Baker Hughes, Ford, and Prudential Insurance. Job rotation did not entirely live up to its expectations, however.[5] The problem again was narrowly defined, routine jobs. That is, if a rotation cycle takes workers through the same old jobs, the workers simply experience several routine and boring jobs instead of just one. Although a worker may begin each job shift with a bit of renewed interest, the effect usually is short-lived.

Rotation may also decrease efficiency. For example, it clearly sacrifices the proficiency and expertise that grow from specialization. At the same time, job rotation is an effective training technique because a worker rotated through a variety of related jobs acquires a larger set of job skills. Thus, there is increased flexibility in transferring workers to new jobs. Many U.S. firms now use job rotation for training or other purposes, but few rely on it to motivate workers. For instance, Pilgrim's Pride, one of the largest chicken-processing firms in the United States, uses job rotation, but not for motivation. Workers in a chicken-processing plant are subject to cumulative trauma injuries such as carpal tunnel syndrome, and managers at Pilgrim's believe that rotating workers across different jobs can reduce these injuries. The TSA also rotates airport security screeners across different tasks every 20–30 minutes to help prevent boredom and to keep them focused on their jobs.

Job enlargement involves giving workers more tasks to perform.

Job Enlargement **Job enlargement**, or horizontal job loading, is expanding a worker's job to include tasks previously performed by other workers. For instance, if job enlargement were introduced at a Cross pen plant, the four tasks noted above might be combined into two "larger" ones. Hence, one set of workers might each test cartridges and then insert them into barrels (old steps 1 and 2); another set of workers might then attach caps to the barrels and put the pens into boxes (old steps 3 and 4). The logic behind this change is that the increased number of tasks in each job reduces monotony and boredom.

Maytag was one of the first companies to use job enlargement.[6] In the assembly of washing machine water pumps, for example, jobs done sequentially by six workers at a conveyor belt were modified so that each worker completed an entire pump alone. Other organizations that implemented job enlargement included AT&T, the U.S. Civil Service, and Colonial Life Insurance Company.

Unfortunately, job enlargement also failed to have the desired effects. Generally, if the entire production sequence consisted of simple, easy-to-master tasks, merely doing more of them did not significantly change the worker's job. If the task of putting two bolts on a piece of machinery was "enlarged" to putting on three bolts and connecting two wires, for example, the monotony of the original job essentially remained.

Job Enrichment

Job enrichment entails giving workers more tasks to perform and more control over how to perform them.

Job rotation and job enlargement seemed promising but eventually disappointed managers seeking to counter the ill effects of extreme specialization. They failed partly because they were intuitive, narrow approaches rather than fully developed, theory-driven methods. Consequently, a new, more complex approach to task design—job enrichment—was developed. **Job enrichment** is based on the dual-structure theory of

Many managers would consider it difficult—if not impossible—to enrich jobs such as those performed by janitors, lawn maintenance workers, and so forth. But Texas Instruments achieved positive results when the firm started letting their janitors have control over their schedules and gave them the responsibility for ordering their own cleaning supplies.

motivation, which is discussed in Chapter 4. That theory contends that employees can be motivated by positive job-related experiences such as feelings of achievement, responsibility, and recognition. To achieve these, job enrichment relies on vertical job loading—not only adding more tasks to a job, as in horizontal loading, but also giving the employee more control over those tasks.[7]

AT&T, Texas Instruments, IBM, and General Foods have all used job enrichment. For example, AT&T utilized job enrichment in a group of eight people who were responsible for preparing service orders. Managers believed turnover in the group was too high and performance too low. Analysis revealed several deficiencies in the work. The group worked in relative isolation, and any service representative could ask them to prepare work orders. As a result, they had little client contact or responsibility, and they received scant feedback on their job performance. The job enrichment program focused on creating a process team. Each member of the team was paired with a service representative, and the tasks were restructured: Ten discrete steps were replaced with three more complex ones. In addition, the group members began to get specific feedback on performance, and their job titles were changed to reflect their greater responsibility and status. As a result of these changes, the number of orders delivered on time increased from 27 percent to 90 percent, accuracy improved, and turnover decreased significantly.[8]

One of the first published reports on job enrichment told how Texas Instruments had used this technique to improve janitorial jobs. The company had given janitors more control over their schedules and let them sequence their own cleaning jobs and purchase their own supplies. As a direct result, turnover dropped, cleanliness improved, and the company reported estimated initial cost savings of approximately $103,000.[9]

At the same time, we should note that many job enrichment programs have failed. Some companies have found job enrichment to be cost ineffective, and others believe that it simply did not produce the expected results.[10] Several programs at Prudential Insurance, for example, were abandoned because managers believed they were benefiting neither employees nor the firm. Some of the criticism is associated with the dual-structure theory of motivation on which job enrichment is based: The theory confuses employee satisfaction with motivation, is fraught with methodological flaws, ignores situational factors, and is not convincingly supported by research.

Because of these and other problems, job enrichment recently has fallen into disfavor among managers. Yet some valuable aspects of the concept can be salvaged. The efforts of managers and academic theorists ultimately have led to more complex and sophisticated viewpoints. Many of these advances are evident in the job characteristics theory, which we consider next.

The **job characteristics theory** identifies five motivational properties of tasks and three critical psychological states of people.

The Job Characteristics Theory

The **job characteristics theory** focuses on the specific motivational properties of jobs. The theory, diagrammed in Figure 5.2, was developed by Hackman and Oldham.[11] At

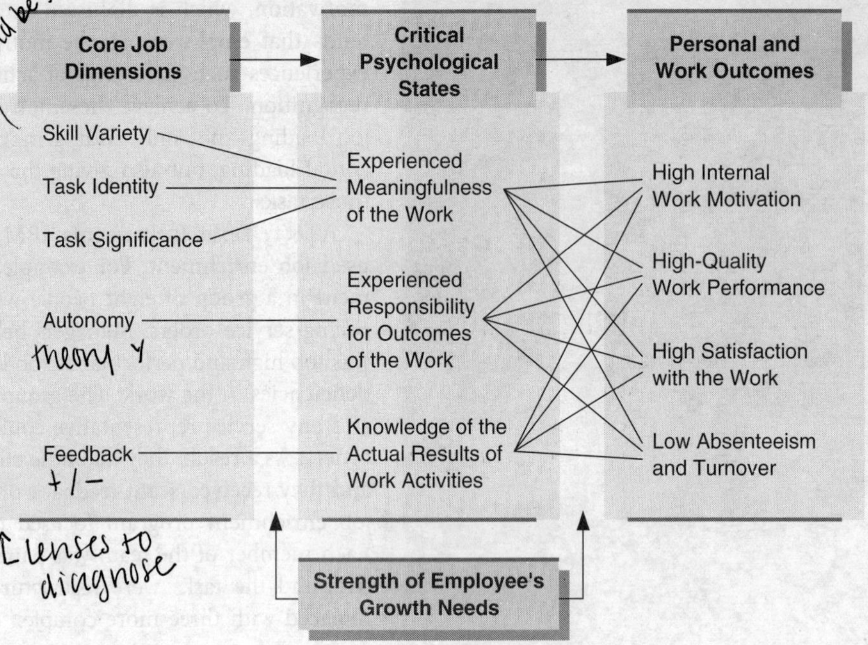

FIGURE 5.2

The Job Characteristics Theory

The job characteristics theory is an important contemporary model of how to design jobs. By using five core job characteristics, managers can enhance three critical psychological states. These states, in turn, can improve a variety of personal and work outcomes. Individual differences also affect how the job characteristics affect people.

Reference: Reprinted from Organizational Behavior and Human Performance, vol. 16, J. R. Hackman and G. R. Oldham, "Motivation Through the Design of Work: Test of a Theory," pp. 250–279. Copyright 1976, with permission from Elsevier.

the core of the theory is the idea of critical psychological states. These states are presumed to determine the extent to which characteristics of the job enhance employee responses to the task. The three critical psychological states are:

1. *Experienced meaningfulness of the work*—the degree to which the individual experiences the job as generally meaningful, valuable, and worthwhile
2. *Experienced responsibility for work outcomes*—the degree to which individuals feel personally accountable and responsible for the results of their work
3. *Knowledge of results*—the degree to which individuals continuously understand how effectively they are performing the job

If employees experience these states at a sufficiently high level, they are likely to feel good about themselves and to respond favorably to their jobs. Hackman and Oldham suggest that the three critical psychological states are triggered by the following five characteristics of the job, or core job dimensions:

1. *Skill variety*—the degree to which the job requires a variety of activities that involve different skills and talents
2. *Task identity*—the degree to which the job requires completion of a "whole" and an identifiable piece of work; that is, the extent to which a job has a beginning and an end with a tangible outcome
3. *Task significance*—the degree to which the job affects the lives or work of other people, both in the immediate organization and in the external environment
4. *Autonomy*—the degree to which the job allows the individual substantial freedom, independence, and discretion to schedule the work and determine the procedures for carrying it out
5. *Feedback*—the degree to which the job activities give the individual direct and clear information about the effectiveness of his or her performance

Figure 5.2 shows that these five job characteristics, operating through the critical psychological states, affect a variety of personal and work outcomes: high internal work motivation (that is, intrinsic motivation), high-quality work performance, high satisfaction with the work, and low absenteeism and turnover. The figure also suggests that individual differences play a role in job design. People with strong needs for personal growth and development will be especially motivated by the five core job characteristics. On the other hand, people with weaker needs for personal growth and development are less likely to be motivated by the core job characteristics.

Figure 5.3 expands the basic job characteristics theory by incorporating general guidelines to help managers implement it.[12] Managers can use such means as forming natural work units (that is, grouping similar tasks together), combining existing tasks into more complex ones, establishing direct relationships between workers and clients, increasing worker autonomy through vertical job loading, and opening feedback channels. Theoretically, such actions should enhance the motivational properties of each task. Using these guidelines, sometimes in adapted form, several firms, including 3M, Volvo, AT&T, Xerox, Texas Instruments, and Motorola, have successfully implemented job design changes.[13]

Much research has been devoted to this approach to job design.[14] This research has generally supported the theory, although performance has seldom been found to

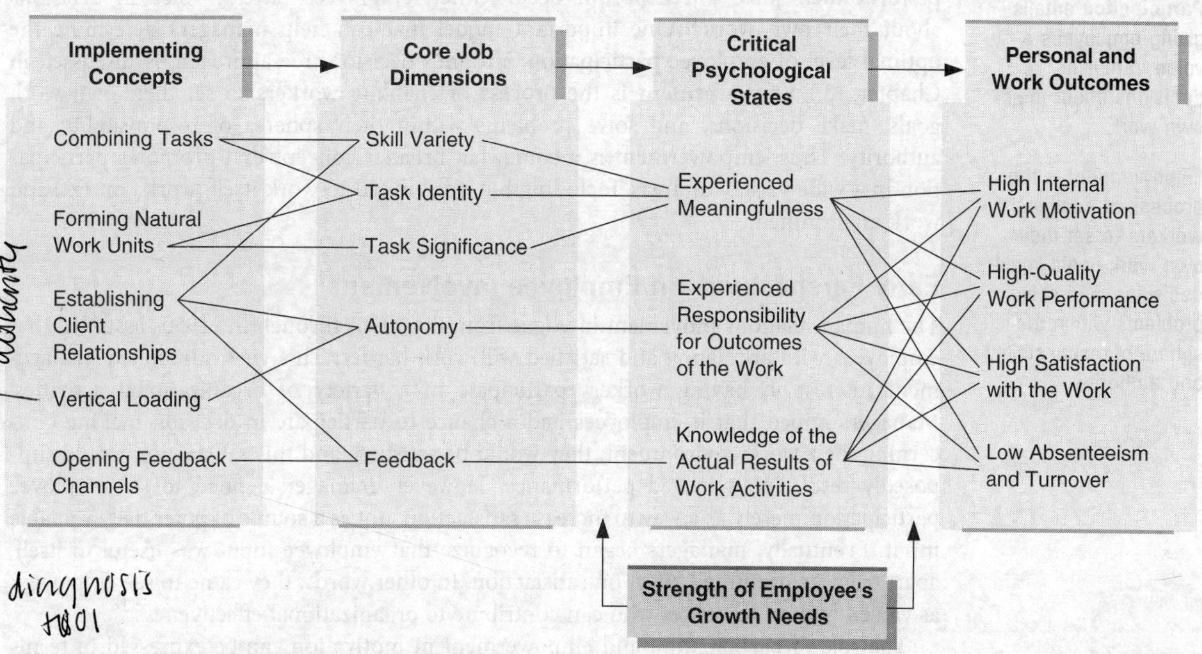

FIGURE 5.3

Implementing the Job Characteristics Theory

Managers should use a set of implementation guidelines if they want to apply the job characteristics theory in their organization. This figure shows some of these guidelines. For example, managers can combine tasks, form natural work units, establish client relationships, vertically load jobs, and open feedback channels.

Reference: From J. R. Hackman, G. R. Oldham, R. Janson, and K. Purdy, "A New Stage for Job Enrichment." Copyright © 1975 by The Regents of the University of California. Reprinted from *California Management Review*, vol. 17, no. 4. By permission of The Regents.

correlate with job characteristics.[15] Several apparent weaknesses in the theory have also come to light. First, the measures used to test the theory are not always as valid and reliable as they should be. Further, the role of individual differences frequently has not been supported by research. Finally, guidelines for implementation are not specific, so managers usually tailor them to their own particular circumstances. Still, the theory remains a popular perspective on studying and changing jobs.[16]

The *Diversity* box on page 135 shows that one of the problems in making workers as happy and productive as possible is the fact the workforce has always consisted of people from different walks of life.

EMPLOYEE INVOLVEMENT AND MOTIVATION

Employees' involvement in their work can also play an important role in motivation. Involvement is most often enhanced through what are called participative management and empowerment. In most cases, managers who use these techniques are attempting to enhance employee motivation. In a sense, participation and empowerment are extensions of job design because each fundamentally alters how employees in an organization perform their jobs. **Participation** occurs when employees have a voice in decisions about their own work. (One important model that can help managers determine the optimal level of employee participation, Vroom's decision-tree approach, is discussed in Chapter 13.) **Empowerment** is the process of enabling workers to set their own work goals, make decisions, and solve problems within their spheres of responsibility and authority. Thus, empowerment is a somewhat broader concept that promotes participation in a wide variety of areas, including but not limited to work itself, work context, and work environment.[17]

Participation entails giving employees a voice in making decisions about their own work.

Empowerment is the process of enabling workers to set their own work goals, make decisions, and solve problems within their sphere of responsibility and authority.

Early Perspectives on Employee Involvement

The human relations movement in vogue from the 1930s through the 1950s assumed that employees who are happy and satisfied will work harder. This view stimulated management interest in having workers participate in a variety of organizational activities. Managers hoped that if employees had a chance to participate in decision making concerning their work environment, they would be satisfied, and this satisfaction would supposedly result in improved performance. However, managers tended to see employee participation merely as a way to increase satisfaction, not as a source of potentially valuable input. Eventually, managers began to recognize that employee input was useful in itself, apart from its presumed effect on satisfaction. In other words, they came to see employees as valued human resources who can contribute to organizational effectiveness.[18]

The role of participation and empowerment in motivation can be expressed in terms of both the need-based perspectives and the expectancy theory discussed in Chapter 4. Employees who participate in decision making may be more committed to executing decisions properly. Furthermore, successfully making a decision, executing it, and then seeing the positive consequences can help satisfy one's need for achievement, provide recognition and responsibility, and enhance self-esteem. Simply being asked to participate in organizational decision making may also enhance an employee's self-esteem. In addition, participation should help clarify expectancies (as a component of expectancy theory, as discussed in Chapter 4). That is, by participating in decision making, employees may better understand the linkage (expectancy) between their performance and the rewards they want most.

SERVICE Empowerment

One of the major challenges in managing people who co-produce service experiences with customers is that they often must make decisions about how to customize experiences in ways that meet the expectations of each unique customer. Even when the service is fairly structured and straightforward, such as those provided by a restaurant server, retail store clerk, or bank customer service representative, the inevitable variation in customers' personalities, capabilities, experiences, and expectations will mean that each will require some individual tailoring of the service encounter by the employee providing the service. Thus, the organization relies not only on that employee's ability to serve the meal, ring up a sale, or open an account (or otherwise perform whatever tasks frame the service experience being provided) but also on that person's ability to accurately diagnose the customer's mood, personality, and capabilities to ensure that the customer's co-production requirements to obtain the service experience are performed in a way that adds value to the service. It is one thing to order the right meal, buy the sweater that fits, or successfully open a new bank account, but what turns a simple commercial transaction into an experience that customers find memorable is the way the server delivered them. Service organizations, therefore, rely on their employees' ability to figure out what the customer wants, needs, and expects and then provide it during that experience. This means that empowerment is a necessity in services, as there is no way to fully prepare, train, or teach an employee how to perform the tasks required in the way that each customer expects.

Instead, service organizations use empowerment extensively. Empowerment works because supervisors can't be everywhere all the time to answer questions, coach correct employee behavior, or prepare their employees for every possible variation that customers will bring to the service encounter. An even more critical reason that empowerment is necessary is that service failures are inevitable. Thus, employees have to be ready, willing, and able to correct those situations in which the service hasn't gone the way the customer expected and something must be done to fix the service failure. The research on service failures tells us that the faster a service failure is resolved, the better the outcome for company and customer. The customer is happier, as the problem is resolved—and are sometimes even happier than if there had been no problem in the first place. The company is happier, as happy customers are more likely to return as repeat customers. Best of all, the server is happier, as most customer encounters with failures are not pleasant, and having the ability to resolve a failure in a positive, quick way leads to a more positive experience for the employee as well as the customer. As one final benefit, most people feel that when they are hired they are supposed to do the jobs for which they were employed and greatly appreciate the opportunity to do them well. When empowered to add value to the customer's experience by personalizing the transaction, service employees feel they have more control over how to perform their jobs, more awareness of the business and their contribution to its success, and more accountability for their own performance.

Successful empowerment requires satisfying five assumptions. First, that the employee has the training, capability, and motivation to do what is needed in the service experience. Second, that the outcome can be measured in some way. Third, that the employee is committed to the organization's mission to provide excellent service and cares about sustaining his or her role in the organization's success. Fourth, that the manager is comfortable with allowing the employee to use discretion in performing the job. Finally, that the organization has a strong culture that can guide the employee on doing the right thing when the right thing is an on-the-spot decision the employee must make as to what should be done to respond to a customer. Thus, both company and employee have to be ready, willing, and able to do what the customer wants when the customer wants it.

Discussion Question: Why is it important to empower an employee in producing service experiences?

Areas of Employee Involvement

At one level, employees can participate in addressing questions and making decisions about their own jobs. Instead of just telling them how to do their jobs, for example, managers can ask employees to make their own decisions about how to do them. Based on their own expertise and experience with their tasks, workers might be able to improve their own productivity. In many situations, they might also be well qualified to make decisions about what materials to use, which tools to use, and so forth.

Chaparral Steel, a small steel producer near Dallas, allows its workers considerable autonomy in how they perform their jobs. For example, when the firm needed a new rolling mill lathe, it budgeted $1 million for its purchase and then put the purchase decision in the hands of an operating machinist. This machinist, in turn, investigated various options, visited other mills in Japan and Europe, and then recommended an alternative piece of machinery costing less than half of the budgeted amount. The firm also helped pioneer an innovative concept called "open-book management"—any employee at Chaparral can see any company document, record, or other piece of information at any time and for any reason.

It might also help to let workers make decisions about administrative matters, such as work schedules. If jobs are relatively independent of one another, employees might decide when to change shifts, take breaks, go to lunch, and so forth. A work group or team might also be able to schedule vacations and days off for all of its members. Furthermore, employees are getting increasing opportunities to participate in broader issues of product quality. Involvement of this type has become a hallmark of successful Japanese and other international firms, and many U.S. companies have followed suit.

Techniques and Issues in Employee Involvement

In recent years many organizations have actively sought ways to extend employee involvement beyond the traditional areas. Simple techniques such as suggestion boxes and question-and-answer meetings allow a certain degree of participation, for example. The basic motive has been to better capitalize on the assets and capabilities inherent in all employees. Thus, many managers today prefer the term "empowerment" to "participation" because it implies a more comprehensive level of involvement.

One method some firms use to empower their workers is the use of work teams. This method grew out of early attempts to use what Japanese firms call "quality circles." A *quality circle* is a group of employees who voluntarily meet regularly to identify and propose solutions to problems related to quality. Quality circles quickly evolved into a broader and more comprehensive array of work groups, now generally called "work teams." These teams are collections of employees empowered to plan, organize, direct, and control their own work. Their supervisor, rather than being a traditional "boss," plays more the role of a coach. We discuss work teams more fully in Chapter 10.

The other method some organizations use to facilitate employee involvement is to change their overall method of organizing. The basic pattern is for an organization to eliminate layers from its hierarchy, thereby becoming much more decentralized. Power, responsibility, and authority are delegated as far down the organization as possible, so control of work is squarely in the hands of those who actually do it.

Regardless of the specific technique used, however, empowerment only enhances organizational effectiveness if certain conditions exist. First, the organization must be sincere in its efforts to spread power and autonomy to lower levels of the organization. Token efforts to promote participation in just a few areas are unlikely to succeed. Second, the organization must be committed to maintaining participation and empowerment. Workers will be resentful if they are given more control only to later have it reduced or taken away altogether. Third, the organization must be systematic and patient in its efforts to empower workers. Turning over too much control too quickly can spell disaster. Finally, the organization must be prepared to increase its commitment to training. Employees who are given more freedom concerning how they work are likely to need additional training to help them exercise that freedom most effectively.

The *Diversity* box entitled "The Law of Diminishing Motivation," discusses some of the challenges faced by women in the legal profession, as well as some of the practices among law firms that have made them difficult to overcome.

DIVERSITY The Law of Diminishing Motivation

©vlad_star/shutterstock

The enrollment of women in U.S. law schools took off after 1970, and women have been graduating at the same rate as men for more than 30 years. Today, however, the census of American law firms still counts relatively few women *partners*—typically, the veteran lawyers who are joint owners and directors. Currently, for example, 34.4 percent of all lawyers are women, yet only 17.8 percent of law firm partners are women. Most female lawyers are *associates*—paid employees with the prospect of becoming partners. Moreover, the further up the law-firm ladder you look, the greater the disparity. According to the National Association of Women Lawyers, 92 percent of all *managing partners* (who run the business end of a firm) are men; men occupy 85 percent of the seats on the governing committees that control a firm's policies, and they hold 84 percent of all *equity partnerships* (which come with ownership and profit sharing). At this rate, women will achieve parity with male colleagues in approximately 2088.

> ***"You have a given population of people who were significantly motivated to go through law school with a certain career goal in mind. What de-motivates them to want to continue working in the law?"***
>
> —ATTORNEY BETTINA B. PLEVAN

So what happens between the time women get job offers and the time firms hand out promotions and partnerships? Do they become less involved? Bettina B. Plevan, an employment-law specialist and partner in the Manhattan firm of Proskauer Rose, believes that, somewhere along the way, female lawyers lose the kind of motivation necessary to get ahead in a law office. "You have a given population of people," she observes, "who were significantly motivated to go through law school with a certain career goal in mind. What de-motivates them," she asks, "to want to continue working in the law?"

The problem, says Karen M. Lockwood, a former partner in the Washington DC firm Howrey and founder of the Lockwood Group, a consultancy specializing in professional diversity, is neither discrimination nor lack of opportunity. "Law firms," she says, "are way beyond discrimination. Problems with advancement and retention are grounded in biases, not discrimination." In part, these biases issue from institutional inertia. Lauren Stiller Rikleen, a former lawyer and currently executive-in-residence at the Center for Work and Family in the Boston College Carroll School of Management, points out that most law firms are "running on an institutional model that's about 200 years old." Many of them, she adds, "do a horrible job of managing their personnel, in terms of training them and communicating with them." One consequence of these practices, in turn, may be less employee involvement. Such problems, of course, affect men as well as women, but because of lingering preconceptions about women's attitudes, values, and goals, women bear the brunt of the workplace burden. In practical terms, they face less adequate mentoring, poorer networking opportunities, lower-grade case assignments, and unequal access to positions of committee control.

To all of these barriers to success Lockwood adds the effect of what she calls the "maternal wall": Male partners, she says, assume that women who return to the firm after having children will be less willing to work hard and less capable of dedicating themselves to their jobs when they return.

Like firms in many other industries, law firms have experimented with such flexible-work options as flexible scheduling and parental leave. More and more, however, they report that such measures have not been as effective as they'd hoped. Says Edith R. Matthai, founder with her husband of the Los Angeles firm Robie & Matthai: "We're very accommodating with leaves and flexible schedules, and even with that we still lose women." The "pressures on women from spouses, family, peers, schools, and others is huge," she adds. The situation has improved over the last 30 years, but "we have a long way to go.... I think the real solution is a reassessment of the role that women play in the family. One thing we need is a sense of shared responsibilities for the household and, most importantly, shared responsibilities for taking care of the kids."

References: Patricia Gillette, "Lack of Self-Promotion Hurts Women in Large Firms," *The AmLaw Daily*, July 9, 2009, http://amlawdaily.typepad.com on April 18, 2012; Lizz O'Donnell, "Women in Law Firms: Stuck in the Middle," *The Glass Hammer*, July 23, 2009, www.theglasshammer.com on April 18, 2012; Timothy L. O'Brien, "Why Do So Few Women Reach the Top of Big Law Firms?" *New York Times*, March 19, 2006, *www.nytimes.com* on April 18, 2012; Lynne Marek, "Women Lawyers Find Their Own Paths as Law Firms Struggle to Keep Them," *Law.com*, June 25, 2007, *www.law.com* on April 18, 2012.

FLEXIBLE WORK ARRANGEMENTS

Beyond the actual redesigning of jobs and the use of employee involvement, many organizations today are experimenting with a variety of flexible work arrangements. These arrangements are generally intended to enhance employee motivation and performance by giving workers more flexibility about how and when they work. Among the more popular flexible work arrangements are variable work schedules, flexible work schedules, extended work schedules, job sharing, and telecommuting.[19]

Variable Work Schedules

There are many exceptions, of course, but the traditional professional work schedule in the United States has long been days that start at 8:00 or 9:00 in the morning and end at 5:00 in the evening, five days a week (and, of course, managers and other professionals often work many additional hours outside of these times). Although the exact starting and ending times vary, most companies in other countries have also used a well-defined work schedule. But such a schedule makes it difficult for workers to attend to routine personal business—going to the bank, seeing a doctor or dentist for a checkup, having a parent-teacher conference, getting an automobile serviced, and so forth. Employees locked into this work schedule may find it necessary to take a sick or vacation day to handle these activities. On a more psychological level, some people may feel so powerless and constrained by their job schedules that they grow resentful and frustrated.

In a **compressed work schedule**, employees work a full forty-hour week in fewer than the traditional five days.

To help counter these problems, one alternative some businesses use is a **compressed work schedule.**[20] An employee following a compressed work week schedule works a full forty-hour week in fewer than the traditional five days. Most typically, this schedule involves working ten hours a day for four days, leaving an extra day off. Another alternative is for employees to work slightly less than ten hours a day but to complete the forty hours by lunchtime on Friday. And a few firms have tried having employees work twelve hours a day for three days, followed by four days off. Firms that have used these forms of compressed workweeks include Recreational Equipment (REI), USAA, Edward Jones, and Mercedes-Benz USA.[21] One problem with this schedule is that if everyone in the organization is off at the same time, the firm may have no one on duty to handle problems or deal with outsiders on the off day. On the other hand, if a company staggers days off across the workforce, people who don't get the more desirable days off (Monday and Friday, for most people) may be jealous or resentful. Another problem is that when employees put in too much time in a single day, they tend to get tired and perform at a lower level later in the day.

A popular schedule some organizations are beginning to use is called a "nine-eighty" schedule. Under this arrangement, an employee works a traditional schedule one week and a compressed schedule the next, getting every other Friday off. That is, they work eighty hours (the equivalent of two weeks of full-time work) in nine days. By alternating the regular and compressed schedules across half of its workforce, the organization is staffed at all times but still gives employees two additional full days off each month. Chevron and Marathon Oil are two businesses that currently use this schedule.

Extended Work Schedules

An **extended work schedule** is one that requires relatively long periods of work followed by relatively long periods of paid time off.

In certain cases, some organizations use another type of work scheduling called an **extended work schedule**. An extended work schedule is one that requires relatively long periods of work followed by relatively long periods of paid time off. These schedules are most often used when the cost of transitioning from one worker to another is high and there are efficiencies associated with having a small workforce.

For instance, KBR is a large defense contractor that manages U.S. military installations in foreign countries, including Iraq and Afghanistan. KBR's civilian employees handle maintenance, logistics, and communications, as well as food, laundry, and mail services, among other things. The typical work schedule for a KBR employee is 12 hours a day, 7 days a week. Extended schedules such as this allow the firm to function with a smaller workforce than would be the case under a more traditional approach to work scheduling. In order to motivate employees to accept and maintain this kind of schedule, the firm pays them a compensation premium and provides them with

Marco Di Lauro/Getty Images

KBR, a major defense contractor, makes extensive use of extended work schedules. For instance, these KBR employees in Afghanistan work 12 hours a day, 7 days a week, for 120 consecutive days. They then get 16 days of paid vacation time and an airline ticket to any major destination in the world. After the 16 day period is over, they repeat the cycle again.

16 days of paid vacation and an airline ticket to any major destination in the world after every 120-day work period.

Other work settings that are conducive to this kind of extended work schedule include offshore petroleum-drilling platforms, transoceanic cargo ships, research labs in distant settings such as the South Pole, and movie crews filming in remote locations. While the specific number of hours and days and the amount of vacation time vary, most of these job settings are characterized by long periods of work followed by an extended vacation plus premium pay. Offshore drilling platform workers at ExxonMobil, for instance, generally work five weeks and then have two weeks off.

Flexible Work Schedules

Flexible work schedules, or flextime, give employees more personal control over the hours they work each day.

Another promising alternative work arrangement is **flexible work schedules**, sometimes called **flextime**. The compressed work schedules previously discussed give employees time off during "normal" working hours, but they must still follow a regular and defined schedule on the days when they do work. Flextime, however, usually gives employees less say about what days they work but more personal control over the times when they work on those days.[22]

Figure 5.4 illustrates how flextime works. The workday is broken down into two categories: flexible time and core time. All employees must be at their workstations during core time, but they can choose their own schedules during flexible time. Thus, one employee may choose to start work early in the morning and leave in mid-afternoon, another to start in the late morning and work until late afternoon, and a third to start early in the morning, take a long lunch break, and work until late afternoon.

The major advantage of this approach, as already noted, is that workers get to tailor their workday to fit their personal needs. A person who needs to visit the dentist in the late afternoon can just start work early. A person who stays out late one night can start work late the next day. And the person who needs to run some errands during lunch can take a longer midday break. On the other hand, flextime is more difficult to manage because others in the organization may not be sure when a person will be available for

FIGURE 5.4

Flexible Work Schedules

Flexible work schedules are an important new work arrangement used in some organizations today. All employees must be at work during "core time." In the hypothetical example shown here, core time is from 9 to 11 a.m. and 1 to 3 p.m. The other time, then, is flexible—employees can come and go as they please during this time, as long as the total time spent at work meets organizational expectations.

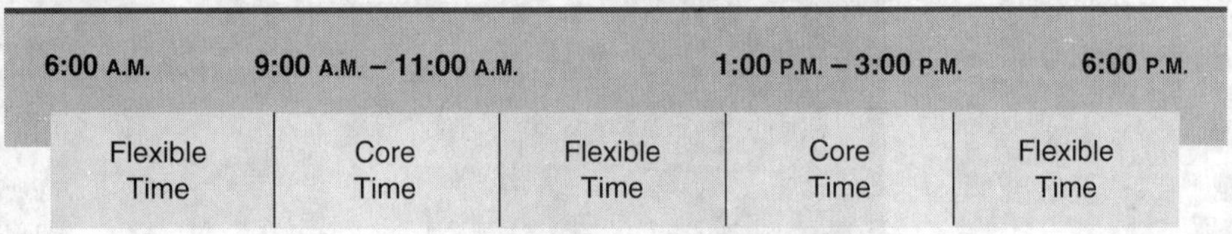

meetings other than during the core time. Expenses such as utilities will also be higher since the organization must remain open for a longer period each day. And as noted earlier in the *Diversity* box, flexible work schedules don't always achieve the desired outcomes.

Some organizations have experimented with a plan in which workers set their own hours but then must follow that schedule each day. Others allow workers to modify their own schedule each day. Organizations that have used the flexible work schedule method for arranging work include Sun Microsystems, KPMG, Best Buy, Pricewaterhouse Coopers, and some offices in the U.S. government. One survey found that as many as 43 percent of U.S. workers have the option to modify their work schedules; most of those who choose to do so start earlier than normal so as to get off work earlier in the day.[23] A more recent study found that approximately 27 million full-time workers in the United States have some degree of flexibility in when they begin and end their work days.[24]

Job Sharing

In **job sharing**, two or more part-time employees share one full-time job.

Yet another potentially useful alternative work arrangement is job sharing. In **job sharing**, two part-time employees share one full-time job. Job sharing may be desirable for people who only want to work part time or when job markets are tight. For its part, the organization can accommodate the preferences of a broader range of employees and may benefit from the talents of more people. Perhaps the simplest job-sharing arrangement to visualize is that of a receptionist. To share this job, one worker would staff the receptionist's desk from, say, 8:00 a.m. to noon each day; the office might close from noon to 1:00 p.m., and a second worker would staff the desk from 1:00 p.m. in the afternoon until 5:00 p.m. To the casual observer or visitor to the office, the fact that two people serve in one job is essentially irrelevant. The responsibilities of the job in the morning and responsibilities in the afternoon are not likely to be interdependent. Thus, the position can easily be broken down into two or perhaps even more components.

Organizations sometimes offer job sharing as a way to entice more workers to the organization. If a particular kind of job is difficult to fill, a job-sharing arrangement might make it more attractive to more people. There are also cost benefits for the organization. Since the employees may be working only part-time, the organization does not have to give them the same benefits that full-time employees receive. The organization can also tap into a wider array of skills when it provides job-sharing arrangements. The firm gets the advantage of the two sets of skills from one job.

Some workers like job sharing because it gives them flexibility and freedom. Certain workers, for example, may only want part-time work. Stepping into a shared job may also give them a chance to work in an organization that otherwise only wants to hire full-time employees. When the job sharer isn't working, she or he may attend school, take care of the family, or simply enjoy leisure time.

Job sharing does not work for every organization, and it isn't attractive to all workers, but it has produced enough success stories to suggest that it will be around for a long time. CNN, Wegmans, Google, SAS, and DreamWorks Animation all allow job sharing.[25] Each of these organizations, and dozens more like them, report that job sharing has become a critically important part of its human resource system. Although job sharing has not been scientifically evaluated, it appears to be a useful alternative to traditional work scheduling.[26]

Telecommuting

Telecommuting is a work arrangement in which employees spend part of their time working off-site.

Another approach to alternative work arrangements that is surging in popularity is **telecommuting**—allowing employees to spend part of their time working off-site, usually at home. By using e-mail, web interfaces, and other technology, many employees can maintain close contact with their organization and do as much work at home as they could in their offices. The increased power and sophistication of modern communication technology—laptops and smartphones, among others—is making telecommuting easier and easier.[27] (Other terms used to describe this concept are e-commuting and working from home.)

On the plus side, many employees like telecommuting because it gives them added flexibility. By spending one or two days a week at home, for instance, they have the same kind of flexibility to manage personal activities as is afforded by flextime or compressed schedules. Some employees also feel that they get more work done by staying at home because they are less likely to be interrupted. Organizations may benefit for several reasons as well: (1) they can reduce absenteeism and turnover since employees will need to take less "formal" time off, and (2) they can save on facilities such as parking spaces because fewer people will be at work on any given day. There are also environmental benefits, given that fewer cars are on the highways.

The ability to work from remote locations, including home, has become not only popular but commonplace today. Telecommuting offers both advantages and challenges to both employees and their organizations, but on balance the pluses generally outnumber the minuses. This manager is working at home but has a Skype conference with his boss.

On the other hand, although many employees thrive under this arrangement, others do not. Some feel isolated and miss the social interaction of the workplace. Others simply lack the self-control and discipline to walk away from the breakfast table to their desk and start working. Managers may also encounter coordination difficulties in scheduling meetings and other activities that require face-to-face contact.

Another issue with telecommuting involves workplace safety. In 2000, the Department of Labor, operating under the Occupational Safety and Health Act, began to require employers to take a proactive stance on home safety. Among other things, employers had to inspect workers' homes to ensure that all safety requirements were being met. For example, the employer had to verify that there were two external exits, that no lead paint had been used on the walls, that the employee's chairs were ergonomically sound, and that the indoor air quality met OSHA standards. This stipulation led to somewhat absurd decisions, such as corporations' allowing their employees to use home telephones but not home computers if the employees' monitors did not meet low-radiation requirements. The employer could also be held accountable for employees' unsafe behaviors, such as plugging too many electrical devices into one power outlet or standing on a chair rather than on a ladder to change a light bulb. Employers complained that the requirements were too burdensome, especially as more workers began telecommuting. Employees, too, objected to the requirements as being too intrusive, invading the privacy of their homes.

In 2001, the ruling was lifted. A number of legal issues remain, however, and some firms still find it best to take at least some role in assessing home safety for their telecommuting employees. And there is now a new area of growing concern—cybercrime. Is a company liable if a client's confidential information is stolen because an employee's home computer didn't have hacker protection? What if the employee uses a home computer for business and also peddles online pornography?

Given the trends and pressures toward telecommuting and the associated legal issues, there will no doubt continue to be significant changes in this area in the future.[28]

SYNOPSIS

Managers seek to enhance employee performance by capitalizing on the potential for motivated behavior to improve performance. Methods often used to translate motivation into performance involve work design, participation and empowerment, alternative work arrangements, performance management, goal setting, and rewards.

The essence of work design is job design—how organizations define and structure jobs. Historically, there was a general trend toward increasingly specialized jobs, but more recently the movement has consistently been away from extreme specialization. Two early alternatives to specialization were job rotation and job enlargement. Job enrichment approaches stimulated considerable interest in job design.

The job characteristics theory grew from early work on job enrichment. One basic premise of this theory is that jobs can be described in terms of a specific set of motivational characteristics. Another is that managers should work to enhance the presence of those motivational characteristics in jobs but should also take individual differences into account.

Employee involvement using participative management and empowerment can help improve employee motivation in many business settings. New management practices such as the use of various kinds of work teams and of flatter, more decentralized methods of organizing are intended to empower employees throughout the organization. Organizations that want to empower their employees need to understand a variety of issues as they go about promoting participation.

Flexible work arrangements are commonly used today to enhance motivated job performance. Among the more popular alternative arrangements are compressed workweeks, flexible work schedules, extended work schedules, job sharing, and telecommuting.

DISCUSSION QUESTIONS

1. What are the primary advantages and disadvantages of job specialization? Were they the same in the early days of mass production?
2. Under what circumstances might job enlargement be especially effective? Especially ineffective? How about job rotation?
3. Do any trends today suggest a return to job specialization?
4. What are the strengths and weaknesses of job enrichment? When might it be useful?
5. Do you agree or disagree that individual differences affect how people respond to their jobs? Explain.
6. What are the primary similarities and differences between job enrichment and the approach proposed by job characteristics theory?
7. What are the motivational consequences of increased employee involvement from the frame of reference of expectancy and equity theories?
8. What motivational problems might result from an organization's attempt to set up work teams?
9. Which form of a flexible work schedule might you prefer?
10. How do you think you would like telecommuting?

HOW DO YOU SEE IT?

Food for Managerial Thought

"We attempt to hire grownups."

—ANDY PFORZHEIMER, COFOUNDER OF BARCELONA RESTAURANT GROUP

In an early section of our video, we find ourselves in the midst of a managers meeting at Barcelona Restaurant Group. Tapping his pen on a projected slide, company president Andy Pforzheimer draws everyone's attention to a section on "technical skills," which he defines as "your ability to do your job. [Over] the last two months," he announces, "it sucked." There ensues some back and forth about the price of suckling pig, with one manager objecting to the implication that he doesn't keep a close eye on his costs. Pforzheimer complains about "29 percent food cost" at the manager's restaurant, but the manager replies, "That's only for the last two months. My last six months were the lowest in the company." In the middle of the room, chief operating officer Scott Lawton rocks back and forth as if in agreement with the aggrieved manager.

We then cut back to Pforzheimer as he admits to the interviewer that "I can be difficult to work for." After some reflection, however, he adds, as if confirming that the encounter with his manager was more contributory than confrontational, "I am very interested in having other people's opinions thrown at me. I like managers who talk back."

Before the video is over, we find that Pforzheimer has a lot of theories about running restaurants and what he wants out of his managers and other employees. First of all, he wants people who respond better to responsibility than to authority: "We tell them when we hire people, 'Look—this is *your* restaurant.... If the place does well, you get all the credit. If the place does badly, it's your fault.' They have to be very comfortable with taking complete ownership. Some of our best managers," explains Pforzheimer,

> *come from very highly regulated large restaurant companies where they were told how to answer the phone and how to set a table and how to greet a guest, and it's all in giant books that they have to memorize.*
>
> *We don't do that. We attempt to hire grownups.*

"We give some basic guidelines as to what our philosophy is," adds Lawton, "… but we have to trust [employees] to work within those confines and make the right choice. They might not always make the choice that *I* would make, [but] sometimes they make a *better* one." For Lawton, who's also done a lot of thinking about the best way to run a restaurant, the key to success is the *possibility* of that better choice. If you dictate choices from the top, you may be right and you may get your desired results. At the same time, however, you forfeit any chance of *better* results. "To give [managers] a correct answer to every question," he suspects,

> *is impossible, and I think it doesn't work. I think, in fact, that you're actually limiting your ability to get better.*
>
> *We, as a company, have gotten better … because we've brought in more brain power, more creativity, and we've allowed people to use it.*

Pforzheimer, who spent 15 years in the kitchens of some of the country's finest restaurants, is also convinced that "restaurants in general are not run terribly professionally." So when he and Sasa Mahr-Batuz, a former tennis pro and veteran restaurateur, decided to launch Barcelona in 1995, they were determined "to inject some professionalism into the restaurant industry." A lot of the literature on how to motivate employees, says Pforzheimer, tends to distort the basic employer-employee-customer linkage, "as in 'If you take care of your employees, then they'll be happy and they'll turn around and take care of your customers.' I don't believe that." As far as he's concerned, the equation doesn't reflect the optimum means of meeting the primary goal of any restaurant: "We are here for the customers," says Pforzheimer:

> *We're here for the customer experience. Everything else is secondary to that. If it makes the manager's life miserable, I don't care. If it makes the waiter's life miserable, I don't care. If it makes the chef miserable, I don't care. If it makes me miserable, I don't care.*
>
> *It's a job. It's work. … It's not always fun. But we're not here to have fun. We're here so that other people can have fun. That's our job.*

The employer's job, in other words, is focused on satisfying customers and doesn't leave much time or energy for satisfying employees. Lawton explains that it's all a matter of how you look at *empowerment*, which, as we learn in this chapter, means letting employees make decisions and solve problems in the organization's best interest. For Barcelona employees, Lawton emphasizes, being "empowered" means being able to "take care of their guests and focus on doing something that's just satisfying [for customers]. That's why you're in this business." The key, he concludes, is simply a little tweaking of your thinking about the employer-employee-customer linkage and the way in which it produces "happiness" all around:

> *If we can empower [employees] to make the guests happy, they're going to make money, the vibe in the restaurant is going to be a ton of fun, so everybody's going to enjoy the shift, and they're going to be proud of what they've done, and they are happy. It's a by-product.*

CASE QUESTIONS

1. If the model of performance-enhancement methods encapsulated in Figure 5.1 is valid, Barcelona's top managers believe that employees can potentially be motivated to enhance performance. Judging from the video, which *perspective on motivation* do you think they prefer—*need*, *process*, or *learning based*? Why? Given this preference, what forms of *potential for motivated behavior* do you think that they prefer to focus on? Which methods of enhancing performance—*job design*, *employee participation*, etc.—are they most likely to use?
2. Would the top managers at Barcelona be averse to applying the criteria of *job characteristics theory* to their policies and practices for motivating employees? Think about each criterion—*experienced meaningfulness of the work*, *experienced responsibility for work outcomes*, and *knowledge of results*—separately as well as collectively.
3. Do top managers at Barcelona appear to encourage *participation* as a motivational strategy, at least for some employees? Consider the specific factors in the chapter's definition of *empowerment*—*setting goals*, *making decisions*, and *solving problems*. In what ways does this definition help to explain the approach to empowerment at Barcelona? In what ways do Barcelona's top managers appear to play variations on these factors?

ADDITIONAL SOURCES

Valerie Schroth, "Success Stories: Barcelona Finds the Formula," *Connecticut Magazine*, January 2012, www.connecticutmag.com on June 27, 2012; Barcelona Restaurant Group, "About Us" (2012), www.barcelonawinebar.com on June 27, 2012; Andrews McMeel Publishing, "About Sasa Bahr-Batuz and Andy Pforzheimer" (May 2012), http://cookbooks.andrewsmcmeel.com on June 27, 2012; James Cooper, "Chef Interview: Andrew Pforzheimer of the Barcelona Restaurant Group," *Examiner.com*, January 27, 2010, www.examiner.com on June 27, 2012; Connecticut Restaurant Association, "Barcelona Restaurant Group's Andy Pforzheimer and Sasa Bahr-Batuz Receive Restaurateurs of the Year Award," *StamfordPlus.com*, December 7, 2010, www.stamfordplus.com on June 27, 2012.

EXPERIENCING ORGANIZATIONAL BEHAVIOR

Learning About Job Design

Purpose: This exercise will help you assess the processes involved in designing jobs to make them more motivating.

Format: Working in small groups, you will diagnose the motivating potential of an existing job, compare its motivating potential to that of other jobs, suggest ways to redesign the job, and then assess the effects of your redesign suggestions on other aspects of the workplace.

Procedure: Your instructor will divide the class into groups of three or four people each. In assessing the characteristics of jobs, use a scale value of 1 ("very little") to 7 ("very high").

1. Using the scale values, assign scores on each core job dimension used in the job characteristics theory (see below) to the following jobs: secretary, professor, food server, auto mechanic, lawyer, short-order cook, department store clerk, construction worker, and newspaper reporter.
2. Researchers often assess the motivational properties of jobs by calculating their motivating potential score (MPS). The usual formula for MPS is

$$\frac{(\text{Variety} + \text{Identity} + \text{Significance})}{3} \times \text{Autonomy} \times \text{Feedback}$$

   Use this formula to calculate the MPS for each job in step 1.
3. Your instructor will now assign your group one of the jobs from the list. Discuss how you might reasonably go about enriching the job.
4. Calculate the new MPS score for the redesigned job and check its new position in the rank ordering.
5. Discuss the feasibility of your redesign suggestions. In particular, look at how your recommended changes might necessitate changes in other jobs, in the reward system, and in the selection criteria used to hire people for the job.
6. Briefly discuss your observations with the rest of the class.

Follow-Up Questions

1. How might your own preexisting attitudes explain some of your own perceptions in this exercise?
2. Are some jobs simply impossible to redesign?

BUILDING MANAGERIAL SKILLS

Exercise Overview Communication skills are your ability to convey ideas and information to other people. They also involve the ways in which you receive ideas and information conveyed *to you*. This exercise puts you on the receiving end of an e-mail that directs you to motivate others but which may not be very effective in motivating you to perform the task. As a result, you may be called upon to exercise not only your own communication skills but other managerial skills as well.

Exercise Background Albert Q. Fixx, the founder and CEO of your company, a small manufacturer of auto parts, has long been committed to the continuous improvement of the firm's management practices through the application of modern management techniques. It seems that Mr. Fixx spent the past weekend at a seminar conducted by a nationally respected consultant on management effectiveness. The principal speaker and the group sessions focused squarely on the use of employee participation as means of improving company-wide productivity and enhancing employees' commitment to their jobs.

So inspired was Mr. Fixx by his weekend experience that he went straight back to his office on Sunday night, where he composed and sent an e-mail that all managers would find in their inboxes bright and early on Monday morning. After recapping his eye-opening weekend, he wrote the following:

> I am convinced that participative management is the key to improving productivity at this company. Because you did not have the advantage of attending

the same seminar that I did, I am attaching copies of all the handouts that were given to participants. They explain everything you need to know about practicing participative management, and I expect all of you to begin putting these principles into practice, starting this week. As of now, both I myself and this company are committed to participative management. Those of you who do not undertake the application of participative-management principles in your departments will find it very difficult to remain with a forward-looking company like A.Q. Fixx.

Exercise Task Your instructor will divide the class into groups of four to seven people. Each member of the group will pretend to be a manager at A.Q. Fixx, and your group of "managers" will discuss each of the following issues. Be prepared to discuss the group's thinking on each issue, even if the group doesn't reach a consensus.

1. What are the chances that Mr. Fixx's e-mail will spur effective participative management at the company? Are the odds better or worse than 50/50?
2. How has each individual manager responded to the e-mail? Is your response consistent with that of most group members, or do you find yourself taking a stance that's different, even if only slightly so? If you've taken a different stance, do you think it's worthwhile trying to convince the group to come around to your way of thinking? Why or why not?
3. What is the group's opinion of Mr. Fixx's approach to implementing participative management at the company? If you don't regard his approach as the best way of implementing participative practices—or his e-mail as the best means of introducing the subject—discuss some ways in which he could he have improved his approach.

SELF-ASSESSMENT EXERCISE

The Job Characteristics Inventory

The following questionnaire was developed to measure the central concepts of the job characteristics theory. Answer the questions in relation to the job you currently hold or the job you most recently held.

Skill Variety

1. How much *variety* is there in your job? That is, to what extent does the job require you to do many different things at work, using a variety of your skills and talents?

1	2	3	4	5	6	7
Very little; the job requires me to do the same routine things over and over again.			Moderate variety			Very much; the job requires me to do many different things, using a number of different skills and talents.

2. The job requires me to use a number of complex or high-level skills.

How accurate is the statement in describing your job?

1	2	3	4	5	6	7
Very inaccurate	Mostly inaccurate	Slightly inaccurate	Uncertain	Slightly accurate	Mostly accurate	Very accurate

3. The job is quite simple and repetitive.*

How accurate is the statement in describing your job?

1	2	3	4	5	6	7
Very inaccurate	Mostly inaccurate	Slightly inaccurate	Uncertain	Slightly accurate	Mostly accurate	Very accurate

Task Identity

1. To what extent does your job involve doing a *"whole" and identifiable piece of work*? That is, is the job a complete piece of work that has an obvious beginning and end? Or is it only a small *part* of the overall piece of work, which is finished by other people or by automatic machines?

1	2	3	4	5	6	7
My job is only a tiny part of the overall piece of work; the results of my activities cannot be seen in the final product or service.			My job is a moderate-sized "chunk" of the overall piece of work; my own contribution can be seen in the final outcome.			My job involves doing the whole piece of work, from start to finish; the results of my activities are easily seen in the final product or service.

2. The job provides me a chance to completely finish the pieces of work I begin.

How accurate is the statement in describing your job?

1	2	3	4	5	6	7
Very inaccurate	Mostly inaccurate	Slightly inaccurate	Uncertain	Slightly accurate	Mostly accurate	Very accurate

3. The job is arranged so that I do *not* have the chance to do an entire piece of work from beginning to end.*

How accurate is the statement in describing your job?

1	2	3	4	5	6	7
Very inaccurate	Mostly inaccurate	Slightly inaccurate	Uncertain	Slightly accurate	Mostly accurate	Very accurate

Task Significance

1. In general, how significant or important is your job? That is, are the results of your work likely to significantly affect the lives or well-being of other people?

1	2	3	4	5	6	7
Not very significant; the outcomes of my work are not likely to have important effects on other people.			Moderately significant			Highly significant; the outcomes of my work can affect other people in very important ways.

2. This job is one in which a lot of people can be affected by how well the work gets done.

How accurate is the statement in describing your job?

1	2	3	4	5	6	7
Very inaccurate	Mostly inaccurate	Slightly inaccurate	Uncertain	Slightly accurate	Mostly accurate	Very accurate

3. The job itself is *not* very significant or important in the broader scheme of things.*

How accurate is the statement in describing your job?

1	2	3	4	5	6	7
Very inaccurate	Mostly inaccurate	Slightly inaccurate	Uncertain	Slightly accurate	Mostly accurate	Very accurate

Autonomy

1. How much *autonomy* is there in your job? That is, to what extent does your job permit you to decide *on your own* how to go about doing your work?

1	2	3	4	5	6	7
Very little; the job gives me almost no personal "say" in how and when the work is done.			Moderate autonomy; many things are standardized and not under my control, but I can make some decisions about the work.			Very much; the job gives me almost complete responsibility for deciding how and when the work is done.

2. The job gives me considerable opportunity for independence and freedom in how I do the work.

How accurate is the statement in describing your job?

1	2	3	4	5	6	7
Very inaccurate	Mostly inaccurate	Slightly inaccurate	Uncertain	Slightly accurate	Mostly accurate	Very accurate

3. The job denies me any chance to use my personal initiative or judgment in carrying out the work.*

How accurate is the statement in describing your job?

1	2	3	4	5	6	7
Very inaccurate	Mostly inaccurate	Slightly inaccurate	Uncertain	Slightly accurate	Mostly accurate	Very accurate

Feedback

1. To what extent does *doing the job itself* provide you with information about your work performance? That is, does the actual *work itself* provide clues about how well you are doing—aside from any "feedback" coworkers or supervisors may provide?

1	2	3	4	5	6	7
Very little; the job itself is set up so I could work forever without finding out how well I am doing.			Moderately; sometimes doing the job provides feedback to me, and sometimes it does not.			Very much; the job is set up so that I get almost constant "feedback" as I work about how well I am doing.

2. Just doing the work required by the job provides many chances for me to figure out how well I am doing.

How accurate is the statement in describing your job?

1	2	3	4	5	6	7
Very inaccurate	Mostly inaccurate	Slightly inaccurate	Uncertain	Slightly accurate	Mostly accurate	Very accurate

3. The job itself provides very few clues about whether or not I am performing well.*

How accurate is the statement in describing your job?

1	2	3	4	5	6	7
Very inaccurate	Mostly inaccurate	Slightly inaccurate	Uncertain	Slightly accurate	Mostly accurate	Very accurate

Scoring: Responses to the three items for each core characteristic are averaged to yield an overall score for that characteristic. Items marked with an asterisk (*) should be scored as follows: 1 = 7; 2 = 6; 3 = 5; 4 = 4; 5 = 3; 6 = 2; 7 = 1.

Once you have calculated the score for each core characteristic, calculate the motivating potential score (MPS) of your job using this formula:

$$\text{MPS} = \frac{(\text{Skill variety} + \text{Task identity} + \text{Task significance})}{3} \times \text{Autonomy} \times \text{Feedback}$$

Finally, compare your MPS with those of your classmates and discuss why some scores are higher or lower than others.

CHAPTER 6

Motivating Employee Performance Through Rewards

Chapter Outline

- Goal Setting and Motivation
- Performance Management in Organizations
- Individual Rewards in Organizations
- Managing Reward Systems

Chapter Learning Objectives

After studying this chapter, you should be able to:

1. Describe goal setting and relate it to motivation.
2. Discuss performance management in organizations.
3. Identify the key elements in understanding individual rewards in organizations.
4. Describe the issues and processes involved in managing reward systems.

Whole Foods and Nothing but Whole Foods

"There's way more going on here than 'health insurance.'"

—Anonymous former executive at Whole Foods Market

Whole Foods Market (WFM) started out in 1980 as 1 store with 19 employees in Austin, Texas. Today, with 350 stores and 54,000 employees in North America and Great Britain, it's the leading natural and organic foods supermarket (and ninth-largest food and drug chain in the United States). Along the way, it's also gained a considerable reputation as a socially responsible company and a good

AP Photo/Richard Drew

Whole Foods is often considered one of the best places to work, in part because of the strong benefits programs it offers to employees. Founder John Mackey, however, recently caused a controversy by stating that people do not have a right to health care.

place to work. WFM's motto is "Whole Foods, Whole People, Whole Planet," and its guiding "core value," according to co-CEO Walter Robb, is "customers first, then team members, balanced with what's good for other stakeholders.... If I put our mission in simple terms," Robb continues, "it would be, No. 1, to change the way the world eats and, No. 2, to create a workplace based on love and respect."

WFM made *Fortune* magazine's very first list of the "100 Best Companies to Work For" in 1998 and is one of 13 organizations to have made it every year since. Citations have acknowledged the company's growth (which means more jobs), salary-cap limits (the top earner gets no more than 19 times the average full-time salary), and generous health plan. The structure of the company's current health care program, which revolves around high deductibles and so-called *health savings accounts (HSAs)*, was first proposed in 2003. Under such a plan, an employee (a "team member," in WFM parlance) pays a deductible before his or her expenses are covered. Meanwhile, the employer funds a special account (an HSA) for each employee, who can spend the money to cover health-related expenditures. The previous WFM plan had covered 100 percent of all expenses, and when some employees complained about the proposed change, the company decided to put it to a vote. Nearly 90 percent of the workforce went to the polls, with 77 percent voting for the new plan. In 2006, employees voted to retain the plan, which now carries a deductible of around $1,300; HSAs may go as high as $1,800 (and accrue for future use). The company pays 100 percent of the premiums for eligible employees (about 89 percent of the workforce).

High-deductible plans save money for the employer (the higher the deductible, the lower the premium), and more importantly—at least according to founder and co-CEO John Mackey—they also make employees more responsible consumers. When the first $1,300 of their medical expenses comes out of their own pockets (or their own HSAs), he argues, people "start asking how much things cost. Or they get a bill and say, 'Wow, that's expensive.' They begin to ask questions. They may not want to go to the emergency room if they wake up with a hangnail in the middle of the night. They may schedule an appointment now."

Mackey believes that "the individual is the best judge of what's right for the individual," and he's so convinced of the value of plans like the one offered by his company that in August 2009 he wrote an op-ed article in the *Wall Street Journal* in which he recommended "The Whole Foods Alternative to ObamaCare." Health care, he wrote, "is a service that we all need, but just like food and shelter, it is best provided through voluntary and mutually beneficial market exchanges." Going a step further, Mackey argued against an "intrinsic right to health care," and on this point he stirred up a reaction among his customers that ran the gamut from surprise to boycotting. "I'm boycotting [Whole Foods]," said one customer who'd been shopping WFM several times a week, "because all Americans need health care. While Mackey is worried about health care and stimulus spending, he doesn't seem too worried about expensive wars and tax breaks for the wealthy and big businesses such as his own that contribute to the [national] deficit."

Consumer advocates and HR specialists also attacked Mackey's proposals and policies. "High-deductible plans for low-wage workers," says Judy Dugan, research director of Consumer Watchdog, "are the next best thing to being uninsured: The upfront costs are so high that workers have to weigh getting health care against paying the rent (to the detriment of their health)." A former WFM executive points out, for example, that the firm's plan entails "astronomical deductibles and co-pays." The $1,300 deductible, he explains,

> *means that you, minimum-wage-earning worker, must pay $1,300 of your own money before you get any coverage applied for medical services. After that, for in-network visits, the rate is 20/80, up to a maximum of $4,600 out of pocket for the year. This means that if you get charged $10,000 for a special hospital test … you are still liable for … $2,000!*

As for the HSA, it has to cover all co-pays and all expenses not covered by the plan (such as mental health care). "There's way more going on here than 'health insurance,'" concludes the anonymous former executive "… [The] system has massive hidden charges that routinely threaten and undermine the financial stability and, ultimately, [the] well-being of the employees."

Responding to the backlash against Mackey's *WSJ* piece, the WFM Customer Communications Team hastened to point out that "our team members vote on our plan … to make sure they continue to have a voice in our benefits." Mackey's intent, said the press release, "was to express his personal opinions—not those of Whole Foods Market team members or our company as a whole." The release also offered an apology for having "offended some of our customers," but for many onetime WFM loyalists, the apology was too little too late. "I will no longer be shopping at Whole Foods," announced one New Jersey shopper, explaining that "a CEO should take care that if he speaks about politics, his beliefs reflect at least the majority of his clients'." In fact, WFM had become, in the words of one reporter, "the granola set's chain of choice," and much of its customer base consists of people whose opinions on such issues as health care reform are quite different from Mackey's. His *WSJ* article, declared a contributor to the company's online forum, was "an absolute slap in the face to the millions of progressive-minded consumers that have made [Whole Foods] what it is today."

The potential repercussions weren't lost on the WFM board. In late August, following the appearance of the *WSJ* op-ed piece, shareholder activists called for Mackey's removal. The CEO, they charged, had "attempted to capitalize on the brand reputation of Whole Foods to champion his personal political views but has instead deeply offended a key segment of Whole Foods consumer base." The company's stock had also slipped 30 percent over the previous five-year period, and in December, the board compromised by convincing Mackey to step down as chairman of the board.

What Do You Think?

1. How important would benefits like those offered by Whole Foods be to you if you were working there to put yourself through school or to collect a paycheck while looking for a position in your chosen field?
2. Would the publicized opinions of a CEO be likely to influence your behavior as a current or potential customer of his or her company? Under what circumstances would your behavior most likely be affected?

References: John Stossel et al., "Health Savings Accounts: Putting Patients in Control," *ABC News*, September 14, 2007, http://abcnews.go.com on May 23, 2012; John Mackey, "The Whole Foods Alternative to ObamaCare," *Wall Street Journal*, August 11, 2009, http://online.wsj.com on May 23, 2012; Judy Dugan, "Whole Foods' Crummy Insurance: What John Mackey Means by 'Choice,'" *Consumer Watchdog*, August 20, 2009, www.consumerwatchdog.org on May 23, 2012; Emily Friedman, "Health Care Stirs Up Whole Foods CEO John Mackey, Customers Boycott Organic Grocery Store," *ABC News*, August 14, 2009, http://abcnews.go.com on May 23, 2012; Nick Paumgarten, "Food Fighter," *The New Yorker*, January 4, 2010, www.newyorker.com on May 23, 2012; "Whole Foods CEO John Mackey Stepping Down as Chairman," *Huffington Post*, December 25, 2009, www.huffingtonpost.com on May 23, 2012.

For decades, management experts have advocated providing meaningful rewards for employees. Most managers initially focused on pay as the basic reward offered to employees, but now many people understand that employees actually seek and respond to a variety of rewards from their work. And, as is apparent at Whole Foods, the perceptions and impact of rewards can vary. As we established at the beginning of Chapter 5, in order to capitalize on the potential for motivated behavior, managers can use a number of strategies directed at enhanced performance to transform that potential into actual enhanced performance. Subsequent discussions in that chapter identified various work-related elements that can help with that transformation.

In this chapter we examine several other organizational methods and elements that can promote enhanced performance. We begin with a discussion of goals and how they relate to both motivation and performance. Next, we describe performance management per se, as well as how performance relates to total quality management. Individual rewards are then introduced and related to motivated performance. Finally, we conclude with a discussion of a variety of issues that affect the management of reward systems.

GOAL SETTING AND MOTIVATION

A **goal** is a desirable objective.

Goal setting is a very useful method of enhancing employee performance.[1] From a motivational perspective, a **goal** is a meaningful objective. Goals are used for two purposes in most organizations. First, they provide a useful framework for managing motivation. Managers and employees can set goals for themselves and then work toward them. Thus, if the organization's overall goal is to increase sales by 10 percent, a manager can use individual goals to help attain that organizational goal. Second, goals are an effective control device (*control* meaning the monitoring by management of how well the organization is performing). Comparing people's short-term performances with their goals can be an effective way to monitor the organization's longer-term performance.

Social learning theory perhaps best describes the role and importance of goal setting in organizations.[2] This perspective suggests that feelings of pride or shame about performance are a function of the extent to which people achieve their goals. A person who achieves a goal will be proud of having done so, whereas a person who fails to achieve a goal will feel personal disappointment and perhaps even shame. People's degree of pride or disappointment is affected by their **self-efficacy**, the extent to which they feel that they can still meet their goals even if they failed to do so in the past.

Our **self-efficacy** is the extent to which we believe we can accomplish our goals even if we failed to do so in the past.

Goal-Setting Theory

Social learning theory provides insights into why and how goals can motivate behavior. It also helps us understand how different people cope with failure to reach their goals. The research of Edwin Locke and his associates most clearly established the utility of goal-setting theory in a motivational context.[3]

Locke's goal-setting theory of motivation assumes that behavior is a result of conscious goals and intentions. Therefore, by setting goals for people in the organization, a manager should be able to influence their behavior. Given this premise, the challenge is to develop a thorough understanding of the processes by which people set their goals and then work to reach them. In the original version of goal-setting theory, two specific goal characteristics—goal difficulty and goal specificity—were expected to shape performance.

Goal difficulty is the extent to which a goal is challenging and requires effort.

Goal Difficulty **Goal difficulty** is the extent to which a goal is challenging and requires effort. If people work to achieve goals, it is reasonable to assume that they will work harder to achieve more difficult goals. But a goal must not be so difficult that it is unattainable. If a new manager asks her sales force to increase sales by 300 percent, the group may ridicule her charge as laughable because they regard it as impossible to reach. A more realistic but still difficult goal—perhaps a 20 percent increase in sales—would probably be a better objective.

A substantial body of research supports the importance of goal difficulty.[4] In one study, managers at Weyerhaeuser set difficult goals for truck drivers hauling loads of timber from cutting sites to wood yards. Over a nine-month period, the drivers increased the quantity of wood they delivered by an amount that would have required $250,000 worth of new trucks at the previous per-truck average load.[5] Reinforcement also fosters motivation toward difficult goals. A person who is rewarded for achieving a difficult goal will be more inclined to strive toward the next difficult goal than will someone who received no reward for reaching the first goal.

Goal specificity is the clarity and precision of a goal.

Goal Specificity **Goal specificity** is the clarity and precision of the goal. A goal of "increasing productivity" is not very specific, whereas a goal of "increasing productivity by 3 percent in the next six months" is quite specific. Some goals, such as those involving costs, output, profitability, and growth, can easily be stated in clear and precise terms. Other goals, such as improving employee job satisfaction and morale, company image and reputation, ethical behavior, and social responsibility, are much harder to state in specific or measurable terms.

Like difficulty, specificity has been shown to be consistently related to performance. The study of timber truck drivers previously mentioned also examined goal specificity. The initial loads the truck drivers were carrying were found to be 60 percent of the maximum weight each truck could haul. The managers set a new goal for drivers of 94 percent, which the drivers were soon able to reach. Thus, the goal was quite specific as well as difficult.

Locke's theory attracted widespread interest and research support from both researchers and managers; so Locke, together with Gary Latham, eventually proposed an expanded model of the goal-setting process. The expanded model, shown in Figure 6.1, attempts to capture more fully the complexities of goal setting in organizations.

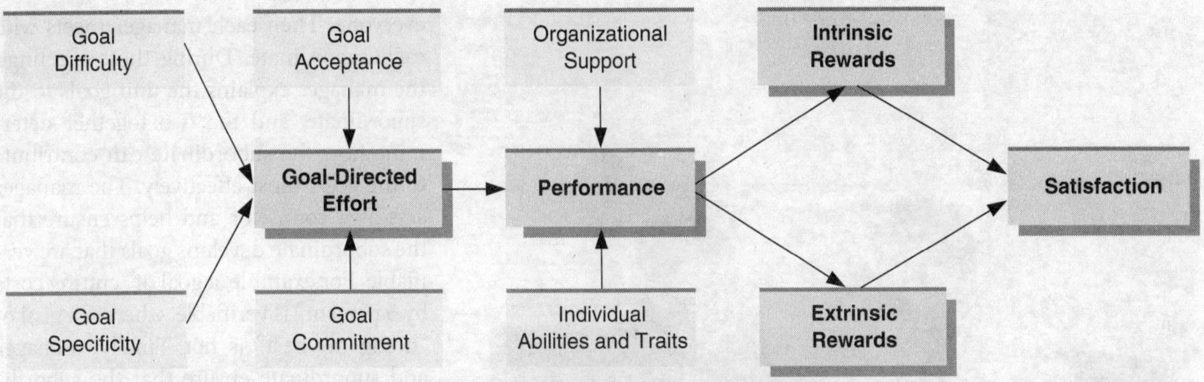

FIGURE 6.1

The Goal-Setting Theory of Motivation

The goal-setting theory of motivation provides an important means of enhancing the motivation of employees. As illustrated here, appropriate goal difficulty, specificity, acceptance, and commitment contribute to goal-directed effort. This effort, in turn, has a direct impact on performance.

Reference: Reprinted from Organizational Dynamics, Autumn 1979, Gary P. Latham et al., "The Goal-Setting Theory of Motivation." Copyright 1979, with permission from Elsevier.

Goal acceptance is the extent to which a person accepts a goal as his or her own.

Goal commitment is the extent to which a person is personally interested in reaching a goal.

The expanded theory argues that goal-directed effort is a function of four goal attributes: difficulty and specificity (previously discussed), and acceptance and commitment. **Goal acceptance** is the extent to which a person accepts a goal as his or her own. **Goal commitment** is the extent to which he or she is personally interested in reaching the goal. The manager who vows to take whatever steps are necessary to cut costs by 10 percent has made a commitment to achieving the goal. Factors that can foster goal acceptance and commitment include participating in the goal-setting process, making goals challenging but realistic, and believing that goal achievement will lead to valued rewards.[6]

The interaction of goal-directed effort, organizational support, and individual abilities and traits determines actual performance. Organizational support is whatever the organization does to help or hinder performance. Positive support might mean providing whatever resources are needed to meet the goal; negative support might mean failing to provide such resources, perhaps due to cost considerations or staff reductions. Individual abilities and traits are the skills and other personal characteristics necessary to do a job. As a result of performance, a person receives various intrinsic and extrinsic rewards that in turn influence satisfaction. Note that the latter stages of this model are quite similar to those of the Porter and Lawler expectancy model discussed in Chapter 4.

Broader Perspectives on Goal Setting

Management by objectives (MBO) is a collaborative goal-setting process through which organizational goals cascade down throughout the organization.

Some organizations undertake goal setting from the somewhat broader perspective of **management by objectives**, or **MBO**. The MBO approach is essentially a collaborative goal-setting process through which organizational goals systematically cascade down through the organization. Our discussion describes a generic approach, but many organizations adapt MBO to suit their own purposes and use a variety of names for it. (Indeed, most firms today use other names. However, since no other generic label has emerged, we will continue to refer to this approach as MBO.)

A successful MBO program starts with top managers' establishing overall goals for the organization. After these goals have been set, managers and employees throughout the organization collaborate to set subsidiary goals. First, the overall goals are communicated to

Performance review meetings are an integral part of effective goal setting. People need to have a voice in setting their goals and need feedback about how well they are achieving them. This manager, for example, is meeting with one of her subordinates to discuss his performance. She is proving him with specific details about where he is meeting expectations and where he needs to improve.

everyone. Then each manager meets with each subordinate. During these meetings, the manager explains the unit goals to the subordinate, and the two together determine how the subordinate can contribute to the goals most effectively. The manager acts as a counselor and helps ensure that the subordinate develops goals that are verifiable. For example, a goal of "cutting costs by 5 percent" is verifiable, whereas a goal of "doing my best" is not. Finally, manager and subordinate ensure that the subordinate has the resources needed to reach his or her goals. The entire process flows downward as each subordinate manager meets with his or her own subordinates to develop their goals. Thus, as we noted earlier, the initial goals set at the top cascade down through the entire organization.

During the time frame set for goal attainment (usually one year), the manager periodically meets with each subordinate to check progress. It may be necessary to modify goals in light of new information, to provide additional resources, or to take some other action. At the end of the specified time period, managers hold a final evaluation meeting with each subordinate. At this meeting, manager and subordinate assess how well goals were met and discuss why. This meeting often serves as the annual performance review as well, determining salary adjustments and other rewards based on reaching goals. This meeting may also serve as the initial goal-setting meeting for the next year's cycle.

Evaluation and Implications

Goal-setting theory has been widely tested in a variety of settings. Research has demonstrated fairly consistently that goal difficulty and specificity are closely associated with performance. Other elements of the theory, such as acceptance and commitment, have been studied less frequently. A few studies have shown the importance of acceptance and commitment, but little is currently known about how people accept and become committed to goals. Goal-setting theory may also focus too much attention on the short run at the expense of long-term considerations. Despite these questions, however, goal setting is clearly an important way for managers to convert motivation into actual improved performance.

From the broader perspective, MBO remains a very popular technique. Alcoa, Tenneco, Black & Decker, General Foods, and DuPont, for example, have used versions of MBO with widespread success. The technique's popularity stems in part from its many strengths. For one thing, MBO clearly has the potential to motivate employees because it helps implement goal-setting theory on a systematic basis throughout the organization. It also clarifies the basis for rewards, and it can stimulate communication. Performance appraisals are easier and more clear-cut under MBO. Further, managers can use the system for control purposes.

However, using MBO also presents pitfalls, especially if a firm takes too many shortcuts or inadvertently undermines how the process is supposed to work. Sometimes, for instance, top managers do not really participate; that is, the goals are actually established in the middle of the organization and may not reflect the real goals of top management. If employees believe this situation to be true, they may become cynical, interpreting the lack of participation by top management as a sign that the goals are not important and that their own involvement is therefore a waste of time. MBO also has a tendency to overemphasize quantitative goals to enhance verifiability. Another potential liability is that an MBO system requires a great deal of information processing and record keeping since every goal must be documented. Finally, some managers do not really let subordinates participate in goal setting but instead merely assign goals and order subordinates to accept them.

On balance, MBO is often an effective and useful system for managing goal setting and enhancing performance in organizations. Research suggests that it can actually do many of the things its advocates claim but that it must also be handled carefully. In particular, most organizations need to tailor it to their own unique circumstances. Properly used, MBO can also be an effective approach to managing an organization's reward system. It does require, however, individual, one-on-one interactions between each supervisor and each employee; and these one-on-one interactions can often be difficult because of the time they take and the likelihood that at least some of them will involve critical assessments of unacceptable performance.

PERFORMANCE MANAGEMENT IN ORGANIZATIONS

As described earlier, most goals are oriented toward some element of performance. Managers can do a variety of things to enhance employee motivation and performance, including redesigning jobs, allowing greater participation, creating alternative work arrangements, and setting goals. However, they may also fail to do things that might have improved motivation and performance, and they might even inadvertently do things that reduce motivation and performance. Thus, it is clearly important that performance be approached as something that can and should be managed.[7]

Performance measurement, or performance appraisal, is the process by which someone (1) evaluates an employee's work behaviors by measurement and comparison with previously established standards, (2) documents the results, and (3) communicates the results to the employee.

A performance management system (PMS) comprises the processes and activities involved in performance appraisals.

The Nature of Performance Management

The core of performance management is the actual measurement of the performance of an individual or group. **Performance measurement**, or **performance appraisal**, is the process by which someone (1) evaluates an employee's work behaviors by measurement and comparison with previously established standards, (2) documents the results, and (3) communicates the results to the employee.[8] A **performance management system (PMS)** comprises the processes and activities involved in performance appraisals, as shown in Figure 6.2.

Simple performance appraisal involves a manager and an employee, whereas the PMS incorporates the total quality management context along with the organizational policies, procedures, and resources that support the activity being evaluated. The timing and frequency of evaluations, choice of who appraises whom, measurement procedures, methods of recording the evaluations, and storage and distribution of information are all aspects of the PMS.

Purposes of Performance Measurement

Performance measurement may serve many purposes. The ability to provide valuable feedback is one critical purpose. Feedback, in turn, tells the employee where she or he

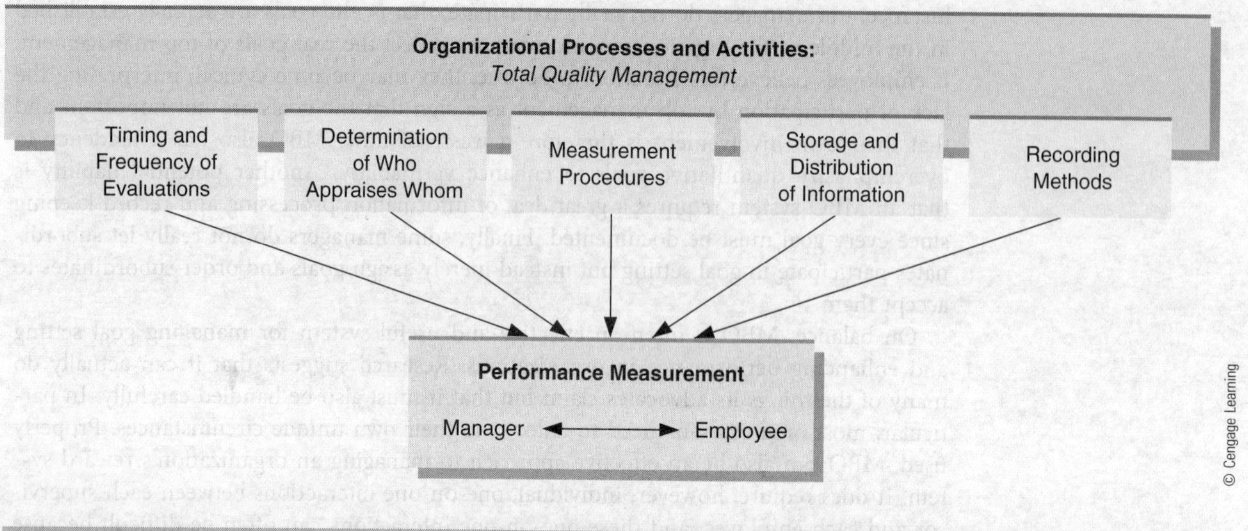

FIGURE 6.2

The Performance Management System

An organization's performance management system plays an important role in determining its overall level of effectiveness. This is especially true when the organization is attempting to employ total quality management. Key elements of a performance management system, as shown here, include the timing and frequency of evaluations, the choice of who does the evaluation, the choice of measurement procedures, the storage and distribution of performance information, and the recording methods. These elements are used by managers and employees in most organizations.

stands in the eyes of the organization. Appraisal results, of course, are also used to decide and justify reward allocations. Performance evaluations may be used as a starting point for discussions of training, development, and improvement. Finally, the data produced by the performance appraisal system can be used to forecast future human resource needs, to plan management succession, and to guide other human resource activities such as recruiting, training, and development programs.

Providing job performance feedback is the primary use of appraisal information. Performance appraisal information can indicate that an employee is ready for promotion or that he or she needs additional training to gain experience in another area of company operations. It may also show that a person does not have the skills for a certain job and that another person should be recruited to fill that particular role. Other purposes of performance appraisal can be grouped into two broad categories, judgment and development, as shown in Figure 6.3.

Performance appraisals with a judgmental orientation focus on past performance and are concerned mainly with measuring and comparing performance and with the uses of this information. Appraisals with a developmental orientation focus on the future and use information from evaluations to improve performance. If improved future performance is the intent of the appraisal process, the manager may focus on goals or targets for the employee, on eliminating obstacles or problems that hinder performance, and on future training needs.

Performance Measurement Basics

Employee appraisals are common in every type of organization, but how they are performed may vary. Many issues must be considered in determining how to conduct an appraisal. Three of the most important issues are who does the appraisals, how often they are done, and how performance is measured.

FIGURE 6.3

Purposes of Performance Management

Performance measurement plays a variety of roles in most organizations. This figure illustrates that these roles can help managers judge an employee's past performance and help managers and employees improve future performance.

Basic Purpose of Performance Measurement: Provide Information About Work Performance

Judgment of Past Performance	*Development of Future Performance*
Provide a basis for reward allocation	Foster work improvement
Provide a basis for promotions, transfers, layoffs, and so on	Identify training and development opportunities
Identify high-potential employees	Develop ways to overcome obstacles and performance barriers
Validate selection procedures	Establish supervisor–employee agreement on expectations
Evaluate previous training programs	

The Appraiser In most appraisal systems, the employee's primary evaluator is the supervisor. This stems from the obvious fact that the supervisor is presumably in the best position to be aware of the employee's day-to-day performance. Further, it is the supervisor who has traditionally provided performance feedback to employees and determined performance-based rewards and sanctions. Problems often arise, however, if the supervisor has incomplete or distorted information about the employee's performance. For example, the supervisor may have little firsthand knowledge of the performance of an employee who works alone outside the company premises, such as a salesperson making solo calls on clients or a maintenance person handling equipment problems in the field. Similar problems may arise when the supervisor has a limited understanding of the technical knowledge involved in an employee's job.

One solution to these problems is a multiple-rater system that incorporates the ratings of several people familiar with the employee's performance. One possible alternative, for example, is to use the employee as an evaluator. Although they may not actually do so, most employees are actually very capable of evaluating themselves in an unbiased manner.

360-degree feedback is a performance management system in which people receive performance feedback from those on all sides of them in the organization—their boss, their colleagues and peers, and their own subordinates.

One of the more interesting approaches being used in some companies today is something called **360-degree feedback**—a performance management system in which people receive performance feedback from those on all "sides" of them in the organization—their boss, their colleagues and peers, and their own subordinates. Thus, the feedback comes from all around them, or from 360 degrees. This form of performance evaluation can be very beneficial to managers because it typically gives them a much wider range of performance-related feedback than a traditional evaluation provides. That is, rather than focusing narrowly on objective performance, such as sales increases or productivity gains, 360-degree feedback often focuses on such things as interpersonal relations and style. For example, one person may learn that she stands too close to other people when she talks, another that he has a bad temper. These are the kinds of things a supervisor might not even be aware of, much less report as part of a performance appraisal. Subordinates or peers are much more willing to provide this sort of feedback.

Of course, for a manager to benefit from 360-degree feedback, he or she must have a thick skin. The manager is likely to hear some personal comments on sensitive topics, which may be threatening. Thus, a 360-feedback system must be carefully managed so that its focus remains on constructive rather than destructive criticism.[9] Because of its potential advantages and in spite of its potential shortcomings, many companies today are using this approach to performance feedback. AT&T, Nestlé, Pitney Bowes, and JPMorgan Chase are a few of the major companies today using 360-degree feedback to help managers improve a wide variety of performance-related behaviors.[10]

SERVICE Mystery Shopper Performance Review

©rangizzz/Shutterstock

You are a restaurant server in the middle of a performance review with your boss. After listening to her make several observations about your performance as a server, you start wondering to yourself whether she has ever really observed what you do. In your mind, you have performed well, your customers seem satisfied, your tips average among the highest in the restaurant, and the mystery shoppers that have reported on your service have uniformly acknowledged your skill and genuine hospitality. Thus, your own assessment of your performance is very high and your belief in the value of the feedback from your boss is very low. As you reflect on this conversation, you think about how much better it would be if your performance evaluation was entirely driven by mystery shoppers.

So what do mystery shoppers do and why is their feedback valued by employees? A mystery shopper is exactly that—a person who comes to a service experience and evaluates it systematically. The employing firm generally will recruit shoppers who fit their clients' targeted customer profiles and send them to a service operation to see whether the service provided is what the organization intends. Thus, the first step in using mystery shoppers is to identify the service expectations of the client organization's customers and find a way to translate those expectations into a set of measureable service standards. If a restaurant's customers' service expectations, for example, include not waiting in long lines for seating, being greeted promptly and warmly upon seating, and eating well-prepared, good-tasting food in reasonable quantities for a fair price in a clean facility, then a set of standards can be established for each of these components of the restaurant experience against which the restaurant and its employees can be systematically assessed by a mystery shopper.

Consequently, that restaurant's mystery shopper will note the time it took to get seated upon arrival; how many minutes it took to be waited on and served; the quality and quantity of the food; the cleanliness of the facility; the warmth, responsiveness, and friendliness of the server; and the price paid for the experience. This report is submitted to the company, which in turn sends it to the restaurant's management. The manager of the restaurant will then use this report as an assessment of the quality of the restaurant, the management of the customer experience, and the performance of the employees.

In one study in which the restaurant used daily mystery shoppers, it created a mystery shopper schedule that captured the value of variable ratio feedback. Although the staff of about 30 servers had no idea when any one of them would be evaluated by a mystery shopper, they did know that they would be shopped on the average of once every 30 days. Moreover, they knew that their manager would be sitting with either them or one of the other servers each day to review the mystery shopper's report for the previous day. The benefit gained was that the employees could see the manager reporting what the shopper said to some employee every day instead of having a traditional annual formal performance review based on the manager's opinion and interpretation of facts. Moreover, the feedback was entirely derived from an external observer. The direct benefit of this system was seen in an increase in repeat customer visits and higher mystery shopper evaluations of employee performance. The indirect benefit was that the mission of customer service was reinforced daily by managers sitting with employees in plain sight of all to talk about the mystery shopper reports. It was visibly obvious that the restaurant company and its mangers took excellent customer service seriously. The second indirect benefit was that it allowed managers to reposition themselves as performance coaches discussing third-party and relatively objective performance feedback instead of acting in the traditional and somewhat subjective supervisory roles of performance judge and jury.

Employees saw these types of performance reviews as fairer and more objectively anchored to their actual behaviors rather than as based on a boss's opinion. The managers were taught to focus on the positive and offer help in correcting any negative. This mystery shopper process rewarded desired behaviors on a variable ratio interval that confirmed the many lab studies on the value of this reinforcement technique and opens the door to using this technique in a wide variety of situations in which employees have internal or external customers that can provide relatively objective performance feedback.

Discussion Question: How would you set up a mystery shopper performance feedback system for your course in organizational behavior? What would you measure as performance standards, and what standards would you create? Do you think such a system would make a positive impact on teaching effectiveness? Why or why not?

Sozaijiten/Datacraft/Imagenavi/Jupiter Images

In general, Japan has a collectivistic culture that puts the group before the individual. As result, it is common for performance appraisal systems in that country to assess and reward group performance as opposed to individual performance.

Frequency of the Appraisal Another important issue is the frequency of appraisals. Regardless of the employee's level of performance, the type of tasks being performed, or the employee's need for information on performance, the organization usually conducts performance appraisals on a regular basis, typically once a year. Annual performance appraisals are convenient for administrative purposes such as record keeping and maintaining a level of routine that helps keep everyone comfortable. Some organizations also conduct appraisals semiannually.[11] Several systems for monitoring employee performance on an "as-needed" basis have been proposed as an alternative to the traditional annual system.

Managers in international settings must ensure that they incorporate cultural phenomena into their performance-appraisal strategies. For example, in highly individualistic cultures such as that of the United States, appraising performance at the individual level is both common and accepted. But in collectivistic cultures such as Japan, performance appraisals almost always need to be focused more on group performance and feedback. And in countries where people put a lot of faith in destiny, fate, or some form of divine control, employees may not be receptive to performance feedback at all, believing that their actions are irrelevant to the results that follow them.

Measuring Performance The cornerstone of a good PMS is the method for measuring performance. Detailed descriptions of the many different methods for measuring performance are beyond the scope of this book; they are more appropriately covered in a course in human resource management or a specialized course in performance appraisal. However, we can present a few general comments about how to measure performance.

The measurement method provides the information managers use to make decisions about salary adjustment, promotion, transfer, training, and discipline. The courts and Equal Employment Opportunity guidelines have mandated that performance measurements be based on job-related criteria rather than on some other factor such as friendship, age, sex, religion, or national origin. In addition, to provide useful information for the decision maker, performance appraisals must be valid, reliable, and free of bias. They must not produce ratings that are consistently too lenient or too severe or that all cluster in the middle.[12] They must also be free of perceptual and timing errors.

Some of the most popular methods for evaluating individual performance are graphic rating scales, checklists, essays or diaries, behaviorally anchored rating scales, and forced-choice systems. These systems are easy to use and familiar to most managers. However, two major problems are common to all individual methods: a tendency to rate most individuals at about the same level, and the inability to discriminate among variable levels of performance.

Comparative methods evaluate two or more employees by comparing them with each other on various performance dimensions. The most popular comparative methods are ranking, forced distribution, paired comparisons, and the use of multiple raters in making comparisons. Comparative methods, however, are more difficult to use than the individual methods, are unfamiliar to many managers, and may require sophisticated development procedures and a computerized analytical system to extract usable information.

The Balanced Scorecard Approach to Performance Management

The **balanced scorecard**, or **BSC**, is a relatively structured performance management technique that identifies financial and nonfinancial performance measures and organizes them into a single model.

A relatively new and increasingly popular form of performance management system is the balanced scorecard approach. The **balanced scorecard**, or **BSC**, is a structured performance management technique that identifies financial and nonfinancial performance measures and organizes them into a single model.[13] The basic BCS is shown in Figure 6.4.

At the core of the BSC is organizational vision and strategy. These must be clearly established and communicated throughout the organization by the top management team. Next, managers establish a small number of objective goals and measures to support four key components of organizational success. These components are customer perceptions, financial performance, internal business processes, and innovation and learning. All subsequent performance measures are derived from this framework.

For instance, suppose that top managers have determined that they want customers to see the firm as a preferred provider of high-quality, premium-priced fashion watches (for example, Rolex). Goals and measures to support this component might be to maintain a 50 percent market share and 98 percent customer satisfaction index within the chosen market segment. One major area of individual performance evaluation, then, would focus on the extent to which a person is contributing market share, customer satisfaction, and/or a closely related area.

FIGURE 6.4

The Balanced Scorecard

The balanced scorecard is a structured performance management technique. In its most basic form, managers establish both goals and measures for how they want to assess customer perceptions, financial performance, internal business process, and innovation and learning. Each of these sets of goals and measures need to be consistent with each other as well as with the organization's overall vision and strategy.

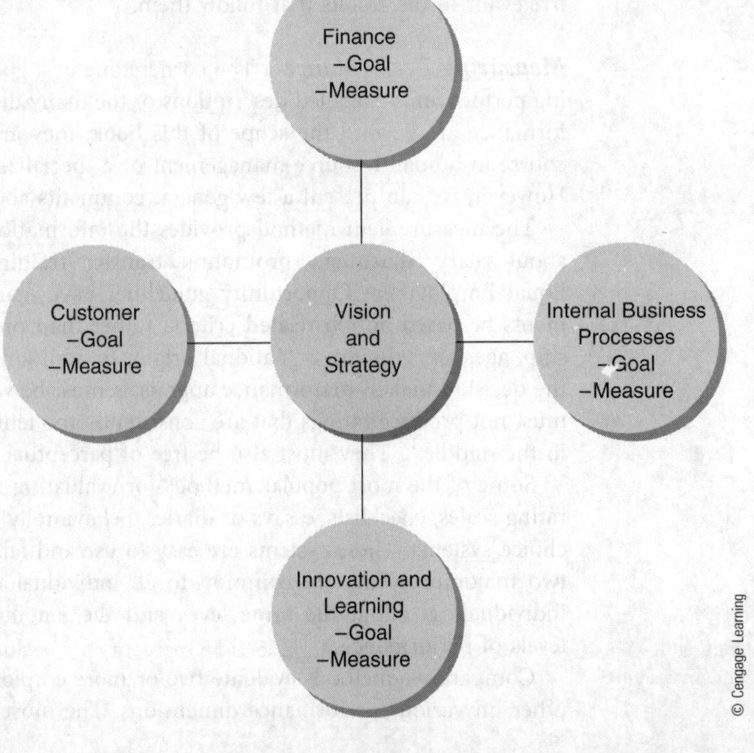

Not surprisingly, there are now a number of commercially available business software systems that help support the balanced scorecard approach. Moreover, a wide array of businesses report using the original BSC, a newer revised version of the BSC, or an alternative model that is patterned after the BSC. On the other hand, most of the evidence used to support the validity of the BSC is anecdotal in nature. That is, its value as a performance management system has not been demonstrated in a rigorous and empirical manner.

INDIVIDUAL REWARDS IN ORGANIZATIONS

As noted earlier, one of the primary purposes of performance management is to provide a basis for rewarding employees. We now turn our attention to rewards and their impact on employee motivation and performance. The **reward system** consists of all organizational components—including people, processes, rules and procedures, and decision-making activities—involved in allocating compensation and benefits to employees in exchange for their contributions to the organization.[14] As we examine organizational reward systems, it is important to keep in mind their role in psychological contracts (as discussed in Chapter 3) and employee motivation (as discussed in Chapter 4). Rewards constitute many of the inducements that organizations provide to employees as their part of the psychological contract, for example. Rewards also satisfy some of the needs employees attempt to meet through their choice of work-related behaviors.

The **reward system** consists of all organizational components, including people, processes, rules and procedures, and decision-making activities, involved in allocating compensation and benefits to employees in exchange for their contributions to the organization.

Roles, Purposes, and Meanings of Rewards

The purpose of the reward system in most organizations is to attract, retain, and motivate qualified employees. The organization's compensation structure must be equitable and consistent to ensure equality of treatment and compliance with the law. Compensation should also be a fair reward for the individual's contributions to the organization, although in most cases these contributions are difficult, if not impossible, to measure objectively. Given this limitation, managers should be as fair and as equitable as possible. Finally, the system must be competitive in the external labor market for the organization to attract and retain competent workers in appropriate fields.[15]

Beyond these broad considerations, an organization must develop its philosophy of compensation based on its own conditions and needs, and this philosophy must be defined and built into the actual reward system. For example, Walmart has a policy that none of its employees will be paid the minimum wage. Even though it may pay some people only slightly more than this minimum, the firm nevertheless wants to communicate to all workers that it places a higher value on their contributions than just having to pay them the lowest wage possible.

The organization needs to decide what types of behaviors or performance it wants to encourage with a reward system because what is rewarded tends to recur. Possible behaviors include performance, longevity, attendance, loyalty, contributions to the "bottom line," responsibility, and conformity. Performance measurement, as described earlier, assesses these behaviors, but the choice of which behaviors to reward is a function of the compensation system. A reward system must also take into account volatile economic issues such as inflation, market conditions, technology, labor union activities, and so forth.

It is also important for the organization to recognize that organizational rewards have many meanings for employees. Intrinsic and extrinsic rewards carry both surface and symbolic value. The **surface value** of a reward to an employee is its objective meaning or worth. A salary increase of 5 percent, for example, means that an individual has 5 percent more spending power than before, whereas a promotion, on the surface, means new duties and responsibilities. But managers must recognize that rewards also

The **surface value** of a reward to an employee is its objective meaning or worth.

The **symbolic value** of a reward to an employee is its subjective and personal meaning or worth.

carry **symbolic value.** If a person gets a 3 percent salary increase when everyone else gets 5 percent, one plausible meaning is that the organization values other employees more. But if the same person gets 3 percent and all others get only 1 percent, the meaning may be just the opposite—the individual is seen as the most valuable employee. Thus, rewards convey to people not only how much they are valued by the organization but also their importance relative to others. Managers need to tune in to the many meanings rewards can convey—not only the surface messages but the symbolic messages as well.

Types of Rewards

An individual's **compensation package** is the total array of money (wages, salary, commission), incentives, benefits, perquisites, and awards provided by the organization.

Most organizations use several different types of rewards. The most common are base pay (wages or salary), incentive systems, benefits, perquisites, and awards. These rewards are combined to create an individual's **compensation package.**

Base Pay For most people, the most important reward for work is the pay they receive. Obviously, money is important because of the things it can buy, but as we just noted, it can also symbolize an employee's worth. Pay is very important to an organization for a variety of reasons. For one thing, an effectively planned and managed pay system can improve motivation and performance. For another, employee compensation is a major cost of doing business—well over 50 percent in many organizations—so a poorly designed system can be an expensive proposition. Finally, since pay is considered a major source of employee dissatisfaction, a poorly designed system can result in problems in other areas such as turnover and low morale.

Incentive systems are plans in which employees can earn additional compensation in return for certain types of performance.

Incentive Systems **Incentive systems** are plans in which employees can earn additional compensation in return for certain types of performance. Examples of incentive programs include the following:

1. *Piecework programs*, which tie a worker's earnings to the number of units produced
2. *Gain-sharing programs*, which grant additional earnings to employees or work groups for cost-reduction ideas
3. *Bonus systems*, which provide managers with lump-sum payments from a special fund based on the financial performance of the organization or a unit
4. *Long-term compensation*, which gives managers additional income based on stock price performance, earnings per share, or return on equity
5. *Merit pay plans*, which base pay raises on the employee's performance
6. *Profit-sharing plans*, which distribute a portion of the firm's profits to all employees at a predetermined rate
7. *Employee stock option plans*, which set aside stock in the company for employees to purchase at a reduced rate

Plans oriented mainly toward individual employees may cause increased competition for the rewards and some possibly disruptive behaviors, such as sabotaging a coworker's performance, sacrificing quality for quantity, or fighting over customers. A group incentive plan, on the other hand, requires that employees trust one another and work together. Of course, all incentive systems have advantages and disadvantages.

Long-term compensation for executives is particularly controversial because of the large sums of money involved and the basis for the payments. Indeed, executive compensation is one of the more controversial subjects that U.S. businesses have had to face in recent years. News reports and the popular press seem to take great joy in telling stories about how this or that executive has just received a huge windfall from his or her organization. Clearly, successful top managers deserve significant rewards. The job of a senior executive, especially a CEO, is grueling and stressful and takes talent and decades of hard work to reach. Only a small handful of managers ever attain a top position in a major

Peter Foley/Bloomberg/Getty Images

Executive compensation remains a controversial subject today. Jerry del Missier was until recently chief operating officer for Barclays Bank. He resigned during a recent investigation into some of Barclay's business practices but still received a large pay off.

corporation. The question is whether some companies are overrewarding such managers for their contributions to the organization.[16]

When a firm is growing rapidly and its profits are also growing rapidly, relatively few objections can be raised to paying the CEO well. However, objections arise when an organization is laying off workers, its financial performance is perhaps less than might be expected, and the CEO is still earning a huge amount of money. It is these situations that dictate that a company's board of directors take a closer look at the appropriateness of its executive compensation decisions.[17]

Indirect Compensation Another major component of the compensation package is **indirect compensation**, also commonly referred to as the employee benefits plan. Typical **benefits** provided by businesses include the following:

1. *Payment for time not worked*, both on and off the job. On-the-job free time includes lunch, rest, coffee breaks, and wash-up or get-ready time. Off-the-job time not worked includes vacation, sick leave, holidays, and personal days.
2. *Social Security contributions*. The employer contributes half the money paid into the system established under the Federal Insurance Contributions Act (FICA). The employee pays the other half.
3. *Unemployment compensation*. People who have lost their jobs or are temporarily laid off get a percentage of their wages from an insurance-like program.
4. *Disability and workers' compensation benefits*. Employers contribute funds to help workers who cannot work due to occupational injury or ailment.
5. *Life and health insurance programs*. Most organizations offer insurance at a cost far below what individuals would pay to buy insurance on their own.
6. *Pension or retirement plans*. Most organizations offer plans to provide supplementary income to employees after they retire.

Indirect compensation, or **benefits**, are an important element in most compensation plans.

A company's Social Security, unemployment, and workers' compensation contributions are set by law. But deciding how much to contribute for other kinds of benefits is up to each company. Some organizations contribute more to the cost of these benefits than others. Some companies pay the entire cost; others pay a percentage of the cost of certain benefits, such as health insurance, and bear the entire cost of other benefits. Offering benefits beyond wages became a standard component of compensation during World War II as a way to increase employee compensation when wage controls were in effect. Since then, competition for employees and employee demands (expressed, for instance, in union bargaining) have caused companies to increase these benefits. In many organizations today, benefits now account for 30 to 40 percent of the payroll.

Moreover, many technology companies today find it necessary to offer extravagant benefits to attract high-talent workers. For example, Google provides its employees with gourmet food, free massages, and a spa. Facebook employees also get gourmet food, plus wash-and-fold laundry services, free haircuts, four weeks of paid vacation, and 100 percent company-paid medical, dental, and vision insurance. Zynga provides on-site dog care, including free grooming service.[18]

But the burden of providing employee benefits is growing heavier for many old-line firms in the United States than it is for organizations in other countries, especially among unionized firms. For example, consider the problem that General Motors faces. Long-time workers at GM's brake factory in Dayton, Ohio, earn an average of $27 an hour in wages. They also earn another $16 an hour in benefits, including full health care coverage with no deductibles, full pension benefits after 30 years of service, life and disability insurance, and legal services. Thus, GM's total labor costs per worker at the factory average $43 an hour. A German rival, Robert Bosch GmbH, meanwhile, has a nonunionized brake plant in South Carolina. It pays its workers an average of $18 an hour in wages, and its hourly benefit cost is around $5. Bosch's total hourly labor costs per worker, therefore, are only $23. Bosch's benefits include medical coverage with a $2,000 deductible, 401(k) retirement plans with employee participation, and life and disability coverage. Toyota, Nissan, and Honda buy most of their brakes for their U.S. factories from Bosch, whereas General Motors must use its own factory to supply brakes. Thus, foreign competitors realize considerable cost advantages over GM in the brakes they use, and this pattern runs across a variety of other component parts as well.[19] To help cope with problems such as this, in early 2008 General Motors offered many of its highest paid hourly workers substantial cash buyouts if they would retire. New labor contracts also now give GM the flexibility to hire new workers at much lower rates in order to help cut costs. Likewise, Ford reached an agreement with the UAW that allows it to hire new workers at hourly rates and benefits lower than those earned by its existing workers.

Perquisites are special privileges awarded to selected members of an organization, usually top managers.

Perquisites **Perquisites** are special privileges awarded to selected members of an organization, usually top managers. For years, the top executives of many businesses were allowed privileges such as unlimited use of the company jet, motor home, vacation home, and executive dining room. In Japan, a popular perquisite is a paid membership in an exclusive golf club; a common perquisite in England is first-class travel. In the United States, the Internal Revenue Service has recently ruled that some "perks" constitute a form of income and thus can be taxed. This decision has substantially changed the nature of these benefits, but they have not entirely disappeared, nor are they likely to. Today, however, many perks tend to be more job-related. For example, popular perks currently include a car and driver (so that the executive can presumably work while being transported to and from work) and BlackBerries, iPhones, or similar devices (so that the executive can conduct business anywhere). More than anything else, though, perquisites seem to add to the status of their recipients and thus may increase job satisfaction and reduce turnover.[20]

Awards At many companies, employees receive awards for everything from seniority to perfect attendance, from zero defects (quality work) to cost reduction suggestions. Award programs can be costly in the time required to run them and in money if cash awards are given. But award systems can improve performance under the right conditions. In one medium-size manufacturing company, careless work habits were pushing up the costs of scrap and rework (the cost of scrapping defective parts or reworking them to meet standards). Management instituted a zero-defects program to recognize employees who did perfect or near-perfect work. During the first month, two workers in shipping caused only one defect in over two thousand parts handled. Division management called a meeting in the lunchroom and recognized each worker with a plaque and a ribbon. The next month, the same two workers had two defects, so there was no award. The following month, the two workers had zero defects, and once again top management called a meeting to give out plaques and ribbons. Elsewhere in the plant, defects, scrap, and rework decreased dramatically as workers evidently sought recognition for quality work. What worked in this particular plant may or may not work in others.[21]

The *Ethics* box on the next page entitled "'What Are They Going to Do—Cut My Pension in Half?'" shows how long-term compensation and indirect-compensation programs, such as pension and retirement plans, can become like perks—special privileges reserved for selected members of an organization.

ETHICS "What Are They Going to Do—Cut My Pension in Half?"

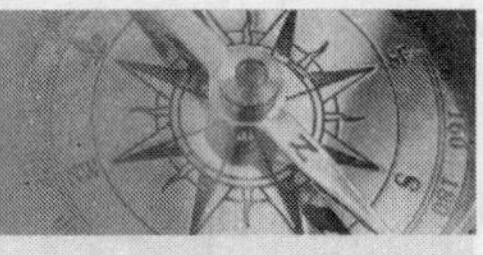

©Trifonov_Evgeniy/iStockphoto

When Ellen Saracini's husband Victor, a pilot for United Airlines, was killed in a crash in 2001, she had his life insurance to protect her house and she could count on her widow's pension to pay for the two biggest expenses looming in her life—college tuition for her daughters and assisted living for her elderly parents. A little over a year after Victor Saracini's death, however, United filed for bankruptcy. In 2005, a federal judge allowed United to default on its pension obligations and turn them over to the Pension Benefit Guaranty Corporation (PBGC), a federal agency that pays pension-fund participants when their employers can't. Ellen Saracini's financial prospects were about to change.

> ***"I call it legalized crime. I lost all my United stock value in the bankruptcy, and here's another part of the retirement I was promised that's gone.... You feel brutalized by the system."***
>
> —FORMER UAL EMPLOYEE KLAUS MEYER

United's pension plan, it seems, was underfunded by $7.8 billion, and its obligations—the money that it owed to workers and retirees—came to $9.8 billion. Because of caps on the amount that it can pay out, PBGC picked up only $6.6 billion of that obligation. The remaining $3.2 billion—roughly $267,000 for every current or retired United pilot, flight attendant, and mechanic—was simply wiped out. A pilot, for example, who had earned a yearly pension of $125,000 was now entitled to no more than the $45,000 maximum amount payable by PBGC at the time. Ellen Saracini was among 122,000 United workers and dependents affected by the new math: She stood to lose 50 to 70 percent of her projected pension. Why so much? Like Social Security, PBGC pays maximum amounts to those who retire at age 65 (or 66) and lesser amounts to those who, for whatever reason, leave pension plans earlier. As it happens, Victor Saracini was only 51 when his plane, United Flight 175, was crashed into the World Trade Center by terrorists on September 11, 2001.

Ellen Saracini was also one of about 2,000 United employees and pensioners who e-mailed their stories of sexagenarian job hunting, unaffordable medical costs, uprooted families, and lost retirement funds to Rep. George Miller of California, who was investigating such agreements as the United default and their effects on the finances of PBGC. Pilot Klaus Meyer, who was 47 at the time of the default, was another of those people. "I call it legalized crime," said Meyer. "I lost all my United stock value in the bankruptcy, and here's another part of the retirement I was promised that's gone. And now," he added, "my Social Security is at risk. Where does it all end? You feel brutalized by the system." According to Meyer, he'd agreed to cooperate with Miller's office despite warnings from fellow workers that United might retaliate against current employees. "What are they going to do," he replied, "cut my pension in half?"

Meanwhile, United CEO Glenn Tilton (now retired) was in the process of collecting $4.5 million in benefits, ostensibly to replace those he'd lost when he left his former employer, Texaco. Asked why he hadn't felt moved by the plight of his employees to pare back his own benefits package, Tilton told a Senate committee looking into the United bankruptcy, "It's part of my contract." The company, he explained, had not only promised it but had guaranteed it. "Why is the promise made to him understandable," wondered a retired pilot whose pension had been cut by 70 percent, "and the one made to me can go by the wayside?"

As for the (moderately) good news, the PBGC announced in December 2011 that, due to flawed accounting of UAL's assets, it had been underpaying many retirees and other pension-plan members. The PBGC said that it would make good the shortfalls with interest, and about 4,400 retired UAL employees could see their monthly benefits jump by $25.

References: Dale Russakoff, "Human Toll of a Pension Default," *Washington Post,* June 13, 2005, www.washingtonpost.com on May 22, 2012; "While Worker Pensions Fail, CEOs Get Rich," *CBS News.com,* November 19, 2009, www.cbsnews.com on May 22, 2012; Pension Benefit Guaranty Corporation, *2009 Annual Management Report,* November 13, 2009, www.pbgc.gov on May 22, 2012; Barbara Hollingsworth, "Pilots: United Airlines Bankruptcy Never Should Have Happened," *Washington Examiner,* March 9, 2010, http://washingtonexaminer.com on May 22, 2012; John Crawley, "U.S. Oversight of UAL Pension Audits Questioned," Reuters, July 23, 2010, www.reuters.com on May 22, 2012; Michael Corkery, "United Retirees May Be Due More," *WSJ.com,* December 2, 2011, http://online.wsj.com on May 22, 2012.

MANAGING REWARD SYSTEMS

Much of our discussion on reward systems has focused on general issues. As Table 6.1 shows, however, the organization must address other issues when developing organizational reward systems. The organization must consider its ability to pay employees at certain levels, economic and labor market conditions, and the impact of the pay system on organizational financial performance. In addition, the organization must consider the relationship between performance and rewards as well as the issues of reward system flexibility, employee participation in the reward system, pay secrecy, and expatriate compensation.

Linking Performance and Rewards

For managers to take full advantage of the symbolic value of pay, there must be a perception on the part of employees that their rewards are linked to their performance. For example, if everyone in an organization starts working for the same hourly rate and then receives a predetermined wage increase every six months or year, there is clearly no relationship between performance and rewards. Instead, the organization is indicating that all entry-level employees are worth the same amount, and pay increases are tied solely to the length of time an employee works in the organization. This holds true whether the employee is a top, average, or mediocre employee. The only requirement is that the employee works well enough to avoid being fired.

Table 6.1 Issues to Consider in Developing Reward Systems

ISSUE	IMPORTANT EXAMPLES
PAY SECRECY	• Open, closed, partial • Link with performance appraisal • Equity perceptions
EMPLOYEE PARTICIPATION	• By human resource department • By joint employee/management committee
FLEXIBLE SYSTEM	• Cafeteria-style benefits • Annual lump sum or monthly bonus • Salary versus benefits
ABILITY TO PAY	• Organization's financial performance • Expected future earnings
ECONOMIC AND LABOR MARKET FACTORS	• Inflation rate • Industry pay standards • Unemployment rate
IMPACT ON ORGANIZATIONAL PERFORMANCE	• Increase in costs • Impact on performance
EXPATRIATE COMPENSATION	• Cost-of-living differentials • Managing related equity issue

At the other extreme, an organization might attempt to tie all compensation to actual performance. Thus, each new employee might start at a different wage, as determined by his or her experience, education, skills, and other job-related factors. After joining the organization, the individual then receives rewards based on actual performance. One employee, for example, might start at $15 an hour because she has ten years of experience and a good performance record at her previous employer. Another might start the same job at a rate of $10.50 an hour because he has only four years' experience and an adequate but not outstanding performance record. Assuming the first employee performs up to expectations, she might also get several pay increases, bonuses, and awards throughout the year whereas the second employee might get only one or two small increases and no other rewards. Of course, organizations must ensure that pay differences are based strictly on performance (including seniority), and not on factors that do not relate to performance (such as gender, ethnicity, or other discriminatory factors).

In reality, most organizations attempt to develop a reward strategy somewhere between these two extremes. Because it is really quite difficult to differentiate among all the employees, most firms use some basic compensation level for everyone. For example, they might start everyone performing a specific job at the same rate, regardless of experience. They might also work to provide reasonable incentives and other inducements for high performers while making sure that they don't ignore the average employees. The key fact for managers to remember is simply that if they expect rewards to motivate performance, employees must see a clear, direct link between their own job-related behaviors and the attainment of those rewards.[22]

Executive compensation has come under close scrutiny and, in many cases, criticism in recent years. Part of the concern is that the absolute levels of compensation—often millions of dollars per year and sometimes much more—simply seem to be excessive. More substantive concerns, though, relate to the relationship between CEO compensation and firm performance. For instance, most shareholders would accept high compensation for CEOs if those CEOs were delivering high firm performance, thereby making the value of investments in those firms increase. But consider the case of Rex Tillerson, CEO of ExxonMobil. In 2009 he was paid $27,168,317, putting him among the top 10 highest-paid CEOs in the United States. But that same year shareholder returns for those holding ExxonMobil stock declined by 12.6 percent. Indeed, one recent study found virtually no correlation between CEO compensation and firm performance.[23]

Flexible Reward Systems

A **flexible reward system** allows employees to choose the combination of benefits that best suits their needs.

Flexible, or cafeteria-style, reward systems are a recent and increasingly popular variation on the standard compensation system. A **flexible reward system** allows employees, within specified ranges, to choose the combination of benefits that best suits their needs. For example, a younger worker just starting out might prefer to have especially strong health care coverage with few deductibles. A worker with a few years of experience might prefer to have more childcare benefits. A midcareer employee with more financial security might prefer more time off with pay. And older workers might prefer to have more rewards concentrated into their retirement plans.

Some organizations are starting to apply the flexible approach to pay. For example, employees sometimes have the option of taking an annual salary increase in one lump sum rather than in monthly increments. General Electric recently implemented such a system for some of its managers. UNUM Corporation, a large insurance firm, allows all of its employees the option of drawing a full third of their annual compensation in the month of January. This makes it easier for them to handle such major expenses as purchasing a new automobile, buying a home, or covering college education costs for their children. Obviously, the administrative costs of providing this level of flexibility are greater, but many employees value this flexibility and may develop strong loyalty and attachment to an employer who offers this kind of compensation package.

Participative Pay Systems

In keeping with the current trend toward worker involvement in organizational decision making, employee participation in the pay process is also increasing. A participative pay system may involve the employee in the system's design, administration, or both. A pay system can be designed by staff members of the organization's human resources department, a committee of managers in the organization, an outside consultant, the employees, or a combination of these sources. Organizations that have used a joint management employee task force to design the compensation system have generally succeeded in designing and implementing a plan that managers could use and that employees believed in. Employee participation in administering the pay system is a natural extension of having employees participate in its design. Examples of companies that have involved employees in the administration of the pay system include Romac Industries, where employees vote on the pay of other employees; Graphic Controls, where each manager's pay is determined by a group of peers; and the Friedman-Jacobs Company, where employees set their own wages based on their perceptions of their performance.[24]

Pay Secrecy

When a company has a policy of open salary information, the exact salary amounts for employees are public knowledge. State governments, for instance, make public the salaries of everyone on their payrolls. A policy of complete secrecy means that no information is available to employees regarding other employees' salaries, average or percentage raises, or salary ranges. The National Labor Relations Board recently upheld an earlier ruling that an employer's starting or enforcing a rule that forbids "employees to discuss their salaries" constitutes interference, restraint, and coercion of protected employee rights under the National Labor Relations Act. Although a few organizations have completely public or completely secret systems, most have systems somewhere in the middle.

Michal Kowalski/Shutterstock.com

Pay secrecy remains a source of contention in some settings. While some businesses allow people to discuss their salaries (and a few even share information openly), many firms discourage employees from discussing their pay with others inside the organization.

Expatriate Compensation

Expatriate compensation is yet another important issue in managing reward systems.[25] Consider, for example, a manager living and working in Houston currently making $450,000 a year. That income allows the manager to live in a certain kind of home, drive a certain kind of car, have access to certain levels of medical care, and live a certain kind of lifestyle. Now suppose the manager is asked to accept a transfer to Tokyo, Geneva, Moscow, or London, cities where the cost of living is considerably higher than in Houston. The same salary cannot begin to support a comparable lifestyle in those cities. Consequently, the employer is almost certain to redesign the manager's compensation package so that the employee's lifestyle in the new location will be comparable to that in the old.

FIGURE 6.5

The Expatriate Compensation Balance Sheet

Organizations that ask employees to accept assignments in foreign locations usually must adjust their compensation levels to account for differences in cost of living and similar factors. Amoco uses the system shown here. The employee's domestic base salary is first broken down into the three categories shown on the left. Then adjustments are made by adding compensation to the categories on the right until an appropriate, equitable level of compensation is achieved.

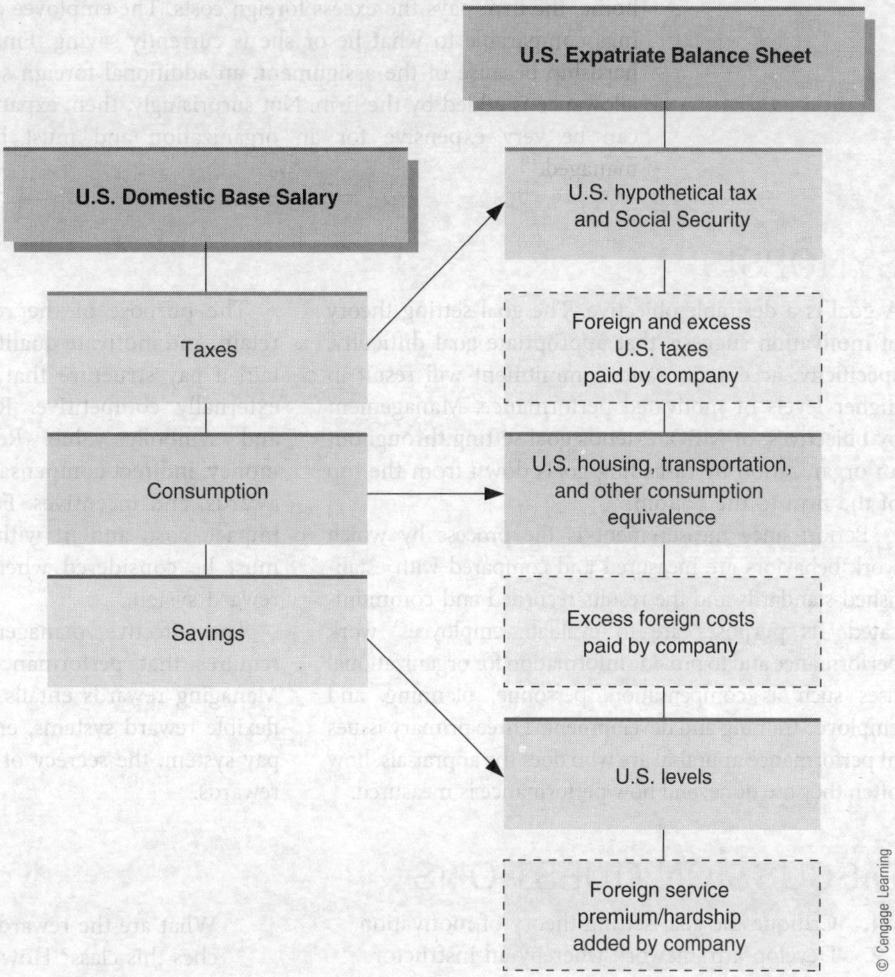

Now consider a different scenario. Suppose the same manager is asked to accept a transfer to an underdeveloped nation. The cost of living in this nation might be quite low by U.S. standards. But there may also be relatively few choices in housing, poorer schools and medical care, a harsh climate, greater personal danger, or similar unattractive characteristics. The firm will probably have to pay the manager some level of additional compensation to offset the decrement in quality of lifestyle. Thus, developing rewards for expatriates is a complicated process.

Figure 6.5 illustrates the approach to expatriate compensation used by one major multinational corporation. The left side of the figure shows how a U.S. employee currently uses her or his salary—part of it goes for taxes, part is saved, and the rest is consumed. When a person is asked to move abroad, a human resource manager works with the employee to develop an equitable balance sheet for the new compensation package. As shown on the right side of the figure, the individual's compensation package will potentially consist of six components. First, the individual will receive income to cover what his or her taxes and Social Security payments in the United States will be. The individual may also have to pay foreign taxes and additional U.S. taxes as a result of the move, so the company covers these as well.

Next, the firm also pays an amount adequate to the employee's current consumption levels in the United States. If the cost of living is greater in the foreign location than at home, the firm pays the excess foreign costs. The employee also receives income for savings comparable to what he or she is currently saving. Finally, if the employee faces a hardship because of the assignment, an additional foreign service premium or hardship allowance is added by the firm. Not surprisingly, then, expatriate compensation packages can be very expensive for an organization and must be carefully developed and managed.[26]

SYNOPSIS

A goal is a desirable objective. The goal-setting theory of motivation suggests that appropriate goal difficulty, specificity, acceptance, and commitment will result in higher levels of motivated performance. Management by objectives, or MBO, extends goal setting throughout an organization by cascading goals down from the top of the firm to the bottom.

Performance measurement is the process by which work behaviors are measured and compared with established standards and the results recorded and communicated. Its purposes are to evaluate employees' work performance and to provide information for organizational uses such as compensation, personnel planning, and employee training and development. Three primary issues in performance appraisal are who does the appraisals, how often they are done, and how performance is measured.

The purpose of the reward system is to attract, retain, and motivate qualified employees and to maintain a pay structure that is internally equitable and externally competitive. Rewards have both surface and symbolic value. Rewards take the form of money, indirect compensation or benefits, perquisites, awards, and incentives. Factors such as motivational impact, cost, and fit with the organizational system must be considered when designing or analyzing a reward system.

The effective management of a reward system requires that performance be linked with rewards. Managing rewards entails dealing with issues such as flexible reward systems, employee participation in the pay system, the secrecy of pay systems, and expatriate rewards.

DISCUSSION QUESTIONS

1. Critique the goal-setting theory of motivation.
2. Develop a framework whereby an instructor could use goal setting in running a class such as this one.
3. Why are employees having their performance measured and evaluated all the time instead of simply being left alone to do their jobs?
4. In what ways is your performance as a student evaluated?
5. How is the performance of your instructor measured? What are the limitations of this method?
6. Can performance on some jobs simply not be measured? Why or why not?
7. What conditions make it easier for an organization to achieve continuous improvement? What conditions make it more difficult?
8. As a student in this class, what "rewards" do you receive in exchange for your time and effort? What are the rewards for the professor who teaches this class? How do your contributions and rewards differ from those of some other student in the class?
9. Do you expect to obtain the rewards you discussed in question 8 on the basis of your intelligence, your hard work, the number of hours you spend in the library, your height, your good looks, your work experience, or some other personal factor?
10. What rewards are easiest for managers to control? What rewards are more difficult to control?
11. Often institutions in federal and state governments give the same percentage pay raise to all their employees. What do you think is the effect of this type of pay raise on employee motivation?

HOW DO YOU SEE IT?

Food for Managerial Thought (Second Course)

"We invest all of our resources in controlling quality. There's really nothing else we do except fix broken refrigerators."

—ANDY PFORZHEIMER, COFOUNDER OF BARCELONA RESTAURANT GROUP

We learned something about the philosophy of management and motivation at Barcelona Restaurant Group in the *Video Case* for Chapter 5. Perhaps most importantly, we found out that cofounder Andy Pforzheimer doesn't agree with the widely held theory that "if you take care of your employees, then they'll be happy and they'll turn around and take care of your customers." In Pforzheimer's opinion, the best way of taking care of customers is to provide them with consistently high *quality*, and when it comes to motivation, he's less interested in "taking care" of his employees than in directing them to deliver quality. "We invest all of our resources in controlling quality," says Pforzheimer. "There's really nothing else we do except fix broken refrigerators."

Pforzheimer adds that "half" of the company's quality-control energies go into meeting "the expectation that we've built. Whatever business you have," he explains, "you've created an expectation," and if Barcelona slips below the customer's high expectation of quality, "we've disappointed our core customer—which you never want to do. That will kill your business."

What's the key to knowing whether or not you're meeting customer expectations? Noting that 85 percent of all restaurants go out of business for reasons that no one—not even owners—seem to be able to fathom, Pforzheimer offers the following opinion: Restaurants, he says, go out of business because of "a lack of self-knowledge," and he believes that the kind of "self-knowledge" that you need to stay in business comes from acting on two managerial imperatives: "really probing" and "wanting to know"—in short, committing yourself to collecting truly useful *information* that can be put to truly effective use.

"From a very, very early point," says Pforzheimer, "we made it clear we wanted to *know*. And that's one of the primary purposes of the secret shopper reports"—that is, reports submitted by anonymous customers who are paid to visit Barcelona outlets and evaluate their performance. Like Pforzheimer, COO Scott Lawton also depends heavily on intelligence gathering, including secret shopper reports. "The most critical components to my approach to managing the restaurants," says Lawton, "are feedback loops"—the responses he gets to active intelligence-seeking techniques—"because that's where we get our information.... The more information I can get, the [more] I actually rely on technology. E-mails, texts, video cameras, secret shopper reports that get e-mailed to me—all of these things are my fingers on the pulse" of the company.

How do Pforzheimer and Lawton use all of this information to motivate employees? Through meetings, says Lawton:

> *Every Wednesday, we have what we call the "war room," where all of the general managers and the chefs come in and we have a meeting. We review numbers, we review shoppers' reports, we interact about what our managers are hearing from the guests. And it's also a great chance for one restaurant to learn from the other.*

Interactions, Lawton admits, often become "intense," as upper management critiques the performance of various restaurants and personnel over the previous weekend. As we see in the meeting excerpted in the video, for example, Pforzheimer admonishes the manager of one outlet that her 2 percent increase in food costs "represents about 8,000 bucks. That sucks."

Lawton is quick to add that "we also try and support" employees, although support is apparently conditional on the admission of on-the-job missteps: Top management, it seems, is most forthcoming with direction when restaurant managers and chefs "admit what they've done wrong." Otherwise, the purpose of the "war room" seems to be to encourage group efforts to solve common problems. The function of top management, suggests Lawton, is to facilitate discussion when employees are "willing to look at" a problem and "when they're willing to have a sort of collaborative attitude towards how we're going to fix it."

As for additional motivational strategies, Barcelona seems to rely on what, in Chapter 16, we characterize as *conflict stimulation*—the constructive use of *conflict* that occurs when people feel that they're working in opposition to each other. In the "war room," explains Lawton,

> *the chefs ... are looking at their labor costs ... [and] their food costs comparatively. And they are the most competitive when it comes to beating out the other chefs. They're artists. They want to be the best, and so they're chasing everything from quality to numbers. The more I can put them in a room together, the better.*

CASE QUESTIONS

1. In what sense does *goal setting* play a role in Barcelona's methods for enhancing performance? Judging from the video, how would you respond to the following questions: What kind of goals does Barcelona set for its managers and chefs? Are those goals *difficult*? Does the company's level of *goal difficulty* seem to enhance performance? Do the company's goals seem *specific*? Does its level of *goal specificity* seem to enhance performance? How might you improve Barcelona's application of *goal-setting theory*?
2. Pforzheimer says that his own motivation comes from

   > *my willingness to come to work in the morning. It's not a particularly easy or lucrative line of work ..., and if we didn't provide the best possible experience just because that's who we were, we couldn't do this. You couldn't pay me enough to do this if I didn't actually care that everybody that walked out of the door had ... as great a time as possible.*

   How—if at all—does this attitude bear upon the motivation of Pforzheimer's employees? Is there a basis here for some kind of *management by objectives (MBO)* approach to motivating employees? Do you think that this attitude can be developed into a "goal-setting process" that's made to "cascade down through the organization"? Why or why not?
3. Lawton admits that many restaurants include *bonuses* in the *compensation packages* of their chefs. Barcelona, however, does not. Why not? Do you agree with this approach, or do you think it entails significant drawbacks, whether for the employer, the employee, or both? (*Hint:* Before responding to this question, be sure that you have a good idea of what Barcelona chefs do.)
4. Let's say that you own a restaurant very much like an average Barcelona outlet.* For several years, you've been your own onsite manager, but now you feel that you need to spend more time attending to marketing and finances. You've decided to hire a general manager, so you're faced with the question of how much to pay for the position. *What*, you ask yourself, *are the industry averages for manager compensation?* You ask a consultant in the field, who replies, "Industry averages are useless in figuring out how much to pay a general manager." Why do you think this is so? What factors should you consider in deciding how much to pay a general manager?

ADDITIONAL SOURCES

Valerie Schroth, "Success Stories: Barcelona Finds the Formula," *Connecticut Magazine*, January 2012, www.connecticutmag.com on June 27, 2012; Barcelona Restaurant Group, "About Us" (2012), www.barcelonawinebar.com on June 27, 2012; Andrews McMeel Publishing, "About Sasa Bahr-Batuz and Andy Pforzheimer" (May 2012), http://cookbooks.andrewsmcmeel.com on June 27, 2012; James Cooper, "Chef Interview: Andrew Pforzheimer of the Barcelona Restaurant Group," *Examiner.com*, January 27, 2010, www.examiner.com on June 27, 2012; Connecticut Restaurant Association, "Barcelona Restaurant Group's Andy Pforzheimer and Sasa Bahr-Batuz Receive Restaurateurs of the Year Award," *StamfordPlus.com*, December 7, 2010, www.stamfordplus.com on June 27, 2012.

*This question is based on Brandon O'Dell, "Restaurant Operations: What Should You Pay a Restaurant Manager?" *Restaurant Report*, (1997–2012), www.restaurantreport.com on July 11, 2012.

EXPERIENCING ORGANIZATIONAL BEHAVIOR

Using Compensation to Motivate Workers

Purpose The purpose of this exercise is to illustrate how compensation can be used to motivate employees.

Format You will be asked to review eight managers and make salary adjustments for each.

Procedure Listed below are your notes on the performance of eight managers who work for you. Either individually or as a group, depending on your instructor's choice, recommend salary increases for eight managers who have just completed their first year with the company and are now to be considered for their first annual raise. Keep in mind that you may be setting precedents and that you need to keep salary costs down. However, there are no formal company restrictions on the kind of raises you can give. Indicate the sizes of the raises that you would like to give each manager by writing a percentage next to each name.

Variations The instructor might alter the situation in one of several ways. One way is to assume that all of the eight managers entered the company at the same salary, say $30,000, which gives a total salary expense of $240,000. If upper management has allowed a salary raise pool of 10 percent of the current salary expenses, then you as the manager have $24,000 to give out as raises. In this variation, students can deal with actual dollar amounts rather than just percentages for the raises. Another interesting variation is to assume that all of the managers entered the company at different salaries, averaging $30,000. (The instructor can create many interesting possibilities for how these salaries might vary.) The students can then suggest salaries for the different managers.

_____ % Abraham McGowan. Abe is not, as far as you can tell, a good performer. You have checked your view with others, and they do not feel that he is effective either. However, you happen to know he has one of the toughest work groups to manage. His subordinates have low skill levels, and the work is dirty and hard. If you lose him, you are not sure whom you could find to replace him.

_____ % Benjy Berger. Benjy is single and seems to live the life of a carefree bachelor. In general, you feel that his job performance is not up to par, and some of his "goofs" are well known to his fellow employees.

_____ % Clyde Clod. You consider Clyde to be one of your best subordinates. However, it is obvious that other people do not consider him to be an effective manager. Clyde has married a rich wife, and as far as you know, he does not need additional money.

_____ % David Doodle. You happen to know from your personal relationship with "Doodles" that he badly needs more money because of certain personal problems he is having. As far as you are concerned, he also happens to be one of the best of your subordinates. For some reason, your enthusiasm is not shared by your other subordinates, and you have heard them make joking remarks about his performance.

_____ % Ellie Ellesberg. Ellie has been very successful so far in the tasks she has undertaken. You are particularly impressed by this because she has a hard job. She needs money more than many of the other people, and you are sure that they respect her because of her good performance.

_____ % Fred Foster. Fred has turned out to be a very pleasant surprise to you. He has done an excellent job, and it is generally accepted among the others that he is one of the best people at the company. This surprises you because he is generally frivolous and does not seem to care very much about money and promotion.

_____ % Greta Goslow. Your opinion is that Greta is just not cutting the mustard. Surprisingly enough, however, when you check to see how others feel about her, you discover that her work is very highly regarded. You also know that she badly needs a raise. She was recently widowed and is finding it extremely difficult to support her household and her young family of four.

_____ % Harry Hummer. You know Harry personally, and he just seems to squander his money continually. He has a fairly easy job assignment, and your view is that he does not do it particularly well. You are, therefore, quite surprised to find that several of the other new managers think that he is the best of the new group.

After you have made the assignments for the eight people, you will have a chance to discuss them either in groups or in the larger class.

Follow-Up Questions

1. Is there a clear difference between the highest and lowest performer? Why or why not?
2. Did you notice differences in the types of information that you had available to make the raise decisions? How did you use the different sources of information?
3. In what ways did your assignment of raises reflect different views of motivation?

Reference

Edward E. Lawler III, "Motivation Through Compensation," adapted by D. T. Hall, in *Instructor's Manual for Experiences in Management and Organizational Behavior* (New York: John Wiley & Sons, 1975). Reprinted by permission of the author.

BUILDING MANAGERIAL SKILLS

Exercise Overview Communication skills refer to your ability to convey ideas and information to other people. In this exercise, you'll get some practice communicating effective goals to someone who, if not exactly a "subordinate," is willing to work with you in achieving the objectives that you develop.

Exercise Background You'll need to review the section on "Goal Setting and Motivation" in this chapter, especially the subsections on *management by objectives*, or *MBO* ("Broader Perspectives on Goal Setting"), and "Evaluation and Implications." In addition, you'll need to consider the following material—a series of sequential steps that will help you get the best results from your goal-setting project:

1. *Integrate goals and overall objectives.* Goals for every individual should be coordinated with overall organizational objectives and strategy. They should also be compatible with the goals of everyone else whose activities may be affected by them.
2. *Be sure that goals are specific.* Explain what each individual should accomplish and describe the tasks needed to accomplish his or her goals. Also be sure to explain the level of performance that you expect of each individual.
3. *Get people to commit to the goals you set for them.* Appeal to each individual's values and needs. Show how achieving organizational goals will help the individual achieve his or her personal goals.
4. *Prioritize goals.* When more than one goal is involved, rank them in order of importance. Encourage individuals to devote the most time and energy to the goals with the biggest payoffs.
5. *Explain how you'll measure performance.* Standards can be quantitative (e.g., units of production) or measured in terms of time (e.g., meeting schedules).
6. *Provide feedback.* Individuals must know whether or not they're on the right track. The best time to provide feedback is while individuals are in the process of working toward goals.

   Feedback can take the form of memos, charts, reports, or personal interaction.

Exercise Task Once you've considered the material above, your instructor will divide the class into groups of five or six members each. Then do the following:

1. Spend a few minutes discussing the nature of your instructor's job. What does he or she do? What do you think constitutes a good performance in his or her job? What factors contribute to a good performance in the job?
2. Now develop a series of five goals that, in the group's opinion, could be used to develop an MBO program for classes in the business curriculum at your college. Try to select goals that are most critical in the performance of your instructor's job. [*Note:* As your chapter says, the most effective MBO goals are usually set in collaboration between "superiors" and "subordinates." For the sake of convenience, we're bypassing this part of the process.]
3. Select a group leader to share the group's list of goals with the whole class.
4. One group at a time, the class will then discuss the goals presented to it. The focus should be on the following criteria:
   - specificity
   - measurability
   - importance
   - motivational qualities
5. When the goals of all groups have been discussed, your instructor will share his or her opinions.

Reference

Phillip L. Hunsaker, *Management: A Skills Approach*, 2nd ed. (Upper Saddle River, NJ: Prentice Hall, 2005), pp. 169–71, 179.

SELF-ASSESSMENT EXERCISE

Assessing Your Feedback Style*

This exercise was designed to help you understand the dynamics of performance appraisal feedback. Diagnosing performance is critical to effective management. Performance appraisal involves both diagnosis and motivation and so is critical to the effective functioning of organizations. One of the difficulties with most performance appraisal systems is that the supervisor or manager feels uncomfortable providing feedback in a one-to-one encounter. The result often is employee vagueness about what the performance appraisal really means, what it is designed to do, and how it can improve performance. The supervisor or manager fails to address those concerns because he or she did not adequately diagnose the situation and therefore lacks an understanding of how subordinates respond to performance feedback or lacks the skill necessary to provide valuable feedback.

Instructions: Below is a list of feedback behaviors. Read the description of each behavior carefully, then select the response that best reflects the extent to which that behavior describes what you do or think you would do. Indicate your choice by circling the response. The possible responses are as follows:

Possible Responses

Y̲ = *Yes, this definitely describes me.*

Y = *Yes I'm fairly sure this describes me.*

? = *I'm not sure.*

N = *No, I'm fairly sure this doesn't describe me.*

N̲ = *No, this definitely doesn't describe me.*

1. When communicating, I try to seek feedback from the receiver to determine whether I'm being understood.
   1. Y̲ 2. Y 3. ? 4. N 5. N̲
2. Whenever possible, I try to ensure that my point of view is accepted and acted upon.
   1. Y 2. Y 3. ? 4. N 5. N̲
3. I can easily handle and accept counterarguments to my ideas.
   1. Y̲ 2. Y 3. ? 4. N 5. N̲
4. When a communication problem occurs between another person and myself, it's usually his or her fault.
   1. Y̲ 2. Y 3. ? 4. N 5. N̲
5. I make sure the other person understands that I know what I am talking about.
   1. Y̲ 2. Y 3. ? 4. N 5. N̲
6. If someone comes to me with a personal problem, I try to listen objectively without being judgmental.
   1. Y̲ 2. Y 3. ? 4. N 5. N̲
7. When listening to someone questioning or criticizing my procedures, I often find myself engaging in mental counterarguments—thinking about my response while the person is talking.
   1. Y̲ 2. Y 3. ? 4. N 5. N̲
8. I let the other person finish an idea before intervening or finishing it for him or her.
   1. Y̲ 2. Y 3. ? 4. N 5. N̲
9. When listening to someone, I find that I can easily restate (paraphrase) that person's point of view.
   1. Y̲ 2. Y 3. ? 4. N 5. N̲
10. I try not to prejudge the speaker or the message.
    1. Y̲ 2. Y 3. ? 4. N 5. N̲
11. Whenever I provide information to someone, I prefer using facts and data.
    1. Y̲ 2. Y 3. ? 4. N 5. N̲
12. Communicating empathy for the feelings of the receiver tends to indicate weakness.
    1. Y̲ 2. Y 3. ? 4. N 5. N̲
13. I try to ensure that others know how I view their actions: good, bad, strong, weak, etc.
    1. Y̲ 2. Y 3. ? 4. N 5. N̲
14. In order to get people to do things properly, you have to tell them what to do.
    1. Y̲ 2. Y 3. ? 4. N 5. N̲
15. When talking with someone, I like saying, "What do you think?" to introduce more acceptance of the issue.
    1. Y̲ 2. Y 3. ? 4. N 5. N̲
16. If you are the boss, people expect you to tell them what to do.
    1. Y̲ 2. Y 3. ? 4. N 5. N̲
17. I try to use probing, nondirective questions in discussions with individuals.
    1. Y̲ 2. Y 3. ? 4. N 5. N̲
18. In providing negative feedback, I want to be certain the receiver knows how I view the situation.
    1. Y̲ 2. Y 3. ? 4. N 5. N̲

19. I try to listen with empathy. I listen both to what is being said and to what I think the sender is trying to say.
    1. Y 2. Y 3. ? 4. N 5. N

20. Whenever I provide someone with feedback, I usually want to persuade him or her to act on it.
    1. Y 2. Y 3. ? 4. N 5. N

Scoring:

(1) For the items listed, score your responses as follows:

Item Score	*Scoring*
1. _____	Y = 2
3. _____	
6. _____	Y = 1
8. _____	
9. _____	? = 0
10. _____	
11. _____	N = −1
15. _____	
17. _____	N = −2
19. _____	
TOTAL _____	

(2) For the items listed, the scoring system is reversed:

Item Score	*Scoring*
2. _____	Y = −2
4. _____	
5. _____	Y = −1
7. _____	
12. _____	? = 0
13. _____	
14. _____	N = 1
16. _____	
18. _____	N = 2
20. _____	
TOTAL _____	

**Source:* From VECCHIO, S/G ORGANIZATIONAL BEHAVIOR, 1E. © 1988 Cengage Learning.

CHAPTER 7

Managing Stress and the Work-Life Balance

Chapter Outline

- The Nature of Stress
- Individual Differences and Stress
- Common Causes of Stress
- Consequences of Stress
- Managing Stress in the Workplace
- Work-Life Linkages

Chapter Learning Objectives

After studying this chapter, you should be able to:

1. Define and describe the nature of stress.
2. Identify basic individual differences related to stress.
3. Identify and describe common causes of stress.
4. Discuss the central consequences of stress.
5. Describe various ways that stress can be managed.
6. Discuss work-life linkages and their relation to stress.

Is Anybody in Control Here?

"Air traffic control is like playing chess at high speed."

—Controller Pete Rogers

The media called it the "Miracle on the Hudson." On the wintry afternoon of January 15, 2009, just minutes after takeoff from New York's LaGuardia Airport, U.S. Airways Flight 1549 struck a flock of birds. Both engines were knocked out, and pilot Chesley "Sully" Sullenberger had no choice but to land his 81-ton Airbus A320 in the frigid Hudson River on the west side of Manhattan. It was the first crash-landing of a major aircraft in the water in some 50 years, but all of the 155 people on board survived. "It was intense," said one passenger. "… You've got to give it to the pilot."

Steven Day/AP Photos

The jobs of airline pilot and air traffic controller are both very stressful. Following the miraculous landing of US Airways flight 1549 in the Hudson River in 2009 both Caption Chesley Sullenberger and air traffice controller Patrick Harten, who helped guide the plane down, suffered symptoms of posttraumatic stress.

(Interestingly, the passengers on Flight 1549 had no way of knowing that Sullenberger's salary was about 40 percent less than it had been just a couple of years earlier, before his employer, United Airlines, had declared bankruptcy. A month after the crash, Sullenberger informed a Congressional subcommittee that United had also defaulted on his pension, which had been taken over by a government agency at "pennies on the dollar." United's pilots and their families, he said, had been placed "in an untenable financial position." We discuss the United pension-plan default in the *Ethics* box in Chapter 6.)

As for Sullenberger, he remembered "the worst sickening, pit-of-your-stomach, falling-through-the-floor feeling" that he'd ever experienced. For weeks after the crash, he suffered symptoms of posttraumatic stress, including sleeplessness and flashbacks, but acknowledged that his condition had improved after a month or two. No wonder Sullenberger experienced some repercussion from the stress, says Patrick Harten, the LaGuardia air traffic controller who was on the other end of the line when Sullenberger radioed his intention to put down in the river. "I thought it was his own death sentence," recalled Harten. "I believed at that moment I was going to be the last person to talk to anyone on that plane alive.... I felt like I'd been hit by a bus." For his own part, says Harten, "the trauma of working an airplane that crash-landed" didn't begin to subside until about a year later.

Interestingly, if Sullenberger, who was 57 at the time of the crash, had been an air traffic controller instead of a pilot, he would probably have been required to retire a year before Flight 1549 took off. Both jobs, of course, are extremely stressful, and the Federal Aviation Administration (FAA) mandates retirement ages for both. Pilots, however, can stay on the job until they're 65, whereas controllers must in most cases call it quits at age 56. Why? Because being an air traffic controller, it seems, is *more* stressful. According to *Health* magazine, it's the fourth-most-stressful job in the United States, just behind police officer (#2) and miner (#3); pilot comes in at a relatively nerve-calming #22. "In a one-hour sitting," explains one member of the profession, "an air traffic controller may be responsible for more money and lives than an average person during [his] entire lifetime." (At the top of the magazine's list, by the way, is inner-city high school teacher.)

At any given moment, there are about 5,000 airplanes in the skies over the United States. The National Air Traffic Controllers Association (NATCA) reports that on an average day, controllers handle 87,000 flights. In a year, they manage 64 million takeoffs and landings. And that's just sheer volume of traffic. Needless to say, all that traffic is also very complex. "Air traffic control is like playing chess at high speed," says Pete Rogers, who helps manage 52,000 flights a year to and from (and over) Martha's Vineyard, Massachusetts.

Not all aircraft, of course, are traveling at the same speed (or at the same altitude), and very few of them are traveling at a steady perpendicular to the ground. Once they learn to "see traffic," according to New York controller Christopher Tucker, controllers "have to learn how to solve the conflicts, preferably in the simplest … manner. It can be as simple as stopping someone's climb/descent to pass below/above converging traffic or issuing speed assignments to ensure constant spacing." Needless to say, however, it's rarely that simple. For example, explains Tucker, "newer aircraft with highly efficient wings cannot descend quickly while going slow, so that has to be taken into account when setting up an intrail operation where arrivals must be descended as well as slowed down."

And then there's the weather. Controllers record weather data every hour and have to be constantly aware of changing conditions. "We have to make sure we don't launch somebody into a thunderstorm," says Rogers. A contributor to Stuck Mic, a website for controllers and other aviation professionals, observes that "a busy day at an air traffic control facility is one thing, [but] when weather moves into the area, it creates even bigger problems. In fact," he explains, "a significant weather system is similar to a giant wall as far as pilots and controllers are concerned…. [T]he effects of an aircraft flying into a storm system can be catastrophic…. Controllers [have to] monitor and re-route traffic so hazardous weather is avoided at all costs." Moreover, because storm systems often appear on radar with little or no notice, controllers must also be able to make quick decisions. According to Tucker, "the ability to run through possible solutions and quickly choose the best one" is a necessary skill for any controller, and so is "being able to make a bad situation work after having made a poor decision." Last but not least, he recommends that would-be controllers cultivate "the ability to maintain some semblance of calm during busy stressful periods." Asked what he did to help Sullenberger land Flight 1549 in the Hudson River, Patrick Harten replied:

> *The best thing I did that day was not to further stress Sully. Pilots and controllers can feel stress in our voices. We both sounded calm, which made it easier to focus on the task at hand. I didn't bother him with standard emergency questions such as fuel remaining and persons on board, knowing he had enough to deal with already.*

At present, there are about 11,000 fully trained air traffic controllers in the United States—the lowest number in 18 years. The total number of positions is slated to increase by 13 percent between now and 2018, but that rate won't keep pace with the projected increase in the number of aircraft that will be in the skies—not to mention vying for air and runway space at the nation's airports. At lower-traffic airports, cost considerations already require controllers to work eight-hour shifts by themselves, performing the jobs of all tower positions, communicating with aircraft in the sky and on the ground, and coordinating the activities of perhaps three separate facilities.

"And so we have a rise in operational errors," both at regional and national airports, admits Melvin Davis, who's been directing air traffic in southern California for more than 20 years. "It's a business decision," he says, arguing that the current situation at the nation's airports is

> clearly the result of a reduction in staffing, a decline in experience, and an increase in the use of employee overtime, which leads to increased fatigue. The result is a 300 percent to 400 percent increase in operational errors ... which results in two bullet trains coming together at 600 miles an hour.

What Do You Think?

1. What kind of stress do you contend with on your job or in your school work—or, of course, as a combination of both? How much of it "comes with the territory"? How much of it do you bring with you as a facet of your personality?
2. In your opinion, how has the situation with air traffic controllers reached what appears to be such a dangerous level?

References: "'Miracle on the Hudson': All Safe in Jet Crash," *MSNBC.com*, January 15, 2009, www.msnbc.msn.com on May 24, 2012; "Chesley 'Sully' Sullenberger to Congress: My Pay Has Been Cut 40 Percent in Recent Years, Pension Terminated," *Huffington Post*, March 27, 2009, www.huffington-post.com on May 24, 2012; Phil Derner Jr., "One Year after the 'Miracle on the Hudson,' an Exclusive Interview with Air Traffic Controller Patrick Harten," *NYCAviation.com*, January 18, 2010, www.nycaviation.com on May 24, 2012; Steve Myrick, "Air Traffic Control—'Chess at High Speed,'" *Martha's Vineyard Times*, December 24, 2009, www.mvtimes.com on May 24, 2012; Alex Altman and Tiffany Sharples, "Air Traffic Controller Sounds Alarm," *Time*, April 26, 2008, www.time.com on May 24, 2012; Christopher Tucker, "I Am an Air Traffic Controller," *Daily Speculations*, March 15, 2009, www.dailyspeculations.com on May 24, 2012; "Air Traffic Control—Stress," *Stuck Mic*, August 27, 2008, www.stuckmic.com on May 24, 2012.

In several of our earlier chapters, we discussed motivational forces and organizational methods that might lead people to be more motivated. However, there are also dark sides to these same perspectives. Many people today work long hours, face constant deadlines, and are subject to pressure to produce more and more. Organizations and the people who run them are under constant pressure to increase income while keeping costs in check. To do things faster and better—but with fewer people—is the goal of many companies today. An unfortunate effect of this trend is to put too much pressure on people—operating employees, other managers, and oneself. The results can indeed be increased performance, higher profits, and faster growth. But stress, burnout, turnover, aggression, and other unpleasant side effects can also occur.

In this chapter, we examine how and why stress occurs in organizations and how to better understand and control it. First, we explore the nature of stress. Then we look at such important individual differences as Type A and Type B personality profiles and their role in stress. Next, we discuss a number of causes of stress and consider its potential consequences. We then highlight several things people and organizations can do to manage stress at work. We conclude by discussing an important factor related to stress—linkages between work and nonwork parts of people's lives.

THE NATURE OF STRESS

Many people think of stress as a simple problem. In reality, however, stress is complex and often misunderstood.[1] To learn how job stress truly works, we must first define it and then describe the process through which it develops.

Stress Defined

Stress is a person's adaptive response to a stimulus that places excessive psychological or physical demands on that person.

Stress has been defined in many ways, but most definitions say that stress is caused by a stimulus, that the stimulus can be either physical or psychological, and that the individual responds to the stimulus in some way.[2] Therefore, we define **stress** as a person's adaptive response to a stimulus that places excessive psychological or physical demands on him or her.

Given the underlying complexities of this definition, we need to examine its components carefully. First is the notion of adaptation. As we discuss presently, people may adapt to stressful circumstances in any of several ways. Second is the role of the stimulus. This stimulus, generally called a *stressor*, is anything that induces stress. Third, stressors can be either psychological or physical. Finally, the demands the stressor places on the individual must be excessive for stress to actually result. Of course, what is excessive for one person may be perfectly tolerable for another. The point is simply that a person must perceive the demands as excessive or stress will not actually be present.

There has been a marked increase in stress reported by airline workers in the last few years. A combination of increased pressure for salary and benefit reductions, threats to pensions, demotions, layoffs, and heavier workloads have all become more pronounced since September 11. And today's rising energy prices are likely to increase these pressures. As a result, more airline workers than ever before are seeking counseling services; turnover and absenteeism are also on the rise.[3]

The Stress Process

Much of what we know about stress today can be traced to the pioneering work of Dr. Hans Selye.[4] Among Selye's most important contributions were his identification of the general adaptation syndrome and the concepts of *eustress* and *distress*.

The **general adaptation syndrome (GAS)** identifies three stages of response to a stressor: alarm, resistance, and exhaustion.

General Adaptation Syndrome Figure 7.1 offers a graphical representation of the **general adaptation syndrome** (GAS). According to this model, each of us has a normal level of resistance to stressful events. Some of us can tolerate a great deal of stress and others much less, but we all have a threshold at which stress starts to affect us.

The GAS begins when a person first encounters a stressor. The first stage is called "alarm." At this point, the person may feel some degree of panic and begin to wonder how to cope. The individual may also have to resolve a "fight-or-flight" question: "Can I deal with this, or should I run away?" For example, suppose a manager is assigned to

FIGURE 7.1

The General Adaptation Syndrome

The general adaptation syndrome (GAS) perspective describes three stages of the stress process. The initial stage is called alarm. As illustrated here, a person's resistance often dips slightly below the normal level during this stage. Next comes actual resistance to the stressor, usually leading to an increase above the person's normal level of resistance. Finally, in stage 3, exhaustion may set in, and the person's resistance declines sharply below normal levels.

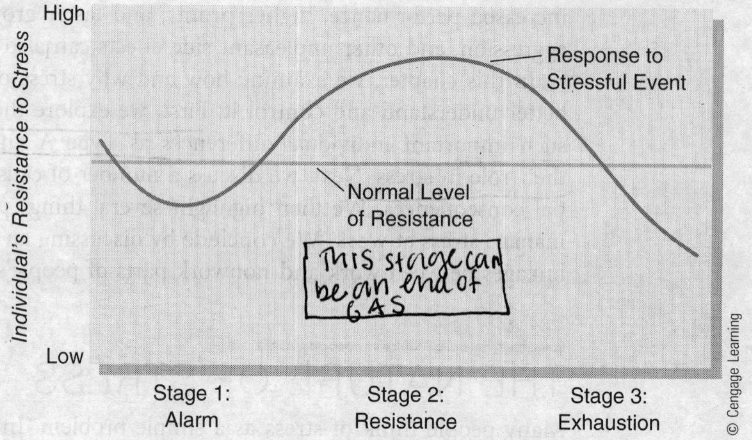

write a lengthy report overnight. Her first reaction may be, "How will I ever get this done by tomorrow?"

If the stressor is too extreme, the person may simply be unable to cope with it. In most cases, however, the individual gathers his or her strength (physical or emotional) and begins to resist the negative effects of the stressor. The manager with the long report to write may calm down, call home to tell her kids that she's working late, roll up her sleeves, order out for dinner, and get to work. Thus, at stage 2 of the GAS, the person is resisting the effects of the stressor.

Often, the resistance phase ends the GAS. If the manager completes the report earlier than she expected, she may drop it in her briefcase, smile to herself, and head home tired but happy. On the other hand, prolonged exposure to a stressor without resolution may bring on phase 3 of the GAS: exhaustion. At this stage, the person literally gives up and can no longer fight the stressor. For example, the manager may fall asleep at her desk at 3 a.m. and fail to finish the report.

stress not always bad

Distress and Eustress Selye also pointed out that the sources of stress need not be bad. For example, receiving a bonus and then having to decide what to do with the money can be stressful. So can getting a promotion, making a speech as part of winning a major award, getting married, and similar "good" things. Selye called this type of stress **eustress**. As we will see later, eustress can lead to a number of positive outcomes for the individual. Of course, there is also negative stress. Called **distress**, this is what most people think of when they hear the word *stress*. Excessive pressure, unreasonable demands on our time, and bad news all fall into this category. As the term suggests, this form of stress generally results in negative consequences for the individual. For purposes of simplicity, we will continue to use the simple term *stress* throughout this chapter. But as you read and study the chapter, remember that stress can be either good or bad. It can motivate and stimulate us, or it can lead to any number of dangerous side effects.

* **Eustress** is the pleasurable stress that accompanies positive events.

* **Distress** is the unpleasant stress that accompanies negative events.

INDIVIDUAL DIFFERENCES AND STRESS

We have already alluded to the fact that stress can affect different people in different ways. Given our earlier discussion of individual differences back in Chapter 3, of course, this should come as no surprise.[5] The most fully developed individual difference relating specifically to stress is the distinction between Type A and Type B personality profiles.

Type A and B Personality Profiles

Type A and Type B profiles were first observed by two cardiologists, Meyer Friedman and Ray Rosenman.[6] They first got the idea when a worker repairing the upholstery on their waiting-room chairs commented on the fact that many of the chairs were worn only on the front. After further study, the two cardiologists realized that many of their heart patients were anxious and had a hard time sitting still—they were literally sitting on the edges of their seats!

Using this observation as a starting point, Friedman and Rosenman began to study the phenomenon more closely. They eventually concluded that their patients were exhibiting one of two very different types of behavior patterns. Their research also led them to conclude that the differences were based on personality. They labeled these two behavior patterns Type A and Type B.

Type A people are extremely competitive, highly committed to work, and have a strong sense of time urgency.

The extreme **Type A** individual is extremely competitive, very devoted to work, and has a strong sense of time urgency. Moreover, this person is likely to be aggressive, impatient, and highly work oriented. He or she has a lot of drive and motivation and wants to accomplish as much as possible in as short a time as possible.

Type B people are less competitive, less committed to work, and have a weaker sense of time urgency.

The extreme **Type B** person, in contrast, is less competitive, is less devoted to work, and has a weaker sense of time urgency. This person feels less conflict with either people or time and has a more balanced, relaxed approach to life. He or she has more confidence and is able to work at a constant pace.

A commonsense expectation might be that Type A people are more successful than Type B people. In reality, however, this is not necessarily true—the Type B person is not necessarily any more or less successful than the Type A. There are several possible explanations for this. For example, Type A people may alienate others because of their drive and may miss out on important learning opportunities in their quest to get ahead. Type B's, on the other hand, may have better interpersonal reputations and may learn a wider array of skills.

Friedman and Rosenman pointed out that most people are not purely Type A or Type B; instead, people tend toward one or the other type. For example, an individual might exhibit marked Type A characteristics much of the time but still be able to relax once in a while and even occasionally forget about time. Likewise, even the most laid-back Type B person may occasionally spend some time obsessing about work.

Friedman and Rosenman's initial research on the Type A and Type B profile differences yielded some alarming findings. In particular, they suggested that Type A's were much more likely to get coronary heart disease than were Type B's. In recent years, however, follow-up research by other scientists has suggested that the relationship between Type A behavior and the risk of coronary heart disease is not all that straightforward.

Although the reasons are unclear, recent findings suggest that Type A's are much more complex than originally believed. For example, in addition to the characteristics already noted, they are also more likely to be depressed and hostile. Any one of these characteristics or a combination of them can lead to heart problems. Moreover, different approaches to measuring Type A tendencies have yielded different results.

Finally, in one study that found Type A's to actually be less susceptible to heart problems than Type B's, the researchers offered an explanation consistent with earlier thinking: Because Type A's are relatively compulsive, they may seek treatment earlier and are more likely to follow their doctors' orders![7]

Hardiness and Optimism

Two other important individual differences related to stress are hardiness and optimism. Research suggests that some people have what are termed *hardier* personalities than

Hardiness is a person's ability to cope with stress. Hardiness is especially important when people work in high-stress occupations. Take this doctor, for example. She has to work long hours and must help her patients make complex medical decisions that have long-lasting effects. She also must deal with an increasingly complex legal system and new health care reforms. Her demeanor, a partial reflection of hardiness, suggests she has the capacity to handle these pressures.

others.[8] Hardiness is a person's ability to cope with stress. People with hardy personalities have an internal locus of control, are strongly committed to the activities in their lives, and view change as an opportunity for advancement and growth. Such people are seen as relatively unlikely to suffer illness if they experience high levels of pressure and stress. On the other hand, people with low hardiness may have more difficulties in coping with pressure and stress.

Another potentially important individual difference is optimism. Optimism is the extent to which a person sees life in positive or negative terms. A popular expression used to convey this idea concerns the glass "half filled with water." A person with a lot of optimism will tend to see it as half full, whereas a person with less optimism (a pessimist) will often see it as half empty. Optimism is also related to positive and negative affectivity, as discussed earlier in Chapter 3. In general, optimistic people tend to handle stress better. They will be able to see the positive characteristics of the situation and recognize that things may eventually improve. In contrast, less optimistic people may focus more on the negative characteristics of the situation and expect things to get worse, not better.

Cultural differences are also important in determining how stress affects people. For example, research suggests that American executives may experience less stress than executives in many other countries, including Japan and Brazil. The major causes of stress also differ across countries. In Germany, for example, major causes of stress are time pressure and deadlines. In South Africa, long work hours more frequently lead to stress. And in Sweden, the major cause of stress is the encroachment of work on people's private lives.[9]

Hardiness is a person's ability to cope with stress.

Optimism is the extent to which a person sees life in relatively positive or negative terms.

Other research suggests that women are perhaps more prone to experience the psychological effects of stress, whereas men may report more physical effects.[10] Finally, some studies suggest that people who see themselves as complex individuals are better able to handle stress than people who view themselves as relatively simple.[11] We should add, however, that the study of individual differences in stress is still in its infancy. It would therefore be premature to draw rigid conclusions about how different types of people handle stress.

COMMON CAUSES OF STRESS

Many things can cause stress. Figure 7.2 shows two broad categories: organizational stressors and life stressors. It also shows three categories of stress consequences: individual consequences, organizational consequences, and burnout.

Organizational Stressors

Organizational stressors are various factors in the workplace that can cause stress. Four general sets of organizational stressors are task demands, physical demands, role demands, and interpersonal demands.

FIGURE 7.2

Causes and Consequences of Stress

The causes and consequences of stress are related in complex ways. As shown here, most common causes of stress can be classified as either organizational stressors or life stressors. Similarly, common consequences include individual and organizational consequences, as well as burnout.

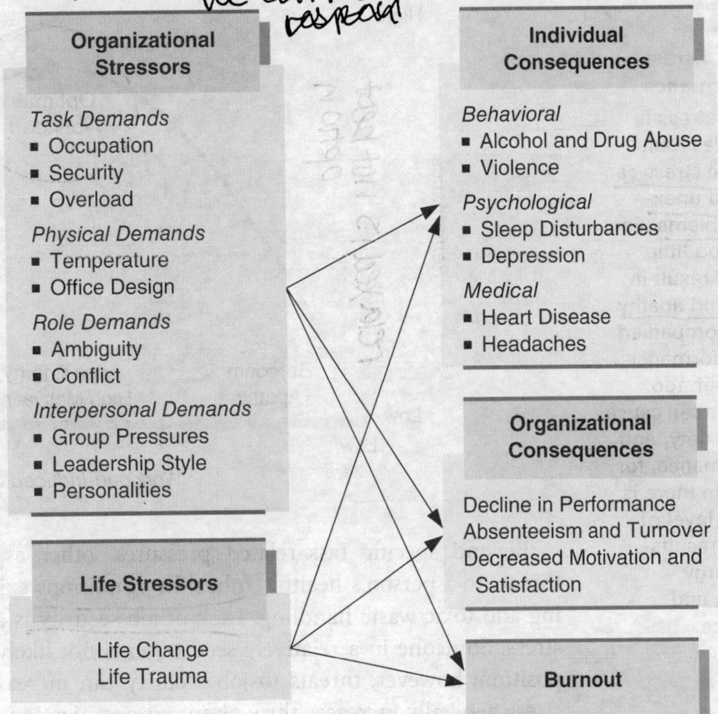

Reference: Adapted from James C. Quick and Jonathan D. Quick, *Organizational Stress and Preventive Management* (McGraw-Hill, 1984) pp. 19, 44, and 76. Used by permission of James C. Quick.

Task demands are stressors associated with the specific job a person performs.

Task Demands Task demands are stressors associated with the specific job a person performs. Some occupations are by nature more stressful than others. Table 7.1 lists a representative sample of relative high- and low-stress jobs, based on one study. As you can see, the jobs of surgeon and commercial airline pilot are among the most stressful, while the jobs of actuary and dietitian are among the least stressful jobs.

Table 7.1 Most and Least Stressful Jobs

TOP MOST STRESSFUL JOBS	TOP LEAST STRESSFUL JOBS
1. Surgeon	1. Actuary
2. Commercial airline pilot	2. Dietitian
3. Photojournalist	3. Computer systems analyst
4. Advertising account executive	4. Statistician
5. Real estate agent	5. Astronomer
6. Physician (general practice)	6. Mathematician
7. Reporter (newspaper)	7. Historian
8. Physician assistant	8. Software engineer

Source: www.careercast.com/jobs/content/StressfulJobs_page1, accessed on April 5, 2010.

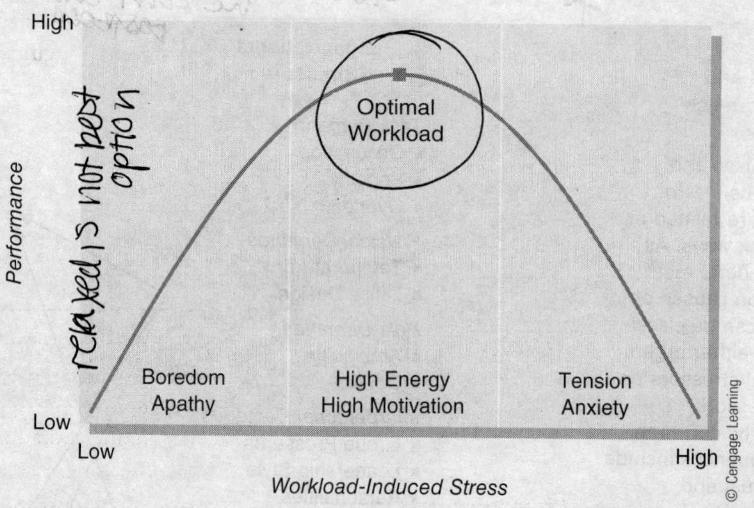

FIGURE 7.3

Workload, Stress, and Performance

Too much stress is clearly undesirable, but too little stress can also lead to unexpected problems. For example, too little stress may result in boredom and apathy and be accompanied by low performance. And although too much stress can cause tension, anxiety, and low performance, for most people there is an optimal level of stress that results in high energy, motivation, and performance.

Beyond specific task-related pressures, other aspects of a job may pose physical threats to a person's health. Unhealthy conditions exist in occupations such as coal mining and toxic waste handling. Lack of job security is another task demand that can cause stress. Someone in a relatively secure job is not likely to worry unduly about losing that position; however, threats to job security can increase stress dramatically. For example, stress generally increases throughout an organization during a period of layoffs or immediately after a merger with another firm. This has been observed at a number of organizations, including AT&T, Safeway, and Digital Equipment.

A final task demand stressor is overload. Overload occurs when a person simply has more work than he or she can handle. The overload can be either quantitative (the person has too many tasks to perform or too little time to perform them) or qualitative (the person may believe he or she lacks the ability to do the job). We should note that the opposite of overload may also be undesirable. As Figure 7.3 shows, low task demands can result in boredom and apathy just as overload can cause tension and anxiety. Thus, a moderate degree of workload-related stress is optimal, because it leads to high levels of energy and motivation.

Physical demands are stressors associated with the job's physical setting, such as the adequacy of temperature and lighting and the physical requirements the job makes on the employee.

Physical Demands The **physical demands** of a job are its physical requirements on the worker; these demands are a function of the physical characteristics of the setting and the physical tasks the job involves. One important element is temperature. Working outdoors in extreme temperatures can result in stress, as can working in an improperly heated or cooled office. Strenuous labor such as loading heavy cargo or lifting packages can lead to similar results. Office design can be a problem, as well. A poorly designed office can make it difficult for people to have privacy or promote too much or too little social interaction. Too much interaction may distract a person from his or her task, whereas too little may lead to boredom or loneliness. Likewise, poor lighting, inadequate work surfaces, and similar deficiencies can create stress. And shift work can cause disruptions for people because of the way it affects their sleep and leisure-time activities.

Role demands are stressors associated with the role a person is expected to play.

A **role** is a set of expected behaviors associated with a particular position in a group or organization.

Role Demands **Role demands** can also be stressful to people in organizations. A **role** is a set of expected behaviors associated with a particular position in a group or organization. As such, it has both formal (i.e., job-related and explicit) and informal (i.e., social and implicit) requirements. People in an organization or work group expect a person in a particular role to act in certain ways. They transmit these expectations both formally and informally. Individuals perceive role expectations with varying degrees of accuracy and then attempt to enact that role. However, "errors" can creep into this process, resulting in stress-inducing problems called role ambiguity, role conflict, and role overload.

Role ambiguity arises when a role is unclear.

Role ambiguity arises when a role is unclear. If your instructor tells you to write a term paper but refuses to provide more information, you will probably experience ambiguity. You do not know what the topic is, how long the paper should be, what format to use, or when the paper is due. In work settings, role ambiguity can stem from poor job descriptions, vague instructions from a supervisor, or unclear cues from coworkers. The result is likely to be a subordinate who does not know what to do. Role ambiguity can thus be a significant source of stress.

Role conflict occurs when the messages and cues constituting a role are clear but contradictory or mutually exclusive.

Interrole - work v. home

Intrarole - Pam v. John E

Intrasender - John E

person-role - ethical

Role conflict occurs when the messages and cues from others about the role are clear but contradictory or mutually exclusive.[12] One common form is *interrole conflict*—conflict between roles. For example, if a person's boss says that to get ahead one must work overtime and on weekends, and the same person's spouse says that more time is needed at home with the family, conflict may result. *Intrarole conflict* may occur when a person gets conflicting demands from different sources within the context of the same role. A manager's boss may tell her that she needs to put more pressure on subordinates to follow new work rules. At the same time, her subordinates may indicate that they expect her to get the rules changed. Thus, the cues are in conflict, and the manager may be unsure about which course to follow.

Intrasender conflict occurs when a single source sends clear but contradictory messages. This might occur if the boss says one morning that there can be no more overtime for the next month but after lunch tells someone to work late that same evening. *Person-role conflict* results from a discrepancy between the role requirements and the individual's personal values, attitudes, and needs. If a person is told to do something unethical or illegal, or if the work is distasteful (for example, reprimanding or firing a close friend), person-role conflict is likely. Role conflict of all varieties is of particular concern to managers. Research has shown that conflict may occur in a variety of situations and may lead to a variety of adverse consequences, including stress, poor performance, and rapid turnover.

Role overload occurs when expectations for the role exceed the individual's capabilities.

A final consequence of a conflicting role structure is **role overload**, which occurs when expectations for the role exceed the individual's capabilities. When a manager gives an employee several major assignments at once while increasing the person's regular workload, the employee will probably experience role overload. Role overload may also result when an individual takes on too many roles at one time. For example, a person trying to work extra hard at his job, run for election to the school board, serve on a committee in church, coach Little League baseball, maintain an active exercise program, and be a contributing member to his family will probably encounter role overload.

Interpersonal demands are stressors associated with group pressures, leadership, and personality conflicts.

Interpersonal Demands A final set of organizational stressors consists of three **interpersonal demands**: group pressures, leadership, and interpersonal conflict. Group pressures may include pressure to restrict output, pressure to conform to the group's norms, and so forth. For instance, as we have noted before, it is quite common for a work group to arrive at an informal agreement about how much each member will produce. Individuals who produce much more or much less than this level may be pressured by the group to get back in line. An individual who feels a strong need to vary from the group's expectations (perhaps to get a pay raise or promotion) will experience a great deal of stress, especially if acceptance by the group is also important to him or her.

Leadership style also may cause stress. Suppose an employee needs a great deal of social support from his leader. The leader, however, is quite brusque and shows no concern or compassion for him. This employee will probably feel stressed. Similarly, assume an employee feels a strong need to participate in decision making and to be active in all aspects of management. Her boss is very autocratic and refuses to consult subordinates about anything. Once again stress is likely to result.

SERVICE Fries with That?

©rangizzz/Shutterstock

How many times can you ask "Would you like fries with that?" before you go out of your mind? Service scholars have been wrestling with this question for some time. The answer lies in understanding that laboring in a service job can be not only physically tiring but emotionally tiring as well. Not only is it tiring to say the same thing over and over again with a big smile and a sincere hello, but it is even more difficult for most people to smile at a customer when they just found out that their mortgage is overdue or that their mammogram reveals a potential problem or some other unpleasant news. It is also hard to focus on doing your job when you are a nurse caring for a young child with a terminal illness, an emergency medical technician on the scene of a bad traffic crash, or a call center employee asking the next person for a generous donation to the alma mater after the last one called yelled obscenities. All of these are examples of people doing work that has more than just a physical element to it. Smiling, caring, focusing, and staying consistent require the ability to perform tasks that have emotional aspects along with the physical.

Managing people who perform jobs with emotional labor components requires awareness of and sensitivity to the demands made upon employees by their interaction with customers. Coping strategies can help those who are faced with demands that tax their emotions. One strategy is to invent roles for employees to play. If the work of a street sweeper at a theme park is demeaning to a person who wondered why he went through four years of college to pick up spilled popcorn and trash, the manager can explain the importance of the role of a street sweeper as a cast member in a theatrical production designed to promote a fun customer environment. Thus, the supervisor would explain, the task is to see how well you can act by playing the role of the excellent street sweeper in a theatrical production. The employee now can see himself as an actor playing a role that requires skill, training, and dedication to the role as opposed to simply being a street sweeper. The ability to "play the role" is a skill that elevates the person performing it above the actual task in ways that protect egos and themselves while enhancing their performance of the role. This is surface acting, and it is similar to the smile you get when the fast food employee asks whether you "would like fries with that."

Sometimes employees become so committed to their roles in surface acting that they take on the behaviors and attitudes associated with those roles. This is called deep acting. It is when the employee acts in the role so convincingly that the displayed emotion becomes authentic. Thus, we have employees in customer contact jobs who may not have started their careers caring that much about how authentically interested and concerned they were with the customers but over time began to really feel that way. People also use surface acting to protect themselves from emotional involvement, which can detract from their ability to perform their jobs. A nurse, an emergency tech, and even a chef all have professional roles to play that allow them to use their professional norms to protect themselves against getting so deeply involved in the pain, suffering, or boredom that they can't perform their jobs with the necessary attention and focus, or even burn out when the emotional labor of doing their jobs gets to them.

Discussion Question: What ideas do you have as a manager of employees performing jobs with emotional labor content in them to help them cope? Using a telephone solicitor employee as an example, what might you do to help that person to deal with the frequent hang-ups and abusive calls that they will inevitably encounter when calling people?

Conflicting personalities and behaviors may cause stress. Conflict can occur when two or more people must work together even though their personalities, attitudes, and behaviors differ. For example, a person with an internal locus of control—that is, who always wants to control how things turn out—might get frustrated working with a person with an external locus who likes to wait and just let things happen. Likewise, an employee who likes to have a quiet and peaceful work environment may experience stress if the adjacent office is assigned to someone whose job requires him or her to talk on the telephone much of the day.[13]

Finally, we should also note that in today's world many job holders experience stress from a variety of sources simultaneously. One clear example is an airport security screener. These individuals must deal with myriad carry-on articles, some of them potentially dangerous. They face pressure from travelers to perform their job as quickly as possible but also are constantly reminded of the potential consequences of an error. Indeed, many individuals involved in security-related jobs face higher stress levels today than ever before.

Life Stressors

Stress in organizational settings also can be influenced by events that take place outside the organization. Life stressors can be categorized in terms of life change and life trauma.

A **life change** is any meaningful change in a person's personal or work situation; too many life changes over a short period of time can lead to health problems.

Life Change Holmes and Rahe first developed and popularized the notion of life change as a source of stress.[14] A **life change** is any meaningful change in a person's personal or work situation. Holmes and Rahe reasoned that major changes in a person's life can lead to stress and eventually to disease. Table 7.2 summarizes their findings on major life change events. Note that several of these events relate directly (fired from work or retirement) or indirectly (change in residence) to work.

Each event's point value supposedly reflects the event's impact on the individual. At one extreme, a spouse's death, assumed to be the most traumatic event considered, is assigned a point value of 100. At the other extreme, minor violations of the law rank only 11 points. The points themselves represent life change units, or LCUs. Note also that the list includes negative events (divorce and trouble with the boss) as well as positive ones (marriage and vacations).

Holmes and Rahe argued that a person can handle a certain threshold of LCUs but that beyond that level, problems can set in. In particular, they suggest that people who encounter more than 150 LCUs in a given year will experience a decline in their health the following year. A score of between 150 and 300 LCUs supposedly carries a 50 percent chance of major illness, while the chance of major illness is said to increase to 70 percent if the number of LCUs exceeds 300. These ideas offer some interesting insights into the potential cumulative impact of various stressors and underscore our limitations in coping with stressful events. However, research on Holmes and Rahe's proposals has provided only mixed support. Moreover, the work context for many people has changed since this early work was published.

A **life trauma** is any upheaval in an individual's life that alters his or her attitudes, emotions, or behaviors.

Life Trauma Life trauma is similar to life change, but it has a narrower, more direct, and shorter-term focus. A **life trauma** is any upheaval in an individual's life that alters his or her attitudes, emotions, or behaviors. To illustrate, according to the life change view, a divorce adds to a person's potential for health problems in the following year. At the same time, the person will obviously also experience emotional turmoil during the actual divorce process itself. This turmoil is a form of life trauma and will clearly cause stress, much of which may spill over into the workplace.[15]

Major life traumas that may cause stress include marital problems, family difficulties, and health problems initially unrelated to stress. For example, suppose a person learns she has developed arthritis that will limit her favorite activity, skiing. Her dismay over the news may translate into stress at work. Similarly, a worker coping with the traumatic aftermath of the death of her or his child will almost certainly go through difficult periods, some of which will affect her or his job performance. And millions of individuals experienced traumatic stress in the wake of the September 11th terrorist attacks.

2.10.19

Table 7.2 Life Changes and Life Change Units

RANK	LIFE EVENT	MEAN VALUE	RANK	LIFE EVENT	MEAN VALUE
1	Death of spouse	100	23	Son or daughter leaving home	29
2	Divorce	73	24	Trouble with in-laws	29
3	Marital separation	65	25	Outstanding personal achievement	28
4	Jail term	63	26	Spouse beginning or ending work	26
5	Death of close family member	63	27	Beginning or ending school	26
6	Personal injury or illness	53	28	Change in living conditions	25
7	Marriage	50	29	Revision of personal habits	24
8	Fired at work	47	30	Trouble with boss	23
9	Marital reconciliation	45	31	Change in work hours or conditions	20
10	Retirement	45	32	Change in residence	20
11	Change in health of family member	44	33	Change in schools	20
12	Pregnancy	40	34	Change in recreation	19
13	Sex difficulties	39	35	Change in church activities	19
14	Gain of new family member	39	36	Change in social activities	18
15	Business readjustment	39	37	Small mortgage or loan	17
16	Change in financial state	38	38	Change in sleeping habits	16
17	Death of close family friend	37	39	Change in the number of family get-togethers	15
18	Change to different line of work	36	40	Change in eating habits	15
19	Change in number of arguments with spouse	35	41	Vacation	13
20	Large mortgage	31	42	Christmas or other major holiday	12
21	Foreclosure of mortgage or loan	30	43	Minor violations of the law	11
22	Change in responsibilities of work	29			

The amount of life stress that a person has experienced in a given period of time, say one year, is measured by the total number of life change units (LCUs). These units result from the addition of the values (shown in the right-hand column) associated with events that the person has experienced during the target time period.

Reference: Reprinted from Journal of Psychosomatic Research, vol. 11, Thomas H. Holmes and Richard H. Rahe, "The Social Adjustment Rating Scale," Copyright © 1967, with permission from Elsevier.

CONSEQUENCES OF STRESS

Stress can have a number of consequences. As we already noted, if the stress is positive, the result may be more energy, enthusiasm, and motivation. Of more concern, of course, are the negative consequences of stress. Referring back to Figure 7.2, we see that stress can produce individual consequences, organizational consequences, and burnout.

We should first note that many of the factors listed are obviously interrelated. For example, alcohol abuse is shown as an individual consequence, but it also affects the organization the person works for. An employee who drinks on the job may perform poorly and create a hazard for others. If the category for a consequence seems somewhat arbitrary, be aware that each consequence is categorized according to the area of its primary influence.

Individual Consequences

The individual consequences of stress, then, are the outcomes that mainly affect the individual. The organization also may suffer, either directly or indirectly, but it is the individual who pays the real price.[16] Stress may produce behavioral, psychological, and medical consequences.

Behavioral Consequences The behavioral consequences of stress may harm the person under stress or others. One such behavior is smoking. Research has clearly documented that people who smoke tend to smoke more when they experience stress. There is also evidence that alcohol and drug abuse are linked to stress, although this relationship is less well documented. Other possible behavioral consequences are accident proneness, aggression and violence, and appetite disorders. The *Change* box entitled "A Disturbance in the Work Force," discusses the possible role of the current economic downturn as a contributing factor in recent incidents of workplace violence.

CHANGE A Disturbance in the Work Force

©Kesu/Shutterstock

In November 2009, Jason Rodriguez, a former employee of an engineering firm in Orlando, Florida, entered the company's offices and opened fire with a handgun, killing one person and wounding five others. Rodriguez had been fired from Reynolds, Smith and Hills less than two years earlier and told police that he thought the firm was hindering his efforts to collect unemployment benefits. "They left me to rot," he told a reporter who asked him about his motive.

"Tough times will cause people to do crazy things."

—SECURITY SPECIALIST KENNETH SPRINGER

According to the U.S. Department of Labor, the incidence of workplace violence has actually been trending down over the past few years, in part because employers have paid more attention to the problem and taken successful preventive measures. More and more companies, for example, have set up *employee assistance programs* (*EAPs*) to help workers deal with various sources of stress, but EAP providers report that, in the current climate of economic uncertainty, they're being asked to deal with a different set of problems than the ones they've typically handled in the past.

In particular, financial problems have replaced emotional problems as employees' primary area of concern, and with unemployment totals having hit nearly 30-year highs, American workers appear to be more worried about the future than about such conventional stressors as pressing deadlines and demanding bosses. Today, says Sandra Naiman, a Denver-based career coach, "off- and on-the-job stresses feed into one another" to elevate stress levels all around, and workplace stress during the current recession may reflect this unfamiliar convergence of stressors.

There are as of yet no hard data to connect workplace violence with economic downturns, but many professionals and other experts in the field are convinced that the connection is real. ComPsych Corp., an EAP provider in Chicago, reports that calls are running 30 percent above normal, and according to Rick Kronberg of Perspectives Ltd., another Chicago-based EAP provider, "with the layoffs and the general financial picture, we're getting a lot of reaction ... [from] people with a high degree of stress." Adds Tim Horner, a managing director at Kroll Inc., a security consulting firm: "There are signs out there that something's going on. It's not unusual that somebody snaps." Kenneth Springer, another security specialist whose job now includes keeping an eye on potentially dangerous ex-employees for their former employers, agrees: "Tough times," he says, "will cause people to do crazy things."

By the same token, says Laurence Miller, a forensic psychologist and author of *From Difficult to Disturbed: Understanding and Managing Dysfunctional Employees*, economic stress alone won't turn someone into a killer, nor is the average coworker likely to turn violent without warning. "People shouldn't be sitting around wondering if someone they've been working with for years who's been a regular guy [with] no real problems is going to suddenly snap and go ballistic on them," says Miller. "It's usually somebody," he warns, "that's had a long streak of problems." Unfortunately, that profile fits Jason Rodriguez, who'd been struggling for years with marital and mental health problems, unemployment, debt, and smoldering anger. "He was a very, very angry man," reports his former mother-in-law.

In January 2012, a judge ruled that Rodriguez was not yet fit to stand trial. His attorney cited his client's conviction that any proceedings should be a forum for exposing the people who'd been "brain-hacking" him since 2005.

References: Mark Trumbull, "Orlando Shooting Comes as Trend in Workplace Violence Drops," *Christian Science Monitor*, November 7, 2009, www.csmonitor.com on April 13, 2012; Ellen Wulhorst, "Recession Fuels Worries of Workplace Violence," Reuters, April 22, 2009, www.reuters.com on April 13, 2012; Scott Powers and Fernando Quintero, "Jason Rodriguez Profile: 'He Was a Very, Very Angry Man,'" *OrlandoSentinel.com*, November 6, 2009, www.orlandosentinel.com on April 14, 2011; Laurence Miller, *From Difficult to Disturbed: Understanding and Managing Dysfunctional Employees* (New York: AMACOM, 2008), http://books.google.com on April 13, 2012; Jeff Weiner, "Jason Rodriguez: Accused Downtown Shooter Not Competent, Judge Says," *Orlando Sentinel*, January 11, 2012, http://articles.orlando-sentinel.com on April 13, 2012.

Psychological Consequences The psychological consequences of stress relate to a person's mental health and well-being. When people experience too much stress at work, they may become depressed or find themselves sleeping too much or not enough.[17] Stress may also lead to family problems and sexual difficulties.

Medical Consequences The medical consequences of stress affect a person's physical well-being. Heart disease and stroke, among other illnesses, have been linked to stress. Other common medical problems resulting from too much stress include headaches, backaches, ulcers and related stomach and intestinal disorders, and skin conditions such as acne and hives.

Organizational Consequences

Clearly, any of the individual consequences just discussed can also affect the organization. Other results of stress have even more direct consequences for organizations. These include decline in performance, withdrawal, and negative changes in attitudes.

Performance One clear organizational consequence of too much stress is a decline in performance. For operating workers, such a decline can translate into poor-quality work or a drop in productivity. For managers, it can mean faulty decision making or disruptions in working relationships as people become irritable and hard to get along with.[18]

Pawel Gaul/Photos.com

Excessive stress can result in a variety of individual consequences. These can be grouped as behavioral, psychological, and medical in nature. This manager, for example, appears to be suffering a headache. She may also experience a backache, be irritable, and have trouble sleeping when she gets home.

Withdrawal Withdrawal behaviors also can result from stress. For the organization, the two most significant forms of withdrawal behavior are absenteeism and quitting. People who are having a hard time coping with stress in their jobs are more likely to call in sick or consider leaving the organization for good. Stress can also produce other, more subtle forms of withdrawal. A manager may start missing deadlines or taking longer lunch breaks. An employee may withdraw psychologically by ceasing to care about the organization and the job. As noted above, employee violence is a potential individual consequence of stress. This also has obvious organizational implications, especially if the violence is directed at another employee or at the organization in general.[19]

Attitudes Another direct organizational consequence of employee stress relates to attitudes. As we just noted, job satisfaction, morale, and organizational commitment can all suffer, along with motivation to perform at high levels. As a result, people may be more prone to complain about unimportant things, do only enough work to get by, and so forth.

Burnout

Burnout is a general feeling of exhaustion that develops when an individual simultaneously experiences too much pressure and has too few sources of satisfaction.

Burnout, another consequence of stress, has clear implications for both people and organizations. **Burnout** is a general feeling of exhaustion that develops when a person simultaneously experiences too much pressure and has too few sources of satisfaction.[20]

People with high aspirations and strong motivation to get things done are prime candidates for burnout under certain conditions. They are especially vulnerable when the organization suppresses or limits their initiative while constantly demanding that they serve the organization's own ends.

In such a situation, the individual is likely to put too much of himself or herself into the job. In other words, the person may well keep trying to meet his or her own agenda while simultaneously trying to fulfill the organization's expectations. The most likely effects of this situation are prolonged stress, fatigue, frustration, and helplessness under the burden of overwhelming demands. The person literally exhausts his or her aspirations and motivation, much as a candle burns itself out. Loss of self-confidence and psychological withdrawal follow. Ultimately, burnout may be the result. At this point, the individual may start dreading going to work in the morning, may put in longer hours but accomplish less than before, and may generally display mental and physical exhaustion.[21]

MANAGING STRESS IN THE WORKPLACE

Given that stress is widespread and so potentially disruptive in organizations, it follows that people and organizations should be concerned about how to manage it more effectively. And in fact they are. Many strategies have been developed to help manage stress in the workplace. Some are for individuals, and others are geared toward organizations.[22]

FIGURE 7.4

Individual and Organizational Coping Strategies

Just as individual and organizational factors can cause stress, there are individual and organizational strategies for coping with stress. This figure shows the individual coping mechanisms most experts recommend and several institutional and collateral organizational programs.

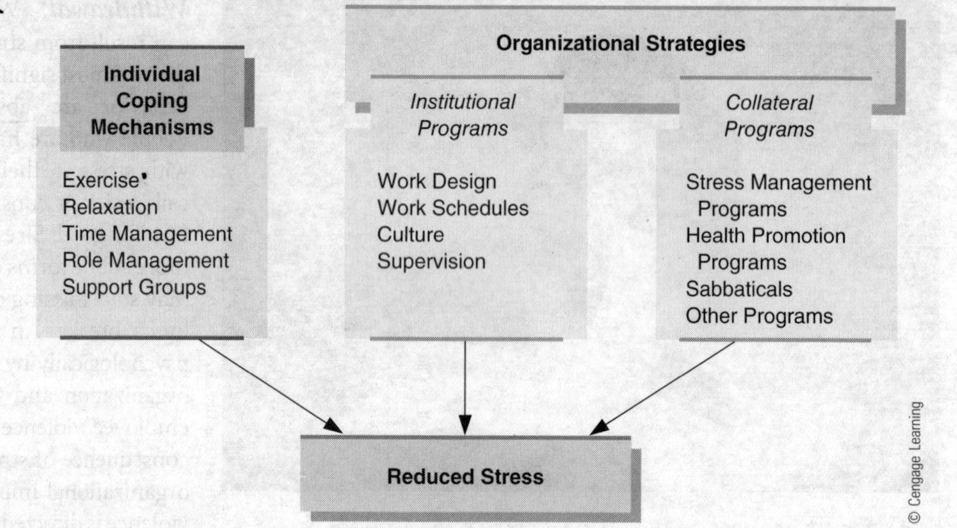

Individual Coping Strategies

Many strategies for helping individuals manage stress have been proposed. Figure 7.4 lists five of the more popular.

Exercise Exercise is one method of managing stress. People who exercise regularly are less likely to have heart attacks than inactive people. More directly, research has suggested that people who exercise regularly feel less tension and stress, are more self-confident, and show greater optimism. People who do not exercise regularly feel more stress, are more likely to be depressed, and experience other negative consequences.

Relaxation A related method of managing stress is relaxation. We noted at the beginning of the chapter that coping with stress requires adaptation. Proper relaxation is an effective way to adapt. Relaxation can take many forms. One way to relax is to take regular vacations. One study found that people's attitudes toward a variety of workplace characteristics improved significantly following a vacation.[23] People can also relax while on the job. For example, it has been recommended that people take regular rest breaks during their normal workday.[24] A popular way of resting is to sit quietly with closed eyes for ten minutes every afternoon. (Of course, it might be necessary to have an alarm clock handy!)

StockLite/Shutterstock

Relaxation is an effective method for coping with stress. Taking vacations, balancing work and non-work activities, and getting a full night of sleep are often recommended approaches to managing stress. Some managers, such as this one, also find time to take a few minutes at work every few hours to meditate or just rest.

Time Management Time management is often recommended for managing stress. The idea is that many daily pressures can be eased or eliminated if a person does a better job of managing time. One popular approach to time management is to make a list every morning of the things to be done that day. Then you group the items on the list into three categories: critical activities that must be performed, important activities that should be performed, and optional or trivial things that can be delegated or postponed. Then, of course, you do the things on the list in their order of importance. This strategy helps people get more of the important things done every day. It also encourages delegation of less important activities to others.

Role Management Somewhat related to time management is the idea of role management, in which the individual actively works to avoid overload, ambiguity, and conflict. For example, if you do not know what is expected of you, you should not sit and worry about it. Instead, ask for clarification from your boss. Another role management strategy is to learn to say "no." As simple as saying "no" might sound, a lot of people create problems for themselves by always saying "yes." Besides working in their regular jobs, they agree to serve on committees, volunteer for extra duties, and accept extra assignments. Sometimes, of course, we have no choice but to accept an extra obligation (if our boss tells us to complete a new project, we will probably have to do it). In many cases, however, saying "no" is an option.[25]

Support Groups A final method for managing stress is to develop and maintain support groups. A support group is simply a group of family members or friends with whom a person can spend time. Going out after work with a couple of coworkers to a basketball game, for example, can help relieve the stress that builds up during the day. Supportive family and friends can help people deal with normal stress on an ongoing basis. Support groups can be particularly useful during times of crisis. For example, suppose an employee has just learned that she did not get the promotion she has been working toward for months. It may help her tremendously if she has good friends to lean on, be it to talk to or to yell at.

Organizational Coping Strategies

Organizations are also increasingly realizing that they should be involved in managing their employees' stress.[26] There are two different rationales for this view. One is that because the organization is at least partly responsible for creating the stress, it should help relieve it. The other is that workers experiencing lower levels of harmful stress will function more effectively. Two basic organizational strategies for helping employees manage stress are institutional programs and collateral programs.

Institutional Programs *Institutional programs* for managing stress are undertaken through established organizational mechanisms. For example, properly designed jobs and work schedules (both discussed in Chapter 5) can help ease stress. Shift work, in particular, can cause major problems for employees, because they constantly have to adjust their sleep and relaxation patterns. Thus, the design of work and work schedules should be a focus of organizational efforts to reduce stress.

The organization's culture (covered in Chapter 18) also can be used to help manage stress. In some organizations, for example, there is a strong norm against taking time off or going on vacation. In the long run, such norms can cause major stress. Thus, the organization should strive to foster a culture that reinforces a healthy mix of work and nonwork activities.

Finally, supervision can play an important institutional role in managing stress. A supervisor can be a major source of overload. If made aware of their potential for assigning stressful amounts of work, supervisors can do a better job of keeping workloads reasonable.

Collateral Programs In addition to institutional efforts aimed at reducing stress, many organizations are turning to collateral programs. A *collateral stress program* is an organizational program specifically created to help employees deal with stress. Organizations have adopted stress management programs, health promotion programs, and other

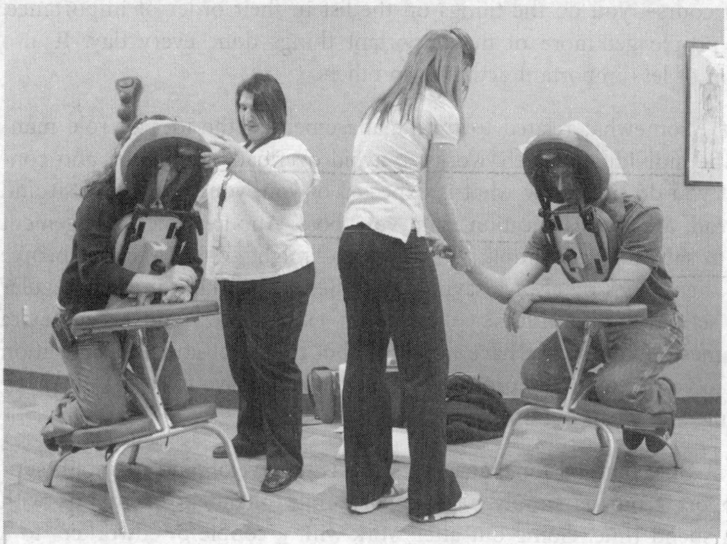

ZUMA Wire Service/Alamy Limited

Some organizations today actively help their employees cope with stress. Intel, for example, has established a wellness facility called the Health for Life Center. These Intel employees are getting professional massages at the Center to help them relax.

kinds of programs for this purpose. More and more companies are developing their own programs or adopting existing programs of this type. For example, Lockheed Martin offers screening programs for its employees to detect signs of hypertension.

Many firms today also have employee fitness programs. These programs attack stress indirectly by encouraging employees to exercise, which is presumed to reduce stress. On the negative side, this kind of effort costs considerably more than stress management programs because the firm must invest in physical facilities. Still, more and more companies are exploring this option.[27] L. L. Bean, for example, has state-of-the-art fitness centers for its employees. And many technology companies such as Google and Facebook provide on-site massages and gyms for their employees.

Finally, organizations try to help employees cope with stress through other kinds of programs. For example, existing career development programs, such as the one at General Electric, are used for this purpose. Other companies use programs promoting everything from humor to massage to yoga as antidotes for stress.[28] Of course, little or no research supports some of the claims made by advocates of these programs. Thus, managers must take steps to ensure that any organizational effort to help employees cope with stress is at least reasonably effective.

For example, the Republic of Tea is a small, privately held company that promotes healthy lifestyles centered around the consumption of tea. The firm recently added a comprehensive program called the Health Ministry to help its employees live healthier lives. A nutritionist provides free counseling to employees about their diet and weight, employees get a $500 credit for gym memberships, and a workday walking program encourages all employees to take 10- to 15-minute walks on company time. Employees were even provided with high-quality walking shoes. The firm says that its health management efforts have boosted its order processing efficiency by 11 percent, increased order accuracy by 7 percent, and decreased employee absenteeism.[29]

WORK-LIFE LINKAGES

At numerous points in this chapter we have alluded to relationships between a person's work and life. In this final brief section we will make these relationships a bit more explicit.

Fundamental Work-Life Relationships

Work-life relationships can be characterized in any number of ways. Consider, for example, the basic dimensions of the part of a person's life tied specifically to work. Common dimensions would include such things as an individual's current job (including working hours, job satisfaction, and so forth), his or her career goals (the person's aspirations, career trajectory, and so forth), interpersonal relations at work (with the supervisor, subordinates, coworkers, and others), and job security.[30]

Part of each person's life is also distinctly separate from work. These dimensions might include the person's spouse or life companion, dependents (such as children or elderly parents), personal life interests (hobbies, leisure-time interests, religious affiliations, community involvement), and friendship networks.

Work-life relationships are interrelationships between a person's work life and personal life.

Work-life relationships, then, include any relationships between dimensions of the person's work life and the person's personal life. For example, a person with numerous dependents (a nonworking spouse or domestic partner, dependent children, dependent parents, etc.) may prefer a job with a relatively high salary, fewer overtime demands, and less travel. On the other hand, a person with no dependents may be less interested in salary and more receptive to overtime, and enjoy job-related travel.

Stress will occur when there is a basic inconsistency or incompatibility between a person's work and life dimensions. For example, if a person is the sole care provider for a dependent elderly parent but has a job that requires considerable travel and evening work, stress is likely to result.

Balancing Work-Life Linkages

Balancing work-life linkages is, of course, no easy thing to do. Demands from both sides can be extreme, and people may need to be prepared to make trade-offs. The important thing is to recognize the potential trade-offs in advance so that they can be carefully weighed and a comfortable decision made. Some of the strategies for doing this were discussed earlier. For example, working for a company that offers flexible work schedules may be an attractive option.[31]

Individuals must also recognize the importance of long-term versus short-term perspectives in balancing their work and personal lives. For example, people may have to respond a bit more to work demands than to life demands in the early years of their careers. In mid-career, they may be able to achieve a more comfortable balance. And in later career stages, they may be able to put life dimensions first by refusing to relocate, working shorter hours, and so forth.

People also have to decide for themselves what they value and what trade-offs they are willing to make. For instance, consider the dilemma faced by a dual-career couple when one partner is being transferred to another city. One option is for one of the partners to subordinate her or his career for the other partner, at least temporarily. For example, the partner being transferred can turn the offer down, risking a potential career setback or the loss of the job. Or the other partner may resign from his or her current position and seek another one in the new location. The couple might also decide to live apart, with one moving and the other staying. The partners might also come to realize that their respective careers are more important to them than their relationship and decide to go their separate ways.[32]

SYNOPSIS

Stress is a person's adaptive response to a stimulus that places excessive psychological or physical demands on that person. According to the general adaptation syndrome perspective, the three stages of response to stress are alarm, resistance, and exhaustion. Two important forms of stress are eustress and distress.

Type A personalities are more competitive and time-driven than Type B personalities. Initial evidence suggested that Type A's are more susceptible to coronary heart disease, but recent findings provide less support for this idea. Hardiness, optimism, cultural context, and gender may also affect stress.

Stress can be caused by many factors. Major organizational stressors are task demands, physical demands, role demands, and interpersonal demands. Life stressors include life change and life trauma.

Stress has many consequences. Individual consequences can include behavioral, psychological, and medical problems. On the organizational level, stress can affect performance and attitudes or cause withdrawal. Burnout is another possibility.

Primary individual mechanisms for managing stress are exercise, relaxation, time management, role management, and support groups. Organizations use both institutional and collateral programs to control stress.

People have numerous dimensions to their work and personal lives. When these dimensions are interrelated, individuals must decide for themselves which are more important and how to balance them.

DISCUSSION QUESTIONS

1. Describe two recent times when stress had both good and bad consequences for you.
2. Describe a time when you successfully avoided stage 3 of the GAS and another time when you got to stage 3.
3. Do you consider yourself a Type A or a Type B person? Why?
4. Can a person who is a Type A change? If so, how?
5. What are the major stressors for a student?
6. Which is likely to be more powerful, an organizational stressor or a life stressor?
7. What consequences are students most likely to suffer as a result of too much stress?
8. Do you agree that a certain degree of stress is necessary to induce high energy and motivation?
9. What can be done to prevent burnout? If someone you know is suffering burnout, how would you advise that person to recover from it?
10. Do you practice any of the stress reduction methods discussed in the text? Which ones? Do you use others not mentioned in the text?
11. Has the work-life balance ever been an issue in your life?

HOW DO YOU SEE IT?

Planting the Seeds of Structure

"I want them to take care of it, but I want them to take care of it the way I would take care of it myself."

—TERESA CARLEO, FOUNDER AND PRESIDENT OF PLANT FANTASIES

Teresa Carleo freely admits that she didn't go quietly when she left the corporate world. She had a good job, she reports, and worked "really really really hard" until an opportunity for promotion came up. "And my boss brought in somebody from the outside instead of considering me for the job. So I got pissed, and we had a fight, and she fired me." Her self-respect was intact, but "I was faced with what am I going to do."

Carleo enjoyed doing two things—cooking and gardening—and designing spaces with living things won out over boiling pots of water in a hot kitchen. In 1987, she started a landscape contracting business called Plant Fantasies. "I just made the decision. I just went for it," she recalls, but she did so with a good deal of either prudence or trepidation. For seven years, she operated out of her Manhattan apartment, and to this day, she considers the availability of this risk-free option a key factor in her decision to take on the burden of business ownership: "I didn't have to worry about paying rent," she says, "and I think that's an important part of the puzzle in terms of making a decision to go out on my own.

"The decision to start the business," she says in retrospect, "was exciting. The determination to *stay* with the business was excruciating." For a while, she had just one customer (who was worth $100 a month), and so the conjunction of home and work in the eleventh-floor apartment that she shared with her husband didn't cause much of a ripple in her daily life, most of which was spent pounding the pavement in search of more clients. Once she'd acquired a few more accounts, she hired "a man with a van" to take her around to worksites, where she'd personally handle the installation and maintenance of plants. By the time she had a fuller client list and a payroll of four, Carleo was finally ready to move into an 800-square-foot loft, but the daunting prospect of having to pay $700 a month in rent prompted her to add a few noncore services, such as putting up clients' Christmas decorations and mowing their lawns.

By 2010—the company's twenty-third year in business—Plant Fantasies had a workforce of forty to sixty (depending on the season) and revenues of around $5 million. Carleo is now a full-service contractor, and her client list is a veritable Who's Who of New York's real estate industry (her core business). "I'm really crazy about losing accounts," she says. "I think I still have almost every account that I started out with 24 years ago. And I feel like I do that because I really try to get into what they want … and get into their mindset. Because it's not about me," she adds. "It's really about them."

One gets the impression, however, that it's really about Carleo's confidence in her personal ability to satisfy her customers. According to Stephen Chapman, president of Craven Management Corp., an early and still major client, "Teresa doesn't supervise from afar. She's here. She pulls it all together and does much of the work herself." "There are times," Carleo admits, "that I have to *think* for" my customers, and she's clearly happiest when everything, from design to implementation and maintenance, is being run from her end: "It's much easier when we're the landscape designers," Carleo explains, "because we're picking the plant material, we have a sense of what … we feel comfortable with, we have faith in our design, we have faith in our choices."

Needless to say, Carleo's work life got busier as her company grew, and she tacitly admits that, when you're a sole proprietor, "we" usually means "I." "At one point," she says,

> *I'm opening every piece of mail. I'm dealing with every phone call that comes in, dealing with all the sales, all the designs, all the flowers. I'm not really doing them, but I'm kind of overseeing them.*
>
> *It's a lot. It's a lot.*
>
> *And all the field work and the maintenance and "Is the shrub cut straight or is it cut crooked? Did you pull out the weeds or did you pull out the flowers?"*
>
> *There's so many kinds of problems and little issues, minutiae, in a business like this.... It's all detail.*

Carleo also admits that she's a stickler when it comes to taking care of all these details. She has employees to cut the shrubs and pull the weeds, and, she says, "I want them to take care of it. But," she adds, "I want them to take care of it the way I would take care of it myself."

After 25 years, however, Carleo seems to have come to the realization that a mature company has some form of *organizational structure*—some system of task and authority relationships that governs the way it does its work (see Chapter 16). "I do like *some* structure," she says, and she's taking steps to let her company's structure relieve her of some of the burden of doing its work: "More and more, as I'm trying to grow the company," she reports, "I'm trying to get my team to be more independent of me, and cut the umbilical cord, and having them take care of [more] stuff. I don't *want* to know every single thing. I don't feel I *need* to know every single thing."

CASE QUESTIONS

1. Would you say that Carleo is *primarily* a *Type A* or a *Type B personality*? If—like most people—she exhibits behavior patterns typical of both types, what are her most prominent Type A and Type B behavior patterns?
2. How would you rank Carleo in terms of *hardiness*? In terms of *optimism*? Be specific in applying the criteria for each behavior pattern. For example, refer to Chapter 3 in applying such criteria as *locus of control* and *affectivity*.
3. Carleo's work and life dimensions seem to be pretty consistent or compatible. What factors in both her work and her life seem to contribute to this balance? Which factors might threaten it?
4. According to one motivational consultant:*

   For the individual who has given birth to a business, whose Herculean efforts have sustained its life through the critical and tumultuous early years, you better believe it's often hard to let go of your baby or even to share caretaking and growth-producing responsibilities.

   This attitude often leads to a "hands-in (everything)" as opposed to "hands-on" approach to managing, which can in turn threaten the continued success of a business. What do you think the individual can and ought to do if he or she succumbs to this approach and it does in fact threaten his or her business? In what ways might possible solutions to this problem affect the individual's work-life balance?

ADDITIONAL SOURCES

Cara S. Trager, "Top Entrepreneurs 2010: Plant Fantasies," *Crain's New York Business.com*, May 1, 2010, *www.crainsnewyork.com* on June 26, 2012; Plant Fantasies, "Teresa Carleo Founded Plant Fantasies in 1987 and Has Been Greening Manhattan from Courtyards to Rooftops Ever Since," *New York Real Estate Journal*, May 11–24, 2010 (press release), *www.plantfantasies.com* on June 26, 2012; "Green Comes Naturally to Teresa Carleo of Plant Fantasies," *New York Real Estate Journal*, July 22, 2008, http://nyrej.com on June 26, 2010; Erin Casey, "From Minimum Wage to Rooftop Gardens," *SUCCESS for Women*, October 21, 2009, *www.sfwmag.com* on June 26, 2010.

*Mark Gorkin, "The Stress Doc's Q and A: Work Stress," *The Stress Doc* (2012), www.stressdoc.com on June 27, 2012.

EXPERIENCING ORGANIZATIONAL BEHAVIOR

Rating Yourself from "Bored" to "Panicked"

Purpose This exercise is designed to help you find out just how stressed you are at the moment.

Format The checklist below consists of a number of symptoms that may indicate the presence of stress in your life. The five columns measure the relative severity of each symptom. By filling in the checklist and figuring your score, you can get some idea of how well you are (or aren't) responding to the stress that you're currently experiencing.

Procedure Check the box that most closely describes how often you have experienced each symptom *during the past month*. Then calculate your score.

2.10.19

Symptom	Never	Rarely	Sometimes	Often	Always
Constant fatigue	[ ]	[ ]	[ ]	[ ]	[ ]
Low energy level	[ ]	[ ]	[ ]	[ ]	[ ]
Recurring headaches	[ ]	[ ]	[ ]	[ ]	[ ]
Gastrointestinal disorders	[ ]	[ ]	[ ]	[ ]	[ ]
Bad breath	[ ]	[ ]	[ ]	[ ]	[ ]
Sweaty hands or feet	[ ]	[ ]	[ ]	[ ]	[ ]
Dizziness	[ ]	[ ]	[ ]	[ ]	[ ]
High blood pressure	[ ]	[ ]	[ ]	[ ]	[ ]
Pounding heart	[ ]	[ ]	[ ]	[ ]	[ ]
Constant inner tension	[ ]	[ ]	[ ]	[ ]	[ ]
Inability to sleep	[ ]	[ ]	[ ]	[ ]	[ ]
Temper outbursts	[ ]	[ ]	[ ]	[ ]	[ ]
Hyperventilation	[ ]	[ ]	[ ]	[ ]	[ ]
Moodiness	[ ]	[ ]	[ ]	[ ]	[ ]
Irritability	[ ]	[ ]	[ ]	[ ]	[ ]
Inability to concentrate	[ ]	[ ]	[ ]	[ ]	[ ]
Increased aggression	[ ]	[ ]	[ ]	[ ]	[ ]
Compulsive eating	[ ]	[ ]	[ ]	[ ]	[ ]
Chronic worrying	[ ]	[ ]	[ ]	[ ]	[ ]
Anxiety	[ ]	[ ]	[ ]	[ ]	[ ]
Inability to relax	[ ]	[ ]	[ ]	[ ]	[ ]
Feeling inadequate	[ ]	[ ]	[ ]	[ ]	[ ]
Increase in defensiveness	[ ]	[ ]	[ ]	[ ]	[ ]
Dependence on tranquilizers	[ ]	[ ]	[ ]	[ ]	[ ]
Excessive use of alcohol	[ ]	[ ]	[ ]	[ ]	[ ]
Excessive smoking	[ ]	[ ]	[ ]	[ ]	[ ]
Totals	5 × 0	1 × 1	8 × 2	10 × 3	2 × 4
	0 +	[1] +	16 +	30 +	[8] = 55

How to score: Tally the number of checks that you made in each column. Next, multiply the column totals by the factor indicated (0 through 4). Add the products to get your symptoms score. Finally, compare your total to the following scale.

Score	*Stress state*
Below 20 =	Bored
20–30 =	Relaxed
31–40 =	Alert
41–50 =	Tense
51–60 =	Stressed
Over 60 =	Panicked

Reference

Hunsaker, Phillip L., *Management: A Skills Approach,* 2nd Edition, © 2005. Reprinted by permission of Pearson Education, Inc. Upper Saddle River, NJ

BUILDING MANAGERIAL SKILLS

Exercise Overview Time management skills help people to prioritize work, to work more efficiently, and to delegate appropriately. Poor time management may result in stress. This exercise will help you relate time management skills to stress reduction.

Exercise Background Make a list of several of the major things that cause stress for you. Stressors might involve school (e.g., hard classes, too many exams), work (e.g., financial pressures, demanding work schedule), and/or personal circumstances (e.g., friends, romance, family). Try to be as specific as possible. Also try to identify at least ten different stressors.

Exercise Task Using the list developed above, do each of the following.

1. Evaluate the extent to which poor time management on your part plays a role in how each stressor affects you. For example, do exams cause stress because you delay studying?
2. Develop a strategy for using time more efficiently in relation to each stressor that relates to time.
3. Note interrelationships among different kinds of stressors and time. For example, financial pressures may cause you to work, but work may interfere with school. Can any of these interrelationships be more effectively managed vis-à-vis time?
4. Assess how you manage the stress in your life. Is it possible to manage stress in a more time-effective manner?

SELF-ASSESSMENT EXERCISE

Stress and Time Management

This self-assessment allows you to understand better the traits that may cause stress for you as you attempt to manage your time.

Instructions: Each of us displays certain kinds of behaviors and thought patterns of personal characteristics. For each of the 21 descriptions below, circle the number that you feel best describes where you are between each pair. The best answer for each set of descriptions is the response that most nearly describes the way you feel, behave, or think. Respond in terms of your regular or typical behavior, thoughts, or characteristics.

Descriptions

1. I'm always on time for appointments.	7 6 5 4 3 2 1	I'm never quite on time.
2. When someone is talking to me, chances are I'll anticipate what he or she is going to say by nodding, interrupting, or finishing sentences.	7 6 5 4 3 2 1	I listen quietly without showing impatience.
3. I frequently try to do several things at once.	7 6 5 4 3 2 1	I tend to take things one at a time.
4. When it comes to waiting in line (at banks, theaters, etc.), I really get impatient and frustrated.	7 6 5 4 3 2 1	It simply doesn't bother me.
5. I always feel rushed.	7 6 5 4 3 2 1	I never feel rushed.
6. When it comes to my temper, I find it hard to control at times.	7 6 5 4 3 2 1	I just don't seem to have one.
7. I tend to do most things like eating, walking, and talking rapidly	7 6 5 4 3 2 1	Slowly.

TOTAL SCORE 1–7 = ______ = S [The interpretation of "S" will be made at the end of the chapter.]

8. Quite honestly, the things I enjoy most are job-related activities.	7 6 5 4 3 2 1	Leisure-time activities.
9. At the end of a typical workday, I usually feel like I needed to get more done than I did.	7 6 5 4 3 2 1	I accomplished everything I needed to.
10. Someone who knows me very well would say that I would rather work than play.	7 6 5 4 3 2 1	I would rather play than work.
11. When it comes to getting ahead at work, nothing is more important.	7 6 5 4 3 2 1	Many things are more important.
12. My primary source of satisfaction comes from my job.	7 6 5 4 3 2 1	I regularly find satisfaction in non-job pursuits, such as hobbies, friends, and family.
13. Most of my friends and social acquaintances are people I know from work.	7 6 5 4 3 2 1	Not connected with my work.
14. I'd rather stay at work than take a vacation.	7 6 5 4 3 2 1	Nothing at work is important enough to interfere with my vacation.

TOTAL SCORE 8–14 = ______ = J [The interpretation of "J" will be made at the end of the chapter.]

15. People who know me well would describe me as hard-driving and competitive.	7 6 5 4 3 2 1	Relaxed and easy-going.
16. In general, my behavior is governed by a desire for recognition and achievement.	7 6 5 4 3 2 1	What I want to do—not by trying to satisfy others.
17. In trying to complete a project or solve a problem, I tend to wear myself out before I'll give up on it.	7 6 5 4 3 2 1	I tend to take a break or quit if I'm feeling fatigued.
18. When I play a game (tennis, cards, etc.), my enjoyment comes from winning.	7 6 5 4 3 2 1	The social interaction.
19. I like to associate with people who are dedicated to getting ahead.	7 6 5 4 3 2 1	Easy-going and take life as it comes.

20. I'm not happy unless I'm always doing something.	7 6 5 4 3 2 1 (7 circled)	Frequently, "doing nothing" can be quite enjoyable.
21. What I enjoy doing most are competitive activities.	7 6 5 4 3 2 1 (1 circled)	Noncompetitive pursuits.

TOTAL SCORE 15–21 = 4? = *H [The interpretation of "H" will be made at the end of the chapter.]*

Source: From John M. Ivancevich and Michael T. Matteson, *Organizational Behavior and Management*, 3rd ed., pp. 274–276. © 1990, 1993 by Richard D. Irwin, Inc. Reprinted by permission of the publisher.

Are You Type A or Type B?

This test will help you develop insights into your own tendencies toward Type A or Type B behavior patterns. Answer the questions honestly and accurately about either your job or your school, whichever requires the most time each week. Then calculate your score according to the instructions that follow the questions. Discuss your results with a classmate. Critique each other's answers and see whether you can help each other develop a strategy for reducing Type A tendencies.

Choose from the following responses to answer the questions that follow:

a. Almost always true
b. Usually true
c. Seldom true
d. Never true

A 1. I do not like to wait for other people to complete their work before I can proceed with mine.
B 2. I hate to wait in most lines.
C 3. People tell me that I tend to get irritated too easily.
d 4. Whenever possible, I try to make activities competitive.
B 5. I have a tendency to rush into work that needs to be done before knowing the procedure I will use to complete the job.
A 6. Even when I go on vacation, I usually take some work along.
A 7. When I make a mistake, it is usually because I have rushed into the job before completely planning it through.
B 8. I feel guilty about taking time off from work.
d 9. People tell me I have a bad temper when it comes to competitive situations.
C 10. I tend to lose my temper when I am under a lot of pressure at work.
A 11. Whenever possible, I will attempt to complete two or more tasks at once.
A 12. I tend to race against the clock.
D 13. I have no patience with lateness.
B 14. I catch myself rushing when there is no need.

Score your responses according to the following key:

- *An intense sense of time urgency* is a tendency to race against the clock, even when there is little reason to. The person feels a need to hurry for hurry's sake alone, and this tendency has appropriately been called hurry sickness. Time urgency is measured by items 1, 2, 8, 12, 13, and 14. Each *a* or *b* answer to these six questions scores one point. 𝍸
- *Inappropriate aggression and hostility* reveal themselves in a person who is excessively competitive and who cannot do anything for fun. This inappropriately aggressive behavior easily evolves into frequent displays of hostility, usually at the slightest provocation or frustration. Competitiveness and hostility are measured by items 3, 4, 9, and 10. Each *a* or *b* answer scores one point. Ø
- *Polyphasic behavior* refers to the tendency to undertake two or more tasks simultaneously at inappropriate times. It usually results in wasted time because of an inability to complete the tasks. This behavior is measured by items 6 and 11. Each *a* or *b* answer scores one point. ||
- *Goal directedness without proper planning* refers to the tendency of an individual to rush into work without really knowing how to accomplish the desired result. This usually results in incomplete work or work with many errors, which in turn leads to wasted time, energy, and money. Lack of planning is measured by items 5 and 7. Each *a* or *b* response scores one point. ||

TOTAL SCORE 9

If your score is 5 or greater, you may possess some basic components of the Type A personality.

Reference: Girdano, Daniel A.; Dusek, Dorothy E.; Everly, Georges., *Controlling Stress and Tension*, 6th Edition, © 2001. p. 94. Reprinted by permission of Pearson Education, Inc., Upper Saddle River, NJ

CHAPTER 8 Decision Making and Problem Solving

Chapter Outline

- The Nature of Decision Making
- The Rational Approach to Decision Making
- The Behavioral Approach to Decision Making
- Creativity, Problem Solving, and Decision Making

Chapter Learning Objectives

After studying this chapter, you should be able to:

1. **Describe the nature of decision making and distinguish it from problem solving.**
2. **Discuss the rational approach to decision making.**
3. **Identify and discuss the primary behavioral aspects of decision making.**
4. **Discuss the nature of creativity and relate it to decision making and problem solving.**

The Creative Imprint at Bigfoot

"What was I going to do—buy more boats, buy more houses? I discovered there's a creative side in me."

—Michael Gleissner, founder of Bigfoot Entertainment

Have you seen *Midnight Movie*? You wouldn't have caught it in a theater because it went straight to DVD, but that doesn't prevent hard-core horror film fans from tracking it down—after all, it was selected as the Best Feature Film at the 10th Annual Chicago Horror Film Festival. It also found an audience outside the United States, with producer Bigfoot selling distribution rights in such countries as Germany, Greece, Thailand, and Japan. How about *3 Needles*, a Canadian-made movie about the worldwide AIDS crisis? It was no blockbuster, but it was endorsed

Izumi Hasegawa/HollywoodNewsWire Hollywood News Wire/Newscom

Most successful entertainment companies like Bigfoot rely heavily on creative people and bold decision makers to succeed.

by the United Nations and did well enough at international film festivals to find distributors in such countries as Australia, New Zealand, and Brazil. Bigfoot CEO Kacy Andrews was pleased with the film's reception: "The positive response from critics and audiences," she said, "... once again affirms our conviction to promote independent filmmakers."

Bigfoot Entertainment is responsible for a host of independently produced films, many of which follow similar distribution paths to venues and audiences around the world. The company, says Andrews, "is dedicated to the community of filmmakers who possess the vision and passion to create critically acclaimed independent films." It was founded in 2004 by a German serial entrepreneur named Michael Gleissner, who is in some ways a model for the sort of creative people that Bigfoot likes to back. He was certainly the model for the hero of *Hui Lu*, a 2007 Bigfoot film that Gleissner wrote and directed about a highly successful young entrepreneur who sells his company but finds himself pushed to the edge despite his millions. "What was I going to do," Gleissner replied when asked about his unusual career move, "buy more boats, buy more houses? I discovered there's a creative side in me."

Gleissner was an e-commerce pioneer in Germany, where he founded Telebook, Germany's number one online bookstore, and WWW-Service GmbH, the country's first, and one of its most successful, web-hosting companies. In 1998 he sold Telebook to Amazon.com, where he served two years as a VP before cashing in and, in 2001, moving to Asia as a base for a new round of entrepreneurial activities. When he bought Bigfoot, it was an e-mail management firm, but Gleissner quickly re-created it as an international entertainment company whose main business, according to its mission statement, is producing and financing "innovative entertainment content, including independent feature films, television series, and reality shows." As head of Bigfoot, Gleissner served as executive producer on *Midnight Movie* and *3 Needles*, as well as on *Irreversi*, his second effort at writing and directing, and on *Shanghai Kiss*, in which he also tried his hand at acting.

Bigfoot maintains offices in Los Angeles and a small production facility in Venice, California, but the centerpiece of its operations is Bigfoot Studios, which opened in 2004 on the island of Mactan, in Cebu, home to the second-largest city in the Philippines. The state-of-the-art facility features six large soundstages, fully equipped editing suites and sound-mixing studios, and the latest in high-tech cameras and other equipment. In 2007, under the auspices of Bigfoot Properties, Gleissner expanded Bigfoot Studios as the first phase of Bigfoot Center, a complex that will eventually house not only film and TV production facilities but Bigfoot Executive Hotel, an array of restaurants, boutiques, and sidewalk shops, and an eleven-story office building (home to Bigfoot Outsourcing, which specializes in business-process services). The Bigfoot Center in the Philippines, by the way, should not be confused with the twenty-six-story Bigfoot Centre in Hong Kong, where Bigfoot Properties is headquartered.

Gleissner's goal is to turn Cebu into a destination of choice for filmmakers who want to cut costs by shooting and finishing movies outside the United States, and when Bigfoot Entertainment finds a film suitable for financing and development, the deal usually requires the director to do some production work at the Cebu facility. By the time the studio opened in 2004, the Philippines were already an attractive location for animators looking for cheap postproduction help, but the pool of talent available for work on live-action films was quite limited. Gleissner's solution? He founded the International Academy of Film and Television (IAFT), not only to staff Bigfoot Studios but to train what executive director Keith Sensing calls "the next generation of global filmmakers." IAFT, says Sensing, looks for creative people who "have a desire for adventure" and "an education that will set them apart from people who have a strictly Hollywood background."

IAFT enrollment is currently 60 percent international and 40 percent Filipino, but "all of our students," says Sensing, "have the opportunity to participate in real projects going on at Bigfoot Studios.... Many IAFT graduates," he adds, "have gone on to write, produce, and direct their own films" and often follow in Bigfoot's steps by finding distribution for their independent features on the international festival circuit. Three recent graduates landed jobs on Gleissner's most recent project, a Philippines-set thriller revolving around a female diver. Gleissner not only cowrote and directed *Deep Gold* but drew on his experience as an underwater photographer to shoot key scenes in Bigfoot's specially designed 170,000-gallon Underwater Studio.

In 2010, Bigfoot moved to expand into the areas of acquisition, distribution, and foreign sales with the purchase of Ascendant Pictures. Much like Bigfoot itself, Ascendant carved out its niche in the industry by integrating the budgeting sensibility of "indie" producers with the marketing skills of larger studios. "Our schools are profitable," explains Kacy Andrews, "but overall we're not profitable yet. We're hoping the distribution side will get us there in one or two years."

The new unit, called Bigfoot Ascendant Distribution, will buy four to six English-language movies annually—"genre films," says Andrews, "horror and action that will sell well internationally and play well theatrically, too." In order to bolster its ability to get its films into theaters (most of the company's features have gone straight to DVD or sold to cable TV), Bigfoot has also become the largest shareholder in Carmike Cinemas, the fourth-largest theater chain in the United States.

In 2010 it also purchased the historic Majestic Crest theater in Los Angeles. The acquisition, says Andrews, goes hand in hand with Bigfoot's purchase of Ascendant: "We wanted a great theater to showcase our films—not only ones we produce but ones we plan to acquire. Everyone knows the Crest," she adds. "It gives us a lot of prestige." In 2011 Bigfoot announced that the Crest would be home to its first annual Singafest, an international film festival celebrating Asian cinema.

What Do You Think?

1. What does the Bigfoot story tell us about the tensions between creativity and innovation on the one hand and financial considerations—such as budgets and control processes—on the other?

2. When you make decisions, do you tend to lean toward the creative (and perhaps risky) side or to the conservative side? Why do you think this is so?

References: Kellen Merrill, "The Big Imprint in the Film Industry," *inmag.com*, 2010, www.inmag.com on May 25, 2012; Stephanie N. Mehta, "Hollywood, South Pacific-Style," *CNNMoney.com*, June 8, 2006, http://money.cnn.com on May 25, 2012; Marlene Rodriguez, "Bigfoot Entertainment's International Academy of Film and Television in Mactan Island, Cebu," *NEDA Knowledge Emporium*, November 5, 2007, www.neda.gov.ph on May 25, 2012; Josh Elmets with Rebecca Pahle, "International Academy of Film and TV Flourishes in the Philippines," *MovieMaker*, January 29, 2010, www.moviemaker.com on May 25, 2012; Jonathan Landreth, "Bigfoot Entertainment Expands, Launches Distribution Company," *Hollywood Reporter*, November 2, 2010, www.hollywoodreporter.com on May 25, 2012; Richard Verrier, "Indie Filmmaker Bigfoot Has an Insider Track to Theater," *Los Angeles Times*, October 6, 2010, http://articles.latimes.com on May 25, 2012; Bigfoot Entertainment, "Inaugural Singafest Asian Film Festival Unveils 2011 Selections," press release, May 25, 2011, http://singafest.com on May 25, 2012.

Managers routinely make both tough and easy decisions. Regardless of which decisions are made, though, it is almost certain that some observers will criticize and others will applaud. Indeed, in the rough-and-tumble world of business, there are few simple or easy decisions to make. Some managers claim to be focused on the goal of what is good for the company in the long term and make decisions accordingly. Others clearly focus on the here and now. Some decisions deal with employees, some with investors, and others with dollars and cents. But all require careful thought and consideration.

This chapter describes many different perspectives of decision making. We start by examining the nature of decision making and distinguishing it from problem solving. Next, we describe several different approaches to understanding the decision-making process. We then identify and discuss related behavioral aspects of decision making. Finally, we discuss creativity, a key ingredient in many effective decisions.

THE NATURE OF DECISION MAKING

Decision making is the process of choosing from among several alternatives.

Problem solving is finding the answer to a question; it is also a form of decision making in which the issue is unique and alternatives must be developed and evaluated without the aid of a programmed decision rule.

Decision making is choosing one alternative from among several. Consider a game of football, for example. The quarterback can run any of perhaps a hundred plays. With the goal of scoring a touchdown always in mind, he chooses the play that seems to promise the best outcome. His choice is based on his understanding of the game situation, the likelihood of various outcomes, and his preference for each outcome.

Problem solving, on the other hand, involves finding the answer to a question. Suppose after running a play the quarterback sees that a referee has thrown a flag to signal a rules infraction. The referee explains to the quarterback that the defensive team committed a foul, and that the offense has the choice of accepting the play that was just run without a sanction against the defense or else they can impose the sanction and then run the play again. If the play resulted in a thirty-yard gain, whereas the penalty would mean only five yards, the answer is to refuse the penalty and take the play. But if the play had resulted in a big loss, the penalty would be accepted.

Note that in some situations decision making and problem solving start out alike. Suppose the issue is to identify the best location for a new plant. If after evaluating each of the primary locations only one viable choice remains, then there is really no decision left to make. But if three locations each meet the firm's basic requirements and

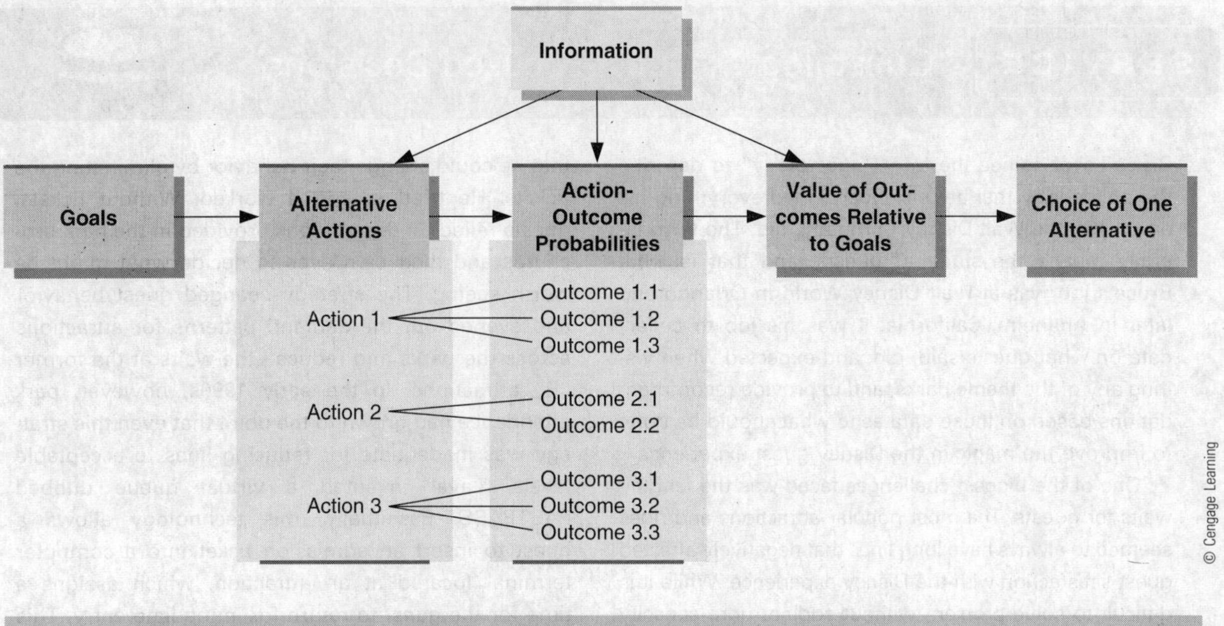

FIGURE 8.1

Elements of Decision Making

A decision maker has a goal, evaluates the outcomes of alternative courses of action in terms of the goal, and selects one alternative to be implemented.

have different relative strengths, the manager will then have to make a decision from among the options. Most of our interest relates to decision making. However, we will identify implications for problem solving as relevant.

Figure 8.1 shows the basic elements of decision making. A decision maker's actions are guided by a goal. Each of several alternative courses of action is linked with various outcomes. Information is available on the alternatives, on the likelihood that each outcome will occur, and on the value of each outcome relative to the goal. The decision maker chooses one alternative on the basis of his or her evaluation of the information.

Decisions made in organizations can be classified according to frequency and to information conditions. In a decision-making context, frequency is how often a particular decision situation recurs, and information conditions describe how much information is available about the likelihood of various outcomes.

Types of Decisions

A **programmed decision** is a decision that recurs often enough for a decision rule to be developed.

A **decision rule** is a statement that tells a decision maker which alternative to choose based on the characteristics of the decision situation.

The frequency of recurrence determines whether a decision is programmed or nonprogrammed. A **programmed decision** recurs often enough for decision rules to be developed. A **decision rule** tells decision makers which alternative to choose once they have predetermined information about the decision situation. The appropriate decision rule is used whenever the same situation is encountered. Programmed decisions usually are highly structured; that is, the goals are clear and well known, the decision-making procedure is already established, and the sources and channels of information are clearly defined.[1]

Airlines use established procedures when an airplane breaks down and cannot be used on a particular flight. Passengers may not view the issue as a programmed decision because they experience this situation relatively infrequently. But the airlines know that equipment problems that render a plane unfit for service arise regularly. Each airline has its own set of clear and defined procedures to use in the event of equipment problems. A given flight may be delayed, canceled, or continued on a different plane, depending on

SERVICE "Guestology": Guest-Focused Decisions

©rangizz/Shutterstock

Bruce Laval coined the term "guestology" to describe the philosophy that he felt underpinned everything his employer, the Walt Disney Company, did. The term literally means the study of guests, and that is what Bruce's job was at Walt Disney World in Orlando and later in Anaheim, California. It was his job to collect data on what guests said, did, and expected when visiting any of the theme parks, and to provide recommendations based on those data as to what should be done to improve the magic in the Disney guest experience.

One of the biggest challenges faced was the lengthy waits for guests. The most popular attractions and rides seemed to always have long lines that negatively affected guest satisfaction with the Disney experience. While it is difficult to solve problem without adding more capacity to the theme parks or reducing the number of guests allowed in them at any one time, it was a problem that needed solving. Bruce had done several things in the past to address this problem. He had, for example, eliminated the tickets that had been the original method of allocating attraction capacity. From his study of customer behavior, he discovered that these tickets were distorting demand for the attractions. For example, the famous "E" tickets were the highest value, and guests used the ticket value to guide their in-park utilization patterns. Thus, guests thought of the "E" ticket attractions as "must-sees," and they would line up for hours to make sure that their limited time in Disney World included these attractions.

Laval recognized that guests were using the ticket price information to direct their behavior and believed that he could change their behavior by eliminating the tickets. He tried it, and it worked. Without tickets, guests relied on descriptions provided in the park brochures and their own eyes to decide what might be worth seeing. The strategy changed guest behavior and evened out the demand patterns for attractions across the parks and reduced the waits at the former "E" attractions. In the early 1990s, however, park attendance had grown to the point that even this strategy was inadequate for reducing lines to acceptable levels. Laval invented a virtual queue dubbed FASTPASS. Essentially, this technology allows a guest to insert an admission ticket into a computer terminal located at an attraction, which assigns a time for the guest to return for immediate entry. This allows guests to do other things, such as stand in another attraction line, go shopping, or eat while awaiting the assigned time to return. In effect, FASTPASS allowed guests to stand in two lines at the same time. The impact of this technique on guest satisfaction was significant. By using guestology to discover what its customers said, expected, and actually did, Disney was able to design a waiting system that allows customers to do more and helps Disney meet their expectations.

Discussion Question: Recall a wait for some service. What did the organization do, or what should it do, to make the experience go by more quickly? What makes a wait more or less enjoyable? Can you think of a wait you didn't mind? Why didn't you mind it?

the nature of the problem and other circumstances (such as the number of passengers booked, the next scheduled flight for the same destination, and so forth).

When a problem or decision situation has not been encountered before, however, a decision maker cannot rely on previously established decision rules. Such a decision is called a **nonprogrammed decision**, and it requires problem solving. Problem solving is a special form of decision making in which the issue is unique—it often requires developing and evaluating alternatives without the aid of a decision rule.[2] Nonprogrammed decisions are poorly structured because information is ambiguous, there is no clear procedure for making the decision, and the goals are often vague. Many of the decisions that had to be made by government, military, and business leaders in the wake of the events of September 11, 2001, were clearly of this type. One key element of nonprogrammed decisions is that they require good judgment on the part of leaders and decision makers.[3]

A **nonprogrammed decision** is a decision that recurs infrequently and for which there is no previously established decision rule.

Table 8.1 summarizes the characteristics of programmed and nonprogrammed decisions. Note that programmed decisions are more common at the lower levels of the

Table 8.1 Characteristics of Programmed and Nonprogrammed Decisions

CHARACTERISTICS	PROGRAMMED DECISIONS	NONPROGRAMMED DECISIONS
Type of Decision	Well structured	Poorly structured
Frequency	Repetitive and routine	New and unusual
Goals	Clear, specific	Vague
Information	Readily available	Not available, unclear channels
Consequences	Minor	Major
Organizational Level	Lower levels	Upper levels
Time for Solution	Short	Relatively long
Basis for Solution	Decision rules, set procedures	Judgment and creativity

organization, whereas a primary responsibility of top management is to make the difficult, nonprogrammed decisions that determine the organization's long-term effectiveness. By definition, the strategic decisions for which top management is responsible are poorly structured, nonroutine, and have far-reaching consequences.[4] Programmed decisions, then, can be made according to previously tested rules and procedures. Nonprogrammed decisions generally require that the decision maker exercise judgment and creativity. In other words, all problems require a decision, but not all decisions require problem solving.

Decision-Making Conditions

Decisions are made to bring about desired outcomes, but the information available about those outcomes varies. The range of available information can be considered as a continuum whose endpoints represent complete certainty—when all alternative outcomes are known—and complete uncertainty, when all alternative outcomes are unknown. Points between the two extremes create risk—the decision maker has some information about the possible outcomes and may be able to estimate the probability of their occurrence.

Under the **condition of certainty**, the manager knows what the outcomes of each alternative of a given action will be but has enough information to estimate the probabilities of various outcomes.

Under a **condition of risk**, the decision maker cannot know with certainty what the outcome of a given action will be but has enough information to estimate the probabilities of various outcomes.

Different information conditions present different challenges to the decision maker.[5] For example, suppose the marketing manager of PlayStation is trying to determine whether to launch an expensive promotional effort for a new video game (see Figure 8.2). For simplicity, assume there are only two alternatives: to promote the game or not to promote it. Under a **condition of certainty**, the manager knows the outcomes of each alternative. If the new game is promoted heavily, the company will realize a $10 million profit. Without promotion, the company will realize only a $2 million profit. Here the decision is simple: Promote the game. (Note: These figures are created for the purposes of this example and are not actual profit figures for any company.)

Under a **condition of risk**, the decision maker cannot know with certainty what the outcome of a given action will be but has enough information to estimate the probabilities of various outcomes. Thus, working from information gathered by the market research department, the marketing manager in our example can estimate the likelihood of each outcome in a risk situation. In this case, the alternatives are defined by the size of the market. The probability for a large video game market is 0.6, and the probability for

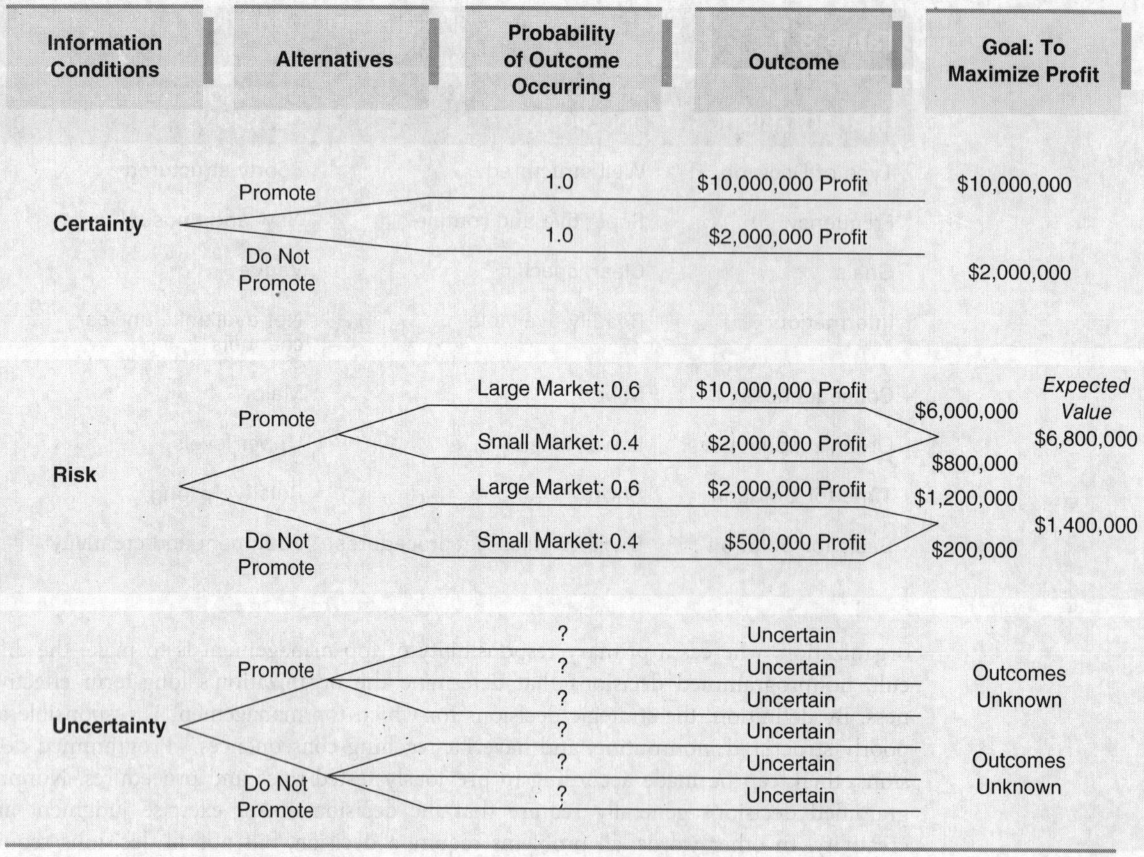

FIGURE 8.2

Alternative Outcomes Under Different Decision-Making Conditions

The three decision-making conditions of certainty, risk, and uncertainty for the decision about whether to promote a new video game to the market.

a small market is 0.4. The manager can calculate the expected value of the promotional effort based on these probabilities and the expected profits associated with each. To find the expected value of an alternative, the manager multiplies each outcome's value by the probability of its occurrence. The sum of these calculations for all possible outcomes represents that alternative's expected value. In this case, the expected value of alternative 1—to promote the new game—is as follows:

$$
\begin{aligned}
0.6 \times \$10{,}000{,}000 &= \$6{,}000{,}000 \\
+0.4 \times \$2{,}000{,}000 &= \$800{,}000 \\
\text{Expected value of alternative 1} &= \$6{,}800{,}000
\end{aligned}
$$

The expected value of alternative 2—not to promote the new game—is $1,400,000 (see Figure 8.2). The marketing manager should choose the first alternative, because its expected value is higher. The manager should recognize, however, that although the numbers look convincing, they are based on incomplete information and are only estimates of probability.

Under the **condition of uncertainty**, the decision maker lacks enough information to estimate the probability of possible outcomes.

The decision maker who lacks enough information to estimate the probability of outcomes (or perhaps even to identify the outcomes at all) faces a **condition of uncertainty**.

Baronefire/Dreamstime.com

When companies such as Sony launch new products or extend existing ones like the PSVITA handheld console the conditions they face may range from certainty to risk to uncertainty. In fact, few business decisions are made under a condition of certainty, so managers must understand how to assess risk and uncertainty for most of their significant decisions.

In the PlayStation example, this might be the case if sales of video games had recently collapsed and it was not clear whether the precipitous drop was temporary or permanent, nor when information to clarify the situation would be available. Under such circumstances, the decision maker may wait for more information to reduce uncertainty or rely on judgment, experience, and intuition to make the decision. Of course, it is also important to remember that decision making is not always so easy to classify in terms of certainty, risk, and uncertainty.

Several approaches to decision making offer insights into the process by which managers arrive at their decisions. The rational approach is appealing because of its logic and economy. Yet these very qualities raise questions about this approach because decision making often is not a wholly rational process. The behavioral approach, meanwhile, attempts to account for the limits on rationality in decision making. Of course, as we will see, many managers combine rationality with behavioral process when making decisions. The sections that follow explore these approaches in more detail.

THE RATIONAL APPROACH TO DECISION MAKING

The **rational decision-making approach** is a systematic, step-by-step process for making decisions.

The **rational decision-making approach** assumes that managers follow a systematic, step-by-step process. It further assumes that the organization is dedicated to making logical choices and doing what makes the most sense economically and that it is managed by decision makers who are entirely objective and have complete information.[6]

Steps in Rational Decision Making

Figure 8.3 identifies the steps of the process, starting with stating a goal and running logically through the process until the best decision is made, implemented, and controlled.

State the Situational Goal The rational decision-making process begins with the statement of a situational goal—that is, a goal for a particular situation. The goal of a marketing department, for example, may be to obtain a certain market share by the end of the year. (Some models of decision making do not start with a goal. We include it, however, because it is the standard used to determine whether there is a decision to be made.)

Identify the Problem The purpose of problem identification is to gather information that bears on the goal. If there is a discrepancy between the goal and the actual state, action may be needed. In the marketing example, the group may gather information about the company's actual market share and then compare it with the desired market share. A difference between the two represents a problem that necessitates a decision.

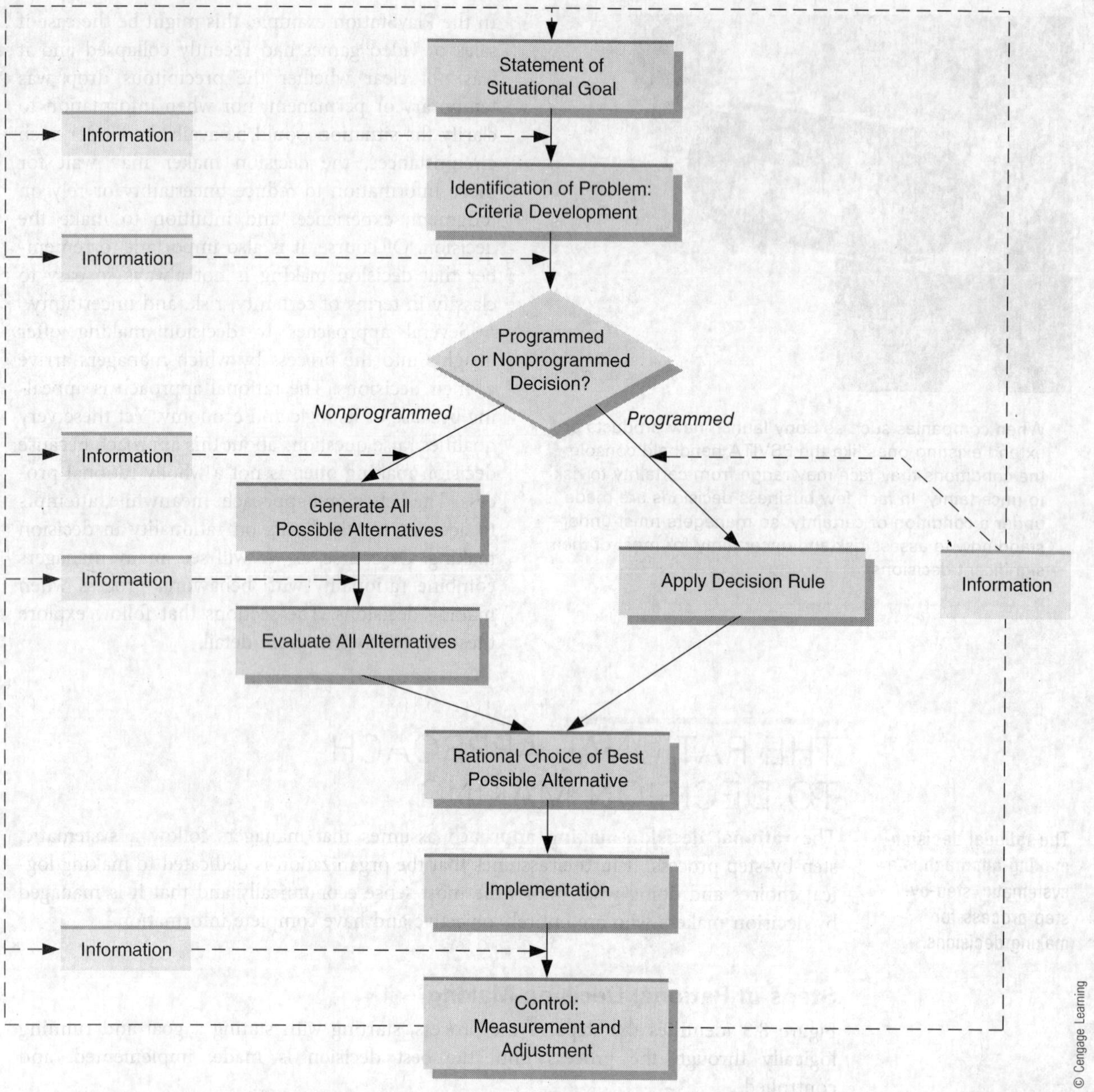

FIGURE 8.3

The Rational Decision-Making Approach

The rational model follows a systematic, step-by-step approach from goals to implementation, measurement, and control.

Reliable information is very important in this step. Inaccurate information can lead to an unnecessary decision or to no decision when one is required.

Determine the Decision Type Next, the decision makers must determine whether the problem represents a programmed or a nonprogrammed decision. If a programmed decision is needed, the appropriate decision rule is invoked, and the process moves on to the choice among alternatives. A programmed marketing decision may be called for if analysis reveals that competitors are outspending the company on print advertising. Because creating print advertising and buying space for it are well-established functions of the marketing group, the problem requires only a programmed decision.

Although it may seem simple to diagnose a situation as programmed, apply a decision rule, and arrive at a solution, mistakes can still occur. Choosing the wrong decision rule or assuming the problem calls for a programmed decision when a nonprogrammed decision actually is required can result in poor decisions. The same caution applies to the determination that a nonprogrammed decision is called for. If the situation is wrongly diagnosed, the decision maker wastes time and resources seeking a new solution to an old problem, or "reinventing the wheel."

Generate Alternatives The next step in making a nonprogrammed decision is to generate alternatives. The rational process assumes that decision makers will generate all the possible alternative solutions to the problem. However, this assumption is unrealistic because even simple business problems can have scores of possible solutions. Decision makers may rely on education and experience as well as knowledge of the situation to generate alternatives. In addition, they may seek information from other people such as peers, subordinates, and supervisors. Decision makers may analyze the symptoms of the problem for clues or fall back on intuition or judgment to develop alternative solutions.[7] If the marketing department in our example determines that a nonprogrammed decision is required, it will need to generate alternatives for increasing market share.

Evaluate Alternatives Evaluation involves assessing all possible alternatives in terms of predetermined decision criteria. The ultimate decision criterion is "Will this alternative bring us nearer to the goal?" In each case, the decision maker must examine each alternative for evidence that it will reduce the discrepancy between the desired state and the actual state. The evaluation process usually includes (1) describing the anticipated outcomes (benefits) of each alternative, (2) evaluating the anticipated costs of each alternative, and (3) estimating the uncertainties and risks associated with each alternative.[8] In most decision situations, the decision maker does not have perfect information regarding the outcomes of all alternatives. At one extreme, as shown earlier in Figure 8.2, outcomes may be known with certainty; at the other, the decision maker has no information whatsoever, so the outcomes are entirely uncertain. But risk is the most common situation.

Choose an Alternative Choosing an alternative is usually the most crucial step in the decision-making process. Choosing consists of selecting the alternative with the highest possible payoff, based on the benefits, costs, risks, and uncertainties of all alternatives. In the PlayStation promotion example, the decision maker evaluated the two alternatives by calculating their expected values. Following the rational approach, the manager would choose the alternative with the largest expected value.

Even with the rational approach, however, difficulties can arise in choosing an alternative. First, when two or more alternatives have equal payoffs, the decision maker must obtain more information or use some other criterion to make the choice. Second, when no single alternative will accomplish the objective, some combination of two or three alternatives may have to be implemented. Finally, if no alternative or combination of alternatives will solve the problem, the decision maker must obtain more information, generate more alternatives, or change the goals.[9]

Contingency plans are alternative actions to take if the primary course of action is unexpectedly disrupted or rendered inappropriate.

An important part of the choice phase is the consideration of **contingency plans**—alternative actions that can be taken if the primary course of action is unexpectedly disrupted or rendered inappropriate.[10] Planning for contingencies is part of the transition between choosing the preferred alternative and implementing it. In developing contingency plans, the decision maker usually asks such questions as "What if something unexpected happens during the implementation of this alternative?" or "If the economy goes into a recession, will the choice of this alternative ruin the company?" or "How can we alter this plan if the economy suddenly rebounds and begins to grow?"

Implement the Plan Implementation puts the decision into action. It builds on the commitment and motivation of those who participated in the decision-making process (and may actually bolster individual commitment and motivation). To succeed, implementation requires the proper use of resources and good management skills. Following the decision to promote the new PlayStation game heavily, for example, the marketing manager must implement the decision by assigning the project to a work group or task force. The success of this team depends on the leadership, the reward structure, the communications system, and group dynamics. Sometimes the decision maker begins to doubt a choice already made. This doubt is called *post-decision dissonance* or, more generally, **cognitive dissonance**.[11] To reduce the tension created by the dissonance, the decision maker may seek to rationalize the decision further with new information.

Cognitive dissonance is doubt about a choice that has already been made.

Control: Measure and Adjust In the final stage of the rational decision-making process, the outcomes of the decision are measured and compared with the desired goal. If a discrepancy remains, the decision maker may restart the decision-making process by setting a new goal (or reiterating the existing one). The decision maker, unsatisfied with the previous decision, may modify the subsequent decision-making process to avoid another mistake. Changes can be made in any part of the process, as Figure 8.3 illustrates by the arrows leading from the control step to each of the other steps. Decision making therefore is a dynamic, self-correcting, and ongoing process in organizations.

Suppose a marketing department implements a new print advertising campaign. After implementation, it constantly monitors market research data and compares its new market share with the desired market share. If the advertising has the desired effect, no changes will be made in the promotion campaign. If, however, the data indicate no change in the market share, additional decisions and implementation of a contingency plan may be necessary.

Strengths and Weaknesses of the Rational Approach The rational approach has several strengths. It forces the decision maker to consider a decision in a logical, sequential manner, and the in-depth analysis of alternatives enables the decision maker to choose on the basis of information rather than emotion or social pressure. But the rigid assumptions of this approach often are unrealistic.[12] The amount of information available to managers usually is limited by either time or cost constraints, and most decision makers have limited ability to process information about the alternatives. In addition, not all alternatives lend themselves to quantification in terms that will allow for easy comparison. Finally, because they cannot predict the future, it is unlikely that decision makers will know all possible outcomes of each alternative. In the *Technology* box entitled "What Went Wrong with Wesabe?" on page 217, one of the founders of a seemingly successful web startup attributes its early demise to a decision that seemed rational at the time but which turned out to have unforeseen consequences.

Evidence-based management (EBM) is the commitment to identify and utilize the best theory and data available to make decisions.

Evidence-Based Decision Making

While rational decision making perspectives have been around for decades, some experts (most notably Jeffrey Pfeffer and Robert Sutton) have recently called for a renewed focus on rationality.[13] This new focus has been called evidence-based management. **Evidence-based management (EBM)** is defined as the commitment to identify and utilize the best

TECHNOLOGY What Went Wrong with Wesabe?

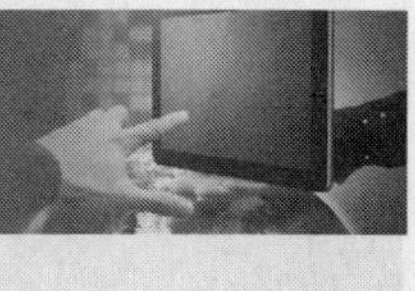

©watcharakun/Shutterstock

As far as U.S. small business was concerned, the first quarter of 2010 could have been worse: There was a net loss of only 96,000 companies with fewer than 100 employees. As a matter of fact, the first quarter of 2009 *was* worse—a *lot* worse: By the end of the quarter, there were 400,000 fewer small businesses than there had been at the beginning.

> ***"We just didn't build it nearly fast enough. That one mistake ... was probably enough to kill Wesabe alone."***
>
> —WESABE COFOUNDER MARC HEDLUND, ON HIS COMPANY'S HESITATION IN BUILDING ONE OPERATIONAL SYSTEM

One of the companies that shut down in 2010 was Wesabe, which had launched in 2006 as an online site to help people manage their money and make better financial decisions. It was one of the first companies to enter the financial sector of what's often referred to as *Web 2.0*—the world of web applications that allow users to interact and collaborate on content that they create themselves. The idea was to let customers access data from several financial institutions and then compare their own money management practices to those of online peers.

Wesabe actually got off to a reasonably good start. Within the first year, founders Marc Hedlund and Jason Knight secured venture capital totaling $4.7 million and attracted 150,000 members. The first signs of trouble appeared in the second year, just after a competitor called Mint.com came online. Nine months after its launch, Mint.com boasted $17 million in venture capital and 300,000 users. In 2009, Intuit, a creator of financial and tax-preparation software, purchased Mint.com for $170 million. Wesabe held on until mid-2010, when Hedlund and Knight announced that the company could no longer handle users' highly sensitive data "with shoestring operations and security staff."

So what went wrong? Naturally, there's no single reason for Wesabe's failure, but both Hedlund, who blogged a postmortem shortly after the shutdown, and independent observers point to one crucial business decision as a key factor. In the early stages of the startup process, Hedlund and Knight rejected a partnership with a firm called Yodlee, which had already developed a system for accessing transaction data from banks. But because the Yodlee process worked with users' passwords, Wesabe considered it too great a security risk and proceeded to work on its own process, which, though more secure, was also more cumbersome.

"Everyone—I mean 90-percent-plus of everybody," says Hedlund, "told me that they would never in a million years use a startup website that asked them for their bank passwords." When Mint came online in 2007, it was using Yodlee technology, password-access included, and Hedlund acknowledges that he'd made a mistake by relying on his own informal market research: "We should have known," he admits, "that somebody would go with Yodlee, and we should have aimed at [Yodlee] as what we needed to achieve." By 2008, Wesabe, too, was accepting users' passwords in order to simplify the process of pulling bank data into its system.

"We just didn't build it nearly fast enough," says Hedlund of Wesabe's own data-access system. "That one mistake—not using or replacing Yodlee before Mint had a chance to launch on Yodlee—was probably enough to kill Wesabe alone."

References: Eilene Zimmerman, "How Six Companies Failed to Survive 2010," *New York Times*, January 5, 2011, www.nytimes.com on June 2, 2012; Anthony Ha, "Personal Finance Startup Wesabe to Shut Down," *VentureBeat*, June 30, 2010, http://venturebeat.com on June 2, 2012; Marc Hedlund, "Why Wesabe Lost to Mint," *Marc Hedlund's Blog*, October 1, 2010, http://blog.precipice.org on June 2, 2012; "Some Lessons Learned from the Rise and Fall of Wesabe," *Credit Union Journal*, December 16, 2010, www.cunatechnologycouncil.org on June 2, 2012.

theory and data available to make decisions. Advocates of this approach encourage the use of five basic "principles":

1. Face the hard facts and build a culture in which people are encouraged to tell the truth, even if it's unpleasant.
2. Be committed to "fact-based" decision making—which means being committed to getting the best evidence and using it to guide actions.

3. Treat your organization as an unfinished prototype—encourage experimentation and learning by doing.
4. Look for the risks and drawbacks in what people recommend (even the best medicine has side effects).
5. Avoid basing decisions on untested but strongly held beliefs, what you have done in the past, or uncritical "benchmarking" of what winners do.

EBM advocates are particularly persuasive when they use EBM to question the outcomes of decisions based on "untested but strongly held beliefs" or on "uncritical 'benchmarking.'" Take, for instance, the popular decision to pay high performers significantly more than low performers. Pfeffer and Sutton's research shows that pay-for-performance policies get good results when employees work solo or independently. But it's another matter altogether when it comes to collaborative teams—the kind of teams that make so many organizational decisions today. Under these circumstances, the greater the gap between highest- and lowest-paid executives, the weaker the firm's financial performance. Why? According to Pfeffer and Sutton, wide disparities in pay often weaken both trust among team members and the social connectivity that contributes to strong team-based decision making.

Or consider another increasingly prevalent decision for evaluating and rewarding talent. Pioneered at General Electric by the legendary Jack Welch, the practice of "forced ranking" divides employees into three groups based on performance—the top 20 percent, middle 70 percent, and bottom 10 percent—and terminates those at the bottom. Pfeffer and Sutton found that, according to many HR managers, forced ranking impaired morale and collaboration and ultimately reduced productivity. They also concluded that automatically firing the bottom 10 percent resulted too often in the unnecessary disruption of otherwise effective teamwork. That's how they found out that 73 percent of the errors committed by commercial airline pilots occur on the first day that reconfigured crews work together.[14]

THE BEHAVIORAL APPROACH TO DECISION MAKING

The **administrative model** of decision making argues that managers use bounded rationality, rules of thumb, suboptimizing, and satisficing in making decisions.

Whereas the rational approach assumes that managers operate logically and rationally, the behavioral approach acknowledges the role and importance of human behavior in the decision-making process. Herbert A. Simon was one of the first experts to recognize that decisions are not always made with rationality and logic.[15] Simon was subsequently awarded the Nobel Prize in economics. Rather than prescribing how decisions should be made, his view of decision making, now called the **administrative model**, describes how decisions often actually are made. (Note that Simon was not advocating that managers use the administrative model but was instead describing how managers actually make decisions.)

Bounded rationality is the idea that decision makers cannot deal with information about all the aspects and alternatives pertaining to a problem and therefore choose to tackle some meaningful subset of it.

The Administrative Model

One crucial assumption of the administrative model is that decision makers operate with bounded rationality rather than with the perfect rationality assumed by the rational approach. **Bounded rationality** is the idea that although individuals may seek the best solution to a problem, the demands of processing all the information bearing on the problem, generating all possible solutions, and choosing the single best solution are beyond the capabilities of most decision makers. Thus, they accept less-than-ideal solutions based on a process that is neither exhaustive nor entirely rational.

Herbert A. Simon won the Nobel Prize in economics for his groundbreaking work in behavioral decision making. Simon is shown here (on the left) receiving his award from Sweden's King Carl Gustaf in 1978.

For example, one recent study found that under time pressure, groups usually eliminate all but the two most favorable alternatives and then process the remaining two in great detail.[16] Thus, decision makers operating with bounded rationality limit the inputs to the decision-making process and base decisions on judgment and personal biases as well as on logic.[17]

The administrative model is characterized by (1) the use of procedures and rules of thumb, (2) suboptimizing, and (3) satisficing. Uncertainty in decision making can initially be reduced by relying on procedures and rules of thumb. If, for example, increasing print advertising has increased a company's market share in the past, that linkage may be used by company employees as a rule of thumb in decision making. When the previous month's market share drops below a certain level, the company might increase its print advertising expenditures by 25 percent during the following month.

Suboptimizing is knowingly accepting less than the best possible outcome to avoid unintended negative effects on other aspects of the organization.

Suboptimizing is knowingly accepting less than the best possible outcome. Frequently, given organizational constraints, it is not feasible to make the ideal decision in a real-world situation. The decision maker often must suboptimize to avoid unintended negative effects on other departments, product lines, or decisions.[18] An automobile manufacturer, for example, can cut costs dramatically and increase efficiency if it schedules the production of one model at a time. Thus, the production group's optimal decision is single-model scheduling. But the marketing group, seeking to optimize its sales goals by offering a wide variety of models, may demand the opposite production schedule: short runs of entirely different models. The groups in the middle—design and scheduling—may suboptimize the benefits the production and marketing groups seek by planning long runs of slightly different models. This is the practice of the large auto manufacturers such as General Motors and Ford, which make multiple body styles in different models on the same production line.

Satisficing is examining alternatives only until a solution that meets minimal requirements is found.

The final feature of the behavioral approach is **satisficing**: examining alternatives only until a solution that meets minimal requirements is found and then ceasing to look for a better one.[19] The search for alternatives usually is a sequential process guided by procedures and rules of thumb based on previous experiences with similar problems. The search often ends when the first minimally acceptable choice is encountered. The resulting choice may narrow the discrepancy between the desired and the actual states, but it is not likely to be the optimal solution. As the process is repeated, incremental improvements slowly reduce the discrepancy between the actual and desired states.

Other Behavioral Forces in Decision Making

In addition to those behavioral elements identified in the administrative model, the manager should also be aware of other behavioral forces that can affect decision making as

Ken C. Horner/Getty Images Sport/Getty Images

While managers are generally advised to use logic and rationality to make decisions, intuition is also sometimes appropriate. The New York Yankees once asked the major shoe manufacturers to bid on providing athletic shoes to their players. While Nike and Reebok were carefully analyzing this opportunity, managers at Adidas simply "knew" it was the right thing to do, moved in quickly and aggressively, and won the contract.

well. These include political forces, intuition, escalation of commitment, risk propensity, and ethics. Prospect theory is also relevant.

Political Forces in Decision Making Political forces can play a major role in how decisions are made. We cover political behavior in Chapter 14, but one major element of politics, coalitions, is especially relevant to decision making. A **coalition** is an informal alliance of individuals or groups formed to achieve a common goal. This common goal is often a preferred decision alternative. For example, coalitions of stockholders frequently band together to force a board of directors to make a certain decision. Indeed, many of the recent power struggles between management and dissident shareholders at Disney Corporation have relied on coalitions as each side tried to gain the upper hand against the other.[20] The impact of coalitions can be either positive or negative. They can help astute managers get the organization on a path toward effectiveness and profitability, or they can strangle well-conceived strategies and decisions. Managers must recognize when to use coalitions, how to assess whether coalitions are acting in the best interests of the organization, and how to constrain their dysfunctional effects.[21]

A **coalition** is an informal alliance of individuals or groups formed to achieve a common goal.

Intuition is innate belief about something without conscious consideration.

Intuition **Intuition** is an innate belief about something without conscious consideration. Managers sometimes decide to do something because it "feels right" or they have a hunch. This feeling is usually not arbitrary, however. Rather, it is based on years of experience and practice in making decisions in similar situations. An inner sense may help managers make an occasional decision without going through a full-blown rational sequence of steps. The recent best-selling book by Malcolm Gladwell entitled *Blink: The Power of Thinking Without Thinking* made strong arguments that intuition is both used more commonly and results in better decisions than had previously been believed. On the other hand, some experts challenge this view and suggest that underlying understanding and experience make intuition mask the true processes used to make quick decisions.[22]

The New York Yankees once contacted three major sneaker manufacturers, Nike, Reebok, and Adidas, and informed them that they were looking to make a sponsorship deal. While Nike and Reebok were carefully and rationally assessing the possibilities, managers at Adidas quickly realized that a partnership with the Yankees made a lot of sense for them. They responded very quickly to the idea, and ended up hammering out a contract while the competitors were still analyzing details.[23] Of course, all managers, but most especially inexperienced ones, should be careful not to rely on intuition too heavily. If rationality and logic are continually flouted for what "feels right," the odds are that disaster will strike one day.

Escalation of commitment occurs when a decision maker stays with a decision even when it appears to be wrong.

Escalation of Commitment Another important behavioral process that influences decision making is **escalation of commitment** to a chosen course of action. In particular, decision makers sometimes make decisions and then become so committed to the course of action suggested by that decision that they stay with it, even when it appears to have been wrong.[24] For example, when people buy stock in a company, they sometimes refuse to sell it even after repeated drops in price. They chose a course of action—buying the stock in anticipation of making a profit—and then stay with it even in the face of increasing losses.

For years Pan American World Airways ruled the skies and used its profits to diversify into real estate and other businesses. But with the advent of deregulation, Pan Am began to struggle and lose market share to other carriers. When Pan Am managers finally realized how ineffective the airline operations had become, the "rational" decision would have been, as experts today point out, to sell off the remaining airline operations and concentrate on the firm's more profitable businesses. But because they still saw the company as being first and foremost an airline, they instead began to slowly sell off the firm's profitable holdings to keep the airline flying. Eventually, the company was left with nothing but an ineffective and inefficient airline, and then had to sell off its more profitable routes before eventually being taken over by Delta. Had Pan Am managers made the more rational decision years earlier, chances are the firm could still be a profitable enterprise today, albeit one with no involvement in the airline industry.[25]

Thus, decision makers must walk a fine line. On the one hand, they must guard against sticking with an incorrect decision too long. To do so can bring about financial decline. On the other hand, managers should not bail out of a seemingly incorrect decision too soon, as Adidas did several years ago. Adidas once dominated the market for professional athletic shoes. It subsequently entered the market for amateur sports shoes and did well there also. But managers incorrectly interpreted a sales slowdown as a sign that the boom in athletic shoes was over. They thought that they had made the wrong decision and ordered drastic cutbacks. The market took off again with Nike at the head of the pack, and Adidas could not recover. Fortunately, a new management team has changed the way Adidas makes decisions and, as illustrated earlier, the firm is again on its way to becoming a force in the athletic shoe and apparel markets.

Risk propensity is the extent to which a decision maker is willing to gamble in making a decision.

Risk Propensity and Decision Making The behavioral element of **risk propensity** is the extent to which a decision maker is willing to gamble when making a decision. (Recall that we introduced risk propensity back in Chapter 3.) Some managers are cautious about every decision they make. They try to adhere to the rational model and are extremely conservative in what they do. Such managers are more likely to avoid mistakes, and they infrequently make decisions that lead to big losses. Other managers are extremely aggressive in making decisions and are willing to take risks.[26] They rely heavily on intuition, reach decisions quickly, and often risk big investments on their decisions. As in gambling, these managers are more likely than their conservative counterparts to achieve big successes with their decisions; they are also more likely to incur greater losses.[27] The organization's culture is a prime ingredient in fostering different levels of risk propensity.

Ethics are a person's beliefs about what constitutes right and wrong behavior.

Ethics and Decision Making **Ethics** are a person's beliefs about what constitutes right and wrong behavior. Ethical behavior is that which conforms to generally accepted social norms; unethical behavior does not conform to generally accepted social norms. Some decisions made by managers may have little or nothing to do with their own personal ethics, but many other decisions are influenced by the manager's ethics. For example, decisions involving such disparate issues as hiring and firing employees, dealing with customers and suppliers, setting wages and assigning tasks, and maintaining one's expense account are all subject to ethical influences. And, of course, managers can make fatal personal decisions simply because they choose to ignore the difference between right and wrong.

In general, ethical dilemmas for managers may center on direct personal gain, indirect personal gain, or simple personal preferences. Consider, for example, a top executive contemplating a decision about a potential takeover. His or her stock option package may result in enormous personal gain if the decision goes one way, even though stockholders may benefit more if the decision goes the other way. An indirect personal gain may result when a decision does not directly add value to a manager's personal worth but does enhance her or his career. Or the manager may face a choice about relocating a company facility in which one of the options is closest to his or her residence.

Managers should carefully and deliberately consider the ethical context of every one of their decisions. The goal, of course, is for the manager to make the decision that is in the best interest of the firm, as opposed to the best interest of the manager. Doing this requires personal honesty and integrity. Managers also find it helpful to discuss potential ethical dilemmas with colleagues. Others can often provide an objective view of a situation that may help a manager avoid unintentionally making an unethical decision.

Prospect theory argues that when people make decisions under a condition of risk they are more motivated to avoid losses than they are to seek gains.

Prospect Theory and Decision Making Finally, prospect theory also offers useful insights into how people make decisions.[28] Essentially, **prospect theory** focuses on decisions under a condition of risk. The theory argues that such decisions are influenced more by the potential value of gains or losses than the final outcome itself. The theory further argues that, all else being equal, people are more motivated to avoid losses than they are to seek gains. Stated another way, people may be more motivated by the threat of losing something they have than they are by the prospect of gaining something they do not have.

For instance, one recent study investigated this hypothesis in a sample of public school teachers in Chicago. One group of teachers was told that they could receive a bonus of up to $8,000 at the end of the school year if their students met certain test score targets. The other group was given an upfront bonus of $4,000 at the beginning of the school year. These teachers were told that if their students did not meet test score targets they would have to pay back some or all of the bonus; however, if their students met targets they could keep the bonus plus earn up to another $4,000 in a year-end bonus. Students of the second group of teachers had higher test scores at the end of the year. The researchers inferred that the teachers who had something to lose (some or all of the $4,000 up-front bonus) were more motivated to improve their students' test scores than were the teachers who could not lose anything.[29]

An Integrated Approach to Decision Making

Because of the unrealistic demands of the rational approach and the limited, short-term orientation of the behavioral approach, neither is entirely satisfactory. However, the worthwhile features of each can be combined into a practical approach to decision making, shown in Figure 8.4. The steps in this process are the same as in the rational approach; however, the conditions recognized by the behavioral approach are added to provide a more realistic process. For example, the **integrated approach** suggests that rather than generating all alternatives, the decision maker should try to go beyond rules of thumb and satisficing limitations and generate as many alternatives as time, money, and other practicalities of the situation allow. In this synthesis of the two other approaches, the rational approach provides an analytical framework for making decisions, whereas the behavioral approach provides a moderating influence.

The **integrated approach** to decision making combines the steps of the rational approach with the conditions in the behavioral approach to create a more realistic approach for making decisions in organizations.

In practice, decision makers use some hybrid of the rational, behavioral, and integrated approaches to make the tough day-to-day decisions in running organizations. Some decision makers use a methodical process of gathering as much information as possible, developing and evaluating alternatives, and seeking advice from knowledgeable people before making a decision. Others fly from one decision to another, making seemingly hasty decisions and barking out orders to subordinates. The second group would

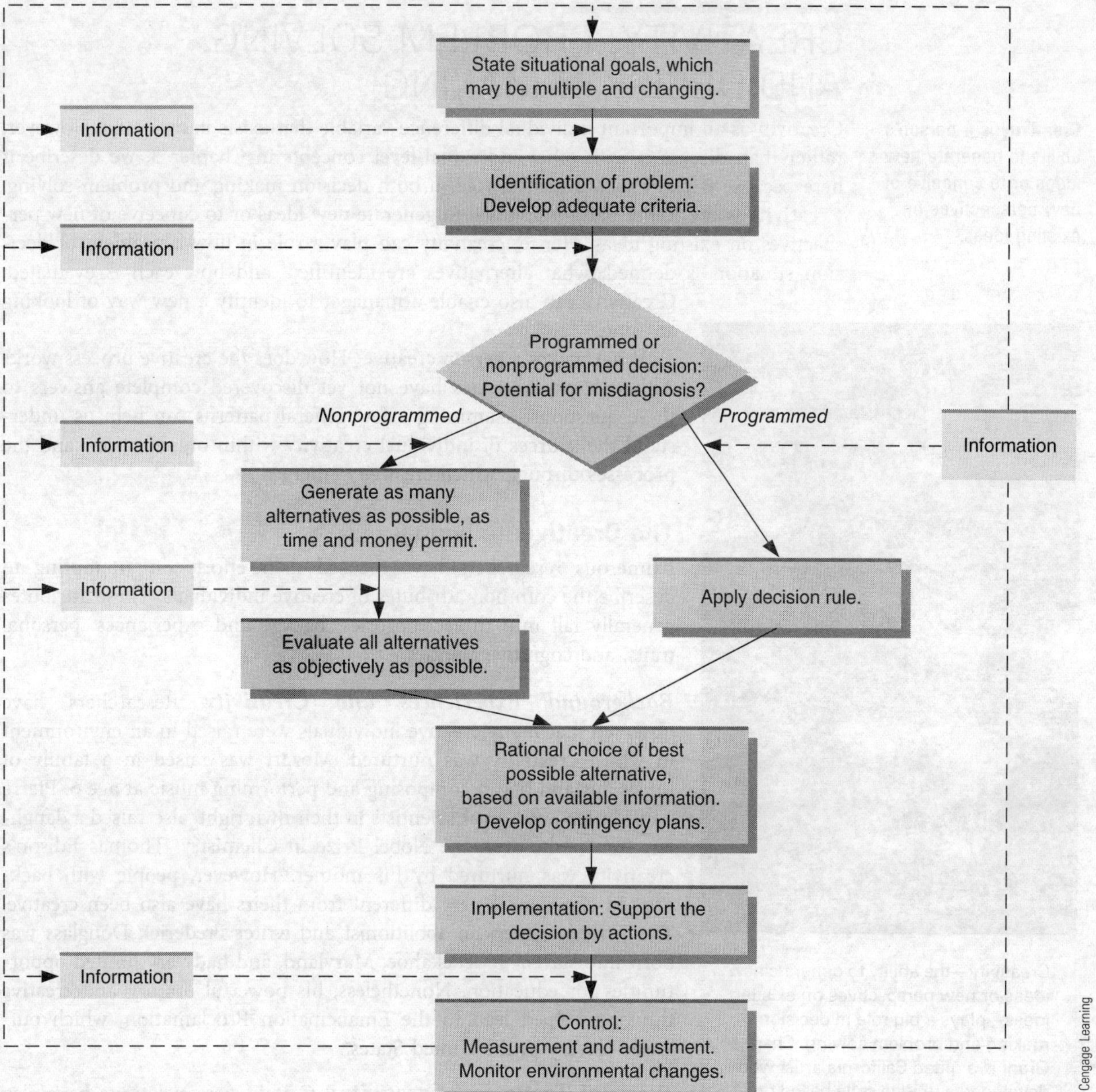

FIGURE 8.4

Practical Approach to Decision Making with Behavioral Guidelines

The practical model applies some of the conditions recognized by the behavioral approach to the rational approach to decision making. Although similar to the rational model, the practical approach recognizes personal limitations at each point (or step) in the process.

seem not to use much information or a rational approach to making decisions. Recent research, however, has shown that managers who make decisions very quickly probably are using just as much, or more, information and generating and evaluating as many alternatives as slower, more methodical decision makers.[30]

CREATIVITY, PROBLEM SOLVING, AND DECISION MAKING

Creativity is a person's ability to generate new ideas or to conceive of new perspectives on existing ideas.

Creativity is an important individual difference variable that exists in everyone. However, rather than discuss it with other individual-level concepts in Chapter 3, we describe it here because it plays such a central role in both decision making and problem solving. **Creativity** is the ability of an individual to generate new ideas or to conceive of new perspectives on existing ideas. Hence, creativity can play a role in how a problem or decision situation is defined, what alternatives are identified, and how each is evaluated. Creativity can also enable a manager to identify a new way of looking at things.[31]

Michael Newman/PhotoEdit

Creativity—the ability to generate new ideas or new perspectives on existing ideas—plays a big role in decision making and problem solving. Charles Grant is a gifted California artist who developed a unique style based on traditional African motifs. He made a decision to start his own shop, a combination gift shop and gallery in Pasadena. His shop carries both inexpensive souvenirs like coffee mugs, post cards, and scarves while also carrying more upscale items such as limited edition prints and original oil paintings. With the African motif as the unifying thread, his business appeals to both tourists looking for trinkets to take home and serious collectors who buy the paintings and prints.

What makes a person creative? How does the creative process work? Although psychologists have not yet discovered complete answers to these questions, examining a few general patterns can help us understand the sources of individual creativity within organizations and the processes through which creativity emerges.[32]

The Creative Individual

Numerous researchers have focused their efforts on attempting to describe the common attributes of creative individuals. These attributes generally fall into three categories: background experiences, personal traits, and cognitive abilities.

Background Experiences and Creativity Researchers have observed that many creative individuals were raised in an environment in which creativity was nurtured. Mozart was raised in a family of musicians and began composing and performing music at age 6. Pierre and Marie Curie, great scientists in their own right, also raised a daughter, Irene, who won the Nobel Prize in Chemistry. Thomas Edison's creativity was nurtured by his mother. However, people with background experiences very different from theirs have also been creative. The African American abolitionist and writer Frederick Douglass was born into slavery in Tuckahoe, Maryland, and had very limited opportunities for education. Nonetheless, his powerful oratory and creative thinking helped lead to the Emancipation Proclamation, which outlawed slavery in the United States.

Personal Traits and Creativity Certain personal traits have also been linked to creativity in individuals. The traits shared by most creative people are openness, an attraction to complexity, high levels of energy, independence and autonomy, strong self-confidence, and a strong belief that one is, in fact, creative. Individuals who possess these traits are more likely to be creative than are those who do not have them.

Cognitive Abilities and Creativity Cognitive abilities are an individual's power to think intelligently and to analyze situations and data effectively. Intelligence may be a precondition for individual creativity—but, although most creative people are highly intelligent, not all intelligent people necessarily are creative. Creativity is also linked with the ability to think divergently and convergently.

FIGURE 8.5

The Creative Process

The creative process generally follows the four steps illustrated here. Of course, there are exceptions, and the process is occasionally different. In most cases, however, these steps capture the essence of the creative process.

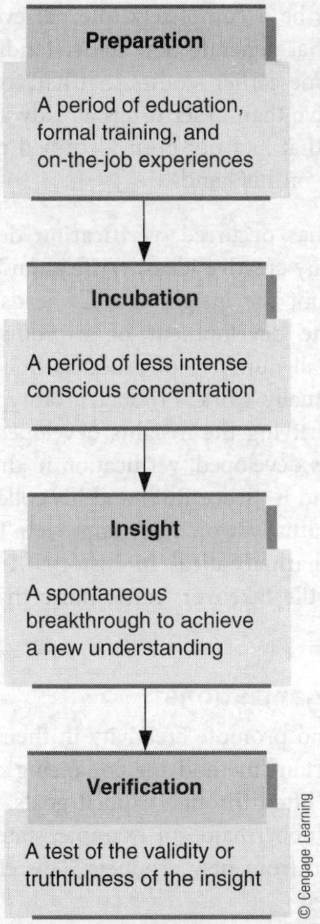

Divergent thinking is a skill that allows people to see differences between situations, phenomena, or events. *Convergent thinking* is a skill that allows people to see similarities between situations, phenomena, or events. Creative people are generally very skilled at both divergent and convergent thinking.

The Creative Process

Although creative people often report that ideas seem to come to them "in a flash," individual creative activity actually tends to progress through a series of stages. Figure 8.5 summarizes the major stages of the creative process. Not all creative activity has to follow these four stages, but much of it does.

Preparation, usually the first stage in the creative process, includes education and formal training.

Preparation The creative process normally begins with a period of **preparation**. Formal education and training are usually the most efficient ways of becoming familiar with a vast amount of research and knowledge. To make a creative contribution to business management or business services, individuals must usually receive formal training and education in business. This is one reason for the strong demand for undergraduate and master's level business education. Formal business education can be an effective way for an individual to get "up to speed" and begin making creative contributions quickly.

Experiences that managers have on the job after their formal training has finished can also contribute to the creative process. In an important sense, the education and training of creative people never really ends. It continues as long as they remain interested in the world and curious about the way things work. One such individual is Bruce Roth, who earned a Ph.D. in chemistry and then spent years working in the pharmaceutical industry learning more and more about chemical compounds and how they work in human beings.

Incubation is the stage of less intense conscious concentration during which a creative person lets the knowledge and ideas acquired during preparation mature and develop.

Incubation The second phase of the creative process is **incubation**—a period of less intense conscious concentration during which the knowledge and ideas acquired during preparation mature and develop. A curious aspect of incubation is that it is often helped along by pauses in concentrated rational thought. Some creative people rely on physical activity such as jogging or swimming to provide a "break" from thinking. Others may read or listen to music. Sometimes sleep may even supply the needed pause. Bruce Roth eventually joined Warner-Lambert, an up-and-coming drug company, to help develop medication to lower cholesterol. In his spare time, Roth read mystery novels and hiked in the mountains. He later acknowledged that this was when he did his best thinking.

Insight is the stage in the creative process in which all the scattered thoughts and ideas that were maturing during incubation come together to produce a breakthrough.

Insight Usually occurring after preparation and incubation, insight is a spontaneous breakthrough in which the creative person achieves a new understanding of some problem or situation. **Insight** represents a coming together of all the scattered thoughts and ideas that were maturing during incubation. It may occur suddenly or develop slowly over time. Insight can be triggered by some external event—such as a new experience or an encounter with new data that forces the individual to think about old issues and problems in new ways—or it can be a completely internal event in which patterns of thought finally coalesce in ways that generate new understanding. One day Bruce Roth was reviewing some data from some earlier studies that had found the new drug under development to be no more effective than other drugs already available. But this time he saw some statistical relationships that had not been identified previously. He knew then that he had a major breakthrough on his hands.

In **verification**, the final stage of the creative process, the validity or truthfulness of the insight is determined.

Verification Once an insight has occurred, **verification** determines the validity or truthfulness of the insight. For many creative ideas, verification includes scientific experiments to determine whether or not the insight actually leads to the results expected. Verification may also include the development of a product or service prototype. A prototype is one (or a very small number) of products built just to see whether the ideas behind this new product actually work. Product prototypes are rarely sold to the public but are very valuable in verifying the insights developed in the creative process. Once the new product or service is developed, verification in the marketplace is the ultimate test of the creative idea behind it. Bruce Roth and his colleagues set to work testing the new drug compound and eventually won FDA approval. The drug, named Lipitor, has become the largest-selling pharmaceutical in history. And Pfizer, the firm that bought Warner-Lambert in a hostile takeover, earns more than $10 billion a year on the drug.[33]

Enhancing Creativity in Organizations

Managers who wish to enhance and promote creativity in their organizations can do so in a variety of ways.[34] One important method for enhancing creativity is to make it a part of the organization's culture, often through explicit goals. Firms that truly want to stress creativity, such as 3M and Rubbermaid, for example, state goals that some percent of future revenues are to be gained from new products. This clearly communicates that creativity and innovation are valued.

Another important part of enhancing creativity is to reward creative successes, while being careful to not punish creative failures. Many ideas that seem worthwhile on paper fail to pan out in reality. If the first person to come up with an idea that fails is fired or otherwise punished, others in the organization will become more cautious in their own work. And as a result, fewer creative ideas will emerge.

SYNOPSIS

Decision making is the process of choosing one alternative from among several. Problem solving is finding the answer to a question. The basic elements of decision making include choosing a goal; considering alternative courses of action; assessing potential outcomes of the alternatives, each with its own value relative to the goal; and choosing one alternative based on an evaluation of the outcomes. Information is available regarding the alternatives, outcomes, and values.

Programmed decisions are well-structured, recurring decisions made according to set decision rules. Nonprogrammed decisions involve nonroutine, poorly structured situations with unclear sources of information; these decisions cannot be made according to existing decision rules. Decision making may also be classified based on salient conditions that exist. The classifications—certainty, risk, and uncertainty—reflect the amount of information available regarding the outcomes of alternatives.

The rational approach views decision making as a completely rational process in which goals are established, a problem is identified, alternatives are generated and evaluated, a choice is made and implemented, and control is exercised. Evidence-based decision making is a recent restatement of the need for rationality when making decisions.

The use of procedures and rules of thumb, suboptimizing, and satisficing characterize the behavioral model. A variety of other behavioral processes also influence decision making in organizations. Political activities by coalitions, managerial intuition, and the tendency to become increasingly committed to a chosen course of action are all important. Risk propensity is also an important behavioral perspective on decision making. Ethics also affect how managers make decisions. Prospect theory suggests that people are more motivated to avoid losses than to make gains. The rational and behavioral views can be combined into an integrated model.

Creativity is the capacity to generate new ideas. Numerous individual and background factors are likely to influence any given individual's level of creativity. The creative process itself generally involves four phases: preparation, incubation, insight, and verification. Managers can enhance or reduce creativity in their organizations through various means.

DISCUSSION QUESTIONS

1. Some have argued that people, not organizations, make decisions and that the study of "organizational" decision making is therefore pointless. Do you agree with this argument? Why or why not?
2. What information did you use in deciding to enter the school you now attend?
3. When your alarm goes off each morning, you have a decision to make: whether to get up and go to school or work, or to stay in bed and sleep longer. Is this a programmed or nonprogrammed decision? Why?
4. Describe at least three points in the decision-making process at which information plays an important role.
5. How does the role of information in the rational model of decision making differ from the role of information in the behavioral model?
6. Why does it make sense to discuss several different models of decision making?
7. Can you think of a time when you satisficed when making a decision? Have you ever suboptimized?
8. Describe a situation in which you experienced escalation of commitment to an ineffective course of action. What did you do about it? Do you wish you had handled it differently? Why or why not?
9. How comfortable or uncomfortable are you in making risky decisions?
10. Do you consider yourself to be relatively more or less creative? Recall an instance in which you made a discovery using the four phases of the creative process.

HOW DO YOU SEE IT?

Shedding Some Light on Decision Making

"Ultimately, the market is going to tell us where to put our energies."

—SCOTT PEARL, SALES CONSULTANT, MODERN SHED

Husband and wife Ryan Grey Smith and Ahna Holder both graduated from the University of Southern California's architecture program in the mid-1990s. When they moved to Seattle in 1998, they bought a 1940s-era house advertised in industry parlance as a "teardown"—something that could be demolished with no regrets and the land put to better use. Being architects, however, the couple decided to renovate instead. As the house had neither basement nor attic, nor even a garage, one obvious problem was storage, and their solution wasn't all that uncommon: They put up a shed. But this was no garden-variety shed: A sloping roof, for example, let in light at the ceiling, and the chic modern design and finished interior made the 10 × 12-foot structure suitable for working and relaxing as well as storage. Smith and Holder called it a "studio shed."

Today, Smith and Holder's company (which was launched in 2005) will sell you a 10 × 12-foot shed for anywhere from $9,349 to $17,535. It all depends on whether you want birch interior wall paneling and finished cedar open-joint siding along with your standard insulated roof, fir-plywood ceiling liner, and framed transom glass. Obviously, the Modern Shed is not your grandfather's shed: It's a sleekly designed, functionally equipped alternative to adding a room to your house—or even adding another dwelling to your dwelling. People use Modern Shed structures as studios, offices, guestrooms, backyard getaways, and even as alternatives to apartments for family members or live-in employees. Modern Shed options range from 6×10 to 16×40, with larger models (ranging in price to $23,000) accommodating plumbing and kitchen amenities. All Modern Shed buildings are custom designed by clients and are shipped flat along with tool kits for assembly on the buyer's property.

The market and industry are still fairly small, and Smith's "big-picture goal" includes getting out the message about the industry in general and his own product line in particular. "I'd love for everyone to know what Modern Shed is," he says. "I would love for Modern Shed to be *the* source for prefabricated structures in the United States." Meanwhile, his sales consultant, Scott Pearl, is busy looking specifically at "high-net-worth neighborhoods that have mid-century modern architecture," because he's convinced that they represent the company's best sales prospects, at least for the foreseeable future.

"As an independent contractor," says Pearl, "I constantly have to stay focused on the most likely opportunities for me to make sales.... Ultimately, the market is going to tell us where to put our energies." And for Pearl, a former marketing consultant with a background in real estate, the current market is pointing to dual-income families needing housing for nannies and au pairs and would-be first-time homeowners wanting to take advantage of Seattle's severely depressed market for residential land. "Modern Shed," he explains, "has been really popular with folks who are doing backyard offices, studios, guestrooms. But the potential in the residential arena is really once in a lifetime." Thus the most recent adjustment in Pearl's sales strategy for Modern Shed: "Rather than selling the smaller structures that we've been [selling], I've actually set the goal of every fourth structure [being] one of our dwelling structures."

Smith clearly values Pearl's creativity in thinking up and searching out original sales ideas: "He's always ... coming to the table with these really fascinating proposals and thinking out of the box," says Smith, who also appreciates the practical approach that Pearl brings to the "big-picture perspective." He also likes the results that Pearl gets by taking a measured approach to getting things done: Pearl, he reports, "has this really subtle way of being incredibly effective.... He has this kind of steady, thoughtful ..., focused approach to [achieving a] goal."

For Pearl, the methodical approach simply makes sense because implementing a business strategy is primarily a matter of "prioritizing" resources—namely, time and money, which, as he points out, are the "two sorts of resources that are in short supply" at every company. Thus the first thing he did at Modern Shed was "analyze the sales that they had had locally because I wanted to see what product type had been selling and at what velocity." With that information in hand, the next step was formulating a practical near-term goal: "I felt that two structures a month would meet *my* goals," he recalls, "and it would certainly meet the *company*'s goals. We've achieved that now," and so it's on to the next near-term goal of ensuring that larger structures constitute 25 percent of all sales.

From Pearl's perspective, making sales—and knowing whether or not you've made enough of them—all depends on setting measurable goals that you can evaluate on a regular basis: "For me," he says, "it's making sure I'm dedicating the right amount of time to near-term goals [and] making sure that the long-term goals are at least being addressed on a weekly basis." From that point on, he admits, it's often necessary to play it by ear, especially with a young and growing company like Modern Shed. "The *more* long-term goals," he admits, "are something that, as a team ..., we really need to pick and choose."

CASE QUESTIONS

1. According to Pearl, what are the most important factors about which every business has to make critical decisions? Does this principle apply to the "business" of managing your life? Explain your answer in as much detail as possible.
2. Explain how Pearl's approach to optimizing sales at Modern Shed combines *decision making* with *problem solving*. To what extent can the model of decision making in Figure 8.1 be applied to the decisions that Pearl has made at Modern Shed?
3. To what extent does the *rational approach* to the *decision-making process* characterize Pearl's approach to optimizing sales at Modern Shed? Explain your answer by going through the steps of the process. Which steps definitely seem applicable? Which steps may or may not be applicable?
4. For each of the following questions, explain how your response is consistent with everything else you've said about Pearl: To what extent does *intuition* probably play a role in his approach to optimizing sales at Modern Shed? Do you see any danger of *escalation of commitment* in his approach (or his personality)? Why or why not? What level of *risk propensity* would you assign to Pearl—high, moderate, low?

ADDITIONAL SOURCES

Aria Shepherd, "Modern Shed: A Chic Outdoor Space," *Seattle Times*, September 13, 2008, http://seattletimes.nwsource.com on June 25, 2012; Modern Shed, "About Us," "Models" (2006), www.modern-shed.com on June 25, 2012; Michael Cannell, "Instead of Trading Up, Adding a High-Style Shed," *New York Times*, September 11, 2008, www.nytimes.com on June 25, 2012; Debra Prinzing, "Elegant, Stylish ... and Prefabricated," *Debra Prinzing*, August 15, 2008, www.debraprinzing.com on June 25, 2012; *Debra Prinzing*, "In Praise of the Modern Shed," Debra Prinzing, September 15, 2008, www.debraprinzing on June 25, 2012; Jonathan Lambert, "Prefab Sheds—The Solution to a Hectic Lifestyle," *Ezine Articles*, June 7, 2011, http://ezinearticles.com on June 25, 2012.

EXPERIENCING ORGANIZATIONAL BEHAVIOR

Programmed and Nonprogrammed Decisions

Purpose This exercise will allow you to take part in making a hypothetical decision and help you understand the difference between programmed and nonprogrammed decisions.

Format You will be asked to perform a task both individually and as a member of a group.

Procedure The following is a list of typical organizational decisions. Your task is to determine whether they are programmed or nonprogrammed. Number your paper 1 through 10, and write *P* for programmed or *N* for nonprogrammed next to each number.

Your instructor will divide the class into groups of four to seven. All groups should have approximately the same number of members. Your task as a group is to make the determinations just outlined. In arriving at your decisions, do not use techniques such as voting or negotiating ("Okay, I'll give in on this one if you'll give in on that one.") The group should discuss the difference between programmed and nonprogrammed decisions and each decision situation until all members at least partly agree with the decision.

Decision List

1. Hiring a specialist for the research staff in a highly technical field
2. Assigning workers to daily tasks
3. Determining the size of the dividend to be paid to shareholders in the ninth consecutive year of strong earnings growth
4. Deciding whether to officially excuse an employee's absence for medical reasons
5. Selecting the location for another branch of a 150-branch bank in a large city
6. Approving the appointment of a new law school graduate to the corporate legal staff
7. Making annual assignments of graduate assistants to faculty
8. Approving an employee's request to attend a local seminar in his or her special area of expertise
9. Selecting the appropriate outlets for print advertisements for a new college textbook
10. Determining the location for a new fast-food restaurant in a small but growing town on the major interstate highway between two very large metropolitan areas

Follow-Up Questions

1. To what extent did group members disagree about which decisions were programmed and which were nonprogrammed?
2. What primary factors did the group discuss in making each decision?
3. Were there any differences between the members' individual lists and the group lists? If so, discuss the reasons for the differences.

BUILDING MANAGERIAL SKILLS

Exercise Overview Decision-making skills are the ability to recognize and define problems and opportunities correctly and then to select an appropriate course of action for solving the problems or capitalizing on the opportunities. In this exercise, you're asked to apply your decision-making skills to a situation calling for both good business sense and a sense of personal values.

Exercise Background You're the owner of a company that makes dress and casual shoes at two small factories, each with a workforce of 40 people. One is located in Smallville, Illinois, and the other in Modesto, Texas (both small towns). You've been in business for 40 years, and both factories have long been profitable. Unfortunately, however, competitive conditions in the industry have changed in recent years. In particular, you're now facing stiff competition from Italian firms whose shoes not only sell for less money but boast higher quality.

You're confident that you can close the quality gap with new high-tech equipment, but your overhead is still 30 percent higher than that of your Italian competitors. At the moment, you feel that your best option is to close the Smallville factory and lay off the workers, but you're a little reluctant to do so. You're the major employer in Smallville, which is dependent on your factory and has just spent a good deal of money to improve its utility service and highway access. In addition, most of your employees are older people who have lived most of their lives in Smallville.

Exercise Task

1. Your instructor will divide the class into groups of three or four people each. Each group will meet as a management team responsible for deciding the fate of the Smallville plant.
2. The team may decide to close the plant or to keep it open, but the goal of the decision-making process is twofold: (1) to keep the company viable and (2) to reflect the team's individual and group values.
3. If the team decides to close the plant, it must draw up a list of the factors on which it based its decision and be prepared to justify it.
4. If the team decides to keep the plant open, it must draw up a plan explaining how the company can still remain competitive.
5. Each member of each team should be prepared to explain the choices that he or she made in helping the group reach its decision.

SELF-ASSESSMENT EXERCISE

Rational versus Integrated Approaches to Decision Making

Managers need to recognize and understand the different models that they use to make decisions. They also need to understand the extent to which they are predisposed to be relatively autocratic or relatively participative in making decisions. To develop your skills in these areas, perform the following activity.

First, assume you are the manager of a firm that is rapidly growing. Recent sales figures strongly suggest the need for a new plant to produce more of your firm's products. Key issues include where the plant might be built and how large it might be (for example, a small, less expensive plant to meet current needs that could be expanded in the future versus a large and more expensive plant that might have excess capacity today but could better meet long-term needs).

Using the rational approach diagrammed in Figure 8.3, trace the process the manager might use to make the decision. Note the kinds of information that might be required and the extent to which other people might need to be involved in making a decision at each point.

Next, go back and look at various steps in the process where behavioral processes might intervene and affect the overall process. Will bounded rationality come into play? How about satisficing?

Finally, use the integrated approach shown in Figure 8.4 and trace through the process again. Again note where other input may be needed. Try to identify places in the process where the rational and integrated approaches are likely to result in the same outcome and places where differences are most likely to occur.

CHAPTER 9 Foundations of Interpersonal and Group Behavior

Chapter Outline

- The Interpersonal Nature of Organizations
- The Nature of Groups
- Types of Groups
- Stages of Group Development
- Group Performance Factors
- Intergroup Dynamics
- Group Decision Making in Organizations

Chapter Learning Objectives

After studying this chapter, you should be able to:

1. **Discuss the interpersonal nature of organizations.**
2. **Define a group and illustrate their importance in organizations.**
3. **Identify and discuss the types of groups commonly found in organizations.**
4. **Describe the general stages of group development.**
5. **Discuss the major group performance factors.**
6. **Discuss intergroup dynamics.**
7. **Describe group decision making in organizations.**

Managing by Clowning Around

"It's difficult to be creative in isolation."

—Lyn Heward, former president of Cirque du Soleil's Creative Content Division

Fourteen-year-old Guy Laliberté dropped out of high school in Québec, Canada, because he wanted to see the world. "I decided to go into street performing because it was a traveling job," he recalls, and although his skills were limited to playing the accordion and telling stories, they were enough to get him to London by the time he was 18. From there he not only extended his travels to Europe but broadened his repertoire to include fire breathing, juggling, magic, and stilt walking. "It was just an adventure," he admits, "and I was planning to go back to school and

Effective teamwork contributes to both the business success and the onstage artistry of Cirque du Soleil.

have a regular life," but his nearly decade-long adventure had only deepened his passion for street performing. When he returned to Canada, he joined a stilt-walking troupe, and in 1984, when he was 23 years old, Laliberté partnered with another high school dropout to form their own street-performance company. Today, he still runs that company, and as 80 percent owner of Cirque du Soleil, he's one of the richest people in Canada.

Cirque du Soleil, which is French for *circus of the sun* ("The sun," explains Laliberté, "stands for energy and youth, which is what I thought the circus should be about"), has completely transformed the traditional three-ring spectacle with trapeze artists, clowns, and lion tamers. Laliberté calls Cirque a "transdiciplinary experience"—an amalgam of breathtaking stunt work, dazzling stagecraft, surreal costumes, and pulsing music. There are currently 20 different Cirque shows, each developed around a distinctive theme and story arc, such as "the urban experience in all its myriad forms" (*Saltimbanco*) and "a tribute to the nomadic soul" (*Varekai*). Headquartered in Montreal, Canada, the company now employs 5,000 people, including more than a 1,300 artists, and its shows have been seen by 100 million spectators. Profits for 2011 were $250 million on revenues of $1 billion.

The key to this success, according to Laliberté, is creativity: "I believe that the profits will come from the quality of your creative products," he says. "Since the beginning, I've always wanted to develop a self-feeding circle of creative productions: The positive financial returns from one show would be used to develop and create a new show, and so on." He's also convinced that his job is to provide a working environment that fosters collective creativity: "I believe in nurturing creativity and offering a haven for creators, enabling them to develop their ideas to the fullest. With more and more talented creators being drawn to Cirque in an environment that fulfills them, these [conditions] are ideal to continue developing great new shows."

Lyn Heward, former president of Cirque's Creative Content Division, calls the company's process of training and integrating talented people "creative transformation": "Everyone," she says, "when they come to Cirque as an employee, even an accountant, comes there because it's a creative and admired company, and they want to be able to contribute something creatively." From her experience at Cirque, Heward drew up a nine-point guide to "creative transformation," and at the heart of her list is a commitment to the value of teamwork. In fact, the fifth item on her list says, "Practice teamwork. True creativity requires stimulation and collaboration. It's difficult to be creative in isolation." Item 6 picks up the same theme: "Keep creativity fresh with hard-working bosses who constantly encourage and receive employees' ideas and feedback and accept that there are often different ways of getting the same end result."

"No matter what your product," Heward argues, "whether it's computers, cars, or anything else, your results [depend on] having a passionate strong team of people." In any workplace, she explains, "our most natural resource is the people we work with—the people we build our product with. Unless there's a strong commitment to teambuilding passionate leadership, and creativity, even at Cirque it would not happen." Heward is willing to admit that "incredible freedom is a problem for most people because it requires us to think differently," but she's also confident that getting people committed to teamwork is the best way to get them to develop their creativity. Take Igor Jijikine, a Russian-born acrobat-actor who helped to train performers for *Mystère*, Cirque's permanent show at Las Vegas' Treasure Island Hotel and Casino. "[T]he really challenging thing," he says,

> *is to change the mentality of the performers I work with. Many of our performers are former competitive gymnasts. Gymnastics is essentially an individual sport. Gymnasts never have to think creatively or be a part of a true team. They got here by being strong individuals. So, right from the start, we really challenge ourselves to erase the lines between athletics and artistry, between individuals and the group. We need to transform an individual into a team player everyone else can count on, literally with their lives.*

Finally, Heward acknowledges that you can't imbue employees with the Cirque du Soleil culture and "then tell them to go work in their cubicles." The space in which they work, she says, "has to reflect [Cirque's] values and vision." All Cirque du Soleil productions are created and developed by teams working at the Montreal facility, which the company calls "the Studio" and describes as "a full-fledged creation, innovation, and training laboratory." In addition to administrative space—"eight floors of uniquely designed office spaces and relaxation areas conducive to inspiration"—the complex boasts acrobatic, dance, and theatrical studios, and the effect of the whole, says Heward, is that of "a fantastical playground." Creativity, she explains,

> *is fostered in work groups where people first get to know each other and then learn to trust one another. And in this playground, we recognize that a good idea can emerge from anywhere in the organization or from within a team. We make our shows from this collective creativity.*

Cirque CEO Daniel Lamarre has a succinct way of explaining the company's success: "We let the creative people run it." As for Laliberté, he, too, is content to trust his creative people—an instinct, he says, that he learned in his days as a street performer: "In the street, you have to develop that instinct of trusting people and reading people because that instinct is your lifesaver." He lists himself as "Artistic Guide" in production notes and tries "not to be too involved in the beginning and during the process," the better to keep his perspective "fresh" and to "be able to give constructive recommendation on the final production." He also wants to do the same thing that he wanted to do when he was 14: "I still want to travel, I still want to entertain, and I most certainly still want to have fun."

To see how technology can also be a lifesaver in the world of Cirque du Soleil, see the *Technology* box on "Teaming Technology and Artistry" on page 246.

What Do You Think?

1. Cirque du Soleil depends on both creativity and the delegation of responsibility at all levels. What do you suppose are some of the problems involved in maintaining this balance?
2. If for some reason Cirque du Soleil moved toward a process that depended less on team decision making and control, what difficulties would probably arise?

References: "Stick to Your Dream—Guy Laliberté," *Young Entrepreneur*, July 8, 2008, www.youngentrepreneur.com on June 3, 2012; "Business Lessons from Poker—Guy Laliberté," *Young Entrepreneur*, July 8, 2008, www.youngentrepreneur.com on June 3, 2012; Jason Zinoman, "Defiant Showman Demands His 'Wow,'" *New York Times*, June 3, 2011, www.nytimes.com on June 3, 2012; "Laliberté, Guy," *eNotes.com*, 2006, www.enotes.com on June 3, 2012; Cirque du Soleil, "Cirque du Soleil at a Glance" (2012), http://static01.cirquedusoleil.com on June 3, 2012; Lyn Heward and John U. Bacon, *Spark: Igniting the Creative Fire That Lives Within Us All* (Toronto: Doubleday Canada, 2006); Arupa Tesolin, "Igniting the Creative Spark at Cirque du Soleil," *Self-Growth.com*, September 12, 2007, www.selfgrowth.com on June 3, 2012; Geoff Keighly, "The Phantasmagoria Factory," *CNNMoney.com*, January 1, 2004, http://money.cnn.com on June 3, 2012; Glenn Collins, "Run Away to the Circus? No Need. It's Staying Here," *New York Times*, April 29, 2009, www.nytimes.com on June 3, 2012.

In Chapter 1 we noted the pervasiveness of human behavior in organizations and the importance of interactions among people as critical to achieving important outcomes for organizations. Indeed, a great deal of all managerial work involves interacting with other people, both directly and indirectly and both inside and outside the organization. This chapter is the first of seven that deal primarily with interpersonal processes in organizations. We begin by reinforcing the interpersonal nature of organizations. We then introduce and describe numerous elements of one important aspect of interpersonal relations, group dynamics. In subsequent chapters we discuss other forms of interpersonal activity in organizations, such as work teams (Chapter 10); interpersonal communication (Chapter 11); leadership (Chapters 12 and 13); power, politics, and workplace justice (Chapter 14); and conflict and negotiation (Chapter 15).

THE INTERPERSONAL NATURE OF ORGANIZATIONS

The schedule that follows is a typical day for the president of a Houston-based company, part of a larger firm headquartered in California. He kept a log of his activities for several different days so you could better appreciate the nature of managerial work.

- 7:45–8:15 a.m. Arrive at work; review hard-copy mail sorted by assistant; review and respond to e-mail; discuss day's schedule with assistant.
- 8:15–8:30 a.m. Scan *The Wall Street Journal* and online financial news sources.

- 8:30–9:00 a.m. Meet with labor officials and plant manager to resolve minor labor disputes.
- 9:00–9:30 a.m. Review internal report; read and respond to new e-mail.
- 9:30–10:00 a.m. Meet with two marketing executives to review advertising campaign; instruct them to fax approvals to advertising agency.
- 10:00–11:30 a.m. Meet with company executive committee to discuss strategy, budgetary issues, and competition (this committee meets weekly).
- 11:30 a.m.–12:00 p.m. Send several e-mails; read and respond to new e-mail.
- 12:00–1:15 p.m. Lunch with the financial vice president and two executives from another subsidiary of the parent corporation. Primary topic of discussion is the Houston Rockets basketball team. Place three business calls from Blackberry en route to lunch, and receive one business call en route back to office. Receive and read four e-mails on Blackberry during lunch.
- 1:15–1:45 p.m. Meet with human resources director and assistant about a recent OSHA inspection; establish a task force to investigate the problems identified and to suggest solutions.
- 1:45–2:00 p.m. Read and respond to new e-mail.
- 2:00–2:30 p.m. Video conference call with four other company presidents.
- 2:30–3:00 p.m. Meet with financial vice president about a confidential issue that came up at lunch (unscheduled).
- 3:00–3:30 p.m. Work alone in office; read and respond to new e-mail; send several e-mails.
- 3:30–4:15 p.m. Meet with a group of sales representatives and the company purchasing agent.
- 4:15–5:30 p.m. Make telephone call to company CEO in California to discuss various organizational issues; work alone in office.
- 5:30–7:00 p.m. Play racquetball at nearby athletic club with marketing vice president.
- 9:00–9:30 p.m. Read and respond to e-mail from home; send e-mail to assistant about an emergency meeting to be scheduled for the next day.

How did this manager spend his time? He spent most of it interacting with other people. This set of other people included people who report to him, his own boss, and various other groups. And this compressed daily schedule does not include several other short telephone calls, quick conversations with his assistant, and brief meetings with other managers. Moreover, myriad other meetings, conversations, and other interpersonal exchanges were taking place throughout the organization simultaneously during that same day. Clearly, interpersonal relations and group processes are a pervasive part of all organizations and a vital part of all managerial activities.[1]

Interpersonal Dynamics

Interpersonal relations in an organization are as varied as the individual members themselves. At one extreme, interpersonal relations can be personal and positive. This occurs when the two parties know each other, have mutual respect and affection, and enjoy interacting with one another.[2] Two managers who have known each other for years, play golf together on weekends, and are close personal friends will likely interact at work in a positive fashion. At the other extreme, interpersonal dynamics can be personal but negative. This is most likely when the parties dislike one another, do not have mutual respect, and do not enjoy interacting with one another. Suppose a manager has fought openly for years to block the promotion of another manager within the organization. Over the objections of the first manager, however, the other manager is eventually promoted to the same rank. When the two of them must interact, it will most likely be in a negative manner.

Most interactions fall between these extremes, as members of the organization interact in a professional way focused primarily on goal accomplishment. The interaction deals with the job at hand, is relatively formal and structured, and is task-directed. Two managers may respect each other's work and recognize the professional competence that each brings to the job. However, they may also have few common interests and little to talk about besides the job they are doing. These different types of interaction may occur between individuals, between groups, or between individuals and groups, and they can change over time. The two managers in the second scenario, for example, might decide to bury the hatchet and adopt a detached, professional manner. The two managers in the third example could find more common ground than they anticipated and evolve to a personal and positive interaction.

The nature of interactions depends in part on the relative goals of the parties involved. What might happen, for example, if a doctor becomes the owner of a hospital in which he or she must interact with staff, patients, and other health care providers? Similarly, suppose two friends work together as colleagues in the office of the district attorney, where they prosecute people who break the law. But if one friend leaves the DA's office and joins a private firm specializing in legal defense, the two friends now have goals that will generally conflict with one another. While in theory both should really want to seek the truth, in reality they may occasionally look at that truth through different lenses.

Outcomes of Interpersonal Behaviors

A variety of things can happen as a result of interpersonal behaviors. Recall from Chapter 4, for example, that numerous perspectives on motivation suggest that people have social needs. Interpersonal relations in organizations can be a primary source of need satisfaction for many people. For people with a strong need for affiliation, high-quality interpersonal relations can be an important positive element in the workplace. However, when this same person is confronted with poor-quality working relationships, the effect can be just as great in the opposite direction.

Interpersonal relations also serve as a solid basis for social support. Suppose that an employee receives a poor performance evaluation or is denied a promotion. Others in the organization can lend support because they share a common frame of reference—an understanding of the causes and consequences of what happened. Good interpersonal relations throughout an organization can also be a source of synergy. People who support one another and who work well together can accomplish much more than people who do not support one another and who do not work well together.[3] Another outcome, implied earlier, is conflict—people may leave an interpersonal exchange feeling angry or hostile. Understanding how and why people interact with one another is a complex process—whether the interaction occurs in a sports team, a work group, or a school committee. This is especially true when those individuals are members of the same group.

Figure 9.1 presents a three-phase model of group dynamics. In the first phase, the reasons for forming the group determine what type of group it will be. A four-step process of group development occurs during the second stage; the precise nature of these steps depends on four primary group performance factors. In the final phase, a mature, productive, adaptive group has evolved. As the model shows, mature groups interact with other groups, meet goals, and sometimes have conflicts with other groups. This model serves as the framework for our discussion of groups in this chapter.

FIGURE 9.1

A General Model of Group Dynamics

This model serves as the framework for this chapter. In phase one, the reasons for group formation determine what type of group it will be. In the second phase, groups evolve through four stages under the influence of four performance factors. Finally, a mature group emerges that interacts with other groups and can pursue organizational goals; conflicts with other groups sometimes occur.

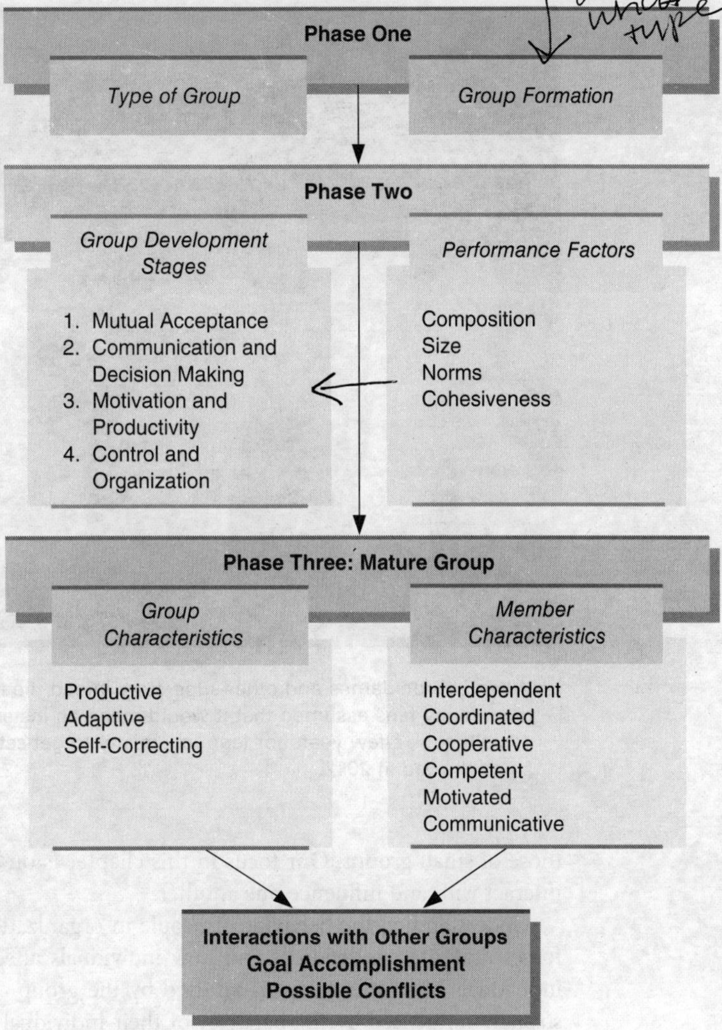

THE NATURE OF GROUPS

Definitions of the term *group* are as abundant as studies of groups. Groups can be defined in terms of perceptions, motivation, organization, interdependencies, and interactions. We will define a **group** as two or more persons who interact with one another such that each person influences and is influenced by each other person.[4] Two people who are physically near each other are not a group unless they interact and have some influence on each other. Coworkers may work side by side on related tasks—but if they do not interact, they are not a group.

A **group** is two or more people who interact with one another such that each person influences and is influenced by each other person.

Although groups often have goals, our definition does not state that group members must share a goal or motivation. This omission implies that members of a group may identify little or not at all with the group's goal. People can be a part of a group and enjoy the benefits of group membership without wanting to pursue any group goal. Members may satisfy needs just by being members, without pursuing anything. Of course, the quality of the interactions and the group's performance may be affected by members' lack of interest in the group goal. Our definition also suggests a limit on group size. A collection of people so large that its members cannot interact with and influence one another does not meet this definition. And in reality, the dynamics of large assemblies of people usually differ significantly from

When LeBron James and other superstars joined the Miami Heat professional basketball team many fans assumed that it would mean an instant NBA championship. However, it actually took a few years for team chemistry to get settled and the Heat's first championship followed in 2012.

those of small groups. Our focus in this chapter is on small groups in which the members interact with and influence one another.

Understanding the behavior of people in organizations requires that we understand the forces that affect individuals and how individuals affect the organization. The behavior of individuals both affects and is affected by the group. The accomplishments of groups are strongly influenced by the behavior of their individual members. For example, adding one key all-star player to a basketball team may make the difference between a bad season and a league championship. At the same time, groups have profound effects on the behaviors of their members. Group pressure, for instance, is often cited as a reason people give for lying or cheating—activities they claim they would not have chosen on their own.

From a managerial perspective, the work group is the primary means by which managers coordinate individuals' behavior to achieve organizational goals. Managers direct the activities of individuals, but they also direct and coordinate interactions within groups. For example, efforts to boost salespersons' performance have been shown to have both individual and group effects.[5] Therefore, the manager must pay attention to both the individual and the group when trying to improve employee performance. Managers must be aware of individual needs and interpersonal dynamics to manage groups effectively and efficiently, because the behavior of individuals is key to the group's success or failure.[6]

TYPES OF GROUPS

Our first task in understanding group processes is to develop a typology of groups that provides insight into their dynamics. Groups may be loosely categorized according to their degrees of formalization (formal or informal) and permanence (relatively permanent or relatively temporary). Table 9.1 shows this classification scheme.

included in pwrpnt

Table 9.1 Classification Scheme for Types of Groups

	RELATIVELY PERMANENT	RELATIVELY TEMPORARY	
FORMAL	**Command Groups**	**Task Groups**	**Affinity Groups**
	Quality-assurance department Cost-accounting group	Search committee for a new school superintendent Task force on new-product quality	New-product development group
INFORMAL	**Friendship Groups**	**Interest Groups**	
	Friends who do many activities together (attend the theater, play games, travel)	Bowling group Women's network	

Formal Groups

A **formal group** is formed by an organization to do its work.

A **command group** is a relatively permanent, formal group with functional reporting relationships and is usually included in the organization chart.

managers?

A **task group** is a relatively temporary, formal group established to do a specific task. - SUA.

Affinity groups are collections of employees from the same level in the organization who meet on a regular basis to share information, capture emerging opportunities, and solve problems.

Formal groups are established by the organization to do its work. Formal groups include command (or functional) groups, task groups, and affinity groups. A **command group** is relatively permanent and is characterized by functional reporting relationships such as having both a group manager and those who report to the manager. Command groups are usually included in the organization chart. A **task group** is created to perform a specific task, such as solving a particular quality problem, and is relatively temporary. **Affinity groups** are relatively permanent collections of employees from the same level in the organization who meet on a regular basis to share information, capture emerging opportunities, and solve problems.[7]

In business organizations, most employees work in command groups, as typically specified on an official organization chart. The size, shape, and organization of a company's command groups can vary considerably. Typical command groups in organizations include the quality-assurance department, the industrial engineering department, the cost-accounting department, and the personnel department. Other types of command groups include work teams organized as in the Japanese style of management, in which subsections of manufacturing and assembly processes are each assigned to a team of workers. The team members decide among themselves who will perform each task.

Teams are becoming widespread in automobile manufacturing. For instance, General Motors has organized most of its highly automated assembly lines into work teams of between five and twenty workers. Federal Express organized its clerical workers into teams that manage themselves. However, although participative teams are becoming more popular, command groups, whether entire departments or sophisticated work teams, are still the dominant type of work group in organizations.

com liasons/ managers meetings

Task (or special-project) groups are usually temporary and are often established to solve a particular problem. The group usually dissolves once it solves the problem or makes recommendations. People typically remain members of their command groups, or functional departments, while simultaneously serving in a task group and continuing to carry out the normal duties of their jobs. The members' command group duties may be temporarily reduced if the task group requires a great deal of time and effort. Task groups exist in all types of organizations around the world.

For example, the Pope once used a special task force of cardinals to study the financial structure of the Vatican and develop new ways to raise money.[8]

Affinity groups are a special type of formal group: They are set up by the organization, yet they are not really part of the formal organization structure. They are not really command groups because they are not part of the organizational hierarchy, yet they are not task groups because they stay in existence longer than any one task. Affinity groups are groups of employees who share roles, responsibilities, duties, and interests, and which represent horizontal slices of the normal organizational hierarchy. Because the members share important characteristics such as roles, duties, and levels, they are said to have an affinity for one another. The members of affinity groups usually have very similar job titles and similar duties but are in different divisions or departments within the organization.

Affinity groups meet regularly, and members have assigned roles such as recorder, reporter, facilitator, and meeting organizer. Members follow simple rules such as communicating openly and honestly, listening actively, respecting confidentiality, honoring time agreements, being prepared, staying focused, being individually accountable, and being supportive of each other and the group. The greatest benefits

SERVICE Customer Created Groups

©rangizz/Shutterstock

Today's customers know a great deal and are not reluctant to tell organizations what they know. In fact, many now expect not only to participate in the experience in ways the organization does not expect and in many cases is unprepared for but also to participate in the creation of the experience itself as part of the organization's creative team. Service organizations have long asked customers their opinions to learn what customers wanted from them. Many use focus groups to solicit information about the services they provide or should provide in the future. Today's well-informed, web-enabled customers want and expect far greater involvement and find ways to get it. Two current trends are examples of this.

The first trend is customer management of a networked team, which is increasingly found in health care. The availability of the Internet and the interest of people in their own health means that many patients arrive at their doctor's office not only with a lot of information about their ailment but also with an ability to identify and assemble their own support group of doctors, family and friends, and health care professionals. These people want to be actively engaged in managing their own health care and enter the doctor's office expecting to involve members of their existing wellness group. They help integrate their primary care physician with the referred specialists and freely add in other specialists whom they learn about via chat rooms, public rankings of doctors, and other disease-specific websites. While the historic model in health care had the family physician assembling a treatment and care team, the modern model is a proactive patient who assembles and actively manages a group of health care providers.

The second example of customer groups collaborating with an organization can be seen in the phenomena of crowdsourcing. Although asking the crowd for help is as old as the wanted posters on post office walls, the web has expanded this concept greatly as it can connect people anywhere in the world who want to be involved. Many newer business models are built on their ability to provide platforms for participation. Many people use crowdsourced Wikipedia as their only encyclopedia and the customer recommendations provided by Amazon, TripAdvisor, OpenTable, and Yelp as their guide for what to read and where to go, eat, or shop.

In the simplest form of crowdsourcing, a crowd is assembled, usually online, to solve a problem or engineer a solution. One classic illustration is described by Tapscott and Williams in their book *Wikinomics.* They write of a struggling Canadian gold mining firm,

Goldcorp, that decided to release all its proprietary geological data about its property to the public and offered a $575,000 prize for anyone who could develop a better way to locate gold on that property. The winning team from Australia gave them an answer that enabled them to increase their production of gold from just over 50,000 ounces annually at a cost of $360 an ounce to over a half million ounces annually at a cost of $59 an ounce. Successful examples of crowdsourcing like this one have generated much interest among others seeking solutions to problems that traditional methods don't seem to solve well. By building a web platform and posing a problem in a way that will interest potential participants, a crowd can be attracted. For example, Threadless uses its website to engage anyone wishing to participate in creating new shirt designs. The U.S. Defense Department offers people an opportunity to help test its software, the Library of Congress asked Flickr users to help identify people in its photo collection, and Walmart asks customers to vote on which new products it should stock.

In all these cases, the organization is creating a nonemployee group that it must manage sometimes without even knowing who the members are. The company generally pays little or nothing for participation. The individuals participating often interact with each other to argue the merits of proposed solutions. IKEA manages a website where it not only solicits new ideas for its stores but where customers can share solutions to each other's problems. Organizations using crowdsourcing must provide a problem in a manner that can be comprehended by potential participants, an interactive web platform that can be found by those knowledgeable and interested in the topic, and some process for identifying success and recognition of contribution when the problem is resolved.

The point is that organizations increasingly must manage groups that they don't employ or even know who is in them. These groups are often customers involved in product innovation or their own health care but can also be computer gamers testing software or suggesting new code or anyone with an expertise and willingness to participate in the problem the organization wishes to solve. Crowd management will require learning new skills beyond those used for managing employees.

Discussion Question: Reflect on websites you have visited where your opinion or input is requested or even expected. How do they manage this to encourage you to participate, or reward you for your contributions? What could they do to get better participation?

of affinity groups are that they cross existing boundaries of the organization and facilitate better communication among diverse departments and divisions throughout the organization.

Informal Groups

An **informal group** is established by its members.

A **friendship group** is relatively permanent and informal and draws its benefits from the social relationships among its members.

An **interest group** is relatively temporary and informal and is organized around a common activity or interest of its members.

Whereas formal groups are established by an organization, **informal groups** are formed by their members and consist of friendship groups, which are relatively permanent, and interest groups, which may be shorter-lived. **Friendship groups** arise out of the cordial relationships among members and the enjoyment they get from being together. **Interest groups** are organized around a common activity or interest, although friendships may develop among members.

Good examples of interest groups are the networks of working women that have developed over the last few decades. Many of these groups began as informal social gatherings of women who wanted to meet with other women working in male-dominated organizations, but they soon developed into interest groups whose benefits went far beyond their initial social purposes. The networks became information systems for counseling, job placement, and management training. Some networks were eventually established as formal, permanent associations; some remained informal groups based more on social relationships than on any specific interest; others were dissolved. These groups may be partly responsible for the dramatic increase in the percentage of women in managerial and administrative jobs.

STAGES OF GROUP DEVELOPMENT

Groups are not static. They typically develop through a four-stage process: (1) mutual acceptance, (2) communication and decision making, (3) motivation and productivity, and (4) control and organization.[9] The stages and the activities that typify them are shown in Figure 9.2. We treat the stages as separate and distinct. It is difficult to pinpoint exactly when a group moves from one stage to another, however, because the activities in the phases tend to overlap.

Mutual Acceptance

The **mutual acceptance stage** of group development is characterized by members' sharing information about themselves and getting to know each other.

In the **mutual acceptance stage** of group development, the group forms, and members get to know one another by sharing information about themselves. They often test one another's opinions by discussing subjects that have little to do with the group, such as the weather, sports, or recent events within the organization. Some aspects of the group's task, such as its formal objectives, may also be discussed at this stage. However, such discussion probably will not be very productive because the members are unfamiliar with one another and do not know how to evaluate one another's comments. If the members do happen to know one another already, this stage may be brief, but it is unlikely to be skipped altogether because this is a new group with a new purpose. Besides, there are likely to be a few members whom the others do not know well or at all.

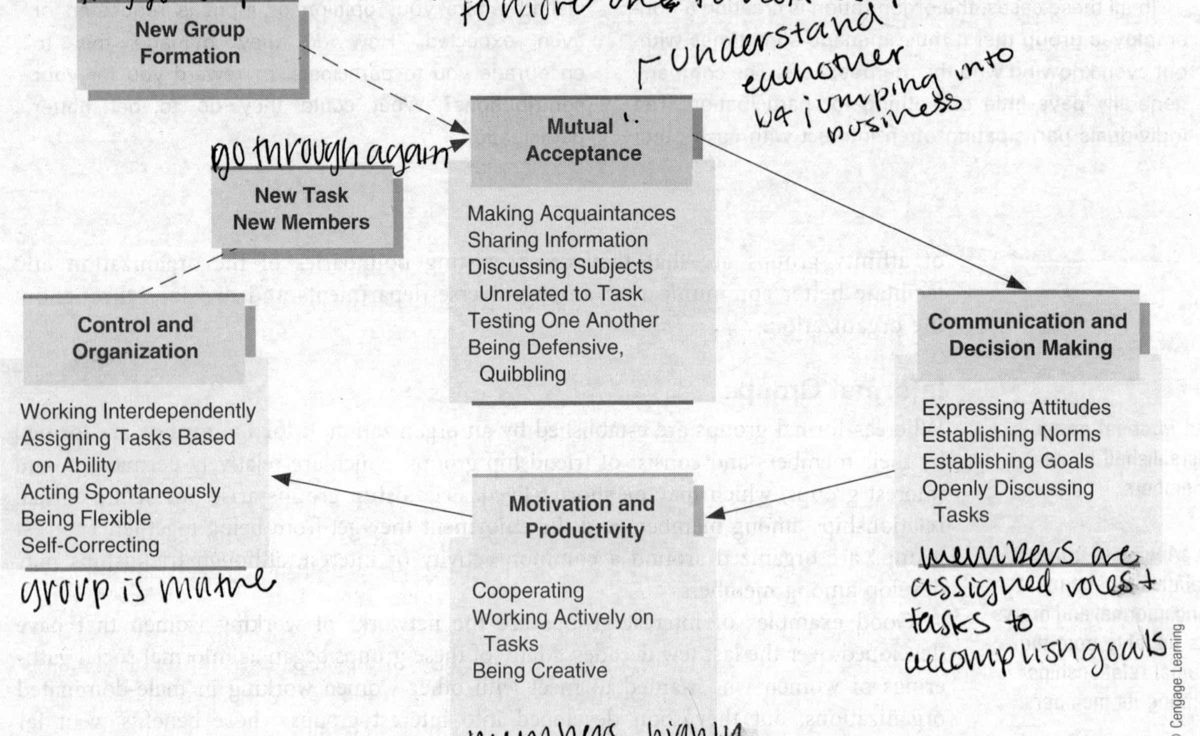

FIGURE 9.2

Stages of Group Development

This figure shows the stages of evolution from a newly formed group to a mature group. Note that as new members are added or an existing group gets a new task, the group needs to go through the stages again.

As the members get to know one another, discussion may turn to more sensitive issues, such as the organization's politics or recent controversial decisions. At this stage, members may have minor arguments and feud a bit as they explore one another's views on various issues and learn about each other's reactions, knowledge, and expertise. From the discussion, members come to understand how similar their beliefs and values are and the extent to which they can trust one another. Members may discuss their expectations about the group's activities in terms of their previous group and organizational experience.[10] Eventually, the conversation turns to the business of the group. When this discussion becomes serious, the group is moving to the next stage of development: communication and decision making.

Communication and Decision Making

In the **communication and decision-making stage** of group development, members discuss their feelings more openly and agree on group goals and individual roles in the group.

The group progresses to the **communication and decision-making stage** once group members have begun to accept one another. In this stage, members discuss their feelings and opinions more openly; they may show more tolerance for opposing viewpoints and explore different ideas to bring about a reasonable solution or decision. The membership usually begins to develop norms of behavior during this stage. Members discuss and eventually agree on the group's goals. Then they are assigned roles and tasks to accomplish the goals.

Motivation and Productivity

In the **motivation and productivity stage** of group development, members cooperate, help each other, and work toward accomplishing tasks.

In the next stage, **motivation and productivity**, the emphasis shifts away from personal concerns and viewpoints to activities that will benefit the group. Members perform their assigned tasks, cooperate with each other, and help others accomplish their goals. The members are highly motivated and may carry out their tasks creatively. In this stage, the group is accomplishing its work and moving toward the final stage of development.

Control and Organization

In the **control and organization stage** of group development, the group is mature; members work together and are flexible, adaptive, and self-correcting.

In the final stage, **control and organization**, the group works effectively toward accomplishing its goals. Tasks are assigned by mutual agreement and according to ability. In a mature group, the members' activities are relatively spontaneous and flexible rather than subject to rigid structural restraints. Mature groups evaluate their activities and potential outcomes and take corrective actions if necessary. The characteristics of flexibility, spontaneity, and self-correction are very important if the group is to remain productive over an extended period.

Not all groups, however, go through all four stages. Some groups disband before reaching the final stage. Others fail to complete a stage before moving on to the next one. Rather than spend the time necessary to get to know one another and build trust, for example, a group may cut short the first stage of development because of pressure from its leader, from deadlines, or from an outside threat (such as the boss).[11] If members are forced into activities typical of a later stage while the work of an earlier stage remains incomplete, they are likely to become frustrated: The group may not develop completely and may be less productive than it could be.[12] Group productivity depends on successful development at each stage. A group that evolves fully through the four stages of development usually becomes a mature, effective group.[13] Its members are interdependent, coordinated, cooperative, competent at their jobs, motivated to do them, self-correcting, and in active communication with one another.[14] The process does not take a long time if the group makes a good, solid effort and pays attention to the processes.

Finally, as working conditions and relationships change, either through a change in membership or when a task is completed and a new task is begun, groups may need to

ZUMA Press, Inc./Alamy

Following an NFL strike during which some players crossed picket lines and others did not coaches for the San Francisco Forty-Niners were unsure of how to restore team unity. The team used a combination of challenging focused workouts and informal social activities to reduce tension and rebuild commaraderie. Their redevelopment into a mature team once again led to two Superbowl victories.

re-experience one or more of the stages of development to maintain the cohesiveness and productivity characteristic of a well-developed group. The San Francisco Forty-Niners, for example, once returned from an NFL strike to an uncomfortable and apprehension-filled period. Their coach conducted rigorous practices but also allowed time for players to get together to air their feelings. Slowly, team unity returned, and players began joking and socializing again as they prepared for the rest of the season.[15] Their redevelopment as a mature group resulted in two subsequent Super Bowl victories.

Although these stages are not separate and distinct in all groups, many groups make fairly predictable transitions in activities at about the midpoint of the period available to complete a task.[16] A group may begin with its own distinctive approach to the problem and maintain it until about halfway through the allotted time. The midpoint transition is often accompanied by a burst of concentrated activity, reexamination of assumptions, dropping old patterns of activity, adopting new perspectives on the work, and making dramatic progress. Following these midpoint activities, the new patterns of activity may be maintained until close to the end of the period allotted for the activity. Another transition may occur just before the deadline. At this transition, groups often go into the completion stage, launching a final burst of activity to finish the job.

GROUP PERFORMANCE FACTORS

The performance of any group is affected by several factors other than its reasons for forming and the stages of its development. In a high-performing group, a group synergy often develops in which the group's performance is more than the sum of the individual contributions of its members. Several additional factors may account for this accelerated performance.[17] The four basic group performance factors are composition, size, norms, and cohesiveness.

Group Composition

Group composition is the degree of similarity or difference among group members on factors important to the group's work.

Group performance factors—composition, size, norms, and cohesiveness—affect the success of the group in fulfilling its goals.

The composition of a group plays an important role in determining group productivity.[18] **Group composition** is most often described in terms of the homogeneity or heterogeneity of the members. A group is *homogeneous* if the members are similar in one or several ways that are critical to the work of the group, such as in age, work experience, education, technical specialty, or cultural background. In *heterogeneous* groups, the members differ in one or more ways that are critical to the work of the group. Homogeneous groups often are created in organizations when people are assigned to command groups based on a similar technical specialty. Although the people who work in such command groups may differ in some ways, such as in age or work experience, they are homogeneous in terms of a critical work performance variable: technical specialty.[19]

Much research has explored the relationship between a group's composition and its productivity. The group's heterogeneity in terms of age and tenure with the group has been shown to be related to turnover: Groups with members of different ages and experiences with the group tend to experience frequent changes in membership.[20] A homogeneous group is likely to be more productive when the group task is simple, cooperation is necessary, the group tasks are sequential, or quick action is required. A heterogeneous group is more likely to be productive when the task is complex, requires a collective effort (that is, each member does a different task, and the sum of these efforts constitutes the group output), and demands creativity, and when speed is less important than thorough deliberations. For example, a group asked to generate ideas for marketing a new product probably needs to be heterogeneous to develop as many different ideas as possible.

To see how Cirque du Soleil teams two very different groups of people—both of them highly heterogeneous—to put on complex, artistically coherent shows, see the *Technology* box entitled "Teaming Technology and Artistry" on page 246.

The link between group composition and type of task is explained by the interactions typical of homogeneous and heterogeneous groups. A homogeneous group tends to have less conflict, fewer differences of opinion, smoother communication, and more interactions. When a task requires cooperation and speed, a homogeneous group is therefore more desirable. If, however, the task requires complex analysis of information and creativity to arrive at the best possible solution, a heterogeneous group may be more appropriate because it generates a wide range of viewpoints. More discussion and more conflict are likely, both of which can enhance the group's decision making.

Group composition becomes especially important as organizations become increasingly more diverse.[21] Cultures differ in the importance they place on group membership and in how they view authority, uncertainty, and other important factors. Increasing attention is being focused on how to deal with groups made up of people from different cultures.[22] In general, a manager in charge of a culturally diverse group can expect several things. First, members will probably distrust one another. Stereotyping will present a problem, and communication problems will almost certainly arise. Thus, managers need to recognize that such groups will seldom function smoothly, at least at first. Managers may therefore need to spend more time helping a culturally diverse group through the rough spots as it matures, and they should allow a longer-than-normal time before expecting it to carry out its assigned task.

TECHNOLOGY Teaming Technology and Artistry

©watcharakun/Shutterstock

Canadian gymnast Natasha Chao joined Cirque du Soleil in 1993. From 1999 to 2003, she performed the role of the Red Bird in *Mystère*, a production permanently staged at Treasure Island Hotel and Casino in Las Vegas. According to the show's production notes, the character of the flightless Red Bird (who is male though the performer needn't be) "leaps ever higher in his futile attempts to take to the skies. Still convinced he can fly, he struggles against his fate." As choreographed, his fate consists of a 60-foot headfirst freefall into a hidden net. "One thing all ... Cirque artists share in common," says *Mystère* choreographer Debra Brown, "is a passion for doing art. Circus performers, who risk their lives, are the most passionate," she adds, and Chao is no exception. Working without an understudy, however, she couldn't afford to get hurt, and, passion for her art notwithstanding, she was understandably cautious in performing the stunt.

In addition to maintaining her impeccable timing and keen spatial awareness, the key for Chao was to curve her spine upright at the final moment before contact with the net. The tension in the net was continuously monitored by technicians working the theater's motion-control system, and it should come as no surprise that all of an artist's skill, preparation, and caution can do little to prevent injury if he or she doesn't get the type of support for which armies of Cirque technicians are responsible every night. Executing a stunt like the plunge of the Red Bird, says another Cirque choreographer, Jacques Heim, "is extremely exciting, but it's ... exciting because it's terrifying." And that's why, he explains, every Cirque performance really consists of two shows: the one that the performers are putting on in front of the audience and the one that the technicians are performing behind the scenes.

Heim did the choreography for *KÀ*, an Egyptian-themed Cirque extravaganza in residence at the MGM Grand Hotel & Casino, also in Las Vegas. Premiering in 2005 at a cost of $220 million, *KÀ* was at the time, both theatrically and technologically, the most ambitious production that Cirque du Soleil had ever mounted. "In *KÀ*," says technical director Matthew Whelan, "the machinery is so impressive that their movement becomes a [dance] number in itself.... The audience does see the lift movements"—the computer-controlled manipulation of the decks that comprise the mobile "stage"—"but there's also a complete other show going on in the pit where the lifts move out of sightline to allow scenic pieces to move from level to level in a specific choreography to manage limited floor space." The interaction of technicians and performers is even more critical than in most Cirque productions because, as stage architect Mark Fisher puts it, the technologically managed scenery is "actually part of the landscape in which the performers live and move to create their show."

"Cirque du Soleil is always about the artist and humanity, and the tools we use—no matter how advanced—must serve the human artists."

—KEITH WRIGHT, OPERATIONS PRODUCTION MANAGER AT CIRQUE DU SOLEIL

"There's a constant risk of artists' falling," admits equipment designer Jaque Paquin, and Cirque du Soleil depends on its technology and the people who run it not only to enhance the performance of its artists but to protect them as well. Paquin, after all, is also responsible for the retractable safety net that's programmed into position beneath *KÀ*'s centerpiece scene—an aerial-acrobatics spectacle—by the theater's modular, multiuser NOMAD control system. Keith Wright, *KÀ*'s operations production manager, sees the technician's twofold responsibility as a basic reflection of Cirque du Soleil's mission: "Cirque du Soleil," he says, "is always about the artist and humanity, and the tools we use—no matter how advanced—must serve the human artists."

References: John Scott Lewinski, "Cirque du Soleil's Sophisticated *Kà* Evolves with New Tech," *Wired*, February 16, 2010, www.wired.com on June 4, 2012; Joe Hunkins, "Cirque du Soleil: Dramatic Technologies," *Technology Report*, December 15, 2009, http://technology-report.com on June 4, 2012; Victoria Looseleaf, "Cirque du Soleil's Magic," *Dance Magazine*, December 2007, www.dancemagazine.com on June 4, 2012; Gigi Berardi, "Circus +Dance=Cirque du Soleil," *Dance Magazine*, September 1, 2002, www.thefreelibrary.com on May 3, 2011; Stephanie Gooch, "Industrial-Scale Technology in Cirque du Soleil's *KÀ*," *Designfax*, February 1, 2005, www.thefreelibrary.com on May 3, 2011.

Many organizations are creating joint ventures and other types of alliances with organizations from other countries. Joint ventures have become common in the automobile and electronics industries, for example. However, managers from the United States tend to exhibit individualistic behaviors in a group setting, whereas managers from more collectivistic countries, such as the People's Republic of China, tend to exhibit more group-oriented behaviors. Thus, when these two different types of managers work together in a joint venture, the managers must be trained to be cautious and understanding in their interactions and in the types of behaviors they exhibit.

Group Size

Group size is the number of members of the group; group size affects the number of resources available to perform the task.

A group can have as few as two members or as many members as can interact and influence one another. **Group size** can have an important effect on performance. A group with many members has more resources available and may be able to complete a large number of relatively independent tasks. In groups established to generate ideas, those with more members tend to produce more ideas, although the rate of increase in the number of ideas diminishes rapidly as the group grows.[23] Beyond a certain point, the greater complexity of interactions and communication may make it more difficult for a large group to achieve agreement.

Social loafing is the tendency of some members of groups to put forth less effort in a group than they would when working alone.

Interactions and communication are much more likely to be formalized in larger groups. Large groups tend to set agendas for meetings and to follow a protocol or parliamentary procedure to control discussion. As a result, time that otherwise might be available to work on tasks is taken up in administrative duties such as organizing and structuring the interactions and communications within the group. Also, the large size may inhibit participation of some people and increase absenteeism; some people may stop trying to make a meaningful contribution and may even stop coming to group meetings if their repeated attempts to contribute or participate are thwarted by the sheer number of similar efforts by other members. Furthermore, large groups present more opportunities for interpersonal attraction, leading to more social interactions and fewer task interactions. **Social loafing** is the tendency of some members of groups not to put forth as much effort in a group situation as they would working alone. Social loafing often results from the assumption by some members that if they do not work hard, other members will pick up the slack. How much of a problem this becomes depends on the nature of the task, the characteristics of the people involved, and the ability of the group leadership to be aware of the potential problem and do something about it.

The most effective size of a group, therefore, is determined by the group members' ability to interact and influence each other effectively. The need for interaction is affected by the maturity of the group, the tasks of the group, the maturity of individual members, and the ability of the group leader or manager to manage the communication, potential conflicts, and task activities. In some situations, the most effective group size is three or four; other groups can function effectively with fifteen or more members.

Group Norms

A **norm** is a standard against which the appropriateness of a behavior is judged.

A **norm** is a standard against which the appropriateness of a behavior is judged. Thus, norms determine the behavior expected in a certain situation. Group norms usually are established during the second stage of group development (communication and decision making) and are carried forward into the maturity stage. By providing a basis for predicting others' behaviors, norms enable people to behave in a manner consistent with and acceptable to the group. Without norms, the activities in a group would be chaotic.

Norms result from the combination of members' personality characteristics, the situation, the task, and the historical traditions of the group.[24] Lack of conformity to group

Group norms are standards of behavior that define appropriate behavior for members of the group. The two group members in the background are hard at work on a major project, while the group member in the foreground is relaxing. One possible explanation for these behaviors is that the group's norms allow a member to take a few minutes to relax when she or he has been putting in extra hours on a project. Another possibility is that he is violating group norms and will subsequently be sanctioned by other group members.

norms may result in verbal abuse, physical threats, ostracism, or ejection from the group. Group norms are enforced, however, only for actions that are important to group members. For example, if the office norm is for employees to wear suits to convey a professional image to clients, a staff member who wears blue jeans and a sweatshirt violates the group norm and will hear about it quickly. But if the norm is that dress is unimportant because little contact with clients occurs in the office, the fact that someone wears blue jeans may not even be noticed.

Norms serve four purposes in organizations. First, they help the group survive. Groups tend to reject deviant behavior that does not help meet group goals or contribute to the survival of the group if it is threatened. Accordingly, a successful group that is not under threat may be more tolerant of deviant behavior. Second, they simplify and make more predictable the behaviors expected of group members. Because they are familiar with norms, members do not have to analyze each behavior and decide on a response. Members can anticipate the actions of others on the basis of group norms, usually resulting in increased productivity and goal attainment. Third, norms help the group avoid embarrassing situations. Group members often want to avoid damaging other members' self-images and are likely to avoid certain subjects that might hurt a member's feelings. And finally, norms express the central values of the group and identify the group to others. Certain clothes, mannerisms, or behaviors in particular situations may be a rallying point for members and may signify to others the nature of the group.[25]

Group Cohesiveness

Group cohesiveness is the extent to which a group is committed to staying together.

Group cohesiveness is the extent to which a group is committed to remaining together; it results from forces acting on the members to remain in the group. The forces that create cohesiveness are attraction to the group, resistance to leaving the group, and motivation to remain a member of the group.[26] As shown in Figure 9.3, group cohesiveness is related to many aspects of group dynamics that we have already discussed—maturity, homogeneity, manageable size, and frequency of interactions.

The figure also shows that group cohesiveness can be increased by competition or by the presence of an external threat. Either factor can focus members' attention on a clearly defined goal and increase their willingness to work together. Finally, successfully reaching goals often increases the cohesiveness of a group because people are proud to be identified with a winner and to be thought of as competent and successful. This may be one reason behind the popular expression "Success breeds success." A group that is successful may become more cohesive and hence possibly even more successful. Of course,

FIGURE 9.3

Factors That Affect Group Cohesiveness and Consequences of Group Cohesiveness

The factors that increase and decrease cohesiveness and the consequences of high and low cohesiveness indicate that although it is often preferable to have a highly cohesive group, in some situations the effects of a highly cohesive group can be negative for the organization.

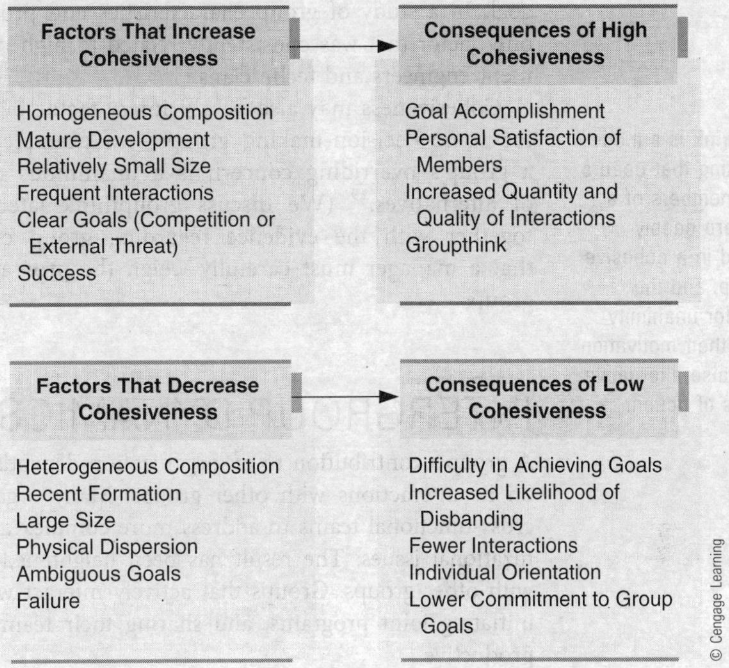

other factors can get in the way of continued success, such as personal differences, egos, and the lure of more individual success in other activities.

Research on group performance factors has focused on the relationship between cohesiveness and group productivity.[27] Highly cohesive groups appear to be more effective at achieving their goals than groups that are low in cohesiveness, especially in research and development groups in U.S. companies.[28] However, highly cohesive groups will not necessarily be more productive in an organizational sense than groups with low cohesiveness. As Figure 9.4 illustrates, when a group's goals are compatible with the organizational goals, a cohesive group probably will be more productive than one that is not cohesive. In other words, if a highly cohesive group has the goal of contributing

FIGURE 9.4

Group Cohesiveness, Goals, and Productivity

This figure shows that the best combination is for the group to be cohesive and for the group's goals to be congruent with the organization's goals. The lowest potential group performance also occurs with highly cohesive groups when the group's goals are not consistent with the organization's goals.

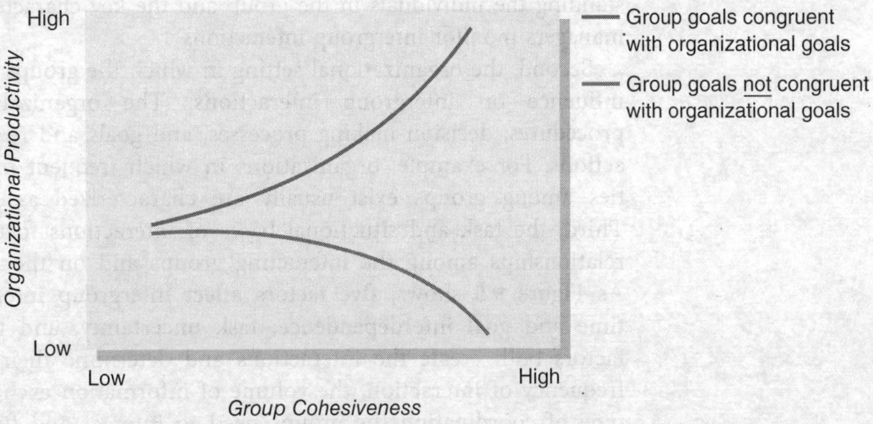

to the good of the organization, it is very likely to be productive in organizational terms. But if such a group decides on a goal that has little to do with the business of the organization, it will probably achieve its own goal even at the expense of any organizational goal. In a study of group characteristics and productivity, group cohesiveness was the only factor that was consistently related to high performance for research and development engineers and technicians.

Groupthink is a mode of thinking that occurs when members of a group are deeply involved in a cohesive in-group, and the desire for unanimity offsets their motivation to appraise alternative courses of action.

Cohesiveness may also be a primary factor in the development of certain problems for some decision-making groups. An example is **groupthink**, which occurs when a group's overriding concern is a unanimous decision rather than critical analysis of alternatives.[29] (We discuss groupthink later in this chapter.) These problems, together with the evidence regarding group cohesiveness and productivity, mean that a manager must carefully weigh the pros and cons of fostering highly cohesive groups.

INTERGROUP DYNAMICS

A group's contribution to an organization depends not only on its productivity but also on its interactions with other groups. Many organizations are expanding their use of cross-functional teams to address more complex and increasingly more important organizational issues. The result has been heightened emphasis on the teams' interactions with other groups. Groups that actively interact with other groups by asking questions, initiating joint programs, and sharing their team's achievements are usually the most productive.

Interactions are the key to understanding intergroup dynamics. The orientation of the groups toward their goals takes place under a highly complex set of conditions that determine the relationships among the groups. The most important of these factors are presented in the model of intergroup dynamics in Figure 9.5. The model emphasizes three primary factors that influence intergroup interactions: group characteristics, organizational setting, and task and situational bases of interaction.

First, we must understand the key characteristics of the interacting groups. Each group brings to the interaction its own unique features. As individuals become a part of a group, they tend to identify so strongly with the group that their views of other groups become biased, so harmonious relationships with other groups may be difficult to achieve.[30] Furthermore, the individuals in the group contribute to the group processes, and these contributions in turn influence the group's norms, size, composition, and cohesiveness; all of these factors affect the interactions with other groups. Thus, understanding the individuals in the group and the key characteristics of the group can help managers monitor intergroup interactions.

Second, the organizational setting in which the groups interact can have a powerful influence on intergroup interactions. The organization's structure, rules and procedures, decision-making processes, and goals and reward systems all affect interactions. For example, organizations in which frequent interactions occur and strong ties among groups exist usually are characterized as low-conflict organizations.[31] Third, the task and situational bases of interactions focus attention on the working relationships among the interacting groups and on the reasons for the interactions. As Figure 9.5 shows, five factors affect intergroup interactions: location, resources, time and goal interdependence, task uncertainty, and task interdependence. These factors both create the interactions and determine their characteristics, such as the frequency of interaction, the volume of information exchange among groups, and the type of coordination the groups need to interact and function. For example, if two groups depend heavily on each other to perform a task about which much uncertainty exists, they need a great deal of information from each other to define and perform the task.

FIGURE 9.5

Factors That Influence Intergroup Interactions

The nature of the interactions between groups depends on the characteristics of the groups involved, the organizational setting, and the task and situational setting for the interaction.

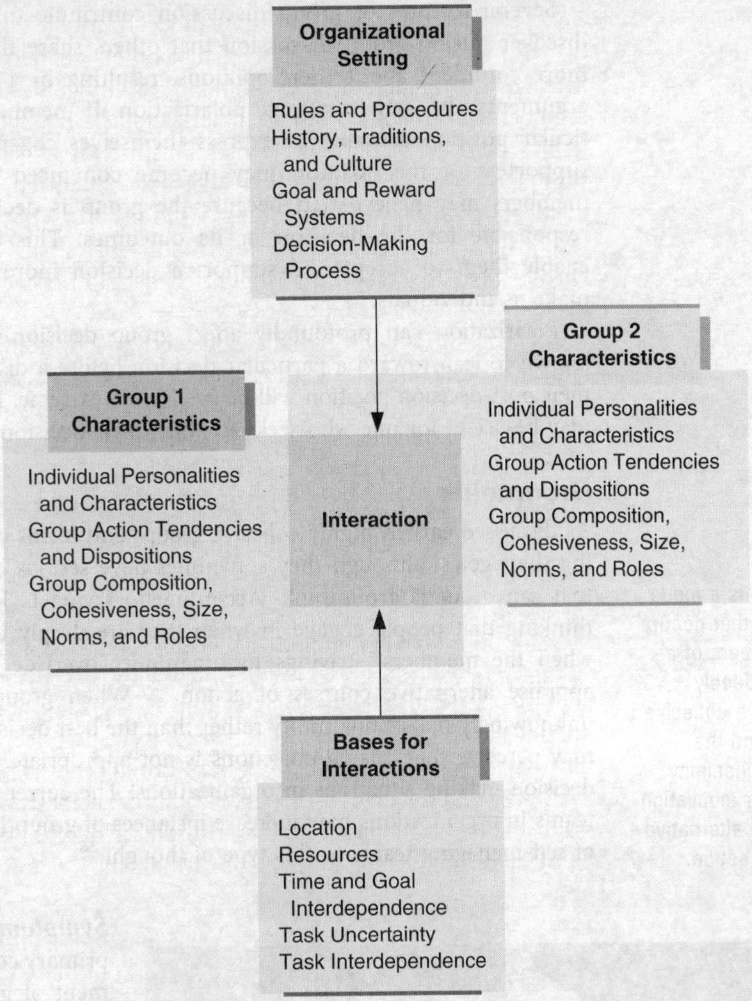

GROUP DECISION MAKING IN ORGANIZATIONS

People in organizations work in a variety of groups—formal and informal, permanent and temporary. Most of these groups make decisions that affect the welfare of the organization and the people in it. Here we discuss several issues surrounding how groups make decisions: group polarization, groupthink, and group problem solving.

Group Polarization

Group polarization is the tendency for a group's average post-discussion attitudes to be more extreme than its average pre-discussion attitudes.

Members' attitudes and opinions with respect to an issue or a solution may change during group discussion. Some studies of this tendency have showed the change to be a fairly consistent movement toward a more risky solution, called "risky shift."[32] Other studies and analyses have revealed that the group-induced shift is not always toward more risk; the group is just as likely to move toward a more conservative view.[33] Generally, **group polarization** occurs when the average of the group members' post-discussion attitudes tends to be more extreme than average pre-discussion attitudes.[34]

Several features of group discussion contribute to polarization. When individuals discover during group discussion that others share their opinions, they may become more confident about their opinions, resulting in a more extreme view. Persuasive arguments also can encourage polarization. If members who strongly support a particular position are able to express themselves cogently in the discussion, less avid supporters of the position may become convinced that it is correct. In addition, members may believe that because the group is deciding, they are not individually responsible for the decision or its outcomes. This diffusion of responsibility may enable them to accept and support a decision more radical than those they would make as individuals.

Polarization can profoundly affect group decision making. If group members are known to lean toward a particular decision before a discussion, it may be expected that their post-decision position will be even more extreme. Understanding this phenomenon may be useful for one who seeks to affect their decision.

Groupthink

Groupthink is a mode of thinking that occurs when members of a group are deeply involved in a cohesive in-group, and the desire for unanimity offsets their motivation to appraise alternative courses of action.

As discussed earlier, highly cohesive groups and teams often are very successful at meeting their goals, although they sometimes have serious difficulties as well. One problem that can occur is groupthink. According to Irving L. Janis, **groupthink** is "a mode of thinking that people engage in when they are deeply involved in a cohesive in-group, when the members' strivings for unanimity override their motivation to realistically appraise alternative courses of action."[35] When groupthink occurs, then, the group unknowingly makes unanimity rather than the best decision its goal. Individual members may perceive that raising objections is not appropriate. Groupthink can occur in many decision-making situations in organizations. The current trend toward increasing use of teams in organizations may increase instances of groupthink because of the susceptibility of self-managing teams to this type of thought.[36]

Jose Luis Pelaez Inc/Jupiter Images

Groupthink creates an illusion of unanimity. This team of workers seems unified in their confidence and would probably argue they are all "on the same page." While this may, in fact, be true, it is also quite possible that they have deceived themselves into only thinking they agree--and are instead experiencing groupthink.

Symptoms of Groupthink The three primary conditions that foster the development of groupthink are cohesiveness, the leader's promotion of his or her preferred solution, and insulation of the group from experts' opinions. Based on analysis of the disaster associated with the explosion of the space shuttle *Challenger* in 1986, the original idea of groupthink symptoms was enhanced to include the effects of increased time pressure and the role of the leader in not stimulating critical thinking in developing the symptoms of groupthink.[37] Figure 9.6 outlines the revised groupthink process.

A group in which groupthink has taken hold exhibits eight well-defined symptoms:

1. An *illusion of invulnerability*, shared by most or all members, that creates excessive optimism and encourages extreme risk taking

FIGURE 9.6

The Groupthink Process

Groupthink can occur when a highly cohesive group with a directive leader is under time pressure; it can result in a defective decision-making process and low probability of successful outcomes.

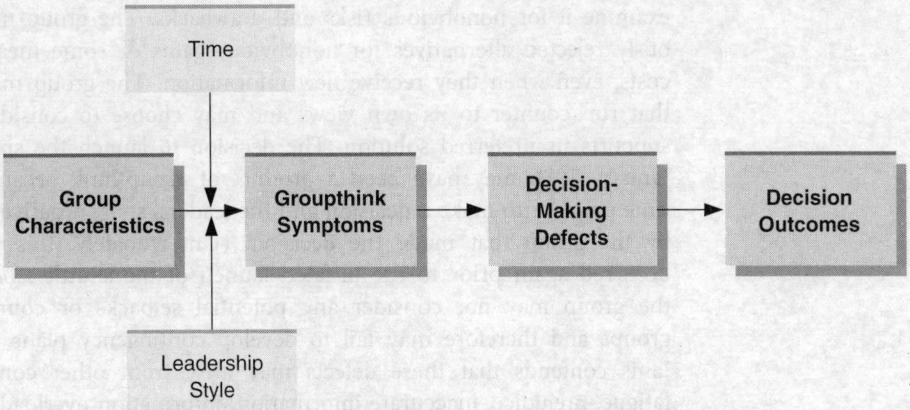

Reference: Gregory Moorhead, Richard Ference, and Chris P. Neck, "Group Decision Fiascoes Continue: Space Shuttle *Challenger* and a Revised Groupthink Framework," *Human Relations,* 1991, vol. 44, pp. 539–550.

2. *Collective efforts to rationalize or discount warnings* that might lead members to reconsider assumptions before recommitting themselves to past policy decisions
3. An *unquestioned belief in the group's inherent morality,* inclining members to ignore the ethical and moral consequences of their decisions
4. *Stereotyped views of "enemy" leaders* as too evil to warrant genuine attempts to negotiate or as too weak or stupid to counter whatever risky attempts are made to defeat their purposes
5. *Direct pressure on a member* who expresses strong arguments against any of the group's stereotypes, illusions, or commitments, making clear that such dissent is contrary to what is expected of loyal members
6. *Self-censorship of deviations* from the apparent group consensus, reflecting each member's inclination to minimize the importance of his or her doubts and counterarguments
7. A *shared illusion of unanimity,* resulting partly from self-censorship of deviations, augmented by the false assumption that silence means consent.[38]
8. *The emergence of self-appointed "mindguards,"* members who protect the group from adverse information that might shatter their shared complacency about the effectiveness and morality of their decisions[39]

Janis contends that the members of the group involved in the Watergate cover-up during President Richard Nixon's administration and reelection campaign—Nixon himself, H. R. Haldeman, John Ehrlichman, and John Dean—may have been victims of groupthink. Evidence of most of the groupthink symptoms can be found in the unedited transcripts of the group's deliberations.[40] More recently, it seems very likely that the recent scandal at Penn State involving its long-time coach Joe Paterno grew at least in part from groupthink.[41] For example, the leadership at the university seemed to have an illusion of invulnerability, they rationalized or discounted warnings, they believed in their own inherent morality, they had an illusion of unanimity, and they tolerated mindguards.

Decision-Making Defects and Decision Quality When groupthink dominates group deliberations, the likelihood increases that decision-making defects will occur. The group is less likely to survey a full range of alternatives and may focus on only a few (often one or two). In discussing a preferred alternative, the group may fail to examine it for nonobvious risks and drawbacks. The group may not reexamine previously rejected alternatives for nonobvious gains or some means of reducing apparent costs, even when they receive new information. The group may reject expert opinions that run counter to its own views and may choose to consider only information that supports its preferred solution. The decision to launch the space shuttle *Challenger* in January 1986 may have been a product of groupthink because, due to the increased time pressure to make a decision and the leaders' style, negative information was ignored by the group that made the decision. (Unfortunately, this same pattern apparently occurred again prior to the ill-fated launch of the shuttle *Columbia* in 2003.) Finally, the group may not consider any potential setbacks or countermoves by competing groups and therefore may fail to develop contingency plans. It should be noted that Janis contends that these defects may arise from other common problems as well: fatigue, prejudice, inaccurate information, information overload, and ignorance.[42]

Defects in decision making do not always lead to bad outcomes or defeats. Even if its own decision-making processes are flawed, one side can win a battle because of the poor decisions made by the other side's leaders. Nevertheless, decisions produced by defective processes are less likely to succeed. Although the arguments for the existence of groupthink are convincing, the hypothesis has not been subjected to rigorous empirical examination. Research supports parts of the model but leaves some questions unanswered.[43]

Prevention of Groupthink Several suggestions have been offered to help managers reduce the probability of groupthink in group decision making. Summarized in Table 9.2, these prescriptions fall into four categories, depending on whether they apply to the leader, the organization, the individual, or the process. All are designed to facilitate the critical evaluation of alternatives and discourage the single-minded pursuit of unanimity.

Participation

A major issue in group decision making is the degree to which employees should participate in the process. Early management theories, such as those of the scientific management school, advocated a clear separation between the duties of managers and workers:

Table 9.2 Prescriptions for Preventing Groupthink

A. Leader prescriptions
1. Assign everyone the role of critical evaluator.
2. Be impartial; do not state preferences.
3. Assign the devil's advocate role to at least one group member.
4. Use outside experts to challenge the group.
5. Be open to dissenting points of view.

B. Organizational prescriptions
1. Set up several independent groups to study the same issue.
2. Train managers and group leaders in groupthink prevention techniques.

C. Individual prescriptions
1. Be a critical thinker.
2. Discuss group deliberations with a trusted outsider; report back to the group.

D. Process prescriptions
1. Periodically break the group into subgroups to discuss the issues.
2. Take time to study external factors.
3. Hold second-chance meetings to rethink issues before making a commitment.

Management was to make the decisions, and employees were to implement them.[44] Other approaches have urged that employees be allowed to participate in decisions to increase their ego involvement, motivation, and satisfaction.[45] Numerous research studies have shown that whereas employees who seek responsibility and challenge on the job may find participation in the decision-making process to be both motivating and enriching, other employees may regard such participation as a waste of time and a management imposition.[46]

Whether employee participation in decision making is appropriate depends on the situation. In tasks that require an estimation, a prediction, or a judgment of accuracy—usually referred to as "judgmental tasks"—groups typically are superior to individuals simply because more people contribute to the decision-making process. However, one especially capable individual may make a better judgment than a group.

In problem-solving tasks, groups generally produce more and better solutions than do individuals. But groups take far longer than individuals to develop solutions and make decisions. An individual or very small group may be able to accomplish some things much faster than a large, unwieldy group or organization. In addition, individual decision making avoids the special problems of group decision making such as groupthink or group polarization. If the problem to be solved is fairly straightforward, it may be more appropriate to have a single capable individual concentrate on solving it. On the other hand, complex problems are more appropriate for groups. Such problems can often be divided into parts and the parts assigned to individuals or small groups who bring their results back to the group for discussion and decision making.

An additional advantage of group decision making is that it often creates greater interest in the task. Heightened interest may increase the time and effort given to the task, resulting in more ideas, a more thorough search for solutions, better evaluation of alternatives, and improved decision quality.

The Vroom decision tree approach to leadership (discussed in Chapter 12) is one popular way of determining the appropriate degree of subordinate participation.[47] The model includes decision styles that vary from "decide" (the leader alone makes the decision) to "delegate" (the group makes the decision, with each member having an equal say). The choice of style rests on seven considerations that concern the characteristics of the situation and the subordinates.

Participation in decision making is also related to organizational structure. For example, decentralization involves delegating some decision-making authority throughout the organizational hierarchy. The more decentralized the organization, the more its employees tend to participate in decision making. Whether one views participation in decision making as pertaining to leadership, organization structure, or motivation, it remains an important aspect of organizations that continues to occupy managers and organizational scholars.[48]

Group Problem Solving

A typical interacting group may have difficulty with any of several steps in the decision-making process. One common problem arises in the generation-of-alternatives phase: The search may be arbitrarily ended before all plausible alternatives have been identified. Several types of group interactions can have this effect. If members immediately express their reactions to the alternatives as they are first proposed, potential contributors may begin to censor their ideas to avoid embarrassing criticism from the group. Less confident group members, intimidated by members who have more experience, higher status, or more power, also may censor their ideas for fear of embarrassment or punishment. In addition, the group leader may limit idea generation by enforcing requirements concerning time, appropriateness, cost, feasibility, and the like. To improve the generation of alternatives, managers may employ any of three techniques to stimulate the group's problem-solving capabilities: brainstorming, the nominal group technique, or the Delphi technique.

Brainstorming is a technique used in the idea-generation phase of decision making that assists in development of numerous alternative courses of action.

Brainstorming **Brainstorming** is most often used in the idea-generation phase of decision making and is intended to solve problems that are new to the organization and have major consequences. In brainstorming, the group convenes specifically to generate alternatives. The members present ideas and clarify them with brief explanations. Each idea is recorded in full view of all members, usually on a flip chart. To avoid self-censoring, no attempts to evaluate the ideas are allowed. Group members are encouraged to offer any ideas that occur to them, even those that seem too risky or impossible to implement. (The absence of such ideas, in fact, is evidence that group members are engaging in self-censorship.) In a subsequent session, after the ideas have been recorded and distributed to members for review, the alternatives are evaluated.

The intent of brainstorming is to produce totally new ideas and solutions by stimulating the creativity of group members and encouraging them to build on the contributions of others. Brainstorming does not provide the resolution to the problem, an evaluation scheme, or the decision itself. Instead, it should produce a list of alternatives that is more innovative and comprehensive than one developed by the typical interacting group.

With a **nominal group technique,** group members follow a generate-discuss-vote cycle until they reach a decision.

The Nominal Group Technique The **nominal group technique** is another means of improving group decision making. Whereas brainstorming is used primarily to generate alternatives, this technique may be used in other phases of decision making, such as identification of the problem and of appropriate criteria for evaluating alternatives. To use this technique, a group of individuals convenes to address an issue. The issue is described to the group, and each individual writes a list of ideas; no discussion among the members is permitted. Following the five- to ten-minute idea-generation period, individual members take turns reporting their ideas, one at a time, to the group. The ideas are recorded on a flip chart, and members are encouraged to add to the list by building on the ideas of others. After all ideas have been presented, the members may discuss them and continue to build on them or proceed to the next phase. This part of the process can also be carried out without a face-to-face meeting or by mail, telephone, or computer. A meeting, however, helps members develop a group feeling and puts interpersonal pressure on the members to do their best in developing their lists.

After the discussion, members privately vote on or rank the ideas or report their preferences in some other agreed-upon way. Reporting is private to reduce any feelings of intimidation. After voting, the group may discuss the results and continue to generate and discuss ideas. The generation-discussion-vote cycle can continue until an appropriate decision is reached.

The nominal group technique has two principal advantages. It helps overcome the negative effects of power and status differences among group members, and it can be used to explore problems to generate alternatives, or to evaluate them. Its primary disadvantage lies in its structured nature, which may limit creativity.

The **Delphi technique** is a method of systematically gathering judgments of experts for use in developing forecasts.

The Delphi Technique The **Delphi technique** was originally developed by Rand Corporation as a method for systematically gathering the judgments of experts for use in developing forecasts. It is designed for groups that do not meet face to face. For instance, the product development manager of a major toy manufacturer might use the Delphi technique to probe the views of industry experts to forecast developments in the dynamic toy market.

The manager who wants the input of a group is the central figure in the process. After recruiting participants, the manager develops a questionnaire for them to complete.

The questionnaire is relatively simple in that it contains straightforward questions that deal with the issue, trends in the area, new technological developments, and other factors the manager is interested in. The manager summarizes the responses and reports back to the experts with another questionnaire. This cycle may be repeated as many times as necessary to generate the information the manager needs.

The Delphi technique is useful when experts are physically dispersed, anonymity is desired, or the participants are known to have trouble communicating with one another because of extreme differences of opinion. This method also avoids the intimidation problems that may exist in decision-making groups. On the other hand, the technique eliminates the often fruitful results of direct interaction among group members.

SYNOPSIS

Interpersonal dynamics are a pervasive element of all organizations. Interpersonal relations can vary from positive to negative and from personal to professional. Numerous outcomes can result from various forms of interpersonal relations, including different levels of need satisfaction, social support, synergy, performance, and conflict.

A group is two or more people who interact such that they influence one another. It is important to study groups because they can profoundly affect individual behavior and because the behavior of individuals in a group is key to the group's success or failure. The work group is the primary means by which managers coordinate individual behavior to achieve organizational goals. Individuals form or join groups because they expect to satisfy personal needs.

Groups may be differentiated on the bases of relative permanence and degree of formality. The three types of formal groups are command, task, and affinity groups. Friendship and interest groups are the two types of informal groups. Command groups are relatively permanent work groups established by the organization and usually are specified on an organization chart. Task groups, although also established by the organization, are relatively temporary and exist only until the specific task is accomplished. Affinity groups are formed by the organization, are composed of employees at the same level and doing similar jobs, and come together regularly to share information and discuss organizational issues. In friendship groups, the affiliation among members arises from close social relationships and the enjoyment that comes from being together. The common bond in interest groups is the activity in which the members engage.

Groups develop in four stages: mutual acceptance, communication and decision making, motivation and productivity, and control and organization. Although the stages are sequential, they may overlap. A group that does not fully develop within each stage will not fully mature as a group, resulting in lower group performance.

Four additional factors affect group performance: composition, size, norms, and cohesiveness. The homogeneity of the people in the group affects the interactions that occur and the productivity of the group. The effect of increasing the size of the group depends on the nature of the group's tasks and the people in the group. Norms help people function and relate to one another in predictable and efficient ways. Norms serve four purposes: They facilitate group survival, simplify and make more predictable the behaviors of group members, help the group avoid embarrassing situations, and express the central values of the group and identify the group to others.

To comprehend intergroup dynamics, we must understand the key characteristics of groups: that each group is unique, that the specific organizational setting influences the group, and that the group's task and setting have an effect on group behavior. Interactions among work groups involve some of the most complex relationships in organizations. They are based on five factors: location, resources, time and goal interdependence, task uncertainty, and task interdependence. The five bases of intergroup interactions determine the characteristics of the interactions among groups, including their frequency, how much information is exchanged, and what type of interaction occurs. Being physically near one another naturally increases groups' opportunities for interactions. If groups use the same or similar resources, or if one group can affect the availability of the resources needed by another group, the potential for frequent interactions increases. The nature of the tasks that groups perform—including time and goal orientation, the uncertainties of group tasks, and group interdependencies—influences how groups interact.

Group decision making involves problems as well as benefits. One possible problem is group polarization, the shift of members' attitudes and opinions to a more extreme position following group discussion. Another difficulty is groupthink, a mode of thinking in which the urge toward unanimity overrides the critical appraisal of alternatives. Yet another concern involves employee participation in decision making. The appropriate degree of participation depends on the characteristics of the situation.

DISCUSSION QUESTIONS

1. Why is it useful for a manager to understand group behavior? Why is it useful for an employee?
2. Our definition of a group is somewhat broad. Would you classify each of the following collections of people as a group? Explain why or why not.
   a. Seventy thousand people at a football game
   b. Students taking this course
   c. People in an elevator
   d. People on an escalator
   e. Employees of IBM
   f. Employees of your local college bookstore
3. List four groups to which you belong. Identify each as formal or informal.
4. Explain why each group you listed in question 3 formed. Why did you join each group? Why might others have decided to join each group?
5. In which stage of development is each of the four groups listed in question 3? Did any group move too quickly through any of the stages? Explain.
6. Analyze the composition of two of the groups to which you belong. How are they similar in composition? How do they differ?
7. Are any of the groups to which you belong too large or too small to get their work done? If so, what can the leader or the members do to alleviate the problem?
8. List two norms each for two of the groups to which you belong. How are these norms enforced?
9. Discuss the following statement: "Group cohesiveness is the good, warm feeling we get from working in groups and is something that all group leaders should strive to develop in the groups they lead."
10. Consider one of the groups to which you belong and describe the interactions that group has with another group.
11. Recall a situation in which you may have encountered or observed groupthink (either as member of a group or as a target or as a simple observer).

HOW DO YOU SEE IT?

The Scoop on Teamwork

"You really need everybody on the same page."

—LEE KNOWLTON, SR. VP, COLD STONE CREAMERY

According to Vice President of Marketing Kevin Myers, teamwork at Cold Stone Creamery, a chain of some 1,400 ice cream outlets, has a lot to do with something called "the customer pyramid": "Teamwork," he says, "is the only way to cut through … to the customer and work with all the elements of what we call the 'customer pyramid' to deliver innovation and happiness to our ice cream lovers." Generally speaking, of course, a strong customer orientation is hardly unusual in a business like Cold Stone, but what, exactly, is the "customer pyramid"—and why is teamwork so important in using it to reach the customer?

The "customer pyramid" is a tool for helping companies manage their existing customers. In the diagram below, for instance, we've divided a pyramid into four levels. At the peak level, we've identified our "top" customers (say, the 1 percent of our most valuable customers), and in the next three levels, we've designated our "large," "medium," and "small" customers, respectively. Most businesses find that the top three levels of the pyramid (*top-large-medium*) account roughly for only 20 percent of their customers. But here's the catch: That 20 percent usually accounts for about 80 percent of the businesses' revenues. Where would you focus your efforts to enhance customer value?

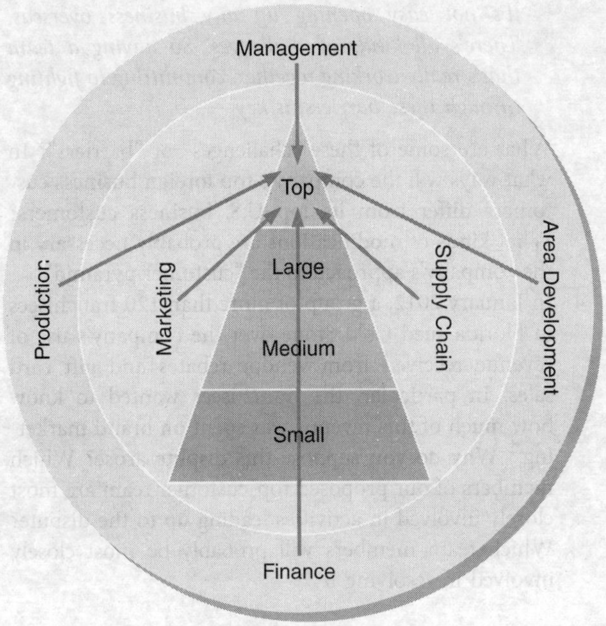

The Customer Pyramid

Myers gives us a broader look at the functions of the pyramid by putting it in context—namely, by suggesting how it's been configured to fit the organizational needs of Cold Stone Creamery. Note that Cold Stone is a *franchise* business and that Myers thus includes franchisees in his informal list of customers. "We work from the customer back," he explains. "When you work from the customer back in the franchise world, you've got the customer, you've got the crew, you have the franchisee, you have the area developer, you've got members of the creamery, and then you have marketing." This variety of people, divisions, and tasks, Myers emphasizes, is why "teamwork is critical at Cold Stone Creamery."

Ultimately, it's largely a matter of *focus* and *coordination*—of ensuring that a broad range of organizational efforts is devoted to reaching the same goal: namely, getting the most value out of your best customers. One way of looking at the application of teamwork to the customer pyramid at Cold Stone is shown in our diagram, where we have two concentric circles surrounding our pyramid. In the outer ring, we've included certain organizational *functions*—departments responsible for similar activities: *management*, *production*, *area development*, and *finance* (see Chapter 16). In the inner ring, we've included two more functions—*marketing* and *supply chain*. The difference between the inner and outer rings comes down simply to *closeness of contact*: People performing inner-ring functions work *more closely* with Cold Stone's top customers than do those performing outer-ring functions.

Finally, we've used arrows to underscore the fact that, at franchiser Cold Stone itself,* *one or more people in each of these departments are responsible for working with the customers at the top of the company's customer pyramid.* When we gather all of these people together, we have what we might call Cold Stone's *top-customer team*. (There would, of course, be *large-*, *medium-*, and *small-customer teams* as well.) Senior Vice President Lee Knowlton seconds Kevin Myers' statement about the importance of teamwork at Cold Stone when he says that "you really need everybody on the same page," but if that sounds a little vague—even like little more than an empty, overused figure of speech—remember that executives who use it typically mean business: They mean that everyone who's been assigned to a team is responsible for using his or her contacts with a customer or group of customers to achieve a specific set of goals that have been determined by top-level management.

What are those goals? The Cold Stone website asks us to

> *consider the first five words of our Mission Statement: "We will make people happy." … From the energetic Cold Stone Creamery crew singing your praises when they hear that "cha-ching" in the tip jar, to the laughter of a family enjoying an after-dinner treat—if it has to do with being happy, you'll find it at your local Cold Stone Creamery.*

"From an operational perspective," explains Knowlton, "you've got crew members that will focus on the operational component. And they've got to teamwork with … the entertainment director … along with those serving the ice cream." On a very basic level, the strategy sounds coherent and (relatively) easy to implement—cultivate teamwork in both corporate dealings with business customers and in serving in-store consumers.

But remember: Cold Stone is a *franchiser*, and its *franchisees*—the people who buy the right to use the Cold Stone brand and sell Cold Stone products—are independent businesspeople who run their own outlets. *They* hire the members of the teams who take care of business in "your local Cold Stone Creamery."

Our video informs us that in-store employees at a Cold Stone outlet perform one of two sets of activities (with a good deal of crossover):

1. "Task specialists" prepare and deliver the "innovative" products by which Cold Stone seeks to differentiate itself from its competitors.
2. Other employees perform "social/emotional roles," creating the atmosphere of "happiness" that Cold Stone considers critical to the customer experience.

That's why Lee Knowlton stresses that the function of teamwork at Cold Stone is to "deliver innovation and happiness to our ice cream lovers."

Thus, one goal of any Cold Stone customer-pyramid team is to work with the franchisee in developing the kind of team-oriented organization that will best succeed in meeting the franchiser-set goal of delivering both "innovative" products and a "happy" customer experience.

CASE QUESTIONS

1. Both the video and the case written to accompany it consistently use the terms *team* or *teamwork.* In Chapter 10, we use four criteria to characterize a team as

   a small number of people with complementary skills who are committed to a common purpose, common performance goals, and an approach for which they hold themselves mutually responsible.

   This chapter, however, focuses on *groups* rather than *teams* and characterizes a *formal group* as being "formed by an organization to do its work." Would *group* be a better term than *team* for characterizing the relevant activities at Cold Stone Creamery? If so, why? If not, why not? [*Hint:* Which of the four criteria for a *team* specified in Chapter 10 seems least applicable to the nature and function of a customer "team" at Cold Stone?]
2. In what ways might Cold Stone's top-customer team function as a *formal group*? As a *command group*? A *task group*? An *affinity group*? In what ways might it make use of the various forms of *group problem solving—brainstorming,* the *nominal group technique,* and the *Delphi technique*?
3. Cold Stone has been opening foreign outlets since 2007, when it launched its first store in Japan, and now boasts more than 1,500 locations in 16 countries.[†] "Internationally," says Lee Knowlton, "we do the same thing" when it comes to designing operations around teamwork. At the same time, he admits that

   it's not easy opening up any business overseas. There's all kinds of challenges. So having a team that's really working together, committing to fighting through these barriers, is key.

   What are some of these "challenges" or "barriers"? In what ways will the company's top foreign business customers differ from its top U.S. business customers? What kinds of modifications are probably necessary in the company's approach to the "customer pyramid"?
4. In January 2012, a group of more than 120 franchisees in Florida sued Cold Stone over the company's use of revenue received from vendor rebates and gift card sales. In particular, the franchisees wanted to know how much of this revenue was spent on brand marketing.[‡] Why do you suppose this dispute arose? Which members of our proposed top-customer team are most closely involved in activities leading up to the dispute? Which team members will probably be most closely involved in resolving it?

ADDITIONAL SOURCES

Cold Stone Creamery, "About Cold Stone Creamery," "The Cold Stone Culture," "The Cold Stone Story" (2012), www.coldstonecreamery.com on September 5, 2012; Jay Curry with Adam Curry, *CRM Concepts for Small and Medium Size Companies* (The Customer Marketing Institute, 2000), www.crmodyssey.com on September 12, 2012; Expert Program Management, "Customer Marketing and Relationship Management: Curry's Pyramid" (June 2011), www.expertprogrammanagement.com on September 12, 2012; Kahala Franchising LLC, "Brands," "Company Structure" (2012), www.kahalamgmt.com on September 15, 2012.

*In 2007, Cold Stone, which was founded in 1988, was sold to Kahala Franchising LLC, which holds 17 franchise brands with a total of some 4,000 outlets in nearly 20 countries. Like all companies in the Kahala portfolio, Cold Stone develops and markets its own brand and establishes its own operating system.

[†]Cold Stone Creamery, "Cold Stone Creamery Expands into Three New Countries in 2011," *Business Wire,* March 8, 2011 (press release), www.businesswire.com on September 5, 2012.

[‡]Sam Oches, "Cold Stone Franchisees File Lawsuit against Company," *QSR,* January 27, 2012, www.qsrmagazine.com on September 11, 2012.

EXPERIENCING ORGANIZATIONAL BEHAVIOR

Learning the Benefits of a Group

Purpose This exercise demonstrates the benefits a group can bring to a task.

Format You will be asked to do the same task both individually and as part of a group.

Procedure You will need a pen or pencil and full-size sheet of paper. Working alone, do the following:

Part 1

1. Write the letters of the alphabet in a vertical column down the left side of the paper: A–Z.
2. Your instructor will randomly select a sentence from any written document and read out loud the first twenty-six letters in that sentence. Write these letters in a vertical column immediately to the right of the alphabet column. Everyone should have an identical set of twenty-six two-letter combinations.
3. Working alone, think of a famous person whose initials correspond to each pair of letters, and write the name next to the letters—for example, "MT Mark Twain." You will have ten minutes. Only one name per set is allowed. One point is awarded for each legitimate name, so the maximum score is twenty-six points.
4. After time expires, exchange your paper with another member of the class and score each other's work. Disputes about the legitimacy of names will be settled by the instructor. Keep your score for use later in the exercise.

Part 2

Your instructor will divide the class into groups of five to ten people. All groups should have approximately the same number of members. Each group now follows the procedure given in Part 1. Again write the letters of the alphabet down the left side of the sheet of paper, this time in reverse order: Z–A. Your instructor will dictate a new set of letters for the second column. The time limit and scoring procedure are the same. The only difference is that the groups will generate the names.

Part 3

Each team identifies the group member who came up with the most names. The instructor places these "best" students into one group. Then all groups repeat Part 2, but this time the letters from the reading will be in the first column and the alphabet letters will be in the second column.

Part 4

Each team calculates the average individual score of its members on Part 1 and compares it with the team score from Parts 2 and 3, kept separately. Your instructor will put the average individual score and team scores from each part of each group on the board.

Follow-Up Questions

1. Are there differences in the average individual scores and the team scores? What are the reasons for the differences, if any?
2. Although the team scores in this exercise usually are higher than the average individual scores, under what conditions might individual averages exceed group scores?

Reference

Adapted from The Handbook for Group Facilitators, pp. 19–20, John E. Jones and J. William Pfeiffer (eds.), Copyright © 1979 Pfeiffer. Reproduced with permission of John Wiley & Sons, Inc.

BUILDING MANAGERIAL SKILLS

Exercise Overview A manager's interpersonal skills are her or his ability to understand how to motivate individuals and groups. Clearly, then, interpersonal skills play a major role in determining how well a manager can interact with others in a group setting. This exercise will allow you to practice your interpersonal skills in relation to just such a setting.

Exercise Background You have just been hired as project manager supervising a group of five employees at a remote job site. The company that hired you is fairly small and has few rules and regulations. Unfortunately, the lack of rules and regulations is creating a problem that you must now address.

Specifically, two of the group members are nonsmokers. They are becoming increasingly more vocal about the fact that two other members of the group smoke at work. These two workers feel that the secondary smoke in the workplace is endangering their health and want to establish a no-smoking policy like those of many large businesses today.

The two smokers, however, argue that since the firm did not have such a policy when they started working there, it would be unfair to impose such a policy now. One of them, in particular, says that he turned down an attractive job with another company because he wanted to work in a place where he could smoke.

The fifth worker is also a nonsmoker but says that she doesn't care if others smoke. Her husband smokes at home anyway, she says, so she is used to being around smokers. You suspect that if the two vocal nonsmokers are not appeased, they may leave. At the same time, you also think that the two smokers will leave if you mandate a no-smoking policy. All five workers do good work, and you do not want any of them to leave.

Exercise Task

With this information as context, do the following:

1. Explain the nature of the conflict that exists in this work group.
2. Develop a course of action for dealing with the situation.

Reference

Ricky W. Griffin, *Management*, 10th ed. (Cengage Learning, 2011), p. 605.

SELF-ASSESSMENT EXERCISE

Group Cohesiveness

Introduction You are probably a member of many different groups: study groups for school, work groups, friendship groups within a social club such as a fraternity or sorority, and interest groups. You probably have some feel for how tightly knit or cohesive each of those groups is. This exercise will help you diagnose the cohesiveness of one of those groups.

Instructions First, pick one of the small groups to which you belong for analysis. Be sure that it is a small group, say between three and eight people. Next, rate on the following scale of 1 (poorly) to 5 (very well) how well you feel the group works together.

1	2	3	4	5
Poorly	Not Very Well	About Average	Pretty Well	Very Well

How well does this group work together?

Now answer the following six questions about the group. Put a check in the blank next to the answer that best describes how you feel about each question.

1. How many of the people in your group are friendly toward each other?
   ___ (5) All of them
   ___ (4) Most of them
   ___ (3) Some of them
   ___ (2) A few of them
   ___ (1) None of them
2. How much trust is there among members of your group?
   ___ (1) Distrust
   ___ (2) Little trust
   ___ (3) Average trust
   ___ (4) Considerable trust
   ___ (5) A great deal of trust
3. How much loyalty and sense of belonging is there among group members?
   ___ (1) No group loyalty or sense of belonging
   ___ (2) A little loyalty and sense of belonging
   ___ (3) An average sense of belonging
   ___ (4) An above-average sense of belonging
   ___ (5) A strong sense of belonging
4. Do you feel that you are really a valuable part of your group?
   ___ (5) I am really a part of my group.
   ___ (4) I am included in most ways.
   ___ (3) I am included in some ways but not others.
   ___ (2) I am included in a few ways but not many.
   ___ (1) I do not feel I really belong.

5. How friendly are your fellow group members toward each other?

___ (1) Not friendly

___ (2) Somewhat friendly

___ (3) Friendly to an average degree

___ (4) Friendlier than average

___ (5) Very friendly

6. If you had a chance to work with a different group of people doing the same task, how would you feel about moving to another group?

___ (1) I would want very much to move.

___ (2) I would rather move than stay where I am.

___ (3) It would make no difference to me.

___ (4) I would rather stay where I am than move.

___ (5) I would want very much to stay where I am.

Now add up the numbers you chose for all six questions and divide by 6. Total from all six questions =/ 6 =. This is the group cohesiveness score for your group.

Compare this number with the one you checked on the scale at the beginning of this exercise about how well you feel this group works together. Are they about the same, or are they quite different? If they are about the same, then you have a pretty good feel for the group and how it works. If they are quite different, then you probably need to analyze what aspects of the group functioning you misunderstood. (This is only part of a much longer instrument; it has not been scientifically validated in this form and is to be used for class discussion purposes only.)

Reference: The six questions were taken from the Groupthink Assessment Inventory by John R. Montanari and Gregory Moorhead, "Development of the Groupthink Assessment Inventory," *Educational and Psychological Measurement*, 1999, vol. 39, pp. 209–219. Reprinted by permission of Gregory Moorhead.

CHAPTER 10

Using Teams in Organizations

Chapter Outline

- Differentiating Teams from Groups
- Benefits and Costs of Teams in Organizations
- Types of Teams
- Implementing Teams in Organizations
- Promoting Team Success

Chapter Learning Objectives

After studying this chapter, you should be able to:

1. Differentiate teams from groups.
2. Identify and discuss the benefits and costs of teams in organizations.
3. Identify and describe various types of teams.
4. Describe how organizations implement the use of teams.
5. Identify essential conditions for promoting team success.

Tracking Carbon Footprints Across Scientific Borders

"Teams now produce the exceptionally high-impact research, even where that distinction was once the domain of solo authors."

—*Study on "The Increasing Dominance of Teams in Production of Knowledge"*

If you're one of the world's 700 million richest people, you're probably a "high emitter" living a "carbon-intensive" lifestyle (at least statistically speaking). In plain English, because your lifestyle probably includes air travel, the use of a car, and a house to heat and cool, you're probably responsible for releasing more than your share of CO_2—carbon dioxide—into the earth's atmosphere.

"We estimate that … half the world's emissions come from just 700 million people," explains Shoibal Chakravarty, lead author of a 2009 study conducted by researchers at Princeton University. "It's mischievous," admits coauthor Robert Socolow, "but it's meant to be a logjam-breaking concept," and the proposals for

Vadym Zaitsev/Shutterstock

Decades of air and water pollution from factories like this have led to an increased awareness of the need to better protect our environment and to the emergence of teams like the Carbon Mitigation Initiative.

cutting CO_2 emissions offered by the Princeton team have been widely praised for the fairness that they inject into a debate that's been stalemated for 20 years.

The research team's report, entitled "Sharing Global CO_2 Emission Reductions Among One Billion High Emitters," appeared in the July 2009 *Proceedings of the National Academy of Sciences* under the names of six coauthors. Shoibal Chakravarty, a physicist specializing in CO_2 emissions, is a research associate at the Princeton Environmental Institute (PEI), an interdisciplinary center for environmental research and education. Also associated with PEI is Massimo Tavoni, an economist who studies international policies on climate change. Stephen Pacala, the director of PEI, is a professor of ecology and evolutionary biology who focuses on the interactions of climate and the global biosphere. Robert Socolow, a professor of mechanical and aerospace engineering, studies global carbon management. Ananth Chikkatur, of Harvard's Belfer Center for Science and International Affairs, is a physicist who specializes in energy policy and technology innovation. Heleen de Coninck, a chemist, works on international climate policy and technology at the Energy Research Centre of the Netherlands.

Needless to say, the carbon footprint team was a diverse group in terms of academic discipline (not to mention nationality). Its innovative approach to the problem of CO_2 emissions—one that shows that it's possible to cut emissions and reduce poverty at the same time—resulted from an approach to high-level scientific problem solving that's typically called *interdisciplinary* or *multidisciplinary research*. The global footprint study, says Pacala, "represents a collaboration among young people from disparate disciplines—physics, economics, political science.... The team," he stresses, "worked together to formulate a novel approach to a long-standing and intractable problem," and its interdisciplinary approach to that problem reflects the prevailing model for the study of today's most complex and daunting issues, such as AIDS, terrorism, and global climate change.

To determine the extent to which team-based research has supplanted individual research among academics, a group at Northwestern University examined nearly 20 million papers published over a period of five decades. They found that

> *teams increasingly dominate solo authors in the production of knowledge. Research is increasingly done in teams across virtually all fields. Teams typically produce more highly cited research than individuals do, and this advantage is increasing over time. Teams now also produce the exceptionally high-impact research, even where that distinction was once the domain of solo authors.*

Not surprisingly, the shift from the individual to the team-based model of research has been most significant in the sciences, where there's been, says the Northwestern study, "a substantial shift toward collective research." One reason for the shift, suggest the authors, may be "the increasing capital intensity of research" in laboratory sciences, where the growth of collaboration has been particularly striking.

The increasing tendency toward specialization may be another reason: As knowledge grows in a discipline, scientists tend to devote themselves to specialty areas, the discipline itself becomes fragmented into "finer divisions of labor," and studies of larger issues in the discipline thus require greater collaboration.

And what about collaboration that extends beyond the confines of Academia? As it happens, Robert Socolow and Stephen Pacala, in addition to working on the carbon footprint team, are codirectors of the Carbon Mitigation Initiative (CMI), a partnership among Princeton, Ford, and BP, the world's third-largest oil company. BP picks up 75 percent of the tab for research whose goal, according to CMI's mission statement, is "a compelling and sustainable solution of the carbon and climate change problem." CMI seeks "a novel synergy across fundamental science, technological development, and business principles that accelerates the pace of discovery," and collaboration is essential to its work because it crosses the borders between scientific, technological, and business interests.

It's also crucial because CMI's research is geared toward what Socolow calls a "whole-system" approach to the problem of reducing carbon emissions. "If BP takes a whole-system view of the problem," explains Socolow, "and as a supplier pays attention to the use of its products and finds ways of improving their efficiency during the use phase, that may be the most important thing this company can do over the next 10 years to save carbon."

A whole-system approach may include, for example, research into a process called *CCS*, for *carbon capture and storage*, which involves capturing CO_2 emissions from a major source, such as a power plant, and storing it somewhere away from the atmosphere, perhaps in a deep geological formation, such as an oil field or a seam of coal. Accordingly, CMI is divided into research groups, including the Capture Group, which works on technologies for capturing emissions from fossil fuels, and the Storage Group, which investigates the potential risks of injecting CO_2 underground. Taking advantage of the diverse perspectives provided by CMI, BP has been able to launch a CCS trial at a gas-development facility in Algeria.

What Do You Think?

1. What's your experience with teamwork? In what ways did it make the outcome of the project more successful than it would have been had you undertaken the project by yourself? Which aspects of the work process did you find unfamiliar and hardest to adapt to?
2. Do you see any potential problems with the combination of academic and business interests in such collaborations as CMI?

References: Robert Socolow, "7 Billion People, 30 Gigatons of CO_2, 1 Warming Planet: Population and Climate in the 21st Century," *Discover*, November 18, 2011, http://blogs.discovermagazine.com on June 5, 2012; Douglas Fischer, "Solving the Climate Dilemma One Billion Emitters at a Time," *Daily Climate*, July 6, 2009, wwwp.thedailygreen.org on June 5, 2012; Kitta McPherson, "New Princeton Method May Help Allocate Carbon Emissions Responsibility among Nations," *News at Princeton*, July 6, 2009, www.princeton.edu on June 5, 2012; Shoibal Chakravarty et al., "Sharing

Global CO_2 Emission Reductions among One Billion High Emitters," *Proceedings of the National Academy of Sciences*, vol. 106 (July 2009), www.pnas.org on June 5, 2012; Stefan Wuchty et al., "The Increasing Dominance of Teams in Production of Knowledge," *Sciencexpress*, April 12, 2009, www.kellogg.northwestern.edu on April 30, 2011; Carbon Mitigation Initiative, "About the Carbon Mitigation Initiative," Princeton University, May 23, 2012, http://cmi.princeton.edu on June 5, 2012; Carbon Mitigation Initiative, "Eleventh Annual Report Executive Summary," Princeton University, March 21, 2012, http://cmi.princeton.edu on June 5, 2012.

Teams are an integral part of the management process in many organizations today. But the notion of using teams as a way of organizing work is not new. Neither is it an American or Japanese innovation. Indeed, one of the earliest uses and analyses of teams was the work of the Tavistock Institute in the late 1940s in the United Kingdom.[1] Major companies such as Hewlett-Packard, Xerox, Procter & Gamble, General Motors, and General Mills have been using teams as a primary means of accomplishing tasks for many years. The popular business press, such as *Fortune*, *Business Week*, *Forbes*, and the *Wall Street Journal*, regularly reports on the use of teams in businesses around the world. The use of teams is not a fad of the month or some new way to manipulate workers into producing more at their own expense to enrich owners. Managers and experts agree that using teams can be among the best ways to organize and manage successfully in the twenty-first century.

This chapter presents a summary of many of the current issues involving teams in organizations. First, we define what "team" means and differentiate teams from normal work groups. We then discuss the rationale for using teams, including both the benefits and the costs. Next, we describe six types of teams in use in organizations today. Then we present the steps involved in implementing teams. Finally, we take a brief look at three conditions that are essential for team success.

DIFFERENTIATING TEAMS FROM GROUPS

Teams have been used, written about, and studied under many names and organizational programs: self-directed teams, self-managing teams, autonomous work groups, participative management, and many other labels. Groups and teams are not exactly the same thing, however, although the two words are often used interchangeably in popular usage. A brief look at a dictionary shows that "group" usually refers to an assemblage of people or objects gathered together whereas "team" usually refers to people or animals organized to work together. Thus, a "team" places more emphasis on concerted action than a "group" does. In common, everyday usage, however, terms such as "committee," "group," "team," and "task force" are often used interchangeably.

In organizations, teams and groups may also be quite different. As we noted in Chapter 9, a group is two or more persons who interact with one another such that each person influences and is influenced by each other person. We specifically noted that individuals interacting and influencing each other need not have a common goal. The collection of people who happen to report to the same supervisor or manager in an organization can be called a "work group." Group members may be satisfying their own needs in the group and have little concern for a common objective. This is where a team and a group differ. In a team, all team members are committed to a common goal.

> A **team** is a small number of people with complementary skills who are committed to a common purpose, common performance goals, and an approach for which they hold themselves mutually accountable.

We could therefore simply say that a team is a group with a common goal. But teams differ from groups in other ways, too, and most experts are a bit more specific in defining teams. A more complete definition is "A **team** is a small number of people with complementary skills who are committed to a common purpose, performance goals, and approach for which they hold themselves mutually accountable."[2] Several facets of this definition warrant further explanation. A team typically includes few people because the interaction and influence processes needed for the team to function can only occur when the number of members is small. When many people are involved, they have difficulty interacting and influencing each other, utilizing their complementary skills, meeting goals, and holding themselves accountable. Regardless of the name, by our definition, mature, fully developed teams are self-directing, self-managing, and autonomous. If they are not, then someone from outside the group must be giving directions, so the group cannot be considered a true team.[3]

Teams include people with a mix of skills appropriate to the tasks to be done. Three types of skills are usually required in a team. First, the team needs to have members with the technical or functional skills to do the jobs. Some types of engineering, scientific, technological, legal, or business skills may be necessary. Second, some team members need to have problem-solving and decision-making skills to help the team identify problems, determine priorities, evaluate alternatives, analyze trade-offs, and make decisions about the direction of the team. Third, members need interpersonal skills to manage communication flow, resolve conflict, direct questions and discussion, provide support, and recognize the interests of all members of the team. Not all members will have all of the required skills, especially when the team first convenes; different members will have different skills. However, as the team grows, develops, and matures, team members will come to have more of the necessary skills.[4]

Having a common purpose and common performance goals sets the tone and direction of the team. A team comes together to take action to pursue a goal, unlike a work group, in which members merely report to the same supervisor or work in the same department. The purpose becomes the focus of the team, which makes all decisions and takes all actions in pursuit of the goal. Teams often spend days or weeks establishing the reason for their existence, an activity that builds strong identification and fosters commitment to the team. This process also helps team members develop trust in one another.[5] Usually, the defining purpose comes first, followed by development of specific performance goals.

For example, a team of local citizens, teachers, and parents may come together for the purpose of making the local schools the best in the state. The team then establishes specific performance goals to serve as guides for decision making, to maintain the focus on action, to differentiate this team from other groups who may want to improve schools, and to challenge people to commit themselves to the team. One study looked at more than thirty teams and found that demanding, high-performance goals often challenge members to create a real team—as opposed to being merely a group—because when goals are truly demanding, members must pull together, find resources within themselves, develop and use the appropriate skills, and take a common approach to reach the goals.[6]

Agreeing on a common approach is especially important for teams because it is often the approach that differentiates one team from others. The team's approach usually covers how work will be done, social norms regarding dress, attendance at meetings, tardiness, norms of fairness and ethical behavior, and what will and will not be included in the team activities.

Finally, the definition states that teams hold themselves mutually accountable for results—rather than merely meeting a manager's demands for results, as in the traditional approach. If the members translate accountability to an external manager into internal, or mutual, accountability, the group moves toward acting like a team. Mutual accountability is essentially a promise that members make to each other to do everything possible to achieve their goals, and it requires the commitment and trust of all members. It is the promise of each member—to hold herself or himself accountable for the team's goals—that earns each individual the right to express her or his views and expect them to get a fair and constructive hearing. With this promise, members maintain and strengthen the trust necessary for the team to succeed. The clearly stated high-performance goals and the common approach serve as the standards to which the team holds itself. Because teams are mutually accountable

Teams are becoming increasingly common in organizations today. This team, for example, is developing a new ad campaign for a client. Two members of the team have expertise in design layout, another in media, and the other in the product market itself. By pooling their knowledge and working together they can approach the new ad campaign from an integrated and comprehensive perspective.

for meeting performance goals, two other differences between groups and teams become important. These are job categories and authority.

Job categories for conventional groups are usually described in terms of highly specialized jobs that require minimal training and moderate effort. Tens or even hundreds of people may have similar job descriptions and see little relationship between their effort and the end result or finished product. In teams, on the other hand, members have many different skills that fit into one or two broad job categories. Neither workers nor management worries about who does what job as long as the team puts out the finished product or service and meets its performance goals.[7]

In terms of authority, in conventional work groups the supervisor directly controls the daily activities of workers. In teams, however, the team discusses what activities need to be done and determines for itself who in the team has the necessary skills and who will do each task. The team, rather than the supervisor, makes the decisions. If a "supervisor" remains on the team, that person's role usually changes to that of coach, facilitator, or one who helps the team make decisions, rather than remaining the traditional role of decision maker and controller.

BENEFITS AND COSTS OF TEAMS IN ORGANIZATIONS

With the popularity of teams increasing so rapidly around the world, it is possible that some organizations are starting to use teams simply because everyone else is doing it—which is obviously the wrong reason. The reason for a company to create teams should be that teams make sense for that particular organization. The best reason to start teams in any organization is to recap the positive benefits that can result from a team-based

Table 10.1 Benefits of Teams in Organizations

TYPE OF BENEFIT	SPECIFIC BENEFIT	ORGANIZATIONAL EXAMPLES
ENHANCED PERFORMANCE	Increased productivity	Ampex: On-time customer delivery rose 98%.
	Improved quality	K Shoes: Rejects per million dropped from 5,000 to 250.
	Improved customer service	Eastman: Productivity rose 70%.
EMPLOYEE BENEFITS	Quality of work life	Milwaukee Mutual: Employee assistance program usage dropped to 40% below industry average.
	Lower stress	
REDUCED COSTS	Lower turnover, absenteeism	Kodak: Reduced turnover to one-half the industry average.
	Fewer injuries	Texas Instruments: Reduced costs more than 50%.
		Westinghouse: Costs down 60%.
ORGANIZATIONAL ENHANCEMENTS	Increased innovation, flexibility	IDS Mutual Fund Operations: Improved flexibility to handle fluctuations in market activity. Hewlett-Packard: Innovative order-processing system.

References: Adapted from Richard S. Wellins, William C. Byham, and George R. Dixon, *Inside Teams* (San Francisco: Jossey-Bass, 1994); Charles C. Manz and Henry P. Sims Jr., *Business Without Bosses* (New York: Wiley, 1993).

environment: enhanced performance, employee benefits, reduced costs, and organizational enhancements. Four categories of benefits and some examples are shown in Table 10.1.

Enhanced Performance

Enhanced performance can come in many forms, including improved productivity, quality, and customer service. Working in teams enables workers to avoid wasted effort, reduce errors, and react better to customers, resulting in more output for each unit of employee input. Such enhancements result from pooling of individual efforts in new ways and from continuously striving to improve for the benefit of the team.[8] For example, a General Electric plant in North Carolina experienced a 20 percent increase in productivity after team implementation.[9] K Shoes reported a 19 percent increase in productivity and significant reductions in rejects in the manufacturing process after it started using teams.

Reduced Costs

As empowered teams reduce scrap, make fewer errors, file fewer worker compensation claims, and reduce absenteeism and turnover, organizations based on teams are showing significant cost reductions. Team members feel that they have a stake in the outcomes, want to make contributions because they are valued, and are committed to their team and do not want to let it down. Wilson Sporting Goods reported saving $10 million per year for five years thanks to its teams. Colgate-Palmolive reported that technician turnover was extremely low—more than 90 percent of technicians were retained after five years—once it changed to a team-based approach.

Other Organizational Benefits

Other improvements in organizations that result from moving from a hierarchically based, directive culture to a team-based culture include increased innovation, creativity, and flexibility.[10] Use of teams can eliminate redundant layers of bureaucracy and flatten the hierarchy in large organizations. Employees feel closer and more in touch with top management. Employees who think their efforts are important are more likely to make significant contributions. In addition, the team environment constantly challenges teams to innovate and solve problems creatively. If the "same old way" does not work, empowered teams are free to throw it out and develop a new way. With increasing global competition, organizations must constantly adapt to keep abreast of changes. Teams provide the flexibility to react quickly. One of Motorola's earliest teams challenged a long-standing top-management policy regarding supplier inspections in an effort to reduce the cycle times and improve delivery of crucial parts.[11] After several attempts, management finally allowed the team to change the system and consequently reaped the expected benefits.

Sometimes, of course, organizational enhancements and adaptive measures don't work out as well as planned, and organizations find that they must "readapt."

Employee Benefits

Employees tend to benefit as much as organizations in a team environment. Much attention has been focused on the differences between the baby-boom generation and the "postboomers" in their attitudes toward work, its importance to their lives, and what they want from it. In general, younger workers tend to be less satisfied with their work and the organization, tend to have lower respect for authority and supervision, and tend to want more than a paycheck every week. Teams can provide the sense of self-control, human dignity, identification with work, and sense of self-worth and self-fulfillment for which current workers seem to strive. Rather than relying on the traditional, hierarchical, manager-based system, teams give employees the freedom to grow and to gain respect and dignity by managing themselves, making decisions about their work, and really making a difference in the world around them.[12] As a result, employees have a better work life, face less stress at work, and make less use of employee assistance programs.

Costs of Teams

The costs of teams are usually expressed in terms of the difficulty of changing to a team-based organization. Managers have expressed frustration and confusion about their new roles as coaches and facilitators, especially if they developed their managerial skills under the traditional hierarchical management philosophy. Some managers have felt as if they were working themselves out of a job as they turned over more and more of their directing duties to a team.[13]

Employees may also feel like losers during the change to a team culture. Some traditional staff groups, such as technical advisory staffs, may feel that their jobs are in jeopardy as teams do more and more of the technical work formerly done by technicians. New roles and pay scales may need to be developed for the technical staff in these situations. Often, technical people have been assigned to a team or a small group of teams and become members who fully participate in team activities.

Another cost associated with teams is the slowness of the process of full team development. As discussed elsewhere in this chapter, it takes a long time for teams to go through the full development cycle and become mature, efficient, and effective. If top management is impatient with the slow progress, teams may be disbanded, returning the organization to its original hierarchical form with significant losses for employees, managers, and the organization.

Probably the most dangerous cost is premature abandonment of the change to a team-based organization. If top management gets impatient with the team change process and cuts it short, never allowing teams to develop fully and realize benefits, all the hard work of employees, middle managers, and supervisors is lost. As a result, employee confidence in management in general and in the decision makers in particular may suffer for a long time.[14] The losses in productivity and efficiency will be very difficult to recoup. Management must therefore be fully committed before initiating a change to a team-based organization.

TYPES OF TEAMS

Many different types of teams exist in organizations today. Some evolved naturally in organizations that permit various types of participative and empowering management programs. Others have been formally created at the suggestion of enlightened management. One easy way to classify teams is by what they do; for example, some teams make or do things, some teams recommend things, and some teams run things. The most common types of teams are quality circles, work teams, and problem-solving teams; management teams are also quite common. These are summarized in Table 10.2.

Quality Circles

Quality circles are small groups of employees from the same work area who regularly meet to discuss and recommend solutions to workplace problems.

Quality circles (QCs) are small groups of employees from the same work area who meet regularly (usually weekly or monthly) to discuss and recommend solutions to workplace problems.[15] QCs were the first type of team created in U.S. organizations, becoming most popular during the 1980s in response to growing Japanese competition. QCs had some success in reducing rework and cutting defects on the shop floors of many manufacturing plants. Some attempts have been made to use QCs in offices and service operations, too. They exist alongside the traditional management structure and are relatively permanent. The role of QCs is to investigate a variety of quality problems that might come up in the workplace. They do not replace the work group or make decisions about how the work is done. The usage of QCs has declined in recent years, although many companies still have them.[16] QCs are teams that make recommendations.

Work teams include all the people working in an area, are relatively permanent, and do the daily work, making decisions regarding how the work of the team is done.

Work Teams

Work teams tend to be permanent, like QCs, but they are, rather than auxiliary committees, the teams that do the daily work.[17] The nurses, orderlies, and various technicians responsible for all patients on a floor or wing in a hospital comprise a work team. Rather than investigate a specific problem, evaluate alternatives, and recommend a solution or change, a work team does the actual daily work of the unit. The difference between a

Table 10.2 Types of Teams in Organizations

Quality Circles: small groups of employees from the same work area who meet regularly to discuss and recommend solutions to workplace problems
Work Teams: teams that do the daily work of an organization
Problem-Solving Teams: temporary teams established to tackle specific problems in the workplace
Management Teams: managers from different areas who coordinate work teams
Product Development Teams: combinations of work teams and problem-solving teams that create new designs for products or services
Virtual Teams: teams that work together from remote locations using digital technologies

SERVICE Teaming with Customers to Coproduce

©rangizzz/Shutterstock

Recall the last time you went to a doctor, a class, or even a discount store. As the patient, student, or customer, you had to do something to get the service expected. At the doctor's office, you had to tell the doctor what hurts to get treatment. In the classroom, you had to study the material to learn it. At the local Walmart, you had to grab a cart, fill it with things you selected, and find a way to pay. Sometimes you even take any of these one step further by going online to find a medical diagnosis for what hurts, using a learning tool available online to help learn, or going through the self-checkout at Walmart to save time. In other words, many times you have to do something yourself to coproduce your own service.

In order to get full value from nearly any service they desire, customers must typically do something as part of getting it. Whether this something is as simple as making a phone call to have someone come out to mow their lawn or something fairly complicated, such as going through an orthopedic rehab program for a hip replacement, the customer has to do something to make the experience happen. Service organizations need to plan for the role that customers must play to successfully obtain the service experience they want. This planning entails studying the tasks that the customers will have to perform and the knowledge, skills, and abilities (KSAs) that the customers will likely bring to the organization, as well as what motivates the customers to perform. In other words, the service organization has to figure out not only the KSAs required of its own employees but the KSAs required of its customers and what motivates them to perform their coproduction roles.

The idea of coproduction is one that service organizations have introduced to managers concerned with organizational behavior. As if it were not challenging enough to understand the behaviors, attitudes, motivations, and expectations of their own employees, service managers also have to understand the behaviors, attitude, motivations, and expectations of their customers. In other words, they must learn how to manage people who are paying them to be managed and expect to be managed well. Moreover, these managers are supervising employees whose job descriptions also include a responsibility to successfully manage coproducing customers. What makes this even more challenging is that each customer is uniquely qualified to coproduce the desired experience and will have different beliefs as to what the customer's role in coproducing the experience should be.

Managers therefore have several tasks to perform in the service organization that are not typically part of the jobs of their counterparts in manufacturing. With regard to their own employees, they must not only ensure that their workforce has the needed skills, abilities, and knowledge to do whatever tasks are part of their job responsibilities, but they must also be able to quickly forge relationships with customers, diagnose their KSAs, and then coach them to successfully perform their coproducing roles. Unlike their manufacturing counterparts, managers in service organizations must prepare employees not only to do their jobs but also to interact with customers to determine the best way to coproduce with them given each's unique needs, wants, expectations and capabilities to perform. Reading customer body language, listening to answers to questions about capabilities, and watching actual coproduction performances are skills that few employees come to the organization possessing. An even more difficult skill to find is the ability to not only do these well but also use the information to make good decisions about which customer needs what kind of coproduction assistance and then be able to provide that assistance to the customer in a way that the customer finds valuable. While a refrigerator doesn't care if it coproduces anything with your employees as it rolls down the assembly line, the next customer in line might care deeply about how and when to coproduce something in obtaining the desired service experience. Customers viewing a FASTPASS dispenser at Disney, attempting to check in at the airport, or renewing their prepaid cell phone plans online can be divided into those who know they can do what is required to coproduce, those who know they can't, and those who think they can but can't. The organization has to plan for these variations, train its employees to recognize the different types, and also train them on how to train customers to be successful.

Discussion Question: How is managing people making things different from managing people managing customer experiences?

traditional work group of nurses and the patient care team is that the latter has the authority to decide how the work is done, in what order, and by whom; the entire team is responsible for all patient care. When the team decides how the work is to be organized or done, it becomes a self-managing team, to which accrue all of the benefits described in this chapter. Work teams are teams that make or do things.

Problem-Solving Teams

Problem-solving teams are temporary teams established to attack specific problems in the workplace.

Problem-solving teams are temporary teams established to attack specific problems in the workplace. Teams can use any number of methods to solve the problem, as discussed in Chapter 9. After solving the problem, the team is usually disbanded, allowing members to return to their normal work. One survey found that 91 percent of U.S. companies utilize problem-solving teams regularly.[18] High-performing problem-solving teams are often cross-functional, meaning that team members come from many different functional areas. Crisis teams are problem-solving teams created only for the duration of an organizational crisis and are usually composed of people from many different areas. Problem-solving teams are teams that make recommendations for others to implement.

Management Teams

Management teams consist of managers from various areas; they coordinate work teams.

Management teams, consisting of managers from various areas, coordinate work teams. They are relatively permanent because their work does not end with the completion of a particular project or the resolution of a problem. Management teams must concentrate on the teams that have the most impact on overall corporate performance. The primary job of management teams is to coach and counsel other teams to be self-managing by making decisions within the team. The second most important task of management teams is to coordinate work between work teams that are interdependent in some manner. Digital Equipment Corporation abandoned its team matrix structure because the matrix of teams was not well organized and coordinated. Team members at all levels reported spending hours and hours in meetings trying to coordinate among teams, leaving too little time to get the real work done.[19]

Top-management teams may have special types of problems. First, the work of the top-management team may not be conducive to teamwork. Vice presidents or heads of divisions may be in charge of different sets of operations that are not related and do not need to be coordinated. Forcing that type of top-management group to be a team may be inappropriate. Second, top managers often have reached high levels in the organization because they have certain characteristics or abilities to get things done. For successful managers, altering their style, pooling resources, and sacrificing their independence and individuality can be very difficult.[20]

Product Development Teams

Product development teams are combinations of work teams and problem-solving teams that create new designs for products or services that will satisfy customer needs.

Product development teams are combinations of work teams and problem-solving teams that create new designs for products or services that will satisfy customer needs. They are similar to problem-solving teams because when the product is fully developed and in production, the team may be disbanded. As global competition and electronic information storage, processing, and retrieving capabilities increase, companies in almost every industry are struggling to cut product development times. The primary organizational means of accomplishing this important task is the "blue-ribbon" cross-functional team. Boeing's team that developed the 787 commercial airplane and the platform teams of Chrysler are typical examples. The rush to market with new designs can lead to numerous problems for product development teams. The primary problems of poor communication and poor coordination of typical product development processes in organizations can be rectified by creating self-managing, cross-functional product development teams.[21]

Virtual Teams

Virtual teams work together by computer and other electronic communication utilities; members move in and out of meetings and of the team itself as the situation dictates.

Virtual teams are teams that may never actually meet together in the same room—their activities take place on the computer via teleconferencing and other electronic information systems. Engineers in the United States can directly connect audibly and visually with counterparts all around the globe, sharing files via Internet, electronic mail, and other communication utilities. All participants can look at the same drawing, print, or specification, so decisions are made much faster. With electronic communication systems, team members can move in or out of a team or a team discussion as the issues warrant. The *Technology* box entitled "What to Do When the Surgeon Asks for a Joystick" discusses a special kind of virtual team that depends on cutting-edge technology.

TECHNOLOGY What to Do When the Surgeon Asks for a Joystick

©watcharakun/Shutterstock

In September 2001, surgeons removed the gall bladder of a 68-year-old woman in Strasbourg, France. Gall-bladder removal is a pretty routine procedure, the standard of care in the use of "minimally invasive surgery." The surgery is made possible by the laproscope—a thin, lighted tube that allows doctors to see what they're doing with remote-controlled instruments inserted into the patient's body through small incisions. The patient in Strasbourg left the hospital after 48 hours and had an uneventful recovery. The only noteworthy aspect of the operation was the fact that the surgeon wasn't in Strasbourg. In fact, he wasn't even in a hospital: He was in the U.S. offices of France Télécom in New York, 4,300 miles away. The operation was the first complete "remote surgery" performed on a human patient—the result of a hands-on collaboration (so to speak) among Dr. Jacques Marescaux, director of the European Institute of Telesurgery; Computer Motion Inc., a maker of medical devices located in California; France Télécom, the biggest telecommunications company in France; and surgeons at Strasbourg's Hôpitaux Universitaires.

> ***"Having a world expert from the United States looking over our shoulder ... greatly enhanced our comfort level and provided the best care for the patient."***
>
> —ARGENTINE SURGEON WHO PERFORMED TRANSCONTINENTAL TELESURGERY

This particular operation wasn't necessarily a qualitative leap forward from conventional laproscopic surgery. Surgeons had been performing computer-assisted procedures since the mid-1990s, though always in the same theaters with their patients. *Remote surgery*, or *telesurgery*, simply adds the technology that allows surgeons and patients to be in different places, and the breakthrough made in the 2001 New York–Strasbourg procedure was largely a matter of distance. In demonstrating "the feasibility of a transatlantic procedure," said Marescaux, his team had achieved merely "a richly symbolic milestone."

Even so, the benefits of remote surgery—say, having a world-class surgeon perform an operation on one patient in Europe in the morning and on another in South America in the afternoon—are fairly obvious. Some doctors also refer to a related benefit that Marescaux calls "telecompanionship"—the opportunity for surgeons to hone their skills and learn new ones by watching acknowledged experts at work.

In 2007, for example, Dr. Alex Gandsas, a surgeon at Sinai Hospital in Baltimore, used a telesurgery system to enable physicians in Argentina to perform a procedure for the treatment of obesity. Dr. Sergio Cantarelli had originally contacted Gandsas about the possibility of coming to the United States to learn the procedure. "He had never done this type of surgery before," recalls Gandsas, but "in practice, it wasn't possible for him to come over and train here." That's when

Gandsas got the idea of mentoring Cantarelli remotely, and for nearly three months, Cantarelli and a colleague, Dr. Gabriel Egidi, studied the procedure by participating in surgeries performed in the United States.

At the end of the training period, Cantarelli and Egidi performed the operation in Argentina by means of a "remote-presence robot" that allowed Gandsas, controlling a joystick in Baltimore, to monitor the procedure and mentor the surgeons in the actual operating room 5,400 miles away. "During the surgery," explains Gandsas, "the robot allowed me to zoom in on the patient and the monitors to assess the situation" while the Argentine doctors operated on the patient, a 39-year-old woman. Meanwhile, Cantarelli and Egidi, who had never met their American colleague personally, reported that the long-distance collaboration benefited everyone involved. "Having a world expert from the United States looking over our shoulder," said Cantarelli, "... greatly enhanced our comfort level and provided the best care for the patient."

References: J[acques] Marescaux, "Code Name: Lindbergh Operation," *WebSurg*, January 2002, www.websurg.com on June 5, 2012; Vicki Brower, "The Cutting Edge in Surgery," *EMBO Reports*, vol. 3 (2002), www.nature.com on June 5, 2012; Vitor da Silva et al., "Telementoring and Telesurgery: Future or Fiction?" *Robot Surgery*, ed. Seung Hyuk Baik (InTech, 2010), Chap. 3; "Remote Surgery between U.S. and Argentina," *The Medical News*, October 4, 2007, www.news-medical.net on June 5, 2012; Matthew Knight, "Virtual Surgery Becoming a Reality," *CNN.com*, October 18, 2007, http://edition.cnn.com on June 5, 2012; "Robot Teaches World's First Remote Surgery," *Physorg.com*, October 3, 2007, www.physorg.com on June 5, 2012.

IMPLEMENTING TEAMS IN ORGANIZATIONS

Implementing teams in organizations is not easy; it takes a lot of hard work, time, training, and patience. Changing from a traditional organizational structure to a team-based structure is much like other organizational changes (which we discuss in Chapter 19). It is really a complete cultural change for the organization. Typically, the organization is hierarchically designed to provide clear direction and control. However, many organizations need to be able to react quickly to a dynamic environment. Team procedures artificially imposed on existing processes are a recipe for disaster. In this section we present several essential elements peculiar to an organizational change to a team-based situation.

Planning the Change

The change to a team-based organization requires a lot of analysis and planning before it is implemented; the decision cannot be made overnight and then quickly implemented. It is such a drastic departure from the traditional hierarchy and authority-and-control orientation that significant planning, preparation, and training are prerequisites. The planning actually takes place in two phases, the first leading to the decision about whether to move to a team-based approach and the second while preparing for implementation.

Making the Decision Prior to making the decision, top management needs to establish the leadership for the change, develop a steering committee, conduct a feasibility study, and then make the go/no-go decision. Top management must be sure that the team culture is consistent with its strategy, as we discuss in Chapter 18. Quite often the leadership for the change is the chief executive officer, the chief operating officer, or another prominent person in top management. Regardless of the position, the person leading the change needs to (1) have a strong belief that employees want to be responsible for their own work, (2) be able to demonstrate the team philosophy, (3) articulate a coherent vision of the team environment, and (4) have the creativity and authority to overcome obstacles as they surface.

The leader of the change needs to put together a steering committee to help explore the organization's readiness for the team environment and lead it through the planning and preparation for the change. The steering committee can be of any workable size, from two to ten people who are influential and know the work and the organization. Members may include plant or division managers, union representatives, human resource department representatives, and operational-level employees. The work of the steering committee includes visits to sites that might be candidates for utilizing work teams, visits to currently successful work teams, data gathering and analysis, low-key discussions, and deliberating and deciding whether to use a consultant during the change process.

A feasibility study is a necessity before making the decision to use teams. The steering committee needs to know whether the work processes are conducive to team use, whether the employees are willing and able to work in a team environment, whether the managers in the unit to be converted are willing to learn and apply the hands-off managerial style necessary to make teams work, whether the organization's structure and culture are ready to accommodate a team-based organization, whether the market for the unit's products or services is growing or at least stable enough to absorb the increased productive capacity that teams will be putting out, and whether the community will support the transition teams. Without answers to these questions, management is merely guessing and hoping that teams will work—and may be destined for many surprises that could doom the effort.

After the leadership has been established, the steering committee has been set up, and a feasibility study has been conducted, the go/no-go decision can be made. The committee and top management will need to decide jointly to go ahead if conditions are right. On the other hand, if the feasibility study indicates that questions exist as to whether the organizational unit is ready, the committee can decide to postpone implementation while changes are made in personnel, organizational structure, and organizational policies, or until market conditions improve. The committee could also decide to implement training and acculturation for employees and managers in the unit in preparation for later implementation.

AP Photo/Roberto Borea

W. L. Gore, best known for its Gore-Tex fabric, uses a team organization approach to business. The firm has no job titles or fixed hierarchies, and workers (called "associates") collaborate in small teams. W. L Gore believes this model fuels creativity and innovation. Potential new employees are carefully screened to ensure they fit the Gore culture. Associates are responsible to one another for the success of their projects.

Preparing for Implementation

Once the decision is made to change to a team-based organization, much needs to be done before implementation can begin. Preparation consists of the following five steps: clarifying the mission, selecting the site for the first work teams, preparing the design team, planning the transfer of authority, and drafting the preliminary plan.

The mission statement is simply an expression of purpose that summarizes the long-range benefits the company hopes to gain by moving to a team environment. It must be consistent with the organization's strategy as it establishes a common set of assumptions for executives, middle managers, support staff, and the teams. In addition, it sets the parameters or boundaries within which the change will take place. It may identify which divisions or plants will be involved or what levels will be converted to teams. The mission statement attempts to stimulate and focus the energy of those people who need to be involved in the change. The mission can focus on continuous improvement, employee involvement, increasing performance, competition, customer satisfaction, and contributions to society. The steering committee should involve many people from many different areas to foster fuller involvement in the change.

Once the mission is established, the steering committee needs to decide where teams will be implemented first. Selection of the first site is crucial because it sets the tone for the success of the total program. The best initial site would be one that includes workers from multiple job categories, one where improving performance or reaching the targets set in the mission is feasible, and one where workers accept the idea of using teams. Also valuable are a tradition or history of success and a staff that is receptive to training, especially training in interpersonal skills. One manufacturing company based its choice of sites for initial teams not on criteria such as these but on the desire to reward the managers of successful divisions or to "fix" areas performing poorly. Team implementation in that company consequently was very slow and not very successful.[22] Initial sites must also have a local "champion" of the team concept.

Once the initial sites have been identified, the steering committee needs to set up the team that will design the other teams. The design team is a select group of employees, supervisors, and managers who will work out the staffing and operational details to make the teams perform well. The design team selects the initial team members, prepares members and managers for teams, changes work processes for use with the team design, and plans the transition from the current state to the new self-managed teams. The design team usually spends the first three months learning from the steering committee, visiting sites where teams are being used successfully, and spending a significant amount of time in classroom training. Considering the composition of the teams is one of the most important decisions the design team has to make.

Planning the transfer of authority from management to teams is the most important phase of planning the implementation. It is also the most distinctive and difficult part of moving to a team-based organization. It is difficult because it is so different from the traditional hierarchical organization management system. It is a gradual process, one that takes from two to five years in most situations. Teams must learn new skills and make new decisions related to their work, all of which takes time. It is, essentially, a cultural change for the organization.

The last stage of planning the implementation is to write the tentative plan for the initial work teams. The draft plan combines the work of the steering and design committees and becomes the primary working document that guides the continuing work of the design teams and the first work teams. The draft plan (1) recommends a process for selecting the people who will be on the first teams; (2) describes roles and responsibilities for all the people who will be affected (team members, team leaders, facilitators, support teams, managers, and top management); (3) explains what training the several groups will need; (4) identifies specifically which work processes will be involved; (5) describes what other organizational systems will be affected; and (6) lays out a preliminary master schedule for the next two to three years. Once the steering committee and top management approve the preliminary plan, the organization is ready to start the implementation.

Phases of Implementation

Implementation of self-managing work teams is a long and difficult process, often taking two to five years. During this period, the teams go through a number of phases

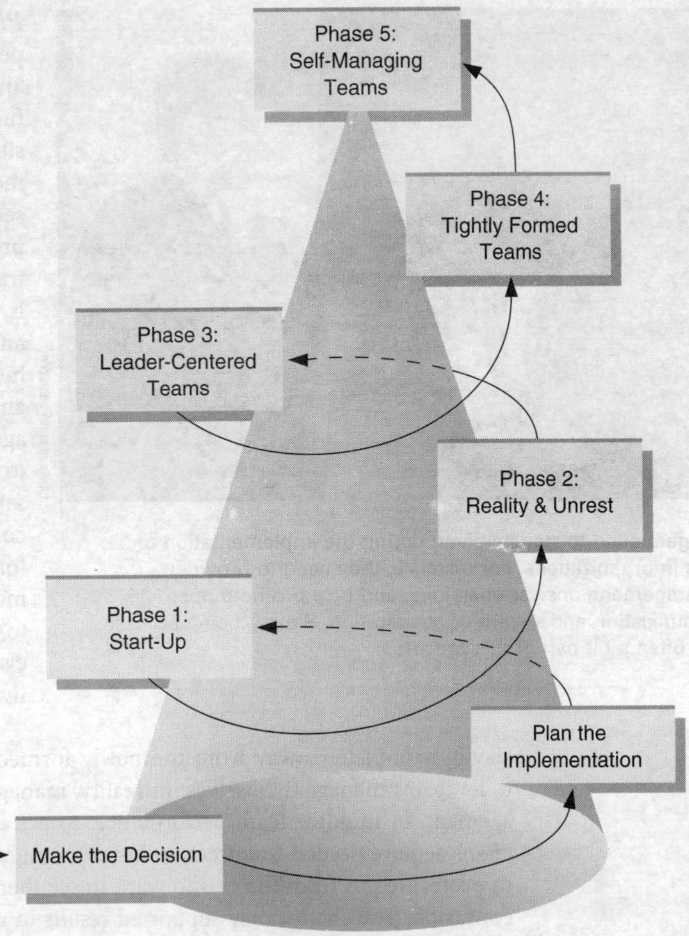

© Cengage Learning

FIGURE 10.1

Phases of Team Implementations

Implementation of teams in organizations is a long and arduous process. After the decision is made to initiate teams, the steering committee develops the plans for the design team, which plans the entire process. The goal is for teams to become self-managing. The time it takes for each stage varies with the organization.

(Figure 10.1); these phases are not, however, readily apparent at the times the team is going through them.

Phase 1: Start-Up In phase 1, team members are selected and prepared to work in teams so that the teams have the best possible chance of success. Much of the initial training is informational or "awareness" training that sends the message that top management is firmly committed to teams and that teams are not experimental. The steering committee usually starts the training at the top, and the training and information are passed down the chain to the team members. Training covers the rationale for moving to a team-based organization, how teams were selected, how they work, the roles and responsibilities of teams, compensation, and job security. In general, training covers the technical skills necessary to do the work of the team, the administrative skills necessary for the team to function within the organization, and the interpersonal skills necessary to work with people in the team and throughout the organization. Sometimes the interpersonal skills are important. Perhaps most important is establishing the idea that teams are not "unmanaged" but are "differently managed." The difference is that the new teams manage themselves. Team boundaries are also identified, and the preliminary plan is adjusted to fit the particular team situations. Employees typically feel that much is changing during the first few months, enthusiasm runs high, and the anticipation of employees is quite positive. Performance by teams increases at start-up because of this initial enthusiasm for the change.

Jupiterimages/Photos.com

Managers need to stay involved during the implementation of teams in organizations. For instance, they need to provide encouragement, answer questions, and help promote open communication and a spirit of cooperation. Simply being accessible is often a bit part of this process.

Phase 2: Reality and Unrest After perhaps six to nine months, team members and managers report frustration and confusion about the ambiguities of the new situation. For employees, unfamiliar tasks, more responsibility, and worry about job security replace hope for the opportunities presented by the new approach. All of the training and preparation, as important as it is, is never enough to prepare for the storm and backlash. Cummins Engine Company held numerous "prediction workshops" in an effort to prepare employees and managers for the difficulties that lay ahead, all to no avail. Its employees reported the same problems that employees of other companies did. The best advice is to perform phase 1 very well and then make managers very visible, continue to work to clarify the roles and responsibilities of everyone involved, and reinforce the positive behaviors that do occur.

Some managers make the mistake of staying completely away from the newly formed teams, thinking that the whole idea is to let teams manage themselves. In reality, managers need to be visible to provide encouragement, to monitor team performance, to act as intermediaries between teams, to help teams acquire needed resources, to foster the right type of communication, and sometimes to protect teams from those who want to see them fail. Managers, too, feel the unrest and confusion. The change they supported results in more work for them. In addition, there is the real threat, at least initially, that work will not get done, projects may not get finished, or orders will not get shipped on time and that they will be blamed for the problems.[23] Managers also report that they still have to intervene and solve problems for the teams because the teams do not know what they are doing.

Phase 3: Leader-Centered Teams As the discomfort and frustrations of the previous phase peak, teams usually long for a system that resembles the old manager-centered organizational structure (see Figure 10.1). However, members are learning about self-direction and leadership from within the team and usually start to focus on a single leader in the team. In addition, the team begins to think of itself as a unit as members learn to manage themselves. Managers begin to get a sense of the positive possibilities of organizing in teams and begin to withdraw slowly from the daily operation of the unit to begin focusing on standards, regulations, systems, and resources for the team.[24] This phase is not a setback to team development—although it may seem like one—because development of and reliance on one internal leader is a move away from focusing on the old hierarchy and traditional lines of authority.

The design and steering committees need to be sure that two things happen during this phase. First, they need to encourage the rise of strong internal team leaders. The new leaders can either be company appointed or team appointed. Top management sometimes prefers the additional control they get from appointing the team leaders, assuming that production will continue through the team transition. On the other hand, if the company-appointed leaders are the former managers, team members have trouble believing that anything has really changed. Team-appointed leaders can be a problem if the leaders are not trained properly and oriented toward team goals.

If the team-appointed leader is ineffective, the team usually recognizes the problem and makes the adjustments necessary to get the team back on track. Another possibility for team leadership is a rotating system in which the position changes every quarter, month, week, or even day. A rotating system fosters professional growth of all members of the team and reinforces the strength of the team's self-management.

The second important issue for this phase is to help each team develop its own sense of identity. Visits to observe mature teams in action can be a good step for newly formed teams. Recognizing teams and individuals for good performance is always powerful, especially when the teams choose the recipients. Continued training in problem-solving steps, tools, and techniques is imperative. Managers need to push as many problem-solving opportunities as possible down to the team level. Finally, as team identity develops, teams develop social activities and display T-shirts, team names, logos, and other items that show off their identity. All of these are a sure sign that the team is moving into phase 4.

Phase 4: Tightly Formed Teams In the fourth phase of team implementation, teams become tightly formed to the point that their internal focus can become detrimental to other teams and to the organization as a whole. Such teams are usually extremely confident of their ability to do everything. They are solving problems, managing their schedule and resources, and resolving internal conflicts. However, communication with external teams begins to diminish, the team covers up for underperforming members, and interteam rivalries can turn sour, leading to unhealthy competition.

To avoid the dangers of the intense team loyalty and isolation inherent in phase 4, managers need to make sure that teams continue to do the things that have enabled them to prosper thus far. First, teams need to keep the communication channels with other teams open through councils of rotating team representatives who meet regularly to discuss what works and what does not; teams who communicate and cooperate with other teams should be rewarded. At the Digital Equipment plant in Connecticut, team representatives meet weekly to share successes and failures so that all can avoid problems and improve the ways their teams operate.[25] Second, management needs to provide performance feedback through computer terminals in the work area that give up-to-date information on performance, or via regular feedback meetings. At TRW plants, management introduced peer performance appraisal at this stage of the team implementation process. It found that in phase 4, teams were ready to take on this administrative task but needed significant training in how to perform and communicate appraisals. Third, teams need to follow the previously developed plan to transfer authority and responsibility to the teams and to be sure that all team members have followed the plan to get training in all of the skills necessary to do the work of the team. By the end of phase 4, the team should be ready to take responsibility for managing itself.

Phase 5: Self-Managing Teams Phase 5 is the end result of the months or years of planning and implementation. Mature teams are meeting or exceeding their performance goals. Team members are taking responsibility for team-related leadership functions. Managers and supervisors have withdrawn from the daily operations and are planning and providing counseling for teams. Probably most important, mature teams are flexible—taking on new ideas for improvement; making changes as needed to membership, roles, and tasks; and doing whatever it takes to meet the strategic objectives of the organization. Although the teams are mature and functioning quite well, several things need to be done to keep them on track. First and foremost, individuals and teams need to continue their training in job skills and team and interpersonal skills. Second, support systems need to be constantly improved to facilitate team development and productivity. Third, teams always need to improve their internal customer and supplier relationships within the organization. Partnerships among teams throughout the organization can help the internal teams continue to meet the needs of external customers.

PROMOTING TEAM SUCCESS

This chapter has described the many benefits of teams and the process of changing to a team-based organization. Teams can be utilized in small and large organizations, on the shop floor and in offices, and in countries around the world. Teams must be initiated for performance-based business reasons, and proper planning and implementation strategies must be used. In this section we discuss three essential issues that cannot be overlooked as organizations move to a team-based setup.

Top-Management Support

The question of where to start in team implementation is really no issue at all. Change starts at the top in every successful team implementation. Top management has three important roles to play. First, top management must decide to go to a team-based organization for sound business performance–related reasons. A major cultural change cannot be made because it is the fad, because the boss went to a seminar on teams, or because a quick fix is needed. Second, top management is instrumental in communicating the reasons for the change to the rest of the organization. Third, top management

Polka Dot Images/Photos.com

Top management support is essential for successful implementation of work teams. Among other things, top managers need to stress that there are sound business reasons for the use of teams and be prepared for some setbacks during the transition to teams. This executive is meeting with her direct reports to explain the process through which their firm is going to move toward a team-based structure.

has to support the change effort during the difficult periods. As discussed previously, performance usually goes down in the early phases of team implementation. Top-management support may involve verbal encouragement of team members, but organizational support systems for the teams are also needed. Examples of support systems for teams include more efficient inventory and scheduling systems, better hiring and selection systems, improved information systems, and appropriate compensation systems.

Understanding Time Frames

Organizations often expect too much too soon when they implement teams. In fact, things often get worse before they get better.[26] Figure 10.2 shows how, shortly after implementation, team performance often declines and then rebounds to rise to the original levels and above. Management at Investors Diversified Services, a financial services firm in Minneapolis, Minnesota (and now a part of American Express), expected planning for team start-up to take three or four months. The actual planning took eight and a half months.[27] It often takes a year or more before performance levels return to at least their before-team levels. If teams are implemented without proper planning, their performance may never return to prior levels. The long lead time for improving performance can be discouraging to managers who reacted to the fad for teams and expected immediate returns.

The phases of implementation discussed in the previous sections correspond to key points on the team performance curve. At the start-up, performance is at its normal levels, although sometimes the anticipation of, and enthusiasm for, teams cause a slight increase in performance. In phase 2, reality and unrest, teams are often confused and frustrated with the training and lack of direction from top management, to the point that actual performance may decline. In phase 3, leader-centered teams become more comfortable with the team idea and refocus on the work of the team. They once again have established leadership, although it is with an internal leader rather than an external manager or supervisor. Thus, their performance usually returns to at least their former levels. In phase 4, teams are beginning to experience the real potential of teamwork and

FIGURE 10.2

Performance and Implementation of Teams

The team performance curve shows that performance initially drops as reality sets in, and team members experience frustration and unrest. However, performance soon increases and rises to record levels as the teams mature and become self-managing.

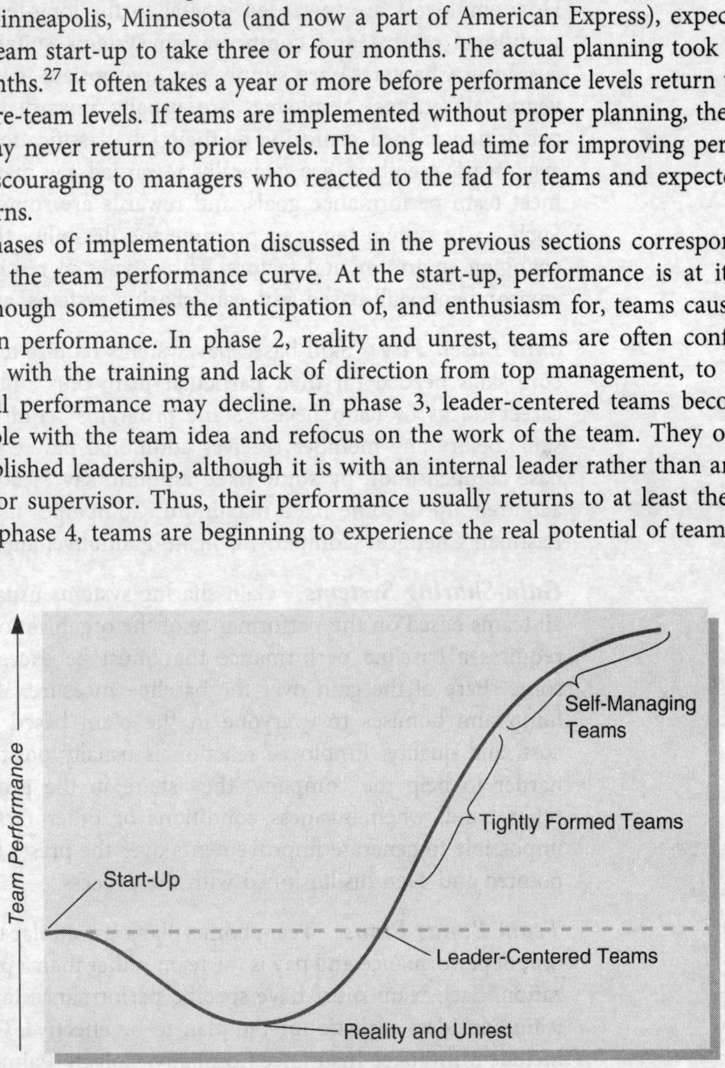

Reference: Reprinted by permission of Harvard Business School Press. From The Wisdom of Teams: Creating the High Performance Organization by Jon R. Katzenbach and Douglas K. Smith. Boston, MA, 1993, p. 84. Copyright by the Harvard Business School Publishing Corporation; all rights reserved.

are producing above their prior levels. Finally, in phase 5, self-managing teams are mature, flexible, and usually setting new records for performance.

Organizations changing to a team-based arrangement need to recognize the time and effort involved in making such a change. Hopes for immediate, positive results can lead to disappointment. The most rapid increases in performance occur between the leader-centered phase and the team-centered phase because teams have managed to get past the difficult, low-performance stages, have had a lot of training, and are ready to utilize their independence and freedom to make decisions about their own work. Team members are deeply committed to each other and to the success of the team. In phase 5, management needs to make sure that teams are focused on the strategic goals of the organization.

Changing Organizational Reward

How employees are rewarded is vital to the long-term success of an organization. The traditional reward and compensation systems suitable for individual motivation (discussed in Chapter 4) are simply not appropriate in a team-based organization. In conventional settings, employees are usually rewarded on the basis of their individual performance, their seniority, or their job classification. In a team-based situation, however, team members are generally rewarded for mastering a range of skills needed to meet team performance goals, and rewards are sometimes based on team performance. Such a pay system tends to promote the flexibility that teams need to be responsive to changing environmental factors. Three types of reward systems are common in a team environment: skill-based pay, gain-sharing systems, and team bonus plans.

Skill-Based Pay Skill-based pay systems require team members to acquire a set of the core skills needed for their particular team plus additional special skills, depending on career tracks or team needs. Some programs require all members to acquire the core skills before any member receives additional pay. Usually employees can increase their base compensation by some fixed amount, say $0.50 per hour for each additional skill acquired, up to some fixed maximum. Companies using skill-based pay systems include Eastman Chemical Company, Colgate-Palmolive, and Pfizer.

Gain-Sharing Systems Gain-sharing systems usually reward all team members from all teams based on the performance of the organization, division, or plant. Such a system requires a baseline performance that must be exceeded for team members to receive some share of the gain over the baseline measure. Westinghouse gives equal one-time, lump-sum bonuses to everyone in the plant based on improvements in productivity, cost, and quality. Employee reaction is usually positive because when employees work harder to help the company, they share in the profits they helped generate. On the other hand, when business conditions or other factors beyond their control make it impossible to generate improvements over the preset baseline, employees may feel disappointed and even disillusioned with the process.

Team Bonus Plans Team bonus plans are similar to gain-sharing plans except that the unit of performance and pay is the team rather than a plant, a division, or the entire organization. Each team must have specific performance targets or baseline measures that the team considers realistic for the plan to be effective. Companies using team bonus plans include Milwaukee Insurance Company, Colgate-Palmolive, and Harris Corporation.

Changes in an organizational compensation system can be traumatic and threatening to most employees. However, matching the reward system to the way that work is organized and accomplished can have very positive benefits. The three types of team-based reward systems presented can be used in isolation for simplicity or in some combination to address different types of issues for each organization.

SYNOPSIS

Groups and teams are not the same. A team is a small number of people with complementary skills who are committed to a common purpose, common performance goals, and a common approach for which they hold themselves mutually accountable. Teams differ from traditional work groups in their job categories and authority.

Teams are used because they make sense for a specific organization. Organizational benefits include enhanced performance, reduced costs, and employee benefits, among others.

Many different types of teams exist in organizations. Quality circles are small groups of employees from the same work area who meet regularly to discuss and recommend solutions to workplace problems. Work teams perform the daily operations of the organization and make decisions about how to do the work. Problem-solving teams are temporarily established to solve a particular problem. Management teams consist of managers from various areas; these teams are relatively permanent and coach and counsel the new teams. Product development teams are teams assigned the task of developing a new product or service for the organization. Members of virtual teams usually meet via teleconferencing, may never actually sit in the same room together, and often have a fluid membership.

Planning the change entails all the activities leading to the decision to utilize teams and then preparing the organization for the initiation of teams. Essential steps include establishing leadership for the change, creating a steering committee, conducting a feasibility study, and making the go/no-go decision. After the decision to utilize teams has been made, preparations include clarifying the mission of the change, selecting the site for the first teams, preparing the design team, planning the transfer of authority, and drafting the preliminary plan.

Implementation includes five phases: start-up, reality and unrest, leader-centered teams, tightly formed teams, and self-managing teams. Implementation of teams is really a cultural change for the organization.

For teams to succeed, the change must start with top management, who must decide why the change is needed, communicate the need for the change, and support the change. Management must not expect too much too soon because team performance tends to decrease before it returns to prior levels and then increases to record levels. Reward systems may also need to be changed.

DISCUSSION QUESTIONS

1. Why is it important to make a distinction between "group" and "team"? What kinds of behaviors might be different in these assemblages?
2. How are other organizational characteristics different for a team-based organization?
3. Some say that changing to a team-based arrangement "just makes sense" for organizations. What are the four primary reasons why this might be so?
4. If employees are happy working in the traditional boss-hierarchical organization, why should a manager even consider changing to a team-based organization?
5. How are the six types of teams related to each other?
6. Explain the circumstances under which a cross-functional team is useful in organizations.
7. Which type of team is the most common in organizations? Why?
8. Why is planning the change important in the implementation process?
9. What can happen if your organization prematurely starts building a team-based organization by clarifying the mission and then selecting the site for the first work teams?
10. What are two of the most important issues facing team-based organizations?

HOW DO YOU SEE IT?

Position Players

"We just kept adding people that are better than us."

—MIKEY LEBLANC, COFOUNDER OF HOLDEN OUTERWEAR

We introduced Holden Outerwear in our *Video Case* for Chapter 2, where we focused on product design and global distribution.* The video introduced cofounder Mikey LeBlanc, who launched Holden in 2002 with partner Scott Zergebel. The founders hired a CEO, former Adidas executive Ben Pruess, in 2011, and LeBlanc currently serves as "marketing director." Zergebel, who doesn't appear in the first video but who does make an uncredited cameo in this one, is identified as "creative director."

This video is all about the approach to *teamwork* among Holden managers, and LeBlanc gets things started with the inevitable sports analogy. His sentiments are pretty much in line with those of most contemporary managers:

> *You can watch an NBA quote/unquote team that's got this superstar that totally just wants to be the stud and doesn't work well with anybody else. Or you can watch a great team that really works together, and that's what we're trying to have here at Holden.*

At last count, Holden, which outsources manufacturing and distribution, had only ten employees, and the payroll had climbed to double digits because LeBlanc (who was a professional snowboarder) and Zergebel (a clothing designer) needed a broader spectrum of talents: "We just kept adding people that were better than us," explains LeBlanc, who admits that "we just started using the word *team* in the last six months because our sales manager started using it. I kind of like the word. So, yeah, we're totally team players. You have to be," he adds. "If you're fighting with anybody internally, it means that things aren't happening."

How does LeBlanc know a team player when he's working with one? It's not hard, he suggests, when there are so few people in the office and each has a definitive area of responsibility, such as "marketing director," "design director," "sales manager," "director of European distribution," and "general counsel." "It's important to have a team," says LeBlanc, because employees need to know "*that's their job*: It's a real thing that needs to be handled." For Nikki Brush, whose official title is Design and Development Manager, what LeBlanc is getting at is more than just job *responsibility* (the obligation to do something): It's also a matter of job *ownership*, which means, among other things, a willingness to understand what an organization does, to develop knowledge and skills that will contribute to its success, and to perform one's job as if it were critical to that success.

Brush remembers exercises in college which tended to *group* people to complete a project but failed in getting them to act as a *team*: "One person," she recalls, "would make the pattern; one person would then have to cut out the fabric; then the next person would have to sew it. And I just never really felt like anyone else really felt responsible or took ownership of the project." After being laid off from her previous job, Brush did design work as a *freelancer*—a self-employed worker with no long-term commitment to any given employer—and she found the experience frustrating because it made job ownership virtually impossible and task performance more difficult: "Freelance is interesting," she says, "because you're not invested in the company. You don't know 100 percent where they've been and where they're going. As a freelancer … they don't divulge that information to you all the time."

LeBlanc reports that he and Zergebel decided to let Brush "design some pieces and worked with her through the process, and she ended up designing my favorite piece in the line." (What are now called "Nikki Pants" simulate embossed leather and feature special Swiss-made zippers.) At the time, Holden didn't outsource very many operations because, as LeBlanc puts it, "we thought we just wanted to do it all ourselves." As the company grew, however, "we came to the realization that we're going to need more employees that are talented." Brush did freelance work with Zergebel for about nine months, "and I really think we just clicked as far as what our design aesthetic is, and our goals."

Brush was added to the select Holden team in November 2010. "Bringing people in is always scary," says LeBlanc, who seems to be as much concerned about access to trade secrets as about person-job and player-team fit. "I mean, you're opening up your secrets," he explains. "You're opening up the way you do your process." In Brush's case, she'd already worked so closely on product designs that "we had to get her back in here after the freelance work and just really dig deeper and find out who she was as a person and whether she could work well with the team."

For her part, Brush wanted to join the team, but she didn't want to have to play out of position. In fact, she says that the original job she was offered wasn't necessarily "the best fit. I didn't want to go somewhere where I also didn't feel it was a good fit, and I wanted to feel like they wanted me." Some tweaking was done to create the position of Design and Development Manager, and Brush is happy about the outcome. After all, she says, "I think that what I bring is my strong attention to detail as far as both development and design go."

CASE QUESTIONS

1. Think about Brush's recollection of a group-based project in college. Explain why she's essentially accurate in characterizing the participants as a *group* rather than a *team*. Now assume that you're a college teacher (you can teach any subject you want). Think up a project for your class that asks students to work together, being sure that you provide certain guidelines that require them to work as *teams*.
2. However informal it may be in practice, in what ways does Holden appear to have a *hierarchical structure*—one in which employees occupy different *levels* within the organization? In what ways does that structure appear to affect its *culture*? In what specific ways does its *team-based culture* appear to override or offset Holden's hierarchical structure/culture?
3. What sort of *organizational enhancements* does Holden try to gain from fostering a team-based culture? **Judging from the video**, describe any apparent enhancements in *innovation*, *creativity*, and *flexibility*.
4. Among *essential team issues*, the chapter discusses the importance of *top management* in implementing a team-based structure/culture. In what ways has top management at Holden played one of the three key roles in implementing such a structure/culture—namely, basing the decision to shift to a team-based orientation on sound business-related reasons?
5. On the one hand, *job ownership* at Holden requires employees to devote their skills and energies to the performance of a specific series of tasks (those of "marketing manager," those of "designer/developer," and so forth). On the other hand, the company's *team-based structure/culture* requires employees to contribute their efforts to organization-wide performance. This would appear to be a *paradox*—a seemingly contradictory state of affairs which can nevertheless prevail under the right circumstances. In what ways does Holden appear to resolve the contradictory elements of this paradox so that they can simultaneously contribute to organizational performance?

ADDITIONAL SOURCES

Holden Outerwear, "Holden History" (2012), www.holdenouterwear.com on June 5, 2012; Allan Brettman, "Holden Outerwear Exits Portland in Search of New Markets, Lower Expenses," *OregonLive.com*, May 2, 2012, http://blog.oregonlive.com on June 5, 2012; Scott Zergebel, "My Inspiration Comes from Trying to Live My Life to the Fullest," *SIA's Latest*," March 28, 2012, www.snowsports.com on June 5, 2012; Mike Lewis, "Holden Announces Three Major New Hires," *Transworld Business*, September 28, 2010, http://business.transworld.net on June 5, 2012; "Holden Gets Sporty," *YoBeat.com*, January 4, 2012, www.yobeat.com on June 5, 2012.

*Check the Chapter 2 *Video Case* to refresh your memory about Holden's product line, operations, and recent initiatives.

EXPERIENCING ORGANIZATIONAL BEHAVIOR

Team Problem Solving with the Fishbone Diagram

Introduction The use of groups and teams is becoming more common in organizations throughout the world. The following exercise teaches you a problem-solving technique that can be used effectively by teams.

Instruction Read "The Fishbone Instructions" that follow. Working in a small group, choose one of the topics for analysis. (Alternatively, your professor may assign topics to groups. You can also write your own topic, but be sure that every student has some experience and understanding of the topic.) Perform the analysis and present your findings to the class.

Topics

a. Student parking on campus is inadequate.
b. Required courses are not offered at convenient, varied, or flexible times.
c. There are too few business elective courses offered.
d. There are not enough sections of required courses to meet student demand.
e. Some business courses have too many students in them to optimize leaning.
f. Faculty are not available for student assistance and office hours.
g. Students do not receive adequate counseling on academic matters and scheduling.

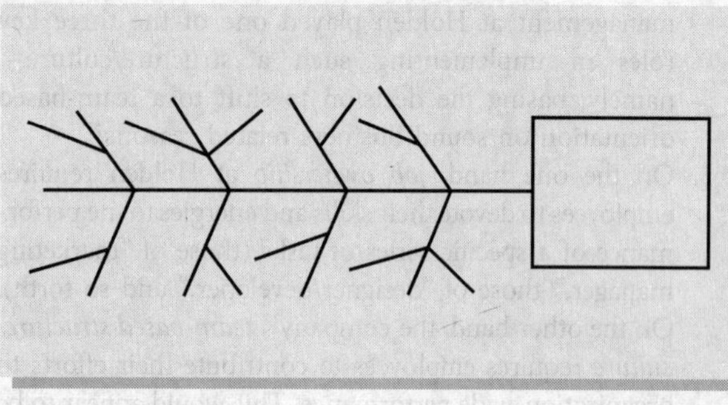

The structure of your completed fishbone diagram will look something like this.

The Fishbone Instructions

1. Write the problem in the "head" of the fish.
2. Brainstorm the major causes of the problem and list them on the fish "bones."
3. Analyze each main cause and write in contributing factors on bone sub-branches.
4. Reach consensus on the one or two most important causes of the problem.
5. Explore ways to correct or remove the major cause(s).

Reference

Adapted from Linda Morable, *Exercises in Management*, Houghton Mifflin Company, Boston, Copyright © 2005, to accompany *Management*, 8th edition, by Ricky Griffin, Houghton Mifflin Company, Boston, Copyright © 2005.

BUILDING MANAGERIAL SKILLS

Exercise Overview Groups and teams are becoming ever more important in organizations. This exercise will allow you to practice your conceptual skills as they apply to work teams in organizations.

Exercise Background A variety of highly effective groups exists outside the boundaries of typical business organizations. For example, each of the following represents a team:

1. A basketball team
2. An elite military squadron
3. A government policy group such as the presidential cabinet
4. A student planning committee

Exercise Task

1. Identify an example of a real team, such as one just listed. Choose one team (1) that is not part of a normal business and (2) that you can argue is highly effective.
2. Determine the reasons for the team's effectiveness.
3. Determine how a manager could learn from this particular team and use its success determinants in a business setting.

SELF-ASSESSMENT EXERCISE

How Well Do You Add Up as a Team Member?

Think about a group or team that you've been a part of. Answer the following questions about the nature of your participation by selecting the option that's most accurate. There are no right or wrong answers. You may have to be "hypothetical" in responding to a few items, and in some cases you might have to rely on "composite" answers reflecting your experience in more than one group or teamwork setting.

1. I offer information and opinions …
   a. Very frequently
   b. Frequently
   c. Sometimes
   d. Rarely
   e. Never
2. I summarize what's happening in the group …
   a. Very frequently
   b. Frequently
   c. Sometimes
   d. Rarely
   e. Never

3. When there's a problem, I try to identify what's happening …
a. Very frequently
b. Frequently
c. Sometimes
d. Rarely
e. Never

4. I start the group working …
a. Very frequently
b. Frequently
c. Sometimes
d. Rarely
e. Never

5. I suggest directions that the group can take …
a. Very frequently
b. Frequently
c. Sometimes
d. Rarely
e. Never

6. I listen actively …
a. Very frequently
b. Frequently
c. Sometimes
d. Rarely
e. Never

7. I give positive feedback to other members of the group …
a. Very frequently
b. Frequently
c. Sometimes
d. Rarely
e. Never

8. I compromise …
a. Very frequently
b. Frequently
c. Sometimes
d. Rarely
e. Never

9. I help relieve tension …
a. Very frequently
b. Frequently
c. Sometimes
d. Rarely
e. Never

10. I talk …
a. Very frequently
b. Frequently
c. Sometimes
d. Rarely
e. Never

11. I help to ensure that meeting times and places are arranged …
a. Very frequently
b. Frequently
c. Sometimes
d. Rarely
e. Never

12. I try to observe what's happening in the group …
a. Very frequently
b. Frequently
c. Sometimes
d. Rarely
e. Never

13. I try to help solve problems …
a. Very frequently
b. Frequently
c. Sometimes
d. Rarely
e. Never

14. I take responsibility for ensuring that tasks are completed …
a. Very frequently
b. Frequently
c. Sometimes
d. Rarely
e. Never

15. I like the group to be having a good time …
a. Very frequently
b. Frequently
c. Sometimes
d. Rarely
e. Never

How to score: Award yourself points according to the values shown in the following table. An answer of "b" on Question 5, for example, is worth 1 point, while a "b" on Question 6 is worth 3 points. To get your total score, add up all the numbers in your "Score" column.

Question	a	b	c	d	e	Score
1	1	2	3	2	1	
2	1	2	3	2	1	
3	1	2	3	2	1	
4	2	2	3	1	0	
5	0	1	3	1	0	
6	3	3	2	1	0	
7	3	3	2	1	0	
8	2	3	3	1	0	
9	1	2	3	1	0	
10	0	0	3	2	1	
11	2	3	3	1	0	
12	3	3	2	1	0	
13	2	3	3	1	0	
14	2	2	3	1	0	
15	1	1	2	1	1	
		TOTAL				

41–45 = Very effective team person

35–40 = Effective team person

Under 35 = Person who probably needs to work on his or her teamwork skills

Reference

Adapted from University of South Australia, "Test Your Effectiveness as a Team Member." *"Working in Teams" Online Workshop.* Handout: "Teamwork Skills Questionnaire." March 24, 2010 at www.unisanet.unisa.edu.au.

CHAPTER 11

Communication in Organizations

Chapter Outline

- The Nature of Communication in Organizations
- Methods of Communication
- The Communication Process
- Digital Information Processing and Telecommunications
- Communication Networks
- Managing Communication

Chapter Learning Objectives

After studying this chapter, you should be able to:

1. **Discuss the nature of communication in organizations.**
2. **Identify and describe the primary methods of communication.**
3. **Describe the communication process.**
4. **Note how information technology affects communication.**
5. **Identify and discuss the basic kinds of communication networks.**
6. **Discuss how communication can be managed in organizations.**

You Can't Make This Stuff Up

"You can't make this stuff up. Well, I guess you could."

—Barbara Mikkelson, cofounder of Snopes.com

Let's say that there was a time when, like about 15 percent of all Americans, your connectivity needs required you to be on your cell phone for more than 1,000 minutes per month, or just over 30 minutes a day. Like just about everybody else in the same segment of the population, you were happy to report that both your business affairs and your personal life had improved significantly.

Snopes.com provides many vivid examples—both very good and very bad—about communication and its role in modern society.

Then you ran across an article in a British Internet magazine called *Wymsey Village*. Entitled "Weekend Eating: Mobile Cooking," it showed you how to cook an egg using two cell phones. At first, you marveled at what they had in fact thought of next, but not long afterward, someone e-mailed you a copy of an article in which, complete with photographs, two Russian journalists explained how they'd replicated the process by propping a hard-boiled egg between two activated cell phones for an hour. This time, however, the article ended on an ominous note: "If the microwave radiation emitted by the mobile phones is capable of modifying the proteins in an egg, imagine what it can do to the proteins in our brains." At that point, you ditched your cell phone and had your landline reinstalled (although you routinely use the speakerphone and stay as far away as possible from the unit itself). Last but not least, you did your civic duty by e-mailing both articles to everybody you know.

Perhaps you should have Snopesed the information that you were relying on when you trashed your cell phone and urged all your friends to do the same. Had you queried the fact checkers at Snopes.com—and a lot of people did—you would have found that the *Wymsey Village* article was a spoof and the article from the Russian tabloid a hoax. "The stories that arise the most," says Snopes cofounder David Mikkelson, "are those that pose a threat to readers.... The things that take off have to hit a nerve we're all thinking about." It's not that hard to debunk them, Mikkelson adds, if you "start off with the thought that extraordinary claims require extraordinary proof," but even so, he admits, "most rumors never die completely." The *Wymsey Village* "article," for example, is still out there, and his only regret, says the unmasked author, "is that I didn't get a dime for every hit on that page."

Snopes.com started out in 1995 as a hobby for David Mikkelson and his wife Barbara, who share a passion for "urban legends," which they define as a "tale" that "circulates widely, is told and retold with differing details (or exists in multiple versions), and is *said* to be true." The site, which they operate from their California home, now attracts 7 to 8 million visitors a month. Two full-time employees manage the enormous amount of e-mail. "We quickly became the place where people mailed anything that was questionable," explains David. "If they needed verification, they'd ask us." A tech columnist for the *New York Times* has called Snopes "the Internet's authority on e-mailed myths," and Richard Roeper, a film critic and amateur myth buster, declares that "Snopes is like having your own army of fact checkers sniffing out a million wacko leads."

"Most of what we deal with," says David Mikkelson, "exists outside traditional media," but he's quick to point out that traditional media sources could perform much the same service as Snopes. "Our approach," he explains, "is going to be that something outrageous is going to be a hoax. But that's unfortunately not what a lot of people in the media do. They say, 'This is real, and we'll see if there's proof it isn't.'" Take, for instance, the famous "Hunting for Bambi" case, in which a Las Vegas TV station did a four-part story on a local outfit offering hunters the chance to shoot paintballs at naked women for a fee of $10,000. "In this case," reports Mikkelson,

> *we [said] is there anything that demonstrates it's real. The first thing you notice is that it's rather improbable that naked women wearing no protection whatsoever, not even helmets or goggles, will run around in front of guys with unmodified paintball guns with nothing more than a vague promise they won't shoot above the waist.*

"You can't make this stuff up," adds Barbara Mikkelson, who pauses before adding, "Well, I guess you could. But if you do, I'm sure we'll get to the bottom of it."

The advent of the Internet is, of course, a key factor in the growth of the hoax and misinformation business, but the Internet, says David, "has made it easier to debunk hoaxes while at the same time making it easier to perpetrate them…. Really widespread Internet-based hoaxes," he adds, "are fairly uncommon. Most of them are just, 'I'm going to put up this gag and see if anyone falls for it.' Having someone go through the time and effort to do a really thought-out hoax is pretty rare, maybe happening once or twice a year." Mikkelson admits that "there's a lot on the Internet that you can't trust," but he's also well aware that "there's a lot on your bookshelf and the library shelves that you can't trust either…. There's never been a medium that you could inherently trust. You still have to look at who's telling you this…. The concept hasn't changed…. Nothing's really changed but the technology."

Fortunately, the Mikkelsons aren't alone in the online fact-checking business. During the Presidential election of 2008, an e-mail began circulating under the head "PLEASE READ!!!!!!! VERY IMPORTANT—SNOPES EXPOSED." The anonymous e-mailer proceeded to reveal that Snopes was "owned by a flaming liberal … in the tank for Obama" and warned everyone receiving his urgent news that "you cannot and should not trust Snopes.com … for anything that remotely resembles the truth." In the spring of 2009, FactCheck.org, which describes itself as "a nonpartisan, nonprofit 'consumer advocate' for voters that aims to reduce the level of deception and confusion in U.S. politics," set out to investigate the allegations against Snopes. Researchers revealed that Barbara Mikkelson is a nonvoting Canadian citizen and that David Mikkelson, though now an independent, had last registered his party affiliation as Republican. The anti-Snopes e-mail, concluded the FactCheck report, "contains a number of false claims about the urban-legend-busting Snopes.com and its proprietors."

It would appear, then, that it is indeed safe to do your fact checking at Snopes.com, where you'll continue to find thorough reviews of widely circulating information—and misinformation—of all kinds. For the record, Walmart has never authorized illegal immigration raids at its stores, and, no, if you're accosted by a mugger at your ATM machine, entering your PIN backwards won't summon the police.

What Do You Think?

1. What kinds of information do you typically collect from the Internet? Has it ever turned out to be less reliable than you had expected it to be?
2. Have you ever received Internet-based "information" (such as the cell phone and the egg phenomenon) that you found suspect? Did you check it out? If so, how?

References: "Oeuf the Wall," *Snopes.com*, March 17, 2009, www.snopes.com on July 18, 2012; "Weekend Eating: Mobile Cooking," *Wymsey Weekend*, 2008, www.wymsey.co.uk on July 18, 2012; Snopes.com, "Frequently Asked Questions" (1995–2012), www.snopes.com on July 18, 2012; David Hochman, "Rumor Detectives: True Story or Online Hoax?" *Reader's Digest*, April 2009, www.rd.com on July 18, 2012; "For Snopes.com, Debunking the Bambi Hoax Was All in a Day's Work," *Online Journalism Review*, July 31, 2003, www.ojr.org on July 18, 2012; Brian Stelter, "Debunkers of Fictions Sift the Net," *New York Times*, April 4, 2010, www.nytimes.com on July 18, 2012; David Pogue, "Tech Tips for the Basic Computer User," *New York Times*, October 2, 2008, http://pogue.blogs.nytimes.com on July 18, 2012; Viveca Novak, "Snopes.com," *FactCheck.org*, April 10, 2009, www.factcheck.org on March 11, 2010.

Communication is something that most of us take for granted—indeed, we have been communicating for so long that we really pay little attention to the actual process. Even at work, we often focus primarily on doing our jobs and pay little attention to how we communicate with others about those jobs. However, since methods of communication play such a pervasive role in affecting behavior in organizations and represent another vital underpinning of interpersonal processes, we need to pay more attention to the processes that effectively link what we do to others in the organization.

In this chapter, we focus on interpersonal communication and information processing. First, we discuss the importance of communication in organizations and some important aspects of international communication. Next, we describe the methods of organizational communication and examine the basic communication process. Then we examine the potential effects of computerized information technology and telecommunications. Next, we explore the development of communication networks in organizations. Finally, we discuss several common problems of organizational communication and methods of managing communication.

THE NATURE OF COMMUNICATION IN ORGANIZATIONS

Communication is the social process in which two or more parties exchange information and share meaning.

Communication is the social process in which two or more parties exchange information and share meaning. Communication has been studied from many perspectives. In this section, we provide an overview of the complex and dynamic communication process and discuss some important issues relating to international communication in organizations.

The Purposes of Communication in Organizations

Communication among individuals and groups is vital in all organizations. Some of the purposes of organizational communication are shown in Figure 11.1. The primary purpose is to achieve coordinated action.[1] Just as the human nervous system responds to stimuli and coordinates responses by sending messages to the various parts of the body, communication coordinates the actions of the parts of an organization. Without communication, an organization would be merely a collection of individual workers doing separate tasks. Organizational action would lack coordination and would be oriented toward individual rather than organizational goals.

A second purpose of communication is information sharing. The most important information relates to organizational goals, which give members a sense of purpose and direction. Another information-sharing function of communication is to give specific task directions to individuals. Whereas information on organizational goals gives employees a sense of how their activities fit into the overall picture, task communication tells them what their job duties are (and are not). Employees must also receive information on the results of their efforts, as in performance appraisals.

Communication is essential to the decision-making process as well, as we discuss in Chapter 8. Information and information sharing are needed to define problems, generate and evaluate alternatives, implement decisions, and control and evaluate results. Finally, communication expresses feelings and emotions. Organizational communication is far from merely a collection of facts and figures. People in organizations, like people anywhere else, often need to communicate emotions such as happiness, anger, displeasure, confidence, and fear.

FIGURE 11.1

Three Purposes of Organizational Communication

Achieving coordinated action is the prime purpose of communication in organizations. Sharing information properly and expressing emotions help achieve coordinated action.

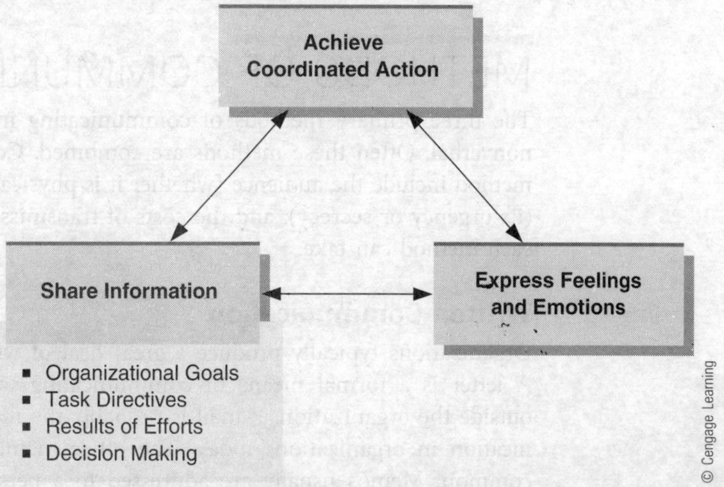

Communication Across Cultures

Communication is an element of interpersonal relations that obviously is affected by the international environment, partly because of language issues and partly because of coordination issues.

Language Differences in languages are compounded by the fact that the same word can mean different things in different cultures. For example, Chevrolet once tried to export a line of cars to Latin America that it called the "Nova" in the United States, but then found that "no va" means "doesn't go" in Spanish—not the best name for an automobile! Similarly, just as KFC was about to launch a major new advertising campaign in China a local manager pointed out that the firm's long-time American slogan "Finger Lickin' Good" meant "Eat Your Fingers Off" when translated directly into Chinese. Fortunately for KFC it had time to revise its slogan before the new advertising campaign was started. On a more effective note, Akio Morita and his business partner Masaru Ibuka named their firm "Sony" because their research found that the word has no specific meaning in any language.

Elements of nonverbal communication also vary across cultures. Colors and body language can convey quite a different message from one culture to another. For example, the American sign for "OK" (making a loop with thumb and first finger) is considered rude in Spain and vulgar in Brazil. Managers should be forewarned that they can take nothing for granted in dealing with people from other cultures. They must take the time to become as fully acquainted as possible with the verbal and nonverbal languages of a culture. And newer forms of communication technology such as e-mail and tweets are actually changing language itself.

Coordination International communication is closely related to issues of coordination. For example, an American manager who wants to speak with his or her counterpart in Hong Kong, Singapore, Rome, or London must contend not only with language differences but also with a time difference of many hours. When the American manager needs to talk on the telephone, the Hong Kong executive may be home asleep. Consequently, organizations are employing increasingly innovative methods for coordinating their activities in scattered parts of the globe. Merrill Lynch, for example, has its own satellite-based telephone network to monitor and participate in the worldwide money and financial markets. And, of course, the Internet makes it easier than ever to communicate across different parts of the world.

METHODS OF COMMUNICATION

The three primary methods of communicating in organizations are written, oral, and nonverbal. Often these methods are combined. Considerations that affect the choice of method include the audience (whether it is physically present), the nature of the message (its urgency or secrecy), and the costs of transmission.[2] Figure 11.2 shows various forms each method can take.

Written Communication

Organizations typically produce a great deal of written communication of many kinds. A letter is a formal means of communicating with an individual, generally someone outside the organization. E-mail is probably the most common form of written communication in organizations today. The office memorandum, or memo, is also still very common. Memos usually are addressed to a person or group inside the organization.

FIGURE 11.2

Methods of Communication in Organizations

The three methods of communication in organizations are related to each other. Each one supplements the other, although each can also stand alone.

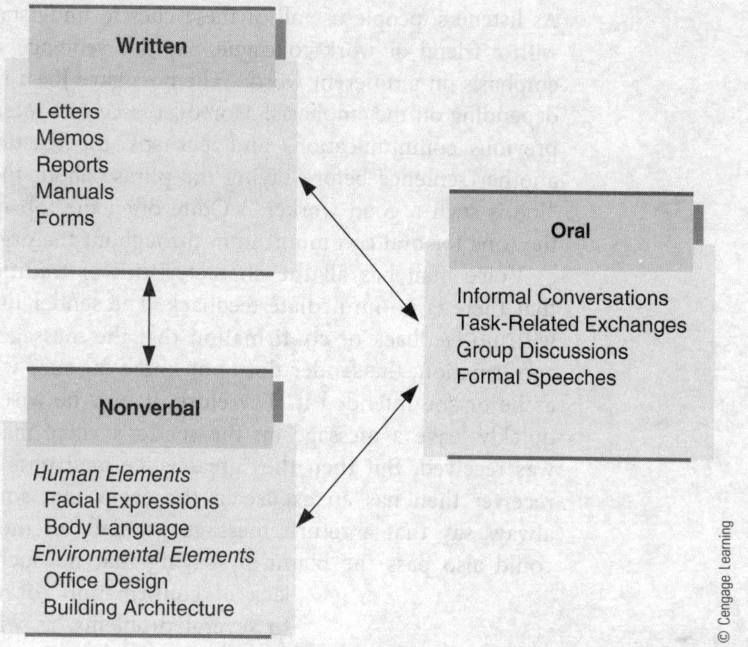

They tend to deal with a single topic and are more impersonal (as they often are destined to reach more than one person) but less formal than letters. Most e-mail is similar to the traditional memo, although it is even less formal.

Other common forms of written communication include reports, manuals, and forms. Reports generally summarize the progress or results of a project and often provide information to be used in decision making. Manuals have various functions in organizations. Instruction manuals tell employees how to operate machines; policy and procedures manuals inform them of organizational rules; operations manuals describe how to perform tasks and respond to work-related problems. Forms are standardized documents on which to report information. As such, they represent attempts to make communication more efficient and information more accessible. A performance appraisal form is an example. We should also note that although many of these forms of written communication have historically been used in a paper-based environment, they are increasingly being put on websites and intranets in many companies today.

Oral Communication

The most prevalent form of organizational communication is oral. Oral communication takes place everywhere—in informal conversations, in the process of doing work, in meetings of groups and task forces, and in formal speeches and presentations. Some studies have suggested that oral communication skills may be the number one criterion for hiring new college graduates.[3] Business school leaders have also been urged by industry to develop better communication skills in their graduates.[4] Even in Europe, employers have complained that the number one problem with current graduates is the lack of oral communication skills, citing cultural factors and changes in the educational process as primary causes.[5]

Oral forms of communication are particularly powerful because they include not only speakers' words but also their changes in tone, pitch, speed, and volume and may be accompanied by facial expressions and gestures (as discussed further in the next section).

As listeners, people use all of these cues to understand oral messages. Try this example with a friend or work colleague. Say this sentence several times, each time placing the emphasis on a different word: "The boss gave Joe a raise." See how the meaning changes depending on the emphasis! Moreover, receivers interpret oral messages in the context of previous communications and, perhaps, the reactions of other receivers. (Try saying another sentence before saying the phrase about the boss—such as "Joe is so lazy" or "Joe is such a good worker.") Quite often the top management of an organization sets the tone for oral communication throughout the organization.

Voice mail has all the characteristics of traditional verbal communication except that there is no immediate feedback. The sender just leaves a message on the network with no feedback or confirmation that the message was, or will be, received. With no confirmation, the sender does not know for sure whether the message will be received as he or she intended it. Therefore, it may be wise for the receiver of a voice mail to quickly leave a message on the sender's voice mail saying that the original message was received. But then the "great voice mail phone tag" is on at its worst! Also, the receiver then has an excuse in the event that something goes wrong later and can always say that a return message was left on the sender's voice mail! The receiver could also pass the blame by saying that no such voice message was received. The lack of confirmation (or two-way communication) can lead to several problems, as will be discussed in later sections of this chapter.

Dana Heinemann/Shutterstock.com

Nonverbal communication can convey a great deal of information. This man, for example, has just read some bad financial news and is venting his anger and frustration by tearing the paper in half. His facial expression also makes his feelings clear.

Nonverbal Communication

Nonverbal communication includes all the elements associated with human communication that are not expressed orally or in writing. Sometimes nonverbal communication conveys more meaning than words do. Human elements of nonverbal communication include facial expressions and physical movements, both conscious and unconscious. Facial expressions have been categorized as (1) interest-excitement, (2) enjoyment-joy, (3) surprise-startle, (4) distress-anguish, (5) fear-terror, (6) shame-humiliation, (7) contempt-disgust, and (8) anger-rage. The eyes are generally the most expressive component of the face.

Physical movements and "body language" are also highly expressive human elements. Body language includes both actual movement and body positions during communication. The handshake is a common form of body language. Other examples include making eye contact, which expresses a willingness to communicate; sitting on the edge of a chair, which may indicate nervousness or anxiety; and sitting back with arms folded, which may convey an unwillingness to continue the discussion.

Environmental elements such as buildings, office space, and furniture can also convey messages. A spacious office, expensive draperies, plush carpeting, and elegant furniture can combine to remind employees or visitors that they are in the office of the president and CEO of the firm. Similarly, the small metal desk set in the middle of the shop floor accurately communicates the organizational rank of a first-line supervisor. Thus, office arrangements convey status, power, and prestige and create an atmosphere for doing business. The physical setting can also be instrumental in the development of communication networks because a centrally located person can more easily control the flow of task-related information.

As digital communication has become more widespread, nonverbal elements are commonly used there as well. For instance, adding digital characters to indicate humor or unhappiness can help the receiver better appreciate the intended meaning of an e-mail. An e-mail that reads "You're fired," for example, followed quickly by a "smiley face" has a much different meaning than just the words alone. The *Services* box provides other illustrations underscoring the important of nonverbal communication.

SERVICE A Smile Says a Lot

©rangizzz/Shutterstock

Isn't it great when someone smiles at you? That simple facial expression communicates a number of important things to the person receiving the smile. It says, "Welcome," "I'm glad you're here," and "I am anxious to listen and help if I can." Service organizations spend considerable time and effort encouraging their employees to smile at their customers. This simple act can be an important part of the success of almost any service experience. The question arises, though: Why is this so important? The answer can be attributed to several human characteristics. The most discussed answer is based on our tendency to like those that like us. Thus, a person who smiles at us is sending a nonverbal signal that the person finds us to be like him or her and is a friend, not a foe. If a service employee smiles at us, we tend to smile back. In other words, we use mimicry to enhance the quality and value of the service experience. There is some interesting research that gives us some insight into the value of mimicry. People being mimicked will like those who mimic them. Moreover, they respond more generously toward people who mimic them. This has been termed the "chameleon effect." Service employees such as restaurant servers can increase the amount of their tips by mimicking the behaviors of their customers in rate of speech, accents, word choice, and syntax. Even mimicking behaviors such as rubbing their face, laughing, and other behaviors when mimicked influence our liking of others.

The second aspect of service with a smile is based on its impact on our emotions. If we see the smile as authentic, it has more impact on us than if it is seen as somehow fake. A "fake" smile will affect our feelings about the person smiling at us. In other words, we have both a mimicking reaction to someone smiling at us as we will automatically and subconsciously respond to behaviors of those we want to interact with, and we will make judgments as to the authenticity of those behaviors. Thus, service managers seek to find ways to encourage their employees to smile in ways that feel authentic to their customers. These strategies can be simple such as posting small mirrors on checkout cash registers so that employees can self-monitor their behaviors and be happily smiling when customers enter their work space. Another strategy puts considerable emphasis on creating fun work environments so that employees have fun that leads them to be genuinely smiling when customers appear. Gaylord's Opryland Hotel, for example, uses a variety of strategies to create a fun work environment. It has a character called DiVine who is dressed like a vine. She stands motionless in the tropical atrium area until some unsuspecting person stands alongside her. Then, without warning, she will reach out and touch the person or suddenly move which leads to surprised laughter. Employees enjoy this performance as well and helps make the workplace fun for them while providing an extra surprise for the guests.

Discussion Question: Recall a recent service experience you've had where the employees seemed to be having fun, what did you see or hear that made that work setting fun?

THE COMMUNICATION PROCESS

Communication is a social process in which two or more parties exchange information and share meaning. The process is social because it involves two or more people. It is a two-way process and takes place over time rather than instantaneously. The communication process illustrated in Figure 11.3 shows a loop between the source and the receiver.[6] Note the importance of the feedback portion of the loop; upon receiving the message, the receiver responds with a message to the source to verify the communication. Each element of the basic communication process is important. If one part is faulty, the message may not be communicated as it was intended. A simple organizational example might be when a manager attempts to give direction to an employee regarding the order in which to perform two tasks. (We refer to this example again in later discussions.) The manager wants to send a message and have the employee understand precisely the meaning she intends. Each part of the communication process is described next.

Source

The **source** is the individual, group, or organization interested in communicating something to another party.

The **source** is the individual, group, or organization interested in communicating something to another party. In group or organizational communication, an individual may send the message on behalf of the organization. The source is responsible for preparing the message, encoding it, and entering it into the transmission medium. In some cases, the receiver chooses the source of information, as when a decision maker seeks information from trusted and knowledgeable individuals.[7] The source in organizational communication is often the manager giving directions to employees.

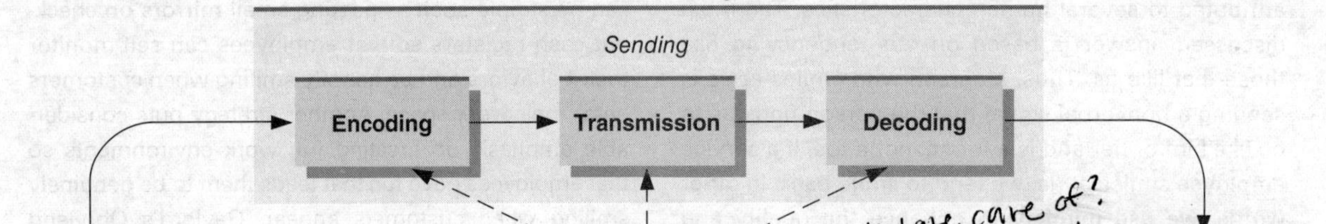

FIGURE 11.3

The Communication Process

The communication process is a loop that connects the sender and the receiver and operates in both directions. Communication is not complete until the original sender knows that the receiver understands the message.

Encoding

Encoding is the process by which the message is translated from an idea or thought into transmittable symbols.

Encoding is the process by which the message is translated from an idea or thought into symbols that can be transmitted. The symbols may be words, numbers, pictures, sounds, or physical gestures and movements. In a simple example, the manager may use words in English as the symbols, usually spoken or written. The source must encode the message in symbols that the receiver can decode properly; that is, the source and the receiver must attach the same meaning to the symbols. When we use the symbols of a common language, we assume those symbols have the same meaning to everyone who uses them. However, the inherent ambiguity of symbol systems can lead to decoding errors. In verbal communication, for example, some words have different meanings for different people. Parents and children often use the same word, but the differences in their positions and ages may lead them to interpret words quite differently. If a manager only speaks Spanish and an employee only speaks German, the message is unlikely to be understood. The meanings of words used by the sender may differ depending on the nonverbal cues, such as facial expression, that the sender transmits along with them.

Transmission

Transmission is the process through which the symbols that represent the message are sent to the receiver.

The **medium** is the channel, or path, through which the message is transmitted.

Transmission is the process through which the symbols that carry the message are sent to the receiver. The **medium** is the channel, or path, of transmission. The medium for face-to-face conversation is sound waves. The same conversation conducted over the telephone involves not only sound waves but also electrical impulses and the lines or networks that connect the two phones. To tell the employee in what order to perform tasks, the manager could tell the employee face-to-face or use the telephone, a memo, e-mail, or voice mail.

Communications media range from interpersonal media, such as talking or touching, to mass media, such as newspapers, magazines, or television broadcasts. Different media have different capacities for carrying information. For example, a face-to-face conversation generally has more carrying capacity than a letter because it allows the transmission of more than just words. In addition, the medium can help determine the effect the message has on the receiver. Calling a prospective client on the telephone to make a business proposal is a more personal approach than sending a letter and is likely to elicit a different response. It is important that a sender choose the medium that is most likely to correspond to the type of message that needs to be sent and understood.

Decoding

Decoding is the process by which the receiver of the message interprets its meaning.

The **receiver** is the individual, group, or organization that perceives the encoded symbols; the receiver may or may not decode them to try to understand the intended message.

Decoding is the process by which the receiver of the message interprets its meaning. The receiver uses knowledge and experience to interpret the symbols of the message; in some situations, he or she may consult an authority such as a dictionary or a code book. Up to this point, the receiver has been relatively inactive, but the receiver becomes more active in the decoding phase. The meaning the receiver attaches to the symbols may be the same as—or different from—the meaning intended by the source. If the meanings differ, of course, communication breaks down and misunderstanding is likely. In our example, if the employee does not understand the language or a particular word, then the employee will not comprehend the same meaning as the sender (manager) and may do the tasks in the wrong order or not do them at all.

Receiver

The **receiver** of the message may be an individual, a group, an organization, or an individual acting as the representative of a group. The receiver decides whether to decode the message, whether to make an effort to understand it, and whether to respond. Moreover, the intended receiver may not get the message at all, whereas an unintended receiver might get it, depending on the medium and the symbols used by the source and the attention level of potential receivers. Also, an employee may share the same language (know the symbols) used by the manager but not want to get the sender's meaning.

The key skill for proper reception of the message is good listening. The receiver may not concentrate on the sender, the message, or the medium such that the message is lost. Listening is an active process that requires as much concentration and effort from the receiver as sending the message does for the sender. The expression of emotions by the sender and receiver enters into the communication process at several points. First, the emotions may be part of the message, entering into the encoding process. If the manager's directions are encoded with a sense of emotional urgency—for example, if they are given with a high-pitched or loud voice—the employee may move quickly to follow the directions. However, if the message is urgent but the manager's tone of voice is low and does not send urgent signals, employees may not engage in quick action. Second, as the message is decoded, the receiver may let his or her emotions perceive a message different from what the sender intended. Third, emotion-filled feedback from the intended receiver can cause the sender to modify her or his subsequent message.

Feedback

Feedback is the process in which the receiver returns a message to the sender that indicates receipt of the message.

Feedback is the receiver's response to the message. Feedback verifies the message by telling the source whether the receiver received and understood the message. The feedback may be as simple as a phone call from the prospective client expressing interest in the business proposal, or as complex as a written brief on a complicated point of law sent from an attorney to a judge. In our example, the employee can respond to the manager's directions by a verbal or written response indicating that he or she does or does not understand the message. Feedback could also be nonverbal, as when, in our example, the employee does not do either task. With typical voice mail, the feedback loop is missing or delayed, which can lead to many communication problems.

Noise

Noise is any disturbance in the communication process that interferes with or distorts communication.

Channel noise is a disturbance in communication that is primarily a function of the medium.

Noise is any disturbance in the communication process that interferes with or distorts communication. Noise can be introduced at virtually any point in the communication process. The principal type, called **channel noise**, is associated with the medium.[8] A dropped cell phone call, an e-mail virus, and a traditional letter getting lost in the mail are all examples of channel noise. When noise interferes in the encoding and decoding processes, poor encoding and decoding can result. An employee may not fully hear the directions given by the manager owing to noisy machinery on the shop floor or competing input from other people. Emotions that interfere with an intended communication may also be considered a type of noise.

Effective communication occurs when information or meaning has been shared by at least two people. Therefore, communication must include the response from the receiver back to the sender. The sender cannot know whether the message has been conveyed as intended if there is no feedback from the receiver, as when we leave voice mail. Both parties are responsible for the effectiveness of the communication. The evolution of new technology in recent years presents novel problems in ensuring that communications work as sender and receiver expect them to.

DIGITAL INFORMATION PROCESSING AND TELECOMMUNICATIONS

Communications-related changes in the workplace are occurring at a rapid clip. Many recent innovations are based on new technologies—computerized information processing systems, telecommunication systems, the Internet, organizational intranets and extranets, and various combinations of these technologies. Managers send and receive memos and other documents to and from one person or a group scattered around the world from their computers using the Internet, and they can do so in their cars or via their notebook computers and cellular phones on the commuter train. Wireless devices such as smartphones and Wi-Fi hotspots are making these activities even more commonplace. Indeed, many employees telecommute from home rather than going to the office every day. And whole new industries are developing around information storage, transmission, and retrieval that were not even dreamed of a few years ago.

The "office of the future" is here, but it just may not be in a typical office building. Every office now has a facsimile (fax) machine, a copier, and personal computers, most of them linked to a single integrated system and to numerous databases and digital mail systems. Automobile companies advertise that their cars and trucks have equipment for your cellular telephone, computer, and fax machine. The digital office links managers, clerical employees, professional workers, and sales personnel—and often suppliers and customers as well—in a worldwide communication network that uses a combination of digital data storage, retrieval, and transmission systems.

Ken Seet/Flame/Corbis

Technology has made it easier—and therefore much more common—for people to work remotely. Indeed, many people today routinely work from home and/or while they are commuting to or from their office. We check our email, text messages, and so forth as easily and casually as people once looked at their notebooks or address books. For instance, this man is checking his voice mail and text messages while waiting for his airplane to take off. Just a few years ago this communication capability did not exist.

In fact, the computer-integrated organization has become commonplace. Ingersol Milling Machine of Rockford, Illinois, boasts a totally computer-integrated operation in which all major functions—sales, marketing, finance, distribution, and manufacturing—exchange operating information quickly and continuously via computers. For example, product designers can send specifications directly to machines on the factory floor, and accounting personnel receive online information about sales, purchases, and prices instantaneously. The computer system parallels and greatly speeds up the entire process.[9]

Computers are facilitating the increase in telecommuting across the United States and reducing the number of trips people make to the office to get work done. Several years ago IBM provided many of its employees with notebook computers and told them not to come to the office but instead to use the computers to work out in the field and interface with the firm digitally.[10] Other companies, such as Motorola and AT&T, have also encouraged telecommuting by employees. Employees report increased productivity, less fatigue caused by commuting, reduced commuting expenses, and increased personal freedom. In addition, telecommuting may reduce air pollution and overcrowding. Some employees have reported, however, that they miss the social interaction of the office. Some managers have also expressed concerns about the quantity and quality of the work that telecommuting employees do when away from the office.

Research conducted among office workers using a new digital office system indicated that attitudes toward the system were generally favorable. On the other hand, other research also suggests that a reduction of face-to-face meetings may depersonalize the office. Some observers are also concerned that companies are installing digital systems with little consideration for the social structures of the office. As departments rely more heavily on computerized information systems, the activities of work groups throughout the organization are likely to become more interdependent, a situation that may alter power relationships among the groups. Most employees quickly learn the system of power, politics, authority, and responsibility in the office. A radical change in work and personal relationships caused by new office technology may disrupt normal ways of accomplishing tasks, thereby reducing productivity. A related problem may occur when an entire network goes out of service, causing most work in an organization to come to a halt. Other potential problems include information overload, loss of records in a "paperless" office, and the dehumanizing consequences of using digital equipment. In effect, new information processing and transmission technologies mean new media, symbols, message transmission methods, and networks for organizational communication.

The real increases in organizational productivity due to information technology may come from the ability to communicate in new and different ways rather than from simply speeding up existing communication patterns. For example, to remain competitive in a very challenging global marketplace, companies will need to be able to generate, disseminate, and implement new ideas more effectively. In effect, organizations will become "knowledge-based" learning organizations that are continually generating new ideas to improve themselves. This can only occur when expert knowledge is communicated and available throughout the organization. FedEx credits its highly developed and integrated internal and external communications networks as being a cornerstone of its long-term success.[11]

One of these new ways of communicating is idea sharing, or knowledge sharing, by sharing information on what practices work best. A computer-based system is necessary to store, organize, and then make available to others the best practices from throughout the company.[12] For example, Eli Lilly, a large pharmaceutical company, uses a company-wide intranet for all of its 16,000 employees. This system makes available internal e-mail, corporate policies, and corporate directories and enables information sharing throughout the organization.[13] Digital technology is, therefore, speeding up existing communication and developing new types of organizational communication processes with potential new benefits and problems for managers.

COMMUNICATION NETWORKS

Communication links individuals and groups in a social system. Initially, task-related communication links develop in an organization so that employees can get the information they need to do their jobs and coordinate their work with that of others in the system. Over a long period, these communication relationships become a sophisticated social system composed of both small-group communication networks and a larger organizational network. These networks structure both the flow and the content of communication and support the organizational structure.[14] The pattern and content of communication also support the culture, beliefs, and value systems that enable the organization to operate. (We should also note that this discussion is based on theory and

FIGURE 11.4

Small-Group Communication Networks

These four types of communication networks are the most common in organizations. The lines represent the most frequently used communication links in small groups.

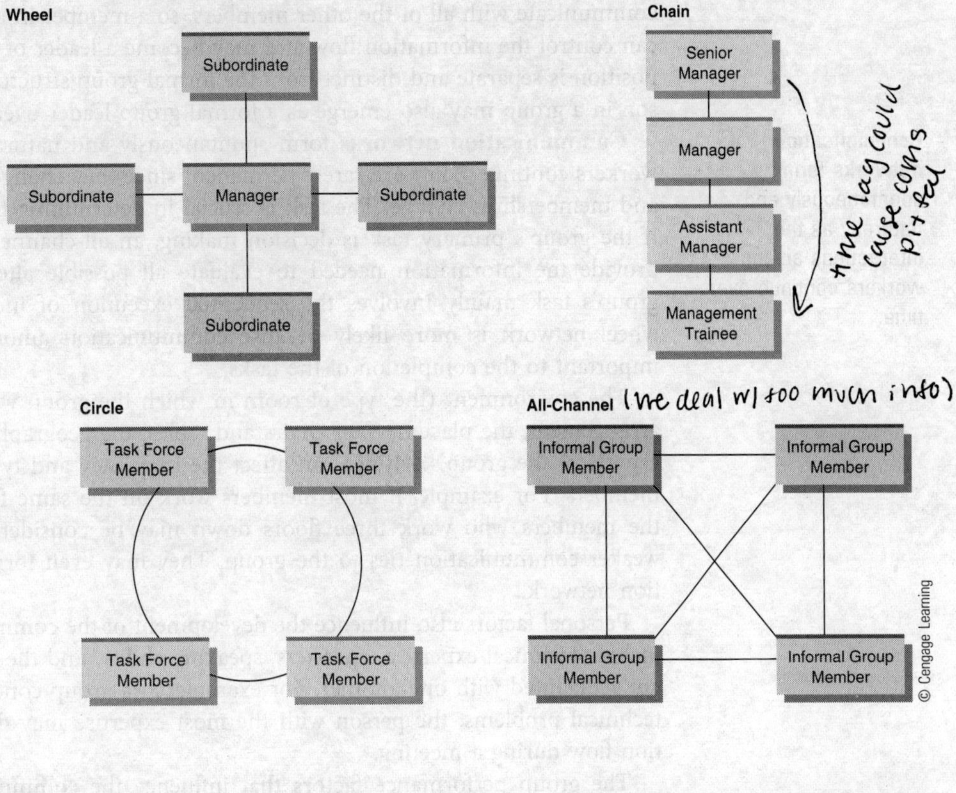

research associated with face-to-face group dynamics. Web-based social networking tools such as MySpace and Facebook reflect networks as well, but these have not been studied in an organizational context.)

In a **wheel network**, information flows between the person at the end of each spoke and the person in the middle.

In a **chain network**, each member communicates with the person above and below, except for the individuals on each end, who communicate with only one person.

In a **circle network**, each member communicates with the people on either side but with no one else.

In an **all-channel network**, all members communicate with all other members.

Small-Group Networks

To examine interpersonal communication in a small group, we can observe the patterns that emerge as the work of the group proceeds and information flows from some people in the group to others.[15] Four such patterns are shown in Figure 11.4. The lines identify the communication links most frequently used in the groups.

A **wheel network** is a pattern in which information flows between the person at the end of each spoke and the person in the middle. Those on the ends of the spokes do not communicate with each other directly. The wheel network is a feature of the typical work group, in which the primary communication occurs between the members and the group manager. In a **chain network**, each member communicates with the person above and below, except for the individuals on each end, who communicate with only one person. The chain network is typical of communication in a vertical hierarchy, in which most communication travels up and down the chain of command. Each person in a **circle network** communicates with the people on either side but not with anyone else. The circle network often is found in task forces and committees. Finally, in an all-channel network, all members communicate with all the other members. The **all-channel network** often is found in informal groups that have no formal structure, leader, or task to accomplish.

Communication may be more easily distorted by noise when much is being communicated or when the communication must travel a great distance. Improvements in digital communication technology, such as computerized mail systems and intranets, are reducing this effect. A relatively central position gives a person an opportunity to communicate with all of the other members, so a member in a relatively central position can control the information flow and may become a leader of the group. This leadership position is separate and distinct from the formal group structure, although a central person in a group may also emerge as a formal group leader over a long period.

Communication networks form spontaneously and naturally as the interactions among workers continue over time.

Communication networks form spontaneously and naturally as interactions among workers continue. They are rarely permanent since they change as the tasks, interactions, and memberships change. The task is crucial in determining the pattern of the network. If the group's primary task is decision making, an all-channel network may develop to provide the information needed to evaluate all possible alternatives. If, however, the group's task mainly involves the sequential execution of individual tasks, a chain or wheel network is more likely because communication among members may not be important to the completion of the tasks.

The environment (the type of room in which the group works or meets, the seating arrangement, the placement of chairs and tables, the geographical dispersion, and other aspects of the group's setting) can affect the frequency and types of interactions among members. For example, if most members work on the same floor of an office building, the members who work three floors down may be considered outsiders and develop weaker communication ties to the group. They may even form a separate communication network.

Personal factors also influence the development of the communication network. These include technical expertise, openness, speaking ability, and the degree to which members are acquainted with one another. For example, in a group concerned mainly with highly technical problems, the person with the most expertise may dominate the communication flow during a meeting.

The group performance factors that influence the communication network include composition, size, norms, and cohesiveness. For example, group norms in one organization may encourage open communication across different levels and functional units, whereas the norms in another organization may discourage such lateral and diagonal communication. These performance factors are discussed in Chapter 9.

Because the outcome of the group's efforts depends on the coordinated action of its members, the communication network strongly influences group effectiveness. Thus, to develop effective working relationships in the organization, managers need to make a special effort to manage the flow of information and the development of communication networks. Managers can, for example, arrange offices and work spaces to foster communication among certain employees. Managers may also attempt to involve members who typically contribute little during discussions by asking them direct questions such as "What do you think, Tom?" or "Maria, tell us how this problem is handled in your district." Methods such as the nominal group technique, also discussed in Chapter 9, can also encourage participation.

CREATISTA/Shutterstock.com

Communication networks are a common feature in virtually all organizations. And as businesses move more toward open office arrangements interactions among colleagues also becomes easier. These co-workers, for example, are sharing a joke in an open office setting.

One other factor that is becoming increasingly more important in the development of communication networks is the advent of virtual groups fostered by digital distribution lists, chat rooms, discussion boards, and other computer networking systems. This form of communication results in a network of people who may have little or no face-to-face communication but still may be considered a group communication network. For example, your professor is probably a member of a virtual group of other professors who share an interest in the topic of this course. Through the virtual group, they keep up with new ideas in the field.

Organizational Communication Networks

An organization chart shows reporting relationships from the line worker up to the CEO of the firm. The lines of an organization chart may also represent channels of communication through which information flows, yet communication may also follow paths that cross traditional reporting lines. Information moves not only from the top down—from CEO to group members—but also upward from group members to the CEO. In fact, a good flow of information to the CEO is an important determinant of the organization's success.

Several companies have realized that the key to their continuing success was improved internal communication. General Motors was known for its extremely formal, top-down communication system. But as the firm's performance suffered, the formality of its system came under fire from virtually all of its stakeholders. GM's response was to embark on a massive communication improvement program that included sending employees to public-speaking workshops, improving the more than 350 publications that it sends out, providing videos of management meetings to employees, and using satellite links between headquarters and field operations to establish two-way conversations around the world.

Downward communication generally provides directions, whereas upward communication provides feedback to top management. Communication that flows horizontally or crosses traditional reporting lines usually is related to task performance. For example, a design engineer, a manufacturing engineer, and a quality engineer may communicate about the details of a particular product design, thus making the product one that is easy to manufacture and inspect. Horizontal communication often travels faster than vertical communication because it need not follow organizational protocols and procedures.

Organizational communication networks may diverge from reporting relationships as employees seek better information with which to do their jobs. Employees often find that the easiest way to get their jobs done or to obtain the necessary information is to go directly to employees in other departments rather than through the formal channels shown on the organization chart. Figure 11.5 shows a simple organization chart and the organization's real communication network. The communication network links the individuals who most frequently communicate with one another; the firm's CEO, for example, communicates most often with employee 5. (This does not mean that individuals who are not linked in the communication network never communicate, only that their communications are relatively infrequent.) Perhaps the CEO and the employee interact frequently outside of work, in church, in service organizations such as Kiwanis, or at sporting events. Such interactions may lead to close friendships that carry over into business relationships. The figure also shows that the group managers do not have important roles in the communication network, contrary to commonsense expectations.

The roles that people play in organizational communication networks can be analyzed in terms of their contribution to the functioning of the network.[16] The most important

FIGURE 11.5

Comparison of an Organization Chart and the Organization's Communication Network

Comparing a single organization chart with actual communication patterns reveals quite different reporting relationships from those shown in the organization chart.

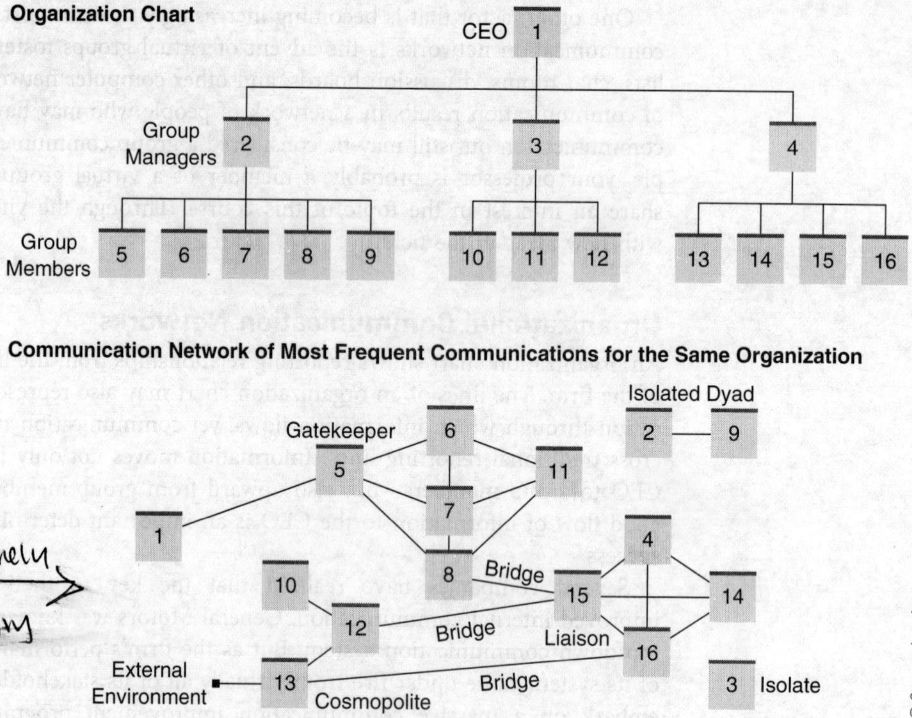

How do we prevent?
*all on same page in timely manner
-create more bridges
*coms are not automatically guaranteed

roles are labeled in the bottom portion of Figure 11.5. A **gatekeeper** (employee 5) has a strategic position in the network that allows him or her to control information moving in either direction through a channel. A **liaison** (employee 15) serves as a bridge between groups, tying groups together and facilitating the communication flow needed to integrate group activities. Employee 13 performs the interesting function of **cosmopolite**, who links the organization to the external environment by, for instance, attending conventions and trade shows, keeping up with outside technological innovations, and having more frequent contact with sources outside the organization. This person may also be an opinion leader in the group. Finally, the **isolate** (employee 3) and the **isolated dyad** (employees 2 and 9) tend to work alone and have little interaction and communication with others.

The **gatekeeper** has a strategic position in the network that allows him or her to control information moving in either direction through a channel.

The **liaison** serves as a bridge between groups, tying groups together and facilitating the communication flow needed to integrate group activities.

The **cosmopolite** links the organization to the external environment and may also be an opinion leader in the group.

The **isolate** and the **isolated dyad** tend to work alone and to interact and communicate little with others.

Each of these roles and functions plays an important part in the overall functioning of the communication network and in the organization as a whole. Understanding these roles can help both managers and group members facilitate communication. For instance, the manager who wants to be sure that the CEO receives certain information is well advised to go through the gatekeeper. If the employee who has the technical knowledge necessary for a particular project is an isolate, the manager can take special steps to integrate the employee into the communication network for the duration of the project.

Recent research has indicated some possible negative impacts of communication networks. Employee turnover has been shown to occur in clusters related to employee communication networks.[17] That is, employees who communicate regularly in a network may share feelings about the organization and thus influence one another's intentions to stay or quit. Communication networks therefore may have both positive and negative consequences.[18]

As we discuss in Chapter 16, a primary function of organizational structure is to coordinate the activities of many people doing specialized tasks. Communication networks in organizations provide this much-needed integration. In fact, in some ways communication patterns influence organizational structure. Some companies are finding that the need for better communication forces them to create smaller divisions. The reduced number of managerial levels and improved team spirit of these divisions tend to enhance communication flows.

MANAGING COMMUNICATION

As simple as the process of communication may seem, messages are not always understood. The degree of correspondence between the message intended by the source and the message understood by the receiver is called **communication fidelity**. Fidelity can be diminished anywhere in the communication process, from the source to the feedback. Moreover, organizations may have characteristics that impede the flow of information.

Communication fidelity is the degree of correspondence between the message intended by the source and the message understood by the receiver.

Improving the Communication Process

To improve organizational communication, one must understand potential problems. Using the basic communication process, we can identify several ways to overcome typical problems.

Source The source may intentionally withhold or filter information on the assumption that the receiver does not need it to understand the communication. Withholding information, however, may render the message meaningless or cause an erroneous interpretation. For example, during a performance appraisal interview, a manager may not tell the employee all of the sources of information being used to make the evaluation, thinking that the employee does not need to know them. If the employee knew, however, he or she might be able to explain certain behaviors or otherwise alter the manager's perspective of the evaluation and thereby make it more accurate. Filtering may be more likely to occur in digital communication such as e-mail or voice mail since they carry an implied emphasis on brevity and conciseness. Selective filtering may cause a breakdown in communication that cannot be repaired, even with good follow-up communication.

To avoid filtering, the communicator needs to understand why it occurs. Filtering can result from a lack of understanding of the receiver's position, from the sender's need to protect his or her own power by limiting the receiver's access to information, or from doubts about what the receiver might do with the information. The sender's primary concern, however, should be the message. In essence, the sender must determine exactly what message he or she wants the receiver to understand, send the receiver enough information to understand the message but not enough to create an overload, and trust the receiver to use the information properly.

Encoding and Decoding Encoding and decoding problems occur as the message is translated into or translated from the symbols used in transmission. Such problems can relate to the meaning of the symbols or to the transmission itself. Encoding and decoding problems include lack of common experience between source and receiver, problems related to semantics and the use of jargon, and difficulties with the medium.

Clearly, the source and the receiver must share a common experience with the symbols that express the message if they are to encode and decode them in exactly the same way. People who speak different languages or come from different cultural backgrounds may experience problems of this sort. But even people who speak the same language can misunderstand each other.

Semantics is the study of language forms.

Semantics is the study of language forms, and semantic problems occur when people attribute different meanings to the same words or language forms. For example, J. Edgar Hoover, the legendary former director of the FBI, once jotted "watch the borders" on a memo he had received and sent it back to the senior agency manager who had written it. Only after dispatching several dozen agents to guard the border between the United States and Mexico did the agency manager learn what Hoover had actually meant—the margins on the memo were too narrow! Similarly, when discussing a problem employee, the division head may tell her assistant, "We need to get rid of this problem." The division head may have meant that the employee should be scheduled for more training or transferred to another division. However, the assistant may interpret the statement differently and fire the problem employee.

Jargon is the specialized or technical language of a trade, profession, or social group.

The specialized or technical language of a trade, field, profession, or social group is called **jargon**. Jargon may be a hybrid of standard language and the specialized language of a group. For example, experts in the computer field use terms such as "gigs," "megs," "RAM," and "bandwidth" that have little or no meaning to those unfamiliar with computers. The use of jargon makes communication within a close group of colleagues more efficient and meaningful, but outside the group it has the opposite effect. Sometimes a source person comfortable with jargon uses it unknowingly in an attempt to communicate with receivers who do not understand it, thus causing a communication breakdown. In other cases, the source may use jargon intentionally to obscure meaning or to show outsiders that he or she belongs to the group that uses the language.

The use of jargon is acceptable (and, indeed, efficient) if the receiver is familiar with it; otherwise, it should be avoided. Repeating a jargon-laden message in clearer terms should help the receiver understand it. In general, the source and the receiver should clarify the set of symbols to be used before they communicate. Also, the receiver can ask questions frequently and, if necessary, ask the source to repeat all or part of the message. The source must send the message through a medium appropriate to the message itself and to the intended receiver. For example, a commercial run on a traditional radio station will not have its intended effect if the people in the desired market segment listen primarily to satellite radio.

Comstock/Jupiter Images

Semantics and jargon can be major problems in the communication process. For example, these three business people are trying to understand how to navigate a new web application their firm is using but are having trouble understanding some of the technical terms associated with the application.

Largely influenced by the Enron debacle, many investors are increasingly beginning to scrutinize the financial reporting systems of larger companies. Coca-Cola, for instance, has recently seen its own accounting practices criticized in the media. These critics contend that the firm is using increasingly complex reporting methods to make its earnings seem higher than they would have been if simpler and more straightforward accounting practices had been used.[19]

Receiver Several communication problems originate in the receiver, including problems with selective attention, value judgments, source credibility, and overload. Selective attention exists when the receiver attends only to selected parts of a message—a frequent occurrence with oral communication. For example, in a college class, some students may hear only part of the professor's lecture as their minds wander to other topics. To focus receivers' attention on the message, senders often engage in attention-getting behaviors such as varying the volume, repeating the message, and offering rewards.

Value judgments are influenced by the degree to which a message reinforces or challenges the receiver's basic personal beliefs. If a message reinforces the receiver's beliefs, he or she may pay close attention and believe it completely, without examination. On the other hand, if the message challenges those beliefs, the receiver may entirely discount it. Thus, if a firm's sales manager predicts that the demand for new baby-care products will increase substantially over the next two years, he or she may be ignoring reports that the birthrate is declining.

The receiver may also judge the credibility of the source of the message. If the source is perceived to be an expert in the field, the listener may pay close attention to the message and believe it. Conversely, if the receiver has little respect for the source, he or she may disregard the message. The receiver considers both the message and the source in making value judgments and determining credibility. An expert in nuclear physics may be viewed as a credible source if the issue is building a nuclear power plant, yet the same person's evaluation of the birthrate may be disregarded, perhaps correctly. This is one reason that trial lawyers ask expert witnesses about their education and experience at the beginning of their testimony: to establish credibility.

A receiver experiencing communication overload is receiving more information than she or he can process. In organizations, this can happen very easily; a receiver can be bombarded with computer-generated reports and messages from superiors, peers, and sources outside the organization. It is not unusual for middle managers or telecommuters to receive a hundred e-mail messages per day. Unable to take in all the messages, decode them, understand them, and act on them, the receiver may use selective attention and value judgments to focus on the messages that seem most important. Although this type of selective attention is necessary for survival in an information-glutted environment, it may mean that vital information is lost or overlooked.[20]

The *Technology* box on page 312 entitled "The Medical Uses of Viral E-mail" shows how value judgments, particularly when combined with selective attention, can influence a receiver's assessment of message content regardless of the perceived credibility of the source.

Verification is the feedback portion of communication in which the receiver sends a message to the source indicating receipt of the message and the degree to which he or she understood the message.

Feedback The purpose of feedback is **verification**, in which the receiver sends a message to the source indicating receipt of the message and the degree to which it was understood. Lack of feedback can cause at least two problems: First, the source may need to send another message that depends on the response to the first; if the source receives no feedback, the source may not send the second message or may be forced to send the original message again. Second, the receiver may act on the unverified message; if the receiver misunderstood the message, the resulting act may be inappropriate.

Because feedback is so important, the source must actively seek it, and the receiver must supply it. Often it is appropriate for the receiver to repeat the original message as an introduction to the response, although the medium or symbols used may be different. Nonverbal cues can provide instantaneous feedback. These include body language and facial expressions such as anger and disbelief.

The source needs to be concerned with the message, the symbols, the medium, and the feedback from the receiver. Of course, the receiver is concerned with these things, too, but from a different point of view. In general, the receiver needs to be source oriented just as the source needs to be receiver oriented. Table 11.1 gives specific suggestions for improving the communication process.

TECHNOLOGY | The Medical Uses of Viral E-mail

Dr. William H. Parker, a clinical professor of obstetrics and gynecology at the UCLA School of Medicine, says there's a certain patient question that he answers almost every day. It concerns a blood test known as CA-125, which is used to monitor the status of ovarian cancer in women diagnosed with the disease. "I probably answer maybe five or six patients a week who come in saying, 'I read this e-mail that says I'm supposed to get this test.' ... I don't mind educating my patients," Parker explains, but the e-mail "is based on bad information." When he investigated the online message that had spurred the concerns of so many patients, Parker discovered that it had been circulating for nearly 10 years.

> ***"I thought to myself, 'I need to do what they did. I need to get an e-mail out there that will take on a life of its own.'"***
>
> —DR. WILLIAM H. PARKER, ON COMBATING ONLINE MISINFORMATION

It was written by a woman named Carolyn Benivegna, who'd had a bad experience with the diagnosis of a disease quite similar to ovarian cancer. Dispatched in July 1998, Benivegna's chain letter emphasized that her cancer could have been treated more effectively if doctors had ordered the CA-125 test earlier in the lengthy diagnostic process. She urged everyone who received her message "to give it or send it via e-mail to everybody you know." She also added: "Beware that their doctors might try to talk them out of it. Don't take no for an answer." Before long, Benivegna's warning was on a decade-long journey through cyberspace—"a full-blown viral message with seemingly unstoppable momentum," according to one medical journalist.

Hence Dr. Parker's dilemma. "To explain to [patients] why this test is not reliable, without brushing off their concerns," he says, "I have to launch into a 15-minute discussion about the science and why this e-mail presents the wrong information. And," he adds, "I still have to quell their anxiety about it." Parker can, for example, explain "the science" (and often does), but he quickly discovered that his calm recitation of the data didn't have nearly the impact of Benivegna's cautionary tale.*

"So one day," he says, "I thought to myself, 'I need to do what they did. I need to get an e-mail out there that will take on a life of its own and be passed from woman to woman.'" So Parker composed an anti-misinformation e-mail and ran it by Carla Dionne, the executive director of a nonprofit women's health organization. "It needed a lot of work," recalls Dionne. "It was extremely passive and written from the clinician's perspective. It was calm, educated, and careful. The whole business of catching attention seemed somewhat offensive to him."

Ironically, she advised Parker to consult Benivegna's original message to see how he should compose his own, and Parker came back with a revised version of his e-mail message, charging it with some emotion and putting the important information up front. It promised to be much more effective. "The content of the message," explains Jeanne Jennings, an e-mail marketing consultant in Washington, D.C., "has to be of intense interest to your target audience. Women, of course, are naturally looking out for each other. So if there's a health concern or a danger, they'll naturally pass it on to their network of friends and relatives."

Parker's revised e-mail message went out in January 2008. It took a couple of weeks before a patient mentioned it, but at least Parker knew that it was making the rounds. He keeps copies of it, along with a write-up in the *New York Times*, in his waiting room, and now, he says, "when patients ask about the test, I refer them to the e-mail and the article. Then, if they have more questions, I talk to them. It just makes my life much easier this way."

References: John McCormack, "Rumor Control: How to Battle Online Misinformation," *American Medical News*, March 17, 2008, www.ama-assn.org on July 19, 2012; "CA-125 Screening for Ovarian Cancer," *BreakTheChain.org*, June 27, 2002/September 27, 2008, www.breakthechain.org on April 30, 2011; Tara Parker-Pope, "Doctors Take On a Notorious E-mail," *New York Times*, January 18, 2008, http://well.blogs.nytimes.com on July 18, 2012; "CA-125," *Snopes.com*, March 11, 2009, www.snopes.com on July 18, 2012; "A Much-Forwarded E-mail about an Ovarian Cancer Test Is Revised," The Health Sciences Institute, February 11, 2009, http://hsionline.com on July 19, 2012.

*When she learned in 2002 that she had inadvertently passed along potentially harmful misinformation, Benivegna hastened to circulate a corrective e-mail. Unfortunately, the follow up has never attained the popularity of the original. Benivegna died of ovarian cancer in September 2008.

Table 11.1 Improving the Communication Process

FOCUS	SOURCE QUESTION	CORRECTIVE ACTION	RECEIVER QUESTION	CORRECTIVE ACTION
Message	What idea or thought are you trying to get across?	Give more information. Give less information. Give entire message.	What idea or thought does the sender want you to understand?	Listen carefully to the entire message, not just to part of it.
Symbols	Does the receiver use the same symbols, words, jargon?	Say it another way. Employ repetition. Use receiver's language or jargon. Before sending, clarify symbols to be used.	What symbols are being used—for example, foreign language, technical jargon?	Clarify symbols before communication begins. Ask questions. Ask sender to repeat message.
Medium	Is this a channel that the receiver monitors regularly? Sometimes? Never?	Use multiple media. Change medium. Increase volume (loudness).	What medium or media is the sender using?	Monitor several media.
Feedback	What is the receiver's reaction to your message?	Pay attention to the feedback, especially nonverbal cues. Ask questions.	Did you correctly interpret the message?	Repeat message.

Improving Organizational Factors in Communication

Organizational factors that can create communication breakdowns or barriers include noise, status differences, time pressures, and overload. As previously stated, disturbances anywhere in the organization can distort or interrupt meaningful communication. Thus, the noise created by a rumored change in a firm's financial situation can disrupt the orderly flow of task-related information. For instance, rumors about a possible bankruptcy may cause a firm's stock to plummet (this actually happened once to retailer Kmart).[21] Similarly, rumors about a potential merger or acquisition can cause share prices to jump or fall, depending on the market's perceptions of the rumored new deal.

Status differences between source and receiver can cause some of the communication problems just discussed. For example, a firm's chief executive officer may pay little attention to communications from employees far lower on the organization chart, and employees may pay little attention to communications from the CEO. Both are instances of selective attention prompted by the organization's status system. Time pressures and communication overloads are also detrimental to communication. When the receiver is not allowed enough time to understand incoming messages, or when there are too many messages, he or she may misunderstand or ignore some of them. Effective organizational communication provides the right information to the right person at the right time and in the right form.

The **grapevine** is an informal system of communication that coexists with the formal system.

Reduce Noise Noise is a primary barrier to effective organizational communication. A common form of noise is the rumor **grapevine**, an informal system of communication that coexists with the formal system. The grapevine usually transmits information faster than official channels do. Because the accuracy of this information often is quite low, however, the grapevine can distort organizational communication. Management can reduce the effects of the distortion by using the grapevine as an additional channel for disseminating information and by constantly monitoring it for accuracy.

Foster Informal Communication Communication in well-run companies was once described as "a vast network of informal, open communications."[22] Informal communication fosters mutual trust, which minimizes the effects of status differences. Open communication can also contribute to better understanding between diverse groups in an organization. Monsanto Company created fifteen-member teams in its Agricultural Group, the primary objective being to increase communication and awareness among various diverse groups. Its Chemical Group set up diversity pairs of one supervisor and one worker to increase communication and awareness. In both cases, Monsanto found that increasing communication between people who were different paid handsome dividends for the organization.[23] Open communication also allows information to be communicated when it is needed rather than when the formal information system allows it to emerge. Some experts describe communication in effective companies as chaotic and intense, supported by the reward structure and the physical arrangement of the facilities. This means that the performance appraisal and reward system, offices, meeting rooms, and work areas are designed to encourage frequent, unscheduled, and unstructured communication throughout the organization.

Develop a Balanced Information Network Many large organizations have developed elaborate formal information networks to cope with the potential problems of information overload and time pressures. In many cases, however, the networks have created problems instead of solving them. Often they produce more information than managers and decision makers can comprehend and use in their jobs. The networks also often use only formal communication channels and ignore various informal lines of communication. Furthermore, they frequently provide whatever information the computer program is set up to provide—information that may not apply to the most pressing problem at hand. The result of all these drawbacks is loss of communication effectiveness.

Organizations need to balance information load and information-processing capabilities. In other words, they must take care not to generate more information than people can handle. It is useless to produce sophisticated statistical reports that managers have no time to read. In response to these problems, many systems now use a view-at-a-glance "dashboard" to convey essential information in a logical and condensed manner. Furthermore, the new technologies that are making more information available to managers and decision makers must be unified to produce usable information. Information production, storage, and processing capabilities must be compatible with one another and, equally important, with the needs of the organization.

Some companies—for example, General Electric, Anheuser-Busch, and McDonald's—have formalized an upward communication system that uses a corporate "ombudsperson" position. A highly placed executive who is available outside the formal chain of command to hear employees' complaints usually holds this position. The system provides an opportunity for disgruntled employees to complain without fear of losing their jobs and may help some companies achieve a balanced communication system.

SYNOPSIS

Communication is the process by which two parties exchange information and share meaning. It plays a role in every organizational activity. The purposes of communication in organizations are to achieve coordinated action, to share information, and to express feelings and emotions.

People in organizations communicate through written, oral, and nonverbal means. Written communications include letters, memos, e-mail, reports, and the like. Oral communication is the type most commonly used. Personal elements, such as facial expressions and body language, and environmental elements, such as office design, are forms of nonverbal communication.

Communication among individuals, groups, or organizations is a process in which a source sends a message and a receiver responds. The source encodes a message into symbols and transmits it through a medium to the receiver, who decodes the symbols. The receiver then responds with feedback, an attempt to verify the meaning of the original message. Noise—anything that distorts or interrupts communication—may interfere at virtually any stage of the process.

The fully integrated communication-information office system—the digital office—links people in a communication network through a combination of computers and digital transmission systems. The full range of effects of such systems has yet to be fully realized.

Communication networks are systems of information exchange within organizations. Patterns of communication emerge as information flows from person to person in a group. Typical small-group communication networks include the wheel, chain, circle, and all-channel networks.

The organizational communication network, which constitutes the real communication links in an organization, usually differs from the arrangement on an organization chart. Roles in organizational communication networks include those of gatekeeper, liaison, cosmopolite, and isolate.

Managing communication in organizations involves understanding the numerous problems that can interfere with effective communication. Problems may arise from the communication process itself and from organizational factors such as status differences.

DISCUSSION QUESTIONS

1. How is communication in organizations an individual process as well as an organizational process?
2. Discuss the three primary purposes of organizational communication.
3. Describe a situation in which you tried to carry on a conversation when no one was listening. Were any messages sent during the "conversation"?
4. A college classroom is a forum for a typical attempt at communication as the professor tries to communicate the subject to the students. Describe classroom communication in terms of the basic communication process outlined in the chapter.
5. Is there a communication network (other than professor-to-student) in the class in which you are using this book? If so, identify the specific roles that people play in the network. If not, why has no network developed? What would be the benefits of having a communication network in this class?
6. Why might educators typically focus most communication training on the written and oral methods and pay little attention to the nonverbal methods? Do you think that more training emphasis should be placed on nonverbal communication? Why or why not?
7. Is the typical classroom means of transferring information from professor to student an effective form of communication? Where does it break down? What are the communication problems in the college classroom?
8. Who is responsible for solving classroom communication problems: the students, the professor, or the administration?
9. Have you ever worked in an organization in which communication was a problem? If so, what were some causes of the problem?

10. What methods were used, or should have been used, to improve communication in the situation you described in question 9?

11. Would the use of advanced computer information processing or telecommunications have helped solve the communications problem you described in question 9?

12. What types of communication problems will new telecommunications methods probably be able to solve? Why?

13. What types of communications would NOT be appropriate to send by e-mail? Or by voice mail?

14. Which steps in the communication process are usually left out, or at the very least poorly done, when e-mail and voice mail are used for communication?

HOW DO YOU SEE IT?

Seeding Connections

"I don't think you can ever be too annoying."

—STEVE MARTUCCI, OPERATIONS MANAGER, PLANT FANTASIES

We discussed Plant Fantasies, a New York landscape contractor, in our *Video Case* for Chapter 7, and you can go there for background details on the company and founder Teresa Carleo. In this episode, we're introduced to Sales Director (and now Operations Manager) Steve Martucci, who joined the firm in 2003. Martucci handles 60-80 accounts, or about half of the company's client list. President/CEO Carleo manages the rest.

Landscape contracting, admits Martucci, "wasn't my first choice, but it's worked out well for me." It's worked out well for Carleo, too. "Steve," she says, "is like my right-hand man in selling and handling customers…. We're good together." For one thing, the relationship works out well when it comes to gathering information from clients: "I think we listen differently," explains Martucci. Teresa will "hear some of it, and I'll hear other things. So we both take away different things…. Teresa tends to really get into the relationship, and I'm more into specifics."

For both, listening is a critical managerial skill. "First," says Martucci (in another interview), "we listen very carefully. We hear what the customer has to say. Then we use our experience to create the look they want." The informal "teamwork" approach to message decoding seems to get good results. In 2008, for example, Plant Fantasies was hired to create rooftop gardens for Manhattan House, which Andy Attinson, an executive at owner O'Connor Capital Partners, describes as "a one-of-a-kind 'New York original,' a building that has often been copied but never duplicated." For the landscaping project, Attinson explains, "R-E-S-P-E-C-T was our mantra: respect for the environment, respect for the original design, respect for its sense of history and place. Plant Fantasies," he reports, "embraced this mantra and were sensitive to nuances in a way that many [contractors] are not."

Carleo and Martucci have also found that skillful encoding is crucial to effective communication. On any given day, Plant Fantasies may be actively involved in as many as 15 jobs, each requiring an allotment of trucks, tools, plants, and workers. "Each job," says Carleo, "requires so many different things. And it needs to be coordinated." Both understand that coordination is a matter of effective downward internal communication. For Carleo, the key is clarity: "I'm a big communicator," she says. "I think I'm really clear. I do get the feeling that no one listens to me sometimes," she admits, "but I think I'm pretty clear." Martucci, on the other hand, apparently prefers the virtues of getting straight to the point. When necessary, he recommends, "just be really blunt." Perhaps the sometimes subtle difference between the two approaches emerges in the following exchange:

> CARLEO: *We do need to communicate on what we're sending out this week, because I'm a little nervous that the flower department doesn't exactly know what the new design is.*
>
> MARTUCCI: *I don't think they do.*
>
> CARLEO: *How does that happen? I thought I went over it.*
>
> MARTUCCI: *… They tell you they understand when they don't actually understand.*

Carleo worries that "I maybe communicate too much…. That would be a fault of mine," she admits, but it's one that she's been working on: "I used to email like all night sometimes. But then I started to feel like it was … not being fair to my employees. So now I write the emails and I save them. And then in the morning, I shoot them all out." Martucci isn't quite so sure that one can overcommunicate—"I don't think you can ever be too annoying"—but he agrees that "email is probably the best way to get the basic information across." For many communications, however, he prefers the phone: "For me, the back and forth on email for a conversation you could have on the phone that would take a minute is a waste of time. I'd rather just make the phone call and get the right information and just move forward."

Even better, argues Martucci, is face to face,

> *when you can do it and when there's time.... It's good for the customer, too. You want them to see you. You want them to remember you. You want them to see that you went through the time to come there. You didn't just shoot them an email in a cab going somewhere else. They want to feel important.*

Carleo, too, realizes that, while it's efficient, email isn't always the best way to handle business communications. She reports that, in order to let her customers know about an award that the company has received, she's decided on a more personal touch:

> *I am hand-writing a note to each of my clients and putting it in an envelope. Remember those? And I'm mailing it. Because I think I have a better chance of my potential customers and existing customers opening that envelope than I would doing an eblast.... In terms of all these emails and eblasts, I feel that it's more significant and meaningful to make a connection with somebody.*

CASE QUESTIONS

1. Review Figure 11.1 in the section on the *purposes of communication in organizations*. Of the three main purposes diagrammed in the figure, which is the most important at Plant Fantasies? How does it relate to the two other purposes identified in the diagram? In answering both questions, be specific in citing examples from the video.
2. When it comes to *methods of communication*, which type does Carleo seem to prefer? How about Martucci? On what points do they appear to be most in agreement? On what points do they seem to differ the most? If you were a client of Plant Fantasies, which of the two would you rather deal with directly—Carleo or Martucci? Why?
3. Plant Fantasies manages its operations by using groups of employees from different departments to work on individual projects. In your opinion, which type of *small-group network* would probably work best at Plant Fantasies—*wheel*, *chain*, *circle*, or *all-channel*? Might the best type be some kind of hybrid created out of two or more of these types? Explain your answer.
4. "I do get the feeling," Carleo admits, "that no one listens to me sometimes." She says that she's working on the problem, but, **judging from the video**, perhaps you can give her some advice on improving her *communication fidelity*. Focusing on the roles of *source* and *receiver*, identify some of the factors that may contribute to Carleo's perceived communication problems and suggest some things that she might do to deal with them.
5. Describe the video as a whole in terms of the *communication process*: Identify the role of each factor in the process—*source*, *encoding*, *transmission*, *decoding*, *receiver*, *noise*, and, if appropriate, *feedback*—in the presentation and use of the video in your class. Which factor seemed most important? Most successful? On the whole, was the use of the video effective in meeting its apparent communication goals? Why or why not?

ADDITIONAL SOURCES

Cara S. Trager, "Top Entrepreneurs 2010: Plant Fantasies," *Crain's New York Business.com*, May 1, 2010, www.crainsnewyork.com on June 26, 2012; Plant Fantasies (2012), "Teresa Carleo Founded Plant Fantasies in 1987 and Has Been Greening Manhattan from Courtyards to Rooftops Ever Since," *New York Real Estate Journal*, May 11-24, 2010 (press release), www.plantfantasies.com on June 26, 2012; Plant Fantasies (2012), "Plant Fantasies: Greening Manhattan from Courtyards to Rooftops," *Mann Report*, n.d. (press release), www.plantfantasies.com on August 28, 2012; Plant Fantasies (2012), "Plant Fantasies Merges Interior, Exterior Landscapes," *Real Estate Weekly*, November 5, 2008 (press release), www.plantfantasies.com on August 28, 2012.

EXPERIENCING ORGANIZATIONAL BEHAVIOR

The Importance of Feedback in Oral Communication

Purpose This exercise demonstrates the importance of feedback in oral communication.

Format You will be an observer or play the role of either a manager or an assistant manager trying to tell a coworker where a package of important materials is to be picked up. The observer's role is to make sure the other two participants follow the rules and to observe and record any interesting occurrences.

Procedure The instructor will divide the class into groups of three. (Any extra members can be roving observers.) The three people in each group will take the roles of manager, assistant manager, and observer. In the second trial, the manager and the assistant manager will switch roles.

Trial 1: The manager and the assistant manager should turn their backs to each other so that neither can see the other. Here is the situation: The manager is in another city that he or she is not familiar with but that the assistant manager knows quite well. The manager needs to find the office of a supplier to pick up drawings of a critical component of the company's main product. The supplier will be closing for the day in a few minutes; the drawings must be picked up before closing time. The manager has called the assistant manager to get directions to the office. However, the connection is faulty; the manager can hear the assistant manager, but the assistant manager can hear only enough to know the manager is on the line. The manager has redialed once, but there was no improvement in the connection. Now there is no time to lose. The manager has decided to get the directions from the assistant without asking questions.

Just before the exercise begins, the instructor will give the assistant manager a detailed map of the city that shows the locations of the supplier's office and the manager. The map will include a number of turns, stops, stoplights, intersections, and shopping centers between these locations. The assistant manager can study it for no longer than a minute or two. When the instructor gives the direction to start, the assistant manager describes to the manager how to get from his or her present location to the supplier's office. As the assistant manager gives the directions, the manager draws the map on a piece of paper.

The observer makes sure that no questions are asked, records the beginning and ending times, and notes how the assistant manager tries to communicate particularly difficult points (including points about which the manager obviously wants to ask questions) and any other noteworthy occurrences.

After all pairs have finished, each observer "grades" the quality of the manager's map by comparing it with the original and counting the number of obvious mistakes. The instructor will ask a few managers who believe they have drawn good maps to tell the rest of the class how to get to the supplier's office.

Trial 2: In trial 2, the manager and the assistant manager switch roles, and a second map is passed out to the new assistant managers. The situation is the same as in the first trial except that the telephones are working properly and the manager can ask questions of the assistant manager. The observer's role is the same as in trial 1—recording the beginning and ending times, the methods of communication, and other noteworthy occurrences.

After all pairs have finished, the observers grade the maps, just as in the first trial. The instructor then selects a few managers to tell the rest of the class how to get to the supplier's office. The subsequent class discussion should center on the experiences of the class members and the follow up questions.

Follow-Up Questions

1. Which trial resulted in more accurate maps? Why?
2. Which trial took longer? Why?
3. How did you feel when a question needed to be asked but could not be asked in trial 1? Was your confidence in the final result affected differently in the two trials?

Source: "Diagnosing Your Listening Skills," from Ethel C. Glenn and Elliott A. Pond, "Listening Self-Inventory," *Supervisory Management,* January 1989, pp. 12–15.

BUILDING MANAGERIAL SKILLS

Exercise Overview Communications skills refer to your ability to convey ideas and information to other people. The task is easier, of course, when the person with whom you're communicating is familiar with the same language as you are. In an increasingly diverse business environment, however, you won't always have the luxury of expressing yourself strictly on your own terms. This exercise asks you to communicate information by carefully crafting the terms in which you express yourself.

Exercise Background Because more than half the information in any face-to-face exchange is conveyed by nonverbal means, body language is a significant factor in any interpersonal communication. Consider, for example, the impact of a yawn or a frown (never mind a shaken fist!). At the same time, however, most people pay relatively little conscious attention to the nonverbal elements of an exchange, especially the more subtle ones. And if you misread the complete set of signals that someone is sending you, you're not likely to receive that person's message in the way that's intended.

In this exercise, you'll examine some interactions between two people from which we've eliminated sound; in other words, you'll have only visual clues to help you decipher the meaning of the messages being sent and received. Then you'll be asked to examine those same interactions with both visual and verbal clues intact.

Exercise Task

1. Observe a silent video segment (you can find it on the student website). For each segment, describe the nature of the relationship and interaction between the two individuals. What nonverbal clues did you rely on in reaching your conclusions?
2. Next, observe the same video segments with audio included. Describe the interaction again, this time indicating any verbal clues that you relied on.
3. How accurate were your assessments when you had only visual information? Explain why you were or were not accurate in your assessment of the situation.
4. What does this exercise show you about the role of nonverbal factors in interpersonal communication? What advice would you now give managers about the importance of these factors?

SELF-ASSESSMENT EXERCISE

Diagnosing Your Listening Skills

Introduction Good listening skills are essential for effective communication and are often overlooked when communication is analyzed. This self-assessment questionnaire examines your ability to listen effectively.

Instructions Go through the following statements, checking "Yes" or "No" next to each one. Mark each question as truthfully as you can in light of your behavior in the last few meetings or gatherings you attended.

Yes	*No*	
___	___	1. I frequently attempt to listen to several conversations at the same time.
___	___	2. I like people to give me only the facts and then let me make my own interpretation.
___	___	3. I sometimes pretend to pay attention to people.
___	___	4. I consider myself a good judge of nonverbal communications.
___	___	5. I usually know what another person is going to say before he or she says it.
___	___	6. I usually end conversations that don't interest me by diverting my attention from the speaker.
___	___	7. I frequently nod, frown, or in some other way let the speaker know how I feel about what he or she is saying.

___ ___ 8. I usually respond immediately when someone has finished talking.

___ ___ 9. I evaluate what is being said while it is being said.

___ ___ 10. I usually formulate a response while the other person is still talking.

___ ___ 11. The speaker's delivery style frequently keeps me from listening to content.

___ ___ 12. I usually ask people to clarify what they have said rather than guess at the meaning.

___ ___ 13. I make a concerted effort to understand other people's point of view.

___ ___ 14. I frequently hear what I expect to hear rather than what is said.

___ ___ 15. Most people feel that I have understood their point of view when we disagree.

Scoring: The correct answers according to communication theory are as follows:

No for statements 1, 2, 3, 5, 6, 7, 8, 9, 10, 11, and 14.
Yes for statements 4, 12, 13, and 15.

If you missed only one or two responses, you strongly approve of your own listening habits and are on the right track to becoming an effective listener in your role as manager. If you missed three or four responses, you have uncovered some doubts about your listening effectiveness, and your knowledge of how to listen has some gaps. If you missed five or more responses, you probably are not satisfied with the way you listen, and your friends and coworkers may not feel you are a good listener, either. Work on improving your active listening skills.

Reference

"Diagnosing Your Listening Skills," from Ethel C. Glenn and Elliott A. Pond, "Listening Self-Inventory," *Supervisory Management*, January 1989, pp. 12–15. Reprinted with permission of American Management Association via Copyright Clearance Center.

CHAPTER 12

Traditional Models for Understanding Leadership

Chapter Outline

- The Nature of Leadership
- Early Approaches to Leadership
- The Emergence of Situational Leadership Models
- The LPC Theory of Leadership
- The Path-Goal Theory of Leadership
- Vroom's Decision Tree Approach to Leadership

Chapter Learning Objectives

After studying this chapter, you should be able to:

1. Characterize the nature of leadership.
2. Trace the early approaches to leadership.
3. Discuss the emergence of situational theories and models of leadership.
4. Describe the LPC theory of leadership.
5. Discuss the path-goal theory of leadership.
6. Describe Vroom's decision tree approach to leadership.

Two Facets of Jamie Dimon's Leadership at JPMorgan

"It was Jamie who saw all the pieces."

—JPMorgan executive, 2008

"It was all about the money, not the client."

—Former JPMorgan mutual funds manager, 2012

In October 2006, the head of the JPMorgan mortgage-servicing department, which collects payments on home loans, informed CEO Jamie Dimon that late payments were increasing at an alarming rate. When Dimon reviewed the report, he confirmed not only that late payments were a problem at Morgan, but that things were even worse for other lenders. "We concluded," recalls Dimon, "that underwriting standards were deteriorating across the industry." Shortly thereafter, Dimon was informed that the cost of insuring securities backed by subprime mortgages was going up even though ratings agencies persisted in classifying them *AAA*. At the time, creating securities backed by subprime mortgages was the hottest and most profitable business on Wall Street, but by the end of the year, Dimon had decided to get out of it. "We saw no profit, and lots of risk," reports Bill Winters, co-head of Morgan's investment arm. "It was Jamie," he adds, "who saw all the pieces."

Dimon's caution—and willingness to listen to what his risk-management people were telling him—paid off in a big way. Between July 2007 and July 2008, when the full force of the crisis hit the country's investment banks, Morgan recorded losses of $5 billion on mortgage-backed securities. That's a lot of money, but relatively little compared to the losses sustained by banks that didn't see the writing on the wall—$33 billion at Citibank, for example, and $26 billion at Merrill Lynch. Citi is still in business, thanks to $45 billion in cash infusions from the federal government, but Merrill Lynch isn't—it was forced to sell itself to Bank of America. Morgan, though hit hard, weathered the storm and is still standing on its own Wall Street foundations. "You know," said President-elect Barack Obama as he surveyed the damage sustained by the U.S. banking industry in 2008, "… there are a lot of banks that are actually pretty well managed, JPMorgan

Jamie Dimon, CEO of JPMorgan Chase, plays a strong leadership role at the financial giant.

being a good example. Jamie Dimon … is doing a pretty good job managing an enormous portfolio."

That was then. In May 2012, Dimon announced that Morgan expected to lose $2 billion on a "stupid" series of trades involving corporate debt and high-yield securities—the so-called "London Whale" deals. Two months later, the total loss from one of the bank's biggest blunders ever stood at nearly $6 billion, but Dimon was able to announce that Morgan had nevertheless reached its expected earnings goal for the second quarter. How? Apparently, through the creative efforts of the accounting department.

Like most of us, banks can write off losses at tax time—that is, deduct them from the bottom line and factor them into their tax bills. Dimon explained that Morgan planned to write off nearly $2 billion of the London Whale loss, or almost 38 percent. That percentage isn't out of line with the U.S. corporate tax rate, but it should be noted that companies rarely *pay* taxes at that rate, which apparently comes in handy only in *reducing* a tax bill. In any case, Morgan had managed to finesse the loss from $6 billion to $4 billion, and, through a few more esoteric moves, it was able to make that $4 billion go away, too.

Unfortunately, bank insiders realized that total losses from the London Whale fiasco might be closer to $9 billion, and to make matters worse, the *New York Times* charged that Morgan, which is also one of the country's largest mutual funds managers, was "making up for lost profit" by steering customers toward its own investment products and away from better options offered by its competitors. As one former Morgan trader told the *Times*, "I was selling JPMorgan funds that often had weak performance records, and I was doing it for no other reason than to enrich the firm." "It was all about the money, not the client," reports another ex-Morgan broker.

How, exactly, does the practice of pushing its own funds benefit Morgan? Fund managers collect fees for managing the funds that it creates, and the more investors' money that goes into its own funds, the more money it collects in fees. Moreover, Morgan was charging a fee of 1.6 percent of fund value, as opposed to the typical industry rate of 1 percent. According to the *Times*, Dimon had originally "balked at the idea of pushing the bank's investments" but ultimately compromised with executives who wanted to strengthen the policy of increasing the emphasis on the bank's proprietary funds over non-Morgan funds. The bank, says the newspaper, has continued to reinforce this policy and, on top of that, has exaggerated the performance of its own funds in its marketing efforts.

The fallout from all the missteps, cover-up maneuvers, and media coverage included a serious blow to Jamie Dimon's once vaunted credibility. In particular, Dimon has been at the forefront of efforts to fight precisely the kind of regulatory changes that would have limited a bank's ability to take the risky steps that got JPMorgan in trouble in the first place.

What Do You Think?

1. What appear to be the key functions of leadership at an organization such as JPMorgan?
2. How would you explain the apparent discrepancy in Dimon's actions between 2006 and 2012? In your opinion, is there anything inherent in the nature of organizational processes that might account for such a discrepancy?

References: Roger Lowenstein, "Jamie Dimon: America's Least-Hated Banker," *New York Times*, December 1, 2010, www.nytimes.com on July 28, 2012; Duff McDonald, "The Banker Who Saved Wall Street," *Newsweek*, September 11, 2009, www.thedailybeast.com on July 28, 2012; Shawn Tully, "How J.P. Morgan Steered Clear of the Credit Crunch," *CNNMoney.com*, September 2, 2008, http://money.cnn.com on July 28, 2012; Mike Taylor, "Hardest-Hitting Jamie Dimon Profile Ever Still Concludes He's Pretty Great," *The New York Observer*, November 2, 2010, http://observer.com on July 28, 2012; Stephen Gandel, "How Jamie Dimon Hid the $6 Billion Loss," *CNNMoney*, July 13, 2012, http://finance.fortune.cnn.com on July 26, 2012; Maureen Farrell, "Who's Paying for JPMorgan's Loss?" *CNNMoney*, July 14, 2012, http://money.cnn.com on July 19, 2012; Jessica Silver-Greenberg and Susanne Craig, "JPMorgan Trading Loss May Reach $9 Billion," *New York Times*, June 28, 2012, http://dealbook.nytimes.com on July 19, 2012; Craig and Silver-Greenberg, "Former Brokers Say JPMorgan Favored Selling Bank's Own Funds Over Others," *New York Times*, July 2, 2012, http://dealbook.nytimes.com on July 19, 2012.

The mystique of leadership makes it one of the most widely debated, studied, and sought-after properties of organizational life. Managers talk about the characteristics that make an effective leader and the importance of leadership to organizational success, while organizational scientists have extensively studied leadership and myriad related phenomena for decades. Paradoxically, however, while leadership is among the most widely studied concepts in the entire field of management, many unanswered questions remain. Why, then, should we continue to study leadership? First, leadership is of great practical importance to organizations. Second, in spite of many remaining mysteries, researchers have isolated and verified some key variables that influence leadership effectiveness.[1]

This chapter, the first of two devoted to leadership, introduces the fundamental traditional models that are commonly used as a basis for understanding leadership. We start with a discussion of the meaning of leadership, including its definition and the distinctions between leadership and management. Then we turn to historical views of leadership, focusing on the trait and behavioral approaches. Next, we examine three contemporary leadership theories that have formed the basis for most leadership research: the LPC theory developed by Fiedler, the path-goal theory, and Vroom's decision tree approach to leadership. In our next chapter, we explore several contemporary and emerging views of leadership.

THE NATURE OF LEADERSHIP

Because "leadership" is a term that is often used in everyday conversation, you might assume that it has a common and accepted meaning. In fact, just the opposite is true—like several other key organizational behavior terms such as "personality" and "motivation," "leadership" is used in a variety of ways. Thus, we first clarify its meaning as we use it in this book.

The Meaning of Leadership

Leadership is both a process and a property. As a *process*, leadership involves the use of noncoercive influence. As a *property*, leadership is the set of characteristics attributed to someone who is perceived to use influence successfully.

Influence is the ability to affect the perceptions, beliefs, attitudes, motivation, and/or behaviors of others.

We will define **leadership** in terms of both process and property.[2] As a process, leadership is the use of noncoercive influence to direct and coordinate the activities of group members to meet a goal. As a property, leadership is the set of characteristics attributed to those who are perceived to use such influence successfully.[3] **Influence**, a common element of both perspectives, is the ability to affect the perceptions, beliefs, attitudes, motivation, and/or behaviors of others. From an organizational viewpoint, leadership is vital because it has such a powerful influence on individual and group behavior.[4] Moreover, because the goal toward which the group directs its efforts is often the desired goal of the leader, it may or may not mesh with organizational goals.

Leadership involves neither force nor coercion. A manager who relies solely on force and formal authority to direct the behavior of subordinates is not exercising leadership. Thus, as discussed more fully in the next section, a manager or supervisor may or may not also be a leader. It is also important to note that on one hand, a leader may actually possess the characteristics attributed to him or her; on the other, the leader may merely be perceived as possessing them. The Service box illustrates some of the complex issues that follow from leadership processes and properties.

Leadership versus Management

From these definitions, it should be clear that leadership and management are related, but they are not the same. A person can be a manager, a leader, both, or neither.[5] Some of the basic distinctions between the two are summarized in Table 12.1. On the left side of the table are four elements that differentiate leadership from management. The two columns show how each element differs when considered from a management and a leadership point of view. For example, when executing plans, managers focus on monitoring results, comparing them with goals, and correcting deviations. In contrast, the leader focuses on energizing people to overcome bureaucratic hurdles to help reach goals.

To further underscore the differences, consider the various roles that might typify managers and leaders in a hospital setting. The chief of staff of a large hospital is clearly a manager by virtue of the position itself. At the same time, this individual may not be respected or trusted by others and may have to rely solely on the authority vested in the position to get people to do things. But an emergency-room nurse with no formal authority may be quite effective at taking charge of a chaotic situation and directing others in how to deal with specific patient problems. Others in the emergency room may respond because they trust the nurse's judgment and have confidence in the nurse's decision-making skills.

And the head of pediatrics, supervising a staff of twenty other doctors, nurses, and attendants, may also enjoy the staff's complete respect, confidence, and trust. They readily take her advice and follow directives without question, and often go far beyond what

Table 12.1 Kotter's Distinctions Between Management and Leadership

ACTIVITY	MANAGEMENT	LEADERSHIP
CREATING AN AGENDA	**Planning and budgeting.** Establishing detailed steps and timetables for achieving needed results; allocating the resources necessary to make those needed results happen	**Establishing direction.** Developing a vision of the future, often the distant future, and strategies for producing the changes needed to achieve that vision
DEVELOPING A HUMAN NETWORK FOR ACHIEVING THE AGENDA	**Organizing and staffing.** Establishing some structure for accomplishing plan requirements, staffing that structure with individuals, delegating responsibility and authority for carrying out the plan, providing policies and procedures to help guide people, and creating methods or systems to monitor implementation	**Aligning people.** Communicating the direction by words and deeds to all those whose cooperation may be needed to influence the creation of teams and coalitions that understand the vision and strategies and accept their validity
EXECUTING PLANS	**Controlling and problem solving.** Monitoring results vs. plan in some detail, identifying deviations, and then planning and organizing to solve these problems	**Motivating and inspiring.** Energizing people to overcome major political, bureaucratic, and resource barriers to change by satisfying very basic, but often unfulfilled, human needs
OUTCOMES	Produces a degree of predictability and order and has the potential to consistently produce major results expected by various stakeholders (e.g., for customers, always being on time; for stockholders, being on budget)	Produces change, often to a dramatic degree, and has the potential to produce extremely useful change (e.g., new products that customers want, new approaches to labor relations that help make a firm more competitive)

References: Adapted with the permission of The Free Press, a Division of Simon & Schuster Inc., from *A Force for Change: How Leadership Differs from Management*, by John P. Kotter.

is necessary to help carry out the unit's mission. Thus, being a manager does not ensure that a person is also a leader—any given manager may or may not also be a leader. Similarly, a leadership position can also be formal, as when someone appointed to head a group has leadership qualities, or informal, as when a leader emerges from the ranks of the group according to a consensus of the members. The chief of staff described earlier is a manager but not really a leader. The emergency-room nurse is a leader but not a manager. And the head of pediatrics is likely both.

Organizations need both management and leadership if they are to be effective. For example, leadership is necessary to create and direct change and to help the organization get through tough times.[6] And management is necessary to achieve coordination and systematic results and to handle administrative activities during times of stability and predictability. Management in conjunction with leadership can help achieve planned orderly change, and leadership in conjunction with management can keep the organization properly aligned with its environment.

In addition, managers and leaders also play a major role in establishing the moral climate of the organization and in determining the role of ethics in its culture.[7] Maintaining one's ethical balance while discharging other leadership duties can sometimes require an executive to walk a fairly fine line. For instance, consider a CEO who knows that her firm will need to lay off several thousand workers in a few months. On the one hand, divulging this information too early may result in devaluing the firm's stock and causing

SERVICE Who's the Boss?

©rangizzz/Shutterstock

You are a manager at a popular local pub. Your bartenders are a good group but seem to have problems always following the house rules. You have learned, for example, that some customers have asked for and received double shots, which are expressly prohibited by company policy. While you have repeatedly reminded your bartenders of this policy, you know they don't always follow your leadership. It is too tempting for them to do what the customers ask because so much of their organizationally derived rewards come from customers in the form of tips and positive feedback. You realize that much of their pay is made up of tips from customers who happily tip well when they get what they ask for and don't tip so well when company policy gets in their way. Since you have just finished a course in OB at the local university, you decide to flip back through your books to see if there is anything there that can help. In specific, you review motivation theory to see if you are using the knowledge in the book. You remember that employees work for a variety of incentives and that leaders provide desired incentives to employees in order to motivate them to perform their jobs with diligence, enthusiasm, and commitment.

You know your bartenders seek financial rewards, interesting jobs, and opportunities to do what they do well. You have provided them with a better than competitive wage, you know that the people you've hired find bartending to be an interesting job with lots of opportunities to meet interesting people, and you have trained them well to perform their jobs. In other words, you've done what you have learned that should motivate the bartenders, and they still pour double shots in defiance of bar policy.

You decide to look deeper into this situation and think about what it was like when you were a bartender. You recall how much fun it was to talk to people who came back time and time again. You also recall that some of these folks asked for special favors (like double shots) that you accommodated from time to time not only because you liked these people but because they would tip you well for your "special treatment." You remember how much you enjoyed it when they told you what a good job you did and how much they appreciated your excellent and skilled service. As these memories linger in your mind, it hits you. Your bartenders are just like you. Their desired incentives don't come entirely from your leadership skills, company rewards, or your feedback. Equally important to most of them, they receive praise from their customers, direct and immediate performance feedback in the form of tips, and the social value of customer interactions. In other words, the incentives you offer your bartenders as their formal leader are only a part of what they seek and gain from these direct customer interactions. No wonder you can't get them to follow the rules all the time the way you wish.

Discussion Question: How does this idea of customer as leader support or change the traditional models of leadership in the chapter?

top employees to look for other jobs. But delaying the news until the last minute might result in longer periods of unemployment for the workers who lose their jobs.

EARLY APPROACHES TO LEADERSHIP

Although leaders and leadership have profoundly influenced the course of human events, careful scientific study of them began only about a century ago. Early studies focused on the traits, or personal characteristics, of leaders.[8] Later research shifted to examine actual leader behaviors.

Trait Approaches to Leadership

Lincoln, Napoleon, Joan of Arc, Hitler, and Gandhi are names that most of us know quite well. Early researchers believed that leaders such as these had some unique set of

The **trait approach** to leadership attempted to identify stable and enduring character traits that differentiated effective leaders from nonleaders.

qualities or traits that distinguished them from their peers. Moreover, these traits were presumed to be relatively stable and enduring. Following this **trait approach**, these researchers focused on identifying leadership traits, developing methods for measuring them, and using the methods to select leaders.

Hundreds of studies guided by this research agenda were conducted during the first several decades of the twentieth century. The earliest writers believed that important leadership traits included intelligence, dominance, self-confidence, energy, activity, and task-relevant knowledge. The results of subsequent studies gave rise to a long list of additional traits. Unfortunately, the list quickly became so long that it lost any semblance of practical value. In addition, the results of many studies were inconsistent.

For example, one early argument was that effective leaders such as Lincoln tended to be taller than ineffective leaders. But critics were quick to point out that Hitler and Napoleon, both effective leaders in their own way, were not tall. Some writers have even tried to relate leadership to such traits as body shape, astrological sign, or handwriting patterns. The trait approach also had a significant theoretical problem in that it could neither specify nor prove how presumed leadership traits are connected to leadership per se. For these and other reasons, the trait approach was all but abandoned several decades ago.

In recent years, however, the trait approach has received renewed interest. For example, some researchers have sought to reintroduce a limited set of traits into the leadership literature. These traits include emotional intelligence, drive, motivation, honesty and integrity, self-confidence, cognitive ability, knowledge of the business, and charisma (which is discussed in Chapter 13).[9] Some people even believe that biological factors may play a role in leadership. Although it is too early to know whether these traits have validity from a leadership perspective, it does appear that a serious and scientific assessment of appropriate traits may further our understanding of the leadership phenomenon. And unfortunately, traits may even play a role in people's not having opportunities to engage in leadership activities. Regardless of the reasons (including prejudice, stereotypes, or other factors), women, African Americans, and Hispanics are still significantly underrepresented among top management teams and boards of directors in the largest American businesses. The *Diversity* box on page 328, entitled "Getting on Board with Diversity," discusses diversity as a lingering issue in the composition of U.S. boards of directors.

The **behavioral approach** to leadership tried to identify behaviors that differentiated effective leaders from nonleaders.

Behavioral Approaches to Leadership

In the late 1940s, most researchers began to shift away from the trait approach and started to look at leadership as an observable process or activity. The goal of the so-called **behavioral approach** was to determine what behaviors are associated with effective leadership.[10] The researchers assumed that the behaviors of effective leaders differed somehow from the behaviors of less effective leaders and that the behaviors of effective leaders would be the same across all situations. The behavioral approach to the study of leadership included the Michigan studies, the Ohio State studies, and the leadership grid.

The **Michigan leadership studies** defined job-centered and employee-centered leadership as opposite ends of a single leadership dimension.

The Michigan Studies The **Michigan leadership studies** were a program of research conducted at the University of Michigan.[11] The goal of this work was to determine the pattern of leadership behaviors that results in effective group performance. From interviews with supervisors and subordinates of high- and low-productivity groups in several organizations, the researchers collected and analyzed descriptions of supervisory behavior to determine how effective supervisors differed from ineffective ones. Two basic forms of leader behavior were identified—job-centered and employee-centered—as shown in the top portion of Figure 12.1.

Job-centered leader behavior involves paying close attention to the work of subordinates, explaining work procedures, and demonstrating a strong interest in performance.

The leader who exhibits **job-centered leader behavior** pays close attention to the work of subordinates, explains work procedures, and is mainly interested in

DIVERSITY Getting on Board with Diversity

©vlad_star/shutterstock

"It's been proven again and again," says Carl Brooks, CEO of the Executive Leadership Council, a network of senior African American executives, "that companies with board members who reflect gender and ethnic diversity also tend to have better returns on equity and sales." According to Marc H. Morial, CEO of the National Urban League, which promotes economic empowerment for African Americans, a minority presence on corporate boards is also necessary to protect the interests of minority consumers and other stakeholders: "African American voices and perspectives," he argues, "are needed on corporate boards to ensure that business decisions affecting Black America are both responsible and sensitive to the needs of our communities."

Unfortunately, says Morial, "African Americans still represent a miniscule fraction of board-level corporate leadership in America." Citing a 2009 study by the Executive Leadership Council, Morial points out that the number of blacks on Fortune 500 boards has actually *declined* in recent years: Even though blacks comprise 13 percent of the U.S. population, representation on corporate boards stands at "a meager 7 percent."

The same trend was confirmed with the release, in August 2010, of the U.S. Senate Democratic Hispanic Task Force report on minority and women representation on Fortune 500 boards and executive teams (CEOs plus their direct reports). Here are some of the survey's findings:

- Women comprise 18 percent of all board members and just under 20 percent of executive team members (roughly 1 in 5). Those figures, of course, are far below the 50-percent proportion of women in the population.
- Minorities comprise 14.5 percent of all directors—about 1 out of every 7—and an even smaller percentage of executive-team members. That's less than half of their 35-percent proportion of the population.
- Although African Americans boast the highest minority representation on boards—8.8 percent—that's equivalent to only 69 percent of their total proportion of the population. Representation on executive teams is only 4.2 percent.
- Hispanics fared worse than any other minority. Although they represent 15 percent of the U.S. population, they comprise only 3.3 percent of board members and 3 percent of executive-team members.

The report, says task force chair Robert Menendez (the lone Hispanic member of the U.S. Senate),

> *clearly confirms what we had suspected all along—that American corporations need to do better when it comes to having the board rooms on Wall Street reflect the reality on Main Street. We need to change the dynamic and make it commonplace for minorities to be part of the American corporate structure. It is not just about doing what's right, but it's a good business decision that will benefit both corporations and the communities they're tapping into and making investments in.*

References: "African Americans Lost Ground on Fortune 500 Boards," *Savoy*, August 2009, http://savoynetwork.com on July 23, 2012; Marc H. Morial, "National Urban League Trains African Americans for Corporate Boards," *Philadelphia Tribune*, April 14, 2011, www.phillytrib.com on April 25, 2011; "Results of Menendez's Major Fortune 500 Diversity Survey: Representation of Women and Minorities on Corporate Boards Still Lags Far Behind National Population," August 4, 2010, Senator Robert Menendez's website (press release), www.menendez.senate.gov on July 23, 2012.

Employee-centered leader behavior involves attempting to build effective work groups with high performance goals.

performance. The leader's primary concern is efficient completion of the task. The leader who engages in **employee-centered leader behavior** attempts to build effective work groups with high performance goals. The leader's main concern is with high performance, but that is to be achieved by paying attention to the human aspects of the group. These two styles of leader behavior were presumed to be at opposite ends of a single dimension. Thus, the Michigan researchers suggested that any given leader could exhibit either job-centered or employee-centered leader behavior, but not both at the same time. Moreover, they suggested that employee-centered leader behavior was

FIGURE 12.1

Early Behavioral Approaches to Leadership

Two of the first behavioral approaches to leadership were the Michigan and Ohio State studies. The results of the Michigan studies suggested that there are two fundamental types of leader behavior, job-centered and employee-centered, which were presumed to be at opposite ends of a single continuum. The Ohio State studies also found two kinds of leadership behavior, "consideration" and "initiating-structure." These behaviors are somewhat parallel to those found in the Michigan studies but this research suggested that these two types of behavior were actually independent dimensions.

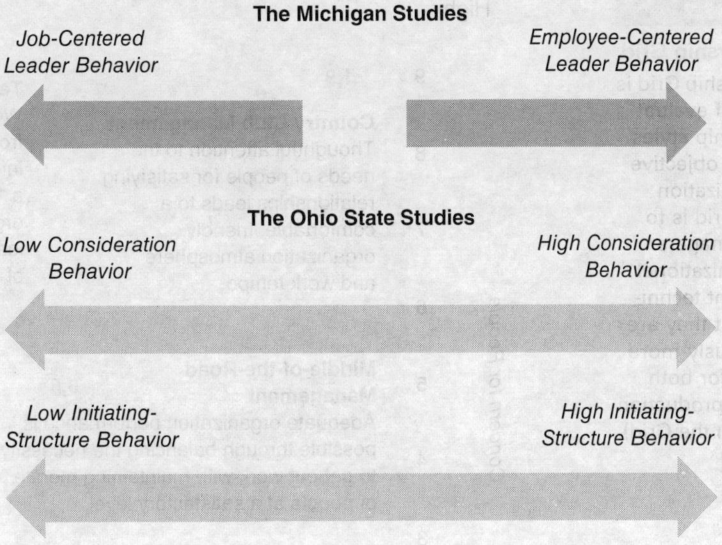

more likely to result in effective group performance than was job-centered leader behavior.

The Ohio State Studies The **Ohio State leadership studies** were conducted at about the same time as the Michigan studies (in the late 1940s and early 1950s).[12] During this program of research, behavioral scientists at Ohio State University developed a questionnaire, which they administered in both military and industrial settings, to assess subordinates' perceptions of their leaders' behavior. The Ohio State studies identified several forms of leader behavior but tended to focus on the two most significant ones: consideration and initiating-structure.

When engaging in **consideration behavior**, the leader is concerned with the subordinates' feelings and respects subordinates' ideas. The leader-subordinate relationship is characterized by mutual trust, respect, and two-way communication. When using **initiating-structure behavior**, on the other hand, the leader clearly defines the leader-subordinate roles so that subordinates know what is expected of them. The leader also establishes channels of communication and determines the methods for accomplishing the group's task.

Unlike the employee-centered and job-centered leader behaviors, consideration and initiating structure were not thought to be on the same continuum. Instead, as shown in the bottom portion of Figure 12.1, they were seen as independent dimensions of the leader's behavioral repertoire. As a result, a leader could exhibit high initiating-structure behavior and low consideration or low initiating-structure behavior and high consideration. A leader could also exhibit high or low levels of each behavior simultaneously. For example, a leader may clearly define subordinates' roles and expectations but exhibit little concern for their feelings. Alternatively, she or he may be concerned about subordinates' feelings but fail to define roles and expectations clearly. But the leader might also demonstrate concern for performance expectations and employee welfare simultaneously.

The Ohio State researchers also investigated the stability of leader behaviors over time. They found that a given individual's leadership pattern appeared to change little as long as the situation remained fairly constant.[13] Another topic they looked at was the combinations of leader behaviors that were related to effectiveness. At first, they

The **Ohio State leadership studies** defined leader consideration and initiating-structure behaviors as independent dimensions of leadership.

Consideration behavior involves being concerned with subordinates' feelings and respecting subordinates' ideas.

Initiating-structure behavior involves clearly defining the leader-subordinate roles so that subordinates know what is expected of them.

FIGURE 12.2

The Leadership Grid

The Leadership Grid is a method of evaluating leadership styles. The overall objective of an organization using the Grid is to train its managers using organizational development techniques so that they are simultaneously more concerned for both people and production (9,9 style on the Grid).

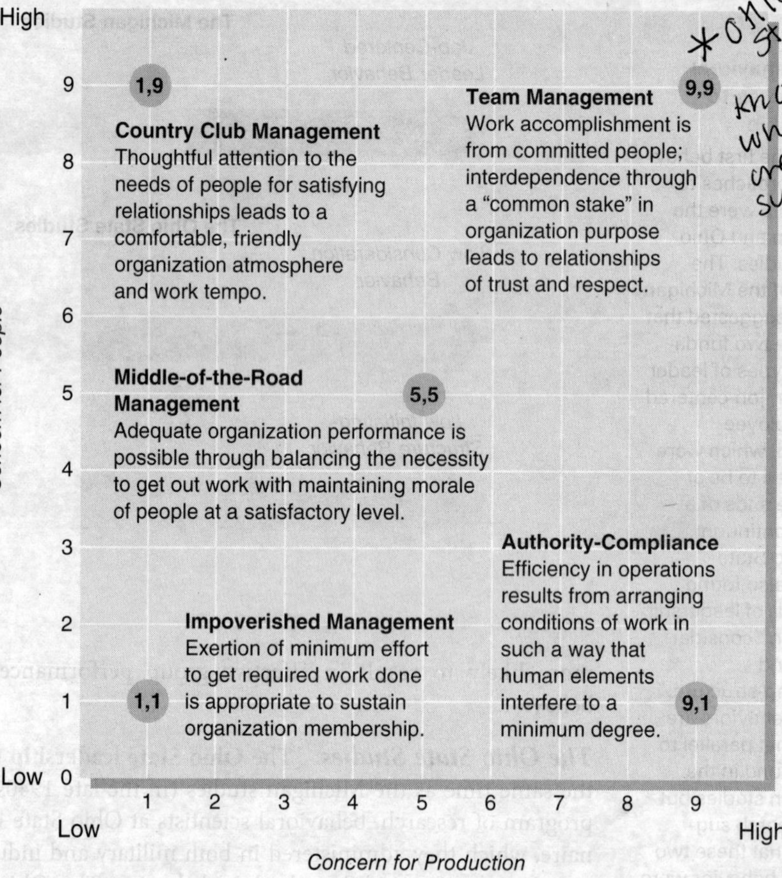

Source: The Leadership Grid Figure from *Leadership Dilemmas—Grid Solutions* by Robert R. Blake and Anne Adams McCanse. (Formerly *The Managerial Grid* by Robert R. Blake and Jane S. Mouton.) Houston: Gulf Publishing Company, p. 29. Copyright © 1997 by Grid International, Inc. Reproduced by permission of Grid International, Inc.

believed that leaders who exhibit high levels of both behaviors would be most effective. An early study at International Harvester (now Navistar Corporation), however, found that employees of supervisors who ranked high on initiating-structure behavior were higher performers but also expressed lower levels of satisfaction. Conversely, employees of supervisors who ranked high on consideration had lower performance ratings but also had fewer absences from work.[14] Later research showed that these conclusions were misleading because the studies did not consider all the important variables. Nonetheless, the Ohio State studies represented another important milestone in leadership research.[15]

Leadership Grid Yet another behavioral approach to leadership is the Leadership Grid (originally called the Managerial Grid).[16] The Leadership Grid provides a means for evaluating leadership styles and then training managers to move toward an ideal style of behavior. The most current version of the Leadership Grid is shown in Figure 12.2. The horizontal axis represents *concern for production* (similar to job-centered and initiating-structure behaviors), and the vertical axis represents *concern for people* (similar to employee-centered and consideration behavior). Note the five extremes of leadership behavior: the 1,1 manager (impoverished management), who exhibits minimal concern for both production and people; the 9,1 manager (authority-compliance), who is highly concerned about production but exhibits little concern for people; the 1,9 manager (country club management), who has the exact opposite concerns from the 9,1 manager; the 5,5 manager (middle of the road management), who maintains adequate concern for both people and production; and the 9,9 manager (team management), who exhibits maximum concern for both people and production.

According to this approach, the ideal style of leadership is 9,9. The developers of this model thus created a multiphase training and development program to assist managers in achieving this style of behavior. A.G. Edwards, Westinghouse, the FAA, Equicor, and other companies have used the Leadership Grid, and anecdotal evidence seems to confirm its effectiveness in some settings. However, there is little published scientific evidence regarding its true effectiveness and the extent to which it applies to all managers or to all settings. Indeed, as we discuss next, such evidence is not likely to actually exist.

THE EMERGENCE OF SITUATIONAL LEADERSHIP MODELS

The leader-behavior theories have played an important role in the development of more realistic, albeit more complex, approaches to leadership. In particular, they urge us not to be so preoccupied with what properties may be possessed by leaders (the trait approach), but to instead concentrate on what leaders actually do (their behaviors). Unfortunately, these theories also make universal generic prescriptions about what constitutes effective leadership. When we are dealing with complex social systems composed of complex individuals, however, few if any relationships are consistently predictable, and certainly no formulas for success are infallible.

Yet the behavior theorists tried to identify consistent relationships between leader behaviors and employee responses in the hope of finding a dependable prescription for effective leadership. As we might expect, they often failed. Other approaches to understanding leadership were therefore needed. The catalyst for these new approaches was the realization that although interpersonal and task-oriented dimensions might be useful to describe the behavior of leaders, they were not useful for predicting or prescribing it. The next step in the evolution of leadership theory was the creation of situational models.

Situational models assume that appropriate leader behavior varies from one situation to another. The goal of a situational theory, then, is to identify key situational factors and to specify how they interact to determine appropriate leader behavior. Before discussing the major situational theories, we first discuss an important early model that in many ways laid the foundation for these theories. In a seminal article about the decision-making process, Robert Tannenbaum and Warren H. Schmidt proposed a continuum of leadership behavior. Their model is much like the original Michigan framework.[17] Besides purely job-centered behavior (or "boss-centered" behavior, as they termed it) and employee-centered ("subordinate-centered") behavior, however, they identified several

Bob Pearson/EPA/Landov Media

Leadership behaviors sometimes emerges during a time of crisis. For example, both during and in the aftermatch of the Auroroa, Colorado movie shootings brave people helped other people avoid the shooter inside the theater and helped maintain calm outside the theater.

intermediate behaviors that a manager might consider. These are shown on the leadership continuum in Figure 12.3.

This continuum of behavior ranges from the one extreme of having the manager make the decision alone to the other extreme of having the employees make the decision with minimal guidance from the leader. Each point on the continuum is influenced by characteristics of the manager, subordinates, and the situation. Managerial characteristics include the manager's value system, confidence in subordinates, personal inclinations, and feelings of security. Subordinate characteristics include the subordinates' need for independence, readiness to assume responsibility, tolerance for ambiguity, interest in the problem, understanding of goals, knowledge, experience, and expectations. Situational characteristics that affect decision making include the type of organization, group effectiveness, the problem itself, and time pressures.

Hence, the leadership continuum acknowledged for the first time that leader behaviors represent a continuum rather than discrete extremes, and that various characteristics and elements of any given situation would affect the success of any given leadership style. Although this framework pointed out the importance of situational factors, it was, however, only speculative. It remained for others to develop more comprehensive and integrated theories. In the following sections, we describe three of the most important and widely accepted situational theories of leadership: the LPC theory, the path-goal theory, and Vroom's decision tree approach.

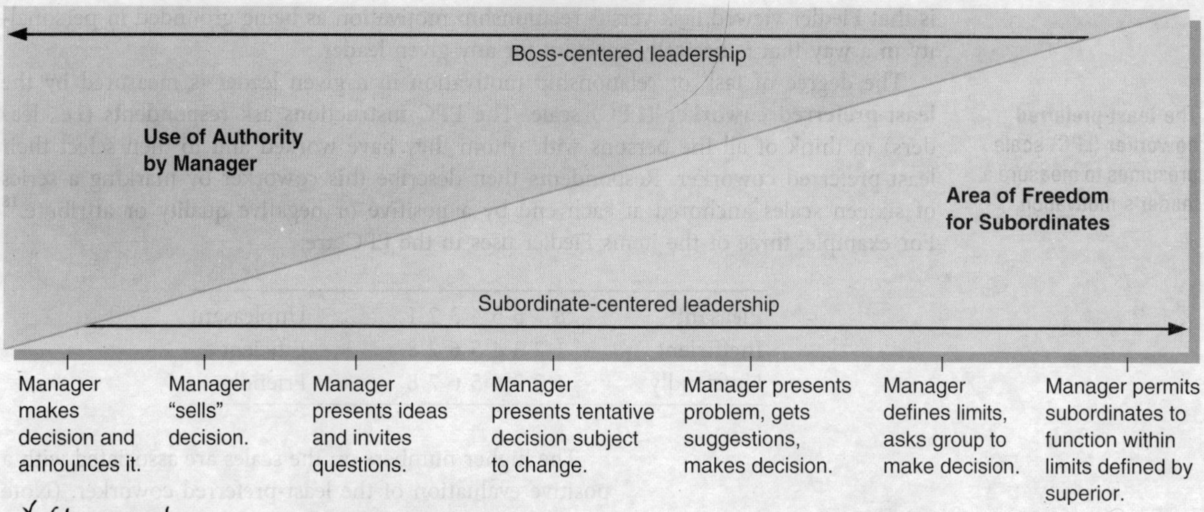

FIGURE 12.3

Tannenbaum and Schmidt's Leadership Continuum

The Tannenbaum and Schmidt leadership continuum was an important precursor to modern situational approaches to leadership. The continuum identifies seven levels of leadership, which range between the extremes of boss-centered and subordinate-centered leadership.

Source: Reprinted by permission of the *Harvard Business Review.* An exhibit from "How to Choose a Leadership Pattern" by Robert Tannenbaum and Warren Schmidt (May–June 1973). Copyright by the Harvard Business School Publishing Corporation; all rights reserved.

THE LPC THEORY OF LEADERSHIP

The **LPC theory of leadership** suggests that a leader's effectiveness depends on the situation.

Fred Fiedler developed the **LPC theory of leadership**. The LPC theory attempts to explain and reconcile both the leader's personality and the complexities of the situation. (This theory was originally called the "contingency theory of leadership." However, because this label has come to have generic connotations, new labels are being used to avoid confusion. "LPC" stands for "least-preferred coworker," a concept we explain later in this section.) The LPC theory contends that a leader's effectiveness depends on the situation and, as a result, some leaders may be effective in one situation or organization but not in another. The theory also explains why this discrepancy may occur and identifies leader-situation matches that should result in effective performance.

Task versus Relationship Motivation

Fiedler and his associates maintain that leadership effectiveness depends on the match between the leader's personality and the situation. Fiedler devised special terms to describe a leader's basic personality traits in relation to leadership: "task motivation" versus "relationship motivation." He also conceptualized the situational context in terms of its favorableness for the leader, ranging from highly favorable to highly unfavorable.

In some respects, the ideas of task and relationship motivation resemble the basic concepts identified in the behavioral approaches. Task motivation closely parallels job-centered and initiating-structure leader behavior, and relationship motivation is similar to employee-centered and consideration leader behavior. A major difference, however, is that Fiedler viewed task versus relationship motivation as being grounded in personality in a way that is basically constant for any given leader.

The **least-preferred coworker (LPC)** scale presumes to measure a leader's motivation.

The degree of task or relationship motivation in a given leader is measured by the **least-preferred coworker (LPC)** scale. The LPC instructions ask respondents (i.e., leaders) to think of all the persons with whom they have worked and to then select their least-preferred coworker. Respondents then describe this coworker by marking a series of sixteen scales anchored at each end by a positive or negative quality or attribute.[18] For example, three of the items Fiedler uses in the LPC are:

Pleasant	8 7 6 5 4 3 2 1	Unpleasant
Inefficient	1 2 3 4 5 6 7 8	Efficient
Unfriendly	1 2 3 4 5 6 7 8	Friendly

The higher numbers on the scales are associated with a positive evaluation of the least-preferred coworker. (Note that the higher scale numbers are associated with the more favorable term and that some items reverse both the terms and the scale values. The latter feature forces the respondent to read the scales more carefully and to provide more valid answers.) Respondents who describe their least-preferred coworker in relatively positive terms receive a high LPC score, whereas those who use relatively negative terms receive a low LPC score.

Fiedler assumed that these descriptions actually say more about the leader than about the least-preferred coworker. He believed, for example, that everyone's least preferred coworker is likely to be equally "unpleasant," and that differences in descriptions actually reflect differences in personality traits among the leaders responding to the LPC scale. Fiedler contended that high-LPC leaders are basically more concerned with interpersonal relations whereas low-LPC leaders are more concerned with task-relevant problems. Not surprisingly, controversy has always surrounded the LPC scale. Researchers have offered several interpretations of the LPC score, arguing that it may be an index of behavior, personality, or some other unknown factor. Indeed, the LPC measure and its interpretation have long been among the most debated aspects of this theory.

Curt Walstead/Imagezoo/Jupiter Images

Situational leadership models suggest that what constitutes effective leader behavior varies with the situation. In some cases, for example, the leader needs to stand apart from followers in order to best guide and direct them. In other cases, though, the leader may need to dive in with her or his followers and help shoulder the load. Not recognizing the differences can be a recipe for disaster!

Situational Favorableness

Fiedler also identified three factors that determine the favorableness of the situation. In order of importance (from most to least important), these factors are leader-member relations, task structure, and leader position power.

Leader-member relations refers to the personal relationship that exists between subordinates and their leader. It is based on the extent to which subordinates trust, respect, and have confidence in their leader, and vice versa. A high

Table 12.2 The LPC Theory of Leadership

LEADER-MEMBER RELATIONS	GOOD				POOR			
	STRUCTURED		UNSTRUCTURED		STRUCTURED		UNSTRUCTURED	
TASK STRUCTURE POSITION POWER	HIGH	LOW	HIGH	LOW	HIGH	LOW	HIGH	LOW
SITUATIONAL FAVORABLENESS	Very favorable ↓		Moderately favorable ↓				Very unfavorable ↓	
RECOMMENDED LEADER BEHAVIOR	Task-oriented behavior		Person-oriented behavior				Task-oriented behavior	

*inflexability of leader bhv   *need for ~~organization~~ motivation   Tigermom ex.

degree of mutual trust, respect, and confidence obviously indicates good leader-member relations, and a low degree indicates poor leader-member relations.

Task structure is the second most important determinant of situational favorableness. A structured task is routine, simple, easily understood, and unambiguous. The LPC theory presumes that structured tasks are more favorable because the leader need not be closely involved in defining activities and can devote time to other matters. On the other hand, an unstructured task is one that is nonroutine, ambiguous, and complex. Fiedler argues that this task is more unfavorable because the leader must play a major role in guiding and directing the activities of subordinates.

Finally, *leader position power* is the power inherent in the leader's role itself. If the leader has considerable power to assign work, reward and punish employees, and recommend them for promotion, position power is high and favorable. If, however, the leader must have job assignments approved by someone else, does not control rewards and punishment, and has no voice in promotions, position power is low and unfavorable; that is, many decisions are beyond the leader's control.

Leader Motivation and Situational Favorableness Fiedler and his associates conducted numerous studies examining the relationships among leader motivation, situational favorableness, and group performance. Table 12.2 summarizes the results of these studies.

To begin interpreting the results, let's first examine the situational favorableness dimensions shown in the table. The various combinations of these three dimensions result in eight different situations, as arrayed across the first three lines of the table. These situations in turn define a continuum ranging from very favorable to very unfavorable situations from the leader's perspective. Favorableness is noted in the fourth line of the table. For example, good relations, a structured task, and either high or low position power result in a very favorable situation for the leader. But poor relations, an unstructured task, and either high or low position power create very unfavorable conditions for the leader.

The table also identifies the leadership approach that is supposed to achieve high group performance in each of the eight situations. These linkages are shown in the bottom line of the table. A task-oriented leader is appropriate for very favorable as well as very unfavorable situations. For example, the LPC theory predicts that if leader-member relations are poor, the task is unstructured, and leader position power is low, a task-oriented leader will be effective. It also predicts that a task-oriented leader will be effective if leader-member relations are good, the task is structured, and leader position power is high. Finally, for situations of intermediate favorableness, the theory suggests that a person-oriented leader will be most likely to achieve high group performance.

Leader-Situation Match What happens if a person-oriented leader faces a very favorable or very unfavorable situation, or if a task-oriented leader faces a situation of intermediate favorableness? Fiedler considers these leader-situation combinations to be "mismatches." Recall that a basic premise of his theory is that leadership behavior is a personality trait. Thus, the mismatched leader cannot readily adapt to the situation and achieve effectiveness. Fiedler contends that when a leader's style and the situation do not match, the only available course of action is to change the situation through "job engineering."[19]

For example, Fiedler suggests that if a person-oriented leader ends up in a situation that is very unfavorable, the manager should attempt to improve matters by spending more time with subordinates to improve leader-member relations and by laying down rules and procedures to provide more task structure. Fiedler and his associates have also developed a widely used training program for supervisors on how to assess situational favorableness and to change the situation, if necessary, to achieve a better match.[20] Weyerhaeuser and Boeing are among the firms that have experimented with Fiedler's training program.

Evaluation and Implications

The validity of Fiedler's LPC theory has been heatedly debated because of the inconsistency of the research results. Apparent shortcomings of the theory are that the LPC measure lacks validity, the theory is not always supported by research, and Fiedler's assumptions about the inflexibility of leader behavior are unrealistic.[21] The theory itself, however, does represent an important contribution because it returned the field to a study of the situation and explicitly considered the organizational context and its role in effective leadership.

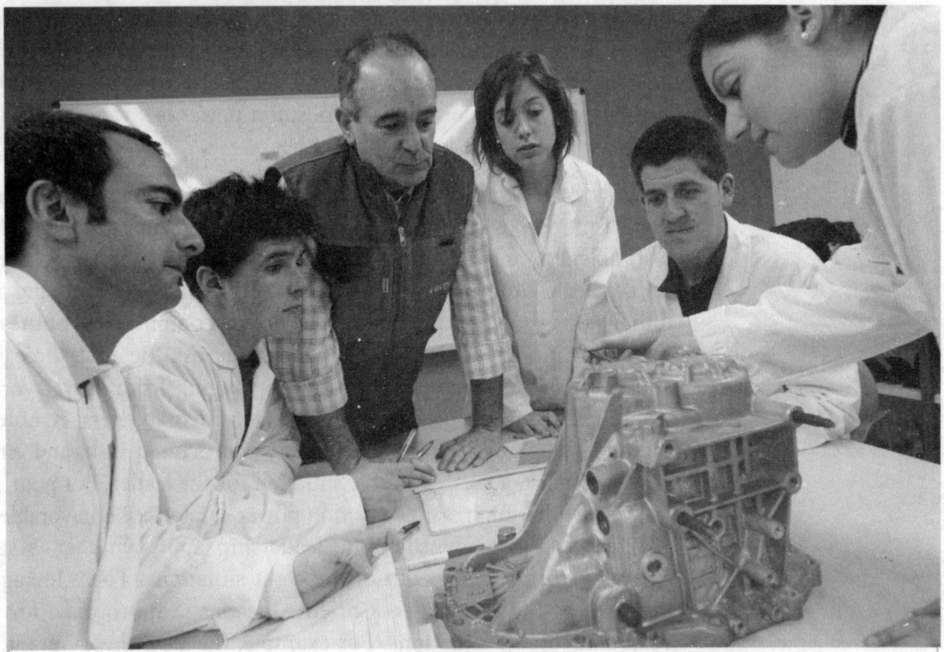

Javier Larrea/AGE Fotostock

Leadership training is very popular in many organizations today. This trainer, for example, is using a complex piece of machinery to help leaders develop creativity and brainstorming techniques. After the training is complete the leaders will, hopefully, be better prepared to help their own teams be more creative.

THE PATH-GOAL THEORY OF LEADERSHIP

Another important contingency approach to leadership is the path-goal theory. Developed jointly by Martin Evans and Robert House, the path-goal theory focuses on the situation and leader behaviors rather than on fixed traits of the leader.[22] In contrast to the LPC theory, the path-goal theory suggests that leaders can readily adapt to different situations.

Basic Premises

The path-goal theory of leadership suggests that effective leaders clarify the paths (behaviors) that will lead to desired rewards (goals).

The path-goal theory has its roots in the expectancy theory of motivation discussed in Chapter 4. Recall that expectancy theory says that a person's attitudes and behaviors can be predicted from the degree to which the person believes job performance will lead to various outcomes (expectancy) and the value of those outcomes (valences) to the individual. The **path-goal theory of leadership** argues that subordinates are motivated by their leader to the extent that the behaviors of that leader influence their expectancies. In other words, the leader affects subordinates' performance by clarifying the behaviors (paths) that will lead to desired rewards (goals). Ideally, of course, getting a reward in an organization depends on effective performance. Path-goal theory also suggests that a leader may behave in different ways in different situations.

Leader Behaviors As Figure 12.4 shows, path-goal theory identifies four kinds of leader behavior: directive, supportive, participative, and achievement-oriented. With *directive leadership*, the leader lets subordinates know what is expected of them, gives specific guidance as to how to accomplish tasks, schedules work to be done, and maintains definitive standards of performance for subordinates. A leader exhibiting *supportive leadership* is friendly and shows concern for subordinates' status, well-being, and needs. With *participative leadership*, the leader consults with subordinates about issues and takes their suggestions into account before making a decision. Finally, *achievement-oriented leadership* involves setting challenging goals, expecting subordinates to perform at their highest level, and showing strong confidence that subordinates will put forth effort and accomplish the goals. Unlike the LPC theory, path-goal theory assumes that leaders can change their behavior and exhibit any or all of these leadership styles.

FIGURE 12.4

The Path-Goal Theory of Leadership

The path-goal theory of leadership specifies four kinds of leader behavior: directive, supportive, participative, and achievement-oriented. Leaders are advised to vary their behaviors in response to such situational factors as personal characteristics of subordinates and environmental characteristics.

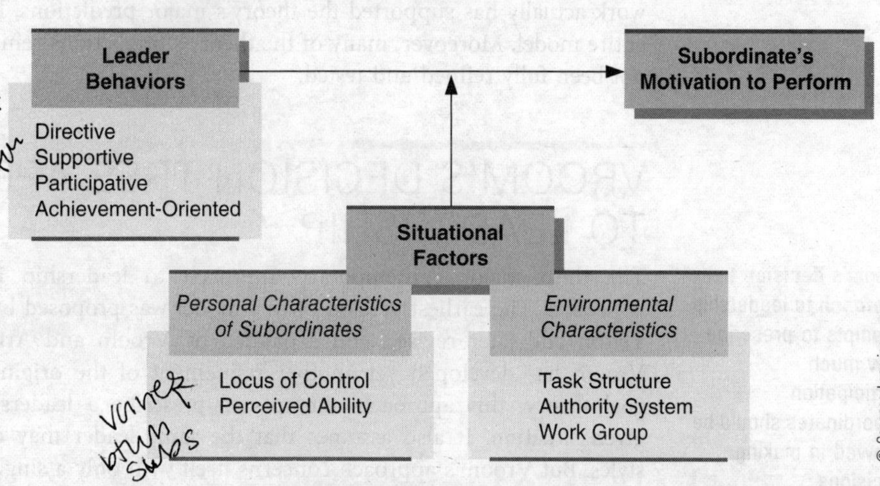

The theory also predicts that the appropriate combination of leadership styles depends on situational factors.

Situational Factors The path-goal theory proposes two types of situational factors that influence how leader behavior relates to subordinate satisfaction: the personal characteristics of the subordinates and the characteristics of the environment (see Figure 12.4).

Two important personal characteristics of subordinates are locus of control and perceived ability. Locus of control, discussed in Chapter 3, refers to the extent to which individuals believe that what happens to them results from their own behavior or from external causes. Research indicates that individuals who attribute outcomes to their own behavior may be more satisfied with a participative leader (since they feel their own efforts can make a difference) whereas individuals who attribute outcomes to external causes may respond more favorably to a directive leader (since they think their own actions are of little consequence). Perceived ability pertains to how people view their own ability with respect to the task. Employees who rate their own ability relatively highly are less likely to feel a need for directive leadership (since they think they know how to do the job), whereas those who perceive their own ability to be relatively low may prefer directive leadership (since they think they need someone to show them how to do the job).

Important environmental characteristics are task structure, the formal authority system, and the primary work group. The path-goal theory proposes that leader behavior will motivate subordinates if it helps them cope with environmental uncertainty created by those characteristics. In some cases, however, certain forms of leadership will be redundant, decreasing subordinate satisfaction. For example, when task structure is high, directive leadership is less necessary and therefore less effective; similarly, if the work group gives the individual plenty of social support, a supportive leader will not be especially attractive. Thus, the extent to which leader behavior matches the people and environment in the situation is presumed to influence subordinates' motivation to perform.

Evaluation and Implications

The path-goal theory was designed to provide a general framework for understanding how leader behavior and situational factors influence subordinate attitudes and behaviors. But the intention of the path-goal theorists was to stimulate research on the theory's major propositions, not to offer definitive answers. Researchers hoped that a more fully developed, formal theory of leadership would emerge from continued study. Further work actually has supported the theory's major predictions, but it has not validated the entire model. Moreover, many of the theory's predictions remain overly general and have not been fully refined and tested.

VROOM'S DECISION TREE APPROACH TO LEADERSHIP

Vroom's decision tree approach to leadership attempts to prescribe how much participation subordinates should be allowed in making decisions.

The third major contemporary approach to leadership is **Vroom's decision tree approach**. The earliest version of this model was proposed by Victor Vroom and Philip Yetton and later revised and expanded by Vroom and Arthur Jago.[23] Most recently, Vroom has developed yet another refinement of the original model.[24] Like the path-goal theory, this approach attempts to prescribe a leadership style appropriate to a given situation. It also assumes that the same leader may display different leadership styles. But Vroom's approach concerns itself with only a single aspect of leader behavior: subordinate participation in decision making.

Basic Premises

Vroom's decision tree approach assumes that the degree to which subordinates should be encouraged to participate in decision making depends on the characteristics of the situation. In other words, no one decision-making process is best for all situations. After evaluating a variety of problem attributes (characteristics of the problem or decision), the leader determines an appropriate decision style that specifies the amount of subordinate participation.

Vroom's current formulation suggests that managers should use one of two different decision trees.[25] To do so, the manager first assesses the situation in terms of several factors. This assessment involves determining whether the given factor is "high" or "low" for the decision that is to be made. For instance, the first factor is decision significance. If the decision is extremely important and may have a major impact on the organization (i.e., choosing a location for a new plant), its significance is high. But if the decision is routine and its consequences not terribly important (i.e., selecting a logo for the firm's softball team uniforms), its significance is low. This assessment guides the manager through the paths of the decision tree to a recommended course of action. One decision tree is to be used when the manager is primarily interested in making the decision on the most timely basis possible; the other is to be used when time is less critical and the manager wishes to help subordinates improve and develop their own decision-making skills.

The two decision trees are shown in Figures 12.5 and 12.6. The problem attributes (situational factors) are arranged along the top of the decision tree. To use the model, the decision maker starts at the left side of the diagram and assesses the first problem attribute (decision significance). The answer determines the path to the second node on

Leaders sometimes have to decide how much participation they should allow others to have when making decisions. This team of firefighters has been asked by their crew chief for their opinions on how best to evacuate a neighborhood in the path of a slow-moving forest fire and save as much property as possible. The crew chief will listen to their ideas and then make a decision.

*developed into leadership software

* go over?

PROBLEM STATEMENT	Decision Significance	Importance of Commitment	Leader Expertise	Likelihood of Commitment	Group Support	Group Expertise	Team Competence	
				H	-	-	-	Decide
							H	Delegate
						H		
			H		H		L	
				L				
						L	-	Consult (Group)
					L	-	-	
							H	Facilitate
						H		
		H			H		L	
				H				
						L	-	Consult (Individually)
					L	-	-	
	H		L					
							H	Facilitate
						H		
					H		L	
				L				
						L	-	Consult (Group)
					L	-	-	
			H	-	-	-	-	Decide
							H	Facilitate
						H		
		L			H		L	
			L	-				
						L	-	Consult (Individually)
					L	-	-	
				H	-	-	-	Decide
		H	-				H	Delegate
	L			L	-	-		
							L	Facilitate
		L	-	-	-	-	-	Decide

How to make a decision - not big picture

FIGURE 12.5

Vroom's Time-Driven Decision Tree

This matrix is recommended for situations in which time is of the highest importance in making a decision. The matrix operates like a funnel. You start at the left with a specific decision problem in mind. The column headings denote situational factors that may or may not be present in that problem. You progress by selecting High or Low (H or L) for each relevant situational factor. Proceed down from the funnel, judging only those situational factors for which a judgment is called for, until you reach the recommended process.

Reference: Victor H. Vroom's Time-Driven Model from *A Model of Leadership Style*, copyright 1998.

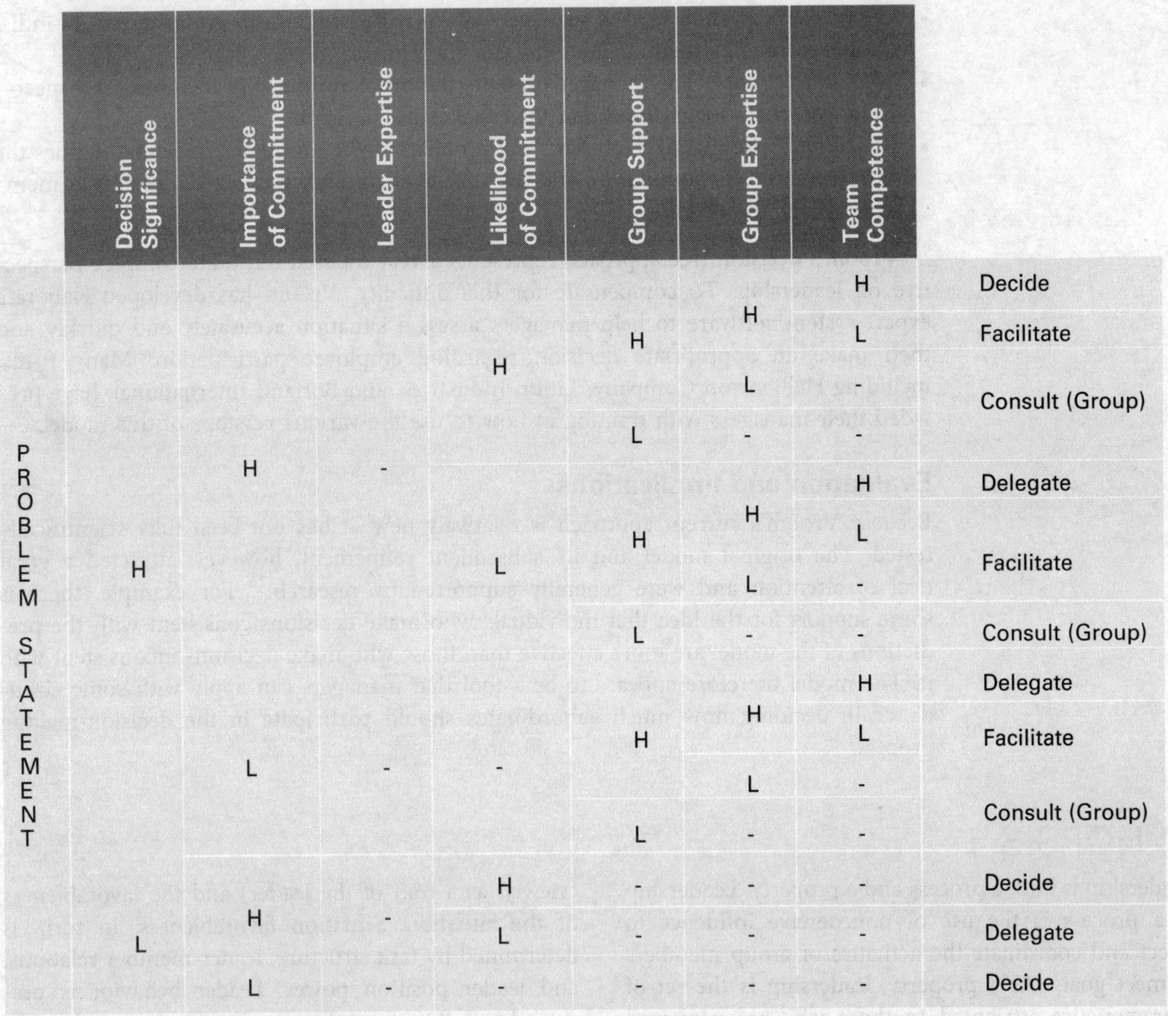

FIGURE 12.6

Vroom's Development-Driven Decision Tree

This matrix is to be used when the leader is more interested in developing employees than in making the decision as quickly as possible. Just as with the time-driven tree shown in Figure 12.5, the leader assesses up to seven situational factors. These factors, in turn, funnel the leader to a recommended process for making the decision.

Reference: Victor H. Vroom's Development-Driven Model from *A Model of Leadership Style,* copyright 1998.

the decision tree, where the next attribute (importance of commitment) is assessed. This process continues until a terminal node is reached. In this way, the manager identifies an effective decision-making style for the situation.

The various decision styles reflected at the ends of the tree branches represent different levels of subordinate participation that the manager should attempt to adopt in a given situation. The five styles are defined as follows:

- *Decide:* The manager makes the decision alone and then announces or "sells" it to the group.
- *Delegate*: The manager allows the group to define for itself the exact nature and parameters of the problem and then develop a solution.

- *Consult (Individually):* The manager presents the program to group members individually, obtains their suggestions, and then makes the decision.
- *Consult (Group):* The manager presents the problem to group members at a meeting, gets their suggestions, and then makes the decision.
- *Facilitate*: The manager presents the problem to the group at a meeting, defines the problem and its boundaries, and then facilitates group member discussion as members make the decision.

Vroom's decision tree approach represents a very focused but quite complex perspective on leadership. To compensate for this difficulty, Vroom has developed elaborate expert system software to help managers assess a situation accurately and quickly and then make an appropriate decision regarding employee participation. Many firms, including Halliburton Company, Litton Industries, and Borland International, have provided their managers with training in how to use the various versions of this model.

Evaluation and Implications

Because Vroom's current approach is relatively new, it has not been fully scientifically tested. The original model and its subsequent refinement, however, attracted a great deal of attention and were generally supported by research.[26] For example, there is some support for the idea that individuals who make decisions consistent with the predictions of the model are more effective than those who make decisions inconsistent with it. The model therefore appears to be a tool that managers can apply with some confidence in deciding how much subordinates should participate in the decision-making process.

SYNOPSIS

Leadership is both a process and a property. Leadership as a process is the use of noncoercive influence to direct and coordinate the activities of group members to meet goals. As a property, leadership is the set of characteristics attributed to those who are perceived to use such influence successfully. Leadership and management are related but distinct phenomena.

Early leadership research primarily attempted to identify important traits and behaviors of leaders. The Michigan and Ohio State studies each identified two kinds of leader behavior, one focusing on job factors and the other on people factors. The Michigan studies viewed these behaviors as points on a single continuum, whereas the Ohio State studies suggested that they were separate dimensions. The Leadership Grid further refined these concepts.

Newer situational theories of leadership attempt to identify appropriate leadership styles on the basis of the situation. The leadership continuum first proposed by Tannenbaum and Schmidt was the catalyst for these theories.

Fiedler's LPC theory states that leadership effectiveness depends on a match between the leader's style (viewed as a trait of the leader) and the favorableness of the situation. Situation favorableness, in turn, is determined by task structure, leader-member relations, and leader position power. Leader behavior is presumed to reflect a constant personality trait and therefore cannot easily be changed.

The path-goal theory focuses on appropriate leader behavior for various situations. The path-goal theory suggests that directive, supportive, participative, or achievement-oriented leader behavior may be appropriate, depending on the personal characteristics of subordinates and the characteristics of the environment. Unlike the LPC theory, this view presumes that leaders can alter their behavior to best fit the situation.

Vroom's decision tree approach suggests appropriate decision-making styles based on situation characteristics. This approach focuses on deciding how much subordinates should participate in the decision-making process. Managers assess situational attributes and follow a series of paths through a decision tree that subsequently prescribes for them how they should make a particular decision.

DISCUSSION QUESTIONS

1. How would you define "leadership"? Compare and contrast your definition with the one given in this chapter.
2. Cite examples of managers who are not leaders and of leaders who are not managers. What makes them one and not the other? Also, cite examples of both formal and informal leaders.
3. What traits do you think characterize successful leaders? Do you think the trait approach has validity?
4. Recent evidence suggests that successful managers (defined by organizational rank and salary) may indeed have some of the same traits originally ascribed to effective leaders (such as an attractive appearance and relative height). How might this finding be explained?
5. What other forms of leader behavior besides those cited in the chapter can you identify?
6. Critique Fiedler's LPC theory. Are other elements of the situation important? Do you think Fiedler's assertion about the inflexibility of leader behavior makes sense? Why or why not?
7. Do you agree or disagree with Fiedler's assertion that leadership motivation is basically a personality trait? Why?
8. Compare and contrast the LPC and path-goal theories of leadership. What are the strengths and weaknesses of each?
9. Of the three major leadership theories—the LPC theory, the path-goal theory, and Vroom's decision tree approach—which is the most comprehensive? Which is the narrowest? Which has the most practical value?
10. How realistic do you think it is for managers to attempt to use Vroom's decision tree approach as prescribed? Explain.

HOW DO YOU SEE IT?

Top Dog

"What Americans love … is consistency."

—HEIDI GANAHL, FOUNDER AND CEO OF CAMP BOW WOW

We first met Sue Ryan in the *Video Case* for Chapter 1, where we saw how she manages things at Camp Bow Wow, a care facility for dogs in Boulder, Colorado. A veteran of the corporate ranks, Ryan focuses her leadership skills on mentoring younger managers on the finer points of human and customer relations and puts the rest of her energy into trying to turn a profit while fostering a "relaxed culture." Because it's a *franchise*, however, certain managerial tasks at Camp Bow Wow fall to managers who work directly for the *franchiser*—the company that permits Ryan to use its brand name and sell its products. The franchiser, for example, sponsors an interactive Facebook game called *Bad to the Bone* and pays a PR firm to keep the brand "constantly barked about" in media ranging from the *Today Show* to the *New York Times*.

That's where Heidi Ganahl comes in. Ganahl founded Camp Bow Wow in 2000 with $83,000 in savings. She began franchising her brand in 2003 and has since awarded more than 200 franchises in 40 states (41 percent of which, according to the company, are women owned).* Ryan explains that she has "a unique relationship" with Ganahl, not only because she was an early franchisee but because she bought the Boulder location directly from Ganahl, who'd owned it since it opened in 2001. They've known and worked with each other for about 10 years, and they're obviously on close terms. But Ryan recalls that there was "a transition period. We both kind of had to find our way … and figure out how much space to give each other." Ryan, confirms Ganahl, had to work her way through an "initial stage of getting the camp where *she* wanted it to be rather than where corporate wanted it to be," and, together, they "had to work at negotiating what was best for her versus what was best for us when we were running the camp."

The negotiations were successful, reports Ryan, because Ganahl's "leadership skills were great in terms of focusing on the right things [and] being pretty clear with me about expectations. And being open to letting go of some of [her expectations] as I got my feet under me and I got more solid with how I was running the camp.… She was able to back off and give me some latitude."

For her part, Ganahl is well aware that such give-and-take is crucial in leading a company whose most important resource is a diverse group of independent businesspeople. "One of the most important things about franchising," she explains,

is being able to duplicate and replicate the original business and, as it evolves, keep everybody on the same page, all the facilities looking the same, the service the same, and the attributes of the brand the same.... What Americans love—and the great thing about franchising—is consistency. Keeping everything the same no matter which location you go to.

By the same token, Ganahl hastens to add, her role is challenging "because when you get all of these 200 people that have all these creative, cool ideas—even though they know they bought into a franchise—they still want to tap into [their own] creativity and add their own bent to the business." Her main job, then, is balancing the need for brand consistency "with the 200 franchisees and the 2,000 employees ... and just really trying to temper their wonderful ideas with what's best for the brand."

How does Ganahl manage this critical balancing act? It's a matter of leadership style:

I've found that the best way of getting people committed to a vision ... and executing that vision is to have an open-door policy and let people communicate their ideas and be part of the growth ... of the brand. And if you do that, you'll come up with some amazing things that you wouldn't have if you weren't open to involving your team and your franchisees and their staffs.

She admits, however, that her leadership style wasn't always so relaxed: "As the company's grown," she explains, "my ability to lead [it] has shifted from very intense micromanagement of day-to-day details to a more strategic look at what's best for the company and growing the brand." She's also discovered the advantages of delegating authority, and, fortunately, the company's success has permitted her to hire "some key folks" to whom she can confidently delegate things—management-level personnel "that I couldn't afford or didn't have the resources [for] in the beginning. And it's been wonderful. It's allowed me to focus on what's best for the brand and the vision of the company, rather than 'How do I get through the day and get through all the things that need to be done?'... My vision for Camp Bow Wow continues to grow and expand," she adds, although she admits that, occasionally, "I drive my team and my franchisees a little bit nuts because I'm always thinking of new creative ways that we can leverage the Camp Bow Wow brand and do more for our customers."

CASE QUESTIONS

1. What do you think of when you think of a *brand*? In what ways can Camp Bow Wow be considered a brand? Clearly, Ganahl's primary focus as a manager is *brand management*—the application of marketing techniques to her product or brand. Why is her commitment to brand management so strong? In what ways does her approach to leadership reflect her commitment to brand management?
2. In what ways might the *trait approach to leadership* help explain Ganahl's approach to dealing with her most important concerns as a manager? [*Hint:* You'll probably want to refer to the section on "Personality and Organizations" in Chapter 3.] Assuming that Ganahl is an effective leader (Sue Ryan says that she is), how might each of the *behavioral approaches to leadership* discussed in the chapter—the *Michigan* and *Ohio State studies* and the *leadership grid*—help to explain her success?
3. How might the various *situational leadership models* discussed in the chapter—*the LPC theory*, the *path-goal theory*, and *Vroom's decision tree*—help to explain Ganahl's success as a leader? And since we're on the subject, how would you characterize Ganahl's own criteria for success in leading Camp Bow Wow?
4. Would you want to work for Ganahl at Camp Bow Wow's corporate headquarters? Why or why not? Would you feel comfortable working with Ganahl as one of her franchisees? Why or why not?

ADDITIONAL SOURCES

"Heidi Ganahl, Founder & CEO, Camp Bow Wow," *SmartGirls Way*, August 4, 2011, http://smartgirlsway.com on September 3, 2012; Camp Bow Wow, "About Us: Camp Bow Wow," 2000-2011, www.campbowwow.com on September 3, 2012; Sramana Mitra, "The 1M/1M Deal Radar: Camp Bow Wow, Boulder," *Sramana Mitra on Strategy*, February 4, 2011, www.sramanamitra.com on September 3, 2012; Tamara Chapman, "Dog Days," *DU Today*, September 1, 2011, http://blogs.du.edu on September 3, 2012; "Camp Bow Wow Launches Facebook Game" (press release), *Marketwire*, April 13, 2012, www.marketwatch.com on September 3, 2012.

**A brief note on how franchising works.* The company that Ganahl runs out of Broomfield, Colorado, has established an *operating system* by which every Camp Bow Wow location must be run, with terms and conditions set out in a contractual agreement. Ryan, however, is an independent businessperson who controls the process by which the franchiser's operating system is managed at her location. She decides whom to hire and how much to pay them and how much to charge for services, and all of these decisions affect her bottom line. If she succeeds, it's a plus for the franchiser's brand, and if she fails, it's probably a negative factor in the franchiser's efforts to expand the brand.

EXPERIENCING ORGANIZATIONAL BEHAVIOR

Understanding Successful and Unsuccessful Leadership

Purpose This exercise will help you better understand the behaviors of successful and unsuccessful leaders.

Format You will be asked to identify contemporary examples of successful and unsuccessful leaders and then to describe how these leaders differ.

Procedure

1. Working alone, each student should list the names of ten people he or she thinks of as leaders in public life. Note that the names should not necessarily be confined to "good" leaders but instead should also identify "strong" leaders.
2. Next, students should form small groups and compare their lists. This comparison should focus on common and unique names as well as on the kinds of individuals listed (i.e., male or female, contemporary or historical, business or nonbusiness, and so on).
3. From all the lists, choose two leaders whom most people would consider very successful and two who would be deemed unsuccessful.
4. Identify similarities and differences between the two successful leaders and between the two unsuccessful leaders.
5. Relate the successes and failures to at least one theory or perspective discussed in the chapter.
6. Select one group member to report your findings to the rest of the class.

Follow-Up Questions

1. What role does luck play in leadership?
2. Are there factors about the leaders you researched that might have predicted their success or failure before they achieved leadership roles?
3. What are some criteria of successful leadership?

BUILDING MANAGERIAL SKILLS

Exercise Overview Conceptual skills refer to the manager's ability to think in the abstract. This exercise will enable you to apply your conceptual skills to better understanding the distinction between leadership and management.

Exercise Task First, identify someone who currently occupies a management and/or leadership position. This individual can be a manager in a large business, the owner of a small business, the president of a campus organization, or any other similar kind of position. Next, interview this individual and ask him or her the following questions:

1. Name three recent tasks or activities that were primarily management in nature, requiring little or no leadership.
2. Name three recent tasks or activities that were primarily leadership in nature, requiring little or no management.
3. Do you spend most of the time working as a manager or a leader?
4. How easy or difficult is it to differentiate activities on the basis of them being management versus leadership?

Finally, after you have completed the interview, break up into small groups with your classmates and discuss your results. What have you learned about leadership from this activity?

SELF-ASSESSMENT EXERCISE

Are You Ready to Lead?

This exercise is designed to help you assess both your current readiness for leadership and your current preference in leadership style. The 10 statements in the table below reflect certain preferences in the nature of work performance. Indicate the extent to which you agree or disagree with each statement by circling the number in the appropriate column.

Statement of preference	***Strongly agree***				***Strongly disagree***
1. I like to stand out from the crowd.	1	2	3	4	5
2. I feel proud and satisfied when I influence others to do things my way.	1	2	3	4	5
3. I enjoy doing things as part of a group rather than achieving results on my own.	1	2	3	4	5
4. I have a history of becoming an officer or captain in clubs or organized sports.	1	2	3	4	5
5. I try to be the one who is most influential in tasks groups at school or work.	1	2	3	4	5
6. In groups, I care most about good relationships.	1	2	3	4	5
7. In groups, I most want to achieve task goals.	1	2	3	4	5
8. In groups, I always show consideration for the feelings and needs of others.	1	2	3	4	5
9. In groups, I always structure activities and assignments to help get the job done.	1	2	3	4	5
10. In groups, I shift between being supportive of others' needs and pushing task accomplishment.	1	2	3	4	5

How to score: Follow the instructions in the following table to enter the numbers that you've circled:

Leadership Readiness Score	Add the numbers that you circled on items 1–5: ___
Leadership Style Score	
Task Preference Score	Add the numbers that you circled on items 7 and 9: ___
Relationship Preference Score	Add the numbers that you circled on items 6 and 8: ___
	Difference between Task and Relationship scores: ___
	Check the higher score: Task ___ Relationship ___
Adaptability Score	Your score on item 10 ___

How to interpret your scores:

Leadership Readiness: If your total score on items 1–5 is 20 or more, you'll probably enjoy a leadership role. If your score is 10 or less, you're probably more interested in personal achievement—*at least at this point in your life.* If you've scored somewhere in the middle range, your leadership potential is still flexible—you could go either way, depending on circumstances.

Leadership Style: Your responses to items 6–10 reflect your leadership style, which may *be task oriented, relationship oriented,* or *flexible.* Your current *leadership-style preference* is determined by the higher of your two scores on the dimensions of task and relationship. The strength of your preference is indicated by the difference between your scores on the two dimensions.

Leadership Style Adaptability: A score of 4 or 5 on item 10 suggests that you're likely to adapt to circumstances as they arise.

Reference: Adapted from Phillip L. Hunsaker, *Management: A Skills Approach,* 2nd ed. (Upper Saddle River, NJ: Pearson Education, 2005), 419–20.

CHAPTER 13

Contemporary Views of Leadership in Organizations

Chapter Outline

- Contemporary Situational Theories
- Leadership Through the Eyes of Followers
- Alternatives to Leadership
- The Changing Nature of Leadership
- Emerging Issues in Leadership

Chapter Learning Objectives

After studying this chapter, you should be able to:

1. Identify and describe contemporary situational theories of leadership.
2. Discuss leadership through the eyes of followers.
3. Identify and describe alternatives to leadership.
4. Describe the changing nature of leadership.
5. Identify and discuss emerging issues in leadership.

When to Stand on Your Head and Other Tips from the Top

"[Leadership is] a game of pinball, and you're the ball."

—*U.S. Senator John McCain*

It isn't easy leading a U.S. business these days. Leaving aside the global recession, the passion for "lean and mean" operations means that there are fewer workers to do more work. Globalization means keeping abreast of cross-cultural differences. Knowledge industries present unique leadership challenges requiring better communication skills and greater flexibility. Advances in technology have opened unprecedented channels of communication. Now more than ever, leaders must be able to do just about everything and more of it. As U.S. Senator and former presidential candidate John McCain puts it, "[Leadership is] a game of pinball, and you're the ball." Fortunately, a few of corporate America's veteran leaders have some tips for those who still want to follow in their increasingly treacherous footsteps.

First of all, if you think you're being overworked—that your hours are too long and your schedule too demanding—odds are you're right: Most people—including executives—*are* overworked. And in some industries, they're *particularly* overworked. U.S. airlines, for example, now service 100 million more passengers annually than they did just five years ago—with 70,000 fewer workers. "I used to manage my time," quips one airline executive. "Now I manage my energy." In fact, many high-ranking managers have realized that energy is a key factor in their ability to complete tasks on tough schedules. Most top corporate leaders work 80 to 100 hours a week, and a lot of them have found that regimens that allow them to refuel and refresh make it possible for them to keep up the pace.

Carlos Ghosn, who's currently CEO and chairman of both Renault and Nissan, believes in regular respites from his workweek routine. "I don't bring my work home. I play with my four children and spend time with my family on weekends," says Ghosn. "I come up with good ideas as a result of becoming stronger after being recharged." Yahoo! CEO/president Marissa Mayer admits that "I can get by on four to six hours of sleep," but she also takes a weeklong vacation three times a

REUTERS/Andrew Burton

Carlos Ghosn, CEO and chairman of both Renault and Nissan, uses a variety of techniques to manage his time and maintain a degree of work-life harmony.

year. Global HR consultant Robert Freedman devotes two minutes every morning to doodling on napkins. Not only does it give him a chance to meditate, but he's thinking about publishing both his doodles and his meditations in a coffee-table book.

Many leaders report that playing racquetball, running marathons, practicing yoga, or just getting regular exercise helps them to recover from overwork. Hank Greenberg, currently chairman and CEO of the financial services firm C.V. Starr & Co., plays tennis for most of the year and skis in the winter months. "I'm addicted to exercise," he says, because it "unwinds me." PayPal cofounder Max Levchin prefers "80 or 90 hard miles on a road bike . . . starting early on Saturday mornings." Eighty-nine-year-old Sumner Redstone, chairman of the parent company of CBS, Viacom, MTV, and Paramount Pictures, rises at 5 a.m. and hits both the exercise bike and the treadmill before the markets open. (Redstone also recommends "lots of fish and plenty of antioxidants.") Finally, Strauss Zelnick, CEO and chairman of Take-Two Interactive Software, is *really* serious about exercise:

> *I try to book my exercise like a meeting and try hard never to cancel it. . . . Generally I try to do an exercise class at the gym once a week; I train for an hour with a trainer once or twice a week; I cycle with a group of friends for an hour once to three times a week, and I lift weights with a friend or colleague twice or three times a week.*

Effective leaders also take control of information flow—which means managing it, not reducing the flow until it's as close to a trickle as they can get it. Like most executives, for example, Mayer can't get by without multiple sources of information: "I always have my laptop with me," she reports, and "I adore my cell phone." Starbucks chairman/CEO Howard Schultz receives a morning voicemail summarizing the previous day's sales results and reads three newspapers a day. Mayer watches the news all day, and Bill Gross, a securities portfolio manager, keeps an eye on six monitors displaying real-time investment data.

On the other hand, Gross stands on his head to force himself to take a break from communicating. When he's upright again, he tries to find time to concentrate. "Eliminating the noise," he says, "is critical. . . . I only pick up the phone three or four times a day. . . . I don't want to be connected—I want to be disconnected."

Ghosn, whose schedule requires weekly intercontinental travel, uses bilingual assistants to screen and translate information—one assistant for information from Europe (where Renault is), one for information from Japan (where Nissan is), and one for information from the United States (where Ghosn often has to be when he doesn't have to be in Europe or Japan). Clothing designer Vera Wang also uses an assistant to filter information. "The barrage of calls is so enormous," she says, "that if I just answered calls I'd do nothing else. . . . If I were to go near email, there'd be even more obligations, and I'd be in [a mental hospital] with a white jacket on."

Not surprisingly, Microsoft chairman Bill Gates integrates the role of his assistant into a high-tech information-organizing system:

On my desk I have three screens, synchronized to form a single desktop. I can drag items from one screen to the next. Once you have that large display area, you'll never go back, because it has a direct impact on productivity.

The screen on the left has my list of emails. On the center screen is usually the specific email I'm reading and responding to. And my browser is on the right-hand screen. This setup gives me the ability to glance and see what new has come in while I'm working on something and to bring up a link that's related to an email and look at it while the email is still in front of me.

At Microsoft, email is the medium of choice. . . . I get about 100 emails a day. We apply filtering to keep it to that level. Email comes straight to me from anyone I've ever corresponded with, anyone from Microsoft, Intel, HP, and all the other partner companies, and anyone I know. And I always see a write-up from my assistant of any other email, from companies that aren't on my permission list or individuals I don't know. . . .

We're at the point now where the challenge isn't how to communicate effectively with email—it's ensuring that you spend your time on the email that matters most. I use tools like "in-box rules" and search folders to mark and group messages based on their content and importance.

What Do You Think?

1. In what ways does information technology appear to be changing the work of leaders?
2. In what ways do you think that the work of leaders will change in the future? In your opinion, what types of people will probably make the best leaders in the future?

References: Geoffrey Colvin, "Catch a Rising Star," *CNNMoney*, February 6, 2006, http://money.cnn.com on July 23, 2012; Klaus Kneale, "Stress Management for the CEO," *Forbes.com*, April 17, 2009, www.forbes.com on July 23, 2012; Susan Berfield, "The Real Effects of Workplace Anxiety," *Bloomberg Businessweek*, July 24, 2009, www.businessweek.com on July 23, 2012; Berfield, "How

Executives Manage Stress," *Bloomberg Businessweek*, July 24, 2009, http://images.businessweek.com on July 23, 2012; Jerry Useem, "Making Your Work Work for You," *CNNMoney*, March 15, 2006, http://money.cnn.com on July 23, 2012; Bill Gates, "How I Work," *CNNMoney*, April 7, 2006, http://money.cnn.com on July 23, 2012.

The three major situational theories of leadership discussed in Chapter 12 altered everyone's thinking about leadership. No longer did people feel compelled to search for the one best way to lead. Nor did they continue to seek universal leadership prescriptions or relationships. Instead, both researchers and practicing managers turned their attention to a variety of new approaches to leadership. These new approaches, as well as other current emerging leadership issues, are the subject of this chapter. We first describe two relatively new situational theories, as well as recent refinements to the earlier theories. We then examine leadership through the eyes of followers. Recent thinking regarding potential alternatives to traditional leadership are then explored. Next we describe the changing nature of leadership. We conclude this chapter with a discussion of several emerging issues in leadership.

CONTEMPORARY SITUATIONAL THEORIES

The LPC theory, the path-goal theory, and Vroom's decision tree approach together redirected the study of leadership. Not surprisingly, then, other situational theories have also been developed. Moreover, there continue to be changes and refinements to the original situational models.

The **leader-member exchange model (LMX)** of leadership stresses the importance of variable relationships between supervisors and each of their subordinates.

The Leader-Member Exchange Model

The **leader-member exchange model** (LMX) of leadership, conceived by George Graen and Fred Dansereau, stresses the importance of variable relationships between supervisors and each of their subordinates.[1] Each superior-subordinate pair is referred to as a "vertical dyad." The model differs from earlier approaches in that it focuses on the differential relationship leaders often establish with different subordinates. Figure 13.1 shows the basic concepts of the leader-member exchange theory.

The **in-group** often receives special duties requiring more responsibility and autonomy; they may also receive special privileges, such as more discretion about work schedules.

Members of the **out-group** receive less of the supervisor's time and attention and are likely to be assigned the more mundane tasks the group must perform and not be "in the loop" when information is being shared.

The model suggests that supervisors establish a special relationship with a small number of trusted subordinates referred to as the "in-group." The **in-group** often receives special duties requiring more responsibility and autonomy; they may also receive special privileges, such as more discretion about work schedules. Members of the in-group are also likely to be privy to sensitive information and are likely to know about upcoming events before others. They may also receive more rewards and generally stronger support from the leader.

Subordinates who are not a part of this group are called the **out-group**, and they receive less of the supervisor's time and attention. Members of the out-group are likely to be assigned the more mundane tasks the group must perform and not be "in the loop" insofar as information is being shared. They may also receive fewer rewards and overall weaker support from the leader.

Note in the figure that the leader has a dyadic, or one-to-one, relationship with each of the five subordinates. Early in his or her interaction with a given subordinate, the supervisor initiates either an in-group or out-group relationship. It is not clear how a leader selects members of the in-group, but the decision may be based on personal

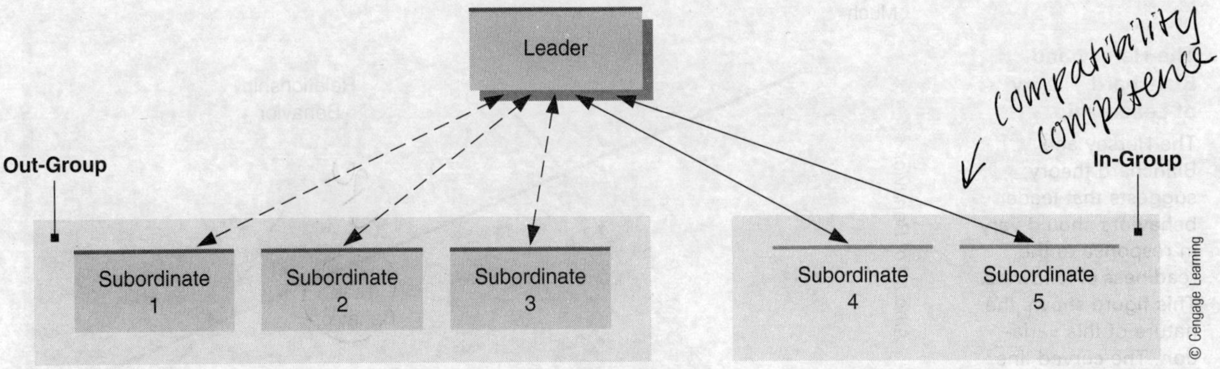

FIGURE 13.1

The Leader-Member Exchange (LMX) Model

The LMX model suggests that leaders form unique independent relationships with each of their subordinates. As illustrated here, a key factor in the nature of this relationship is whether the individual subordinate is in the leader's out-group or in-group.

compatibility and subordinates' competence. Research has confirmed the existence of in-groups and out-groups. In addition, studies generally have found that in-group members tend to have a higher level of performance and satisfaction than out-group members.[2]

The Hersey and Blanchard Model

Another recent situational perspective, especially popular among practicing managers, is the Hersey and Blanchard model. Like the leadership grid discussed in the previous chapter, this model was also developed as a consulting tool. The **Hersey and Blanchard model** is based on the notion that appropriate leader behavior depends on the "readiness" of the leader's followers.[3] In this instance, readiness refers to the subordinate's degree of motivation, competence, experience, and interest in accepting responsibility. Figure 13.2 shows the basic model.

The Hersey and Blanchard model is based on the premise that appropriate leader behavior depends on the "readiness" of the leader's followers. In this instance, readiness refers to the subordinate's degree of motivation, competence, experience, and interest in accepting responsibility.

The figure suggests that as the readiness of followers improves, the leader's basic style should also change. When subordinate readiness is low, for example, the leader should rely on a "telling" style by providing direction and defining roles. When low to moderate readiness exists, the leader should use a "selling" style by offering direction and role definition accompanied by explanation and information. In a case of moderate to high follower readiness, the leader should use a "participating" style, allowing followers to share in decision making. Finally, when follower readiness is high, the leader is advised to use a "delegating" style by allowing followers to work independently with little or no overseeing.

Refinements and Revisions of Other Theories

In addition to these somewhat newer models, the three dominant situational theories have also continued to undergo various refinements and revisions. For instance, while the version of the LPC theory presented in Chapter 12 is still the dominant model, researchers have made several attempts to improve its validity. Recently, for example, Fiedler has added the concept of stress as a major element of situational favorableness. He also argued that the leader's intelligence and experience play a major role in enabling her or him to cope with various levels of stress that characterize any particular situation.[4]

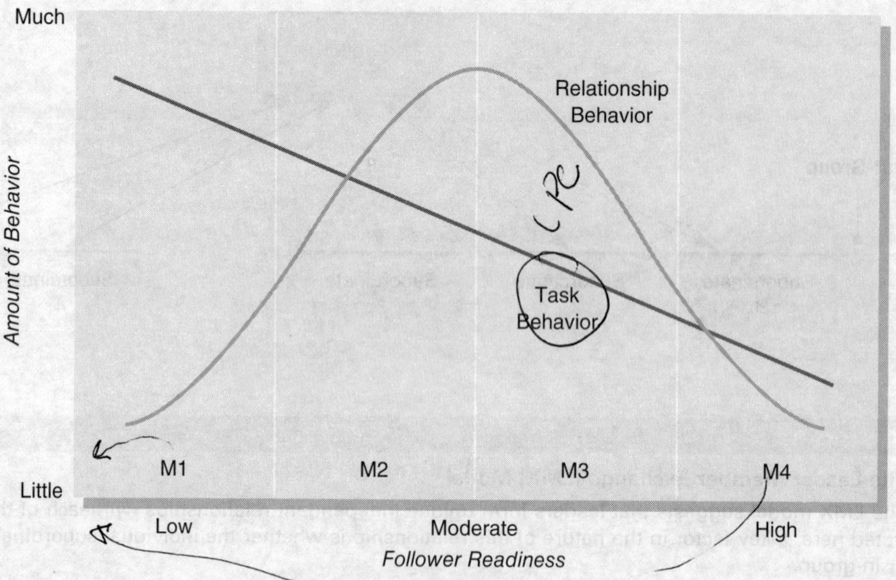

FIGURE 13.2

The Hersey and Blanchard Theory of Leadership

The Hersey and Blanchard theory suggests that leader behaviors should vary in response to the readiness of followers. This figure shows the nature of this variation. The curved line suggests that a leader's relationship behavior should start low, gradually increase, but then decrease again as follower readiness increases. But the leader's task behavior, shown by the straight line, should start high when followers lack readiness and then continuously diminish as they gain readiness.

References: The Situational Leadership® Model is the registered trademark of the Center for Leadership Studies, Escondido, CA. Excerpt from P. Hersey, *Management of Organizational Behavior: Utilizing Human Resources*, 3rd ed., 1977, p. 165.

The path-goal theory has also undergone major refinements over the years. Its original formulation included only two forms of leader behavior. A third was later added and then, most recently, the theory evolved to include the four forms of leader behavior discussed in Chapter 12. While there has been relatively little research on this theory in recent years, its intuitive logic and general research support make it highly likely that it will again one day emerge as a popular topic for research.

Finally, Vroom's decision tree approach also continues to evolve. The version presented in Chapter 12 was the third published version. Moreover, Vroom and his associates have continued to develop training and assessment materials to better enable managers to understand their own "natural" decision-making styles. In addition, there are software versions of the various models that now can quickly help managers determine the optimal level of participation in any given situation.

LEADERSHIP THROUGH THE EYES OF FOLLOWERS

Another recent perspective that has been adopted by some leadership experts focuses on how leaders are seen through the eyes of followers. That is, in what ways and to what extent is it important that followers and other observers attribute leadership to others? The three primary approaches to leadership through the eyes of followers are transformational leadership, charismatic leadership, and attributions of leadership.

Transformational Leadership

Transformational leadership focuses on the basic distinction between leading for change and leading for stability.[5] According to this viewpoint, much of what a leader does occurs in the course of normal, routine, work-related transactions—assigning work, evaluating performance, making decisions, and so forth. Occasionally, however, the leader has to initiate and manage major change, such as managing a merger, creating a work group, or defining the organization's culture. The first set of issues involves transactional leadership, whereas the second entails transformational leadership.[6]

Recall from Chapter 12 the distinction between management and leadership. *Transactional leadership* is essentially the same as management in that it involves routine, regimented activities. Closer to the general notion of leadership, however, is **transformational leadership**, the set of abilities that allows the leader to recognize the need for change, to create a vision to guide that change, and to execute the change effectively. Only a leader with tremendous influence can hope to perform these functions successfully. Some experts believe that change is such a vital organizational function that even successful firms need to change regularly to avoid complacency and stagnation; accordingly, leadership for change is also important.[7]

Transformational leadership refers to the set of abilities that allows the leader to recognize the need for change, to create a vision to guide that change, and to execute the change effectively.

Another hallmark of effective leadership is the ability to see which approach is needed. Following the death of Steve Jobs in 2011, Apple executive Tim Cook was elevated to the position of CEO. At the time Apple was racking in enormous profits, was becoming the most valuable company in the world, and had a strong and robust pipeline of new products and technologies in development. Hence, Cook saw little need for dramatic change. While he has changed a few things, such as paying shareholder dividends for the first time in years, Apple today is essentially the same as it was during Jobs' tenure. On the other hand, when Marissa Mayer was recruited from Google to lead Yahoo! in 2012, the need for dramatic change was obvious. While Yahoo! had once been as successful as other technology firms like Google, Microsoft, Apple, and Facebook, it was falling behind these and other high-tech giants and headed toward irrelevance. Consequently, she embarked on a series of major strategic initiatives in an attempt to revitalize the firm.

Robert Galrait/REUTERS

Steve Jobs was a passionate and visionary CEO. When he died in 2012 he left Apple in such good shape that his successor, Tim Cook, had no need to make dramatic changes. The firm's product portfolio and innovation pipelines were strong and the firm's finances were stable, so Cook has been able to think about long-term strategic issues rather than addressing a lot of short-term problems.

Leaders may also find it necessary to transition from either transformational or transactional leadership to the other. For instance, when Alan Mulally assumed the leadership role at Ford Motor, the firm was in desperate straits. Its production facilities were outmoded, its costs were too high, and its product line was stale and had a reputation for poor quality. Using dramatic transformational leadership, Mulally managed to completely overhaul the firm, revitalizing it along every major dimension and transforming it into the healthiest of the Big Three U.S. automakers. Indeed, while General Motors and Chrysler needed federal bailout funds in 2009, Ford was able to maintain operations on its own without government assistance and posted a large profit in the first quarter of 2010 and for the full years of 2011 and 2012. Now that the transformation is complete, Mulally has transitioned to a transactional role and continues to lead the firm toward higher revenues, market share, and profits.[8] In the event of another major crisis, though, Mulally may need to move back toward transformational leadership.

Charismatic Leadership

Charisma is a form of interpersonal attraction that inspires support and acceptance.

Charismatic leadership is a type of influence based on the leader's personal charisma.

Perspectives based on charismatic leadership, like the trait theories discussed in Chapter 12, assume that charisma is an individual characteristic of the leader. **Charisma** is a form of interpersonal attraction that inspires support and acceptance.

Charismatic leadership is accordingly a type of influence based on the leader's personal charisma. All else being equal, someone with charisma is more likely to be able to influence others than someone without charisma. For example, a highly charismatic supervisor will be more successful in influencing subordinate behavior than a supervisor who lacks charisma. Thus, influence is again a fundamental element of this perspective.[9]

Robert House first proposed a theory of charismatic leadership based on research findings from a variety of social science disciplines.[10] His theory suggests that charismatic leaders are likely to have a lot of self-confidence, firm confidence in their beliefs and ideals, and a strong need to influence people. They also tend to communicate high expectations about follower performance and to express confidence in their followers. Herb Kelleher, legendary CEO of Southwest Airlines (now retired), is an excellent example of a charismatic leader. Kelleher skillfully blended a unique combination of executive skill, honesty, and playfulness. These qualities attracted a group of followers at Southwest who were willing to follow his lead without question and to dedicate themselves to carrying out his decisions and policies with unceasing passion.[11] Other individuals who are or were seen as charismatic leaders include Condoleezza Rice, Mary Kay Ash, Steve Jobs, Ted Turner, Martin Luther King, Jr., and Pope John Paul II. Unfortunately, however, charisma can also empower leaders in other directions. Adolf Hitler had strong charismatic qualities that appealed to some followers, for instance, as did Osama bin Laden.

AF archive/Alamy

Arguably the most charismatic President of the United States, John F. Kennedy came from a powerful family, and was blessed with good looks in addition to his personal charisma.

Figure 13.3 portrays the three elements of charismatic leadership in organizations that most experts acknowledge today.[12] First, charismatic leaders are able to envision likely future trends and patterns, to set high expectations for themselves and for others, and to model behaviors consistent with meeting those expectations. Next, charismatic leaders are able to energize others by demonstrating personal excitement, personal confidence, and consistent patterns of success. Finally, charismatic leaders enable others by supporting them, empathizing with them, and expressing confidence in them.[13]

Charismatic leadership ideas are quite popular among managers today and are the subject of numerous books and articles.[14] Unfortunately, few studies have specifically attempted to test the meaning and impact of charismatic leadership. Lingering ethical concerns about charismatic leadership also trouble some people. They stem from the fact that some charismatic leaders inspire such blind faith in their followers that they may engage in inappropriate, unethical, or even illegal behaviors just because the leader instructed them to do so. This tendency likely played a role in the unwinding of both Enron and Arthur Andersen as people followed orders from their charismatic

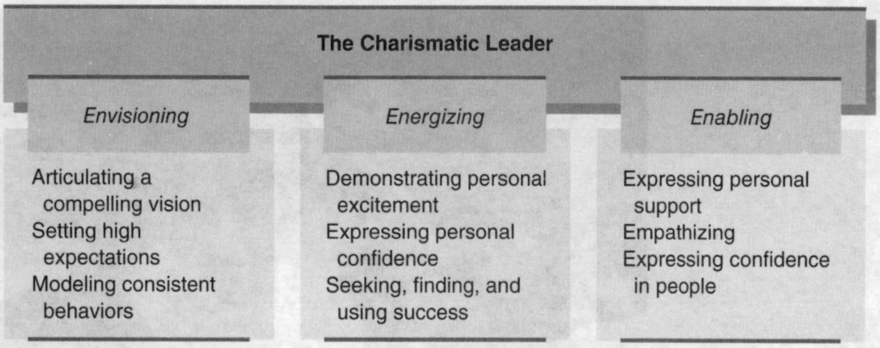

FIGURE 13.3

The Charismatic Leader

The charismatic leader is characterized by three fundamental attributes. As illustrated here, these are behaviors resulting in envisioning, energizing, and enabling. Charismatic leaders can be a powerful force in any organizational setting.

References: David A. Nadler and Michael L. Tushman, "Beyond the Charismatic Leader: Leadership and Organizational Change," *California Management Review,* Winter, 1990, pp. 70–97.

bosses to hide information, shred documents, and mislead investigators. Taking over a leadership role from someone with substantial personal charisma is also a challenge. For instance, the immediate successors to very successful charismatic football coaches like Vince Lombardi (Green Bay Packers), Steve Spurrier (University of Florida), and Tom Osborne (University of Nebraska) each failed to measure up to his predecessor's legacy and was subsequently fired.

Attribution and Leadership

We discussed attribution theory back in Chapter 3 and noted then that people tend to observe behavior and then attribute causes (and hence meaning) to it. There are clear implications for attribution theory and leadership, especially when leadership is framed through the eyes of followers. Basically, then, the **attribution perspective** holds that when behaviors are observed in a context associated with leadership, others may attribute varying levels of leadership ability or power to the person displaying those behaviors.

The **attribution perspective** on leadership holds that when behaviors are observed in a context associated with leadership, others may attribute varying levels of leadership ability or power to the person displaying those behaviors.

For example, suppose we observe an individual behaving confidently and decisively; we also observe that others are paying close attention to what this person says and does and that they seem to defer to and/or consult with her on various things. We might subsequently conclude that this individual is a leader because of both her behavior and the behaviors of others. However, in a different setting we observe that a person seems to not be especially confident or decisive; we also observe that others seem relatively indifferent to what she has to say and that she is not routinely consulted about things. In this case we are more likely to assume that this person is not really a leader.

The attributions we make subsequently affect both our own behavior and the actual capacity of an individual to behave like a leader. For instance, suppose after observing the first group described above we then become a member of that group; since we have attributed leadership qualities to a certain person, we are somewhat likely to mimic the behaviors of others and treat this person like our own leader. Moreover, the fact that we and others do this reinforces this person's confidence in continuing the leadership role.

To further put this into perspective, assume that a group of strangers is trapped in an elevator. One person in the group immediately steps forward and takes charge. He appears confident, has a reassuring, calming effect on others, and says that he knows

These people are trapped in an elevator. The woman peering through the door is relaying information to the others that a rescue team is outside and that they will be freed soon. Her demeanor and this information are helping people remain calm.

how to call for help and what to do until that help arrives. In all likelihood, the others in the elevator will acknowledge his leadership, will respond positively to his behavior, and would later credit him with helping them get through the unpleasant experience. On the other hand, if in the same setting someone tries to take charge but clearly lacks confidence and/or clearly exhibits ignorance of what to do, others will quickly pick up on this, pay little attention to what the person subsequently says, and perhaps look to someone else for leadership.

The attribution perspective on leadership is especially clear during presidential campaigns. Candidates and their handlers strive to make sure that they are always shown in the best possible light—demonstrating confidence, being sympathetic, knowing what to do, looking poised and well-groomed, and so forth. George W. Bush received a lot of media attention when during the early stages of the war with Iraq he landed in a jet plane on an aircraft carrier, jumped out of the cockpit, and boldly walked toward the cameras under a banner proclaiming "mission accomplished." Supporters of Bush saw this as an illustration of his strong leadership. But his critics no doubt saw it as a carefully orchestrated media event designed solely to make him look strong and leader-like. Hence, each camp attributed things about Bush's leadership based on the same objective reality but heavily influenced by their own attitudes and predispositions.

One context in which followers pay especially close attention to a leader's behavior is during a time of crisis, particularly if followers perceive that their own best interests are directly at stake. The *Change* box on page 357, entitled "Tips for Tough Times," presents some advice from executives on how to lead employees during an economic downturn.

CHANGE Tips for Tough Times

How does one go about leading in a recession like the one we're currently going through? What adjustments do you have to make when money is scarce, markets are volatile, and morale needs boosting? Dennis Carey, vice chairman of Korn Ferry International, an executive-search firm, suggests that top managers start by acknowledging that leading in extreme circumstances means calling into question everything they do under normal circumstances. "You can't rely on a peacetime general to fight a war," he reminds fellow executives. "The wartime CEO prepares for the worst so that his or her company can take market share away from players who haven't." Hire away your competitors' best people, advises Carey, and keep *them* from grabbing *yours*. Or buy up their assets while they can be had at bargain prices.

> "Communicate, communicate, communicate.'"
>
> —JIM DONALD, CEO OF EXTENDED STAY HOTELS

Jack Hayhow, consultant and founder of Opus Training and ReallyEasyHR, adds that leaders need to make sure that their employees know why they're making changes: "Clearly state to your people that we are in a recession . . . [and that] very little of what [they've] assumed to be true in the past will be true in the future. [Tell them]: 'You must understand that this is no longer business as usual.' . . . My suggestion," says Hayhow, "would be [something like]: 'Quit worrying about the things you can't control and focus on what you can. Find ways to contribute . . . and make it really hard for the company to let you go. . . .' If you have people who argue or debate, show them the door."

Hayhow also realizes that "when things are as bad as they are [in a recession], motivation is critical. . . . If you create an environment conducive to people motivating themselves," he contends, "you'll be able to motivate in these changing times." How do you create such an environment? "Start by matching talent with the task," says Hayhow. "Play to your employees' strengths. Figure out who does what and make sure they're spending their time where they can best utilize their talents." And don't forget to "give people some choice. . . . When people have even a little choice over what they do or how they do it, they're more committed and enthusiastic about the task." Let employees decide how to do something "or maybe even who they work with to get the job done."

Ex-Starbucks CEO Jim Donald, who's now CEO of Extended Stay Hotels, makes a fairly simple recommendation: "Communicate, communicate, communicate. Especially at a time of crisis," he advises, "make sure your message reaches all levels, from the very lowest to the uppermost." Kip Tindell, who's been CEO of the Container Store since its founding in 1978, agrees. That's why his managers "run around like chickens relentlessly trying to communicate everything to every single employee at all times." He admits that, practically speaking, it's an impossible task, but he's also convinced that the effort is more important than ever in times of crisis. He also contends that his company is in a better position to ride out the economic storm "because we're so dedicated to the notion that communication and leadership are the same thing." At the very least, he says, "we're fortunate to be minus the paranoia that goes with employees who feel they don't know what's going on."

References: Emily Thornton, "Managing through a Crisis: The New Rules," *Bloomberg Businessweek*, January 8, 2009, www.businessweek.com on July 23, 2012; Anthony Portuesi, "Leading in a Recession: An Interview with Jack Hayhow," *Driven Leaders*, February 24, 2009, http://drivenleaders.com on April 24, 2011; Jim Donald, "Guest Post: Former Starbucks CEO's Tips for Tough Times," *CNNMoney*, April 1, 2009, http://postcards.blogs.fortune.cnn.com on July 23, 2012; Ellen Davis, "Retail Execs Offer Insights on Leadership in Tough Economic Times," *Retail's BIG Blog*, January 15, 2009, http://blog.nrf.com on July 23, 2012.

ALTERNATIVES TO LEADERSHIP

Another perspective on leadership that has received considerable attention in recent years has focused on alternatives to leadership. In some cases, circumstances may exist that render leadership unnecessary or irrelevant. The factors that contribute to these circumstances are called leadership substitutes. In other cases, factors may exist that neutralize or negate the influence of a leader even when that individual is attempting to exercise leadership.

Leadership Substitutes

Leadership substitutes are individual, task, and organizational characteristics that tend to outweigh the leader's ability to affect subordinates' satisfaction and performance.

Leadership substitutes are individual, task, and organizational characteristics that tend to outweigh the leader's ability to affect subordinates' satisfaction and performance.[15] In other words, if certain factors are present, the employee will perform his or her job capably without the direction of a leader. Unlike traditional theories, which assume that hierarchical leadership in one form or another is always important, the premise of the leadership substitutes perspective is that leader behaviors may be irrelevant in some situations. Several basic leadership substitutes are identified in Table 13.1.

Consider, for example, what happens when an ambulance with a critically injured victim screeches to the door of a hospital emergency room. Do the ER employees stand around waiting for someone to take control and instruct them on what to do? The answer is obviously no—they are highly trained and well-prepared professionals who know how to respond, who to depend on, who to communicate with, how to work together as a team, and so forth. In short, they are fully capable of carrying out their jobs without someone playing the role of leader.

Individual ability, experience, training, knowledge, motivation, and professional orientation are among the characteristics that may substitute for leadership. Similarly, a task characterized by routine, a high degree of structure, frequent feedback, and intrinsic satisfaction may also render leader behavior unnecessary. Thus, if the task gives the subordinate enough intrinsic satisfaction, she or he may not need support from a leader.

Explicit plans and goals, rules and procedures, cohesive work groups, a rigid reward structure, and physical distance between supervisor and subordinate are organizational characteristics that may substitute for leadership. For example, if job goals are explicit, and there are many rules and procedures for task performance, a leader providing directions may not be necessary. Research has provided support for the concept of leadership substitutes, but additional research is needed to identify other potential substitutes and their impact on leadership effectiveness.[16]

Table 13.1 Substitutes and Neutralizers for Leadership

Individual	**Group**
Individual professionalism	Group norms
Motivation	Group cohesiveness
Experience and training	
Indifference to rewards	
Job	**Organization**
Structured/automated	Rigid procedures and rules
Highly controlled	Explicit goals and objectives
Intrinsically satisfying	Rigid reward system
Embedded feedback	

Leadership Neutralizers

Leadership neutralizers are factors that render ineffective a leader's attempts to engage in various leadership behaviors.

In other situations, even if a leader is present and attempts to engage in various leadership behaviors, those behaviors may be rendered ineffective—neutralized—by various factors. These factors are referred to as **leadership neutralizers**. Suppose, for example, that a relatively new and inexperienced leader is assigned to a work group comprised of very experienced employees with long-standing performance norms and a high level of group cohesiveness. The norms and cohesiveness of the group may be so strong that there is nothing the new leader can do to change things. Of course, this pattern may also work in several different ways. The norms may dictate acceptable but not high performance, and the leader may be powerless to improve things because the group is so cohesive. Or the norms may call for very high performance, such that even a bungling and ineffective leader cannot cause any damage. In both cases, however, the process is the same—the leader's ability to alter the situation is neutralized by elements in that situation.

In addition to group factors, elements of the job itself may also limit a leader's ability to "make a difference." Consider, for example, employees working on a moving assembly line. Employees may only be able to work at the pace of the moving line, so performance quantity is constrained by the speed of the line. Moreover, if performance quality is also constrained (say, by simple tasks and/or tight quality control procedures), the leader may again be powerless to influence individual work behaviors.

Finally, organizational factors can also neutralize at least some forms of leader behavior. Suppose a new leader is accustomed to using merit pay increases as a way to motivate people. But in her or his new job, pay increases are dictated by union contracts and are based primarily on employee seniority and cost of living. Or suppose that an employee is already at the top of the pay grade for his or her job. In either case, the leader's previous approach to motivating people has been neutralized and so new approaches will have to be identified.

THE CHANGING NATURE OF LEADERSHIP

Various alternatives to leadership aside, though, many settings still call for at least some degree of leadership, although the nature of that leadership continues to evolve.[17] The Service box helps underscore this point. Among the recent changes in leadership that managers should recognize are the increasing role of leaders as coaches and gender and cross-cultural patterns of leader behavior.

Leaders as Coaches

Whereas leaders were once expected to control situations, direct work, supervise people, closely monitor performance, make decisions, and structure activities, many leaders today are being asked to change how they manage people—to become **coaches**.

We noted in Chapter 10 that many organizations today are using teams. And many other organizations are attempting to become less hierarchical—that is, to eliminate the old-fashioned command-and-control mentality often inherent in bureaucratic organizations and to motivate and empower individuals to work independently. In each case, the role of leaders is also changing. Whereas leaders were once expected to control situations, direct work, supervise people, closely monitor performance, make decisions, and structure activities, many leaders today are being asked to change how they manage people. Perhaps the best description of this new role is that the leader is becoming a **coach** instead of an overseer.[18]

Consider the metaphor from the standpoint of the coach of an athletic team. The coach plays a role in selecting the players for the team and deciding on the general direction to take (such as emphasizing offense versus defense). The coach also helps develop

SERVICE | Leadership by Mission

©rangizzz/Shutterstock

A family with a young daughter was visiting Orlando's Walt Disney Resort's Magic Kingdom. For reasons known only to her, the young girl's favorite character was Captain Hook. The family, knowing that Disney's characters could be found inside the theme parks at certain times to sign autographs and have their pictures taken, sought out the ill-mannered Captain. When they found him, they stood in the line to get his picture with their daughter. Unfortunately, there is a time limit on character appearances, and before the little girl got her turn, Captain Hook was escorted "offstage." The girl was devastated. Later that evening the family was dining in one of the resort hotels. The server saw the sad look on the girl's face and asked if everything was all right. Dad told her about the disappointment in their day and what that meant to the little girl. The server left the table and went directly to her supervisor to explain the situation.

Because of Disney employees' commitment to the company's service mission and the company's empowerment of employees to make things right if they can, the supervisor picked up the phone to call the character supervisor to request a special visit from Captain Hook to the restaurant. As she dialed the number, a thought occurred to her and she hung up the phone. Turning to the server, she asked if Captain Hook would do anything as nice as showing up with an apology? They both agreed that this was totally out of character and thought they should find a better solution to fixing this little girl's disappointment. And they did. They went to the stockroom and found a plush doll of Captain Hook. They took it to the hotel's housekeeping department to have someone place it on the little girl's bed along with a note. On the note they wrote, "Dear Sally: I am sorry that Captain Hook was mean to you today but he is sometimes like that. Next time I see him I will tell him he shouldn't be so mean to our guests. (signed) Peter Pan." The little girl was thrilled and the parents not only wrote a letter to Disney management telling of their appreciation for creating this magical solution to their daughter's disappointment, they vowed to tell everyone they knew how a Disney server saved their day.

The question is what leadership model would predict this outcome? In the service sector, employees are so often out of any supervisor's vision that organizations must rely on something other than a leader's direct supervision to elicit the employee behaviors and actions desired. What these companies realize is that a strong organizational mission can drive employee behavior, and they work hard to translate strong missions into terms that will guide employee actions. Disney, for example, has a strong mission of providing fun to its guests. It tells its employees that they should be guided by four overarching principles in decisions they make when interacting with guests. These are, in their descending order of importance to the mission, safety, courtesy, show, and efficiency. Thus, employees are expected to use these four as they interact with guests anywhere on Disney property, whether a supervisor is watching or not.

Since a manager can't be everywhere and see everything, organizations that provide services must rely on their employees to deliver the experience that customers expect. When experiences exist only in customers' minds, empowering employees in services is a necessity to ensure that the service expected is delivered when and where it is desired. The point here is that service employees must figure out what to do and how to do it on the spot and the organizations that employs them must ensure that they not only have the training and ability to do their jobs but are empowered to flexibly respond to the unique needs, wants, and behaviors that each customer has in ways that meet each's expectations.

Discussion Question: How can managers define jobs in ways that enable their employees to effectively meet the different expectations of different customers when there is no boss around to ask?

player talent and teaches them how to execute specific plays. But at game time, the coach stays on the sidelines; it's up to the players themselves to execute plays and get the job done. And while the coach may get some of the credit for the victory, he or she didn't actually score any of the points.

Likewise, then, from the standpoint of an organizational leader, a coaching perspective would call for the leader to help select team members and other new employees, to provide some general direction, to help train and develop the team and the skills of its members, and to help the team get the information and other resources it needs. The leader may also have to help resolve conflict among team members and mediate other disputes that arise. And coaches from different teams may need to play important roles in linking the activities and functions of their respective teams. But beyond these activities, the leader keeps a low profile and lets the group get its work done with little or no direct oversight from the leader.

Within the coaching role, some leaders have also excelled at taking on more responsibilities as a **mentor**—helping a less experienced person learn the ropes to better prepare himself or herself to advance within the organization.

Of course, some managers long accustomed to the traditional approach may have trouble changing to a coaching role. But others seem to make the transition with little or no difficulty. Moreover, companies such as Texas Instruments, Halliburton, and Yum! Brands have developed very successful training programs to help their managers learn how to become better coaches. Within the coaching role, some leaders have also excelled at taking on more responsibilities as a **mentor**—the role of helping a less experienced person learn the ropes to better prepare himself or herself to advance within the organization. Texas Instruments has maintained a very successful mentoring program for years.

Gender and Leadership

Another factor that is clearly changing the nature of leadership is the growing number of women advancing to higher levels in organizations. Given that most leadership theories and research studies have focused on male leaders, developing a better understanding of how females lead is clearly an important next step. For example, do women and men tend to lead differently? Some early research suggests that there are indeed fundamental differences in leadership as practiced by women and men.[19]

For instance, in contrast to original stereotypes, female leaders are not necessarily more nurturing or supportive than are male leaders. Likewise, male leaders are not systematically more harsh, controlling, or task focused than are female leaders. The one difference that does seem to arise in some cases is that women have a tendency to be slightly more democratic in making decisions, whereas men have a similar tendency to be somewhat more autocratic.[20]

There are two possible explanations for this pattern. One possibility is that women may tend to have stronger interpersonal skills than men and are hence better able to effectively involve others in making decisions. Men, on the other hand, may have weaker interpersonal skills and thus have a tendency to rely on their own judgment. The other possible explanation is that women may encounter more stereotypic resistance to their occupying senior roles. If this is the case, they may actively work to involve others in making decisions so as to help minimize any hostility or conflict. Clearly, however, much more work needs to be done in order to better understand the dynamics of gender and leadership. It is obvious, of course, that high-profile and successful female leaders such as Marissa Mayer (CEO of Yahoo!), Sheryl Sandberg (COO of Facebook), Indra Nooyi (CEO of PepsiCo), and Hillary Clinton (Secretary of State) are demonstrating the effectiveness with which women can be truly exceptional leaders.

Cross-Cultural Leadership

Another changing perspective on leadership relates to cross-cultural issues. In this context, culture is used as a broad concept to encompass both international differences and diversity-based differences within a single culture. However, we will examine international differences in the next section, so at this point we focus first on intra-country cultural

Peter Steiner/The New Yorker Collection

"Do you have any problem being fired by a woman?"

The role of gender in leadership has become an interesting topic in recent years. For example, some people think that women and men tend to lead in different ways. Similarly, as illustrated here, there is interest in the possibility that followers may respond differently to men versus women leaders. In reality, of course, both women and men have the capacity to be strong leaders.

issues. And actually, given our previous discussions of diversity, social interactions, and so forth, the extension of these topics to cross-cultural leadership should be obvious.

For instance, cross-cultural factors clearly play a growing role in organizations as their workforces become more and more diverse. Most leadership research, for instance, has been conducted on samples or case studies involving white male leaders (since until several years ago most business leaders were white males!). But as African Americans, Asian Americans, Hispanics, and members of other ethnic groups achieve leadership positions, it may be necessary to reassess how applicable current theories and models of leadership are when applied to an increasingly diverse pool of leaders.

Religion is also a potential issue in leadership. A Jewish or Christian leader, for example, leading a group with Islamist members may face a variety of complex issues; and, of course, those issues would also exist if the roles were reversed. There are cross-cultural issues even when leaders and followers have less visible indicators of diversity. A manager who has spent his or her entire career in, say, Texas or Alabama will likely face some adjustment issues if promoted to a leadership position in New York or San Francisco.

International Leadership and Project GLOBE

Cross-cultural issues are also obvious in international contexts. For instance, when a Japanese firm sends an executive to head up the firm's operation in the United States, that person will likely need to become acclimated to the cultural differences that exist between the two countries and consider adjusting his or her leadership style accordingly. Japan is generally characterized by collectivism, while the United States is based more on individualism. The Japanese executive, then, will find it necessary to recognize the importance of individual contributions and rewards and the differences in individual and group roles that exist in Japanese and U.S. businesses. And, obviously, similar issues will result if an American leader is posted to Asia.

To learn more about international leadership, a global team of researchers has been working on a series of studies under the general heading of Project GLOBE (Global Leadership and Organizational Behavior Research Project). GLOBE was initiated by Robert House, and research is still being conducted under its auspices.[21] GLOBE identified six leader behaviors that can be observed and assessed across a variety of cultures. These behaviors are:

- *Charismatic/value-based leadership*: the ability to inspire, to motivate, and to promote high performance; includes being visionary, self-sacrificing, trustworthy, decisive, and performance oriented.
- *Team-oriented leadership*: emphasizes team building and creating a sense of common purpose; includes being collaborative, diplomatic, and administratively competent.

- *Participative leadership*: the extent to which leaders involve others in making decisions; being participative and nonautocratic.
- *Humane-oriented leadership*: being supportive, considerate, compassionate, and generous; displaying modesty and sensitivity.
- *Autonomous leadership*: refers to being independent and individualist; being autonomous and unique.
- *Self-protective leadership*: includes behaviors intending to ensure the safety and security of the leader and the group; includes being self-centered, status conscious, conflict inducing, and face saving.

These behaviors have been—and are being—studied in 62 global societies. These societies are mostly separate countries, but when there are markedly different societies with a country (such as Black and White South Africa), each is examined separately. Based on the preliminary results, the original 62 societies were condensed into 10 cultural clusters—societies that yielded highly similar results to one another. For instance, the Nordic Europe cluster includes Finland, Sweden, Denmark, and Norway, and the Southern Asia cluster consists of India, Indonesia, Malaysia, Thailand, and Iran.

In general, the findings of GLOBE suggest that within any cultural cluster, followers react in similar ways to various leader behaviors. For example, employees in Nordic Europe generally want their leaders to be inspiring and to involve others in decision making but are less concerned with status and similar self-centered attributes. Therefore, charismatic/value-based and participative leadership are most important and humane-oriented and self-protective leadership are least important. In Southern Asia, however, most employees want their leaders to be collaborative, sensitive to other people's needs, and concerned with status and face saving. Consequently, self-protective and charismatic/value-based leadership are most important in these countries, while autonomous and participative leadership are least important.[22] Of course, as noted earlier, this research is still ongoing, and it would be premature to draw overly strong generalizations at this point.

EMERGING ISSUES IN LEADERSHIP

Finally, there are also three emerging issues in leadership that warrant discussion. These issues are strategic leadership, ethical leadership, and virtual leadership.

Strategic Leadership

Strategic leadership is the capability to understand the complexities of both the organization and its environment and to lead change in the organization so as to achieve and maintain a superior alignment between the organization and its environment.

Strategic leadership is a new concept that explicitly relates leadership to the role of top management.[23] We will define **strategic leadership** as the capability to understand the complexities of both the organization and its environment and to lead change in the organization so as to achieve and maintain a superior alignment between the organization and its environment. In some ways, then, strategic leadership may be seen as an extension of the transformational leadership role discussed earlier. However, this recent focus has more explicitly acknowledged and incorporated the importance of strategy and strategic decision making. That is, while both transformational and strategic leadership include the concept of change, transformational leadership implicitly emphasizes the ability to lead change as the central focus. Strategic leadership, on the other hand, puts greater weight on the leader's ability to think and function strategically.

To be effective in this role, a manager needs to have a thorough and complete understanding of the organization—its history, its culture, its strengths, and its weaknesses. In addition, the leader needs a firm grasp of the organization's environment. This understanding must encompass current conditions and circumstances as well as significant trends and issues on the horizon. The strategic leader also needs to recognize how the firm is currently aligned with its environment—where it relates effectively with that environment, and where it relates less effectively. Finally, looking at environmental trends and issues, the strategic leader works to improve not only the current alignment but also the future alignment.

Marissa Mayer (CEO of Yahoo!), Michael Dell (founder and CEO of Dell Computer), and A. G. Lafley (former CEO of Procter & Gamble) have all been recognized as strong strategic leaders. Reflecting on the dramatic turnaround he led at Procter & Gamble, for instance, Lafley commented, "I have made a lot of symbolic, very physical changes so people understand we are in the business of leading change." On the other hand, Jurgen Schrempp (former CEO of DaimlerChrysler), Raymond Gilmartin (former CEO of Merck), and Scott Livengood (former CEO of Krispy Kreme) have been singled out for their poor strategic leadership (and note the consistent description of "former"!).[24]

Ethical Leadership

Now more than ever, high standards of **ethical conduct** are being held up as a prerequisite for effective leadership. Top managers are being called upon to maintain high ethical standards for their own conduct, to unfailingly exhibit ethical behavior, and to hold others in their organizations to the same standards.

Most people have long assumed that top managers are ethical people. But in the wake of recent corporate scandals at firms such as Lehman Brothers, Toyota, BP, and Goldman Sachs, faith in top managers has been shaken. Hence, perhaps now more than ever, high standards of **ethical conduct** are being held up as a prerequisite for effective leadership. More specifically, top managers are being called upon to maintain high ethical standards for their own conduct, to unfailingly exhibit ethical behavior, and to hold others in their organizations to the same standards.

The behaviors of top leaders are being scrutinized more than ever, and those responsible for hiring new leaders for a business are looking more and more closely at the backgrounds of those being considered. The emerging pressures for stronger corporate governance models are likely to further increase the commitment to select only those individuals with high ethical standards for leadership positions in business, and to hold them more accountable than in the past for both their actions and the consequences of those actions.[25]

Virtual Leadership

Virtual leadership is emerging as an important issue for organizations.

Finally, **virtual leadership** is also emerging as an important issue for organizations. In earlier times, leaders and their employees worked together in the same physical location and engaged in personal (i.e., face-to-face) interactions on a regular basis. But in today's world, both leaders and their employees may work in locations that are far from one another. Such arrangements might include people who telecommute from a home office one or two days a week and people who actually live and work far from company headquarters and see one another in person only very infrequently.

How, then, do managers carry out leadership when they do not have regular personal contact with their followers? And how do they help mentor and develop others? Communication between leaders and their subordinates will still occur, of course, but it may be largely by telephone and e-mail. Hence, one implication may be that leaders in these situations simply need to work harder at creating and maintaining relationships with their employees that go beyond simply words on a computer screen. While nonverbal communication such as smiles and handshakes may not be possible online, managers can instead make a point of adding a few personal words in an e-mail (whenever appropriate) to convey appreciation, reinforcement, or constructive feedback. Building on this, managers should then also take advantage of every single opportunity whenever they are in face-to-face situations to go further than they might have done under different circumstances to develop a strong relationship.

But beyond these simple prescriptions, there is no theory or research to guide managers functioning in a virtual world. Hence, as electronic communications continues to pervade the workplace, researchers and managers alike need to work together to help frame the appropriate issues and questions regarding virtual leadership, and then collaborate to help address those issues and answer those questions.[26]

SYNOPSIS

There are two contemporary situation theories. The leader-member exchange model (LMX) of leadership stresses the importance of variable relationships between supervisors and each of their subordinates. Each superior-subordinate pair is referred to as a "vertical dyad." The Hersey and Blanchard model argues that appropriate leader behavior depends on the subordinate's degree of motivation, competence, experience, and interest in accepting responsibility. In addition to these somewhat newer models, the three dominant situational theories have also continued to undergo various refinements and revisions.

There are three primary approaches to leadership through the eyes of followers. Transformational leadership focuses on the basic distinction between leading for change and leading for stability. Perspectives based on charismatic leadership assume that charisma is an individual characteristic of the leader. Charisma is a form of interpersonal attraction that inspires support and acceptance. The attribution perspective holds that when behaviors are observed in a context associated with leadership, others may attribute varying levels of leadership ability or power to the person displaying those behaviors.

Another perspective on leadership that has received considerable attention in recent years has focused on alternatives to leadership. In some cases, circumstances may exist that render leadership unnecessary or irrelevant. The factors that contribute to these circumstances are called leadership substitutes. In other cases, factors may exist that neutralize or negate the influence of a leader even when that individual is attempting to exercise leadership.

The nature of leadership continues to evolve. Among recent changes in leadership that managers should recognize is the increasing role of leaders as coaches. The most frequent instance of this arrangement is when an organization uses self-managing teams. Gender differences in leader behavior are also becoming more important, especially given the increasing numbers of women advancing up the organizational ladder. Cross-cultural patterns of leadership both between and within national boundaries are also taking on growing importance. Project GLOBE is shedding new light on international leadership.

Finally, there are three emerging issues in leadership. Strategic leadership is a new concept that explicitly relates leadership to the role of top management. In addition, leaders in all organizations are being called upon to maintain high ethical standards for their own conduct, to unfailingly exhibit ethical behavior, and to hold others in their organizations to the same standards. And the growing importance of virtual leadership needs to be further studied.

DISCUSSION QUESTIONS

1. Compare and contrast the leader-member exchange and the Hersey and Blanchard models of leadership.
2. Are you now or have you ever been a member of an in-group? An out-group? If so, in what ways did your experiences differ?
3. Which of the three traditional situational theories discussed in Chapter 12 is most similar to the leader-member exchange model? To the Hersey and Blanchard model?
4. Identify an individual who could serve as an example of a transformational leader. How successful or unsuccessful has this person been?
5. Name the three people today whom you consider to be the most charismatic. How well do they or might they function as a leader?
6. In your opinion, is it possible for someone with little or no charisma to become charismatic? If so, how? If not, why?

7. Have you ever made direct leadership attributions about someone based on the context in which you observed them?
8. What are some of the substitutes and neutralizers to leadership that might exist in your classroom?
9. Do you believe that men and women differ in how they lead? If so, what are some of the factors that might account for the differences?
10. In what ways does strategic leadership differ from "non-strategic" leadership?
11. Some people have held that highly successful managers and leaders all face situations in which they cannot be entirely truthful and still succeed. For instance, a politician who personally believes that a tax increase is inevitable may feel that to fully disclose this belief will result in a significant loss of votes. Do you agree or disagree with the idea that sometimes people cannot be entirely truthful and still succeed?

HOW DO YOU SEE IT?

Managing by Knowing What You're Talking About

"One big misconception is that a manager is someone that oversees activity."

—DANNIELLE OVIEDO, DISTRIBUTION CENTER MANAGER, NUMI ORGANIC TEA

On the day that our video crew arrived at the Numi Organic Tea distribution center in Oakland, California, a crisis was brewing. It all came down to *containers*—those big steel bins used to store and transport products by rail or water. According to Customer Service Manager Cindy Graffort, the problem involved a very important customer—a large distributor of Numi products to retailers in the United Kingdom. This customer, explains Graffort, "has been sitting on a very large order [from retailer customers] that will need to ship via a container, and we don't have a container here yet. Prior to this, I would have to say to the customer, 'No'"—as in "No, we can't get the products to you in the timely fashion that you expect" or "No, we can't satisfy the business needs that we told you we could satisfy."

Up to a point, Graffort isn't surprised by the nature of the problem: "We ha[d] heard loud and clear . . . from our customers," she admits, ". . . that our lead times were not competitive and that they would, without hesitation, go to a competitor." As Graffort also implies, however, Numi has taken steps to improve its performance on *lead time*—the passage of time between the receipt of a customer's order and the customer's receipt of the products ordered. One of the things it did was hire Dannielle Oviedo, a ten-year veteran of distribution management, to take over its distribution center.

Graffort is convinced that the biggest difference between Oviedo and her predecessor is "flexibility"—the ability to make changes that keep up with the changing demands on a growing business. In particular, indicates one shipping clerk, "everything seems to be getting out a lot faster," and Graffort is quick to confirm that everything is in fact getting out a lot faster. "Before Dannielle got here," she says, "orders that shipped via containers would take up to fifteen days from the time the customer approved the order before we could actually get it on the water or on the rails." Now, she says, "we're averaging five days."

Unfortunately, that overall improvement in efficiency won't necessarily be of any use to Graffort in solving the current problem with her U.K. customer. "I was anticipating the worst," she admits, "when I went to [Dannielle] with this challenge." Graffort is pleasantly surprised, however, to learn that Oviedo has initiated a process called "live load." "Live load," explains Graffort, "means that when the container gets here, [Dannielle] has her team set to have it loaded within an hour. Which is," she hastens to add, "amazing. I was surprised to learn that she had implemented that type of drastic change to a very critical part of our business."

In short, Dannielle Oviedo is very good at conceiving and executing "efficiencies"—a skill that, according to Graffort, requires "finding processes and/or introducing technologies. . . . It's constantly reviewing the processes that are in place [and improving them]. By improving your efficiencies, you open up *time*, and time is what's needed to be effective." What's more, Oviedo is good at finding efficiencies in times of what Graffort calls "turbulence." Director of Operations Brian Durkee seems a little less surprised by Oviedo's particular complement of competencies. "I really rely on . . . Dannielle," he says, "to be innovative any way she can to make this process efficient. So a big part of her job, and what I look to her for, is [the ability] to create saneness out of chaos.

"The experience is really key," adds Durkee, but Dannielle is "a calm and assertive leader, and that calmness and that assertiveness [are the traits that] people really grabbed on to and followed." Noting that Oviedo has more direct reports than any other manager in the company, Durkee believes that "her leadership is really the primary thing that's changed how the organization runs in regards to distribution."

And what about Oviedo? How does she go about managing and leading? She says that she hones her own efficiency by "always looking ahead with as much information as possible," and she's convinced that people are more likely to follow a leader who knows what she's talking about than one who's always telling them what to do: "One thing that I try to do," she explains, "is to do what I ask folks to do. So if I assign you something, I've done it before, myself, and I have a good idea as to how long it will take [and] what your challenges will be when you're doing it."

It's an approach that also makes her subordinates look upon her as a team member who's working to discover practical knowledge that everyone needs rather than a superior giving orders to the next available subordinate: "One big misconception," she says, "is that a manager is someone that *oversees* activity. . . . If you just assign a task and walk away," she explains, "then you don't experience what your team member [does], and you don't gain any knowledge. You'll do it the same over and over and over." And so will your staff. Developing solutions collectively, on the other hand, makes efficiency possible, because all processes require the participation of groups of employees. Oviedo goes a step further by getting her staff involved not only in work processes but in the *changes* being made to them:

> *They'll feel that they're involved, and they'll be faster. . . . I think that the way I've drawn people into the big picture here at Numi is [that] when you're adjusting to a change, you need to make sure that your staff is aware of the reason behind it. That way, when they go to execute it, they understand the importance behind it.*

CASE QUESTIONS

1. How can each of the two *contemporary situational theories* of leadership discussed in the chapter—the *leader-exchange model (LMX)* and the *Hersey and Blanchard model*—help to explain Oviedo's success as a leader at Numi? Which of the two is *more* useful? Why?
2. Use the concept of *transformational leadership* to explain as fully as possible Oviedo's approach to leadership and the reasons for her success. Can the model of *charismatic leadership* or the *attribution perspective* on leadership be used to provide any additional insights into Oviedo's approach and success?
3. How does the idea of the *leader as coach* help to explain Oviedo's approach to leadership? **Judging from the video**, would you say that Oviedo's *gender* plays a role in her success as a leader? If so, how so?

ADDITIONAL SOURCES

"Dannielle Oviedo," "Cindy Graffort," LinkedIn (2012), www.linkedin.com on September 16, 2012; Inner City Advisors, "Case Study: Numi Organic Teas" (2010), http://innercityadvisors.org on September 15, 2012; Stacey R. Louiso, "Numi Equals Puri-Tea," *Attribute Magazine*, July 6, 2009, www.attributemagazine.com on September 16, 2012.

EXPERIENCING ORGANIZATIONAL BEHAVIOR

Understanding Leadership Substitutes

Purpose This exercise will help you assess the possibilities and limitations of leadership substitutes in organizations.

Format Working in small groups, you will identify several factors that can substitute for and/or neutralize leadership in different settings.

Procedures Your instructor will divide the class into small groups of four to five members each. Working as a team, do the following:

1. Identify two jobs, one that is relatively simple (perhaps a custodian or a fast food cook) and one that is much more complex (such as an airline pilot or software engineer).

2. For each job, identify as many potential leadership substitutes and neutralizers as possible.
3. Next, exchange one of your lists with one group and the other list with a different group.
4. Review the two new lists and look for areas where you agree or disagree.
5. Exchange lists once again to get back your original lists.
6. Discuss among yourselves whether there is a discernable pattern as to the types of job groups in which leadership might be most easily substituted or neutralized.

Follow-Up Questions

1. To what extent did your own experiences affect how you performed this exercise?
2. Are there some jobs for which there are no substitutes for leadership? Provide examples.
3. Should managers actively seek substitutes for leadership? Why or why not?

BUILDING MANAGERIAL SKILLS

Exercise Overview Interpersonal skills are a manager's ability to communicate with, understand, and motivate individuals and groups. This exercise will help you develop your interpersonal skills as they relate to leadership.

Exercise Background As noted in the chapter, virtual leadership is an emerging phenomenon about which little is known. Begin this exercise by partnering with three of your classmates (that is, create groups of four). Spend some time with your group members getting to know each other and exchanging e-mail addresses.

Next, create a hypothetical work team. The team should identify one of you as the leader and the other three as employees. Develop relatively detailed roles for yourselves—gender, age, work experiences, motivations and aspirations, and so forth, as well as some detail about a work project that the team has been assigned.

Between now and the next class meeting, you should all exchange numerous e-mails about your hypothetical work project. The leader should be especially active in the process and send a wide array of messages. Specifically, the leader should be sure to provide some encouragement, respond to questions, relay some information, provide some criticism, and so forth. The leader should also maintain a written log of what the intention was of each e-mail that was sent. Employees can communicate among yourselves, but also be sure to communicate with your leader—ask questions, relay information, and so forth.

During the process of exchanging e-mails, it is virtually certain that you will need to "make up some things." Try to maintain realism, however, and try to be consistent with things that have already transpired. For example, an employee might "create" a problem and ask the leader's advice. However, the problem should be realistic, and it should be reasonable for the leader to be able to answer the question. For her or his part, the leader should also make a realistic effort to answer the question. During subsequent exchanges, remember to account for the question and the answer if and when appropriate. You can end the exercise whenever several exchanges have taken place and you sense that the group has "run out of steam."

Exercise Task At the next class meeting, reconvene with your team members and respond to the following questions:

1. The leader should first recount each e-mail that was sent and then convey his or her intended meaning; the recipient(s) should then convey how the message was actually interpreted. Were there any differences between the intended message and how it was interpreted?
2. To what extent did interactions among those playing the roles of employees affect how they interpreted messages from the leader?
3. What, if anything, could the leader have done to improve communication?

SELF-ASSESSMENT EXERCISE

What Are Your Skills Leading Up To?

Now that you're more than halfway through this book, you've probably come to recognize a number of interesting facts about today's organizations and the people who lead them. One of these is—or ought to be—the fact that conditions are in the process of changing rapidly: Hierarchies are flatter and more fluid. Teams are more vital, though sometimes virtual. Workforces are accustomed to doing more with less, and workers want a more workable balance between work and nonwork life. Only when managers manage well under these conditions do organizations manage to operate effectively.

So here's an important question that you might want to ask yourself: Are you the kind of person who's likely to succeed in making the necessary adjustments for leading in the twenty-first century—or are you just gearing up to drive your grandfather's organization?

The following quiz—which is by no means exhaustive—is designed to provide you with a very informal answer to this question by assessing the degree to which you possess a few specific skills. On some items, you'll have to assess your personality and skills without the benefit of real-life experience, but you should know yourself fairly well by now. Remember: The more honest you are, the more useful the results will be.

For each of the 11 skill areas on the quiz, ask yourself *how others would characterize you* and put the *number* corresponding to the best answer in the appropriate blank space:

1. Do I have a **need to exceed**?
Do I demonstrate a sustained passion to succeed? Willingly step up to significant challenges? Set high standards? Convey a sense of urgency? Hold myself accountable for adding value? Am I driven to achieve results?
___ A This is not me (1)
___ B Sometimes this is me (3)
___ C This is definitely me (5)

2. Do I **help others succeed**?
Do I support others by providing constructive feedback or coaching? Do I provide developmental resources and try to see that others are developed?
___ A This is not me (1)
___ B Sometimes this is me (3)
___ C This is definitely me (5)

3. Am I **courageous**?
Am I willing to stand up and be counted? Do I step forward to address difficult issues? Put myself on the line to deal with important problems? Stand firm when necessary? Am I willing to hold back nothing that needs to be said? Am I willing to take negative action when appropriate?
___ A This is not me (1)
___ B Sometimes this is me (3)
___ C This is definitely me (5)

4. Do I **lead**?
Do I try to offer a vision and purpose that others buy into and share? Do I take actions that inspire confidence in my vision? Do I set clear and compelling goals that serve as a unifying focal point of joint efforts? Do I encourage team spirit? Do I believe that "good enough" never is?
___ A This is not me (1)
___ B Sometimes this is me (3)
___ C This is definitely me (5)

5. Am I **customer focused**?
Do I try to create sustained partnerships with customers (internal and external) based on a thorough firsthand understanding of what creates value for them? Do I continually search for ways to increase customer satisfaction?
___ A This is not me (1)
___ B Sometimes this is me (3)
___ C This is definitely me (5)

6. Am I a **relationship builder**?
Do I initiate and develop relationships with others as a key priority? Use informal networks to get things done? Rely more on ability than on hierarchical relationships to influence people?
___ A This is not me (1)
___ B Sometimes this is me (3)
___ C This is definitely me (5)

7. Am I a **team builder**?
Do I champion teamwork? Do I try to create an environment in which teams are used appropriately, their development is supported, and they

are generally successful? Do I foster collaboration among team members and among teams and create a feeling of belonging among members?

___ A This is not me (1)
___ B Sometimes this is me (3)
___ C This is definitely me (5)

8. Am I **principled**?
Do I inspire trust through ethical behavior? Show consistency among my principles, values, and behavior? Consistently live, breathe, and express my principles in all that I do?

___ A This is not me (1)
___ B Sometimes this is me (3)
___ C This is definitely me (5)

9. Am I a **change agent**?
Do I act as a catalyst for change and stimulate others to change? Challenge the status quo and champion new initiatives? Effectively manage the implementation of change?

___ A This is not me (1)
___ B Sometimes this is me (3)
___ C This is definitely me (5)

10. Am I an **eager learner**?
Do I learn from experience? Learn quickly? Actively pursue learning and self-development? Am I a versatile learner?

___ A This is not me (1)
___ B Sometimes this is me (3)
___ C This is definitely me (5)

11. Do I **value others**?
Do I show and foster respect and appreciation for everyone, regardless of background, race, age, gender, values, or lifestyle? Do I make others feel valued for their ideas and contributions? Do I seek other people's point of view? Do I recognize the contributions of others and make them feel appreciated?

___ A This is not me (1)
___ B Sometimes this is me (3)
___ C This is definitely me (5)

How to score: Add up all the numbers that you put in the blank spaces and compare your score to the following scale:

11–21 You're an **obsolete manager**.

If you're presently a manager, you're probably quite frustrated and yearn for the good old days. Sorry, but they weren't that good in the first place, and they aren't coming back. Have you considered a nonmanagerial position?

21–43 You're a **closet twenty-first-century manager**.

You may be torn between the impulse to hold on to the past and perpetuate the skills of your old masters and the desire to join your more progressive contemporaries. Sometimes you go one way, sometimes another. What you need is more consistency. Start by trusting yourself: You're at a fork in the road, but you know which way you need to go. Look for opportunities to sharpen your skills so that you can develop more confidence in relying on them.

45–55 You're a **twenty-first-century manager**.

Your skills should stand you in good stead in the future. Don't relax, however, and keep learning and adapting. You never know what the future has in store, but it's a pretty safe bet that it's going to be something different. Besides, a constant willingness to learn and adapt is a handy personality trait under any circumstances characterized by change.

Reference: Matt M. Starcevich, Center for Coaching and Mentoring, Inc., "Are You Ready to Manage in the 21st Century?" 2009, www.work911.com. Accessed June 1, 2010. Used by permission of Matt M. Starcevich, Ph.D.

CHAPTER 14 Power, Politics, and Organizational Justice

Chapter Outline

- Influence in Organizations
- Power in Organizations
- Politics and Political Behavior
- Organizational Justice

Chapter Learning Objectives

After studying this chapter, you should be able to:

1. Define and discuss influence in organizations.
2. Describe the types and uses of power in organizations.
3. Discuss politics and political behavior in organizations.
4. Describe the various forms and implications of justice in organizations.

Arrested Development in the Workplace

"This stuff happens all the time."

—Employee-rights lawyer Ellen Simon

At first glance, it doesn't seem too hard to figure out what sort of behavior constitutes *sexual harassment* in the workplace. The U.S. Equal Employment Opportunity Commission (EEOC), the federal agency that investigates complaints of workplace discrimination, offers the following explanation:

> *Unwelcome sexual advances, requests for sexual favors, and other verbal or physical conduct of a sexual nature constitutes sexual harassment when submission to or rejection of this conduct explicitly or implicitly affects an individual's employment, unreasonably interferes with an individual's work performance, or creates an intimidating, hostile, or offensive work environment.*

If you still have questions, the EEOC is happy to clarify a few of the legal fine points. Sexual harassment, for example, can occur in a variety of circumstances, including but not limited to the following:

- The victim as well as the harasser may be a woman or a man. The victim does not have to be of the opposite sex.
- The harasser can be the victim's supervisor, an agent of the employer, a supervisor in another area, a coworker, or a nonemployee.
- The victim does not have to be the person harassed but could be anyone affected by the offensive conduct.
- Unlawful sexual harassment may occur without economic injury to or discharge of the victim.

What does all of this mean in a practical sense—if, let's say, you're a woman who must go to court to assert your rights against workplace discrimination, as

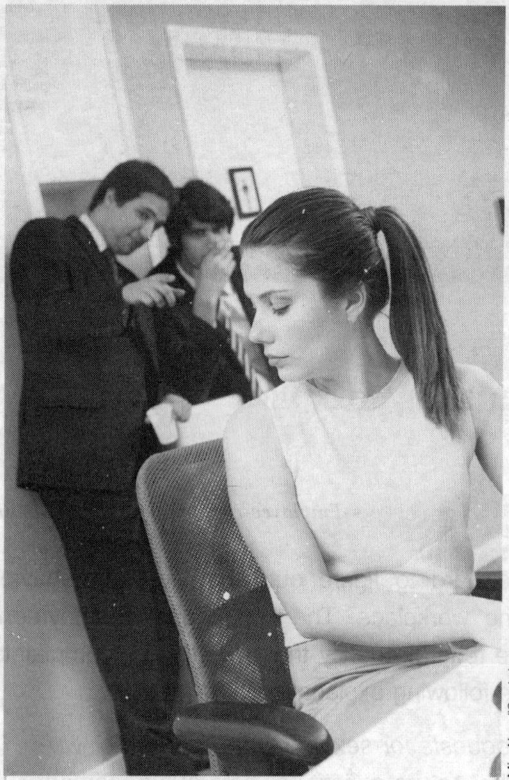

Sexual harassment and bullying are all too common in today's workplace. In many instances they involve power differentials between people.

defined by Title VII of the Civil Rights Act of 1964 (and subsequent court decisions)? According to employee-rights attorney Ellen Simon, you'll have to establish four facts:

1. That you're a member of a protected class (female)
2. That you were subjected to harassment through either words or actions, based on sex
3. That the harassment had the effect of unreasonably interfering with your work performance and creating an objectively intimidating, hostile, or offensive work environment
4. That there exists some basis for liability on the part of your employer

Consider the case of Julie Gallagher, who held a sales position in the Cleveland office of C. H. Robinson Worldwide Inc., which provides freight transportation and other supply chain–management services. According to Gallagher, a typical workday in the Robinson office included the widespread use of foul language and what one employee-rights lawyer familiar with the case calls "male arrested-development behavior." Women were regularly called "sluts," "bitches," and other epithets that you won't find in the index to the average OB textbook; coworkers displayed nude photos of girlfriends, traded dirty jokes, and engaged in graphic discussions of sexual fantasies and preferences. Gallagher herself was often referred to as a "bitch" and once as a "heifer with milking udders." The work space consisted of cubicles separated by short dividers and grouped in pods on an open floor plan, making it impossible for her to avoid exposure to such behavior. When she complained to the branch manager—who not only had witnessed some of this behavior but had actually participated in it—things only got worse.

"I have been hearing these stories—and they haven't seemed to change that much—for the past thirty years," says Simon. "This stuff happens all the time." Like about 12,000 other female workers that year, Gallager sought a legal resolution to her story and filed charges of sexual harassment against C. H. Robinson. Judge Dan A. Polster of the U.S. District Court for the Northern District of Ohio threw her case out of court. Why? "For reasons that I am at a complete loss to genuinely understand," says Simon, who nevertheless boils down the judge's reasoning to three key being played out as well:

1. The conduct in the Robinson office was not "based on sex." Both men and women were regularly present, and because the behavior in question was "indiscriminate," Gallagher could not argue that it discriminated against her.
2. The behavior in the office was not severe enough to satisfy the legal requirements of sexual harassment: Most of it wasn't directed at Gallagher, her work performance didn't suffer, and it wasn't "objectively" hostile. In other words, Gallagher was being "unreasonable" or "hypersensitive" in perceiving the level of hostility.
3. The actions that took place in its office did not make the employer, C. H. Robinson, liable for sexual harassment. Gallagher had not followed the firm's established harassment policies; the company itself received no notice of her complaints, and she was being unreasonable in expecting things to change after complaining only to the branch manager.

Gallagher appealed the district court's ruling, and the outcome is reported in the *Ethics* box entitled "Ruling Out Corporate Lunacy" on page 380.

What Do You Think?

1. Have you ever witnessed sexual harassment in a workplace? What conditions in the workplace contributed to the environment in which the harassment took place?
2. What is an employer's responsibility when there are charges of sexual harassment in a workplace? What should employers do to reduce the likelihood of the offensive behavior?

References: U.S. Equal Employment Opportunity Commission, "Sexual Harassment," "Facts about Sexual Harassment" (Washington, D.C., 2012), www.eeoc.gov on July 29, 2012; EEOC, "Sexual Harassment Charges EEOC & FEPAs Combined: FY 1997–FY 2009" (Washington, D.C., 2010), www1.eeoc.gov on April 8, 2010; Ellen Simon, "Harassed Female Wins 'Locker Room' Hostile Environment Case," *Employee Rights Post*, June 2, 2009, www.employeerightspost.com on July 29, 2012; Paul Mollica, "*Gallagher v. C. H. Robinson Worldwide, Inc.*, No. 08-3337 (6th Cir., May 22, 2009)," *Daily Developments in EEO Law*, May 21, 2009, www.employmentlawblog.info on July 29, 2012; Simon, "Gender-Based Profanity Constitutes Sexual Harassment," *Employee Rights Post*, January 27, 2010, www.employeerightspost.com on July 29, 2012.

As we learned in Chapters 12 and 13, leadership is a powerful, complex, and amorphous concept. This chapter explores a variety of forces and processes in organizations that are often related to—but at the same time distinct from—leadership. These forces and processes may precede, follow from, undermine, and/or reinforce a leader's ability to function effectively. They may also occur independently of leadership and its other associated activities.

We begin by briefly revisiting the concept of influence. While we introduced influence at the beginning of Chapter 12 as a basis for defining leadership, we now examine influence a bit more completely, and also describe a specific form of influence known as impression management. We then discuss power in its myriad forms in organizations. Politics and political behavior are then introduced and described in detail. Finally, we discuss organizational justice. (Some authors treat justice in the context of motivation, but given its close association with influence, power, and politics, it seems most reasonable to cover it here.)

INFLUENCE IN ORGANIZATIONS

Recall that in Chapter 12 we defined leadership (from a process perspective) as the use of noncoercive influence to direct and coordinate the activities of group members to meet goals. We then described a number of leadership models and theories based variously on leadership traits, behaviors, and contingencies. Unfortunately, most of these models and theories essentially ignore the influence component of leadership. That is, they tend to focus on the characteristics of the leader (traits, behaviors, or both) and the responses from followers (satisfaction, performance, or both, for instance) with little regard for how the leader actually exercises influence in an effort to bring about the desired responses from followers.

But influence should actually be seen as the cornerstone of the process of one person attempting to affect another. For instance, regardless of the leader's traits or behaviors, leadership only matters if influence actually occurs. That is, a person's effectiveness in affecting the behavior of others through influence is the ultimate determinant of whether she or he is really a leader. No one can truly be a leader without the ability to influence others. And if someone does have the ability to influence others, he or she clearly has the potential—at least—to become a leader.

The Nature of Influence

Influence is the ability to affect the perceptions, attitudes, or behaviors of others.

Influence is defined as the ability to affect the perceptions, attitudes, or behaviors of others.[1] If a person can make another person recognize that her working conditions are more hazardous than she currently believes them to be (change in perceptions), influence has occurred. Likewise, if an individual can convince someone else that the organization is a much better place to work than he currently believes it to be (change in attitude), influence has occurred. And if someone can get others to work harder or to file a grievance against their boss (change in behavior), influence has occurred.[2]

Influence can be dramatic or subtle. For instance, a new leader may be able to take a group of disenchanted employees working on a flawed and poorly conceived project and energize them to work harder while simultaneously enhancing the nature and direction of their project so as to make it much more worthwhile. As a result, the group will enjoy much greater success. In a different setting, however, a specific disgruntled employee may be very unhappy and on the verge of resigning. One morning a supervisor makes an innocuous comment that the unhappy employee perceives to be a criticism. That one comment, taken alone, might objectively be seen as very trivial. But on top of the

Influence is the ability to affect the perceptions, attitudes, or behaviors of others. These business colleagues are trying to influence one another through discussion and persuasion.

employee's current feelings and attitudes, it's enough to prompt an immediate resignation.

We should also point out that both the source and the target of influence might be either a person or a group. For instance, the efforts and success of a work team might so inspire other teams as to cause them to work harder. Further, influence might be intentional or unintentional. If one employee starts coming to work dressed more casually than has been the norm, others might follow suit even though the actions of the first employee were not meant to influence others in any way but only to be more comfortable.

Note, too, that influence can be used in ways that are beneficial or harmful. Someone can be influenced to help clean up a city park on the weekend as part of a community service program, for example. Operating employees can be influenced to work harder, engineers can be influenced to become more creative and innovative, and teams can be influenced to increase their efficiency. But people can also be influenced to use or sell drugs or to smoke. Employees can be influenced to care less about the quality of their work, engineers can be influenced to not explore or advocate new ideas, and teams can be influenced to be less efficient. Hence, influence is a major force in organizations that managers cannot afford to ignore.

Impression Management

Impression management is a special—and occasionally subtle—form of influence that deserves special mention. **Impression management** is a direct, intentional effort by someone to enhance his or her image in the eyes of others. People engage in impression management for a variety of reasons. For one thing, they may do so to further their own careers. By making themselves look good, they think they are more likely to receive rewards, attractive job assignments, and promotions. They may also engage in impression management to boost their own self-esteem. When people have a positive image in an organization, others make them aware of it through their compliments, respect, and so forth. Another reason people use impression management is to acquire more power and thus more control.

Impression management is a direct and intentional effort by someone to enhance his or her own image in the eyes of others.

People attempt to manage how others perceive them through a variety of mechanisms. Appearance is one of the first things people think of. A person motivated by impression management will pay close attention to choice of attire, selection of language, and the use of manners and body posture. People interested in impression management are also likely to jockey to be associated only with successful

Impression management is a form of influence. Take this manager, for example. The way she is dressed and the confident manner in which she is presenting her ideas, combined with the substance of those ideas, will interact to help her influence a decision being contemplated by this group of her colleagues.

projects. By being assigned to high-profile projects led by highly successful managers, a person can begin to link his or her own name with such projects in the minds of others.

In its most basic sense, of course, there is nothing wrong with impression management. After all, most people want to create a positive—and honest—image of themselves in the eyes of others. Sometimes, however, people motivated too strongly by impression management become obsessed by it and resort to dishonest or unethical means. For example, a person may start to take credit for the work of others in an effort to make herself or himself look better. People may also exaggerate or even falsify their personal accomplishments in an effort to enhance their image. Hence, while there is clearly nothing wrong with "putting your best foot forward," people should be cognizant of the impressions they are attempting to create and make sure they are not using inappropriate methods.

POWER IN ORGANIZATIONS

Influence is also closely related to the concept of power. Power is one of the most significant forces that exist in organizations. Moreover, it can be an extremely important ingredient in organizational success—or organizational failure. In this section we first describe the nature of power. Then we examine the types and uses of power.

The Nature of Power

Power is the potential ability of a person or group to exercise control over another person or group.

Power has been defined in dozens of different ways; no one definition is generally accepted. Drawing from the more common meanings of the term, we define **power** as the potential ability of a person or group to exercise control over another person or group.[3] Power is distinguished from influence due to the element of control—the more powerful control the less powerful. Thus, power might be thought of as an extreme form of influence.

One obvious aspect of our definition is that it expresses power in terms of potential; that is, we may be able to control others but may choose not to exercise that control. Nevertheless, simply having the potential may be enough to influence others in some settings. We should also note that power may reside in individuals (such as managers and informal leaders), in formal groups (such as departments and committees), and in informal groups (such as a clique of influential people). Finally, we should note the direct link between power and influence. If a person can convince another person to change his or her opinion on some issue, to engage in or refrain from some behavior, or to view circumstances in a certain way, that person has exercised influence—and used power.

Considerable differences of opinion exist about how thoroughly power pervades organizations. Some people argue that virtually all interpersonal relations are influenced by power, whereas others believe that the exercise of power is confined only to certain situations. Whatever the case, power is undoubtedly a pervasive part of organizational life. It affects decisions ranging from the choice of strategies to the color of the new office carpeting. It makes or breaks careers. And it enhances or limits organizational effectiveness.

Types of Power

Within the broad framework of our definition, there obviously are many types of power. These types usually are described in terms of bases of power and position power versus personal power. Table 14.1 identifies and summarizes the most common forms of power.

Bases of Power The most widely used and recognized analysis of the bases of power is the classic framework developed by John R. P. French and Bertram Raven.[4] French and Raven identified five general bases of power in organizational settings: legitimate, reward, coercive, expert, and referent power.

Legitimate power is power that is granted by virtue of one's position in the organization.

Legitimate power, essentially the same thing as authority, is granted by virtue of one's position in an organization. Managers have legitimate power over their subordinates. The organization specifies that it is legitimate for the designated individual to direct the activities of others. The bounds of this legitimacy are defined partly by the formal nature of the position involved and partly by informal norms and traditions. For example, it was once commonplace for managers to expect their secretaries not only to perform work-related activities such as typing and filing but also to run personal errands such as picking up laundry and buying gifts. In highly centralized, mechanistic, and bureaucratic organizations such as the military, the legitimate power inherent in each position is closely specified, widely known, and strictly followed. In more organic organizations, such as research and development labs and software firms, the lines of legitimate power often are blurry. Employees may work for more than one boss at the same time, and leaders and followers may be on a nearly equal footing.

Table 14.1	Common Forms of Power in Organizations
LEGITIMATE POWER	Power that is granted by virtue of one's position in the organization
REWARD POWER	Power that exists when one person controls rewards that another person values
COERCIVE POWER	Power that exists when one person has the ability to punish or physically or psychologically harm someone else
EXPERT POWER	Power that exists when one person controls information that is valuable to someone else
REFERENT POWER	Power that exists when one person wants to be like or imitates someone else
POSITION POWER	Power that resides in a position, regardless of who is filling that position
PERSONAL POWER	Power that resides in the person, regardless of the position being filled

Reward power is the extent to which a person controls rewards that another person values.

Reward power is the extent to which a person controls rewards that are valued by another. The most obvious examples of organizational rewards are pay, promotions, and work assignments. If a manager has almost total control over the pay his or her subordinates receive, can make recommendations about promotions, and has considerable discretion to make job assignments, he or she has a high level of reward power. Reward power can extend beyond material rewards. As we noted in our discussions of motivation theory in Chapters 4 and 5, people work for a variety of reasons in addition to pay. For instance, some people may be motivated primarily by a desire for recognition and acceptance. To the extent that a manager's praise and acknowledgment satisfy those needs, that manager has even more reward power.

Coercive power is the extent to which a person has the ability to punish or physically or psychologically harm someone else.

Coercive power exists when someone has the ability to punish or physically or psychologically harm another person. For example, some managers berate subordinates in front of their peers and colleagues, belittling their efforts and generally making their work lives miserable. Certain forms of coercion may also be more subtle than this example. In some organizations, a particular division may be notorious as a resting place for people who have no future with the company. Threatening to transfer someone to a dead-end branch or some other undesirable location is thus a form of coercion. Clearly, the more negative the sanctions a manager can bring to bear on others, the stronger is that manager's coercive power. At the same time, the use of coercive power carries a considerable cost in terms of employee resentment and hostility. It may also entail legal consequences, as you can see from the *Ethics* box entitled "Ruling Out Corporate Lunacy" on page 380.

Expert power is the extent to which a person controls information that is valuable to someone else.

Control over expertise or, more precisely, over information is another source of power in an organization. For example, to the extent that an inventory manager has information that a sales representative needs, the inventory manager has **expert power** over the sales representative. The more important the information and the fewer the alternative sources for getting it, the greater the power. Expert power can reside in many niches in an organization; it transcends positions and jobs.[5] Although legitimate, reward, and coercive power may not always correspond exactly to formal authority, they often do. Expert power, on the other hand, may be much less associated with formal authority.

Upper-level managers usually decide on the organization's strategic agenda, but individuals at lower levels in the organization may have the expertise those managers need to do the tasks. A research scientist may have crucial information about a technical breakthrough of great importance to the organization and its strategic decisions. Or an assistant may take on so many of the boss's routine and mundane activities that the manager loses track of such details and comes to depend on the assistant to keep things running smoothly. In other situations, lower-level participants are given power as a way to take advantage of their expertise. For instance, some airlines have given their flight service managers more say over whether to delay a flight based on catering problems. The logic is that the flight attendants on board a plane may be in the best position to judge their ability to handle a shortage of, say, ice or beverage cups.

Referent power exists when one person wants to be like or imitates someone else.

Referent power is power through identification. If Jose is highly respected by Adam, Jose has referent power over Adam. Like expert power, referent power does not always correlate with formal organizational authority. In some ways, referent power is similar to the concept of charisma in that it often involves trust, similarity, acceptance, affection, willingness to follow, and emotional involvement. Referent power usually surfaces as imitation. For example, suppose a new department manager is the youngest person in the organization to have reached that rank. Further, it is widely believed that she is being groomed for the highest levels of the company. Other people in the department may begin to imitate her, thinking that they too may be able to advance. They may begin dressing like her, working the same hours, and trying to pick up as many work-related pointers from her as possible.

Position versus Personal Power The French and Raven framework is only one approach to examining the origins of organizational power. Another approach categorizes power in organizations in terms of position or personal power.

Position power resides in the position, regardless of who is filling that position.

Position power is power that resides in the position, regardless of who holds it. Thus, legitimate, reward, and some aspects of coercive and expert power can all contribute to position power. Position power is thus similar to authority. In creating a position, the organization simultaneously establishes a sphere of power for the person filling that position. He or she will generally have the power to direct the activities of subordinates in performing their jobs, to control some of their potential rewards, and to have a say in their punishment and discipline. There are, however, limits to a manager's position power. A manager cannot order or control activities that fall outside his or her sphere of power, for instance, directing a subordinate to commit crimes, to perform personal services, or to take on tasks that clearly are not part of the subordinate's job.

Personal power resides in the person, regardless of the position being filled.

Personal power is power that resides with an individual, regardless of his or her position in the organization. Thus, the primary bases of personal power are referent and some elements of expert, coercive, and reward power. Charisma is also likely to contribute to personal power. Someone usually exercises personal power through rational persuasion or by playing on followers' identification with him or her. An individual with personal power often can inspire greater loyalty and dedication in followers than someone who has only position power. The stronger influence stems from the fact that the followers are acting more from choice than from necessity (as dictated, for example, by their organizational responsibilities) and thus will respond more readily to requests and appeals. Of course, the influence of a leader who relies only on personal power is limited, because followers may freely decide not to accept his or her directives or orders.

The distinctions between formal and informal leaders are also related to position and personal power. A formal leader will have, at minimum, position power. And an informal leader will similarly have some degree of personal power. Just as a person may be

ETHICS Ruling Out Corporate Lunacy

Let's revisit the case of Julie Gallagher, which we introduced as the opening vignette earlier in this chapter. Gallagher appealed the decision of the district court judge to the U.S. Court of Appeals for the Sixth Circuit, which delivered its opinion in May 2009. To appreciate fully the court's attention to detail, it will help to recall the four facts which, according to employee-rights attorney Ellen Simon, Gallagher had to establish in her suit against her former employer, C. H. Robinson Worldwide (italics added):

> ***"The 'equal opportunity abuser' defense is on the way out."***
>
> —EMPLOYMENT LAWYER FRANK STEINBERG

1. That she was a member of a *protected class* (female)
2. That she was subjected to harassment either through words or actions, *based on sex*
3. That the harassment had the effect of *unreasonably interfering with her work performance* and creating *an objectively intimidating, hostile, or offensive work environment*
4. That there existed some basis for *liability on the part of her employer*

As you'll recall, District Judge Dan A. Polster had rejected Gallagher's suit for three reasons. Here's a point-by-point summary of the appeals court's response to Polster's decision in *Gallagher v. C. H. Robinson Worldwide, Inc.*:

- First, the judges ruled that the conduct of Gallagher's coworkers was indeed "based on sex": Even though both men and women were exposed to the offensive conduct, that conduct, said the court, was "patently degrading and anti-female" in nature; thus, "it stands to reason that women would suffer … greater disadvantage in the terms and conditions of their employment than men."
- Second, the appeals court rejected the district judge's opinion that the harassment was not sufficiently severe or pervasive. Even if the offensive conduct was not directed specifically at Gallagher, the nature of the office layout meant that "she had no means of escaping [and] was unavoidably exposed to it." In addition, any "reasonable person" would have found the "vulgar language, demeaning conversations and images, and palpable anti-female animus" of the C. H. Robinson office "objectively hostile"—in other words, just as hostile as Gallagher found it; her reaction, therefore, was not "unreasonable, exaggerated, or hypersensitive." The court also deemed it reasonable to accept her claim that the abusive conduct "rendered her work more difficult."
- Third, the appeals court panel ruled that C. H. Robinson could be held liable for creating a sexually hostile workplace environment. The facts showed that the branch manager knew about the offensive behavior and about Gallagher's objections to it, and the law holds that the company itself is also aware of any situation which is known to "any supervisor or department head who has been authorized … to receive and respond to or forward such complaints to management." Moreover, said the court, "a reasonable jury" should be given the opportunity to determine whether Robinson had responded to Gallagher's complaints "with manifest indifference."

The ruling of the district court judge was reversed and the case sent back to district court for reconsideration. It hasn't yet been settled, but many lawyers believe that the appeals court delivered a clear message to both employers and lower-court judges. According to Frank Steinberg, an attorney who handles sexual harassment and other employment-related cases, C. H. Robinson's conduct in the entire matter is an "illustration of self-destructive corporate lunacy…. So if you run a business," he advises,

> *don't be lulled into a false sense of security by the fact that you curse at women and men with equal gusto. The "equal opportunity abuser" defense is on the way out. And don't think that the work environment is not hostile to women just because some women are acting like the boys.*

References: Ellen Simon, "Harassed Female Wins 'Locker Room' Hostile Environment Case," *Employee Rights Post*, June 2, 2009, www.employeerightspost.com on July 29, 2012; "Preventing Sexual Harassment: A Fact Sheet for Employees," *SexualHarassmentLawFirms.com*, November 17, 2004, http://informationtips.wordpress.com on July 29, 2012; United States Court of Appeals for the Sixth Circuit, *Gallagher v. C .H. Robinson Worldwide, Inc.*, No. 08 3337, May 22, 2009, www.ca6.uscourts.gov/opinions.pdf on July 28, 2012; Frank Steinberg, "Sexual Harassment: Workplace Loaded with Pornography and Bad Language," *New Jersey Employment Law Blog*, June 24, 2009 http://employment.lawfirmnewjersey.com on July 29, 2012.

FIGURE 14.1

Position Power and Personal Power

Position power resides in a job whereas personal power resides in an individual. When these two types of power are broken down into high and low levels and related to one another, the two-by-two matrix shown here is the result. For example, the upper-right cell suggests that a leader with high levels of both position and personal power will have the highest overall level of power. Other combinations result in differing levels of overall power.

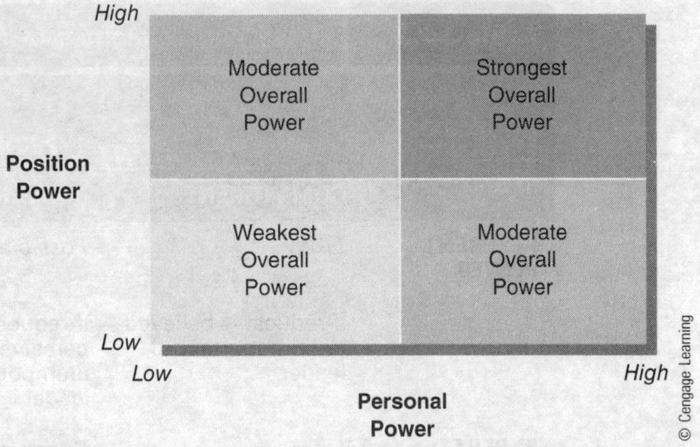

both a formal and an informal leader, he or she can have both position and personal power simultaneously. Indeed, such a combination usually has the greatest potential influence on the actions of others. Figure 14.1 illustrates how personal and position power may interact to determine how much overall power a person has in a particular situation. An individual with both personal and position power will have the strongest overall power. Likewise, an individual with neither personal nor position power will have the weakest overall power. Finally, when either personal or position power is high but the other is low, the individual will have a moderate level of overall power.

The Uses of Power in Organizations

Power can be used in many ways in an organization. But because of the potential for its misuse and the concerns that it may engender, it is important that managers fully understand the dynamics of using power. Gary Yukl has presented a useful perspective for understanding how power may be wielded.[6] His perspective includes two closely related components. The first relates power bases, requests from individuals possessing power, and probable outcomes in the form of prescriptions for the manager. Table 14.2 indicates the three outcomes that may result when a leader tries to exert power. These outcomes depend on the leader's base of power, how that base is operationalized (for example, using coercive power in an abusive manner versus applying it in an instructional manner), and the subordinate's individual characteristics (for example, personality traits or past interactions with the leader).

Commitment will probably result from an attempt to exercise power if the subordinate accepts and identifies with the leader. Such an employee will be highly motivated by requests that seem important to the leader. For example, a leader might explain that a new piece of software will greatly benefit the organization if it is developed soon. A committed subordinate will work just as hard as the leader to complete the project, even if that means working overtime. Sam Walton once asked all Walmart employees to start greeting customers with a smile and an offer to help. Because Walmart employees generally were motivated by and loyal to Walton, most of them complied with his request. This simple gesture, in turn, played a big role Walmart's dramatic surge to become the world's largest retailer.

Compliance means the subordinate is willing to carry out the leader's wishes as long as doing so will not require extraordinary effort. That is, the person will respond to normal, reasonable requests that are perceived to clearly be within the normal boundaries of the job. But the person will not be inclined to do anything extra or to go beyond the normal expectations for the job. Thus, the subordinate may work at a reasonable pace

Table 14.2 Uses and Outcomes of Power

SOURCE OF LEADER INFLUENCE	TYPE OF OUTCOME		
	COMMITMENT	COMPLIANCE	RESISTANCE
REFERENT POWER	*Likely*	*Possible*	*Possible*
	If request is believed to be important to leader	If request is perceived to be unimportant to leader	If request is for something that will bring harm to leader
EXPERT POWER	*Likely*	*Possible*	*Possible*
	If request is persuasive and subordinates share leader's task goals	If request is persuasive but subordinates are apathetic about leader's task goals	If leader is arrogant and insulting, or subordinates oppose task goals
LEGITIMATE POWER	*Possible*	*Likely*	*Possible*
	If request is polite and very appropriate	If request or order is seen as legitimate	If arrogant demands are made or request does not appear proper
REWARD POWER	*Possible*	*Likely*	*Possible*
	If used in a subtle, very personal way	If used in a mechanical, impersonal way	If used in a manipulative, arrogant way
COERCIVE POWER	*Very Unlikely*	*Possible*	*Likely*
		If used in a helpful, nonpunitive way	If used in a hostile or manipulative way

References: From Dorwin P. Cartwright (ed.), *Studies in Social Power*, 1959. Reprinted with permission from the Institute for Social Research, University of Michigan, Ann Arbor, Michigan.

but refuse to work overtime, insisting that the job will still be there tomorrow. Many ordinary requests from a boss meet with compliant responses from subordinates.

Resistance occurs when the subordinate rejects or fights the leader's wishes. For example, suppose an unpopular leader asks employees to volunteer for a company-sponsored community activity project. The employees may reject this request, largely because of their feelings about the leader. A resistant subordinate may even deliberately neglect the project to ensure that it is not done as the leader wants. Continental Airlines once had a very unpopular CEO named Frank Lorenzo; some employees routinely disobeyed his mandates as a form of protest against his leadership of the firm.

Table 14.3 suggests ways for leaders to use various kinds of power most effectively. By effective use of power we mean using power in the way that is most likely to engender

Table 14.3 Guidelines for Using Power

BASIS OF POWER	GUIDELINES FOR USE
REFERENT POWER	Treat subordinates fairly Defend subordinates' interests Be sensitive to subordinates' needs, feelings Select subordinates similar to oneself Engage in role modeling
EXPERT POWER	Promote image of expertise Maintain credibility Act confident and decisive Keep informed Recognize employee concerns Avoid threatening subordinates' self-esteem
LEGITIMATE POWER	Be cordial and polite Be confident Be clear and follow up to verify understanding Make sure request is appropriate Explain reasons for request Follow proper channels Exercise power regularly Enforce compliance Be sensitive to subordinates' concerns
REWARD POWER	Verify compliance Make feasible, reasonable requests Make only ethical, proper requests Offer rewards desired by subordinates Offer only credible rewards
COERCIVE POWER	Inform subordinates of rules and penalties Warn before punishing Administer punishment consistently and uniformly Understand the situation before acting Maintain credibility Fit punishment to the infraction Punish in private

References: Yukl, Gary A., *Leadership in Organizations*, 5th Edition, © 2002, pp. 144–152. Adapted by permission of Pearson Education, Inc., Upper Saddle River, NJ.

commitment (or at least compliance) and that is least likely to engender resistance. For example, to suggest a somewhat mechanistic approach, managers may enhance their referent power by choosing subordinates with backgrounds similar to their own. They might, for instance, build a referent power base by hiring several subordinates who went to the same college they did. A more subtle way to exercise referent power is through role modeling: The leader behaves as she or he wants subordinates to behave. As noted earlier, because subordinates relate to and identify with the leader with referent power, they may subsequently attempt to emulate that person's behavior.

In using expert power, managers may subtly make others aware of their education, experience, and accomplishments as they apply to current circumstances. But to maintain credibility, a leader should not pretend to know things that he or she really does not know. A leader whose pretensions are exposed will rapidly lose expert power. A confident and decisive leader demonstrates a firm grasp of situations and takes charge when circumstances dictate. Managers should also keep themselves informed about developments related to tasks that are valuable to the organization and relevant to their expertise.

A leader who recognizes employee concerns works to understand the underlying nature of these issues and takes appropriate steps to reassure subordinates. For example, if employees feel threatened by rumors that they will lose office space after an impending move, the leader might ask them about this concern and then find out just how much office space there will be and tell the subordinates. Finally, to avoid threatening the self-esteem of subordinates, a leader should be careful not to flaunt expertise or behave like a "know-it-all."

In general, a leader exercises legitimate power by formally requesting that subordinates do something. The leader should be especially careful to make requests diplomatically if the subordinate is sensitive about his or her relationship with the leader. This might be the case, for example, if the subordinate is older or more experienced than the leader. But although the request should be polite, it should be made confidently. The leader is in charge and needs to convey his or her command of the situation. The request should also be clear. Thus, the leader may need to follow up to ascertain that the subordinate has understood it properly. To ensure that a request is seen as appropriate and legitimate to the situation, the leader may need to explain the reasons for it. Often subordinates do not understand the rationale behind a request and consequently are unenthusiastic about it. It is important, too, to follow proper channels when dealing with subordinates.

Suppose a manager has asked a subordinate to spend his day finishing an important report. Later, while the manager is out of the office, the manager's boss comes by and asks the subordinate to drop that project and work on something else. The subordinate will then be in the awkward position of having to choose which of two higher-ranking individuals to obey. Exercising authority regularly will reinforce its presence and legitimacy in the eyes of subordinates. Compliance with legitimate power should be the norm, because if employees resist a request, the leader's power base may diminish. Finally, the leader exerting legitimate power should attempt to be responsive to subordinates' problems and concerns in the same ways we outlined for using expert power.

Reward power is in some respects the easiest base of power to use. Verifying compliance simply means that leaders should find out whether subordinates have carried out their requests before giving rewards; otherwise, subordinates may not recognize the link between their performance and subsequent reward. The request that is to be rewarded must be both reasonable and feasible, of course, because even the promise of a reward will not motivate a subordinate who thinks a request should not or cannot be carried out.

The same can be said for a request that seems improper or unethical. Among other things, the follower may see a reward linked to an improper or unethical request, such as a bribe or other shady offering. Finally, if the leader promises a reward that subordinates know she or he cannot actually deliver, or if they have little use for a reward the manager can deliver, they will not be motivated to carry out the request. Further, they may grow skeptical of the leader's ability to deliver rewards that are worth something to them.

Coercion is in many ways the most difficult form of power to exercise. Because coercive power is likely to cause resentment and to erode referent power, it should be used infrequently, if at all. Compliance is about all one can expect from using coercive power, and even that much can be expected only if the power is used in a helpful, nonpunitive way—that is, if the sanction is mild and fits the situation and if the subordinate learns from it. In most cases, resistance is the most likely outcome, especially if coercive power is used in a hostile or manipulative way.

The first guideline for using coercive power—that subordinates should be fully informed about rules and the penalties for violating them—will prevent accidental violations of a rule, which pose an unpalatable dilemma for a leader. Overlooking an infraction on the grounds that the perpetrator was ignorant may undermine the rule or the leader's legitimate power, but carrying out the punishment probably will create resentment. One approach is to provide reasonable warning before inflicting punishment, responding to the first violation of a rule with a warning about the consequences of another violation. Of course, a serious infraction such as a theft or violence warrants immediate and severe punishment.

Stockbroker/Alamy

A leader can use power in a variety of ways. Take this chef, for example. He is training a protégé in the proper way to apply a topping to a steak. He clearly has expert power, but is also drawing upon referent, reward, and legitimate power as well.

The disciplinary action needs to be administered consistently and uniformly, because doing so shows that punishment is both impartial and clearly linked to the infraction. Leaders should obtain complete information about what has happened before they punish, because punishing the wrong person or administering uncalled-for punishment can stir great resentment among subordinates. Credibility must be maintained, because a leader who continually makes threats but fails to carry them out loses both respect and power. Similarly, if the leader uses threats that subordinates know are beyond his or her ability to impose, the attempted use of power will be fruitless. Obviously, too, the severity of the punishment generally should match the seriousness of the infraction. Finally, punishing someone in front of others adds humiliation to the penalty, which reflects poorly on the leader and makes those who must watch and listen uncomfortable as well.

POLITICS AND POLITICAL BEHAVIOR

Organizational politics are activities carried out by people to acquire, enhance, and use power and other resources to obtain their desired outcomes.

A concept closely related to power in organizational settings is politics, or political behavior. **Organizational politics** are activities people perform to acquire, enhance, and use power and other resources to obtain their preferred outcomes in a situation where there is uncertainty or disagreement. Thus, political behavior is the general means by which people attempt to obtain and use power. Put simply, the goal of such behavior is to get one's own way about things.[7]

Politics and political behavior often play a role in making critical decisions. These managers, for example, are informally discussing a new project under review by their division. They are likely trying to influence each other's thinking through persuasion and other techniques. There may also be political agendas involved.

The Pervasiveness of Political Behavior

One important survey provides some interesting insights into how managers perceive political behavior in their organizations.[8] Roughly one-third of the 428 managers who responded to this survey believed political behavior influenced salary decisions in their organizations, while 28 percent felt it affected hiring decisions. Moreover, three-quarters of them also believed political behavior to be more prevalent at higher levels of the organization than at lower levels. More than half believed that politics is unfair, unhealthy, and irrational but also acknowledged that successful executives must be good politicians and that it is necessary to behave politically to get ahead. The survey results suggest that managers see political behavior as an undesirable but unavoidable facet of organizational life.

Politics often are viewed as synonymous with dirty tricks or backstabbing and therefore as something distasteful and best left to others. But the results of the survey just described demonstrate that political behavior in organizations, like power, is pervasive. Thus, rather than ignoring or trying to eliminate political behavior, managers might more fruitfully consider when and how organizational politics can be used constructively.

Figure 14.2 presents an interesting model of the ethics of organizational politics.[9] In the model, a political behavior alternative (PBA) is a given course of action, largely political in character, in a particular situation. The model considers political behavior ethical and appropriate under two conditions: (1) if it respects the rights of all affected parties and (2) if it adheres to the canons of justice (that is, to a commonsense judgment of what is fair and equitable). Even if the political behavior does not meet

FIGURE 14.2

A Model of Ethical Political Behavior

Political behavior can serve both ethical and unethical purposes. This model helps illustrate circumstances in which political behavior is most and least likely to have ethical consequences. By following the paths through the model, a leader concerned about the ethics of an impending behavior can gain insights into whether ethical considerations are really a central part of the behavior.

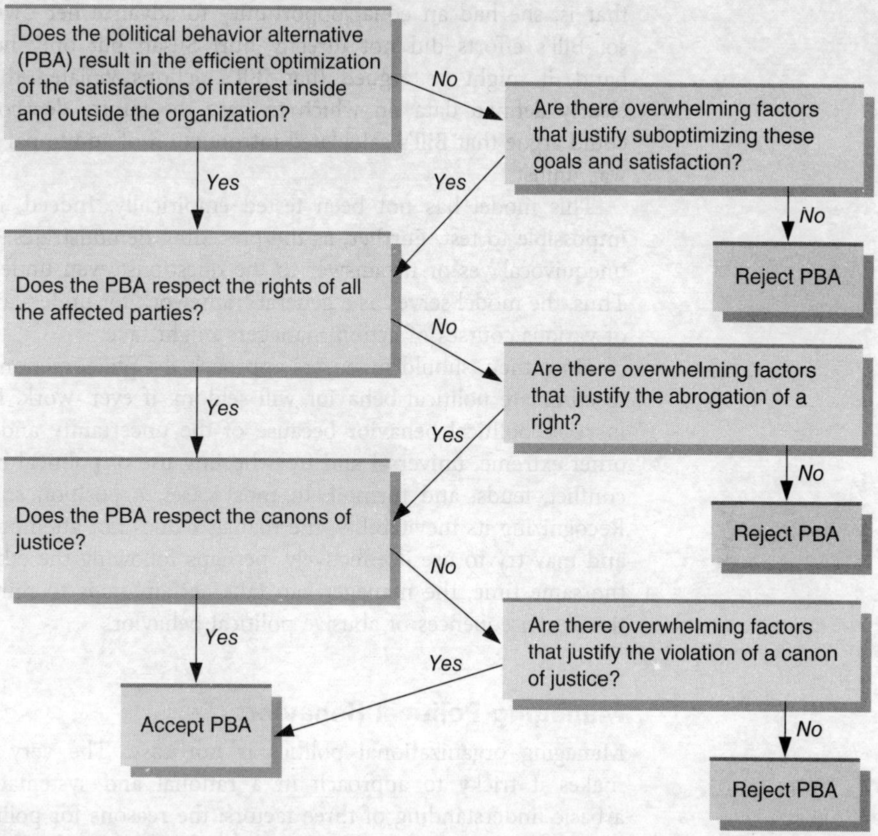

Reference: Gerald E. Cavanaugh, Dennis J. Moberg, and Manuel Velasques, "The Ethics of Organizational Politics," *Academy of Management Review*, July 1981, p. 368. Used with permission.

these tests, it may be ethical and appropriate under certain circumstances. For example, politics may provide the only possible basis for deciding which employees to let go during a recessionary period of cutbacks. In all cases where nonpolitical alternatives exist, however, the model recommends rejecting political behavior that abrogates rights or justice.

To illustrate how the model works, consider Susan Jackson and Bill Thompson, both assistant professors of English at a private university. University regulations and a budget reduction stipulate that only one of the assistant professors may be tenured; the other must be let go (some universities actually follow this practice!). Both Susan and Bill submit their credentials for review. By most objective criteria, such as number of publications and teaching evaluations, the two faculty members' qualifications are roughly the same. Because he fears termination, Bill begins an active political campaign to support a tenure decision favoring him. For instance, he reminds the tenured faculty of his intangible contributions, such as his friendship with influential campus administrators, and points out his family ties to the university. Susan, on the other hand, decides to say nothing and let her qualifications speak for themselves. The department ultimately votes to give Bill tenure and let Susan go.

Was Bill's behavior ethical? Assuming that his comments about himself were accurate and that he said nothing to disparage Susan, his behavior did not affect her rights;

that is, she had an equal opportunity to advance her own cause but chose not to do so. Bill's efforts did not directly hurt Susan but only helped himself. On the other hand, it might be argued that Bill's actions violated the canons of justice because clearly defined data on which to base the tenure decision were available. Thus, one could argue that Bill's calculated introduction of additional information into the decision was unjust.

This model has not been tested empirically. Indeed, its very nature may make it impossible to test. Further, as the preceding demonstrates, it often is difficult to give an unequivocal yes or no answer to the questions, even under the simplest circumstances. Thus, the model serves as a general framework for understanding the ethical implications of various courses of action managers might take.

How, then, should managers approach the phenomenon of political behavior? Trying to eliminate political behavior will seldom, if ever, work. In fact, such action may well increase political behavior because of the uncertainty and ambiguity it creates. At the other extreme, universal and freewheeling use of political behavior probably will lead to conflict, feuds, and turmoil. In most cases, a position somewhere in between is best: Recognizing its inevitability, the manager does not attempt to eliminate political activity and may try to use it effectively, perhaps following the ethical model just described. At the same time, the manager can take certain steps to minimize the potential dysfunctional consequences of abusive political behavior.

Managing Political Behavior

Managing organizational politics is not easy. The very nature of political behavior makes it tricky to approach in a rational and systematic way. Success will require a basic understanding of three factors: the reasons for political behavior, common techniques for using political behavior, and strategies for limiting the effects of political behavior.

Reasons for Political Behavior Political behavior occurs in organizations for five basic reasons: ambiguous goals, scarce resources, technology and environment, nonprogrammed decisions, and organizational change (see Figure 14.3).

Most organizational goals are inherently ambiguous. Organizations frequently espouse goals such as "increasing our presence in certain new markets" or "increasing our market share." The ambiguity of such goals provides an opportunity for political behavior because people can view a wide range of behaviors as helping meet the goal. In reality, of course, many of these behaviors may actually be designed for the personal gain of the individuals involved. For example, a top manager might argue that the corporation should pursue its goal of entry into a new market by buying out another firm instead of forming a new division. The manager may appear to have the good of the corporation in mind—but what if his or her spouse owns some of the target firm's stock and stands to make money on a merger or acquisition?

Whenever resources are scarce, some people will not get everything they think they deserve or need. Thus, they are likely to engage in political behavior as a means of inflating their share of the resources. In this way, a manager seeking a larger budget might present accurate but misleading or incomplete statistics to inflate the perceived importance of her department. Because no organization has unlimited resources, incentives for this kind of political behavior are often present.

Technology and environment may influence the overall design of the organization and its activities. The influence stems from the uncertainties associated with nonroutine

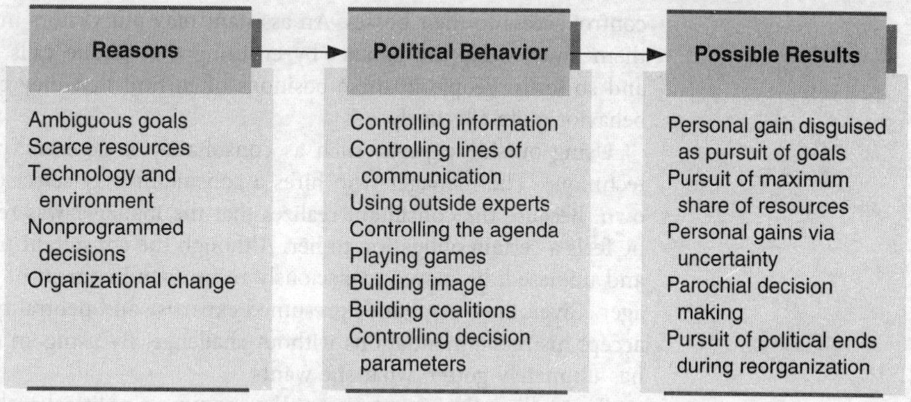

© Cengage Learning

FIGURE 14.3

Uses of Political Behavior: Reasons, Techniques, and Possible Consequences

People choose to engage in political behavior for many reasons. Depending on the reasons and circumstances, a person interested in using political behavior can employ a variety of techniques, which will produce a number of intended—and possibly unintended—consequences.

technologies and dynamic, complex environments. These uncertainties favor the use of political behavior because in a dynamic and complex environment it is imperative that an organization respond to change. An organization's response generally involves a wide range of activities, from purposeful activities to uncertainty to a purely political response. In the last case, a manager might use an environmental shift as an argument for restructuring his or her department to increase his or her own power base.

Political behavior is also likely to arise whenever many nonprogrammed decisions need to be made. Nonprogrammed-decision situations involve ambiguous circumstances that allow ample opportunity for political maneuvering. The two faculty members competing for one tenured position is an example. The nature of the decision allowed political behavior, and in fact, from Bill's point of view, the nonprogrammed decision demanded political action.

As we discuss in Chapter 19, changes in organizations occur regularly and can take many forms. Each such change introduces some uncertainty and ambiguity into the organizational system, at least until it has been completely institutionalized. The period during which this is occurring usually affords much opportunity for political activity. For instance, a manager worried about the consequences of a reorganization may resort to politics to protect the scope of his or her authority.

The Techniques of Political Behavior Several techniques are used in practicing political behavior. Unfortunately, because these techniques have not been systematically studied, our understanding of them is based primarily on informal observation and inference.[10] To further complicate this problem, the participants themselves may not even be aware that they are using particular techniques. Figure 14.3 summarizes the most frequently used techniques.[11]

One technique of political behavior is to control as much information as possible. The more critical the information and the fewer the people who have access to it, the larger the power base and influence of those who do. For example, suppose a top manager has a report compiled as a basis for future strategic plans. Rather than distributing the complete report to peers and subordinates, he shares only parts of it with the few managers who must have the information. Because no one but the manager has the complete picture, he has power and is engaging in politics to control decisions and activities according to his own ends.

Similarly, some people create or exploit situations to control lines of communication, particularly access to others in the organization. Administrative assistants frequently control access to their bosses. An assistant may put visitors in contact with the boss, send them away, delay the contact by ensuring that phone calls are not returned promptly, and so forth. People in these positions often find that they can use this type of political behavior quite effectively.

Using outside experts, such as consultants or advisers, can be an effective political technique. The manager who hires a consultant may select one whose views match her own. Because the consultant realizes that the manager was responsible for selecting him, he feels a certain obligation to her. Although the consultant truly attempts to be objective and unbiased, he may unconsciously recommend courses of action favored by the manager. Given the consultant's presumed expertise and neutrality, others in the organization accept his recommendations without challenge. By using an outside expert, the manager has ultimately gotten what she wants.

Controlling the agenda is another common political technique. Suppose a manager wants to prevent a committee from approving a certain proposal. The manager first tries to keep the decision off the agenda entirely, claiming that it is not yet ready for consideration, or attempts to have it placed last on the agenda. As other issues are decided, he sides with the same set of managers on each decision, building up a certain assumption that they are a team. When the controversial item comes up, he can defeat it through a combination of collective fatigue, the desire to get the meeting over with, and the support of his carefully cultivated allies. This technique, then, involves group polarization. A less sophisticated tactic is to prolong discussion of prior agenda items so that the group never reaches the controversial one. Or the manager may raise so many technical issues and new questions about the proposal that the committee decides to table it. In any of these cases, the manager will have used political behavior for his or her own ends.

"Game playing" is a complex technique that may take many forms. When playing games, managers simply work within the rules of the organization to increase the probability that their preferred outcomes will come about. Suppose a manager is in a position to cast the deciding vote on an upcoming issue but does not want to alienate either side by voting on it. One game she might play is to arrange to be called out of town on a crucial business trip when the vote is to take place. Assuming that no one questions the need for the trip, she will successfully maintain her position of neutrality and avoid angering either opposing camp.

Another game would involve using any of the techniques of political behavior in a purely manipulative or deceitful way. For example, a manager who will soon be making recommendations about promotions tells each subordinate, in "strictest confidence," that he or she is a leading candidate and needs only to increase his or her performance to have the inside track. Here the manager is using his control over information to play games with his subordinates. A power struggle at the W.R. Grace Company clearly illustrates manipulative practices. One senior executive fired the CEO's son and then allegedly attempted to convince the board of directors to oust the CEO and to give him the job. The CEO, in response, fired his rival and then publicly announced that the individual had been forced out because he had sexually harassed other Grace employees.[12]

The technique of building coalitions has as its general goal convincing others that everyone should work together to accomplish certain things. A manager who believes she does not control enough votes to pass an upcoming agenda item may visit with other managers before the meeting to urge them to side with her. If her preferences are in the best interests of the organization, this may be a laudable strategy for her to follow. But if she herself is the principal beneficiary, the technique is not desirable from the organization's perspective.

At its extreme, coalition building, which is frequently used in political bodies, may take the form of blatant reciprocity. In return for Roberta Kline's vote on an issue that concerns him, Jose Montemayor agrees to vote for a measure that does not affect his group at all but is crucial to Kline's group. Depending on the circumstances, this practice may benefit or hurt the organization as a whole.

The technique of controlling decision parameters can be used only in certain situations and requires much subtlety. Instead of trying to control the actual decision, the manager backs up one step and tries to control the criteria and tests on which the decision is based. This allows the manager to take a less active role in the actual decision but still achieve his or her preferred outcome. For example, suppose a district manager wants a proposed new factory to be constructed on a site in his region. If he tries to influence the decision directly, his arguments will be seen as biased and self-serving. Instead, he may take a very active role in defining the criteria on which the decision will be based, such as target population, access to rail transportation, tax rates, distance from other facilities, and the like. If he is a skillful negotiator, he may be able to influence the decision parameters such that his desired location subsequently appears to be the ideal site as determined by the criteria he has helped shape. Hence, he gets just what he wants without playing a prominent role in the actual decision.

Limiting the Effects of Political Behavior Although it is virtually impossible to eliminate political activity in organizations, managers can limit its dysfunctional consequences. The techniques for checking political activity target both the reasons it occurs in the first place and the specific techniques that people use for political gain.

Open communication is one very effective technique for restraining the impact of political behavior. For instance, with open communication the basis for allocating scarce resources will be known to everyone. This knowledge, in turn, will tend to reduce the propensity to engage in political behavior to acquire those resources, because people already know how decisions will be made. Open communication also limits the ability of any single person to control information or lines of communication.

A related technique is to reduce uncertainty. Several of the reasons political behavior occurs—ambiguous goals, nonroutine technology, an unstable environment, and organizational change—and most of the political techniques themselves are associated with high levels of uncertainty. Political behavior can be limited if the manager can reduce uncertainty. Consider an organization about to transfer a major division from Florida to Michigan. Many people will resist the idea of moving north and may resort to political behavior to forestall their own transfer. However, the manager in charge of the move could announce who will stay and who will go at the same time that news of the change spreads throughout the company, thereby curtailing political behavior related to the move.

The adage "forewarned is forearmed" sums up one final technique for controlling political activity. Simply being aware of the causes and techniques of political behavior can help a manager check their effects. Suppose a manager anticipates that several impending organizational changes will increase the level of political activity. As a result of this awareness, the manager quickly infers that a particular subordinate is lobbying for the use of a certain consultant only because the subordinate thinks the consultant's recommendations will be in line with his own. Attempts to control the agenda, engage in game playing, build a certain image, and control decision parameters often are transparently obvious to the knowledgeable observer. Recognizing such behaviors for what they are, an astute manager may be able to take appropriate steps to limit their impact.

ORGANIZATIONAL JUSTICE

Organizational justice is an important phenomenon that has recently been introduced into the study of organizations. Justice can be discussed from a variety of perspectives, including motivation, leadership, and group dynamics. We choose to discuss it here because it is also likely to be related to power and political behavior in organizations. The *Services* box provides additional insights into the role of justice as it relates to power and political behavior. Basically, **organizational justice** refers to the perceptions of people in an organization regarding fairness.[13] As illustrated in Figure 14.4, there are four basic forms of organizational justice.

Organizational justice refers to the perceptions of people in an organization regarding fairness.

Distributive Justice

Distributive justice refers to people's perceptions of the fairness with which rewards and other valued outcomes are distributed within the organization. Obviously related to the

SERVICE — Don't Let an Unfair Customer Spill Over to the Next in Line

©rangizzz/Shutterstock

If you've ever stood in line at a store waiting your turn while the person in front of you is being rude and yelling at the clerk, you know the sense of dread that all who have been in this situation face. Will the server be able to overlook the bad behavior of the person in front of you and treat you well, or will the bad feelings the clerk must have after that unpleasant encounter spill over into how you are treated? That is the question, and it is an important one for managers to answer because each customer expects to be treated with dignity, empathy, responsiveness, and respect. It is very hard for people to go from an emotionally charged situation where they are being yelled at to smiling pleasantly at the next in line.

Managers of service organizations know this and work hard to ensure that their employees are taught how to avoid the spilling over of any negative emotions created by one customer onto another customer or even onto their boss and coworkers. It is all too easy for a bad customer to cause an employee to become so shaken that he or she feels the need to get away and blow off some steam. Thus, managers who know this rely on tools and techniques to relieve stress for their employees so they can face the next in line with a smile.

These techniques have three types of issues. The first is to decouple the employee from the problem. This can be done through teaching employees how to respond to bad customers via role playing and teaching them that the customer isn't attacking them as a person but as a representative of an organization that has somehow done something that is seen as frustrating or wrong by that customer. The second strategy a manager can take is to help create a separate persona to deal with a negative situation. This can be done through teaching the employee to pretend to be someone else, establishing a professional norm that insulates the person from the attack. The third strategy is to shift the customer to a manager or someone else after a level of frustration is reached by the employee. Here employees are told that when the customer starts to get to them, they should call in a manager to take over.

The point is that the employee who is being attacked by a customer will respond, and it is the organization's responsibility to help find a way to respond that does not lead to any further problems for the employee, the organization, the customer, or any others that the employee encounters after having a bad experience with a customer.

Discussion Question: Using the text's description of interactional justice, what strategies can you suggest managers use to help employees deal with unfair customers?

FIGURE 14.4

Four Basic Forms of Organizational Justice

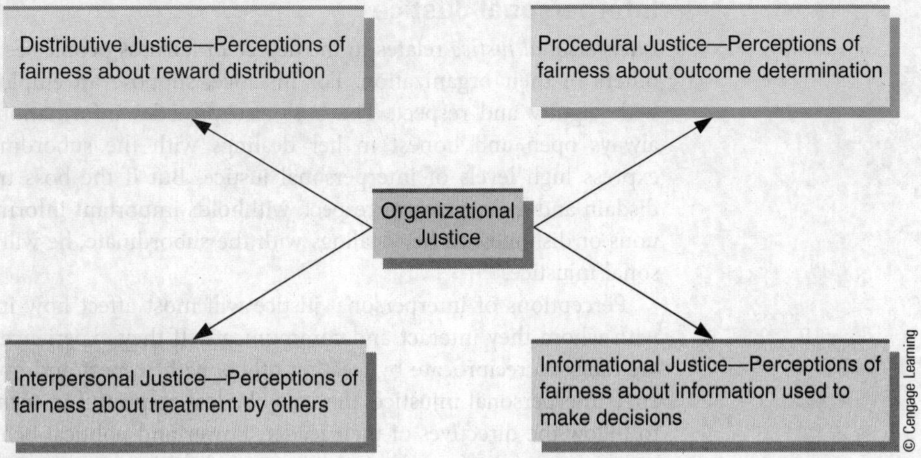

equity theory of motivation discussed back in Chapter 4, distributive justice takes a more holistic view of reward distribution than simply a comparison between one person and another. For instance, the compensation paid to top managers (especially the CEO), to peers and colleagues at the same level in an organization, and even to entry-level hourly workers can all be assessed in terms of their relative fairness vis-à-vis anyone else in the organization.

Perceptions of distributive justice affect individual satisfaction with various work-related outcomes such as pay, work assignments, recognition, and opportunities for advancement. Specifically, the more *just* people see the rewards to be distributed as being, the more satisfied they will be with those rewards; the more *unjust* they see the rewards to be distributed as being, the less satisfied they will be. Moreover, individuals who feel that rewards are not distributed justly may be inclined to attribute such injustice to misuse of power and/or to political agendas.

Procedural Justice

Another important form of organizational justice is *procedural justice*—individual perceptions of the fairness of the process used to determine various outcomes. For instance, suppose an employee's performance is evaluated by someone very familiar with the job being performed. Moreover, the evaluator clearly explains the basis for the evaluation and then discusses how that evaluation will translate in other outcomes such as promotions and pay increases. The individual will probably see this set of procedures as being fair and just. But if the evaluation is conducted by someone unfamiliar with the job who provides no explanation as to how the evaluation is being done nor what it will mean, the individual is likely to see that process as less fair and just.

When workers perceive a high level of procedural justice, they are somewhat more likely to be motivated to participate in activities, to follow rules, and to accept relevant outcomes as being fair. But if workers perceive more procedural injustice, they tend to withdraw from opportunities to participate, to pay less attention to rules and policies, and to see relevant outcomes as being unfair. In addition, perceptions of procedural injustice may be accompanied by interpretations based on the power and political behaviors of others.

Interpersonal Justice

Interpersonal justice relates to the degree of fairness people see in how they are treated by others in their organization. For instance, suppose an employee is treated by his boss with dignity and respect. The boss also provides information on a timely basis and is always open and honest in her dealings with the subordinate. The subordinate will express high levels of interpersonal justice. But if the boss treats her subordinate with disdain and a clear lack of respect, withholds important information, and is often ambiguous or dishonest in her dealings with the subordinate, he will experience more interpersonal injustice.

Perceptions of interpersonal justice will most affect how individuals feel about those with whom they interact and communicate. If they experience interpersonal justice, they are likely to reciprocate by treating others with respect and openness. But if they experience interpersonal injustice, they may be less respectful in turn, and may be less inclined to follow the directives of their leader. Power and political behaviors are also again likely to be seen as playing roles in interpersonal justice.

Informational Justice

Finally, *informational justice* refers to the perceived fairness of information used to arrive at decisions. If someone feels that a manager made a decision based on relatively complete and accurate information, and that the information was appropriately processed and considered, the person will likely experience informational justice even if he or she does not completely agree with the decisions. But if the person feels that the decision was based on incomplete and inaccurate information and/or that important information was ignored, the individual will experience less informational justice.

Power and political behaviors are likely to play an important role in perceptions of informational justice. Recall, for example, our earlier discussion of information control as a political tactic. To the extent that people believe that informational justice is lacking, they may very well see power and political behaviors as having played a major role in the decision-making process.[14]

SYNOPSIS

Influence can be defined as the ability to affect the perceptions, attitudes, or behaviors of others. Influence is a cornerstone of leadership. Impression management is a direct, intentional effort by someone to enhance his or her image in the eyes of others. People engage in impression management for a variety of reasons and use a variety of methods to influence how others see them.

Power is the potential ability of a person or group to exercise control over another person or group. The five bases of power are legitimate power (granted by virtue of one's position in the organization); reward power (control of rewards valued by others); coercive power (the ability to punish or harm); expert power (control over information that is valuable to the organization); and referent power (power through personal identification). Position power is tied to a position regardless of the individual who holds it. Personal power is power that resides in a person regardless of position. Attempts to use power can result in commitment, compliance, or resistance.

Organizational politics are activities people perform to acquire, enhance, and use power and other resources to obtain their preferred outcomes in a situation where uncertainty or disagreement exists. Research indicates that most managers do not advocate use of political behavior but acknowledge that it is a necessity of organizational life. Because managers cannot eliminate political activity in the organization, they must learn to cope with it. Understanding how to manage political behavior requires understanding why it occurs, what techniques it employs, and strategies for limiting its effects.

Organizational justice refers to the perceptions of people in an organization regarding fairness. There are four basic forms of organizational justice:

distributive, procedural, interpersonal, and informational. Power and political behaviors are likely to be assumed when any or all of these forms of justice are seen as being deficient.

DISCUSSION QUESTIONS

1. Can a person without influence be a leader? Does having influence automatically make someone a leader?
2. Have you ever engaged in impression management? What did you hope to accomplish?
3. What might happen if two people, each with significant, equal power, attempt to influence each other?
4. Cite examples based on a professor–student relationship to illustrate each of the five bases of organizational power.
5. Is there a logical sequence in the use of power bases that a manager might follow? For instance, should the use of legitimate power usually precede the use of reward power, or vice versa?
6. Cite examples in which you have been committed, compliant, and resistant as a result of efforts to influence you. Think of times when your attempts to influence others led to commitment, compliance, and resistance.
7. Do you agree or disagree with the assertion that political behavior is inevitable in organizational settings?
8. The term "politics" is generally associated with governmental bodies. Why do you think it has also come to be associated with the behavior in organizations described in this chapter?
9. Recall examples of how you have either used or observed others using the techniques of political behavior identified in the chapter. What other techniques can you suggest?
10. Recall an instance when you have experienced each of the four forms of organizational justice in either a positive or a negative manner.

HOW DO YOU SEE IT?

Fair Tradeoffs

"If they want to work for us … they must see that these are Numi's values."

—BRIAN DURKEE, DIRECTOR OF OPERATIONS, NUMI ORGANIC TEA

Now that we've been on the subject of organizational behavior for some time, perhaps this video provides a good opportunity to make sure that we know just what an "organization" is. For an official definition, we need only glance ahead to Chapter 16, where we find that an *organization* is a goal-directed group of people who perform activities according to certain processes and systems. A further look ahead, to Chapter 17, informs us that organizations exist in *environments*, which include all of the elements, from people to economic conditions, that lie *outside* the organization. One of these environments, the *task environment*, includes all the specific organizations and groups that can *influence* an organization.

So far, so good. In order to understand the issues being discussed in this video, we need to know just two more things:

1. The task environment includes *suppliers*—other organizations that provide the resources that an organization needs to conduct its operations.
2. An organization's suppliers belong to its *supply chain*—the chain of operations stretching from the organization's purchase of needed resources to the sale of its finished products to consumers.

Its supply chain, then, lies *outside* the organization, but it must be managed from *within*. In effect, managing its supply chain extends an organization's influence beyond its own boundaries and into the realm of its external environment.

At Numi Organic Tea, which specializes in premium-quality, full-leaf organic teas, the person responsible for managing the supply chain is Director of Operations Brian Durkee. Numi's supply chain begins in Asia—primarily, though by no means exclusively, in China—and Durkee says that one of his "biggest challenges in China is getting the people … and the managers of the factories to understand how we want things done." How *does* Numi want things done? Or, to put the same question another way: What does it require its suppliers to do? "We're a triple-bottom-line company," says Durkee. "Our focus is on people, planet, and profit.... [We want] to make sure that our quality is there," but it's also imperative that tea suppliers "meet the level of sustainability we expect in the supply chain." *Sustainability*—fostering conditions under which natural resources are available to meet the social and economic needs of both present and future generations—ranks very high on Numi's list of policies that the company and its business partners must practice.

"My personal goal for Numi," says Durkee, "is to become among the elite as far as how we manage our supply chain. We're looking at the most sustainable methods of packaging our goods, transporting our goods, and producing our goods." If suppliers, he adds, "want to work for us ... they must see that these are Numi's values.... How are they handling their waste? How are they packaging our products? How are they treating their workers?" In short, setting standards for sustainability is an important tool for supply chain management at Numi.

Not surprisingly, says cofounder Ahmed Rahim, putting this principle into practice isn't always easy and often entails troublesome tradeoffs. If, for example, "you're working with chemicals but you're taking care of the farmers with the chemicals"—i.e., protecting their crops and making them more productive—"then you're polluting the farmers with the chemicals." Such decisions, adds Rahim, must be made in "every single aspect of the supply chain," and whenever such decisions have to be made, there's always a possibility for conflict. For one thing, such decisions usually involve tradeoffs in managing costs—that is, your own and/or somebody else's money. "You're trying to spend money to improve the sustainability of your product [and] to improve Fair Trade*," says Durkee, but you can never be sure that a supply chain partner regards the extra cost as important as you do.

Coercive power, Durkee observes, isn't really an option in resolving conflicts with suppliers, domestic or foreign. "It's really important," he explains, "for them to understand *why* you're [insisting on sustainability] and for them to really buy into it and get excited about it." Durkee is quick to add that

> *we don't do business overseas to reduce cost and ... exploit a system.... We're not trying to change their culture by any means, but we are trying to improve the standard of living for them.... That's ... why we spend a lot of time in Asia ... meeting with factory managers, meeting with the workers, doing our own discovery process with the workers.*

In a sense, then, Numi strives to leverage its organizational "vision" as a supply chain–management tool. Among the tenets of that vision is the belief that "all people should be paid an equitable wage that allows their families to thrive," and Durkee emphasizes that empowerment, rather than the exercise of economic power, is the most effective means to that end. He tells the story, for example, of Numi's dealings with a Chinese supplier of bamboo, which the company uses in the packaging for gift items:

> *We spent a lot of time out there ... helping him improve his factory and providing him with money ... to get better workers ... and better work conditions and to get a better factory in place. And he's starting to implement changes himself. That's when we're having some success: If we can leave a mark, then we can leave the situation and have it continue to improve itself.*

CASE QUESTIONS

1. The introduction to the case explains that when we consider an organization as the anchor of a supply chain, we extend the boundaries of the organization itself. Brian Durkee, for example, manages the members of Numi's supply chain, which are *external* to the organization, in much the same way that, we assume, he manages the company's *internal* units. **Judging from the video**, how would you characterize the nature of the *organizational politics* in this extended organization? Applying Figure 14.2 to what the video tells us about Numi's *political behavior* in this extended organization, summarize the role and nature of ethical considerations in this behavior.
2. A type of conflict called *interorganizational conflict* can occur between two organizations, such as the members of a supply chain. Can you think of two or three different forms that interorganizational conflict between Numi and a supplier might take (e.g., a disagreement over worker wages)? What might be the most likely causes of a given conflict? The most likely consequences? [*Hint:* In trying to imagine possible forms of conflict, you might go back to Chapter 2 and think about issues that could arise from *cross-cultural differences* or *diversity* among the people involved in Numi's supply chain.]
3. In the event of conflict in this extended organization, what role in resolving it might be played by each form of *organizational justice* discussed in the chapter—*distributive, procedural, interpersonal, and informational*? In your opinion, which form or combination of forms is most likely to be effective? Explain your answer.
4. Fair Trade products such as tea are priced in roughly the same range as other high-quality specialty-food items, such as organic products. The quality is in fact typically higher because many Fair Trade importers,

such as Numi, encourage higher quality.[†] Assuming that you're in a position to afford it (and assuming that you have a consumer preference for high-quality tea), would you pay the premium—the portion of the price above the price charged for non-specialty brands—for Fair Trade tea products like those sold by Numi? Why or why not?

5. Now suppose that you read the results of a study that claims the following:

   Even analysts sympathetic to the [Fair Trade] movement have suggested that only 25 percent of the premium reaches producers. No study ever produced has shown that the benefit to producers … matches the premium paid.[‡]

   Although you're not in the habit of taking everything you read at face value, you're now more skeptical about Fair Trade promises than you were before reading the article. If you answered *yes* or *probably* to question 4, how (if at all) would your purchase decision change? In your opinion, what role does the politics of the extended organization play in the distribution of revenue from Fair Trade products? What role might it play in addressing any injustices in the Fair Trade system?

ADDITIONAL SOURCES

Numi Organic Tea, "Numi's Vision," "Founder's Story," "Celebrating People," "Fair Trade Certified" (2005–2012), www.numitea.com on September 24, 2012; Inner City Advisors, "Case Study: Numi Organic Teas" (2010), http://innercityadvisors.org on September 15, 2012; Stacey R. Louiso, "Numi Equals Puri-Tea," *Attribute Magazine*, July 6, 2009, www.attributemagazine.com on September 16, 2012.

*"Fair Trade" is not just a casual slogan. The term refers to programs designed to ensure that export-dependent farmers in developing countries receive fair prices for their crops. Numi is Fair Trade Certified by Fair Trade Labelling Organizations International, a global nonprofit network of fair trade groups headquartered in Germany. "We're very big on Fair Trade," says Brian Durkee, "and we insist on that in our supply chain model."

[†]Tyler Gage, "The Central Benefit of Fair Trade: Price or Premium?" *T Ching*, November 28, 2011, www.tching.com on September 25, 2012.

[‡]HarryWallop, "Fair Trade Does Not Help the Poorest, Report Says," *The Telegraph*, November 4, 2010, www.telegraph.co.uk on September 25, 2012.

EXPERIENCING ORGANIZATIONAL BEHAVIOR

Power Bases

Purpose This exercise will give you practice in identifying power bases associated with various formal and informal positions in organizations.

Format You will name and explain the power bases individually. Then you will meet in a small group or as a class to discuss your responses and to answer the follow-up questions.

Procedure For each of the following positions, decide which of the five power bases are present (legitimate, reward, coercive, referent, and expert power). There may be more than one power base for an occupation. Then, for each power base that is present, write a sentence to explain or give a brief example.

- Top-performing salesperson
- Professor
- Popular campus athlete
- Small business owner
- Corporate CEO
- Research scientist heading corporate R&D
- Administrative assistant to a corporate CEO
- The U.S. president

Follow-Up Questions

1. Did class members find it easy to agree on the answers? If not, why not?
2. To what extent would more knowledge of a specific individual change your answers? To what extent would more knowledge of a specific situation change your answers?
3. Based on each position's power base(s), what outcomes would a person in this position be likely to experience if he or she were acting as a leader?

BUILDING MANAGERIAL SKILLS

Exercise Overview Diagnostic skills help a manager visualize appropriate responses to a situation. One situation managers often face is whether to use power to solve a problem. This exercise will help you develop your diagnostic skills as they relate to using different types of power in different situations.

Exercise Background Several methods have been identified for using power. These include:

1. Legitimate request—The manager requests that the subordinate comply because the subordinate recognizes that the organization has given the manager the right to make the request. Most day-to-day interactions between manager and subordinate are of this type.
2. Instrumental compliance—In this form of exchange, a subordinate complies to get the reward the manager controls. Suppose that a manager asks a subordinate to do something outside the range of the subordinate's normal duties, such as working extra hours on the weekend, terminating a relationship with a long-standing buyer, or delivering bad news. The subordinate complies and, as a direct result, reaps praise and a bonus from the manager. The next time the subordinate is asked to perform a similar activity, that subordinate will recognize that compliance will be instrumental in her getting more rewards. Hence the basis of instrumental compliance is clarifying important performance-reward contingencies.
3. Coercion—This is used when the manager suggests or implies that the subordinate will be punished, fired, or reprimanded if he does not do something.
4. Rational persuasion—This is when the manager can convince the subordinate that compliance is in the subordinate's best interest. For example, a manager might argue that the subordinate should accept a transfer because it would be good for the subordinate's career. In some ways, rational persuasion is like reward power except that the manager does not really control the reward.
5. Personal identification—This is when a manager who recognizes that she has referent power over a subordinate can shape the behavior of that subordinate by engaging in desired behaviors: The manager consciously becomes a model for the subordinate and exploits personal identification.
6. Inspirational appeal—This is when a manager can induce a subordinate to do something consistent with a set of higher ideals or values through inspirational appeal. For example, a plea for loyalty represents an inspirational appeal.

Exercise Task With these ideas in mind, do the following:

1. Relate each of the uses of power listed above to the five types of power identified in the chapter. That is, indicate which type(s) of power are most closely associated with each use of power, which type(s) may be related to each use of power, and which type(s) are unrelated to each use of power.
2. Is a manager more likely to be using multiple forms of power at the same time, or using a single type of power?
3. Identify other methods and approaches to using power.
4. What are some of the dangers and pitfalls associated with using power?

SELF-ASSESSMENT EXERCISE

How to Gain Power and Influence People

This exercise is designed to help you assess the ways in which your approach to your work will be effective in gaining power and influence. If you have a job, consider that your work; if you're a student, apply this exercise to your schoolwork.

The twenty-eight statements below reflect approaches that people can take toward their work, both personally and in their relationships with others. Using the following scale, indicate the extent to which, in your opinion, each statement is true of you.

1. Strongly disagree
2. Disagree
3. Slightly disagree
4. Slightly agree
5. Agree
6. Strongly agree

In a situation in which it is important to obtain more power:

_______1. I strive to become highly proficient in my line of work.

_______2. I express friendliness, honesty, and sincerity toward those with whom I work.

_______3. I put forth more effort and take more initiative than expected in my work.

_______4. I support organizational and ceremonial events and activities.

_______5. I form a broad network of relationships with people at all levels throughout the organization.

_______6. I send personal notes to others when they accomplish something significant or when I pass along important information to them.

_______7. In my work, I strive to generate new ideas, initiate new activities, and minimize routine tasks.

_______8. I try to find ways to be an external representative for my unit or organization.

_______9. I am continually upgrading my skills and knowledge.

______10. I strive to enhance my personal appearance.

______11. I work harder than most of my coworkers.

______12. I encourage new members to support important organizational values by both their words and their actions.

______13. I gain access to important information by becoming central in communications networks.

______14. I strive to find opportunities to make reports about my work, especially to senior people.

______15. I maintain variety in the tasks that I perform.

______16. I keep my work connected to the central mission of the organization.

When trying to influence someone for a specific purpose:

______17. I emphasize reason and factual information.

______18. I feel comfortable using a variety of different influence techniques, matching them to specific circumstances.

______19. I reward others for agreeing with me, thereby establishing a condition of reciprocity.

______20. I use a direct, straightforward approach rather than an indirect or manipulative one.

______21. I avoid using threats or demands to impose my will on others.

When resisting an inappropriate influence attempt directed at me:

______22. I use resources and information I control to equalize demands and threats.

______23. I refuse to bargain with individuals who use high-pressure negotiation tactics.

______24. I explain why I can't comply with reasonable-sounding requests by pointing out how the consequences would affect my responsibilities and obligations.

When trying to influence those above me in the organization:

______25. I help determine the issues to which they pay attention by effectively selling the importance of those issues.

______26. I convince them that the issues on which I want to focus are compatible with the goals and future success of the organization.

______27. I help them solve problems that they didn't expect me to help them solve.

______28. I work as hard to make them look good and be successful as I do for my own success.

How to score: Add up the numbers that you put down in the left-hand column. The maximum possible score is 168. You should compare your score with the scores of other students in the class and with those of 1,500 business school students summarized as follows:

Score	Ranking
134.9	mean
145 or above	top quartile
136–144	second quartile
126–135	third quartile
125 or below	bottom quartile

Reference: Whetten, David A; Cameron, Kim S., *Developing Management Skills*, 7th Edition, © 2007. pp. 284–85, 324. Reprinted by permission of Pearson Education, Inc., Upper Saddle River, NJ.

CHAPTER 15

Conflict and Negotiation in Organizations

Chapter Outline

- The Nature of Conflict in Organizations
- Common Forms and Causes of Conflict
- Reactions to Conflict
- Managing Conflict
- Negotiation in Organizations

Chapter Learning Objectives

After studying this chapter, you should be able to:

1. **Define and discuss the nature of conflict in organizations.**
2. **Identify and describe the common forms and causes of conflict.**
3. **Discuss the most frequent reactions to conflict in organizations.**
4. **Describe how conflict can be managed.**
5. **Define negotiation in organizations and discuss its underlying processes.**

When Conflict Becomes a Head-On Collision

"I want the world to know what happened."

—Ex-Toyota employee and whistle-blower Dimitrios Biller

"Mr. Biller's actions and the timing of his lawsuit do not support his claim that he is motivated by the public interest."

—Toyota Motor Corp.

When the Toyota Corolla in which they were driving with their young daughter was rear-ended by an SUV, Raul and Diana Lopez sued Toyota, charging that the driver's seat recliner had failed, causing the seat to strike their daughter and leaving her blind in one eye. The Toyota defense team was led by Dimitrios Biller, the automaker's National Managing Counsel for accident litigation, and Todd Tracy, the Lopezes' Texas attorney, was forced to settle the suit for much less than he was asking. There was apparently no love lost between the two lawyers in the case. "He was hard-nosed, almost obsessive-compulsive, about cases," says Tracy, who'd faced Biller in court twenty-five times. "People on the plaintiff side," he adds, "thought that he was a mean-spirited bastard." Not so, responded Biller, who claims that he sometimes cried after winning personal-injury cases because he "just felt a lot of empathy" for the plaintiffs.

Biller remained with Toyota until September 2007, when he left with a $3.7 million severance package, and it now appears that the parting wasn't exactly amicable. Biller also left with some 6,000 company documents related to vehicle-safety defects, charging that he was "forced" to resign because he resisted the company's "calculated conspiracy to prevent the disclosure of damaging evidence" in about 300 personal-injury lawsuits. Biller claimed that his superiors at Toyota had subjected him to "intimidation, harassment, and an uncertain future" and that he had suffered "a complete mental and physical breakdown." His severance package, he said, was "hush money," and he took the internal documents because of legal and ethical obligations to turn over "clearly discoverable material."

In 2008, Toyota, alleging that Biller had disclosed some of these internal company documents, sued its former in-house lawyer, arguing that he had violated

Problems with Toyota Camry's accelerator pedals led to several crashes. Ex-Toyota employee and whistleblower Dimitros Biller helped raise awareness of this problem by telling his story to the media.

the confidentiality clause of his severance agreement. "In our view," said Toyota, "Mr. Biller has repeatedly breached his ethical and professional obligations, both as an attorney and in his commitments to us, by violating attorney-client privilege."

In July 2009, Biller responded by filing a whistle-blower suit against Toyota and several of his former supervisors, claiming that they had acted to "stop, prevent, and delay" his efforts to "search, collect, preserve, review, and produce" documents for disclosure in litigation brought against the company. "I did as much as I could as a lawyer for a client" to prevent the client from breaking the law, said Biller. "I wrote email after email, memo after memo, explaining the legal obligations Toyota … needed to fill." He had filed his suit, Biller said, because "I want the world to know what happened." His former employer, however, was skeptical: Biller's "actions and the timing of his lawsuit," replied Toyota, "do not support his claim that he is motivated by the public interest. [His] actions have been motivated by his own personal financial interests."

And what about those 6,000 documents that Biller took with him when he parted company with Toyota? What kind of information did they contain? "Trade secrets," said the automaker, but Biller maintained that the documents could be used "to establish liability against Toyota in product liability and negligence cases." Toyota secured a court order to keep the documents confidential, but at this point in the proceedings, Biller was joined by an unlikely ally in his battle to disclose his potentially incriminating evidence. In October 2009, Biller turned over his cache of documents to a federal judge in Texas. Why Texas? It seems that Todd Tracy, spurred by the revelations promised in Biller's suit against Toyota, had decided to refile seventeen of the personal-injury lawsuits that he'd originally lost to Biller, starting with the case of Raul and Diana Lopez. The documents provided by Biller, declared Tracy, clearly contained "information that Toyota does not want the public to see…. Toyota's accident victims need to see [this] information … to find out if the Japanese auto giant perverted the course of American justice."

Two months later, however, Tracy announced that he was withdrawing his petition to reopen his seventeen cases. "After reviewing … the Biller documents," said Tracy, "I did not see any type of concealment, destruction, or pattern of discovery abuse that had affected my cases…. I did not see a smoking gun," Tracy added. "I didn't even see a smoldering gun." Meanwhile, a federal judge had responded to Toyota's complaint that Biller had violated the terms of his severance agreement by referring Biller to the California State Bar for investigation. A month later, another federal judge dismissed his allegations against Toyota's in-house lawyers and sent the case to arbitration.

Then, in March 2010, the strange case of *Dimitrios Biller v. Toyota Motor Corp.* took yet another unexpected turn. Meeting to hear complaints of uncontrolled-acceleration problems in Toyota vehicles, the Congressional Committee on Oversight and Government Reform had subpoenaed the documents in Biller's possession, and committee chairman Ed Towns had apparently found them much more interesting than Todd Tracy had. "We have reviewed these documents," wrote Towns in a letter to Toyota officials, "and found evidence that Toyota deliberately withheld relevant electronic records that it was legally required to produce in response to discovery orders in litigation." In particular, the chairman cited a memo from in-house attorney Dimitrios Biller urging his supervisor to turn over electronic information relating to vehicle design flaws. "The Biller documents," Congressman Towns concluded, "indicate a systematic disregard for the law and routine violation of court discovery orders in litigation."

At least part of the dispute was settled in January 2011, when the arbitrator to whom the case had been turned over in 2010 delivered his ruling. He ordered Biller to pay Toyota $2.6 million in damages, finding that Biller had violated contractual, statutory, and ethical duties. The decision was upheld by a federal Court of Appeals. "We feel this award," said a Toyota spokesman, "is an appropriate consequence of [Biller's] actions and completely discredits his meritless attacks on our company and our people." The ruling, however, does *not* settle the question of whether Biller's allegations against his former employer are true. "I have not given up on this mission," insists Biller. "I'll tell you this right now: I'm not finished."

For another perspective on the complexities of whistle-blowing as a special form of legal conflict, read the *Change* box entitled "Whistle-blowing in the Dark" on page 407.

What Do You Think?

1. Is conflict more or less inevitable in an organization as large as Toyota?
2. From a strictly legal standpoint, which party do you think is right—Biller or Toyota? Would you have done what Biller did? If so, why? If not, what would you have done?

References: Deborah Feyerick and Sheila Steffen, "Ex-Toyota Lawyer Says Documents Prove Company Hid Damaging Information," *CNN U.S.*, March 10, 2010, http://articles.cnn.com on August 6, 2012; Zusha Elinson, "Ex-Toyota Lawyer Holds Tight to Whistleblower Suit," *Law.com*, October 22, 2009, www.law.com on August 6, 2012; Michelle Massey, "Tracy Refiles Toyota Suit as Whistle-blower Faces Sanctions," *The Southeast Texas Record*, October 30, 2009, www.setexasrecord.com on August 6, 2012; Rob Riggs, "Dallas Attorney Todd Tracy Dismisses Suit to Reopen Toyota Accident Cases," *PR Web*, December 26, 2009, www.prweb.com on August 6, 2012; Peter Valdes-Dapena, "Oversight Chief Says Toyota Withheld Documents," *CNNMoney*, February 26, 2010, http://money.cnn.com on August 6, 2012; Valdes-Dapena, "Toyota Chalks a Win against 'Whistleblower,'" *CNNMoney*, January 6, 2011, http://money.cnn.com on August 6, 2012; Matthew Heller, "Dimitrios Biller: Inside Out," *California Lawyer*, August 2012, www.callalawyer.com on August 6, 2012.

Organizations like Toyota constantly face myriad instances of conflict—employees disagreeing with their boss, two executives disagreeing over a new marketing campaign, arguments between labor leaders and company representatives at the negotiating table, and many more. As we have seen throughout this book, when people work together in organizational settings, a variety of consequences can result. For instance, people may leave work each day feeling happy and energized for having done a great job; they can be frustrated and unhappy because of some problem they encountered; or they can feel stressed because of the pressures being imposed upon them. Another possible outcome that occurs with regularity is conflict, the subject of this chapter. We begin with a discussion of the nature of conflict. We then examine its most common forms and the things that cause it in the first place. We then discuss reactions to conflict and how it can be managed. We conclude with a discussion of a related organizational process, negotiation.

THE NATURE OF CONFLICT IN ORGANIZATIONS

Conflict is a process resulting in the perceptions of two parties that they are working in opposition to each other in ways that produce feelings of discomfort and/or animosity.

Conflict is a common occurrence in organizations. While there are numerous definitions of **conflict**, we will define it as a process resulting in the perceptions of two parties that they are working in opposition to each other in ways that result in feelings of discomfort and/or animosity. There are several elements of this definition that warrant additional comment.

First, note that conflict is a process, not a singular event. It evolves over time and draws upon previous events. While it may emerge as a result of a specific event, more than likely it has been brewing for some time. Further, the parties have to actually perceive it to exist in order for conflict to be real. If an observer witnesses what appears to be an argument between two other individuals but those people do not perceive their dialog to be conflictual, then conflict does not really exist. Finally, discomfort or animosity must occur in order for the conflict to be real. For example, a group of friends who play each other in a friendly game of softball may be competing for victory but are not in conflict.

We should also note that the parties involved in conflict may be individuals, groups, and/or organizations. Hence, conflict may involve one person in opposition to another, one group in opposition to another, or one organization in opposition to another. Conflict may also exist across levels, for example when an individual is in conflict with a group. Conflict may also result from the anticipation of future problems. For example,

FIGURE 15.1

The Nature of Organizational Conflict

Either too much or too little conflict can be dysfunctional for an organization. In either case, performance may be low. However, an optimal level of conflict that sparks motivation, creativity, innovation, and initiative can result in higher levels of performance.

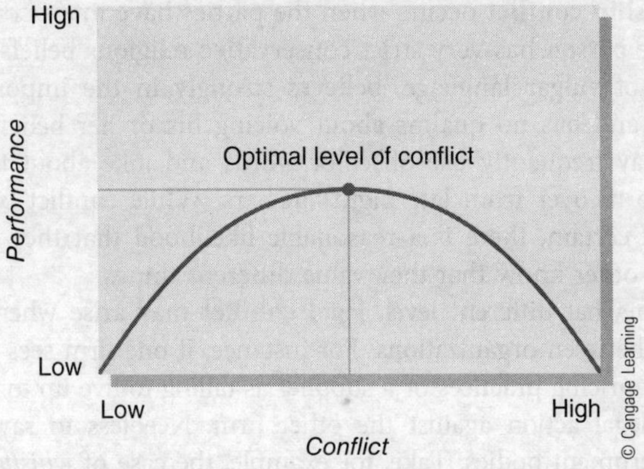

a person may behave antagonistically toward another person whom he or she expects to pose obstacles to goal achievement.[1]

Although conflict often is considered harmful and thus something to avoid, it can also have some benefits. A total absence of conflict can lead to apathy and lethargy. A moderate degree of focused conflict, on the other hand, can stimulate new ideas, promote healthy competition, and energize behavior. In some organizations, especially profit-oriented ones, many managers believe that conflict is dysfunctional. On the other hand, many managers in not-for-profit organizations often view conflict as beneficial and conducive to higher-quality decision making.[2] In many cases, the impact of conflict on performance may take the form shown in Figure 15.1. Either too little or too much conflict may result in low performance, while a moderate level of conflict may lead to higher performance.[3]

COMMON FORMS AND CAUSES OF CONFLICT

Conflict may take a number of forms. In addition, it may be caused by a wide array of factors in an organization.

Common Forms of Conflict

In general, there are three basic forms of conflict that exist within an organization. There are additional forms that can relate to conflict between organizations. **Task conflict** refers to conflict regarding the goals and content of the work. For instance, suppose one manager believes that the firm should strive to maximize profits and hence shareholder value. This individual will feel strongly that the organization should avoid social causes and instead focus its efforts on increasing revenues and/or lowering costs to the exclusion of most other activities. Another manager in the same firm, however, may believe the business should have a pronounced social agenda and be an active participant in relevant social programs. While this manager recognizes the importance of profits, he or she also sees the importance of corporate citizenship. To the extent that their differences lead to disagreements over substantive issues, it represents task conflict.

Task conflict refers to conflict regarding the goals and content of the work.

Process conflict occurs when the parties agree on the goals and content of work but disagree on how to achieve the goals and actually do the work. For example, suppose the two executives noted above actually both believe in the importance of a social agenda and support the concept of sharing corporate profits with society. Hence, they have no task conflict. However, one thinks the best way to do this is to simply give a portion of the firm's profits to one or more social causes. The other thinks the company should be more active; for instance, she or he wants the firm to sponsor ongoing building projects through Habitat for Humanity. While they share the same goals, they see different processes being the best way to achieve those goals.

Process conflict occurs when the parties agree on the goals and content of work but disagree on how to achieve the goals and actually do the work.

Relationship conflict occurs when the parties have interpersonal issues.

Relationship conflict occurs when the parties have interpersonal issues. For instance, suppose one person has very strict conservative religious beliefs. This person is offended by the use of vulgar language, believes strongly in the importance of regular church attendance, and has no qualms about voicing his or her beliefs to others. A coworker, however, may frequently use off-color words and joke about the need to sleep late on weekends to recover from late nights in bars. While conflict between these two individuals is not certain, there is a reasonable likelihood that they will at least occasionally each let the other know that they value different things.

Legal conflict may arise when there are differences in perceptions between organizations.

At a somewhat different level, **legal conflict** may arise when there are differences in perceptions between organizations. For instance, if one firm sees a competitor as engaging in predatory pricing practices or a supplier as failing to live up to the terms of a contract, it may bring legal action against the other firm. Needless to say, legal conflict may also involve government bodies. Take, for example, the case of *whistle-blowing*, which refers to the disclosure by an employee of illegal or unethical conduct on the part of an organization. By its very nature, whistle-blowing presupposes a significant level of process conflict between employee and employer; however, whistle-blowers are protected from retaliation by a variety of state and federal laws, and many companies have found themselves embroiled in legal conflicts resulting not only from activities disclosed by whistle-blowers but from actions they've taken to retaliate against them. As we saw in our chapter opener, laws—and legal conflicts—can get complicated and acrimonious, both for employers and whistle-blowers. For a good example, see the *Change* box entitled "Whistle-Blowing in the Dark" on page 407.

AP Photo/Matt Dunham

WikiLeaks founder Julian Assange is a controversial figure. He has recently been embroiled in a legal battle in Sweden, where has been accused of sexual abuse by two women there. Legal conflict is a major concern for managers and entrepreneurs everywhere.

Causes of Conflict

Interpersonal Conflict Conflict between two or more individuals is almost certain to occur in any organization, given the great variety in perceptions, goals, attitudes, and so forth among its members. William Gates, founder and CEO of Microsoft, and Kazuhiko Nishi, a former business associate from Japan, ended a long-term business relationship because of interpersonal conflict. Nishi accused Gates of becoming too political, while Gates charged that Nishi became too unpredictable and erratic in his behavior.[4]

A frequent source of interpersonal conflict in organizations is what many people call a personality clash—when two people distrust each others' motives, dislike one another, or for some other reason simply can't get along.[5] Conflict may also arise between people who have different beliefs or perceptions about some aspect of their work or their organization. For example, one manager may want the organization to require that all employees use Microsoft Office software to promote standardization. Another manager may believe a variety of software packages should be allowed in order to recognize individuality. Similarly, a male manager may disagree with his female colleague over whether the organization is guilty of discriminating against women in promotion decisions. Former Defense Secretary Donald Rumsfeld frequently had conflicts with others because of his abrasive and confrontational style.[6]

CHANGE Whistle-Blowing in the Dark

©Kesu/Shutterstock

In 2008 Joseph Burke, a former manager at the advertising firm Ogilvy & Mather (O&M), filed a complaint with the Occupational Safety and Health Administration (OSHA), which is responsible for enforcing the whistle-blower protection provisions of the Sarbannes-Oxley Act (SOX). Burke charged that, in violation of SOX, he had been fired for cooperating with a federal investigation into his employer's billing practices. The story (at least so far) may seem straightforward, but it raises two fairly obvious questions:

"Otherwise, a company that wants to do something shady could just do it in a subsidiary."

—U.S. SENATOR PATRICK LEAHY, ON THE INTENDED BREADTH OF SOX

1. Why SOX? Enacted in 2002 in the wake of corporate scandals involving such companies as Enron and Worldcom, SOX protects people who blow the whistle on firms that are registered or required to file reports with the Securities and Exchange Commission (SEC). The law states in part that covered companies "may not discharge or in any manner retaliate against an employee because he or she ... assisted in an investigation by ... a federal regulatory or law enforcement agency."
2. Why OSHA? Under the direction of the U.S. Department of Labor (DOL), OSHA is responsible for enforcing the whistle-blowing statutes of SOX. A complaint like Joseph Burke's goes first to an OSHA official, where it may be upheld or dismissed. It may then be appealed to a DOL administrative law judge (ALJ) and again appealed to the DOL's Administrative Review Board (ARB).

Burke's complaint didn't get very far: It was dismissed by OSHA, whose decision was upheld by an ALJ. As it happens, Burke had a lot of company in his frustration. In the decade after SOX became law, the OSHA-DOL process ruled in favor of just 21 corporate whistle-blowers—out of nearly 1,500 complaints. And almost 1,000 others were dismissed before reaching an ALJ. Why this overwhelming preponderance in favor of corporate defendants? Under the Bush administration, DOL lawyers issued a directive declaring that there is "no legal basis for the argument that subsidiaries of covered corporations are automatically covered" by SOX; after all, said administration lawyers, the law nowhere "expressly" says "subsidiaries." Joseph Burke, as an employee of O&M, worked for a *non-public subsidiary* of publicly traded WPP Group PLC. Thus, according to the ALJ who presided over it, his case fell short because "only employees of publicly traded companies are protected" and Burke had "not established, by a preponderance of evidence, that he is an employee of a company covered under" SOX.

Not surprisingly, many people, both in government and the legal profession, were opposed to the DOL's strict interpretation of SOX. At least one ALJ, recalling the era of unchecked corporate fraud under which the law was passed, reminded his colleagues that "subsidiaries were the vehicles through which the fraud was facilitated or accomplished" in the first place. Also adamant about the broader intent of SOX was U.S. Senator Patrick Leahy, who coauthored the law's whistle-blowing provisions. Why *wouldn't* SOX cover subsidiaries? he asked. "Otherwise, a company that wants to do something shady could just do it in a subsidiary."

As Congress eventually moved to close the loophole, OSHA took steps to enforce the whistle-blowing provisions of SOX more vigorously: In March 2010, the agency issued awards totaling more than $1.6 million, plus reinstatement, to two whistle-blowers. In April 2011, the DOL's Administrative Review Board ruled that SOX does in fact protect employees of non-publicly traded companies.

References: Jennifer Levitz, "Shielding the whistleblower," *Wall Street Journal*, December 1, 2009, http://online.wsj.com on August 6, 2012; David Nolte, "DOL Continues to Ignore and Rewrite SOX's whistleblower Law," *Fulcrum Inquiry*, September 2008, www.fulcrum.com on August 6, 2012; Squire, Sanders & Dempsey LLP, "Sarbannes-Oxley whistleblower Complaints against Non-Public Subsidiaries Routinely Dismissed by OSHA," September 2008, www.squiresanders.com on August 6, 2012; Jennifer Levitz, "whistleblowers Are Left Dangling," *Wall Street Journal*, September 4, 2008, http://online.wsj.com on August 6, 2012; Seyfarth Shaw LLP, "OSHA Steps Up Enforcement of Sarbannes-Oxley whistleblower Claims," March 24, 2010, www.seyfarth.com on April 30, 2011; Richard Renner, "ARB Holds That SOX Covers Subsidiaries," *whistleblower Protection Blog*, April 1, 2011, www.whistleblowersblog.org on August 6, 2012.

Conflict also can result from excess competitiveness among individuals. Two people vying for the same job, for example, may resort to political behavior in an effort to gain an advantage. If either competitor sees the other's behavior as inappropriate, accusations are likely to result. Even after the "winner" of the job is determined, such conflict may continue to undermine interpersonal relationships, especially if the reasons given in selecting one candidate are ambiguous or open to alternative explanation. Robert Allen had to resign as CEO of Delta Airlines because of his disagreement with other key executives over how best to reduce the carrier's costs. After he began looking for a replacement for one of his rivals without the approval of the firm's board of directors, the resultant conflict and controversy left him no choice but to leave.[7]

Intergroup Conflict Conflict between two or more organizational groups is also quite common. For example, the members of a firm's marketing group may disagree with the production group over product quality and delivery schedules. Two sales groups may disagree over how to meet sales goals, and two groups of managers may have different ideas about how best to allocate organizational resources.

At a J. C. Penney department store, conflict arose between stockroom employees and sales associates. The sales associates claimed that the stockroom employees were slow in delivering merchandise to the sales floor so that it could be priced and shelved. The stockroom employees, for their part, claimed that the sales associates were not giving them enough lead time to get the merchandise delivered and failed to understand that they had additional duties besides carrying merchandise to the sales floor.

Just like people, different departments often have different goals. Further, these goals may often be incompatible. A marketing goal of maximizing sales, achieved partially by offering many products in a wide variety of sizes, shapes, colors, and models, probably conflicts with a production goal of minimizing costs, achieved partially by long production runs of a few items. Reebok confronted this very situation. One group of managers wanted to introduce a new sportswear line as quickly as possible, while other managers wanted to expand more deliberately and cautiously. Because the two groups were not able to reconcile their differences effectively, conflict between the two factions led to quality problems and delivery delays that plagued the firm for months.

Competition for scarce resources can also lead to intergroup conflict. Most organizations—especially universities, hospitals, government agencies, and businesses in depressed industries—have limited resources. In one New England town, for example, the public works department and the library battled over funds from a federal construction grant. The Buick and Chevrolet divisions of General Motors have frequently fought over the rights to manufacture various new products developed by the company. And in some firms, such as Boeing, the corporate culture may breed competition to the point that conflict is an ever-present phenomenon.[8]

Conflict Between Organization and Environment Conflict that arises between one organization and another is called interorganizational conflict. A moderate amount of interorganizational conflict resulting from business competition is, of course, expected—but sometimes conflict becomes more extreme. For example, the owners of Jordache Enterprises, Inc., and Guess?, Inc., battled in court for years over ownership of the Guess label, allegations of design theft, and several other issues. Similarly, General Motors and Volkswagen went to court to resolve a bitter conflict that spanned more than four years. It all started when a key GM executive, José Ignacio López de Arriortúa, left for a position at Volkswagen. GM claimed that he took with him key secrets that could benefit its German competitor. After the messy departure, dozens of charges and countercharges were made by the two firms, and only a court settlement was able to put the conflict to an end. And in 2012 Apple won a lawsuit against Samsung, charging that its Korean competitor had infringed on its patent rights for technologies and designs used in the iPhone.

Conflict can also arise between an organization and other elements of its environment. For example, a business organization may conflict with a consumer group over claims it makes about its products. McDonald's faced this problem a few years ago when it published nutritional information about its products that omitted unhealthy details about fat content. A manufacturer might conflict with a governmental agency such as OSHA. For example, the firm's management may believe it is in compliance with OSHA regulations, while officials from the agency itself feel that the firm is not in compliance. Or a firm might conflict with a supplier over the quality of raw materials. The firm may think the supplier is providing inferior materials, while the supplier thinks the materials are adequate. Finally, individual managers may obviously have disagreements with groups of workers. For example, a manager may think her workers are doing poor-quality work and that they are unmotivated. The workers, on the other hand, may believe they are doing a good job and that the manager is doing a poor job of leading them.

Task Interdependence Task interdependence can also result in conflict across any of the levels noted previously. The greater the interdependence between departments, the greater the likelihood that conflict will occur. There are three major forms of interdependence: pooled, sequential, and reciprocal.[9]

Pooled interdependence represents the lowest level of interdependence, and therefore results in the least amount of conflict.

Pooled interdependence represents the lowest level of interdependence and therefore results in the least amount of conflict. Units with pooled interdependence operate with little interaction—the output of the units is pooled at the organizational level. The Gap clothing stores operate with pooled interdependence. Each store is considered a "department" by the parent corporation. Each has its own operating budget, staff, and so forth. The profits or losses from each store are "added together" at the organizational level. The stores are interdependent to the extent that the financial success or failure of one store affects the others, but they do not generally interact on a day-to-day basis.

In **sequential interdependence**, the output of one unit becomes the input for another in a sequential fashion; this creates a moderate level of interdependence and a somewhat higher potential for conflict.

In **sequential interdependence**, the output of one unit becomes the input for another in a sequential fashion. This creates a moderate level of interdependence and a somewhat higher potential for conflict. At Nissan, for example, one plant assembles engines and then ships them to a final assembly site at another plant, where the cars are completed. The plants are interdependent in that the final assembly plant must have the engines from the engine assembly plant before it can perform its primary function of producing finished automobiles. But the level of interdependence is generally one-way—the engine plant is not necessarily dependent on the final assembly plant. In this example, though, if the engine assembly plant is constantly late with its deliveries, it will quickly encounter problems with managers at the final assembly plant.

Reciprocal interdependence exists when activities flow both ways between units; this form has the highest potential for conflict.

Reciprocal interdependence exists when activities flow both ways between units. This form is clearly the most complex, and hence has the highest potential for conflict. Within a Marriott Hotel, for example, the reservations department, front-desk check-in, and housekeeping are all reciprocally interdependent. Reservations has to provide front-desk employees with information about how many guests to expect each day, and housekeeping needs to know which rooms require priority cleaning. If any of the three units does not do its job properly, the others will all be affected. And as a result, routine conflict is almost inevitable. Another example is the reciprocal interdependence between the Hollywood studios, which produce and distribute movies and TV shows, and the guilds of artists who write, direct, and act in them.

SERVICE Fixing a Customer Failure

©rangizzz/Shutterstock

A Scandinavian Airways System (SAS) flight was delayed, and the waiting passengers were getting hungry, restless, and frustrated. Because the gate agent knew that the philosophy of SAS was to do whatever it could to satisfy its customers, she thought that it would be helpful to defuse the growing anger with some snacks and beverages. She went to the catering manager, who held a higher organizational position, and asked for enough servings of coffees and biscuits to serve the passengers. The catering manager checked her records and found that this flight's food allotment had already been spent and denied the request. The gate agent could have accepted this decision but choose not to. Instead, she noticed that at the next gate was a Finnair gate agent. Because the SAS agent knew that Finnair purchased its food and drink from SAS, she asked the Finnair agent to order the food she wanted to provide to her SAS passengers. SAS's catering department was required by company policy to fill any Finnair requests, the biscuits and coffee were delivered, the SAS agent paid the Finnair agent for the food out of her petty cash account, and the passengers got a welcome snack.

Conflict between departments over meeting the customer service mission was resolved in this case by a creative solution invented by a mission-driven employee. While this gate agent's action allowed the airline to overcome a conflict between a company purchasing policy and a customer service mission and at least partially address a service failure, it illustrates the challenges that the service sector has in finding and fixing failures in meeting customer expectations for service. Being stuck in the snow is a simple illustration of a service failure, but everyone has been in a situation where the service provided was different from the service expected. This is typically a perceptual difference, as the provider may think the service was perfect but, because quality and value are determined by the customer, the customer has the final vote. These differences in perception lead to conflict between the customer and the customer facing employee representing the organization.

Such conflicts between an employee and a customer over whether a service experience met the customer's expectations are relatively common occurrences in the service industry. Since all experiences are subjectively evaluated by the customer, there is room for disagreement. When disagreements occur, the service industry considers these as service failures that should be fixed. Service organizations seek to train and reward employees to not only solicit failure information from customers but figure out how to fix the failures, as well.

Consequently, the best service providers teach their employees how to identify and resolve these differences quickly and fairly so that the customer comes back (repatronizes). These organizations have calculated the value of a lifetime customer and know that resolving a complaint in the customer's favor may cost more in the short run but will yield long-run benefits as that now-satisfied customer returns to buy again. Whether it is a Cadillac, insurance policy, or pizza, service providers balance the lifetime value of a customer against the cost of a service recovery from a failure to deliver the experience expected.

Service organizations therefore, expect their employees to find and fix any service failures that may cause conflict with customers. While this sometimes feels unfair to employees when customers complain about things that are beyond their organization's control, it is nonetheless part of the job expectations. Service organizations know that unhappy customers not only are likely never to return but are likely to find creative ways to express their anger with the perceived failure by posting complaints on websites, advising friends to avoid the company or even seeking to retaliate in some way. Thus, these companies teach their employees to observe customers for evidence of dissatisfaction and then ask if there is a problem. Quick, proactive, flexible, and fair resolution of a customer failure is the most effective way to prevent the failure escalating into the kind of major conflict that leads to a loss of future business. As was said at Wendy's, "A hamburger tossed is better than a customer lost."

Discussion Question: When you had a conflict with an organization over whether or not it had met your expectations, how was it resolved and how did you feel about it?

REACTIONS TO CONFLICT

The most common reactions to conflict are avoidance, accommodation, competition, collaboration, and compromise.[10] Whenever conflict occurs between groups or organizations, it is really the people who are in conflict. In many cases, however, people are acting as representatives of the groups to which they belong. In effect, they work together, representing their group as they strive to do their part in helping the group achieve its goals. Thus, whether the conflict is between people acting as individuals or people acting as representatives of groups, the five types of interactions can be analyzed in terms of relationships among the goals of the people or the groups they represent.

Reactions to conflict can be differentiated along two dimensions: how important each party's goals are to that party and how compatible the goals are, as shown in Figure 15.2. The importance of reaching a goal may range from very high to very low. The degree of **goal compatibility** is the extent to which the goals can be achieved simultaneously. In other words, the goals are compatible if one party can meet its goals without preventing the other from meeting its goals. The goals are incompatible if one party's meeting its goals prevents the other party from meeting its goals. The goals of different groups may be very compatible, completely incompatible, or somewhere in between.

The degree of **goal compatibility** is the extent to which the goals can be achieved simultaneously.

Avoidance **Avoidance** occurs when an interaction is relatively unimportant to either party's goals, and the goals are incompatible, as in the bottom left corner of Figure 15.2. Because the parties to the conflict are not striving toward compatible goals and the issues in question seem unimportant, the parties simply try to avoid interacting with one another. For example, one state agency may simply ignore another agency's requests for information. The requesting agency can then practice its own form of avoidance by not following up on the requests.

Avoidance occurs when an interaction is relatively unimportant to either party's goals and the goals are incompatible.

Accommodation **Accommodation** occurs when the goals are compatible but the interactions are not considered important to overall goal attainment, as in the bottom right corner of Figure 15.2. Interactions of this type may involve discussions of how the parties can accomplish their interdependent tasks with the least expenditure of time and effort. This type of interaction tends to be very friendly. For example, during a college's course scheduling period, potential conflict may exist between the marketing and management departments. Both departments offer morning classes. Which department is allocated the 9:00 a.m. time slot and which one the 10:00 a.m. time slot may not be that important to either group. Their overall goal is for the classes to be scheduled so that students will be able to take courses.

Accommodation occurs when the goals are compatible but the interactions are not considered important to overall goal attainment.

Competition **Competition** occurs when the goals are incompatible, and the interactions are important to each party's meeting its goals, as in the top left corner of Figure 15.2. If all parties are striving for a goal but only one can reach the goal, the parties will be in competition. As we noted earlier, if a competitive situation gets out of control, as when overt antagonism occurs, and there are no rules or procedures to follow, then competition can result in conflict. Sometimes, however, conflict can also change to competition if the parties agree to rules to guide the interaction and conflicting parties agree not to be hostile toward each other.

Competition occurs when the goals are incompatible and the interactions are important to each party's meeting its goals.

In one freight warehouse and storage firm, the first, second, and third shifts each sought to win the weekly productivity prize by posting the highest productivity record. Workers on the winning shift received recognition in the company newspaper. Because the issue was important to each group and the interests of the groups were incompatible, the result was competition.

FIGURE 15.2

Five Types of Reactions to Conflict

The five types of reactions to conflict stem from the relative importance of interaction to goal attainment and the degree of goal compatibility.

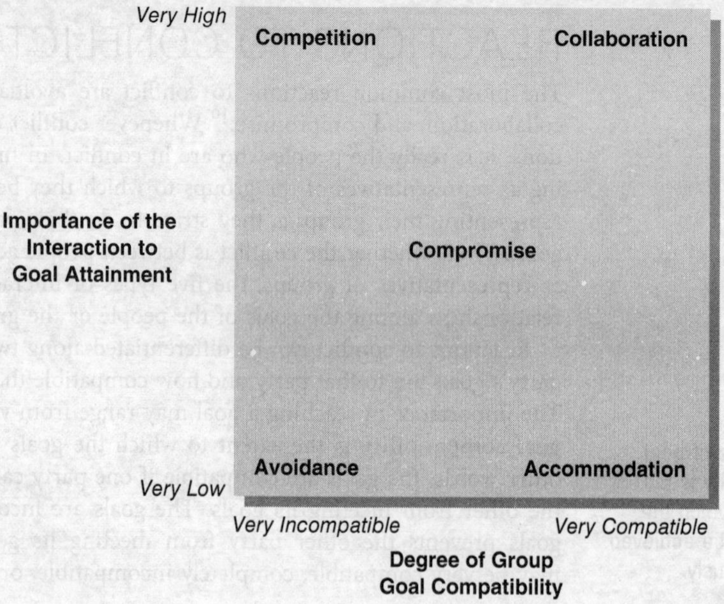

Reference: Adapted from Kenneth Thomas, "Conflict and Conflict Management," in Marvin Dunnette (Ed.), *Handbook of Industrial and Organizational Psychology* (Chicago: Rand McNally, 1976), pp. 889–935. Reprinted by permission.

The competition among the shifts encouraged each shift to produce more per week, which increased the company's output and eventually improved its overall welfare (and thus the welfare of each group). Both the company and the groups benefited from the competition because it fostered innovative and creative work methods, which further boosted productivity. After about three months, however, the competition got out of control. The competition among the groups led to poorer overall performance as the groups started to sabotage other shifts and inflate records. The competition became too important, open antagonism resulted, rules were ignored, and the competition changed to open conflict, resulting in actual decreases in work performance.[11]

Collaboration occurs when the interaction between groups is very important to goal attainment and the goals are compatible.

Collaboration **Collaboration** occurs when the interaction between groups is very important to goal attainment and the goals are compatible, as in the top right corner of Figure 15.2. In the class scheduling situation mentioned earlier, conflict may arise over which courses to teach in the first semester and which ones in the second. Both departments would like to offer specific courses in the fall. However, by discussing the issue and refocusing their overall goals to match students' needs, the marketing and economics departments can collaborate on developing a proper sequence of courses. At first glance, this may seem to be simple interaction in which the parties participate jointly in activities to accomplish goals after agreeing on the goals and their importance. In many situations, however, it is no easy matter to agree on goals, their importance, and especially the means for achieving them. In a collaborative interaction, goals may differ but be compatible. Parties to a conflict may initially have difficulty working out the ways in which all can achieve their goals. However, because the interactions are important to goal attainment, the parties are willing to continue to work together to achieve the goals. Collaborative relationships can lead to new and innovative ideas and solutions to differences among the parties.

Compromise is sometimes used to resolve conflict and disagreement. President Barack Obama is shown here discussing issues with Senate Minority Leader Mitch McConnell. The leadership of the Republican and Democratic parties often compromise on issues about which they cannot reach full agreement.

Compromise **Compromise** occurs when the interactions are moderately important to goal attainment and the goals are neither completely compatible nor completely incompatible. In a compromise situation, parties interact with others striving to achieve goals, but they may not aggressively pursue goal attainment in either a competitive or collaborative manner because the interactions are not that important to goal attainment. On the other hand, the parties may neither avoid one another nor be accommodating because the interactions are somewhat important. Often each party gives up something, but because the interactions are only moderately important, they do not regret what they have given up.

Compromise occurs when the interactions are moderately important to goal attainment and the goals are neither completely compatible nor completely incompatible.

Contract negotiations between union and management are usually examples of compromise. Each side brings numerous issues of varying importance to the bargaining table. The two sides frequently give and take on the issues through rounds of offers and counteroffers. The complexity of such negotiations increases as negotiations spread to multiple plants in different countries. Agreements between management and labor in a plant in the United States may be unacceptable to either or both parties in Canada. Weeks of negotiations ending in numerous compromises usually result in a contract agreement between the union and management.

In summary, when groups are in conflict, they may react in several different ways. If the goals of the parties are very compatible, the parties may engage in mutually supportive interactions—that is, collaboration or accommodation. If the goals are very incompatible, each may attempt to foster its own success at the expense of the other, engaging in competition or avoidance.

MANAGING CONFLICT

Managers must know when to stimulate conflict and when to resolve it if they are to avoid its potentially disruptive effects.[12] As we noted earlier, too little conflict and too much conflict are each dysfunctional in their own ways. Hence, if there is too little conflict, managers many need to stimulate a moderate degree of conflict. If conflict is excessive, however, it may need to be reduced. Figure 15.3 introduces some of the basic techniques for stimulating and resolving conflict.

Stimulating Conflict

A complete absence of conflict may indicate that the organization is stagnant and that employees are content with the status quo. It may also suggest that work groups are not motivated to challenge traditional and well-accepted ideas. **Conflict stimulation** is the creation and constructive use of conflict by a manager. Its purpose is to bring about situations in which differences of opinion are exposed for examination by all.

Conflict stimulation is the creation and constructive use of conflict by a manager.

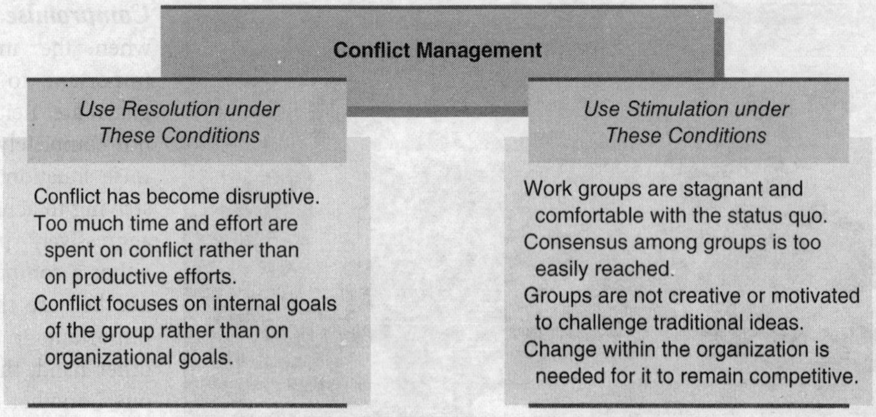

FIGURE 15.3

Conflict Management Alternatives

Conflict management may involve resolution or stimulation of conflict, depending on the situation.

For example, if competing organizations are making significant changes in products, markets, or technologies, it may be time for a manager to stimulate innovation and creativity by challenging the status quo. Conflict may give employees the motivation and opportunity to reveal differences of opinion that they previously kept to themselves. When all parties to the conflict are interested enough in an issue to challenge other groups, they often expose their hidden doubts or opinions. These in turn allow the parties to get to the heart of the matter and often to develop unique solutions to the problem. Indeed, the interactions may lead the groups to recognize that a problem in fact does exist. Conflict, then, can be a catalyst for creativity and change in an organization.

Several methods can be used to stimulate conflict under controlled conditions. These include altering the physical location of groups to stimulate more interactions, forcing more resource sharing, and implementing other changes in relationships among groups. In addition, training programs can be used to increase employee awareness of potential problems in group decision making and group interactions. Adopting the role of "devil's advocate" in discussion sessions is another way to stimulate conflict among groups. In this role, a manager challenges the prevailing consensus to ensure that all alternatives have been critically appraised and analyzed. Although this role is often unpopular, employing it is a good way to stimulate constructive conflict.

Conflict Resolution

Conflict resolution is a managed effort to reduce or eliminate harmful conflict.

When a potentially harmful conflict situation exists, however, a manager needs to engage in **conflict resolution**. Conflict needs to be resolved when it causes major disruptions in the organization and absorbs time and effort that could be used more productively. Conflict should also be resolved when its focus is on the group's internal goals rather than on organizational goals.

When attempting to resolve conflict, managers should first attempt to determine the source of the conflict. If the source of destructive conflict is a particular person or two, it might be appropriate to alter the membership of one or both groups. If the conflict is due to differences in goals, perceptions of the difficulty of goal attainment, or the importance of the goals to the conflicting parties, then the manager can attempt to move the conflicting parties into one of the five types of reactions to conflict, depending on the nature of the conflicting parties.

To foster collaboration, it might be appropriate to try to help people see that their goals are really not as different as they seem to be. The manager can help groups view

A **superordinate goal** is a goal of the overall organization and is more important to the well-being of the organization and its members than the more specific goals of the conflicting parties.

their goals as part of a **superordinate goal** to which the goals of both conflicting parties can contribute. A superordinate goal is a goal of the overall organization and is more important to the well-being of the organization and its members than the more specific goals of the conflicting parties. If the goals are not really that important and are very incompatible, the manager may need to develop ways to help the conflicting parties avoid each other. Similarly, accommodation, competition, or compromise might be appropriate for the conflicting parties.

Using Structure to Manage Conflict

Beyond the methods noted above, managers can also rely heavily on elements of organization structure to manage conflict. Among the more common methods are the hierarchy, rules and procedures, liaison roles, and task forces.

The Managerial Hierarchy Organizations that use the hierarchy to manage conflict place one manager in charge of people, groups, or departments in conflict. In Walmart distribution centers, major activities include receiving and unloading bulk shipments from railroad cars and loading other shipments onto trucks for distribution to retail outlets. The two groups (receiving and shipping) are interdependent and may experience conflict in that they share the loading docks and some equipment. To ensure coordination and minimize conflict, one manager is in charge of the whole operation.

Rules and Procedures Routine conflict management can be handled via rules and standard procedures. In the Walmart distribution center, an outgoing truck shipment has priority over an incoming rail shipment. Thus, when trucks are to be loaded, the shipping unit is given access to all of the center's auxiliary forklifts. This priority is specifically stated in a rule. But as useful as rules and procedures often are in routine situations, they are not particularly effective when coordination problems and conflict are complex or unusual.

Liaison Roles We introduced the liaison role of management in Chapter 1. As a device for managing conflict, a manager in a liaison role coordinates activities, acting as a common point of contact. This individual may not have any formal authority over the groups but instead simply facilitates the flow of information between parties. Two engineering groups working on component systems for a large project might interact through a liaison. The liaison maintains familiarity with each group as well as with the overall project. She can answer questions and otherwise serve to integrate the activities of all the groups. Since the groups do not directly interact with one another, there is less chance of conflict.

Task Forces A task force may be created when the need for conflict management is acute. When interdependence is complex and several groups and/or individuals are involved, a single liaison person may not be sufficient. Instead, a task force might be assembled by drawing one representative from each group. The conflict management function is thus spread across several individuals, each of whom has special information about one of the groups involved. When the project is completed, task force members return to their original positions. For example, a college overhauling its degree requirements might establish a task force made up of representatives from each department affected by the change. Each person retains her or his regular departmental affiliation and duties but also serves on the special task force. After the new requirements are agreed on, the task force is dissolved.

Team-building activities are intended to enhance the effectiveness and satisfaction of individuals who work in groups or teams and to promote overall group effectiveness; they should lead to a decrease in conflict among members of the team.

In **survey feedback**, each employee responds to a questionnaire intended to measure perceptions and attitudes (for example, satisfaction and supervisory style).

Using Interpersonal Techniques to Manage Conflict

There are also several techniques that focus on interpersonal processes that can be used to manage conflict. These often fall under the heading of organization development, discussed in Chapter 19. Consequently, we mention only a few of these here.

Team Building **Team-building activities** are intended to enhance the effectiveness and satisfaction of individuals who work in groups or teams and to promote overall group effectiveness; they should lead to a decrease in conflict among members of the team. Given the widespread use of teams today, these activities have taken on increased importance. Caterpillar used team building as one method for changing the working relationships between workers and supervisors from confrontational to cooperative. An interesting approach to team building involves having executive teams participate in group cooking classes to teach them the importance of interdependence and coordination.[13]

Survey Feedback In **survey feedback**, each employee responds to a questionnaire intended to measure perceptions and attitudes (for example, satisfaction and supervisory style). Everyone involved, including the supervisor, receives the results of the survey. The aim of this approach is usually to change the behavior of supervisors by showing them how their subordinates view them. After the feedback has been provided, workshops may be conducted to evaluate results and suggest constructive changes.

David Madison/Ivy/Corbis

Team building is a common method used by organizations to help overcome conflict and promote collaboration among employees. Outward Bound was a pioneer in developing unique and challenging outdoor exercises for teams. The idea is that by spending time together in demanding situations and having to rely on each other to accomplish their goals, team members will develop improved working relationships. That is, trust and respect developed during the outdoors exercises will (in theory, at least) carry over back at work. This group of professionals has just gone through team-building exercises as part of a hiking and camping excursion in Vermont.

Third-Party Peacemaking A somewhat more extreme form of interpersonal conflict management is **third-party peacemaking**, which is most often used when substantial conflict exists within the organization. Third-party peacemaking can be appropriate on the individual, group, or organization level. A third party, usually a trained external facilitator, uses a variety of mediation or negotiation techniques to resolve problems or conflicts between individuals or groups.

Third-party peacemaking, primarily used to address extreme conflict, involves bringing in an outsider to facilitate conflict resolution.

Negotiated Conflict Management

Finally, conflict solutions are sometimes negotiated in advance. For instance, a labor agreement often spells out in detail how union members must report a grievance, how management must respond, and how the dispute will be resolved. Conflict is thus avoided by preestablishing exactly how it will be addressed. The following discussion of negotiation also has other implications for conflict management.

NEGOTIATION IN ORGANIZATIONS

Negotiation is the process in which two or more parties (people or groups) reach agreement on an issue even though they have different preferences regarding that issue. In its simplest form the parties involved may be two individuals who are trying to decide who will pay for lunch. A little more complexity is involved when two people, such as an employee and manager, sit down to decide on personal performance goals for the next year against which the employee's performance will be measured. Even more complex are the negotiations that take place between labor unions and the management of a company or between two companies as they negotiate the terms of a joint venture. The key issues in such negotiations are that at least two parties are involved, their preferences are different, and they need to reach agreement.

Negotiation is the process in which two or more parties (people or groups) reach agreement on an issue even though they have different preferences regarding that issue.

Approaches to Negotiation

Interest in negotiation has grown steadily in recent years.[14] Four primary approaches to negotiation have dominated this study: individual differences, situational characteristics, game theory, and cognitive approaches. Each of these is briefly described in the following sections.

Individual Differences Early psychological approaches concentrated on the personality traits of the negotiators.[15] Traits investigated have included demographic characteristics and personality variables. Demographic characteristics have included age, gender, and race, among others. Personality variables have included risk taking, locus of control, tolerance for ambiguity, self-esteem, authoritarianism, and Machiavellianism. The assumption of this type of research was that the key to successful negotiation was selecting the right person to do the negotiating, one who had the appropriate demographic characteristics or personality. This assumption seemed to make sense because negotiation is such a personal and interactive process. However, the research rarely showed the positive results expected because situational variables negated the effects of the individual differences.[16]

Situational Characteristics Situational characteristics are the context within which negotiation takes place. They include such things as the types of communication between negotiators, the potential outcomes of the negotiation, the relative power of the parties (both positional and personal), the time frame available for negotiation, the number of people representing each side, and the presence of other parties. Some of this research

Jochen Tack/Alamy

Negotiation is a process for reaching an agreement between two or more parties. While more dramatic than typical business negotiations, hostage negotiations are a vivid example. This is not a real crime scene, but instead a training session to help a SWAT negotiator refine his negotiation skills. Similarly, business leaders in charge of sensitive negotiations often undergo training as well.

has contributed to our understanding of the negotiation process. However, the shortcomings of the situational approach are similar to those of the individual characteristics approach. Many situational characteristics are external to the negotiators and beyond their control. Often the negotiators cannot change their relative power positions or the setting within which the negotiation occurs. So, although we have learned a lot from research on the situational issues, we still need to learn much more about the process.

Game theory was developed by economists using mathematical models to predict the outcome of negotiation situations.

Game Theory Game theory was developed by economists using mathematical models to predict the outcome of negotiation situations (as illustrated in the Academy Award–winning movie *A Beautiful Mind*). It requires that every alternative and outcome be analyzed with probabilities and numerical outcomes reflecting the preferences for each outcome. In addition, the order in which different parties can make choices and every possible move are predicted, along with associated preferences for outcomes. The outcomes of this approach are exactly what negotiators want: A predictive model of how negotiation should be conducted. One major drawback is that it requires the ability to describe all possible options and outcomes for every possible move in every situation before the negotiation starts. This is often very tedious, if possible at all. Another problem is that this theory assumes that negotiators are rational at all times. Other research in negotiation has shown that negotiators often do not act rationally. Therefore, this approach, although elegant in its prescriptions, is usually unworkable in a real negotiation situation.

Cognitive Approaches The fourth approach is the cognitive approach, which recognizes that negotiators often depart from perfect rationality during negotiation; it tries to predict how and when negotiators will make these departures. Howard Raiffa's decision analytic approach focuses on providing advice to negotiators actively involved in negotiation.[17] Bazerman and Neale have added to Raiffa's work by specifying eight ways in which negotiators systematically deviate from rationality.[18] The types of deviations they describe include escalation of commitment to a previously selected course of action, overreliance on readily available information, assuming that the negotiations can produce fixed-sum outcomes, and anchoring negotiation in irrelevant information. These cognitive approaches have advanced the study of negotiation a long way beyond the early individual and situational approaches. Negotiators can use them to attempt to predict in advance how the negotiation might take place.

Win-Win Negotiation

In addition to the approaches to negotiation previously described, a group of approaches proposed by consultants and advisors is meant to give negotiators a specific model to use in carrying out difficult negotiations. One of the best of these is the "Win-Win Negotiator."[19] The Win-Win approach does not treat negotiation as a game in which there are winners and losers. Instead, it approaches negotiation as an opportunity for both sides to be winners, to get what they want out of the agreement. The focus is on both parties' reaching agreement such that both are committed to fulfilling their own end of the agreement and to returning for more agreements in the future. In other words, both parties want to have their needs satisfied. In addition, this approach does not advocate either a "tough guy" or a "nice guy" approach to negotiation, both of which are popular in the literature. It assumes that both parties work together to find ways to satisfy both parties at the same time.

The **PRAM model** is four-step approach to negotiation that proposes that proper planning, building relationships, getting agreements, and maintaining the relationships are the key steps to successful negotiation.

The Win-Win approach is a four-step approach illustrated in the **PRAM model** shown in Figure 15.4. The PRAM four-step approach proposes that proper planning, building relationships, getting agreements, and maintaining the relationships are the key steps to successful negotiation.

Planning requires that each negotiator set his or her own goals, anticipate the goals of the other, determine areas of probable agreement, and develop strategies for reconciling areas of probable disagreement.

Developing Win-Win *relationships* requires that negotiators plan activities that enable positive personal relationships to develop, cultivate a sense of mutual trust, and allow

FIGURE 15.4

The Pram Model of Negotiation

The PRAM model shows the four steps in setting up negotiation so that both parties win.

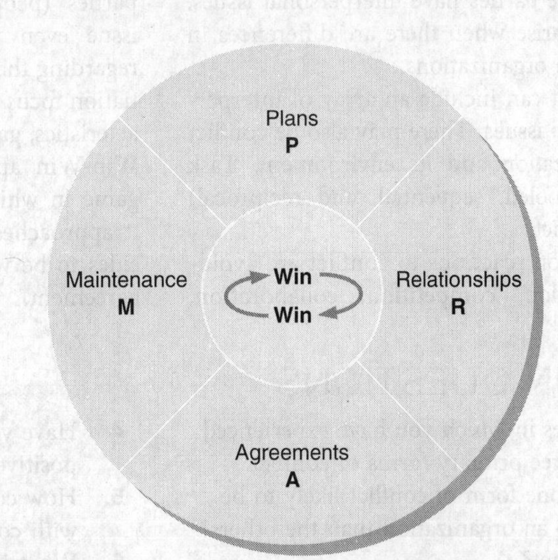

Reference: Brian G. Long, Ph.D., and Ross R. Reck, Ph.D., *The Win-Win Negotiatior: How to Negotiate Favorable Agreements That Last*. Copyright © 1985, 1987 by Brian G. Long and Ross R. Reck. Reprinted with permission of Ross R. Reck, Ph.D.

relationships to develop fully before discussing business in earnest. The development of trust between the parties is probably the single most important key to success in negotiation.

Forming Win-Win *agreements* requires that each party confirm the other party's goals, verify areas of agreement, propose and consider positive solutions to reconcile areas of disagreement, and jointly resolve any remaining differences. The key in reaching agreement is to realize that both parties share many goals. The number of areas of disagreement is usually small.

Finally, Win-Win *maintenance* entails providing meaningful feedback based on performance, each of the parties holding up an end of the agreement, keeping in contact, and reaffirming trust between the parties. The assumption is that both parties want to keep the relationship going so that future mutually beneficial transactions can occur. Both parties must uphold their ends of the agreement and do what they said they would do. Finally, keeping in touch is as easy as making a telephone call or meeting for lunch.

SYNOPSIS

Conflict is a process resulting in the perceptions of two parties that they are working in opposition to each other in ways that result in feelings of discomfort and/or animosity. Although conflict often is considered harmful, and thus something to avoid, it can also have some benefits.

There are three basic forms of conflict that exist within an organization. Task conflict refers to conflict regarding the goals and content of the work. Process conflict occurs when the parties agree on the goals and content of work but disagree on how to achieve the goals and actually do the work. Relationship conflict occurs when the parties have interpersonal issues. Legal conflict may arise when there are differences in perceptions between organizations.

Causes of conflict can include an array of interpersonal and intergroup issues. There may also be conflict between an organization and its environment. Task interdependence (pooled, sequential, and reciprocal) can also cause conflict.

The most common reactions to conflict are avoidance, accommodation, competition, collaboration, and compromise. Reactions to conflict can be differentiated along two dimensions: how important each party's goals are to that party and how compatible the goals are.

Managers must know when to stimulate conflict and when to resolve it if they are to avoid its potentially disruptive effects. There are a variety of methods that can be used to either stimulate or resolve conflict. Organization structure and various interpersonal methods may also be useful in managing conflict. Conflict resolution may also be negotiated in advance.

Negotiation is the process in which two or more parties (people or groups) reach agreement on an issue even though they have different preferences regarding that issue. Four primary approaches to negotiation focus on individual differences, situational characteristics, game theory, and cognitive approaches. The Win-Win approach does not treat negotiation as a game in which there are winners and losers. Instead, it approaches negotiation as an opportunity for both sides to be winners, to get what they want out of the agreement.

DISCUSSION QUESTIONS

1. Recall instances in which you have experienced each of the three primary forms of conflict.
2. In general, is one form of conflict likely to be more costly to an organization than the others? Why or why not?
3. Are certain forms of conflict more likely than others to be associated with each level of interdependence? In what way?
4. Have you ever been a party to conflict that had positive benefits? What were the details?
5. How comfortable are you personally in dealing with conflict?
6. What is the primary risk of trying to stimulate moderate levels of conflict in a situation characterized by lethargy?

7. Relate the various methods of resolving conflict to the primary forms of conflict. That is, for example, what conflict resolution methods are most likely to be useful in dealing with task conflict?
8. Describe various ways in which conflict and negotiations may be related.
9. Recall an instance in which you negotiated something and describe it in terms of the discussion of negotiation in this chapter.
10. Why don't people engaged in all negotiation situations try to adopt a Win-Win mentality?

HOW DO YOU SEE IT?

Food for Managerial Thought (Third Course)

"We're always hiring. And we're always firing."

—SCOTT LAWTON, COO OF BARCELONA RESTAURANT GROUP

Throughout the video for this case, Scott Lawton, COO of Barcelona Restaurant Group,* talks about the company's approach to human resources (HR), which is, he says, "the biggest thing we do." At the very end of the video, the interviewer asks him if he would hire himself for a managerial position at Barcelona. "That's a good question. I think I would," he replies, but after a moment's hesitation, he reconsiders his initial response. "Well, I don't know," he says. "I don't know if I would have the floor presence that I demand out of my managers. I'm not sure that I'd be a great floor manager for Barcelona."

What does a floor manager do? Typically, the floor manager in a restaurant is a jack of all trades. He or she must train and schedule employees and ensure operational efficiency by managing employees and controlling inventories and cash. Above all, however, a floor manager is responsible for customer service—making sure that customers come first and that every employee understands that dictum. And that's why, according to Lawton, HR—particularly, the approach to hiring people—is critical at Barcelona: "For any company that's involved in customer service," he says, "hav[ing] the right people in front of your customers is the most important thing you can do."

So, why would Lawton—at least in his own opinion—not be the right person to hire as a floor manager at one of his own restaurants? Perhaps it's something in his perception of his personality. Training people to do certain jobs is always a major task in HR management, but Lawton is skeptical about training as an effective method of developing exactly the right people for Barcelona. "We can train people all day," he explains, "but we can't find happy people with good attitudes. We can't train that into people. Either they are or they aren't.... You can't train people to be enthusiastic, nice, fun, great people.

"You have to *hire* that," he argues, and the Barcelona approach to finding the right people to deliver the required level of customer service seems to be hiring new employees until the person-job fit clicks. And, of course, firing employees who don't fit. "We're always hiring," says Lawton. "And we're always firing." Very few managers, he reports, actually quit Barcelona, but he notes that, in his three years with the company, "we've turned over 60-70 percent of management.... And that is because we're not afraid to let people go. We demand a certain level of quality, and we're continually raising the bar on what our expectations are."

And not only does the bar go up, but employee agility often goes down. "This is a high-burnout business," explains Lawton. "... Somebody who is great a year ago may not be great this year." Take DJ, whom we never meet but whose name comes up in a managers' meeting. After reminding managers that they're "famous for friendly service," Lawton alludes to some reports that he's received about DJ's performance: "I'm getting some signs," he says, that customers "did not feel welcome by DJ. They love Barcelona, but they said [DJ's attitude] just didn't feel like Barcelona." DJ's manager agrees that customer perceptions were probably accurate at the time but hastens to add that, on other occasions, "I saw him hustling and doing a good job."

"Well, let's put it another away," interjects cofounder and CEO Andy Pforzheimer. "DJ *can* be good. Right now, he's not. So have somebody else there or make him real good real fast."

In any case, when it comes to upgrading the work force through firing and hiring, there's always the fallback position of paring away the bottom 20 percent. "We're always hiring," Lawton tells his managers, because "we're always culling out the bottom 20 percent. There's always somebody better out there than our worst servers." He himself conducts hiring interviews every day and advises his managers to do the same: "That's how you get better. You hire your way out of your problems." In the last stage of his own hiring process, explains Lawton, he asks prospective employees to "pretend that you've worked for us for six months. I want to see who you are. I want to see you commanding the floor, making friends with the guests, talking to the staff. I want to see who you'd be for me."

CASE QUESTIONS

1. Would you be enthusiastic, nice, and fun if you worked for Barcelona? Why or why not?
2. Focusing on the issue that's central to this video—HR strategies and processes—explain why *conflict* is liable to arise at Barcelona. **Judging from the video**, what types of *reactions to conflict—avoidance, accommodation, competition, collaboration*, or *compromise*—are *most* likely to be evident, whether at individual outlets or within the managerial ranks?
3. Consider your answer to question 2. Does top management at Barcelona tend to depend more on *stimulating conflict* or on *conflict resolution*? Do you approve of the preference, or do you think that the other approach—or some combination of the two—would be more effective? In other words, how would you go about achieving the *optimal level of conflict* summarized in Figure 15.1?
4. For what reasons might *intergroup conflict* develop at Barcelona? [*Hint:* Recall the managers' meeting excerpted in *Video Case 5*.] Be as specific as you can in describing the nature of this potential conflict.
5. Here's an excerpt from the kind of advertising that Scott Lawton talks about in the video:[†]

Extremely Busy Restaurants in Connecticut's Fairfield County are Looking for a General Manager

Job Responsibilities

Responsibilities include but are not limited to the following:

- Oversee management and operations at your locations.
- Execute company-wide strategic plans & implement processes to achieve them.
- Ensure our high standards of guest service are upheld.
- Develop, coach, mentor and evaluate performance of the management staff.
- Execute operating procedures to ensure uniform performance throughout the company.
- Drive Sales, Profitability and Guest Satisfaction results in the market.

Given what you know about Barcelona's HR policies, do you think that you have the right personality for a job like this one? Do you have, or would you be interested in developing, the skills for such a job? What reservations might you have about the job? (*Note:* The starting salary for a General Manager at Barcelona is "$100,000 +++.")

ADDITIONAL SOURCES

Valerie Schroth, "Success Stories: Barcelona Finds the Formula," *Connecticut Magazine*, January 2012, www.connecticutmag.com on June 27, 2012; Barcelona Restaurant Group, "About Us" (2012), www.barcelonawinebar.com on June 27, 2012; James Cooper, "Chef Interview: Andrew Pforzheimer of the Barcelona Restaurant Group," *Examiner.com*, January 27, 2010, www.examiner.com on June 27, 2012.

*Barcelona is also the subject of *Video Case 5*, which introduces us to the company's top managers and their philosophy for managing employees ("We attempt to hire grownups"), and *Video Case 6*, which discusses their strategies for motivating employees and gathering information about the level of customer service at Barcelona outlets.

[†]"General Manager/Director of Food & Beverage," *careerbuilder.com*, September 4, 2012, www.careerbuilder.com on September 29, 2012.

EXPERIENCING ORGANIZATIONAL BEHAVIOR

Learning Negotiation Skills

Purpose This exercise will help you learn more about how to prepare for and participate in a negotiation.

Format You will participate in this exercise with one of your classmates. The two of you will attempt to negotiate an understanding regarding a hypothetical assignment.

Procedure Assume that your instructor has assigned the two of you an out-of-class project. The hypothetical project consists of the following activities:

1. You are to interview a total of five managers in your local community. Each interview should last about an hour. The purpose of the interviews is to learn more about the nature and substance of managerial work. You will ask each manager a set of predetermined questions about their jobs.
2. The results of the interviews are to be synthesized into a single discussion of what managers do. Detailed analyses of the responses to each question are to be carefully studied and integrated into a single overall description.
3. The description is to be written up in the form of a paper of approximately ten pages. In addition to its content, issues such as language, grammar, spelling, and format will all be considered when the paper is graded.
4. Finally, the content of the paper must also be organized for an in-class presentation. The presentation needs to be of professional quality, make use of PowerPoint slides and other visual aids, and be formally presented to a group of visiting executives.
5. Your instructor is indifferent as to how the assignment is completed. That is, you and your partner can divide the work up in any way that you see fit. However, you will each receive the same overall grade on the project regardless of what you each do.

Now, you and your partner should negotiate what you will each do. Be as specific as possible when deciding how to divide up the work involved in completing the project.

Follow-Up Questions

1. What factors did you consider as you reached agreement on how to divide up the work?
2. How comfortable were you with the final division of labor?
3. If this were a real assignment, what concerns would you have about reaching a successful outcome? What steps, if any, might you use to offset those concerns?

BUILDING MANAGERIAL SKILLS

Exercise Overview A manager's interpersonal skills are her or his ability to understand how to motivate individuals and groups. Clearly, then, interpersonal skills play a major role in determining how well a manager can interact with others in a group setting. This exercise will allow you to practice your interpersonal skills in relation to just such a setting.

Exercise Background You have just been transferred to a new position supervising a group of five employees. The business you work for is fairly small and has few rules and regulations. Unfortunately, the lack of rules and regulations is creating a problem that you must now address.

Specifically, two of the group members are nonsmokers. They are becoming increasingly more vocal about the fact that two other members of the group smoke at work. These two workers feel that the secondary smoke in the workplace is endangering their health and want to establish a no-smoking policy like those of many large businesses today.

The two smokers, however, argue that since the firm did not have such a policy when they started working there, it would be unfair to impose such a policy now. One of them, in particular, says that he turned down an attractive job with another company because he wanted to work in a place where he could smoke.

The fifth worker is also a nonsmoker but says that she doesn't care if others smoke. Her husband smokes at home anyway, she says, so she is used to being around smokers. You suspect that if the two vocal nonsmokers are not appeased, they may leave. At the same time, you also think that the two smokers will leave if you mandate a no-smoking policy. All five workers do good work, and you do not want any of them to leave.

Exercise Task With this information as context, do the following:

1. Explain the nature of the conflict that exists in this work group.
2. Develop a course of action for dealing with the situation.

SELF-ASSESSMENT EXERCISE

What Do You Do When Interests Conflict?

This exercise is designed to help you assess your level of competency in managing conflict. If you have a job, consider that your work; if you're a student, apply this exercise to your school work.

The twenty-four statements below reflect approaches that people can take toward managing workplace conflict. Using the following scale, indicate the extent to which, in your opinion, each statement is true of you.

1. Strongly disagree
2. Disagree
3. Slightly disagree
4. Slightly agree
5. Agree
6. Strongly agree

When I see someone doing something that needs correcting:

_______1. I avoid making personal accusations and attributing self-serving motives to the other person.

_______2. I present my concerns as my problems.

_______3. I succinctly describe problems in terms of the behavior that occurred, its consequences, and my feelings about it.

_______4. I specify the expectations and standards that have been violated.

_______5. I make a specific request, detailing a more acceptable solution.

_______6. I persist in explaining my point of view until it is understood by the other person.

_______7. I encourage two-way interaction by inviting the respondent to express his or her perspective and to ask questions.

_______8. I approach multiple concerns incrementally, starting with the simple and easy issues and then progressing to those that are more complex and difficult.

When someone complains about something that I've done:

_______9. I look for our common areas of agreement.

_______10. I show genuine concern and interest, even when I disagree.

_______11. I avoid justifying my actions and becoming defensive.

_______12. I seek additional information by asking questions that provide specific and descriptive information.

_______13. I focus on one issue at a time.

_______14. I find some aspects of the complaint with which I can agree.

_______15. I ask the other person to suggest more acceptable actions.

_______16. I reach agreement on a remedial plan of action.

When two other people are in conflict and I'm the mediator:

_______17. I acknowledge that conflict exists and treat it as serious and important.

_______18. I help to create an agenda for a problem-solving meeting by identifying the issues to be discussed, one at a time.

_______19. I don't take sides, but remain neutral.

_______20. I help focus the discussion on the impact of the conflict on work performance.

_______21. I keep the interaction focused on problems instead of personalities.

_______22. I make certain that neither party dominates the conversation.

_______23. I help the parties generate multiple alternatives.

_______24. I help the parties find areas on which they agree.

How to score: Add up the numbers that you put down in the left-hand column. The maximum possible score is 144. You should compare your score with the scores of other students in the class and with those of 1,500 real-world managers and business school students:

Score	Ranking
113.20	mean
122 or above	top quartile
114–121	second quartile
105–113	third quartile
104 or below	bottom quartile

Reference: Whetten, David A; Cameron, Kim S., *Developing Management Skills*, 7th Edition, © 2007. pp. 378–79, 438–39. Reprinted by permission of Pearson Education, Inc., Upper Saddle River, NJ.

CHAPTER 16

Foundations of Organization Structure

Chapter Outline

- **The Nature of Organization Structure**
- **Classic Views of Structure**
- **Structural Configuration**
- **Structure and Operations**
- **Responsibility and Authority**

Chapter Learning Objectives

After studying this chapter, you should be able to:

1. **Define organization structure and discuss its purpose.**
2. **Describe the classic views of organization structure.**
3. **Describe structural configuration and summarize its four basic dimensions.**
4. **Discuss two structural policies that affect operations.**
5. **Explain the dual concepts of authority and responsibility.**

Delayering as a Defense Mechanism

"I know what it is that we need to do."

—Anglo American CEO Cynthia Carroll

In October 2009, Anglo American PLC, the world's fourth-largest diversified mining company, announced that it was *delayering*—eliminating a layer of organizational structure. Analysis of its "operating model," reported the company (referring to itself as "the Group"), had resulted in "an organizational simplification and delayering across the Group, with the divisional co-ordinating level across … Coal and Ferrous Metals being removed." Previously, the company had been organized into two global divisions—Coal and Ferrous Metals, each with its own CEO, both of whom reported directly to the CEO of Anglo American. Below the divisional level were Anglo's various global business operations, each dealing with a different commodity (e.g., coal, platinum, iron ore) and each headed by its own CEO and functional support staff. The CEOs of these units reported directly to the CEOs of their respective divisions.

As a result of "simplification and delayering," these businesses were reorganized into seven "commodity business units" (BUs), each of which is now "profit accountable"—that is, responsible for its own performance. The major criteria for this reorganization were geography and asset status. The platinum unit, for example, is headquartered in South Africa (which is also home to the parent company), the copper unit in Chile, and the metallurgical-coal unit in Australia.

In addition, Anglo now maintains BUs only for its *core assets*—operations that are essential to producing revenue, cash flow, or profit. Going hand in hand with the company's delayering strategy is thus a strategy to divest itself of its non-core assets: Having already shed its interests in gold and aluminum, Anglo also intends to sell its holdings in such commodities as phosphates and zinc and a company that manufactures steel products for the construction industry. The decision to delayer and divest, says chairman Sir John Parker, "represents an important step in creating a more streamlined business, with enhanced focus on operational effectiveness…. We have a truly world-class portfolio of assets, and these initiatives further improve our ability to deliver its full potential."

Anglo American CEO Cynthia Carroll discusses Anglo American's culture, strategy and the resource industry as well as her leadership style and the challenges she has faced as a leading businesswoman, at the GIBS (Gordon Institute of Business Science) business school in Illovo, Johannesburg, South Africa on 27 October 2010.

Streamlining and efficiency, of course, are common and logical reasons for restructuring an organization, but if we look a little more closely at the recent history of Anglo American, we will find that these strategies also play a key role in a much more complicated game of corporate competition and, perhaps, even survival.

The year 2009 had already been a hectic one for Anglo. In February, CEO Cynthia Carroll admitted that the organization, like many companies, was starting to feel the impact of the global recession: "The breadth and severity of the global downturn [is] difficult to understate," she said in announcing that Anglo would cut 19,000 jobs—about a tenth of its workforce—and suspend dividend payments accrued in 2008. Carroll also reported that earnings per share had fallen from $4.40 to $4.36 and that operating profit had dropped by 0.3 percent. The slippage was hardly catastrophic, but analysts had predicted an increase of 13 percent in earnings per share and had expected operating profit to at least remain flat.

Carroll's appointment as CEO in 2007 had already been a shock to many people in what the *Times of London* calls "an irredeemably macho industry." Not only was she not a man, she was neither a mining-industry veteran nor a South African (she is American). When her appointment was announced, Anglo's stock immediately dropped $0.80 per share. The dice, observed the *Times*, were "probably loaded against her from the start," and to make her job even more difficult, she was soon forced to embark upon a $2 billion efficiency program involving a number of changes guaranteed to rile the old guard of the 91-year-old company. Her whirlwind campaign to cut costs by $450 million in the first half of 2009 earned her the nickname "Cyclone Cynthia," but many analysts and investors were unimpressed by the savings: Because the entire industry was struggling with high costs during the recession, Carroll's cost cutting was seen as little more than the logical and obvious strategy to pursue.

Then, in June 2009, the Swiss-British mining company Xstrata proposed a merger with Anglo—a move that would create a $68 billion firm to compete with industry giants such as BHP Billiton, Vale, and Rio Tinto. Xstrata said in a statement that it was seeking "a merger of equals that would realize significant value for both companies' shareholders" and cited "substantial operational synergies" that could amount to savings of $1 billion a year in combined costs.

*did their best to survive
decentralization
larger span of control
less hierarchy
feedback
more formalized
less b/c org #↓
*if we don't change orgs are doomed to dissapear

From Anglo's perspective, there were drawbacks to the deal—the value of its portfolio was greater than Xstrata's and would be diluted by a merger of the two—but the appeal to Anglo shareholders was clear: Depending on how the new company distributed the cost savings among its investors, Anglo shareholders stood to realize an increase in the market value of their holdings of 26 to 37 percent.

Carroll and the Anglo board quickly rejected Xstrata's offer as "totally unacceptable," and in August Carroll presented both Anglo's mid-year financial results and its argument for remaining independent. Once again, however, the numbers were underwhelming: Because of the global economy, profits were off 69 percent and revenues 38 percent. Anglo investors wanted to know what management was doing to deliver the kind of returns promised by the Xstrata merger, and an analyst at Barclays Capital, Britain's biggest investment bank, announced that, "in our view, Anglo American has not yet presented a strong argument as to why a merger with Xstrata is not strategically sensible and value-creating for its shareholders." "Frankly," replied Carroll,

> *I know what it is that we need to do.... We have a strategy, we have clear goals, we have tremendous assets ... in the most attractive commodities in the world. The opportunities are massive.... We're well aware of what Xstrata does, but I'm very confident of what we can do in the future.*

In October, Xstrata withdrew its offer in the face of resistance from the Anglo board. Anglo, said a company spokesman, "can now move forward and run our business without further distraction." One analyst predicted that Anglo "will likely show a renewed sense of urgency ... and pull out all the stops to win shareholders over," and exactly one week later, Carroll announced her "simplification and delayering" plan. In making the announcement, she asked shareholders for more time to develop the firm's assets and prove its value as an independent company. "The portfolio changes we have announced," she argued, "... will position Anglo American well for sustained, profitable growth in the commodities we have identified as being the most attractive."

What Do You Think?

1. Assume that you are an investor in Anglo American. Would you have supported the stance of Carroll and the board when Xstrata first made its merger bid? What about now?
2. Assume that you are an Anglo employee. What would you do if the company's restructuring required you to move to another part of the world? What advantages and disadvantages would weigh most heavily on your decision?

References: Jeffrey Sparshott, "Miner Anglo to Sell Assets in Shake-Up," *Wall Street Journal*, October 22, 2009, http://online.wsj.com on August 7, 2012; Kate Holton et al., "Xstrata Seeks $68 Billion Merger with Anglo," Reuters, June 21, 2009, www.reuters.com on August 7, 2012; Julia Werdigier, "Xstrata Makes a New Move for Merger with Anglo," *New York Times*, June 25, 2009, www.nytimes.com on August 7, 2012; Martin Waller and David Robinson, "Business Big Shot: Cynthia Carroll of Anglo American," *Times* (London) *Online*, August 1, 2009, http://business.timesonline.co.uk on March 14, 2011; Andrew Cave, "Cynthia Carroll Digs Deep for Anglo," *Telegraph*, August 1, 2009, www.telegraph.co.uk on August 12, 2012; Julia Werdigier, "Xstrata Ends Bid for Rival in London," *New York Times*, October 16, 2009, www.nytimes.com on August 7, 2012.

These days, it is not unusual for businesses to change their organization structure as they struggle to remain competitive in a rapidly changing world. Facing a downturn in the economy and their business, Anglo American PLC changed its organization structure by removing layers, simplifying reporting relationships, and selling off non-core assets. This chapter introduces many of the key concepts of organization structure and sets the stage for understanding the many aspects of developing the appropriate organization design, which is discussed in Chapter 17.

THE NATURE OF ORGANIZATION STRUCTURE

In other chapters we discuss key elements of the individual and the factors that tie the individual and the organization together. In a given organization, these factors must fit together within a common framework: the organization's structure.

Organization Defined

An **organization** is a goal-directed social entity with deliberate processes and systems.

An **organization** is a goal-directed social entity with deliberate processes and systems.[1] In other words, an organization is a collection of people working together to accomplish something better than they could working separately.[2] Organizations are social actors, influencing and being influenced by their environments and affecting the behaviors of individuals in them. As social actors, organizations are different from two other entities, those being individuals and the government or state. Organizations influence and are influenced by other organizations, as well as individuals and the state.[3] Top management determines the direction of the organization by defining its purpose or mission, establishing goals to meet that purpose, and formulating strategies to achieve the goals.[4] The definition of its purpose gives the organization reason to exist; in effect, it answers the question "What business are we in?"

Organizational goals are objectives that management seeks to achieve in pursuing the firm's purpose.

Establishing goals converts the defined purpose into specific, measurable performance targets. **Organizational goals** are objectives that management seeks to achieve in pursuing the purpose of the firm. Goals motivate people to work together. Although each individual's goals are important to the organization, it is the organization's overall goals that are most important. Goals keep the organization on track by focusing the attention and actions of the members. They also give the organization a forward-looking orientation. They do not address past success or failure; rather, they force members to think about and plan for the future.

Finally, strategies are specific action plans that enable the organization to achieve its goals and thus its purpose. Pursuing a strategy involves developing an organization structure and the processes to do the organization's work.

Organization Structure

Organization structure is the system of task, reporting, and authority relationships within which the organization does its work.

Organization structure is the system of task, reporting, and authority relationships within which the work of the organization is done. Thus, structure defines the form and function of the organization's activities. Structure also defines how the parts of an organization fit together, as is evident from an organization chart.

The purpose of an organization's structure is to order and coordinate the actions of employees to achieve organizational goals. The premise of organized effort is that people can accomplish more by working together than they can separately. The work must be coordinated properly, however, if the potential gains of collective effort are to be realized. Consider what might happen if the thousands of employees at Dell Computers worked without any kind of structure. Each person might try to build a computer that he or she thought would sell. No two computers would be alike, and each would take months or years to build. The costs of making the computers would be so high that no one would be able to afford them. To produce computers that are both competitive in the marketplace and profitable for the company, Dell must have a structure in which its employees and managers work together in a coordinated manner. When Intel changed its organization structure from a product-centered structure to a customer-focused model, it did so to better coordinate its efforts to serve its customers.[5]

The task of coordinating the activities of thousands of workers to produce microprocessors and computers that do the work expected of them and that are guaranteed and

Vario images GmbH & Co.KG/Alamy

These employees at the Dell Service Center in Halle Germany are meeting to coordinate the work they do. In this case they are structurally and physically located near each other to foster better coordination and improved service.

easy to maintain may seem monumental. Yet whether the goal is to mass-produce computers or to make soap, the requirements of organization structure are similar. First, the structure must identify the various tasks or processes necessary for the organization to reach its goals. This dividing of tasks into smaller parts is often called "division of labor." Even small organizations (those with fewer than one hundred employees) use a division of labor.[6] Second, the structure must combine and coordinate the divided tasks to achieve a desired level of output. The more interdependent the divided tasks, the more coordination is required.[7] Every organization structure addresses these two fundamental requirements.[8] The various ways of approaching these requirements are what make one organization structure different from another.

In this chapter we first describe three of the classical views of organizations that strongly influence how organizations are still viewed today. Then we break down the various components of organization structure. Organization structure can be analyzed in three ways: First, we can examine its configuration—that is, its size and shape—as depicted on an organization chart. Second, we can analyze its operational aspects or characteristics, such as separation of specialized tasks, rules and procedures, and decision making. Finally, we can examine responsibility and authority within the organization. In this chapter, we describe organization structure from all three points of view.

CLASSIC VIEWS OF STRUCTURE

The earliest views of organization structure have often been called "classical organization theory" and include Max Weber's concept of the ideal bureaucracy, the classic organizing principles of Henri Fayol, and the human organization view of Rensis Likert. All three approaches attempt to describe an organization structure that is universally applicable across organizations, and thus are called universal approaches, yet their concerns and structural prescriptions differ significantly.

Ideal Bureaucracy

Weber's **ideal bureaucracy** is characterized by a hierarchy of authority and a system of rules and procedures designed to create an optimally effective system for large organizations.

In the early 1900s, Max Weber, a German sociologist, proposed a "bureaucratic" structure that he believed would work for all organizations. Weber's **ideal bureaucracy** was an organizational system characterized by a hierarchy of authority and a system of rules and procedures that, if followed, would create a maximally effective system for large organizations. Weber, writing at a time when organizations were inherently inefficient, claimed that the bureaucratic form of administration is superior to other forms of management with respect to stability, control, and predictability of outcomes.[9]

Weber's ideal bureaucracy had seven essential characteristics: rules and procedures, division of labor, a hierarchy of authority, technical competence, separation of ownership, rights and property differentiation, and documentation, as shown in Table 16.1. These characteristics utilize several of the building blocks discussed later in this chapter. Weber intended these characteristics to ensure order and predictability in relationships among people and jobs in the bureaucracy. But it is easy to see how the same features can lead to sluggishness, inefficiency, and red tape. The administrative system can easily break down if any of the characteristics are carried to an extreme or are violated. For example, if endless arrays of rules and procedures bog down employees who must find the precise rule to follow every time they do something, responses to routine client or customer requests may slow to a crawl. Moreover, subsequent writers have said that Weber's view of authority is too rigid and have suggested that the bureaucratic organization may impede creativity and innovation and result in a lack of compassion for the individual in the organization.[10] In other words, the impersonality that is supposed to

Table 16.1 Elements of Weber's Ideal Bureaucracy

ELEMENTS	COMMENTS
1. Rules and Procedures	A consistent set of abstract rules and procedures should exist to ensure uniform performance.
2. Distinct Division of Labor	Each position should be filled by an expert.
3. Hierarchy of Authority	The chain of command should be clearly established.
4. Technical Competence	Employment and advancement should be based on merit.
5. Segregation of Ownership	Professional managers rather than owners should run the organization.
6. Rights and Properties of the Position	These should be associated with the organization, not with the person who holds the office.
7. Documentation	A record of actions should be kept regarding administrative decisions, rules, and procedures.

foster objectivity in a bureaucracy may result in serious difficulties for both employees and the organization. However, some organizations retain some characteristics of a bureaucratic structure while remaining innovative and productive.

Paul Adler has recently countered the currently popular movements of "bureaucracy busting" by noting that large-scale, complex organizations still need some of the basic characteristics that Weber described—hierarchical structure, formalized procedures, and staff expertise—to avoid chaos and ensure efficiency, quality products and services, and timeliness. Adler further proposes a second type of bureaucracy that essentially serves an enabling function in organizations.[11] The need for bureaucracy is not relegated to the past. Bureaucracy, or at least some of its elements, is still critical for designing effective organizations.

The Classic Principles of Organizing

Also at the beginning of the twentieth century, Henri Fayol, a French engineer and chief executive officer of a mining company, presented a second classic view of the organization structure. Drawing on his experience as a manager, Fayol was the first to classify the essential elements of management—now usually called **management functions**—as planning, organizing, command, coordination, and control.[12] In addition, he presented fourteen principles of organizing that he considered an indispensable code for managers (see Table 16.2).

The **management functions** set forth by Henri Fayol include planning, organizing, command, coordination, and control.

Fayol's principles have proved extraordinarily influential; they have served as the basis for the development of generally accepted means of organizing. For example, Fayol's "unity of command" principle means that employees should receive directions from only one person, and "unity of direction" means that tasks with the same objective should have a common supervisor. Combining these two principles with division of labor, authority, and responsibility results in a system of tasks and reporting and authority relationships that is the very essence of organizing. Fayol's principles thus provide the framework for the organization chart and the coordination of work.

The classic principles have been criticized on several counts. First, they ignore factors such as individual motivation, leadership, and informal groups—the human element in

Table 16.2 Fayol's Classic Principles of Organizing

PRINCIPLE	FAYOL'S COMMENTS
1. Division of work	Individuals and managers work on the same part or task.
2. Authority and responsibility	Authority—right to give orders; power to exact obedience; goes with responsibility for reward and punishment.
3. Discipline	Obedience, application, energy, behavior. Agreement between firm and individual.
4. Unity of command	Employee receives orders from one superior.
5. Unity of direction	One head and one plan for activities with the same objective.
6. Subordination of individual interest to general interest	Objectives of the organization come before objectives of the individual.
7. Remuneration of personnel	Pay should be fair to the organization and the individual; discussed various forms.
8. Centralization	Proportion of discretion held by the manager compared to that allowed to subordinates.
9. Scalar chain	Line of authority from lowest to top.
10. Order	A place for everyone and everyone in his or her place.
11. Equity	Combination of kindness and justice; equality of treatment.
12. Stability of tenure of personnel	Stability of managerial personnel; time to get used to work.
13. Initiative	Power of thinking out and executing a plan.
14. Esprit de corps	Harmony and union among personnel is strength.

Reference: From *General and Industrial Management*, by Henri Fayol. Copyright © Lake Publishing 1984, Belmont, CA 94002. Used with permission.

organizations. This line of criticism asserts that the classic principles result in a mechanical organization into which people must fit, regardless of their interests, abilities, or motivations. The principles have also been criticized for their lack of operational specificity in that Fayol described the principles as universal truths but did not specify the means of applying many of them. Finally, Fayol's principles have been discounted because they were not supported by scientific evidence; Fayol presented them as universal principles, backed by no evidence other than his own experience.[13]

Human Organization

In the 1960s Rensis Likert developed an approach to organization structure he called "human organization."[14] Because Likert, like others, had criticized Fayol's classic principles for overlooking human factors, it is not surprising that his approach centered on the principles of supportive relationships, employee participation, and overlapping work groups.

The term "supportive relationships" suggests that in all organizational activities, individuals should be treated in such a way that they experience feelings of support, self-worth, and importance. By "employee participation," Likert meant that the work group needs to be involved in decisions that affect it, thereby enhancing the employees' sense of supportiveness and self-worth. The principle of "overlapping work groups" means that work groups are linked, with managers serving as the "linking pins." Each manager (except the highest ranking) is a member of two groups: a work group that he or she supervises and a management group composed of the manager's peers and their supervisor. Coordination and communication grow stronger when the managers perform the linking function by sharing problems, decisions, and information both upward and downward in the groups to which they belong. The **human organization** concept rests on the assumption that people work best in highly cohesive groups oriented toward organizational goals. Management's function is to make sure the work groups are linked for effective coordination and communication.

Rensis Likert's **human organization** approach is based on supportive relationships, participation, and overlapping work groups.

Likert described four systems of organizing, which he called management systems, whose characteristics are summarized in Table 16.3. System 1, the exploitive authoritative system, can be characterized as the classic bureaucracy. System 4, the participative group, is the organization design Likert favored. System 2, the benevolent authoritative system, and system 3, the consultative system, are less extreme than either system 1 or system 4.

Likert described all four systems in terms of eight organizational variables: leadership processes, motivational forces, communication processes, interaction-influence processes, decision-making processes, goal-setting processes, control processes, and performance goals and training. Likert believed that work groups should be able to overlap horizontally as well as vertically where necessary to accomplish tasks. This feature is directly contrary to the classic principle that advocates unity of command. In addition, rather than the hierarchical chain of command, Likert favored the linking-pin concept of overlapping work groups for making decisions and resolving conflicts.

Research support for Likert's human organization emanates primarily from Likert and his associates' work at the Institute for Social Research at the University of Michigan. Although their research has upheld the basic propositions of the approach, it is not entirely convincing. One review of the evidence suggested that although research has shown characteristics of system 4 to be associated with positive worker attitudes and, in some cases, increased productivity, it is not clear that the characteristics of the human organization "caused" the positive results.[15] It may have been that positive attitudes and high productivity allowed the organization structure to be participative and provided the atmosphere for the development of supportive relationships. Likert's design has also been criticized for focusing almost exclusively on individuals and groups and not dealing extensively with structural issues. Overall, the most compelling support for this approach is at the individual and work-group levels. In some ways, Likert's system 4 is much like the team-based organization popular today.

Thus, the classic views of organization embody the key elements of organization structure. Each view, however, combined these key elements in different ways and with other management elements. These three classic views are typical of how the early writers attempted to prescribe a universal approach to organization structure that would be best in all situations. In the following sections, we break down the various elements of organization structure to examine how they contribute to coordinating the tasks and people who perform those tasks toward goal accomplishment.

Table 16.3 Characteristics of Likert's Four Management Systems

CHARACTERISTIC	SYSTEM 1: EXPLOITIVE AUTHORITATIVE	SYSTEM 2: BENEVOLENT AUTHORITATIVE	SYSTEM 3: CONSULTATIVE	SYSTEM 4: PARTICIPATIVE GROUP
Leadership				
• Trust in subordinates	None	None	Substantial	Complete
• Subordinates' ideas	Seldom used	Sometimes used	Usually used	Always used
Motivational Forces				
• Motives tapped	Security, status	Economic, ego	Substantial	Complete
• Level of satisfaction	Overall dissatisfaction	Some moderate satisfaction	Moderate satisfaction	High satisfaction
Communication				
• Amount	Very little	Little	Moderate	Much
• Direction	Downward	Mostly downward	Down, up	Down, up, lateral
Interaction-Influence				
• Amount	None	None	Substantial	Complete
• Cooperative teamwork	None	Virtually none	Moderate	Substantial
Decision Making				
• Locus	Top	Policy decided at top	Broad policy decided at top	All levels
• Subordinates involved	Not at all	Sometimes consulted	Usually consulted	Fully involved
Goal Setting				
• Manner	Orders	Orders with comments	Set after discussion	Group participation
• Acceptance	Covertly resisted	Frequently resisted	Sometimes resisted	Fully accepted
Control Processes				
• Level	Top	None	Some below top	All levels
• Information	Incomplete, inaccurate	Often incomplete, inaccurate	Moderately complete, accurate	Complete, accurate
Performance				
• Goals and training	Mediocre	Fair to good	Good	Excellent

Reference: Adapted from Rensis Likert, *New Patterns of Management* (New York: McGraw-Hill, 1961), pp. 223–233; and Rensis Likert, *The Human Organization* (New York: McGraw-Hill, 1967), pp. 197, 198, 201, 203, 210, and 211.

STRUCTURAL CONFIGURATION

An **organization chart** is a diagram showing all people, positions, reporting relationships, and lines of formal communication in the organization.

The **configuration** of an organization is its shape, which reflects the division of labor and the means of coordinating the divided tasks.

The structure of an organization is most often described in terms of its organization chart. See Figure 16.1 for an example. A complete **organization chart** shows all people, positions, reporting relationships, and lines of formal communication in the organization. (However, as we discussed in Chapter 11, communication is not limited to these formal channels.) For large organizations, several charts may be necessary to show all positions. For example, one chart may show top management, including the board of directors, the chief executive officer, the president, all vice presidents, and important headquarters staff units. Subsequent charts may show the structure of each department and staff unit. Figure 16.1 depicts two organization charts for a large firm; top management is shown in the upper portion of the figure and the manufacturing department in the lower portion. Notice that the structures of the different manufacturing groups are given in separate charts.

An organization chart depicts reporting relationships and work-group memberships and shows how positions and small work groups are combined into departments, which together make up the configuration, or shape, of the organization. The **configuration** of organizations can be analyzed in terms of how the two basic requirements of structure—division of labor and coordination of the divided tasks—are fulfilled.

FIGURE 16.1

Examples of Organizational Charts

These two charts show the similarities between a top-management chart and a department chart. In each, managers have four other managers or work groups reporting to them.

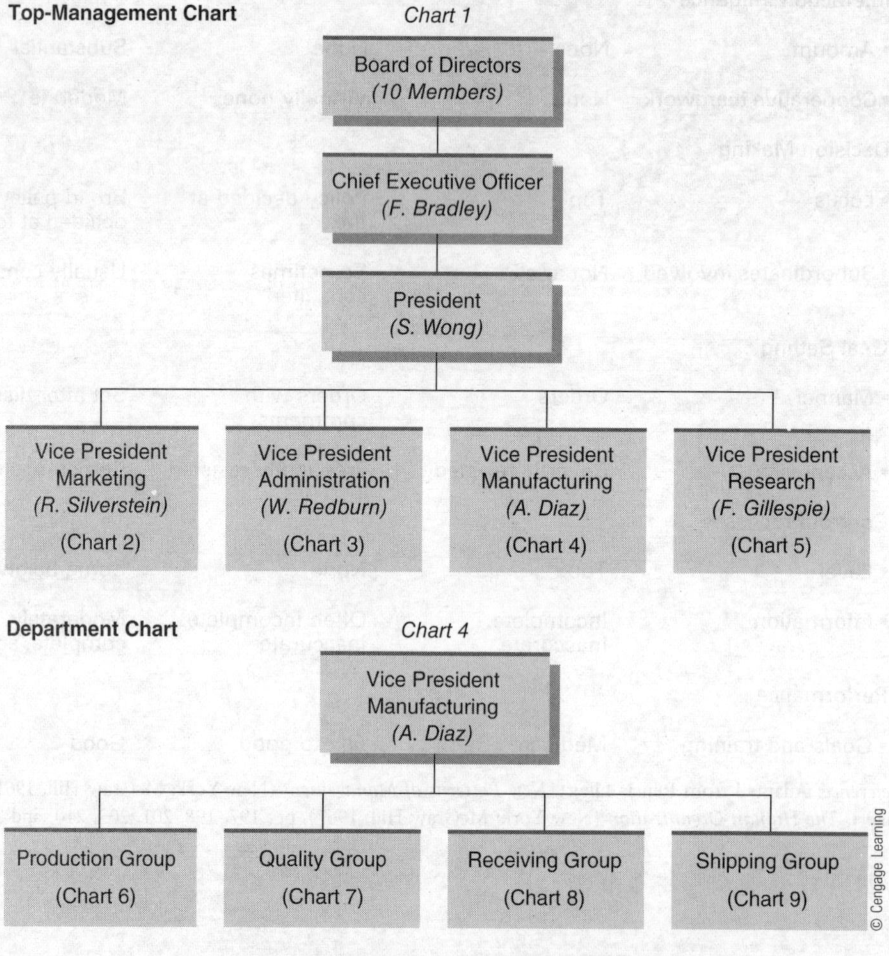

Division of Labor

Division of labor is the way the organization's work is divided into different jobs to be done by different people. Division of labor is often referred to as **specialization.**

Differentiation is the process of establishing the division of labor and tasks throughout the organization.

Division of labor is the extent to which the organization's work is separated into different jobs to be done by different people and is often referred to as **specialization**, which we discussed in Chapter 5 on motivation and work design. The more people become divided doing different tasks, the more differentiated they become, thus requiring more coordination. **Differentiation** is the process of establishing the division of labor and tasks throughout the organization. While division of labor is one of the seven primary characteristics of structuring described by Max Weber[16] discussed earlier in this chapter, the concept can be traced back to eighteenth-century economist Adam Smith, who used a study of pin making to promote the idea of dividing production work to increase productivity.[17] Division of labor grew more popular as large organizations became more prevalent in a manufacturing society. This trend has continued, and most research indicates that large organizations usually have more division of labor than smaller ones.[18] Division of labor has been found to have both advantages and disadvantages (see Table 16.4). Modern managers and organization theorists are still struggling with the primary disadvantage: division of labor often results in repetitive, boring jobs that undercut worker satisfaction, involvement, and commitment.[19] In addition, extreme division of labor may be incompatible with new, integrated computerized manufacturing technologies that require teams of highly skilled workers.[20]

However, division of labor need not result in boredom. Visualized in terms of a small organization such as a basketball team, it can be quite dynamic. A basketball team consists of five players, each of whom plays a different role on the team. In professional basketball the five positions typically are center, power forward, small forward, shooting guard, and point guard. The tasks of the players in each position are quite different, so players of different sizes and skills are on the floor at any one time. The teams that win championships, such as the Miami Heat and the Los Angeles Lakers, use division of labor by having players specialize in doing specified tasks, and doing them impeccably. Similarly, organizations must have specialists who are highly trained and know their specific jobs very well.

Integration is the process of coordinating the various tasks and roles in the organization to achieve goal accomplishment.

Coordinating the Divided Tasks

Divided tasks need to be properly coordinated to achieve the potential productivity gains expected from specialization of tasks. The problem of differentiation must be balanced with proper integration. **Integration** is the process of coordinating the various tasks

Table 16.4 Advantages and Disadvantages of Division of Labor

ADVANTAGES	DISADVANTAGES
Efficient use of labor	Routine, repetitive jobs
Reduced training costs	Reduced job satisfaction
Increased standardization and uniformity of output	Decreased worker involvement and commitment
Increased expertise from repetition of tasks	Increased worker alienation
	Possible incompatibility with computerized manufacturing technologies

Dmitry Argunov/Alamy

On the USA Women's National Basketball Team the various tasks required to win games are divided among the players who have different skills, abilities, and physical attributes. Coordinating these skills and abilities and the various tasks are necessary for the team to succeed.

and roles to achieve goal accomplishment. Three basic mechanisms are used to help coordinate the divided tasks: departmentalization, span of control, and administrative hierarchy. These mechanisms focus on grouping tasks in some meaningful manner, creating work groups of manageable size, and establishing a system of reporting relationships among supervisors and managers. When companies reorganize, they are usually changing the ways in which the divided labor is coordinated. To some people affected by reorganization, it may seem that things are still just as disorganized as they were before. But there really is a purpose for such reorganization efforts. Top management expects that the work will be better coordinated under the new system.

Departmentalization **Departmentalization** is the manner in which divided tasks are combined and allocated to work groups. It is a consequence of the division of labor if coordinated action is to be achieved. Because employees engaged in specialized activities can lose sight of overall organizational goals, their work must be coordinated to ensure that it contributes to goal accomplishment for the organization.

Departmentalization is the manner in which divided tasks are combined and allocated to work groups.

There are many possible ways to group, or departmentalize, tasks. The five groupings most often used are business function, process, product or service, customer, and geography. The first two, function and process, derive from the internal operations of the organization; the others are based on external factors. Most organizations tend to use a combination of methods, and departmentalization often changes as organizations evolve.[21]

Departmentalization by business function is based on traditional business functions such as marketing, manufacturing, and human resource administration (see Figure 16.2). In this configuration, employees most frequently associate with those engaged in the same function, a situation that helps in communication and cooperation. In a functional group, employees who do similar work can learn from one another by sharing ideas about opportunities and problems they encounter on the job. Abercrombie & Fitch (A&F) is one of five brands owned by Ohio-based A&F Corporation. The company's other brands include abercrombie ("classic cool" for preteens), Hollister ("SoCal" for teenagers), RUEHL 925 (a higher-priced brand for post-collegiates 22 to 30), and Gilly Hicks (Australian-themed lounge- and underwear for women). Obviously, A&F's businesses are related, and although its overall corporate strategy is designed to take advantage of this linkage, it does not reflect the *divisionalized form* of organization favored by most companies that operate multiple related businesses. Rather, A&F relies on a structure based on *functional* departments—that is, groups responsible for specific company or management functions. At A&F every employee is assigned to one of eight basic business functions, such as planning, purchasing, distribution, or stores, each of which is headed by a

FIGURE 16.2

Departmentalization by Business Function and by Process

These two charts compare departmentalization by business function and by process. "Functions" are the basic business functions, whereas "processes" are the specific categories of jobs that people do.

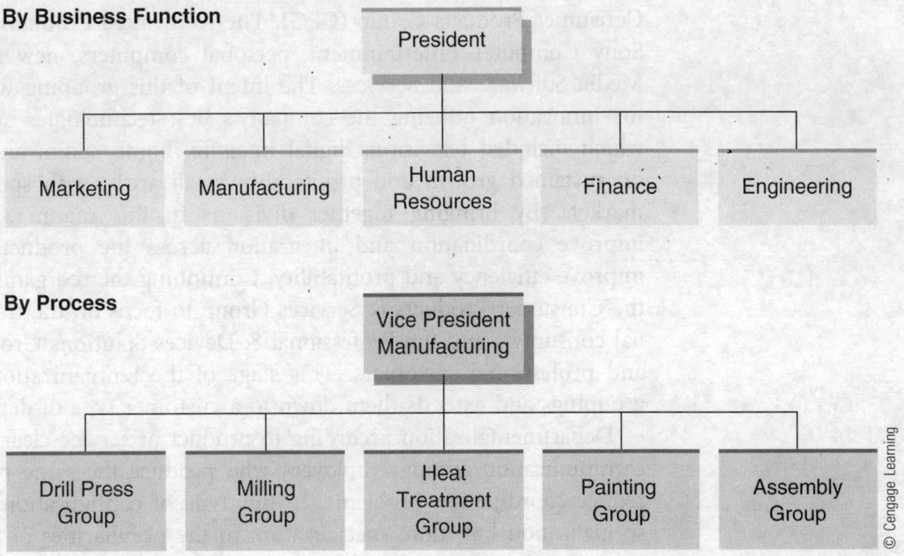

president. A&F wants every employee to develop highly specialized skills within a functional area. In addition, this design is obviously more effective in coordinating activities within a function.[22]

Although functional groups usually have good communication and coordination within the group, functional groups lack an automatic mechanism for coordinating the flow of work through the organization.[23] In other words, employees in a functional structure tend to associate little with those in other parts of the organization. The result can be a narrow focus that limits the coordination of work among functional groups, as when the engineering department fails to provide marketing with product information because it is too busy testing materials to think about sales. Organizations with functional structures must rely on management to focus and coordinate the functional groups.

Departmentalization by process is similar to functional departmentalization except the focus is much more on specific jobs grouped according to activity. Thus, as Figure 16.2 illustrates, the firm's manufacturing jobs are divided into certain well-defined manufacturing processes: drilling, milling, heat treatment, painting, and assembly. Hospitals often use process departmentalization, grouping the professional employees such as therapists according to the types of treatment they provide.

Process groupings encourage specialization and expertise among employees, who tend to concentrate on a single operation and share information with departmental colleagues. A process orientation may develop into an internal career path and managerial hierarchy within the department. For example, a specialist might become the "lead" person for that specialty—that is, the lead welder or lead designer. As in functional grouping, however, narrowness of focus can be a problem. Employees in a process group may become so absorbed in the requirements and execution of their operations that they disregard broader considerations such as overall product flow.[24]

Departmentalization by product or service occurs when employees who work on a particular product or service are members of the same department regardless of their business function or the process in which they are engaged. In 2009 Sony Corporation began a multiyear project to reorganize by product category. They started by creating two new product groupings: the Networked Products & Services Group and the New

Consumer Products Group (CPG). The Networked Products & Services Group included Sony Computer Entertainment, personal computers, new mobile products, and Sony Media Software and Services. The intent of this grouping was to increase the potential for innovation utilizing the company's best technologies and service platforms. CPG, which included television, digital imaging, home audio, and video businesses, focuses on sustained growth and profitability in all areas, with special emphasis on emerging markets. By bringing together divisions in this manner, the company expected to improve coordination and integration across the products and services, as well as improve efficiency and profitability. Continuing the reorganization in 2012, they created the Consumer Products & Services Group to focus on the traditional home and individual consumers and the Professional & Devices Solutions Group to focus on the business and professional customers. This stage of the reorganization takes the product/service groupings and extends them down to a customer type of departmentalization.[25]

Departmentalization according to product or service clearly enhances interaction and communication among employees who produce the same product or service and may reduce coordination problems. In this type of configuration, there may be less process specialization but more specialization in the peculiarities of the specific product or service. The disadvantage is that employees may become so interested in their particular product or service that they miss technological improvements or innovations developed in other departments.

In contrast, Intel reorganized away from product lines by creating five new customer-oriented divisions. Their new organization chart at the executive level is shown in Figure 16.3. In the past, Intel's corporate structure reflected the product-centered business model, with departments focused on microprocessors, networking equipment, communications equipment, and services. In 2005 the firm switched its attention from the technology to the consumers who use that technology. Intel felt it needed to pay more attention to customer needs to continue growing. Each of the newly created departments focuses on a specific group of customers, their needs, and how they use their computers. The new structure creates more variety among the departments. As each unit responds to a particular set of buyers, a unique set of solutions and devices is developed. For example, the Health Group invents technology to help individuals better manage their health. Among dozens of innovative products, one system supports individuals with Alzheimer's disease, prompting them to eat meals and displaying

FIGURE 16.3

Departmentalization by Customer

Intel changed its departmentalization scheme by creating five new product groups. They expect the new structure will group together complementary business segments and improve the way technology is used.

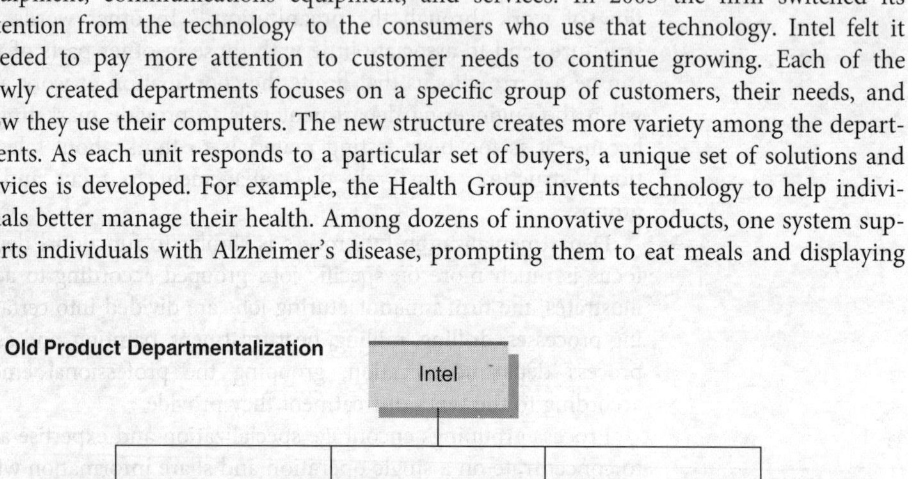

detailed cooking instructions for forgetful seniors. Another system provides monitoring of seniors and a warning system to alert at-home caregivers when help is required. In the new structure, computing, communications, networking, and services staff are merged into every new department. Intel expected the new alignment would allow all employees, from designers to manufacturing workers to marketing experts, to become specialists in a particular type of customer so they would be better able to meet specific customer needs.[26]

Departmentalization by customer is often called "departmentalization by market." Many lending institutions in Texas, for example, have separate departments for retail, commercial, agriculture, and petroleum loans similar to those shown in Figure 16.4. When significant groups of customers differ substantially from one another, organizing along customer lines may be the most effective way to provide the best products or services possible. This is why hospital nurses often are grouped by the type of illness they handle; the various maladies demand different treatment and specialized knowledge.[27] Deutsche Bank changed its organization structure from a regional structure to one based on client groups in order to expand its international presence and to appeal to more international investors.[28]

With customer departmentalization there is usually less process specialization because employees must remain flexible to do whatever is necessary to enhance the relationship with customers. This configuration offers the best coordination of the workflow tailored to the customer's needs; however, it may isolate employees from others in their special areas of expertise. For example, if each of a company's three metallurgical specialists is assigned to a different market-based group, these individuals are unlikely to have many opportunities to discuss the latest technological advances in metallurgy.

Departmentalization by geography means that groups are organized according to a region of the country or world. Sales or marketing groups often are arranged by geographic region. As Figure 16.4 illustrates, the marketing effort of a large multinational corporation can be divided according to major geographical divisions. Using a geographically based configuration may result in significant cost savings and better market coverage. On the other hand, it may isolate work groups from activities in the organization's home office or in the organization's technological community because the focus of the work group is solely on affairs within the region. Such a regional focus may foster loyalty

FIGURE 16.4

Departmentalization by Customer and by Geographic Region

Departmentalization by customer or by geographic region is often used in marketing or sales departments to focus on specific needs or locations of customers.

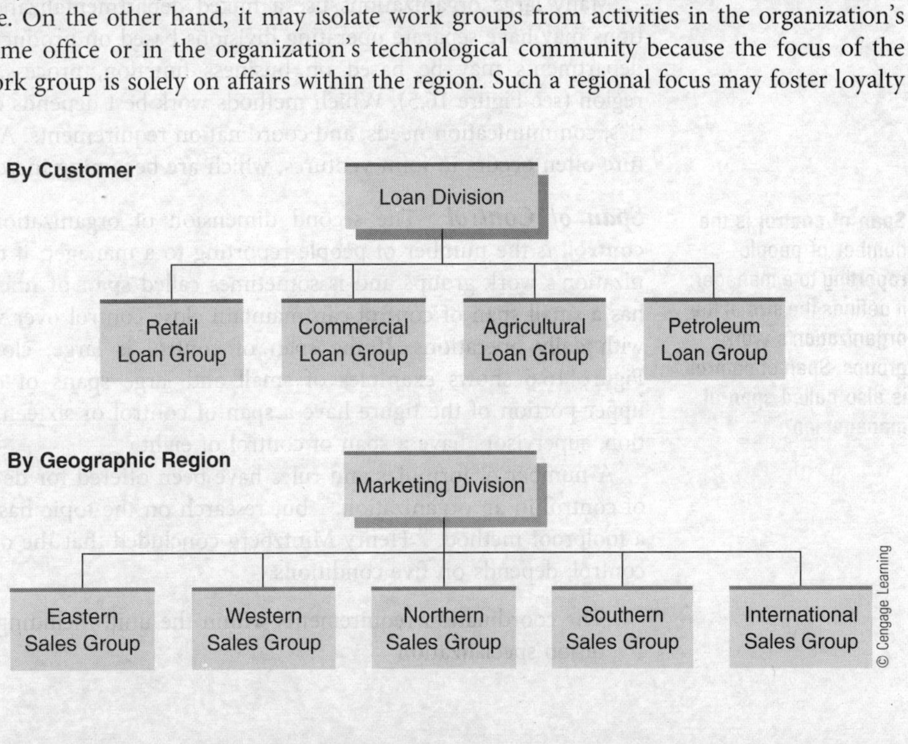

FIGURE 16.5

Mixed Departmentalization

A mixed departmentalization scheme is often used in very large organizations with more complex structures. Headquarters is organized based on products. Industrial products and consumer products are departmentalized on the basis of function. The manufacturing department is based on process. Sales is based on customers. Marketing is based on geographical regions.

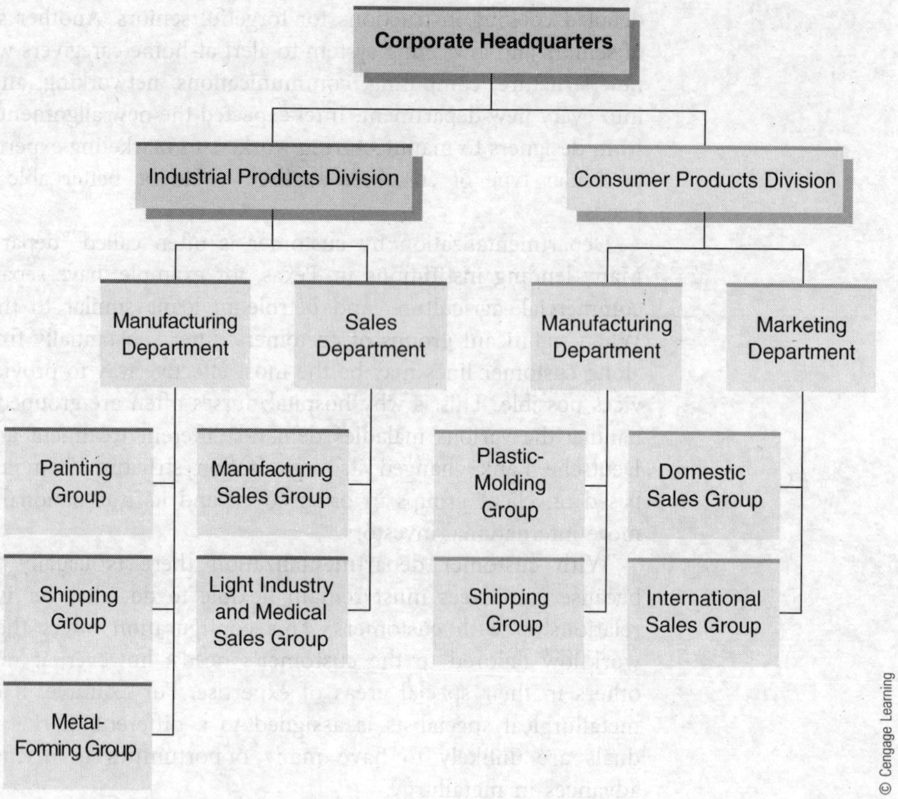

to the work group that exceeds commitment to the larger organization. In addition, work-related communication and coordination among groups may be somewhat inefficient.

Many large organizations use a mixed departmentalization scheme. Such organizations may have separate operating divisions based on products, but within each division, departments may be based on business function, process, customers, or geographic region (see Figure 16.5). Which methods work best depends on the organization's activities, communication needs, and coordination requirements. Another type of mixed structure often occurs in joint ventures, which are becoming increasingly popular.

Span of control is the number of people reporting to a manager; it defines the size of the organization's work groups. Span of control is also called **span of management**.

Span of Control The second dimension of organizational configuration, **span of control**, is the number of people reporting to a manager; it defines the size of the organization's work groups and is sometimes called **span of management**. A manager who has a small span of control can maintain close control over workers and stay in contact with daily operations. If the span of control is large, close control is not possible. Figure 16.6 shows examples of small and large spans of control. Supervisors in the upper portion of the figure have a span of control of sixteen, whereas in the lower portion, supervisors have a span of control of eight.

A number of formulas and rules have been offered for determining the optimal span of control in an organization,[29] but research on the topic has not conclusively identified a foolproof method.[30] Henry Mintzberg concluded that the optimal unit size, or span of control, depends on five conditions:

1. The coordination requirements within the unit, including factors such as the degree of job specialization

FIGURE 16.6

Span of Control and Levels in the Administrative Hierarchy

These charts show how span of control and the number of levels in the administrative hierarchy are inversely related. The thirty-two first-level employees are in two groups of sixteen in the top chart and in four groups of eight in the bottom chart. Either may be appropriate, based on the work situation.

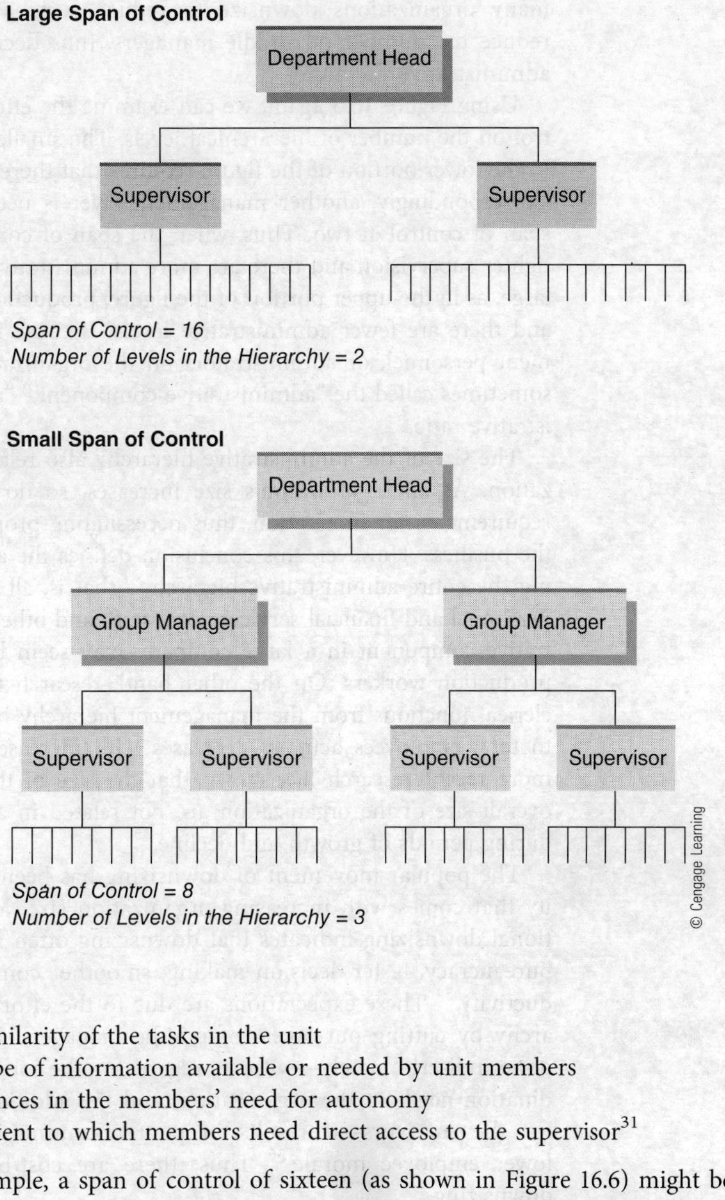

2. The similarity of the tasks in the unit
3. The type of information available or needed by unit members
4. Differences in the members' need for autonomy
5. The extent to which members need direct access to the supervisor[31]

For example, a span of control of sixteen (as shown in Figure 16.6) might be appropriate for a supervisor in a typical manufacturing plant in which experienced workers do repetitive production tasks. On the other hand, a span of control of eight or fewer (as shown in Figure 16.6) might be appropriate in a job shop or custom-manufacturing facility in which workers do many different things and the tasks and problems that arise are new and unusual.[32]

The **administrative hierarchy** is the system of reporting relationships in the organization, from the lowest to the highest managerial levels.

Administrative Hierarchy The **administrative hierarchy** is the system of reporting relationships in the organization, from the first level up through the president or CEO. As another facet of integration, it results from the need for supervisors and managers to coordinate the activities of employees. The size of the administrative hierarchy is inversely related to the span of control: organizations with a small span of control have many managers in the hierarchy; those with a large span of control have a smaller administrative hierarchy. Companies often rearrange their administrative hierarchies to achieve more efficient operations. In difficult economic times when many organizations downsize to reduce costs and attempt to survive, they often reduce the number of middle managers, thus decreasing the number of levels in the administrative hierarchy.

Using Figure 16.6 again, we can examine the effects of small and large spans of control on the number of hierarchical levels. The smaller span of control for the supervisors in the lower portion of the figure requires that there be four supervisors rather than two. Correspondingly, another management layer is needed to keep the department head's span of control at two. Thus, when the span of control is small, the workers are under tighter supervision and there are more administrative levels. When the span of control is large, as in the upper portion of the figure, production workers are not closely supervised and there are fewer administrative levels. Because it measures the number of management personnel, or administrators, in the organization, the administrative hierarchy is sometimes called the "administrative component," "administrative intensity," or "administrative ratio."

The size of the administrative hierarchy also relates to the overall size of the organization. As an organization's size increases, so do its complexity, differentiation, and requirements for integration, thus necessitating proportionately more people to manage the business. However, this conclusion defines the administrative component as including the entire administrative hierarchy—that is, all of the support staff groups, such as personnel and financial services, legal staff, and others. Defined in this way, the administrative component in a large company may seem huge compared with the number of production workers. On the other hand, research that separates the support staff and clerical functions from the management hierarchy has found that the ratio of managers to total employees actually decreases with increases in the organization's size. Other, more recent research has shown that the size of the administrative hierarchy and the overall size of the organization are not related in a straightforward manner, especially during periods of growth and decline.[33]

The popular movement of downsizing has been part of a reaction to the complexity that comes with increasing organization size. Much of the literature on organizational downsizing indicates that downsizing often results in lower overhead costs, less bureaucracy, faster decision making, smoother communications, and increases in productivity.[34] These expectations are due to the effort to reduce the administrative hierarchy by cutting out layers of middle managers. Unfortunately, when downsizing is done indiscriminately—without regard for the jobs that people actually do, the coordination needs of the organization, and the additional training that may be necessary for the survivors—it results in poorer communication, reduced productivity, and lower employee morale.[35] Thus, there are cost/benefit tradeoffs for organizational downsizing.

The impact of downsizing on organizational performance may not be as straightforward as early studies suggested and may be contingent on the nature of the industry and industry economic conditions. A recent study of manufacturing firms in many different industries has noted the negative effects of downsizing on firm performance across industries but has shown these effects to be most pronounced in research and development–intensive industries (pharmaceuticals, biotech, and electronic components) as well as in fast-growth industries where the market is expanding.[36] Not only does the loss of human capital in knowledge-intensive industries and fast-growing industries result in the lost potential productivity of those let go, but also the survivors may experience lower morale, reduced commitment, and thus lower performance. In difficult economic times as have been experienced in recent years, firms may have to make workforce reductions to stay in business, but they must recognize that such reductions may have other long-term performance implications.

STRUCTURE AND OPERATIONS

Some important aspects of organization structure do not appear on the organization chart and thus are quite different from the configurational aspects discussed in the previous section. In this section, we examine the structural policies that affect operations and prescribe or restrict how employees behave in their organizational activities.[37] The two primary aspects of these policies are centralization of decision making and formalization of rules and procedures.

Centralization

Centralization is a structural policy in which decision-making authority is concentrated at the top of the organizational hierarchy.

Decentralization is a structural policy in which decisions are made throughout the hierarchy.

The first structural policy that affects operations is **centralization**, wherein decision-making authority is concentrated at the top of the organizational hierarchy. At the opposite end of the continuum is **decentralization**, in which decisions are made throughout the hierarchy.[38] Increasingly, decentralization is being discussed in terms of participation in decision making.[39] In decentralized organizations, lower-level employees participate in making decisions. The changes that Jack Smith made in 1993 and 1996 at General Motors were intended to decentralize decision making throughout the company. Smith dismantled the old divisional structure, created a single unit called North American Operations, and did away with a tangle of management committees that slowed down decision making. Managers were then encouraged to make decisions on new designs and pricing that used to take weeks to circulate through the committee structure on their way to the top.[40] Following the bankruptcy and government bailout, current Chief Executive Dan Akerson is planning on eliminating the four regional divisions (North America, South America, Europe, and International Operations), returning to a more functional organization with global heads of manufacturing, purchasing, and marketing.[41]

Decision making in organizations is more complex than the simple centralized/decentralized classification indicates. In Chapter 8 we discussed organizational decision making in more depth. One of the major distinctions we made there was that some decisions are relatively routine and require only the application of a decision rule. These decisions are programmed decisions, whereas those that are not routine are nonprogrammed. The decision rules for programmed decisions are formalized for the organization. This difference between programmed and nonprogrammed decisions tends to cloud the distinction between centralization and decentralization. For even if decision making is decentralized, the decisions themselves may be programmed and tightly circumscribed.

SpxChrome/iStockphoto.com

This organization chart shows the President/CEO reporting to the Board of Directors indicating the CEO is responsible to the Board for everything that happens in the organization. Does responsibility stop there? To whom is the Board responsible? Certainly the President/CEO has a lot of authority based on the position shown, but the organization chart does not reveal much about that authority and how it is used or delegated.

If there is little employee participation in decision making, then decision making is centralized, regardless of the nature of the decisions being made. At the other extreme, if individuals or groups participate extensively in making nonprogrammed decisions, the structure can be described as truly decentralized. If individuals or groups participate extensively in decision making but mainly in programmed decisions, the structure is called "formalized decentralization." Formalized decentralization is a common way to provide decision-making involvement for employees at many different levels in the organization while maintaining control and predictability.

Participative management is a total management system in which people throughout the organization are involved in the daily decision making and management of the organization.

Participative management is a total management system in which people throughout the organization are involved in the daily decision making and management of the organization. It builds on the motivational aspects of employee involvement, as discussed in Chapter 5 on motivation. As part of an organization's culture, participative management can contribute significantly to the long-term success of an organization.[42] It has been described as effective and, in fact, morally necessary in organizations. Thus, for many people, participation in decision making has become more than a simple aspect of organization structure. Caution is required, however, because if middle managers are to make effective decisions, as participative management requires, they must have sufficient information.[43] One of the highly touted benefits of the "Information Age" was that all employees throughout the organization would have more information and would therefore be able to participate more in decisions affecting their work, thus creating more decentralized organizations. However, some have suggested that all of this new information in organizations has had the opposite effect by enabling top managers to have more information about the organization's operations and keep decision making to themselves, thus creating more centralized organizations.[44]

Formalization is the degree to which rules and procedures prescribe the jobs and activities of employees.

Formalization is the degree to which rules and procedures prescribe employees' jobs and activities. The purpose of formalization is to predict and control how employees behave on the job.[45] Rules and procedures can be both explicit and implicit. Explicit rules are set down in job descriptions, policy and procedures manuals, or office memos. Implicit rules may develop as employees become accustomed to doing things in a certain way over a period of time.[46] Though unwritten, these established ways of getting things done become standard operating procedures and have the same effect on employee behavior as written rules.

We can assess formalization in organizations by looking at the proportion of jobs that are governed by rules and procedures and the extent to which those rules permit variation. More formalized organizations have a higher proportion of rule-bound jobs and less tolerance for rule violations.[47] Increasing formalization may affect the design of jobs throughout the organization,[48] as well as employee motivation[49] and work group interactions.[50] The specific effects of formalization on employees are still unclear, however.[51]

Organizations tend to add more rules and procedures as the need for control of operations increases. Some organizations have become so formalized that they have rules for how to make new rules! One large university created such rules in the form of a three-page document entitled "Procedures for Rule Adoption" that was added to the four-inch-thick *Policy and Procedures Manual.* The new policy first defines terms such as "university," "board," and "rule" and lists ten exceptions that describe when this policy on rule adoptions does not apply. It then presents a nine-step process for adopting a new rule within the university.

Other organizations are trying to become less formalized by reducing the number of rules and procedures employees must follow. In this effort, Chevron cut the number of its rules and procedures from over four hundred to eighteen. Highly detailed procedures for hiring were eliminated in favor of letting managers make hiring decisions based on common sense.[52]

Another approach to organizational formalization attempts to describe how, when, and why good managers should bend or break a rule.[53] Although rules exist in some form in almost every organization, how strictly they are enforced varies significantly from one organization to another and even within a single organization. Some managers argue that "a rule is a rule" and that all rules must be enforced to control employee behaviors and prevent chaos in the organization. Other managers act as if "all rules are made to be broken" and see rules as stumbling blocks on the way to effective action. Neither point of view is better for the organization; rather, a more balanced approach is recommended.

The test of a good manager in a formalized organization may be how well he or she uses appropriate judgment in making exceptions to rules. A balanced approach to making exceptions to rules should do two things. First, it should recognize that individuals are unique and that the organization can benefit from making exceptions that capitalize on exceptional capabilities. For example, suppose an engineering design department with a rule mandating equal access to tools and equipment acquires a limited amount of specialized equipment such as new computers with cutting-edge design software. The department manager decides to make an exception to the equal-access rule by assigning the computers to the designers the manager believes will use them the most and with the best results instead of making them available for use by all. Second, a balanced approach should recognize the commonalities among employees. Managers should make exceptions to rules only when there is a true and meaningful difference between individuals rather than base exceptions on features such as race, sex, appearance, or social factors.

SERVICE Customer-Centric Structures

©rangizzz/Shutterstock

Early writers on organization theory spent considerable time and effort focused on the boundary that separated the organization from its surrounding environment. In its simplest form, their idea was that top management managed the boundary between the external and internal environments. Its responsibilities included sensing all that took place external to the organization, pondering the implications of the world outside the organization on what was taking place inside the production core, and setting a strategic direction for the organization based on what it saw. Meanwhile, the production core or those responsible for actually producing whatever the organization was created to produce was deep inside the boundary, buffered from the forces outside by middle managers. These managers were responsible for translating what top management had concluded in its survey of what was changing outside the organization's boundary into formalized policies and procedures that would allow the operating core to adapt to these changes without major disruption. In other words, top management figured out the organization's strategic direction based on its boundary-spanning activities while middle management translated this strategy into operational plans that would optimally merge the existing operating core's capabilities and resources with the need to adapt to whatever the changes were that top management saw in the environment. Meanwhile, the protected operating core could carry on with its standardized procedures for producing the refrigerators, clothes, furniture, tires, or rocket ships with minimal interruptions from any external forces.

The service sector turns this organizational model on its head. Imagine, as examples, a retail store clerk, reservationist for a hotel, restaurant server, or amusement park ride attendant. These employees are not only the operating core of the service organization producing customer experiences; they are also the people who sit at the boundary of the organization, interacting with the external environment through their continuing contact with customers. It is these employees who learn from their contact with customers what the organization's problems are with its current service products, what the competition offers that customers prefer, and what changes are happening in customer attitudes, preferences, capabilities, and expectations. Every time they serve a customer, they are in touch with the external environment and operating in the boundary-spanning role traditionally performed by top management. Indeed, in these customer-centric organizations, the operating core learns before top management what is happening in the external environment.

The importance of this transformation from a production core that is protected from external intrusions to a production core that is directly involved in external interactions is profound. The service organization's division of labor now includes the assignment of responsibility to all customer contact employees to discover what the customers are thinking, considering, and concerned about. It is everyone's responsibility to listen and report what is in customer's minds and not just a market research department or top managers talking to the market experts. Departments need to be established to collect and analyze this information gleaned from customers. More interestingly, authority has to be assigned to the customer contact employee to ensure that any customer problems are immediately resolved instead of waiting until a critical web site is discovered or a negative entry is found on a customer blog by top managers. Because it is so important to fix what is not right while the customer is still involved in coproducing a service experience, considerable decision-making responsibility must be given to employees who can correct a service failure on the spot, quickly and fairly. The test of a good manager in service organizations is how well he or she prepares employees to make good decisions when customers ask for help, have a problem, or need some extra accommodation.

Organizations also need to design information flows that are as efficient at sending information up the chain of command as they have been in sending information down. Because they are no longer the primary boundary spanners to the external environment, top managers must enable their customer contact employees to deliver timely and useful information they are gathering from their customers up the chain to those who are still responsible for interpreting this information into strategic direction. Middle managers become responsible for collecting and organizing information coming from below instead of only translating top management decisions and strategic direction into operational policy and procedures. Service organizations know there is no one better to ask about the organization's competitive environment than those who serve, talk to, and observe customers every day.

Discussion Question: Thinking about the importance of customer contact employees in discovering what is happening about changes in the external environment from interacting with customers, assess what, if any, parts of classical organization theory discussed in this chapter might now require revision. What revisions would you make?

RESPONSIBILITY AND AUTHORITY

Responsibility and authority are related to both configurational and operational aspects of organization structure. For example, the organization chart shows who reports to whom at all levels in the organization. From the operational perspective, the degree of centralization defines the locus of decision-making authority in the organization. However, often there is some confusion about what responsibility and authority really mean for managers and how the two terms relate to each other.

Responsibility

Responsibility is an obligation to do something with the expectation of achieving some act or output.

Responsibility is an obligation to do something with the expectation that some act or output will result. For example, a manager may expect an employee to write and present a proposal for a new program by a certain date; thus, the employee is responsible for preparing the proposal. Responsibility ultimately derives from the ownership of the organization. The owners hire or appoint a group, often a board of directors, to be responsible for managing the organization, making the decisions, and reaching the goals set by the owners. A downward chain of responsibility is then established. The board hires a chief executive officer (CEO) or president to be responsible for running the organization. The CEO or president hires more people and holds them responsible for accomplishing designated tasks that enable her or him to produce the results expected by the board and the owners. Jack Welch became famous for the way he ran GE for twenty years. Over the years he hired many managers and assigned responsibility for running various parts of the business. However, in the end, Jack Welch was responsible for all of the activities of the organization.

The chain extends throughout the organization because each manager has an obligation to fulfill: to appropriately employ organizational resources (people, money, and equipment) to meet the owners' expectations. Although managers can assign responsibility to others and expect them to achieve results, each manager is still held responsible for the outputs of those to whom he or she assigns the tasks.

A manager responsible for a work group assigns tasks to members of the group. Each group member is then responsible for doing his or her task, yet the manager still remains responsible for each task and for the work of the group as a whole. This means that managers can take on the responsibility of others but cannot shed their own responsibility onto those below them in the hierarchy.

Authority

Authority is power that has been legitimized within a particular social context.

Authority is power that has been legitimized within a specific social context.[54] (Power is discussed in Chapter 14.) Only when power is part of an official organizational role does it become authority. Authority includes the legitimate right to use resources to accomplish expected outcomes. As we discussed in the previous section, the authority to make decisions may be restricted to the top levels of the organization or dispersed throughout the organization.

One increasingly important form of such authority is the authority to enforce an organization's principles of ethical conduct. To see how one well-known organization handles this authority, see the *Ethics* box entitled "A Panel of Your Peers" on page 450.

Like responsibility, authority originates in the ownership of the organization. The owners establish a group of directors who have the authority to utilize certain resources and are responsible for managing the organization's affairs. The directors, in turn, authorize people in the organization to make decisions and to use organizational resources. Thus, they delegate authority, or power in a social context, to others.

Authority is linked to responsibility because a manager responsible for accomplishing certain results must have the authority to use resources to achieve those results.[55] The relationship between responsibility and authority must be one of parity; that is, the authority over resources must be sufficient to enable the manager to meet the output expectations of others.

But authority and responsibility differ in significant ways. Responsibility cannot be delegated down to others (as discussed in the previous section), but authority can. One complaint often heard from employees is that they have too much responsibility but not enough authority to get the job done. This indicates a lack of parity between responsibility and authority. Managers usually are quite willing to hold individuals responsible for specific tasks but are reluctant to delegate enough authority to do the job. In effect, managers try to rid themselves of responsibility for results (which they cannot do), yet they rarely like to give away their cherished authority over resources.

Brooks Kraft/Corbis

Jack Welch, former Chairman and CEO of General Electric, hired and fired many employees and reshaped the organization's businesses and its structure. During his tenure at GE, the company's value rose 4000% and was the most valuable company in the world. In 2006 Welch's net worth was estimated at $720 million.

ETHICS A Panel of Your Peers

©Trifonov_Evgeniy/iStockphoto

Kathleen Edmond is chief ethics officer at Best Buy, the world's largest consumer-electronics retailer. With a legal background, Edmond first came to Best Buy in 2002, when she joined a newly established ethics office whose original purpose was to assist corporate officers in dealing with laws designed to regulate their behavior. The position, however, sparked Edmond's interest in the broader concerns of ethical business culture, and she stayed on to build an ethics office that works to encourage employees at all levels to give careful thought to ethics-related issues and activities.

In January 2009 Edmond posted the following exercise (which we have edited slightly) on her website at www.kathleenedmond.com:

> In 2008, a Best Buy supervisor (a department manager responsible for seeing that merchandising and pricing standards are met) told a direct-report employee to put an "open item" tag on an unused, undamaged product. The tag would indicate that the product might later be priced at a markdown. The supervisor explained that he was thinking about buying the product but was not sure and instructed the employee to put the "open item" price tag beneath a regular price tag until he had made up his mind. The supervisor did not buy this particular item but did buy other products at markdowns of 55–65 percent. As it happens, the employee who had been told to place the "open item" price tag on the new product rang up these purchases. He reported that when another manager was called to the register to authorize the markdowns, he was assured by the supervisor that the store's product process manager (a higher-level manager responsible for merchandising, inventory, and loss prevention for the whole store) knew about the transaction. When questioned later about the purchases, the supervisor confirmed that he had spoken about them to the product process manager. The product process manager said that the supervisor had indeed expressed an interest in buying some products but had provided no specifics about products or pricing.

At the end of this summary, Edmond addressed the following questions to Best Buy employees:

- What ethical missteps do you see in this story?
- Which of the supervisor's actions were most alarming to you, and why?
- Are there procedures in place that could prevent this from happening at your store?

Following established procedure, Edmond referred the dispute, at the supervisor's request, to a peer review panel, which examined statements from all employees involved as well as the company's policy on inappropriate conduct. After a decision had been reached by the panel, Edmond posted its decision summary:

1. The discount applied was not consistent with other pricing of open-box items.
2. The pricing of the supervisor's purchases seemed to be based on the fact that the supervisor was purchasing them rather than on the condition of the products themselves.
3. Management was not involved in these pricing decisions.
4. The instructions to the subordinate to hide a price were considered.

So, what do you think? Given the factors considered by the peer review panel, what action should the company have taken?*

References: Ethics and Compliance Officer Association, "Kathleen Edmond, Chief Ethics Officer, Best Buy," Board of Directors, 2012, www.theecoa.org on August 7, 2012; Best Buy Inc., *Code of Business Ethics*, 2005, http://media.corporate-ir.net on August 7, 2012; Kathleen Edmond, "Supervisor Takes Massive Discounts," Kathleen Edmond, Best Buy's Chief Ethics Officer, January 13, 2009, www.kathleenedmond.com on August 7, 2012.

*In order to avoid prolonging what little suspense we have managed to build, we can report that the supervisor was terminated. In the interest of full disclosure, we also confess that we have slightly reconstructed the story: The decision to terminate the supervisor was originally made by his superiors, and his request for a hearing before the peer review panel was actually made as an appeal to this decision.

Delegation is the transfer to others of authority to make decisions and use organizational resources.

Delegation is the transfer to others of authority to make decisions and use organizational resources. Delegation of authority to lower-level managers to make decisions is common in organizations today. The important thing is to give lower-level managers authority to carry out the decisions they make. Managers typically have difficulty delegating successfully. In the Self-Assessment Exercise at the end of this chapter, you will have a chance to practice delegation.

An Alternative View of Authority

So far we have described authority as a "top-down" function in organizations; that is, authority originates at the top and is delegated downward as the managers at the top consider appropriate. In author Chester Barnard's alternative perspective, authority is seen as originating in the individual, who can choose whether or not to follow a directive from above. The choice of whether to comply with a directive is based on the degree to which the individual understands it, feels able to carry it out, and believes it to be in the best interests of the organization and consistent with personal values. This perspective has been called the **acceptance theory of authority** because it means that the manager's authority depends on the subordinate's acceptance of the manager's right to give the directive and to expect compliance.

The **acceptance theory of authority** says that the authority of a manager depends on the subordinate's acceptance of the manager's right to give directives and to expect compliance with them.

For example, assume that you are a marketing analyst and your company has a painting crew in the maintenance department. For some reason, your manager has told you to repaint your own office over the weekend. You probably would question your manager's authority to make you do this work. In fact, you would probably refuse to do it. If you received a similar request to work over the weekend to finish a report, you would be more likely to accept it and carry it out. Thus, by either accepting or rejecting the directives of a supervisor, workers can limit or expand supervisory authority. In most organizational situations, employees accept a manager's right to expect compliance on normal, reasonable directives because of the manager's legitimate position in the organizational hierarchy or in the social context of the organization. They may choose to disobey a directive and must accept the consequences if they do not accept the manager's right. It is important to note that the range of a manager's authority may differ significantly across cultures. In some cultures, employees may be expected to follow a manager's directive without question, regardless of the appropriateness or inappropriateness of the order. On the other hand, in other cultures employees may be expected to question various directives of managers if employees believe it to be in the best interest of the organization. Therefore, employees and managers who move to work in a culture different from their own may need to be watchful about how authority and responsibility are viewed.

SYNOPSIS

The structure of an organization is the system of task, reporting, and authority relationships within which the organization does its work. The purpose of organization structure is to order and coordinate the actions of employees to achieve organizational goals. Every organization structure addresses two fundamental issues: dividing available labor according to the tasks to be performed, and combining and coordinating divided tasks to ensure that tasks are accomplished.

Weber's ideal bureaucracy, Fayol's classic principles of organizing, and Likert's human organization cover many of the key features of organization structure. Weber's bureaucratic form of administration was intended to ensure stability, control, and predictable outcomes. Rules and procedures, division of labor, a hierarchy of authority, technical competence, separation of ownership, rights and property differentiation, and documentation characterize the ideal bureaucracy.

Fayol's classic principles included, among others, departmentalization, unity of command, and unity of direction; they came to be generally accepted as a means of organizing. Taken together, the fourteen principles provided the basis for the modern organization chart and for coordinating work.

Likert's human organization was based on the principles of supportive relationships, employee participation, and overlapping work groups. Likert described the human organization in terms of eight variables based on the assumption that people work best in highly supportive and cohesive work groups oriented toward organization goals.

An organization chart shows reporting relationships, work-group memberships, departments, and formal lines of communication. In a broader sense, an organization chart shows the configuration, or shape, of the organization. Configuration has four dimensions: division of labor, departmentalization, span of control, and administrative hierarchy. Division of labor is the separation of work into different jobs to be done by different people. Departmentalization is the manner in which the divided tasks are combined and allocated to work groups for coordination. Tasks can be combined into departments on the basis of business function, process, product, customer, and geographic region. Span of control is the number of people reporting to a manager; it also defines the size of work groups and is inversely related to the number of hierarchical levels in the organization. The administrative hierarchy is the system of reporting relationships in the organization.

Structural policies prescribe how employees should behave in their organizational activities. Such policies include formalization of rules and procedures and centralization of decision making. Formalization is the degree to which rules and procedures shape employees' jobs and activities. The purpose of formalization is to predict and control how employees behave on the job. Explicit rules are set down in job descriptions, policy and procedures manuals, and office memos. Implicit rules develop over time as employees become accustomed to doing things in certain ways.

Centralization concentrates decision-making authority at the top of the organizational hierarchy; under decentralization, decisions are made throughout the hierarchy.

Responsibility is an obligation to do something with the expectation of achieving some output. Authority is power that has been legitimized within a specific social context. Authority includes the legitimate right to use resources to accomplish expected outcomes. The relationship between responsibility and authority needs to be one of parity; that is, employees must have enough authority over resources to meet the expectations of others.

DISCUSSION QUESTIONS

1. Define "organization structure" and explain its role in the process of managing the organization.
2. What is the purpose of organization structure? What would an organization be like without a structure?
3. In what ways are aspects of the organization structure analogous to the structural parts of the human body?
4. How is labor divided in your college or university? In what other ways could your college or university be departmentalized?
5. What types of organizations could benefit from a small span of control? What types might benefit from a large span of control?
6. Discuss how increasing formalization might affect the role conflict and role ambiguity of employees.
7. How might the impact of formalization differ for research scientists, machine operators, and bank tellers?
8. How might centralization or decentralization affect the job characteristics specified in job design?
9. When a group makes a decision, how is responsibility for the decision apportioned among the members?
10. Why do employees typically want more authority and less responsibility?
11. Consider the job you now hold or one that you held in the past. Did your boss have the authority to direct your work? Why did he or she have this authority?
12. Describe at least four features of organization structure that were important parts of the classic view of organizing.

HOW DO YOU SEE IT?

Shedding Some Light on Adaptability

"It's the way business goes. It'll all come and go like that."

—RYAN GREY SMITH, FOUNDER OF MODERN SHED

The first major hint of Ryan Grey Smith's acute sense of adaptability in business came in the early 2000s. He and his wife, both architects, had started Grey Design Studio, which handled both interior design and larger renovation projects in the Seattle area. As Smith tells it, a client had come to see them about his 100-year-old house. "We were going to tear out the basement," he recalls, "or lift up the house, or do an addition, and we were talking about something that was \$150-, \$175,000." The client, however, noticed the shed that Smith and his wife had designed and put up on their own property—a modern 10-x-12-foot structure with a sloping roof to let light in and a finished interior that made it suitable for working and relaxing as well as storage. "He looked at our shed," reports Smith, "and he said, 'I just need this in the backyard and I can work.'

"Modern Shed really came from that," says Smith, who readily adapted to apparent conditions in the local market for architectural products and services by spinning off a whole new company. As we saw in *Video Case 8*,* Modern Shed, which was launched in 2005, provides structures that can be used as studios, offices, guestrooms, backyard getaways, and even alternatives to apartments for family members or live-in employees. Perhaps most importantly, all Modern Shed buildings are custom-designed by clients, and because the company's operations are pegged so closely to the specific but unpredictable patterns of customer needs, Smith is quite sensitive to fluctuations in demand for his product. "We'd get busy one month, and the next month we weren't *as* busy. It's the way business goes," he says philosophically. "It'll all come and go like that."

It is this understanding of "the way business goes" that underlies Smith's approach to organizing Modern Shed. Very few operations are conducted "in house," he explains, because

you'd have to have the accounting position [and] you'd have to have the organizing position, the person that's going to answer the phone, and the people that are going to make the things [you sell]. You'd have to have all these positions, and you just can't do that when you start a company. It absolutely doesn't make sense.

If he had started out with even his current modest in-house staff, says Smith, "we definitely would not be the same today. Or even, possibly, *here*.... So the most logical way to start anything is to just find the people who can help you out and work out an arrangement." Today, seven years later, Smith employs only 12 to 14 full-time employees and contracts out all of the other activities that he would otherwise have to "organize." Sales and distribution, for example, are handled by networks of 12 sales reps and 35 dealers located around the country.

Even Scott Pearl, who, as he himself puts it, "handles sales and marketing with Modern Shed," is an outside consultant who works with other clients as well. If Pearl is a particularly good fit for Modern Shed, it may be because he, too, is particularly sensitive to the ups and downs of business cycles. Pearl originally hooked up with Modern Shed, he admits, because "I needed a job." A specialist in real estate marketing, he had been caught up in "the turbulence of the 'eighties savings and loan fiasco," in which rising inflation and interest rates closed down 23 percent of the nation's savings and loan associations, which are chartered to underwrite home mortgages. Pearl thus found himself a refugee from an industry that had "absolutely been decimated," and he was attracted to Modern Shed because the company was "essentially insulated from what is going on in the general marketplace.... Interestingly enough," he points out, "Modern Shed has not been affected by the [current] downturn. In fact, if anything, our sales are increasing."

How has Ryan Smith's company managed to "insulate" itself from the current economic crisis? For one thing, structures like those offered by Modern Shed are an increasingly attractive option when it comes to adding or renovating dwelling space: Larger models, which can be equipped with plumbing and kitchen amenities, can be purchased for \$23,000 or less.

More important, however, are the effects of the company's tight organizational structure on its bottom line. Modern Shed, says Pearl, "is very lean and unstructured" because it does its work through "independent contractors" rather than in-house employees who occupy "organized positions." The firm's dealer network, for example, "is set up to take advantage of markets that we think we've got an initial logical fit with. The dealers are essentially folks that also represent other products." They are positioned in related industries, explains Pearl, but they "aren't directly competitive with Modern Shed."

The arrangement is much the same with "fabricator" Eric Johnson, an expert in *panelization*—the development of prefabricated wall, floor, and roof sections ("panels") that are assembled at building sites (all Modern Shed structures are shipped flat along with tool kits for assembly on the customer's property). Pearl sums up the advantages of "organizing" the company's operations around partners like Johnson:

He's actually set up to support not only Modern Shed, but other companies that have a panelization component. He actually comes from the world of panelization for home *builders. Because that industry has really fallen off because of the economy, we [also] become a solution for Eric.... So it works out really well with the fabrication being something that's third party, offsite, and we have no financial interest in.*

CASE QUESTIONS

1. How would you summarize Smith's *organizational goals* for Modern Shed? How would you summarize the company's *organizational structure*? Are its goals and structure compatible? If so, why? If not, why not?
2. What are the *divided tasks* that Modern Shed must perform in offering its products and delivering customer service? How would you characterize Smith's role in *coordinating* these tasks? In other words, how would you characterize his *responsibility* and *authority*? [*Hint:* Review *Video Case 8* to find out more about the company's products and marketing strategy.]
3. Consider Pearl's explanation of why Modern Shed's arrangement with Eric Johnson works so well. Focus on his three criteria for a desirable arrangement—namely, one that involves a "third party," relies on tasks performed "offsite," and avoids any "financial interest" on the part of Modern Shed. Explain why each of these criteria is compatible with the company's *organizational goals* and *structure*.

ADDITIONAL SOURCES

Aria Shepherd, "Modern Shed: A Chic Outdoor Space," *Seattle Times*, September 13, 2008, http://seattletimes.nwsource.com on June 25, 2012; Modern Shed, "About Us," "Models" (2006), www.modern-shed.com on June 25, 2012; Michael Cannell, "Instead of Trading Up, Adding a High-Style Shed," *New York Times*, September 11, 2008, www.nytimes.com on June 25, 2012; Debra Prinzing, "Elegant, Stylish … and Prefabricated," *Debra Prinzing*, August 15, 2008, www.debraprinzing.com on June 25, 2012; Debra Prinzing, "In Praise of the Modern Shed," *Debra Prinzing*, September 15, 2008, www.debraprinzing on June 25, 2012; Jonathan Lambert, "Prefab Sheds—The Solution to a Hectic Lifestyle," *Ezine Articles*, June 7, 2011, http://ezinearticles.com on June 25, 2012.

*See *Video Case 8* for an overview of Modern Shed's product line and strategies for marketing it.

EXPERIENCING ORGANIZATIONAL BEHAVIOR

Understanding Organization Structure

Purpose: This exercise will help you understand the configurational and operational aspects of organization structure.

Format: You will interview at least five employees in different parts of either the college or university you attend or a small- to medium-sized organization and analyze its structure. (You may want to coordinate this exercise with the exercise in Chapter 17.)

Procedure: If you use a local organization, your first task is to find one with fifty to five hundred employees. The organization should have more than two hierarchical levels, but it should not be too complex to understand in a short period of study. You may want to check with your professor before contacting the company. Your initial contact should be with the highest-ranking manager, if possible. Be sure that top management is aware of your project and gives its approval.

If you use your local college or university, you could talk to professors, secretaries, and other administrative staff in the admissions office, student services department, athletic department, library, or many other areas. Be sure to represent a variety of jobs and levels in your interviews.

Using the material in this chapter, interview employees to obtain the following information on the structure of the organization:

1. The type of departmentalization (business function, process, product, customer, geographic region)
2. The typical span of control at each level of the organization
3. The number of levels in the hierarchy
4. The administrative ratio (ratio of managers to total employees and ratio of managers to production employees)

5. The degree of formalization (to what extent are rules and procedures written down in job descriptions, policy and procedures manuals, and memos?)
6. The degree of decentralization (to what extent are employees at all levels involved in making decisions?)

Interview three to five employees of the organization at different levels and in different departments. One should hold a top-level position. Be sure to ask the questions in a way that is clear to the respondents; they may not be familiar with the terminology used in this chapter.

Students should produce a report with a paragraph on each configurational and operational aspect of structure listed in this exercise as well as an organization chart of the company, a discussion of differences in responses from the employees interviewed, and a description of any unusual structural features (for example, a situation in which employees report to more than one person or to no one). You may want to send a copy of your report to the company's top management.

Follow-Up Questions

1. Which aspects of structure were the hardest to obtain information about? Why?
2. If there were differences in the responses of the employees you interviewed, how do you account for them?

BUILDING MANAGERIAL SKILLS

Exercise Overview: Managers typically inherit an existing organization structure when they are promoted or hired into a position as manager. Often, however, after working with the existing structure for a while, they feel the need to rearrange the structure to increase the productivity or performance of the organization. This exercise provides you with the opportunity to restructure an existing organization.

Exercise Background: Recall the analysis you did in the "Experiencing Organizational Behavior" exercise above, in which you analyzed the structure of an existing organization. In that exercise you described the configurational and operational aspects of the structure of a local organization or a department at your college or university.

Exercise Task: Develop a different organization structure for that organization. You may utilize any or all of the factors described in this chapter. For example, you could alter the span of control, the administrative hierarchy, and the method of departmentalization as well as the formalization and centralization of the organization. Remember, the key to structure is to develop a way to coordinate the divided tasks. You should draw a new organization chart and develop a rationale for your new design.

Conclude by addressing the following questions:

1. How difficult was it to come up with a different way of structuring the organization?
2. What would it take to convince the current head of that organization to go along with your suggested changes?

SELF-ASSESSMENT EXERCISE

Making Some Sense of Yourself

As we saw in Chapter 5, *participation* and *empowerment* go hand in hand as techniques for motivating employees by getting them involved in an organization's decision-making processes. We also pointed out that both may be regarded as extensions of job design because both fundamentally affect how employees perform their jobs.

This exercise is designed to help you determine how much empowerment you feel in your own work, whether at a job or in school. If you have a job, consider that your work; if you are a student, apply this exercise to your school work.

The twenty statements below reflect attitudes that people can have toward their work. Using the following scale, indicate the extent to which, in your opinion, each statement is true of you.

1. Very strongly disagree
2. Strongly disagree
3. Disagree
4. Neutral

5. Agree
6. Strongly agree
7. Very strongly agree

_______ 1. The work that I do is very important to me.

_______ 2. I am confident about my ability to do my work.

_______ 3. I have significant autonomy in determining how I do my work.

_______ 4. I have significant impact on what happens in my work unit.

_______ 5. I trust my coworkers to be completely honest with me.

_______ 6. My work activities are personally meaningful to me.

_______ 7. My work is within the scope of my competence and capabilities.

_______ 8. I can decide how to go about doing my own work.

_______ 9. I have a great deal of control over what happens in my work unit.

_______ 10. I trust my coworkers to share important information with me.

_______ 11. I care about what I do in my work.

_______ 12. I am confident about my capabilities to perform my work successfully.

_______ 13. I have considerable opportunity for independence and freedom in how I do my work.

_______ 14. I have significant influence over what happens in my work unit.

_______ 15. I trust my coworkers to keep the promises they make.

_______ 16. The work I do has special meaning and importance to me.

_______ 17. I have mastered the skills necessary to do my work.

_______ 18. I have a chance to use personal initiative in carrying out my work.

_______ 19. My opinion counts in my work unit's decision making.

_______ 20. I believe that my coworkers care about my well-being.

How to score: Each of the twenty statements in this exercise falls into one of five skill areas. You will therefore be calculating your score in each of these areas. Scoring requires two steps:

1. Total up your scores for the four items in each skill area.
2. Divide your total score in each area by 4 to find your mean score.

Scoring Key

Skill Area	Statements	(Total ÷ 4)
Self-efficacy—your sense of personal competence	2, 7, 12, 17	
Self-determination—your sense of personal choice	3, 8, 13, 18	
Personal consequence—your sense of having impact	4, 9, 14, 19	
Meaningfulness—your sense of value in your activities	1, 6, 11, 16	
Trust—your sense of security	5, 10, 15, 20	

Once you have determined your mean scores, you can compare them to the findings recorded in the following table, which reflect the scores of about 3,000 U.S. middle managers.

Comparison Data

Skill Area	Mean	Top Third	Bottom Third
Self-efficacy	5.76	>6.52	<5.00
Self-determination	5.50	>6.28	<4.72
Personal consequence	5.49	>6.34	<4.64
Meaningfulness	5.88	>6.65	<5.12
Trust	5.33	>60.3	<4.73

Reference

David A. Whetten and Kim S. Cameron, *Developing Management Skills,* 7th ed. (Upper Saddle River, NJ: Prentice Hall, 2007), 445–46, 451, 489–90.

CHAPTER 17

Organization Design

Chapter Outline

- Contingency Approaches to Organization Design
- Strategy, Structural Imperatives, and Strategic Choice
- Organizational Designs
- Contemporary Organization Design Processes

Chapter Learning Objectives

After studying this chapter, you should be able to:

1. **Describe the basic premise of contingency approaches to organization design.**
2. **Discuss how strategy and the structural imperatives combine to affect organization design.**
3. **Summarize five types of organization designs.**
4. **Explain several contemporary approaches to organization design.**

Codesharing the Wealth

"American [Airlines] helped originate the whole idea of alliances and partnerships. If somebody should be good at it, you could make the argument they should be."

—Investment analyst George Van Horn

Assume you are a businessperson in New York who needs to fly to Hong Kong. Logging on to Orbitz, you find that American Airlines (AMR) offers a nonstop round-trip flight for $2,692. Because Orbitz recommends that you "Act Fast! Only 1 ticket left at this price!" you buy your ticket online. On your departure date, you arrive at the American Airlines ticket desk, only to be referred to the Cathay Pacific Airways counter. Your flight, the ticket agent informs you, is actually operated by Cathay, and she points to the four-digit "codeshare number" on your ticket. Bewildered but hoping that you are still booked on a flight to Hong Kong, you hustle to the Cathay counter, where your ticket is in fact processed. Settled into your seat a few hours later, you decide to get on your laptop to see if you can figure out why you are and are not on the flight that you booked. Going back to Orbitz, you find that, like American, Cathay does indeed offer a nonstop round-trip flight to and from its home city of Hong Kong—for $1,738. It dawns on you that if you had bought your ticket directly from Cathay, you would be sitting in the same seat on the same airplane for almost $1,000 less.

If this scenario sounds confusing, that is because it is, even to veteran flyers. What is confusing about it is the practice of *codesharing*, which works like this: You buy a ticket from Airline A for a flight operated by Airline B on a route that Airline A does not otherwise serve. This practice is possible if both airlines, like AMR and Cathay, belong to the same *airline alliance* (in this case, Oneworld).

On the surface, the advantages to the airlines may seem mostly a matter of perception: An airline *seems* to be serving certain markets that it does not actually serve and flying certain routes more frequently than it actually does. The networks formed by codesharing agreements, however, are real, and the breadth of an airline's network is a real factor in attracting high-margin corporate travelers. In fact, the spread of codesharing has led directly to the formation of much

Frances Roberts/Alamy

Although the merger between United and Continental was official May 2010, these pilots conducted an informational picket outside the New York Stock Exchange and reminded us that the merger is far more than new logos painted on planes or a legal arrangement. The key to a successful merger is in how the people and tasks are coordinated in the new organization.

larger "alliances" of carriers who cooperate on a substantial level, including codesharing and shared frequent-flyer programs. The three largest airline alliances are the Star Alliance, which includes United Airlines, US Airways, Air Canada, Air China, and Scandinavian Airlines; SkyTeam, which includes Delta, Air France, Alitalia, and Dutch-based KLM; and Oneworld, which includes AMR, Cathay, Qantas, British Airways, and Japan's JAL.

An airline alliance is a good example of a *virtual organization*—a temporary alliance formed by two or more organizations to pursue a specific venture or to exploit a specific opportunity. Although each member remains an independently owned and managed organization, alliance members can save money by sharing sales, maintenance, and operational facilities and staff (such as check-in, boarding, and other on-the-ground personnel), and they can also cut costs on purchases and investments by negotiating volume discounts. The chief advantages, however, are breadth of service and geographical reach—in short, size (both perceived and real). Star Alliance, for example, operates more than 21,000 daily flights to 1,356 airports in 193 countries. In 2011, its members carried 679 million passengers for a total of 1.3 trillion *revenue passenger kilometers* (1 *rpk* means that 1 paying passenger was flown 1 kilometer). Based on *rpk* (which is really a measure of sales volume), Star commands 25.8 percent of global market share in the airline industry—just slightly less than the combined market share of all airlines that do not belong to any of the three major alliances.

Note that our definition of a *virtual organization* indicates a "*temporary* alliance," and shifts by members of airline alliances are not unheard of. In January 2009, for example, a few months after merger talks had broken down with United Airlines, Continental Airlines, a member of SkyTeam since 2004, announced that it was joining United in the Star Alliance. According to one analyst, the move, which took effect in October 2009, "was obviously a precursor to a full-blown merger," and, sure enough, Continental and United merged in May 2010 under a parent company called United Continental Holdings. The new airline remains a member of the Star Alliance.

The Continental–United merger was particularly bad news for both AMR, a member of Oneworld and the country's largest stand-alone airline, and US Airways Group, a member of SkyTeam and the fifth-largest U.S. carrier. With the merger of Continental and United, observed Vaughn Cordle, chief analyst at Airline Forecasts, a specialist in industry investment research, "the odds of … bankruptcy for US Airways and American increase because it will be too difficult, if not impossible, for them to remain viable as stand-alone businesses…. [W]ithout a new strategic direction and significant changes in the industry's structure," Cordle predicted, AMR and US Airways "will continue on the slow … path to failure."

Cordle recommended consolidation, and many analysts reported that AMR management had begun considering its options even before the Continental–United merger. Who is the most likely partner if AMR decides to consolidate? John Kasarda, an aviation expert at the University of North Carolina's Kenan-Flagler Business School, suggested that an AMR–US Airways merger was not out of the question: "It would be more out of necessity," he admitted, but both airlines had been "asleep at the switch" and could expect their respective shareholders to demand some kind of action. A merger, however, would have required US Airways to leave the Star Alliance, and US Airways announced that "we highly value our membership in Star and maintain that it is the strongest alliance."

In any case, observers agreed that AMR needed to make some kind of strategic move. Once the world's largest airline, it had dropped to number 3, behind the new Continental–United and Delta Airlines. Among U.S. airlines, AMR had the lowest margins and highest costs, and it was also the only U.S. airline that lost money in 2010. But George Van Horn, an analyst at the research firm IBISWorld, pointed out that AMR had considerable experience at the kind of deal making in question: American, he reminded potential investors, "helped originate the whole idea of alliances and partnerships. If somebody should be good at it, you could make the argument they should be."

But "they"—namely, AMR Chairman/CEO Tom Horton and his management team—decided not to merge with US Airways or anybody else, and in November 2011 AMR filed for Chapter 11 bankruptcy protection. Moreover, the airline has since resisted any further merger proposals, with Horton insisting—despite evidence that AMR's market share is eroding—that the airline will not only emerge from bankruptcy independently but will also recover its former position in the industry. Most observers, however, continue to promote a merger as AMR's best strategy. "It's not an option," says one. "It's not an alternative. It's inevitable." Not surprisingly, AMR's most avid suitor is US Airways, which became a player in the company's bankruptcy proceedings by buying up some of AMR's debt in July 2012. Other possible merger partners include JetBlue and Frontier Airlines.

What Do You Think?

1. Do you think such practices as codesharing are fair to consumers?
2. In the long run, do you think that the shakeout in the airline industry—with companies merging and forming alliances—will benefit consumers? Why or why not?

References: "Orbitz: Flights," *Orbitz.com*, May 3, 2010, www.orbitz.com on May 3, 2010; Star Alliance, "Facts and Figures" (2012), www.staralliance.com on August 16, 2012; Andrew Clark, "United and Continental Merge to Create World's Biggest Airline," *The Guardian*, September 17, 2010, www.guardian.co.uk on August 16, 2012; Susanna Ray, "AMR May Seek Alliances as Mergers Erase Lead in Size," Bloomberg, May 3, 2010, www.bloomberg.com on August 16, 2012; Andrew Ross Sorkin, "Airlines Dance around a Merger," *New York Times*, July 10, 2012, http://query.nytimes.com on August 16, 2012; Mike Spector, Susan Carey, and Anupreeta Das, "American Airlines Opens Its Door to a Merger," *Wall Street Journal*, July 10, 2012, http://online.wsj.com on August 16, 2012; Mary Schlangenstein, "US Airways Gets Voice in AMR Bankruptcy by Buying Debt," Bloomberg, July 13, 2012, www.bloomberg.com on August 16, 2012.

Most organizations struggle to find the best organizational design in order to survive in an ever-changing environment. Airlines are no exception. In their case, however, they often look outside of themselves to larger alliances in order to compete effectively. These alliances become temporary arrangements that allow them to share the benefits of larger target markets and reduced costs. Many companies are constantly reorganizing to try to increase their performance, productivity, and response times—or just to survive. The primary issue is how to determine which organizational form is right for a given organization at this point in time to position the organization for the future. In this chapter we describe several approaches to organization design.

CONTINGENCY APPROACHES TO ORGANIZATION DESIGN

In the **universal approach** to organization design, prescriptions or propositions are designed to work in any circumstances.

Under the **contingency approach** to organization design, the desired outcomes for the organization can be achieved in several ways.

Organization designs vary from rigid bureaucracies to flexible matrix systems. Most theories of organization design take either a universal or a contingency approach. A **universal approach** is one whose prescriptions or propositions are designed to work in any situation. Thus, a universal design prescribes the "one best way" to structure the jobs, authority, and reporting relationships of the organization, regardless of factors such as the organization's external environment, the industry, and the type of work to be done. The classical approaches discussed in Chapter 16 are all universal approaches: Weber's ideal bureaucracy, Fayol's classic principles of organizing, and Likert's human organization. A **contingency approach**, on the other hand, suggests that organizational efficiency and effectiveness can be achieved in several ways. In a contingency design, specific conditions such as the environment, technology, and the organization's workforce determine the structure. Figure 17.1 shows the distinction between the universal and contingency approaches. This distinction is similar to the one between universal and contingency approaches to motivation (Chapter 4), job design (Chapter 5), and leadership (Chapters 12 and 13). Although no one particular form of organization is generally accepted, the contingency approach most closely represents current thinking.

Weber, Fayol, and Likert (see Chapter 16) each proposed an organization design that is independent of the nature of the organization and its environment. Although each of their approaches contributed to our understanding of the organizing process and the practice of management, none has proved to be universally applicable. In this chapter

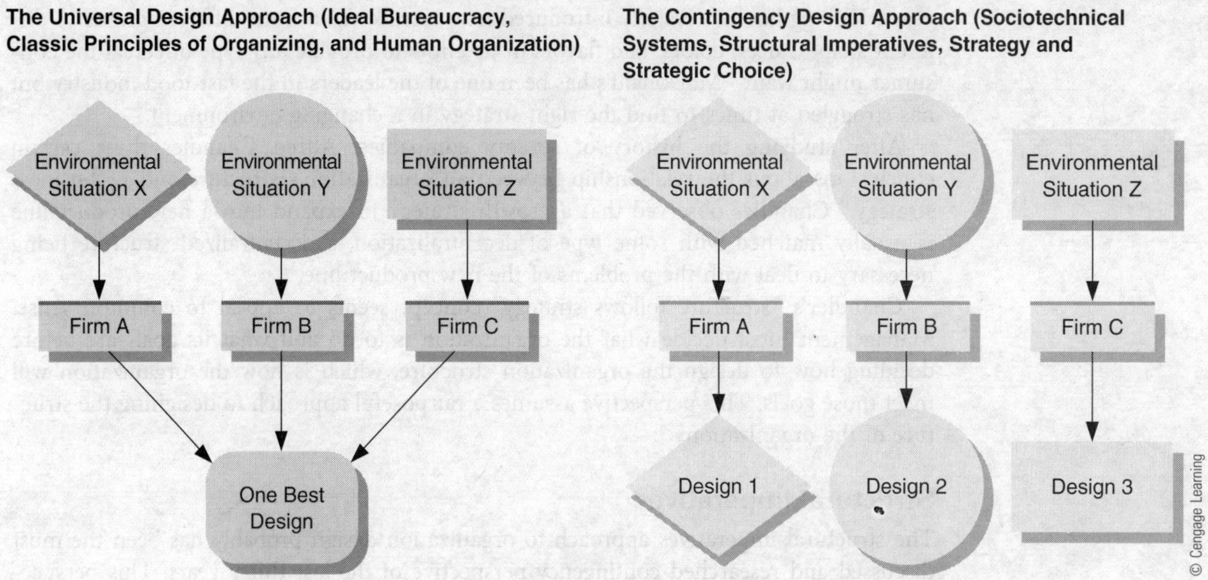

FIGURE 17.1

Universal and Contingency Approaches to Organizational Design

The universal approach looks for the single best way to design an organization regardless of situational issues. The contingency approach designs the organization to fit the situation.

we turn to several contingency designs, which attempt to specify the conditions, or contingency factors, under which they are likely to be most effective. The contingency factors include such things as the strategy of the organization, its technology, the environment, the organization's size, and the social system within which the organization operates.

The contingency approach has been criticized as being unrealistic because managers are expected to observe a change in one of the contingency factors and then to make a rational structural alteration. On the other hand, Lex Donaldson has argued that it is reasonable to expect organizations to respond to lower organizational performance, which may result from a lack of response to some significant change in one or several contingency factors.[1]

STRATEGY, STRUCTURAL IMPERATIVES, AND STRATEGIC CHOICE

The decision about how to design the organization structure is based on numerous factors. In this section, we present several views of the determinants of organization structure and integrate them into a single approach. We begin with the strategic view.

Strategy

Strategy is the set of plans and actions necessary to achieve organizational goals.

A **strategy** is the set of plans and actions necessary to achieve organizational goals.[2] Every organization tries to develop a strategy that will enable it to meet its goals. Kellogg, for example, has attempted to be the leader in the ready-to-eat cereal industry by pursuing a strategy that combines product differentiation and market segmentation. Over the years, Kellogg has successfully introduced new cereals made from different grains in different shapes, sizes, colors, and flavors in its effort to provide any type of cereal the consumer might want.[3] McDonald's has been one of the leaders in the fast-food industry but has struggled at times to find the right strategy in a changing environment.[4]

After studying the history of seventy companies, Alfred Chandler drew certain conclusions about the relationship between an organization's structure and its business strategy.[5] Chandler observed that a growth strategy to expand into a new product line is usually matched with some type of decentralization, a decentralized structure being necessary to deal with the problems of the new product line.

Chandler's "structure follows strategy" concept seems to appeal to common sense. Management must decide what the organization is to do and what its goals are before deciding how to design the organization structure, which is how the organization will meet those goals. This perspective assumes a purposeful approach to designing the structure of the organization.

Structural Imperatives

The structural-imperatives approach to organization design probably has been the most discussed and researched contingency perspective of the last thirty years. This perspective was not formulated by a single theorist or researcher, and it has not evolved from a systematic and cohesive research effort. Rather, it gradually emerged from a vast number of studies that sought to address the question "What are the compelling factors that determine how the organization must be structured to be effective?" As Figure 17.2 shows, the three factors that have been identified as **structural imperatives** are size, technology, and environment.

Structural imperatives —size, technology, and environment—are the three primary determinants of organization structure.

Size The size of an organization can be gauged in many ways. Usually it is measured in terms of total number of employees, value of the organization's assets, total sales in the previous year (or number of clients served), or physical capacity. The method of measurement is very important, although the different measures usually are correlated.[6]

Generally, larger organizations have a more complex structure than smaller ones. Peter Blau and his associates concluded that large size is associated with greater specialization of labor, a larger span of control, more hierarchical levels, and greater formalization.[7] These multiple effects are shown in Figure 17.3. Increasing size leads to more specialization of labor within a work unit, which increases the amount of differentiation among work units and the number of levels in the hierarchy, resulting in a need for more intergroup formalization. With greater specialization within the unit, there is less need for coordination within groups; thus, the span of control can be larger. Larger spans of control mean fewer first-line managers, but the need for more intergroup coordination may require

FIGURE 17.2

The Structural-Imperatives Approach

Organizational size, environment, and technology determine how an organization should be structured to be effective.

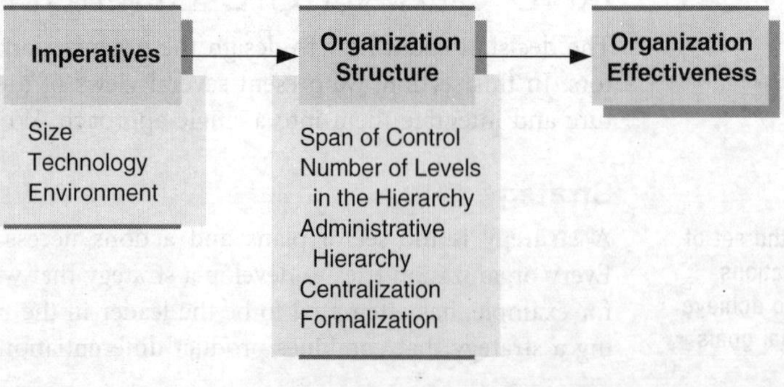

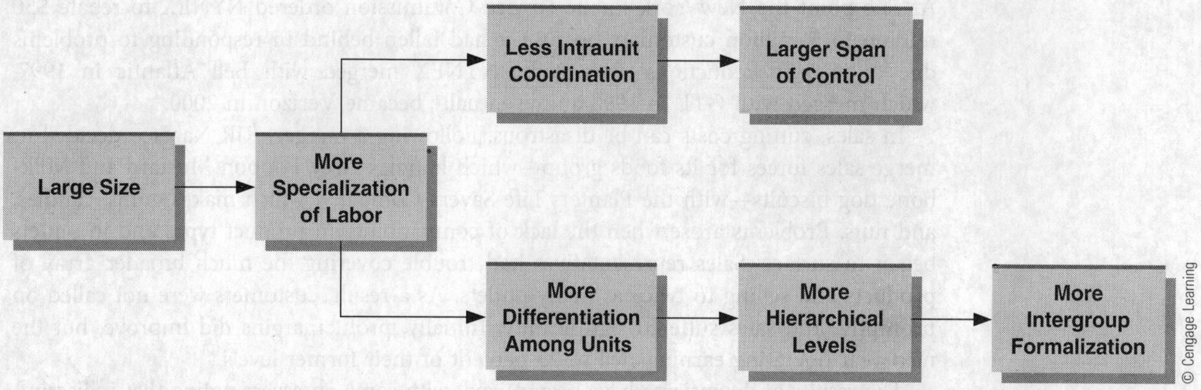

FIGURE 17.3

Impact of Large Size on Organization Structure

As organizations grow larger, their structures usually change in predictable ways. Larger organizations tend to have more complex structures, larger spans of control, and more rules and procedures.

more second- and third-line managers and staff personnel to coordinate them. Large organizations may therefore be more efficient because of their large spans of control and reduced administrative overhead; however, the greater differentiation among units makes the system more complex. Studies by researchers associated with the University of Aston in Birmingham, England, and others have shown similar results.[8]

Economies of scale are another advantage of large organizations. In a large operation, fixed costs—for example, plant and equipment—can be spread over more units of output, thereby reducing the cost per unit. In addition, some administrative activities such as purchasing, clerical work, and marketing can be accomplished for a large number of units at the same cost as for a small number. Their cost can then be spread over the larger number of units, again reducing unit cost.

Companies such as W. L. Gore, AT&T Technologies, General Electric's Aircraft Engines products group, and S. C. Johnson & Son have gone against the conventional wisdom that larger is always better in manufacturing plants. They cite as their main reasons the smaller investment required for smaller plants, the reduced need to produce a variety of products, and the desire to decrease organizational complexity (that is, reduce the number of hierarchical levels and shorten lines of communication). In a number of instances, smaller plants have resulted in increased team spirit, improved productivity, and higher profits.[9] Other studies have found that the relationship between size and structural complexity is less clear than the Blau results indicate. These studies suggest that size must be examined in relation to the technology of the organization.[10]

Traditionally, as organizations have grown, several layers of advisory staff have been added to help coordinate the complexities inherent in any large organization. However, even in good times, some organizations have gone through significant staff reductions. Known as **organizational downsizing** and discussed briefly in Chapter 16, this popular trend is aimed primarily at reducing the size of corporate staff and middle management to reduce costs.

Organizational downsizing is a popular trend aimed at reducing the size of corporate staff and middle management to reduce costs.

Companies such as NYNEX and RJR Nabisco have made cutbacks with disastrous results, and NYNEX had to hire back hundreds of employees who had taken an early retirement program to try to build back its reputation for customer service. NYNEX Corporation, the telephone company in the northeastern region of the United States in the 1980s and early 1990s, had made massive cutbacks and layoffs in order to survive.

At one point the New York Public Service Commission ordered NYNEX to rebate $50 million to 5 million customers because it had fallen behind in responding to problems due to its staff reductions. Eventually, NYNEX merged with Bell Atlantic in 1997, which merged with GTE in 1998 and eventually became Verizon in 2000.

In sales, cutting costs can be disastrous. Following a merger, RJR Nabisco decided to merge sales forces for its foods group—which handles Grey Poupon Mustard and Milk-bone dog biscuits—with the Planters Life Savers Company, which makes gums, candies, and nuts. Problems arose when the lack of compatibility in product types and in outlets began to surface. Sales representatives had trouble covering the much broader array of products and selling to twice as many outlets. As a result, customers were not called on promptly, and sales suffered significantly. Initially, profit margins did improve, but the next year operating earnings fell to 25 percent of their former levels.[11]

The results of downsizing have been mixed, with some observers noting that indiscriminate across-the-board cuts may leave the organization weak in certain key areas. However, positive results often include quicker decision making because fewer layers of management must approve every decision. One review of research on organizational downsizing found that it had both psychological and sociological impacts. Studies suggest that in a downsizing environment, size affects organization design in very complex ways.[12]

In difficult economic periods such as those recently experienced worldwide, many companies have been forced to reduce the number of employees throughout the organization through large-scale layoffs. Several years ago, during a significant economic downturn, sales for Honeywell International, Inc., fell 11 percent in two years. Honeywell responded with massive layoffs of more than 31,000 employees and canceled plans for many new products and other global expansion plans. Executives now claim those moves were disastrous for the company when the economy turned around. During the most recent recession, when their sales fell 15 percent and profits dropped 23 percent, Honeywell took a more measured response by limiting layoffs to 6,000 and using benefit cuts and furloughs to reduce expenses.[13] This time they expect to be ready for the rebound with hundreds of new products and a full workforce.

Organizational technology refers to the mechanical and intellectual processes that transform inputs into outputs.

Technology **Organizational technology** consists of the mechanical and intellectual processes that transform raw materials into products and services for customers. For example, the primary technology employed by major oil companies transforms crude oil (input) into gasoline, motor oil, heating oil, and other petroleum-based products (outputs). Prudential Insurance uses actuarial tables and information-processing technologies to produce its insurance services. Of course, most organizations use multiple technologies. Oil companies use research and information-processing technologies in their laboratories, where new petroleum products and processes are generated.

Although there is general agreement that organizational technology is important, the means by which this technology has been evaluated and measured have varied widely. Five approaches to examining the technology of the organization are shown in Table 17.1. For convenience, we have classified these approaches according to the names of their proponents.

In an early study of the relationship between technology and organization structure, Joan Woodward categorized manufacturing technologies by their complexity: unit or small-batch, large-batch or mass production, and continuous process.[14] Tom Burns and George Stalker proposed that the rate of change in technology determines the best method of structuring the organization.[15] Charles Perrow developed a technological continuum, with routine technologies at one end and nonroutine technologies at the other, and claimed that all organizations could be classified on his routine-to-nonroutine continuum.[16] Thompson claimed that all organizations could be classified into one of three

Table 17.1 Summary of Approaches to Technology

APPROACH	CLASSIFICATION OF TECHNOLOGY	EXAMPLE
Woodward (1958 and 1965) (cit. no. 13)	Unit or small-batch	Customized parts made one at a time
	Large-batch or mass production	Automobile assembly line
	Continuous process	Chemical plant, petroleum refinery
Burns and Stalker (1961) (cit. no. 14)	Rate of technological change	Slow: large manufacturing; rapid: computer industry
Perrow (1967) (cit. no. 15)	Routine	Standardized products (Procter & Gamble, General Foods)
	Nonroutine	New technology products or processes (computers, telecommunications)
Thompson (1967) (cit. no. 16)	Long-linked	Assembly line
	Mediating	Bank
	Intensive	General hospital
Aston studies: Hickson, Pugh, and Pheysey (1969) (cit. no. 17)	Workflow integration; operations, materials, and knowledge technologies	Technology differs in various parts of the organization

technological categories: long-linked, mediating, and intensive.[17] Finally, a group of English researchers at the University of Aston developed three categories of technology based on the type of workflow involved: operations, material, and knowledge.[18] These perspectives on technology are somewhat similar in that all (except the Aston typology) address the adaptability of the technological system to change. Large-batch or mass production, routine, and long-linked technologies are not very adaptable to change. At the opposite end of the continuum, continuous-process, nonroutine, and intensive technologies are readily adaptable to change.

The effect of technology in organizations often is a function of the extent to which the technology creates or demands that tasks be interdependent in order to be accomplished. The more interdependent the tasks, the more coordination is required. Conversely, when the technology allows tasks to be more independent, less coordination is required. This effect may seem to be most pronounced in knowledge work, where engineers or analysts may appear to work independently; however, a closer examination reveals that their tasks are highly interdependent and require very close coordination.[19]

One major contribution of the study of organizational technology is the recognition that organizations have more than one important "technology" that enables them to accomplish their tasks. Instead of examining technology in isolation, the Aston group recognized that size and technology are related in determining organization structure.[20] They found that in smaller organizations, technology had more direct effects on the structure. In large organizations, however, they, like Blau, found that structure depended less on the operations technology and more on size considerations such as the number of employees. In large organizations, each department or division may have a different technology that

Chinese workers assemble cars at a plant of Beijing Hyundai in Beijing, China. In many manufacturing plants the technology of the manufacturing process often dictates much about how the organization is structured.

determines how that department or division should be structured. In short, in small organizations the structure depended primarily on the technology, whereas in large organizations the need to coordinate complicated activities was the most important factor. Thus, both organizational size and technology are important considerations in organization design.

Global technology variations come in two forms: variations in available technology and variations in attitudes toward technology. The technology available affects how organizations can do business. Many developing countries, for example, lack electric power sources, telephones, and trucking equipment, not to mention computers and robots. A manager working in such a country must be prepared to deal with many frustrations. Some Brazilian officials convinced a U.S. company to build a high-tech plant in their country. Midway through construction, however, the government of Brazil decided it would not allow the company to import some highly accurate measuring instruments that it needed to produce its products. The new plant was abandoned before it opened.[21]

The **organizational environment** is everything outside an organization and includes all elements—people, other organizations, economic factors, objects, and events—that lie outside the boundaries of the organization.

The **general environment** includes the broad set of dimensions and factors within which the organization operates, including political-legal, sociocultural, technological, economic, and international factors.

The **task environment** includes specific organizations, groups, and individuals who influence the organization.

Attitudes toward technology also vary across cultures. Surprisingly, Japan only began to support basic research in the 1980s. For many years, the Japanese government encouraged its companies to take basic research findings discovered elsewhere (often in the United States) and figure out how to apply them to consumer products (applied research). In the mid-1980s, however, the government changed its stance and started to encourage basic research as well.[22] Most Western nations have a generally favorable attitude toward technology, whereas until the 1990s, China and other Asian countries (with the exception of Japan) did not.

Despite all of the emphasis on technology's role as a primary determinant of structure, there is some support for viewing it from the perspective that the strategy and structure of the organization determine what types of technology are appropriate. For example, Walmart and Dell Computers are careful to use new information technology only in ways that support their strategy and structure. Walmart's information systems keep track of its inventory from receipt to shelf placement to purchase, and Dell uses technology to optimize its manufacturing processes. Because both companies started with low-tech processes and then adopted new technologies over time, the technology clearly was a result of each firm's structure and strategy, and not the other way around.[23]

Environment The **organizational environment** includes all of the elements—people, other organizations, economic factors, objects, and events—that lie outside the boundaries of the organization. The environment is composed of two layers: the general environment and the task environment. The **general environment** includes all of a broad set of dimensions and factors within which the organization operates, including political-legal, social, cultural, technological, economic, and international factors. The **task environment** includes specific organizations, groups, and individuals who influence the organization. People in the task environment include customers, suppliers, donors, regulators, inspectors, and shareholders. Among the organizations in the task environment are competitors, legislatures, and regulatory agencies. Economic factors in the task environment might include interest rates, international trade factors, and the unemployment rate in a particular area. Objects in the task environment include such things as buildings, vehicles, and trees. Events that may affect organizations include weather, elections, or war.

It is necessary to determine the boundaries of the organization to understand where the environment begins. These boundaries may be somewhat elusive, or at least changeable, and thus difficult to define. Many companies are spinning off some business units but then continuing to do business with them as suppliers. Therefore, one day a manager may be a member of an organization and the next day might be a part of that organization's environment. But for the most part, we can say that certain people, groups, or buildings are either in the organization or in the environment. For example, a college student shopping for a personal computer is part of the environment of HP, Dell, IBM, and other computer manufacturers. However, if the student works for one of these computer manufacturers, he or she is not part of that company's environment but is within the boundaries of the organization.

This definition of organizational environment emphasizes the expanse of the environment within which the organization operates. It may give managers the false impression that the environment is outside their control and interest. But because the environment completely encloses the organization, managers must be constantly concerned about it. Most managers these days are aware that the environment is changing rapidly. The difficulty for most is to determine how those changes affect the company.

The manager, then, faces an enormous, only vaguely specified environment that somehow affects the organization. Managing the organization within such an environment may seem like an overwhelming task. The alternatives for the manager are to (1) ignore the environment because of its complexity and focus on managing the internal operations of the company, (2) exert maximum energy in gathering information on every part of the environment and in trying to react to every environmental factor, and (3) pay attention to specific aspects of the task environment, responding only to those that most clearly affect the organization.

To ignore environmental factors entirely and focus on internal operations leaves the company in danger of missing major environmental shifts such as changes in customer preferences, technological breakthroughs, and new regulations. To expend large amounts of energy, time, and money exploring every facet of the environment may take more out of the organization than the effort may return.

The third alternative—to carefully analyze segments of the task environment that most affect the organization and to respond accordingly—is the most prudent course. The issue, then, is to determine which parts of the environment should receive the manager's attention. In the remainder of this section, we examine two perspectives on the organizational environment: the analysis of environmental components and environmental uncertainty.

Forces in the environment have different effects on different companies. For example, all organizations in the healthcare industry in the United States are quite concerned about the direction of the government's involvement in health care. It is not that various individuals and organizations are for or against any given proposal; their primary concern is how the various proposals will affect their operations. In fact, many industry leaders have been involved in consulting and lobbying activities in efforts to influence the final outcome. In effect, these organizations are trying to change the relevant environment, and will then have to determine how their organizations will be affected. It is most likely that it will take several years for organizations to fully adapt to new regulations. Quite different environmental forces, on the other hand, affect McDonald's—consumer demand, disposable income, the cost of meat and bread, and gasoline prices. Thus, the task environment, the specific set of environmental forces that influence the operations of an organization, varies among organizations.

The one environmental characteristic that brings together all of these different environmental influences and appears to have the most effect on the structure of the organization is uncertainty. **Environmental uncertainty** exists when managers do not have sufficient information about environmental factors, and thus they have difficulty predicting the impact of these factors on the organization.[24] Uncertainty has been described as resulting from complexity and dynamism in the environment. **Environmental complexity** is the number of environmental components that factor into organizational decision making. **Environmental dynamism** is the degree to which important environmental components change.

Environmental uncertainty exists when managers have little information about environmental events and their impact on the organization.

Environmental complexity is the number of environmental components that factor into organizational decision making.

Environmental dynamism is the degree to which environmental components that factor into organizational decision making change.

In a low-uncertainty environment, there are few important components and they change infrequently. A company in the cardboard container industry might have a highly certain environment when demand is steady, manufacturing processes are stable, and government regulations have remained largely unchanged. In contrast, in highly uncertain environments there are many important components involved in decision making that often change. The environment of health care in the United States is now highly uncertain with the new healthcare bill and the likelihood of continuing changes in the future. The toy industry also is in a highly uncertain environment. As they develop new toys, toy companies must stay in tune with movies, television shows, and cartoons, as well as with public sentiment. Between 1983 and 1988, Saturday morning cartoons were little more than animated stories about children's toys. Recently, however, due to the disappointing sales of many toys presented in cartoons designed to promote them, most toy companies have left the toy-based cartoon business. Many toys that are now sold are based on movies.[25]

Environmental characteristics and uncertainty have been important factors in explaining organization structure, strategy, and performance. For example, the characteristics of the environment affect how managers perceive the environment, which in turn affects how they adapt the structure of the organization to meet environmental demands.[26] The environment has also been shown to affect the degree to which a firm's strategy enhances its performance.[27] That is, a certain strategy will enhance organizational performance to the extent that it is appropriate for the environment in which the organization operates. Finally, the environment is directly related to organizational performance.[28] The environment and the organization's response to it are crucial to success.

An organization attempts to continue as a viable entity in a dynamic environment. The environment completely encloses the organization, and managers must be constantly concerned about it. The organization as a whole, as well as departments and divisions within it, are created to deal with different challenges, problems, and uncertainties. James Thompson suggested that organizations design a structure to protect the dominant technology of the organization, smooth out any problems, and keep down coordination costs.[29] Thus, organization structures are designed to coordinate relevant technologies and protect them from outside disturbances. Structural components such as inventory, warehousing, and shipping help buffer the technology used to transform inputs into outputs. For instance, demand for products usually is cyclical or seasonal and is subject to many disturbances, but warehousing inventory helps the manufacturing system function as if the environment accepted output at a steady rate, maximizing technological efficiency and helping the organization respond to fluctuating demands of the market. On the other hand, warehousing inventory

Rob Kim/Everett/Photoshot

Many toys are now based on movies. Children see the movie and then beg their parents to buy the action figures based on the movies. The Toy Story movies have spawned huge sales of the Jessie doll and other action figures for Mattel. Barbie and Ken have even found new life with Toy Story 3 and you can have the Barbie and Ken gift set for only $24.99!

costs money, so managers must balance costs of inventory with costs of shipping, labor costs, and many other factors.

Organizations with international operations must contend with additional levels of complexity and dynamism, both within and across cultures. Many cultures have relatively stable environments. For example, the economies of Sweden and the United States are fairly stable. Although competitive forces within each country's economic system vary, each economy remains strong. In contrast, the environments of other countries are much more dynamic. For example, France's policies on socialism versus private enterprise tend to change dramatically with each election. At present, far-reaching changes in the economic and management philosophies of most European countries make their environments far more dynamic than that of the United States. Managers of global corporations have experienced even more concerns as the worldwide recession in recent years has had many differential effects around the globe.

Environments also vary widely in terms of their complexity. The Japanese culture, which is fairly stable, is also quite complex. Japanese managers are subject to an array of cultural norms and values that are far more encompassing and resistant to change than those U.S. managers face. India, too, has an extremely complex environment that continues to be influenced by its old caste system—in contrast to India's outstanding educational system, which produces a wealth of excellent engineering talent. Although the business potential is great in China, the many environmental uncertainties faced by foreign firms who want to do business there make it a difficult proposition. Infrastructure problems, language and cultural differences, governmental regulations, inconsistent suppliers, customs issues, and irregular copyright protection make it a difficult environment at best.[30]

Strategic Choice

The previous two sections described how structure is affected by the strategy of the organization and by the structural imperatives of size, technology, and environment. These approaches may seem to contradict each other since both approaches attempt to specify the determinants of structure. This apparent clash has been resolved by refining the strategy concept to include the role of the top management decision maker in determining the organization's structure.[31] In effect, this view inserts the manager as the decision maker who evaluates the imperatives and the organization strategy and then designs the organization structure.

The importance of the role of top management can be understood by comparing Figure 17.4 with Figure 17.2. Figure 17.4 shows structural imperatives as

FIGURE 17.4

The Strategic Choice Approach to Organization Design

The integration of the structural-imperative approach to organization design with the strategic choice approach takes into account the role of the manager, whose perspective on contextual factors and the organization, along with personal preferences, values, and experience, help determine the structure of the organization.

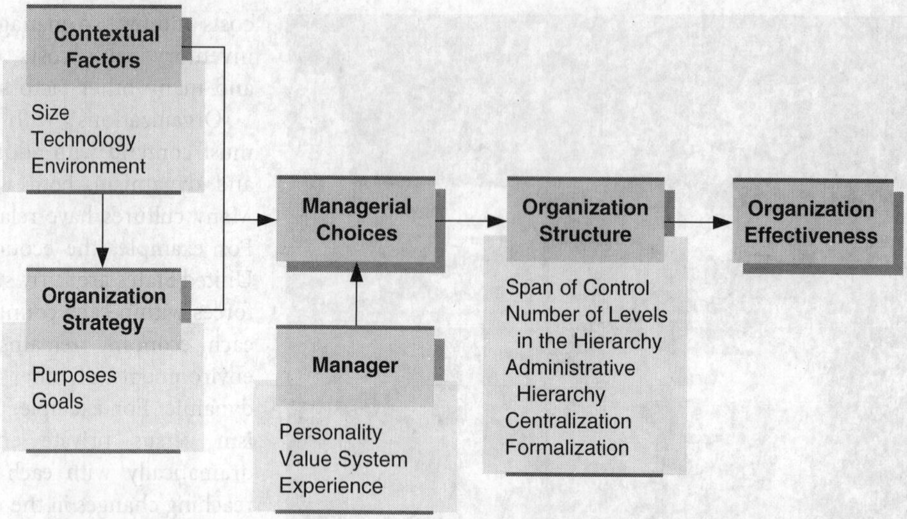

contextual factors—within which the organization must operate—that affect the purposes and goals of the organization. The manager's choices for organization structure are affected by the organization's strategy (purposes and goals), the imperatives (contextual factors), and the manager's personal value system and experience.[32] Organizational effectiveness depends on the fit among the size, the technology, the environment, the strategies, and the structure.

Another perspective on the link between strategy and structure is that the relationship may be reciprocal; that is, the structure may be set up to implement the strategy, but the structure may then affect the process of decision making, influencing such matters as the centralization or decentralization of decision making and the formalization of rules and procedures.[33] Thus, strategy determines structure, which in turn affects strategic decision making. A more complex view, suggested by Herman Boschken, is that strategy is a determinant of structure and long-term performance, but only when the subunits doing the planning have the ability to do the planning well.[34]

The relationship between strategic choice and structure is actually more complicated than the concept that "structure follows strategy" conveys. However, this relationship has received less research attention than the idea of structural imperatives. And, of course, some might view strategy simply as another imperative, along with size, technology, and environment. But the strategic-choice view goes beyond the imperative perspective because it is a product of both the analyses of the imperatives and the organization's strategy. As an example, when Daimler-Benz merged with Chrysler, Daimler CEO Juergen Schrempp claimed it was a merger of equals. Very quickly, however, it became clear that was not accurate as Chrysler became just another division of the German automaker. Mr. Schrempp finally admitted that this was the structure he wanted all along.[35] Within only a few years, Chrysler was sold by Daimler to an investment group, went bankrupt, and was subsequently picked up by Fiat, the Italian automotive giant.[36]

ORGANIZATIONAL DESIGNS

The previous section described several factors that determine how organizations are structured. In this section we present several different organizational designs that have been created to adapt organizations to the many contingency factors they face. We discuss mechanistic and organic structures, the sociotechnical system perspective, Mintzberg's designs, matrix designs, and virtual organizations.

Table 17.2	Mechanistic and Organic Organization Designs	
CHARACTERISTIC	MECHANISTIC	ORGANIC
Structure	Hierarchical	Network based on interests
Interactions, Communication	Primarily vertical	Lateral throughout
Work Directions, Instructions	From supervisor	Through advice, information
Knowledge, Information	Concentrated at top	Throughout
Membership, Relationship with Organization	Requires loyalty, obedience	Commitment to task, progress, expansion

A **mechanistic structure** is primarily hierarchical; interactions and communications typically are vertical, instructions come from the boss, knowledge is concentrated at the top, and loyalty and obedience are required to sustain membership.

An **organic structure** is set up like a network; interactions and communications are horizontal, knowledge resides wherever it is most useful to the organization, and membership requires a commitment to the organization's tasks.

Mechanistic and Organic Designs

As we discussed in the previous section, most organizational scholars believe that organizations need to be able to adapt to changes in the technology of that organization. For example, if the rate of change in technology is slow, the most effective design is bureaucratic or, to use Burns and Stalker's term, "mechanistic." As summarized in Table 17.2, a **mechanistic structure** is primarily hierarchical in nature, interactions and communications are mostly vertical, instructions come from the boss, knowledge is concentrated at the top, and continued membership requires loyalty and obedience.

But if the technology is changing rapidly, the organization needs a structure that allows more flexibility and faster decision making so that it can react quickly to changes. This design is called "organic." An **organic structure** resembles a network—interactions and communications are more lateral, knowledge resides wherever it is most useful to the organization, and membership requires a commitment to the tasks of the organization. An organic organization is generally expected to be faster at reacting to changes in the environment.

A **system** is an interrelated set of elements that function as a whole.

An **open system** is a system that interacts with its environment.

The **sociotechnical systems approach** to organization design views the organization as an open system structured to integrate the technical and social subsystems into a single management system.

A **technical (task) subsystem** is the means by which inputs are transformed into outputs.

Sociotechnical Systems Designs

The foundation of the sociotechnical systems approach to organizing is systems theory, discussed in Chapter 1. There we defined a **system** as an interrelated set of elements that function as a whole. A system may have numerous subsystems, each of which, like the overall system, includes inputs, transformation processes, outputs, and feedback. An **open system** is one that interacts with its environment. A complex system is made up of numerous subsystems in which the outputs of some are the inputs to others. The **sociotechnical systems approach** views the organization as an open system structured to integrate the two important organizational subsystems: the technical (task) subsystem and the social subsystem.

The **technical (task) subsystem** is the means by which inputs are transformed into outputs. The transformation process may take many forms. In a steel machine shop, it would entail the way steel is formed, cut, drilled, chemically treated, and painted. In an insurance company or financial institution, it would be the way information is processed. Often, significant scientific and engineering expertise is applied to these transformation processes to get the highest productivity at the lowest cost. The transformation process usually is regarded as technologically and economically driven; that is, whatever process is most productive and costs the least is generally the most desirable.

A few products, however, are built to standards rather than prices. The *Change* box entitled "A Marriage of Technique and Technology" on page 472 shows how renowned piano maker Steinway applies modern time- and labor-saving technology to a transformation process geared toward traditional standards of quality.

CHANGE A Marriage of Technique and Technology

In 1883, the great composer and piano virtuoso Franz Liszt wrote Heinrich Steinway, founder of Steinway & Sons, to praise the Steinway grand piano. In particular, Liszt had good things to say about the tonal effect of the piano's *scale*—the arrangement of its strings. Thirty years earlier, Henry Steinway Jr. had patented a technique for scaling called *overstringing*: Instead of running them parallel to the piano's treble strings, he fanned the bass strings above and diagonally to create a second tier of strings. As a result, he was able to improve the instrument's tone by using longer strings with superior vibratory quality.

Another feature developed by Steinway in the mid-19th century made it possible to use strings that were also bigger—and thus louder. If you look under a piano, you will see a cast-iron plate. This component was once made of wood fortified by metal braces, but Steinway had made the cast-iron plate a regular feature by the 1840s. The metal plate, of course, is much stronger and allowed the piano maker to apply much greater tension to the strings; in turn, the ability to increase string tension made it possible to tune the piano to more exacting standards of pitch.

Steinway was the first piano maker to combine the cast-iron plate with the technique of overstringing, and very little has changed in the construction of a grand piano since these and a few other facets of traditional technology were first introduced. This is not to say, however, that you will not find any modern technology in the present Steinway factory.

Take, for example, the soundboard, which you will see if you open up a grand piano and look inside. A solid wooden "diaphragm" located between the strings and the metal plate, the *soundboard* is a marvel of deceptively simple design that vibrates to amplify the sound of the strings while withstanding the 1,000 pounds of pressure that they place on it. Because they are constructed by hand, no two soundboards are exactly the same size. Nor is any one piano *case*—the curved lateral surface that runs around the whole instrument—the same size as any other.

"We're talking about wood here," says Andrew Horbachevsky, Steinway's director of manufacturing. "This [case] could be 1/16th from that one." The important thing is that the case is fitted—and fitted *precisely*—to a soundboard. "We don't want ... a foundation that twists," explains Horbachevsky.

> ***"We're talking about wood here."***
>
> —ANDREW HORBACHEVSKY, DIRECTOR OF MANUFACTURING, STEINWAY & SONS

Because the soundboard is measured first and the case then fitted to it, there is only one case for each soundboard. To ensure a satisfactory fit between case and soundboard, the case must be *frazed*—sawed and planed to specification. Performed by hand, this task took 14 hours, but today it is done in 1½ hours by a CNC (for *computer numerically controlled*) milling machine—a system in which a computerized storage medium issues programmed commands to a variety of specialized tools.

Granted, CNC technology is fairly new at Steinway—the million-dollar milling machine and several other pieces of CNC technology were introduced between 2000 and 2005. Most of Steinway's CNC tools are highly specialized, and the company custom-built many of them. Obviously, such technology leads to a lot of labor saving, but Steinway officials are adamant about the role of technology in maintaining rather than supplanting Steinway tradition: Some people, says Director of Quality Robert Berger, "think that Steinway is automating to save on labor costs or improve productivity. But these investments are all about quality. We're making a few specific technology investments in areas where we can improve the quality of our product."

References: Steinway & Sons, "Steinway History: Leadership through Craftsmanship and Innovation," *German American Pioneers*, www.germanamericanpioneers.org on August 17, 2012; Steinway & Sons, "Online Factory Tour," Steinway Hall, www.steinwaypianos.com on August 17, 2012; Victor Verney, "88 Keys: The Making of a Steinway Piano," *All About Jazz*, June 18, 2006, www.allaboutjazz.com on August 17, 2012; WGBH (Boston), "Note by Note: The Making of Steinway L1037," 1995–2012, www.wgbh.org on August 17, 2012; M. Eric Johnson, Joseph Hall, and David Pyke, "Technology and Quality at Steinway & Sons," Tuck School of Business at Dartmouth, May 13, 2005, http://mba.tuck.dartmouth.edu on March 29, 2011.

A **social subsystem** includes the interpersonal relationships that develop among people in organizations.

Autonomous work groups are used to integrate an organization's technical and social subsystems for the benefit of the larger system.

The **social subsystem** includes the interpersonal relationships that develop among people in organizations. Employees learn one another's work habits, strengths, weaknesses, and preferences while developing a sense of mutual trust. The social relationships may be manifested in personal friendships and interest groups. Communication, about both work and employees' common interests, may be enhanced by friendship or hampered by antagonistic relationships. The Hawthorne studies, conducted between 1927 and 1932 at Western Electric's Hawthorne plant near Chicago, were the first serious studies of the social subsystems in organizations.[37]

The sociotechnical systems approach was developed by members of the Tavistock Institute of England as an outgrowth of a study of coal mining. The study concerned new mining techniques that were introduced to increase productivity but failed because they entailed splitting up well-established work groups.[38] The Tavistock researchers concluded that the social subsystem had been sacrificed to the technical subsystem. Thus, improvements in the technical subsystem were not realized because of problems in the social subsystem.

The Tavistock group proposed that an organization's technical and social subsystems could be integrated through autonomous work groups. The aim of **autonomous work groups** is to make technical and social subsystems work together for the benefit of the larger system. These groups are developed using concepts of task design—particularly job enrichment—and ideas about group interaction, supervision, and other characteristics of organization design. To structure the task, authority, and reporting relationships around work groups, organizations should delegate to the groups themselves decisions regarding job assignments, training, inspection, rewards, and punishments. Management is responsible for coordinating the groups according to the demands of the work and task environment. Autonomous work groups often evolve into self-managing teams, as was discussed in Chapter 10.

Mirrorpix/Newscom

These mineworkers must carefully work together and coordinate their efforts in order make the mechanized mining techniques work. The pit-prop is cut to the length required, and then hammered home into position, wedged under the steel roof-supports. It is essential that the steel bars are exactly horizontal. The blend between the social and technical subsystems enables this process to work.

Organizations in turbulent environments tend to rely less on hierarchy and more on the coordination of work among autonomous work groups. Sociotechnical systems theory asserts that the role of management is twofold: to monitor the environmental factors that impinge on the internal operations of the organization and to coordinate the social and technical subsystems. Although the sociotechnical systems approach has not been thoroughly tested, it has been tried with some success in the General Foods plant in Topeka, Kansas; the Saab-Scania project in Sweden; and the Volvo plant in Kalmar, Sweden.[39] The development of the sociotechnical systems approach is significant in its departure from the universal approaches to organization design and in its emphasis on jointly harnessing the technical and human subsystems. The popular movements in management today include many of the principles of the sociotechnical systems design approach. The development of cross-functional teams to generate and design new products and services is a good example (see Chapter 10).

FIGURE 17.5

Mintzberg's Five Coordinating Mechanisms

Mintzberg described five methods of coordinating the actions of organizational participants. The dashed lines in each diagram show the five different means of coordination: (1) mutual adjustment; (2) direct supervision; and standardization of (3) input skills, (4) work processes, and (5) outputs.

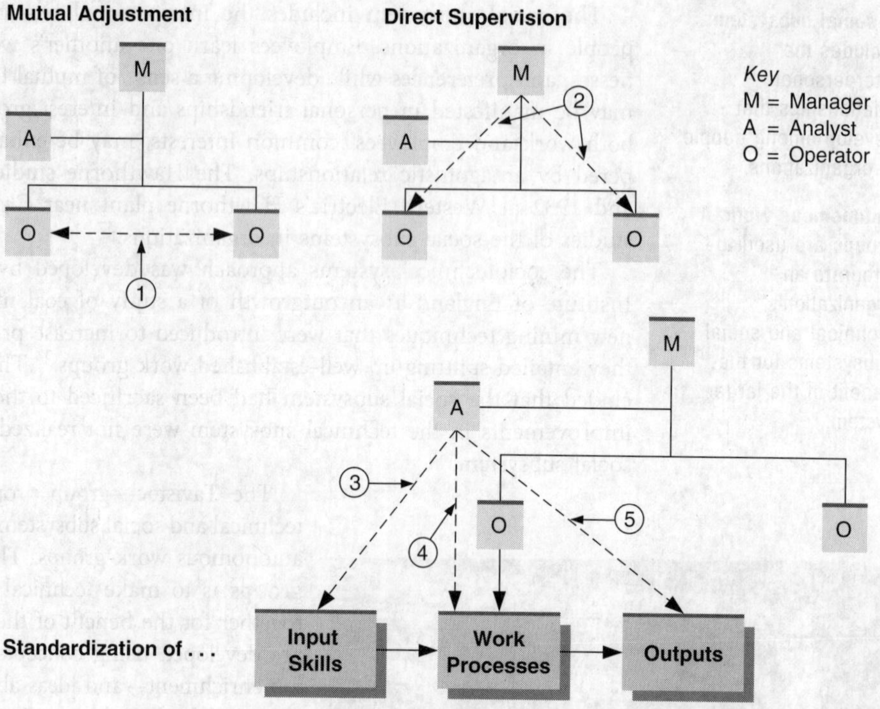

Reference: Henry Mintzberg, The Structuring of Organizations: A Synthesis of the Research, © 1979, p. 4. Reprinted by permission of Prentice Hall, Inc., Upper Saddle River, NJ.

Mintzberg's Designs

In this section we describe five specific organization designs proposed by Henry Mintzberg. The universe of possible designs is large, but fortunately we can divide designs into a few basic forms. Mintzberg proposed that the purpose of organizational design was to coordinate activities, and he suggested a range of coordinating mechanisms that are found in operating organizations.[40] In Mintzberg's view, organization structure reflects how tasks are divided and then coordinated. He described five major ways in which tasks are coordinated: by mutual adjustment; by direct supervision; and by standardization of worker (or input) skills, work processes, or outputs (see Figure 17.5). These five methods can exist side by side within an organization.

Coordination by mutual adjustment (1 in Figure 17.5) simply means that workers use informal communication to coordinate with one another, whereas *coordination by direct supervision* (2 in Figure 17.5) means that a manager or supervisor coordinates the actions of workers. As noted, *standardization* may be used as a coordination mechanism in three different ways: (1) We can standardize the *input skills* (3 in Figure 17.5)—that is, standardize the worker skills that are inputs to the work process; (2) we can standardize the *work processes* themselves (4 in Figure 17.5)—that is, standardize the methods workers use to transform inputs into outputs; and (3) we can standardize the *outputs* (5 in Figure 17.5)—that is, standardize the products or services or the performance levels expected of workers. Standardization usually is developed by staff analysts and enforced by management such that skills, processes, and output meet predetermined standards.

Mintzberg further suggested that the five coordinating mechanisms roughly correspond to stages of organizational development and complexity. In the very small organization, individuals working together communicate informally, achieving coordination by mutual adjustment. As more people join the organization, coordination needs become more complex, and direct supervision is added. For example, two or three people working in a small fast-food business can coordinate the work simply by talking to each other about the incoming orders for hamburgers, fries, and drinks. However, direct supervision becomes necessary in a larger restaurant with more complex cooking and warming equipment and several shifts of workers.

In large organizations, standardization is added to mutual adjustment and direct supervision to coordinate the work. The type of standardization depends on the nature of the work situation—that is, the organization's technology and environment. Standardization of work processes may achieve the necessary coordination when the organization's tasks are fairly routine. Thus, the larger fast-food outlet may standardize the making of hamburger patties: the meat is weighed, put into a hamburger press, and compressed into a patty. McDonald's is well known for this type of standardized process. Analysis of the success of McDonald's shows that some part of its success is due to the degree of standardization.

In other complex situations, standardization of the output may allow employees to do the work in any appropriate manner as long as the output meets specifications. Thus, the cook may not care how the hamburger is pressed, only being concerned that the right amount of meat is used and that the patty is the correct diameter and thickness. In other words, the worker may use any process as long as the output is a standard burger.

A third possibility is to coordinate work by standardizing worker skills. This approach is most often adopted in situations in which processes and outputs are difficult to standardize. In a hospital, for example, each patient must be treated as a special situation; the hospital process and output therefore cannot be standardized. Similar diagnostic and treatment procedures may be used with more than one patient, but the hospital relies on the skills of the physicians and nurses (which are standardized through their professional training) to coordinate the work. Organizations may have to depend on workers' mutual adjustment to coordinate their own actions in the most complex work situations or when the most important elements of coordination are the workers' professional training and communication skills. In effect, mutual adjustment can be an appropriate coordinating mechanism in both the simplest and the most complex situations.

Mintzberg pointed out that the five methods of coordination could be combined with the basic components of structure to develop five structural forms: the simple structure, the machine bureaucracy, the professional bureaucracy, the divisionalized form, and the adhocracy. Mintzberg called these structures pure or ideal types of designs.

The simple structure, typical of relatively small or new organizations, has little specialization or formalization; power and decision making are concentrated in the chief executive.

Simple Structure The **simple structure** characterizes relatively small, usually young organizations in a simple, dynamic environment. The organization has little specialization and formalization, and its overall structure is organic. Power and decision making are concentrated in the chief executive, often also the owner-manager, and the flow of authority is from the top down. The primary coordinating mechanism is direct supervision. The organization must adapt quickly to survive because of its dynamic and often hostile environment. Most small businesses—a car dealership, a locally owned retail clothing store, or a candy manufacturer with only regional distribution—have a simple structure.

In a **machine bureaucracy**, which typifies large, well-established organizations, work is highly specialized and formalized, and decision making is usually concentrated at the top.

Machine Bureaucracy The **machine bureaucracy** is typical of large, well-established companies in simple, stable environments. Work is highly specialized and formalized, and decision making is usually concentrated at the top. Standardization of work processes is the primary coordinating mechanism. This highly bureaucratic structure does not have to adapt quickly to changes because the environment is both simple and stable. Examples include large mass-production firms such as Container Corporation of America, large meatpacking companies, and providers of services to mass markets, such as insurance companies.

A **professional bureaucracy** is characterized by horizontal specialization according to professional areas of expertise, little formalization, and decentralized decision making.

Professional Bureaucracy Usually found in a complex and stable environment, the **professional bureaucracy** relies on standardization of skills as the primary means of coordination. There is much horizontal specialization by professional areas of expertise but little formalization. Decision making is decentralized and takes place where the expertise is. The only means of coordination available to the organization is standardization of skills—those of the professionally trained employees.

Although it lacks centralization, the professional bureaucracy stabilizes and controls its tasks with rules and procedures developed in the relevant profession. Hospitals, universities, and consulting firms are examples.

The **divisionalized form**, typical of old, very large organizations, is divided according to the different markets served; horizontal and vertical specialization exists between divisions and headquarters, decision making is divided between headquarters and divisions, and outputs are standardized.

Divisionalized Form The **divisionalized form** is characteristic of old, very large firms operating in a relatively simple, stable environment with several diverse markets. It resembles the machine bureaucracy except that it is divided according to the various markets it serves. There is some horizontal and vertical specialization between the divisions (each defined by a market) and headquarters. Decision making is clearly split between headquarters and the divisions, and the primary means of coordination is standardization of outputs. The mechanism of control required by headquarters encourages the development of machine bureaucracies in the divisions.

The classic example of the divisionalized form is General Motors, which in a reorganization during the 1920s adopted a design that created divisions for each major car model.[41] Although the divisions have been reorganized and the cars changed several times, the concept of the divisionalized organization is still very evident at GM.[42] General Electric uses a two-tiered divisionalized structure, dividing its numerous businesses into strategic business units, which are then further divided into sectors.[43]

In an **adhocracy**, typically found in young organizations in highly technical fields, decision making is spread throughout the organization, power resides with the experts, horizontal and vertical specialization exists, and there is little formalization.

Adhocracy The **adhocracy** is typically found in young organizations engaged in highly technical fields in which the environment is complex and dynamic. Decision making is spread throughout the organization, and power is in the hands of experts. There is horizontal and vertical specialization but little formalization, resulting in a very organic structure. Coordination is by mutual adjustment through frequent personal communication and liaison. Specialists are not grouped together in functional units but are instead deployed into specialized market-oriented project teams.

The typical adhocracy is usually established to foster innovation, something to which the other four types of structures are not particularly well suited. Numerous U.S. organizations—Whole Foods, W. L. Gore, and Google, for example—are known for their innovation and constant stream of new products.[44] These companies have minimal hierarchies, are built around teams, and are known as some of the most innovative companies in the world.

Another type of adhocracy is the "boss-less" or "boss-free" organization in which there is no hierarchy of managers, departments, and levels. Employees decide what projects to work on, determine each other's pay, and direct their own activities every day. Valve Corp. established its boss-free organization when it was founded in 1996, and since then has created no managerial positions, letting employees recruit others

RALPH BARRERA/MCT/Landov

Whole Foods employees Mark Ehrnstein, right, global vice president for team member services and Nikki Newman, left, receptionist at corporate HQ offices, high-five one another after a brief conversation at the main entrance to their offices, June 21, 2012, in Austin, Texas. Whole Foods has a rule requiring executive pay go no higher than 19 times that of the lowest paid employee.

to work on projects and put their desks on wheels so work groups can rearrange themselves as needed to get the work done. This is similar to W. L. Gore, which calls its management structure a lattice structure based on teams rather than managers and departments. Boss-free organizations can be a little chaotic to work in, and they require employees who are ready for the freedom and motivated to take responsibility for their actions. It sometimes takes new employees a few months to get acclimated to the lack of a boss.[45]

Mintzberg believed that fit among parts is the most important consideration in designing an organization. Not only must there be a fit among the structure, the structural imperatives (technology, size, and environment), and organizational strategy, but the components of structure (rules and procedures, decision making, specialization) must also fit together and be appropriate for the situation. Mintzberg suggested that an organization could not function effectively when these characteristics are not put together properly.[46]

Matrix Organization Design

One other organizational form deserves attention here: the matrix organization design. Matrix design is consistent with the contingency approach because it is useful only in certain situations. One of the earliest implementations of the matrix design was at TRW Systems Group in 1959.[47] Following TRW's lead, other firms in aerospace and high-technology fields created similar matrix structures.

The **matrix design** combines two different designs to gain the benefits of each; typically combined are a product or project departmentalization scheme and a functional structure.

The **matrix design** attempts to combine two different designs to gain the benefits of each. The most common matrix form superimposes product or project departmentalization on a functional structure (see Figure 17.6). Each department and project has a manager; each employee, however, is a member of both a functional department and a project team. The dual role means that the employee has two supervisors: the department manager and the project leader.

A matrix structure is appropriate when three conditions exist:

1. There is external pressure for a dual focus, meaning that factors in the environment require the organization to focus its efforts equally on responding to multiple external factors and on internal operations.
2. There is pressure for a high information-processing capacity.
3. There is pressure for shared resources.[48]

In the aerospace industry in the early 1960s, all these conditions were present. Private companies had a dual focus: their customers, primarily the federal government, and the complex engineering and technical fields in which they were engaged. Moreover, the environments of these companies were changing very rapidly. Technological sophistication and competition were increasing, resulting in growing environmental uncertainty

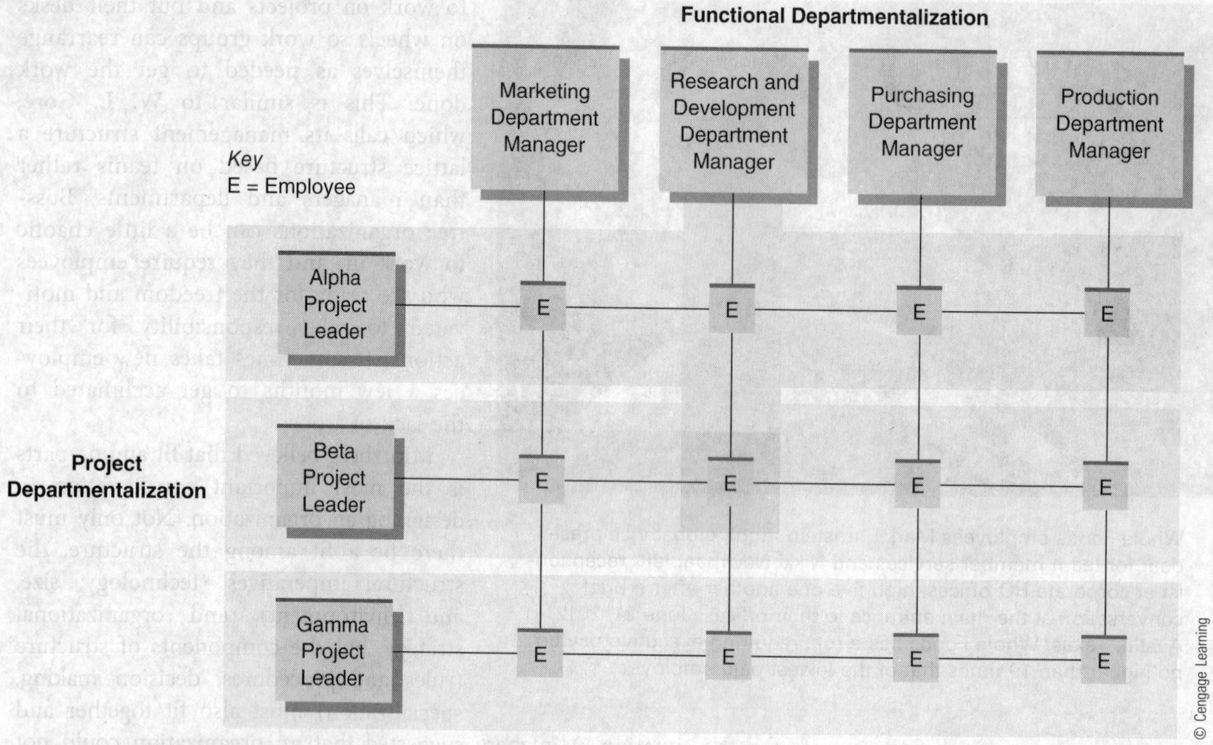

FIGURE 17.6

A Matrix Organization Design

A matrix organization design superimposes two different types of departmentalization onto each other—for example, a functional structure and a project structure.

and an added need for information processing. The final condition stemmed from the pressure on the companies to excel in a very competitive environment despite limited resources. The companies concluded that it was inefficient to assign their highly professional—and highly compensated—scientific and engineering personnel to just one project at a time.

Built into the matrix structure is the capacity for flexible and coordinated responses to internal and external pressures. Members can be reassigned from one project to another as demands for their skills change. They may work for a month on one project, be assigned to the functional home department for two weeks, and then be reassigned to another project for the next six months. The matrix form improves project coordination by assigning project responsibility to a single leader rather than dividing it among several functional department heads. Furthermore, it improves communication because employees can talk about the project with members of both the project team and the functional unit to which they belong. In this way, solutions to project problems may emerge from either group. Many different types of organizations have used the matrix form of organization, notably large-project manufacturing firms, banks, and hospitals.[49]

The matrix organizational form thus provides several benefits for the organization. It is not, however, trouble-free. Typical problems include the following:

1. The dual reporting system may cause role conflict among employees.
2. Power struggles may occur over who has authority on which issues.

3. Matrix organization often is misinterpreted to mean that a group must make all decisions; as a result, group decision-making techniques may be used when they are not appropriate.
4. If the design involves several matrices, each laid on top of another, there may be no way to trace accountability and authority.[50]

Only under the three conditions listed earlier is the matrix design likely to work. In any case, it is a complex organizational system that must be carefully coordinated and managed to be effective.

Virtual Organizations

A **virtual organization** is a temporary alliance formed by two or more organizations to pursue a specific venture or to exploit a specific opportunity.

The **virtual company** is an organization that allows employees the freedom to do their work anywhere they want or can, relaxing the requirement that employees go to the same location every day.

There are multiple meanings for the term "virtual organizations." The earliest usage, which we call the **virtual organization**, meant a relatively temporary alliance or network created by two or more organizations who agree to work together to complete a specific venture. A second usage of the term, which we call the **virtual company**, has come to refer to any organization where everyone telecommutes to work from different places rather than go to work at a central office space. This allows workers to work from a coffee shop, from home, from a park somewhere, or from a different country, yet stay in touch with coworkers via electronic telecommunications technology. In this section we describe the organizational issues involved in both types of virtual organizations, starting with the earlier usage.

Virtual Organizations as Networks Some companies do one or two things very well, such as sell to government clients, but struggle with most others, such as manufacturing products with very tight precision. Other companies might be great at close-tolerance manufacturing but lousy at reaching out to certain types of clients. What is needed is some way for those two organizations to get together to utilize each other's strengths yet still retain their independence. They can, and many are doing so in what are called "virtual organizations."

A virtual organization in this sense is a relatively temporary alliance or network created by two or more organizations who agree to work together to accomplish a specific venture. Each partner contributes to the partnership what it does best. The opportunity is usually something that needs a quick response to maximize the market opportunity. A slow response will probably result in losses. Therefore, a virtual organization allows different organizations to bring their best capabilities together without worrying about learning how to do something that they have never done before. Thus, the reaction time is faster, mistakes are fewer, and profits are quicker. Sharing of information among partners is usually facilitated by electronic technology such as computers, faxes, electronic mail, and electronic file-sharing systems, thereby avoiding the expenses of renting new office space for the venture or costly travel time between companies.

There are no restrictions on how large or small organizations or projects need to be to take advantage of this type of alliance. In fact, some very small organizations are working together quite well. In Phoenix, Arizona, a public relations firm, a graphic design firm, and a management consulting firm are working together on projects that have multiple requirements beyond those offered by any single firm. Rather than turn down the business or try to hire additional staff to do the extra work, the three firms work together to better serve client needs. The clients like the arrangement because they get high-quality work and do not have to shop around for someone to do little pieces of work. The networking companies feel that the result is better creativity, more teamwork, more efficient use of resources, and better service for their clients.

More typically, however, large companies create virtual organizations. Corning is involved in nineteen partnerships on many different types of projects, and it is pleased with most of its ventures and plans to do more. Intel worked with two Japanese organizations to manufacture flash memory chips for computers. One of the Japanese companies was not able to complete its part of the project, leaving Intel with a major product-delivery problem. Intel's chairman at the time, Andrew Grove, was not too happy about that venture.[51]

The virtual organization is not just another management fad. It has become one way to deal with the rapid changes brought about by evolving technology and global competition. Management scholars have mixed opinions on the effectiveness of such arrangements. Although it may seem odd, this approach can produce substantial benefits in some situations.

The Virtual Company as Telecommuters with No Office In this alternate use of the term, the virtual company is an organization that allows employees the freedom to do their work anywhere they want or can, relaxing the requirement that employees go to the same location every day. With social networking tools, many different types of group/team software, instant messaging, videoconferencing and teleconferencing, cloud computing, and the standard e-mail, it has become very common for employees not to have to go to "the office" every day to complete their work. Many companies allow

Table 17.3 Lessons Learned from a Month as a Virtual Company

FOR THE COMPANY
• Lower costs for office space and utilities
• Company may have increased cost of computer equipment, software, video/teleconferencing, but employees may already have the basics at home.
• Company may save on costs of telephone switching, serves, expensive enterprise software licensing
• Potential loss of culture and standard ways of doing things
• May be an asset in recruiting efforts
• Loss of positive benefits of collaboration, depending on the nature of the project
FOR EMPLOYEES
• Save the costs of commuting, time, fuel, bus/train fares, eating out for lunch, and laundry
• Can be at home for important family time and events, birthdays, piano practice
• Work-life balance has to be readjusted
• Some forgot to eat lunch, while others ate all the time
• May work more hours (no commuting and no defined "leave the office" at 6)
• Must set up rules for when family time is and when work time is
• May have to upgrade the office chair for better ergonomics
• Loss of face-to-face relationships
• Workers can stay focused for longer periods with fewer interruptions
• Loss of stimulation created by collaborative work

Source: Max Chafkin, "The Case, and the Plan, for the Virtual Company," Inc.com, April 1, 2010, accessed online April 25, 2010 at http://www.inc.com/magazine/20100401/the-case-and-the-plan-for-the-virtual-company.html.

individual employees in certain types of jobs to work from home one or a few days per week, requiring them to be at the office the other days. However, the fullest extension of this model is one where there is no office and all employees work from home. Many knowledge workers, such as designers, writers, professors who teach online, software developers, and numerous others have the capability of working this way.

The company considering becoming a virtual company needs to examine many issues. Other than the obvious reductions in the cost of office space, reduced utilities, and reduced computer/server costs, the company needs to consider the culture of the organization, the role of collaboration (which may be a necessary part of what makes the company and its products/services unique and have value), and the type of employees and their relationships with each other. Managers often have difficulty giving up the sense of control they may have by being able to visually observe their employees at work.

One interesting example of the fully virtual company is the editorial staff of *Inc.* magazine, which did an experiment in which the editorial staff and writers did not go to the office for an entire month, doing their work from home, coffee shops, and other non-office places.[52] A summary of what they learned in shown in Table 17.3. The virtual company may be the wave of the future as communication technologies improve, fuel costs go higher, and concern for the environment becomes more intense. There is no clear mandate that all companies can or should "go virtual." The benefits, however, could be great for some companies.

CONTEMPORARY ORGANIZATION DESIGN PROCESSES

The current proliferation of design theories and alternative forms of organization gives practicing managers a dizzying array of choices. The task of the manager or organization designer is to examine the entity and its situation and to design a form of organization that meets its needs. A partial list of contemporary alternatives includes such approaches as downsizing, rightsizing, reengineering the organization, team-based organizations, and the virtual company. These approaches often make use of total quality management, employee empowerment, employee involvement and participation, reduction in force, process innovation, and networks of alliances. Managers must deal with the new terminology, the temptation to treat such new approaches as fads, and their own organizational situation before making major organization design shifts. In this section we describe two popular approaches—reengineering and rethinking the organization—as well as global organization structure and design issues. We conclude with a summary of the dominant themes in contemporary organization design.

Reengineering the Organization

Reengineering is the radical redesign of organizational processes to achieve major gains in cost, time, and provision of services.

Reengineering is the radical redesign of organizational processes to achieve major gains in cost, time, and provision of services. It forces the organization to start from scratch to redesign itself around its most important, or core, processes rather than beginning with its current form and making incremental changes. It assumes that if a company had no existing structure, departments, jobs, rules, or established ways of doing things, reengineering would design the organization as it should be for future success. The process starts with determining what the customers actually want from the organization and then developing a strategy to provide it. Once the strategy is in place, strong leadership from top management creates teams of people to design an organizational system to achieve the strategy.[53] The aim of reengineering is to fundamentally change the way everybody in the organization conceives his or her role. Rather than view their role as a position in a hierarchy, reengineering creates a horizontal flow of teams that focus on core processes that deliver the product or service. Throughout a decade of reengineering, the forces of change have been intensified by information technology—the Internet—that has accelerated all of these processes and led to what some have called "X-engineering," which takes these same reengineering processes across organizational boundaries, searching for new efficiencies from suppliers to distributors.[54]

Rethinking the Organization

Rethinking the organization means looking at organization design in totally different ways, perhaps even abandoning the classic view of the organization as a pyramid.

Also currently popular is the concept of rethinking the organization. **Rethinking** the organization is also a process for restructuring that throws out traditional assumptions that organizations should be structured with boxes and horizontal and vertical lines. Robert Tomasko makes some suggestions for new organizational forms for the future.[55] He suggests that the traditional pyramid shape of organizations may be inappropriate for current business practices. Traditional structures, he contends, may have too many levels of management arranged in a hierarchy to be efficient and to respond to dynamic changes in the environment.

Rethinking organizations might entail thinking of the organization structure as a dome rather than a pyramid, the dome being top management, which acts as an umbrella, covering and protecting those underneath but also leaving them alone to do their work. Internal units underneath the dome would have the flexibility to interact with each other and with environmental forces. Companies such as Microsoft Corporation and Royal Dutch Petroleum have some of the characteristics of this dome approach to organization design. American Express Financial Advisors restructured from a vertical organization into a horizontal organization as a result of its rethinking everything about the ways it needed to meet customers' needs.[56]

Global Organization Structure and Design Issues

Managers working in an international environment must consider not only similarities and differences among firms in different cultures but also the structural features of multinational organizations.

Between-Culture Issues "Between-culture issues" are variations in the structure and design of companies operating in different cultures. As might be expected, such companies have both differences and similarities. For example, one study compared the structures of fifty-five U.S. and fifty-one Japanese manufacturing plants. Results suggested that the Japanese plants had less specialization, more "formal" centralization (but less "real" centralization), and taller hierarchies than their U.S. counterparts. The Japanese structures were also less affected by their technology than the U.S. plants.[57]

Many cultures still take a traditional view of organization structure not unlike the approaches used in this country during the days of classical organization theory. For example, Tom Peters, a leading U.S. management consultant and coauthor of *In Search of Excellence*, spent some time lecturing to managers in China. They were not interested in his ideas about decentralization and worker participation, however. Instead, the most frequently asked question concerned how a manager determined the optimal span of control.[58] However, managers in global companies may have to understand the differential interaction patterns among employees in different countries and not draw the wrong conclusions from culturally based interactions.[59]

In contrast, many European companies are increasingly patterning themselves after successful U.S. firms, a move stemming in part from corporate raiders in Europe emulating their U.S. counterparts and partly from the managerial workforce becoming better educated. Together, these two factors have caused many European firms to become less centralized and to adopt divisional structures by moving from functional to product departmentalization.[60]

SERVICE This Place Feels Right

©rangizz/Shutterstock

Have you ever noticed that some places you go or have worked seem to feel warm and welcoming while others feel cold and unfriendly? The environment makes a difference for both customer and employees. Warm colors, open spaces, softened noises, pleasant aromas, and proper lighting make a place feel welcoming, whereas the opposites do not. Studies have identified the key factors in the environment and how they impact both customers and employees. Several organizations have recognized the value of treating their employees like customers in terms of their physical setting. They have learned that it is a contradiction to tell employees "Our people are the most important in the world because they make the difference" when the employee entrance is located behind the building next to the dumpster. These organizations create beautifully appointed break rooms, rest rooms that equate to anything provided customers, and employee entrances that feel welcoming and as special as those used by customers. In other words, an organization that recognizes the value of backing up its statements about employee importance with a physical facility that reinforces this idea will send a consistent message that it does believe that its people are important and make the difference.

The concern for managers is in identifying the constituent elements of a beneficial environment. One scholar suggests there are five factors that comprise a setting that lead to a cognitive, emotional, and/or physiological response. First are ambient conditions. These are what we experience with our senses. What we see, smell, taste, hear, and touch will help determine our response to an environment. If we work or are a customer in a dirty, smelly, noisy, and dark store, bank, or medical facility, we will form a different impression from the one we will form if the place is clean, fresh smelling, quiet, and well lit. The ambient conditions influence how we feel about a place and the benchmark service organizations manage these appropriately for both customer and employees. The second factor that influences the feeling of a place is the way space is laid out and the feeling that it is functionally well designed. Open spaces feel more friendly than cramped ones, wide paths seem easier to navigate than narrow ones, well-lit spaces feel safer than dark ones, and neatly ordered spaces with properly functioning equipment feel more organized. The third environmental aspect is signs, symbols, and artifacts. These are physical objects that provide interpretations and guidance as to what the environment is like, helping customers and employees interpret the environment and navigate it easily. Thus, signs provide wayfinding or directional help to make it easy to get around or to engage whatever is needed. Symbols offer interpretations of the physical environment so people can see that the person with the big desk in a corner office is probably someone who can make the decision, or that the doctor with a diploma on the wall has a real medical degree, or that the person wearing a name badge with the company logo is the one who will provide answers to questions. Finally, the last component of the environment is other people. How other people in the environment look and dress tells a lot about the setting. If everyone looks somber while dressed in suits and pantsuits, the environment will feel more formal than if everyone is smiling in jeans and flip-flops.

The point is simple. The components that make up an environment communicate to employees and customers what it feels like to be there. Thus, an environment that is hot and humid will affect us physiologically. If it is also dark with scary music, it will also have an emotional impact. Finally, if it is full of dangerous-looking people who we know can hurt us, it will have a cognitive impact as well. In a more positive light, it feels a whole lot different being around people in a temperature-controlled climate who are all smiling on a bright, sunny corporate campus from being in a work team in a cramped, dark seam of an underground coal mine.

Discussion Question: Reflect on the various classrooms you have been in across your academic experience. Identify their environmental factors and describe how each contributed to the feeling of the setting.

Multinational Organizations More and more firms have entered the international arena and have found it necessary to adapt their designs to better cope with different cultures.[61] For example, after a company has achieved a moderate level of international activity, it often establishes an international division, usually at the same organizational level as other major functional divisions. Levi-Strauss uses this organization design. One division, Levi-Strauss International, is responsible for the company's business activities in Europe, Canada, Latin America, and Asia.

For an organization that has become more deeply involved in international activities, a logical form of organization design is the international matrix. This type of matrix arrays product managers across the top. Project teams headed by foreign-market managers cut across the product departments. A company with three basic product lines, for example, might establish three product departments (of course, it would include domestic advertising, finance, and operations departments as well). Foreign-market managers can be designated for, say, Canada, Japan, Europe, Latin America, and Australia. Each foreign-market manager is then responsible for all three of the company's products in his or her market.[62]

Finally, at the most advanced level of multinational activity, a firm might become an international conglomerate. Nestlé and Unilever N.V. fit this type. Each has an international headquarters (Nestlé in Vevey, Switzerland, and Unilever in Rotterdam, the Netherlands) that coordinates the activities of businesses scattered around the globe. Nestlé has factories in fifty countries and markets its products in virtually every country in the world. Over 96 percent of its business is done outside of Switzerland, and only about 7,000 of its 160,000 employees reside in its home country.

Recently, several organizations are moving major product group headquarters closer to the growing markets in the Asia-Pacific region. One of these, Proctor & Gamble Company (P&G), is relocating its global skin, cosmetics, and personal-care unit to Singapore from its headquarters in Ohio. A very centralized company, P&G will take two years to move employees and manufacturing facilities closer to the important markets in Asia. In addition, for the first time it promoted an Asian leader to be in charge of an Asian business group. Other companies joining the move to the Asia-Pacific region include General Electric, which is moving its x-ray unit from Waukesha, Wisconsin, to Beijing, China; DSM Engineering Plastics, moving its global headquarters from the Netherlands to Singapore; and Rolls-Royce PLC, moving its global Marine headquarters to Singapore from London.[63] Clearly, major multinational companies are making significant structural shifts to take advantage of changes in the international marketplace.

Dominant Themes of Contemporary Designs

The four dominant themes of current design strategies are (1) the effects of technological and environmental change, (2) the importance of people, (3) the necessity of staying in touch with the customer, and (4) the global organization. Technology and the environment are changing so fast and in so many unpredictable ways that no organization structure will be appropriate for long. The changes in electronic information processing, transmission, and retrieval alone are so vast that employee relationships, information distribution, and task coordination need to be reviewed almost daily.[64] The emphasis on productivity through people that was energized by Thomas Peters and Robert Waterman Jr. in the 1980s continues in almost every aspect of contemporary organization design.[65] In addition, Peters and Nancy Austin further emphasized the importance of staying in touch with customers at the initial stage in organization design.[66] Superimposed over these four dominant themes are the rapid changes in technology, competition, and globalization. Organizations must be adaptive to new circumstances in order to survive.[67]

These popular contemporary approaches and the four dominant factors argue for a contingency design perspective. Unfortunately, there is no "one best way." Managers must consider the impact of multiple factors—sociotechnical systems, strategy, the structural imperatives, changing information technology, people, global considerations, and a concern for end users—on their particular organization, and then design the organization structure accordingly.

SYNOPSIS

Universal approaches to organization design attempt to specify the one best way to structure organizations for effectiveness. Contingency approaches, on the other hand, propose that the best way to design organization structure depends on a variety of factors. Important contingency approaches to organization design center on the organizational strategy, the determinants of structure, and strategic choice.

Initially, strategy was seen as the determinant of structure: the structure of the organization was designed to implement its purpose, goals, and strategies. Taking managerial choice into account in determining organization structure is a modification of this view. The manager designs the structure to accomplish organizational goals, guided by an analysis of the contextual factors, the strategies of the organization, and personal preferences.

The structural imperatives are size, technology, and environment. In general, large organizations have more complex structures and usually more than one technology. The structures of small organizations, on the other hand, may be dominated by one core operations technology. The structure of the organization is also established to fit with the environmental demands and buffer the core operating technology from environmental changes and uncertainties.

Organization designs can take many forms. A mechanistic structure relies on the administrative hierarchy for communication and directing activities. An organic design is structured like a network; communications and interactions are horizontal and diagonal across groups and teams throughout the organization.

In the sociotechnical systems view, the organization is an open system structured to integrate two important subsystems: the technical (task) subsystem and the social subsystem. According to this approach, organizations should structure the task, authority, and reporting relationships around the work group, delegating to the group decisions on job assignments, training, inspection, rewards, and punishments. The task of management is to monitor the environment and coordinate the structures, rules, and procedures.

Mintzberg's ideal types of organization design were derived from a framework of coordinating mechanisms. The five types are simple structure, machine bureaucracy, professional bureaucracy, divisionalized form, and adhocracy. Most organizations have some characteristics of each type, but one is likely to predominate. Mintzberg believed that the most important consideration in designing an organization is the fit among parts of the organization.

The matrix design combines two types of structure (usually functional and project departmentalization) to gain the benefits of each. It usually results in a multiple command and authority system. Benefits of the matrix form include better use of skilled personnel and increased flexibility, cooperation, and communication. Typical problems are associated with the dual reporting system and the complex management system needed to coordinate work.

Virtual organizations are temporary alliances between several organizations that agree to work together on a specific venture. Reaction time to business opportunities can be very fast with these types of alliances. In effect, organizations create a network of other organizations to enable them to respond to changes in the environment. A virtual company is an organization that allows employees the freedom to do their work anywhere they want or can, relaxing the requirement that employees go to the same location every day.

Contemporary organization design is contingency oriented. Current popular design strategies are reengineering the organization and rethinking the organization. Four factors influencing design decisions are the changing technological environment, concern for people as valued resources, the need to keep in touch with customers, and global impacts on organizations.

DISCUSSION QUESTIONS

1. What are the differences between universal approaches and contingency approaches to organization design?
2. Define "organizational environment" and "organizational technology." In what ways do these concepts overlap?
3. Identify and describe some of the environmental and technological factors that affect your college or university. Give specific examples of how they affect you as a student.
4. How does organization design usually differ for large and small organizations?
5. What might be the advantages and disadvantages of structuring the faculty members at your college or university as an autonomous work group?
6. What do you think are the purposes, goals, and strategies of your college or university? How are they reflected in its structure?
7. Which of Mintzberg's pure forms is best illustrated by a major national political party (Democratic or Republican)? A religious organization? A football team? The U.S. Olympic Committee?
8. In a matrix organization, would you rather be a project leader, a functional department head, or a highly trained technical specialist? Why?
9. Discuss what you think the important design considerations will be for organization designers in the year 2020.
10. How would your college or university be different if you rethought or reengineered the way in which it is designed?

HOW DO YOU SEE IT?

The Sweet Strategy of Success

"When push comes to shove, it's really a volume game."

—DEBRA MUSIC, VP OF SALES AND MARKETING AT THEO CHOCOLATE

Joe Whinney was a conservation volunteer in Central America when he decided to see what he could do to improve the livelihood of local cocoa farmers. Helping them sell their crops was an obvious place to start, so in 1994 he started importing organic cocoa beans into the United States. Equally important was making sure that farmers got fair prices for their crops, so Joe also worked to promote Fair Trade practices among U.S. businesses that used cocoa beans. In the back of his mind, however, was the idea of a much more direct involvement in the cocoa industry and with the people at the head of its supply chain: He wanted to start up a factory for making chocolate out of organic Fair Trade cocoa beans.* And he wanted to introduce chocolate lovers to such exotic flavors as coconut curry in milk chocolate.

In 2004, Whinney moved from his home in Massachusetts to Seattle, Washington, where he spent two years developing his business model and converting an old brewery into a chocolate factory. As we see in the video, he also insisted that his ex-wife come along with him to help run the business. Theo Chocolate was launched in 2006. Today, Whinney is CEO, and Debra Music, with a background in social marketing and consumer-brand building, is VP of Sales and Marketing.

When your business plan has gestated as long as Whinney's, "the strategy," as he puts it, may indeed seem to be "the easy part," and his current strategy—or, perhaps more precisely, his vision—is still the same as it was in 2004: "I want[ed] to build a chocolate company that other companies can look at and emulate." Toward that end, he reports, "we produced products that really excited us, and we put them in packaging that we liked." Theo's target market, says Music, consisted of "green consumers or people who were really 'foodies'—meaning that they're adventurous eaters…. We had a really, really great launch," she adds, "and garnered accolades from both the press and food critics."

That initial promise of success, she now suspects, was "partly because of the uniqueness" of the firm's original strategy, and when it became clear that Theo's growth was not living up to the potential implied by its launch, "we decided to apply some science to what we were doing." A little market research revealed the problem, but Music now knows that simply listening to customers should have provided an important clue:

> *We had people coming into our store all the time saying, "Can't you just do chocolate with mint?" And so we thought, "Well, yeah, we definitely can do chocolate with mint." We weren't especially* excited *about doing chocolate with mint, but we realized, "Why wouldn't we do that if our customers were asking for it?"*

"When push comes to shove," she admits, "it's really a volume game, and we needed to be selling a lot more chocolate." Theo needed to tweak its strategy. In order to appeal to "a more mainstream group of consumers," explains Whinney, "we had to produce products where the flavors were easily understood, in packaging that was easy for consumers to read on the shelf."

What Theo needed, as Music puts it, was "a more accessible product line, [plus] we needed to be selling in places where people just wanted a milk chocolate bar." Theo needed to be in such mainstream retailers as supermarket and drugstore chains, but this particular shift in strategy entailed another problem: "There was already a lot of this kind of product … on the shelf," explains Music, "and retailers have limited space.… Probably the single most important thing that was beyond our control was whether or not retailers were going to be willing to give us some shelf placement."

As it turns out, they did. Why? Both Music and Whinney think that it was primarily because of "our reputation"—a reputation based on the quality of the Theo product, whether specialty (spicy chili) or mainstream (chocolate with orange). "Just being organic and Fair Trade," explains Whinney, "isn't enough. We'll spark consumers' interest because of our certifications … but if it doesn't taste good—if people don't enjoy it—it really doesn't matter. So we put *as much* or *more* emphasis on *quality* because, without that, nothing else really matters."

Ironically, then, the success of Theo's revised strategy hinged on at least one facet of its original strategy—making a product differentiated by quality as well as unusual ingredients. In fact, according to Music, that facet of Theo's strategy is linked to another, equally important factor in Whinney's original strategic approach to building his kind of chocolate company: the uniqueness not simply of its product, but of its *supply chain management*—of the chain of operations stretching from an organization's purchase of needed resources to the sale of its finished products to consumers. "What's most unique about us," she says,

> *is that we are the only organic Fair Trade brand that's actually making the product that we sell. So, we're the only vertically integrated product on the shelf. We're the only product where we're controlling the supply chain from start to finish. We work with the farmers, we import the beans and all of our other ingredients, we make the product in our own facility. So, we're able to control not only all those relationships … but the entire manufacturing process. And that's what sets us apart.*

CASE QUESTIONS

1. Our video opens with Joe Whinney's statement that "strategy is actually the easy part." As it unfolds, however, the video suggests that Whinney may have overstated the case. **Judging from the video**, explain Whinney's original strategy in your own words: Exactly what kind of chocolate company did he want to build? In precisely what ways was Whinney's vision of his company a matter of *strategic choice*? Which of Whinney's strategic choices eventually had to be revised? Why?
2. **Judging from the video**, describe Theo Chocolate's *organization design* in your own words. Now address the following questions: What does the motto "structure follows strategy" mean? Is it helpful in understanding the organization design of Theo Chocolate? Why or why not?
3. Music says that Theo Chocolate is "the only vertically integrated product on the shelf." What is *vertical integration*? How is it relevant to both Theo's organization and strategy? What role did Theo's vertically integrated design play in the revision of its strategy?
4. What role does Theo's *organizational environment* play in the events described in the video? What affects does it have on the company's strategy? In particular, which members of Theo's *task environment* figure most prominently in the story of Theo's strategy revision?

ADDITIONAL SOURCES

Theo Chocolate, "Our Story," "Our Mission" (2012), at www.theochocolate.com on October 6, 2012; "Debra Music and Joe Whinney—Doing Well While Doing Good: The Sweet Story of Theo Chocolate," *TEDXSeattle*, April 16, 2010, http://tedxseattle.com on October 6, 2012; John Trybus, "The Social Strategist Part IV: Theo Chocolate's Joe Whinney, and Profitability with Principles," *The Social Strategist*, December 29, 2011, at https://blogs.commons.georgetown.edu on October 6, 2012; "Joseph Whinney: 2012 Krista Foundation GCA Honoree—Developing World" (Krista Foundation, February 12, 2012), at www.kristafoundation.org on October 6, 2012; Greg Lamm, "Seattle's Theo Chocolate Making Organic Products in Old Red Hook Brewery in Fremont," *Puget Sound Business Journal*, February 10, 2008, at www.bizjournals.com on October 6, 2012.

*Organic-certified products satisfy a variety of criteria that vary from country to country. Basically, *organic certification* means that synthetic chemicals and certain types of fertilizer have not been used in producing the ingredients of final food products. Organic certification in the United States is overseen by the U.S. Department of Agriculture. As we pointed out in *Video Case 14*, "Fair Trade" refers to programs designed to ensure that export-dependent farmers in developing countries receive fair prices for their crops. Theo Chocolate is Fair Trade certified by TransFair USA, a nonprofit organization based in Oakland, California.

EXPERIENCING ORGANIZATIONAL BEHAVIOR

Studying a Real Organization

Purpose: This exercise will help you understand the factors that determine the design of organizations.

Format: You will interview at least five employees in different parts of the college or university that you attend or employees of a small- to medium-sized organization and analyze the reasons for its design. (You may want to coordinate this exercise with the "Experiencing Organizational Behavior" exercise in Chapter 16.)

Procedure: If you use a local organization, your first task is to find one with between fifty and five hundred employees. If you did the exercise for Chapter 16, you can use the same company for this exercise. The organization should have more than two hierarchical levels, but it should not be too complex to understand within a short period of study. You may want to check with your professor before contacting the company. Your initial contact should be with the highest-ranking manager you can reach. Make sure that top management is aware of your project and gives its approval.

If you use your local college or university, you could talk to professors, secretaries, and other administrative staff in the admissions office, student services department, athletic department, library, and many others. Be sure to include employees from a variety of jobs and levels in your interviews.

Using the material in this chapter, you will interview employees to obtain the following information on the structure of the organization:

1. What is the organization in business to do? What are its goals and its strategies for achieving them?
2. How large is the company? What is the total number of employees? How many work full-time? How many work part-time?
3. What are the most important components of the organization's environment?
4. Is the number of important environmental components large or small?
5. How quickly or slowly do these components change?
6. Would you characterize the organization's environment as certain, uncertain, or somewhere in between? If in between, describe approximately how certain or uncertain.
7. What is the organization's dominant technology; that is, how does it transform inputs into outputs?
8. How rigid is the company in its application of rules and procedures? Is it flexible enough to respond to environmental changes?
9. How involved are employees in the daily decision making related to their jobs?
10. What methods are used to ensure control over the actions of employees?

Interview at least five employees of the college or company at different levels and in different departments. One should hold a top-level position. Be sure to ask the questions in a way the employees will understand; they may not be familiar with some of the terminology used in this chapter.

The result of the exercise should be a report describing the technology, environment, and structure of the company. You should discuss the extent to which the structure is appropriate for the organization's strategy, size, technology, and environment. If it does not seem appropriate, you should explain the reasons. If you also used this company for the exercise in Chapter 16, you can comment further on the organization chart and its appropriateness for the company. You may want to send a copy of your report to the cooperating company.

Follow-Up Questions

1. Which aspects of strategy, size, environment, and technology were the most difficult to obtain information about? Why?
2. If there were differences in the responses of the employees you interviewed, how do you account for them?
3. If you were the president of the organization you analyzed, would you structure it in the same way? Why or why not? If not, how would you structure it differently?
4. How did your answers to questions 2 and 3 differ from those in the exercise in Chapter 16?

BUILDING MANAGERIAL SKILLS

Exercise Overview: When organizations utilize a matrix organizational structure (see Figure 17.6), every employee and manager in the system has dual reporting relationships, a situation that puts additional pressure on the managerial skills of everybody in the system. This exercise provides you with an opportunity to analyze some of the managerial requirements for success in a matrix organizational structure.

Exercise Background: The matrix organizational structure was initially established to overcome the inadequacies of traditional structures when the environment and technology of certain organizations required additional information-processing capabilities. It has been hailed as a great innovation in certain situations, but it has also caused some problems when utilized in other organizations.

Exercise Task: Working alone, look again at the managerial roles and critical managerial skills described in Chapter 2. See if you can describe how each of these managerial roles and skills is affected when an organization uses a matrix structure. Go through each role and each skill, first listing each one along with a simple one-sentence description. Then reread the section on matrix organizations in this chapter and write a description of the roles and skills required of managers in a matrix structure.

Exchange papers with a classmate or share papers in a small group. Make notes about how others saw the roles and skills differently than you did. Discuss the differences and similarities that you find.

Conclude by addressing the following questions:

1. To what extent does the matrix organization structure put additional pressure on managers?
2. What should organizations using a matrix structure do to help their managers be prepared for those additional pressures?
3. Would you like to work in a matrix organizational structure? Why or why not?

SELF-ASSESSMENT EXERCISE

Finding Your Comfort Level

This exercise is designed to help you determine whether you are more comfortable working in an organization with a mechanistic structure or one with an organic structure. The fifteen statements below reflect preferences that people can have in workplace structure and environment. Using the following scale, indicate the extent to which each statement accurately describes your preference:

5 Strongly agree

4 Agree somewhat

3 Undecided

2 Disagree somewhat

1 Strongly disagree

I prefer to work in an organization in which:

_______1. Goals are defined by those at higher levels.

_______2. Work methods and procedures are specified.

_______3. Top management makes important decisions.

_______4. My loyalty counts as much as my ability to do the job.

_______5. Clear lines of authority and responsibility are established.

_______6. Top management is decisive and firm.

_______7. My career is pretty well planned out for me.

_______8. I can specialize.

_______9. My length of service is almost as important as my level of performance.

_______10. Management is able to provide the information I need to do my job well.

_______11. The chain of command is well established.

_______12. Rules and procedures are adhered to equally by everyone.

_______13. People accept the authority of a leader's position.

_______14. People do as they've been instructed.

_______15. People clear things with their bosses before going over their heads.

How to score: Find your score by adding the numbers that you assigned to the fifteen statements. Interpret your score as follows:

- The higher your score above 64, the more comfortable you are with a mechanistic structure.
- The lower your score *below* 48, the more comfortable you are with an organic structure.
- Scores between 48 and 64 can go either way.

Reference: John F. Veiga and John N. Yanousa, *The Dynamics of Organization Theory: Gaining a Macro Perspective* (St. Paul, MN: West, 1979).

CHAPTER 18

Organization Culture

Chapter Outline

- The Nature of Organization Culture
- Creating the Organization Culture
- Approaches to Describing Organization Culture
- Emerging Issues in Organization Culture
- Managing Organization Culture

Chapter Learning Objectives

After studying this chapter, you should be able to:

1. **Define organization culture, explain how it affects employee behavior, and understand its historical roots.**
2. **Describe how to create organization culture.**
3. **Describe two different approaches to culture in organizations.**
4. **Identify emerging issues in organization culture.**
5. **Discuss the important elements of managing the organizational culture.**

The NetApp Approach to Net Satisfaction

"Funny, no one mentions wanting free M&Ms."

—Consultant George Brymer on what NetApp employees do and don't want

NetApp, a computer storage and data management company headquartered in Sunnyvale, California, is no stranger to best-places-to-work lists. Since 2005, it has consistently been ranked among the top fifteen Best Multinational Work Places in the world. In 2012, it came in sixth on *Fortune* magazine's list of the "100 Best Companies to Work For" in the United States—a drop from first place in 2009 but the firm's tenth consecutive appearance on the list. *Fortune* also ranked NetApp among the top five in Japan, Canada, Switzerland, the United Kingdom, Australia, France, and the Netherlands.

NetApp likes to cite employee-survey scores as a key reason for its regular appearance on the annual list compiled by *Fortune* and the Great Place to Work Institute. According to the company's website, worker surveys reflect "our employees' experiences and opinions about our culture and values, trust in leadership, integrity and fairness, teamwork, and camaraderie." High on the list of things that keep workers satisfied and motivated seems to be a culture that encourages employee input and the sharing of ideas. The "most impressive thing … about the company," says one engineer, "is the open-door culture. I can approach any other engineer with technical issues, product marketing with new ideas, and anyone in management with any questions." Also highly satisfying appears to be the collaborative approach to work processes. "Cooperation is the … actual norm," reports one another worker. "This company is unique in my experience for avoiding the politics and empire building typical in growing companies." "The focus is on the issues," adds another employee, "and in most cases, you find that the issues aren't owned by one particular function," such as marketing or operations. "The focus is on team problem solving."

Most of all, NetApp employees seem happy with the level of freedom that they are given in the pursuit of both organizational and personal goals. In particular, says one worker, "I have … lots of freedom to implement my ideas to make things better, and [I'm] also able to make decisions in order to get the job done." Another employee

Kris Tripplaar/TRIPPLAAR KRISTOFFER/SIPA/Newscom

This the headquarters of NetApp in Silicon Valley in Sunnyvale, California. As attractive as the headquarters building of NetApp is, the outside is not what is so important about NetApp. Within the headquarters building the top management team of NetApp develops the policies and procedures and creates the culture in effect in every building that houses NetApp employees.

thinks that "the most unique thing about NetApp … is that they give us a lot of the free stuff—*free* as in *freedom*, not 'free beer.'" Granted, he adds, "there's a lot of 'free beer' here—free gifts, goodies, lunches. But I think giving 'free beer' to keep employees happy works only as long as the company is [riding] high. Freedom lasts forever." Or at least as long as it is embedded in the company culture, according to George Brymer, founder and president of All Square Inc., a provider of managerial training programs. Brymer, who is also the author of *Vital Integrities: How Values-Based Leaders Acquire and Preserve Their Credibility*, contrasts the role of "free beer" at NetApp with its more highly publicized counterpart at Google. "Among the perks enjoyed by Google employees," he writes,

> *are onsite haircuts, free laundry facilities, workout and massage rooms, in-house childcare, and car washes. And then there's the free food. The campus has eleven cafeterias serving everything from gourmet meals to M&Ms….*
>
> *Unlike Google, which got to the top [of the* Fortune *list of "100 Best Companies to Work For" in 2007 and 2012] largely by providing employees with lots of goodies, NetApp earned [its] spot because of its culture of trust. NetApp's leaders promote an atmosphere of openness and honesty, and they go out of their way to proactively share information with workers….*
>
> *For their part, NetApp employees say they appreciate how easy it is to share ideas, get answers to questions, meet with senior leaders, and find opportunities to take responsibility. Funny, no one mentions wanting free M&Ms.*

In placing NetApp on its "UK's 50 Best Workplaces" and "100 Best Workplaces in Europe" lists, the Great Place to Work Institute cited employees' opinions that company management is approachable and easy to talk to, is forthcoming with straight answers to reasonable questions, and keeps workers informed about important issues and changes.

In addition, the principle of trust at NetApp extends beyond management's confidence in the ability of informed employees to make good operational decisions: It also applies to management's confidence that satisfied employees will live up to item number seven on the company's list of "living values"—namely, that they will "Get Things Done!" "What I appreciate most about NetApp," says one worker,

> *is that I'm respected—to manage my time, my day, my workload. No one's telling me to be at my desk by a certain time or gives me a strange look if I'm leaving the office early. It's expected that you get your work done, and if you do that late at night or early in the morning, that's your choice.... No one's watching your movements. It's about performance, achieving goals....*

When things get done—when individuals and teams perform and achieve goals—NetApp has a number of programs in place to recognize them. The SHARE Rewards program, for instance, offers incentives for knowledge sharing; a program called Total Customer Experience Champions offers rewards for enhancing customer views of the company, and the NetApp Patent Award program distributes up to $15,000 to employees involved in projects that produce patents. NetApp is also ranked among *Fortune*'s list of "25 Top-Paying Companies." In order to recruit and retain top talent, it regularly monitors the competitiveness of its pay rates among high-tech companies, and in one recent year, 98 percent of all employees received incentive bonuses totaling $47 million.

What Do You Think?

1. Compare NetApp's culture with that of Wegmans, the grocery chain discussed in the vignette opening Chapter 1. In what ways are their cultures similar? Given the difference in the companies' industries, in what ways are the similarities most surprising?
2. Why do you suppose that the number of companies with cultures like those of NetApp and Wegmans are on the rise in today's business environment? Will the trend continue? Why or why not?

References: "100 Best Companies to Work For: Top 100," *Fortune*, February 6, 2012, http://money.cnn.com on August 20, 2012; "100 Best Companies to Work For: Big Pay," *Fortune*, February 6, 2012, http://money.cnn.com on August 20, 2012; Amy Lyman, *NetApp: Culture—Values—Leadership* (San Francisco: Great Place to Work® Institute, 2009), http://resources.greatplacetowork.com on August 20, 2012; George Brymer, "NetApp: A Great Place to Work," *Vital Integrities*, April 2009, http://allsquareinc.blogspot.com on August 20, 2012; J. P. Gallagher, "I Work for One of the 10 Best Companies," *Fortune*, January 21, 2010, http://money.cnn.com on August 20, 2012; NetApp, "NetApp Is a Great Place to Work Worldwide!" *ThaibizPR*, May 17, 2010, www.thaibizpr.com on August 20, 2012.

THE NATURE OF ORGANIZATION CULTURE

In the early 1980s, organization culture became a central concern in the study of organizational behavior. Hundreds of researchers began to work in this area. Numerous books were published, important academic journals dedicated entire issues to the discussion of culture, and, almost overnight, organizational behavior textbooks that omitted culture as a topic of study became obsolete.

Interest in organization culture was not limited to academic researchers. Businesses expressed a far more intense interest in culture than in other aspects of organizational behavior. *Business Week, Fortune,* and other business periodicals published articles that touted culture as the key to an organization's success and suggested that managers who could manage through their organization's culture almost certainly would rise to the top.[1]

The study of organization culture remains important, although the enthusiasm of the early 1980s has waned somewhat. The assumption is that organizations with a strong culture perform at higher levels than those without a strong culture.[2] For example, studies have shown that organizations with strong cultures that are strategically appropriate and that have norms that permit the organization to change actually do perform well.[3] Other studies have shown that different functional units may require different types of cultures.[4] The research on the impact of culture on organizational performance is mixed, however, depending on how the research is done and what variables are measured.

Many researchers have begun to weave the important aspects of organization culture into their research on more traditional topics. Now there are fewer headline stories in the popular business press about culture and culture management, but organization culture can have powerful effects on organizational performance, as the opening case about NetApp illustrates. The enormous amount of research on culture completed in the last twenty years has fundamentally altered the way academics and managers alike look at organizations. Some of the concepts developed in the analysis of organization culture have become basic parts of the business vocabulary, and the analysis of organization culture is one of the most important specialties in the field of organizational behavior.

What Is Organization Culture?

A surprising aspect of the recent rise in interest in organization culture is that the concept, unlike virtually every other concept in the field, has no single widely accepted definition. Indeed, it often appears that authors feel compelled to develop their own definitions, which range from very broad to highly specific. For example, T. E. Deal and A. A. Kennedy define a firm's culture as "the way we do things around here."[5] This very broad definition presumably could include the way a firm manufactures its products or creates its service, pays its bills, treats its employees, and performs any other organizational operation. More specific definitions include those of E. H. Schein ("the pattern of basic assumptions that a given group has invented, discovered, or developed in learning to cope with its problems of external adaptation and internal integration"[6]) and Tom Peters and Robert Waterman ("a dominant and coherent set of shared values conveyed by such symbolic means as stories, myths, legends, slogans, anecdotes, and fairy tales"[7]). Table 18.1 lists these and other important definitions of organization culture.

Table 18.1 Definitions of Organization Culture

DEFINITION	SOURCE
"A belief system shared by an organization's members"	J. C. Spender, "Myths, Recipes and Knowledge-Bases in Organizational Analysis" (Unpublished manuscript, Graduate School of Management, University of California at Los Angeles, 1983), p. 2.
"Strong, widely shared core values"	C. O'Reilly, "Corporations, Cults, and Organizational Culture: Lessons from Silicon Valley Firms" (Paper presented at the Annual Meeting of the Academy of Management, Dallas, Texas, 1983), p. 1.
"The way we do things around here"	T. E. Deal and A. A. Kennedy, *Corporate Cultures: The Rites and Rituals of Corporate Life* (Reading, MA: Addison-Wesley, 1982), p. 4.
"The collective programming of the mind"	G. Hofstede, *Culture's Consequences: International Differences in Work-Related Values* (Beverly Hills, CA: Sage, 1980), p. 25.
"Collective understandings"	J. Van Maanen and S. R. Barley, "Cultural Organization: Fragments of a Theory" (Paper presented at the Annual Meeting of the Academy of Management, Dallas, Texas, 1983), p. 7.
"A set of shared, enduring beliefs communicated through a variety of symbolic media, creating meaning in people's work lives"	J. M. Kouzes, D. F. Caldwell, and B. Z. Posner, "Organizational Culture: How It Is Created, Maintained, and Changed" (Presentation at OD Network National Conference, Los Angeles, October 9, 1983).
"A set of symbols, ceremonies, and myths that communicates the underlying values and beliefs of that organization to its employees"	W. G. Ouchi, *Theory Z: How American Business Can Meet the Japanese Challenge* (Reading, MA: Addison-Wesley, 1981), p. 41.
"A dominant and coherent set of shared values conveyed by such symbolic means as stories, myths, legends, slogans, anecdotes, and fairy tales"	T. J. Peters and R. H. Waterman Jr., *In Search of Excellence: Lessons from America's Best-Run Companies* (New York: Harper & Row, 1982), p. 103.
"The pattern of basic assumptions that a given group has invented, discovered, or developed in learning to cope with its problems of external adaptation and internal integration"	E. H. Schein, "The Role of the Founder in Creating Organizational Culture," *Organizational Dynamics,* Summer 1985, p. 14.

Despite the apparent diversity of these definitions, a few common attributes emerge. First, all the definitions refer to a set of values held by individuals in an organization. These values define good or acceptable behaviors and bad or unacceptable behavior. In some organizations, for example, it is unacceptable to blame customers when problems arise. Here the value "the customer is always right" tells managers what actions are acceptable (not blaming the customer) and what actions are not acceptable (blaming the customer). In other organizations, the dominant values might support blaming customers for problems, penalizing employees who make mistakes, or treating employees as the organization's most valuable assets. In each case, values help members of an organization understand how they should act.

A second attribute common to many of the definitions in Table 18.1 is that the values that make up an organization's culture are often taken for granted; that is, they are basic assumptions made by the firm's employees rather than prescriptions written in a book or made explicit in a training program. It may be as difficult for an organization to articulate these basic assumptions as it is for people to express their personal beliefs and values. Several authors have argued that organization culture is a powerful influence on individuals in organizations precisely because it is not explicit but instead becomes an implicit part of employees' values and beliefs.[8]

Some organizations have been able to articulate the key values in their cultures. Some have even written down these values and made them part of formal training procedures. Whole Foods Market stands out from the rest of the supermarket industry. In 2004, the 160-store chain earned $137 million, while Kroger, the nation's largest supermarket chain, lost $100 million. Whole Foods has a unique organization culture, described by CEO John Mackey as "a fast-breaking basketball team. We're driving down the court, but we don't exactly know how the play is going to evolve." Many experts attribute the differences in performance to its unique organization culture that is democratic, participative, egalitarian, innovative, team-based, and transparent.[9]

Even when organizations can articulate and describe the basic values that make up their cultures, however, the values most strongly affect actions when people in the organization take them for granted. An organization's culture is not likely to influence behavior powerfully when employees must constantly refer to a handbook to remember what the culture is. When the culture becomes part of them—when they can ignore what is written in the book because they already have embraced the values it describes—the culture can have an important impact on their actions.

The final attribute shared by many of the definitions in Table 18.1 is an emphasis on the symbolic means through which the values in an organization's culture are communicated. Although, as we noted, companies sometimes could directly describe these values, their meaning is perhaps best communicated to employees through the use of stories, examples, and even what some authors call "myths" or "fairy tales." Stories typically reflect the important implications of values in an organization's culture. Often they develop a life of their own. As they are told and retold, shaped and reshaped, their relationship to what actually occurred becomes less important than the powerful impact the stories have on the way people behave every day. Nike uses a group of technical representatives called "Ekins" ("Nike" spelled backwards) who run a nine-day training session for large retailers, telling them stories about Nike's history and traditions, such as the stories about CEO Phil Knight selling shoes from the trunk of his car and cofounder Bill Bowerman using the family's waffle iron to create the first waffle-soled running shoe.[10]

Some organization stories have become famous. At E*Trade, CEO Christos Cotsakos has done many things that have since become famous around the company because he did not follow the rules for the typical investment company. To make people move faster, he organized a day of racing in Formula One cars at speeds of around 150 miles per hour. To create a looser atmosphere around the office, he had employees carry around rubber chickens or wear propeller beanies. To bond the employees together, he organized gourmet-cooking classes.[11] The stories of these incidents and others are told to new employees and are spread throughout the company, thus affecting the behavior of many more people than those who actually took part in each event.

David Madison/The Image Bank/Getty Images

Would this be fun—to drive a Formula One race car on a track with your coworkers? This is a great way to spend the day with coworkers, racing Formula One cars and getting a feel for what working faster really means!

We can use the three common attributes of definitions of culture just discussed to develop a definition with which most authors probably could agree: **Organization culture** is the set of shared values, often taken for granted, that help people in an organization understand which actions are considered acceptable and which are considered unacceptable. Often these values are communicated through stories and other symbolic means.

Historical Foundations

Although research on organization culture exploded onto the scene in the early 1980s, the antecedents of this research can be traced to the origins of social science. Understanding the contributions of other social science disciplines is particularly important in the case of organization culture because many of the dilemmas and debates that continue in this area reflect differences in historical research traditions.

Anthropological Contributions Anthropology is the study of human cultures.[12] Of all the social science disciplines, anthropology is most closely related to the study of culture and cultural phenomena. Anthropologists seek to understand how the values and beliefs that make up a society's culture affect the structure and functioning of that society. Many anthropologists believe that to understand the relationship between culture and society, it is necessary to look at a culture from the viewpoint of the people who practice it—from the "native's point of view."[13] To reach this level of understanding, anthropologists immerse themselves in the values, symbols, and stories that people in a society use to bring order and meaning to their lives. Anthropologists usually produce book-length descriptions of the values, attitudes, and beliefs that underlie the behaviors of people in one or two cultures.[14]

Organization culture is the set of values that helps the organization's employees understand which actions are considered acceptable and which are unacceptable.

Whether the culture is that of a large, modern corporation or a primitive tribe in New Guinea or the Philippines, the questions asked are the same: How do people in this culture know what kinds of behavior are acceptable and what kinds are unacceptable? How is this knowledge understood? How is this knowledge communicated to new members? Through intense efforts to produce accurate descriptions, the values and beliefs that underlie actions in an organization become clear. However, these values can be fully understood only in the context of the organization in which they developed. In other words, a description of the values and beliefs of one organization is not transferable to those of other organizations; each culture is unique.

Sociological Contributions Sociology is the study of people in social systems such as organizations and societies. Sociologists have long been interested in the causes and consequences of culture. In studying culture, sociologists have most often focused on informal social structure. Émile Durkheim, an important early sociologist, argued that the study of myth and ritual is an essential complement to the study of structure and rational behavior in societies.[15] By studying rituals, Durkheim argued, we can understand the most basic values and beliefs of a group of people.

Many sociological methods and theories have been used in the analysis of organization cultures. Sociologists use systematic interviews, questionnaires, and other quantitative research methods rather than the intensive study and analysis of anthropologists. Practitioners using the sociological approach generally produce a fairly simple typology of cultural attributes and then show how the cultures of a relatively large number of firms can be analyzed with this typology.[16] The major pieces of research on organization culture that later spawned widespread business interest—including Ouchi's *Theory Z,* Deal and Kennedy's *Corporate Cultures,* and Peters and Waterman's *In Search of Excellence*[17]—used sociological methods. Later in this chapter, we review some of this work in more detail.

Social Psychology Contributions Social psychology is a branch of psychology that includes the study of groups and the influence of social factors on individuals. Although most research on organization culture has used anthropological or sociological methods and approaches, some has borrowed heavily from social psychology. Social psychological theory, with its emphasis on the creation and manipulation of symbols, lends itself naturally to the analysis of organization culture.

For example, research in social psychology suggests that people tend to use stories or information about a single event more than they use multiple observations to make judgments.[18] Thus, if your neighbor had trouble with a certain brand of automobile, you will probably conclude that the brand is bad even though the car company can generate reams of statistical data to prove that the situation with your neighbor's car was a rarity. Today, it does not even have to be sharing stories with a neighbor because the proliferation of websites, blogs, and product reviews on the Internet enables everyone to share stories/reviews of all kinds of products and services.

The impact of stories on decision making suggests an important reason that organization culture has such a powerful influence on the people in an organization. Unlike other organizational phenomena, culture is best communicated through stories and examples, and these become the basis that individuals in the organization use to make judgments. If a story says that blaming customers is a bad thing to do, then blaming customers is a bad thing to do. This value is communicated much more effectively through the cultural story than through some statistical analysis of customer satisfaction.[19]

Economics Contributions The influence of economics on the study of organization culture is substantial enough to warrant attention, though it has been less significant than the influence of anthropology and sociology. Economic analysis treats organization culture as one of a variety of tools that managers can use to create some economic advantage for the organization.

The economics approach attempts to link the cultural attributes of firms with their performance rather than simply describing the cultures of companies as the sociological and anthropological perspectives do. In *Theory Z,* for example, Ouchi does not just say that Type Z companies differ from other kinds of companies—he asserts that Type Z firms outperform other firms.[20] When Peters and Waterman say they are in search of excellence, they define "excellence," in part, as consistently high financial performance.[21] These authors are using cultural explanations of financial success.

Researchers disagree about the extent to which culture affects organization performance. Several authors have investigated the conditions under which organization culture is linked with superior financial performance.[22] This research suggests that under some relatively narrow conditions, a link between culture and performance may exist. However, the fact that a firm has a culture does not mean it will perform well; indeed, a variety of cultural traits can actually hurt performance. For example, a firm could have a culture that includes values such as "customers are too ignorant to be of much help," "employees cannot be trusted," "innovation is not important," and "quality is too expensive." The firm would have a strong culture, but the culture might impair its performance. Walmart, known for its retailing expertise and its culture of respect for individuals, is also becoming known as a company whose culture does not lead to success for women.[23]

In some cases the culture of an organization may lead to its success and its downfall at the same time: Toyota may be a good example. For decades Toyota had been known for the quality and dependability of its cars and trucks, partially due to its unique organization culture—the "Toyota way"—which led to lean manufacturing and very close relationships with suppliers. However, one of the distinguishing features of the culture is its secretive nature. Very few outsiders were allowed access to key processes within the company. For several years, some car owners had experienced difficulties with sticking gas pedals causing their Toyotas to suddenly accelerate. The company dismissed the problem as simply floor mats pressing against the gas pedals. Toyota claimed it was working with the National Highway Traffic Safety Administration (NHTSA) to address the problem—but in fact they were really stalling and not cooperating. Some have claimed that the secretive nature of its culture, although one reason for its success, may also have been the cause of its 2.3 million vehicle recall and the NHTSA order to Toyota to temporarily stop selling cars.[24] The relationship between culture and performance depends, to some extent at least, on the values expressed in the organization's culture.

Culture versus Climate

In the thirty years since the concept of organization culture became popular, managers have often asked about the similarities and differences between organization culture and organization climate. Some people, managers and researchers alike, have argued that they are really the same thing, although their research bases are different, as we explain next.

The two concepts are similar in that both are concerned with the overall work atmosphere of an organization. In addition, they both deal with the social context in organizations, and both are assumed to affect the behaviors of people who work in organizations.[25]

The two concepts differ in several significant ways, however. Much of the study of climate was based in psychology, whereas the study of organization culture was based in anthropology and sociology. **Organization climate** is based on individual perceptions and is often defined as the recurring patterns of behavior, attitudes, and feelings that characterize life in the organization; it refers to current situations in an organization and the linkages among work groups, employees, and work performance.[26] Climate, therefore, is usually more easily manipulated by management to directly influence the behavior of employees. Organization culture, on the other hand, usually refers to the historical context within which a situation occurs and the impact of this context on the behaviors of employees. Organization culture is generally considered much more difficult to alter in short-run situations because it has been defined over the course of years of history and tradition.

Organization climate is based on individual perceptions; is often defined as the recurring patterns of behavior, attitudes, and feelings that characterize life in the organization; and refers to current situations in an organization and the linkages among work groups, employees, and work performance.

The two concepts also differ in their emphases. Organization culture is often described as the means through which people in the organization learn and communicate what is acceptable and unacceptable in an organization—its values and norms.[27] Most descriptions of organization climate do not deal with values and norms. Therefore, descriptions of organization climate are concerned with the current atmosphere in an organization, whereas organization culture is based on the history and traditions of the organization and emphasizes values and norms about employee behavior.

CREATING THE ORGANIZATION CULTURE

To the entrepreneur who starts a business, creating the culture of the company may seem secondary to the basic processes of creating a product or service and selling it to customers or clients. However, as the company grows and becomes successful, it usually develops a culture that distinguishes it from other companies and that is one of the

Table 18.2	Creating Organization Culture
Step 1—Formulate Strategic Values	
Step 2—Develop Cultural Values	
Step 3—Create Vision	
Step 4—Initiate Implementation Strategies	
Step 5—Reinforce Cultural Behaviors	

reasons for its success. In other words, a company succeeds as a result of what the company does (its strategy), and how the company does it (its culture). The culture is linked to the strategic values, whether one is starting up a new company or trying to change the culture of an existing company.[28] The process of creating an organization culture is really a process of linking its strategic values with its cultural values, much as the structure of the organization is linked to its strategy, as we described in Chapter 17. The process is shown in Table 18.2.

Establish Values

Strategic values are the basic beliefs about an organization's environment that shape its strategy.

Cultural values are the values that employees need to have and act on for the organization to act on the strategic values.

The first two steps in the process involve establishing values. First, management must determine the strategic values of the organization. **Strategic values** are the basic beliefs about an organization's environment that shape its strategy. They are developed following an environmental scanning process and strategic analysis that evaluate economic, demographic, public policy, technological, and social trends to identify needs in the marketplace that the organization can meet. Strategic values, in effect, link the organization with its environment. Dell Computer believed that customers would, if the price was right, buy computers from a catalogue rather than go to computer stores as the conventional wisdom dictated they would. A $6.8 billion business resulted.[29] The second set of required values includes the cultural values of the organization. **Cultural values** are the values employees need to have and to act on for the organization to carry out its strategic values. They should be grounded in the organization's beliefs about how and why the organization can succeed. Organizations that attempt to develop cultural values that are not linked to their strategic values may end up with an empty set of values that have little relationship to their business. In other words, employees need to value work behaviors that are consistent with and support the organization's strategic values: low-cost production, customer service, or technological innovation. Herb Kelleher, former CEO and one of the early leaders of Southwest Airlines, believed that the culture, the "esprit de corps," was the most valuable asset of the company.[30]

Tony Hsieh (pronounced *Shay)* starting selling shoes online (Zappos.com) in 1999 and booked $1 billion in sales in 2008, but he believes the business is about one thing: happiness. He simply wanted to make customers and employees feel really, really good. His strategic values were that he believed shoes could be sold online with free shipping and free returns. Zappos now has ten core values that include "Be humble," "Create fun and a little weirdness," and "Deliver WOW through service." Hsieh's basic cultural value is to make everyone happy.[31]

Create Vision

After developing its strategic and cultural values, the organization must establish a vision of its direction. This "vision" is a picture of what the organization will be like at some point in the future. It portrays how the strategic and cultural values will combine to create the future. For example, an insurance company might establish a vision of "protecting the lifestyles of 2 million families by the year 2020." In effect, it synthesizes both the strategic and cultural values as it communicates a performance target to employees. The conventional wisdom has been that the vision statement is written first, but experience suggests that, for the vision to be meaningful, the strategic and cultural values must be established first. Mr. Hsieh, of Zappos, envisions big things for his company as long as he can provide a service that makes people happy. He is creating an outsourcing service to handle customer service, selling and shipping for other companies, and has initiated a website to provide training and education for small businesses.[32]

Initiate Implementation Strategies

The next step, initiating implementation strategies, builds on the values and initiates the action to accomplish the vision. The strategies cover many factors, from developing the organization design to recruiting and training employees who share the values and will carry them out. Consider a bank that has the traditional orientation of handling customer loans, deposits, and savings. If the bank changes, placing more emphasis on customer service, it may have to recruit a different type of employee, one who is capable of building relationships. The bank will also have to commit to serious, long-term training of its current employees to teach them the new service-oriented culture. The strategic and cultural values are the stimuli for the implementation practices.

Zappos fully implemented its cultural values in many ways. Zappos hires people who fit the culture, pays them average wages, and provides them lots of training on topics ranging from the initial two-week orientation to current business books, how to Twitter, public speaking, and financial planning—all intended to help people grow and think and be ready to be a senior leader in the company. Sales from the previous day are on a chart in the lobby of the headquarters building with a computer printout in the hallway showing how many shoes are in the warehouse. Call center reps are left to make decisions on their own, do not read from scripts, do not have their call times recorded, and are encouraged to create personal emotional connections (PEC) with customers. Managers are required to spend 10–20 percent of their time goofing off with the people they manage, and "hanging out with your people" is highly encouraged.

Reinforce Cultural Behaviors

The final step is to reinforce the behaviors of employees as they act out the cultural values and implement the organization's strategies. Reinforcement can take many forms. First, the formal reward system in the organization must reward desired behaviors in ways that employees value. Second, stories must be told throughout the organization about employees who engaged in behaviors that epitomize the cultural values. Third, the organization must engage in ceremonies and rituals that emphasize employees doing the things that are critical to carrying out the organization's vision. In effect, the organization must "make a big deal out of employees doing the right things." For example, if parties are held only for retirement or to give out longevity and service pins, the employees get the message that retirement and length of service are the only things that matter. On the other hand, holding a ceremony for a group of employees who provided exceptional customer service reinforces desirable employee behaviors. Reinforcement practices are the final link between the strategic and cultural values and the creation of the organization culture. Zappos reinforces the culture every single day as employees come to work happy, leave happy, and often go out with their coworkers and managers after work. It becomes a way of life for them.[33]

SERVICE Creating a Service Culture

©rangizzz/Shutterstock

John Caparella was hired to be the opening manager of the 1,400-room Gaylord Palms located in Orlando, Florida. John had become convinced in his earlier hotel jobs that an organization's culture should be thought of as the operating "software" for service organizations. He believed, therefore, that in opening this new hotel he should spend considerable effort on creating a sustainable culture that would focus his employees on how to provide excellent customer service. John began by assembling a leadership team that thought as he did and would be willing to teach and model the cultural values and beliefs he wanted employees to adopt. They then interviewed applicants from a labor pool that had been attracted by the excitement of working in a new hotel that was part of a company, Gaylord Entertainment, that also owned Nashville's iconic Grand Ole Opry. Since the labor pool was so large, the people that were selected were termed "10's" as they were the one out of ten candidates that were actually hired. To further build a language that would reinforce the cultural values, John's team invented the term "STARS" as a word to describe all employees, hourly or management. STARS stood for Smiles, Teamwork, Attitude, Reliability, and Service with a passion. The idea was to use language to constantly remind employees about the cultural beliefs.

To teach employees the cultural values of what customers should expect at the Palms, John believed in the power of telling stories. He wrote a letter that would represent what he hoped the hotel would get from guests once the hotel was opened. He knew the power of stories, legends, and heroes in teaching culture and wanted to provide a strong example of a service hero in the letter that would establish a benchmark of what excellent service looked like to a customer. Eventually, once the hotel had been open long enough to receive feedback from real guests, that benchmark would be adjusted based on their comments. He also knew the power of teaching culture through what was rewarded and what was punished. He provided bonuses to employees based on the percent of "5's"—the highest possible mark—they received on a five-point customer scoring of service quality. John figured that only the best would do for his hotel. Finally, he included fun as one of the core values of the company.

A fun work culture is obviously more smile inducing for both employees and customers, so John promoted activities that would be seen as fun. Besides the typical family activities and company-sponsored sports teams, Gaylord combined fun activities with significant opportunities to teach the culture. For example, there were quarterly celebrations of the seven Gaylord values (service, citizenship, integrity, respect, excellence, creativity, and passion) that recognized one person as best representing each value. The celebrations were highly anticipated events, with employees competing for the right to provide the entertainment. Another celebratory event was the promotion celebrations in which the manager responsible for a newly promoted employee would pedal the employee around the hotel in a pedicab, often with a parade of employees with noisemakers that attracted hotel guests to join in the fun. Perhaps one of the most unusual parts of teaching the culture was the offer of an employment guarantee to every employee. Newly hired employees were told that if the job were not what was promised, they should call the general manager directly to tell him about it. Obviously, this promoted supervisory responsiveness to all employee concerns and consideration across the entire organization. The obvious question is whether all this culture building was worth it. It would seem so: the hotel was honored in multiple years as a best place to work, it was considered an outstanding place to hold meetings and events winner, and it made good profits. Building a service culture guided employees to fill in the gaps between what they could be trained to do and what needed to be done in successfully dealing with many different customers.

Discussion Question: Based on your knowledge of culture, what ways can you see to create a positive work environment that is attractive to both employees and customers?

APPROACHES TO DESCRIBING ORGANIZATION CULTURE

The models discussed in this section provide valuable insights into the dimensions along which organization cultures vary. No single framework for describing the values in organization cultures has emerged; however, several frameworks have been suggested. Although these frameworks were developed in the 1980s, their ideas about organization culture are still influential today. Some of the "excellent" companies that they described are not as highly lauded today, but the concepts are still in use in companies all over the world. Managers should evaluate the various parts of the frameworks described and use the parts that fit the strategic and cultural values of their own organizations.

The **Type Z firm** is committed to retaining employees; evaluates workers' performance based on both qualitative and quantitative information; emphasizes broad career paths; exercises control through informal, implicit mechanisms; requires that decision making occur in groups and be based on full information sharing and consensus; expects individuals to take responsibility for decisions; and emphasizes concern for people.

The Ouchi Framework

One of the first researchers to focus explicitly on analyzing the cultures of a limited group of firms was William G. Ouchi. Ouchi analyzed the organization cultures of three groups of firms, which he characterized as (1) typical U.S. firms, (2) typical Japanese firms, and (3) Type Z U.S. firms.[34]

Through his analysis, Ouchi developed a list of seven points on which these three types of firms can be compared. He argued that the cultures of typical Japanese firms and Type Z U.S. firms are very different from those of typical U.S. firms, and that these differences explain the success of many Japanese firms and Type Z U.S. firms as well as the difficulties faced by typical U.S. firms. The seven points of comparison developed by Ouchi are presented in Table 18.3.

Commitment to Employees According to Ouchi, typical Japanese and Type Z U.S. firms share the cultural value of trying to keep employees. Thus, both types of firms lay off employees only as a last resort. In Japan, the value of "keeping employees on" often takes the form of lifetime employment, although some Japanese companies, reacting to the economic troubles of the past few years, are challenging this value. A person who begins working at some Japanese firms usually has a virtual guarantee that he or she will never be fired. In Type Z U.S. companies, this cultural value is manifested in a commitment to what Ouchi called "long-term employment." Under the Japanese system of

Table 18.3 The Ouchi Framework

CULTURAL VALUE	EXPRESSION IN JAPANESE COMPANIES	EXPRESSION IN TYPE Z U.S. COMPANIES	EXPRESSION IN TYPICAL U.S. COMPANIES
COMMITMENT TO EMPLOYEES	Lifetime employment	Long-term employment	Short-term employment
EVALUATION	Slow and qualitative	Slow and qualitative	Fast and quantitative
CAREERS	Very broad	Moderately broad	Narrow
CONTROL	Implicit and informal	Implicit and informal	Explicit and formal
DECISION MAKING	Group and consensus	Group and consensus	Individual
RESPONSIBILITY	Group	Individual	Individual
CONCERN FOR PEOPLE	Holistic	Holistic	Narrow

lifetime employment, employees usually cannot be fired. Under the U.S. system, workers and managers can be fired, but only if they are not performing acceptably.

Ouchi suggested that typical U.S. firms do not have the same cultural commitment to employees that Japanese firms and Type Z U.S. firms do. In reality, U.S. workers and managers often spend their entire careers in a relatively small number of companies. Still, there is a cultural expectation that if there is a serious downturn in a firm's fortunes, a change of ownership, or a merger, workers and managers will be let go. For example, when Wells Fargo Bank bought First Interstate Bank in Arizona, it expected to lay off about 400 employees in Arizona and 5,000 in the corporation as a whole. However, eight months after the purchase, Wells Fargo had eliminated over 1,000 employees in Arizona alone and had laid off a total of 10,800 workers. Wells Fargo already had a reputation as a vicious job cutter following takeovers and seemed to be living up to it.[35]

Evaluation Ouchi observed that in Japanese and Type Z U.S. companies, appropriate evaluation of workers and managers is thought to take a very long time—up to ten years—and requires the use of qualitative as well as quantitative information about performance. For this reason, promotion in these firms is relatively slow, and promotion decisions are made only after interviews with many people who have had contact with the person being evaluated. In typical U.S. firms, on the other hand, the cultural value suggests that evaluation can and should be done rapidly and should emphasize quantitative measures of performance. This value tends to encourage short-term thinking among workers and managers.

Careers Ouchi next observed that the careers most valued in Japanese and Type Z U.S. firms span multiple functions. In Japan, this value has led to very broad career paths, which may lead to employees' gaining experience in six or seven distinct business functions. The career paths in Type Z U.S. firms are somewhat narrower.

However, the career path valued in typical U.S. firms is considerably narrower. Ouchi's research indicated that most U.S. managers perform only one or two different business functions in their entire careers. This narrow career path reflects, according to Ouchi, the value placed on specialization that is part of so many U.S. firms.

Control All organizations must exert some level of control to achieve coordinated action. Thus, it is not surprising that firms in the United States and Japan have developed cultural values related to organizational control and how to manage it. Most Japanese and Type Z U.S. firms assume that control is exercised through informal, implicit mechanisms. One of the most powerful of these mechanisms is the organization's culture. In contrast, typical U.S. firms expect guidance to come through explicit directions in the form of job descriptions, delineation of authority, and various rules and procedures, rather than from informal and implicit cultural values.

From a functional perspective, organization culture could be viewed as primarily a means of social control based on shared norms and values.[36] Control comes from knowing that someone who matters is paying close attention to what we do and will tell us if our actions are appropriate or not. In organizations, control can come from formal sources, such as the organization structure or a supervisor, or from social sources, such as the organization's culture. In Ouchi's view, control is based in formal organizational mechanisms in typical U.S. firms, whereas control in Japanese and Type Z U.S. firms is more social in nature and derived from the organization culture's shared norms and values.

Decision Making Japanese and Type Z U.S. firms have a strong cultural expectation that decision making occurs in groups and is based on principles of full information sharing and consensus. In most typical U.S. firms, individual decision making is considered appropriate.

Responsibility Closely linked to the issue of group versus individual decision making are ideas about responsibility. Here, however, the parallels between Japanese firms and Type Z U.S. firms break down. Ouchi showed that in Japan, strong cultural norms support collective responsibility; that is, the group as a whole, rather than a single person, is held responsible for decisions made by the group. In both Type Z U.S. firms and typical U.S. firms, individuals expect to take responsibility for decisions.

Linking individual responsibility with individual decision making, as typical U.S. firms do, is logically consistent. Similarly, group decision making and group responsibility, the situation in Japanese firms, seem to go together. But how do Type Z U.S. firms combine the cultural values of group decision making and individual responsibility?

Ouchi suggested that the answer to this question depends on a cultural view we have already discussed: slow, qualitative evaluation. The first time a manager uses a group to make a decision, it is not possible to tell whether the outcomes associated with that decision resulted from the manager's influence or from the quality of the group. However, if a manager works with many groups over time, and if these groups consistently do well for the organization, it is likely that the manager is skilled at getting the most out of the groups. This manager can be held responsible for the outcomes of group decision-making processes. Similarly, managers who consistently fail to work effectively with the groups assigned to them can be held responsible for the lack of results from the group decision-making process.

Concern for People The last cultural value examined by Ouchi deals with a concern for people. Not surprisingly, in Japanese firms and Type Z firms, the cultural value that dominates is a holistic concern for workers and managers. Holistic concern extends beyond concern for a person simply as a worker or manager to concern about that person's home life, hobbies, personal beliefs, hopes, fears, and aspirations. In typical U.S. firms, the concern for people is a narrow one that focuses on the workplace. A culture that emphasizes a strong concern for people, rather than one that emphasizes a work or task orientation, can decrease worker turnover.[37]

AP Photo/Eric Gay

Toyota Motor Manufacturing Texas, Inc. employees cheer during the Tundra Line-off Celebration at the plant in San Antonio, Texas. Toyota Motor Corp.'s latest effort in the U.S. automotive industry is considered its most important, and what a place for it: deep in the heart of Texas, where American pickups have crowded back roads and highways for decades.

Theory Z and Performance Ouchi argued that the cultures of Japanese and Type Z firms help them outperform typical U.S. firms. Toyota imported the management style and culture that succeeded in Japan into its manufacturing facilities in North America. Toyota's success has often been attributed to the ability of Japanese and Type Z firms to systematically invest in their employees and operations over extended periods, resulting in steady and significant improvements in long-term performance.

Table 18.4 The Peters and Waterman Framework

ATTRIBUTES OF AN EXCELLENT FIRM	
1. Bias for action	5. Hands-on management
2. Stay close to the customer	6. Stick to the knitting
3. Autonomy and entrepreneurship	7. Simple form, lean staff
4. Productivity through people	8. Simultaneously loose and tight organization

The Peters and Waterman Approach

Tom Peters and Robert Waterman, in their best seller *In Search of Excellence,* focused even more explicitly than Ouchi on the relationship between organization culture and performance. Peters and Waterman chose a sample of highly successful U.S. firms and sought to describe the management practices that led to their success.[38] Their analysis rapidly turned to the cultural values that led to successful management practices. These "excellent" values are listed in Table 18.4.

Bias for Action According to Peters and Waterman, successful firms have a bias for action. Managers in these firms are expected to make decisions even if not all the facts are in. Peters and Waterman argued that for many important decisions, all the facts will never be in.

Delaying decision making in these situations is the same as never making a decision. Meanwhile, other firms probably will have captured whatever business initiative existed. On average, according to these authors, organizations with cultural values that include a bias for action outperform firms without such values.

Stay Close to the Customer Peters and Waterman believe that firms whose organization cultures value customers over everything else outperform firms without this value. The customer is a source of information about current products, a source of ideas about future products, and the ultimate source of a firm's current and future financial performance. Focusing on the customer, meeting the customer's needs, and pampering the customer when necessary all lead to superior performance.

Autonomy and Entrepreneurship Peters and Waterman maintained that successful firms fight the lack of innovation and the bureaucracy usually associated with large size. They do this by breaking the company into smaller, more manageable pieces and then encouraging independent, innovative activities within smaller business segments. Stories often exist in these organizations about the junior engineer who takes a risk and influences major product decisions, or of the junior manager, dissatisfied with the slow pace of a product's development, who implements a new and highly successful marketing plan.

Productivity Through People Like Ouchi, Peters and Waterman believe successful firms recognize that their most important assets are their people—both workers and managers—and that the organization's purpose is to let its people flourish. It is a basic value of the organization culture—a belief that treating people with respect and dignity is not only appropriate but essential to success.

Hands-On Management Peters and Waterman noted that the firms they studied insisted that senior managers stay in touch with the firms' essential business. It is an expectation, reflecting a deeply embedded cultural norm, that managers should manage not from behind the closed doors of their offices but by "wandering around" the plant, the design facility, the research and development department, and so on.

Stick to the Knitting Another cultural value characteristic of excellent firms is their reluctance to engage in business outside their areas of expertise. These firms reject the concept of diversification, the practice of buying and operating businesses in unrelated industries. This notion is currently referred to as relying on the company's "core competencies," or what the company does best. While there are certainly many good examples, one of the best is what happened when Lee Raymond ascended to the CEO position at Exxon Mobil Corporation. He promptly ended all of the company's investments in alternative energy methodologies in favor of sticking with what EXXON knew best—petroleum.[39]

Simple Form, Lean Staff According to Peters and Waterman, successful firms tend to have few administrative layers and relatively small corporate staff groups. In excellently managed companies, importance is measured not only by the number of people who report to a manager but also by the manager's impact on the organization's performance. The cultural values in these firms tell managers that what is important is their staff's performance, not its size.

Simultaneously Loose and Tight Organization The final attribute of organization culture identified by Peters and Waterman appears contradictory. How can firms be simultaneously loosely and tightly organized? The resolution of this apparent paradox is found in the firms' values. These firms are tightly organized because all their members understand and believe in the firms' values. This common cultural bond is strong glue that holds the firms together. At the same time, however, the firms are loosely organized because they tend to have less administrative overhead, fewer staff members, and fewer rules and regulations. The result is increased innovation and risk taking and faster response times.

The loose structure is possible only because of the common values held by people in the firm. When employees must make decisions, they can evaluate their options in terms of the organization's underlying values—whether the options are consistent with a bias for action, service to the customer, and so on. By referring to commonly held values, employees can make their own decisions about what actions to take. In this sense, the tight structure of common cultural values makes possible the loose structure of fewer administrative controls.

EMERGING ISSUES IN ORGANIZATION CULTURE

As the implementation of organization culture continues, it inevitably changes and develops new perspectives. Many new ideas about productive environments build on earlier views such as those of Ouchi, Peters and Waterman, and others. Typical of these approaches are the total quality management movement, worker participation, procedural justice, and team-based management, which were discussed in earlier chapters. Three other movements are briefly discussed in this section: innovation, empowerment, and appropriate cultures.

Innovation is the process of creating and doing new things that are introduced into the marketplace as products, processes, or services.

Innovation

Innovation is the process of creating and doing new things that are introduced into the marketplace as products, processes, or services. Innovation involves every aspect of the organization, from research through development, manufacturing, and marketing. One of the organization's biggest challenges is to bring innovative technology to the needs of the marketplace in the most cost-effective manner possible.[40] Note that innovation does not just involve the technology to create new products: true organizational innovation is pervasive throughout the organization. According to *Fortune* magazine, the most admired organizations are those that are the most innovative.[41] Those companies are innovative in every way—staffing, strategy, research, and business processes. 3M has long been one of those companies known for its creativity and innovation. However, a few years ago it was sued for age discrimination by an employee group (ages 54–64) claiming that various organizational processes, such as performance evaluations, selection for training programs, and promotion opportunities, placed more emphasis on innovation and creativity by younger employees. They claimed that older workers can be just as creative and innovative as younger employees.[42]

Many risks are associated with being an innovative company. The most basic is the risk that decisions about new technology or innovation will backfire. As research proceeds, and engineers and scientists continue to develop new ideas or solutions to problems, there is always the possibility that innovations will fail to perform as expected. For this reason, organizations commit considerable resources to testing innovations.[43] A second risk is the possibility that a competitor will make decisions enabling it to get an innovation to the market first. The marketplace has become a breeding ground for continuous innovation.

In all fairness some authors have suggested that the term, "innovation," has become a cliché from overuse by companies and consultants. As companies create positions, such as chief innovation officer, and consultants sell their services for hundreds of thousands of dollars, some claim that creating new products barely different from old ones or increasing production by small percentages may not deserve to be called innovations. They call for the term to be reserved for major disruptive or radical shifts in products, services, or processes.[44]

While these criticisms may have some merit, organizations still need to be wary of simply maintaining the status quo and risk getting surpassed by more innovative practices by their competition or new technological breakthroughs. For evidence, one needs only to examine the demise of the Blackberry by Research in Motion (RIM), which dominated the market for cell phone and e-mail devices from 2003 to 2009. Apple's iPhone and the Google Android devices, initially introduced in 2007 and 2008, along with thousands of applications (apps), have pushed RIM to the brink of collapse.[45] Another area that's experiencing the effects of technological breakthrough is the home entertainment industry. As you can see from the *Technology* box entitled "TV Gets Personal" on page 509, mass-market TV may be on the way out as home entertainment providers increasingly target-market personal preferences and cater to growing consumer demand for customized products.

Radical innovation (sometimes called disruptive innovation) is a major breakthrough that changes or creates whole industries.

Systems innovation creates a new functionality by assembling parts in new ways.

Incremental innovation continues the technical improvement and extends the applications of radical and systems innovations.

Types of Innovation Innovation can be radical, systems, or incremental. A **radical innovation** (sometimes called disruptive innovation) is a major breakthrough that changes or creates whole industries. Examples include xerography (which was invented by Chester Carlson in 1935 and became the hallmark of Xerox Corporation), steam engines, and the internal combustion engine (which paved the way for today's automobile industry). **Systems innovation** creates a new functionality by assembling parts in new ways. For example, the gasoline engine began as a radical innovation and became a systems innovation when it was combined with bicycle and carriage technology to create automobiles. **Incremental innovation** continues the technical improvement and extends the applications of radical and systems innovations. There are many more

TECHNOLOGY TV Gets Personal

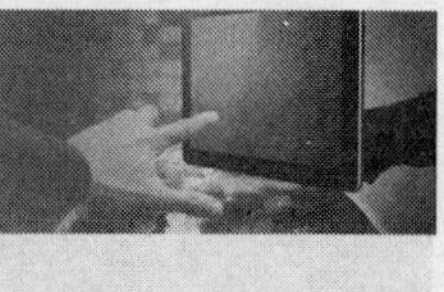
©watcharakun/Shutterstock

Personalized phone service? Tailor-made blue jeans? Coffee concoctions brewed to your personal taste? Just a few years ago, products like these would have been props in a science fiction movie. Today, however, the ability to personalize just about every feature of every product and service on the market has become so important to consumers that virtually every industry worth its customer orientation has been shaken to its mass-market core.

"We're creating a new way to reach audiences in an era where the traditional TV time slot doesn't exist anymore."

—YOUTUBE COFOUNDER CHAD HURLEY

Consider, for example, the distribution of programming for home viewing—which, today, means via TV or computer. About 20 years ago, when the advent of digital cable made 500 TV channels a reality, specialized broadcasters began developing content-specific programming for targeted audiences. If your passion was auto racing, for example, you could subscribe to the Speed Channel; for military buffs, there was the Military Channel, and for animal lovers, there was Animal Planet. It was not long before cable and satellite systems were filled up, but newer technology was soon available to handle the overflow of special-interest programming that *Wired* magazine dubbed "the long tail" of the home-viewing market. The key, of course, was the Internet. Along with the ease of digital video production, the Internet provided an impetus for thousands of producers wanting to reach small but dedicated audiences with special-interest programming. The *New York Times* coined the term "slivercasting" to characterize the new sector of the media industry, and today there is slivercasting for vegans (VegTV), sailboat enthusiasts (Sail.tv), lovers of classic TV comedy (Yuks TV), the betrothed (The Knot TV), and even surgery buffs (OR Live).

Online revenue streams are also beginning to flow more smoothly. TV advertising grew by 9.7 percent in 2010, but that followed an 11.3 percent drop-off in 2009, and it increased by only 2.5 percent in 2011. Meanwhile, online ad revenues grew by 14.5 percent in 2010 and by nearly 25 percent in 2011.

In 2010, Google, the world's leading online search company, entered yet another sector of the emerging industry—delivering programming through Internet-connected TV sets. Partnering with such content providers as HBO, CNBC, Turner Broadcasting, Twitter, and Netflix, Google TV is only the latest (albeit the most prominent) company to announce the proposed marriage of the two media. "One of our goals," says Google TV product manager Ambarish Kenghe, "... is to finally open up the living room and enable new innovation from content creators, programmers, [and] developers." And, of course, advertisers: Analysts predict that there will be 43 million Internet-connected TV sets in the United States by 2015 and that online advertising revenue will surpass TV ad revenue in the following year.

Perhaps the most popular medium for home viewing, however, is the social website that allows users to distribute videos that they have made themselves. One of the most successful of these sites is YouTube, which was founded in 2005 by three 20-something friends who wanted to share party videos. After just one year of operation, YouTube was screening 30 million videos per day. In October 2006, when that number reached 100 million, its founders sold the company to Google for $1.65 billion. Today it is estimated that users post about 830,000 videos every day. Those videos attract more than 2 billion views a day, with the average user looking in about 900 seconds per day. Boasts YouTube cofounder Chad Hurley, "We're creating a new way to reach audiences in an era where the traditional TV time slot doesn't exist anymore."

References: Heather Green, "Way Beyond Home Videos," *Bloomberg Businessweek*, April 10, 2006, www.businessweek.com on August 20, 2010; Greg Sterling, "IAB: 2010 Online Advertising Worth $26 Billion, Search 46 Percent," *Search Engine Land*, April 13, 2011, http://searchengineland.com on August 20, 2012; Stephanie Reese, "Quick Stat: Television Ad Spending Expected to Reach $60.5 Billion in 2011," *eMarketer*, May 16, 2011, www.emarketer.com on August 20, 2012; Dawn C. Chmielewski, "Online Advertising to Reach $31 Billion in 2011," *Los Angeles Times*, June 8, 2011, http://latimesblogs.latimes.com on August 20, 2012; Robert Hof, "Online Ad Spend to Overtake TV by 2016," *Forbes*, August 26, 2011, www.forbes.com on August 20, 2012; Saul Hansell,"As Internet TV Aims at Niche Audiences, the Slivercast Is Born," *New York Times*, March 12, 2006, www.nytimes.com on August 20, 2012; Claire Miller and Brian Stelter, "Google TV Announces Its Programming Partners, but the Top Networks Are Absent," *New York Times*, October 4, 2010, www.nytimes.com on August 20, 2012.

incremental innovations than there are radical and systems innovations. In fact, several incremental innovations are often necessary to make radical and systems innovations work properly. Incremental innovations force organizations to continuously improve their products and keep abreast or ahead of the competition.

New Ventures New ventures based on innovations require entrepreneurship and good management to work. The profile of the entrepreneur typically includes a need for achievement, a desire to assume responsibility, a willingness to take risks, and a focus on concrete results. Entrepreneurship can occur inside or outside large organizations. Outside entrepreneurship requires all of the complex aspects of the innovation process. Inside entrepreneurship occurs within a system that usually discourages chaotic activity.

Large organizations typically do not accept entrepreneurial types of activities. Thus, for a large organization to be innovative and develop new ventures, it must actively encourage entrepreneurial activity within the organization. This form of activity, often called **intrapreneurship**, usually is most effective when it is a part of everyday life in the organization and occurs throughout the organization rather than in the research and development department alone.

Intrapreneurship is entrepreneurial activity that takes place within the context of a large corporation.

Corporate Research The most common means of developing innovation in the traditional organization is through corporate research, or research and development. Corporate research is usually set up to support existing businesses, provide incremental innovations in the organization's businesses, and explore potential new technology bases. It often takes place in a laboratory, either on the site of the main corporate facility or some distance away from normal operations.

Corporate researchers are responsible for keeping the company's products and processes technologically advanced. Product life cycles vary a great deal, depending on how fast products become obsolete and whether substitutes for the product are developed. Obviously, if a product becomes obsolete or some other product can be substituted for it, the profits from its sales will decrease. The job of corporate research is to prevent this from happening by keeping the company's products current.

Jacob Kepler/Bloomberg/Getty Images

If you think of Scotch tape and Post-it notes when you think of 3M Co. products, think again. New products include the 3M Co. PocketProjector MP180 micro projector shown on display during the 2011 International Consumer Electronics Show (CES) in Las Vegas, Nevada, U.S., on Friday, Jan. 7, 2011, and Scotch brand Magic eco-friendly tape.

The corporate culture can be instrumental in fostering an environment in which creativity and innovation occur. For example, 3M is a company known for its innovation. From 1914 to 1966 its scientists developed masking tape, Scotch tape, Scotchguard fabric protector, and Thinsulate material. The company allowed employees to spend up to 15 percent of their paid time on any projects they chose. By 2001, however, it was taking years for new products to come to market, manufacturing was inefficient, and profits were almost nonexistent. A new CEO, Jim McNerney, was brought onboard; his new initiatives included Six Sigma quality training, forced performance rankings, and cost efficiency measures throughout the company. Problems soon arose: the new approach reduced not just costs but innovation as well. The number of new products on the market slowed even more, and by 2005 Mr. McNerney left the company, replaced by George Buckley. Mr. Buckley immediately increased the research and development budget by 20 percent, but his most important task is to restore the innovative culture that is the company's heritage.[46]

Empowerment

One of the most popular buzzwords in management today is "empowerment." Almost every new approach—to quality, meeting the competition, getting more out of employees, productivity enhancement, and corporate turnaround—deals with employee empowerment. As we discussed in Chapter 5, **empowerment** is the process of enabling workers to set their own goals, make decisions, and solve problems within their spheres of responsibility and authority. Fads are often dismissed as meaningless and without substance because they are misused and overused, and the concept of empowerment can likewise be taken too lightly.

Empowerment is the process of enabling workers to set their own work goals, make decisions, and solve problems within their sphere of responsibility and authority.

Empowerment is simple and complex at the same time. It is simple in that it tells managers to quit bossing people around so much and to let them do their jobs. It is complex in that managers and employees typically are not trained to do that. A significant amount of time, training, and practice may be needed to truly empower employees. In Chapter 5 we discussed some techniques for utilizing empowerment and conditions in which empowerment can be effective in organizations.

Empowerment can be much more than a motivational technique, however. In some organizations it is the cornerstone of the organization's culture. W. L. Gore & Associates is built around a lattice framework (rather than a hierarchy) in which there are no bosses who tell others what to do. Ideas are championed by sponsors and leaders, and associates can choose what project teams to work on. People are free to experiment and are empowered to commit themselves to projects rather than being assigned to projects. W. L. Gore is extremely successful with this management model, considering that it was founded on these principles in 1958, has annual sales of $2.1 billion, and has 8,000 employees in 45 plants. Empowerment, as part of a unique management model, is no fad.[47]

Empowerment can be viewed as liberating employees, but sometimes "empowerment" entails little more than delegating a task to an employee and then watching over the employee too closely. Employees may feel that this type of participation is superficial and that they are not really making meaningful decisions. The concept of liberating employees suggests that they should be free to do what they think is best without fear that the boss is standing by to veto or change the work they do.[48]

Appropriate Cultures

Much of the literature on organization culture has focused on describing the concept of organization culture, linking culture to performance, and then creating an organization culture. For example, the Peters and Waterman framework described eight attributes that successful firms all had, the implication being that those same attributes would be desirable in all organizations. But one need only examine a few successful organizations—such as Southwest Airlines, General Electric, and Microsoft, all with vastly different cultures—to legitimately question the appropriateness of one culture for all organizations. Rob Goffee and Gareth Jones have questioned the idea that there is one best organization culture and instead propose that there are only "appropriate cultures."[49] After all, flying airplanes and moving people from one place to another at the lowest possible cost is vastly different from writing new software for personal computers. Goffee and Jones suggest that the nature of the value chain and the dynamism of the environment are two factors that may determine what type of culture is appropriate for a particular organization. The determining factors may prove to be quite elusive, however, as nobody has been able to successfully copy Southwest Airlines, although many have tried. Much more research is needed on the prospect of a contingency theory of organization culture.

Whole Foods Markets has created a culture that is right for it and quite different from the rest of the commercial food retail industry. Starting with a small natural food store in Austin, Texas, founder and CEO John Mackey studied Japanese management techniques and created a culture that is democratic, participative, egalitarian, innovative, team-based, and transparent. It is democratic in that employees created their "Declaration of Interdependence" and vote on whether or not new employees get to join the team. It is participative in that decisions regarding store design, selection of products that will sell in the local store, and price setting are made by the people who have to implement the decisions. It is egalitarian in that average pay is respectable, no executive can make more than 19 times the average hourly wage, and employees get stock options, 93 percent of which go to nonexecutive personnel. It is innovative in that everyone is encouraged to experiment without asking permission. Store managers can spend up to $100,000 a year to try new ideas. It is team-based because each department is a team with the right to run their area, vote on new members to the team, and be responsible for team profit, to which team pay is tied. It is transparent because the company releases almost all financial data to everyone in the company and everyone knows how their team performed compared to all other teams and how much everyone in the company gets paid.[50] This culture of Whole Foods works for it and is counter to the rest of the industry. In other words, it is appropriate and fits Whole Foods.

MANAGING ORGANIZATION CULTURE

The work of Ouchi, Peters and Waterman, and many others demonstrates two important facts. First, organization cultures differ among firms; second, these different organization cultures can affect a firm's performance. Based on these observations, managers have become more concerned about how to best manage the cultures of their organizations. The three elements of managing organization culture are (1) taking advantage of the existing culture, (2) teaching the organization culture, and (3) changing the organization culture.

Taking Advantage of the Existing Culture

Most managers are not in a position to create an organization culture; rather, they work in organizations that already have cultural values. For these managers, the central issue in managing culture is how best to use the existing cultural system. It may be easier and faster to alter employee behaviors within the culture in place than it is to change the history, traditions, and values that already exist.[51]

To take advantage of an existing cultural system, managers must first be fully aware of the culture's values and what behaviors or actions those values support. Becoming fully aware of an organization's values usually is not easy, however. It involves more than reading a pamphlet about what the company believes in. Managers must develop a deep understanding of how organizational values operate in the firm—an understanding that usually comes only through experience.

This understanding, once achieved, can be used to evaluate the performances of others in the firm. Articulating organizational values can be useful in managing others' behaviors. For example, suppose a subordinate in a firm with a strong cultural value of "sticking to its knitting" develops a business strategy that involves moving into a new industry. Rather than attempting to argue that this business strategy is economically flawed or conceptually weak, the manager who understands the corporate culture can point to the company's organizational value: "In this firm, we believe in sticking to our knitting."

Senior managers who understand their organization's culture can communicate that understanding to lower-level individuals. Over time, as these lower-level managers begin to understand and accept the firm's culture, they will require less direct supervision. Their understanding of corporate values will guide their decision making.

Teaching the Organization Culture: Socialization

Socialization is the process through which individuals become social beings.

Organizational socialization is the process through which employees learn about the firm's culture and pass their knowledge and understanding on to others.

Socialization is the process through which individuals become social beings.[52] As studied by psychologists, it is the process through which children learn to become adults in a society—how they learn what is acceptable and polite behavior and what is not, how they learn to communicate, how they learn to interact with others, and so on. In complex societies, the socialization process takes many years.

Organizational socialization is the process through which employees learn about their organization's culture and pass their knowledge and understanding on to others. Employees are socialized into organizations, just as people are socialized into societies; that is, they come to know over time what is acceptable in the organization and what is not, how to communicate their feelings, and how to interact with others. They learn both through observation and through efforts by managers to communicate this information to them. Research into the process of socialization indicates that for many employees, socialization programs do not necessarily change their values, but instead they make employees more aware of the differences between personal and organization values and help them develop ways to cope with the differences.[53]

A variety of organizational mechanisms can affect the socialization of workers in organizations. Probably the most important are the examples that new employees see in the behavior of experienced people. Through observing examples, new employees develop a repertoire of stories they can use to guide their actions. When a decision needs to be made, new employees can ask, "What would my boss do in this situation?" This is not to suggest that formal training, corporate pamphlets, and corporate statements about organization culture are unimportant in the socialization process. However, these factors tend to support the socialization process based on people's close observations of the actions of others.

auremar/Shutterstock

Employees working together provide excellent opportunities to share the culture with new employees or learn the culture from veterans. Observation of others' work habits often says more about what is expected in organizations than an employee handbook or hours of classroom training.

In some organizations, the culture described in pamphlets and presented in formal training sessions conflicts with the values of the organization as they are expressed in the actions of its people. For example, a firm may say that employees are its most important asset but treat employees badly. In this setting, new employees quickly learn that the rhetoric of the pamphlets and formal training sessions has little to do with the real organization culture. Employees who are socialized into this system usually come to accept the actual cultural values rather than those formally espoused.

Changing the Organization Culture

Much of our discussion to this point has assumed that an organization's culture enhances its performance. When this is the case, learning what an organization's cultural values are and using those values to help socialize new workers and managers is very important, for such actions help the organization succeed. However, as Ouchi's and Peters and Waterman's research indicates, not all firms have cultural values that are consistent with high performance. Ouchi found that Japanese firms and Type Z U.S. firms have performance-enhancing values. Peters and Waterman identified performance-enhancing values associated with successful companies. By implication, some firms not included in Peters and Waterman's study must have had performance-reducing values. What should a manager who works in a company with performance-reducing values do?

The answer to this question is, of course, that top managers in such firms should try to change their organization's culture. However, this is a difficult thing to do.[54] Organization culture resists change for all the reasons that it is a powerful influence on behavior—it embodies the firm's basic values, it is often taken for granted, and it is typically most effectively communicated through stories or other symbols. When managers attempt to change organization culture, they are attempting to change people's basic assumptions about what is and is not appropriate behavior in the organization. Changing from a traditional organization to a team-based organization (discussed in Chapter 10) is one example of an organization culture change. Another is the attempt by 3M to change from its low-cost and efficiency culture to return to its roots as an innovative culture.[55]

Despite these difficulties, some organizations have changed their cultures from performance-reducing to performance-enhancing.[56] This change process is described in more detail in Chapter 19. The earlier section on creating organization culture describes the importance of linking the strategic values and the cultural values in creating a new organization culture. We briefly discuss other important elements of the cultural change process in the following sections.

Managing Symbols Research suggests that organization culture is understood and communicated through the use of stories and other symbolic media. If this is correct, managers interested in changing cultures should attempt to substitute stories and myths that support new cultural values for those that support old ones. They can do so by creating situations that give rise to new stories.

Suppose an organization traditionally has held the value "employee opinions are not important." When management meets in this company, the ideas and opinions of lower-level people—when discussed at all—are normally rejected as foolish and irrelevant. The stories that support this cultural value tell about subordinate managers who tried to make a constructive point only to have that point lost in personal attacks from superiors.

An upper-level manager interested in creating a new story, one that shows lower-level managers that their ideas are valuable, might ask a subordinate to prepare to lead a discussion in a meeting and follow through by asking the subordinate to take the lead when the topic arises. The subordinate's success in the meeting will become a new story, one that may displace some of the many stories, suggesting that the opinions of lower-level managers do not matter.

The Difficulty of Change Changing a firm's culture is a long and difficult process. A primary problem is that upper-level managers, no matter how dedicated they are to implementing some new cultural value, may sometimes inadvertently revert to old patterns of behavior. This happens, for example, when a manager dedicated to implementing the value that lower-level employees' ideas are important vehemently attacks a subordinate's ideas.

This mistake generates a story that supports old values and beliefs. After such an incident, lower-level managers may believe that although the boss seems to want employee input and ideas, in fact, nothing could be further from the truth. No matter what the boss says or how consistent his/her behavior is in the future, some credibility has been lost, and cultural change has been made more difficult.

The Stability of Change The processes of changing a firm's culture start with a need for change and move through a transition period in which efforts are made to adopt new values and beliefs. In the long run, a firm that successfully changes its culture will find that the new values and beliefs are just as stable and influential as the old ones. Value systems tend to be self-reinforcing. Once they are in place, changing them requires an enormous effort. Thus, if a firm can change its culture from performance-reducing to performance-enhancing, the new values are likely to remain in place for a long time.

SYNOPSIS

Organization culture has become one of the most discussed subjects in the field of organization behavior. It burst on the scene in the 1980s with books by Ouchi, Peters and Waterman, and others. Interest has not been restricted to academics, however. Practicing managers are also interested in organization culture, especially as it relates to performance.

There is little agreement about how to define organization culture. A comparison of several important definitions suggests that most have three things in common: They define culture in terms of the values that individuals in organizations use to prescribe appropriate behaviors; they assume that these values are usually taken for granted; and they emphasize the stories and other symbolic means through which the values are typically communicated.

Current research on organization culture reflects various research traditions. The most important contributions have come from anthropology and sociology. Anthropologists have tended to focus on the cultures of one or two organizations and have used detailed descriptions to help outsiders understand organization culture from the "natives' point of view." Sociologists typically have used survey methods to study the cultures of larger numbers of organizations. Two other influences on current work in organization culture are social psychology, which emphasizes the manipulation of symbols in organizations, and economics. The economics approach sees culture both as a tool used to manage and as a determinant of performance.

Creating organization culture is a four-step process. It starts with formulating strategic and cultural values for the organization. Next, a vision for the organization is created, followed by the institution of implementation strategies. The final step is reinforcing the cultural behaviors of employees.

Although no single framework for describing organization culture has emerged, several have been suggested. The most popular efforts in this area have been Ouchi's comparison of U.S. and Japanese firms and Peters and Waterman's description of successful firms in the United States. Ouchi and Peters and Waterman suggested several important dimensions along which organization values vary, including treatment of employees, definitions of appropriate means for decision making, and assignment of responsibility for the results of decision making.

Emerging issues in the area of organization culture include innovation, employee empowerment, and appropriate cultures. Innovation is the process of creating and doing new things that are introduced into the marketplace as products, processes, or services. The organization culture can either help or hinder innovation. Employee empowerment, in addition to being similar to employee participation as a motivation technique, is now viewed by some as a type of organization culture. Empowerment occurs when employees make decisions, set their own work goals, and solve problems in their own area of responsibility. Finally, experts are beginning to suggest that there are cultures that are appropriate for particular organizations rather than there being any one best type of culture.

Managing the organization culture requires attention to three factors. First, managers can take advantage of cultural values that already exist and use their knowledge to help subordinates understand them. Second, employees need to be properly socialized, or trained, in the cultural values of the organization, either through formal training or by experiencing and observing the actions of higher-level managers. Third, managers can change the culture of the organization through managing the symbols, addressing the extreme difficulties of such a change, and relying on the durability of the new organization culture once the change has been implemented.

DISCUSSION QUESTIONS

1. A sociologist or anthropologist might suggest that the culture in U.S. firms simply reflects the dominant culture of the society as a whole. Therefore, to change the organization culture of a company, one must first deal with the inherent values and beliefs of the society. How would you respond to this claim?
2. Psychology has been defined as the study of individual behavior. Organizational psychology is the study of individual behavior in organizations. Many of the theories described in the early chapters of this book are based in organizational psychology. Why was this field not identified as a contributor to the study of organization culture along with anthropology, sociology, social psychology, and economics?
3. Describe the culture of an organization with which you are familiar. It might be one in which you currently work, one in which you have worked, or one in which a friend or family member works. What values, beliefs, stories, and symbols are significant to employees of the organization?
4. Discuss the similarities and differences between the organization culture approaches of Ouchi and Peters and Waterman.
5. Describe how organizations use symbols and stories to communicate values and beliefs. Give some examples of how symbols and stories have been used in organizations with which you are familiar.
6. What is the role of leadership (discussed in Chapters 12 and 13) in developing, maintaining, and changing organization culture?
7. Review the characteristics of organization structure described in earlier chapters and compare them with the elements of culture described by Ouchi and Peters and Waterman. Describe the similarities and differences, and explain how some characteristics of one may be related to characteristics of the other.
8. Discuss the role of organization rewards in developing, maintaining, and changing the organization culture.
9. Describe how the culture of an organization can affect innovation.

HOW DO YOU SEE IT?

Dogged Determination

"It's kind of like a video game: You never know what's going to come at you."

—HEIDI GANAHL, FOUNDER AND CEO OF CAMP BOW WOW

We were introduced to Heidi Ganahl,* founder and CEO of Camp Bow Wow, in *Video Case 12*, which profiled her approach to leading her company. In this video, she provides a glimpse into her past, and when it comes to understanding an organization that so thoroughly reflects its founder's personal vision for it, a little biography can be a useful thing. As Ganahl explains, she and her first husband came up with the idea for Camp Bow Wow, an alternative to traditional kennelling for dogs, in the 1990s. Her husband, however, was killed in a plane crash before they could launch the business, and Ganahl tucked the plan away in a drawer while she struggled to regain control of her life. "[I] got a pretty good settlement from the plane crash," she reports, but I "managed to screw that up pretty well and blow it on loans to family and friends and buying things I shouldn't have." A single mother, she took a part-time job as a pharmaceuticals rep, and although the job paid well enough, it did little to reenergize her entrepreneurial ambitions ("I called it the 'golden handcuffs,'" she says elsewhere).

Five years, one ill-considered marriage, and two failed business ventures later, her brother urged her to revisit the Camp Bow Wow plan. As Ganahl recalls, "I thought, 'Well, [I] might as well risk it all'"—meaning the $83,000 left from her $1 million insurance settlement—"'and put it all into starting my dream, and if it doesn't work, it doesn't work.' ... It was a crazy road—a lot of twists and turns," she adds. "... It's kind of like a video game: You never know what's going to come at you." Camp Bow Wow finally launched in 2000 and began franchising in 2003.

As the chapter tells us, an organization's *culture* is often communicated and reinforced by the stories that embody and explain its values, and Ganahl's story is certainly a key part of both Camp Bow Wow's history and its culture. Everyone connected with the company, she says, "knows the gist of how we got here. It really does give them a different way to look at our company and a different perspective on things. And I definitely think it's been a big part of our culture," she adds, because, "ultimately, at the end of the day, [your culture] is what the outside world *perceives* of you." Ganahl wants people to perceive a "very scrappy" company whose chief *value* is the ability to overcome challenges—an organization with a "we-can-get-through-anything," "we-can-conquer-all" attitude. She believes that it is important to keep "the 'folklore' of Camp Bow Wow alive" so that when people "hear the story and ... specifically how we overcame different challenges," they will have "a lot more respect for where we are today."

"As business owners," confirms Sue Ryan, a franchisee in Boulder, Colorado, "we all experience, not the tragedy that [Heidi] did, but a lot of the tough stuff that she did" in getting the franchise off the ground. Ryan also offers a somewhat more practical perspective on the Camp Bow Wow culture: Culture, she says,

> *is an interesting question in a franchise because you have different layers of it. I've got the layer of culture that I'm trying to establish here with myself and my staff to make it a fun place for people to show up and work ... and ... work well as a team.*
>
> *Then we've got the culture among the different franchisees and what that feels like and ... the culture of the franchisees and the corporate offices* together. *So there [are] all these different layers. I think they're all individual and unique, and in a perfect situation, they all complement each other.*

Ganahl agrees. "One of the challenges for franchise companies," she says, "is to get everybody, when you have a couple hundred people that have bought into the brand, on the same page and committed to one vision—one way of getting there." *Vision* is an operative term for Ganahl. "Beginning to franchise," she admits, "wasn't something I originally had in the plan, but it was the perfect fit for me because it allowed me to be the visionary and not handle the day-to-day operations. I love the visionary part. The day-to-day operations, not so much." What is the "visionary part"? For one thing, it means finding ways of extending the company's mission and brand. Take, for example, the Bow Wow Buddies Foundation, which Ganahl created to find foster and lifetime homes for unwanted animals and invest in research into pet diseases. Home Buddies, an in-home pet-care service, was launched in 2009.

Meanwhile, franchising presents a way of taking on reliable partners, not only to handle the day-to-day operations but to complement Ganahl's strategic vision with their own visions for the company on the operational level. However, keeping everyone committed to the vision and the brand, says Ganahl, "is a very tenuous thing"—a process, as she puts it in *Video Case 12*, of balancing the need for brand consistency with the creative urges of 200 franchisees and "trying to temper their wonderful ideas with what's best for the brand." In order to perform that balancing act, she explains, "you have to have a very strong culture, and a very creative culture—one that doesn't allow for people to color outside the lines but yet taps into *their* creativity and their innovation."

CASE QUESTIONS

1. Review Table 18.1. Which definitions of *organization culture* seem to be most applicable to the culture of Camp Bow Wow? Explain your choice(s).
2. In what ways has Ganahl worked to *create an organization culture*? What *values* has she tried to establish? What *vision* has she tried to create? What *strategies* has she tried to initiate? What does she do to reinforce *cultural behaviors*? Which of these efforts seems most important to her?
3. In what ways is the *Peters and Waterman approach* to describing organization culture useful in characterizing the culture of Camp Bow Wow?
4. "I am seen as a pretty laid-back CEO and leader of the company," says Ganahl, "until somebody messes with the brand or ... [my] vision for the company." What role does the Camp Bow Wow brand play in the establishment of its culture? In Ganahl's vision for the company? In her conviction that company has to be innovative?

ADDITIONAL SOURCES

"Heidi Ganahl, Founder & CEO, Camp Bow Wow," *SmartGirls Way*, August 4, 2011, http://smartgirlsway.com on September 3, 2012; Camp Bow Wow, "About Us: Camp Bow Wow," 2000–2011, www.campbowwow.com on September 3, 2012; Sramana Mitra, "The 1M/1M Deal Radar: Camp Bow Wow, Boulder," *Sramana Mitra on Strategy*, February 4, 2011, www.sramanamitra.com on September 3, 2012; Tamara Chapman, "Dog Days," *DU Today*, September 1, 2011, http://blogs.du.edu on September 3, 2012; Noelle Pechar Hale, "Heidi Flammang: To Dog, Camp Bow Wow," *Ladies Who Launch*, February 11, 2008, at www.ladieswholaunch.com on October 15, 2012; Megan L. Reese, "Heidi Ganahl: Founder and CEO—Camp Bow Wow," *Ladies Who Launch*, October 26, 2009, at www.ladieswholaunch.com on October 15, 2012.

*The name *Manogue*, which appears in the subtitles of the video, is due to an error in transcription.

EXPERIENCING ORGANIZATIONAL BEHAVIOR

Culture of the Classroom

Purpose: This exercise will help you appreciate both the fascination and the difficulty of examining culture in organizations.

Format: The class will divide into groups of four to six. Each group will analyze the organization culture of a college class. Students in most classes that use this book will have taken many courses at the college they attend and therefore should have several classes in common.

Procedure: The class is divided into groups of four to six on the basis of classes the students have had in common.

1. Each group should first decide which class it will analyze. Each person in the group must have attended the class.
2. Each group should list the cultural factors to be discussed. Items to be covered should include
   a. Stories about the professor
   b. Stories about the exams
   c. Stories about the grading
   d. Stories about other students
   e. The use of symbols that indicate the students' values
   f. The use of symbols that indicate the instructor's values
   g. Other characteristics of the class as suggested by the frameworks of Ouchi and Peters and Waterman.
3. Students should carefully analyze the stories and symbols to discover their underlying meanings. They should seek stories from other members of the group to ensure that all aspects of the class culture are covered. Students should take notes as these items are discussed.
4. After twenty to thirty minutes of work in groups, the instructor will reconvene the entire class and ask each group to share its analysis with the rest of the class.

Follow-Up Questions

1. What was the most difficult part of this exercise? Did other groups experience the same difficulty?
2. How did your group overcome this difficulty? How did other groups overcome it?
3. Do you believe your group's analysis accurately describes the culture of the class you selected? Could other students who analyzed the culture of the same class come up with a very different result? How could that happen?
4. If the instructor wanted to try to change the culture in the class you analyzed, what steps would you recommend that he or she take?

BUILDING MANAGERIAL SKILLS

Exercise Overview: Typically, managers are promoted or selected to fill jobs in an organization with a given organization culture. As they begin to work, they must recognize the culture and either learn how to work within it or figure out how to change it. If the culture is a performance-reducing one, managers must figure out how to change the culture to a performance-enhancing one. This exercise will give you a chance to develop your own ideas about changing organization culture.

Exercise Background: Assume that you have just been appointed to head the legislative affairs committee of your local student government. As someone with a double major in business management and government, you are eager to take on this assignment and really make a difference. This committee has existed at your university for several years, but it has done little because the members use the committee as a social group and regularly throw great parties. In all the years of its existence, the committee has done nothing to affect the local state legislature in relation to the issues important to university students, such as tuition. You know that the issue of university tuition will come before the state legislature during the current legislative session, and you know that many students could not afford a substantial raise in tuition, so you are determined to use this committee to ensure that any tuition increase is as small as possible. However, you are worried that the party culture of the existing committee may make it difficult for you to use it to work for your issues. You also know that you cannot "fire" any of the volunteers on the committee and can add only two people to the committee.

Exercise Task: Using this information as context, do the following:

1. Design a strategy for utilizing the existing culture of the committee to help you influence the legislature regarding tuition.
2. Assuming that the existing culture is a performance-reducing culture, design a strategy for changing it to a performance-enhancing culture.

SELF-ASSESSMENT EXERCISE

Refining Your Sense of Culture

This exercise is designed to help you assess what you now know about organization culture. The ten statements in the following table reflect certain opinions about the nature of work performed in the context of organization culture. Indicate the extent to which you agree or disagree with each opinion by circling the number in the appropriate column.

Statement of Opinion	Strongly Agree				Strongly Disagree
1. If a person can do well in one organization, he or she can do well in any organization.	1	2	3	4	5
2. Skills and experience are all that really matter; how a job candidate will "fit in" is not an important factor in hiring.	1	2	3	4	5
3. Members of an organization explicitly tell people how to adhere to its culture.	1	2	3	4	5
4. After appropriate study, astute managers can fairly quickly change a corporate culture.	1	2	3	4	5
5. A common culture is important for unifying employees but does not necessarily affect the firm's financial health.	1	2	3	4	5
6. Conscientious workers are not really influenced by an organization's culture.	1	2	3	4	5
7. Strong organization cultures are not necessarily associated with high organization performance.	1	2	3	4	5
8. Members of a subculture share the common values of the subculture but not those of the dominant organization culture.	1	2	3	4	5
9. Job candidates seeking to understand a prospective employer's culture can do so by just asking the people who interview them.	1	2	3	4	5
Your Total Score					

How to score: To get your total score, add up the values of the numbers that you have circled. You can then interpret your score as follows:

Your Score	
40–50	You have excellent instincts about organization cultures and how people respond to them.
30–39	You show average or above-average awareness of the principles of organization culture.
20–29	You have some sense of how cultures affect workers, but you need to improve your knowledge.
0–19	You definitely need to bolster your knowledge before thinking further about assessing or modifying an organization culture.

Reference

Hunsaker, Phillip L, *Management: A Skills Approach*, 2nd Edition, © 2005. Reprinted by permission of Pearson Education, Inc., Upper Saddle River, NJ.

CHAPTER 19

Organization Change and Development

Chapter Outline

- Forces for Change
- Processes for Planned Organization Change
- Organization Development
- Resistance to Change
- Managing Successful Organization Change and Development

Chapter Learning Objectives

After studying this chapter, you should be able to:

1. **Summarize the dominant forces for change in organizations.**
2. **Describe the process of planned organization change.**
3. **Discuss several approaches to organization development.**
4. **Explain resistance to change.**
5. **Identify the keys to managing successful organization change and development.**

Shifting Gears in the Auto Industry

"We've been sticking to our guns, and it's worked well so far."

—Chrysler Group CEO Sergio Marchionne on his strategy for reviving Chrysler

In November 2008, U.S. automaker Chrysler announced that it was cutting 25 percent of its workforce and acknowledged that domestic sales had dropped 35 percent in 12 months. CEO Robert Nardelli also admitted that the company could survive only by means of an alliance with another automaker and an infusion of government cash. In December, Chrysler announced that it would shut down all production through January 2009, that it planned to file for bankruptcy, and that it ultimately expected to cease production permanently. Federal aid to both Chrysler and General Motors was authorized in the same month and had topped $17 billion by March 2009, when the Obama administration gave Chrysler 30 days to finalize a previously announced merger agreement with the Italian carmaker Fiat or face the loss of another $6 billion in government subsidies.

Fiat? Things, it seems, had changed since the days when, for many American car buyers, *Fiat* stood for "*F*ix *i*t *a*gain, *T*ony." As recently as 2005, GM had been only too happy to pay $2 billion to bail out of a joint venture with Fiat, which was wallowing in debt after accumulated losses of $14 billion. A year later, however, Fiat had actually shown a profit—its first since 2000—and its stock price had doubled. By 2009, it was on *Fortune* magazine's list of the "World's Most Admired Companies." It is now Europe's third-largest car company, behind only Volkswagen and Peugeot Citroën and ahead of Renault, Daimler (Mercedes Benz), and BMW, and number nine in the world, producing more cars than Hyundai or Mitsubishi.

The credit for this remarkable turnaround goes to CEO Sergio Marchionne, an accountant and industry outsider who, in 2004, became Fiat's fifth CEO in two years. Billie Blair, a consultant specializing in corporate change management, reports that Marchionne brought an "unconventional approach" to the task of managing a car company in the twenty-first century. In the process, she says—citing Marchionne's own explanation of his success at Fiat—he "revolutionized the [Fiat] culture in a way that will keep the company competitive in the long term." Adds David Johnston, whose Atlanta-based marketing company has worked with

ZUMA Wire Service/Alamy

A new Fiat 500 rolls out of the Van Nuys Fiat dealership. Fiat of Van Nuys was the number 2 Fiat dealer in the US over the Memorial Day weekend. The Italian auto manufacturer is pinning its future in the U.S. on its popular Fiat 500 model. The new Fiat 500 is a modernized version of the original Fiat 500, referred to in Italy as the Cinque Cento, which was one of the most popular Fiats of all time.

Chrysler, Marchionne "has been able to garner respect for Fiat again after its down years and reestablish it as a business leader."

What was Marchionne's "unconventional approach"? It is the same approach that he is trying to bring to Chrysler. Taking over Fiat after nearly 15 years of continuously poor performance, Marchionne was forced to lay off employees, but he focused his job-cutting strategy on longer-term goals: He cut 10 percent of the company's white-collar workforce of about 20,000, stripping away layers of management and making room for a younger generation of managers with experience in brand marketing rather than engineering. Refocusing the company on market-driven imperatives, he cut the design-to-market process from 4 years to 18 months, and, even more importantly, he spurred the introduction of a slew of new products. The Grande Punto, which was launched in mid-2005, was the best-selling subcompact in Western Europe a year later and spearheaded the firm's resurgence. The Fiat Nuova 500, a subcompact with a distinctive retro look (think Volkswagen New Beetle), was first introduced in 2007. Both the car and its marketing launch were designed with heavy customer involvement, and the 500, like the Grande Punto, was an immediate success, with first-year sales outstripping Fiat's original target by 160 percent.

Under the merger agreement reached with Fiat in June 2009, the 500 became one of at least seven Fiat vehicles that Chrysler will begin building and selling in the United States by 2014. Produced in four versions—hatchback, sporty hatchback, convertible, and station wagon—the U.S. adaptation of the 500 went to market in 2011, and Marchionne was convinced that, with a full range of body styles, "the 500 … will be a smash if we do it right." Strategically, Marchionne knew that he had to reposition Chrysler from a maker of clunky gas guzzlers to a marketer of stylish, energy-efficient technology, and the 500, which one marketing association in Japan has declared "the sexiest car in the world," has been designated the flagship of Fiat Chrysler's new North American fleet.

Many analysts, however, remained skeptical about Marchionne's prospects for turning Chrysler around even if the 500 turned out to be "a smash." A big issue, they say, is time: Can "New Chrysler" (officially Chrysler Group LLC) hang on financially until projected new-product revenues start filling the company coffers? Completely new and improved Chryslers will not hit showrooms until 2013, but the new management has managed to roll out some new products, including a revamped Jeep Compass and an all-new Chrysler 300 sedan. "We've attacked the bulk of the product portfolio," says Marchionne. "What we've got now is a commercially viable set of products in the marketplace." He also points out that Chrysler sales are ahead of internal targets and claims that he is more confident now about the prospects for a turnaround than he had been when the merger plans were being drawn up. "We've been sticking to our guns," he says, "and it's worked well so far."

In the interest of balanced reporting, we should point out that things have not continued to work out *quite* as well as Marchionne had hoped—at least not at first. Introduced in 2011, the 500 sold only 26,000 units in North America. Fiat executives blamed their marketing strategy in general and their ad agency in particular: "I don't think we have a car problem," said chief marketing officer Oliver Francois. "… I think we have an awareness problem." The ad agency was fired, and a revamped marketing strategy was in place for 2012. Early returns show promising results: Thanks largely to the high-performance 500 Arboth, which had sold out by June, sales of Fiat models in the United States were up by 432 percent through the month of May.

What Do You Think?

1. Assume that you are an employee at Chrysler. Do you think that your attitudes and behavior will change as Fiat's new organizational goals and processes are put in place? Why or why not?
2. Would you expect any resistance among Chrysler employees to the changes that will come with the Fiat takeover? If so, what kinds of resistance? What can Fiat do to meet resistance most effectively?

References: Dale Buss, "Fiat CEO Marchionne Has Led Unlikely Turnaround," *Edmunds Auto Observer*, January 21, 2009, www.autoobserver.com on February 10, 2011; Leslie Wayne, "Sergio Marchionne," *New York Times*, May 1, 2009, http://topics.nytimes.com on February 10, 2011; "Fiat Plays Double or Quits with Chrysler," *The Economist*, November 25, 2010, www.economist.com on August 22, 2012; Deepa Seetharaman, "Fiat Raises Chrysler Stake, Readies for IPO," Reuters, January 10, 2011, www.reuters.com on August 22, 2012; Steven J. Ewing, "Fiat Sales in U.S. Not Meeting Expectations amidst Marketing Meltdown," *Autoblog*, September 27, 2011, www.autoblog.com on August 22, 2012; Tommaso Ebhardt and Craig Trudell, "Fiat Tries Again in the U.S.," *Bloomberg Businessweek*, March 8, 2012, www.businessweek.com on August 22, 2012; "Fiat Arboth Sells Out in US," *Daily News* (New York), June 6, 2012, http://articles.nydailynews.com on August 22, 2012.

The auto industry is typical of the predicament in which many organizations find themselves. They have a good business model that works and makes them a lot of money, possibly for many years. Then the environment changes, and the former business model no longer works. Companies that change appropriately can continue as viable businesses. Those that do not make the right changes cease to exist by going out of business or by being gobbled up by a larger organization. This chapter is about how organizations need to face the prospect of change and develop processes to ensure their viability in a complex, ever-changing global environment. The chapter begins with a discussion of some of the forces that create pressures for change followed by a detailed explanation of the complex change process. Then we describe organization development and sources of resistance to change, finishing with a summary view of how to manage change in organizations.

FORCES FOR CHANGE

An organization is subject to pressures for change from far more sources than can be discussed here. Moreover, it is difficult to predict what types of pressures for change will be most significant in the next decade because the complexity of events and the rapidity of change are increasing. However, it is possible—and important—to discuss the broad categories of pressures that probably will have major effects on organizations. The four areas in which the pressures for change appear most powerful involve people, technology, information processing and communication, and competition. Table 19.1 gives examples of each of these categories.

People

Approximately 56 million people were born in the United States between 1945 and 1960. These baby boomers differed significantly from previous generations with respect to education, expectations, and value systems.[1] As this group has aged, the median age of

Table 19.1 Pressures for Organization Change

CATEGORY	EXAMPLES	TYPE OF PRESSURE FOR CHANGE
People	Generation X, Y, Millennials Global labor supplies Senior citizens Workforce diversity	Demands for different training, benefits, workplace arrangements, and compensation systems
Technology	Manufacturing in space Internet Global design teams	More education and training for workers at all levels, more new products, products move faster to market
Information Processing and Communication	Computer, satellite communications Global Sourcing Videoconferencing Social networking	Faster reaction times, immediate responses to questions, new products, different office arrangements, telecommuting, marketing, advertising, recruiting on social networking sites
Competition	Global markets International trade agreements Emerging nations	Global competition, more competing products with more features and options, lower costs, higher quality

the U.S. population has gradually increased, passing 32 for the first time in 1988[2] and further increasing to 37.3 in 2011.[3] The special characteristics of baby boomers show up in distinct purchasing patterns that affect product and service innovation, technological change, and marketing and promotional activities.[4] Employment practices, compensation systems, promotion and managerial succession systems, and the entire concept of human resource management are also affected.

Other population-related pressures for change involve the generations that sandwich the baby boomers: the increasing numbers of senior citizens and those born after 1960. The parents of the baby boomers are living longer, healthier lives than previous generations, and today they expect to live the "good life" that they missed when they were raising their children. The impact of the large number of senior citizens is already evident in part-time employment practices, in the marketing of everything from hamburgers to packaged tours of Asia, and in service areas such as health care, recreation, and financial services. The post-1960 generation of workers who entered the job market in the 1980s—often called Generation X—was different from the baby-boom generation. Sociologists and psychologists have identified a new group, often called Millennials, born from roughly between 1980 and 2000 (experts differ on start and end dates from as early as 1977 to as late as 2002), who seem to be experiencing a distinct and separate life stage in between adolescence and adulthood in which young people may jump from job to job and relationship to relationship, often living at home with few responsibilities and experimenting with life. Millennials are putting off marriage, childbearing, home purchases, and most adult responsibilities.[5] However, they seem to be much more group oriented, celebrate diversity, are optimistic, and assimilate technology very fast.[6] On the job, Millennials seem to prefer positive reinforcement, like clarity in job assignments, want more flexibility in how to do their jobs, and want to be treated as different individuals rather than everyone's being treated the same.[7] These changes in demographics extend to the composition of the workforce, family lifestyles, and purchasing patterns worldwide.

The increasing diversity of the workforce in coming years will mean significant changes for organizations. This increasing diversity was discussed in some detail in Chapter 2. In addition, employees are facing a different work environment in the twenty-first century. The most descriptive word for this new work environment is "change." Employees must be prepared for constant change. Change is occurring in organizations' cultures, structures, work relationships, and customer relationships, as well as in the actual jobs that people do. People will have to be completely adaptable to new situations while maintaining productivity under the existing system.[8]

Technology

Not only is technology changing, but the rate of technological change is also increasing. In 1970, for example, all engineering students owned slide rules and used them in almost every class. By 1976, slide rules had given way to portable electronic calculators. In the mid-1980s, some universities began issuing personal computers to entering students or assumed that those students already owned them. In 1993, the Scholastic Aptitude Test (SAT), which many college-bound students take to get into college, allowed calculators to be used during the test. Today students cannot make it through the university without owning or at least having ready access to a personal computer in the form of a laptop, notebook, or iPad. Entire campuses at most universities are wired for direct computer access for e-mail and class assignments and for connection to the Internet. Many schools, from kindergarten to graduate schools, are now BYOT—"bring your own technology"—and utilize online educational tools throughout the curriculum.[9] With 3G and 4G technology, people have Internet access from just about anywhere. Technological development is increasing so rapidly in almost every field that it is quite difficult to predict which products will dominate ten years from now. DuPont is an example of a company that is making major changes due to new technological developments. Although its business had been based on petrochemicals since the end of the nineteenth century, DuPont changed its basic business strategy as new technology developed in the life sciences. It reorganized its eighty-one business units into only three and invested heavily in agrichemicals and the life sciences. Realizing that a biotechnology-based business changes much more rapidly than a petrochemical-based business, DuPont's former chairman from 1998 to 2008, Chad Holliday, had to make cultural changes in addition to the structural ones to make the strategy work.[10]

Interestingly, organization change is self-perpetuating. With the advances in information technology, organizations generate more information, and it circulates faster. Consequently, employees can respond more quickly to problems, so the organization can respond more quickly to demands from other organizations, customers, and competitors. Toyota, long known as a leader in developing and using new technologies in its plants, has introduced new advanced robots, "kokino robotto," in its efforts improve efficiency in its plants and reduce its costs to the level of China's.[11]

New technology will affect organizations in ways we cannot yet predict. Gesture technology may eliminate all controls in your home, from your AV system remote to your thermostat, and replace them with your own gestures with your hands and fingers. HP's TouchSmart technology allows people to touch things without actually touching them, and could drive innovations in medicine and education in a decade. Sensawaft technology will allow people to control devices such as smart phones and ATMs using exhaled breath—which could dramatically increase mobility and control for people with limited mobility.[12]

Several companies are developing systems to manufacture chemicals and exotic electronic components in space. The Internet, the World Wide Web, and cloud computing are changing the way companies and individuals communicate, market, buy, and distribute faster than organizations can respond. Thus, as organizations react more quickly to change, change occurs more rapidly, which in turn necessitates more rapid responses.

Information Processing and Communication

Advances in information processing and communication have paralleled each other. A new generation of computers, which will mark another major increase in processing power, is being designed. Satellite systems for data transmission are already in use. Today people carry a device in their pocket that serves as their portable computer, e-reader, pocket-size television, camera, video recorder, music player, and personal communication device (telephone), all in one device. And they work all over the world.

Social networking may be the most radical and fastest-growing aspect of the advances in information processing and communication. Through such sites as Facebook, Twitter, LinkedIn, Ning, Yammer, Bebo, Viadeo, Skype, FaceTime, and many others, people are networking with others exploring common interests. People are spending hours reading about others and updating their own sites. Business uses of this phenomenon include advertising, marketing, market research and test marketing, recruiting, and more. And everyone looking for a job starts with Monster.com, Jobing.com, and similar sites.[13]

Employees do not need offices because they work with computers and communicate through new data transmission devices. Increasingly, people are working from home instead of going to the office every day. In 2011 more than 22 million corporate workers

TECHNOLOGY You, Too, Can Afford a Place in the Sun

Darin Budwig, a registered nurse in Glendale, California, wanted to do the green thing by going solar. Price, however, was a problem: "I wanted to do the right thing for the environment," says Budwig, "but I really had to ask whether it was worth taking on $30,000 in debt." According to Lyndon Rive, CEO of SolarCity, a provider of solar-energy systems located in Foster City, California, the average cost is actually closer to $20,000, but he understands Budwig's reservations in any case. "Even those who really want to make an environmental change," admits Rive, "can't part with $20,000.... The solution is just too costly for them."

> ***"Even those who really want to make an environmental change can't part with $20,000."***
>
> —SOLARCITY CEO LYNDON RIVE

That is why Rive revamped his business model to make solar panels affordable for a much broader range of environmentally conscious consumers. He realized that he could put solar panels on roofs in much the same way that automakers put more expensive vehicles in their garages: by leasing them rather than selling them outright. So instead of borrowing $20,000, Darin Budwig only had to put $1,000 down and agree to lease a SolarCity system for 15 years. At a cost of $73 a month, Budwig figured to save about $95 a month and recoup his $1,000 in less than a year. Too good to be true? "We hear that a lot," says Rive. "But we do save you money, and it doesn't cost you a cent to go solar." With leasing, he adds, "we can essentially make it so that everybody can now afford clean power."

At the same time, however, Rive understands that price is not the only consideration for potential customers like Darin Budwig. "Widespread adoption," he admits, "will come if you can take away the complexity and hassle of installing solar." SolarCity thus made things easier for Budwig by lining up building permits, financing, and tax breaks. The company also streamlined costs by using innovative computer automation to custom-design Budwig's installation, which was based on satellite images of his rooftop. SolarCity even compiled utility-rate data to estimate Budwig's return on his solar investment.

In 2010 the company added another automated service to its innovative product line. With the acquisition of Building Solutions, a firm specializing in software-controlled home energy audits, SolarCity entered the market for home-efficiency upgrades. Company auditors now come into a house armed with duct blowers, infrared cameras, and combustion analyzers to check for leaks and test heaters. The data are then analyzed to determine what can be done at what cost and to calculate the homeowner's best return on his or her upgrade investment. COO Peter Rive (Lyndon's older brother) is especially optimistic about the company's ability to combine panel-installation services with such services as energy audits and building-envelope sealing (sealing leaks in walls, doors, and windows). "As of right now," he points out, "there aren't residential energy-efficiency providers with any serious scale. We're going to be able to bring serious economies of scale" to bear on the costs to both the provider and the customer.

Like Darin Budwig, Google engineer Michael Flaster leased a SolarCity system for his home in Menlo Park, California. He saves $100 a month on his energy bill and expects to save more than $16,000 over the 15 years of his lease. His employers at Google, a longtime supporter of clean-energy innovations, were impressed and, in June 2011, announced a $280 million fund to help SolarCity finance installations across the country.

References: Pete Engardio and Adam Aston, "The Next Energy Innovators," *Bloomberg Businessweek*, July 16, 2009, www.businessweek.com on August 22, 2012; "Solar Power for Less Than Your Cable Bill," *Renewable Energy Information*, April 24, 2008, http://renewenergy.wordpress.com on August 22, 2012; Julie Schmidt, "SolarCity Aims to Make Solar Power More Affordable," *USA Today*, November 10, 2009, www.usatoday.com on August 22, 2012; Eric Wesoff, "SolarCity Adds Energy Efficiency to Solar Finance, Design and Monitoring," *Greentech Media*, October 14, 2010, www.solarcity.com on August 22, 2012; David A. Hill, "Solar City Takes Aim at Home Energy Audit Market," *Colorado Energy News*, May 14, 2010, http://coloradoenergynews.com on June 14, 2011; Rick Needham, "Helping Homeowners Harness the Sun," *The Official Google Blog*, June 14, 2011, http://googleblog.blogspot.com on August 22, 2012.

ZUMA Wire Service/Alamy

Many companies are now creating shared workspaces for telecommuters to use on days they go into the office. Although such spaces appear relatively Spartan and may lack the personalized feel of normal offices or cubicles, telecommuters usually get accustomed to it pretty quickly. Some telecommuters bring in a few personal items to personalize the shared space for the day. Either way, companies are reporting reductions in costs of renting and maintaining office space and employees like the freedom and responsibility to work from anywhere.

were working from home at least one day a month, and that number has been increasing by more than 20 percent a year since 2007.[14] Depending on the company and the type of work, some employees actually go into the office only a few days a month. Taking advantage of this trend, some companies are reconfiguring traditional space by minimizing offices dedicated to one individual and creating communal spaces, unassigned cubicles, and shared spaces. In addition to saving on office space costs, these types of shared spaces seem to be creating new ways for employees to collaborate and get work done. American Express estimates that 20 percent of their five-thousand-person workforce are in the office at their headquarters in New York more than a few days a week. GlaxoSmithKline estimates it is saving almost $10 million a year in real estate costs by using unassigned seating that is made possible by having more and more employees who work somewhere other than the traditional office.[15]

Flexible work stations, both inside and outside of offices, are more electronic than paper and pencil. For years, the capability has existed to generate, manipulate, store, and transmit more data than managers could use, but the benefits were not fully realized. Now the time has come to utilize all of that information-processing potential, and companies are making the most of it. Typically, companies received orders by mail in the 1970s, by toll-free telephone numbers in the 1980s, by fax machine in the late 1980s and early 1990s, and by electronic data exchange in the mid-1990s. Orders used to take a week; now they are placed instantaneously, and companies can and must be able to respond immediately, all because of changes in information processing and communication.[16] Zappos.com (discussed in more detail in Chapter 18) can ship a pair of shoes in as little as eight minutes from receiving an order.[17] Suppliers and end users in some industries now have the parts systems integrated so closely that new parts shipments sometimes are not even ordered—they just show up at the receiving dock when they are needed.

Competition

Although competition is not a new force for change, competition today has some significant new twists. First, most markets are global because of decreasing transportation and communication costs and the increasing export orientation of business.[18] The adoption of trade agreements such as the North American Free Trade Agreement (NAFTA) and the presence of the World Trade Organization (WTO) have changed the way business operates. In the future, competition from industrialized countries such as Japan and Germany will take a back seat to competition from the booming industries of developing nations such as China and India. The Internet is creating new competitors overnight in ways that could not have been imagined five years ago. Companies in developing nations may soon offer different, newer, cheaper, or higher-quality products while enjoying the benefits of low labor costs, abundant supplies of raw materials, expertise in certain areas of production, and financial protection from their own governments that may not be available to firms in older industrialized states.

Consider, for example, the market for cell phones or smart phones. Once consumers simply compared calling plans and phone costs and chose a phone available from a provider with the best deal and coverage in their primary area of usage. Currently, the choices are far more complex: we now have platforms in addition to manufacturers and carriers or service providers. Manufacturers include Apple, Blackberry, Motorola, Samsung, Sony Ericsson, HTC, LG, Nokia, Palm, Toshiba, and others. Carriers include Verizon, T-Mobile, AT&T, Sprint, Alltel, Bell, Orange, O2, Vodafone, and others. Platforms include Android, MacOS, Java, Linux, Palm OS, Symbian, Windows Mobile, and others. For consumers the choices are seemingly endless and extremely confusing. Manufacturers have to develop new equipment and software combinations to work on various platforms for a variety of carriers. Carriers must decide which instruments and platform combinations to offer to subscribers. And platform developers must show their platform can do more things, simpler and with fewer errors, with maximum flexibility. And every month there are new combinations of all three to further confuse consumers and industry experts.

PROCESSES FOR PLANNED ORGANIZATION CHANGE

External forces may impose change on an organization. Ideally, however, the organization will not only respond to change but will also anticipate it, prepare for it through planning, and incorporate it in the organization strategy. Organization change can be viewed from a static point of view, such as that of Lewin (see next section), or from a dynamic perspective.

Lewin's Process Model

Planned organization change requires a systematic process of movement from one condition to another. Kurt Lewin suggested that efforts to bring about planned change in organizations should approach change as a multistage process.[19] His model of planned change is made up of three steps—unfreezing, change, and refreezing—as shown in Figure 19.1.

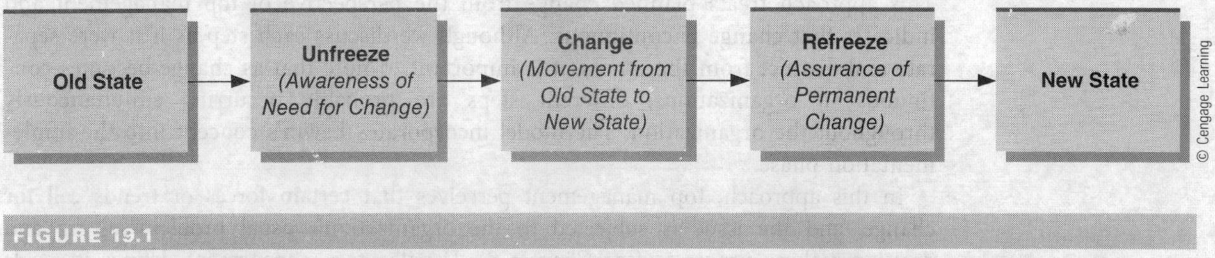

FIGURE 19.1

Lewin's Process of Organization Structure

In Lewin's three-step model, change is a systematic process of transition from an old way of doing things to a new way. Inclusion of an "unfreezing" stage indicates the importance of preparing for the change. The "refreezing" stage reflects the importance of following up on the change to make it permanent.

Unfreezing is the process by which people become aware of the need for change.

Unfreezing is the process by which people become aware of the need for change. If people are satisfied with current practices and procedures, they may have little or no interest in making changes. The key factor in unfreezing is making employees understand the importance of a change and how their jobs will be affected by it. The employees who will be most affected by the change must be made aware of why it is needed, which in effect makes them dissatisfied enough with current operations to be motivated to change. Creating in employees the awareness of the need for change is the responsibility of the leadership of the organization.[20] Following the recent deep recession with so much downsizing, layoffs, restructuring, and takeovers, employees may be weary of the constant pressure and uncertainties of their position and/or organization. Top managers and change agents are urged to make the effort to empathize with employees, acknowledge the difficulties of the past and uncertainties of the present, and provide forums for employees to vent a little, followed up with workshops for information sharing and training. After making the emotional connection with employees, top management can make the intellectual connection and make the business case by sharing economic and marketing data and the short- and long-term visions for the organization, and by involving employees at all levels in translating organizational goals into division, department, and work unit goals.[21]

Change itself is the movement from the old way of doing things to a new way. Change may entail installing new equipment, restructuring the organization, or implementing a new performance appraisal system—anything that alters existing relationships or activities.

Refreezing is the process of making new behaviors relatively permanent and resistant to further change.

Refreezing makes new behaviors relatively permanent and resistant to further change. Examples of refreezing techniques include repeating newly learned skills in a training session and then role playing to teach how the new skill can be used in a real-life work situation. Refreezing is necessary because without it, the old ways of doing things might soon reassert themselves while the new ways are forgotten. For example, many employees who attend special training sessions apply themselves diligently and resolve to change things in their organizations. But when they return to the workplace, they find it easier to conform to the old ways than to make waves. There usually are few, if any, rewards for trying to change the organizational status quo. In fact, the personal sanctions against doing so may be difficult to tolerate. Learning theory and reinforcement theory (see Chapter 4) can play important roles in the refreezing phase.

The Continuous Change Process Model

Perhaps because Lewin's model is very simple and straightforward, virtually all models of organization change use his approach. However, it does not deal with several important issues. A more complex, and more helpful, approach is illustrated in Figure 19.2. This approach treats planned change from the perspective of top management and indicates that change is continuous. Although we discuss each step as if it were separate and distinct from the others, it is important to note that as change becomes continuous in organizations, different steps are probably occurring simultaneously throughout the organization. The model incorporates Lewin's concept into the implementation phase.

In this approach, top management perceives that certain forces or trends call for change, and the issue is subjected to the organization's usual problem-solving and decision-making processes (see Chapter 8). Usually, top management defines its goals in terms of what the organization or certain processes or outputs will be like after the change. Alternatives for change are generated and evaluated, and an acceptable one is selected.

FIGURE 19.2

Continuous Change Process Model of Organization Change

The continuous change process model incorporates the forces for change, a problem-solving process, a change agent, and transition management. It takes a top-management perspective and highlights the fact that in organizations today, change is a continuous process.

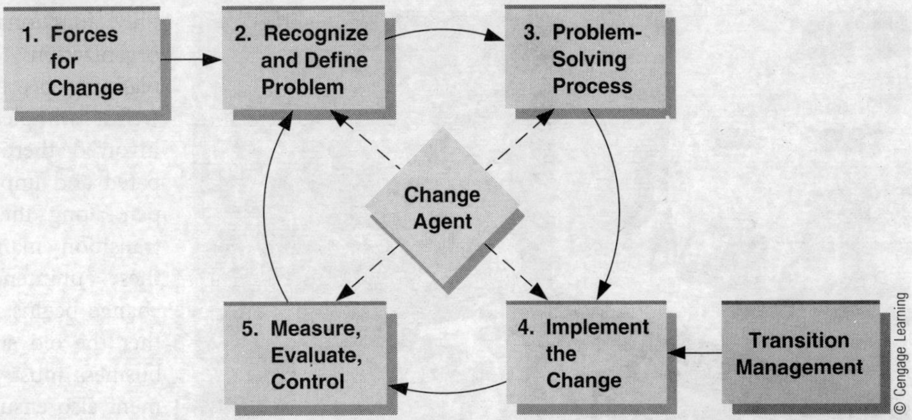

A **change agent** is a person responsible for managing a change effort.

Early in the process, the organization may seek the assistance of a **change agent**—a person who will be responsible for managing the change effort. The change agent may also help management recognize and define the problem or the need for the change and may be involved in generating and evaluating potential plans of action. The change agent may be a member of the organization, an outsider such as a consultant, or even someone from headquarters whom employees view as an outsider. An internal change agent is likely to know the organization's people, tasks, and political situations, which may be helpful in interpreting data and understanding the system; but an insider may also be too close to the situation to view it objectively. (In addition, a regular employee would have to be removed from his or her regular duties to concentrate on the transition.) An outsider, then, is often received better by all parties because of his or her assumed impartiality. Under the direction and management of the change agent, the organization implements the change through Lewin's unfreeze, change, and refreeze process.

The final step is measurement, evaluation, and control. The change agent and the top management group assess the degree to which the change is having the desired effect; that is, they measure progress toward the goals of the change and make appropriate changes if necessary. The more closely the change agent is involved in the change process, the less distinct the steps become. The change agent becomes a "collaborator" or "helper" to the organization as she or he is immersed in defining and solving the problem with members of the organization. When this happens, the change agent may be working with many individuals, groups, and departments within the organization on different phases of the change process. When the change process is moving along from one stage to another, it may not be readily observable because of the total involvement of the change agent in every phase of the project. Throughout the process, however, the change agent brings in new ideas and viewpoints that help members look at old problems in new ways. Change often arises from the conflict that results when the change agent challenges the organization's assumptions and generally accepted patterns of operation.

Through the measurement, evaluation, and control phase, top management determines the effectiveness of the change process by evaluating various indicators of organizational productivity and effectiveness or employee morale. It is expected the organization will be better after the change than before. However, the uncertainties and rapid changes in all sectors of the environment make constant organization change a given for most organizations.

Transition management is the process of systematically planning, organizing, and implementing change.

Transition management is the process of systematically planning, organizing, and implementing change, from the disassembly of the current state to the realization of a

Brian Peterson/ZUMA Press/Newscom

Best Buy has appointed a new CEO, Hubert Joly, to lead the beleaguered electronics retailer. In this photo taken September 6, 2012 Joly was working the floor as a "blue shirt" at the St. Cloud Store in order to better understand what employees in stores actually experience. Through this process Joly is most likely in Stage 2 discovering what the real problems are for the company.

fully functional future state within an organization.[22] No matter how much planning precedes the change and how well it is implemented, because people are involved there will always be unanticipated and unpredictable things that happen along the way.[23] One key role of transition management is to deal with these unintended consequences. Once change begins, the organization is in neither the old state nor the new state, yet business must go on. Transition management also ensures that business continues while the change is occurring; therefore, it must begin before the change occurs. The members of the regular management team must take on the role of transition managers and coordinate organizational activities with the change agent. An interim management structure or interim positions may be created to ensure continuity and control of the business during the transition. Communication about the changes to all involved, from employees to customers and suppliers, plays a key role in transition management.[24]

ORGANIZATION DEVELOPMENT

On one level, organization development is simply the way organizations change and evolve. Organization change can involve personnel, technology, competition, and other areas. Employee learning and formal training, transfers, promotions, terminations, and retirements are all examples of personnel-related changes. Thus, in the broadest sense, organization development means organization change.[25] The term as used here, however, means something more specific. Over the past forty years, organization development has emerged as a distinct field of study and practice. Experts now substantially agree as to what constitutes organization development in general, although arguments about details continue.[26] Our definition of organization development is an attempt to describe a very complex process in a simple manner. It is also an attempt to capture the best points of several definitions offered by writers in the field.

Organization development is a system-wide application of behavioral science knowledge to the planned development and reinforcement of organizational strategies, structures, and processes for improving organizational effectiveness.

Organization Development Defined

"**Organization development** (OD) is a system-wide application of behavioral science knowledge to the planned development and reinforcement of organizational strategies, structures, and processes for improving an organization's effectiveness."[27] Three points in this definition make it simple to remember and use. First, organization development involves attempts to plan organization changes, which excludes spontaneous, haphazard initiatives. Second, the specific intention of organization development is to improve organization effectiveness. This point excludes changes that merely imitate those of another organization, are forced on the organization by external pressures, or are undertaken merely for the sake of changing. Third, the planned improvement must be based on knowledge of the behavioral sciences such as organizational behavior, psychology, sociology, cultural anthropology, and related fields of study rather than on financial or technological considerations. Under this definition, the replacement of manual personnel records with a computerized system would not be considered an instance of organization development. Although such a change has behavioral effects, it is a technology-driven reform rather than a behavioral one. Likewise, alterations in record keeping necessary to support new government-mandated reporting requirements are not a part of organization development because the change is obligatory and the result of an external force. The three most basic types of techniques for implementing organization development are system-wide, task and technological, and group and individual.

At one time in the 1960s and 1970s organization development was treated as a field of study and practiced by specially trained OD professionals. However, as organization change became the order of the day in progressive organizations around the world, it became clear that all organizational leaders needed to become leaders and teachers of change throughout their organizations if their organizations were going to survive. Excellent examples of organizations that have embraced OD are the U.S. Army, General Electric, and Royal Dutch Shell.[28]

System-Wide Organization Development

Structural change is a system-wide organization development involving a major restructuring of the organization or instituting programs such as quality of work life.

The most comprehensive type of organization change involves a major reorientation or reorganization—usually referred to as a **structural change** or a system-wide rearrangement of task division and authority and reporting relationships. A structural change affects performance appraisal and rewards, decision making, and communication and information-processing systems. As we discussed in Chapter 17, reengineering and rethinking the organizations are two contemporary approaches to system-wide structural change. Reengineering can be a difficult process, but it has great potential for organizational improvement. It requires that managers challenge long-held assumptions about everything they do and set outrageous goals and expect that they will be met. An organization may change the way it divides tasks into jobs, combines jobs into departments and divisions, and arranges authority and reporting relationships among positions. It may move from functional departmentalization to a system based on products or geography, for example, or from a conventional linear design to a matrix or a team-based design. Other changes may include dividing large groups into smaller ones or merging small groups into larger ones. In addition, the degree to which rules and procedures are written down and enforced, as well as the locus of decision-making authority, may be altered. Supervisors may become "coaches" or "facilitators" in a team-based organization. The organization will have transformed both the configurational and the operational aspects of its structure if all of these changes are made.

No system-wide structural change is simple.[29] A company president cannot just issue a memo notifying company personnel that on a certain date they will report to a different supervisor and be responsible for new tasks and expect everything to change overnight. Employees have months, years, and sometimes decades of experience in dealing with people and tasks in certain ways. When these patterns are disrupted, employees

Quality of work life programs are aimed at increasing the the ways employees satisfy important personal needs through their work. The employees shown here seem to be enjoying each others' company, probably satisfying needs for interpersonal interaction and fellowship with colleagues.

need time to learn the new tasks and to settle into the new relationships. Moreover, they may resist the change for a number of reasons; we discuss resistance to change later in this chapter. Therefore, organizations must manage the change process.

Ford Motor Company is pretty typical of organizations that have had to make major organization-wide and worldwide changes. Over the years, Ford had developed several regional fiefdoms, such as Ford of Europe, Ford United States, and Ford Australia, which all operated relatively independently. When Jacques Nasser was named CEO, he set out to tear down those regionally based organizations and to create a truly globally integrated car manufacturer. As his plan was unfolding, however, Ford continued to lose market share, so on October 30, 2001, Nasser was replaced as CEO by Ford family member William Clay (Bill) Ford Jr., who is continuing to develop the global integration of the design, development, and manufacture of Ford automobiles. In the years under the leadership of Alan Mulally, Ford has made a stunning turnaround.[30]

Quality of work life is the extent to which workers can satisfy important personal needs through their experiences in the organization.

Another system-wide change is the introduction of quality-of-work-life programs. J. Lloyd Suttle defined **quality of work life** as the "degree to which members of a work organization are able to satisfy important personal needs through their experiences in the organization."[31] Quality-of-work-life programs focus strongly on providing a work environment conducive to satisfying individual needs. The emphasis on improving life at work developed during the 1970s, a period of increasing inflation and deepening recession. The development was rather surprising because an expanding economy and substantially increased resources are the conditions that usually induce top management to begin people-oriented programs. However, top management viewed improving life at work as a means of improving productivity.

Any movement with broad and ambiguous goals tends to spawn diverse programs, each claiming to be based on the movement's goals, and the quality-of-work-life movement is no exception. These programs vary substantially, although most espouse a goal of "humanizing the workplace." Richard Walton divided them into the eight categories shown in Figure 19.3.[32] Obviously, many types of programs can be accommodated by the categories, from changing the pay system to establishing an employee bill of rights that guarantees workers the rights to privacy, free speech, due process, and fair and equitable treatment. The Defense Information Systems Agency (DISA) has a QWL program that includes options for a compressed work schedule, in which employees can work eighty hours in nine workdays over a two-week period, and a "telework" option in which eligible employees may telework at an alternative worksite such as a telework center, at home, or at a satellite office, on a regular and recurring schedule for a maximum of three days per week. The program

FIGURE 19.3

Walton's Categorization of Quality-of-Work-Life Programs

Quality-of-work-life programs can be categorized into eight types. The expected benefits of these programs are increased employee morale, productivity, and organizational effectiveness.

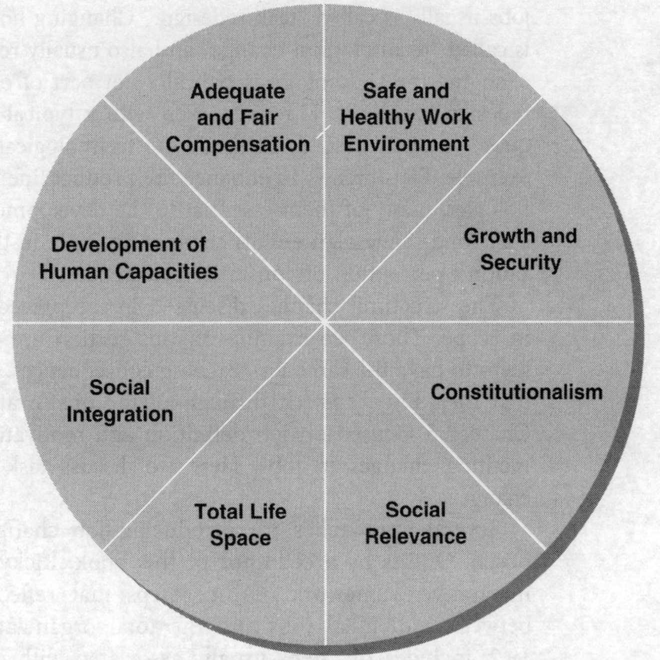

Reference: Adapted from Richard E. Walton, "Quality of Work Life: What Is It?" *Sloan Management Review*, Fall 1973, pp. 11–21, by permission of the publisher. Copyright © 1973 by the Sloan Management Review Association. All rights reserved.

is designed to promote a more beneficial lifestyle for employees both personally and professionally.[33]

Total quality management, which was discussed in several earlier chapters, can also be viewed as a system-wide organization development program. In fact, some might consider total quality management as a broad program that includes both structural change and quality of work life. It differs from quality of work life in that it emphasizes satisfying customer needs by making quality-oriented changes rather than focusing on satisfying employee needs at work. Often, however, the employee programs are very similar to it.

The benefits gained from quality-of-work-life programs differ substantially, but generally they are of three types. A more positive attitude toward the work and the organization, or increased job satisfaction, is perhaps the most direct benefit.[34] Another is increased productivity, although it is often difficult to measure and separate the effects of the quality-of-work-life program from the effects of other organizational factors. A third benefit is increased effectiveness of the organization as measured by its profitability, goal accomplishment, shareholder wealth, or resource exchange. The third gain follows directly from the first two: if employees have more positive attitudes about the organization and their productivity increases, everything else being equal, the organization should be more effective.

Task and Technological Change

Another way to bring about system-wide organization development is through changes in the tasks involved in doing the work, the technology, or both. The direct alteration of jobs usually is called "task redesign." Changing how inputs are transformed into outputs is called "technological change" and also usually results in task changes. Strictly speaking, changing the technology is typically not part of organization development whereas task redesign usually is. However, even with a typical technology-based change, OD techniques are often used to facilitate the technological changes. At the "New Chrysler," for example, Fiat intends to enhance the product line by introducing a number of new technologies, many of them essential to the development of smaller, more fuel-efficient cars. This long-range plan entails changes not only in the product line but also in the organization's perception of consumer preferences.[35]

The structural changes discussed in the preceding section are explicitly system-wide in scope. Those we examine in this section are more narrowly focused and may not seem to have the same far-reaching consequences. It is important to remember, however, that their impact is felt throughout the organization. The discussion of task design in Chapter 5 focused on job definition and motivation and gave little attention to implementing changes in jobs. Here we discuss task redesign as a mode of organization change.

Several approaches to introducing job changes in organizations have been proposed. One is by a coauthor of this book, Ricky W. Griffin. Griffin's approach is an integrative framework of nine steps that reflect the complexities of the interfaces between individual jobs and the total organization.[36] The process, shown in Table 19.2, includes the steps usually associated with change, such as recognizing the need for a change, selecting the appropriate intervention, and evaluating the change. But Griffin's approach inserts four additional steps into the standard sequence: diagnosis of the overall work system and context, including examination of the jobs, workforce, technology, organization design, leadership, and group dynamics; evaluating the costs

Table 19.2 Integrated Framework for Implementation of Task Redesign in Organizations

Step 1: Recognition of a need for a change
Step 2: Selection of task redesign as a potential intervention
Step 3: Diagnosis of the work system and context
a. Diagnosis of existing jobs
b. Diagnosis of existing workforce
c. Diagnosis of technology
d. Diagnosis of organization design
e. Diagnosis of leader behavior
f. Diagnosis of group and social processes
Step 4: Cost-benefit analysis of proposed changes
Step 5: Go/no-go decision
Step 6: Formulation of the strategy for redesign
Step 7: Implementation of the task changes
Step 8: Implementation of any supplemental changes
Step 9: Evaluation of the task redesign effort

Reference: Ricky W. Griffin, *Task Design: An Integrative Framework* (Glenview, IL: Scott, Foresman, 1982), p. 208. Used by permission.

and benefits of the change; formulating a redesign strategy; and implementing supplemental changes.

Diagnosis includes analysis of the total work environment within which the jobs exist. It is important to evaluate the organization structure, especially the work rules and decision-making authority within a department, when job changes are being considered.[37] For example, if jobs are to be redesigned to give employees more freedom in choosing work methods or scheduling work activities, diagnosis of the present system must determine whether the rules will allow that to happen. Diagnosis must also include evaluation of the work group and teams, as well as the intragroup dynamics (discussed in Chapters 9 and 10). Furthermore, it must determine whether workers have or can easily obtain the new skills to perform the redesigned task.

It is extremely important to recognize the full range of potential costs and benefits associated with a job redesign effort. Some are direct and quantifiable; others are indirect and not quantifiable. Redesign may involve unexpected costs or benefits; although these cannot be predicted with certainty, they can be weighed as possibilities. Factors such as short-term role ambiguity, role conflict, and role overload can be major stumbling blocks to a job redesign effort.

Implementing a redesign scheme takes careful planning, and developing a strategy for the intervention is the final planning step. Strategy formulation is a four-part process. First, the organization must decide who will design the changes. Depending on the circumstances, the planning team may consist of only upper-level management or may include line workers and supervisors. Next, the team undertakes the actual design of the changes based on job design theory and the needs, goals, and circumstances of the organization. Third, the team decides the timing of the implementation, which may require a formal transition period during which equipment is purchased and installed, job training takes place, new physical layouts are arranged, and the bugs in the new system are worked out. Fourth, strategy planners must consider whether the job changes require adjustments and supplemental changes in other organizational components such as reporting relationships and the compensation system.

Group and Individual Change

Groups and individuals can be involved in organization change in a vast number of ways. Retraining a single employee can be considered an organization change if the training affects the way the employee does his or her job. Familiarizing managers with the leadership grid or the Vroom decision tree (Chapter 12) in order to improve the way they lead or involve subordinate participation in decision making is an attempt at change. In the first case, the goal is to balance management concerns for production and people; in the second, the goal is to increase the participation of rank-and-file employees in the organization's decision making. In this section, we present an overview of four popular types of people-oriented change techniques: training, management development, team building, and survey feedback.

Training Training generally is designed to improve employees' job skills. Employees may be trained to run certain machines, taught new mathematical skills, or acquainted with personal growth and development methods. Stress management programs are becoming popular for helping employees, particularly executives, understand organizational stress and develop ways to cope with it.[38] Training may also be used in conjunction with other, more comprehensive organization changes. For instance, if an organization is implementing a management-by-objectives program, training in

SERVICE | The Innovation Cocreation Challenge

©rangizz/Shutterstock

A missing ingredient in successful innovation for many organizations is the simple truth that innovation requires both organizations and their customers to change. Simultaneously incorporating the knowledge, skills, and capabilities of both customer and organization through collaboration is the innovation cocreation challenge. Organizations that successfully cocreate innovation ensure that they manage not only the resultant internal changes but the changes required of their customers to successfully coproduce the newly created experience. Two firms that are widely recognized as successful in realizing the value of cocreating innovation for themselves and their customers are the Walt Disney Company and IKEA. They have both demonstrated a sustainable ability to engage their customers in successful co-production of today's experiences and in cocreating innovations for tomorrow's. They systematically cocreate with their customers the new roles and behaviors required by innovation and then teach both their own employees and their customers how to perform in those roles. These companies carefully study what their customers and employees will need to know and do to coproduce the magic at Disney and the real-life solutions at IKEA, and then make sure both have the resources and capabilities needed to successfully perform in their roles.

The starting point for both Disney's and IKEA's innovation cocreation processes is identifying their customers' key value drivers. Key value drivers are those specific activities, interactions, touch-points, or functions that are provided to customers, which, based on how well they are performed, have a direct impact on the overall success of the company and the value of the customer's experience. These are what the innovation literature calls performance attributes. If the customer's rating on a specific activity, interaction, or function has a direct and significant relationship to the overall success of the company, then it is a key value driver.

The most direct way to identify key value drivers is to ask the customers in surveys, focus groups, or individual interviews. Not only can they tell the company a great deal about what it is doing that works or does not work, but they can identify what the key value drivers in the experience are and, consequently, where innovative activity needs to be focused.

Innovating a customer solution is a special challenge for service companies, as experiences exist in customers' imaginations when they cocreate them and in their memories after they coproduce them. Thus, for a newly created intangible service, customers are asked to coproduce an experience that they have never had before. On the other side of coproducing a service innovation is the company, which has to gather and organize its resources and capabilities to coproduce an experience that it has never produced before either. For an elaborate service, this can mean a major investment that does not meet enough customers' needs or adequately match their capabilities to be profitable. Cocreating a cruise ship, information system, or medical service that customers will not or cannot use requires a lot of upfront money only to find out that what seemed like a good innovation in the customer cocreation process, was not.

In any innovation, companies must learn new ways of using their resources and then teach their employees how to provide the service their customers expect. Just as importantly, however, as IKEA and Disney illustrate, companies need to develop strategies and tactics to teach their employees to teach their customers how to coproduce a experience in ways that successfully capture its value. For innovation to be successful, not only must the organization learn new ways of doing things, but it must also ensure that the customers acquire the new knowledge, develop the skills, and possess the abilities an innovation will require of them. Managing the innovation cocreation challenge is about managing both customers and the employees' activities and interactions as they coproduce the experience.

Disney and IKEA have learned that there are degrees of innovation requiring different innovation strategies. Moreover, there are varying levels of customer capabilities that must be planned for, trained, and managed to match the different types of customers with different ways that employees can coproduce the experience. These two exemplars offer several lessons for all organizations that seek to implement successful innovations.

First, the innovation cocreation challenge is exactly that—a cocreation challenge. These two organizations teach us to discover through customer involvement in cocreating what the implications of those changes will be on the customer. If the customer must do something radically new, then the company must anticipate the learning that will be required and provide for it. The introduction of self-service technologies at airline check-ins and retail checkouts has had varying success depending upon the degree to which the organizations have provided employees to educate customers in what is, for many, a radical change in how they interface with the organization.

Second, the organizations that successfully implement innovations account for the impact of innovation on customers as part of who they are. It is in their DNA. If customers need to do new things to enjoy or benefit from the innovation, then the successful organizations try to make learning a worthwhile part of the experience for the customer. When a customer is required, for example, to do new things, these successful organizations make the new things fun or offer a benefit to the customer for doing the new things required by the innovation versus the old. When Disney added the free Magical Express bus service from Orlando's airport to the guest's hotel room, guests felt they were getting a valuable new benefit that saved them the aggravation and cost of finding their way from the airport to their room.

Moreover, organizations that consider their customers as cocreators of innovations put more thought into the customer interface. Whether this is an environmental setting, web site, or personal contact with an employee, when an innovation changes the way the customer interacts with the organization, the point of interaction is very carefully designed with the customer in mind. It is very different to be immersed in an IKEA experience room than it is to visit a traditional furniture store. The successful innovators spend considerable effort in the innovation cocreation process, gathering customer data, input, and feedback to be sure they deliver the "wow" experience their customers expect.

The *final* lesson learned is that cocreation of innovation means that the company must teach its employees how to teach its customers. Few organizations, especially manufacturing organizations, spend enough time teaching their employees to teach their customers. Even when customers cocreate an innovation, there is no guarantee that the innovation will be successful. Innovations, especially radical ones, will require new behaviors of customers just as they will require new behaviors of the organizations' own employees. While most organizations know that innovation requires employee training, too often the need to also train employees to train customers is overlooked. If both employees and customers will have to do different things as a result of an innovation, then both will need to learn new skills and behaviors. And the more radical the change, the more training will be required.

The lessons learned from the successful implementation of innovation by both Disney and IKEA are important and profound. Perhaps the most important is that the innovation requires the customer to coproduce in some way any experience that the innovation creates. The company that fails to recognize and plan for customer participation in that coproduction is not likely to attend to both its own and its customers' learning needs when cocreating the innovation. When that happens, the benefits of the innovation are likely to be unrealized.

Discussion Question: In considering how organizations have to teach you to perform new tasks and roles in coproducing a service experience, relate any examples of what organizations have done to teach you how to do what you had to do to have a successful experience.

establishing goals and reviewing goal-oriented performance is probably needed. One important type of training that is becoming increasingly more common is training people to work in other countries. Companies such as Motorola give extensive training programs to employees at all levels before they start an international assignment. Training includes intensive language courses, cultural courses, and courses for the family.

Among the many training methods, the most common are lecture, discussion, a lecture-discussion combination, experiential methods, case studies, films or videotapes, and the increasingly popular online training modules. Training can take place in a standard classroom, either on company property or in a hotel, at a resort, at a conference center, or online from anywhere. On-the-job training provides a different type of experience in which the trainee learns from an experienced worker. Most training programs

Stephen Shaver/Upi/Landow Media

Training can take many forms, from in-class sessions to simulation drills and practice. China International Search and Rescue (CISAR) teams take part in a search and rescue training exercise at an earthquake training base outside of Beijing February 26, 2010. CISAR is primarily responsible for implementing domestic search and rescue operations and international humanitarian missions for victims of natural disasters. During a disaster there is little time to train teams as lives may be at stake. Therefore, they use simulations and drills to train search and recovery teams.

use a combination of methods determined by the topic, the trainees, the trainer, and the organization.

A major problem of training programs is transferring employee learning to the workplace. Often an employee learns a new skill or a manager learns a new management technique, but upon returning to the normal work situation, he or she finds it easier to go back to the old way of doing things. As we discussed earlier, the process of refreezing is a vital part of the change process, and some way must be found to make the accomplishments of the training program permanent.

Management Development Management development programs, like employee training programs, attempt to foster certain skills, abilities, and perspectives. Often, when a highly qualified technical person is promoted to manager of a work group, he or she needs training in how to manage or deal with people. In such cases, management development programs can be important to organizations, both for the new manager and for his or her subordinates.

Typically, management development programs use the lecture-discussion method to some extent but rely most heavily on participative methods such as case studies and role playing. Participative and experiential methods allow the manager to experience the problems of being a manager as well as the feelings of frustration, doubt, and success that are part of the job. The subject matter of this type of training program is problematic, however, in that management skills, including communication, problem diagnosis, problem solving, and performance appraisal, are not as easy to identify or to transfer from a classroom to the workplace as the skills required to operate a machine.

In addition, rapid changes in the external environment can make certain managerial skills obsolete in a very short time. As a result, some companies are approaching the development of their management team as an ongoing, career-long process and require their managers to periodically attend refresher courses.

Jack Welch was so committed to making cultural changes within GE that he created the now famous Crotonville, New York, training facility to develop an army of change leaders. GE put more than ten thousand managers a year through a three-step workshop series called the Change Acceleration Program (CAP). Leadership was redefined as a teaching activity in which leaders taught their direct reports how to change the way they did their jobs. In order to make the system-wide changes Welch thought were needed, he turned to individual OD.[39]

As corporate America invests hundreds of millions of dollars in management development, certain guiding principles are evolving: (1) management development is a multifaceted, complex, and long-term process to which there is no quick or simple approach; (2) organizations should carefully and systematically identify their unique developmental needs and evaluate their programs accordingly; (3) management development objectives must be compatible with organizational objectives; and (4) the utility and value of management development remain more an article of faith than a proven fact.[40]

Team Building When interaction among group members is critical to group success and effectiveness, team development, or team building, may be useful. Team building emphasizes members working together in a spirit of cooperation and generally has one or more of the following goals:

1. To set team goals and priorities
2. To analyze or allocate the way work is performed
3. To examine how a group is working—that is, to examine processes such as norms, decision making, and communications
4. To examine relationships among the people doing the work[41]

Total quality management efforts usually focus on teams, and the principles of team building must be applied to make them work. Team participation is especially important in the data-gathering and evaluation phases of team development. In data gathering, the members share information on the functioning of the group. The opinions of the group thus form the foundation of the development process. In the evaluation phase, members are the source of information about the effectiveness of the development effort.[42]

Like total quality management and many other management techniques, team building should not be thought of as a one-time experience, perhaps something undertaken on a retreat from the workplace; rather, it is a continuing process. It may take weeks, months, or years for a group to learn to pull together and function as a team. Team development can be a way to train the group to solve its own problems in the future. Research on the effectiveness of team building as an organization development tool so far is mixed and inconclusive. For more details on developing teams in organizations, please refer to Chapter 10.

Survey Feedback Survey feedback techniques can form the basis for a change process. In this process, data are gathered, analyzed, summarized, and returned to those who generated them to identify, discuss, and solve problems. A survey feedback process is often set in motion either by the organization's top management or by a consultant to management. By providing information about employees' beliefs and attitudes, a survey can help management diagnose and solve an organization's problems. A consultant or

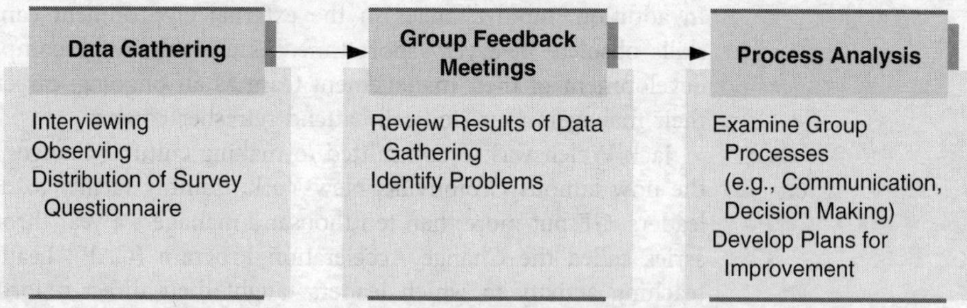

FIGURE 19.4

The Survey Feedback Process

The survey feedback process has three distinct stages, which must be fully completed for the process to be most effective. As an organization development process, its purpose is to fully involve all employees in data analysis, problem identification, and development of solutions.

change agent usually coordinates the process and is responsible for data gathering, analysis, and summary. The three-stage process is shown in Figure 19.4.[43]

The use of survey feedback techniques in an organization development process differs from their use in traditional attitude surveys. In an organization development process, data are (1) returned to employee groups at all levels in the organization and (2) used by all employees working together in their normal work groups to identify and solve problems. In traditional attitude surveys, top management reviews the data and may or may not initiate a new program to solve problems the survey has identified.

In the data-gathering stage, the change agent interviews selected personnel from appropriate levels to determine the key issues to be examined. Information from these interviews is used to develop a survey questionnaire, which is distributed to a large sample of employees. The questionnaire may be a standardized instrument, an instrument developed specifically for the organization, or a combination of the two. The questionnaire data are analyzed and aggregated by group or department to ensure that respondents remain anonymous.[44] Then the change agent prepares a summary of the results for the group feedback sessions. From this point on, the consultant is involved in the process as a resource person and expert.

The feedback meetings generally involve only two or three levels of management. Meetings are usually held serially, first with a meeting of the top management group, which is then followed by meetings of employees throughout the organization. The group manager rather than the change agent typically leads sessions to transfer "ownership" of the data from the change agent to the work group. The feedback consists primarily of profiles of the group's attitudes toward the organization, the work, the leadership, and other topics on the questionnaire. During the feedback sessions, participants discuss reasons for the scores and the problems that the data reveal.

In the process analysis stage, the group examines the process of making decisions, communicating, and accomplishing work, usually with the help of the consultant. Unfortunately, groups often overlook this stage as they become absorbed in the survey data and the problems revealed during the feedback sessions. Occasionally, group managers simply fail to hold feedback and process analysis sessions. Change agents should ensure that managers hold these sessions and that they are rewarded for doing so. The process analysis stage is important because its purpose is to develop action plans to make improvements. Several sessions may be required to discuss the process issues fully and to settle on a strategy for improvements. Groups often find it useful to document the plans as they are discussed and to appoint a member to follow up on implementation. Generally, the follow-up assesses whether communication and communication processes have actually been improved. A follow-up survey can be administered several months to a year later to assess how much these processes have changed since they were first reported.

The survey feedback method is probably one of the most widely used organization change and development interventions. If any of its stages are compromised or omitted, however, the technique becomes less useful. A primary responsibility of the consultant or change agent, then, is to ensure that the method is fully and faithfully carried through.

RESISTANCE TO CHANGE

Change is inevitable; so is resistance to change. Paradoxically, organizations both promote and resist change. As an agent for change, the organization asks prospective customers or clients to change their current purchasing habits by switching to the company's products or services, asks current customers to change by increasing their purchases, and asks suppliers to reduce the costs of raw materials. The organization resists change in that its structure and control systems protect the daily tasks of producing a product or service from uncertainties in the environment. The organization must have some elements of permanence to avoid mirroring the instability of the environment, yet it must also react to external shifts with internal change to maintain currency and relevance in the marketplace.

A commonly held view is that all resistance to change needs to be overcome, but that is not always the case. Resistance to change can be used for the benefit of the organization and need not be eliminated entirely. By revealing a legitimate concern that a proposed change may harm the organization or that other alternatives might be better, resistance may alert the organization to reexamine the change.[45] For example, an organization may be considering acquiring a company in a completely different industry. Resistance to such a proposal may cause the organization to examine the advantages and disadvantages of the move more carefully. Without resistance, the decision might be made before the pros and cons have been sufficiently explored. Some have suggested that change agents may contribute to resistance through their mismanagement of the change process or miscommunication throughout the process.[46]

Resistance may come from the organization, the individual, or both. Determining the ultimate source is often difficult, however, because organizations are composed of individuals. Table 19.3 summarizes various types of organizational and individual sources of resistance.

Organizational Sources of Resistance

Daniel Katz and Robert Kahn have identified six major organizational sources of resistance: overdetermination, narrow focus of change, group inertia, threatened expertise, threatened power, and changes in resource allocation.[47] Of course, not every organization or every change situation displays all six sources.

Overdetermination, or **structural inertia**, occurs because numerous organizational systems are in place to ensure that employees and systems behave as expected to maintain stability.

Overdetermination Organizations have several systems designed to maintain stability. For example, consider how organizations control employees' performance. Job candidates must have certain specific skills so that they can do the job the organization needs them to do. A new employee is given a job description, and the supervisor trains, coaches, and counsels the employee in job tasks. The new employee usually serves some type of probationary period that culminates in a performance review; thereafter, the employee's performance is regularly evaluated. Finally, rewards, punishment, and discipline are administered, depending on the level of performance. Such a system is said to be characterized by **overdetermination**, or **structural inertia**,[48] in that one could probably have the same effect on employee performance with fewer procedures and

Table 19.3 Organizational and Individual Sources of Resistance

ORGANIZATIONAL SOURCES	EXAMPLES
Overdetermination	Employment system, job descriptions, evaluation and reward system, organization culture
Narrow Focus of Change	Structure changed with no concern given to other issues (e.g., jobs, people)
Group Inertia	Group norms
Threatened Expertise	People move out of area of expertise
Threatened Power	Decentralized decision making
Resource Allocation	Increased use of part-time help
INDIVIDUAL SOURCES	**EXAMPLES**
Habit	Altered tasks
Security	Altered tasks or reporting relationships
Economic Factors	Changed pay and benefits
Fear of the Unknown	New job, new boss
Lack of Awareness	Isolated groups not heeding notices
Social Factors	Group norms

safeguards. In other words, the structure of the organization produces resistance to change because it was designed to maintain stability. Another important source of overdetermination is the culture of the organization. As discussed in Chapter 18, the culture of an organization can have powerful and long-lasting effects on the behavior of its employees.

Narrow Focus of Change Many efforts to create change in organizations adopt too narrow a focus. Any effort to force change in the tasks of individuals or groups must take into account the interdependence among organizational elements such as people, structure, tasks, and the information system. For example, some attempts at redesigning jobs fail because the organization structure within which the jobs must function is inappropriate for the redesigned jobs.[49]

Group Inertia When an employee attempts to change his or her work behavior, the group may resist by refusing to change other behaviors that are necessary complements to the individual's altered behavior. In other words, group norms may act as a brake on individual attempts at behavior change.

Threatened Expertise A change in the organization may threaten the specialized expertise that individuals and groups have developed over the years. A job redesign or a structural change may transfer responsibility for a specialized task from the current expert to someone else, threatening the specialist's expertise and building his or her resistance to the change.

Threatened Power Any redistribution of decision-making authority, such as with reengineering or team-based management, may threaten an individual's power relationships with others. If an organization is decentralizing its decision making, managers who wielded their decision-making powers in return for special favors from others may resist the change because they do not want to lose their power base.

Resource Allocation Groups that are satisfied with current resource allocation methods may resist any change they believe will threaten future allocations. Resources in this context can mean anything from monetary rewards and equipment to additional seasonal help to more computer time.

These six sources explain most types of organization-based resistance to change. All are based on people and social relationships. Many of these sources of resistance can be traced to groups or individuals who are afraid of losing something—resources, power, or comfort in a routine.

Individual Sources of Resistance

Individual sources of resistance to change are rooted in basic human characteristics such as needs and perceptions. Researchers have identified six reasons for individual resistance to change: habit, security, economic factors, fear of the unknown, lack of awareness, and social factors (see Table 19.3).[50]

Habit It is easier to do a job the same way every day if the steps in the job are repeated over and over. Learning an entirely new set of steps makes the job more difficult. For the same amount of return (pay), most people prefer to do easier rather than harder work.

Security Some employees like the comfort and security of doing things the same old way. They gain a feeling of constancy and safety from knowing that some things stay the same despite all the change going on around them. People who believe their security is threatened by a change are likely to resist the change.

Economic Factors Change may threaten employees' steady paychecks. Workers may fear that change will make their jobs obsolete or reduce their opportunities for future pay increases.

Fear of the Unknown Some people fear anything unfamiliar. Changes in reporting relationships and job duties create anxiety for such employees. Employees become familiar with their bosses and their jobs and develop relationships with others within the organization, such as contact people for various situations. These relationships and contacts help facilitate their work. Any disruption of familiar patterns may create fear because it can cause delays and foster the belief that nothing is getting accomplished.

Lack of Awareness Because of perceptual limitations such as lack of attention or selective attention, a person may not recognize a change in a rule or procedure and thus may not alter his or her behavior. People may pay attention only to things that support their point of view. As an example, employees in an isolated regional sales office may not notice—or may ignore—directives from headquarters regarding a change in reporting procedures for expense accounts. They may therefore continue the current practice as long as possible.

Social Factors People may resist change for fear of what others will think. As we mentioned before, the group can be a powerful motivator of behavior. Employees may believe change will hurt their image, result in ostracism from the group, or simply make them "different." For example, an employee who agrees to conform to work rules established by management may be ridiculed by others who openly disobey the rules.

MANAGING SUCCESSFUL ORGANIZATION CHANGE AND DEVELOPMENT

In conclusion, we offer seven keys to managing change in organizations. They relate directly to the problems identified earlier and to our view of the organization as a comprehensive social system. Each can influence the elements of the social system and may help the organization avoid some of the major problems in managing the change. Table 19.4 lists the points and their potential impacts.

Consider Global Issues

One factor to consider is how global issues dictate organization change. As we have already noted, the environment is a significant factor in bringing about organization change. Given the additional environmental complexities multinational organizations face, it follows that organization change may be even more critical to them than it is to purely domestic organizations. Dell Computer, for example, owes much of its success to its original strategy of selling directly to consumers. Since 2006, however, it has expanded its distribution activities to include retail sales, and significant system-wide change has eased the company's entry into some key foreign markets.[51]

A second point to remember is that acceptance of change varies widely around the globe. Change is a normal and accepted part of organization life in some cultures. In

Table 19.4 Keys to Managing Successful Organization Change and Development

KEY	IMPACT
Consider global issues.	Keeps in touch with the latest global developments and how change is handled in different cultures
Take a holistic view of the organization.	Helps anticipate the effects of change on the social system and culture
Start small.	Works out details and shows the benefits of the change to those who might resist
Secure top-management support.	Gets dominant coalition on the side of change: safeguards structural change, heads off problems of power and control
Encourage participation by those affected by the change.	Minimizes transition problems of control, resistance, and task redefinition
Foster open communication.	Minimizes transition problems of resistance and information and control systems
Reward those who contribute to change.	Minimizes transition problems of resistance and control systems

other cultures, change causes many more problems. Managers should remember that techniques for managing change that have worked routinely back home may not work at all and may even trigger negative responses if used indiscriminately in other cultures.[52]

Take a Holistic View

Managers must take a holistic view of the organization and the change project. A limited view can endanger the change effort because the subsystems of the organization are interdependent. A holistic view encompasses the culture and dominant coalition as well as the people, tasks, structure, and information subsystems.

Start Small

Peter Senge claims that every truly successful, system-wide change in large organizations starts small.[53] He recommends that change start with one team, usually an executive team. One team can evaluate the change, make appropriate adjustments along the way, and, most importantly, show that the new system works and gets desired results. If the change makes sense, it begins to spread to other teams, groups, and divisions throughout the system. Senge described how significant changes at Shell and Ford started small, with one or two parallel teams, and then spread as others recognized the benefits of the change. When others see the benefits, they automatically drop their inherent resistance and join in. They can voluntarily join and be committed to the success of the change effort.

Secure Top Management Support

The support of top management is essential to the success of any change effort. As the organization's probable dominant coalition, it is a powerful element of the social system, and its support is necessary to deal with control and power problems. For example, a manager who plans a change in the ways in which tasks are assigned and responsibility is delegated in his or her department must notify top management and gain its support. Complications may arise if disgruntled employees complain to high-level managers who have not been notified of the change or do not support it. The employees' complaints may jeopardize the manager's plan—and perhaps her or his job.

Encourage Participation

Problems related to resistance, control, and power can be overcome by broad participation in planning the change. Allowing people a voice in designing the change may give them a sense of power and control over their own destinies, which may help to win their support during implementation.

Foster Open Communication

Open communication is an important factor in managing resistance to change and overcoming information and control problems during transitions. Employees typically recognize the uncertainties and ambiguities that arise during a transition and seek information on the change and their place in the new system. In the absence of information, the gap may be filled with inappropriate or false information, which may endanger the change process. Rumors tend to spread through the grapevine faster than accurate information can be disseminated through official channels. A manager should always be sensitive to the effects of uncertainty on employees, especially during a period of change; any news, even bad news, seems better than no news.

Reward Contributors

Although this last point is simple, it can easily be neglected. Employees who contribute to the change in any way need to be rewarded. Too often, the only people acknowledged after a change effort are those who tried to stop it. Those who quickly grasp new work assignments, work harder to cover what otherwise might not get done during the transition, or help others adjust to changes deserve special credit—perhaps a mention in a news release or the internal company newspaper, special consideration in a performance appraisal, a merit raise, or a promotion. From a behavioral perspective, individuals need to benefit in some way if they are to willingly help change something that eliminates the old, comfortable way of doing the job.

In the current dynamic environment, managers must anticipate the need for change and satisfy it with more responsive and competitive organization systems. These seven keys to managing organization change may also serve as general guidelines for managing organizational behavior because organizations must change or face elimination.

SYNOPSIS

Change may be forced on an organization, or an organization may change in response to the environment or an internal need. Forces for change are interdependent and influence organizations in many ways. Currently, the areas in which the pressures for change seem most powerful involve people, technology, information processing and communication, competition, and social trends.

Planned organization change involves anticipating change and preparing for it. Lewin described organization change in terms of unfreezing, the change itself, and refreezing. In the continuous change process model, top management recognizes forces encouraging change, engages in a problem-solving process to design the change, and implements and evaluates the change.

Organization development is the process of planned change and improvement of organizations through the application of knowledge of the behavioral sciences. It is based on a systematic change process and focuses on managing the culture of the organization. The most comprehensive change involves altering the structure of the organization through reorganization of departments, reporting relationships, or authority systems.

Quality-of-work-life programs focus on providing a work environment in which employees can satisfy individual needs. Task and technological changes alter the way the organization accomplishes its primary tasks. Along with the steps usually associated with change, task redesign entails diagnosis, cost-benefit analysis, formulation of a redesign strategy, and implementation of supplemental changes.

Frequently used group and individual approaches to organization change are training and management development programs, team building, and survey feedback techniques. Training programs are usually designed to improve employees' job skills, to help employees adapt to other organization changes (such as a management-by-objectives program), or to develop employees' awareness and understanding of problems such as workplace safety or stress. Management development programs attempt to foster in current or future managers the skills, abilities, and perspectives important to good management. Team-building programs are designed to help a work team or group develop into a mature, functioning team by helping it define its goals or priorities, analyze its tasks and the way they are performed, and examine relationships among the people doing the work. As used in the organization development process, survey feedback techniques involve gathering data, analyzing and summarizing them, and returning them to employees and groups for discussion and to identify and solve problems.

Resistance to change may arise from several individual and organizational sources. Resistance may indicate a legitimate concern that the change is not good for the organization and may warrant a reexamination of plans.

To manage change in organizations, international issues must be considered, and managers should take a holistic view of the organization and start small. Top management support is needed, and those most affected by the change must participate. Open communication is important, and those who contribute to the change effort should be rewarded.

DISCUSSION QUESTIONS

1. Is most organization change forced on the organization by external factors or fostered from within? Explain.
2. What broad category of pressures for organization change other than the four discussed in the chapter can you think of? Briefly describe it.
3. Which sources of resistance to change present the most problems for an internal change agent? For an external change agent?
4. Which stage of the Lewin model of change do you think is most often overlooked? Why?
5. What are the advantages and disadvantages of having an internal change agent rather than an external change agent?
6. How does organization development differ from organization change?
7. How and why would organization development differ if the elements of the social system were not interdependent?
8. Do quality-of-work-life programs rely more on individual or organizational aspects of organizational behavior? Why?
9. Describe how the job of your professor could be redesigned. Include a discussion of other subsystems that would need to be changed as a result.
10. Which of the seven keys for successfully managing an organizational change effort seem to be the most difficult to manage? Why?

HOW DO YOU SEE IT?

The More Things Change

"And then you say, 'Yes,' and they say, 'No,' and you say, 'Yes—this is how.'"

—MIKEY LEBLANC, COFOUNDER OF HOLDEN OUTERWEAR

Mikey LeBlanc, a professional snowboarder, and Scott Zergebel, a clothing designer, founded Holden Outerwear in 2002 to make pants and jackets for snowboarders. Today, the product line is much broader.* Holden clothing, says LeBlanc, is suitable if "you go snowboarding or skiing, or you just might be in New York City on a rainy day, or it's negative 20 in Quebec, and you just want to feel good."

He attributes the company's success to its strategy of staying ahead of the industry-wide fashion curve. "We've been kind of labeled as … the brand that pushes the style portion of technical outerwear," he says. "… When Holden came out, we were the new and improved outerwear. For the first five or six years … a lot of our accounts [came] in and they [said], 'I can't wait to see the collection. What have you done this year? What new fabrics, what new designs do you have?'" The approach worked, and Holden found itself in the position of being first to market with new designs. "It really affected the industry," recalls LeBlanc. "We had competitors at our big shows, showing pieces in their lines as 'This is our Holden piece.' 'This is our Holden-esque garment.'"

"That's probably what I love most about LeBlanc and Zergebel," says Design and Development Manager Nikki Brush. "The fact that they take cues from fashion and that they're not looking at what everyone else in the outerwear market is doing. They're looking at high fashion and figuring out a way to apply it to a garment that someone would wear up on the hill." She took the job with Holden, says Brush, because "I wanted to do something creative and something that was never the same and that always changed."

Holden is no doubt nimble when it comes to implementing new ideas because it is a small company whose competitive edge depends on differentiating its product on the basis of innovations in style. There are, however, certain obstacles to overcome when you're a small buyer in your market. "We're a small brand," admits LeBlanc. "… We don't own factories. We don't own fabric mills. We can't *fill* a factory [with orders]." So how does Holden deal with its relative lack of leverage in its supply chain?† "We've gotta have really great relationships with all of our vendors," says LeBlanc.

In the beginning, he recalls, "Scott and I wanted to make a natural-fiber, waterproof, breathable fabric which didn't exist…. Every time we'd meet with a fabric supplier, we would say, 'Do you have anything natural, waterproof, breathable?' And they're like, 'Okay, you're crazy.'" Holden had to take the lead in developing the fabric it wanted, and it took three years to come up with just the right "hemp-poly mix" and to locate a mill that was willing to make it. But "we won a ton of awards for it," says LeBlanc, "and we had our major competitors again chasing us right after that."

"That's how we do our business," says Brush. "[We're] able to push our vendors in ways that they aren't pushed. That's how we come up with something new." Granted, she adds, "it's definitely getting harder and harder to push our vendors to do new developments. Costs are going up, and they don't want to develop something that may not get used" by additional clients.

According to LeBlanc, the key to negotiating with factories and mills is jump-starting their own creative capacities:

> *We may go with a new design that they've never seen, and they're like, "Well, that's not possible." And then you say, "Yes," and they say, "No," and you say, "Yes—this is how." And then they're like, "Wow! Cool!" And then their brains start working, and they're like, "Wow, this is great. This is something new our factory can do and offer to other people."*

Not surprisingly, admits LeBlanc, Holden has gone through "a ton of vendors." For Brush, however, the need for constant give-and-take with different suppliers is just another means of keeping her creative energy at a high level: "I have a pretty solid background in both development and design"—thus her job title—"so I actually do get excited about technology and working with the fabric mill or garment manufacturer on taking something that everyone does every day and doing it slightly different." She is also interested in the marketing angle—"how are we going to do it different and how are we going to present it to the market in a way that's still acceptable and functional."

For LeBlanc, at least one aspect of the outerwear market was easy to figure out from the beginning: "The industry," he says, "loves change." So when Holden came out with products that looked "radically different, the industry really embraced it. And also [competing] brands embraced it. They've all basically followed suit.... A lot of brands have followed Holden's lead and gone down that [same] fashion route."

Unfortunately, he adds, a competitive edge can also be a double-edged sword: "There's a lot of ways that people can rip you off," he admits, but he has learned to accept that drawback as part of the cost of doing business the Holden way: "We turn over designs ... and that's the fun thing about Holden.... We're not reacting to current business [trends]. We actually like creating stuff every year. New things. That'll always be part of Holden, and if people want to copy us, they're probably going to sell a lot of pieces. So I don't blame them."

CASE QUESTIONS

1. Holden came into being because its founders wanted to change the type of products offered by a certain industry. Of the four *forces for change* discussed in the chapter—*people, technology, information processing and communication*, and *competition*—which have been the most important in driving strategy at Holden? Rank the four in order of importance and be specific in explaining the role of each in Holden's strategy.
2. What kinds of *internal* changes will Holden probably need to make over time—and especially as it continues to *grow*—in order to maintain and adapt its current strategy? What role is each of the four forces for change likely to play in this process, both in prompting these changes and in presenting challenges to implementing them?
3. What about you? What would your *quality of work life* be in an organization like Holden? Would you, like Nikki Brush, be happy doing "something that was never the same and that always changed"? Or would you prefer doing something that was a little more predictable on a regular basis? Which type of organization would be more likely to foster your morale and productivity? Also consider Figure 19.3. Which of the following factors would probably play a role in determining—or changing—your preference: *growth and security, development of human capacities, total life space, social relevance*?
4. Once again, bear in mind the fact that Holden came into existence to implement changes in an industry. Now consider the criteria for including and excluding strategies for change under the concept of *organizational development (OD)*—for example, planned versus haphazard changes, intrinsic versus imitative changes, behavior-driven versus technology-driven changes. How can OD criteria be used to describe the motives behind the creation of Holden, its continuing approach to fostering change, or both?

ADDITIONAL SOURCES

Holden Outerwear, "Holden History" (2012), www.holdenouterwear.com on June 5, 2012; Scott Zergebel, "My Inspiration Comes from Trying to Live My Life to the Fullest," *SIA's Latest*, March 28, 2012, www.snowsports.com on June 5, 2012; "Holden Gets Sporty," *YoBeat.com*, January 4, 2012, www.yobeat.com on June 5, 2012; Allan Brettman, "Holden Outerwear Exits Portland in Search of New Markets, Lower Expenses," *OregonLive.com*, May 2, 2012, http://blog.oregonlive.com on June 5, 2012.

*Holden is also the subject of *Video Case 2*, which discusses the company's background and business practices, and *Video Case 10*, which focuses on its teamwork approach to product development.

†Recall our definition of a *supply chain* in *Video Case 14* as the chain of operations stretching from an organization's purchase of needed resources to the sale of its finished products to consumers.

EXPERIENCING ORGANIZATIONAL BEHAVIOR

Planning a Change at the University

Purpose: This exercise will help you understand the complexities of change in organizations.

Format: Your task is to plan the implementation of a major change in an organization.

Procedure:

Part 1

The class will divide into five groups of approximately equal size. Your instructor will assign each group one of the following changes:

1. A change from the semester system to the quarter system (or the opposite, depending on the school's current system)
2. A requirement that all work—homework, examinations, term papers, problem sets—be done on computers and submitted via computers
3. A requirement that all students live on campus
4. A requirement that all students have reading, writing, and speaking fluency in at least three languages, including English and Japanese, to graduate
5. A requirement that all students room with someone in the same major

First, decide what individuals and groups must be involved in the change process. Then decide how the change will be implemented using Lewin's process of organization change (Figure 19.1) as a framework. Consider how to deal with resistance to change, using Tables 19.3 and 19.4 as guides. Decide whether a change agent (internal or external) should be used. Develop a realistic timetable for full implementation of the change. Is transition management appropriate?

Part 2

Using the same groups as in Part 1, your next task is to describe the techniques you would use to implement the change described in Part 1. You may use structural changes, task and technology methods, group and individual programs, or any combination of these. You may need to go to the library to gather more information on some techniques.

You should also discuss how you will utilize the seven keys to successful change management discussed at the end of the chapter.

Your instructor may make this exercise an in-class project, but it is also a good semester-ending project for groups to work on outside of class. Either way, the exercise is most beneficial when the groups report their implementation programs to the entire class. Each group should report on which change techniques are to be used, why they were selected, how they will be implemented, and how problems will be avoided.

Follow-Up Questions

Part 1

1. How similar were the implementation steps for each change?
2. Were the plans for managing resistance to change realistic?
3. Do you think any of the changes could be successfully implemented at your school? Why or why not?

Part 2

1. Did various groups use the same technique in different ways or to accomplish different goals?
2. If you did outside research on organization development techniques for your project, did you find any techniques that seemed more applicable than those in this chapter? If so, describe one of them.

BUILDING MANAGERIAL SKILLS

Exercise Overview: Diagnostic skills, which enable a manager to visualize the most appropriate response to a situation, are especially important during periods of organizational change.

Exercise Background: You are the general manager of a hotel situated along a beautiful stretch of beach on a tropical island. One of the oldest of six large resorts in the immediate area, your hotel is owned by a group of foreign investors. For several years, it has been operated as a franchise unit of a large international hotel chain, as are all of the other hotels on the island.

For the past few years, the hotel's franchisee-owners have been taking most of the profits for themselves and putting relatively little back into the hotel. They have also let you know that their business is not in good financial health and that the revenue from the hotel is being used to offset losses incurred elsewhere. In contrast, most of the other hotels on the island have recently been refurbished, and plans for two brand-new hotels have been announced for the near future.

A team of executives from franchise headquarters has just visited your hotel. They are quite disappointed in the property, particularly because it has failed to keep pace with other resorts on the island. They have informed you that if the property is not brought up to standards, the franchise agreement, which is up for review in a year, will be revoked. You realize that this move would be a potential disaster because you cannot afford to lose the franchisor's brand name or access to its reservation system.

Sitting alone in your office, you identified several seemingly viable courses of action:

1. Convince the franchisee-owners to remodel the hotel. You estimate that it will take $5 million to meet the franchisor's minimum standards and another $5 million to bring the hotel up to the standards of the top resort on the island.
2. Convince the franchisor to give you more time and more options for upgrading the facility.
3. Allow the franchise agreement to terminate and try to succeed as an independent hotel.
4. Assume that the hotel will fail and start looking for another job. You have a pretty good reputation but are not terribly happy about the possibility of having to accept a lower-level position (say, as an assistant manager) with another firm.

Having mulled over your options, do the following:

1. Rank-order your four alternatives in terms of probable success. Make any necessary assumptions.
2. Identify alternatives other than those that you have identified above.
3. Ask yourself: Can more than one alternative be pursued simultaneously? Which ones?
4. Develop an overall strategy for trying to save the hotel while protecting your own interests.

SELF-ASSESSMENT EXERCISE

Support for Change

Introduction: The following questions are designed to help people understand the level of support for or opposition to change within an organization. Scores on this scale should be used for classroom discussion only.

Instructions: Think of an organization for which you have worked in the past or an organization to which you currently belong and consider the situation when a change was imposed at some point in the recent past. Then circle the number that best represents your feeling about each statement or question.

1. Values and Vision
(Do people throughout the organization share values or vision?)

1 2 3 4 5 6 7
Low High

2. History of Change
(Does the organization have a good track record in handling change?)

1 2 3 4 5 6 7
Low High

3. Cooperation and Trust
(Do they seem high throughout the organization?)

1 2 3 4 5 6 7
Low High

4. Culture
(Is it one that supports risk taking and change?)

1 2 3 4 5 6 7
Low High

5. Resilience
(Can people handle more?)

1 2 3 4 5 6 7
Low High

6. Rewards
(Will this change be seen as beneficial?)

1 2 3 4 5 6 7
Low High

7. Respect and Face
(Will people be able to maintain dignity and self-respect?)

1	2	3	4	5	6	7
Low						High

8. Status Quo
(Will this change be seen as mild?)

1	2	3	4	5	6	7
Low						High

A Guide to Scoring and explanation is available in the *Instructor's Resource Manual.*

Reference: From Rick Maurer, *Beyond the Wall of Resistance,* 1996 (Austin, TX: Bard Press), pp. 104–105. Used by permission of Bard Press.

Notes

Chapter 1

1. For a classic discussion of the meaning of organizational behavior, see Larry Cummings, "Toward Organizational Behavior," *Academy of Management Review*, January 1978, pp. 90–98. See also Nigel Nicholson, Pino Audia, and Madan Pillutla (eds.), *The Blackwell Encyclopedia of Management Vol. 11, Organizational Behavior* (London: Blackwell Publishing, 2005).
2. "The World's Most Admired Companies," *Fortune*, March 20, 2012, pp. 135–140.
3. Mauro F. Guillen, "The Age of Eclecticism: Current Organizational Trends and the Evolution of Managerial Models," *Sloan Management Review*, Fall 1994, pp. 75–86; see also Jason Colquitt and Cindy Zapata-Phelan, "Trends in Theory Building and Theory Testing: A Five-Decade Study of the *Academy of Management Journal*," *Academy of Management Journal*, 2007, vol. 50, no. 6, pp. 1281–1303.
4. Henry Mintzberg, "The Manager's Job: Folklore and Fact," *Harvard Business Review*, July–August 1975, pp. 49–61.
5. Robert L. Katz, "The Skills of an Effective Administrator," *Harvard Business Review*, September–October 1987, pp. 90–102; see also Morten Hansen, Herminia Ibarra, and Urs Peyer, "The Best-Performing CEOs in the World," *Harvard Business Review*, January–February 2010, pp. 104–113.
6. "SBC Chief Says Deal Preserves an 'Icon,'" *USA Today*, February 1, 2005, pp. 1B, 2B.
7. "Most Important Qualities for a CEO," *USA Today*, March 11, 2002, p. A1.
8. Max Bazerman, "Conducting Influential Research: The Need for Prescriptive Implications," *Academy of Management Review*, January 2005, pp. 25–31; see also Gary Latham, "A Speculative Perspective on the Transfer of Behavioral Science Findings to the Workplace: 'The Times They Are A-Changin,'" *Academy of Management Journal*, 2007, vol. 50, no. 5, pp. 1027–1032.
9. Joseph W. McGuire, "Retreat to the Academy," *Business Horizons*, July–August 1982, pp. 31–37; Kenneth Thomas and Walter G. Tymon, "Necessary Properties of Relevant Research: Lessons from Recent Criticisms of the Organizational Sciences," *Academy of Management Review*, July 1982, pp. 345–353. See also Jeffrey Pfeffer, "The Theory-Practice Gap: Myth or Reality?" *Academy of Management Executive*, February 1987, pp. 31–32; and R. Duane Ireland and David Ketchen, "Interesting Problems and Interesting Research: A Path to Effective Exchanges Between Managers and Scholars," *Business Horizons*, January–February 2008, pp. 65–62.
10. Fremont Kast and James Rosenzweig, "General Systems Theory: Applications for Organization and Management," *Academy of Management Journal*, December 1972, pp. 447–465.
11. See Fremont Kast and James Rozenzweig (eds.), *Contingency Views of Organization and Management* (Chicago: SRA, 1973), for a classic overview and introduction.

12. James Terborg, "Interactional Psychology and Research on Human Behavior in Organizations," *Academy of Management Review*, October 1981, pp. 569–576; Benjamin Schneider, "Interactional Psychology and Organizational Behavior," in Larry Cummings and Barry Staw (eds.), *Research in Organizational Behavior*, vol. 5 (Greenwich, CT: JAI Press, 1983), pp. 1–32; Daniel B. Turban and Thomas L. Keon, "Organizational Attractiveness: An Interactionist Perspective," *Journal of Applied Psychology*, 1993, vol. 78, no. 2, pp. 184–193.

Chapter 2

1. See Adrienne Fox, "At Work in 2020," *HR Magazine*, January 2010, pp. 18–23.
2. M. J. Gent, "Theory X in Antiquity, or the Bureaucratization of the Roman Army," *Business Horizons*, January–February 1984, pp. 53–54.
3. Ricky Griffin and Michael Pustay, *International Business*, 7th ed. (Upper Saddle River, NJ: Prentice Hall, 2012).
4. Ya-Ru Chen, Kwok Leung, and Chao C. Chen, "Bringing National Culture to the Table: Making a Difference with Cross-Cultural Differences and Perspectives," in James Walsh and Arthur Brief (eds.), *The Academy of Management Annals*, vol. 3 (London: Routledge, Taylor & Francis Group, 2009), pp. 217–250. See also Miriam Erez, "Cross-Cultural and Global Issues In Organizational Psychology," in Sheldon Zedeck (ed.), *Handbook of Industrial and Organizational Psychology* (Washington, DC: American Psychological Association, 2010).
5. Simcha Ronen and Oded Shenkar, "Clustering Countries on Attitudinal Dimension: A Review and Synthesis," *Academy of Management Review*, July 1985, pp. 435–454.
6. Nancy J. Adler, Robert Doktor, and Gordon Redding, "From the Atlantic to the Pacific Century," *Journal of Management*, Summer 1986, pp. 295–318.
7. Tamotsu Yamaguchi, "The Challenge of Internationalization," *Academy of Management Executive*, February 1988, pp. 33–36; see also Anne Tsui, "From Homogenization to Pluralism in International Management," *Academy of Management Journal*, 2007, vol. 50, no. 6, pp. 1353–1364.
8. Geert Hofstede, *Culture's Consequences: International Differences in Work-Related Values* (Beverly Hills, CA: Sage Publications, 1980).
9. André Laurent, "The Cultural Diversity of Western Conceptions of Management," *International Studies of Management and Organization*, Spring–Summer 1983, pp. 75–96.
10. Michael L. Wheeler, "Diversity: Making the Business Case," *Business Week*, April 14, 2007; special advertising section.
11. For example, see Joshua Sacco and Neal Schmitt, "A Dynamic Multilevel Model of Demographic Diversity and Misfit Effects," *Journal of Applied Psychology*, 2005, vol. 90, no. 2, pp. 203–232.
12. See Scott Page, "Making the Difference: Applying a Logic of Diversity," *Academy of Management Perspectives*, 2007, vol. 21, no. 4, pp. 6–20.
13. Loden and Rosener, *Workforce America!: Managing Employee Diversity as a Vital Resource* (Homewood, IL: Business One Irwin, 1991), p. 19.
14. Howard N. Fullerton Jr. and Mitra Toossi, "Labor Force Projections to 2010: Steady Growth and Changing Composition," *Monthly Labor Review*, November 2006, pp. 24–35.
15. Ibid, p. 22.
16. Harish C. Jain and Anil Verma, "Managing Workforce Diversity for Competitiveness: The Canadian Experience," *International Journal of Manpower*, April–May 1996, pp. 14–30.
17. "Plenty of Muck, Not Much Money," *Economist*, May 8, 1999, p. 52.
18. Ron Corben, "Thailand Faces a Shrinking Work Force," *Journal of Commerce and Commercial*, December 26, 1996, p. 5a.
19. Susan Meisinger, "Diversity: More Than Just Representation," *HR Magazine*, January 2008, p. 8.
20. Wheeler, "Diversity: Making the Business Case."
21. Orland Richard, B. P. S. Murthi, and Kiran Ismail, "The Impact of Racial Diversity on Intermediate and Long-Term Performance: The Moderating Role of Environmental Context," *Strategic Management Journal*, 2007, vol. 28, no. 12, pp. 1213–1233.
22. Sujin K. Horwitz and Irwin B. Horwitz, "The Effects of Team Diversity on Team Outcomes: A Meta-Analytic Review of Team Demography," *Journal of Management*, 2007, vol. 33, no. 6, pp. 987–1015.
23. See Adrienne Fox, "At Work in 2020," *HR Magazine*, January 2010, pp. 18–23.

24. Employment Projections: 2010–2020 Summary, U.S. Bureau of Labor Statistics, May 2, 2012.
25. Josh Quittner, "The Future of Reading," *Fortune*, March 1, 2010, pp. 62–67.
26. "CareerBuilder Releases Annual List of the Most Unusual Excuses for Calling in Sick, According to U.S. Employers," *CareerBuilder*, October 27, 2010.
27. "Chains' Ties Run Deep on Pharmacy Boards," *USA Today*, December 31, 2008, pp. 1B, 2B.
28. Jeremy Kahn, "Presto Chango! Sales Are Huge," *Fortune*, March 20, 2000, pp. 90–96; "More Firms Falsify Revenue to Boost Stocks," *USA Today*, March 29, 2000, p. 1B.
29. "Diamond Foods Restating Profits After an Audit," *Bloomberg Businessweek*, February 13–February 19, 2012, p. 28.
30. "U.S. Probes Hilton Over Theft Claims," *Wall Street Journal*, April 22, 2009, pp. B1, B4.
31. "Walmart's Discounted Ethics," *Time*, May 7, 2012, p. 19.
32. "How U.S. Concerns Compete in Countries Where Bribes Flourish," *Wall Street Journal*, September 29, 1995, pp. A1, A14; Patricia Digh, "Shades of Gray in the Global Marketplace," *HR Magazine*, April 1997, pp. 90–98.
33. "Alcoa Faces Allegation by Bahrain of Bribery," *Wall Street Journal*, February 28, 2009, p. A2.
34. "How to Fix Corporate Governance," *Business Week*, May 6, 2002, pp. 68–78.
35. Max Boisot, *Knowledge Assets* (Oxford: Oxford University Press, 1998).
36. M. L. Tushman and C. A. O'Reilly, *Winning Through Innovation* (Cambridge, MA: Harvard Business School Press, 1996).
37. M. A. Von Glinow, *The New Professionals* (Cambridge, MA: Ballinger, 1988).
38. T. W. Lee and S. D. Maurer, "The Retention of Knowledge Workers with the Unfolding Model of Voluntary Turnover," *Human Resource Management Review*, 1997, vol. 7, pp. 247–276.
39. G. T. Milkovich, "Compensation Systems in High-Technology Companies," in A. Klingartner and C. Anderson (eds.), *High Technology Management* (Lexington, MA: Lexington Books, 1987).
40. http://www.hewittassociates.com/OutsourcingStudy_2009_Results.pdf, March 21, 2010
41. Rita Zeidner, "Heady Debate—Rely on Temps or Hire Staff?" *HR Magazine*, February 2010, pp. 28–33.
42. "Harley Union Makes Concessions," *Wall Street Journal*, December 3, 2009, p. B3.
43. "Ford to Begin Hiring at New Lower Wages," *Wall Street Journal*, January 26, 2010, p. B1.

Chapter 3

1. Denise M. Rousseau and Judi McLean Parks, "The Contracts of Individuals and Organizations," in Larry L. Cummings and Barry M. Staw (eds.), *Research in Organizational Behavior*, vol. 15 (Greenwich, CT: JAI Press, 1993), pp. 1–43. See also Denise M. Rousseau, "The Individual-Organization Relationship: The Psychological Contract," in Sheldon Zedeck (Ed.), *Handbook of Industrial and Organizational Psychology* (Washington, DC: American Psychological Association, 2010).
2. Denise M. Rousseau, "Changing the Deal While Keeping the People," *Academy of Management Executive*, February 1996, pp. 50–58; see also Violet Ho, "Social Influence on Evaluations of Psychological Contract Fulfillment," *Academy of Management Review*, January 2005, pp. 113–128.
3. Richard A. Guzzo, Katherine A. Noonan, and Efrat Elron, "Expatriate Managers and the Psychological Contract," *Journal of Applied Psychology*, vol. 79, no. 4, pp. 617–626.
4. Amy L. Kristof, "Person–Organization Fit: An Integrative Review of Its Conceptualizations, Measurement, and Implications," *Personnel Psychology*, Spring 1996, pp. 1–49.
5. Oleksandr S. Chernyshenko, Stephen Stark, and Fritz Drasgow, "Individual Differences: Their Measurement and Validity," in Sheldon Zedeck (Ed.), *Handbook of Industrial and Organizational Psychology* (Washington, DC: American Psychological Association, 2010).
6. See Dan McAdams and Bradley Olson, "Personality Development: Continuity and Change Over the Life Course," in Susan Fiske, Daniel Schacter, and Robert Sternberg (Eds.), *Annual Review of Psychology*, vol. 61 (Palo Alto, CA: Annual Reviews, 2010), pp. 517–542.
7. M. R. Barrick and M. K. Mount, "The Big Five Personality Dimensions and Job Performance: A Meta-Analysis," *Personnel Psychology*, 1991, vol. 44, pp. 1–26.
8. See Daniel Goleman, *Emotional Intelligence: Why It Can Matter More Than IQ* (New York: Bantam Books, 1995).

9. Daniel Goleman, "Leadership That Gets Results," *Harvard Business Review*, March–April 2000, pp. 78–90.
10. J. B. Rotter, "Generalized Expectancies for Internal vs. External Control of Reinforcement," *Psychological Monographs*, 1966, vol. 80, pp. 1–28; Bert De Brabander and Christopher Boone, "Sex Differences in Perceived Locus of Control," *Journal of Social Psychology*, 1990, vol. 130, pp. 271–276.
11. See Jeffrey Vancouver, Kristen More, and Ryan Yoder, "Self-Efficacy and Resource Allocation: Support for a Nonmonotic, Discontinuous Model," *Journal of Applied Psychology*, 2008, vol. 93, no. 1, pp. 35–47.
12. T. W. Adorno, E. Frenkel-Brunswick, D. J. Levinson, and R. N. Sanford, *The Authoritarian Personality* (New York: Harper & Row, 1950).
13. "The Rise and Fall of Dennis Kozlowski," *Business Week*, December 23, 2002, pp. 64–77.
14. Patricia C. Smith, L. M. Kendall, and Charles Hulin, *The Measurement of Satisfaction in Work and Behavior* (Chicago: Rand-McNally, 1969).
15. Linda Grant, "Happy Workers, High Returns," *Fortune*, January 12, 1998, p. 81.
16. See Timothy Judge, Carl Thoresen, Joyce Bono, and Gregory Patton, "The Job-Satisfaction–Job Performance Relationship: A Qualitative and Quantitative Review," *Psychological Bulletin*, 2001, vol. 127, no. 3, pp. 376–407.
17. James R. Lincoln, "Employee Work Attitudes and Management Practice in the U.S. and Japan: Evidence from a Large Comparative Study," *California Management Review*, Fall 1989, pp. 89–106.
18. See Michael Riketta, "Attitudinal Organizational Commitment and Job Performance: A Meta-Analysis," *Journal of Organizational Behavior*, 2002, vol. 23, no. 3, pp. 257–266; see also Omar Solinger, Woody van Olffen, and Robert Roe, "Beyond the Three-Component Model of Organizational Commitment," *Journal of Applied Psychology*, 2008, vol. 93, no. 1, pp. 70–83.
19. Lincoln, "Employee Work Attitudes and Management Practice."
20. Leslie E. Palich, Peter W. Hom, and Roger W. Griffeth, "Managing in the International Context: Testing Cultural Generality of Sources of Commitment to Multinational Enterprises," *Journal of Management*, 1995, vol. 21, no. 4, pp. 671–690.
21. For an example of research in this area, see Jennifer M. George and Gareth R. Jones, "The Experience of Mood and Turnover Intentions: Interactive Effects of Value Attainment, Job Satisfaction, and Positive Mood," *Journal of Applied Psychology*, 1996, vol. 81, no. 3, pp. 318–325. For a recent review, see Arthur P. Brief and Howard M. Weiss, "Organizational Behavior: Affect in the Workplace," in *Annual Review of Psychology*, vol. 53 (Palo Alto, CA: Annual Reviews, 2002), pp. 279–307.
22. See Wei-Chi Tsai, Chien-Cheng Chen, and Hui-Lu Liu, "Test of a Model Linking Employee Positive Moods and Task Performance," *Journal of Applied Psychology*, 2007, vol. 92, no. 6, pp. 1570–1583.
23. "One Man's Accident Is Shedding New Light on Human Perception," *Wall Street Journal*, September 30, 1993, pp. A1, A13.
24. William H. Starbuck and John M. Mezias, "Opening Pandora's Box: Studying the Accuracy of Managers' Perceptions," *Journal of Organizational Behavior*, 1996, vol. 17, pp. 99–117.
25. Mark J. Martinko and William L. Gardner, "The Leader/Member Attribution Process," *Academy of Management Review*, April 1987, pp. 235–249; Jeffrey D. Ford, "The Effects of Causal Attributions on Decision Makers' Responses to Performance Downturns," *Academy of Management Review*, October 1985, pp. 770–786.
26. See Peter Hom, Loriann Roberson, and Aimee Ellis, "Challenging Conventional Wisdom About Who Quits: Revelations from Corporate America," *Journal of Applied Psychology*, 2008, vol. 93, no. 1, pp. 1–34; see also Jean Martin and Conrad Schmidt, "How to Keep Your Top Talent," *Harvard Business Review*, May 2010, pp. 54–61.
27. "Chick-fil-A Cuts Job Turnover Rates," *Houston Chronicle*, January 9, 2002, p. B3.
28. Christine Porath and Christine Pearson, "The Cost of Bad Behavior," *Organizational Dynamics*, January–March 2010, pp. 64–71.
29. See Anne O'Leary-Kelly, Ricky W. Griffin, and David J. Glew, "Organization-Motivated Aggression: A Research Framework," *Academy of Management Review*, January 1996, pp. 225–253; see also Ramona Paetzold, Anne O'Leary-Kelly, and Ricky W. Griffin, "Workplace Violence, Employer Liability, and Implications for

Organizational Research," *Journal of Management Inquiry*, 2007, vol. 16, no. 4, pp. 362–370.

30. See Dennis W. Organ, "Personality and Organizational Citizenship Behavior," *Journal of Management*, 1994, vol. 20, no. 2, pp. 465–478. For more recent information, see Jeffrey LePine, Amir Erez, and Diane Johnson, "The Nature and Dimensionality of Organizational Citizenship Behavior: A Critical Review and Meta-Analysis," *Journal of Applied Psychology*, 2002, vol. 87, no. 1, pp. 52–65; and Mark Bolino and William Turnley, "Going the Extra Mile: Cultivating and Managing Employee Citizenship Behavior," *Academy of Management Executive*, 2003, vol. 17, no. 3, pp. 60–70.

Chapter 4

1. See Craig Pinder, *Work Motivation in Organizational Behavior*, 2nd ed. (Upper Saddle River, NJ: Prentice Hall, 2008). See also Robert Lord, James Diefendorff, Aaron Schmidt, and Rosalie Hall, "Self-Regulation at Work," in Susan Fiske, Daniel Schacter, and Robert Sternberg (Eds.), *Annual Review of Psychology*, vol. 61 (Palo Alto: Annual Reviews, 2010), pp. 543–568; and James M. Diefendorff and Megan M. Chandler, "Motivating Employees," in Sheldon Zedeck (Ed.), *Handbook of Industrial and Organizational Psychology* (Washington, DC: American Psychological Association, 2010).
2. Richard M. Steers, Gregory A. Bigley, and Lyman W. Porter, *Motivation and Leadership at Work*, 7th ed. (New York: McGraw-Hill, 2002). See also Ruth Kanfer, "Motivational Theory and Industrial and Organizational Psychology," in M. D. Dunnette and L. M. Hough (Eds.), *Handbook of Industrial and Organizational Psychology*, 2nd ed., vol. 1 (Palo Alto, CA: Consulting Psychologists Press), pp. 75–170; and M. L. Ambrose, "Old Friends, New Faces: Motivation Research in the 1990s," *Journal of Management*, 1999, vol. 25, no. 2, pp. 110–131.
3. Roland E. Kidwell Jr. and Nathan Bennett, "Employee Propensity to Withhold Effort: A Conceptual Model to Intersect Three Avenues of Research," *Academy of Management Review*, July 1993, pp. 429–456; see also Adam Grant, "Does Intrinsic Motivation Fuel the Prosocial Fire? Motivational Synergy in Predicting Persistence, Performance, and Productivity," *Journal of Applied Psychology*, 2008, vol. 93, no. 1, pp. 48–58.
4. Jeffrey Pfeiffer, *The Human Equation* (Boston: Harvard Business School Press, 1998).
5. See Adrienne Fox, "Raising Engagement," *HR Magazine*, May 2010, pp. 35–40.
6. E. L. Deci and R. M. Ryan, "The 'What' and 'Why' of Goal Pursuits: Human Needs and the Self-Determination of Behavior," *Psychological Inquiry*, 2000, vol. 11, no. 4, pp. 227–269.
7. Frederick W. Taylor, *Principles of Scientific Management* (New York: Harper, 1911).
8. Elton Mayo, *The Social Problems of an Industrial Civilization* (Boston: Harvard University Press, 1945); Fritz J. Rothlisberger and W. J. Dickson, *Management and the Worker* (Boston: Harvard University Press, 1939).
9. Gerald R. Salancik and Jeffrey Pfeiffer, "An Examination of Need-Satisfaction Models of Job Attitudes," *Administrative Science Quarterly*, September 1977, pp. 427–456.
10. Teresa Amabile and Steven Kramer, "What Really Motivates Workers," *Harvard Business Review*, January–February 2010, pp. 44–45.
11. Abraham H. Maslow, "A Theory of Human Motivation," *Psychological Review*, 1943, vol. 50, pp. 370–396; Abraham H. Maslow, *Motivation and Personality* (New York: Harper & Row, 1954). Maslow's most famous works include Abraham Maslow, Deborah C. Stephens, and Gary Heil, *Maslow on Management* (New York: John Wiley and Sons, 1998); and Abraham Maslow and Richard Lowry, *Toward a Psychology of Being* (New York: John Wiley and Sons, 1999).
12. See "Professionals Sick of Old Routine Find Healthy Rewards in Nursing," *USA Today*, August 16, 2004, pp. 1B, 2B.
13. See Nancy Adler, *International Dimensions of Organizational Behavior*, 5th ed. (Cincinnati, OH: Southwestern Publishing, 2007).
14. Mahmond A. Wahba and Lawrence G. Bridwell, "Maslow Reconsidered: A Review of Research on the Need Hierarchy Theory," *Organizational Behavior and Human Performance*, April 1976, pp. 212–240.
15. Clayton P. Alderfer, *Existence, Relatedness, and Growth* (New York: Free Press, 1972).
16. Ibid.

17. Frederick Herzberg, Bernard Mausner, and Barbara Synderman, *The Motivation to Work* (New York: John Wiley and Sons, 1959); Frederick Herzberg, "One More Time: How Do You Motivate Employees?" *Harvard Business Review*, January–February 1968, pp. 53–62.
18. Herzberg, Mausner, and Synderman, *The Motivation to Work*.
19. Ibid.
20. Ibid.
21. Ricky W. Griffin, *Task Design: An Integrative Approach* (Glenview, IL: Scott, Foresman, 1982).
22. Pinder, *Work Motivation in Organizational Behavior*.
23. Frederick Herzberg, *Work and the Nature of Man* (Cleveland, OH: World, 1966); Valerie M. Bookman, "The Herzberg Controversy," *Personnel Psychology*, Summer 1971, pp. 155–189; Benedict Grigaliunas and Frederick Herzberg, "Relevance in the Test of Motivation-Hygiene Theory," *Journal of Applied Psychology*, February 1971, pp. 73–79.
24. Marvin Dunnette, John Campbell, and Milton Hakel, "Factors Contributing to Job Satisfaction and Job Dissatisfaction in Six Occupational Groups," *Organizational Behavior and Human Performance*, May 1967, pp. 143–174; Charles L. Hulin and Patricia Smith, "An Empirical Investigation of Two Implications of the Two-Factor Theory of Job Satisfaction," *Journal of Applied Psychology*, October 1967, pp. 396–402.
25. Adler, *International Dimensions of Organizational Behavior*.
26. David McClelland, *The Achieving Society* (Princeton, NJ: Nostrand, 1961). See also David C. McClelland, *Human Motivation* (Cambridge, UK: Cambridge University Press, 1988).
27. Michael J. Stahl, "Achievement, Power, and Managerial Motivation: Selecting Managerial Talent with the Job Choice Exercise," *Personnel Psychology*, Winter 1983, pp. 775–790.
28. Stanley Schachter, *The Psychology of Affiliation* (Palo Alto, CA: Stanford University Press, 1959).
29. As reported in "Best Friends Good for Business," *USA Today*, December 1, 2004, pp. 1B, 2B.
30. David McClelland and David H. Burnham, "Power Is the Great Motivator," *Harvard Business Review*, March–April 1976, pp. 100–110.
31. Pinder, *Work Motivation in Organizational Behavior*; McClelland and Burnham, "Power Is the Great Motivator."
32. J. Stacy Adams, "Toward an Understanding of Inequity," *Journal of Abnormal and Social Psychology*, November 1963, pp. 422–436. See also Richard T. Mowday, "Equity Theory Predictions of Behavior in Organizations," in Richard M. Steers and Lyman W. Porter (Eds.), *Motivation and Work Behavior*, 4th ed. (New York: McGraw-Hill, 1987), pp. 89–110.
33. Priti Pradham Shah, "Who Are Employees' Social Referents? Using a Network Perspective to Determine Referent Others," *Academy of Management Journal*, 1998, vol. 41, no. 3, pp. 249–268.
34. J. Stacy Adams, "Inequity in Social Exchange," in L. Berkowitz (Ed.), *Advances in Experimental Social Psychology*, vol. 2 (New York: Academic Press, 1965), pp. 267–299.
35. Pinder, *Work Motivation in Organizational Behavior*.
36. See Kerry Sauler and Arthur Bedeian, "Equity Sensitivity: Construction of a Measure and Examination of Its Psychometric Properties," *Journal of Management*, 2000, vol. 26, no. 5, pp. 885–910; Mark Bing and Susan Burroughs, "The Predictive and Interactive Effects of Equity Sensitivity in Teamwork-Oriented Organizations," *Journal of Organizational Behavior*, 2001, vol. 22, pp. 271–290.
37. Victor Vroom, *Work and Motivation* (New York: John Wiley and Sons, 1964).
38. Lyman W. Porter and Edward E. Lawler, *Managerial Attitudes and Performance* (Homewood, IL: Dorsey Press, 1968).
39. See Terence R. Mitchell, "Expectancy Models of Job Satisfaction, Occupational Preference, and Effort: A Theoretical, Methodological, and Empirical Appraisal," *Psychological Bulletin*, 1974, vol. 81, pp. 1096–1112; and John P. Campbell and Robert D. Pritchard, "Motivation Theory in Industrial and Organizational Psychology," in Marvin D. Dunnette (Ed.), *Handbook of Industrial and Organizational Psychology* (Chicago, IL: Rand McNally, 1976), pp. 63–130, for reviews.
40. Pinder, *Work Motivation and Organizational Behavior*.
41. Ibid.
42. Campbell and Pritchard, "Motivation Theory in Industrial and Organizational Psychology."
43. Adler, *International Dimensions of Organizational Behavior*.

44. David A. Nadler and Edward E. Lawler, "Motivation: A Diagnostic Approach," in J. Richard Hackman, Edward E. Lawler, and Lyman W. Porter (Eds.), *Perspectives on Behavior in Organizations*, 2nd ed. (New York: McGraw-Hill, 1983), pp. 67–78; see also Anne Fisher, "Turning Clock-Watchers into Stars," *Fortune*, March 22, 2004, p. 60.
45. Ivan P. Pavlov, *Conditional Reflexes* (New York: Oxford University Press, 1927).
46. Albert Bandura, "Social Cognitive Theory: An Agentic Perspective," *Annual Review of Psychology*, 2001, vol. 52, pp. 1–26.
47. B. F. Skinner, *Science and Human Behavior* (New York: Macmillian, 1953); and B. F. Skinner, *Beyond Freedom and Dignity* (New York: Knopf, 1972).
48. Fred Luthans and Robert Kreitner, *Organizational Behavior Modification and Beyond* (Glenview, IL: Scott, Foresman, 1985).
49. Telis Demos, "Motivate Without Spending Millions," *Fortune*, April 12, 2010, pp. 37–38.
50. See Richard Arvey and John M. Ivancevich, "Punishment in Organizations: A Review, Propositions, and Research Suggestions," *Academy of Management Review*, April 1980, pp. 123–132, for a review of the literature on punishment; see also Leanne Atwater, Joan Brett, and Atira Cherise Charles, "The Delivery of Workplace Discipline: Lessons Learned," *Organizational Dynamics*, 2007, vol. 36, no. 4, pp. 392–403.
51. Fred Luthans and Robert Kreitner, *Organizational Behavior Modification* (Glenview, IL: Scott Foresman, 1975); Luthans and Kreitner, *Organizational Behavior Modification and Beyond.*
52. Alexander D. Stajkovic, "A Meta-Analysis of the Effects of Organizational Behavior Modification on Task Performance, 1975–95," *Academy of Management Journal*, 1997, vol. 40, no. 5, pp. 1122–1149.
53. "At Emery Air Freight: Positive Reinforcement Boosts Performance," *Organizational Dynamics*, Winter 1973, pp. 41–50; W. Clay Hamner and Ellen P. Hamner, "Organizational Behavior Modification on the Bottom Line," *Organizational Dynamics*, Spring 1976, pp. 3–21.
54. Hamner and Hamner, "Organizational Behavior Modification on the Bottom Line."
55. Edwin Locke, "The Myths of Behavior Mod in Organizations," *Academy of Management Review*, 1977, vol. 2, pp. 543–553.

Chapter 5

1. Ricky W. Griffin and Gary C. McMahan, "Motivation Through Job Design," in Jerald Greenberg (Ed.), *Organizational Behavior: State of the Science* (New York: Lawrence Erlbaum and Associates, 1994), pp. 23–44; see also Adam M. Grant, Yitzhak Fried, and Tina Juillerat, "Work Matters: Job Design in Classic and Contemporary Perspectives," in Sheldon Zedeck (Ed.), *Handbook of Industrial and Organizational Psychology* (Washington, DC: American Psychological Association, 2010), pp. 417–453.
2. Frederick W. Taylor, *The Principles of Scientific Management* (New York: Harper & Row, 1911).
3. C. R. Walker and R. Guest, *The Man on the Assembly Line* (Cambridge, MA: Harvard University Press, 1952).
4. Jia Lin Xie and Gary Johns, "Job Scope and Stress: Can Job Scope Be Too High?" *Academy of Management Journal*, 1995, vol. 38, no. 5, pp. 1288–1309.
5. Ricky W. Griffin, *Task Design: An Integrative Approach* (Glenview, IL: Scott, Foresman, 1982).
6. H. Conant and M. Kilbridge, "An Interdisciplinary Analysis of Job Enlargement: Technology, Cost, Behavioral Implications," *Industrial and Labor Relations Review*, 1965, vol. 18, no. 7, pp. 377–395.
7. Frederick Herzberg, "One More Time: How Do You Motivate Employees?" *Harvard Business Review*, January–February 1968, pp. 53–62; Frederick Herzberg, "The Wise Old Turk," *Harvard Business Review*, September–October 1974, pp. 70–80.
8. R. N. Ford, "Job Enrichment Lessons from AT&T," *Harvard Business Review*, January–February 1973, pp. 96–106.
9. E. D. Weed, "Job Enrichment 'Cleans Up' at Texas Instruments," in J. R. Maher (Ed.), *New Perspectives in Job Enrichment* (New York: Van Nostrand, 1971).
10. Griffin, *Task Design*; Griffin and McMahan, "Motivation Through Job Design."
11. J. Richard Hackman and Greg Oldham, "Motivation Through the Design of Work: Test of a Theory," *Organizational Behavior and Human Performance*, 1976, vol. 16, pp. 250–279. See also Michael A. Campion and Paul W. Thayer, "Job Design: Approaches, Outcomes, and Trade-Offs," *Organizational Dynamics*, Winter 1987, pp. 66–78.

12. J. Richard Hackman, "Work Design," in J. Richard Hackman and J. L. Suttle (Eds.), *Improving Life at Work: Behavioral Science Approaches to Organizational Change* (Santa Monica, CA: Goodyear, 1977).
13. Griffin, *Task Design*.
14. Griffin, *Task Design*. See also Karlene H. Roberts and William Glick, "The Job Characteristics Approach to Task Design: A Critical Review," *Journal of Applied Psychology*, 1981, vol. 66, pp. 193–217; and Ricky W. Griffin, "Toward an Integrated Theory of Task Design," in Larry L. Cummings and Barry M. Staw (Eds.), *Research in Organizational Behavior* (Greenwich, CT: JAI Press, 1987), vol. 9, pp. 79–120.
15. Ricky W. Griffin, M. Ann Welsh, and Gregory Moorhead, "Perceived Task Characteristics and Employee Performance: A Literature Review," *Academy of Management Review*, October 1981, pp. 655–664.
16. See Timothy Butler and James Waldroop, "Job Sculpting," *Harvard Business Review*, September–October 1999, pp. 144–152; see also the recent special issue of the *Journal of Organizational Behavior* (vol. 31, no. 2–3, February 2010) devoted entirely to job design.
17. David J. Glew, Anne M. O'Leary-Kelly, Ricky W. Griffin, and David D. Van Fleet, "Participation in Organizations: A Preview of the Issues and Proposed Framework for Future Analysis," *Journal of Management*, 1995, vol. 21, no. 3, pp. 395–421; for a recent update, see Russ Forrester, "Empowerment: Rejuvenating a Potent Idea," *Academy of Management Executive*, 2002, vol. 14, no. 1, pp. 67–78.
18. John A. Wagner III, "Participation's Effects of Performance and Satisfaction: A Reconsideration of Research Evidence," *Academy of Management Review*, 1994, vol. 19, no. 2, pp. 312–330.
19. Elizabeth George and Carmen Kaman Ng, "Nonstandard Workers: Work Arrangements and Outcomes," in Sheldon Zedeck (Ed.), *Handbook of Industrial and Organizational Psychology* (Washington, DC: American Psychological Association, 2010), pp. 573–596.
20. A. R. Cohen and H. Gadon, *Alternative Work Schedules: Integrating Individual and Organizational Needs* (Reading, MA: Addison-Wesley, 1978); see also Ellen Ernst Kossek and Jesse S. Michel, "Flexible Work Schedules," in Sheldon Zedeck (Ed.), *Handbook of Industrial and Organizational Psychology* (Washington, DC: American Psychological Association, 2010), pp. 535–572.
21. "100 Best Companies to Work For 2012," www.fortune.com on July 28, 2012.
22. See Barbara Rau and MaryAnne Hyland, "Role Conflict and Flexible Work Arrangements: The Effects on Applicant Attraction," *Personnel Psychology*, 2002, vol. 55, no. 1, pp. 111–136.
23. "Working 9-to-5 No Longer," *USA Today*, December 6, 2004, pp. 1B, 2B.
24. "5 Flextime-Friendly Companies," Jobs & Job Search Advice, Employment & Careers, December 18, 2009, www.careerbuilder.com/Article/CB-632-Job-Search-Strategies-5-Flextime-Friendly-Companies on July 28, 2012.
25. "100 Best Companies to Work For 2012," www.fortune.com on July 28, 2012.
26. See Carolyn Hirschman, "Share and Share Alike," *HR Magazine*, September 2005, pp. 52–57.
27. For a recent analysis, see Sumita Raghuram, Raghu Garud, Batia Wiesenfeld, and Vipin Gupta, "Factors Contributing to Virtual Work Adjustment," *Journal of Management*, 2001, vol. 27, pp. 383–405.
28. See Ravi Gajendran and David Harrison, "The Good, the Bad, and the Unknown About Telecommuting: Meta-Analysis of Psychological Mediators and Individual Consequences," *Journal of Applied Psychology*, 2007, vol. 92, no. 6, pp. 1524–1541.

Chapter 6

1. Jon R. Katzenbach and Jason A. Santamaria, "Firing Up the Front Line," *Harvard Business Review*, May–June 1999, pp. 107–117.
2. A. Bandura, *Social Learning Theory* (Englewood Cliffs, NJ: Prentice Hall, 1977).
3. See Edwin A. Locke, "Toward a Theory of Task Performance and Incentives," *Organizational Behavior and Human Performance*, 1968, vol. 3, pp. 157–189.
4. Gary P. Latham and Gary Yukl, "A Review of Research on the Application of Goal Setting in Organizations," *Academy of Management Journal*, 1975, vol. 18, pp. 824–845.
5. Gary P. Latham and J. J. Baldes, "The Practical Significance of Locke's Theory of Goal Setting,"

Journal of Applied Psychology, 1975, vol. 60, pp. 187–191.

6. Gary P. Latham, "The Importance of Understanding and Changing Employee Outcome Expectancies for Gaining Commitment to an Organizational Goal," *Personnel Psychology*, 2001, vol. 54, pp. 707–720.
7. See Anthea Zacharatos, Julian Barling, and Roderick Iverson, "High-Performance Work Systems and Occupational Safety," *Journal of Applied Psychology*, vol. 90, no. 1, January 2005, pp. 77–94.
8. H. John Bernardin and Richard W. Beatty, *Performance Appraisal: Assessing Human Behavior at Work* (Boston: Kent, 1984); see also Jessica L. Wildman, Wendy L. Bedwell, Eduardo Salas, and Kimberly A. Smith-Jentsch, "Performance Measurement at Work: A Multilevel Perspective," in Sheldon Zedeck (Ed.), *Handbook of Industrial and Organizational Psychology* (Washington, DC: American Psychological Association, 2010), pp. 303–341.
9. See Bruce Pfau and Ira Kay, "Does 360-Degree Feedback Negatively Affect Company Performance?" *HR Magazine*, June 2002, pp. 54–59; see also Angelo S. DeNisi and Shirley Sonesh, "The Appraisal and Management of Performance at Work," in Sheldon Zedeck (Ed.), *Handbook of Industrial and Organizational Psychology* (Washington, DC: American Psychological Association, 2010), pp. 255–279.
10. Joan Brett and Leanne Atwater, "360° Feedback: Accuracy, Reactions, and Perceptions of Usefulness," *Journal of Applied Psychology*, 2001, vol. 86, no. 5, pp. 930–942; Terry Beehr, Lana Ivanitskaya, Curtiss Hansen, Dmitry Erofeev, and David Gudanowski, "Evaluation of 360-Degree Feedback Ratings: Relationships with Each Other and with Performance and Selection Predictors," *Journal of Organizational Behavior*, 2001, vol. 22, pp. 775–788.
11. Vanessa Urch Druskat and Steven B. Wolff, "Effects and Timing of Developmental Peer Appraisals in Self-Managing Work Groups," *Journal of Applied Psychology*, 1999, vol. 84, no. 1, pp. 58–74.
12. Joanne Sammer, "Calibrating Consistency," *HR Magazine*, January 2008, pp. 73–78.
13. See Robert Kaplan and David Norton, *The Balanced Scorecard: Translating Strategy Into Action* (Cambridge, MA: Harvard Business Review Press, 1996); and Robert Kaplan and David Norton, *Alignment: Using the Balanced Scorecard to Create Corporate Synergies* (Cambridge, MA: Harvard Business Review Press, 2006).
14. See Edward E. Lawler, *Pay and Organization Development* (Reading, MA: Addison-Wesley, 1981); see also Joseph J. Martocchio, "Strategic Reward and Compensation Plans," in Sheldon Zedeck (Ed.), *Handbook of Industrial and Organizational Psychology* (Washington, DC: American Psychological Association, 2010), pp. 343–372.
15. Brian Boyd and Alain Salamin, "Strategic Reward Systems: A Contingency Model of Pay System Design," *Strategic Management Journal*, 2001, vol. 22, pp. 777–792.
16. Alfred Rappaport, "New Thinking on How to Link Executive Pay with Performance," *Harvard Business Review*, March–April 1999, pp. 91–99; see also Cynthia Devers, Albert Cannella, Jr., Gregory Reilly, and Michele Yoder, "Executive Compensation: A Multidisciplinary Review of Recent Developments," *Journal of Management*, 2007, vol. 33, no. 6, pp. 1016–1072.
17. Steve Bates, "Piecing Together Executive Compensation," *HR Magazine*, May 2002, pp. 60–69.
18. "Welcome to Silicon Valley: Perksville, USA," *USA Today*, July 5, 2012, p. 1A.
19. "Rich Benefit Plan Gives GM Competitors Cost Edge," *Wall Street Journal*, March 21, 1996, pp. B1, B4.
20. "Painless Perks," *Forbes*, September 6, 1999, p. 138; see also "Does Rank Have Too Much Privilege?" *Wall Street Journal*, February 26, 2002, pp. B1, B4.
21. Charlotte Garvey, "Meaningful Tokens of Appreciation," *HR Magazine*, August 2004, pp. 101–106.
22. John R. Deckop, Robert Mangel, and Carol C. Cirka, "Getting More Than You Pay For: Organizational Citizenship Behavior and Pay-for-Performance Plans," *Academy of Management Journal*, 1999, vol. 42, no. 4, pp. 420–428.
23. "How Much is a CEO Worth?" *Bloomberg Businessweek*, May 10–May 16, 2010, pp. 70–72.
24. Charlotte Garvey, "Steering Teams with the Right Pay," *HR Magazine*, May 2002, pp. 70–80.

25. Andrea Poe, "Selection Savvy," *HR Magazine*, April 2002, pp. 77–80.
26. Ricky W. Griffin and Michael W. Pustay, *International Business—A Managerial Perspective*, 7th ed. (Upper Saddle River, NJ: Pearson, 2012).

Chapter 7

1. For a recent review, see Richard S. DeFrank and John M. Ivancevich, "Stress on the Job: An Executive Update," *Academy of Management Executive*, 1998, vol. 12, no. 3, pp. 55–65.
2. See James C. Quick and Jonathan D. Quick, *Organizational Stress and Preventive Management* (New York: McGraw-Hill, 1984), for a review. See also Mark A. Griffin and Sharon Clarke, "Stress and Well-Being at Work," in Sheldon Zedeck (Ed.), *Handbook of Industrial and Organizational Psychology* (Washington, DC: American Psychological Association, 2010), pp. 359–397.
3. "Job Stress Beginning to Take Toll on Some Airline Workers," *USA Today*, November 30, 2004, pp. 1B, 2B.
4. Hans Selye, *The Stress of Life* (New York: McGraw-Hill, 1976).
5. For example, see Steve M. Jex and Paul D. Bliese, "Efficacy Beliefs as a Moderator of the Impact of Work-Related Stressors: A Multilevel Study," *Journal of Applied Psychology*, 1999, vol. 84, no. 3, pp. 349–361.
6. Meyer Friedman and Ray H. Rosenman, *Type A Behavior and Your Heart* (New York: Knopf, 1974).
7. "Prognosis for the 'Type A' Personality Improves in a New Heart Disease Study," *Wall Street Journal*, January 14, 1988, p. 27.
8. Susan C. Kobasa, "Stressful Life Events, Personality, and Health: An Inquiry Into Hardiness," *Journal of Personality and Social Psychology*, January 1979, pp. 1–11; Susan C. Kobasa, S. R. Maddi, and S. Kahn, "Hardiness and Health: A Prospective Study," *Journal of Personality and Social Psychology*, January 1982, pp. 168–177.
9. Findings reported by Carol Kleiman, *Chicago Times*, March 31, 1988, p. B1.
10. Todd D. Jick and Linda F. Mitz, "Sex Differences in Work Stress," *Academy of Management Review*, October 1985, pp. 408–420; Debra L. Nelson and James C. Quick, "Professional Women: Are Distress and Disease Inevitable?" *Academy of Management Review*, April 1985, pp. 206–218.
11. "Complex Characters Handle Stress Better," *Psychology Today*, October 1987, p. 26.
12. Robert L. Kahn, D. M. Wolfe, R. P. Quinn, J. D. Snoek, and R. A. Rosenthal, *Organizational Stress: Studies in Role Conflict and Role Ambiguity* (New York: Wiley, 1964); see also David M. Sluss, Rolf van Dick, and Bryant S. Thompson, "Role Theory in Organizations: A Relational Perspective," in Sheldon Zedeck (Ed.), *Handbook of Industrial and Organizational Psychology* (Washington, DC: American Psychological Association, 2010), pp. 505–534.
13. David R. Frew and Nealia S. Bruning, "Perceived Organizational Characteristics and Personality Measures as Predictors of Stress/Strain in the Work Place," *Academy of Management Journal*, December 1987, pp. 633–646.
14. Thomas H. Holmes and Richard H. Rahe, "The Social Readjustment Rating Scale," *Journal of Psychosomatic Research*, 1967, vol. 11, pp. 213–218.
15. Evelyn J. Bromet, Mary A. Dew, David K. Parkinson, and Herbert C. Schulberg, "Predictive Effects of Occupational and Marital Stress on the Mental Health of a Male Workforce," *Journal of Organizational Behavior*, 1988, vol. 9, pp. 1–13.
16. Thomas Wright, "The Role of Psychological Well-Being in Job Performance, Employee Retention, and Cardiovascular Health," *Organizational Dynamics*, January–March 2010, pp. 13–23.
17. "I Can't Sleep," *Business Week*, January 26, 2004, pp. 66–74.
18. Edward Hallowell, "Why Smart People Underperform," *Harvard Business Review*, January 2005, pp. 54–62.
19. "Employers on Guard for Violence," *Wall Street Journal*, April 5, 1995, p. 3A; Joel H. Neuman and Robert A. Baron, "Workplace Violence and Workplace Aggression: Evidence Concerning Specific Forms, Potential Causes, and Preferred Targets," *Journal of Management*, 1998, vol. 24, no. 3, pp. 391–419.
20. Raymond T. Lee and Blake E. Ashforth, "A Meta-Analytic Examination of the Correlates of the Three Dimensions of Job Burnout," *Journal of Applied Psychology*, 1996, vol. 81, no. 2, pp. 123–133.

21. For a recent update, see Iain Densten, "Re-thinking Burnout," *Journal of Organizational Behavior*, 2001, vol. 22, pp. 833–847.
22. John M. Kelly, "Get a Grip on Stress," *HR Magazine*, February 1997, pp. 51–57.
23. John W. Lounsbury and Linda L. Hoopes, "A Vacation from Work: Changes in Work and Nonwork Outcomes," *Journal of Applied Psychology*, 1986, vol. 71, pp. 392–401.
24. "Overloaded Staffers Are Starting to Take More Time Off Work," *Wall Street Journal*, September 23, 1998, p. B1.
25. "Eight Ways to Help You Reduce the Stress in Your Life," *Business Week Careers*, November 1986, p. 78. See also Holly Weeks, "Taking the Stress out of Stressful Conversations," *Harvard Business Review*, July–August 2001, pp. 112–116.
26. See Marilyn Macik-Frey, James Campbell Quick, and Debra Nelson, "Advances in Occupational Health: From a Stressful Beginning to a Positive Future," *Journal of Management*, 2007, vol. 33. no. 6, pp. 809–840 for a recent review.
27. Richard A. Wolfe, David O. Ulrich, and Donald F. Parker, "Employee Health Management Programs: Review, Critique, and Research Agenda," *Journal of Management*, Winter 1987, pp. 603–615.
28. "Workplace Hazard Gets Attention," *USA Today*, May 5, 1998, pp. 1B, 2B.
29. "Recession Plans: More Benefits," *Time*, May 10, 2010, p. Global 8.
30. See Sonya Premeaux, Cheryl Adkins, and Kevin Mossholder, "Balancing Work and Family: A Field Study of Multi-Dimensional, Multi-Role, and Work-Family Conflict," *Journal of Organizational Behavior*, 2007, vol. 28, pp. 705–727.
31. "Work and Family," *Business Week*, September 15, 1997, pp. 96–99. See also Leslie B. Hammer and Kristi L. Zimmerman, "Quality of Work Life," in Sheldon Zedeck (Ed.), *Handbook of Industrial and Organizational Psychology* (Washington, DC: American Psychological Association, 2010), pp. 399–431.
32. Samuel Aryee, E. S. Srinivas, and Hwee Hoon Tan, "Rhythms of Life: Antecedents and Outcomes of Work-Family Balances in Employed Parents," *Journal of Applied Psychology*, 2005, vol. 90, no. 1, pp. 132–146.

Chapter 8

1. Herbert Simon, *The New Science of Management Decision* (New York: Harper & Row, 1960), p. 1.
2. See Philip Bromiley and Devaki Rau, "Strategic Decision Making," in Sheldon Zedeck (Ed.), *Handbook of Industrial and Organizational Psychology* (Washington, DC: American Psychological Association, 2010), pp. 161–182.
3. See Noel Tichy and Warren Bennis, *Judgement—How Winning Leaders Make Great Calls* (New York: Penguin Group, 2007).
4. Nandini Rajagopalan, Abdul M. A. Rasheed, and Deepak K. Datta, "Strategic Decision Processes: Critical Review and Future Directions," *Journal of Management*, Summer 1993, vol. 19, no. 2, pp. 349–384.
5. See George P. Huber, *Managerial Decision Making* (Glenview, IL: Scott, Foresman, 1980), pp. 90–115, for a discussion of decision making under conditions of certainty, risk, and uncertainty.
6. See David Garvin and Michael Roberto, "What You Don't Know About Making Decisions," *Harvard Business Review*, September 2001, pp. 108–115.
7. "'90s Style Brainstorming," *Forbes ASAP*, October 25, 1993, pp. 44–61.
8. Henry Mintzberg, Duru Raisinghani, and Andre Thoret, "The Structure of 'Unstructured' Decision Processes," *Administrative Science Quarterly*, June 1976, pp. 246–275; Milan Zeleny, "Descriptive Decision Making and Its Application," *Applications of Management Science*, 1981, vol. 1, pp. 327–388.
9. See E. Frank Harrison, *The Managerial Decision-Making Process*, 5th ed. (Boston: Houghton Mifflin, 1999), pp. 55–60, for more on choice processes.
10. Ari Ginsberg and N. Ventrakaman, "Contingency Perspectives of Organizational Strategy: A Critical Review of the Empirical Research," *Academy of Management Review*, July 1985, pp. 412–434; Donald C. Hambrick and David Lei, "Toward an Empirical Prioritization of Contingency Variables for Business Strategy," *Academy of Management Journal*, December 1985, pp. 763–788.
11. Leon Festinger, *A Theory of Cognitive Dissonance* (Palo Alto, CA: Stanford University Press, 1957).
12. See Harrison, *The Managerial Decision-Making Process*, pp. 74–100, for more on the rational approach to decision making.

13. Jeffrey Pfeffer and Robert I. Sutton, *Hard Facts, DangerousHalf-Truths, and Total Nonsense: Profiting from Evidence-Based Management* (Cambridge, MA: Harvard Business School Press, 2006).
14. Pfeffer and Sutton, 2006.
15. Herbert A. Simon, *Administrative Behavior* (New York: Free Press, 1945). Simon's ideas have been refined and updated in Herbert A. Simon, *Administrative Behavior*, 3rd ed. (New York: Free Press, 1976); and Herbert A. Simon, "Making Management Decisions: The Role of Intuition and Emotion," *Academy of Management Executive*, February 1987, pp. 57–63.
16. Craig D. Parks and Rebecca Cowlin, "Group Discussion as Affected by Number of Alternatives and by a Time Limit," *Organizational Behavior and Human Decision Processes*, 1995, vol. 62, no. 3, pp. 267–275.
17. See James G. March and Herbert A. Simon, *Organizations* (New York: Wiley, 1958), for more on the concept of bounded rationality.
18. Herbert A. Simon, *Administrative Behavior: A Study of Decision Making Processes in Administrative Organizations*, 3rd ed. (New York: Free Press, 1976).
19. Richard M. Cyert and James G. March, *A Behavioral Theory of the Firm* (Englewood Cliffs, NJ: Prentice Hall, 1963), p. 113; Simon, *Administrative Behavior*.
20. Hoover's *Handbook of American Business 2012* (Austin, TX: Hoover's Business Press, 2012), pp. 845–847.
21. Kimberly D. Elsbach and Greg Elofson, "How the Packaging of Decision Explanations Affects Perceptions of Trustworthiness," *Academy of Management Journal*, 2000, vol. 43, no. 1, pp. 80–89.
22. Tichy and Bennis, *Judgment*.
23. Charles P. Wallace, "Adidas—Back in the Game," *Fortune*, August 18, 1997, pp. 176–182.
24. Barry M. Staw and Jerry Ross, "Good Money after Bad," *Psychology Today*, February 1988, pp. 30–33; and D. Ramona Bobocel and John Meyer, "Escalating Commitment to a Failing Course of Action: Separating the Roles of Choice and Justification," *Journal of Applied Psychology*, 1994, vol. 79, pp. 360–363.
25. Mark Keil and Ramiro Montealegre, "Cutting Your Losses: Extricating Your Organization When a Big Project Goes Awry," *Sloan Management Review*, Spring 2000, pp. 55–64.
26. Gerry McNamara and Philip Bromiley, "Risk and Return in Organizational Decision Making," *Academy of Management Journal*, 1999, vol. 42, no. 3, pp. 330–339.
27. See Brian O'Reilly, "What it Takes to Start a Startup," *Fortune*, June 7, 1999, pp. 135–140, for an example.
28. Kahneman, Daniel, and Amos Tversky, "Prospect Theory: An Analysis of Decision under Risk," *Econometrica*, 1979, vol. 47, 263–291.
29. As described by Jordan Weissmann, "A Very Mean (but Maybe Brilliant) Way to Pay Teachers," *The Atlantic Monthly*, July 24, 2012, pp. 44–46.
30. Kathleen M. Eisenhardt, "Making Fast Strategic Decisions in High-Velocity Environments," *Academy of Management Journal*, September 1989, pp. 543–576.
31. Jing Zhou and Christina E. Shalley, "Deepening our Understanding of Creativity in the Workplace: A Review of Different Approaches to Creativity Research," in Sheldon Zedeck (Ed.), *Handbook of Industrial and Organizational Psychology* (Washington, DC: American Psychological Association, 2010), pp. 275–302
32. See Richard W. Woodman, John E. Sawyer, and Ricky W. Griffin, "Toward a Theory of Organizational Creativity," *Academy of Management Review*, April 1993, pp. 293–321; see also Beth Henessey and Teresa Amabile, "Creativity," in Susan Fiske, Daniel Schacter, and Robert Sternberg (Eds.), *Annual Review of Psychology*, vol. 61 (Palo Alto, CA: Annual Reviews, 2010), pp. 569–598.
33. John Simons, "The $10 Billion Pill," *Fortune*, January 20, 2003, pp. 58–68.
34. Christina E. Shalley, Lucy L. Gilson, and Terry C. Blum, "Matching Creativity Requirements and the Work Environment: Effects on Satisfaction and Intentions to Leave," *Academy of Management Journal*, 2000, vol. 43, no. 2, pp. 215–223; see also Filiz Tabak, "Employee Creative Performance: What Makes it Happen?" *The Academy of Management Executive*, vol. 11, no. 1, 1997, pp. 119–122.

Chapter 9

1. See John J. Gabarro, "The Development of Working Relationships," in Jay W. Lorsch (Ed.), *Handbook of Organizational Behavior* (Englewood Cliffs, NJ: Prentice Hall, 1987), pp. 172–189; see also Tara C. Reich and M. Sandy Hershcovis, "Interpersonal Relationships at Work," in

Sheldon Zedeck (Ed.), *Handbook of Industrial and Organizational Psychology* (Washington, DC: American Psychological Association, 2010), pp. 223–248.

2. See Emily Heaphy and Jane Dutton, "Positive Social Interactions and the Human Body at Work: Linking Organizations and Physiology," *Academy of Management Review*, 2008, vol. 33, no. 1, pp. 137–162.
3. See Richard McDermott and Douglas Archibald, "Harnessing Your Staff's Informal Networks," *Harvard Business Review*, March 2010, pp. 82–89.
4. Marvin E. Shaw, *Group Dynamics: The Psychology of Small Group Behavior*, 3rd ed. (New York: McGraw-Hill, 1991), p. 11. See also Janis A. Cannon-Bowers and Clint Bowers, "Team Development and Functioning," in Sheldon Zedeck (Ed.), *Handbook of Industrial and Organizational Psychology* (Washington, DC: American Psychological Association, 2010), pp. 597–650.
5. Francis J. Yammarino and Alan J. Dubinsky, "Salesperson Performance and Managerially Controllable Factors: An Investigation of Individual and Work Group Effects," *Journal of Management*, 1990, vol. 16, pp. 97–106.
6. Rob Cross and Laurence Prusak, "The People Who Make Organizations Go—Or Stop," *Harvard Business Review*, June 2002, pp. 104–114.
7. William L. Sparks, Dominic J. Monetta, and L. M. Simmons Jr., "Affinity Groups: Developing Complex Adaptive Organizations," working paper, The PAM Institute, Washington, DC, 1999.
8. Shawn Tully, "The Vatican's Finances," *Fortune*, December 21, 1997, pp. 29–40.
9. Bernard M. Bass and Edward C. Ryterband, *Organizational Psychology*, 2nd ed. (Boston: Allyn & Bacon, 1979), pp. 252–254. See also Scott Lester, Bruce Meglino, and M. Audrey Korsgaard, "The Antecedents and Consequences of Group Potency: A Longitudinal Investigation of Newly Formed Work Groups," *Academy of Management Journal*, 2002, vol. 45, no. 2, pp. 352–369.
10. Susan Long, "Early Integration in Groups: A Group to Join and a Group to Create," *Human Relations*, April 1994, pp. 311–332.
11. For example, see Mary Waller, Jeffrey Conte, Cristina Gibson, and Mason Carpenter, "The Effect of Individual Perceptions of Deadlines on Team Performance," *Academy of Management Review*, 2001, vol. 26, no. 4, pp. 596–600.
12. Steven L. Obert, "Developmental Patterns of Organizational Task Groups: A Preliminary Study," *Human Relations*, January 1993, pp. 37–52.
13. Bass and Ryterband, *Organizational Psychology*, pp. 252–254.
14. Bernard M. Bass, "The Leaderless Group Discussion," *Psychological Bulletin*, September 1954, pp. 465–492.
15. Jill Lieber, "Time to Heal the Wounds," *Sports Illustrated*, November 2, 1997, pp. 96–91.
16. Connie J. G. Gersick, "Marking Time: Predictable Transitions in Task Groups," *Academy of Management Journal*, 1999, vol. 32, pp. 274–309.
17. James H. Davis, *Group Performance* (Reading, MA: Addison-Wesley, 1964), pp. 92–96.
18. Shaw, *Group Dynamics*; see also Sujin K. Horwitz and Irwin B. Horwitz, "The Effects of Team Diversity on Team Outcomes: A Meta-Analytic Review of Team Demography," *Journal of Management*, 2007, vol. 33, no. 6, pp. 987–1015.
19. Susan E. Jackson and Aparna Joshi, "Work Team Diversity," in Sheldon Zedeck (Ed.), *Handbook of Industrial and Organizational Psychology* (Washington, DC: American Psychological Association, 2010), pp. 651–686.
20. Charles A. O'Reilly III, David F. Caldwell, and William P. Barnett, "Work Group Demography, Social Integration, and Turnover," *Administrative Science Quarterly*, March 1999, vol. 34, pp. 21–37.
21. See Sheila Simsarian Webber and Lisa Donahue, "Impact of Highly and Less Job-Related Diversity on Work Group Cohesion and Performance: A Meta-Analysis," *Journal of Management*, 2001, vol. 27, pp. 141–162.
22. Nancy Adler, *International Dimensions of Organizational Behavior*, 4th ed. (Cincinnati, OH: Thomson Learning, 2002), Chapter 5.
23. Shaw, *Group Dynamics*, pp. 173–177.
24. See Jennifer Chatman and Francis Flynn, "The Influence of Demographic Heterogeneity on the Emergence and Consequences of Cooperative Norms in Work Teams," *Academy of Management Journal*, 2001, vol. 44, no. 5, pp. 956–974.
25. Daniel C. Feldman, "The Development and Enforcement of Group Norms," *Academy of Management Review*, January 1994, pp. 47–53.
26. William E. Piper, Myriam Marrache, Renee Lacroix, Astrid M. Richardson, and Barry D. Jones, "Cohesion as a Basic Bond in Groups," *Human Relations*, February 1993, pp. 93–109.

27. Daniel Beal, Robin Cohen, Michael Burke, and Christy McLendon, "Cohesion and Performance in Groups: A Meta-Analytic Clarification of Construct Relations," *Journal of Applied Psychology*, 2003, vol. 88, no. 6, pp. 989–1004.
28. Robert T. Keller, "Predictors of the Performance of Project Groups in R & D Organizations," *Academy of Management Journal*, December 1996, pp. 715–726.
29. Irving L. Janis, *Groupthink*, 2nd ed. (Boston: Houghton Mifflin, 1992), p. 9.
30. Blake E. Ashforth and Fred Mael, "Social Identity Theory and the Organization," *Academy of Management Review*, January 1999, pp. 20–39.
31. Reed E. Nelson, "The Strength of Strong Ties: Social Networks and Intergroup Conflict in Organizations," *Academy of Management Journal*, June 1999, pp. 377–401.
32. M. A. Wallach, N. Kogan, and D. J. Bem, "Group Influence on Individual Risk Taking," *Journal of Abnormal and Social Psychology*, August 1962, pp. 75–86; James A. F. Stoner, "Risky and Cautious Shifts in Group Decisions: The Influence of Widely Held Values," *Journal of Experimental Social Psychology*, October 1968, pp. 442–459.
33. Dorwin Cartwright, "Risk Taking by Individuals and Groups: An Assessment of Research Employing Choice Dilemmas," *Journal of Personality and Social Psychology*, December 1971, pp. 361–378.
34. S. Moscovici and M. Zavalloni, "The Group as a Polarizer of Attitudes," *Journal of Personality and Social Psychology*, June 1969, pp. 125–135.
35. Irving L. Janis, *Groupthink*, 2nd ed. (Boston: Houghton Mifflin, 1982), p. 9.
36. Gregory Moorhead, Christopher P. Neck, and Mindy West, "The Tendency Toward Defective Decision Making Within Self-Managing Teams: Relevance of Groupthink for the 21st Century," *Organizational Behavior and Human Decision Processes*, February–March 1998, pp. 327–351.
37. Gregory Moorhead, Richard Ference, and Chris P. Neck, "Group Decision Fiascoes Continue: Space Shuttle Challenger and a Revised Groupthink Framework," *Human Relations*, 1991, vol. 44, pp. 539–550.
38. See Robert Cross and Susan Brodt, "How Assumptions of Consensus Undermine Decision Making," *Sloan Management Review*, Winter 2001, pp. 86–95.
39. Irving L. Janis, *Victims of Groupthink* (Boston: Houghton Mifflin, 1972), pp. 197–198.
40. Janis, *Groupthink*.
41. Lawrence J. Cohen and Anthony T. DeBenedet, M.D., "Penn State Cover-Up: Groupthink in Action." Time (http://ideas.time.com/2012/07/17/penn-state-cover-up-group-think-in-action/#ixzz2FVO7vAaI) July 17, 2012.
42. Janis, *Groupthink*, pp. 193–197; Gregory Moorhead, "Groupthink: Hypothesis in Need of Testing," *Group & Organization Studies*, December 1982, pp. 429–444.
43. Gregory Moorhead and John R. Montanari, "Empirical Analysis of the Groupthink Phenomenon," *Human Relations*, May 1986, pp. 399–410; John R. Montanari and Gregory Moorhead, "Development of the Groupthink Assessment Inventory," *Educational and Psychological Measurement*, Spring 1989, pp. 209–219.
44. Frederick W. Taylor, *The Principles of Scientific Management* (New York: Harper & Row, 1911).
45. Chris Argyris, *Personality and Organization* (New York: Harper & Row, 1957); Rensis Likert, *New Patterns of Management* (New York: McGraw-Hill, 1961).
46. Lester Coch and John R. P. French, "Overcoming Resistance to Change," *Human Relations*, 1948, vol. 1, pp. 512–532; N. C. Morse and E. Reimer, "The Experimental Change of a Major Organizational Variable," *Journal of Abnormal and Social Psychology*, January 1956, pp. 120–129.
47. Victor Vroom, "Leadership and the Decision-Making Process," *Organizational Dynamics*, Spring 2000, pp. 82–94.
48. For a recent example, see Carsten K. W. De Dreu and Michael West, "Minority Dissent and Team Innovation: The Importance of Participation in Decision Making," *Journal of Applied Psychology*, 2001, vol. 86, no. 6, pp. 1191–1201.

Chapter 10

1. Eric L. Trist and K. W. Bamforth, "Some Social and Psychological Consequences of the Longwall Method of Coal-Getting," *Human Relations*, February 1951, pp. 3–38; Jack D. Orsburn, Linda Moran, Ed Musselwhite, and John Zenger, *Self-Directed Work Teams: The New American Challenge* (Homewood, IL: Business One Irwin, 1990).
2. See Jon R. Katzenbach and Douglas K. Smith, *The Wisdom of Teams: Creating the High-Performance*

Organization (Boston: Harvard Business School Press, 1993), p. 45.

3. See Ruth Wageman, "How Leaders Foster Self-Managing Team Effectiveness: Design Choices Versus Hands-On Coaching," *Organization Science*, 2001, vol. 12, no. 5, pp. 559–577. See also Janis A. Cannon-Bowers and Clint Bowers, "Team Development and Functioning," in Sheldon Zedeck (Ed.), *Handbook of Industrial and Organizational Psychology* (Washington, DC: American Psychological Association, 2010), pp. 597–650.
4. See Michelle Marks, John Mathieu, and Stephen Zaccaro, "A Temporally Based Framework and Taxonomy of Team Processes," *Academy of Management Review*, 2001, vol. 26, no. 3, pp. 356–376.
5. Michele Williams, "In Whom We Trust: Group Membership as an Affective Context for Trust Development," *Academy of Management Review*, 2001, vol. 26, no. 3, pp. 377–396.
6. Katzenbach and Smith, *The Wisdom of Teams*, p. 3.
7. See Michelle Marks, Mark Sabella, C. Shawn Burke, and Stephen Zaccaro, "The Impact of Cross-Training on Team Effectiveness," *Journal of Applied Psychology*, 2002, vol. 87, no. 1, pp. 3–13.
8. See Ramon Rico, Miriam Sanchez-Manzanares, Francisco Gil, and Christina Gibson, "Team Implicit Knowledge Coordination Processes: A Team Knowledge-Based Approach," *Academy of Management Review*, 2008, vol. 33, no. 1, pp. 163–184.
9. Orsburn, Moran, Musselwhite, and Zenger, *Self-Directed Work Teams*, p. 15.
10. See Deborah Ancona, Henrik Bresman, and Katrin Kaeufer, "The Competitive Advantage of X-Teams," *Sloan Management Review*, Spring 2002, pp. 33–42.
11. Katzenbach and Smith, *The Wisdom of Teams*, pp. 184–189.
12. Manz and Sims, *Business Without Bosses*, pp. 10–11.
13. Manz and Sims, *Business Without Bosses*, pp. 74–76.
14. Jason Colquitt, Raymond Noe, and Christine Jackson, "Justice in Teams: Antecedents and Consequences of Procedural Justice Climate," *Personnel Psychology*, 2002, vol. 55, pp. 83–95.
15. Nigel Nicholson, Pino Audia, and Madan Pillutla (Eds.), *Encyclopedic Dictionary of Organizational Behavior*, 2nd ed. (Cambridge, MA: Blackwell, 2005), pp. 337–338.
16. Brian Dumaine, "The Trouble with Teams," *Fortune*, September 5, 1994.
17. Ibid.
18. Ibid.
19. Ibid.
20. Ellen Hart, "Top Teams," *Management Review*, February 1996, pp. 43–47.
21. Dan Dimancescu and Kemp Dwenger, "Smoothing the Product Development Path," *Management Review*, January 1996, pp. 36–41; see also "The World's 50 Most Innovative Companies," *Fast Company*, March 2008, pp. 72–117
22. Ibid.
23. Manz and Sims, *Business Without Bosses*, pp. 27–28.
24. Ibid., pp. 29–31.
25. Ibid., p. 130.
26. Manz and Sims, *Business Without Bosses*, p. 200; see also Sujin K. Horwitz and Irwin B. Horwitz, "The Effects of Team Diversity on Team Outcomes: A Meta-Analytic Review of Team Demography," *Journal of Management*, 2007, vol. 33, no. 6, pp. 987–1015.
27. Manz and Sims, *Business Without Bosses*, p. 200.

Chapter 11

1. Otis W. Baskin and Craig E. Aronoff, *Interpersonal Communication in Organizations* (Santa Monica, CA: Goodyear, 1980), p. 2. See also Marshall Scott Poole, "Communication," in Sheldon Zedeck (Ed.), *Handbook of Industrial and Organizational Psychology* (Washington, DC: American Psychological Association, 2010), pp. 249–270.
2. See Bruce Barry and Ingrid Smithey Fulmer, "The Medium and the Message: The Adaptive Use of Communication Media in Dyadic Influence," *Academy of Management Review*, 2004, vol. 29, no. 2, pp. 272–292.
3. Jeanne D. Maes, Teresa G. Weldy, and Marjorie L. Icenogle, "A Managerial Perspective: Oral Communication Competency Is Most Important for Business Students in the Workplace," *Journal of Business Communication*, January 1997, pp. 67–80.

4. Melinda Knight, "Writing and Other Communication Standards in Undergraduate Business Education: A Study of Current Program Requirements, Practices, and Trends," *Business Communication Quarterly*, March 1999, p. 10.
5. Robert Nurden, "Graduates Must Master the Lost Art of Communication," *The European*, March 20, 1997, p. 24.
6. See Everett M. Rogers and Rekha Agarwala-Rogers, *Communication in Organizations* (New York: Free Press, 1976), for a brief review of the background and development of the source-message-channel-receiver model of communication.
7. Charles A. O'Reilly III, "Variations in Decision Makers' Use of Information Sources: The Impact of Quality and Accessibility of Information," *Academy of Management Journal*, December 1982, pp. 756–771.
8. See Jerry C. Wofford, Edwin A. Gerloff, and Robert C. Cummins, *Organizational Communication* (New York: McGraw-Hill, 1977), for a discussion of channel noise.
9. Charlie Feld and Donna Stoddard, "Getting IT Right," *Harvard Business Review*, February 2005, pp. 72–81.
10. Kym France, "Computer Commuting Benefits Companies," *Arizona Republic*, August 16, 1993, pp. E1, E4.
11. "The FedEx Edge," *Fortune*, April 3, 2006, pp. 77–84.
12. Paul S. Goodman and Eric D. Darr, "Exchanging Best Practices Through Computer-Aided Systems," *Academy of Management Executive*, May 1996, pp. 7–18.
13. Jenny C. McCune, "The Intranet: Beyond E-mail," *Management Review*, November 1996, pp. 23–27.
14. See Daniel Katz and Robert L. Kahn, *The Social Psychology of Organizations*, 2nd ed. (New York: John Wiley and Sons, 1978), for more about the role of organizational communication networks.
15. For good discussions of small-group communication networks and research on this subject, see Wofford, Gerloff, and Cummins, *Organizational Communication*; and Marvin E. Shaw, *Group Dynamics: The Psychology of Small Group Behavior*, 3rd ed. (New York: McGraw-Hill, 1981), pp. 150–161.
16. See R. Wayne Pace, *Organizational Communication: Foundations for Human Resource Development* (Englewood Cliffs, NJ: Prentice Hall, 1983), for further discussion of the development of communication networks.
17. David Krackhardt and Lyman W. Porter, "The Snowball Effect: Turnover Embedded in Communication Networks," *Journal of Applied Psychology*, February 1986, pp. 50–55.
18. See "Did You Hear the Story About Office Gossip?" *USA Today*, September 10, 2007, pp. 1B, 2B.
19. "Has Coke Been Playing Accounting Games?" *Business Week*, May 13, 2002, pp. 98–99.
20. See "E-mail's Limits Create Confusion, Hurt Feelings," *USA Today*, February 5, 2002, pp. 1B, 2B.
21. "Talk of Chapter 11 Bruises Kmart Stock," *USA Today*, January 3, 2002, p. 1B.
22. Thomas J. Peters and Robert H. Waterman Jr., *In Search of Excellence: Lessons from America's Best-Run Companies* (New York: Harper & Row, 1982), p. 121.
23. Shari Caudron, "Monsanto Responds to Diversity," *Personnel Journal*, November 1990, pp. 72–78; "Trading Places at Monsanto," *Training and Development Journal*, April 1993, pp. 45–49.

Chapter 12

1. Ralph M. Stogdill, *Handbook of Leadership* (New York: Free Press, 1974). See also Bernard Bass and Ruth Bass, *Handbook of Leadership: Theory, Research, and Application*, 4th ed. (Riverside, NJ: Free Press, 2008); Noel Tichy and Warren Bennis, *Judgment: How Winning Leaders Make Great Calls* (New York: Portfolio Press, 2007); and Andrew J. Vinchur and Laura L. Koppes, "A Historical Survey of Research and Practice in Industrial and Organizational Psychology," in Sheldon Zedeck (Ed.), *Handbook of Industrial and Organizational Psychology* (Washington, DC: American Psychological Association, 2010), pp. 3–36.
2. See Gary Yukl and David D. Van Fleet, "Theory and Research on Leadership in Organizations," in M. D. Dunnette and L. M. Hough (Eds.), *Handbook of Industrial and Organizational Psychology*, vol. 3 (Palo Alto, CA: Consulting Psychologists Press, 1992), pp. 148–197. See also Bruce J. Avolio, Fred O. Walumbwa, and Todd J. Weber, "Leadership: Current Theories, Research, and Future Decisions," in Susan T. Fiske, Daniel

L. Schacter, and Robert J. Sternberg (Eds.), *Annual Review of Psychology 2009* (Palo Alto, CA: Annual Reviews, 2009), pp. 421–450.

3. Arthur G. Jago, "Leadership: Perspectives in Theory and Research," *Management Science*, March 1982, pp. 315–336. See also Julian Barling, Amy Christie, and Colette Hoption, "Leadership," in Sheldon Zedeck (Ed.), *Handbook of Industrial and Organizational Psychology* (Washington, DC: American Psychological Association, 2010), pp. 183–240.
4. Melvin Sorcher and James Brant, "Are You Picking the Right Leaders?" *Harvard Business Review*, February 2002, pp. 78–85.
5. See John P. Kotter, "What Leaders Really Do," *Harvard Business Review*, May–June 1990, pp. 103–111. See also Abraham Zaleznik, "Managers and Leaders: Are They Different?" *Harvard Business Review*, March–April 1992, pp.126–135; and John Kotter, "What Leaders Really Do," *Harvard Business Review*, December 2001, pp. 85–94.
6. Ronald Heifetz and Marty Linsky, "A Survival Guide for Leaders," *Harvard Business Review*, June 2002, pp. 65–74.
7. Frederick Reichheld, "Lead for Loyalty," *Harvard Business Review*, July–August 2001, pp. 76–83.
8. David D. Van Fleet and Gary A. Yukl, "A Century of Leadership Research," in D. A. Wren and J. A. Pearce II (Eds.), *Papers Dedicated to the Development of Modern Management* (Chicago, IL: The Academy of Management, 1986), pp. 12–23.
9. Shelly A. Kirkpatrick and Edwin A. Locke, "Leadership: Do Traits Matter?" *Academy of Management Executive*, May 1991, pp. 48–60; see also Robert J. Sternberg, "Managerial Intelligence: Why IQ Isn't Enough," *Journal of Management*, 1997, vol. 23, no. 3, pp. 475–493.
10. Philip M. Podsakoff, Scott B. MacKenzie, Mike Ahearne, and William H. Bommer, "Searching for a Needle in a Haystack: Trying to Identify the Illusive Moderators of Leadership Behaviors," *Journal of Management*, 1995, vol. 21, no. 3, pp. 422–470.
11. Rensis Likert, *New Patterns of Management* (New York: McGraw-Hill, 1961).
12. Edwin Fleishman, E. F. Harris, and H. E. Burtt, *Leadership and Supervision in Industry* (Columbus: Bureau of Educational Research, Ohio State University, 1955).
13. See Edwin A. Fleishman, "Twenty Years of Consideration and Structure," in Edward A. Fleishman and James G. Hunt (Eds.), *Current Developments in the Study of Leadership* (Carbondale, IL: Southern Illinois University Press, 1973), pp. 1–40.
14. Fleishman, Harris, and Burtt, *Leadership and Supervision in Industry.*
15. For a recent update, see Timothy Judge, Ronald Piccolo, and Remus Ilies, "The Forgotten Ones? The Validity of Consideration and Initiating Structure in Leadership Research," *Journal of Applied Psychology*, 2004, vol. 89, no. 1, pp. 36–51.
16. Robert R. Blake and Jane S. Mouton, *The Managerial Grid* (Houston, TX: Gulf Publishing, 1964); Robert R. Blake and Jane S. Mouton, *The Versatile Manager: A Grid Profile* (Homewood, IL: Dow Jones-Irwin, 1981).
17. Robert Tannenbaum and Warren H. Schmidt, "How to Choose a Leadership Pattern," *Harvard Business Review*, March–April 1958, pp. 95–101.
18. From Fred E. Fiedler, *A Theory of Leadership Effectiveness* (New York: McGraw-Hill, 1967). Reprinted by permission of the author.
19. See Fred E. Fiedler, "Engineering the Job to Fit the Manager," *Harvard Business Review*, September–October 1965, pp. 115–122.
20. See Fred E. Fiedler, Martin M. Chemers, and Linda Mahar, *Improving Leadership Effectiveness: The Leader Match Concept* (New York: John Wiley and Sons, 1976).
21. Chester A. Schriesheim, Bennett J. Tepper, and Linda A. Tetrault, "Least Preferred Co-Worker Score, Situational Control, and Leadership Effectiveness: A Meta-Analysis of Contingency Model Performance Predictions," *Journal of Applied Psychology*, 1994, vol. 79, no. 4, pp. 561–573.
22. See Martin G. Evans, "The Effects of Supervisory Behavior on the Path-Goal Relationship," *Organizational Behavior and Human Performance*, May 1970, pp. 277–298; Robert J. House, "A Path-Goal Theory of Leadership Effectiveness," *Administrative Science Quarterly*, September 1971, pp. 321–339; Robert J. House and Terence R. Mitchell, "Path-Goal Theory of Leadership," *Journal of Contemporary Business*, Autumn 1974, pp. 81–98.
23. See Victor H. Vroom and Philip H. Yetton, *Leadership and Decision Making* (Pittsburgh:

University of Pittsburgh Press, 1973); Victor H. Vroom and Arthur G. Jago, *The New Leadership* (Englewood Cliffs, NJ: Prentice Hall, 1988).

24. Victor Vroom, "Leadership and the Decision-Making Process," *Organizational Dynamics*, Spring 2000.
25. Vroom and Jago, *The New Leadership*.
26. See Madeline E. Heilman, Harvey A. Hornstein, Jack H. Cage, and Judith K. Herschlag, "Reaction to Prescribed Leader Behavior as a Function of Role Perspective: The Case of the Vroom-Yetton Model," *Journal of Applied Psychology*, February 1984, pp. 50–60; R. H. George Field, "A Test of the Vroom-Yetton Normative Model of Leadership," *Journal of Applied Psychology*, February 1982, pp. 523–532.

Chapter 13

1. George Graen and J. F. Cashman, "A Role-Making Model of Leadership in Formal Organizations: A Developmental Approach," in J. G. Hunt and L. L. Larson (Eds.), *Leadership Frontiers* (Kent, OH: Kent State University Press, 1975), pp. 143–165; Fred Dansereau, George Graen, and W. J. Haga, "A Vertical Dyad Linkage Approach to Leadership Within Formal Organizations: A Longitudinal Investigation of the Role-Making Process," *Organizational Behavior and Human Performance*, 1975, vol. 15, pp. 46–78; see also Julian Barling, Amy Christie, and Colette Hoption, "Leadership," in Sheldon Zedeck (Ed.), *Handbook of Industrial and Organizational Psychology* (Washington, DC: American Psychological Association, 2010), pp. 183–240.
2. See Charlotte R. Gerstner and David V. Day, "Meta-Analytic Review of Leader-Member Exchange Theory: Correlates and Construct Issues," *Journal of Applied Psychology*, 1997, vol. 82, no. 6, pp. 827–844; John Maslyn and Mary Uhl-Bien, "Leader-Member Exchange and Its Dimensions: Effects of Self-Effort and Others' Effort on Relationship Quality," *Journal of Applied Psychology*, 2001, vol. 86, no. 4, pp. 697–708.
3. Paul Hersey and Kenneth H. Blanchard, *Management of Organizational Behavior: Utilizing Human Resources*, 3rd ed. (Englewood Cliffs, NJ: Prentice Hall, 1977).
4. See Fred Fiedler and Joe Garcia, *New Approaches to Effective Leadership: Cognitive Resources and Organizational Performance* (New York: Wiley, 1987).
5. See James MacGregor Burns, *Leadership* (New York: Harper & Row, 1978); and Karl W. Kuhnert and Philip Lewis, "Transactional and Transformational Leadership: A Constructive/Developmental Analysis," *Academy of Management Review*, October 1987, pp. 648–657. See also Nick Turner, Julian Barling, Olga Epitropaki, Vicky Butcher, and Caroline Milner, "Transformational Leadership and Moral Reasoning," *Journal of Applied Psychology*, vol. 87, no. 3, pp. 304–311.
6. Francis J. Yammarino and Alan J. Dubinsky, "Transformational Leadership Theory: Using Levels of Analysis to Determine Boundary Conditions," *Personnel Psychology*, 1994, vol. 47, pp. 787–800. See also A. N. Pieterse, D. van Knippenberg, M. Schippers, and D. Stam, "Transformational and Transactional Leadership and Innovative Behavior: The Role of Psychological Empowerment," *Journal of Organizational Behavior*, May 2010, pp. 609–623.
7. Vicki Goodwin, J. C. Wofford, and J. Lee Whittington, "A Theoretical and Empirical Extension to the Transformational Leadership Construct," *Journal of Organizational Behavior*, 2001, vol. 22, pp. 759–774; see also Amy Colbert, Amy Kristof-Brown, Bret Bradley, and Murray Barrick, "CEO Transformational Leadership: The Role of Goal Congruence in Top Management Teams," *Academy of Management Journal*, 2008, vol. 51, no. 1, pp. 81–96.
8. *Hoover's Handbook of American Business 2012* (Austin, TX: Hoover's Business Press, 2012, pp. 340–341.
9. Juan-Carlos Pastor, James Meindl, and Margarita Mayo, "A Network Effects Model of Charisma Attributions," *Academy of Management Journal*, 2002, vol. 45, no. 2, pp. 410–420.
10. See Robert J. House, "A 1976 Theory of Charismatic Leadership," in J. G. Hunt and L. L. Larson (Eds.), *Leadership: The Cutting Edge* (Carbondale, IL: Southern Illinois University Press, 1977), pp. 189–207. See also Jay A. Conger and Rabindra N. Kanungo, "Toward a Behavioral Theory of Charismatic Leadership in Organizational Settings," *Academy of Management Review*, October 1987, pp. 637–647.
11. "Play Hard, Fly Right," *Time, Bonus Section: Inside Business*, June 2002, pp. Y15–Y22.

12. David A. Nadler and Michael L. Tushman, "Beyond the Charismatic Leader: Leadership and Organizational Change," *California Management Review*, Winter 1990, pp. 77–97.
13. David A. Waldman and Francis J. Yammarino, "CEO Charismatic Leadership: Levels-of-Management and Levels-of-Analysis Effects," *Academy of Management Review*, 1999, vol. 24, no. 2, pp. 266–285.
14. Jane Howell and Boas Shamir, "The Role of Followers in the Charismatic Leadership Process: Relationships and Their Consequences," *Academy of Management Review*, January 2005, pp. 96–112.
15. See Steven Kerr and John M. Jermier, "Substitutes for Leadership: Their Meaning and Measurement," *Organizational Behavior and Human Performance*, 1978, vol. 22, pp. 375–403. See also Charles C. Manz and Henry P. Sims Jr., "Leading Workers to Lead Themselves: The External Leadership of Self-Managing Work Teams," *Administrative Science Quarterly*, March 1987, pp. 106–129.
16. Jon P. Howell, David E. Bowen, Peter W. Dorfman, Steven Kerr, and Philip Podsakoff, "Substitutes for Leadership: Effective Alternatives to Ineffective Leadership," *Organizational Dynamics*, Summer 1990, pp. 20–38. See also Philip M. Podsakoff, Scott B. Mackenzie, and William H. Bommer, "Transformational Leader Behaviors and Substitutes for Leadership as Determinants of Employee Satisfaction, Commitment, Trust, and Organizational Citizenship Behaviors," *Journal of Management*, 1996, vol. 22, no. 2, pp. 259–298.
17. Tamara Erickson, "The Leaders We Need Now," *Harvard Business Review*, May 2010, pp. 62–67.
18. J. Richard Hackman and Ruth Wageman, "A Theory of Team Coaching," *Academy of Management Review*, April 2005, pp. 269–287; see also David B. Peterson, "Executive Coaching: A Critical Review and Recommendations for Advancing the Practice," in Sheldon Zedeck (Ed.), *Handbook of Industrial and Organizational Psychology* (Washington, DC: American Psychological Association, 2010), pp. 527–566.
19. Russell L. Kent and Sherry E. Moss, "Effects of Sex and Gender Role on Leader Emergence," *Academy of Management Journal*, 1994, vol. 37, no. 5, pp. 1335–1346.
20. A. H. Eagly, M. G. Makhijani, and R. G. Klonsky, "Gender and the Evaluation of Leaders: A Meta-Analysis," *Psychological Bulletin*, 1992, vol. 111, pp. 3–22.
21. House, Robert J. et al. (Eds.), *Culture, Leadership, and Organizations: The GLOBE Study of 62 Societies* (London: Sage, 2004).
22. See Jagdeep S. Chhokar. Felix C. Brodbek, and Robert J. House (Eds.), *Culture and Leadership Across the World* (Hillsdale, NJ: Lawrence Erlbaum Associates, 2008); and Vipin Gupta, Paul J. Hanges, and Peter Dorfman, "Cultural Clusters: Methodology and Findings," *Journal of World Business*, 2002, vol. 37, pp. 11–15 for more details. See also Kwok Leung and Mark F. Peterson, "Managing a Globally Distributed Workforce: Social and Interpersonal Issues," in Sheldon Zedeck (Ed.), *Handbook of Industrial and Organizational Psychology* (Washington, DC: American Psychological Association, 2010), pp. 771–805.
23. Cynthia Montgomery, "Putting Leadership Back Into Strategy," *Harvard Business Review*, January 2008, pp. 54–61.
24. "The Best (& Worst) Managers of the Year," *Business Week*, January 10, 2005, p. 55.
25. See Kurt Dirks and Donald Ferrin, "Trust in Leadership," *Journal of Applied Psychology*, 2002, vol. 87, no. 4, pp. 611–628; see also Christopher Meyer and Julia Kirby, "Leadership in the Age of Transparency," *Harvard Business Review*, April 2010, pp. 38–46.
26. See John Cordery, Christine Soo, Bradley Kirkman, Benson Rosen, and John Mathieu, "Leading Parallel Global Virtual Teams," *Organizational Dynamics*, July–September 2009, pp. 204–216.

Chapter 14

1. Robert W. Allen and Lyman W. Porter (Eds.), *Organizational Influence Processes* (Glenview, IL: Scott, Foresman, 1983).
2. Alan L. Frohman, "The Power of Personal Initiative," *Organizational Dynamics*, Winter 1997, pp. 39–48; see also James H. Dulebohn and Gerald R. Ferris, "The Role of Influence Tactics in Perceptions of Performance Evaluations' Fairness," *Academy of Management Journal*, 1999, vol. 42, no. 3, pp. 288–303.
3. For reviews of the meaning of power, see Henry Mintzberg, *Power in and around*

Organizations (Englewood Cliffs, NJ: Prentice Hall, 1983); Jeffrey Pfeffer, *Power in Organizations* (Marshfield, MA: Pitman Publishing, 1981); John Kenneth Galbraith, *The Anatomy of Power* (Boston: Houghton Mifflin, 1983); Gary A. Yukl, *Leadership in Organizations*, 3rd ed. (Englewood Cliffs, NJ: Prentice Hall, 1994).

4. John R. P. French and Bertram Raven, "The Bases of Social Power," in Darwin Cartwright (Ed.), *Studies in Social Power* (Ann Arbor, MI: University of Michigan Press, 1959), pp. 150–167. See also Philip M. Podsakoff and Chester A. Schriesheim, "Field Studies of French and Raven's Bases of Power: Critique, Reanalysis, and Suggestions for Future Research," *Psychological Bulletin*, 1985, vol. 97, pp. 387–411.
5. See Sze-Sze Wong, Violet Ho, and Chay Hoon Lee, "A Power Perspective to Interunit Knowledge Transfer: Linking Attributes to Knowledge Power and the Transfer of Knowledge," *Journal of Management*, 2008, vol. 34, no. 1, pp. 127–150.
6. Yukl, *Leadership in Organizations*, Chapter X.
7. See Darren Treadway, Wayne Hochwarter, Charles Kacmar, and Gerald Ferris, "Political Will, Political Skill, and Political Behavior," *Journal of Organizational Behavior*, 2005, vol. 26, pp. 229–245.
8. Victor Murray and Jeffrey Gandz, "Games Executives Play: Politics at Work," *Business Horizons*, December 1980, pp. 11–23. See also Jeffrey Gandz and Victor Murray, "The Experience of Workplace Politics," *Academy of Management Journal*, June 1980, pp. 237–251.
9. Gerald F. Cavanaugh, Dennis J. Moberg, and Manuel Valasquez, "The Ethics of Organizational Politics," *Academy of Management Review*, July 1981, pp. 363–374. See also Gerald R. Ferris and Wayne A. Hochwarter, "Organizational Politics," in Sheldon Zedeck (Ed.), *Handbook of Industrial and Organizational Psychology* (Washington, DC: American Psychological Association, 2010), pp. 435–459.
10. Pfeffer, *Power in Organizations*; Mintzberg, *Power in and around Organizations*.
11. The techniques are based on Pfeffer, *Power in Organizations*; Mintzberg, *Power in and around Organizations*; and Galbraith, *Anatomy of Power*.
12. "How the Two Top Officials of Grace Wound Up in a Very Dirty War," *Wall Street Journal*, May 18, 1995, pp. Al, A8.
13. See Jerald Greenberg and Jason Colquitt, *Handbook of Organizational Justice* (Mahwah, NJ: Lawrence Erlbaum Associates, 2004), for a comprehensive discussion and review of the literature on justice in organizations. See also James Lavelle, Deborah Rupp, and Joel Brockner, "Taking a Multifoci Approach to the Study of Justice, Social Exchange, and Citizenship Behavior," *Journal of Management*, 2007, vol. 33, no. 6, pp. 841–866; and Joel Brockner, *A Contemporary Look at Organizational Justice* (New York: Routledge, 2010), for recent updates.
14. See Russell Cropanzano, David Bowen, and Stephen Gilliland, "The Management of Organizational Justice," *Academy of Management Perspectives*, 2007, vol. 21, no. 4, pp. 34–48. See also Jerald Greenberg, "Organizational Justice: The Dynamics of Fairness in the Workplace," in Sheldon Zedeck (Ed.), *Handbook of Industrial and Organizational Psychology* (Washington, DC: American Psychological Association, 2010), pp. 271–327.

Chapter 15

1. See Stephen P. Robbins, *Managing Organizational Conflict* (Englewood Cliffs, NJ: Prentice Hall, 1974), for a classic review. See Carsten K. W. de Dreu, "Conflict at Work: Basic Principles and Applied Issues," in Sheldon Zedeck (Ed.), *Handbook of Industrial and Organizational Psychology* (Washington, DC: American Psychological Association, 2010), pp. 461–493, for a more recent review.
2. Charles R. Schwenk, "Conflict in Organizational Decision Making: An Exploratory Study of Its Effects in For-Profit and Not-for-Profit Organizations," *Management Science*, April 1990, pp. 436–448.
3. See Carsten K. W. De Dreu, "The Virtue and Vice of Workplace Conflict: Food for (Pessimistic) Thought," *Journal of Organizational Behavior*, 2008, vol. 29, no. 1, pp. 5–18; and Dean Tjosvold, "The Conflict-Positive Organization: It Depends on Us," *Journal of Organizational Behavior*, 2008, vol. 29, no. 1, pp. 19–28, for discussions of negative and positive perspectives on conflict.
4. "How Two Computer Nuts Transformed Industry Before Messy Breakup," *Wall Street Journal*, August 27, 1996, pp. A1, A10.

5. Bruce Barry and Greg L. Stewart, "Composition, Process, and Performance in Self-Managed Groups: The Role of Personality," *Journal of Applied Psychology*, vol. 82, no. 1, 1997, pp. 62–78.
6. "Rumsfeld's Abrasive Style Sparks Conflict with Military Command," *USA Today*, December 10, 2002, pp. 1A, 2A.
7. "Delta CEO Resigns After Clashes with Board," *USA Today*, May 13, 1997, p. B1.
8. "Why Boeing's Culture Breeds Turmoil," *Business Week*, March 21, 2005, pp. 34–36.
9. James Thompson, *Organizations in Action* (New York: McGraw-Hill, 1967). For a more recent discussion, see Bart Victor and Richard S. Blackburn, "Interdependence: An Alternative Conceptualization," *Academy of Management Review*, July 1987, pp. 486–498.
10. Kenneth Thomas, "Conflict and Conflict Management," in Marvin Dunnette (Ed.), *Handbook of Industrial and Organizational Psychology* (Chicago, IL: Rand McNally, 1976), pp. 889–935.
11. Alfie Kohn, "How to Succeed Without Even Vying," *Psychology Today*, September 1986, pp. 22–28.
12. See Carsten K. W. De Dreu and Annelies E. M. Van Vianen, "Managing Relationship Conflict and the Effectiveness of Organizational Teams," *Journal of Organizational Behavior*, 2001, vol. 22, pp. 309–328; see also Kristin Behfar, Randall Peterson, Elizabeth Mannix, and William Trochim, "The Critical Role of Conflict Resolution in Teams: A Close Look at the Links Between Conflict Type, Conflict Management Strategies, and Team Outcomes," *Journal of Applied Psychology*, 2008, vol. 93, no. 1, pp. 170–188.
13. "Memo to the Team: This Needs Salt!" *Wall Street Journal*, April 4, 2000, pp. B1, B14.
14. See Kimberly Wade-Benzoni, Andrew Hoffman, Leigh Thompson, Don Moore, James Gillespie, and Max Bazerman, "Barriers to Resolution in Ideologically Based Negotiations: The Role of Values and Institutions," *Academy of Management Review*, 2002, vol. 27, no. 1, pp. 41–57; see also Leigh Thompson, Jiunwen Wang, and Brian Gunia, "Bargaining, Negotiation, Conflict, Social Justice," in Susan Fiske, Daniel Schacter, and Robert Sternberg (Eds.), *Annual Review of Psychology 2010* (Palo Alto, CA: Annual Reviews, 2010), pp. 491–516.
15. J. Z. Rubin and B. R. Brown, *The Social Psychology of Bargaining and Negotiation* (New York: Academic Press, 1975).
16. R. J. Lewicki and J. A. Litterer, *Negotiation* (Homewood, IL: Irwin, 1985). See also Michele J. Gelfand, C. Ashley Fulmer, and Laura Severance, "The Psychology of Negotiation and Meditation," in Sheldon Zedeck (Ed.), *Handbook of Industrial and Organizational Psychology* (Washington, DC: American Psychological Association, 2010), pp. 495–554.
17. Howard Raiffa, *The Art and Science of Negotiation* (Cambridge, MA: Belknap, 1982). See also Leigh L. Thompson, Jiunwen Wang, and Brian C. Gunia, "Bargaining, Negotiation, Conflict, Social Justice," in Susan T. Fiske, Daniel L. Schacter, and Robert J. Sternberg (Eds.), *Annual Review of Psychology 2010* (Palo Alto, CA: Annual Reviews, 2010), pp. 491–516.
18. K. H. Bazerman and M. A. Neale, *Negotiating Rationally* (New York: Free Press, 1992).
19. Ross R. Reck and Brian G. Long, *The Win-Win Negotiator* (Escondido, CA: Blanchard Training and Development, 1985).

Chapter 16

1. See Richard L. Daft, *Organization Theory and Design*, 8th ed. (Mason, OH: South-Western, 2004), p.11, for further discussion of the definition of *organization*.
2. Gareth R. Jones, *Organizational Theory, Design, and Change*, 9th ed. (Upper Saddle River, NJ: Pearson Prentice Hall, 2007), p. 4.
3. Brayden G. King, Teppo Felin, and David A. Whetten, "Perspective—Finding the Organization in Organizational Theory: A Meta-Theory of the Organization as a Social Actor," *Organization Science*, January–February 2010, pp. 290–305, ©2010 INFORMS.
4. Charles W. L. Hill and Gareth R. Jones, *Strategic Management: An Integrated Approach*, 9th ed. (Mason, OH: South-Western Cengage Learning, 2010), p. 12. See also John R. Montanari, Cyril P. Morgan, and Jeffrey S. Bracker, *Strategic Management* (Hinsdale, IL: Dryden Press, 1990), pp. 1–2.
5. "Intel Aligns Around Platforms," "Intel Corporation in Summary," Intel website, appzone.intel.com on February 8, 2005.
6. A. Bryman, A. D. Beardworth, E. T. Keil, and J. Ford, "Organizational Size and Specialization,"

Organization Studies, September 1983, pp. 271–278.
7. Joseph L. C. Cheng, "Interdependence and Coordination in Organizations: A Role System Analysis," *Academy of Management Journal*, March 1983, pp. 156–162.
8. Henry Mintzberg, *The Structuring of Organizations* (Englewood Cliffs, NJ: Prentice Hall, 1979), for further discussion of the basic elements of structure.
9. Max Weber, *The Theory of Social and Economic Organization*, trans. A. M. Henderson and Talcott Parsons (New York: Free Press, 1947).
10. For more discussion of these alternative views, see John B. Miner, *Theories of Organizational Structure and Process* (Hinsdale, IL: Dryden Press, 1982), p. 386.
11. Paul S. Adler, "Building Better Bureaucracies," *Academy of Management Executive*, November 1999, pp. 36–46.
12. This summary of the classic principles of organizing is based on Henri Fayol, *General and Industrial Management*, trans. Constance Storrs (London: Pittman, 1949); Miner, *Theories of Organizational Structure and Process*, pp. 358–381; and the discussions in Arthur G. Bedeian, *Organizations: Theory and Analysis*, 2nd ed. (Chicago, IL: Dryden, 1984), pp. 58–59.
13. Miner, *Theories of Organizational Structure and Process*, pp. 358–381.
14. See Rensis Likert, *New Patterns of Management* (New York: McGraw-Hill, 1961); and Rensis Likert, *The Human Organization: Its Management and Value* (New York: McGraw-Hill, 1967), for a complete discussion of the human organization.
15. Miner, *Theories of Organizational Structure and Process*, pp. 17–53.
16. Weber, *The Theory of Social and Economic Organization*.
17. Adam Smith, *An Inquiry into the Nature and Causes of the Wealth of Nations* (London: Dent, 1910).
18. Nancy M. Carter and Thomas L. Keon, "The Rise and Fall of the Division of Labour, the Past 25 Years," *Organization Studies*, 1986, pp. 54–57.
19. Glenn R. Carroll, "The Specialist Strategy," *California Management Review*, Spring 1984, pp. 126–137.
20. "Management Discovers the Human Side of Automation," *Business Week*, September 29, 1986, pp. 70–75.
21. See Robert H. Miles, *Macro Organizational Behavior* (Santa Monica, CA: Goodyear, 1980), pp. 28–34, for a discussion of departmentalization schemes.
22. Robert Berner, "Flip-Flops, Torn Jeans—and Control," *BusinessWeek*, May 30, 2005, www.businessweek.com on April 20, 2010; Jess Cartner-Morley, "History of Abercrombie & Fitch: Tracing a Line from JFK's Blazer," *The Guardian*, June 24, 2009, www.guardian.com on April 20, 2010; Benoit Denizet-Lewis, "The Man behind Abercrombie & Fitch," *Salon.com*, January 24, 2006, www.salon.com on April 20, 2010; Andria Cheng, "Abercrombie & Fitch Clothed in Green," *MarketWatch*, February 13, 2009, www.marketwatch.com on March 17, 2010.
23. Mintzberg, *The Structuring of Organizations*, p. 125.
24. Miles, *Macro Organizational Behavior*, pp. 122–133.
25. "Sony Corporation Announces Major Reorganization and the New Management Team Led by Howard Stringer," Sony Corporation News Release, February 27, 2009; Erica Orden, "Sony Expected to Reorganize U.S. Entertainment Leadership," *Wall Street Journal*, Updated March 21, 2012, 6:13 pm; and Mark Kurlyandchik, *Wall Street Journal*, March 10, 2011, 8:20 am.
26. "Performance Inside: 2007 Annual Report," "Intel Aligns Around Platforms," "Intel Corporation in Summary," Intel website, www.intel.com on April 21, 2008; Ephraim Schwartz, "The Age of the Industry-Specific PC," *InfoWorld*, January 28, 2005, www.infoworld.com on February 8, 2005; Gary Rivlin and John Markoff, "Can Mr. Chips Transform Intel?" *New York Times*, September 12, 2004, pp. BU1, BU4 (quote); "Intel Corporation," *Hoover's*, www.hoovers.com on March 6, 2005; "Intel Shuffles Key Management Roles," *TechWeb*, October 10, 2000, www.techweb.com on February 8, 2005.
27. Peggy Leatt and Rodney Schneck, "Criteria for Grouping Nursing Subunits in Hospitals," *Academy of Management Review*, March 1984, pp. 150–165.
28. "Fact Sheets," "Organizational Structure," Deutsche Bank website, group.deutsche-bank.de on June 7, 2002; Marcus Walker, "Lean New Guard at Deutsche Bank Sets Global Agenda—But Cultural Rifts Prevent More-Aggressive Cost Cuts—The Traditionalists Haven't Gone Quietly,"

Wall Street Journal, February 14, 2002, www.wsj.com on April 4, 2002; Stephen Graham, "Deutsche Bank Says 2001 Profit Plummeted, Proceeds with Management Shake-Up," *National Business Stream*, January 31, 2002; "Deutsche Bank Names Next CEO, Continuity Seen," *National Business Stream*, September 21, 2000.
29. Lyndall F. Urwick, "The Manager's Span of Control," *Harvard Business Review*, May–June 1956, pp. 39–47.
30. Dan R. Dalton, William D. Tudor, Michael J. Spendolini, Gordon J. Fielding, and Lyman W. Porter, "Organization Structure and Performance: A Critical Review," *Academy of Management Review*, January 1980, pp. 49–64.
31. Mintzberg, *The Structuring of Organizations*, pp. 133–147.
32. See David Van Fleet, "Span of Management Research and Issues," *Academy of Management Journal*, September 1983, pp. 546–552, for an example of research on span of control.
33. John R. Montanari and Philip J. Adelman, "The Administrative Component of Organizations and the Ratchet Effect: A Critique of Cross-Sectional Studies," *Journal of Management Studies*, March 1987, pp. 113–123.
34. D. A. Heenan, "The Downside of Downsizing," *Journal of Business Strategy*, November–December 1989, pp. 18–23.
35. Wayne F. Cascio, "Downsizing: What Do We Know? What Have We Learned?" *Academy of Management Executive*, February 1993, pp. 95–104.
36. James P. Guthrie and Deepak K. Datta, "The Impact of Downsizing on Firm Performance," *Organization Science*, January–February 2008, pp. 108–123, ©2008 INFORMS.
37. Dalton et al.,"Organization Structure and Performance."
38. See John Child, *Organization: A Guide to Problems and Practice*, 2nd ed. (New York: Harper & Row, 1984), pp. 145–153, for a detailed discussion of centralization.
39. Richard H. Hall, *Organization: Structure and Process*, 3rd ed. (Englewood Cliffs, NJ: Prentice Hall, 1982), pp. 87–96.
40. "Can Jack Smith Fix GM?" *Business Week*, November 1, 1993, pp. 126–131; John McElroy, "GM's Brand Management Might Work," *Automotive Industries*, September 1996, p. 132.
41. Sharon Terlep, "GM's Chief Labors to Get Rebuilt Car Maker Into Gear," *Wall Street Journal*, June 12, 2012, p. A1.
42. Daniel R. Denison, "Bringing Corporate Culture to the Bottom Line," *Organizational Dynamics*, Autumn 1984, pp. 4–22.
43. Leonard W. Johnson and Alan L. Frohman, "Identifying and Closing the Gap in the Middle of Organizations," *Academy of Management Executive*, May 1989, pp. 107–114.
44. Michael Schrage, "I Know What You Mean, and I Can't Do Anything About It," *Fortune*, April 2, 2001, p. 186.
45. Mintzberg, *The Structuring of Organizations*, pp. 83–84.
46. Arthur P. Brief and H. Kirk Downey, "Cognitive and Organizational Structures: A Conceptual Analysis of Implicit Organizing Theories," *Human Relations*, December 1983, pp. 1065–1090.
47. Jerald Hage, "An Axiomatic Theory of Organizations," *Administrative Science Quarterly*, December 1965, pp. 289–320.
48. Gregory Moorhead, "Organizational Analysis: An Integration of the Macro and Micro Approaches," *Journal of Management Studies*, April 1981, pp. 191–218.
49. J. Daniel Sherman and Howard L. Smith, "The Influence of Organizational Structure on Intrinsic Versus Extrinsic Motivation," *Academy of Management Journal*, December 1984, pp. 877–885.
50. Eileen Fairhurst, "Organizational Rules and the Accomplishment of Nursing Work on Geriatric Wards," *Journal of Management Studies*, July 1983, pp. 315–332.
51. Fairhurst, "Organizational Rules and the Accomplishment of Nursing Work on Geriatric Wards."
52. "Chevron Corp. Has Big Challenge Coping with Worker Cutbacks," *Wall Street Journal*, November 4, 1986, pp. 1, 25.
53. Neil F. Brady, "Rules for Making Exceptions to Rules," *Academy of Management Review*, July 1987, pp. 436–444.
54. See Jeffrey Pfeiffer, *Power in Organizations* (Boston: Pittman, 1981), pp. 4–6, for a discussion of the relationship between power and authority.
55. Miner, *Theories of Organizational Structure and Process*, p. 360.

56. Chester Barnard, *The Functions of the Executive* (Cambridge, MA: Harvard University Press, 1938), pp. 161–184.
57. Pfeiffer, *Power in Organizations*, pp. 366–367.

Chapter 17

1. Lex Donaldson, "Strategy and Structural Adjustment to Regain Fit and Performance: In Defense of Contingency Theory," *Journal of Management Studies*, January 1987, pp. 1–24.
2. John R. Montanari, Cyril P. Morgan, and Jeffrey Bracker, *Strategic Management* (Hinsdale, IL: Dryden Press, 1990), p. 114.
3. See Arthur A. Thompson Jr. and A. J. Strickland III, *Strategic Management*, 3rd ed. (Plano, TX: Business Publications, 1984), pp. 19–27.
4. David Stires, "Fallen Arches," *Fortune*, April 26, 1999, pp. 146–152.
5. Alfred D. Chandler, *Strategy and Structure: Chapters in the History of the American Industrial Enterprise* (Cambridge, MA: MIT Press, 1962).
6. John R. Kimberly, "Organizational Size and the Structuralist Perspective: A Review, Critique, and Proposal," *Administrative Science Quarterly*, December 1976, pp. 571–597.
7. Peter M. Blau and Richard A. Schoenherr, *The Structure of Organizations* (New York: Basic Books, 1971).
8. The results of these studies are thoroughly summarized in Richard H. Hall, *Organizations: Structure and Process*, 3rd ed. (Englewood Cliffs, NJ: Prentice Hall, 1982), pp. 89–94. For another study in this area, see John H. Cullen and Kenneth S. Anderson, "Blau's Theory of Structural Differentiation Revisited: A Theory of Structural Change or Scale?" *Academy of Management Journal*, June 1986, pp. 203–229.
9. "Small Is Beautiful Now in Manufacturing," *Business Week*, October 22, 1984, pp. 152–156.
10. Richard H. Hall, J. Eugene Haas, and Norman Johnson, "Organizational Size, Complexity, and Formalization," *American Sociological Review*, December 1967, pp. 903–912.
11. Catherine Arnst, "Downsizing: Out One Door and In Another," *Business Week*, January 22, 1996, p. 41; Peter Elstrom, "Dial A for Aggravation," *Business Week*, March 11, 1996, p. 34; Alex Markels and Matt Murray, "Call It Dumbsizing: Why Some Companies Regret Cost-Cutting," *Wall Street Journal*, May 14, 1996, pp. A1, A5.
12. James P. Guthrie and Deepak K. Datta: "The Impact of Downsizing on Firm Performance," *Organization Science*, January–February 2008, pp. 108–123, ©2008 INFORMS; and Robert I. Sutton and Thomas D'Anno, "Decreasing Organizational Size: Untangling the Effects of Money and People," *Academy of Management Review*, May 1989, pp. 194–212.
13. Scott Thurm, "Recalculating the Cost of Big Layoffs," *Wall Street Journal*, May 5, 2010, accessed online, May 6, 2010.
14. Joan Woodward, *Management and Technology: Problems of Progress in Industry*, no. 3 (London: Her Majesty's Stationery Office, 1958); Joan Woodward, *Industrial Organizations: Theory and Practice* (London: Oxford University Press, 1965).
15. Tom Burns and George M. Stalker, *The Management of Innovation* (London: Tavistock, 1961).
16. Charles B. Perrow, "A Framework for the Comparative Analysis of Organizations," *American Sociological Review*, April 1967, pp. 194–208.
17. James D. Thompson, *Organizations in Action* (New York: McGraw-Hill, 1967).
18. David J. Hickson, Derek S. Pugh, and Diana C. Pheysey, "Operations Technology and Organization Structure: An Empirical Reappraisal," *Administrative Science Quarterly*, September 1969, pp. 378–397.
19. Diane E. Bailey, Paul M. Leonardi, and Jan Chong, "Minding the Gaps: Understanding Technology Interdependence and Coordination in Knowledge Work," *Organization Science, Articles in Advance*, September 25, 2009, pp. 1–18. INFORMS.
20. Bailey et al., "Minding the Gaps."
21. Andrew Kupfer, "How to Be a Global Manager," *Fortune*, March 14, 1988, pp. 52–58.
22. "Going Crazy in Japan—In a Break from Tradition, Tokyo Begins Funding a Program for Basic Research," *Wall Street Journal*, November 10, 1986, p. D20.
23. "About Wal-Mart," "Wal-Mart Stores, Inc., at a Glance," Walmart website, www.walmartstores.com on June 12, 2002; "Dell at a Glance," "Dell Worldwide," Dell website, www.dell.com on June 12, 2002; Brian Dumaine, "What Michael Dell Knows That You Don't," *Fortune*, June 3, 2002, www.fortune.com on June 12, 2002; Andy Serwer, "Dell Does Domination," *Fortune*, January 21,

2002, pp. 71–75; Eryn Brown, "America's Most Admired Companies," *Fortune*, March 1, 1999, pp. 68–73 (quotation p. 70).

24. Richard L. Daft, *Organization Theory and Design*, 8th ed. (Cincinnati, OH: South-Western, a division of Thomson Learning, 2004), p. 141.
25. "Toy Makers Lose Interest in Tie-Ins with Cartoons," *Wall Street Journal*, April 28, 1988, p. 29.
26. Masoud Yasai-Ardekani, "Structural Adaptations to Environments," *Academy of Management Review*, January 1986, pp. 9–21.
27. John E. Prescott, "Environments as Moderators of the Relationship Between Strategy and Performance," *Academy of Management Journal*, June 1986, pp. 329–346.
28. Timothy M. Stearns, Alan N. Hoffman, and Jan B. Heide, "Performance of Commercial Television Stations as an Outcome of Interorganizational Linkages and Environmental Conditions," *Academy of Management Journal*, March 1987, pp. 71–90.
29. Thompson, *Organizations in Action*, pp. 51–82.
30. Lori Ioannou, "American Invasion," *Fortune*, May 13, 2002, www.fortune.com on June 12, 2002; Jesse Wong, "How to Start a Business Without a Road Map," *Fortune*, April 1, 2002, www.fortune.com on June 12, 2002; Camilla Ojansivu, "Strategy for a Stronger Market Economy: Corporate Restructuring the PRC," *Business Beijing*, November, 2001, pp. 38–39.
31. For more information on managerial choice, see John Child, "Organizational Structure, Environment, and Performance: The Role of Strategic Choice," *Sociology*, January 1972, pp. 1–22; John R. Montanari, "Managerial Discretion: An Expanded Model of Organizational Choice," *Academy of Management Review*, April 1978, pp. 231–241.
32. H. Randolph Bobbitt and Jeffrey D. Ford, "Decision Maker Choice as a Determinant of Organizational Structure," *Academy of Management Review*, January 1980, pp. 13–23.
33. James W. Frederickson, "The Strategic Decision Process and Organization Structure," *Academy of Management Review*, April 1986, pp. 280–297.
34. Herman L. Boschken, "Strategy and Structure: Reconceiving the Relationship," *Journal of Management*, March 1990, pp. 135–150.
35. "Kerkorian Sues Daimler," *CNN Money*, November 28, 2000, cnnmoney.com on March 10, 2005; Stephen Graham, "DaimlerChrysler to Trim Management," *Detroit Free Press*, February 1, 2003, www.freep.com on March 10, 2005; Danny Hakim, "You Say 'Takeover.' I Say 'Merger of Equals.'" *New York Times*, December 21, 2003, pp. BU1, BU10; Jeffrey K. Liker, "What Was Daimler Thinking?" *Across the Board*, January/February 2005, pp. 12–13.
36. Jerry Flint, "Is Fiat Helping Chrysler—Or Fiat," *Forbes.com*, November 3, 2009, http://www.forbes.com/2009/11/02/chrysler-fiat-automobiles-jerry-flint-business-autos-backseat.html on May 2, 2010.
37. Elton Mayo, *The Human Problems of an Industrial Civilization* (New York: Macmillan, 1933); F. J. Roethlisberger and W. J. Dickson, *Management and the Worker* (Cambridge, MA: Harvard University Press, 1939).
38. Eric L. Trist and K. W. Bamforth, "Some Social and Psychological Consequences of the Longwall Method of Coal-Getting," *Human Relations*, February 1951, pp. 3–38.
39. Richard E. Walton, "How to Counter Alienation in the Plant," *Harvard Business Review*, November–December 1972, pp. 70–81; Pehr G. Gyllenhammar, "How Volvo Adapts Work to People," *Harvard Business Review*, July–August 1977, pp. 102–113; Richard E. Walton, "Work Innovations at Topeka: After Six Years," *Journal of Applied Behavioral Science*, July–September 1977, pp. 422–433.
40. Henry Mintzberg, *The Structuring of Organizations: A Synthesis of the Research* (Englewood Cliffs, NJ: Prentice Hall, 1979).
41. See Harold C. Livesay, *American Made: Men Who Shaped the American Economy* (Boston: Little, Brown, 1979), pp. 215–239, for a discussion of Alfred Sloan and the development of the divisionalized structure at General Motors.
42. Anne B. Fisher, "GM Is Tougher Than You Think," *Fortune*, November 10, 1986, pp. 56–64.
43. Thompson and Strickland, *Strategic Management*, p. 212.
44. Gary Hamel with Bill Breen, *The Future of Management* (Boston, MA: Harvard Business School Press, 2007).
45. Rachel Emma Silverman, "Who's the Boss? There Isn't One," *Wall Street Journal*, June 20, 2012, p. B1.
46. Henry Mintzberg, "Organization Design: Fashion or Fit," *Harvard Business Review*, January–February 1981, pp. 103–116.

47. Harvey F. Kolodny, "Managing in a Matrix," *Business Horizons*, March–April 1981, pp. 17–24.
48. Stanley M. Davis and Paul R. Lawrence, *Matrix* (Reading, MA: Addison-Wesley, 1977), pp. 11–36.
49. Lawton R. Burns, "Matrix Management in Hospitals: Testing Theories of Matrix Structure and Development," *Administrative Science Quarterly*, September 1989, pp. 355–358.
50. Ibid., pp. 129–154.
51. "The Virtual Corporation," *Business Week*, February 8, 1993, pp. 98–102; William H. Carlile, "Virtual Corporation a Real Deal," *Arizona Republic*, August 2, 1993, pp. E1, E4.
52. Max Chafkin, "The Case, and the Plan, for the Virtual Company," *Inc.com*, April 1, 2010, http://www.inc.com/magazine/20100401/the-case-and-the-plan-for-the-virtual-company.html on April 25, 2010. See the following website for a more complete listing of the pros and cons of teleworking: http://www.teleworker.com/pro-con.html.
53. Thomas A. Stewart, "Reengineering: The Hot New Managing Tool," *Fortune*, August 23, 1993, pp. 41–48.
54. James A. Champy, "From Reengineering to X-Engineering," in Subir Chowdhury (Ed.), *Organization 21C: Someday All Organizations Will Lead This Way* (Upper Saddle River, NJ: Financial Times Prentice Hall, 2003), pp. 93–95.
55. Robert Tomasko, *Rethinking the Corporation* (New York: AMA-COM, 1993).
56. Rahul Jacob, "The Struggle to Create an Organization for the 21st Century," *Fortune*, April 3, 1995, pp. 90–99; Gene G. Marcial, "Don't Leave Your Broker Without It?" *Business Week*, February 5, 1996, p. 138; Jeffrey M. Laderman, "Loading Up on No-Loads," *Business Week*, May 27, 1996, p. 138.
57. James R. Lincoln, Mitsuyo Hanada, and Kerry McBride, "Organizational Structures in Japanese and U.S. Manufacturing," *Administrative Science Quarterly*, September 1986, pp. 338–364.
58. "The Inscrutable West," *Newsweek*, April 18, 1988, p. 52.
59. Michael W. Morris, Joel Podolny, and Bilian Ni Sullivan, "Culture and Coworker Relations: Interpersonal Patterns in American, Chinese, German, and Spanish Divisions of a Global Retail Bank," *Organization Science*," July–August 2008, pp. 517–532.
60. Richard I. Kirkland Jr., "Europe's New Managers," *Fortune*, September 29, 1980, pp. 56–60; Shawn Tully, "Europe's Takeover Kings," *Fortune*, July 20, 1987, pp. 95–98.
61. Henry W. Lane and Joseph J. DiStefano, *International Management Behavior* (Ontario: Nelson, 1988).
62. William H. Davison and Philippe Haspeslagh, "Shaping a Global Product Organization," *Harvard Business Review*, July–August 1982, pp. 125–132.
63. Emily Glazer, "P&G Unit Bids Goodbye to Cincinnati, Hello to Asia," *Wall Street Journal*, May 10, 2012, p. B1.
64. John Child, *Organizations: A Guide to Problems and Practice* (New York: Harper & Row, 1984), p. 246.
65. Thomas J. Peters and Robert H. Waterman Jr., *In Search of Excellence: Lessons from America's Best-Run Companies* (New York: Harper & Row, 1982), pp. 235–278.
66. Thomas J. Peters and Nancy K. Austin, "A Passion for Excellence," *Fortune*, May 13, 1985, pp. 20–32.
67. Michael Beer, "Building Organizational Fitness" in Subir Chowdhury (Ed.), *Organization 21C: Someday All Organizations Will Lead This Way* (Upper Saddle River, NJ: Financial Times Prentice Hall, 2003), pp. 311–312.

Chapter 18

1. See "Corporate Culture: The Hard-to-Change Values That Spell Success or Failure," *Business Week*, October 27, 1980, pp. 148–160; Charles G. Burck, "Working Smarter," *Fortune*, June 15, 1981, pp. 68–73.
2. Charles A. O'Reilly and Jennifer A. Chatman, "Culture as Social Control: Corporations, Cults, and Commitment," in Barry M. Staw and L. L. Cummings (Eds.), *Research in Organizational Behavior*, vol. 18 (Stamford, CT: JAI Press, 1996), pp. 157–200.
3. J. P. Kotter and J. L. Heskett, *Corporate Culture and Performance* (New York: Free Press, 1992).
4. Michael Tushman and Charles A. O'Reilly, *Staying on Top: Managing Strategic Innovation and Change for Long-Term Success* (Boston: Harvard Business School Press, 1996).
5. T. E. Deal and A. A. Kennedy, *Corporate Cultures: The Rites and Rituals of Corporate Life* (Reading, MA: Addison-Wesley, 1982), p. 4.

6. E. H. Schein, "The Role of the Founder in Creating Organizational Culture," *Organizational Dynamics*, Summer 1983, p. 14.
7. Thomas J. Peters and Robert H. Waterman Jr., *In Search of Excellence: Lessons from America's Best-Run Companies* (New York: Harper & Row, 1982), p. 103.
8. See M. Polanyi, *Personal Knowledge* (Chicago: University of Chicago Press, 1958); E. Goffman, *The Presentation of Self in Everyday Life* (New York: Doubleday, 1959); and P. L. Berger and T. Luckman, *The Social Construction of Reality* (Garden City, NY: Anchor Books, 1967).
9. "Declaration of Interdependence," Whole Foods Market website, www.wholefoodsmarket.com on May 1, 2005; "David B. Dillon," *Forbes*, www.forbes.com on April 29, 2005; "The Kroger Co.," *Hoover's*, www.hoovers.com on April 29, 2005; Charles Fischman, "The Anarchist's Cookbook," *Fast Company*, July 2004, pp. 70–78; Evan Smith, "John Mackey," *Texas Monthly*, March 2005, pp. 122–132 (quotation); Amy Tsao, "Whole Foods' Natural High," *Business Week*, July 17, 2003, www.businessweek.com on April 30, 2005.
10. Eric Ransdell, "The Nike Story? Just Tell It!" *Fast Company*, January–February 2000, pp. 44–46 (quotation on p. 46); Claude Solnik, "Co-Founder of Nike Dies Christmas Eve," *Footwear News*, January 3, 2000, p. 2; Rosemary Feitelberg, "Bowerman's Legacy Runs On," *WWD*, December 30, 1999, p. 8.
11. Louise Lee, "Tricks of E*Trade," *Business Week E.Biz*, February 7, 2000, pp. EB18–EB31.
12. A. L. Kroeber and C. Kluckhohn, "Culture: A Critical Review of Concepts and Definitions," in *Papers of the Peabody Museum of American Archaeology and Ethnology*, vol. 47, no. 1 (Cambridge, MA: Harvard University Press, 1952).
13. C. Geertz, *The Interpretation of Cultures* (New York: Basic Books, 1973).
14. See, for example, B. Clark, *The Distinctive College* (Chicago, IL: Aldine, 1970).
15. E. Durkheim, *The Elementary Forms of Religious Life*, trans. J. Swain (New York: Collier, 1961), p. 220.
16. See William G. Ouchi, Theory *Z: How American Business Can Meet the Japanese Challenge* (Reading, MA: Addison-Wesley, 1981); and Peters and Waterman, *In Search of Excellence*.
17. See Ouchi, *Theory Z;* Deal and Kennedy, *Corporate Cultures;* and Peters and Waterman, *In Search of Excellence*.
18. E. Borgida and R. E. Nisbett, "The Differential Impact of Abstract vs. Concrete Information on Decisions," *Journal of Applied Social Psychology*, July–September 1977, pp. 258–271.
19. J. Martin and M. Power, "Truth or Corporate Propaganda: The Value of a Good War Story," in Pondy et al., *Organizational Symbolism* (Greenwich, CT: JAI, 1983), pp. 93–108.
20. W. G. Ouchi, "Markets, Bureaucracies, and Clans," *Administrative Science Quarterly*, March 1980, pp. 129–141; A. Wilkins and W. G. Ouchi, "Efficient Cultures: Exploring the Relationship Between Culture and Organizational Performance," *Administrative Science Quarterly*, September 1983, pp. 468–481.
21. Peters and Waterman, *In Search of Excellence*.
22. J. B. Barney, "Organizational Culture: Can It Be a Source of Sustained Competitive Advantage?" *Academy of Management Review*, July 1986, pp. 656–665.
23. Michelle Conlin, "Is Wal-Mart Hostile to Women?" *Business Week*, July 16, 2001, www.businessweek.com on June 21, 2002.
24. Kate Linebaugh, Dionne Searcey, and Norihiko Shirouzu, "Secretive Culture Led Toyota Astray," *Wall Street Journal*, February 8, 2010, accessed online, February 13, 2010.
25. Daniel R. Denison, "What Is the Difference Between Organizational Culture and Organizational Climate? A Native's Point of View on a Decade of Paradigm Wars," *Academy of Management Review*, July 1996, pp. 619–654.
26. S. G. Isaksen and G. Ekvall, *Assessing the Context for Change: A Technical Manual for the Situational Outlook Questionnaire* (Orchard Park, NY: The Creative Problem Solving Group, 2007).
27. O'Reilly and Chatman, "Culture as Social Control."
28. Richard L. Osborne, "Strategic Values: The Corporate Performance Engine," *Business Horizons*, September–October 1996, pp. 41–47.
29. See Osborne, "Strategic Values: The Corporate Performance Engine."; and Gary McWilliams, "Dell's Profit Rises Slightly, As Expected," *Wall Street Journal*, February 11, 2000, p. A3.
30. "The Jack and Herb Show," *Fortune*, January 11, 1999, p. 166.

31. Max Chafkin, "The Zappos Way of Managing," *Inc.com*, May 1, 2009, www.inc.com on April 25, 2010.
32. Ibid.
33. Ibid.
34. Ouchi, *Theory Z.*
35. Catherine Reagor, "Wells Fargo Riding Roughshod in State, Some Say," *Arizona Republic*, September 8, 1996, pp. D1, D4; Catherine Reagor, "Wells Fargo to Cut 3,000 Additional Jobs," *Arizona Republic*, December 20, 1996, pp. E1, E2.
36. O'Reilly and Chatman, "Culture as Social Control."
37. John E. Sheridan, "Organizational Culture and Employee Retention," *Academy of Management Journal*, December 1992, pp. 1036–1056; Lisa A. Mainiero, "Is Your Corporate Culture Costing You?" *Academy of Management Executive*, November 1993, pp. 84–85.
38. Peters and Waterman, *In Search of Excellence.*
39. Steve Coll, *Private Empire: EXXONMOBIL and American Power* (New York: The Penguin Press, 2012).
40. Watts S. Humphrey, *Managing for Innovation: Leading Technical People* (Englewood Cliffs, NJ: Prentice Hall, 1987).
41. Brian O'Reilly, "Secrets of the Most Admired Corporations: New Ideas and New Products," *Fortune*, March 3, 1997, pp. 60–64.
42. Association for the Advancement of Retired Persons, "Now You See It, Now You Don't," November 11, 2005, www.aarp.org on April 25, 2008; State of Minnesota, Employment District Court, Second Judicial District, "Second Amended Complaint," *Clifford L. Whitaker et al., Plaintiffs, v. 3M Company, Defendant*, January 3, 2006, www.sprengerlang.com on May 7, 2010; Julie Foster, "6,000 3M Workers Could Be Part of Age Discrimination Suit," *St. Paul Pioneer Press*, April 15, 2008, www.twincities.com on April 25, 2008.
43. Laurie K. Lewis and David R. Seibold, "Innovation Modification During Intraorganizational Adoption," *Academy of Management Review*, April 1993, vol. 10, no. 2, pp. 322–354.
44. Leslie Kwoh, "You Call That Innovation?" *Wall Street Journal*, May 23, 2012, p. B1.
45. Steve Tobak, "Leadership Lessons from BlackBerry's Demise," *CBS MoneyWatch*, April 2, 2012, http://www.cbsnews.com/8301-505125_162-57407782/leadership-lessons-from-blackberrys-demise/.
46. Brian Hindo, "3M's Culture of Innovation," *Business Week*, June 11, 2007, www.businessweek.com on April 25, 2008; Brian Hindo, "At 3M, a Struggle Between Efficiency and Creativity," *Business Week*, June 11, 2007, www.businessweek.com on January 18, 2008; Brian Hindo, "3M Chief Plants a Money Tree," *Business Week*, June 11, 2007, www.businessweek.com on April 25, 2008.
47. For more discussion of W. L. Gore & Associates, see Gary Hamel (with Bill Breen), *The Future of Management* (Boston: Harvard Business School Press, 2007), pp. 83–100.
48. Oren Harari, "Stop Empowering Your People," *Management Review*, November 1993, pp. 26–29.
49. Rob Goffee and Gareth Jones, "Organizational Culture," in Subir Chowdhury (Ed.), *Organization 21C: Someday All Organizations Will Lead This Way* (Upper Saddle River, NJ: Financial Times Prentice Hall, 2003), pp. 273–290.
50. "Declaration of Interdependence," Whole Foods Market website, www.wholefoodsmarket.com on May 1, 2005; Amy Tsao, "Whole Foods' Natural High," *Business Week*, July 18, 2003, www.businessweek.com on April 30, 2005; Charles Fischman, "The Anarchist's Cookbook," *Fast Company*, July 2004, pp. 70–78; "David B. Dillon," *Forbes*, www.forbes.com on April 29, 2005; Evan Smith, "John Mackey," *Texas Monthly*, March 2005, pp. 122–132.
51. See Warren Wilhelm, "Changing Corporate Culture—Or Corporate Behavior? How to Change Your Company," *Academy of Management Executive*, November 1992, pp. 72–77.
52. "Socialization" has also been defined as "the process by which culture is transmitted from one generation to the next." See J. W. M. Whiting, "Socialization: Anthropological Aspects," in D. Sils (Ed.), *International Encyclopedia of the Social Sciences*, vol. 14 (New York: Free Press, 1968), p. 545.
53. J. E. Hebden, "Adopting an Organization's Culture: The Socialization of Graduate Trainees," *Organizational Dynamics*, Summer 1986, pp. 54–72.
54. J. B. Barney, "Organizational Culture: Can It Be a Source of Sustained Competitive Advantage?" *Academy of Management Review*, July 1986, pp. 656–665.

55. Brian Hindo, "3M's Culture of Innovation."
56. James R. Norman, "A New Teledyne," *Forbes*, September 27, 1993, pp. 44–45.

Chapter 19

1. "Baby Boomers Push for Power," *Business Week*, July 2, 1984, pp. 52–56.
2. "Americans' Median Age Passes 32," *Arizona Republic*, April 6, 1988, pp. A1, A5.
3. Annual Estimates of the Resident Population by Sex and Five-Year Age Group for the United States: April 1, 2010 to July 1, 2011 (NC-EST 2011-01). Source: U.S. Census Bureau, Population Division. Release Date: May 2012, http://www.census.gov/popest/data/national/asrh/2011.
4. Geoffrey Colvin, "What the Baby Boomers Will Buy Next," *Fortune*, October 15, 1984, pp. 28–34.
5. Lev Grossman, "Grow Up? Not So Fast," *Time*, January 24, 2005, p. 42.
6. Diane Thielfoldt and Devon Scheef, "Generation X and the Millennials: What You Need to Know About Mentoring the New Generations," *Law Practice Today*, August 2004, www.abanet.org/lm/lpt/articles/nosearch/mgt08044_print.html on March 11, 2008.
7. Michael A. Olguin, "5 Tips for Managing Millennial Employees," *Inc.com*, April 13, 2012, http://www.inc.com/michael-olguin/5-tips-for-managing-millennial-employees.html on July 20, 2012.
8. John Huey, "Managing in the Midst of Chaos," *Fortune*, April 5, 1993, pp. 38–48.
9. Craig Stanley, "At one school district, the motto is BYOT - Bring Your Own Technology," *NBC News*, May 6, 2012, http://dailynightly.msnbc.msn.com/_news/2012/05/06/11567170-at-one-school-district-the-motto-is-byot-bring-your-own-technology?lite on July 20, 2012.
10. "DuPont Adopts New Direction in China," Xinhua News Agency, September 7, 1999, p. 1008250h0104; Alex Taylor III, "Why DuPont Is Trading Oil for Corn," *Fortune*, April 26, 1999, pp. 154–160; Jay Palmer, "New DuPont: For Rapid Growth, an Old-Line Company Looks to Drugs, Biotechnology," *Barron's*, May 11, 1998, p. 31.
11. "Toyota to Employ Robots," News24.com website, January 6, 2005, www.news24.com on May 4, 2005; "Toyota's Global New Body Line," Toyota Motor Manufacturing website, www.toyotageorgetown.com on May 4, 2005; Burritt Sabin, "Robots for Babies—Toyota at the Leading Edge," Japan.com website, www.japan.com on May 5, 2005.
12. Stephanie Schomer, "Body Language," *Fast Company*, May 2010, pp. 61–66.
13. Tarmo Virki, "Professional Social Networking Booming," bx.businessweek.com, May 18, 2010, bx.businessweek.com on May 24, 2010; and Eric Tsai, "How to Integrate Email Marketing, SEO, and Social Media," bx.businessweek.com, May 20, 2010, bx.businessweek.com on May 24, 2010.
14. Sue Shellenbarger, "'Working From Home' Without Slacking Off," *Wall Street Journal*, July 11, 2012, p. B3.
15. Rachel Emma Silverman and Robin Sidel, "Warming Up to the Officeless Office," *Wall Street Journal*, April 18, 2012, p. B1.
16. Thomas A. Stewart, "Welcome to the Revolution," *Fortune*, December 13, 1993, pp. 66–80.
17. Max Chafkin, "The Zappos Way of Managing," *Inc.com*, May 1, 2009, www.inc.com on April 25, 2010.
18. See Thomas L. Friedman, *The World Is Flat 3.0: A Brief History of the Twenty-First Century* (New York: Farrar, Straus & Giroux, 2007), for an excellent account of the impact of globalization and technology.
19. Kurt Lewin, *Field Theory in Social Science* (New York: Harper & Row, 1951).
20. W. Warner Burke, "Leading Organizational Change," in Subir Chowdhury (Ed.), *Organization 21C: Someday All Organizations Will Lead This Way* (Upper Saddle River, NJ: Financial Times Prentice Hall, 2003), pp. 291–310.
21. Mitchell Lee Marks, "In With the New," *Wall Street Journal*, May 24, 2010, online.wsj.com on May 24, 2010.
22. Linda S. Ackerman, "Transition Management: An In-Depth Look at Managing Complex Change," *Organizational Dynamics*, Summer 1982, pp. 46–66; David A. Nadler, "Managing Transitions to Uncertain Future States," *Organizational Dynamics*, Summer 1982, pp. 37–45.
23. Burke, "Leading Organizational Change."
24. Noel M. Tichy and David O. Ulrich, "The Leadership Challenge—A Call for the

Transformational Leader," *Sloan Management Review*, Fall 1984, pp. 59–68.
25. W. Warner Burke, *Organization Development: Principles and Practices* (Boston: Little, Brown, 1982).
26. Michael Beer, *Organization Change and Development* (Santa Monica, CA: Goodyear, 1980); Burke, *Organization Development*.
27. Cummings and Worley, *Organization Development and Change*, 6th ed. (Cincinnati, OH: South-Western Publishing, 1997), p. 2.
28. Noel M. Tichy and Christopher DeRose, "The Death and Rebirth of Organizational Development," in Subir Chowdhury (Ed.), *Organization 21C: Someday All Organizations Will Lead This Way* (Upper Saddle River, NJ: Financial Times Prentice Hall, 2003), pp. 155–177.
29. Danny Miller and Peter H. Friesen, "Structural Change and Performance: Quantum Versus Piecemeal-Incremental Approaches," *Academy of Management Journal*, December 1982, pp. 867–892.
30. Sharon Silke Carty, "Bill Ford Carries on Family Name with Grace," *USA Today*, February 27, 2005, http://www.usatoday.com/money/autos/2005-02-27-ford-ceo-usat_x.htm on March 12, 2008; "Ford Enters New Era of E-Communication: New Web Sites Connect Dealers, Consumer, Suppliers," *PR Newswire*, January 24, 2000, p. 7433; Suzy Wetlaufer, "Driving Change," *Harvard Business Review*, March–April 1999, pp. 77–85; "Ford's Passing Fancy," *Business Week*, March 15, 1999, p. 42; Bill Saporito, "Can Alan Mulally Keep Ford in the Fast Lane?" *Time*, August 9, 2010, http://www.time.com/time/magazine/article/0,9171,2007401,00.html on August 19, 2010.
31. J. Lloyd Suttle, "Improving Life at Work—Problems and Prospects," in J. Richard Hackman and J. Lloyd Suttle (Eds.), *Improving Life at Work: Behavioral Science Approaches to Organizational Change* (Santa Monica, CA: Goodyear, 1977), p. 4.
32. Richard E. Walton, "Quality of Work Life: What Is It?" *Sloan Management Review*, Fall 1983, pp. 11–21.
33. DISA website, www.disa.mil/careers/worklife, on May 23, 2010.
34. Daniel A. Ondrack and Martin G. Evans, "Job Enrichment and Job Satisfaction in Greenfield and Redesign QWL Sites," *Group & Organization Studies*, March 1987, pp. 5–22.
35. Ben Farmer, "Fiat 500 Is Britain's Sexiest Car," *Telegraph*, September 5, 2008, www.telegraph.co.uk on May 22, 2010; Peter Gumbel, "Chrysler's Sergio Marchionne: The Turnaround Artista," *Time*, www.time.com on May 20, 2010; "Online Extra: Fiat's Sexy Designs on Success," *BusinessWeek*, January 16, 2006, www.businessweek.com on May 20, 2010; Chris Poole, "2011 Fiat 500 Review and Prices," *Consumer Guide Automotive*, July 2, 2009, http://consumerguideauto.howstuffworks.com on May 20, 2010; Shawn Langlois, "Style and Substance," *MarketWatch*, December 3, 2009, www.marketwatch.com on May 24, 2010.
36. Ricky W. Griffin, *Task Design: An Integrative Framework* (Glenview, IL: Scott, Foresman, 1982).
37. Gregory Moorhead, "Organizational Analysis: An Integration of the Macro and Micro Approaches," *Journal of Management Studies*, April 1981, pp. 191–218.
38. James C. Quick and Jonathan D. Quick, *Organizational Stress and Preventive Management* (New York: McGraw-Hill, 1984).
39. Tichy and DeRose, "The Death and Rebirth of Organizational Development."
40. Kenneth N. Wexley and Timothy T. Baldwin, "Management Development," *1986 Yearly Review of Management of the Journal of Management*, in the *Journal of Management*, Summer 1986, pp. 277–294.
41. Richard Beckhard, "Optimizing Team-Building Efforts," *Journal of Contemporary Business*, Summer 1972, pp. 23–27, 30–32.
42. Bernard M. Bass, "Issues Involved in Relations Between Methodological Rigor and Reported Outcomes in Evaluations of Organizational Development," *Journal of Applied Psychology*, February 1983, pp. 197–201; William M. Vicars and Darrell D. Hartke, "Evaluating OD Evaluations: A Status Report," *Group & Organization Studies*, June 1984, pp. 177–188.
43. Beer, *Organization Change and Development*.
44. Jerome L. Franklin, "Improving the Effectiveness of Survey Feedback," *Personnel*, May–June 1978, pp. 11–17.
45. Paul R. Lawrence, "How to Deal with Resistance to Change," *Harvard Business Review*, May–June 1954, reprinted in Gene W. Dalton, Paul R. Lawrence, and Larry E. Greiner (Eds.),

Organizational Change and Development (Homewood, IL: Irwin, 1970), pp. 181–197.

46. Jeffrey D. Ford, Laurie W. Ford, and Angelo D'Amelio, "Resistance to Change: The Rest of the Story," *Academy of Management Review*, April, 2008, pp. 362–377.
47. Daniel Katz and Robert L. Kahn, *The Social Psychology of Organizations*, 2nd ed. (New York: John Wiley and Sons, 1978), pp. 36–68.
48. See Michael T. Hannah and John Freeman, "Structural Inertia and Organizational Change," *American Sociological Review*, April 1984, pp. 149–164, for an in-depth discussion of structural inertia.
49. Moorhead, "Organizational Analysis: An Integration of the Macro and Micro Approaches."
50. G. Zaltman and R. Duncan, *Strategies for Planned Change* (New York: John Wiley and Sons, 1977); David A. Nadler, "Concepts for the Management of Organizational Change," in J. Richard Hackman, Edward E. Lawler III, and Lyman W. Porter (Eds.), *Perspectives on Behavior in Organizations*, 2nd ed. (New York: McGraw-Hill, 1983), pp. 551–561.
51. Dell Inc., "Dell Sees Unrivalled Opportunity in Connected Era and Fast Growing Economies," press release, April 10, 2008, www.dell.com on May 26, 2010; Jack Ewing, "Where Dell Sells with Brick and Mortar," *BusinessWeek*, October 8, 2007, www.businessweek.com on May 26, 2010; "Dell Says Sales in India Grew to $700 Million," *Wall Street Journal*, March 25, 2008, www.wsj.com on April 26, 2008; Bruce Einhorn, "Dell Goes Retail in China with Gome," *BusinessWeek*, September 24, 2007, www.businessweek.com on May 26, 2010; "Microsoft Sees China PC Sales Growing 20% in 2011," *MarketWatch*, March 18, 2010, www.marketwatch.com on August 22, 2010.
52. Alfred M. Jaeger, "Organization Development and National Culture: Where's the Fit?" *Academy of Management Review*, January 1986, pp. 178–190.
53. Alan M. Webber, "Learning for a Change," *Fast Company*, May 1999, pp. 178–188.

Name Index

Company Index

Subject Index

D

P

T